PETER LONGERICH

Peter Longerich is Professor of Modern German History at Royal Holloway University of London, and founder of Royal Holloway's Holocaust Research Centre.

He has published extensively on Nazi Germany, including the acclaimed biography *Heinrich Himmler*, *Holocaust: The Nazi Persecution and Murder of the Jews* and *The Unwritten Order: Hitler's Role in the Final Solution.*

PETER LONGERICH

Goebbels

A Biography

TRANSLATED BY
Alan Bance, Jeremy Noakes, and
Lesley Sharpe

VINTAGE

5 7 9 10 8 6

Vintage
20 Vauxhall Bridge Road,
London SW1V 2SA

Vintage is part of the Penguin Random House group of companies whose
addresses can be found at global.penguinrandomhouse.com.

Copyright © Peter Longerich 2015

Peter Longerich has asserted his right to be identified as the author of this
Work in accordance with the Copyright, Designs and Patents Act 1988

First published in Vintage in 2016
First published in Great Britain in hardback by The Bodley Head in 2015

www.vintage-books.co.uk

A CIP catalogue record for this book is available from the British Library

ISBN 9780099523697

Printed and bound by Clays Ltd, elcograf S.p.A

Penguin Random House is committed to a sustainable future for our
business, our readers and our planet. This book is made from Forest
Stewardship Council certified paper.

MIX
Paper from
responsible sources
FSC® C018179

CONTENTS

PROLOGUE

On April 30, 1945, a few hours after becoming Reich chancellor following Hitler's death, Dr. Joseph Goebbels made a final attempt to delay his suicide, announced so often in advance. Goebbels wrote to the "commander-in-chief of Soviet forces," informing him of Hitler's suicide and of the arrangements for his succession that were now in force. As well as promoting Goebbels to chancellor, the dictator had made Grand Admiral Karl Dönitz president of the Reich. Goebbels proposed a ceasefire and offered to negotiate peace terms with the Soviet commander.

The chief of the general staff, General Hans Krebs, a fluent Russian speaker from his days as military attaché in Moscow, undertook to cross the front line, now only a few hundred yards from the Reich Chancellery. Early in the morning Krebs delivered the letter to Major General Vasily Chuikov, commander of the 8th Guards Army, who had set up his headquarters in Tempelhof. He contacted Marshal Georgy Zhukov, the commander-in-chief of the Soviet Army attacking Berlin. Zhukov in turn informed the Soviet dictator, Joseph Stalin. Moscow delivered its answer some hours later: There could be no question of a ceasefire. The Soviet leader expected the German forces to surrender.[1] When Krebs passed this on to Goebbels on May 1, Goebbels held Krebs responsible for the Russians' refusal to negotiate. Goebbels sent another delegation to Chuikov. But this too was rejected.[2]

Goebbels now decided to inform Dönitz of Hitler's death and the Führer's arrangements regarding succession; he had wisely made his armistice overtures before the new head of state took office. In a discussion of the situation, Goebbels told the staff in the bunker that they were free to break out on their own initiative.[3] He had repeatedly announced in public that if the Third Reich should fall he intended to end his own life and those of his family. In a radio address at the end of February he made it clear that he would regard life after the war as "not worth living, either for myself or for my children."[4] On April 15 he wrote a piece for the magazine *Das Reich* entitled "Staking Your Whole Life" in which he took his leave of readers by posing a rhetorical question: Could anyone "even conceive of continuing their existence in such conditions after an Allied victory?"[5] No more than two weeks later, the end came for the Goebbels family.

Goebbels left his wife to make the arrangements for the long-planned murder of the children. The precise circumstances surrounding their death (and the question of individual responsibility for it) have never been satisfactorily established. After the war the dentist Helmut Kunz repeatedly stated that he gave the children morphine injections, after which Magda Goebbels crushed cyanide capsules in their mouths. Later he changed his statement, ascribing the latter action to Hitler's personal physician, Ludwig Stumpfegger.[6]

By April 28, Magda and Joseph Goebbels had already written farewell letters to Harald Quandt, Magda's son from her first marriage, announcing their intention of killing themselves and their children. They entrusted the letters to the pilot Hanna Reitsch, who managed to fly out of the city that same day. Goebbels wrote that Germany would "recover from this terrible war, but only if presented with examples to give it fresh heart. We want to give such an example."[7] Magda maintained in her letter to Harald that both her husband and Hitler had urged her to leave Berlin. She had refused. She made no secret of her involvement in the plan to murder Harald's half-sisters and brother: "The world after the Führer and National Socialism will not be worth living in, and that is why I have taken the children with me. They are too good for the life that will come after us, and a merciful God will understand my granting them release. [. . .] We have only one aim: faithfulness to the Führer unto death."[8]

Hitler's adjutant, Günther Schwägermann, stated after the war that, on the evening of May 1, Goebbels called him in to tell him that

he and his wife intended to take their own lives. According to Schwägermann's testimony, Goebbels asked that "a shot should be fired to
make sure he was dead" and that the corpses should be burned. With
the preparations made, Goebbels said goodbye to him and gave him
the photograph of the Führer that stood on his desk. Schwägermann
conveys the importance that Goebbels attached to maintaining the
proprieties until the very last minute of his life: "Shortly afterward, at
about 20:30 hours, the minister and his wife came out of the room.
He went calmly to the coat rack, put on his hat and coat, and pulled
on his gloves. He offered his wife his arm and without a word left the
bunker by the garden exit." Not long after this, Schwägermann found
the couple's motionless bodies—both seemed to have taken poison[9]—
in the garden. "As agreed, my companion shot Dr. Goebbels once or
twice. Neither body showed any sign of movement. The gasoline we
had brought with us was then poured over them and ignited. The
corpses were enveloped in flames immediately."[10]

Nearly all the leading officials of the Nazi regime fled the capital as
the Soviet troops advanced, and even the top leadership looked to
save their lives as the Third Reich collapsed. Heinrich Himmler, hoping to pass unnoticed among the millions of defeated Wehrmacht
soldiers, was caught and identified. After Hitler's death, Martin Bormann joined in an armed attempt to break out through the cordon of
enemy troops around the Reich Chancellery and died in the act. Hermann Göring and Albert Speer surrendered to the Allies. Goebbels
was the only member of Hitler's innermost circle to hold out in the
bunker and ultimately follow him in committing suicide—and he
was the only one who dragged his whole family down with him to
their deaths.

This last step was deliberately staged for its effect on posterity. By
merely ending his life along with his wife, he would simply have appeared to be drawing the logical conclusion from a hopeless situation. To his way of thinking, this would have been seen as an
admission of the complete failure of his life's project, as a miserable
exit at the moment when his political work, the work of the previous
twenty years, was about to end in a colossal disaster. What Goebbels
wanted, however, was to create, with his wife, a dramatic grand fi-
nale, to leave posterity with an "example" of the "faithfulness unto
death" his wife had invoked. He could no longer use the resources of
conventional propaganda. But the extreme act of wiping out his en-

tire family seemed to him a way of proving to the whole world that, to the bitter end, he was absolutely committed to Hitler; that he was the only member of Hitler's clique prepared to set aside his most fundamental human obligations in the name of demonstrating his loyalty. He saw in this last step a chance to turn the total failure of his life's course into a life's work that seemed to be utterly consistent and marked by unqualified devotion. At the same time, this last propaganda performance also revealed Goebbels's great psychological dependence on Hitler. With the Führer's suicide, his own life, too, seemed to have lost all meaning. Indeed, for Goebbels and his wife the continuing existence of their own family after Hitler's death was unthinkable, since they regarded their family as Hitler's family, too. This absolute reliance on Hitler was to be made into a virtue by suicide: faithfulness unto death.

Throughout his life Joseph Goebbels was driven by an exceptional craving for recognition by others. He was positively addicted to others' admiration. It was fundamentally impossible for this addiction to be satisfied. It revealed itself, for example, in the delight he continued to take, after so many years in the business, as propaganda minister and overlord of the Third Reich's public sphere, in the fanfares with which the media—controlled by himself—greeted his speeches, and in their appreciative comments on them. He regularly noted such "successes" in his diary.

His character fulfilled all the essential criteria recognized in current psychoanalytic practice as defining a narcissistically disturbed personality.[11] On the one hand, there was the yearning for recognition and the powerful urge to be seen as great and unique, already highly developed in his early years; the megalomaniac fantasies about his future role in the world; the pride and arrogance; the lack of empathy for others; and the tendency to exploit personal relationships with icy detachment for personal ends. On the other hand, there was his readiness to subordinate himself without reservation to some supposedly greater personality and not least the bouts of depression he suffered whenever the anticipated outstanding success failed to materialize. In order to appease this hunger, Goebbels—privately deeply insecure about his impact on others—needed constant praise and recognition from an idol to whom he completely subordinated himself. From 1924 onward, this idol was Adolf Hitler. By constantly confirming Goebbels's exceptional brilliance, Hitler gave him the stability he needed to maintain control over his life, a stability otherwise lacking in this unbalanced personality.

There is no doubt that a narcissistic craving for recognition was the main driving force behind Goebbels's career. He clearly manifested the chief characteristics of this addiction: conceit; a restless obsession with work; unreserved self-subjugation to an idol; disdain for other human relationships; and a willingness to place himself beyond generally accepted moral norms in pursuit of his own ends.

Goebbels's aim in life was to prove that he, Joseph Goebbels, was able to unite the German people behind his own political idol and leader, Adolf Hitler. In seeking to fix this conviction in people's minds, Goebbels produced and left behind a vast amount of material. There is the flood of printed matter, film footage, and audio recordings generated by the propaganda machine he directed; the enormous volume of contemporary reports on the public mood, indicating the success of this propaganda effort; and finally his diaries, edited between 1993 and 2008 by Elke Fröhlich of the Munich Institute for Contemporary History and comprising thirty-two volumes. The diary was above all intended to document his success.[12]

He himself set forth the individual chapters of this success story in full: the rise of a not especially privileged man of the people to the position of spokesman for a "socialist" National Socialist Party in western Germany; the conqueror of "red Berlin" and creator of a "Führer" aura around the figure of Hitler by adroit use of propaganda between 1926 and 1933; the man who united the masses into a "national community" behind Hitler in the years after 1933; and finally the closest supporter of his leader, spurring the German people to a supreme effort in wartime. The core of this autobiographical narrative has survived to this day in various forms, albeit in a negative context. Ever since Goebbels's death, the material created by him and his colleagues has been put to multimedia use and has remained influential. No film, no schoolbook, no popular or academic treatment of the Third Reich can manage without this material. Everyone now knows what is meant by "Goebbels propaganda." No one looking for an explanation for the obvious support the Nazi system enjoyed among the great majority of the German population can afford to overlook Joseph Goebbels.

A particular challenge facing the propaganda minister's biographer is that of questioning the self-portrait so effectively created by

Goebbels and thoroughly revising his historical role. The biographer's chief problem from the outset is, in fact, that the vast mass of material about the propaganda minister and Gauleiter of Berlin originates either with him or with his propaganda machine and was presented for the purpose of demonstrating the preeminence and unique historical success of Joseph Goebbels. However, closer analysis reveals that the large number of texts Goebbels wrote about himself and the wealth of material that his propaganda machine used to document his influence offer a surprising number of starting points for deconstructing the self-image Goebbels projected.

As the author and chief propagandist of the Third Reich, Goebbels was concerned above all to hold up a mirror with which to admire a larger-than-life reflection of himself. Gazing into this mirror, he could give full vent to his narcissistic cravings. Lacking both inner balance and external confidence and profoundly mistrusting his effect on other people, he needed constant affirmation that the magnificent image in the mirror really did represent him, Joseph Goebbels. He derived this affirmation from the leader he had chosen, a leader sent from God, as he supposed, to whom he subordinated himself. The more completely he subjugated himself, the more weight he ascribed to the judgment of this idol.

The mountains of evidence Goebbels left to posterity that demonstrate his self-affirmation and self-adulation in fact serve to bring out very clearly his insecurity, his dependence, and his overwhelming conceit. In this historical biography, first and foremost concerned with the question of the part played by Goebbels in the leadership of the Third Reich, insights gained into the deficiencies of his personality can help to develop wider perspectives. A particular purpose of this biography is to open the way to an analysis of the construction and modus operandi of the Nazi propaganda apparatus.

The conventional approach to the history of organizations and structures cannot quite encompass the position Goebbels built up for himself over time through accumulating and, in part, amalgamating various offices. It was historically unique and completely tailor-made for him, bearing the stamp of his personality through and through. Only a biography, therefore, can make it fully intelligible. He combined the offices of Gauleiter of Berlin, head of propaganda for the Party, and leader of a ministry that was especially invented for him and united the management of the mass media with the National

Socialist control of cultural life. In addition, he was tasked with certain special functions, again tailor-made for him, for example in the area of foreign policy. To the extent that Goebbels succeeded during the war in extending his authority beyond propaganda into other spheres, eventually assuming a central role in the conduct of the non-military side of the war effort, it was—as we shall see—a result of his attempt to shape the public sphere into his desired image, particularly under the conditions of the "total war" he himself propagated. The connections, often quite subtle, among his various responsibilities become apparent only through a description of his life.

A Goebbels biography not only enables us to take a look behind the scenes by bringing together a multiplicity of sources to show how Nazi propaganda was conceived and carried out; it can also question the frequently asserted omnipotence of Goebbels's propaganda. Here, the deconstruction of Goebbels's self-constructed image, as bequeathed to posterity, of the brilliant director of propaganda plays a central role. It will become clear that narcissistic self-elevation not only represented an important aspect of Goebbels's character but was also decisive in creating the image he built up over the years, so powerful that it was by no means demolished even by his death. It will be apparent that Goebbels was not the absolute master of the whole propaganda machine, as he liked to think, but that in some areas, at least, he was obliged to share his responsibilities with other Nazi apparatchiks. Above all, however, we shall see that the enormous impact claimed for propaganda by the National Socialists, and particularly by Goebbels himself, was itself an integral component of Goebbels's propaganda. The importance of a biographical approach is emphasized by the fact that the man who asserted the all-powerful effect of propaganda was a textbook case of self-overestimation who had difficulty distinguishing fact from fiction.

Moreover, biography can make an important contribution to the general history of the Third Reich. Goebbels, with his diaries, has left us the most important insider's chronicle of Nazism and its Führer, from the re-founding of the Party in 1924–25 until the end of the regime. No other source of insight into the inner workings of Nazi power can compare. True, Goebbels often stood outside the decision-making process, but he did have the opportunity to observe at close quarters how decisions were arrived at. With his fixation on Hitler and consequent inability to take a critical view of him, he often gives us a unique and peculiarly authentic perspective on the dictator.

The diaries, the basis of this biography and one of the chief sources for histories of the Third Reich, were transcribed many years ago for publication without notes or commentary. But to give them their full value as a historical source we need to analyze the propaganda minister's personality and ambitions. This book is the product of a double process: evaluating the diaries as a historical source for a biography and interpreting them in the light of the author's personality. Particularly in the early years, the diary was a site of self-reflection and self-criticism for Goebbels. But quite soon it began chiefly to serve the purpose of confirming his successes to himself, consolidating his success story, brushing aside failures and setbacks, constantly reinforcing his own morale, and driving him forward along the path taken. If the self-critical passages are the most interesting parts of the earliest diary, the almost complete absence of self-criticism is perhaps the most conspicuous aspect of the later volumes.

The diaries had a further function as a place for Goebbels to deposit material he would go on to use elsewhere. Textual comparisons reveal how the diary corresponds with his publicity-oriented and literary writing as well as with his private letters. No clear distinctions can be made: The diary is frequently the first draft of a literary treatment, perhaps consisting of colorful descriptions of individuals, dramatized events, evocations of atmosphere, or aphorisms. The writer of the diary was not just a chronicler but also a journalist and a literary author, collecting impressions and trying out various forms. Once he had gained a foothold in politics at the end of the 1920s, his ideas about the secondary uses of the diary became more concrete. It served him now, above all, as the basis for publications centered on the recording of political chronology. Its utility can be seen, for example, in books such as *Kampf um Berlin* (Battle for Berlin, 1931) or *Vom Kaiserhof zur Reichskanzlei* (From the Kaiserhof [Hotel] to the Reich Chancellery, 1934), where he was chiefly concerned with one thing only: the success story of Joseph Goebbels. Eventually, in 1936, he sold the right to publish the diaries—after revision—to the Party's publisher, Max Amann and also planned to draw on them for publications connected with a projected official history of the Third Reich.[13] The variety of ways in which Goebbels proposed to utilize the diaries should be borne in mind when reading them.

Not least, though, the purpose of the diary was to provide an aide-mémoire and logbook of events, and this function increased with the growing range of offices that the propaganda minister acquired. An important turning point was the start of hostilities against the Soviet Union. The entries were now no longer handwritten but dictated to a secretary, with the result that the personal content of the texts was further diminished, and the diary became diffused and inflated by the admixture of other texts—military situation reports, the minister's official correspondence, and whatever else was lying around on his desk.

Comparison with other sources shows that the information about appointments and encounters with other people is very largely reliable and that Goebbels's recall of conversations is in essence generally correct—apart from the exaggeration (especially where his own role is concerned), the dramatizing of certain situations, the omissions, and so forth. But time and again the diaries also feature freely invented strategic assertions from the workshop of Goebbels the propagandist, assertions that he clearly intended to reproduce in his later publications. Such distortions and inventions are particularly valuable for a biography. They provide us with the key to understanding Goebbels's perception and interpretation of certain situations. But to come to terms with them properly, the diaries must, if possible, be weighed against other historical sources. That is the procedure followed by this biography, wherever feasible.

A basic problem of every biographical approach to Goebbels is that, particularly in the early years, for the most part we have only his own testimony to go on, so that we are confronted with the challenge of penetrating the narcissistic front of the author's self-interpretation. Almost everything he tells us about his childhood and youth originated in a deeply depressive phase of his life, between 1923 and 1934, when Goebbels was clearly driven by a manic compulsion to write.

To gain access to these early years, we have to engage closely with these texts and attempt to decipher them. As our entry point into his life story, we have therefore chosen the autumn of 1923, the moment when Goebbels began to keep his regular autobiographical record.

1897—1933

TO ADVANCE AT ANY PRICE

CHAPTER 1

"Rings a Song Eternally /
From Youth's Happy Hours"*

Goebbels on His Childhood and Youth

Neither his handicap nor his academic ambitions seem to have turned him into an isolated loner: Joseph Goebbels (front row, third from left) with his fellow pupils at the high school in Rheydt, about 1914.

"I can't go on suffering like this. I need to write this bitterness out of my soul. Else is giving me a notebook for day-to-day use. So on October 17 I'm going to start my diary."[1]

It was in 1923 that Goebbels came to this decision—a resolve he maintained consistently, right up to the last weeks of his life. The diary became his constant companion.

* Translators' note: The first two lines of a poem/song by Friedrich Rückert (1788–1866) officially recommended by the Prussian government in 1912 for use in the 7th and 8th grades of its schools.

There were many reasons for the pain and bitterness from which Goebbels was suffering in the autumn of 1923. The plain facts are that at this juncture the almost twenty-seven-year-old Joseph Goebbels was an unsuccessful writer who had just been fired from a job he loathed in a Cologne bank and was now completely penniless, having retreated to his parents' home in Rheydt on the Lower Rhine. Else, a young schoolteacher, was his girlfriend. But the relationship was troubled, and after an argument the couple, overshadowed by money worries, had canceled a vacation on the Frisian island of Baltrum. Goebbels saw himself as a "wreck on a sandbank"; he felt "deadly sick." He had spent days in "wild desperation drinking."[2] The general political and economic situation added in no small measure to his depression.

His hometown of Rheydt was part of the territory west of the Rhine that had been occupied by British, Belgian, and French troops since the end of the Great War. Passive resistance to the French army, which since the beginning of the year had extended its occupation beyond the Rhine to the Ruhr, had just collapsed. Inflation had reached its absurd high point: Money earned in the morning was worthless by the evening. Extremist groups of the left and right were gearing up for civil war; separatists in the Rhineland were preparing to secede from the Reich. Rocked by a series of grave crises, the German Republic seemed on the verge of falling apart. "Politics are enough to make you laugh and cry," noted Goebbels.[3]

He had longed for the crisis as for a cleansing fever: "The dollar is climbing like an acrobat. I'm secretly delighted. We need chaos before things can get better."[4] It was to help him cope with this state of personal and political tension that he turned to his diary. After a few months he set about writing a short biographical introduction to it, an outline of his life written in the summer of 1924, hastily thrown together and in part reduced to key words; he called it his "memory pages." This is the most important source of information we possess about Goebbels's early years.[5] It was the same depressed mood in 1923–24 that led him both to take up the diary and to give this short account of his life. In his despair, Goebbels asked himself who he was, what made him the way he was, and what he wanted to achieve in life.

THE RHEYDT YEARS

He began his life story thus: "Born on October 29, 1897, in Rheydt, at that time an up-and-coming little industrial town on the Lower Rhine near Düsseldorf and not far from Cologne." We learn that his father, Fritz Goebbels, born in 1862, was a lowly clerk in a wick factory and that in 1892 he married Katharina Odenhausen, seven years younger than himself and employed at the time as a farmhand. Both came from humble circumstances, artisan families.[6]

The Goebbelses were good Catholics, as they say on the Lower Rhine. They had six children in all: Konrad (b. 1893), Hans (1895), Maria (who died at six months in 1896), Joseph (1897), Elisabeth (1901), and Maria (1910).[7] In 1900 their father managed to acquire a "modest little house" in Dahlenerstrasse.[8]

Joseph's childhood was overshadowed by ill health. Later, as an adult, he recalled among others a protracted illness (inflammation of the lungs with "terrifying delirium"). "And I also remember a long family walk to Geistenbeck one Sunday. The next day on the sofa my old foot complaint returned. [. . .] Excruciating pain." There followed, Goebbels tells us, lengthy treatments and further investigations at the Bonn University Clinic, but "foot lame for life" was the inexorable verdict. The consequences were dire: "My youth from then on pretty blighted. One of the pivotal events of my childhood. I was thrown back on my own devices. Could no longer play with the others. Became solitary, a loner. Maybe for that reason the complete favorite at home. I was not popular with my comrades." Only one friend, Richard Flisges, stood by him.[9]

What Goebbels says about his illness suggests that his "foot complaint" was a case of neurogenic clubfoot, a deformity that is often particularly associated with a metabolic disorder in childhood. His right foot was turned inwards; it was shorter and thicker than his healthy left foot.[10]

Goebbels's account of his elementary education, which began in 1904, makes for equally sorry reading. He remembered a teacher called Hennes, "a lying hound." There was another, Hilgers, who was "a villain and a swine who mistreated us children and made our school life hell. [. . .] My mother once discovered the stripes from his cane across my back when she was bathing me." However, Goebbels did admit that his difficulties at school may have had something to do with his own attitude: "At the time I was so stubborn and independent-minded, a precocious lad the teachers couldn't stand."[11]

In his last year at elementary school he underwent a largely unsuccessful operation on his foot: "When my mother was about to leave, I howled dreadfully. I still have terrible memories of the last half hour before the anesthetic and the trains rattling past the hospital during the night." But there was a positive side to his stay in the hospital: His godmother, Aunt Stina, brought him fairy-tale books, which he "absolutely devoured. My first fairy tales. There wasn't much storytelling at home. Those books awakened my first interest in reading. From then on I consumed everything in print, including newspapers, even politics, without understanding a word." Immediately after his time in hospital, he left elementary school for the grammar school in Rheydt: Thanks to his father's intervention, he recalled, his academic record was considerably enhanced.[12] Although, according to his own estimation, Goebbels was "pretty lazy and lethargic" during his early years at grammar school, he gradually developed into an outstanding and extremely ambitious student, excelling particularly in religion, Greek, and history.[13]

At first sight, it does not seem hard to explain why he was so ambitious: He was trying to compensate for his physical deformity. Goebbels himself put forward this explanation in 1919 in a piece of autobiographical writing entitled *Michael Voormann's Early Years*, a dramatic literary version of his own childhood and youth that was clearly quite consciously modeled on a traditional German form, the novel of development.[14] Michael was "a strange boy. You did not need to know him to see it when he opened his big, gray eyes wide and looked so questioningly at whoever was talking to him. There was something unusual in his gaze, a whole world of questions that no one suspected. You seldom saw him playing with other children." Michael was lazy at school. The teacher "hated him like sin," and his fellow pupils "were not fond of him." "He was so harsh and rude to them, and if anyone asked him to do them a favor, he just turned away with a laugh. Only one person loved him—his mother." Then Goebbels indulged in a description of his parents that made them out to belong to the lumpenproletariat: "She could neither read nor write, because before she married his father—a poor day laborer—she had been a farm girl. She had borne him seven sons, becoming pale and thin as a result. The fourth child was Michael. No one knew anything about his mother's family origins, not even their father." The text describes the father as "an upright, honest man with a highly developed sense of duty" who sometimes treated his mother "harshly and roughly" and from whom he had inherited a certain "tyrannical tendency."

At the age of ten, we are told, Michael suffered from a serious illness that left him with a lame right leg: "Michael was in despair most of the time; eventually he came to terms with it. However, it made him even more withdrawn, and he spent even less time with his comrades." He had now become "eager and industrious at school, for his ambition was to become a great man one day." He had been unpopular with his fellow pupils, and the gulf between them had made him "hard and bitter." It is clear that in the novel Goebbels was trying out an imaginary variation on his autobiography. Unlike Joseph Goebbels, son of a petit bourgeois, Michael Voormann is from the working class, and by excelling at school he tries to make up for the distance from his contemporaries, an isolation initially rooted in his sense of being different and then increased by his disability. Goebbels was testing out a dramatic version of his own life story: rising above the most humble origins, crippled, disdained, solitary, but at the same time highly talented, determined, and successful, even if embittered, cold, and consumed with ambition. In this telling, his later development into a genius is taken for granted. The differences between this and the memoir he composed in his "memory pages" five years later are obvious: Although he certainly describes his disability as the most important factor in his bleak childhood, he no longer wants to represent it as the real force driving him on to higher things. In subsequent literary treatments of his life story, his disability is as inconspicuous as it is in the diary, where it is rarely mentioned, although in fact he needed an orthopedic appliance to help him walk, and medical complications frequently recurred.[15] Can *Michael* therefore be seen as an authentic account of his life? Is this a rare and valuable autobiographical document in which Goebbels for once shows himself capable of honest soul-searching? Is he attempting in *Michael* to break out from his denial of a disability that has become a permanent front to the world and honestly face up to his deformity and its consequences?

His physical disability may well have intensified his adult convic-

tion of a call to higher things, his compulsion as a boy to escape the
narrow confines of his childhood milieu by excelling at schoolwork,
and his self-imposed isolation. But there are other reasons for his
narcissistic streak, his highly developed craving for recognition and
affirmation by others.

Psychoanalysts today see the origins of narcissistic personality
disorders in psychological maladjustments that occur between the
second and third years of life. They refer to a failure to develop autonomy: The child is not capable of detaching itself from a solicitous
and domineering mother, and its own personality fails to develop
fully. The possible reasons for this failure are manifold: temporary
neglect by the mother, for example, or an upbringing where the rules
are inconsistently applied, sending mixed messages to the child,
overprotectiveness on the one hand and excessive discipline on the
other. It is easy to imagine these conditions prevailing in a large and
financially hard-pressed family like the Goebbelses. While it is of
course impossible to reconstruct the young Joseph's upbringing, it is
reasonable to note that there are convincing explanations for his undeniable narcissistic traits.

Joseph Goebbels can serve as a textbook example of failed autonomy. A narcissist like Goebbels constantly looks for a source of recognition in order to strengthen his own identity, which he perceives
as inadequate. In particular he seeks a life partner totally dedicated to
himself, from whom he expects to receive—as he did from his solicitous mother—recognition and affirmation. Narcissists find it difficult to distinguish themselves from those who provide them with
recognition; their personality sometimes seems to merge with that of
another person. In this light, Goebbels's attempt in *Michael Voormann* to construct a variant of his own development is a typical expression of uncertainty about his own identity. In the novel he plays
a game of experimenting with his own biography; it is not self-
revelation.

Narcissists like Goebbels generally have difficulty in distinguishing between daydreams and the real world, appearance and reality,
success and fantasies of success. Their relationship to the world
around them is somewhat underdeveloped, their sense of self not
securely anchored. They live in a self-referential way, tending toward
feelings of superiority and delusions of grandeur. But because of their
weak egos, they are often haunted by fear of loss and separation; they

can easily experience the absence of success as failure, and for this reason they are inclined to suffer from depression.[16] Therefore, Goebbels did not develop his narcissism as compensation for his disability. Thanks to the tendency to overestimate himself and to distort reality that he had acquired in infancy, to a great extent he was actually capable of ignoring his deformity. His sense of self-worth relegated it to a subordinate role.

Reading the "memory pages," it is also apparent that Goebbels did not in any way regard himself in high school as a student isolated by his disability and the ambition it induced in him. On the contrary, he remembered a series of good friends from school, friends who would continually cross his path in later life.[17] According to his memoir, it was the awakening of sexuality and the erotic in him that was foremost in the adolescent's mind and constantly got him into trouble. He wrote that it was the stepmother of a friend who first aroused his "urges toward women": "Eros awakes. Well-informed in a crude way even as a boy." He remembered being in love with a girl for the first time sometime between 1912 and 1914: "Sentimental period. Flowery letters. Poems. Along with love for mature women." There was an embarrassing outcome when love letters Goebbels had written under an assumed name to the object of his desire were traced back to him. It was this episode that made his favorite teacher, Herr Voss—whom he credited with great influence on him throughout his schooldays—refuse to support his application for a competitive scholarship offered by the town. In *Michael Voormann* Goebbels inflates this incident into a minor case of martyrdom.[18]

The summer of 1914 had a powerful impact on the sixteen-year-old: "Outbreak of war. Mobilization. Everyone called to the colors. Pain of not being able to go with them. [. . .] The first of my comrades to be wounded. [. . .] Gradually lots of comrades gone. [. . .] Class beginning to empty."[19] Via the army postal service, he kept in touch with his schoolmates, who were now on active duty.[20] In December 1915 his sister Elisabeth died of tuberculosis; some years later, his father would remind him how after she died the family gathered around her deathbed seeking solace in prayer.[21]

A few of Goebbels's school essays that have survived strike the requisite "patriotic" note, something he later found "tedious."[22] Apart from his German teacher, Herr Voss, he was clearly very taken with the history master, Gerhard Bartels, who taught him in his first years at the grammar school. Bartels's early death was marked by a memorial publication to which Goebbels contributed. He praised above all Bartels's dedicated teaching and especially his tales of heroes, which brought home patriotic ideals to his pupils.[23] Goebbels took his *Abitur* (Baccalaureate) examination in 1917, and as the top student in his class he gave the customary speech at the formal leaving-certificate award ceremony. Naturally, this speech too was full of patriotic sentiments: "The land of poets and thinkers must now prove that it is more than that, that it has a valid claim to lead the world politically and intellectually."[24]

Initially he wanted to study medicine, but his German teacher, Herr Voss, dissuaded him. "So: German and history. It doesn't matter which." But regardless of the choice of subject, what did matter was that he should go to university, not least because by doing so he would avoid civilian service (from 1916 on, all men over seventeen were required to perform "auxiliary service for the Fatherland"). During his last years at school, he acquired a girlfriend, Lene Krage from Rheindalen: "First kiss in Gartenstrasse. [. . .] Wonderful boyhood bliss. Naturally get married. A matter of honor." With his *Abitur* came a "leave-taking from Lene," which he considered temporary: "Shut in the Kaiserpark at night. I kiss her breast for the first time. For the first time, she becomes the loving woman."[25]

All in all, one can say that in his childhood and youth he was by no means deprived of the recognition he so eagerly sought: He had successfully completed his education, finishing at the top of his class, in fact; in spite of his family's straitened circumstances, he was able to choose his subject of study freely; he had friends; and he even had a girlfriend.

A NONE-TOO-ZEALOUS STUDENT

With two friends from school, Goebbels set off to study at the University of Bonn at the beginning of April 1927.[26] His situation was far from favorable: "Money worries. Often hungry. Private lessons for ill-mannered youths." He recorded in his "memory pages" that the university made little impression on him. He seems to have spent less time there than in the Catholic student fraternity, Unitas Sigfridia, which he joined as soon as he arrived in Bonn. He became the *Leib-*

bursche ("buddy") of his new acquaintance Karl Heinz ("Pille") Kölsch, whom he proclaimed his "ideal."[27] In the Sigfridia he adopted the name Ulex (after a character in a novel by Wilhelm Raabe, his favorite author). At the society's gala evening in June 1917 he made his mark with a talk about the writer, whom he had admired ever since he was a schoolboy. Goebbels recommended Raabe as a model to his fellow students as someone "who fought for his ideals, fought for his worldview."[28] Fraternity members spent many such convivial evenings together, in taverns and at celebrations and bowling parties. Group excursions took place on the weekends. Student social life suffered from wartime conditions, however. The number of active members had dwindled to five, and there were complaints in the fraternity magazine about the constantly declining quality of the beer. The coffers were empty, although Goebbels, promoted to secretary of Unitas, had no hesitation in writing to comrades on active service to beg for contributions.[29]

During the university vacation, Goebbels was temporarily enlisted to undertake office work for the Fatherland Auxiliary Service, but he soon managed to free himself from this obligation.[30] A shortage of funds forced him to return to Rheydt. Lene was waiting for him there: "A night in Rheindahlen with her on the sofa. Stayed chaste. I feel myself to be a man." He could not escape his financial woes: "Unpaid bills from Bonn. Argument at home. Father helping out. Intellectual experience at Bonn practically nil."[31] In the end he succeeded in raising some funds. The Catholic Albertus Magnus Society of Cologne agreed to support his studies, eventually loaning him a total of 960 Reichsmarks.[32]

During this time in Rheydt he wrote two novellas: *Bin ein fahrender Schüler, ein wüster Gesell* . . . (I am a wandering scholar, a wild fellow . . .)* and *Die die Sonne lieben* (Those who love the sun). In 1924 he called these efforts "bombastic and sentimental. Almost unbearable." This verdict was shared by the *Kölnische Zeitung*, which declined to publish them.[33] However, *Bin ein fahrender Schüler*, like *Michael Voormann* written in 1919, provides an interesting insight into Goebbels's self-image. The hero is called Karl Heinz Ellip (the nickname of his friend "Pille," to whom he dedicated the novella, spelled backward) but has adopted the name Ulex: Ellip explains that

---

* Translators' note: The title of a student drinking song.

he chose the name because his model was the hero of Raabe's novel, "a true German idealist [. . .] deep, a dreamer, as we Germans are." Ellip/Ulex is "a tall strong lad" characterized by a "sunny, cheerful disposition." The only child of a North German landowner, he is studying (out of pure interest) German and history in Bonn, among other places. Ellip is called back to the family home, Elpenhof, where the mother he loves more than anything in the world is on her death-bed. Profoundly shaken by her final throes of agony, he suffers a fatal heart attack the same night that she dies. He is buried next to her.

Goebbels began his second semester in Bonn in October 1917, sharing a room with Kölsch.[34] His relationship with Lene began to cool, as he was warming to Kölsch's sister Agnes. In the Kölsch parental home, to which he was now quite often invited, he got to know another sister, Liesel. General erotic confusion: "Liesel loves me, I love Agnes. [She] is playing with me." The affair became more complicated in the course of the semester when a classmate, Hassan, also fell in love with Agnes. Hassan had what was known as "hassle-free lodgings": "Agnes in Bonn. A night with her in Hassan's room. I kiss her breast. For the first time she is really good to me. Had left the door open. Lied afterward." Soon there was a rerun with Liesel: "Liesel in Bonn. A night with her in Hassan's room. I spare her. She is really good to me. A good deed that gives me a kind of satisfaction."[35]

"Spent hardly any time at university" was his comment on his academic progress in this semester. "Torment and agitation. Time of ferment. I seek and find nothing."[36] Nonetheless, he signed up in both semesters at Bonn for a whole series of classes on history and German studies, including a lecture on Heinrich Heine which he is known to have attended. He also signed up for courses on art history, psychology, and folklore as well as a lecture on "Venereal diseases, their causes and prevention."[37] After the second semester Goebbels and Kölsch decided to continue their studies elsewhere. Moving around from one university to another was quite normal at the time. Their Unitas comrades were sorry to see them leave: They had done so much to breathe new life into the society with their active and spirited participation.[38]

Goebbels spent his third semester in Freiburg, where he was greeted by Pille Kölsch, who had gone on ahead and was very eager to introduce him to an acquaintance, Anka Stahlherm. "And how deeply and completely I got to know you, Anka Stahlherm!" noted

Goebbels in his "memory pages."³⁹ Goebbels fell in love with Anka, who was three years older than himself⁴⁰ and from a solid bourgeois background. He spent the next few weeks trying to lure her away from his friend.

At Whitsun he went to Lake Constance with Kölsch and two other friends. Anka joined them later. They took several sightseeing trips; Goebbels became jealous of Kölsch, and the feeling grew ever stronger. Back in Freiburg, he recorded various friendly signals from Anka: "Gradual break between Anka and Kölsch. But greater attachment to me." They now met more often alone; he got closer and closer to his goal: "I kiss her [. . .]. Fulfillment without end." His feelings for Anka inevitably led to tensions between him and Kölsch; in the end Goebbels moved out of their shared accommodation. When Anka's brother Willy visited her, Anka did not invite Goebbels to join them: "The first argument. Social differences. I'm a poor devil. Money troubles. Big calamity. Hardly been at the university. [. . .] I'm hardly aware there's a war on anymore."

Anka was uncertain whether to make a final break with Kölsch. Finally there came a "big scene" with Goebbels: "She begs for my love on bended knee. For the first time I see how a woman can suffer. I am shattered." The next morning the tragedy continued, but it ended conclusively: "Anka is mine."⁴¹ He had reached his goal: "Blissful days. Nothing but love. Perhaps the happiest time of my life." Anka asked Kölsch if they could talk. He declined, whereupon, bitterly disappointed, she wrote him a goodbye letter.⁴²

At the end of the semester, Goebbels went back to his parents' house in Rheydt.⁴³ He spent his autumn vacation there in 1918. He had become "pale and thin." In three weeks he "laboriously" worked out an idea for a drama in five acts called *Judas Ischariot*. It was a—not particularly original—reinterpretation of the story of Judas in the New Testament: Judas is represented as a patriot who, although at first a fervent disciple of his Messiah, finally betrays him because Jesus will not lead a revolutionary movement to liberate the Jewish people from the yoke of Rome. After the death of Christ, Judas is ambitious to make himself leader but then recognizes the greatness of Jesus and commits suicide.⁴⁴ Clearly, the first signs of religious doubt were emerging here, but at the prompting of the local chaplain Goebbels decided to put the work away in a drawer. As he wrote to Anka, he did not want to break with his "childhood belief and religion." That he owed his funding to this same chaplain may have reinforced his decision.[45]

Unfortunately, Anka met Agnes, who had been discarded in such an abrupt fashion, and the result was that "Anka doubted me. Letters cold and uncertain." She came to see him, and they talked things over, though much remained unresolved. She wanted to continue her studies in Würzburg, while he told her he felt like moving to Munich. He spent the next few days waiting "desperately" for a message, but in vain.[46] In the end he traveled to Würzburg, set about locating Anka, and found her: "One look, and we were back together again. After a long fight for her I'm staying."[47]

The winter semester of 1918–19 was Joseph Goebbels's fourth semester as a student. In fact, he had not done any serious studying up to this point. It is astonishing that the First World War and politics affected his life so little. He was caught up in his reading, his literary ambitions; he cultivated his friendships and his highly volatile love affair with Anka and enjoyed student life to the fullest. On Goebbels's evidence it is hard to see that the war was making any difference to him, and neither is there any indication that his exclusion from "front line experience" on disability grounds made him feel inferior or bitter.

However, in Würzburg he does seem to have devoted himself more to the academic side of student life. His academic record documents attendance at sessions on ancient history, German literature, philology, archaeology, Romance languages, pedagogy, and the history of architecture.[48] No longer much drawn to fraternity life, he gave up his membership in Unitas.[49] At night he read Dostoyevsky for the first time: Looking back in 1924, he wrote that he had been "shaken" by *Crime and Punishment*.

Significant political events took place in the middle of his Würzburg semester. The armistice of November 11, 1918, sealed the military defeat of the German Reich, the revolution broke out, and the Kaiser abdicated: "The revolution. Disgust. Return of the troops. Anka is crying."[50] He noted that "democratic influences" were spreading. His position was clear: "Conservative, nonetheless." He voted for the Bavarian People's Party (Bayerische Volkspartei), the right-wing party of the Bavarian Catholics. For the most part, however, political developments left him cold. In a letter to his schoolfriend Fritz Prang, he adopted a sanguine view of revolutionary events: The hour would come again when the "base, meaningless throngs" would be calling for "spirit and strength." We would just have to "wait for that hour and not cease to arm ourselves for this struggle through untiring spiritual discipline." Germany might have lost the war, but it seemed to him that "the Fatherland had won nonetheless."[51]

Goebbels's father wrote anxious letters. He would have preferred Joseph to attend a university in his native Rhineland. All he could do was try to support his son financially. Goebbels came back from Würzburg at the end of January 1919.[52] He also spent the summer vacation of 1919 in Rheydt, which in the meantime had become occupied territory. Money worries were pressing, and to earn his keep he took up private tutoring. He spent the rest of the time writing another play, *Heinrich Kämpfert*. The subject sounds familiar: The penniless hero falls in love with a girl from a rich family.

Aside from his efforts as a playwright, he applied himself to writing lyric poetry. His diary and other papers contain some unpublished poems from the wartime and postwar periods. Literature scholar Ralf Georg Czapla has studied this oeuvre, finding them for the most part to be "rather uninspired constructs consisting of effusive phrase-making and empty clichés, with quite defective versification and rhyme schemes in parts." The content consists predominantly of evocations of domestic idylls, descriptions of idealized pastoral scenes, and love poems featuring, according to Czapla, "familiar components drawn from a Biedermeier worldview."[53] The form of Goebbels's poetry was also highly conventional, confined to borrowings from folk poems (the *Volkslied*). He took on more probing subjects, too: his quest for God,[54] his loss of faith (to the point of cursing the Christian God),[55] and his fear of death: "In vielen Nächten sitze ich / Auf meinem Bett / Und lausche. / Dann rechne ich / Wie viele Stunden noch / Vom Tod mich trennen mögen." (Many a night I sit upon my bed / And listen. / Then I count / How many hours may remain / 'Twixt death and me.)[56]

Looking for a political direction, Goebbels attended a meeting of the center-left Deutsche Demokratische Partei (German Democratic Party), where his former history teacher Bartels gave a speech. He liked the style of the address, but its content left him feeling "still more opposed to the Democrats" (he no doubt meant the supporters of this party). "All my classmates are voting Center Party [Zentrum] or German Nationalist [Deutschnational]. I would have voted German Nationalist too."[57] In any case, he thought that a large part of the German public was still politically immature: About 25 percent of ballot papers in his home constituency were spoiled because the voters did not understand the voting system.[58] Politically speaking, he did not feel at home in any party.[59] At the end of the semester break he learned that Anka had moved to Freiburg and that his old rival Kölsch had already arrived there: "So whatever it costs, it's off to Freiburg."[60] In Freiburg he met up with Anka, who, he established with consternation, "was no longer the same person." Finally she admitted that she had cheated on him with Kölsch. There followed jealous scenes, attempts at reconciliation, renewed jealousy. At one point he even borrowed a revolver from a friend. "Past death," he declared enigmatically. He made no significant headway with his studies that semester.[61] Richard Flisges, his friend from grammar school, who had returned from the war as a lieutenant and was his "daily companion," spent some time with him in Freiburg and also registered as a student of *Germanistik* (German literature) there. Flisges now became his closest friend.[62]

At the end of the semester, lacking a valid pass, he could not reenter the occupied zone. He then traveled to Münster, where he rented a cheap room. Every day he telephoned Anka, who was living at home with her parents in Recklinghausen. In Münster Goebbels continued his writing efforts. During his stay in Freiburg he had tried to publish a collection of poetry, but the venture failed because of the substantial subsidy the publishers had asked him to contribute in advance.[63] Now he tried another genre. In Münster he wrote the autobiographical novel *Michael Voormann,* referred to earlier in this chapter: "With anguished soul, I am writing my own story."[64]

Historians have only Parts I and III of this three-part work. In Part I the author gives us a stylized version of his childhood and schooldays, while Part III is concerned with the Freiburg period and his relationship with Anka, who appears here as "Hertha Holk" and who, after a long struggle, eventually becomes submissive to him: "She became a part of him." Thereupon he returns home to write a Christ play. When the work is finished, he again sees Hertha, who confesses that she has been unfaithful to him. He leaves her and burns his play, which he had dedicated to her.[65] The whole thing was obviously written to impress Anka: She could think herself lucky not to be playing the role of Hertha, who clearly bears the blame for ending the relationship with Michael and cutting short a promising literary career.

After finishing *Michael* Goebbels decided—ignoring the lack of a pass—to go home. He succeeded in bribing a sentry and slipped across the demarcation line. He felt "deadly sick" and tried to recover a little in Rheydt before the start of the new semester.[66] Goebbels decided to follow Anka, who was planning to move to Munich in the coming semester. For this purpose he borrowed 1,200 marks from family acquaintances.[67] The couple took the train south together. By chance, breaking the journey in Frankfurt, Goebbels was present at the opening of the book fair by Friedrich Ebert. "Miserable impression," he recalled in 1924.

Goebbels was impressed by Munich: "Stachusplatz. Marienplatz. Odeons-Platz. Pinakotheks. Schack Gallery. Dürer (Apostles), Böcklin, Spitzweg, and Feuerbach."[68] Six months earlier the Munich Soviet Republic, a socialist uprising, had been bloodily suppressed by the Free Corps. Since that time the city had turned into a center of counterrevolution. Paramilitary units, secret radical right-wing organizations, and nationalist groups were engaging in a wide variety of activities. A certain Adolf Hitler, still a lance corporal in the *Reichswehr* (army), made a stir for the first time in February 1920, when he addressed some two thousand people at the first rally of the Deutsche Arbeiterpartei (DAP, German Workers' Party), a small splinter group. Over the next few months he became something of a local attraction.[69]

There is very little about the political turmoil in Goebbels's "memory pages," and neither Hitler nor the DAP is mentioned at all. But he does refer to the outrage among the student body in January 1920 when Anton Arco-Valley—the assassin of Kurt Eisner, leader of the Munich revolution of November 1918—was sentenced to death (the very next day the government commuted his sentence to life imprisonment). There was uproar at the University of Munich.[70]

As the Munich city council had banned non-Bavarian students from moving to the university, Goebbels did not register with the police—normally a requirement—or with the university. Instead, his friend Richard signed him up for lecture courses in Freiburg. His first "argument" with Anka occurred after she had spent a few days in the mountains with friends, a trip from which for obvious reasons he was excluded.[71] In his memoirs he recalled visits to the theater and the opera. Performances included *Carmen, The Flying Dutchman, Siegfried, Elektra,* and *Der Freischütz.* He saw the conductor Bruno Walter as well as the Munich premiere of Strauss's opera *Die Frau ohne Schatten.* At the theaters, apart from classics like *Amphitryon, Antigone,* and *Don Carlos,* he mostly saw modern pieces, such as Walter Hasenclever's *Der Sohn* (The Son); works by Strindberg, Ibsen, and Gustav Meyrink; *Das Gelübde* (The Vow), by Heinrich Lautensack; Hermann Bahr's *Der Unmensch* (The Brute); and *Gas,* by Georg Kaiser. He was quite overwhelmed by it all: "Chaos inside me. Fermentation. Unconscious clarifying [process]." A performance of Tolstoy's last play, *A Light Shines in Darkness,* impressed him particularly. Of this time he later wrote, "Socialism. Spreading only slowly. Social sympathy. Expressionism. Not yet pure and clarified."[72]

He discussed with the Munich literature specialist Arthur Kutscher the possibility of a doctoral thesis on the subject of mime but soon rated the prospects of success for this project—about which he corresponded with Kutscher a few weeks later—as "bleak."[73] He was experiencing financial difficulties once more. He was forced to sell his suits and his watch. Anka subsidized him by pawning her gold watch. By this time he was practically living off her, in any case.[74] Once again he had doubts about his Catholicism and turned for help to his father, who in a long letter of November 1919 offered Joseph comfort and advice, trying to reassure his distraught son: Crises of faith were quite normal among young people; prayer and the sacraments would see him through it. He reminded Joseph of his sister Elisabeth's death in 1915, when the whole family had been helped by praying together. He would not cast him out (as the son had feared he might) even if he turned away from the church, but he had to ask him two questions: Did he mean to write anything incompatible with the Catholic religion, and did he intend to take up work to which the same applied? If this were not the case, then everything would fall back into place again. Goebbels was grateful for this understanding reply, which shows, however, how far he had moved away from the petit bourgeois Catholic milieu of his parents.[75]

His relationship with Anka suffered several crises, but the two always became reconciled again and then felt "closer to each other than before." There were marriage plans, which bumped up against what Goebbels contemptuously referred to as "conventionalities."[76] He asked accusingly in a letter to Anka: "Have other people got a right to despise me and pour shame and disgrace on me because I love you to the point of insanity?"[77] He was now working on a social drama called *The Struggle of the Working Class*. But in Munich he was too restless to finish the manuscript.[78]

At the end of the semester he went home: His brother Hans, a released prisoner of war, had returned as well. Hans brought with him "hatred and aggressive thoughts." For his part, Goebbels records: "Avid reading. Tolstoy, Dostoyevsky, revolution in me. [. . .] Russia."[79] In a letter to Anka he commented on the "sensational news from Berlin": Elements of the extreme right under Wolfgang Kapp had mounted a coup attempt. The "putsch" failed after a few days, but the ultimate outcome was still unclear. Goebbels was skeptical, believing that it was questionable whether "a right-wing government is good for us at this moment." He was going to wait and see how things worked out.[80] Traveling through the Ruhr, Anka was caught unawares by the Kapp putsch and the workers' revolt that followed it: "Red revolution in the Ruhr. She's learning about terror there. I am enthusiastic from afar." It appears that his enthusiasm concerned the revolutionaries' terror, not the comparable terrorism the Free Corps deployed to suppress them.

In this unruly time Goebbels applied for a job as tutor on an estate in Holland as well as one "in East Prussia," but to no avail.[81] Otherwise, his literary work was productive. His new play was a general indictment of the "tainted" and "crumbling" world in which a workers' revolt would sow "the seed"—the play's title—for the "generation that is coming of age, strong and beautiful, that of the new man."[82]

In April, a letter to Anka included a lengthy passage about a question "that is still unresolved between us: the question of communism." It was "rotten and stultifying that a world of so and so many million people is dominated by a single caste, which has the power to lead these millions towards life or death according to its whim. [. . .] This capitalism has learned nothing." It was responsible for the fact that "people with the most brilliant intellectual gifts sink into poverty and go to ruin."[83]

His reading, according to his own report, included intensive engagement with secondary literature on German studies as well as Tolstoy, Goethe, Maeterlinck, Lessing, George, Kālidāsa, Cervantes, Wedekind, Kleist, Hölderlin, and Ibsen. However, there were also Hans Sachs and the *Nibelungenlied*, the Early New High German writer Johann Baptist Fischer, German-speaking authors of the seventeenth and eighteenth centuries, including Spee von Langenfeld, Abraham a Sancta Clara, Heinrich Wilhelm von Gerstenberg, Martin Opitz, Friedrich von Logau, and Paul Fleming as well as the Romantic writer Wilhelm Heinrich Wackenroder. It looked as though he had decided to concentrate on working for his examination.[84]

At Whitsun he met Anka again. She "indignantly" rejected his latest work, *Die Saat,* which had been "enthusiastically" received by his friend Richard.[85] Finally he learned from one of Anka's letters that Theo Geitmann, a friend from Rheydt about whom he had long harbored certain suspicions,[86] had been making advances to her: "Theo has been treacherous. Loves her." Goebbels and Anka met in Karlsruhe, where she also told him about a certain "Herr Mumme." The break came after he—totally misunderstanding the situation—magnanimously proposed that they should get engaged.[87] Surprisingly, there was a reconciliation in Heidelberg, which clearly did not reassure Goebbels. Anka promised once more to be faithful, and they decided to spend the next semester together.

Goebbels simply refused to recognize that she was taking the relationship much less seriously than he was. He spent the holidays in Rheydt, while she was with her parents in the Ruhr. She did not keep his rival, "Herr Mumme in Recklinghausen," at bay.[88] Goebbels composed a farewell letter to Anka; Without her, he would go to pieces: "Love is killing me. If I had you here now, I would grab you and force you to love me, if only for a moment, and then I would kill you. Yes, you can laugh about this, but you know I'm capable of it."[89]

He did contemplate suicide. He wrote a will on October 1, naming his brother Hans as his "literary custodian" and his father as executor. His clothes were to be sold and the proceeds put toward paying off his debts. His brothers should each choose five of his books for themselves, and the rest should be sold, with the income to go to his sister. He also bequeathed her the rest of his few possessions—for example, his alarm clock and his toiletry articles. "I am taking my leave of this world and from all those who have behaved well or ill towards me," he wrote. "I am glad to depart from my life, which for me has been nothing but hell."[90] This theatrical announcement was as far as he went.

For the winter semester he returned to Heidelberg. Contrary to their agreement, he did not find Anka there. His friend Richard tracked her down in Munich, where he spotted her sitting in a café with Mumme. Goebbels went to Munich. He discovered her address but then found that she had left for Freiburg—with her "fiancé," as he was informed. In a desperate state, he returned to Heidelberg. There was a final exchange of letters.[91] On her behalf, Anka's fiancé, Mumme, wrote to request the return of her letters and presents. Goebbels replied with a "categorical" refusal.[92]

GRADUATION WITH A
DOCTORATE BUT FAILED AUTHORSHIP

Back in Heidelberg, Goebbels worked toward his doctorate. His reading matter, Oswald Spengler's *The Decline of the West*, was not calculated to lift his mood. On the contrary, this grand attempt to situate the decline of Europe within a universal history of the rise and fall of the great cultures induced "pessimism" and "despair" in him. Beset by such dark thoughts, he plunged into work on his doctoral dissertation, which he wrote in four months in Rheydt after the end of his Heidelberg semester.[93]

He had originally hoped to write his thesis under the well-known Heidelberg literary historian Friedrich Gundolf. He had reported to Anka that his reception by the great man at the beginning of June had been "extrordinarily kind" and that the professor had given him valuable advice.[94] It did not worry Goebbels that Gundolf was a Jew. The literature expert, who belonged to the elite group around the poet Stefan George, was working at the time on the posthumous reputation of a great historical figure, tracing the influence of Julius Caesar in the history of European literature. Perhaps Gundolf's feeling for historical greatness attracted Goebbels, who in his own mind had already begun his quest for a leader.[95] But Gundolf, who had been relieved of teaching and examining duties, directed Goebbels to his colleague, the associate professor Max von Waldberg. That Goebbels did not see this as an affront is attested by his appreciative comments on Gundolf in a public address he delivered months later.[96] He followed Gundolf's advice and attended Waldberg's seminar, where he gave a presentation and submitted a seminar paper.[97]

At Waldberg's suggestion, Goebbels took the dramatic work of the largely unknown Romantic Wilhelm von Schütz as his dissertation

topic. The thesis, over two hundred pages in length and never published, takes the form of an overview of Schütz's works.[98] Most interesting is the preface, which begins with a quotation from Dostoyevsky,
and then goes on—almost in a kind of declamation—to compare the
Romantic period with "the decade in which we are now living."
Goebbels sees the parallels most strongly in cultural life: "Now as
then, a shallow Enlightenment is spreading, finding its aim and its
purpose in a trite, uninspired atheism. But it is meeting resistance
from a younger generation of God-seekers, mystics, romantics. All
these little people, the smallest, are crying out for leaders, but no
great man appears who will embrace them all."

After submitting his thesis in Heidelberg, Goebbels prepared intensively for the oral examination. He passed in November with a
grade of *rite superato*, which meant that his academic performance
was judged no more than average. Nonetheless, he was now Doctor
of Philosophy Joseph Goebbels.[99] However, for Waldberg, supervising a student who was later to become so prominent brought no returns. Because of his Jewish origins he was obliged to retire in 1933,
and in 1935 his license to teach was revoked. When Goebbels was
being honored with great pomp at the University of Heidelberg in
1942, on the twentieth anniversary of his doctoral examination, there
was no mention of Waldberg, who had died in 1938.[100]

Back in Rheydt, Goebbels once again earned his living by private
tutoring. Early in 1922, however, he succeeded in placing a series of
articles in the local newspaper, the *Westdeutsche Landeszeitung*. The
series, which according to Goebbels caused "a great sensation" and
brought him "enemies in the Rheydt press,"[101] offered him the opportunity to express his deep hatred of prevailing cultural activities and
to give full vent to his feelings about the zeitgeist.

In his first article Goebbels proclaimed briefly and succinctly that
"the German materialism and worship of Mammon that we see before us now in unadulterated form [. . .] are the main cause of the
ruination of our German soul."[102] Goebbels then indulged in an
all-encompassing critique of modern culture and the prevailing cultural tendencies. The main problem of modern culture was the "lack
of a solid, secure sense of style." What was missing above all was "a
great artistic individual who bears this style in himself, [. . .] the
young hothead who will take from the troubles of our time his titanic
'in tyrannos' and hurl it into the world."

The second article, which bore the ambitious title "On the Meaning of Our Time,"[103] contained a passage that the contemporary reader could easily decode as an anti-Semitic polemic: "We pay homage to an internationalism that is opposed to our national character and that alien elements have extolled as the only chance of rescue." His polemic equally targeted enthusiasm about the "Russian spirit" or "the Indian personality." He was also critical of Spengler's book: *The Decline of the West* had only served to reinforce the dominant underlying pessimism, whereas what was needed was, wrote Goebbels with youthful emotion, "books that comforted, raised the spirits, brought to mind those things that were eternal." In this sense, in his next contribution, "The True National Character," he put forward his reflections on "the German soul," which he characterized as "Faustian."[104] The series culminated in a call "for the education of a new public," a kind of affront to the audience: "In many ways these nice art lovers are damned similar to our pack of racketeers and war profiteers."[105]

This article series, with its dogmatic judgments and emotionally charged notions of world improvement, demonstrates one thing above all: the tendency to overestimate oneself, to which the unemployed and unsuccessful author Joseph Goebbels had obviously succumbed in the act of writing. Completely carried away by the opportunity to present himself to the educated bourgeoisie of Rheydt and its surroundings, he even included personal elements. Thus in his last article[106] he described in detail, with a characteristic mixture of retrospective self-pity and self-love, his mood on a lonely Christmas Eve in Munich in 1919. He did not neglect to make frequent references to his years of suffering as a student: Anyone "who had struggled in the same way" would know what "serious academic youth had accomplished in their silent, heroically self-denying struggle" over the previous five years.[107]

In the autumn he made a short guest appearance, based on a trainee contract, as an art critic in the *Landeszeitung*. Losing this position as soon as he did—allegedly because of an internal reorganization—may also have contributed to the rather condescending way in which he commented on the intellectual debates taking place in this provincial town. On the subject of a lecture at the "Society for Foundational Philosophy," for instance, he wrote that the discussion that followed the talk had shown once again "how unprofitable, on the whole, such exchanges are, between a speaker the audience hardly knows and an audience the speaker does not know at all."[108]

That autumn he was also offered the chance to give a talk on "Excerpts from Contemporary German Literature." He used it to settle his score with postwar literature in general ("one pathetic scribbler trying to outdo another") but dealt particularly harshly with the worst excesses of Expressionism, although he did not condemn the movement as a whole. He devoted some space once more to Spengler, taking strong exception to the prevailing "cultural pessimism" reading of Spengler (by which he himself had initially been infected). Goebbels now tended, he confided to his listeners, to read Spengler's study of the rise, growth, and decline of the great world cultures as a "source of consolation, strength, and encouragement." He regarded Spengler's assessment of Russia as the bearer of high culture in the millennium to come as "the magic word," confirming his own positive verdict on the events in Russia.[109]

Toward the end of the year, Goebbels endeavored to establish a drama group in Rheydt within the framework of the *Bühnenvolksbund* (Popular Theater League) that existed throughout the country. It was an attempt to "renew the theater in the spirit of the German-Christian people," founded in opposition to the socialist *Freie Volksbühne* (Free People's Theater).[110]

In Rheydt, meanwhile, Goebbels had met the young schoolteacher Else Janke.[111] What he initially described as a "quiet, platonic love" gradually developed from the summer of 1922 onward into a fully fledged love affair. It can be inferred from what he recalled about 1924 and the surviving correspondence that the relationship was not always harmonious. They argued, for example, because Else "did not want to acknowledge our relationship in public"; and later there was a "falling-out over my foot complaint." She told him her mother was Jewish, a revelation recorded in his words as: "She has confessed her parentage to me. Since then, the first enchantment ruined."[112]

This passage indicates Goebbels's growing anti-Semitism. Up to this point he had not been particularly interested in "the Jewish question." In February 1919, in connection with a critical appreciation of Heinrich Heine in a history of German literature, he had written to Anka: "You know I don't particularly like this exaggerated anti-Semitism. [. . .] I can't say that the Jews are my best friends, but I believe you cannot rid the world of them through cursing and polemics or even through pogroms, and even if you could, it would be demeaning and beneath human dignity."[113] The formulation "exaggerated anti-Semitism" of course carried the implication that a "normal" anti-Jewish attitude was justified. Occasional remarks suggest that Goebbels was prone to a casual, everyday anti-Semitism, but that "the Jewish question" did not occupy a central position in his worldview.[114] Yet now, early in 1923, as the crisis of the German Reich deepened, he was among the many who blamed "the Jews" for the impending catastrophe.[115]

UNBEARABLE DRUDGERY

On January 2, 1923, Goebbels took a job in a bank. Else had strongly urged him to take this step;[116] the doctor of philosophy, as he now was, seemed to have few other professional prospects. But his dislike of this new occupation set in quickly and grew steadily. In the meantime, chaos erupted around him. The French army marched into the Ruhr in January, since the German government had ceased to pay reparations. The Reich government called on the German people to pursue passive resistance, which led to the breakdown of public life in the region, one result among many being that the trains were no longer running, which meant that Goebbels could not get to Rheydt. He spent a few "sweet hours" with Else, who constantly tried in her letters to lift him out of his depression,[117] but there were always heated arguments as well.[118]

Goebbels desperately sought a direction, as he makes clear in his "memory pages," written in 1924: "My vision clarified by necessity. Loathing for the bank and my job. [. . .] The Jews. I am thinking about the money problem."[119] He went to an opera conducted by Otto Klemperer: "The Jewish question in art. Gundolf. Intellectual clarification. Bavaria. Hitler." It is doubtful that in 1923, in the light of his "intellectual clarification," he had already settled on Hitler. Since he only began to gravitate toward National Socialism in the course of 1924, this seems more likely to be a retrospective smoothing out of his biography. During this period he read Thomas and Heinrich Mann. Dostoyevsky once again evoked the strongest emotional response in him. Describing his mood after reading *The Idiot,* he wrote,

"Revolution in me" but also "Pessimism about everything." On Richard Wagner, he noted: "Turning away from internationalism." His reading of Houston Stewart Chamberlain's *Grundlagen des 19. Jahrhunderts* (Foundations of the Nineteenth Century) took him back to "the Jewish question." As an interim result of his quest for a solid ideological standpoint he finally noted: "Communism. Jewry. I am a German communist."[120] We have seen that these notes were written in 1924, and it is altogether likely, and correlates with his somewhat playful literary approach to his biography, that he transposed the politicization he was experiencing at this later date onto the crisis year of 1923.[121]

Affected by the crisis and his increasingly depressed mood, he began to detest his bank job more and more.[122] In June he succeeded in publishing in the *Kölner Tageblatt*, a newspaper regarded as liberal, a lengthy article in which he expatiated on the "fiasco of modern German literature." Goebbels once again used the opportunity to mount a wide-ranging attack on Impressionism and Expressionism as well as various other tendencies of wartime and postwar literature: "The serious talents, struggling tirelessly for the spirit of the new age, are ignored or shouted down."[123]

In the summer he composed something like a confessional account of his life. It was titled "From My Diary," and it seems to have been meant for Else: a thirty-two-page mixture of remarks about his failed life, aphorisms, and poems. This collection expressed above all his depression, which was particularly marked at this time. Among other things, he raged against the misery caused by passive resistance in the Ruhr and against the financial manipulators (not least in his own bank) who were profiting from the crisis.[124] Neither this collection nor his article suggests that he had drawn any firm political conclusions from his negative assessment of the contemporary situation. Else was extremely concerned about him at this time, writing: "Your soul is so sensitive, perhaps too sensitive for this rough time, and so easily crushed and discouraged by this severe distress."[125]

Reporting himself sick, he went off in August 1923 with Else to the coast.[126] But the mood of the couple was constantly spoiled by permanent money worries and increasing tensions. On the North Sea island of Baltrum, news reached him of the death of his close friend Richard Flisges in an industrial accident. Goebbels decided to cancel the vacation.[127] At the end of the year he published an obituary for his friend in the *Rheydter Zeitung.*[128]

Back in the Rhineland, he received his dismissal notice from the bank. Although various literary projects were taking shape in his mind, he went looking for employment. He found none.[129] Finally he relinquished his room in Cologne and, following his parents' advice, moved back to Rheydt.[130] His relationship with Else became less tense, but it was hardly passionate: "Else is my comrade. Eros only now and then." Occasionally he resorted to alcohol to drown his own personal sorrows as well as consternation over recent political and economic events.[131] It was in these circumstances that he began keeping the diary that Else had given him.

CHAPTER 2

"Spare the Rod and Spoil the Child"

Goebbels's Path to National Socialism

Dr. Joseph Goebbels about 1922. The unsuccessful writer and occasional journalist failed to make an impression on the bourgeois intelligentsia. Suffering from depression, he set out on an existential quest for salvation, which he eventually came to believe he had found, not in religion or in cultural revolution but in the politics of the *völkisch* movement.

Goebbels's diaries in the autumn and winter of 1923–24 convey a picture of a man lacking direction, isolated from others, internally conflicted, even despairing, and trying to use the daily entries as a way of bringing his personal crisis under control. The diary was his "best friend," he wrote. "I can confide everything to it. There's nobody else I can tell all this."[1]

In his first diary entry, on October 17, 1923, Goebbels addressed Else directly: "My dear, kind love! You raise me up and give me new courage when despair threatens. I just cannot get my mind around how much I owe you." There follows a kind of snapshot of Rheydt, in those days a town in the occupied Rhineland: "What a miserable experience it is to walk through the town today. There are groups of unemployed people standing on every corner, debating and speculating. It's a time for laughing and for crying." It "looked as though things were moving toward the right," but "it would be completely wrong to see this swing to the right as the non plus ultra of political development." We were on the verge of great developments in world history, he thought, but not everybody was able to recognize them. It was "the poet who is needed today, not the academic; for while the former has insight, the latter merely sees. The academic only knows how to administer small sedatives for the European sickness, whereas the poet can point out the path that leads to great developments."

But where were the poets who were up to the task? "Our so-called writers are nothing but bunglers, intellectual snobs, would-be witty aesthetes and coffee-house heroes. [. . .] No one has found the cry from the heart that expresses the despair of every German." He wished there was just one person "who could once more bring forth an 'in tyrannos.'" Of all European countries, he confessed, he held "holy Russia" in the "deepest respect." This positively rhapsodic veneration of Russia was above all the result of his intensive reading of Russian literature, particularly Dostoyevsky, to whom he had recently returned. The present day in Russia, he wrote, "is just the froth on the surface, the real cleansing liquid lies deeper."

After further dark thoughts, he drew up "ten commandments" designed to snap him out of his mood of depression:

1. *Be good to everybody, especially to mother, father and Else [. . .].*
2. *Do not talk much, think a lot.*
3. *Be alone often.*
4. *Try to make your peace with life.*
5. *Get up at 8 and go to bed at 10.*
6. *Read and write the bitterness out of your soul.*
7. *Take plenty of long walks, especially alone.*
8. *Do not neglect your body.*

9. *Try to come to terms with God.*
10. *Do not despair.*

LONGING FOR "SALVATION"

A few days after this entry, Goebbels's hometown of Rheydt became
the scene of a bloody political clash. On October 21 separatist groups
who enjoyed the support of the French and Belgian occupying powers staged a coup aimed at bringing about an independent Rhenish
state.[2] In Aachen, armed separatists successfully stormed the town
hall, where they proclaimed a "Free Rhineland." For a few hours, they
also managed to occupy the town hall of nearby Mönchengladbach.[3]
The next day the unrest spread to Rheydt. Separatists gathered in the
town, while armed townsfolk flocked together to avert the putsch.[4]
Goebbels witnessed a civil war scenario: "The rabble drives through
the town in stolen cars proclaiming the Free Rhenish Republic. In
Gladbach there are many dead and wounded. In Rheydt people are
forming a 'civil self-defense force' against the separatists." The police
and the self-defense group were preparing to protect the town hall.
Disgusted, Goebbels recorded: "They inspect the weapons, go around
showing them off, and imagine heroic scenes of battle. They talk
about fatalities as casually as you might mention margarine."[5]

The next day, with the attack warded off, the mob exacted their
revenge on the separatists: "They're taking action like vandals against
the autonomists," noted Goebbels, describing the destruction of furniture and household goods. "No one seems to have any restraint.
Vox populi—vox diaboli." Goebbels saw himself as a neutral observer, as a writer living in troubled times able to put his unique impressions to literary use: "I'm beginning to see all this just as material
that is operating upon my inner self. I am the center, and everything
revolves around me."[6]

He found his relationship with Else increasingly problematic. At
this time he often thought "about the Jewish question," and he wrote
that she, like others, was unable to deny her "Jewish blood": There
was something "powerfully destructive" in her character, especially
in the "area of intellect," although this was not particularly overt,
since "her intellect had not yet ripened to fruition." It was not only in

this respect that Else suffered from a comparison with Anka: The latter had been far more generous in her gifts to him than Else: "indiscriminate, without hesitation, just for the pure pleasure of giving."[7]

Else was not prepared to suffer in silence his lack of respect and regard for her; she wrote to tell him that she felt neglected and that his views on the "race question" might be an "obstacle to our future lives together." For she was "firmly convinced that in this respect your thinking is quite definitely exaggerated, so that you tend to interpret all utterances in that sense."[8] It was *her* lack of confidence in their future partnership that was substantially responsible for the breakup that soon followed, whereas his diary entries give the impression that *he* was the one plagued by doubts about whether she was right for him. As so often with Goebbels, however, the break was soon followed by reconciliation.[9] He confessed to himself that Else was simply "so dear and so good that I can't give her up."[10] At the end of the year he wrote, "I love Else and feel myself more deeply connected to her since she gave herself to me." But then his dreams and his feelings reverted to Anka, who, he was convinced at the time, would always remain the greatest love of his life.[11]

In this period Goebbels was once more racked by a profound crisis of faith. In his diary he lamented the loss of "that tremendous corpus of belief that once determined my actions and thinking"; since he had lost his faith he was "sarcastic, ironic, skeptical, prone to relativism" and had forfeited "a huge part of my momentum and my drive."

However, there were two things he still believed in: "the ultimate victory of the truth and myself." He swore to himself that he would hold on to this belief at all costs: He would draw from it "all my strength and all my goodness." And then this noteworthy sentence: "It doesn't matter what we believe in, as long as we believe." He would go on at other points to find a variety of ways of expressing this idea, such as "Every thought is right, you just have to argue it convincingly," or "Every time has its idea, and in every time the idea is right."[12] There is no doubt that Goebbels was urgently seeking an ideology to which he could commit himself, but it would be wrong to take such maxims to mean that in this phase of his life he was ready to subscribe to *any* idea. His intellectual shift toward right-wing radicalism had already gone too far for that—possibly further than he himself was aware.

In any case, he told himself in October 1923, he would "soon have to part company with my God."[13] He wrestled constantly with his religion in these months, but he always returned to the conviction that Christian belief would not fail to bring him the "redemption" for which he so desperately longed.[14]

At the beginning of November, during his temporary break with Else, he started working on the drama "Prometheus," material that had preoccupied him for years and that he was now determined to master.[15] He worked at the writing so frenetically[16] that by November 12 he had finished the play "apart from the last act."[17] He handed the completed manuscript over to Else on November 18.[18] Only fragments of the text have survived, but its subject matter is quite clear: Prometheus, whose origins are half-titanic (that is, divine) and half-human, rebels against the gods of Olympus.[19]

Immersed in his work on "Prometheus," he merely noted from the sidelines the Munich putsch staged by the National Socialists, writing laconically and without great sympathy: "Putsch by nationalists in Munich. Once again Ludendorff just happened to go missing."[20] He was as skeptical as ever about any shift to the right in politics.[21] But only a few days after the putsch, he made some caustic anti-Semitic remarks in his diary in connection with two one-act plays by Curt Goetz he had seen in Rheydt. His verdict on the evening ran: "All in all Jewish claptrap, sneering about the downfall," and then went on to generalize: "The Jews are the poison that is destroying the body of Europe." Would he have been prepared to moderate his declamatory pronouncement on Jewish cultural subversion if he had known that the Curt Goetz whose plays had so inflamed him was *not* a Jew?

A new literary project, entitled "The Wanderer," was again completed very quickly, between November 14 and 28.[22] The plot chimed with his mood of depression and was a further attempt to achieve "redemption": "Christ comes back as a wanderer on earth and accompanies the writer visiting suffering mankind. A kind of dance of death."[23] After finishing the manuscript he wrote that in "The Wanderer" he was "trying depict the sick Europe of today. I have shown the only path to salvation and must recognize with pain and bitterness that this path will never be taken."[24] He offered "The Wanderer" to the Cologne Schauspielhaus and "Prometheus" to the Stadttheater in Düsseldorf.[25] Neither venue was interested. His efforts to place the dramas in Frankfurt and Duisburg were equally unsuccessful.[26]

In mid-December he attended a lecture on Vincent van Gogh, which he found "deeply enjoyable." He wrote that van Gogh was "one of the most modern men in new art, a God-seeker, a Christ-person." He perceived similarities to Dostoyevsky and to his own "Wanderer": "All modern artists—I'm not talking here about half-hearted snobs and epigones—are to a greater or lesser degree teachers, preachers, fanatics, prophets, to a greater or lesser degree insane—like all of us who have active minds." However: "We younger people are being ignored. Perhaps a later generation will be able to capitalize on our broken hearts. How unutterably heavy is the sorrow of the seers!"[27] These lines express his hope that the "redemption" he so fervently sought might arise out of a complete cultural revolution along Christian-socialist lines—and Goebbels was obviously convinced that he was destined to play a prominent role in such an upheaval, as a "prophet" or "seer." He went even further when he noted during the Christmas period: "I can feel myself driven toward the whole, toward men and mankind. If God gives me a long enough lease of life, I shall be a redeemer. Whether for myself, for one or two, or for a whole people, it's all the same. I must become mature enough for the mission."[28]

Craving "redemption," Goebbels now saw himself as the redeemer and no longer just speculated about the godlike nature of the artist[29] but boldly stated: "If God has made me in his image, then I am God like him."[30] Quite clearly he thought he felt a "divine spark" within him, and it seems that he flirted with gnostic speculations (according to which man is able to escape the bonds of his corporeal being and move closer to the Godhead). In the ranks of the *völkisch* (nationalist/racist) movement toward which he was now slowly gravitating, he was by no means alone in this respect.[31] There was a reason for his preoccupation over many years with his "Prometheus problem," as he called it; his preoccupation, that is to say, with a figure who—in his own words—was "half god and half human" and rebelled against the gods in heaven.[32] While indulging in such thoughts, he had nonetheless not relinquished his hope of redemption through religion: "I'll stay calm and await the redeemer," he wrote on January 5, 1924.

Completely wrapped up in his metaphysical speculations, he adopted a scornful view of politics. "To practice politics," he wrote in his diary in January, "is to enchain the spirit, to know when to speak and when to be silent, to lie for the greater good: My God, what a dreadful business."[33] Once more he enjoyed the role of the detached observer disgusted by the times: "Demonstrators are parading through the streets. [...] Who is to blame for all this confusion, all this barbarism? Why can't we settle our differences? Why not all pull together, since the country—in fact, all of Europe—is on its knees?"[34]

It is not the political events of the time that his diary entries predominantly reflect in these months but his own artistic and emotional development. Goebbels was preoccupied by religious-philosophical questions and aesthetic matters and with the concerts he attended regularly over the winter of 1923–24.[35] And he made extensive notes on his reading: the great Russian authors who inspired him, especially Dostoyevsky, the "great soul of Russia";[36] Tolstoy, whose *The Cossacks* and *War and Peace* particularly impressed him;[37] and Gogol, although he thought *Dead Souls* was somewhat "infected by western Europe."[38] Aside from these authors, he mainly read Scandinavian writers: He mentions in particular Selma Lagerlöf's homespun tales;[39] Knut Hamsun, whose novel *The Women at the Pump* now seemed very dated,[40] although Goebbels had clearly read him with profit in earlier years; and Strindberg, to whom his response was mixed.[41]

He approved of naturalistic plays like Max Halbe's *Der Strom* (The River) and Gerhart Hauptmann's *Biberpelz* (The Beaver Coat).[42] He had no time for contemporary German literature. Thomas Mann, whose *Buddenbrooks* he had once admired, now seemed to him a "decadent writer,"[43] and he dismissed the novel *Königliche Hoheit* (Royal Highness) as "cold fish literature."[44] *Nebeneinander* (Side by Side), a drama by the most important German Expressionist playwright, Georg Kaiser, betokening that author's transition to the hard-edged "New Objectivity" movement of the postwar era, was comprehensively demolished in the diary.[45] However, he liked Hermann Hesse. In Hesse's novels *Unterm Rad* (Beneath the Wheel) and *Peter Camenzind,* both dealing with the difficulties experienced by highly gifted young people in finding their place in the world, he found parallels with his own youth.[46]

When it came to pictorial art, he was slightly more receptive to contemporary work. It is true that at exhibitions he tended to fulminate against the dilettantism of modern art, but this did not prevent him from enthusing about a series of Expressionists. He still admired van Gogh, Emil Nolde, and Ernst Barlach.[47]

He found the atmosphere in the family home increasingly oppressive. He wanted to get away, he confessed in late December: "If only I knew where to!" At home he was "the reprobate, [...] the renegade, the apostate, the outlaw, the atheist, the revolutionary." He was "the only one who can't do anything, whose advice is never wanted, whose opinion isn't worth listening to. It's driving me crazy!"[48]

In February he penned a thumbnail sketch of his parents: His mother was described as "open-hearted and good. She can't help loving. [...] My mother is a delightful spendthrift, with everything, whether it be money or the pure goodness of her heart." "The old man" was "a tightwad, but he meant well"; he was "a pedant, small-minded and limited," "a born (dusty) old jurist." It always came down to the wretched subject of money: "For him, money is the thing-in-itself. Money sometimes makes him into a petty domestic despot. [...] He hasn't got a clue about me. Mother has the right instinct where I'm concerned. Why wouldn't she have? I owe the best part of me to her!"[49]

Everything combined to paint a dismal picture: the narrow confines of the house, the lack of recognition, his dissatisfaction over his relationship with Else, his hopelessness concerning his failure as an artist as well as the prevailing conditions of life in postwar Germany, together with his doubts about religion, his despairing search for "redemption," his depression, and his loneliness.

On February 10 his diary refers to a new project: a "novel in diary form," to which he gave the provisional title "Quiet Flames."[50] These reflections eventually produced the diary-style novel "Michel Voormann," a reworking of the autobiographical material he had already written up in 1919. He started at the end of February and completed the work in a week. He worked so intensively that, contrary to his usual practice, he made only brief entries in his diary during this time.[51]

The figure of Michael Voormann is autobiographically based, as in the 1919 novel, but now also bears some of the characteristics of Goebbels's late friend Richard Flisges.[52] Michael returns from the war; takes up studying, though with no great aspirations; falls in love with a fellow student, clearly based on Anka; writes a play about Jesus Christ; loses his lover; and finds "redemption" in hard work in the mines, where an accident eventually costs him his life. His legacy, so the message runs, is to have lived out an exemplary synthesis between working with the hands and with the head, between the working class and the bourgeoisie; his self-sacrificial death; his personal redemption—all of it a precondition for collective salvation, for the emergence of a new and better world.[53] The key statement of the work is "when I redeem myself, I am also the redeemer of mankind."[54] This perspective seems to counterbalance the tragedy of the hero's individual death.

When Goebbels finished the manuscript on March 10, he was tired and apathetic: "I don't feel like doing anything at all."

THE TURN TO POLITICS

In this phase of acute exhaustion early in 1924, Goebbels turned back to the latest political developments. In Munich the trial of the participants in the failed putsch of November 9 had begun. It was the ringleader who particularly aroused his interest, as shown by the first relevant diary entry, on March 13: "I am thinking about Hitler and the National Socialist movement and will obviously have to go on doing so for some time. Socialism and Christ. Ethical foundations. Away from paralyzing materialism. Back to devotion and to God!" The idea that the National Socialists were primarily seekers after God shows how deeply preoccupied he was with religious questions and how far these questions had superimposed themselves on his grasp of politics.

For all his enthusiasm, he had his reservations: "But the Munich people want a fight, not reconciliation, perhaps because they feel that in a general settlement they would lose out. But I haven't given up on it yet." In the next few days his thoughts were very much taken up with Hitler and his "movement."[55] At first his doubts had the upper hand: "The objective may be right, but I am not convinced about the methods. And the Christianity of these people has practically nothing to do with Christ himself." But he also noted, "What is liberating about Hitler is the way he commits himself as a truly upright and honest personality. That is so rare in a world dominated by party interests."[56]

In the end it was not so much the content of Hitler's mind that led to Goebbels's decision to join him as his charisma—all the more alluring for Goebbels because he identified a great many correspondences between Hitler and the protagonist of his autobiographical novel:

> Hitler is an enthusiastic idealist. A man who will bring new belief to the Germans. I'm reading his speech, letting myself be carried away by him and up to the stars. The route runs from the brain to the heart. I keep on coming across the basic motif of "Michael Voormann": "As a Christian, I am not obliged to let myself be cheated." [. . .] Nationalist and socialist consciousness. Away from materialism. New fervor, complete devotion to the one great thing, the Fatherland, Germany. We always ask about the way. But here is a will. He'll find a way, all right.[57]

What he admired about Hitler was not just his "will," "fervor," "devotion," and "belief"; it was also his "wonderful élan," "verve," "enthusiasm," and "German soul." Goebbels at last "once more heard notes coming from the heart."[58] Even if what first drew him was Hitler's personality, while he either misunderstood Nazi ideas or thought them to be secondary—nonetheless, Goebbels's embracing of National Socialism was certainly not just due to chance or the emotional pull of the Munich firebrand.

Goebbels's nationalistic outlook had become ever more firmly entrenched in the preceding years, not least because of the conduct of the Belgian and French occupation. The emotional invocation of "mankind" that he had so ardently represented as recently as the "Michael" manuscript was gradually giving way to his unconditional identification with a threatened nation. The process was not the product of rational political insight but above all of the yearning for salvation and for fusion with a greater whole. "Fatherland! Germany!" he wrote in his diary in April 1924. "I love you like a mother and a lover!"[59]

Furthermore, Goebbels subscribed to resentful anti-Semitic notions that served as a kind of negative pole to his nationalistic ideas, vague as these were. He lamented the general cultural decline but had little time for democracy and modern tendencies in art and culture. However, neither could he stomach the current social inequities, and he even expressed some sympathy with communism. His enthusiasm for Hitler as a political "Führer" corresponded to messianic sentiments common on the right (we shall return to this theme). His political worldview therefore already bore many of the hallmarks of the "New Right" after the Great War. Accordingly, it is highly improbable that if a political leader of the left had happened to cross his path in the spring of 1924 he would have attached himself so enthusiastically to him and to his ideas. In his burgeoning enthusiasm for National Socialism, Goebbels was not alone in the lower-middle-class milieu to which he belonged. Referring to the Reichstag elections scheduled for May 4, he remarked: "All the young people I know are going to vote National Socialist."[60] His maxim of a few months earlier, that it "does not matter what we believe in, as long as we believe," cannot therefore be read as proof that Goebbels was a thoroughgoing relativist or opportunist at this time.

While his interest in Hitler was growing stronger, his attitude to Else was becoming more critical: She was a "mood-killer"; she had "no style, no class, no system." She was a "human dumpling"; he could not hold a conversation with her, and no doubt she felt the same about him.[61] "Else is good, but I don't love her anymore. She is a good friend, nothing more," he wrote. They would "just have to split up."[62] Then he felt sorry for her; after all, the "curse of Jewish blood" lay upon her.[63]

After an argument with Else he hoped finally to be "free of all racial attachments. How often the Jewish part of Else's nature has pained and depressed me." He thought that Else's sister Trude was "a typical Jewish girl who combines in herself in concentrated form all the physical and mental characteristics of her mother's race." It was clear to him, at least: "A bastardized race becomes sterile and must go under. I can't have a hand in that!!!"[64] Once again, though, he wavered: "And yet I love her more than I thought. But I'm becoming more firmly convinced all the time that we must not stay together." Surely making a "radical break was the only cure," but he could not bring himself to do so.[65]

During these months he made various efforts to reenter the world of work. In February 1924 he applied to the newspaper publisher Rudolf Mosse in Berlin. He claimed to "have studied modern theater and press history" and said he was "looking for an appropriate position, suited to my knowledge and abilities, in my actual field of newspapers and publishing."[66] He was obviously not put off by his knowledge that the Mosse publishing house was anathema to the right as a "Jewish" concern. Then he applied—equally unsuccessfully—for a teaching position at a commercial college in Düsseldorf.[67] There are indications of further applications in the following months.[68]

Meanwhile, with his old schoolfriend Fritz Prang he was working on a plan to start a "monthly Rhineland journal for German art and cultural politics" in Düsseldorf: "Then I'll be able to fulfill my greatest desire; freedom of speech and expression without any constraints."[69] The project quickly took shape in his mind: It should be a publication taking a "pro–Greater Germany, anti-international line": "So, something National Socialist, but avoiding all demagoguery and rabble-rousing patriotism. About the sense of national community. Out of the morass of party politics."[70]

Early in April he began to be active in politics, on behalf of the National Socialists he had so recently learned to admire. Thanks to the complete edition of the diaries, we now know precisely when his activism began: April 4, 1924.[71] On this day he wrote, "We have founded a local National Socialist group." Since the NSDAP had been banned in November 1923, the group, involving about a dozen mostly young people from Rheydt, was an illegal organization. The first thing on the agenda was an internal discussion of aims, and one topic predominated, as Goebbels noted of the founding meeting: "We basically talked about anti-Semitism. [. . .] The anti-Semitic idea is a world idea. It brings together Germans and Russians. For the coming millennium, as Michael Voormann says."[72]

Goebbels now preoccupied himself intensively with "the Jewish question," which he held to be "the burning question of the hour."[73] He read Henry Ford's anti-Semitic tract *The International Jew,* which he found illuminating, although he was not prepared to follow the author's train of thought all the way. As ever, he placed great importance on informing himself of the facts and maintaining his critical point of view: "Lenin, Trotsky, [Georgy] Chicherin are Jews. You can sometimes make such stupid judgments about political events if you aren't in command of the material facts." However, it had escaped his attention that Lenin was not a Jew.[74]

His reading of Ford led him to "The Protocols of the Elders of Zion." It is true that he came to the correct conclusion that this all-too-seductive "proof" of the alleged Jewish plan of world domination must be an anti-Semitic forgery—but all the same, he accepted the "inner" authenticity of the protocols.[75] Finally, he summed up his intense preoccupation with "the Jewish question" as follows: "I am on the *völkisch* side: I hate the Jew with my instincts and my reason. He is deeply hateful and repulsive to me."[76] And somewhat later he wrote: "Every 'anti-' aimed at the Jews is a plus for the national community."[77] Unlike with other *völkisch*-oriented people, his anti-Semitism does not seem to have been an integral part of a fully developed racist ideology. His animus against the Jews followed a quite straightforward pattern: The less clear his concept of the desired "national community," the clearer his opposition to all things Jewish. "The Jews" simply stood for all the "subversive," culturally destructive, international forces that prevented the coming together of "the people," *das Volk*. In his nebulous worldview there was now at least one fixed, negative point.

In the elections at the beginning of May—the Rheydters were voting for their local council as well as for the Reichstag—the National Socialists appeared in a list under the umbrella heading *Völkisch-Social Bloc* (VSB).[78] The members of the illegal local group distributed leaflets and put up posters at night.[79] On April 28 they organized a big election meeting. A lawyer called Borries particularly addressed himself to "the Jewish question," although in Goebbels's opinion "pretty half-heartedly." There was a relatively large bloc of communists in the hall, but Goebbels, who was conducting the meeting, saw the event through to the end without incident.[80]

The election campaign exhausted him: "The low points of the election campaign are horribly dry and dusty. But behind it all stands the great idea of a *völkisch* Europe in which a *völkisch* Germany will take a prominent place."[81] On the eve of the election he gave a talk "to an invited audience about our aims and the Semitic danger." He spoke freely for the first time: "Good success. Our idea is catching on, because it's a world idea."[82]

In the elections for the Reichstag the National Socialists—who featured in individual constituencies not only as a part of the *Völkisch*-Social Bloc but also under other groupings—succeeded in gaining thirty-two seats in all throughout the Reich, and 6.6 percent of the vote. In the Rheydt local elections they did rather less well, with 528 votes, or 2.7 percent of the vote. The Catholic Center Party dominated the town as ever, with 30.3 percent, while the bourgeois parties, the German People's Party (DVP) and the German-Nationalist People's Party (DNVP), scored 17.5 and 14.6 percent of the vote, respectively. At least the *Völkisch*-Social Bloc now had one representative on the Town Council.[83]

Political activism restored a sense of purpose to Goebbels's life. He felt "pure joy" that he had found "faith and a new aim." But really he saw himself as an intellectual, a cultural politician. He continued to commit himself wholeheartedly to the plan of a *völkisch*-oriented Rhenish cultural magazine.[84] For a while it seemed as if such a project might be realized with the help of the Schiller Community, a *völkisch* cultural organization headquartered in Vienna that was extending its activities to the Rhineland. "Reawakening of German intellectual life in the spirit of Schiller" and "Excising of all Jewish-international subversion"—such a program was music to Goebbels's ears.[85] But it was the music of the future, and meanwhile he was profoundly dissatisfied with the dull everyday reality of party work. "I've had it up to here with this drudgery for the *völkisch* cause. I must get back to involvement in principles and intellectual matters."[86] What is more, he was uncomfortable with many of his fellow party members, consisting as they did to a large extent of "a wild rabble of ex-convicts, loudmouths, idiots, and informers."[87] "Squabbling" was the order of the day in the local group.[88]

In the middle of May 1924, about two weeks after the elections, he drew up a sobering balance sheet. His "reckless support for the *völkisch* idea" had "ended his last chance of breaking into the press or the theater," and furthermore he had "burned his bridges" with the Center Party people in Rheydt. On the other hand, there were seeds of hope: "Out of the despair and depressing skepticism of the last few years has arisen once again my belief in the nation and in the German spirit. Now I am strong and waiting with more yearning than ever for salvation." Could this ardent search be turned to literary account? "I should write about my intellectual journey from [Ernst] Toller to Hitler. Some of that is already present in 'Michael Voor-

mann.' [. . .] I want to be my own salvation. If a book or a play contributes to my salvation, it will have done its job. After that it can
molder away in my desk drawer."[89]

His political activism on the radical right wing soon exacted its
price: In June he was set upon by a gang. He suspected the "damned
Semites" were behind the attack. He thought he had been fighting for
his life against some six or eight men, although he clearly emerged
unscathed.[90] He received threatening letters (whose senders quickly
turned out to be harmless), there were house searches, and he was
sure he would soon be arrested.[91] In the end he hardly dared venture
out onto the streets.[92]

THE QUEST FOR ORIENTATION

At the end of June he took part in a political conference in Elberfeld
that brought together like-minded people from all over the occupied
territory. Goebbels was deeply disappointed by the leaders of the
völkisch movement in the occupied zone: "All you Jews and French
and Belgian gentlemen need have no fear. You're safe from them. I
have rarely been at a meeting where so much ranting and railing
went on as yesterday. And most of it directed at their own comrades."

In the non-occupied areas, he recorded, a struggle had broken out,
one that he had long expected, between the two organizations competing for the leadership of the radical right, namely "between the
völkisch Freedom Party and the National Socialist Worker's Party." As
he soberly observed, the two did not "belong together at all. The former want Prussian Protestantism (they call it the German Church),
the latter a Greater Germany settlement—possibly with a Catholic
element. Munich and Berlin are locked in combat. You could also say
Hitler and Ludendorff." His allegiance was unambivalent: "I belong
much more with Munich than with Berlin. If only Hitler were free!"

He was concerned that the actually existing *völkisch* movement
had failed to produce a "competent, hard-working, and noble leader."
A few days later he formulated his longings more dramatically: "Germany yearns for the One, the Man, as the earth longs for rain in summer." And then there followed a really fervent cry: "O Lord, give your
German people a miracle! A miracle!! A man!!! Bismarck, arise!"[93]

The call for a leader, a political Messiah, so exaltedly expressed here by Goebbels, was a commonplace of right-wing thinking in those postwar years. The image evoked by Goebbels of the rescuer as a new Bismarck was widespread; hopes were likewise pinned on the return of a Frederick the Great or an Arminius (Hermann). In literature, the press, the youth movement, the Protestant church but also in the humanities, countless voices were raised to express the hope, and even the certainty, that this great personality, "the One," would appear and lead the nation out of defeat and back to honor and self-esteem. Such nationalistic visions of rescue had a high proportion of religious and pseudo-religious content: The future leader would be God-sent and equipped with extraordinary abilities.[94]

We can assume that at the time Goebbels—albeit full of doubts—related the call for a great man above all to himself: "Am I a wastrel or someone sent by God to await His word? Amid all the profound despair there is always one shining light: belief in my own purity and that my great hour must come one day."[95]

His growing involvement in politics led him for a while to engage intensively with the writings of leading socialist thinkers. First he read Karl Marx's *Das Kapital*. He was impressed by the description of the condition of the workers in England but found the style "dry" and "terribly heartless."[96] A few weeks later he moved on to Rosa Luxemburg's *Letters from Prison*. At first he felt entirely sympathetic to "Rosa," as he called her in his diary, but as he read on he became increasingly critical, which by his own admission may have had something to do with his "somewhat one-sided" anti-Semitic attitude.[97] Then he read *From Kiel to Kapp*, the memoirs of the renegade social democrat turned right-winger Gustav Noske, which provoked a fit of hatred toward the "Jewish riff-raff."[98]

Finally he turned to August Bebel's memoirs. Bebel had "appealing features" and an "upright, straight character," but Goebbels was bothered that he was "half-educated."[99] "Bebel's socialism," Goebbels summed up when he had finished the book, was "a healthy reaction in response to the liberalism that was all-powerful at the time" and initially "thoroughly patriotic in attitude," but later it was "contaminated by Jewishness."[100] The humble workers' leader Bebel was, as Goebbels saw it, a tool of the internationally minded Jewish left-intellectuals, hopelessly in thrall to their "phrase-mongering."[101] That Goebbels identified himself with the more "socialist" side of National Socialist policy in the next few years had less to do with the socioeconomic restructuring of society than with creating a racially homogeneous "national community."

A tight-knit group of politically like-minded people was formed in Rheydt, mockingly known to him as the "league of the resolute." Meetings were held to exchange ideas on subjects transcending day-to-day politics; Goebbels's house was frequently the venue.[102] His radical politics meant that ties with old friends were lost. He gradually distanced himself from "the German small-town type" that he saw personified in these "awful windy beggars" who were distinguished by a "lazy, vapid bonhomie," "swine dressed up as gentlemen," "the next bourgeois generation."[103]

The relationship with Else, which had undergone a severe crisis in April 1924, had been restored. The stigma of her "Jewish blood" now no longer seemed to worry him so much: "Many a sweet lovers' tryst with Else," he wrote in May.[104] It may be that for him it was mainly a comfortable arrangement: "Else is a nice, good child. A bit boring. But a loyal, industrious handmaiden. You can rely on her, and she'll do you any kind of favor."[105] In July he wrote that he was "incurably ego-centered as far as women are concerned. Do I give? No, I take; as much as I can. [. . .] I'm sometimes ashamed of myself. If I could marry you, Else, it would solve a lot of problems." But he couldn't marry Else, precisely for "racial" reasons.[106]

Else aside, the image of Anka haunted him as much as ever. He often confided to his diary that his great love, of whom he felt cheated, appeared to him in his dreams. His unfulfilled longing for Anka was highly detrimental to his relationship with the opposite sex: "I'm only half a man for women today. I lack what is best and most consoling: esteem, distance, respect."[107] He concluded: "Why is Eros my tormentor, why can't he be my joy and my strength? Anka, you wicked, lovely woman!"[108]

CRAMPED QUARTERS AND *VÖLKISCH* EUPHORIA

Goebbels lapsed once more into depression. In the summer of 1924 he felt he "lacked the courage to face life" and simply "never left this dump."[109] And there was "no stimulus, no enthusiasm, no belief. Waiting! Waiting! If only I knew what for. I delude myself by sending my Michael to one publisher after another. Nobody wants it. Surprising?"[110]

In August he noted: "Lots of drunken evenings."[111] A few days before this he described an anxiety dream: "A Bulgarian throws a knife at me. The knife's point hits me in the head. I am bleeding. I am losing strength. Fear. Horror. I can feel death approaching. Then I wake up. The man's name was Bolgorovkov."[112]

A review of his circumstances left little room for optimism: "My ideal: to be able to write and live off it. But no one's going to pay me for my rubbish."[113] He wrote the "memory pages," short autobiographical sketches, as an adjunct to the diaries begun in October 1923.[114] As he was leafing through old correspondence with Anka he had a new idea for a project: an epistolary novel about a love affair.[115]

The memory of Anka and the pain of losing her became almost overwhelming. Else had gone off to the Black Forest by herself: He had no money to go with her.[116] He sketched out a wistful letter to Anka lamenting their parting.[117] "All the people I love and will ever love in my life will have to accept less love from me because of what I lavished on Anka Stalherm," he wrote.[118] On the other hand, he longed increasingly for Else: "I have a yearning for her white body."[119] There was something connecting the two women for him. In both of them he rediscovered his mother. He wrote about Anka: "There was something maternal in her love,"[120] and of Else he said that she was "my young mother and lover. I sometimes think of her as a mother."[121] "Mother is good to me," he wrote on the same day. "I have her to thank for nearly everything I am." He branded his father "uniquely lacking in style," a "pub strategist,"[122] a "moaner": He was "peevish, but the soul of goodness at heart,"[123] a "beer-drinking pedant." Earlier, at the beginning of the year, he characterized his father as a pedant and a tyrant: "I can't understand why my mother married the old skinflint."[124]

He participated ever more apathetically in the activities of the *völkisch* group in Rheydt: "I'm only suited to wide-ranging politics, just as I can only take the wider view in my work. Day-to-day work repels me."[125] By contrast, his friend Fritz Prang took part enthusiastically. Goebbels regarded him as a busybody fantasist, an "idealistic ideologue" with too little sense of practical politics who saddled him "week after week with every kind of lout" in his house.[126] All the same, Goebbels was persuaded to accompany him to Weimar[127] to attend a conference from August 15 to 17, 1924, of German-*völkisch* supporters and National Socialists, where a fragile alliance was struck. It was known as the National Socialist Freedom Movement of Greater Germany.[128]

Plans for the journey seemed about to collapse, since Prang initially failed to raise the money. In any case, Goebbels had "lost interest" in the party congress, but when the money came through after all, he set off on the afternoon of August 15.[129] The trip was to make a profound impression on him.

After a tiring overnight journey, he arrived in Weimar the next morning. It was his first visit to the city of German Classicism. The next few days passed in almost unbroken high spirits: He felt he was among his peers, among people whom he regarded as belonging without doubt "to a certain elite." He saw himself in the company of the initiated, in a festive mood, standing out clearly from the run of the population: "It gladdens my heart! Oh, this blessed youth of ours! We enthusiasts! We fanatics! Glow, sacred flame!"

The supporters of the "movement" held their congress in the National Theater, where he found himself facing Erich Ludendorff: "He scrutinized me closely. Very thoroughly. He seemed not displeased." In Weimar he also had his first sighting of other prominent right-extremist figures: Albrecht von Graefe, leader of the German-*völkisch* Freedom Party, whom Goebbels saw as a "born aristocrat" and who reminded him of a "thoroughbred racehorse"; Gregor Strasser ("the affable pharmacist from Bavaria"); Gottfried Feder ("fraternity student"); Wilhelm Kube, who attracted his attention with a "loud and pompous" speech; Ernst Graf zu Reventlow, the "clever, sarcastic Count, the world politician of the movement"; and Julius Streicher, the "fanatic with pursed lips" who seemed to him "somewhat pathological." He talked for a whole hour to Theodor Fritsch, the leading anti-Semitic publicist of Germany, whom he thought of as a "nice old uncle."

For two days Goebbels was swept away by the bustle of the party rally. He was entertained by the parades and the solemn appeals, the emotional addresses, and the communal singing of patriotic songs. He dropped in at the pubs the National Socialists had taken over.[130] But he also found time to visit the houses of Goethe and Schiller. Visiting the Schiller house, full of elevated patriotic emotion, he had a strange experience: Standing before a portrait of Schiller, he thought he could see physical similarities between himself and the writer. As he was inclined to identify himself strongly with Schiller and tended in his imagination to fuse himself with whatever was greater, more significant, and unattainable, such an observation was not surprising in itself. In the same way, he had recently been prompted after reading Richard Wagner's autobiography to contemplate the similarities between himself and the composer.[131] However, what is notable is that, as he recalled, a lady standing next to him also noticed the similarities and reacted "with amazement and with something like horror." Claus-Ekkehard Bärsch has pointed out, in connection with this scene, that for Goebbels his self-loving reflection in the portrait of the great man only had value when it was confirmed by a third person. Goebbels wanted to be as great as Schiller, but above all he wanted to experience this elevation in the eyes of others.[132]

He returned to Rheydt with his "whole heart full of unforgettable impressions."[133] In his mind the relics of German Classicism merged with the *völkisch* mood of national awakening: "The national question is connected to all the questions of spirit and religion. I'm starting to think in a *völkisch* way. This has nothing to do with politics anymore. This is a matter of a worldview. I'm beginning to find firm ground beneath my feet."[134]

THE *VÖLKISCH* JOURNALIST

Still very much under the influence of his Weimar experiences, Goebbels, together with Fritz Prang, founded in Mönchengladbach on August 21, 1924, a local group of the National Socialist Freedom Movement of Greater Germany, which was banned in the occupied zone. Allegedly, twenty members promptly appeared, after Goebbels had spent "one and a half hours explaining the basic problems of the *völkisch* worldview." Prang remarked appreciatively afterward that he was "a born speaker."[135]

Goebbels now regularly gave talks in his local area. On September 3 he addressed a middle-class audience in Wickrath, on the 10th in Mönchengladbach, on the 17th again in Wickrath, this time an audience of farming people, on September 18 workers in Mönchengladbach, on the 25th in Rheydt, on the 27th in Neuss.[136] "It isn't nearly so hard to speak off the cuff as I would have thought," he wrote, "but you've got to practice beforehand, as with everything. And I practice on these small meetings of supporters."[137]

In the foreground of his political work was the project of a nationalistic journal that was to appear in Elberfeld. The plan, first mentioned in his diary in July,[138] slowly took shape, replacing the earlier idea of a cultural-political magazine for the occupied Rhineland. It was agreed with the publisher, Friedrich Wiegershaus, leader of the Freedom Movement in the North Rhineland district, that it would contain "every week a cultural-political essay, a political review of the week, a glossary, and one or two smaller items. [. . .] Payment initially to consist only of idealism and ingratitude." The paper was titled *Völkische Freiheit* (*Völkisch* Freedom).[139]

The first edition of the weekly appeared at the beginning of September.[140] Goebbels proudly reported that he had co-written as much as three quarters of the third issue himself.[141] It was true that the paper was, as he had to admit, "still an insignificant little rag," but he felt "young and bold" enough to make a success of it.[142]

Goebbels wrote lengthy articles; was responsible for the "Political Diary"; wrote, as "Ulex," satirical commentaries under the heading of "Sidelights"; and swept up other items into a column called "From My Daily File." In the second edition, under the title "National and Social," he attempted to formulate a synthesis of the two concepts: "To think nationally," he said, "is to base all your actions, thoughts, and feelings on a sense of responsibility toward the state as a national community."[143] He went on to say: "A feeling for the social is a heightened version of feeling for the family. Everything rises from the heart into the mind. It is the feeling of fateful, racial bonds within the framework of the state. [. . .] The ultimate aim of National Socialism is a strong, healthy people in a strong, healthy state." In another contribution he asserted, clearly influenced by his reading of Spengler's *Preussentum und Sozialismus* (Socialism and the Prussian Way), that "National Socialism is nothing other than a Friderician sense of the state, nothing other than the Kantian imperative."[144]

As one tries to make sense of such utterances, it is evident that Goebbels's socialism had precious little to do with contemporary debates about state control of the means of production or the nationalization of key industries, and neither did it aim to establish a fair and egalitarian social order. "National Socialism" was about the total integration of the individual into a completely organized national community. Since social differences were a second-order matter in an ethnically homogeneous national community absolutely geared to achieving nationalist aims, wherever "national socialism" prevailed the "social question" was solved as far as Goebbels was concerned.

Goebbels, who in the years 1925–26 was one of the most vocal proponents of a "socialist" direction in NSDAP policy, never attempted to explain the sociopolitical and economic consequences "national socialism" would bring about. He played only a marginal role in the debates on the "left" wing of the NSDAP about a future economic order under a National Socialist regime.[145] Admittedly, he did criticize his Gauleiter (district leader), Axel Ripke, in April 1925 for wanting to grant the workers no more than a 49 percent ownership interest, a proposal Goebbels rejected as "reformed capitalism."[146] But he gave nothing away about his own view of ownership. In propagating "national socialism" he was concerned above all to project an image of himself as an utterly uncompromising young radical, the chief representative of an oppositional strand within the Party. The "socialist" attitude was a fanciful pose he liked to strike.

In his contributions to *Völkische Freiheit,* Goebbels had a special penchant for writing on cultural-political questions. In the essay "*Völkisch* Cultural Questions" of October 1924 he expatiated on the subject of the "new man," a figure undoubtedly modeled on his "Michael": "Three great factors have been at work on this [new] man. [...] The war awoke him from his deep slumber; it made him conscious. His spirit troubled him and led him toward catastrophe; it showed him the heights and the depths. Work released him; it made him proud and free."[147]

Under the title "The Nationalist Intelligentsia" a week later, Goebbels sang the praises of "working students," whom he saw as "symbolizing the new direction of a young German intellectual elite."[148] In his paean of praise for "those heroic students" who earned their keep "as workers and clerks in the mines, the factories and the banks," there is another echo of motifs in "Michael."

Goebbels was gradually making a name for himself within the Party. On September 23 he took part in a commemoration of the battle of Tannenberg in Elberfeld. Many leading Party figures made the journey, and he had the opportunity to speak to, among others, Ludendorff, Graefe, Strasser, Ernst Röhm, and Kube.[149] "My reputation as a speaker and cultural-political author is spreading through the ranks of National Socialist supporters throughout the Rhineland. Gratifying!" he wrote proudly in his diary at the end of the month.[150]

Early in October he officially took over as editor of the *Völkisch Freedom,* which meant traveling to Elberfeld two days a week. The rest of the week he spent at home writing articles for the paper, if he was not out and about on *völkisch* business.[151] It seems that Goebbels had at last found a task suited to his interests and abilities.

CHAPTER 3

"Working with the Mind
Is the Greatest Sacrifice"

Maneuvering in the Early NSDAP

From 1924 onward, Goebbels tried to project himself as a representative of a
left-wing tendency in the NSDAP. But Hitler succeeded in splitting up the
group around Gregor Strasser by means of internal Party promotions.
Goebbels—shown here in hat and coat at the end of 1926, at a rally held by
Gregor Strasser in Essen—was soon in conflict with his old mentor.

On October 22, 1924, the Belgian occupation authorities carried out
a search of the Goebbels house in Rheydt. The next day Joseph Goebbels was interrogated by the criminal police. In the afternoon he set
out to leave the occupied zone and decided to stay in Elberfeld for the
time being.[1]

At the beginning of November he traveled for the first time to Berlin to hear a talk. This was at a time when discussions lasting several
days were taking place in the capital among members of the Freedom
Movement, who were at loggerheads: Goebbels was involved, albeit

only on the margins. Rather self-importantly, he noted: "Long negotiations with Ludendorff over the occupied territory. He agrees with
me on all points. Everyone liked my speech."

The trip to Berlin brought him once more into close contact with
other important representatives of the political right: Karl Neuhaus,
Reichstag deputy of the Deutschnationale Volkspartei (German National People's Party, DNVP),[2] Ernst Graf zu Reventlow, and Albrecht
von Graefe, as well as members of the *völkisch* camp such as Reinhold Wulle, deputy of the Nationalsozialistische Freiheitsbewegung
(National Socialist Freedom Movement, NSFB), and Wilhelm Kube.
Goebbels quickly developed distinct preferences: "Wiegershaus gets
on my nerves in the long run. Uneducated. Formless. Plebeian! Ludendorff is the man for me, though." Otherwise, "my impression of
Berlin was in part very dismal. Chasing votes. It damages the idea."[3]
Conflict was building up between himself and Wiegershaus, publisher of the *Völkische Freiheit*. There were an increasing number of
unfavorable comments about his employer in the diary. He was "a
fat, well-favored little man, no revolutionary, feeds off my ideas"—in
short, "an incompetent dolt."[4]

The speaking engagements that he eagerly continued in the
Rhine-Ruhr area[5] now more frequently took Goebbels outside this
sphere of operations. In November he undertook a week's propaganda tour through Pomerania, and at the end of the month and in
early December he made several appearances in Hesse.[6] In Elberfeld
he struck up a close acquaintance with Karl Kaufmann, a former
member of the Free Corps militia and a National Socialist activist.
They soon became friends: "Perhaps he can replace Richard."[7] He
also got to know Axel Ripke, an "educated person" whom he learned
to value.[8] Another name that appears increasingly often in the diary
is that of the dentist and active Party supporter Hellmuth Elbrechter.[9]

However, in the Reichstag elections of December 1924 the Freedom Movement did poorly, receiving only 3 percent of the vote.
Goebbels called the results "disastrous."[10] He published an article in
the *Völkische Freiheit* openly admitting this defeat. "Rally!" was the
slogan by which he hoped to overcome the disappointment of the
result. In the article he distanced himself markedly from the *völkisch*
faction, whom he held responsible for the defeat, and—falling completely into the pose of the "born revolutionary"—declared himself
unambiguously in favor of "socialism."[11] Acting in accordance with

this appeal, the opposition within the Party, which included Goebbels, Kaufmann, and Ripke, set about unseating Wiegershaus. But the plot failed.[12]

"I lack a great love in my life," wrote Goebbels in December. "That's why all my love goes to the great cause."[13] At the end of 1924 he got to know Elisabeth Gensicke: "A bit old, but nice and affectionate. Reminds me very much of Anka."[14] A little affair developed: "Why don't I feel any inner conflict when I leave Elisabeth to go to Else," he asked himself when he set off for Rheydt just before Christmas. But he quickly dispelled such pangs of conscience: "My heart is big enough to hold two women at once."[15] So he spent Christmas and New Year's with Else, and in between a long evening in Elberfeld with Elisabeth.[16] "Tomorrow I'm seeing little Else! Elisabeth on Friday!" he exulted. "Both are looking forward to seeing me, and I'm equally eager to see them! Am I a cheat?"[17]

THE IDOL IS FOUND

On December 20, 1924, Hitler was released early from his Landsberg prison. Goebbels, who in a special edition of *Völkische Freiheit* devoted to Hitler and the anniversary of the November 9 putsch had vehemently demanded Hitler's release and declared himself a "hero-worshipper,"[18] responded enthusiastically: "Adolf Hitler is free! Now we can break away from the reactionary *völkisch* people and be true National Socialists again. Heil, Adolf Hitler!"[19] In the *Völkische Freiheit* he praised him to the skies:

There is a dull longing in us that we cannot name and cannot describe. [...] In strange silence millions of the unredeemed, misled, betrayed, despairing, subjugated, the army of slaves is waiting for a word, a sound. There, rolling in the distance, dull, accusing, clearer—a drumbeat! The outcry of the masses! They call to you from the depths! Drummer, drum for German freedom! The call for salvation! Uncomprehended by all those still stuck in the old forms; meeting the deepest longings of all those who overcame the old model of mankind, who have learned to believe; who are prepared to take the path of sacrifice as if it were a triumphal procession, the apostles, those who cry in the wilderness, who have been set free by the ultimate vision.[20]

The "call for salvation," meant for Hitler's ears, ended a painful quest stretching over many years. Goebbels had reached the culmination of a biographical development that, given the lack of balance in his personality, was in a certain sense the logical outcome. Having struggled with his Catholicism and so desperately sought "redemption," Goebbels himself had initially slipped into the role of "redeemer": first as a writer, then as proponent of a cultural new departure. Then, in symbiosis with his friend Flisges, he had found in the role of Michael, in "redemption" through hard work in the mines, in close connection with working people, a model—immortalized by Flisges's death—for salvation at the national level. He had then transposed his search for a savior onto the *völkisch* movement, undersupplied as it was with leader figures, and once again—flirting with the great exemplars Schiller, Wagner, and others—had fantasized his way into this role. But he had finally reached the conclusion that it was for someone else to be the savior-leader and that his destiny was to be the latter's first disciple.

This transfer of the role of savior to another person, somebody greater, and the desire for the most perfect possible symbiotic fusion with this idol played to Goebbels's narcissistic disorder. He himself could feel great only if he had constant confirmation from an idol he had chosen. Hitler was to be this idol: Celebrated on the extreme right as a martyr since the days of his Landsberg incarceration, he was busy exploiting this role and, as the admired Führer, elbowing aside his remaining rivals in radical right-wing circles. It is not a matter of wild speculation to maintain that in Goebbels's imagination Hitler played the part of the solicitous, protective, and affirming mother. Goebbels himself quite openly confessed as much in his official speech on Hitler's forty-sixth birthday, in 1935: "But the whole nation loves him because it feels as safe in his hands as a child does in the arms of its mother."[21]

With Hitler's release from imprisonment, the time had come for Goebbels not just to idolize the leader but to *declare* himself openly for him. For Hitler's release ensured that the conflicts, so far laboriously swept under the carpet, between the *völkisch* and National

Socialist factions in the Freedom Movement once more broke out into the open. In the Rhineland, similarly, the question was whether to opt for Graefe or for Hitler. For Goebbels, then, his support of Hitler was simultaneously part of a heroic struggle concerning the future of National Socialism in general. In any case, he felt he could smell "fresh morning air"[22] and was convinced that "Hitler would know what was right. We'll help him with his launch."

Goebbels's contribution to this process of clarification was an open letter in the *Völkische Freiheit* addressed to Ernst Graf zu Reventlow, one of the leading figures of the National Socialist Freedom Movement. Goebbels attacked Reventlow for his remark that the NSDAP was not "socialist" but "social," asserting on the contrary, "The social is a stopgap. Socialism is the ideology of the future." In taking up the argument with Reventlow, born in 1869 and one of the figureheads of the *völkisch* movement, Goebbels was above all trying to make himself the spokesman for the "destiny-laden youth of the German future" and conjuring up the "spirit of the west," the modern industrial regions of the Rhine and the Ruhr.[23] His anger was also directed at Reinhold Wulle, who had been "insolent" toward National Socialism and declared that he simply could not understand "the younger generation."[24]

The leading lights of the *völkisch* movement—Reventlow, Graefe, Wulle—were in fact politicians who had already been active during the *Kaiserreich* but had never progressed beyond political sectarianism. In contrast to these figures—Goebbels explicitly made an exception of Ludendorff, who understood "young people"[25]—Goebbels tried to accentuate the youthfulness of the Nazi movement; by this reckoning, only men like Hitler who had previously been young soldiers at the front or members of the generation that had grown up during the war were in a position to fulfill his emotive demand for a "new man." It is within this context of his self-projection as the epitome of youth that his advocacy of "socialist" as against mere "social" policies must be viewed.

In Elberfeld, open revolt against Wiegershaus now erupted: "We've got to checkmate the old, sclerotic big shots."[26] As a result of the turbulence, the *Völkische Freiheit* ceased publication in January, and Goebbels was dismissed.

The affair with Elisabeth, meanwhile, was cramping his relationship with Else. In early February he and Else had "pretty well finished with each other,"[27] but once again he had doubts at the last moment: "Now that I've got to leave Else, I feel I don't love Elisabeth."[28] And in the end there was always the memory of his great love: "Anka, Else, Elisabeth! How can I reconcile you three women in my mind? Anka wronged me. The other two must suffer for that."[29] The problem was solved for him when Elisabeth left Elberfeld at the beginning of March. Since two of the women were now inaccessible, he revived his relationship with the faithful Else.[30]

Finally, on February 12, 1925, the heads of the Freedom movement, the "Reich leadership," stood down, and soon afterward Hitler, confidently expecting the lifting of the ban on the Party, announced the re-founding of the Nazi Party (NSDAP).[31] The *völkisch* group, for their part, formed the Deutschvölkische Freiheitsbewegung (German-*Völkisch* Freedom Movement). Goebbels was already decided, but now he was exercised above all by the question whether "Hitler really would now make pure national socialism his program."[32]

On February 16 the bans on the NSDAP and the *Völkischer Beobachter* were lifted, after Hitler agreed with the Bavarian prime minister, Heinrich Held, that he would make no more putsch attempts.[33] A few days later Gregor Strasser, one of the leading National Socialist politicians, appeared at a rally in Hamm, where the representatives of the old NSDAP together with the National Socialist Freedom Movement from the whole of North Germany "swore their renewed undying allegiance and loyalty" to Hitler.[34] A little later Goebbels learned that he had been "appointed manager of NSDAP affairs for the entire west," with a regular salary. His Gauleiter was to be Axel Ripke,[35] a "great fellow" whom he esteemed highly.[36] A few days later Hitler's long-awaited exhortation to re-found the Party arrived in Elberfeld: "Brilliant in style and content. What a man! We have new courage."[37]

As business manager, Goebbels first of all set about creating designs for Nazi posters, some of which he recommended for wider distribution by local Party groups throughout the Reich. His designs depended entirely on the impact of the written word: Containing about twenty-five lines of print, they addressed passersby who could spare only a minute for a quick read. The coloring was uneven, and the swastika was only lightly indicated. The main message concerned anti-Semitism.[38]

In addition, Goebbels distributed information letters for the local region *(Gau)*[39] as well as his first piece of propaganda writing (*Das kleine ABC des Nationalsozialisten,* A Small ABC for the National Socialist).[40] He continued enthusiastically with his speaking engagements: By his own account of October 1924, he had spoken on 189 occasions in the previous year.[41] Furthermore, he developed a plan for a "National Socialist Freedom League," which would be, so to speak, the "intellectual spearhead of our movement in the west." In line with his suggestion, active Party members were drafted into a separate organization and induced to be particularly generous in their donations.[42]

Hitler's decision to back Ludendorff as a candidate in the upcoming election for president of the Reich on March 29, 1925, was at first received with skepticism by Goebbels, but after a few days he came around completely.[43] However, the vote on March 29, 1925, turned out to be a fiasco for Ludendorff: The *Deutschvölkische Freiheitspartei* supported the candidate of the right, the DVP politician Karl Jarres, and Ludendorff took only 1.1 percent of the vote. The result was considerably worse than that achieved by the united *völkisch* right in the Reichstag election of December 1924. As a leading figure of the extreme right, Ludendorff was totally eliminated—which was no doubt Hitler's plan all along in supporting his candidacy. In the second vote, necessary because none of the candidates had achieved a majority, Jarres was withdrawn as the candidate of the extreme right wing, to be replaced by Paul von Hindenburg, the former field marshal under the Kaiser.

It was not long before there were disagreements between business manager Goebbels and the Gauleiter he had hitherto valued so highly.[44] Goebbels adopted the view that Ripke's "witty remarks" were doing little to advance the cause. Ripke was simply "not an activist"[45] but a "bourgeois in disguise" and not "socialist" enough.[46] Kaufmann supported Goebbels in this dispute. As Goebbels had hoped, Kaufmann was increasingly turning out to be a replacement for his lost friend Flisges.[47] Goebbels sought to bring things to a head by indicting the Gauleiter: In the *völkisch* paper *Deutsche Wochenschau* (Weekly Review) he published a "reckoning with the German bourgeoisie," whom he accused of allowing themselves to be reduced to "slave masters and promoters of the stock market dictatorship."[48] The whole thing was set out as an "open letter" addressed to a "Director General." The "open letter" became one of Goebbels's favorite journalistic ploys in the mid-1920s, allowing him to instigate particularly effective polemical allusions and a good many slurs of varying severity on his political opponents, all under cover of a personal, often quite civil manner.

Meanwhile, the presidential election campaign was coming to an end. Goebbels appeared at several events, supporting Hindenburg's candidacy. When Hindenburg won on April 26, however, Goebbels saw his success as no more than a "stage on the way to the ultimate goal."[49] All the same, he acquired a copy of Hindenburg's 1920 autobiography, *Aus meinem Leben* (From My Life), and arrived at a relatively mild verdict on it: "a great, unassuming man."[50]

After a temporary lull, the dispute with Ripke broke out again at the end of May.[51] Goebbels anticipated clarification from the party leader on the future direction of the NSDAP: "Will he be a nationalist or a socialist? Who is right, Ripke or I? That is what I have pinned my hopes on. Hitler as the leader of German socialists! The world belongs to us!"[52] But Hitler's public pronouncements on this issue were couched in such general terms that they could not be interpreted as support for either side.[53]

A series of articles by Goebbels appeared in the *Völkischer Beobachter* in the following weeks. On May 24 the paper published part of his attack on Reventlow from January,[54] and in June the first of his essays, "Idea and Sacrifice," a declaration of war on the "bourgeois," whom he hated, as he openly conceded, not least because they displayed what "we have not yet conquered in ourselves, a touch of small-mindedness placed by Mother Nature in every German cradle."[55] He harped on the same subject later that month with his contribution "Sclerotic Intelligentsia,"[56] and again in July with "National Community and Class War."[57] This latter article took the form of an open letter to Albrecht von Graefe, leader of the Deutschvölkische Freiheitsbewegung, in which Goebbels described the class war as the repression of the great mass of the people by a very small exploiting class. They and their bourgeois accomplices, their "shameless henchmen" (Graefe and company, in other words), were preventing the formation of a true "national community." He also produced two further open letters in the *Völkischer Beobachter*, to Hanns Hustert, the would-be assassin of the Reich's foreign minister, Gustav Stresemann, who was serving a sentence in military detention—although Goebbels did not mention Hustert by name.[58]

The diary entries around this time are full of vicious remarks about Ripke: "Poor, miserable, cowardly old bellyacher! Arteriosclerosis personified."[59] The article "Sclerotic Intelligentsia," in which Goebbels accused an imaginary "Geheimrat" (privy councilor) of representing a stuffy and "lame" version of socialism, was aimed at Ripke, who was well aware of this.[60]

As ever, the busy journalist was badly beset by money worries.[61] His father wrote that he could no longer support him.[62] When Goebbels told Kaufmann that, because of lack of money and the conflict with Ripke, he was tempted to pack up and leave Elberfeld,[63] Kaufmann had "tears in his eyes": "O God, give me Kaufmann as a friend. He is everything to me, and I to him. Richard was taken away from me, and Kaufmann was sent."[64] In April he made the final break with Elisabeth[65] and then tried to get his relationship with Else back on a proper footing, which he gradually succeeded in doing by May. The couple spent Whitsun in the Westerwald uplands.[66] But as he saw it, there was no future for them together: "I'd love to make her my wife, if only she weren't a half-breed."[67]

It was at the Gau leaders' conference in Weimar on July 12, 1925, that he first saw Hitler in the flesh.[68] After much delay, according to Goebbels, the Party leader finally showed up at the conference venue. Needless to say, Goebbels's enthusiasm knew no bounds: "Weimar was a resurrection in the truest sense of the word. [. . .] What a voice. What gestures, what passion. Just as I wished him to be." He recorded the key words of the speech in his diary: "Organization! No ideal. But unfortunately necessary. In it worldview becomes belief. Struggle! All those with the same aims belong in the organization. Then the way will be found. Communism and bourgeoisie! The idea of the masses! [. . .] Tough on bourgeoisie and capitalism. Freedom! Berserkers of freedom!" Hitler ended with an appeal for trust, while "bright tears ran down his cheeks." The speech made an enduring impression on Goebbels. He was "shaken": "I stand outside by the window and cry like a baby. Away from other people. [. . .] Hitler goes. A handshake. Come again soon." The next morning, back in Elberfeld, he summed it all up: "I'm a different person. Now I know that the man who leads was born to be a leader. I'm ready to sacrifice everything for him."

For Goebbels, the high expectations of Hitler he had formulated six months earlier in the *Völkische Freiheit* as a "call for salvation" had been fulfilled. He saw the Weimar encounter as a "resurrection" and was obviously incapable of scrutinizing Hitler's speech more closely to see where it diverged in terms of policy from his own views.

Invigorated by the Weimar experience, Goebbels, Elbrechter, and Kaufmann continued trying to unseat Ripke. At a series of meetings of leading Nazis in the Gau, he was gradually demolished. Ripke's opponents knew that their move was supported by the Party leadership in Munich. For Ripke belonged to the group of northwest German Gauleiters who had spoken out against the practice, current until then, of issuing NSDAP membership cards from the Munich head office. Their preference was to keep membership lists at Gau headquarters; this would deprive Munich of effective control over access to members' subscriptions. For Goebbels and his associates, these efforts clearly offered a platform for charging Ripke with irregularities.[69] Eventually Ripke requested a disciplinary hearing against himself.[70] He was suspended, and Goebbels was appointed acting Gauleiter.[71] One of his first acts in office was to report the membership figures for the Gau to Munich.[72]

In July he spent a night with Alma Kuppe, Else's best friend, who was on a visit to Elberfeld.[73] Later, his great fear was that the two women would exchange notes.[74] "Is it possible to love two women at the same time?"[75] he asked himself. Full of self-pity, in all these complications he once again saw himself in the role of someone who simply loved everybody and was the victim to the end: "Little Else, when am I going to see you again? Alma, you lovely minx! Anka, I'll never forget you! And yet now I'm utterly alone!"[76]

THE WESTERN BLOC

On August 20 Gregor Strasser came to Elberfeld and reached an agreement in principle with Kaufmann and Goebbels on the formation of a "western bloc" within the Party. The target of this strategy was clear: the "sclerotic big shots in Munich," the "lousy, useless management at the head office" from which they wanted to liberate Hitler.[77]

With this new creation in mind, during the days that followed Goebbels set about reinforcing his relations with two personalities

who were very important for the new setup: He befriended the head
of the Sturmabteilung (stormtroopers, SA) in the Gau, Viktor Lutze,
and finally established with Kaufmann that they should be on a
first-name basis with each other.[78] Apart from this, he was immersed
in reading the first volume of *Mein Kampf,* which had just been published, and about which he was "extremely enthusiastic."[79] On September 10 the decisive meeting took place in Hagen: The NSDAP
Gaus in North and West Germany formed a working association.
Goebbels recorded the significant points: "Single leader (Strasser).
Single headquarters (Elberfeld). Single business manager *(moi).* Fort-
nightly information publication *Nationalsozialistische Briefe* [Na-
tional Socialist Correspondence] (publisher Strasser, editor *moi*)."[80]

From Goebbels's diary notes in these days it clearly emerges where
he saw the dividing line within the Party. In a separate internal session with Party comrades appended to the main meeting, he proposed the following rallying cry: "First salvation through socialism,
followed like a whirlwind by national liberation." But he ran into opposition. The Pomeranian Gauleiter, Professor Theodor Vahlen, for
example, demanded: "First turn the workers into nationalists!" According to Goebbels, Hitler stood between the two camps, but he
held that he was about "to come over to our side completely."[81]

On September 27, at a conference of the leading officials of the
North Rhineland Gau, Goebbels was once more elected business
manager of the Gau; Kaufmann became the Gauleiter. Goebbels was
visibly disappointed. The idea had in fact been to make him Gauleiter, but he had had to decline because of overcommitment. All the
same, though: "A little niggle against Kaufmann in me. I do the work,
and he 'leads.' But I'll get over it!"[82]

A few days later Strasser was back in Elberfeld. The two men had
long discussions, gradually building up to a confidential relationship.
Goebbels learned that there was a notion of moving him to Munich,
but he was not ready for such a step: "I must first complete my mission here in the Rhine and Ruhr." The goal was a general assault on
the "pigsty" in Munich.[83] With Strasser he drafted a paper that was to
serve as the constitution of the working association formed a few
weeks earlier in Hanover: The eight Gaus involved agreed to a united
organization and greater exchange of information.[84]

Meanwhile, his relationship with Else was drifting inexorably toward a final break. He received several "farewell letters" from her which did not, however, lead to any consequences for the time being.[85]

CONFLICT OVER PARTY POLICY

Not only was Goebbels writing for the *Völkischer Beobachter* and the *Deutsche Wochenschau,* but he now also had his own publication, the *Nationalsozialistische Briefe* (National Socialist Correspondence).[86] He used the *Briefe,* above all, to propagate his views on Bolshevism and socialism. Russian Bolshevism, he asserted, should not be seen primarily as a "Jewish" system of government but as an attempt to open up a Russian national path to socialism. However, the battle between Jewish-international and Russian-nationalist forces within the Bolshevik movement was not yet over. Not until there was "a truly nationalist and socialist Russia" would it be possible to "recognize the beginnings of our own declaration for nationalism and socialism."[87]

In November 1925 his article "National Socialism or Bolshevism," which he had already published in mid-October in the *Briefe,* appeared in the *Völkischer Beobachter.* What was highly unusual was that this contribution was accompanied by a response from the chief ideologue of the Party, Alfred Rosenberg. Where Goebbels in his article had tried to bring out the positive aspects of the Bolshevist revolution, Rosenberg vehemently disagreed: Lenin's agrarian reforms had not freed the Russian peasants, he maintained; it was precisely under the Soviet system that they had no freedom whatsoever. The Soviet Union was not "the germ cell of a nationalist restructuring of European states" but its greatest obstacle. Neither was it possible to separate out the role of the Jews in the Soviet Union, as Goebbels had proposed. It was wrong to think, said Rosenberg, that the Soviet communists were supporting the German proletariat in order to safeguard the national existence of Russia; the fact was that "Soviet Judah" was concerned to prevent the "nationalist awakening" of peoples (including the Russians). Rosenberg concluded his response with the words: "The wish has often been the father to belief. We think in this case it has played a little prank on our Party comrade." The Party leadership could not have stated more clearly that Goebbels's assessment of the Soviet Union ran completely counter to the Munich line.[88]

It was inevitable that Hitler observed the activities of the working association, especially of its business manager, with a degree of mistrust. Informed of this by Strasser and patently shocked, Goebbels wrote in his diary on October 12: "Hitler doesn't trust me. He has complained about me. How that hurts." He hoped to clear the air in a one-to-one discussion, but if this were to end in accusations, "then I'll go." He could not "take that as well. Sacrifice everything, only to be accused by Hitler himself."[89]

In the meantime, he had finished reading the first volume of *Mein Kampf*. The book had made an extraordinary impression on him: "Who is this man? Half-plebeian, half-god! Is this really Christ or just John the Baptist?"[90] Despite his veneration of Hitler, he cannot have helped noticing that on two essential points the Party leader's position was completely at odds with his own. If Goebbels had hoped to find in *Mein Kampf* the long-awaited commitment to "socialism," then he was disappointed. What is more, Hitler had put forward a view of future policy toward the east that was completely opposed to Goebbels's image of Russia: Hitler saw Bolshevist rule in Russia as nothing but a tool "of the Jews." He rejected any alliance with Russia; on the contrary, he wanted a colonial land grab of Russian territory.[91]

For Goebbels, the chance to clear the air with Hitler came in early November at a Gau meeting in Braunschweig. Hitler greeted him there like "an old friend. And these large, blue eyes. Like stars. He is pleased to see me. I'm very happy." He was impressed by Hitler's rhetorical talent: "This man has all it takes to become king. A born people's tribune. The coming dictator." Questions of content obviously played no part at all in this encounter. Goebbels was simply happy that Hitler had made no accusations against him and in fact had treated him favorably.[92] He wrote to Gregor Strasser that they were "now completely straightened out with Munich."[93]

Two weeks later, on November 20, Hitler and Goebbels met again, at an event in Plauen where both were speaking. The controversial questions of substance played as little part this time as before. He was once more utterly captivated by his Party boss: "He greets me like an old friend. And treats me with solicitude. How I love him! What a fellow!" He was overwhelmed by Hitler's speech: "How small I am!"[94]

After their meeting Goebbels wrote Hitler one of his open letters,

in which he publicly declared his unconditional submission to the
Party leader: "You showed us once more in our deepest despair the
way to faith. [...] The last time I saw you, in Plauen, after days of
tempestuous struggle, I felt deep in my soul the happiness of standing behind a man who embodies the will to freedom in his very person. Before that you were my leader. But then you became my
friend."[95]

Such personal declarations of loyalty from leading Party comrades
were in fact nothing new since the re-founding of the NSDAP; after
all, Hitler had conceived of the Party as a "Führer party," and his entourage spared no effort to create a "Führer myth" around him. But
what seemed to many Party comrades a dutiful exercise (since the
vague policies of the Party necessitated a powerfully integrative
leader figure) was for Goebbels a highly charged emotional need, beyond all tactical considerations.[96]

On the way back from Plauen, Goebbels stopped off in Hanover,
where another meeting of the working association was taking place,
with representatives from eleven Gaus. Here, Strasser put forward an
outline program, but in the meeting it was decided that Kaufmann
and Goebbels should develop an alternative proposal.[97] Goebbels
had in fact been working intensively on such a manifesto draft since
mid-December 1925, after he had assessed as "unsatisfactory" a revised version of Gregor Strasser's draft, which had proposed partial
socialization.[98] But the deadline originally announced, December 15,
could not be met. On January 6 Goebbels recorded in his diary that
he had pulled the program together under "24 basic demands": Unfortunately, this document no longer exists. But the course taken
later by internal Party debate would go on to show that Goebbels's
position, especially his pro-Russian stance, was largely ignored.

At Christmas Hitler had given the Gau business manager enormous pleasure by sending him a leather-bound copy of *Mein Kampf*,
complete with a personal dedication in which he praised Goebbels's
work as exemplary.[99] Such gestures were to exert a long-term influence on Goebbels.

Meanwhile, negotiations had begun with the goal of combining
the North Rhineland and Westphalian Gaus into a single "Greater
Ruhr Gau." "Then we'll have a pressure group that counts for something," wrote Goebbels in his diary.[100] By January 9 an understanding
had been reached on all essential points with Franz Pfeffer von Salo-

mon, leader of the Westphalian Gau; on January 15, visiting Elberfeld, Strasser confirmed the agreements.[101]

Goebbels now set about further developing and modifying his pro-Russian position. On January 15 he published an article in the *Nationalsozialistische Briefe* on the topic of "Orientation: West or East." His decision was unambiguous: "That is why we place ourselves alongside Russia as equal partners in the struggle for this freedom which means everything to us."[102]

On February 19 he gave a speech in Königsberg on the subject of "Lenin or Hitler?," a topic he had already addressed on November 17, 1925, in Chemnitz.[103] He circulated the text of the carefully prepared Königsberg speech as a printed pamphlet;[104] he spent weeks polishing the final version.[105] As before, he assessed the Soviet agrarian reforms positively but came to the conclusion that Moscow's industrial policy had failed because "the Jewish question" remained unresolved there. That was why—and this was his main concession to the Party line—"no rescue could come from that quarter for the German people [. . .] because communism and Marxism as confederates of the Jewish stock exchange scoundrels never have the will to real freedom." On the other hand, he prophesied a Russian "awakening" that would produce the "socialist nationalist state."[106]

At its next gathering in Hanover on January 24, the working association considered the draft program.[107] An emissary of the Munich Party leadership, Gottfried Feder, also appeared at this meeting. In his diary Goebbels described the arrival of Feder—"lackey. Careerist and first program-writer of the movement"—as a surprise visit even though he had given Goebbels due notice in writing.[108] Evidently, with this description Goebbels was trying to lend a more dramatic air to the meeting. Feder's contribution was "clever, but obstinately dogmatic," says the diary, whereupon "an endless muddle of debates" followed. "And then I wade in. Russia, Germany, Western capitalism, Bolshevism, I talk for half an hour, a whole hour. Everybody listens with bated breath. And then a storm of approval." By Goebbels's reckoning this was the decisive turning point: "We have carried the day. [. . .] Strasser shakes my hand. Feder small and ugly. Period. Period."

In reality the working association agreed to pass on the suggestions made by various comrades to a "working party under [. . .] Gregor Strasser," which would then pass on "the material reviewed [. . .]

to Party headquarters for further utilization." So there was no question of a brilliant victory for Goebbels over the unwelcome guest from Munich.[109]

The decisive debate on the finalized Party program was to take place at a leadership meeting called by Hitler for Sunday February 14 in Bamberg. Hitler, as Goebbels was aware, was "angry about the program." But this did not seem to worry him. He was convinced that he could win the Party leader over to his side, since he had only recently received a letter from Hitler which had given him "great pleasure": "I've got a whole series of new photos of him on my desk. Charming!" Goebbels appeared relaxed, obviously full of optimism about the outcome of the Bamberg conference: "No one believes in Munich anymore. Elberfeld will be the future Mecca of German socialism."[110]

But the conference took a different turn altogether. Shocked, he noted in his diary: "Hitler speaks. 2 hours. I am stunned. What Hitler? A reactionary? Fantastically unskillful and unsure. Russian question: wide of the mark. Italy and England natural allies. Terrible! Our mission is the destruction of Bolshevism. Bolshevism is a Jewish plot! We must become the heirs to Russia!"

He found equally appalling what Hitler had to say on the question of the "princes' settlement," which was the initiative launched by the Kommunistische Partei Deutschlands (German Communist Party, KPD) and adopted by the Sozialdemokratische Partei Deutschlands (German Social Democratic Party, SPD) to expropriate the royal houses of Germany without compensation.[111] In Hanover the working association had spoken out in support of the planned referendum, but to Goebbels's dismay Hitler took the opposite position: "Princes' settlement. The law must remain the law. For the princes, too. Not to disturb the question of private property. Dreadful!"

It disappointed him that Hitler refused to draw up a new program for the Party: "Feder nods, Ley nods, Streicher nods. Esser nods. It pains me to the heart to see you in that company!!!" After a short discussion, Strasser spoke up: "Strasser speaks. Halting, trembling, awkward, good honest Strasser, oh God, we're so ill equipped to deal with those swine down there!" His summary was shattering: "One of the greatest disappointments of my life. I no longer totally believe in Hitler. That's the terrible thing: I've lost my inner conviction. I'm now just half the man I was."[112]

ON HITLER'S SIDE

At the beginning of March, at a special Party conference in Essen, the former Gaus of North Rhineland and Westphalia merged to form the "Greater Ruhr Gau." Goebbels was named along with Kaufmann and Pfeffer as a member of a triumvirate Gau leadership; three months later Kaufmann took over as sole Gauleiter.[113]

The party conference in Essen increased the tension with Munich. Gottfried Feder, then the leading author of the Party program, complained to Hitler after the event that in his publications, especially where the Soviet Union was concerned, Goebbels sounded like a "communist agitator."[114] While Feder was writing this letter, Goebbels was busy preparing "Lenin or Hitler" for the press; he had already begun to adapt his views on the Soviet Union to the Party line, at least in part. On another foreign policy question, too, Goebbels sought to link up with Munich: In March he read Hitler's pamphlet *Die Südtiroler Frage und das deutsche Bündnisproblem* (The South Tyrol Question and the Problem of German Alliances), in which the author, with an eye to an alliance with fascist Italy, argued for renouncing German claims to the South Tyrol. Finding this a "fabulously clear and tolerant booklet,"[115] Goebbels rapidly aligned himself with Hitler's thinking by writing an essay counseling against an economic boycott of Italy.[116]

Early in April Hitler invited the triumvirate leadership of the Greater Ruhr Gau—Goebbels, Kaufmann, and Pfeffer—to Munich. Strasser had instructed Goebbels beforehand to "weigh carefully every single word he uttered, whether in public or in private"; Goebbels made a firm promise to do so.[117] In Munich Hitler courted the West German opposition. "What a splendid reception," commented Goebbels later, delighting in retrospect at having been met by Hitler's driver at the station.[118] The next day Hitler placed his car at their disposal for an outing to Starnberg. In the evening Goebbels gave a speech in the Hackerbräu Beer Hall. In it—in complete contrast to his earlier statements—he ranked the solution of the "social question" as the central challenge facing the NSDAP but resisted giving any clear-cut account of what he understood as "socialism."[119] He had obviously gotten the message: "At the end Hitler embraces me. There are tears in his eyes. You could say I'm happy." On the other hand,

and quite understandably, Kaufmann and Pfeffer reproached him: His speech had "not been good." Goebbels ascribed this criticism to envy on Kaufmann's part.[120]

The next day Goebbels visited the NSDAP headquarters. His thumbnail sketches of the leading figures, who appear in his diary as a collection of ludicrous fuddy-duddies, demonstrate not only arrogance but above all an attempt to account for his differences with Hitler by referring to the leader's incompetent, scheming clique back at headquarters. The three visitors from Wuppertal first of all had to listen in Hitler's office to "a whole catalogue of complaints," albeit "elegantly and nicely expressed." Then the Führer extended his hand in reconciliation: "Let's put it behind us!" In the afternoon he delivered a three-hour lecture to the visitors from the Rhineland. Goebbels was not entirely convinced by the content, but he was once more completely overwhelmed by the Party leader's personality: "It's enough to drive you mad. Italy and England our allies. Russia wants to devour us. All this is in his pamphlet and in the next volume of his 'Kampf.' We wrangle. We question. His answers are brilliant. I love him."

On the "social question," too, Hitler gave Goebbels some completely "new insights": "His ideal—a mixture of collectivism and individualism. The soil, something solid for the people. Productivity, creative, individualistic. Businesses, trusts, finished products. Transport etc. nationalized." Goebbels was convinced of one thing: "A man so brimming with ideas is welcome to be my leader. I bow to the greater man, the political genius!" (So impressed was Goebbels that he went on to adopt Hitler's basic ideas about the mixed economy lock, stock, and barrel for a Party recruiting leaflet.)[121] Finally, Hitler gave the three delegates from the Ruhr his "firm confirmation" of their position in the Party: "And there should be peace between us from now on." While Kaufmann and Pfeffer returned to Essen, Goebbels stopped briefly in Lower Bavaria to report to Gregor Strasser and to fulfill a few speaking engagements. This was where he met Strasser's assistant Heinrich Himmler for the first time: a "good fellow, very intelligent. I like him."[122]

Goebbels then went back to Munich, where he had another long conversation with Hitler. Although impressed by Hitler's arguments, he was by no means convinced as yet. He thought Hitler had "not yet fully grasped the problem of Russia. But I'll to have rethink quite a few things."[123] The two men then traveled to Stuttgart, where they both spoke at several mass meetings.[124] Goebbels felt that Hitler had "taken him into his heart like nobody else." The net effect of the journey was plain: "Adolf Hitler, I love you because you are at once both great and straightforward. What they call a genius."[125] He reported to Strasser on the last few days and asked him to request an interview with Hitler as soon as possible "so that all the points on your side can be cleared up and we can collaborate with full confidence with Munich."[126]

Back in Elberfeld, he wrote an article for the *Briefe* called "The General Staff" in which he urged Hitler in exalted fashion to create a close "Führer circle" around himself, a "General Staff–type organization of the spirit of our movement": "With rigor and discipline a group must be selected from among the best, the bravest, and the most self-sacrificing. Strengthened by a puritanical toughness toward themselves, they must fortify their hearts against that day when more will be asked of us than conviction: brutality, thoroughness, certainty of insight, clarity of vision."[127]

On May 22 he took part in the general meeting of NSDAP members in Munich, at which a change to the Party constitution strengthened the position of Hitler within the Party and the Party program of 1920 was confirmed as "unalterable." Goebbels was pleased that Hitler not only expressed his appreciation of the developments in the Ruhr area but also declared his contentment that "this year a few first-class speakers have once more emerged, above all our friend from Elberfeld, Goebbels."[128]

It is not surprising that this rapprochement between Goebbels and Hitler aroused the distrust and suspicion of the Gau business manager in the Elberfeld head office.[129] For his part, however, since the beginning of 1926 Goebbels had begun to take an increasingly critical view of the way Kaufmann conducted the affairs of the Gau.[130] He suspected that Kaufmann was coming more and more under the influence of Elbrechter, a Party comrade active in the background, and this led to feelings of jealousy on Goebbels's part.[131] In the end, though, he decided to stand by Kaufmann, because "in the depths of my heart I love him."[132]

By June 1926 dissent among the Goebbels-Pfeffer-Kaufmann triumvirate was so far advanced that a reorganization was inevitable. Kaufmann accused Pfeffer of having misrepresented the financial position of his old Gau at the time of their merger. In the internal Party investigation that followed, Goebbels came down on the side of Pfeffer, whereupon Kaufmann turned his attack on Goebbels.[133] In the end Goebbels had to acknowledge ruefully that Kaufmann had gained the upper hand in the conflict. Goebbels was inclined to believe that "political machinations" by leading Party comrades in the Gau lay behind these disputes. He was disappointed to find he had no role to play in the reorganization.[134]

In mid-June Hitler came up to the Rhine-Ruhr area to settle the dispute. Goebbels, who accompanied him on this journey, was once again completely bowled over: "As a speaker he achieves a wonderful coordination of gesture, action, and word. A born demagogue! You could conquer the world with that man."[135]

At the Gau meeting on July 20, in Hitler's presence, the Gau leadership question was resolved at last: "Yesterday we appointed Kaufmann as Gauleiter," wrote Goebbels in his diary on June 21. Although he made positive comments on the outcome, the resolution smarted: "There's something of a split between me and Kaufmann. He's not straight."

For some time Hitler had been preoccupied by much more far-reaching changes in Party personnel. Goebbels noted in this connection that there was a plan to move him to Munich as "general secretary" of the movement. But there was also talk of making him Gauleiter of Berlin.[136]

Early in July the first NSDAP rally was held in Weimar.[137] Goebbels spoke—to great applause, as he wrote—on the subject of "propaganda" and addressed the National Socialist student organization on "Students and Workers."[138] He was deeply moved as he followed the Führer's words to the rally: "Deep and mystical. Almost like a gospel. Shuddering, you walk with him past the abysses of existence."[139]

After the rally Goebbels gave several speeches in Bavaria and then arranged to see Hitler in Berchtesgaden.[140] Accompanied by varying members of the Party elite—Rudolf Hess, Bernhard Rust, Gregor Strasser, and others—the two of them undertook excursions in the surrounding countryside.[141] Goebbels's notes show that he had now fully internalized Hitler's arguments. This applied to the "social question"[142] as much as to "race questions": "He is a genius. The naturally creative instrument of divine destiny. I stand before him deeply moved. That is how he is, like a child, nice, good, kind-hearted. Like a cat, sly, clever, and agile; like a lion, roaring, great, and gigantic. A splendid fellow, a man." He claims to have seen a "white cloud forming a swastika shape" overhead as Hitler spoke: "A blazing light in the sky, which cannot be a star. A sign of destiny!?"[143] The genius of the "Master" seemed inexhaustible: "He talks about the country's future architecture and is the complete master builder; he sketches a new German constitution. And is the complete statesman!"[144] Hitler's parting gesture was to give him a bouquet of "red, red roses," as Goebbels reported happily.[145]

Goebbels could not escape the concentrated charm of Hitler. With the intimacy Goebbels now believed was fully established between them and the recognition and praise bestowed by Hitler on his work, the man he had picked out two years earlier as the "savior" figure was now providing him with the self-confirmation that the narcissist Goebbels demanded. What were differences over policy compared to this? What mattered was to submit to the genius.

Quite obviously, however, the courting of Goebbels was part of the tactics used by Hitler to divide the "northwest German" opposition: give the protagonists new tasks and thus tie them more closely to the Munich leadership. On July 1 he put Strasser in charge of NSDAP propaganda throughout the Reich; Pfeffer was already a spokesman for the SA during discussions and was to take over that office starting on November 1.[146] The proposed "promotion" of Goebbels should be seen in the same light. The very fact that Hitler so ostentatiously lavished attention on him led to growing mistrust among Goebbels's political friends and undermined his position in Elberfeld—which in turn could only serve to bind him more closely to Hitler.

Corresponding at the beginning of August, Strasser and Goebbels "had a forthright exchange about our relationship to each other," but Goebbels still believed he could "straighten things out" with Strasser.[147] He recorded on August 23: "The latest line: People in the movement are noting my Damascus. I have bowed to Hitler and Munich. Gossip-monger: 1. Strasser, and 2. originators: Elbrechter and Kaufmann."

Goebbels dealt with his critics in an open letter that he published in the *Briefe*.[148] The revolution, he said, was no abstract "thing in itself" but a "practical political step on the way to socialism." To stand solidly behind the "Führer," who "is an instrument of the divine will that shapes history," had nothing to do with "Damascus."

At the end of August the Munich office offered him the position of acting Gauleiter of Berlin, with a four-month tenure. But Goebbels was undecided.[149] In mid-September he traveled to the capital, where the incumbent Gauleiter, Ernst Schlange, and his deputy Erich Schmiedicke tried to persuade him to accept the position.[150] In the middle of October he returned to Berlin "with a full heart." His relationship with Else was now breaking down completely, which may have accelerated his decision to move to the capital.[151] Goebbels, after his Elberfeld experience quite unused to being celebrated, clearly enjoyed the Berliners' attempts to recruit him. After three days in the capital he was ready "to take over Berlin and to rule. Period!"[152] The Party leadership dispelled his last doubts at the beginning of November during a stay in Munich.[153] As was Hitler's intention, the working association of the northwestern Gauleiters had meanwhile been quietly dissolved.[154]

CHAPTER 4

"Faith Moves Mountains"

Political Beginnings in Berlin

Goebbels was able to assert himself in the position of Gauleiter of Berlin only because he could
count on the Party leader's protection. This photo
from the Nuremberg Party rally of 1927 clearly
illustrates this relationship of dependency. At this
point, the NSDAP in Berlin-Brandenburg had
been banned for three months. On their return
from the Party rally, the 450-man Berlin contingent was picked up by the police and arrested en
masse.

Conditions in the Berlin NSDAP in the mid-1920s were notoriously
difficult. Right-wing radicalism had certainly enjoyed something of a
heyday until 1923, but with the stabilizing of the Republic the various
groups sank into insignificance. Moreover, there persisted within the

newly founded NSDAP from 1925 onward a strong paramilitary formation, the Frontbann: Jealous of its independence and still wholly
attached to "putschist" tactics, it was reluctant to accept the Munich
leadership's new "legal" strategy. Consequently, the Party did not
participate in the Berlin municipal elections of October 1925—apart
from one district, Spandau, where it gained a grand total of 137 votes
(0.3%). The Party leadership tried to bring the paramilitary element
decisively under its authority by forming a "Sportabteilung" (sports
section), a temporary substitute name for the Sturmabteilung, which
had not yet been officially re-founded after its banning. However,
this SA, as the paramilitaries themselves called it, continued to lead
an independent existence as before: There were 450 men in the SA,
compared to about 200 Party members. The situation was further
complicated by the fact that the Strasser brothers, who called for a
distinct "left-wing" direction for the NSDAP, were powerful within
the Berlin Party. Their publishing house, Kampf-Verlag, was based in
Berlin, and their newspaper, *Der nationale Sozialist,* which appeared
in Berlin as the *Berliner Arbeiterzeitung* (Berlin Workers' Newspaper), was the sole National Socialist press organ there.[1]

In the course of the year the conflict between the Party and the SA
became more acute, such that Gauleiter Ernst Schlange was forced to
hand over responsibility to Erich Schmiedicke. At a Party meeting in
August 1926, the SA leader, Kurt Daluege, managed to install the
former Free Corps commander Oskar Hauenstein as Schlange's successor; in the process there were wild scenes during which Otto
Strasser and Hauenstein slapped each other in the face.[2]

To try to get a grip on the situation, the Munich office sent an outsider to Berlin to calm tempers. Joseph Goebbels seemed to be the
right man for the job.

HITLER'S MAN IN THE CAPITAL

The early days of Goebbels in Berlin have been described more than
once.[3] Most authors follow the line put out by Goebbels himself in his
propaganda publication *Kampf um Berlin* (Struggle for Berlin), first
published in 1931: In the book, he claims that he first of all consolidated the chaotic Party organization in the capital and then through
a series of provocative acts ensured that Berliners took notice of this

political splinter group. This was, he maintains, the precondition for the conquest of "red Berlin" that followed. He asserts that the banning of the NSDAP in May 1927 should be seen in connection with a series of carefully engineered scandals and therefore, in retrospect, as a sign of success. *Trotz Verbot nicht tot* (despite the ban, still alive) ran the slogan.[4]

Goebbels's account of these months in *Kampf um Berlin* is based on a heavily reworked version of his diaries, the original text of which became accessible only with the publication of the new edition of the journal in 2005.[5] The unrevised version shows that, contrary to the stylized and self-serving propaganda account in *Kampf um Berlin*, Goebbels's beginnings in Berlin by no means represented a triumphal progress. The fact was that the Prussian authorities managed very successfully to keep the NSDAP under control through bans and restraints and used the criminal law to maintain considerable pressure on the Gauleiter. Moreover, Goebbels's policies provoked opposition within the Party, which he could only overcome with solid support from Munich. The rise of the NSDAP did not begin in Berlin in 1927–28 but about a year later and mostly in the provinces.

On November 9, 1926, the day he left Elberfeld for Berlin, Goebbels started a new diary. On the first page he wrote: "With this book I begin the struggle for Berlin—how will it end???"[6]

Goebbels's appointment itself had met with disapproval in the Berlin Party organization. "Agitation about the salary" negotiated by Goebbels led the Berlin office to send him the money every month via Munich.[7] What Goebbels took charge of was an expanded Gau, "Berlin-Brandenburg," formed out of the former Gaus "Greater Berlin" and "Potsdam." Hitler launched Goebbels on his new start with special powers: Goebbels was "responsible solely to him [. . .] for the organizational, propagandistic, and political leadership of the Gau"; the local SA and SS were also to come under his "political leadership," and their leaders would be selected by the Party leadership following Goebbels's recommendations.[8]

Goebbels moved in at first "with good old Steiger": At this time Hans Steiger was editor of the newspaper *Berliner Lokal-Anzeiger* (Berlin Local Advertiser) and an active member of the NSDAP who took in paying guests, mostly Party comrades, at his house in the Potsdamer Strasse.[9] The incumbent business manager of the Berlin NSDAP was Franz Gutsmiedl: "A Bavarian. Good-natured, decent, not particularly bright, but extremely useful as an executive officer." However, as the weeks passed, Goebbels's comments on the "decent Bavarian" deteriorated, until he finally parted from him at the end of the year.[10] Goebbels also inherited the deputy Gauleiter Erich Schmiedicke and the treasurer Rudolf Rehm: "They're hard-working but lack initiative."[11]

On the day he arrived, November 9, Goebbels was already giving a speech at a memorial ceremony of the Deutscher Frauenorden (Order of German Women, recognized by the NSDAP that year as the Party's official women's organization); he was criticized in the *Berliner Tageblatt* for praising Hermann Fischer and Erwin Kern, the murderers of Foreign Minister Walther Rathenau, as models of patriotic conviction. Since this cosmopolitan newspaper otherwise largely ignored NSDAP events, Goebbels counted this comment as his "first success."[12]

It was no accident that Hitler came to the capital during the days when his new beacon of hope was taking over office. One day after his arrival he took him to meet the Bechsteins. The piano manufacturer Edwin Bechstein and his wife, Helene, were fervent supporters of Hitler, who made use of their home for discreet political meetings. Hitler turned up in Berlin again a few days later and spent an evening with Goebbels.[13] The latter lost no time in contacting the Strassers, getting together with them often, and setting great store by Gregor in particular: "Good, honest Gregor. I like him."[14]

Goebbels, in a "really combative mood," plunged straight into the work. He held "consultation after consultation, [. . .] discussion after discussion." For the lower-middle-class product of Rheydt who had studied predominantly in comfortable university towns, life in the metropolis was a novelty. He shared the contemporary prejudice of provincials against the capital: "Berlin: city of the intelligentsia and of asphalt,"[15] a "pillar of iniquity and naked wealth."[16] It took him some years to shake off these reservations about the "asphalt desert" of Berlin.[17]

Hardly had he arrived before he shot off a round-robin memo to Party comrades in Berlin in a brusque tone that left no doubt who was in charge: "The Gau office is the workplace of the Gau Berlin-Brandenburg and as such not to be confused with a shelter or a waiting room. [. . .] The Gauleiter is available only for business matters." The local NSDAP branches that had existed so far in Berlin were disbanded. There was now just one Berlin local branch with sections in the various districts. Goebbels also announced that he had appointed Daluege, the powerful head of the Berlin SA, his deputy Gauleiter.[18]

At a meeting of the Berlin NSDAP on November 11, he managed to assert himself against the leader of the opposition: "Hauenstein, my snooping polar opposite, was set on terrorizing and breaking up the meeting yesterday evening; his people had to leave the hall, and as many as 50 men left. I'm rid of the eternal troublemakers and negative critics."[19] With that, as far as he was concerned, the internal Party opposition was "finished. For good and all!"[20]

On November 17, Penitence and Prayer Day (Buss- und Bettag), he held a meeting with "Berlin's finest" and founded, as he had in his old Gau, an "NS-Freedom League," whose members pledged to make a certain monthly donation to the Party coffers.[21] On November 14 the SA staged a propaganda march in the "red" citadel of Neukölln. Not surprisingly, there were violent clashes with the communists. Goebbels noted: "Parade in Neukölln, 4 seriously injured, 4 slightly injured. But we're on the march."[22] On November 20, a Sunday, he held his first "Gau day," an event he staged every month from then on, with the purpose of making the leading Party and SA functionaries commit themselves to his line.[23]

It was not long before the first conflicts arose between Goebbels and Gregor Strasser. He was "in the final analysis a Bavarian bourgeois, not a revolutionary, not ascetic, not a New Man."[24] Goebbels also fell out with Gregor's brother Otto. The latter's whole character displeased him: "There's a lot about him which is decayed and rotten. He has no feeling for the ascetic."[25] After he received a "stupid, illogical letter" from Gregor, he had a long meeting with him to clear the air, in the course of which he settled on his verdict about the brothers, not deviating from it in the following weeks: "Gregor is good, Otto is a rogue."[26]

Goebbels was featured as a speaker in various settings, as for example on November 30 in the Veterans' Association House, and at the National Socialist Christmas festivities on December 11 ("They all love me"). At the Veterans' Association on December 17 he gave what he thought was his "best speech in Berlin."[27] He found that in the new environment his rhetoric was gradually changing: "My way of thinking, speaking and writing has moved toward the graphic and the typical. I never see the particular anymore, just what is typical. I think that's a tremendous gain in itself."[28] For his public engagements he tried in his outward appearance to demonstrate his distance from "bourgeois" politics: Photographs from his "years of struggle" in Berlin show him mostly wearing a leather jacket or a faded trench coat.

He gradually settled down in Berlin. He developed a friendship with the graphic artist Hans Herbert Schweitzer, who designed National Socialist posters under the pseudonym Mjölnir. Goebbels often visited the Schweitzers and posed for the artist.[29] He also had a good relationship with his landlord, Steiger, although he did find the latter "rather too soft."[30] He frequently dropped in on the Bechsteins, because Frau Bechstein was "often like a mother" to him.[31] Christmas was spent with his parents in Rheydt, New Year's with the Schweitzers in Berlin.[32]

Early in 1927, Goebbels arranged for the Party to move into a new office at Lützowstrasse 44. The old headquarters at Potsdamer Strasse 109, "a kind of dirty vaulted cellar at the rear of a building," known as "the opium den" and serving as a meeting place for out-of-work Party comrades to loiter in, hardly seemed conducive to the efficiently functioning office that was extremely important to him.[33] He also set out to create a band, acquired an "official Party car" ("a lovely six-seater Benz"), and reorganized the SA, which was now brought together under three "standards" for the whole region of the Berlin-Potsdam Gau.[34] In addition, he went on speaking at NSDAP events throughout the Reich.[35] One of his trips took him to Munich, where he appeared at the "packed Hacker beer cellar." Afterward he sat with Hitler late into the night: "I think he likes me. I am full of enthusiasm for him."

The next day Rudolf Hess introduced him to Elsa Bruckmann; she and her husband, the publisher Hugo Bruckmann, were two of the most important financial backers of the NSDAP and its Führer in Munich. And during his stay in Munich, to his enormous pleasure Hitler gave him "the first copy of volume two of *Mein Kampf*." On the journey back to Berlin he read "Hitler's book with feverish excitement. Genuine Hitler. Just as he is! Sometimes I feel like shouting for joy. He really is a fellow!"[36]

It is hardly conceivable that Goebbels failed to notice in his reading that Hitler's views differed a good deal from the principles he himself had upheld only a short while before. For example, Hitler quite unmistakably declared the acquisition of *Lebensraum* (living space) at the cost of the Soviet Union to be the central aim of National Socialist policy[37] while carefully avoiding even the most general claim to a socialist direction.

But for Goebbels, questions of content were unimportant; for him *Mein Kampf* was not primarily a political program but the prophecy and revelation of the master—and therefore beyond criticism and discussion.

PROPAGANDA TACTICS

"What drives an ideological movement," Goebbels asserted in a speech to the national Party rally in August 1927, was in essence "not a matter of knowledge but of faith." Besides Jean-Jacques Rousseau's writings and Karl Marx's *Kapital,* he cited as an example above all the Sermon on the Mount.[38] "Christ did not offer proofs in his Sermon on the Mount," wrote Goebbels in an article around this time. "He simply made assertions. Self-evident truths don't have to be proven."[39] It could not have been clearer: Goebbels had no intention of conducting Party propaganda in terms of argument. The only thing that mattered was a successful impact on the masses: "Berlin needs sensations like a fish needs water. This city lives off them, and any political propaganda that fails to recognize this is bound to miss its target."[40] The focus of his activity for the moment was the propaganda generated by posters and meetings.[41] The impact of leaflets depended on massive print runs, and there was no money for them. And the only National Socialist press organ in the city was in the hands of the Strasser brothers, from whom Goebbels maintained an ever-increasing critical distance.

Between August 1926 and the spring of 1927, Goebbels published in the *Briefe* some handy practical tips on propaganda. For the first time, he sought to bring the available propaganda media together in one place.

In August 1926 he suggested that in the coming winter, intensive propaganda should be used to "build up one or two dozen large cities of the Reich into impregnable bulwarks of the movement" and from these fortresses venture forth to conquer the provinces. But an essential precondition for this was that the regional work be subordinated to a "single control center." The core and hub of this propaganda offensive should be public meetings, in connection with which posters and leaflets should play an important part.[42]

In a further series of articles he dealt with various forms of propaganda: the "daily grind"[43] of Party activists, perhaps in their workplace; the "discussion evenings"[44] of local branches; and above all the core activity of Nazi propaganda, the "mass meeting."[45] It was decisively important that such large-scale events should be "prepared in painstaking detail." Political opponents who tried to break into and disrupt the proceedings should be "politely manhandled out of the building" by the SA. If it came to the rough stuff, it would not do to be too fussy, explained Goebbels with a conspiratorial wink: "Compensation for riot damage starts at four hundred marks. I need say no more!"[46] But mass meetings stood or fell by the choice of speaker. Goebbels exhorted his comrades to take good care of their speakers.[47]

In an article on "The Poster," Goebbels set out some design principles: As always, posters carrying texts were given pride of place. A textual poster should coin phrases that "would eventually become slogans." Posters should be "a skillfully formulated series of apparently unmotivated mental leaps." He put forward as an example a Berlin poster design featuring short sentences with exclamation marks, precisely a series of "mental leaps" comprising fifteen lines of text. The whole thing should take no longer than a minute to read. In the case of visual posters, however, aesthetics played a decisive role: "A pictorial poster must be artistically flawless and convincing as propaganda."[48] Naturally, Goebbels added slyly, posters must only be put up where permitted. However, if they should be "purloined by overzealous Party members and posted on empty house walls, garden fences, or perhaps on the windows of Jewish businesses, even being stuck on with water-glass glue," this would be "very regrettable from a moral point of view"—but could not be helped. As far as design was concerned, there was one point to bear in mind above all else: "The color of our movement is a brilliant red. There should be no color in our posters other than this revolutionary one."

Goebbels admitted that his propaganda neither possessed a method of its own nor conformed to any theory: "It has only one aim, and this political aim is always known as 'the conquest of the masses.' All means used to this end are good. And all means that ignore this aim are bad. [. . .] Propaganda methods develop out of the day-to-day struggle."[49] He formulated this thoroughly instrumental and functional approach in many ways,[50] including outright cynicism. In a presentation in August 1929 he contended that the people were "in his view mostly just a gramophone record playing back public opinion. Public opinion [. . .], in its turn, is created by the organs of public opinion such as the press, posters, radio, school, and university and general education. But the government owns these organs."[51]

It seems that in developing these principles Goebbels was not much influenced by contemporary theoretical writings about the much-discussed use of slogans in political propaganda; unlike Hitler, he was not particularly impressed by the propaganda put out by the workers' movement or by British propaganda during the Great War. He took his cue from the model of commercial advertising, and there was nowhere better to study it than the world of everyday Berlin, which in the "Golden Twenties" had become something of a laboratory for advertising experiments.[52]

The commercial advertisement of those days fell more and more under the influence of advertising psychology, developed in the United States and picked up and systematically applied in Germany starting in the early 1920s. Advertising experts experimented to establish fundamental axioms about the readability of various scripts and forms, along with the optimum size, colors, and placement of advertising material; systematic work was done on the cognitive and recognition powers of passersby; and so forth. In accordance with the behaviorism prevalent in psychology at the time, advertising specialists were convinced that consumer behavior could be greatly influenced by relatively simple, partly subliminal stimuli. Much significance was attached to the principle of concentrating and repeating advertisers' messages in the form of campaigns.[53] Such new methods of commercial advertising were widely discussed in the public sphere, and their practical results could be seen in the advertisement columns of newspapers, in cinema advertising, and in the everyday metropolitan scene.

Goebbels took over these models and used them for Party propaganda. In August 1929 he attended an advertising exhibition in Berlin, casting an expert, critical eye over the exhibits: "Quite a few very good things. But most of it still inspired by the bourgeois spirit." Significantly, he noted the absence of "the political poster" at the exhibition.[54] In a leaflet written by his head of propaganda in Berlin, Georg Stark, and published by Goebbels in 1930, commercial advertising was overtly cited as the model to follow.[55] Whether it was a matter of simplification, constant repetition of memorable slogans, or concentration of propaganda material in regular campaigns, the principles of mass advertising could easily be applied to political propaganda.

If the National Socialist movement in general highlighted the significance of inflammatory speech-making among its propaganda methods, this was especially true of the Berlin NSDAP and its Gauleiter. A naturally gifted orator, during his Berlin years Goebbels perfected his rhetorical abilities; any event in which he was announced as a speaker was sure to see a strong turnout.

Joseph Goebbels's effect as a speaker was based on a whole package of abilities. Given his slight build, he had a surprisingly deep voice that projected well, one that was carefully articulated but also capable of modulation.[56] Even if he made extreme demands on his voice—as we know he often did—he generally avoided making it sound overstretched or perceptibly strained to the listener. As a speaker he commanded a relatively wide register of different styles: sometimes a witty conversational tone; biting irony; furious, even desperate accusation; solemn and triumphal pathos; an obituary oration with his voice almost breaking. He had a rich vocabulary at his disposal (sometimes adopting rare, quaintly old-fashioned phrases) and brought in many historical examples and classical quotations. On the other hand, his arguments were always easy to grasp, intelligible to a broad audience.

Unlike Hitler, as a speaker Goebbels always kept himself well under control at every stage of his address, even when completely exhausted. His acting and gestures, carefully practiced, were almost perfectly suited to the speech at hand, their lively and dramatic quality striking contemporary observers as quite Mediterranean.[57] Typical were the light waving motion of his hand that accompanied the expository parts of his speech; the threatening index finger suddenly thrust skyward; the clenched fist, which he moved back and forth to beat his chest to the rhythm of his sentence; the hammering on the lectern; and the posture of arms akimbo, meant to underline the authority of the speaker.

His mildly Rhenish accent reinforced the often measured, solemn tone of his speech. The stretching of certain vowels typical of the Rhineland enabled him to pronounce such key terms as "Führer" or "Deutschland" with particular fervor or to emit with theatrical contempt words such as "Judentum" (Jewry). With his singsong intonation and certain idiosyncratic features of expression and emphasis, he could achieve an effective heightening of his sentence and then bring it to a more or less harmonious conclusion. In short, all this lent Goebbels's language its own rhythm, giving his sentences an unmistakable "tune," often reminiscent of the church preacher, a "heartfelt tone," as one of his later listeners, Victor Klemperer, was to call it.[58] However, this tone could very quickly turn into that of a biting attack. It was precisely this flexibility and versatility that made Goebbels so effective as a speaker.

DOMINATING THE STREETS

If the whole object of Goebbels's highly robust propaganda campaign was to attract attention at any price, he certainly succeeded: "People started talking about us. We could no longer be ignored or passed over in icy contempt. However reluctant and furious they were about it, people couldn't avoid mentioning us." The Party was "suddenly at the center of public interest," and "people now had to decide whether they were for or against."[59]

But getting your name known was just the first step. Using a combination of aggressive propaganda and violent action, Goebbels was out to achieve for the Party what he had called, in an article in the summer of 1926, "domination of the streets": "Anyone who spreads his ideology by terror and brutality against all force will one day gain power and thereby also the right to bring down the state."[60]

Goebbels approached this objective by arranging a series of carefully targeted provocations in quick succession. The Party caused violent confrontations on a grand scale, not only drawing attention to itself but also penetrating districts that had until then been the preserve of the workers' movement.

The first event in this series was a mass meeting in the Seitz ballroom in the red citadel of Spandau. Reportedly, there were five hundred Communist Party (KPD) supporters in the hall, about half of those present. Goebbels himself judged that he spoke "as I've never done before in Berlin. The reds are quite bemused." During the discussion news filtered through that an NSDAP supporter had been knocked down in the street. Goebbels immediately broke off and had his debating opponent forcibly ejected from the building. The National Socialists left in closed ranks. Later there was some brawling with communists on the streets of Spandau.[61]

A few days later Goebbels appeared at a rally in Cottbus. SA members from throughout the Gau area rounded off the proceedings with a propaganda march through the town, where on the same day—surely no coincidence—a trade union rally and a procession by the Reichsbanner (Reich Banner)* were due to take place. The police tried in vain to keep the two groups of supporters apart. The outcome was a pitched battle between the SA and the police.[62]

On February 11 there was another rally, this time in the Pharus rooms in Wedding, another red stronghold. This occasion was conceived as an "open declaration of war" against the left. Goebbels chose his topic, "The Collapse of the Bourgeois Class System," with a working-class audience in mind. The Party chronicler Reinhold Muchow, from the Neukölln district branch, commented that "it was all about making it obvious that National Socialism is absolutely determined to use all necessary force to get to the workers." And it did: During the meeting the SA, clearly in the majority, fought with KPD supporters.[63] These riots publicized the NSDAP, but the "struggle" also consolidated Goebbels's position within the Party: "Quite suddenly these successes secured and established for us the strong, leading authority we had never enjoyed in our Berlin organization," wrote Goebbels, looking back in his propaganda book *Struggle for Berlin*.[64]

On February 15 there was another event in Spandau, where members of the Roter Frontkämpferbund (Red Frontline Fighters' League)† were violently evicted from the hall. On the return trip to the city center, a communist counterattack was anticipated: Some of the SA were armed. Goebbels fancied himself in the role of the daredevil revolutionary: "Home! 6 cars. All full of gunners. Along the whole long Heerstrasse. In the dead of night. War! Revolution!" But the attack never came.[65]

On February 23 Goebbels again arrived in Munich, where "the boss" called on him in person in his hotel the next morning. "I'm

---

* Translators' note: The pro-Republican and predominantly Social Democratic paramilitary force.
† Translators' note: The communist paramilitary organization.

terrifically pleased to see him again. He is so good to me. A true Führer and friend!" They went to Hitler's home, where first of all Goebbels received "a little dressing down" because of an essay he had published a few days earlier openly accusing Wilhelm Frick of jeopardizing National Socialist principles by his politically motivated tactics in the Reichstag.[66] "I tolerated it," Goebbels wrote. But then Hitler suddenly got to his feet. He "gives me both hands, gripping tightly, tears come to his eyes, and then he says: 'You are right.'" Then they discussed a whole series of inner Party figures, and agreed with each other "one hundred percent" on all of them, including their estimation of the Strasser brothers. Together, they went to lunch, to headquarters, to a café, and in the evening to dinner and the theater. They concluded the evening in a pub. On parting, Hitler had said: "You should be with me all the time. [. . .] He expresses my inmost thoughts!"[67] Once again, Goebbels succumbed completely to the Hitler charm offensive.

The most serious clash so far instigated by the NSDAP came on March 20, 1927. At a nighttime event in Trebbin, about eighteen miles from Berlin, celebrating the first anniversary of the official existence of the Berlin SA, Goebbels had made an "incendiary speech." The next day at a rally he raised the temperature still further by making a rabidly anti-Semitic speech from his open car. After a concluding ceremony, as some of the SA contingent were making their way home by train, they came across a troop of Red Frontline Fighters and tried to get access to the communists' carriage via the footboards and the roof of the train. At every station they threw stones at the car until all the windows were smashed. The confrontation escalated at the Lichterfeld Ost Station: A shot rang out from the communist side, badly wounding an SA man. At this point the SA tried to storm the carriage, only to be repulsed by further shots from the communists. Two Nazis and fourteen communists were wounded, some of them seriously.[68]

When Goebbels arrived at the station, having traveled by car, agitated NSDAP supporters were already gathering for a demonstration: "March through the city. Every provocation to be punished with the most extreme severity. Our brave lads pull a Jew down out of a bus. [. . .] The new Germany is demonstrating. I speak in front of 10,000 people in the Wittenbergplatz. With huge success."[69]

On their march the Nazis had indeed abused or knocked down

passersby they took to be Jewish.[70] Two days later the liberal *Berliner Tageblatt* complained about the total ineffectiveness of the police.[71] After this, the police appeared in great strength at two National Socialist meetings and—with some success—searched those present for weapons.[72] Goebbels reviewed the situation: "I'm terrifically pleased about one thing: that we managed to irritate this massive city sufficiently to force it to react. [. . .] The Jew [*sic*] has done me the honor of saying in the *B.T.* and the *News at Eight* that I have succeeded in bringing things out into the open here."[73] According to a Berlin criminal police report, not all Party members approved of Goebbels's brutal methods, but the majority were "in favor of activity." And in March the number of Party members rose by 400 to about 3,000.[74]

On May 4 Goebbels spoke again at the Veterans' Association House. "A fresh heckler was thrown out into the fresh air," he noted laconically in his diary. "At the end the 3–400 people present were searched by two police companies for weapons. Imagine this lunacy."[75] Somebody had indeed heckled Goebbels during his speech and on a signal from the Gauleiter had been seized by a horde of SA men, brutally manhandled, and thrown down the stairs. A journalist from the Scherl publishing house who was discovered in the hall was subjected to the same treatment. A large contingent of police then sealed off the premises and searched every participant individually for weapons.[76]

This occurrence—which has to be seen in the context of the provocative tactics pursued by Goebbels since January—led the head of the Berlin police, Karl Friedrich Zörgiebel, to take a drastic step: On May 5, 1927, just seven months after Goebbels became Gauleiter, the Berlin-Brandenburg organization of the NSDAP was declared to have been dissolved. The reasons cited were the acts of violence by the Nazis and a series of pronouncements by Goebbels that made it clear that the Party was proceeding deliberately to fulfill a plan.[77] But Goebbels was not in the least abashed. On the contrary, "Dissolved. It shows we're on the right path. That's good!" He only narrowly escaped arrest by going to Stuttgart for a while.[78]

Goebbels's policy of provocation was certainly not without its detractors in the Party, and the ban on the Party was not universally acclaimed as a success. Even before the passing of the ban, the internal Party opposition had attacked him severely for his ruthless leadership style. On April 27, 1927, a remarkable article had appeared in the *Berliner Arbeiterzeitung,* the Strassers' newspaper. In it, Party comrade Erich Koch, district leader in Elberfeld, had issued a warning about people who were "marked" by the consequences of miscegenation: "We have enough examples from history in this area. King Richard III of England [. . .] was a model of depravity. [. . .] And there you have it: He was a hunchback with a limp. Like him, the court jester of Francis I of France limped, too; he was notorious, infamous, and hated for his malice, intrigues, and calumnies. [. . .] Talleyrand had a clubfoot. His character is well known." In short, people of this kind, though "intelligent, were boundlessly ambitious, heartless egoists who have never done their people as a whole anything but harm."[79]

Incandescent with rage about these "swine," Goebbels complained to Hitler about Strasser.[80] However, Koch denied that his "clubfoot" remark was in any way aimed at Goebbels.[81] For his part, Goebbels assumed that the forces of opposition in the Berlin Party organization had written the article with the agreement of Otto Strasser and that Koch was nothing but a patsy. He demanded a clear declaration of loyalty from Hitler and threatened to resign if the latter chose merely to pass over the incident in silence.[82] The difficulty of his relationship with the Strassers was further exacerbated by Goebbels's plan to bring out a newspaper of his own in Berlin no later than the end of May, thus competing with the Strassers' Kampf-Verlag. This blatant offensive[83] added even more fuel to the rage of the Strasser brothers.[84] Before the end of the month he was obliged to give up editing the *Nationalsozialistische Briefe.* Goebbels's thoughts turned to revenge.[85]

The conflict became more acute when criticism of the high-handed Gauleiter, expressed so clearly in the article, increased after the ban on the Party. At a meeting of the Party inner circle in Munich, Goebbels was obliged to defend himself against the Strassers' charge that he had unnecessarily provoked the authorities' move by his behavior.[86] At the Berlin Party rally of June 10, 1927, Goebbels read the "clubfoot" article aloud and named the Party comrades in Berlin he thought were behind the attack. His misshapen foot, he declared, was "not an innate defect" but the result of an accident. This was one of the very few occasions when he referred to his deformity in public.

Finally, Goebbels consulted Party headquarters about how to handle the affair. The result was that in the *Völkischer Beobachter* of

June 25, Hitler moved to counter the rumors already circulating widely in the Berlin press of "fraternal strife in the house of Hitler." He reaffirmed that Goebbels enjoyed his full confidence.[87] The very fact that Goebbels needed this support from Munich shows how hard it was for him to deal with the internal Party opposition.

The conflict flared up again in September 1927, and Goebbels found himself once more offering Hitler his resignation.[88] When Hitler came to Berlin shortly afterward, they again spent a great deal of time together—but without discussing the conflict.[89] In the end, with Hitler acting as intermediary, Goebbels in November concluded a "Strasser peace" with the brothers.[90] In December he thought he had obtained Hitler's agreement that the Kampf-Verlag should be moved to Essen.[91] But this did not happen. There was peace for a few months, but then the conflict with the Strassers broke out again.

With all these troubles in the Gau, Goebbels's relations with his friend and landlord, Steiger, had steadily deteriorated.[92] Finally, Steiger left Goebbels's weekly *Der Angriff* (The Attack), moving to the Strassers' *Arbeiterzeitung*. Goebbels thought he saw the "low-bred scoundrel" emerging in Steiger.[93] Under these circumstances it was impossible to remain Steiger's tenant. At the beginning of November he rented an apartment in Friedenau.[94]

During his first months in Berlin, Goebbels had kept loosely in touch with Else, seeing her—although increasingly rarely—when he happened to go to Rheydt.[95] Gradually he began to keep an eye out in Berlin. His eye fell first upon "Fräulein Behr," who had joined the team at the Gau office in the spring of 1927.[96]

In spring 1927 he struck up a flirtation with Dora Hentschel, a young woman from Dessau who had just taken up a teaching position in Potsdam.[97] But hardly had the relationship begun when Goebbels wanted to end it: "I must not make her unhappy. That's why I've got to stop seeing her."[98] A female acquaintance in whose house he had met Dora strongly advised him to marry, but this advice did not appeal to Goebbels: "What's the hurry? I replied rather angrily."[99] He began to see less of Dora.[100] In December 1927, in a "Russian pub," he got to know a "wonderful blonde Russian émigrée," Tamara von Heede.[101] They began their affair in February 1928.[102]

DER ANGRIFF

The strife within the Party and the immobilized Party organization induced Goebbels, who at the end of 1925 had already been pursuing the idea of a national socialist weekly for West Germany, to start up a publication of his own in Berlin, acquiring Hitler's approval for a weekly paper called *Der Angriff* (The Attack).[103] The first issue, appearing in early July, was preceded by a big advertising campaign. Three posters appeared at an interval of a few days on the Berlin streets. The first simply bore the words "The Attack?" and the second proclaimed, "The Attack begins on July 4"; only by the third poster did the public learn that a new magazine would be appearing on Mondays.[104] Goebbels found "many faults" with the first edition.[105] He was much happier with subsequent issues.[106]

Der Angriff projected itself as a modern metropolitan paper taking a shrill, aggressive line. Its slogan, "For the oppressed! Against the exploiters," suggested a socialist alignment; in many ways, the Strassers' *Berliner Arbeiterzeitung* (Berlin Workers' Newspaper) was the model. But since the paper's early editions had a modest print run of about two hundred copies, it hardly reached the proletarian masses.

Goebbels regularly wrote the editorials, and his byline was attached to a column called "The Political Diary." He left the role of editor in chief to Julius Lippert, who had relevant experience in the *völkisch* press. The distinctive caricatures—featuring mostly powerful-looking SA men—were contributed by Goebbels's friend Schweitzer/Mjölnir.

In the editorials Goebbels showed himself to be an accomplished stylist. He turned his hand to a variety of genres: satirical, fairy-tale, saga, conversational, or epistolary.[107] Goebbels enjoyed writing in the vein of a metropolitan tabloid journalist, with the appropriate aggressive and deliberately overblown formulations aimed at the Republic and its press. So, for example, he called the detective assigned to shadow him a "snout-wipe," and the chief commissioner of police the current "token goy at Berlin police headquarters." Foreign Minister Gustav Stresemann appeared as "this politicizing dilettante thrown up by a grotesque quirk of fate out of the chocolate trade into high diplomacy," and the "so-called German Reichstag" was "a pawnbroker tribunal in the service of high finance."[108]

Goebbels also used *Der Angriff* in various ways to publicize his own views, diverging as they did from the official Party line. This applied, for example, to his interpretation of the "Russian question," which held that "Bolshevism" was in the process of a development in which it "purges itself of its Jewish wreckers and begins to pursue nationalist policies beyond party dogma."[109] But he soon dropped this line of argument. In the autumn of 1930 he planned to bring up, in two editorials, the demand for a stronger "socialist" emphasis in the National Socialist program but abandoned the project after the leadership plainly signaled that this was not the direction it had in mind.

One characteristic of *Der Angriff* was its—even by National Socialist standards—strikingly vulgar anti-Semitism. On the death of the Jewish left-liberal publicist Maximilian Harden, for example, the paper said on November 3 that he had been "executed by inflammation of the lungs." With him, "there departed from this world one of the lowest, most vile of individuals, who brought Germany to the brink of the abyss."[110] In its anti-Semitic hate campaign, *Der Angriff* did not even shrink from invoking, in all seriousness, the medieval motif of "Jewish ritual murder."[111]

There was one person above all who was the prime target for anti-Semitic abuse: the lawyer Dr. Bernhard Weiss, appointed deputy commissioner of police in March 1927.[112] In 1927–28 there was only one issue of *Der Angriff* that failed to attack him. In 1928 and 1929, moreover, Goebbels published two anti-Weiss books. In 1929–30 the attacks on Weiss subsided, but they can still be found in more than half of the editions of the paper.[113]

Goebbels—far from the first to do so[114]—dubbed Weiss "Isidor." The supposedly Jewish first name was meant to insinuate that Weiss had changed his name, that for him to use the Germanic "Bernhard" was an affront. In numerous articles and caricatures, "Isidor Weiss" became the anti-Jewish stereotype personified: His appearance was caricatured as "typically Jewish," and he was represented as cowardly, underhanded, overbearing, a ridiculous figure. The object of this distorted image of "Isidor Weiss" was to pillory the alleged predominance of "the Jews" in the Weimar "system." Under the steady barrage of this smear campaign, the person of Weiss became a type and the name "Isidor Weiss" a byword. This confirmed the motto with which

Goebbels prefaced his Isidor book: "Isidor: not a person or an individual in the legal sense. Isidor is a type, a mentality, a face, or rather a phizog."

On September 26, to wild applause from his supporters, Goebbels proclaimed in Hasenheide Park in Neukölln: "We are fighting against men, yes, but in them we are fighting the system. We don't speak like the bourgeois parties of the corruption in Berlin or the Bolshevism of Berlin City Hall. No! All we say is: Isidor Weiss! That's enough!"[115]

Thus Dr. Bernhard Weiss was turned into a caricature. Again and again Weiss was made to serve in Nazi propaganda as a figure, a template "proving" the validity of the anti-Semitic stereotype. Weiss tried to defend himself against his derisive nickname with a flood of complaints, which police headquarters handed on to the state prosecutors. Goebbels came under considerable pressure as a result, and charges against him were upheld, but the publicity generated by all this court activity only made the "Isidor Weiss" stereotype even better known. Thus Goebbels was able to declare disingenuously at an appeal hearing on June 2, 1931, that "the first name Isidor was so familiar to Berliners and was used so often that many people didn't even know Dr. Weiss's real name" and that consequently "no insult can be implied in the use of this name."[116]

Once the "Isidor" sobriquet had been put into circulation, the slightest hint was enough to keep the "Isidor" campaign alive. For example, *Der Angriff* printed the deputy commissioner's real name in quotation marks, and a list of personnel using full names singled Weiss out for the honor of referring to him only by his first name. References to "I. Weiss" or allusions to names in general in connection with the person of the deputy commissioner fulfilled the same purpose. Even where *Der Angriff* used the "respectful" title "Police Commissioner Dr. Bernhard Weiss," it was all part of the same name game. In this game Goebbels was always devising new variations, and Weiss's attempts to defend himself only helped to spread them further. Goebbels asked hypocritically in an editorial in *Der Angriff* in April 1928 why Weiss was so eager to take action against him. "Is it because 'Isidor' is another word for Jew? Does this mean there is something inferior about being Jewish?"[117] In the end, taking legal steps against this campaign proved ineffectual.[118] After one court had established that a caricature donkey did indeed represent Weiss, *Der*

Angriff printed the cartoon again, this time announcing that accord-ing to legal opinion the drawing referred to the deputy police com-missioner, Dr. Bernhard Weiss.[119]

From Goebbels's point of view, this relentless personification of anti-Semitism was the ideal way to denigrate the authority of the Weimar state while also diverting attention from the extreme vague-ness of the NSDAP's policy ideas. This was especially true of the Ber-lin Gauleiter's own ideas: For him, the image of the Jewish enemy represented the counterpart of his very rudimentary notions of "na-tional community" and "socialism." For him, "the Jews" stood for the establishment, for democracy, general moral degeneracy, and cul-tural decline.

LIVING UNDER THE BAN

The Berlin NSDAP, banned in Prussia from the beginning of May 1927, continued an illegal existence, partly in the disguised form of leisure organizations.[120] Time and again Berlin National Socialists provoked incidents. Young Nazis skulked around on the Kurfürsten-damm, looking to jostle and molest passersby they took to be Jewish. A local paper was already voicing its fear that "the brutal activities of National Socialists on the Kurfürstendamm were becoming these youngsters' normal entertainment."[121] In its first issue, *Der Angriff* re-ported the trial of eighteen young National Socialists who in May, "out of justified rage at the unreasonable ban on their meeting," had descended on the Kurfürstendamm. If "Jews behaving arrogantly really had been beaten up there," then the perpetrators were Ger-mans "who had learned at first hand what it means to live under Jewish oppression."[122] When the prison sentences were handed down, Goebbels raged at the verdicts: "There are no judges left in Berlin," he concluded.[123] In an editorial in November he criticized a similar ver-dict,[124] and in his book *Kampf um Berlin* (Struggle for Berlin), pub-lished in 1931, he observed laconically that "the inevitable result of such bans was the constant recurrence of political excesses on the streets. Many a West Berlin Jew found himself getting slapped in these outbursts." Admittedly, some of the people who had been as-saulted had no personal responsibility for the suppression of the

NSDAP, but "the masses do not understand these finer nuances. They grab anyone they can get ahold of."[125]

The Berlin police authorities were not intimidated by such "spontaneous" outbreaks of violence on the part of the National Socialists: They did their best to enforce the ban. On August 22 the Berlin police stopped a train bringing Berlin National Socialists back to the capital from the Nuremberg party rally and arrested 450 men for illegal activities: They were found to possess provisional membership cards.[126] *Der Angriff* then predicted "mass arrests of NSDAP voters and supporters," and in an editorial in the same issue Goebbels proclaimed that the flag confiscated by the police from the arrested comrades was now a fetish, a "sacred cloth."[127]

During the summer of 1927, Goebbels continued to make public appearances in Berlin: As long as the Party did not openly organize an event, the police were powerless to intervene.[128] However, at the end of August—Goebbels had just returned from several weeks of vacation in Bavaria[129]—the Berlin chief commissioner of police pronounced that Goebbels was prohibited from public speaking for more than two months.[130] It was not until November 8 that he gave his next speech, to a meeting of three thousand people in Neukölln.[131] On January 13 he "called the political police to account" in Friedrichshain. Two weeks later the Party succeeded (though not under its own name) in attracting an audience of ten thousand on one evening in two large halls, again in Friedrichshain.[132] In March the NSDAP, still prohibited, staged its "Second Brandenburg Day" in Bernau, near Berlin. Under the noses of the police, who turned out in strength, Goebbels organized a parade in the market square that was followed by an address to the men.[133]

In the early months of 1928, a veritable avalanche of court cases bore down upon Goebbels, who had already been fined in November 1927 for inciting violence.[134] At the end of February 1928 he was sentenced to six weeks' imprisonment for the brutal treatment of a heckler by the SA at the May 4 meeting: This was the incident that earned the Party its ban. In the "Stucke trial," as it was called, the court accepted the state prosecutor's case, perceiving a link between the violent behavior of the SA and one or two relevant "tips" that Goebbels had issued earlier for such situations.[135] "Shameless Terror Tactics Against the N.S.D.A.P.," ran the headline in *Der Angriff*, while Goeb-

bels announced in an article that he regarded prison sentences as
"honors and distinctions" in his battle against the "system."[136]

Goebbels did not have to serve his sentence, as he benefited from
an amnesty brought in by the Reichstag in July 1928. On March 24 he
complained that he had six court cases pending against him: "4 for
insulting Isidor, one for high treason, and one for bodily harm." On
March 29 a Munich court sentenced him to a fine of 1,500 Reichsmarks, once again for an insult to Bernhard Weiss.[137]

Moreover, in March the case concerning the shooting incident in
Lichterfelde came up in court.[138] To avoid giving evidence, Goebbels
planned to go away for the Easter vacation but was remanded and
obliged to appear in court. Eventually, relatively stiff sentences, of
between two and thirty months' imprisonment, were imposed on
five National Socialists.[139] In late April, in another trial, he was again
sentenced to three weeks in jail for an "Isidor" insult, but thanks to
the amnesty law of July 1928, he did not have to serve this sentence
either.[140]

The NSDAP had now been prohibited for almost a year, and the
law had begun seriously to crack down on Goebbels, threatening him
with prison. Within the Party his position was by no means unassail-
able. It seemed that the tactics he had introduced on arriving in Berlin at the end of 1926—especially the use of provocation to draw
attention to the NSDAP at all costs—had led to a dead end.

DIGRESSIONS INTO AUTHORSHIP

Once Goebbels started full-time political activity in 1925, the time
available for reading literature rapidly diminished. His main reading
matter now consisted of the New Right canon, on which he usually
wrote commentaries ranging from benign to enthusiastic. To mention only the best-known titles, these works included Moeller van
den Bruck's *Das Dritte Reich* (The Third Reich), which he had difficulty finishing;[141] Ernst Jünger's *In Stahlgewittern* (Storms of Steel);[142]
Margherita Sarfatti's biography of Mussolini;[143] Houston Stewart
Chamberlain's *Grundlagen des 19. Jahrhunderts* (The Foundations of
the Nineteenth Century);[144] Ernst Röhm's memoir *Geschichte eines
Hochverräters* (The Story of a Traitor);[145] Franz Schauwecker's *Auf-
bruch der Nation* (The Awakening of the Nation);[146] and Alfred

Rosenberg's *Mythos des 20. Jahrhunderts* (Myth of the 20th Century).[147]

Despite all the political turbulence, Goebbels certainly had not given up on his own literary ambitions. Thus he used the period of prohibition to slip once again into his writer persona. In June 1927 he had completed a revised version of his play "The Wanderer."[148] The drama premiered in early November in a "national socialist experimental theater" instituted by the Gau.[149] The piece consisted of eleven "pictures," displayed to the "wanderer" by the "writer," denouncing the failings of the prevailing "system": social misery, exploitation, the stock market (embodied by a Jew, naturally), the alleged mendacity of Marxist party leaders, the rigidity of the "reactionaries." The whole thing climaxed in a final picture solemnly proclaiming the birth of the "Third Reich." The play was an "artless mixture of medieval, Expressionist, and Naturalistic elements," commented a later reviewer who was somewhat puzzled by it.[150]

Goebbels noted with regret that although Hitler was in Berlin during December, he did not choose to attend the performance.[151] Among the reviews, there were two that particularly annoyed Goebbels: A "mean"[152] writeup appeared in the *Nationalsozialistische Briefe,* dismissing the play as "unsatisfactory" and "in the deepest sense untrue to life."[153] The *Berliner Arbeiterzeitung,* published by Otto Strasser, printed what Goebbels called a "miserable" review.[154] In fact, the review by Herbert Blank, one of Otto Strasser's lieutenants, commented that there was much to be said against the play, but he preferred to withhold his criticism in view of its positive reception by "like-minded Berlin friends."[155] Goebbels complained to Hess— and to some effect: He recorded with satisfaction soon afterward that Strasser had been "raked over the coals."[156]

His meager success did not prevent Goebbels from continuing to pursue his literary plans. It was obvious that he wanted to be perceived by the public as a literary man and an intellectual, not just a rabid agitator. In the summer of 1928 he set to work revising his old novel manuscript, "Michael," written in 1924. The book was finally published at the end of 1928,[157] but the literary outpourings of a Nazi Gauleiter passed almost unnoticed.[158]

Goebbels maintained the basic structure of the book: *Michael* is a novel in diary form whose hero, a young war veteran, has autobiographical features as well as some characteristics of his late friend

Richard Flisges. Goebbels extended the idea of merging the two characters by inventing for Michael a friend called Richard, who obtains his Ph.D. at Heidelberg and subsequently works "in a large publishing house."

The novel begins with the return of this "double" Michael from the front. In spring 1919 Michael begins his studies in Heidelberg but is dissatisfied. He falls in love with Hertha Holk, who is unmistakably based on Anka. Michael writes a play about Jesus Christ, studies for another semester in Munich, and loses his beloved Hertha there. He wrestles with his Christian belief, which he finally abandons. He falls more and more under the influence of Ivan Vienurovsky, a revolutionary-minded Russian student of philosophy. Finally he decides to take a job as a miner. Rejected at first by the other workers, he gradually gains their approval, shakes off the influence of Ivan's thinking, and finds his long-sought "salvation" in teamwork. The novel ends with the death of the hero underground. The diary form allows Goebbels, in emotionally charged confessional passages only tenuously related to the plot, to set out his "principled" views on religion, ideology, politics, and literature. Not surprisingly, Michael's diary entries borrow frequently from Goebbels's own diary.

In his 1928 reworking, Goebbels retained the plot and narrative structure but made some changes and additions that had the effect of turning the political and ideological content of the novel on its head. The changes demonstrate two things: First, they show how far Goebbels's ideological standpoint had shifted over the previous few years; and second, they reveal his great skill in making small, calculated alterations to reverse the original message of the work. The revised *Michael* is very much the product of a deeply cynical and highly skilled manipulator of texts.

Goebbels now inserted some biting anti-Semitic passages into the text, whose original version contained hardly any anti-Jewish jibes. He described the Jews as "this abscess on the body of our sick national character," which will "destroy us if we do not neutralize it."[159] "I spend a lot of time sitting in cafés," we read in the older version.[160] "Over a cigarette you can have all sorts of superficial thoughts. You see people. Munich is inconceivable without its cafés."[161] In the book version, Goebbels began the passage in the same conversational tone of the *flâneur* but then gave this short section a completely different turn: "I spend a lot of time sitting in cafés. I get to know people from all over the world. It teaches you to love everything German all the more. This has become so rare in our own fatherland. It's hard to imagine Munich without its snobbish Jews."[162]

He also incorporated a scene of political awakening into the new *Michael:* Michael's first encounter with a real political leader. Michael is sitting in a hall in Munich surrounded by people he doesn't know, the flotsam and jetsam washed up by the lost war. Before he is really aware of it, "somebody is suddenly standing up there and starting to speak. Hesitant and self-conscious at first, as if seeking words for things that are too great to be compressed into narrow forms." But then the speaker gets into his stride: "It's as if he is flooded with light from above. [...] The man up there. Piles up one building-block upon another to build the cathedral of the future. What has been alive in me for years has taken shape here, achieved tangible forms. Revelation! Revelation! [...] That's not a speaker. That's a prophet!"[163] The author has even inserted a dialogue with Hertha Holk where Michael attempts to describe his ideal political leader to her. When she objects that this figure, "the One," will "sacrifice the last flower of our youth," Michael replies coolly: "Geniuses use up people. That's just how it is. But the consolation is that they don't do so for themselves but for their task. It is permissible to use up one youthful generation as long as you open paths to life for a new one."[164]

Throughout the published novel, Goebbels replaces the "love of humanity" pathos of the earlier "Michael" with his new *völkisch* ideal. So the sentence "By redeeming myself, I redeem humanity" now becomes "By redeeming myself, I redeem my *Volk.*"[165] By the same token, "love of humanity" becomes "dedication to the *Volk.*"[166] In the original text he had called for an alliance with Russia. There we read, in a speech ascribed to Ivan (but lifted from his diary): "Within the great problem of Europe lies the old, holy Russia. Russia is the past and the future, but not the present. [...] The solution of the great puzzle that is Europe is burgeoning in the soil of Russia. [...] Ex oriente Lux!"[167] This now became: "The great problem of Europe shares a border with the old, new Russia. Russia is the past and perhaps also the future, but not the present [...]. The solution of its great puzzle is burgeoning in the soil of Russia." Needless to say, he had also deleted the "Ex oriente Lux."[168]

Goebbels even went a step further, turning the vision of fraternal cooperation with Russia that he still harbored in 1924 into a declaration of war. In the old version, he had called out to his Russian friend and intellectual adversary Ivan Vienurovsky as they parted: "You have shown me the path, and I will seek and find the end. Yes, we will cross swords! Over the new man."[169] The 1928 version, however, instead has: "Without wanting to, you have shown me the way. I will find redemption. Yes, we will cross swords, as German and Russian. Teuton and Slav!"[170]

He was to undertake one more literary effort in 1928. In November he began a play he entitled "Die Saat" (The Seed).[171] He had finished the manuscript by February 1929,[172] and the premiere took place in the Nazi experimental theater in March 1929: The one-act drama was now called "Blood Seed."[173] He was angered by the reviews in the "bourgeois press," insisting that they had "missed the point completely."[174] This seems to have been his last attempt to make a name for himself in literature.

CHAPTER 5

"Struggle Is the Father of All Things"

The Gauleiter and the Capital of the Reich

The "conquest of red Berlin"—here Goebbels appears in a proletarian pose in the north of Berlin, 1929—was, in fact, a propaganda invention on Goebbels's part. The NSDAP did not manage to outdo the election results of the two left-wing parties in Berlin: In the Reich capital, the results were always several percentage points below the average for the National Socialists throughout the Reich.

The last session of the Reichstag elected in December 1924 took place on March 31, 1928; a new election was scheduled for May 20. As early as the previous November Hitler had offered Goebbels a place in the list of NSDAP candidates, and after some hesitation Goebbels had accepted: "Although it does my reputation no good, damn it, [it's worth it] if only for the sake of the immunity." The prospect of placing himself beyond the reach of the law was the factor that finally swayed him.[1] In February Hitler had conceived the idea that Goebbels should stand simultaneously for a seat in the Prussian state parliament (the Landtag) and become leader of the parliamentary Party there.[2] Goebbels suspected that the plan was to shunt him off into the Landtag because he was too difficult a customer for his Party comrades in the Reichstag.[3] But the double candidacy project came to nothing.

At the beginning of the election campaign, the Berlin chief commissioner of police lifted the ban on the NSDAP in Berlin.[4] On April 14 the Party was officially re-founded in a solemn ceremony held at the Veteran Soldiers' House.[5] The newly legalized party now moved into new headquarters at Berliner Strasse 77.[6] The SA, too, now appeared openly again in public. Goebbels was forced to take into account the fact that this troop of about a thousand strong (about eight hundred in Berlin and two hundred in Brandenburg)[7] immediately stated its claims on the political organization, for example with regard to the selection of candidates for the Reichstag election.[8]

During the campaign Goebbels organized SA marches through various districts of Berlin; on May 13 they paraded in Wilmersdorf, for instance.[9] On May 17, Ascension Day, they undertook a "march out" to Spandau and subsequently made a wide detour via Tegel to Wedding, where there was a confrontation with communist counter-demonstrators. Goebbels considered it a great success that they managed to force their way through here, in enemy territory, and continue the march despite all attempts to disrupt the proceedings.[10]

In the Reichstag elections on May 20, the National Socialists gained a meager 2.6 percent of the vote in the Reich as a whole and did even worse in Berlin, at 1.6 percent.[11] For Goebbels this was—strange to say—a "fine result, but we earned it by our hard work, after all." The NSDAP had twelve deputies in the Reichstag, among them Joseph Goebbels: "So now I'm an M.d.R. [Mitglied des Reichstags, Member of the Reichstag]. Immune, that's the main thing."[12] In *Der Angriff* he asserted that he was "not a Member of the Reichstag. I am an I.d.I. An I.d.F. A possessor of immunity [Inhaber der Immunität], the holder of a free ticket to ride [Inhaber der Freifahrkarte]."[13]

The Strasser brothers immediately criticized the poor election results in Berlin: Gregor Strasser in the *Berliner Arbeiterzeitung* on May 27, and Otto in the *Nationalsozialistische Briefe* of June 15, where he complained that the NSDAP had attracted lower-middle-class and farming community votes above all but no proletarian ones; this was apparent in the Berlin results, among others.[14] The shaky outcome in Berlin was indeed sobering for Goebbels, who liked to see himself as "socialistic."

Although his immunity as a deputy now protected him from having to serve any future prison sentences, he had to face a series of prosecutions before he could enjoy this protection. Hence at the end of April he was sentenced to three weeks' imprisonment for an "Isidor insult" in *Der Angriff*.[15] On June 6 he was fined 200 marks because of an article in which he called the policemen who testified against him in an earlier trial "White Chekists."[16] On June 8 there was another fine of 20 marks as a result of the so-called department store case (this had to do with a special edition of *Der Angriff* in December 1928),[17] and on June 19 his fine in connection with the Stucke case was reduced to 600 marks. He commented defiantly: "I won't pay a single penny."[18] On July 14, 1928, the Reichstag passed an amnesty law that protected Goebbels from further court cases: "Now I'm as pure as an angel again."[19]

At the beginning of July Goebbels gave his maiden speech in the Reichstag. "When one takes part for the first time as a novice in this democratic swindle," declared the deputy, "it's a horrifying sight." He made use of the topic of the debate—the introduction of a national day—to mount polemical attacks, suggesting August 29 (the day on which the Reichstag had passed a law accepting the revised Dawes Plan for reparation payments) and the Jewish festival of Purim as suitable days to celebrate the nation. His personal summary of the day was: "An endless din as I told those swine what's what until it came out of their ears."[20]

During the summer of 1928 the conflict between Goebbels and the Strasser brothers became increasingly turbulent. Comments about Gregor Strasser proliferated in the diary, which also recorded even more frequently evidence of serious differences of opinion with his brother Otto. In June 1928 Goebbels learned from the Essen Gauleiter, Josef Terboven, that Otto Strasser, Kaufmann, and Reventlow were planning to start a new party "with more emphasis on steering a socialist course."[21] In June Goebbels agreed to support Kaufmann and the Ruhr Gau in publishing a new paper called *Die neue Front* (The New Front), no doubt hoping with this project to land a blow on "the Satan of the whole movement," Otto Strasser.[22] For a while, with

Hitler failing to back him in his confrontation with the Strassers, he even considered resigning his position as Gauleiter. But after a long personal discussion with Hitler in mid-July, in which according to Goebbels Hitler expressed "sharp" views about Otto Strasser, Goebbels dropped the idea.[23]

CONFLICT WITH THE SA

At the end of July Goebbels went alone to Borkum to recuperate. The island was a bastion of *völkisch* sentiment and largely *judenfrei* (free of Jews), which was a source of pride.[24] The campaign to achieve this was led by Pastor Ludwig Münchmeyer, whom Goebbels called on immediately. He respected him for the "enormous battle" he had fought on the island, but he also considered that the anti-Semitic minister had acted "ineptly."[25] During his vacation he gave several speeches on behalf of the Party, and after almost two weeks he felt "fresh and restored. All that's missing is a beautiful woman."[26]

Back in Berlin, he discovered that a serious crisis was building up within the Party. Since April there had been signs of increasing dissatisfaction within the SA—not just in Berlin but throughout the Reich. The ex-military men who headed the SA, Walter Stennes in Berlin and Pfeffer in the Reich, were seeking—so it seemed to Goebbels—to put the leadership of the Party under increasing pressure.[27] Now there were indications that this crisis was becoming more and more acute.[28]

In fact, this conflict represented a systemic problem of the National Socialist movement that was present from its inception: How was the paramilitary wing of the Party, the SA, to be integrated into the NSDAP? This question was to lead to repeated, deep-seated conflicts and was never truly resolved until the problem was "solved" in bloody fashion on June 30, 1934.

The background of the conflict lay in the following complex: While the Party leadership perceived the SA as an auxiliary force useful for providing security at meetings, turning out for propaganda marches, and distributing leaflets, the ambitions of the SA leaders—mostly ex-officers and former Free Corps fighters—went considerably further. They saw themselves as "political soldiers" and the SA as a "military unit," an independent instrument of power that could be used to apply political pressure internally, as well as a military reserve organization with a role to play in the context of the secret expansion of the Reichswehr. The self-confident SA leadership naturally enjoyed cross-connections with the various military outfits on the right and held out political promises to try to attract recruits from the other formations. On the other hand, however, since they were not prepared to allow the Party leadership—mere politicians—any opportunity to scrutinize, let alone control, their possessively guarded "military" sphere of operations, their behavior risked compromising the Party's political line. The "putschism" that was still rife within the SA leadership was bound to jeopardize the Party's policy of operating within the law.

Hitler had suffered as early as 1923 from the substantial limitations imposed on his freedom of action as a politician by what were then the close ties between the SA and the radical right-wing scene in Bavaria. Preparations for a putsch by the military formations, which fully embraced the SA, had developed such an independent momentum that Hitler was left with practically no option but to take part in the risky enterprise of November 9. What he learned from this experience was that in the future the SA should be completely subordinate to the Party and forget about its war games.[29]

Now, in August 1928, just back from his vacation, Goebbels found that the SA was on the brink of open revolt. He managed to eavesdrop on a conversation between Stennes and one of his confidants, noting afterward: "Now I know what I'm dealing with." He resolved to "give these gentlemen a rap on the knuckles before long."[30] But first of all, in fact, he allowed himself another breather. He took a trip to Garmisch, where, not far from the grave of his friend Richard Flisges, he revised the "Michael" manuscript of 1924.[31] In Berlin, meanwhile, the conflict with the SA that had long been festering had now broken out. Stennes and a group of *Standartenführer* ostentatiously resigned from the Party when their financial demands—the SA in Berlin had accumulated debts of over 3,000 Reichsmarks—were not met by the Party leadership in Munich.

Goebbels told himself separation was the answer: "And now there will have to be a split. Party or military unit, revolution or reaction."[32] But his words were bolder than his deeds. For the time being, he saw no reason to cut short his stay in Bavaria. He clearly tried as much as he could to keep out of the dispute between the Party and the SA. It was to be almost two weeks before he returned to the capital. There he found a short-term solution to the crisis by making substantial concessions. He agreed to provide Stennes with additional resources by raising credit and asked Hitler to come and speak more often in Berlin (which, because of a ban on speaking imposed on him in Prussia, he could only do in closed NSDAP meetings).[33]

Reporting to Munich, he found that Hitler regarded Stennes, as well as Pfeffer, as "freebooters"—"Probably rightly." But it was clear to Goebbels that at this moment "a crisis was the last thing they needed" and that it was now important to keep the peace at all costs: "I convince the boss against my own better judgment. But I've got to take this action in order to save the Party." In concrete terms, all that was agreed was that Hitler should appear more often in Berlin to calm unruly spirits.[34] Then Goebbels continued his vacation until the end of the month.[35]

For the Gauleiter of Berlin, whose propaganda campaign depended crucially on "his" SA and who at the same time was doing his utmost to stay in the Party leader's good books, great danger lay in an open conflict between the Party and the SA. So he tried to contain the conflict by offering concessions to the SA leaders, on the one hand, and placating the leadership in Munich, on the other. He came to an agreement with Stennes that from now on they would work "loyally" together.[36]

At the end of August and the beginning of September, Goebbels attended a meeting of the Party elite in Munich that lasted several days. He was repelled by the performance of the top Party functionaries, finding it to be "shocking." Hitler alone was "phenomenal." Goebbels learned here that as part of a regional reorganization of the NSDAP, his Gau was to be divided: He was now responsible only for Berlin, while a new Gau would be formed in Brandenburg. He commented laconically: "Thank God, that takes a lot of trouble off my shoulders."[37]

PARTY WORK IN BERLIN, AUTUMN AND WINTER 1928

At the end of the summer break, Goebbels began to step up the propaganda effort of the Gau. The opening note was struck by *Der An-*

griff on September 24, 1928, with a special issue attacking the Dawes Plan. Reportedly, sixty thousand copies were sold.[38]

At the end of September the NSDAP held its "Third Brandenburg Day" in Teltow, near Berlin. After rapturous events in the capital—Goebbels took to the podium no fewer than five times—participants gathered on the Sunday to parade near the small Brandenburg town. Four thousand SA men from all over the Reich were said to have assembled. In the afternoon they convened to march into the capital, where in the Sportpalast (Palace of Sport) that evening they took part in the largest National Socialist meeting so far in Berlin, with over ten thousand participants. "Blood is the best adhesive," cried Goebbels to his listeners, referring to the many violent clashes that had occurred during the march and in the area around the Sportpalast.[39] Goebbels was delighted when, a few days later, Hitler sent him a letter congratulating him on his success: "Berlin—that is your work."[40] His pleasure was heightened when Hitler appeared unexpectedly in Berlin a few days later, assuring Goebbels of his support in the dispute with Otto Strasser and the SA.[41]

On November 4 the SA marched unhindered through Neukölln, something *Der Angriff* presented as a great triumph.[42] On November 16 Hitler spoke in Berlin, for the first time at a public meeting since the lifting of the speaking ban in Prussia: Once again the Sportpalast was the chosen venue. Goebbels later declared this to be "the greatest success of my work so far."[43] He celebrated the leader's appearance under the headline "When Hitler Speaks": "Where hard work and knowledge and education fail to find the solution, God proclaims it through those he has chosen to speak on his behalf."[44] Even if, with such fulsome praise,[45] Goebbels may have contributed to the "Führer cult" in the NSDAP so heavily promoted by Munich, it would be wrong to think that Goebbels's propaganda efforts in the capital were exclusively concentrated on the person of the Party leader. He focused on quite different topics, which is evident in the Gauleiter's manifold publicity activities: political questions of the day; anti-Semitic agitation, not least against Deputy Police Commissioner Weiss; the constant reassertion of the "socialist" character of the NSDAP; but first and foremost his own "struggle for Berlin."[46]

On the morning after Hitler's appearance, the police found the body of the SA man Hans-Georg Kütemeyer in the Landwehrkanal.

The police assumed that Kütemeyer had committed suicide.[47] The National Socialists, however, maintained that he was the victim of communist terror tactics. Goebbels accused the police and the "Jew press" of covering up a murder and tried to turn Kütemeyer into a National Socialist martyr.[48] The Party placed a bounty on the head of the "murderer," but police headquarters banned the display of posters to this effect.[49] The affair escalated when Deputy Commissioner Weiss prohibited a funeral procession, and a confrontation ensued outside the cemetery—Goebbels had given the funeral oration—between thousands of National Socialists and a large contingent of police.[50]

Relations with Stennes and his SA were to an extent straightened out in autumn 1928.[51] But Goebbels resisted being nominally responsible for the paramilitaries, while the leadership under Franz Pfeffer jealously warded off any interference by Gauleiters in SA business. Goebbels thought this arrangement was fundamentally wrongheaded: "How can I take responsibility for things run by other authorities?" Worse still, "the boss takes the easy way out by staying aloof and leaving it all to the people in charge. And I'm always left holding the bag."[52]

Early in December he came to an understanding with Pfeffer, whom he regarded with a certain amount of skepticism,[53] that "the SA leader shall be deployed with the Gauleiter's agreement."[54] At the leadership conference of the NSDAP, which took place in Weimar in January 1929, this position of Goebbels's was largely accepted.[55] Nonetheless, he found himself in something of a jam, as he confessed in January after a talk with the young SA leader Horst Wessel, who was pressing for more "activism": "If we become more active in Berlin, our people will go around smashing the place up. And then Isidor will enjoy banning us."[56] His attitude to Stennes remained skeptical. In the final analysis, he considered the former police captain a "bourgeois" who could no doubt organize a putsch but lacked the courage and ruthlessness to start a revolution.[57]

Although the NSDAP was still no more than a splinter party with modest results at the polls, there was one sense in which it had succeeded: It was now the only radical right-wing organization of any note surviving in Berlin, and its structures were gradually firming up, even if the position of the SA within the Party as a whole was still problematic.[58] The "Gau days" instituted by Goebbels played an important part in strengthening the organization: Roughly once a month, the Gauleiter called all the leading Party officeholders together. He observed in December that a "leadership cadre" was now gradually taking shape in Berlin, not least thanks to the good work done by the National Socialist functionary Reinhold Muchow, who had been appointed head of the administrative department in July 1928.[59]

Following the model of the German Communist Party (KPD), Muchow introduced a system of street cells led by civilian Party comrades; in this way SA members were released from the organizational work of the Party and freed up for other tasks. By the beginning of 1930 the Berlin NSDAP could count on over nine hundred street cells coordinated by forty sections. The street cells carried out the detailed work of campaigning above all: For example, they distributed "block newspapers" produced independently by the sections themselves. In this system, there were twelve hundred functionaries working for the Party.[60] In 1929, to form a second component in the organization of the Gau—again following the KPD model—Muchow set about building up a cell structure within industry. From these— initially slow—beginnings, the system of National Socialist industry- based cells developed into the NSDAP's employee organization.[61]

The price to be paid for this steadily increasing political success was—something Goebbels himself desired—his gradual isolation from his Party cronies, tending eventually to solitude. Whereas early in his time in Berlin he had struck up friendships with various Party comrades, now he was far more concerned to keep his distance. By October 1928, the only two people he considered friends were Hans Herbert Schweitzer and his driver, Albert Tonak. Five days later he even wrote that he had "no friends." "Everybody makes claims on my person," he complained a few weeks later, "but I have no claim on anyone else. It's lonely at the top!" More than a year later, he felt "how solitary I have become. But perhaps that's a good thing."[62] In August 1931 he explained to a colleague "why I have no close friends in the Gau. I've been disappointed often enough. Business and friendship don't mix."[63]

GOEBBELS AND WOMEN

The many affairs that Goebbels engaged in from spring 1928 on, as the Berlin Party was being re-founded and the Party organization built up, failed to overcome his loneliness. All these affairs were in any case eclipsed by the resumption of the relationship between him and the still-idolized Anka.

His ex-girlfriend made a surprise visit in March to tell him how unhappy she was. Her husband—his old rival Mumme—had cheated on her. She sat at home with her little four-year-old son, "unloved and joyless." In Goebbels the old emotions were immediately rekindled: "You have one great love in your lifetime. Everything else is deception or a business deal: Mine was called Anka."[64] A few weeks later they met up in Thuringia,[65] and a few days after that she was back in Berlin: "Anka loves me, I love her, neither of us says anything about it, but we know it all the same."[66]

In April he met Anka in Weimar. In the evening, as they were sitting together in a wine bar, a former lover of hers, an artist, appeared. Goebbels was forced to listen to the stories told by this "horror": "He's a pacifist and a militarist, anti-Semite and Jew vassal, democrat and aristocrat, enthuses about the East and praises classicism. A dreadful conglomeration. And full of jealousy, too." On top of everything else, Anka took his side against Goebbels: "I give in. I'm too good to be just the tail end of a failed marriage, even if she is called Anka. Farewell, Anka! You will be ruined by sin or bogged down in mundane life. It's a shame about you. But evidently it can't be helped." When Anka turned up in Berlin a few days later, he spurned her. But two weeks later they met again in Weimar and were reconciled.[67]

The reunion with Anka cast a shadow over his relationship with Tamara,[68] who revealed to him a few weeks after his passion for Anka had been reignited that she was now "with the Jew Arnold Zweig."[69] This relationship was now over as far as he was concerned, for "since I've seen Anka again, the beauty of all other women fades before my eyes."[70] Goebbels now constantly fell in love, and with a wide variety of women, often sustaining two or three affairs at a time. The old love for Anka flared up again and again, but he could not bring himself to make her leave her husband. It seems as if he was keeping the affair with Anka up in the air for as long as he could in order to wreak revenge for her earlier unfaithfulness. And yet he did not want to commit himself to other lovers, because all his affairs were overshadowed by Anka. His behavior naturally provoked jealousy and led to many a tearful evening. But he was neither able nor willing to empathize with the injured women. For him there was only one thing that mattered: *his* state of mind. He convinced himself that there was an inherent tragedy hovering over all of his relationships and that it was all Anka's fault. This tragedy, which he invoked constantly, was part of his self-dramatizing narrative: With a glittering career ahead of him, he had to make this sacrifice—and the women had to share his fate.

In his almost total self-absorption he thought women he had met only briefly were in love with him. He was completely sure of their feelings, although not a word was exchanged, not a gesture reciprocated. So, for example, on an outing of Berlin Party employees he sat "next to a lovely girl, and without saying as much, we love each other. Neither of us shows it, but it is so."[71] Less than a week later, he experienced a very special erotic attraction during a theater visit: "During the last act I sit next to a wonderful woman, and we have a little celebration of love, without a word, just two glances, a couple of indrawn breaths."[72]

In August he fell instantly in love with the wife of the right-wing writer Friedrich Wilhelm Heinz but after seeing her a few times came to the conclusion: "Maybe not."[73] On a short visit to Innsbruck, he met Pille Kölsch with his young wife and immediately confessed that "this young woman, this little devil," had him under her spell.[74] In September he met the young Party supporter Hannah Schneider, "a true German girl," with whom he immediately fell in love.[75] But this affair had hardly begun when he received a cry for help from Anka: She had now decided to ask for a divorce.[76] He met her again at the beginning of October. But by then, for the sake of her son, she had already dropped the idea of divorce. Trouble seemed to be looming: "Now she wants to leave Weimar for a few months and come to Berlin. Things could get quite lively."[77]

In October Goebbels broke up with Hannah: The relationship was becoming too complicated for his liking.[78] "A man with a mission can't afford unhappy love affairs," he wrote.[79] Goebbels clearly felt that beautiful women were positively pursuing him: At one of his events in Wilmersdorf, the audience contained "Fräulein Müller from Borkum";[80] his ex-girlfriend Tamara, with whom he spent a few moments after the meeting; and a new "lovely girlfriend" who visited him next evening at home.[81] This was Johanna Polzin, and it would not be the last evening they spent together.[82] And an eighteen-year-old girl, Jutta Lehmann, came into his life one day in December.[83] "She wants to be my loyal comrade. Temptation to escape from the burden of loneliness around me. [. . .] Love and duty in conflict. But I love her all the more because I know I must lose her, just as I've lost all other women, because I must serve my cause. Farewell! Adio! Jutta!"[84] However, in the next few weeks there was no further mention of farewells, and he decided he was "very happy to have her."[85] In February he found that "in the last few days I have not been able to relate properly to Jutta. I don't know whether this is due to my general agitation, or whether I've tired of [the affair] again because of my insatiable need for change."[86] But he did not want to make a real break with her.[87]

Over the winter of 1928–29 he saw Anka when he was passing through Weimar, and from time to time she came to Berlin.[88] He felt as if "she were a good friend to me. With her it feels like being with a mother."[89] She attended a performance of Goebbels's play *Blood Seed*. But afterward they clashed badly over "the Jewish question": "Her thinking is still too bourgeois." Late at night Anka described her difficult private situation, which drew sympathy from him: "What a burden of sorrow and suffering Anka has had to bear!" "Is this fate revenging itself on her for what she did to me?"[90] After many more meetings[91] he believed that she was once again "allowing herself to be formed by me. She is becoming a part of me."[92]

At Easter they took a trip to the Harz Mountains. The party included the Schweitzers, Fräulein Bettge—a Party employee devoted to him—and Anka's husband:[93] "She's wearing a green leather coat and looking wonderful. The Stalherm lady. How did she end up with this man?" Georg Mumme's behavior was odd: "She cold-shoulders him completely, and he puts up with it. [. . .] He doesn't understand Anka at all. And she doesn't love him anymore, either. The man expresses his admiration and respect for me in Anka's presence. Let anyone work that out if they can." They went to see the Kyffhäuser monument, Harzburg, Goslar, and Wernigerode. "This poor, marvelous woman in the hands of that pseudo-educated philistine. Makes you want to wade in." So it was that "retribution came late, but thereby took even crueler revenge. But it's right that it should be so. We were not meant to be together. I had to take the path of action. It was for her to help me as much as she could."

During the car journey they sat "close to each other like lovers. Under cover of the car rug Anka passed a ring to me that her mother gave her. Thank you: so kind! I'll keep it like a talisman." After they had parted company in Aschersleben, his mood was sad: "Why must I forgo happiness?" But he knew the answer of old: "Probably so that all Germans can be happy again one day. A few must sow for many to reap. It's hard, but that's how it has to be."

Between meetings with Anka he sought consolation, and the pattern was always the same. There was, for example, an Anneliese Haegert who loved him "beyond measure": "But I can't decide. Anka always intervenes."[94] One evening in April he was visited by the "lovely Xenia": Her full name was Xenia von Engelhardt, and she told him how she had to suffer at the hands of "her faithless young man." Goebbels offered consolation in a "night vibrant with happiness."[95] He declared on May 20 that he loved her "beyond measure." She was "like Anka in many ways." He was with Anka from late May to early June in Weimar.[96] As Mumme spent a good deal of time away, the two were left completely undisturbed: "We were both happy beyond measure. Anka looked after me like a mother."[97]

But he was not comfortable with the role of "man friend" and occasional lover, either. At the end of July in Weimar he made a decision: "Farewell, you two. I've got to leave you in all your misery and futility. I haven't got the time to give myself completely to women. Greater tasks await me."[98] He was to visit Anka in Weimar again in December and in January 1930, but after that he thought he had gotten over her.[99]

As Xenia had found out in July about his visit to Weimar, their relationship entered a serious crisis.[100] In the meantime, during a vacation in Mecklenburg, he had met Erika Chelius, "daughter of a head forester from Angermünde": "not beautiful, but charming and pleasant" and, most important of all,[101] "so like Anka Stalherm. When she was young and not weighed down by marriage and bourgeois life."[102]

In August Erika accompanied him to the Nuremberg Party rally, where Xenia unexpectedly turned up too.[103] During an excursion he kissed Erika goodbye.[104] Back in Berlin, he found his mind constantly dwelling on his new conquest, although he was certain that "I won't be any more committed to her than to all the others." Gradually he began to feel "pangs of conscience about all these tortuous relation- ships. [. . .] It's enough to make you despair. Women! Women are to blame for nearly everything."[105]

In the following weeks he saw Erika several times in Berlin, or visited her at her parents' place in Grumsin in Mecklenburg, where he spent New Year's.[106] He told Xenia in mid-August that he wanted to end their relationship, and on the same evening he met Julia, with whom he likewise made a final break: "Enough! Enough! [. . .] Oth- erwise I'll end up [wrung out] like a washcloth."[107] But Xenia did not completely disappear from the scene: She came to his place often during the autumn and winter of 1929.[108] Of one particular evening, for example, when he had come home exhausted, he wrote: "Get Xenia to come over, so I'm not quite so alone. [. . .] I've got to have someone to whom I can pour my heart out. Xenia is a good lis- tener."[109]

In February he met Charlotte Streve.[110] "She loves me to distrac- tion," he noted. "But more for what I want than for what I am."[111] In the next few weeks he spent plenty of time with Xenia, too, of whom he wrote almost apologetically in his diary that she was "a welcome counterweight [. . .] to all this mass activity."[112]

Over lunch one day at the beginning of March he talked to Erika Chelius about his relationships with women: "I need women as a counterweight. Particularly on critical days they have an effect on me like balm on a wound. But I must have different types of women around me." Erika reacted "very understandingly" to this avowal. That afternoon he was visited by Xenia: "Made coffee and played around."[113]

CHAPTER 6

"A Life Full of Work and Struggle"

Politics Between Berlin and Munich

The Prussian police and judiciary were far from passive observers of the continual provocations from the Berlin Gauleiter. The constant interrogations, court cases, and convictions visibly affected Goebbels. This picture shows him shortly before being found guilty on account of an article in *Der Angriff* that was judged to be insulting to the Reich president, May 31, 1930.

From spring 1929 onward, Goebbels observed with some suspicion the closer collaboration Hitler was developing with two nationalist groups: a veterans' organization called the Stahlhelm (Steel Helmet) and the Deutschnationale Volkspartei (German National People's Party, DNVP). Central to this cooperation was the Stahlhelm proposal to form a united front of the nationalist right and to organize a plebiscite to bring about fundamental changes in the constitution: The powers of Parliament were to be devolved to the president of the Reich and the Weimar democracy turned into an authoritarian state.[1]

Goebbels was afraid that if Hitler fell for the blandishments of the Stahlhelm and supported what he, Goebbels, regarded as a "pointless referendum," then the Führer would become too deeply embroiled in a right-wing opposition front, and the NSDAP's scope for action would be significantly curtailed.[2]

On March 24 Goebbels wrote in his diary: "I'm scared of a rerun of November 9 [19]23. Nothing connects us either with the right or with the left. Ultimately, we stand absolutely alone. And that is good. We must not forfeit our own preeminence in opposition." One thing that particularly worried him was that "the boss doesn't reply to any inquiries." But at the end of the month he noted with relief that Hess had assured him on Hitler's behalf that there would be nothing more than "friendly relations" between the Party and the Stahlhelm, and there was "no question of going along with the mad policy of the alliance. Especially not the plebiscite."[3] But just a few days later his anxiety returned, above all because of the very receptive attitude shown by the *Völkischer Beobachter* to the Stahlhelm. Commenting on a conversation with Horst Wessel, he wrote: "The Munich circle is intolerable at times. I'm not prepared to go along with a bad compromise [. . .]. I have my doubts about Hitler sometimes. Why doesn't he speak out?"[4]

On his next visit to Berlin, Hitler was able to reassure him: "He too rejects the plebiscite in the sharpest terms, and has even written a cutting critique of it. There can be no question whatsoever of collaborating."[5] Goebbels thought a "fairly crude letter" written by Hitler[6] to the head of the Stahlhelm, Franz Seldte, was not quite adequate: "Our intention is to be, and remain, revolutionaries."[7] In May he ostentatiously published two editorials pillorying "the reactionaries."[8] In May, finally, Hitler attacked the plebiscite plan in a memorandum "which was refreshingly direct about the bourgeois party rabble."[9] For the moment, Goebbels was satisfied.

He went on polemicizing against the "united front of Dawes patriots,"[10] an allusion to the fact that in 1924 some members of the DNVP parliamentary party had voted in favor of the Dawes Plan, the first international agreement to restructure reparation payments. He also declined to take part in a large-scale event staged by the nationalist right on the grounds that he did not want to collaborate with "parties and men who have said 'yes' to Versailles or Dawes, since this means they have accepted the war-guilt lie and appear unfit to conduct an honest campaign against it."[11] But in the meantime a new plebiscitary movement was being launched by the nationalist right, calling for a petition for a referendum on the Young Plan, accepted by the Reich government on July 21, which was designed to make German reparations payments somewhat more manageable but which, according to the nationalists, would actually serve to guarantee the delivery of payments and cement reparations in place.

At the beginning of July Hitler spoke to a rally of National Socialist students in Berlin; during this visit he stated his intention "to go in with the German nationalists" on the plebiscite against Versailles and Young.[12] A terse diary entry for that day concealed a resounding defeat for Goebbels: Although the terms of the proposed petition had been altered, the NSDAP was nonetheless allying itself with the "reactionaries" he disliked so much. He was suspiciously quick to spot a positive side to this setback, however: "But we'll take control and rip the mask away from the D.N.V.P. We're strong enough to dominate any alliance."

On July 9, 1929, Alfred Hugenberg, head of the DNVP, Seldte of the Stahlhelm, Hitler, and Privy Councilor Heinrich Class, the leader of the Alldeutscher Verband (Pan-German League), set up a "Reich Committee for the German People's Petition," actually a comprehensive organization with an administrative network covering the Reich, a common platform for agitation for the whole of the united nationalist right.[13] Goebbels—whose *Angriff* did not deign to notice the setting up of the committee—was less than enthusiastic. "Our job now is to see we're not swindled and to make sure we're in charge of the whole caboodle, with the others behind us."[14]

Goebbels's indecent haste, for all his objections, to join the "united front of Dawes patriots" was mainly due to the fact that Hitler had given him to understand that he, Goebbels, was destined to play the part of his closest collaborator and confidant. It flattered Goebbels, too, that Hitler took him into his confidence concerning his plans for the future: On July 5 they had a long discussion "about the coming constitution." Goebbels's diary notes for this day are among the rare documents from before 1933 that record Hitler expressing himself on the subject of his plans to structure the state after the proposed "seizure of power." In general he avoided being prematurely tied down in this respect by public or internal Party pronouncements. What Hitler wanted, according to Goebbels, was a "tripartite" structure: first, an elected parliament that would debate but not make decisions; second, a "senate of about 60–70 members [. . .] to be augmented by co-opting," where "after clarification in the course of discussion, experts" would make decisions "on their own responsibility"; third, a "corporative parliament for economic questions." By and large, Goebbels agreed with these plans, although he did have some doubts: "Is the political parliament necessary, should there be general elections to it, won't the senate eventually become rigid and bloodless?"[15]

Ultimately, Goebbels's revised attitude to Hitler's alliance policy may well have been due to the prospect of becoming head of propaganda for the Reich based in Munich, which Hitler had held out to him around the end of May and again at the beginning of July. It was an appointment about which he had speculated since at least April.

RAPPROCHEMENT WITH STRASSER

Goebbels's skepticism about the line the Party leadership was taking made it seem expedient in spring 1929 to repair fences with Strasser and the "left" wing of the Party. At the beginning of March he agreed with Strasser that Hitler must be more decisive in his dealings with the SA.[16] Moreover, Goebbels criticized Hitler's leadership style to Party friends and called for the appointment of a deputy as well as other "representatives" of the Party leader who would take some of the burden off his shoulders. In this connection he also gave a glimpse of the way he saw his future in the Party leadership: "My job is propaganda and information. The area of culture and education. That is something which suits me and which I enjoy."[17]

At the end of April, on a return trip together by train from Berlin to Dresden, Gregor Strasser and Goebbels took advantage of the opportunity—now in an entirely "friendly" atmosphere—to have a long talk. They came to an understanding on a whole series of political questions, among them the topic of propaganda: "There's got to be a new appointment in Reich headquarters. I'm the only possible candidate."[18] Strasser's agreement on this point was particularly important, since the Lower Bavarian National Socialist leader had been responsible for Reich propaganda until the end of 1927, after which he had become chief Party organizer for the Reich. In order to document the rapprochement publicly, Goebbels contributed an article to the *Nationalsozialistische Briefe* with the title "From Chaos to Form." He confidently announced in the publication, for which he had not written since 1927, when he was relieved of the editorship: "We are giving the century a meaningful shape."[19]

The idea of putting Goebbels in charge of propaganda for the Reich, conceived during the rail trip to Dresden, was adopted by Hitler in the following months as his own. Twice, at the end of May and the beginning of July, he offered to make Goebbels director of propaganda. This offer was linked to the assumption that Goebbels would spend a good deal of his time in Munich, with a second base there. Instead of accepting immediately, though, Goebbels asked for time to think about it.[20] By the end of July, however, he was assuming he would in fact be taking over as director of propaganda by September.[21] He had also begun to step up the propaganda effort of his own Gau, and in June he created an appropriate local department under Georg Stark.[22]

During the Weimar Party rally, which stretched across the end of July and the beginning of August, he found that rumors were circulating to the effect that he was going to move to Munich, thus relinquishing his office in Berlin. He immediately suspected that this canard was a ploy on the part of Otto Strasser, who was aiming to disempower him in Berlin. Was it possible that Hitler was behind the maneuver? If so—which he thought unlikely, however—then he was ready to drop "the whole business."[23] But Hitler succeeded in calming him down: There was no question of him giving up his Berlin position. He was eventually placated by an "excellent summary" of his propaganda expertise from the mouth of the Führer. Goebbels, seeing himself already as the "boss" of Party propaganda, conducted himself accordingly at the propagandists' conference.[24] In the same month he wrote a report on the reorganization of the Party's propaganda apparatus; with regard to the final "decision about Reich propaganda and Berlin," he expressed himself quite emphatically in writing to Hitler himself.[25] However, it was not until October that he reached an agreement with headquarters over the conditions applying to his takeover of the Reich propaganda machine: "The Party are giving me an apartment there, I'll be going every 2 weeks to Munich, staying for 3 days, and setting up a perfectly functioning office; all propaganda will be centralized and will have a unified style. I'll then be giving a few more talks in Bavaria. They can do with it. Berlin remains unchanged."[26]

In November 1929, Goebbels sat down with Heinrich Himmler, nominally deputy director of Reich propaganda but in practice the acting officeholder, to work out the further details of his future work.[27] But his appointment had still not been announced.

AFTER THE SUMMER BREAK, 1929:
THE RENEWED STRUGGLE FOR THE STREETS

After the break in summer 1929, Goebbels had resumed his fight for domination of the streets. The SA was again in the news with its violence-prone marches. *Der Angriff*, feeling that the "final desperate battle" with the communists had arrived,[28] declared the working-class districts of Wedding, Neukölln, Friedrichshain, Lichtenberg, and Prenzlauer Berg "main combat zones."[29]

On September 7 the SA marched through Schöneberg and Wilmersdorf; during the closing ceremony Goebbels talked himself "hoarse once more."[30] On September 15 there was a propaganda march through Charlottenburg and Moabit, once again capped by a Goebbels speech, this time in the Savignyplatz.[31] The following Sunday, September 22, three standards of the SA marched through Kreuzberg and Neukölln. As Goebbels was inspecting the marchers in front of Görlitz Station he was attacked and only just managed to escape to his car; his driver was injured. In an editorial in *Der Angriff* entitled "On the Front Line," Goebbels supplied his readers with a dramatic account of this assault.[32] And the local news in *Der Angriff* during those weeks did in fact read like reports from the front. Covering a "large-scale battle on the foremost front line," for example, its reporter wrote: "If the Fischerkiez [district] can be taken, it will mean that the backbone of the Red Terror in the central area has been broken."[33] A few weeks later the paper published "front-line accounts" from this disputed territory, while it said of Schöneberg that here "the lowest form of sub-humanity [. . .] was hunting down National Socialist workers."[34]

In October the Berlin NSDAP planned to hold a grand-scale "Hitler Week" with many meetings and propaganda marches. However, the high point, a big SA parade, was banned on short notice by the police.[35] There had been no plans for Hitler to appear at this event: The Party leader appeared only once in public in Berlin during 1929, at the student rally in July mentioned earlier.

Even if Hitler was rarely present in Berlin and the person of the Party leader did not feature prominently in the day-to-day propaganda work of the NSDAP, Goebbels was nonetheless highly dependent on Hitler—and not just in political terms, either, as shown by the following episode in September 1929. Goebbels happened to be in Breslau when, just before he was due to give a speech that evening, he received a telegram signed by Alfred Rosenberg: Hitler had suffered a fatal accident. "I feel completely numb. I am shaken by paroxysms of weeping. I see chaos ahead of me. I'm standing all alone among strangers. Groping my way in endless loneliness." A telephone call to Munich established that Hitler was alive and well and that the telegram was a fake.

Goebbels returned to the rally and gave a two-hour speech: "Suffering dreadfully! My greatest feat of oratory yet. Despite my depression, concentration beyond belief." Then he collapsed, exhausted: "I don't sleep all night. Only now do I realize what Hitler means to me and the movement. Everything! Everything!"[36] The enormous tension took its toll; he was ill for the next three days.[37]

A NATIONALIST ALLIANCE AND LOCAL ELECTIONS

During the summer of 1929, while he was hoping that Hitler would soon confirm his appointment to the job in Munich, Goebbels had been holding back—despite considerable reservations—from criticizing the Party leader's unappealing policy of allying with nationalist forces. He does not seem to have realized, or else found too complicated and too troublesome, the twin-track strategy employed by Hitler—as in several other projects—of wooing the nationalist right while at the same time clearly distancing himself from it.

By September the Reich Committee for the German People's Petition had assembled a bill to put before the Reichstag proposing a plebiscite aimed at preventing the Reich government from taking on any new burdens or commitments under the Versailles Treaty. The government would also be formally obliged to retract the admission of war guilt contained in the treaty, as well as to annul all of the previously accepted commitments arising out of that admission. Government ministers and other representatives of the Reich who ignored these decrees and signed agreements with foreign states could be tried for treason. Goebbels published one of his speeches as a pamphlet, in which agitation against the Young Plan was given a pronounced "socialist" slant: Through reparations the means of production were being expropriated by foreigners, thus making nationalization impossible.[38]

The collection of signatures in support of a petition calling for a plebiscite on the Young Plan was carried out between October 16 and October 29. This drive was boosted by a smoothly functioning propaganda machine, with contributions not only from the participating organizations—the DNVP, the Stahlhelm, the NSDAP—but also from the press network controlled by Hugenberg, as well as a large amount of assorted propaganda material, together with funding, distributed by the Reich Committee to participating organizations.[39]

A common perception that this massive propaganda exposure was crucially important for the NSDAP's transformation into a mass movement does not seem to stand up to scrutiny. The Hugenberg press, for example, was quite reluctant to give the NSDAP space for its propaganda during the referendum drive, and it appears that the Party's participation in the campaign did little to increase sponsorship from industry.[40]

In private, Goebbels was skeptical about the whole venture, as his diary indicates. In particular, his entries at the time are full of complaints about inadequate financial support from the Reich Committee.[41] Hitler's willingness to collaborate with the "reactionaries" still rubbed him the wrong way: "Hitler and Hugenberg shared a platform in Munich. Grr! [. . .] Nothing more can be achieved by parliamentary means. The revolution must be on the march!"[42]

He wavered in his assessment of the outcome of the petition. Around the end of October and the beginning of November, he was sure that the necessary quorum for a petition (10 percent of those eligible to vote) would not be achieved and that the bourgeois parties could be blamed for this defeat.[43] However, when the petition barely gained the necessary support—at 10.02 percent of the vote—to stage a plebiscite, he was cheering: "Hurrah! At least all that work wasn't wasted. So now the dance can continue." He cast aside his doubts: "We'll be the winners, come what may."[44]

The campaign against the Young Plan merged smoothly into the election campaign, in which the SA, aroused by Goebbels's call for "mobilization,"[45] again took a front-line role.[46] In the Prussian local elections on November 17, 1929, the NSDAP in Berlin took 132,000 votes, or 5.8 percent, sending thirteen deputies to the city council. Its greatest successes came in middle-class districts such as Steglitz, Schöneberg, and Zehlendorf, the bastions of the "nationalist" middle class specifically targeted by the anti–Young Plan campaign. It was in proletarian districts such as Wedding, Prenzlauer Berg, and Neu-kölln that the NSDAP did the worst.[47] For almost a year Goebbels took over the leadership of the small NSDAP section in the council, but he did not speak there once, essentially leaving local politics to Julius Lippert.[48]

On December 22 the plebiscite on the Young Plan bill failed: Despite the huge propaganda effort, no more than 13.8 percent of the vote was in favor.[49] But the group that had established the Reich Committee—regarded by Goebbels with the utmost suspicion—did not dissolve it. So he decided to take provocative action that would drive a wedge into the coalition.

On December 29, under the headline "Is Hindenburg Still Alive?," he mounted an attack in *Der Angriff* on the eighty-two-year-old pres-ident, predicting that in the case of the Young Plan, Hindenburg would once more do what "his Jewish and Marxist advisers prompted him" to do. This was accompanied by a cartoon lampooning the pres-ident. Goebbels calculated that, although the nationalists who had launched the plebiscite wanted to pressure the president into refus-ing to sign the Young Plan even if Parliament accepted it, they would not want to target the World War hero directly in their campaign. The calculation proved correct, as he learned early in January: "The Stahlhelm has us in its sights on account of the Hindenburg article. Hitler is completely with me on this."[50]

Relentlessly, Goebbels added fuel to the fire: When the Young Plan was passed into law by the Reichstag on March 12, 1930, and the president immediately added his signature, he asserted in an edito-rial that "starting now we have a new enemy: Hindenburg."[51] In a speech at the Veteran Soldiers' House on March 14 he described the president as the "lackey of this crooked government and of crooked politics,"[52] and he wrote in the next issue of *Der Angriff* that "Herr von Hindenburg" had "given himself the stamp of a Young-patriot."[53]

For his December 1929 article, the Charlottenburg court of lay assessors fined him 800 marks.[54] Goebbels accounted the verdict a moral victory: "A first-class funeral for Hindenburg."[55]

DEATH AND THE DEATH CULT

On November 8, 1929, the Berlin Gau staged a commemorative ceremony in the Veteran Soldiers' House for the dead of the Great War and those of the "movement": Goebbels and Hermann Göring both gave speeches.[56] Two days later there were three further memorial ceremonies, at the graves of Georg Kütemeyer and two other members of the National Socialist movement. "Dr. Goebbels three times made himself the interpreter between the dead and the living," wrote *Der Angriff.*[57]

On these occasions, as so often at that time of year, Goebbels succumbed to melancholy: "It was a bright, sunny autumn day. And a sad sense of mortality came over me."[58]

Two weeks later he heard from his eldest brother, Konrad, that their father, whose health had been a cause of concern for some time,[59] was terminally ill. He went to Rheydt, where he found the dying man "completely emaciated, reduced to a skeleton, whimpering": A week later came the news of his death.[60] When he saw the dead man laid out, he "wept uncontrollably." Commenting on the church funeral service, he observed how "empty and colorless [. . .] all these forms" were. He spent two days in Rheydt with his family, who tried to console themselves by sharing their memories of the deceased.[61]

Goebbels brought his father to mind again in the diary: He praised his morality, his sense of duty, and his devotion to principles. It had not been granted to him "to do great service for his country," but the son found comfort in the thought that his father would "go on living in him and be resurrected in glory," and this idea helped him to suppress his feelings of guilt—had he returned his love sufficiently? had he been ungrateful?—toward his father.[62]

Back in Berlin, a few days later he recorded in his diary a "strange dream" that sheds light on his state of mind at the time: He was "in a school, being pursued along wide corridors by a crowd of East Galician rabbis. They kept on shouting their 'hatred' at me. I was a few steps ahead of them, shouting the same back at them. So it went on for hours. But they never caught up with me."[63]

Repeatedly he had to deliver speeches at commemorative ceremonies: on December 18 at a memorial gathering for the SA man Walter Fischer; a few days later at the same man's funeral; and on December 28 at the burial of Werner Wessel, brother of the SA leader Horst Wessel, who had died in an accident.[64] The concentrated work of mourning in these months may have led him to develop a cult around the dead of the movement, a result of the mounting loss of Party comrades. Early in 1930, the violent clashes in Berlin provided him with a suitable icon for this cult: Horst Wessel. Since the beginning of 1929 Goebbels had often been thrown together with the young SA leader: "A brave lad, student, speaker, SA leader."[65] Raised in a middle-class family, Wessel had abandoned his law studies early, at the age of twenty-two, to devote himself entirely to the National Socialist cause. In May 1929 he had taken charge of an SA troop in the predominantly communist area around the Silesia Station. This troop rapidly evolved into the "SA-Sturm 5," one of the most feared groups of thugs in the Berlin SA. It paraded with a trademark *Schalmei* band,* which was a particular provocation to the communists, as they had made the *Schalmei* their own instrument. Wessel also composed song lyrics, including "Die Fahne hoch" (Raise high the flag), a song that was to acquire practically national-anthem status during the Third Reich.[66]

In January 1930, Wessel was attacked by two communists in his home and sustained a bad gunshot wound.[67] The cause of the attack was a dispute over the rent between Wessel and his landlady, who then called on the local "commune" for assistance. As Wessel's girlfriend was a former prostitute, it was not difficult for communist propaganda to depict the whole affair as a dispute between "pimps." The weeks in the hospital, as Wessel's life slowly ebbed away, and the circumstances of the assault stirred Goebbels's imagination: "Like in a Dostoyevsky novel: the idiot, the workers, the prostitute, the middle-class family, endless pangs of conscience, endless suffering. Such is the life of this 22-year-old visionary idealist."[68]

* Translators' note: A *Schalmei* is a metal wind instrument with multiple trumpet-like "bells" or horns and makes a raucous sound.

Wessel died on February 23, and Goebbels decided to make him the martyr figure of the movement.[69] He had tried to do the same with Kütemeyer in 1928, but the circumstances surrounding his death remained unclear. Walter Fischer, the second National Socialist fatality in Berlin, had resigned from the SA by the time he was murdered, and was therefore effectively ruled out as a role model. But Goebbels was determined to make Wessel into a heroic legend, despite the murky background of his murder. On March 1 Goebbels spoke at his graveside, while communists and National Socialists clashed outside the cemetery.

Using the language of religious symbolism, Goebbels did his utmost to create a cult around the late Horst Wessel that immediately took on sacral overtones. He adapted the Catholic hope of resurrection, which he had encountered some months earlier in his father's church funeral service, to the purposes of National Socialism. Goebbels designated Wessel as a "Christ-socialist," and just as he had done with his friend Flisges in *Michael*, he elevated Wessel to the role of "redeemer" who had sacrificed his life for a Germany that would arise in the not-too-distant future: "Someone must set an example by sacrificing himself. [...] Through sacrifice to redemption [...] through struggle to victory. [...] Wherever Germany is, you are there too, Horst Wessel!"[70] He proclaimed "Die Fahne hoch," the song written by Wessel, to be the anthem of the National Socialist movement.[71] In a contribution to *Der Angriff* Goebbels honored Wessel's life as though summarizing the sufferings of Jesus: He had "drained the chalice of pain to the lees."[72]

A DAILY NEWSPAPER FOR THE BERLIN NSDAP

Goebbels had been making plans for a daily newspaper in Berlin since early 1929,[73] and in the autumn of 1929 it had seemed that the project was in the bag. Goebbels had come to an agreement with Max Amann, head of the Party's own Eher Verlag publishing house: The paper was to be published by Eher in Berlin; Hitler was to be named the publisher and Goebbels editor in chief.[74] Hitler had decided in December that the paper should be printed in Berlin,[75] but in January Goebbels learned to his dismay that the printing presses would not be installed until September 1, 1930. "Those buffoons in Munich ruin every big plan we make," he complained. For the time being, the *Völkischer Beobachter* would carry a special supplementary page for Berlin.[76]

Goebbels was in for another surprise in January 1930: The Strasser brothers' Kampf-Verlag announced it was starting its own daily newspaper on March 1. Goebbels countered this move by proposing to expand *Der Angriff* as rapidly as possible into a daily, which could then be merged with the planned new daily newspaper.[77] But it took Hitler a long time to make up his mind. *Disappointed* hardly does justice to Goebbels's reaction to Hitler's hesitation ("I'm sick of him!"); once more he considered resigning if the Party leader sided with the Strassers in this newspaper war.[78]

Finally, Hitler summoned Goebbels to Munich and decided that the Kampf-Verlag would not be permitted to publish a daily paper. Starting on March 1, he would start up a special Berlin edition of the *Völkischer Beobachter* instead. Both agreed that Goebbels should take over the Reich propaganda machine as early as the following week—eight months had passed since Hitler first held out the prospect of this appointment.[79]

But once again nothing came of it. Not only did the question of the Reich propaganda takeover drag on, but the Kampf-Verlag continued to refer to its forthcoming newspaper. Goebbels thought the reaction of Hitler and the *Völkischer Beobachter* was bush-league and felt himself "completely let down" by this behavior.[80]

In the middle of the month, when the conflict had still not been resolved,[81] he saw "anarchy in the Party"; he blamed Hitler entirely for "not deciding and asserting his authority."[82] In the end Hitler published an appeal in the *Völkischer Beobachter*,[83] writing in favor of Goebbels and against the Kampf-Verlag. When the Strassers then intervened with Hitler, Goebbels immediately feared that he was about to "break his word" yet again.[84] Hitler, he declared after meeting him in Nuremberg on February 21, "promises much and delivers little."[85]

Goebbels was slow to grasp Hitler's strategy in the Strasser crisis. This amounted to avoiding an open breach with the Strasser brothers, which could potentially have divided the Party. So he put up with their waywardness over press policy even at the expense of alienating Goebbels, the ambitious publisher of *Der Angriff*. He placated Goebbels by complaining vociferously about the Strassers and kept him in check by holding out the promise of a daily newspaper and the position of Reich director of propaganda.

Heralded for weeks in advance, the first edition of the Kampf-Verlag's daily newspaper, the *Nationaler Sozialist,* appeared on March 1. Goebbels's disappointment was boundless: "Hitler has openly capitulated to these megalomaniac, cunning little Bavarians and their asphalt [i.e., metropolitan] followers. So I've sent him an urgent letter demanding that he should openly repudiate this insolent move, failing which I offer my resignation."[86] Hitler was extremely angry, but his overriding concern was to avoid choosing between Goebbels and Strasser. He repeated his promise to take steps internally to deal decisively with the Party publishing company and if necessary remove Strasser from his position as head of the Party organization. As usual, nothing actually happened.[87]

By the middle of the month Goebbels had to admit that *Der Angriff* and the *Völkischer Beobachter* in Berlin were being "pushed to the wall" by the Kampf-Verlag, while Hitler looked on passively: "For whatever reason—it doesn't matter why—Hitler has broken his word to me 5 times. [. . .] Hitler stands aside, he makes no decisions, he doesn't lead, he just lets things drift." He "no longer believed Hitler at all," he declared at the end of the month: "What is it going to be like later, when he has to play the dictator in Germany?"[88]

At the beginning of March Hitler had once again—"for the umpteenth time"—told him that he was appointing him head of propaganda but had not acted on his promise.[89] A few weeks later, when Himmler was urging Goebbels finally to take over the new position of propaganda chief, Goebbels was still waiting for the "call from Munich. If Hitler doesn't make the first move, then it's Götz von Berlichingen."*[90] But in spite of all the pressure, the Party leader could not make up his mind to take decisive action against Strasser.[91] Goebbels was so worn down by the dispute that at the end of the month he was once more thinking of resigning as Gauleiter.[92] But he could not bring himself to make the break with his idol.

---

* Translators' note: An allusion to Goethe's eponymous play containing the famous line "He can lick my arse"!

THE END OF THE GRAND COALITION

The end of March 1930 saw the collapse of the grand coalition—consisting of the Center Party (Zentrum), the socialists (SPD), the German Democratic Party (DDP), and the German People's Party (DVP) under the Social Democrat chancellor Hermann Müller—following a disagreement among the parties over the question of funding unemployment pay. The background to this dispute was the dramatic rise in the unemployment figures since the winter: The world economic crisis was having a massive impact on Germany. In this situation Hindenburg called on the Center Party's Heinrich Brüning to form a government, but explicitly told him not to aim at a coalition but rather to resolve any conflicts by using the emergency powers of the president under Article 48 of the Weimar Constitution. There is no doubt that the president's objective was to permanently exclude the Social Democrats from power, make Parliament redundant, and introduce an authoritarian regime subject to his consent.[93]

Early in April, when the SPD confronted the new government—exclusively formed from the bourgeois parties—with a motion for a vote of no confidence, the DNVP was in a position to tip the balance. If it went along with the vote, another election would follow.

After a long discussion with Hindenburg on March 31, this was Hitler's preferred option, as he told Goebbels the same day. Goebbels was delighted with the news: "New elections will give us about 40 seats. That will be amusing!" It seemed to the National Socialists that the rapidly deteriorating economic situation would give their party the opening they were looking for.[94] But in the end the DNVP voted against the no-confidence motion. "The boss is as angry as hell," noted Goebbels. He did manage to find something positive in this turn of events, namely "our withdrawal from the Reich Committee." But he was suspicious about the Party leader's next few maneuvers. "Hitler-Hugenberg talks. Hitler says he's prepared to hold off the announcement about withdrawing for two weeks. Hugenberg plans to bring the cabinet down by then. I don't believe it. The boss is on the wrong wavelength."[95]

When Strasser's *Nationaler Sozialist* ignored Hitler's wishes and publicized the NSDAP's exit from the Reich Committee before the agreed two weeks had elapsed, Goebbels went on the offensive against

Hugenberg and the DNVP in *Der Angriff:* The party was a "superfluous and harmful outfit"; in his last contribution to the Reichstag, the
party's leader had acted out "a tragicomedy about misunderstood
leadership."[96] But the DNVP had also reneged on its agreement with
Hitler: In the decisive vote on the budget on April 12, their parliamentary party voted for the government bill and thus saved Brüning's
government.[97] Goebbels wrote that Hitler, who had come to Berlin,
had no doubt "indulged in too many illusions. But on the other hand
the party [DNVP] is finished. There's bound to be a split. All grist to
our mill."[98]

TAKING OVER AS HEAD OF PROPAGANDA

At the end of April Hitler decided to oppose Strasser publicly and
hand the long-promised control of Reich propaganda over to Goebbels. Hitler used the NSDAP leaders' conference, which took place
on April 26 and 27 in Munich, to stage a fundamental "settling of
accounts" with Gregor Strasser, the Kampf-Verlag, the "drawing-
room Bolsheviks," and other undesirable elements within the Party.
After Hitler's speech Goebbels observed that "Strasser and his circle"
were "shattered." After his tirade, Hitler took the decisive step: As
Goebbels tells it, he "gets to his feet again and amid a breathless hush
announces my appointment as Reich head of propaganda. It serves
the others right. Strasser is as white as a sheet. He stammers out a few
sentences at the end, and then it's all over. We have won all along the
line. [. . .] Goebbels triumphans!"[99] He seems to have forgotten that it
had taken more than a year for the Party leader to confirm his appointment as head of propaganda—which can be traced back ultimately to an agreement between him and Strasser—and that Hitler
only did so when it proved useful to demonstrate his power over
Gregor Strasser and his brother.

Goebbels effectively began to run the Munich propaganda operation in May.[100] As planned, he now traveled every other week to Munich for a few days, working with Himmler on getting the Party
propaganda machine up and running. He hoped to bring it "up to
scratch" by the autumn. In this he relied a good deal at first on
Himmler, whose praises he sang constantly even as he treated him
condescendingly like a kind of servant-pupil.[101] The runup to the

election in Saxony was to be his first test as head of propaganda, but his view of it was quite relaxed: "Well, if it doesn't work out, it's all the Saxons' fault."[102]

As chief of Reich propaganda, he did not by any means have the whole of the Party's propaganda operation under his thumb: The Eher-Verlag under Amann remained independent; Strasser's Reich organization office was responsible for radio, film, and popular education; and Goebbels also had no responsibility for the training of speakers, which duties were under the "Reich propaganda department II." It was thus inevitable that there would be friction with the "megalomaniac Party comrade Fritz Reinhardt," who was responsible for this area of operations.[103]

"THE SOCIALISTS ARE LEAVING THE NSDAP"—BUT GOEBBELS STAYS ON

Goebbels's conviction that he had totally routed the Strassers at the leaders' meeting in April seemed to be corroborated when Hitler visited Berlin on May 2—Goebbels was proud to receive him in the new and greatly extended Gau office[104]—and ostentatiously banned the evening edition of the *Nationaler Sozialist*. Under this pressure, Strasser agreed with Hitler a little later that he would sell his share of the paper to Amann; he finally shut it down on May 20.[105] But to Goebbels's great consternation, the *Nationaler Sozialist* continued to appear after the stated deadline. Hitler was very critical of Otto Strasser, but he was not prepared to deal with him severely.[106]

On May 21 and 22, Hitler had lengthy talks with Otto Strasser, who, as he told Goebbels shortly afterward, made a very bad impression on him. This conversation was an important influence on Strasser's decision to break with the NSDAP for good. After quitting the Party at the beginning of July, he went on to publish a transcript of the discussion, replete with details embarrassing to Hitler.[107]

At the Berlin Gau Day on May 28, Goebbels took a tough line with the *Nationaler Sozialist,* preventing the Party organization from advertising the paper in any way.[108] However, Hitler wanted to postpone a public reckoning—as promised to Goebbels—with the internal opposition until after the Landtag elections in Saxony on June 22. But the deadline came and went, and to Goebbels's chagrin

Hitler took no action.[109] All he did was exclude a few minor rebels from the Berlin Party organization.[110] Hitler did not dare take on Otto Strasser, but he told Goebbels that Gregor had in the meantime very openly distanced himself from his brother.[111] "I don't trust those crafty Lower Bavarians," noted Goebbels.[112] But in fact Gregor Strasser would go on to relinquish his position as publisher of the *Nationaler Sozialist* by the end of June.[113]

At the general meeting of Party members on June 30 and the Gau Day of July 2, Goebbels once more raked the *Nationaler Sozialist* group, the "literati clique," fiercely over the coals.[114] The next day, under the headline "The Socialists Are Leaving the N.S.D.A.P.," Otto Strasser and his supporters announced that they were leaving the Party. Goebbels was relieved: "This clears the air."[115] A few days later he proclaimed the end of the crisis: "Otto Strasser has lost out completely."[116]

CHAPTER 7

"Dare to Live Dangerously!"

Goebbels's Radicalism and Hitler's Policy of "Legality"

Das unnachahmliche Goebbels-Lächeln.

GOEBBELS

CHAPLIN

Chaplin imponiert uns Berlinern nicht. — Wir sind ganz andere Grotesk-Komiker gewöhnt!

Goebbels's public appearances in Berlin were strongly marked by his liking for sensation-loving dramatization and his vain self-presentation. Contemporaries were fully aware of the clownish aspects of his campaigns: "We Berliners are not impressed by Chaplin; we are quite used to other grotesque comedians." Cartoon inspired by Chaplin's visit to Berlin, March 1931.

In mid-July 1930 the Reichstag was close to dissolution: The majority in Parliament rejected Hindenburg's attempt to use his presidential decree under Article 48 to push through Brüning's budget proposals in spite of their failure to gain parliamentary approval. For Goebbels personally, one immediate result would be the loss of his parliamentary immunity from the law: "If the Reichstag is dissolved they'll arrest me right away. It's shitty."[1]

On July 18 a majority in the Reichstag vetoed Hindenburg's emergency decree. The president had previously instructed Brüning to announce the dissolution of Parliament in the event of such a block. Goebbels, now a wanted man again, managed to leave the Reichstag building unhindered. He and Göring took the night train to Munich,[2] where Hitler held a meeting: Apart from Göring and Goebbels, the attendees included Alfred Rosenberg, Wilhelm Frick, Gregor Strasser, Konstantin Hierl, and Franz Ritter von Epp. The discussion centered on the distribution of seats in the next Parliament. A tour of the Palais Barlow on the Königsplatz, bought by the Party in May, had been arranged for the occasion. Once the renovation was complete, it would become the site of the new headquarters. Goebbels found the place "ostentatious and spacious." He took careful note of Hitler's disparaging remarks about Gregor Strasser.[3]

THE ELECTION CAMPAIGN

At headquarters over the next few days Goebbels adjusted to working with the election campaign machine, but the atmosphere of Munich did not suit him: He could "not work in Munich. It's disorderly and disorganized."[4] But he had to stick it out for a few more days, since a meeting of Gauleiters was scheduled for July 27, when the basic decisions about the election campaign would be made. Goebbels was officially entrusted with running the central election campaign, and then discussion moved on to the nomination of candidates. Goebbels boasted in the diary that he had thwarted various maneuvers by Strasser, pushed through the candidacies of his Berlin Party comrade Martin Löppelmann and that of his old boss Axel Ripke, and prevented "many another dubious blessing," though he could do nothing about certain "dead losses." He had spoken out explicitly against Reventlow, but the latter—like his enemy Münchmeyer—was re-nominated.[5]

For the time being, Goebbels swallowed his reservations about Munich. He decided to rent an apartment in the Bavarian capital at the Party's expense and "gradually move to Munich" after the election.[6]

Following the guidelines established at the Gauleiters' meeting, Goebbels now exercised a decisive influence on the election campaign. However, the Reich propaganda department's management of the campaign was far from optimal: The Party's propaganda machine was not yet streamlined enough for that.[7] At Goebbels's suggestion, the whole campaign was fought under a single slogan: "The fight against the Young parties." The plan was to attack the SPD above all, but also the Center Party, the DVP, and the DDP, thus targeting the government parties that had voted in the Reichstag in March for the restructuring of reparations under the Young Plan. In terms of content, then, the new head of Reich propaganda continued along the lines that had been central to the Party's agitation in previous years.

Typical of the campaign was a poster featuring the massive figure of a martial-looking worker wielding a huge hammer with which to smash some creatures representing the "Young parties" ("Pulverize them!") or another showing a caricature of a Social Democrat functionary willingly carrying out the Young Plan by shifting billions of marks abroad: "Stop! That money belongs to hardworking people." Aside from this, the NSDAP's most important campaigning methods consisted of mass rallies and propaganda marches.[8]

While he was working on the campaign, Goebbels was deluged with court cases. On August 12 he had to appear in a court in Hanover to answer a charge of slandering the Prussian prime minister, Otto Braun. Goebbels managed to extract his head from this noose not by denying the remarks, which had been an accusation of corruption, but by claiming that his remarks did not refer to Braun at all but rather to the former Reich chancellor Gustav Bauer. And he actually got away with this charade; the court found him not guilty.[9]

Potentially more threatening was a summons from the Leipzig High Court, which wanted to question him about a speech he had made in 1927 in which he had speculated about a possible SA putsch—or at least, that was how the law perceived it. He was investigated on suspicion of high treason. When cross-examined at the end of July, he pretended that he could not remember the speech. The case was eventually dropped for lack of evidence.[10]

Meanwhile, there was a development in the appeal hearing connected with the "Hindenburg trial." Goebbels had already learned from his defending counsel that Hindenburg had indicated to his state secretary, Otto Meissner, that he wanted to drop charges. Goebbels's lawyer worked with the Reich president's office to draw up a corresponding statement.[11] The hearing was postponed;[12] when it finally took place, on August 14, the state prosecutor revealed to an astonished public a letter from Hindenburg stating that[13] on the basis of the explanation he had received from Goebbels he had concluded that no insult to his person had been intended, so that he was no longer inclined to press charges against the National Socialist politician.[14] Instead of the fine of 800 marks the court had earlier imposed on him, it now brought in a verdict of not guilty: "Hurrah! Great result!"[15]

But Goebbels did not get off so cleanly in every case. On August 16 the court of lay assessors in Charlottenburg ruled against him because of an article in *Der Angriff* in December 1929 in which he called members of the Reich government "hired traitors." However, the court did not wish to sentence him to six months' imprisonment, as the public prosecutor had demanded, but thought that a fine of 600 marks would suffice.[16] On the same day, two other fines were imposed on him.

STENNES'S REVOLT

It was not only the law that was putting pressure on Goebbels at this point but his own people as well. Just as the election campaign was getting under way, a conflict broke out that was extremely dangerous for Goebbels and the NSDAP: The SA was flexing its muscles. On August 7 Goebbels met Stennes and other SA leaders, who bluntly presented him with their demands: "The gentlemen want to be in the Reichstag and don't wish to be subject to Party discipline, and since this has been turned down, they're staging a kind of mini–palace revolution. [. . .] Stennes has told me brazenly and sanctimoniously that if they were to quit, the SA would drop from 15,000 to 3,000 men."[17]

The same day, Goebbels phoned the head of the SA, Franz Pfeffer, who had undertaken a similar initiative, in his case against Hitler himself: "He is subdued. Hitler tore him to shreds. Called the whole move mutiny and conspiracy." Goebbels told the Berlin SA leader Ernst Wetzel that he considered Pfeffer a "schemer" who had led the SA to the point of "rebellion."[18] In the middle of that month, he met Pfeffer, who "surely must have realized" that the SA "had overshot the mark on this question of the nominations."[19]

The SA revolt was to break out openly at the end of the month. On August 27 Goebbels heard "the first report of a rebellion planned by the S.A." His initial reaction was incomprehension: "They propose to give us an ultimatum [parliamentary candidate nominations] and lash out if they don't get their way. In the middle of the battle. [. . .] Stennes squats like a spider behind the scenes."[20] Some hours later—despite the worrisome news, he had gone to a campaigning event in Dresden—he learned that "the affair is worse than I feared. The Standard leaders have joined forces and openly rebelled against [the] Gau and Munich."

Back in Berlin, he jotted down the next day: "Terrible disappointment. Talks with Stennes. He shamelessly states his demands: 3 nominations. Money, political power." Stennes had openly threatened to break up an event planned for the Sportpalast the next day. Goebbels made a decision: "Pretend to give in. Take revenge on September 15." Unfortunately, he was committed to another work trip, this time to Hamburg. After many fruitless attempts, he finally got a call through to Hitler. But the telephone conversation took a disappointing turn: Hitler "hasn't grasped the situation at all. Takes it too lightly."

Only just arrived back in Berlin, he noted on August 29: "Chaos. A shock troop from Standard IV set on demolishing our office and beating up Wilke and Muchow. It takes all my authority to make them see reason. Stennes wilfully lets the affair come to a head and then sees he's out of his depth." Under the circumstances, Stennes was prepared to compromise: "His demands are diminishing by the hour. Endless telephone calls to Munich. Can't get ahold of Hitler. And the others are dimwits."

Goebbels decided to act on Stennes's suggestion that he should address the SA that evening. As *Der Angriff* reported, he used the event in the Sportpalast to "hold [to account] the rumor-mongers in Jewish pay who are now trying to sow discord in the National Socialist ranks just before the election." Furthermore, he wrung a statement out of Stennes that he published in *Der Angriff*: The rumors of a mutiny by the Berlin SA were "all lies"; the SA stood "loyally by the Party and its leader."[21] Goebbels regarded the pledge he had made to Stennes as null and void, since it had been obtained "by coercion and was therefore invalid."

For a while, things seemed to settle down—in any case, Goebbels was determined not to let the Berlin crisis ruin his election campaign plan, so he duly set off for Breslau on August 30. It is tempting to think that in these stormy days his external commitments were not at all unwelcome, as they prevented him from being pulled into the Berlin quagmire. During the last Stennes crisis, in the summer of 1928, he had not even thought it necessary to break off his vacation in Bavaria. However, that night in Breslau he received alarming, if not entirely unexpected, news: "S.A. has stormed and demolished office. S.S. defending, two injured." He decided to return to Berlin. There at midday he met Göring and Hitler: The latter had come up from Bayreuth. In the evening they toured the SA drinking haunts together. Although Hitler was "greeted with enthusiasm" everywhere, the prevailing "mood was subdued."

Late in the evening he received a visit—clearly an unexpected one: "Around 10 o'clock the Berlin SA leaders turn up at my place—Hitler talks to them. He's not in good form." There were signs that the atmosphere was deteriorating: "The vulgar behavior of these people. They tell him what's what." Goebbels could not resist adding, "In many ways they're not entirely wrong. [. . .] Poor Hitler! That's the price you pay for years of negligence." In the end Stennes too had a talk with Hitler; it lasted until dawn but achieved no clear-cut result.

That morning Goebbels had yet another court appearance to make: He received a six-week prison sentence and a fine of 500 marks for his repeated smears against Deputy Police Commissioner Bernhard Weiss.[22] "Went during adjournment to Hitler, who is with Göring. New situation. I urge reconciliation, otherwise we're facing disaster. The rebellion is already spreading to the countryside." A decision was reached at four that afternoon: Hitler dismissed Pfeffer, took over command of the SA himself, and simultaneously decreed an improvement to the SA's finances, to be funded by raising special levies from the Party.[23] The SA leaders accepted the proposal the same afternoon, and Goebbels tried to represent the last-minute compromise as a defeat for the SA: "Revolution is held indoors.* Stennes has submitted."

In the evening there was a gathering in the Veteran Soldiers' House to make a conspicuous show of celebrating the reconciliation. The SA, Goebbels wrote, which "just before had been intent on an explosion, is now sitting horror-stricken and weeping. Hitler speaks." The Berlin police recorded that after a lengthy speech Hitler issued a call for loyalty from the SA, "raising his already strained voice to the

---

* Translators' note: A reference to a line in a Kurt Tucholsky poem of 1928: "Due to bad weather, the revolution will be held indoors."

pitch of an almost hysterical shriek." Following him as speaker, Goebbels had delivered some "sentimental remarks" intended to "draw a line" under the whole affair. Goebbels's own comment on his address was triumphant, however: "I speak. Everything goes fine. That's the end of the Stennes putsch. The consequences will be seen after September 14." But he omitted to say that Stennes spoke after he did, announcing Hitler's new arrangements and proclaiming himself the victor.[24]

A few days later Goebbels conspicuously demonstrated the reconciliation to Berliners. He wrote that he had moved around Berlin with the SA the whole day, from morning until the late evening: "Both a battle march and a triumphal and celebratory procession. It was glorious. Right through the red citadels."[25] On September 10 Hitler spoke at an event in the Sportpalast.[26] It was the high point of the election campaign. Afterward, Goebbels was sitting with the Party leader: "Boss wants me to hang on in Berlin. I must do that, although I don't really feel like it anymore." At least Hitler had recognized that he bore "not an iota of guilt" for the recent events and that it had been more about "a structural flaw in the organization." Now the "influence of the political leaders" would have to increase.[27]

The next day Goebbels had a long discussion with Stennes, with whom he "gradually got into contact."[28] He had no choice: The SA was essential for his strident style of agitation. On the other hand, if he was too closely identified with the SA and overplayed the part of a radical, he would inevitably come into conflict with the Party leadership.

CLASHES OVER THE PARTY LINE

As Goebbels had expected,[29] the NSDAP enjoyed some spectacular results in the election of September 14, 1930, taking 18.3 percent of the vote. Without a doubt, the Party had now become a mass movement. All the same, the results in Berlin were distinctly below average for the Reich as a whole: The Party achieved only 14.6 percent in the capital.[30] Nonetheless, in the Sportpalast on the evening of election day there was an air of "excitement as in 1914."[31] Goebbels celebrated the victory in *Der Angriff* with the assertion that "in the long run a National Socialist government in Germany is inevitable."[32] In his view, now was the moment to draw a line under recent disputes. At the Gau day on September 17 he magnanimously announced a "general amnesty"[33] and put intense effort into reinforcing the settlement between the Party and the SA, on whose loyalty he ultimately depended. On September 20 he had a long, "open and amiable" talk with Stennes,[34] but after a few days he began once more to doubt that Stennes would sustain the peace.[35]

On September 25 Goebbels went to Leipzig with Göring to appear as a witness in the so-called Leipzig Treason Trial. The German public was taking an intense interest in the case: Three Reichswehr officers stationed in Ulm had attempted to organize a National Socialist cell within the army and were now being tried for treason. To clarify where the NSDAP stood in relation to the constitution of the Republic, the court had called in leading National Socialists as witnesses. Coming immediately after the surprising success of the Party in the Reichstag elections, their court appearances promised to give important clues as to the Party's future direction.

Hitler was the first to deliver his testimony. He declared unequivocally that the NSDAP aimed to achieve power purely by legal means. Goebbels was in the public gallery with Göring, listening to Hitler's evidence. He had reason to fear that the state prosecutor's material aimed at disproving Hitler's assertion would include some of his own "revolutionary" writings. This fear proved to be unfounded. In the end, Goebbels was not called as a witness.[36] Once again, any open disclosure of the differences between the "legal" Hitler and the "revolutionary" Goebbels was avoided.

After its election successes, the elite of the NSDAP began—in keeping with their "legal" policy—to sound out the chances of joining a Brüning-led coalition. On one of his visits to Berlin, Hitler let Goebbels know his three conditions. The Party would demand three ministries: "Foreign Affairs (Rosenberg); Ministry of the Interior (Frick); and Ministry of Defense (probably Epp)" as well as the withdrawal of the Center Party from the coalition government in Prussia, which it shared with the SPD and the DDP. It seemed that some quite fantastic vistas were suddenly opening up for Goebbels's personal future: "If we participate, then for a start I'll gain power in Prussia. Then there'll be a clearing-out."[37]

Hitler, seconded by Frick and Strasser, had confidential discussions with Brüning on October 5. The NSDAP drew a blank: There was no possibility of its taking part in a Reich government.[38] Goebbels was one of the first to be told: "We remain in opposition. Thank God."[39] Goebbels still hoped his chance would come with the collapse of the coalition in Prussia, the largest German state.[40] But there was a long way to go before that. Until the opening of the new Reichstag, Goebbels lacked immunity from the law, and the authorities used the situation to increase pressure on him. To avoid imminent arrest, on October 10 Goebbels escaped to Weimar.[41] He was back in Berlin for the opening of the Reichstag on October 13 and managed to evade the agents of the law waiting for him to enter the building. *Der Angriff* revealed some of the details of this hide-and-seek game a few days later.[42] Goebbels's parliamentary privileges were now restored to him.[43]

He soon had a chance to strengthen his position as a publicist. After some unpleasant clashes—"that loathsome Amann! I hate him"[44]—in September he reached an agreement with the Eher Verlag whereby Eher and the Gau would jointly publish *Der Angriff* as a daily paper. Goebbels was jubilant: He was now "in sole charge, commercially and intellectually, I'm completely independent."[45] At the beginning of October 1930 he signed the definitive contract with Amann: "But he'll do the dirty on me all the same."[46] However, starting on November 1 *Der Angriff* did indeed appear as a daily paper.[47]

In November he discovered in Munich what Hitler planned to do about the SA crisis that was still smoldering: "Röhm is coming back. From Bolivia, where he's been working with the army. He's very nice to me, and I like him. An open, straight military type."[48] Röhm came to Berlin at the end of the month. "He's a lovely chap," wrote Goebbels, "but no match at all for Stennes."[49]

Ernst Röhm had actually gone to Bolivia as a military instructor after a disagreement with Hitler in 1925 over the incorporation of his creation, the Frontbann (a surrogate organization for members of the prohibited SA), into the re-founded NSDAP.[50] Hitler's decision to put Röhm in charge of the SA, which he pushed through despite some resistance at the SA leadership conference on November 30 in Munich, was bound to lead to further conflicts over the medium to long term. The self-confident Röhm was not the man to play second fiddle to Hitler. But in the short term, Hitler's aim was to keep Stennes and his henchmen in check by appointing Röhm.[51]

GOEBBELS ACTS RADICAL

Goebbels had his own prescription for keeping the SA under control in Berlin: permanent violent activity to reinforce the internal cohesion of the SA and to satisfy the hunger for action among the young brownshirts, as most of them were unemployed. He hoped that this would give the rapidly expanding and heterogeneous organization some sense of momentum.

In November 1930 he found a new target in his war against the "system": the American film *All Quiet on the Western Front,* based on the 1929 novel of that name by the German antiwar writer Erich Maria Remarque, a realistic description of trench warfare. Goebbels saw the film as an attack on the honor of the German front-line soldier, and it was obvious to him that Jewish machinations lay behind the movie project. The screening of the film in Berlin must be prevented at all costs; that was his aim.

On December 5 he and a large group of supporters went to an evening screening of the film. They swung into action: "After only 10 minutes the cinema is like a madhouse. The police are powerless. The embittered crowd act against the Jews. The first incursion into the west [of the city]. 'Jews out!' 'Hitler is at the gates!' [. . .] Outside, the box offices are under attack. Window panes tinkle. The screening is canceled, and the next one too. We have won."[52]

A few days later, after specific exhortations from *Der Angriff* to do so, National Socialists organized further riots at a screening of the film in the west of Berlin.[53] On the Wittenbergplatz Goebbels addressed more than twenty thousand supporters, by his own estimate (the *Berlin Lokalanzeiger* newspaper put the crowd at about five thousand). A procession of demonstrators formed and succeeded in breaking through the police barrier and on to the Kurfürstendamm.[54] The same scene was repeated the next day. This time the police employed force in an effort to disperse the demonstrators—Goebbels reckoned there were forty thousand of them—trying to gain access to the Kurfürstendamm, and eventually the law officers drew their weapons. The next morning the chief commissioner of police imposed a ban on demonstrations. Goebbels was delighted: "Our ordinary N.S. people dictate government action."[55] In the end the film was banned on the grounds that it "was a threat to German prestige"—

for Goebbels this was a "triumph":[56] "The Republic is enraged by our film victory. [. . .] In the eyes of the public we are the men of strength."[57]

The new year began with further acts of violence by the SA. On January 3 the Gauleiter made a laconic entry in his diary: "2 Reichsbanner shot dead by our people. That creates respect. The others start terror actions; we act only in self-defense." Seeing the film *Afrika* on the same day seems to have confirmed his belief that he was on the right track: "Fight, fight is the cry of the creature. Nowhere is there peace, just murder, just killing, all for the sake of survival. As it is with lions, so it is with human beings. We alone lack the courage to openly admit the way things are. In this respect wild animals are the better human beings."

Around the middle of the month Hitler assured him that the Party in general was in good shape; however, there was "a danger that everything will take too long, so that the Party might lose its dynamic and stall. The answer is to raise the level of activity."[58] This was an endorsement of Goebbels's mode of operation. A few days later, on January 22, a debate with the communist politician Walter Ulbricht in the Friedrichshain hall ended in a brawl.[59] The *Vossische Zeitung* reported that the rioting "was like nothing ever seen before at a political meeting": More than 100 people were injured.[60]

The riot was the prelude to a whole series of violent outbreaks, as reported in *Der Angriff* over the next few days. One public site after another became the setting for a pitched indoor battle. *Der Angriff*—naturally blaming the opposition—declared that it was "open civil war"; force had to be used in confronting the "blood-terror of the communists."[61] "Drop Your Weapons!" demanded the headline of an editorial in the *Vossische Zeitung,* reacting to the violent clashes between National Socialists and communists that took place over the weekends of early February.[62]

With the increasing deployment of the SA, Goebbels felt it advisable to forge closer links with Stennes again. In January he invited Stennes and his wife to an evening gathering in his new apartment and voiced his satisfaction at having "gotten much closer to the SA leader."[63] But a few days later, at an SA parade, Stennes again aroused Goebbels's suspicions.[64] All the same, he supported Stennes's attempts to bring the Berlin SS unambiguously under his control.[65] In February the two men had further talks, after which they were agreed on the basics: "We form a partnership. S.A. and I. That's power."[66]

While he was making approaches to the SA and following an ever more radical course, Goebbels increasingly distanced himself from Göring, who had a special role to play in the capital, above all setting up contacts among the nationalist and conservative elites. From the beginning of the year his complaints about Göring became more voluble. Nonetheless, in the course of 1930—after many difficulties—Goebbels was at least able to establish reasonable personal relations with him.[67] In April 1930 they even went on a vacation to Sweden together.[68]

Early in January 1931, just after a minor dispute brought on by Göring's desire to exclude him from a soirée with the army chief of staff, General Kurt von Hammerstein-Equord,[69] Goebbels heard from a mutual acquaintance that "G. has given way to the vice of morphine again";[70] feigning concern, he passed this information on to Hitler two weeks later.[71] Goebbels eagerly collected negative observations and complaints about Göring;[72] objected that he "went snobbing around too much in alien circles"; criticized Göring for visiting the court of the exiled Kaiser ("what does Doorn mean to us?"); and accused him of being too optimistic about political questions.[73] In a lengthy talk with Hitler, he discovered they were largely of one mind in their unfavorable opinion of his rival, whom Hitler accused of megalomania.[74] In mid-March there was a frank discussion between Goebbels and Göring in which the two initially hurled serious accusations at each other but then parted "as semi-friends."[75]

Goebbels's newly awakened radicalism widened the contrast with Munich. He was not pleased that at this time Hitler seemed completely taken up with the new headquarters in the renovated Brown House (once the Palais Barlow) in a prominent position on the Königsplatz, into which the NSDAP had moved in January.[76] When in February he heard from Stennes that SA leader Röhm was possibly homosexual—the very person whom, a few weeks earlier, Goebbels had warned about a Berlin SA leader with the same reputation![77]—he unleashed even more of his anger on the Party leadership: "Revolting! Hitler not taking enough care again. We can't have this, the Party as the El Dorado of the 175ers."*[78]

In a meeting with Berlin SA leaders in his apartment, Goebbels discerned a "strong antipathy to Munich," but as for himself, he "was

---

* Translators' note: Paragraph 175 was the section of the German Criminal Code relating to homosexuality.

on good terms with the men."[79] In Munich at the beginning of March, he found himself agreeing with the Party leader on many questions, but he also concluded that Hitler was "too weak and too keen on compromise. Wants to achieve power at any price, and wants it right away."[80]

In the Bavarian capital he raised with Röhm the subject of the tensions in the SA, particularly the critical relations between SA and SS. "Röhm sees things the right way, but Hitler won't hear a word against the SS. His hobbyhorse. The bodyguards!" In the dispute between the SA and the Party he saw himself in the noble role of "mediator." He resolved to "support Stennes's legitimate demands on behalf of the SA" but also to combat with all his might any tendency "to mount a putsch against the Party or Hitler."[81]

A few weeks later it was all Goebbels could do to prevent Röhm from dismissing Stennes. As on numerous other visits to Munich, Goebbels convinced himself that the blame for Hitler's less "activist" attitude was due to the insidious influence of his coterie, the terrible "Munich milieu": "Afternoon in the café. Boss as bourgeois. Terrible to see him among these Philistines." On the other hand: "If it comes to a breach, I'll stand by Hitler, although I think there's so much that needs reforming at a lower level."[82] Ultimately, it was because—for all his doubts—he was always determined to stick to Hitler that his relationships with other National Socialist politicians such as Stennes, Göring, and Röhm were so fraught: He was not interested in being drawn into internal Party alliances that might ultimately land him in a confrontation with the Party leader. As he saw it, he owed his place in the NSDAP primarily to his special relationship with Hitler, and in no way would he permit any other political ties within the NSDAP to jeopardize this privileged position.

The extreme adaptability of the Berlin Gauleiter was also apparent in another area. His own view of the Party's economic policy was that it was badly in need of revising. After the September 1930 election he had written two editorials for Der Angriff calling for the Party to be more specific in its pronouncements on economic questions. He held that the Party's twenty-five points, dating from 1920 and declared sacrosanct by Hitler (they included a demand for "a share of large companies' profits" as well as land reform), could only be a "framework." Goebbels called on leading Party comrades to assemble in order to "resolve by discussion and exchange of ideas the problems that are in part still contentious or unclear today."[83] And in fact such a session did come about, in December 1930. After consulting "Hitler and a large number of experts," Goebbels came up with a definition of socialism that immediately met with Hitler's "enthusiastic" approval: "placing the concept of the people above that of the individual." Goebbels was certain that "this will find its way into the program."[84]

However, collective deliberations about a future economic program, let alone concrete policy decisions, were not the style favored by Hitler, who was fundamentally more inclined to take a tactical line on such questions. In January 1930 he set up a new economic policy unit at headquarters under Otto Wagener, who then went to work—in competition with other parts of the NSDAP machine—on an economic program. In March 1931, Wagener submitted a paper envisaging a private-sector economy under the supervision and direction of the state. Goebbels was appalled: "Not a trace of socialism left." He wrote a scathing critique of the paper and tried to encourage Göring to oppose it, but he was not high on socialism. "G. is all about encouraging economic activity," was Goebbels's summary of Göring's pro-business attitude.[85]

What is more, in spring 1931 Hans Reupke, another newly appointed economic adviser, produced a leaflet in which he—Reupke was a board member of the Reich Association of German Industry—clearly departed from the earlier nationalization plans of the NSDAP. For Goebbels this was a "downright betrayal of socialism."[86] A few days later he discussed the economic policy with Hitler and allowed himself to be persuaded that Reupke had already been "shaken off."[87] In reality, Hitler never adopted any precise economic program for the Party. Engaging his consultant, Reupke, to write a paper was a clear signal that he wanted nothing to do with socialist experiments. Goebbels gave up trying to induce the Party to clarify its economic policy. It even seems that on his way to state power he ceased to care very much which economic and sociopolitical concepts were deployed to achieve it.

Goebbels's self-presentation as a radical, engaged in a daily struggle and under constant threat at his position in the front line, is exemplified by an episode he contrived in March 1931. On March 13, he records in the diary, "someone tried to kill me with a bomb."[88] A package that his office thought looked suspicious was found to contain "explosives": No one was injured. The next day *Der Angriff* gave this incident headline treatment.[89] A few weeks later it emerged, either as a result of police inquiries or of a leak by former Party employees, that the assassination attempt had clearly been faked by Goebbels himself—and quite crudely at that. The "explosives" consisted of some jumping jacks and a little gunpowder.[90] That Goebbels wrote up the "assassination attempt" in his diary as a genuine threat shows his relationship to the truth: Having acted out a charade for public consumption, he then recorded it as a fact in his diary.

A NEW STENNES CRISIS

In March 1931 the Republic resorted to tougher measures against the NSDAP. On March 18 the Berlin police imposed a public speaking ban on Goebbels, and on March 20 he discovered shortly before an event in Königsberg that the police had prohibited him from appearing "for fear of a breach of the peace."[91]

When an emergency decree promulgated by the Reich president at the end of March restricted the political parties' right to demonstrate and campaign, therefore limiting the scope for SA activities, it was bound to exacerbate further the conflict between the "activist" political troops and the "legal" course pursued by the Party leadership. Goebbels saw this as a confirmation of his radical approach: "Long live legality! It's sickening! Now we'll have to find other ways of working." Too many mistakes had been made in the past: "Above all getting too close to the enemy. Now he is swindling us. That's Göring's doing. We should have remained an ominous threat and an enigmatic sphinx. Now we're out in the open. [. . .] Change of approach! Back to stubborn opposition. Struggle, work, action, not negotiation."[92]

With such pronouncements Goebbels projected himself as the spokesman of the SA, but as a Party Gauleiter he inevitably found himself caught between the two front lines, engendering mounting suspicion both in Munich and within the Stennes circle: "There's a stink in the SA again. Stennes won't give it a rest. But Munich is making major blunders, too. Headquarters is bringing us down again." He heard from an SA leader that there was a "strong clique" working against him in Munich. "Hierl, Rosenberg etc., but Strasser, too."[93]

On a trip to East Prussia at the end of March he learned from the Danzig Gauleiter, Albert Forster, that there was a similar "stink in the SA" in his area. Stennes, thought Goebbels, was operating everywhere behind the scenes.[94] Goebbels was truly prescient in foretelling "the very grave crisis the Party will one day have to go through."[95] But this did not stop him from leaving the capital in these critical days and fulfilling electioneering engagements in Saxony.

On March 31 Hitler unexpectedly called Goebbels to Weimar. The next day he learned there from Röhm that Stennes had been dismissed for open rebellion. However, Stennes had not reacted passively but had gone on the offensive, sending in the SA to occupy the Party's Berlin headquarters and the editorial offices of Der Angriff. On April 1 the paper carried a statement by Stennes. Berlin, said Goebbels, was "an anthill."[96] But he came down unequivocally on Hitler's side—"despite all criticisms."

Goebbels suspected that behind the Berlin putsch was the figure of Captain Hermann Ehrhardt, a former Free Corps and secret society leader who had placed himself at the head of an oppositional group within the SA. What he was certain of, however, was that this was "the biggest, and perhaps the last, crisis of the Party." In the evening both he and Hitler participated in an event at which Goebbels declared his loyalty "to the leader without reservation."[97] Overnight he drove with Hitler to Munich. The putsch was put down from there. Hitler and Goebbels expressed themselves on the subject in the National Socialist press. In Der Angriff Hitler announced that he had given Goebbels "plenipotentiary powers to cleanse the National Socialist movement of all subversive elements," but the Party newspaper also—to Goebbels's vexation—gave Stennes space to air his views. Goebbels promptly fired the business manager of Der Angriff, Ludwig Weissauer.[98]

The plenipotentiary used the special authority given to him to exclude the "traitors" from the Party. The issue of Der Angriff on April 4 was once again totally under Goebbels's control and appeared with the banner headline "The End of the Mutinous Gang." The page contained a two-column spread by Hitler appealing to Party comrades. Goebbels therefore had good reason to regard the revolt as having been "suppressed" after just a few days. Nonetheless, it stuck in his craw that Göring in Berlin had tried to play the leading role himself in the battle with Stennes: "I'll never forgive Göring for this! People make you despair. He's a lump of frozen shit."[99]

All the same, Goebbels took his time returning to Berlin. He spent Easter with Hitler in Munich and the surrounding area and only set off for the capital again on April 8. He was hoping, therefore, as in the two previous Stennes crises of 1928 and 1930, that his geographical distance from the scene would prevent him from being drawn too much into the conflict. For all his loyalty to Hitler, he had to be careful not to sever his links with the SA completely. Thus on his return to Berlin he declared that he was ill: He kept engagements and issued statements but avoided public appearances.[100]

His collaboration with Stennes's replacement, Paul Schulz, seemed to get off to a good start; moreover, he established that the Party organization had survived practically unaffected by the crisis.[101] He called on the authority of the state, in the form of the police and some bailiffs, to enforce the return of the office furniture Stennes had removed.[102] In *Der Angriff* of April 7 he wrote a long declaration of loyalty to Hitler, embracing his "legal" policy.[103]

During the Stennes putsch he had kept faith with Hitler; now he laid the blame for the insurgency squarely at the door of headquarters in Munich, this "palace party."[104] A few days later, in time-honored fashion, he conspicuously demonstrated reconciliation with the SA by mustering 4,000 of them in the Sportpalast for a "general roll call."[105]

COURT HEARINGS

By amending standing orders, the Reichstag had in February 1931 introduced restrictions on parliamentary immunity and made it easier for the law to prosecute members. Furthermore, Parliament decided to permit the courts to force the Reichstag member Joseph Goebbels to appear before them if he persisted in ignoring official summonses.[106] A new tidal wave of trials was now about to engulf Goebbels.[107]

On April 14 there were two cases to answer: One involved a further insult to the deputy commissioner of police, Bernhard Weiss, for which Goebbels was fined 1,500 Reichsmarks; the other, obstructive public comments on the banning of uniforms, attracting a fine of 200 Reichsmarks.[108] The next case came two days later: "These trials are killing me."[109] He was fined 2,000 and 500 Reichsmarks, respectively, by the Berlin regional court for another "Isidor" insult to Weiss and for incitement to violence against Jews, both of which had appeared in *Der Angriff* the previous June.[110]

When he failed to turn up at a court hearing at the end of April—it concerned still more insults printed in *Der Angriff*—having set off for a conference in Munich instead, the Berlin public prosecutor sent an official by plane to Munich. Goebbels was arrested the same day and brought back to Berlin on the night train in police custody.[111] There he was fined another 1,500 Reichsmarks, and two days later he was sentenced to a fine of the same amount and a month's imprisonment.[112] Two days after that he was fined a further 1,000 marks.[113] Goebbels complained in an editorial in *Der Angriff* about the fines that were piling up. In doing so, he also inadvertently revealed that the law's relentless pursuit of him really was hurting him.[114]

DISPUTES WITHIN THE PARTY

After the elections of September 1930, Goebbels had set about seriously expanding the Reich propaganda machine in Munich. In November 1930 he acquired a deputy there, Heinz Franke, who soon had a staff of around ten. The propaganda department's activities included, among other things, putting out a series of publications, organizing school events, and producing films and gramophone records.[115]

In a circular of January 1931 Goebbels expressed himself highly dissatisfied with the performance of the Gau propaganda offices: "The aim of the Reich propaganda office is to create a first-class apparatus functioning in accordance with headquarters directives like a flawless precision engine, and the Reich office does not intend to allow itself to be diverted from this goal by recalcitrant or incompetent Gau propaganda sections."[116]

After a press and propaganda conference[117] in Munich on April 26, 1931, Goebbels published "Guidelines for NSDAP Propaganda Management" in *Wille und Weg* (Will and Way), the Reich propaganda office's newly founded newsletter. In particular, he described in detail the responsibility of Gau propaganda directors, who "in practical terms" were subordinate to the Reich propaganda office, and he gave instructions for the conduct of meetings, sending Party speakers out to the Party organization around the country, and producing leaflets.[118] His self-confident manner here hardly endeared him to the Party. It was nothing new for him to find at the conference that he had not exactly gone over well among the Party's more senior functionaries, and that he had been the subject of malicious gossip: "Nobody likes me."[119]

After the Munich conference he had a long talk with Hitler. Hitler declared that he was "completely free of suspicion about me, and condemns in the sharpest terms all the agitation against me in the Party. I ask him if he has full confidence in me, and he comes out wholeheartedly on my side. 'Berlin belongs to you, and that's how it will stay!' "[120]

In the following weeks critical remarks about Hitler abounded in his diary. While he considered *Mein Kampf* "honest and courageous," he also found "the style [. . .] sometimes unbearable." Furthermore: "You've got to be tolerant. He writes the way he talks. The effect is direct, but often also inept." Commenting on a meeting with Hitler in the Kaiserhof Hotel a few days later, he wrote: "He hates Berlin and loves Munich. [. . .] But why Munich, exactly? I don't understand it."[121]

In May 1931 the Stennes trial took place, threatening to plunge Hitler into considerable difficulties thanks to a statement Goebbels had made some years earlier. The danger avoided at the Leipzig Treason Trial now appeared to rear its ugly head again. So it was not surprising that Goebbels anticipated Hitler's testimony "with a racing pulse."[122] The situation was that members of the infamous SA Stormtroop 33 were on trial once more; this time the charge was attempted homicide. The secondary charge maintained that the SA violence was systematic and that the leadership of the SA and the Party were ultimately behind it. Among those subpoenaed were Stennes, who was now sidelined, but who had been in charge of the SA in eastern Germany at the time of the assaults in question; and Hitler, as head of the whole Party.

To Goebbels's surprise, Stennes claimed in court that in his time the Party had followed a strictly legal course. Hitler, who gave his evidence quite tamely, was confronted with a passage from *Der*

Nazi-Sozi, a leaflet written by Goebbels, stating that the National Socialists wanted "revolution": "Then we'll send Parliament to hell and
found the state on German muscle and German brain-power!"[123]
Goebbels's radicalism made Hitler uncomfortable: "I did not have all
the contents of the leaflet in mind at the time I appointed Goebbels,"
he responded. "In any case, today he is strictly required to follow the
line laid down by me and nobody but me."[124] In the evening when
they were sitting together in the Kaiserhof, Goebbels remembered
that he had cut the offending passage out of the second edition. "Hitler positively dances with joy. That vindicates us." For the time being,
the danger that Goebbels might be called as a "witness for the Crown"
against Hitler's claim to pursue a law-abiding policy had been
averted.[125]

On June 9 Goebbels participated in an NSDAP leadership conference at the Brown House in Munich, which also included Frick and
the "revolting Göring." The potential for conflict was substantial:
"Strasser opens the attack on Hitler. He wants a General Secretary—
Strasser himself, naturally—to be appointed. He would be in charge
of organization and propaganda. Party to be divided into three areas:
S.A., state (Hierl), and fighting movement (Strasser). Plus a commissar in Prussia. So they want to make the boss honorary chairman and
sideline me." Göring and Hierl had supported Strasser, but Hitler had
defended himself "cleverly and emphatically" and "rejected the move
on its face." Goebbels kept his head down during this attack and
stayed silent, reasoning that "I haven't got many friends in the Party.
Practically no one apart from Hitler. They all envy me my success
and my popularity." After the conference, Hitler assured him that he
was completely behind him.

At the behest of Göring's wife, Carin, the two rivals met in June
and agreed to a kind of ceasefire.[126] But Goebbels was reminded in
the following weeks how insecure his position was within the Party.
At the end of June rumors reached him that Hitler wished to replace
him as Gauleiter of Berlin. He suspected the source was somebody in
Munich headquarters.[127] Finally, he published in *Der Angriff* a short
notice in which he confirmed in ironic fashion his intention of staying in Berlin for the duration: "I am not ill. I could become so by
laughing myself sick over the unholy amount of activity being put
into kindly talking me away from Berlin."[128]

In July he stumbled upon evidence of a "widespread conspiracy":

"S.S. (Himmler) maintains a spy bureau here in Berlin to keep me under surveillance. They are putting out the craziest rumors. I think it's an agent provocateur operation." He decided to try to bring down Himmler, "that crafty swine."[129] A few days later he found an opportunity to bring the affair to Hitler's attention. The latter reacted "with horror" and ordered an "immediate end" to the bureau, not without "assuring [Goebbels] of his full confidence."[130] That seemed to put an end to the rumors of his removal from Berlin. He was clearly not willing to entertain the fairly obvious idea that in spying on him Himmler might be doing the Party leadership's bidding.

In all these disputes it became clear how small Goebbels's power base within the Party actually was during this phase of the NSDAP's rapid expansion into a mass movement. In Berlin he had to appear as a radical hothead in order to keep the SA on board, but this in turn created tensions around his attitude to the "legal" course chosen by the Party leader, upon whose support he was so highly dependent. The conflicts he had to endure with leading Party comrades such as Göring, Strasser, and Himmler showed the danger he ran of isolating himself within the Party.

MAGDA

In the meantime, great changes were occurring in Goebbels's private life. After several affairs, he had at last found a partner he thought worthy of comparison with Anka.

The first mention of her in the diary came on November 7, 1930: "A lovely woman called Quandt is reorganizing my private papers." But it was more than three months, during which Goebbels was involved in a whole series of other affairs, before the couple got closer to each other. On February 15, 1932, he wrote in the diary: "Magda Quandt comes in the evening. And stays for a very long time. And blossoms into an enchanting blond sweetness. You really are my queen." He added a little "1" in brackets, which we can take to indicate that this was the first time he slept with Magda.[131]

Magda Quandt, twenty-nine years old at this point, was a cultivated and well-educated young woman of elegant appearance, self-assured and completely independent. Her mother had divorced her husband, the Berlin building developer Oskar Ritschel, in 1905, and married the leather-goods magnate Richard Friedländer, who adopted Magda. In 1920 Magda met the industrialist Günther Quandt, who was nearly twice her age. The ill-matched pair were married in 1921.[132]

At the end of 1921 her son Harald was born. But the couple soon drifted apart. Quandt was interested in little but the expansion of his business empire, and he neglected his young wife, who was left with the household to run as well as no fewer than six children to bring up. Apart from Harald, there were two sons from Quandt's previous marriage, and he had also taken in the three children of a friend who had died. Overburdened, Magda yearned in vain to play an active part in the cultural and social life of 1920s Berlin.[133]

After Quandt discovered that Magda was having an affair with a student, he separated from her, and in 1929 she succeeded in obtaining a financially advantageous divorce. It was agreed that Harald should live with his mother until he was fourteen, and then—as the future heir to a business empire—live with his father.[134]

The divorcée Frau Quandt had begun to take an interest in the NSDAP in the summer of 1930, had joined the Party, and was looking for some practical activity within the Berlin Gau. Taking over responsibility for the Gauleiter's private papers seemed to her a highly suitable occupation. On February 21 Goebbels took his new lover and a group of other acquaintances on a short trip to Weimar, of all places, where he had an engagement to keep; they stayed for two days. It is no wonder that his brief meeting with Anka during this time in Weimar was a very chilly occasion.[135] Not long afterward, when Magda was visiting him again, they had their "first argument," caused by a "careless word" from him and ending with her leaving his apartment in tears. But they made up the next day.[136] She now visited him often, and the numbers he gives in brackets beneath the dates of her visits show that their evenings together went off very successfully from his point of view: "She goes home late (2:3)," "Magda in the evening (4:5)," "Magda (6:7)."[137]

The relationship was not trouble-free; they often argued, but the new stimulus that had entered his life seemed to suit Goebbels, although he often had to remind himself that this new bond must not be allowed to jeopardize his real mission: "Then Magda came, there was love, an argument, and then love again (8:9). She is a fabulous child. However, I must not lose myself in her. But the work is too great and too momentous for that."[138] It was clear to him: "The Party comes first, then Magda."[139] He got to know her son Harald, and he took her with him on an Easter trip to Munich, where among other things she met Hitler.[140]

In April there was the first serious crisis in their relationship. For days on end he tried in vain to get through to her by telephone. When she finally answered, Goebbels was to discover that her former lover had by no means disappeared from her life: "The man she was in love with before me has shot and seriously injured her in her apartment. Now she's completely finished. I can tell from her voice that I'm going to lose her. I'm plunged into the deepest despair. I see from this how deeply I love Magda."[141] In reality, either Magda had overdramatized the situation or Goebbels's nerves had gotten the better of him. Magda had not suffered any bullet wound. But even so, the next few days were sheer agony for Goebbels:[142] "There is something unspoken between us. I think it's the other man, her former lover. She disputes this. Our arguments are becoming fiercer." She would not let him forbid her to make a farewell visit to her ex-lover, and she left his apartment in tears.[143] But a few days later all was sweetness and light again.[144]

The couple spent Whitsun in Severin, a country estate in Mecklenburg owned by Magda's ex-husband.[145] Eventually the two of them began to make plans for the future: "We have made a solemn vow to each other: When we have conquered the Reich, we will become man and wife. I am very happy."[146]

Anka, informed by him in June about the new relationship, was "quite shattered [. . .] and refuses to believe it. So she thinks she can win me back again. But it's all too late. I am with Magda, and I'm staying with her."[147]

CHAPTER 8

"Now We Must Gain Power ... One Way or Another!"

A Share of Government?

A picnic in summer 1931. In the foreground, Joseph and Magda Goebbels, behind them Julius Schaub, Adolf Hitler, Erna Hoffmann, and Johanna Wolff. Shortly after Goebbels had introduced Magda to Hitler's court, the latter confessed to him that he had fallen in love with Magda. Eventually a solution to the problem was found that was acceptable to all three parties.

Goebbels and Magda spent July 1931 as guests of Magda's grandmother at her house in the Schleswig-Holstein seaside resort of St. Peter-Ording.[1] "Magda is like a mother and a lover to me,"[2] he wrote. "She loves as only a great woman can."[3] He was enjoying himself: "Work, love, sun, and happiness. What more do I want?" But there was a "shadow" over all of this happiness: "Magda loved somebody else before me. That pains me and tortures me."[4]

The man in question was certainly not her ex-husband, Günther Quandt, but Magda's lover from the last years of her marriage. When Magda told him about her past love life, he found her "heartless" and was regularly overcome by fits of jealousy: an argument always ensued.[5] His trust in her was "shaken," he confided to his diary: "She has loved too much and only told me some fragments of it. And now I lie here until the early hours racked by jealousy."[6] He found consolation in his work on *Battle for Berlin,* in which he set out to tell the story of his early years in the capital.[7]

By the beginning of August he was back in Berlin, to find that publication of *Der Angriff,* which had already been halted by the authorities for a week while he was on vacation, was now prohibited once again. Although the ban was lifted the next day, by the end of the month there followed yet another prohibition lasting a further week.[8] The frequent bans were a clear indication that his radical line was meeting with resistance from the state, and this was significant for the future policy of the wider Party beyond Berlin.

Once Goebbels had found his footing as chief of propaganda for the Reich, there began for him—about a year after the landslide electoral success of the NSDAP—a phase in which his focus increasingly shifted from Berlin affairs to the policy of the Party as a whole. This is particularly reflected in his diaries. After autumn 1931, for Goebbels and the Party elite, the question of participating in government or even of seizing power altogether moved into the realm of the politically possible. Even though, until January 1933, Goebbels was not directly involved in the negotiations that were to bring the NSDAP to power (for this purpose, Hitler preferred to be accompanied by Göring, Frick, Röhm, and Strasser), as Gauleiter of Berlin he usually received firsthand information about the outcome of discussions.

The diaries record the tactical maneuvers of the NSDAP leaders at this time, and they reveal above all how much direct and indirect influence the Party exerted on the policies of the presidential cabinets in the final phase of the Brüning government. But they also show how, as Goebbels saw it, increasing proximity to power revealed potential internal divisions within the Party. In particular he was worried that Hitler might be drawn too close to his potential allies in the conservative camp, an orientation that would lead to open conflict within Party ranks. Goebbels therefore continued to profile himself as the representative of a radical course, thereby setting himself against Hitler's emphasis on a "law-abiding" strategy. However, he always managed to survive inner Party conflicts by his ostentatious deference to the Party leader and his vows of personal loyalty to him.

REFERENDUM IN PRUSSIA

In August an important decision was imminent: a referendum in Prussia following the so-called Stahlhelm petition, which the NSDAP supported, if half-heartedly. Goebbels disliked collaborating with bourgeois elements. The referendum concerned the dissolution of the Prussian Landtag, which was dominated by a "Weimar coalition" consisting of the SPD, the Center Party, and the DVP. The aim was ultimately to make the Brüning government's position untenable. A petition in April proposing dissolution had only just achieved the necessary quorum. After the initiative had been rejected by the Prussian Landtag, a referendum (obligatory under the Prussian constitution if a petition was voted down by Parliament) was set to take place on August 9. In addition to the NSDAP, the project was supported by the DVP, the DNVP, and the KPD.[9]

But the referendum failed: Only 36.8 percent of voters on the register were in favor of an early dissolution of the Landtag (50 percent was the required level of support for the project to become law over the head of the Parliament). Goebbels saw this as a "heavy defeat" into which "the Stahlhelm have dragged us." The conclusion he drew—and immediately communicated to Hitler by telephone—was: "So: enough of this bourgeois pap. We must be masterful and more rigorous. National Socialists. There lies redemption." He doubted whether power could be obtained "quite so legally."[10] In *Der Angriff* he declared that "after an action initiated by others which was tactically inept and which therefore failed," the NSDAP must set about "making clear—publicly, not just internally—the factors that led to this debacle."[11]

When he traveled to Munich shortly afterward to check up on things there, he was still fuming about the Party leadership: "This rabble. They've got no initiative in Munich. Party bureaucracy. With-

out the boss [Hitler was away] a dead torso without a head." By contrast, his discussions with Max Amann, head of the Eher Verlag, had
an extremely gratifying outcome: Amann offered him—voluntarily,
as Goebbels took the trouble to emphasize—an advance of 3,000
marks for his *Battle for Berlin*. A new publishing contract for *Der
Angriff* was also agreed on, which reinforced Goebbels's authority.[12]

A few days later he met Hitler in the Berlin Kaiserhof. The Party
leader seemed to him much too optimistic in his conviction that he
could bring about the "breakup" of the Brüning coalition. He found
Hitler's "grand strategy" brilliant but thought he ought to "pay more
attention to the movement. He's too wrapped up in tactics."[13]

Goebbels was obviously not aware at this point that Strasser and
Frick had already been deputed by Hitler to lay the groundwork for
future cooperation between the NSDAP, the Stahlhelm, and the
DNVP. This collaborative venture was to be publicly consolidated at
a combined mass rally planned for autumn 1931.[14]

THE ARRANGEMENT

In the late summer of 1931 Goebbels was for the most part preoccupied with private problems. His relationship with Magda was constantly troubled by outbursts of jealousy. He simply could not get
over her earlier love affair.[15] Furthermore, a real disaster was in the
making: Hitler took a liking to Magda. Though Goebbels was pleased
to hear Hitler's "fabulous verdict"[16] on her, he was less pleased to note
that his interest in Magda did not stop there. On his next visit to Berlin, while Goebbels was away at a memorial ceremony,[17] he settled
down for a few hours in her apartment with his entourage. The next
day Goebbels and Magda got together with Hitler in the Kaiserhof,
and later the leader turned up again at Magda's place with some of his
retinue. To Goebbels's great annoyance, during this visit there was
some flirting between Magda and Hitler: "Magda is letting herself
down somewhat with the boss. It's making me suffer a lot. She's not
quite a lady. Didn't sleep a wink all night. I must do something about
it. I'm afraid I can't be quite sure of her faithfulness. That would be
terrible." Goebbels didn't extend his judgments to Hitler himself:
"However, I don't begrudge the boss a little heart and charm. They
are so lacking in his life."[18]

The next day there followed a tearful heart-to-heart: "At midday Magda came and cried a lot. She is innocent, I'm sure; it was just a slight lapse of decorum. She gave me back the ring, and tears were streaming from her lovely eyes." They were reconciled again, and she got her ring back.[19]

At the beginning of September Goebbels was staying in Hamburg when he once more had cause to doubt Magda's faithfulness, and once again it centered on Hitler: "A call to Magda. Boss on the telephone. Invited himself for a meal. The devil! I'm quite sad. Come if you like." And he continued: "Terrible night. Agonizing jealousy!"[20] Eventually he was able to persuade Magda to join him in Hamburg. It could not go on like this: "Magda will have to invite the boss around and tell him how things stand with us. Otherwise love and stupid jealousy will come between us."[21]

A few days later he called Magda from Bochum and discovered she was not alone: "She's talking to the boss right this minute." He suffered the pangs of hell: "I spend the evening in a state of pointless agitation! [. . .] I can't sleep and keep thinking up crazy, wild tragedies." The pain was all the greater when Magda, having promised to meet him on the way back, begged off because of "toothache."[22] He later cut out various diary entries from this time, for his "great rage at Magda" turned out to be "unjustified."

As soon as he was back in Berlin, they had another discussion. Magda told him that she had met her ex-husband and let him know that she intended to marry Goebbels. But that was not all; she had already told Hitler of her intention: "Then with boss. Said the same to him. He was dumbfounded, too. But won't betray my trust. Nor will Magda." Goebbels was blissful: "Hitler resigned. He really is very lonely. Has no luck with women. Because he's too soft. Women don't like that. They need to know who's in charge. I'm very happy now. Blissful evening." But one thing concerned him still: "Poor Hitler! I'm almost ashamed to be so happy. I hope it doesn't ruin our friendship. He spoke very well of me." Some days later it seemed that this fear had been unfounded: "Hitler asks me to come outside and is quite warm-hearted toward me. Friend and brother. Lucky devil, he says. He loves Magda. But he doesn't begrudge me my happiness. 'A clever and beautiful woman. She won't hold you back, but help you to make progress.' He shakes both my hands and has tears in his eyes. Good luck! I'm quite grateful. He says a lot of good things about me. My honest comrade and leader! We should marry right away."

During this conversation Goebbels found Hitler "somewhat resigned. [. . .] He too is looking for a good woman to marry one day. I have found Magda. Lucky beggar. We will all three be good to each other. He intends to be our most loyal friend. [. . .] When he leaves us on that note, I have a bit of a bad conscience. But he wishes me the best of luck, and he has tears in his big, astonished eyes. I am proud of Magda."[23]

To recapitulate: In September Magda Quandt and Joseph Goebbels decided to move up the date of their wedding, which was originally intended to take place after the NSDAP had gained power. This move was clearly Magda's idea; she told her ex-husband and Hitler about it before informing her future spouse. It emerges from Goebbels's account that, once he had overcome his initial astonishment, Hitler advised them to marry quickly.

It is also worth investigating a different version of the marriage plan. A devotee of Hitler's, Otto Wagener, wrote that the plan of a Goebbels-Quandt marriage was conceived in Hitler's entourage as a way of providing the Party leader with a respectable female partner. According to Wagener, Hitler already had his eye on Magda before he learned to his disappointment that the one he adored was already spoken for by Goebbels.[24] Hitler then developed the notion of building an intimate relationship with Magda, whom he regarded as the ideal "female opposite pole to my purely masculine instincts." Hitler believed that a precondition for this was that Magda should be married. Wagener claims that when he presented this idea to Magda shortly afterward, simultaneously proposing Goebbels as the candidate for marriage; after some time for reflection both accepted the idea.[25]

Wagener's report contains one or two chronological inconsistencies,[26] but it seems entirely plausible that a contributory factor in Magda's surprise decision to marry Goebbels was a desire to place her relationship to the much-admired Hitler on a firm footing. It also seems quite possible that Goebbels took this on board and that he hoped to curry favor with Hitler by going along with the arrangement. Thus a triangular relationship developed among Hitler, Goebbels, and Magda Quandt whereby Magda became the woman who would take her place at Hitler's side, offering him her social skills, her good taste, and her advice but would outwardly be neutralized, erotically speaking, by being married to Goebbels. Goebbels, for his part, swallowed his jealousy and accepted the arrangement for the sake of its promise of undreamed-of influence over Hitler.

The Goebbelses' Berlin apartment became a refuge for Hitler. Often accompanied by members of his entourage, he felt completely at home there.[27] He was such a familiar visitor to the Goebbelses that over the years he became practically a member of their growing family. Hitler was fond of the Goebbels children, all of whose names would begin with the letter h.

What possessed Magda Quandt to enter into this arrangement, even to encourage it? After all, by doing so she forfeited a generous alimony settlement from her divorced husband. Magda was a highly ambitious woman. From what we know of the way her life had gone, it must have been the prospect of coming closer to someone who might in the future be the most powerful man in Germany, thus achieving a position that would eclipse even her previous status as the wife of one of the richest men in the country.

Hardly had the three of them established this relationship, however, when terrible news struck. On the morning of September 19, Hitler's niece, his beloved Geli Raubal, was found shot dead in Hitler's apartment, where she had a room. The bullet came from a revolver belonging to Hitler, who was not in Munich at the time. The circumstances pointed to suicide: "I simply don't dare to look for motives," wrote Goebbels in his diary. "How will the boss ever get over this?"[28]

Geli's death at this point raises a whole series of questions. Was there a connection between the arrangement Hitler had entered into with Goebbels and Magda and the death of Geli? Had Hitler's interest in Magda upset the balance of his relationship with Geli and brought on a crisis between them? Had he perhaps indicated to Geli that only a more mature woman was suitable for him, not a twenty-three-year-old girl?

BRUTALITY ON THE KURFÜRSTENDAMM

In contrast to Hitler, who moved closer to the conservatives, Goebbels continued to advocate a more radical course. What this might look like was demonstrated on September 12, 1931, the Jewish New Year, when the SA started a protest "action" on the Kurfürstendamm. About a thousand SA men in civilian clothes began to jostle, abuse, and beat up passersby they took to be Jews. The head of the Berlin SA, Count Wolf-Heinrich von Helldorf, who was newly appointed in August, was driving his car up and down the Kurfürstendamm when he was arrested and interrogated by the police along with twenty-seven other SA men.[29]

Six days later came the beginning of the so-called Kurfürstendamm trial of thirty-four of the accused; Helldorf and the SA leaders would get a separate trial later. Goebbels feared a ban on the Party: As it happens, *Der Angriff* was suppressed on the day the trial began, but that was because of a cartoon on another topic.[30]

After several days of hearings, a total of twenty-seven National Socialists were given prison sentences.[31] Goebbels complained about the verdicts on the telephone to Reich Minister of Justice Gottfried Treviranus (who allegedly referred in this conversation to a "miscarriage of justice")[32] and to Reich Chancellor Brüning. On September 26 he even called on the chancellor in his office in order to question the way the law had treated the assailants. Goebbels commented on this first meeting with the Center Party politician: "He too finds the sentences intolerable and is very strong in his condemnation of the red terror. There's no question of a ban." Brüning had even instructed Robert Weismann, state secretary in the Prussian State Department, to block everything that might lead to a ban, saying to him: "I've got to be careful. I have let the judge know that I would find a heavy sentence for Helldorf incomprehensible."[33] Goebbels was not impressed: "The eternal ditherer! [. . .] You can't expect anything from Brüning." Finally Brüning directed the state secretary for justice, Curt Joël, who was also present, to "do something" for Helldorf and the other accused.[34]

And in fact the second Kurfürstendamm trial was postponed for a few days. "That's Brüning's work," commented Goebbels on September 30.[35] So his intervention had yielded fruit. But on the same day,

Der Angriff was banned for a further three weeks. It was clear to Goebbels: "This is Severing's work."* The trial began on October 8, and sentences were passed on November 7. Helldorf received a six-month prison sentence but was freed; the other accused were given jail sentences of up to two years.[36]

An appeal hearing took place in January 1932. The prison sentences imposed in November were reduced, and Helldorf was now fined only 100 Reichsmarks, since his role as instigator of the offenses could supposedly no longer be proved conclusively. Goebbels was partly responsible for this lack of evidence. He was called as a witness but refused to testify when confronted with the accusation of jointly planning the violence with Helldorf. His behavior in the courtroom— Goebbels shouted at the state prosecutor and used insulting language in his evidence—earned him a fine of 500 marks for contempt of court.[37]

PATHS TO POWER:
TAKING SOUNDINGS AND DEMONSTRATIONS OF STRENGTH

To return to autumn 1931: At the beginning of October Hitler came to Berlin to conduct various discussions about the possibility of a place in the coalition. These talks took place just a few days before a mass demonstration of the nationalist parties in Harzburg demanding the resignation of the governments of the Reich and of Prussia.[38] Goebbels looked on suspiciously as Hitler and his partners—or competitors—on the political right jockeyed for tactical advantage.

On October 3 Hitler met General Kurt von Schleicher, state secretary at the Reichswehr Ministry and one of Hindenburg's closest confidants. Goebbels learned about this discussion from Hitler, who had already declared that he was prepared to join a Brüning government but only on the condition that new elections were held. He had also stated that the NSDAP was ready to form a single-party government, should the occasion arise.[39] Goebbels's note on Hitler's report continued: "We are willing to renounce Prussia for the time being if we can gain decisive power in the Reich. [. . .] In Prussia we can put in a governor to force the communists to their knees." The deal

---

* Translators' note: Curt Severing was SPD minister of the interior in Prussia.

emerging from talks between Hitler and Schleicher suggested an invitation to the NSDAP to form a Reich government, while in return the Party would be prepared to accept a Reich governor for Prussia nominated by Hindenburg.

On October 10 Hitler met Hindenburg. Immediately afterward he informed Goebbels: "Result: We are respectable. The old man has met us face-to-face. The boss calls him venerable. But what does that mean? In no way is he up to the job. A disaster for Germany."[40]

After these discussions about possible direct routes to government for the NSDAP, during the next few days Hitler increased the pressure. On the evening of October 10 Hitler, Goebbels, and Göring drove to Bad Harzburg, a small town in the state of Braunschweig. Here the NSDAP was already in charge; there was no ban on uniforms here,[41] and that was why the state had been chosen. This was the site for the long-planned mass rally of nationalists, a powerful demonstration by the NSDAP, the Stahlhelm, the DNVP, the Alldeutscher Verband (Pan-German League), and the Reichslandbund (Reich Agricultural League).

The attitude with which Hitler and his National Socialist leadership team approached Bad Harzburg was ambivalent: They were happy enough to make use of their nationalist partners to put the government under pressure, but Hitler had conducted negotiations for a share in government solely on his own behalf. In Harzburg the decision was made to demand the resignation of Brüning's government. Yet only a short while before, Hitler had declared himself ready to participate in a government led by Brüning. The mutual distrust between Hitler and the nationalists, reflected in subsequent entries in Goebbels's diaries, was therefore not without cause.

The first encounter in Harzburg went badly: "Hitler is fuming because they're trying to push us aside [. . .]. I spend an hour talking to him. More distance from the right." The next morning, at a joint meeting of the NSDAP and DNVP parliamentary parties, the mistrust broke out into the open. Hitler, who was not taking part, had previously delivered a declaration put together by himself and Goebbels, the tone of which was a good deal fiercer than that of the agreed-upon joint communiqué.[42] During the ensuing military review he did not wait for the Stahlhelm formation but ostentatiously left the platform after reviewing the SA section.

Goebbels waited impatiently for the outcome of an hour-long dis-

cussion between Hitler and Hugenberg, during which it cost the latter a great effort to prevent Hitler from leaving the rally early. Then
there were speeches by Hugenberg ("an oddball!") and Hitler, who
according to Goebbels was rendered "off form" by sheer rage, followed by, among others, the head of the Stahlhelm; Franz Seldte and
his deputy, Theodor Duesterberg; Eberhard Graf von Kalckreuth,
president of the Reichslandbund; and a surprise guest speaker, the
former president of the Reichsbank, Hjalmar Schacht, who delivered
a stinging attack on the government's financial policy.[43] Goebbels was
inwardly seething: He saw the whole event as nothing but a display of
"organized disloyalty to us." After Harzburg, Hitler and Goebbels
were agreed: "Never again a mass rally. Only a leaders' conference."

On October 13, 1931, having been suspended for more than six
months, the Reichstag reconvened. On October 16 the government
narrowly survived a vote of no confidence on which Hitler had been
pinning high hopes. Then Parliament was adjourned again until the
following February. "We've been conned," was Goebbels's comment.[44]

Goebbels, Magda, and Harald drove to Braunschweig, where a big
National Socialist march was planned for October 18. Harald too
wore his little made-to-measure SA uniform; he looked, said Goebbels, "so sweet" in his "high yellow boots."

On the Schlossplatz in Braunschweig there was a parade lasting
over six hours in which more than a hundred thousand members of
the SA, SS, and Hitler Youth took part; it was followed by a meeting
addressed by Hitler. Goebbels assessed the day—it was in fact the
biggest National Socialist parade before the "seizure of power"—as
"our answer to Harzburg and Brüning," a show of strength that was
meant to blot out the memory of the parliamentary defeat only two
days earlier and the preceding tactical skirmishing with the nationalist parties.[45] In an article in *Der Angriff*, he described Harzburg as a
"tactical half-way stage," while Braunschweig had clearly demonstrated that the "political leadership of the anti-Brüning front was in
the hands of the National Socialist movement."[46]

THE WEDDING

To her horror, in October Magda learned from her mother that she
had been unwed when her daughter was born. Goebbels was afraid

that the blemish of illegitimacy might be exploited by his political opponents. Under these circumstances, was it possible for them to marry at all? A rapid decision was needed: "Only Hitler can decide. She goes back to the Kaiserhof again in the evening." Hitler was quite relaxed about it: "He just laughs at us. He prefers a girl with a child to a woman without a child. Typical of Hitler! I'm so happy we can stay together. Magda is beaming."[47] With this verdict, obtained by Magda and not by Goebbels himself, Hitler had paved the way for the Goebbelses to start a family.

The next day, over a meal, Magda asked Hitler to be a witness at their wedding in December. Hitler agreed, as Goebbels noted, "with pleasure." In this emotional atmosphere Hitler began to talk about Geli: "He loved her very much. She was his 'good comrade.' He had tears in his eyes. [. . .] Magda is very kind to him. Why shouldn't we be? This man, at the height of his success, without personal happiness, simply committed to the happiness of his friends."

Hitler persuaded Goebbels and Magda to go with him to Munich the next day. They stopped off in Weimar, where they went to the theater in the evening. Goebbels then went on to Munich by the sleeper train, reporting that "the others are coming by car."[48] He spent a strenuous day in the propaganda office and met Magda that evening in the hotel where she had just arrived, still chilled to the marrow by the drive in an open car. During dinner, which they ate with Hermann Esser and Prince Philipp von Hessen, she "did not behave very well" and eventually went off to her room. Goebbels then stayed on with Esser until the wee hours in Hitler's favorite haunt, the Café Heck. When he came back to the hotel, an "almighty argument" with Magda followed; she returned her engagement ring and wanted to leave. But they made their peace again.

Goebbels does not divulge what brought this scene on. In fact, the whole journey to Munich is mysterious. It seems that Hitler used this short trip to have an undisturbed talk with Magda—hence the separate journeys from Weimar to Munich. Did Magda and Hitler touch on subjects that triggered the argument with Goebbels that evening?

The next day's lunch was a kind of engagement celebration, attended by Hitler, who had sent an "enormous bouquet" and conducted himself "like a good father." Goebbels later bought Magda an engagement present, a "wonderful convertible" made by the Wanderer company, half financed by "advertising in the V.B. [*Völkischer*

Beobachter]" and half by his "royalty account." A reference to Amann, whose "assistance had been heartwarming," makes it clear that the head of the Eher Verlag had advanced the purchase price. The mention of "advertising in the V.B." can be understood to mean that the Party newspaper carried "unpaid" advertisements for the Wanderer company, but Amann in return accumulated credit in kind with the company to meet half of the price of a private car for the future wife of the Berlin Gauleiter Dr. Joseph Goebbels.

This was, to put it mildly, a fairly corrupt transaction, which would have cost the participants their Party careers if it had become public knowledge. It is scarcely credible that such a deal could have happened without the acquiescence of Hitler, the Party boss. It is also hard to imagine that Goebbels, persuaded by Hitler on the evening of October 30 to go with him to Munich, would simply have marched two days later into a automobile showroom in Munich and used a complicated financial arrangement to buy an expensive sportscar. The whole story only makes sense if you assume that Hitler, having given his blessing to their marriage, issued the invitation to Munich in order to mark the engagement; used the time en route to have a confidential chat at his leisure with Magda; and then, as generous as "a good father," enabled Goebbels to give his fiancée an extravagant engagement present. In other words, Goebbels's rather laconic diary entries point to a triangular relationship that meant for Magda in particular a testing emotional burden and led her occasionally to consider breaking off the engagement to Goebbels. Immediately after returning to Berlin, Magda went into the hospital for a "small operation." Goebbels mentions the reason in his diary: "She wants to have children, and I'm very pleased about it."[49] The operation went "satisfactorily."[50]

Goebbels postponed their plans to rent a house together because he did not want to appear a "big shot."[51] Magda sympathized with these reservations. For the sake of simplicity, in November Goebbels moved into Magda's spacious apartment on the Reichskanzlerplatz (today called Theodor-Heuss-Platz) in Westend, where Magda equipped a study and a bedroom for him.[52] Magda did not leave the hospital until the day after he moved in. Goebbels went to meet her and took her back to the apartment they now shared. He gave two speeches and then returned to the Reichskanzlerplatz. In the meantime, company had arrived: "Boss and Hess already here." Hitler was to keep up the habit of dropping in casually at the Reichskanzlerplatz apartment during his Berlin visits. On this particular evening the atmosphere was relaxed, and Hitler waxed personal: "Boss tells us about women, whom he loves a lot. About the special woman he cannot find. About the hysterical females who pursue him. About Geli, whom he has lost and whom he mourns with all his heart. [. . .] Takes such a sincere pleasure in our happiness that we are almost ashamed. He likes Magda very much, and she's good at dealing with him."[53]

One day in late October Anka surprised him by turning up at the door. She had no inkling of his marriage plans and upon hearing the news became completely distraught. He reflected with a certain satisfaction: "This is revenge for her earlier unfaithfulness. Life goes on."[54]

Shortly before the wedding he met Günther Quandt, Magda's ex-husband. "He's going to donate to the Party. Magda takes him to task. She is our best advocate. [. . .] He's very well disposed. An old man. But clever, energetic, a brutal capitalist, has come over to us completely. Quite right—and he should give us money, too." All the same, it was with a heavy heart that he took Quandt's 200 marks for "people in prison and the wounded." The tone of the conversation was "not as cold as I expected," he noted. No doubt the atmosphere was improved by Quandt's donation but also by his lavish praise for Goebbels's new book, *Battle for Berlin*.[55]

Three days later he burned "packets of old love letters" and commented: "Not an ounce of melancholy." But emotions were running high all the same: "Argument with Magda, of course. We didn't say a word to each other for the rest of the evening."[56]

Just before the wedding, articles appeared in the hostile press asserting that Magda was "born a Jewess." In fact, her stepfather, Richard Friedländer, the second husband her mother had married five years after the birth of Magda, was from a Jewish background. Goebbels took the accusation hard, as his diary shows.[57]

The wedding—Magda was a few weeks pregnant by then—took place on December 19 in Severin, Mecklenburg, where the Quandt family owned an estate. The right of residence there had been conceded to Magda by Quandt as part of the divorce settlement. The nuptials were organized by Walter Granzow, Quandt's brother-in-law and one of the leading National Socialists in Mecklenburg.

The registry-office wedding was conducted by the mayor of the village of Frauenmark. Goebbels was moved by this "village idyll," he records. His witnesses were Hitler and Franz Ritter von Epp. After the ceremony, says Goebbels, Hitler "gave him an emotional hug." "Magda gives him a kiss. He has tears in his eyes." The religious ceremony—which Goebbels was loath to forgo, despite his hostility to the church—took place immediately afterward in the village church in Severin. Goebbels's sister Maria was a bridesmaid, and Magda's son Harald, once more in SA uniform, was Goebbels's "aide" at the altar. The wedding breakfast took place in the nearby manor house, that is to say on Quandt's property—supposedly without the owner's knowledge.[58]

ELECTORAL BATTLE FOR THE PRESIDENCY: HITLER VERSUS HINDENBURG

In November 1931 the leadership of the SA in Munich had merged the previously separate SA troops of Berlin and Brandenburg into a single unit, the "Berlin-Brandenburg SA group," and appointed Helldorf, the organizer of the Kurfürstendamm assaults, to lead it; he had previously headed the Berlin troop. Goebbels supported the appointment.[59]

But on December 8, within the framework of a broader emergency decree issued by the president, the Brüning government imposed a general ban on uniforms and insignia for political organizations. "Reality in Germany. The beginning of the end," Goebbels wrote.[60] Goebbels's appalled reaction did not have to do with the practical effect of the ban, which was negligible. Uniform bans were already in place in several German states, among them Bavaria and Prussia. But with a decree issued at Reich level Brüning had unmistakeably signaled that he personally intended to take a tougher line with the NSDAP. The chancellor underlined this stance in a broadcast speech on December 8, which contained explicit warnings to the Party. The occasion for this was the discovery of the "Boxheim documents," plans drawn up by leading members of the NSDAP in Hesse to seize power by force; this revelation was extremely embarrassing for a movement allegedly committed to taking power legally.[61] Goebbels was not the only one who wondered whether Brüning was planning to "decamp to the SPD."[62] At the same time, as Gauleiter of Berlin, he found the grip of the Prussian authorities as tight as ever. On December 1 *Der Angriff* was banned for a week, and it had only just reappeared, on December 8, when the Prussian minister of the interior imposed another weeklong ban.[63]

On the one hand, in this way the Brüning administration built up a threatening backdrop; on the other, it felt obliged to heed the NSDAP. In the event, at the turn of the year the government faced an increasingly urgent problem: How was it to handle the approaching end of the president's seven-year term of office, which was due to expire in spring 1932?[64]

After taking soundings[65] from the NSDAP leadership and from Hugenberg, on January 5 Hindenburg finally authorized Brüning to initiate talks with the parties about extending his presidency.[66] To this end, Brüning negotiated with an NSDAP delegation led by Hitler,[67] but the latter raised "constitutional objections" to these proposals, thus attempting to represent the chancellor to the president as a man willing to push the head of state into a breach of the constitution.[68]

The tactic Hitler was pursuing emerges from a diary entry dated January 12. Goebbels was always kept informed about these discussions:[69] "Boss sends Hindenburg short memorandum with constitutional reservations about Brüning's proposal. The idea is that as a result the old gentleman declares today that he thinks Brüning's route is impracticable. That kills Brüning off." But the plan failed. Hindenburg was not yet ready to cut Brüning loose, and the maneuver ended in a resounding defeat.[70] On the other hand, the question that now arose was whether Hitler would take up the challenge of pitting himself against Hindenburg in the forthcoming presidential election.

On January 18, 1932, Goebbels went with Magda to Munich, where they met Hitler in the evening. Once again, at the sight of the Goebbelses' happiness, Hitler fell into a sentimental mood: "Hitler talks movingly about his youth. About his strict father and kindly mother. She was exactly as my mother still is. That's why my mother has a special place in his heart. My good Hitler, whom both of us, Magda and I, love dearly."[71]

The next day the couple visited Hitler in his apartment to discuss the "Reich presidency question." Goebbels was able to tell him that just before leaving Berlin he had learned from Arno Kriegsheim, one of the leading functionaries of the Reichslandbund, that his organization would not be supporting Hindenburg.[72] But Hitler could not make up his mind to run. Goebbels's diary entries show how difficult it was to bring the Party leader, plagued by gloomy feelings, to make a political decision. In the evening, at a private reception, Hitler "conversed about questions of marriage": "He feels very lonely. Yearning for the woman he can't find. Moving and touching. He likes Magda very much. We must find him a good wife. Someone like Magda. Then he'll have a counterweight to all these men."[73]

At this time Goebbels spent a lot of time with Hitler: "Discussed and made plans for the future. Boss offers me my later job: Wants me to be minister for popular education. Film, radio, schools, university, art, culture, propaganda. The Prussian Ministry of Culture will then be added. A huge project."[74] A few days later he heard the news that a "Hindenburg committee" had been formed to get the incumbent reelected. Goebbels noted impatiently: "Hitler is taking too long. Brüning will end up checkmating him."[75] After a certain amount of tactically motivated hesitation,[76] on a visit to Berlin on February 22 Hitler "finally" gave him permission to announce his candidacy. Goebbels did so that evening at an event in the Sportpalast. His comment on the news that the Stahlhelm and the DNVP had put up their own candidate—the deputy leader of the Stahlhelm, Theodor Duesterberg—that same day was cheerful: The "Harzburg Front" he so disliked had proved ineffectual.[77]

On February 23 Goebbels gave a speech in the Reichstag whose content he had cleared with Hitler in advance;[78] it was conceived as a reckoning with the Brüning government. When he eventually turned his fire on the president, accusing him of being supported by "the party of deserters," there was uproar in the ranks of the SPD (at whom this jibe was aimed and who included many war veterans and members disabled in combat). The president of the Reichstag, Paul Löbe, interrupted the session and, after consulting the House Advisory Committee, excluded Goebbels from taking any further part in the proceedings on the grounds that he had insulted the head of state. On behalf of the centrist parties, Ernst Lemmer read out a statement distancing them from Goebbels;[79] then the Social Democrat Kurt Schumacher took the floor to rebuke the National Socialists and specifically their head of propaganda, Goebbels: "If there's one thing we

concede to National Socialism, it's the fact that it has succeeded for
the first time in German politics in the total mobilization of stupidity."[80]

Two days later Goebbels was back in the Reichstag to finish his
speech. First of all, he rejected the accusation that he had intended to
insult the Reich president. To "prove" his innocence, he read again
from the parliamentary record the sentence containing the reference
to the "party of deserters" to outraged protests from the Social Democrats, but he was safely protected by standing orders. Then in the rest
of his speech Goebbels embarked on a frontal attack on Chancellor
Brüning, declaring that the coming presidential election would be a
referendum on Brüning's policies. On March 13 the country would
decide "who deserves power in Germany, we or you."[81]

After his speech he went to the Kaiserhof, where, according to
Goebbels, Hitler was highly "enthusiastic" about his performance.
Goebbels also accounted it a triumph for the National Socialist cause
that the Party leader had just acquired German citizenship by virtue
of his appointment as an official in Braunschweig—where the NSDAP
already governed—so that he was now for the first time legally entitled to take public office in the Reich.

For the campaign beginning on February 27, Goebbels temporarily moved part of the Reich propaganda office to Berlin.[82] On February 29 he briefed Hitler on his campaign strategy: "We will conduct
our war mainly through posters and speeches."[83] But Goebbels also
used unconventional methods. He made a gramophone record,
of which 50,000 copies were circulated, as well as a sound film that,
among other things, showed him in action as a speaker.[84]

Goebbels styled the election as a "decisive battle" between the
Weimar "system" and National Socialism, the latter personified by
"the leader of young Germany," the challenger to the aging Hindenburg.[85] Hitler was presented to voters in a double role: as the bringer
of hope and savior of the nation, standing above petty party squab-
bles, but also as a figure to identify with, an ordinary person and a
former front-line soldier. The cult of the leader, prevailing within the
Party since 1922–23 but reinforced after the re-founding of the Party
in 1925, was now systematically used for the first time as a campaigning stratagem.[86]

Goebbels had done everything he could—despite his occasional
doubts about the leader—through his totally Hitler-centered policy

to strengthen the personal position of the latter within the Party, and positively transfigure his role as leader. But focusing Party propaganda entirely on Hitler was a first, even for Goebbels. In keeping with this approach to the campaign, he celebrated Hitler in a series in *Der Angriff* (which was again banned for a week at the beginning of the campaign),[87] as a "political fighter," a "statesman," and not least as a "kind-hearted person" who was "especially child-loving." Hitler was a man of "the finest intellectual taste, of pronounced artistic sensitivity," who "never uttered a word he did not personally believe in."[88]

On March 1 Goebbels embarked on a speaking tour that took him to Magdeburg, Essen, Düsseldorf, and Cologne.[89] On March 6, 1932, right in the middle of the election campaign, the Social Democrat newspaper *Welt am Montag* published some letters from Röhm to Karl-Günther Heimsoth, a doctor and pioneer of the homosexual liberation movement, in which Röhm talked openly about his same-sex proclivities.[90] Goebbels immediately called Röhm, who admitted "that it's true." He also telephoned Hitler, who instructed him to "reject all accusations as downright lies."[91] Disgusted, Goebbels groaned: "Oh, I've had it up to here with all this queer business." When he met Röhm a few days later and found him to be "full of beans," he simply could not believe it.[92] But he was glad to discover a little later that in his rejection of homosexuality Hitler "takes as strong a line as I do. [. . .] Eradicate!"[93]

There was a "big gathering" in the Goebbelses' apartment on the Reichskanzlerplatz on the evening of March 13 to celebrate Hitler's anticipated victory in the presidential election. But it was not to be. "Getting on for 10 o'clock it becomes clear: We're beaten. Terrible prospects!" In fact the NSDAP gained only 11.3 million votes, against more than 18.6 million for Hindenburg, who narrowly missed achieving the absolute majority required to win the first round of voting outright. Goebbels tried to pick himself up again: "Our Party comrades are depressed and discouraged. Now we need to make some big move." "On phone to Hitler. He is terrifically surprised by the result. We set our sights too high. We have all made mistakes." But Hitler showed himself determined to carry on the fight into the second round of voting.[94]

This was also the opinion of the majority of leading National Socialists when they met the next day at the Brown House in Munich:[95]

"We go on fighting." Above all they expected that participating in the second round, even with no prospect of beating Hindenburg, would mobilize voters for the Landtag elections due to take place shortly afterward in Prussia and other states.[96]

After a brief diversion in which they both spoke in Weimar, Hitler and Goebbels returned to Munich to prepare for the rest of the election campaign. Meanwhile, Magda had followed them there from Berlin.[97] It was obvious that Goebbels found it difficult to work effectively in close proximity to the Party leader: "Hitler is always full of new ideas. But around him you can't concentrate on finer details."[98] On March 13 there was a conference of Gauleiters, where it is clear that Goebbels had to take a certain amount of flak for his propaganda work in the previous weeks.[99]

Goebbels returned to Munich with Hitler for the Easter break, once more accompanied by Magda. A few days were spent on the Obersalzberg, near Berchtesgaden, working on the finer points of the propaganda campaign to be employed in contesting the second round of voting. But there was time to relax, too: "In the afternoon the women went for a walk, and Hitler demonstrated his new pistol to us. He's a very good shot."[100]

On March 31 Goebbels was back in Berlin to get the propaganda machine there up and running. He had something special in mind for Hitler: He sent him on a campaign tour by air so that the candidate could appear before mass audiences in three or four cities a day. This "flight over Germany" was hailed by his own propaganda as a triumphal progress, proof of Hitler's closeness to the people. But in a contest with the octogenarian Hindenburg, it also served to reinforce his image as a "modern" politician embracing technological innovations.[101]

Goebbels embarked on another campaign tour of his own on April 3. He spoke in Wiesbaden and Frankfurt but was then unexpectedly recalled to Berlin by Hitler. Both spoke at a rally approved on short notice by the authorities—a general ban on demonstrations was in place until April 1—to a crowd of 200,000 in the Lustgarten (Pleasure Garden), then to 50,000 in the Potsdam Stadium, and finally to an audience of 20,000 in the Sportpalast.[102] The campaign trail took in Weimar, Jena, and Aachen and then finally led back to Berlin.[103]

Goebbels's chief election aim was to "break through into the bour-

geois part of the Hindenburg front." To his Party comrades, he recommended detailed work: "Thus individual units must carefully take
soundings from bakers, butchers, grocers, in pubs, etc., to establish
who voted for Hindenburg for the above-mentioned reasons." The
Reich propaganda office made templates for posters and leaflets
available and published the campaign newspaper *The Flamethrower*
as well as a special anti-Hindenburg leaflet.[104]

Several factors made it a difficult campaign for the NSDAP. On the
eve of the first round of voting, large-scale "maneuvers" by the SA in
the greater Berlin area gave rise to rumors of a National Socialist
putsch.[105] In fact, though, Goebbels warned the Reich Chancellery
on election day itself about alleged plans on the part of the "Stennes
people" to assassinate Brüning. Goebbels's move was later interpreted
as an attempt to intimidate the Reich chancellor.[106] A few days after
the election, on March 17, the police undertook a big search operation throughout Prussia aimed at SA and SS units. A ban on National
Socialist organizations appeared to be in the offing.[107] On March 23
Der Angriff was closed down for a further six days.[108] The business of
Röhm's homosexuality was putting an increasing strain on the Party:
At the beginning of April Goebbels was clear—"the compromising
letters are genuine."[109]

Although the NSDAP gained over two million more votes in the
second round, Hindenburg won comfortably, with more than 53 percent of the total. Goebbels decided to take a positive view of the outcome, interpreting the defeat as a "springboard for the Prussian
election."[110] After 1933, too, despite some objections within the Party,
he would follow the same line of constructing his election campaign
entirely around the person of Hitler as the recipe for gaining power.[111]

The fact is that in spring 1932 the majority of Germans were not
prepared to subscribe to the Führer myth propagated by the NSDAP.
But after 1933, in the heady days of "Führer fever" stoked up by all of
the propaganda methods at Goebbels's disposal, this fact would be
forgotten.

THE BAN ON THE SA AND THE PLOT AGAINST BRÜNING

The searches carried out by the police in several SA offices on March 17 revealed some incriminating evidence. Consequently the minister for defense and the interior, Wilhelm Groener, who had thus far argued against a Reich-wide ban on the SA "for defense policy reasons," dropped his reservations. As Goebbels and other leading Party comrades had expected, the ban came into effect on April 13 at 5 P.M. precisely. The police occupied the meeting places and offices of the SA and the SS and disbanded the organizations. "We have Groener to thank for this," commented Goebbels. The action was particularly directed at Schleicher and his close NSDAP connections: "[H]e's completely shaken. That shit Hindenburg." Needless to say, the SA and the SS got around the ban by continuing their activities in disguised form, for example by starting up sport clubs or hiking associations.[112]

Despite the ban, in the Prussian Landtag election on April 24, 1932, the NSDAP once again achieved an outstanding result, lifting its share of the vote from 1.8 percent (1928) to 36.3 percent to become the strongest party in Prussia. But owing to the poor showing of the other right-wing parties, there was no prospect of forming a government with them.

In Bavaria, Württemberg, and Hamburg, the NSDAP achieved similar results—and faced the same dilemma. Only in Anhalt, aided by other parties of the right, did it represent a parliamentary majority able to form a government. It was not the case, therefore, that the NSDAP's sensational election results betokened a political turning point in the individual states. "Something's got to happen. We've got to get into power. Otherwise our victories will be the death of us," was Goebbels's commentary.[113] He too had gotten the point: By themselves the NSDAP would never gain power, either through elections or through threatening SA marches. The cabinet lists discussed by Goebbels with Hitler and other leading National Socialists—featuring Goebbels himself as a possible Prussian minister of the interior, an idea to which he was gradually warming—had now become redundant.[114] Furthermore, the NSDAP's results in Berlin were considerably below those of the Party in the Reich as a whole.[115]

With the "Harzburg Front," the alliance of the NSDAP, the DNVP, and the Stahlhelm, failing to function in the presidential election—the Stahlhelm and the DNVP had not been able to bring themselves to support Hitler in the second round—the only realistic prospect of gaining power lay in collaboration with the Center Party: "Nothing can be done without the Center Party. Neither in Prussia nor in the Reich."[116]

The diary entry of April 27 marks a striking turning point for Goebbels. Whereas in previous years he had always asserted his opposition to any cooperation with the ultra-conservatives that would dilute NSDAP policy, he was now ready to enter into an alliance with the moderate Center Party, of all parties, a staunch pillar of the hated Republic's constitution. Goebbels, previously always eager to put himself forward as spokesman of the "revolutionary" tendency in the NSDAP, finally fell into line behind Hitler's tactically oriented policy of negotiation. This policy seemed to yield immediate success: The Berlin SA leader Helldorf told Goebbels that he had learned from a discussion with Schleicher that the general was ready for a "change of approach": "Under pressure from him, the Center Party is said to have become compliant. Negotiations in the Reich too. Tolerate the Center Party in Prussia." Schleicher wanted to work with Goebbels, rather than with Strasser and Göring, as Goebbels noted with much satisfaction. Two days later Schleicher received Hitler. Goebbels was told later by Helldorf, who was allowed to accompany Hitler, that the Party leader had "reached an agreement" with Schleicher.[117]

The plot envisaged a role for the Center Party, but not for Chancellor Brüning, and Schleicher set the ball rolling correspondingly. On the night of May 2–3 he informed Brüning about the putative right-wing solution for Prussia and the Reich he had discussed with the NSDAP leadership. When Brüning replied that he wanted to remain in office as chancellor until his Versailles revision policy had been safely passed, Schleicher told him plainly that he did not support such a position.[118]

On May 5, while Goebbels and Magda happened to be visiting Hitler in Berchtesgaden, it was announced that the economics minister, Hermann Warmbold, had stepped down. Goebbels's diary entry makes it clear that this resignation was substantially due to the dismantling of the Brüning government that Schleicher had begun in the last few days: "Schleicher has detonated the bomb."[119]

Goebbels immediately left for Berlin, where on May 7, accompanied by Röhm and Helldorf (both having liaised with Schleicher), Hitler met with Schleicher; the president's state secretary, Otto Meissner; and Hindenburg's son and adjutant, Oskar. Goebbels was informed at first hand after the return of the trio: "Brüning is to fall this week. The old man will withdraw his support from him. Schleicher is pressing strongly for it. [...] Then there'll be a presidential cabinet. Reichstag dissolved. The restraining legislation falls. We are free to agitate and deliver our masterstroke."[120]

Goebbels's entry makes plain the role envisaged for the NSDAP in Schleicher's calculation: It was supposed to tolerate the new government in return for the lifting of the ban on uniforms and the prospect of new elections. In view of the strong performances of the NSDAP in the various states, these concessions were likely to make the NSDAP the biggest party in Parliament.

Finally, the National Socialist leadership contacted Schleicher the same evening by telephone and arranged with him that Brüning's downfall should be speeded up so that he would not have time to put a vote of confidence to the Reichstag. It was agreed that Hitler should leave Berlin in order to avoid speculation about the background of the imminent toppling of the chancellor. The Severin estate seemed a suitable retreat, and Goebbels, Magda, Hitler, Harald, and a few attendants made their way there the same evening. The following day they held discussions about organizing the next election campaign.[121]

On May 12 Goebbels participated in a Reichstag session which took a sensational turn: After a group of National Socialist members had beaten up the journalist Helmuth Klotz—the former National Socialist, who had switched to the SPD, had published the incriminating Röhm letters—in the Reichstag restaurant, Paul Löbe, president of the Reichstag, alerted the police and had four NSDAP members removed from the session. When the latter refused to leave the building, a police squad led by Deputy Police Commissioner Bernhard Weiss arrived to arrest the four. The NSDAP benches erupted, and amid the howling of the NSDAP faction Goebbels could be heard saying: "That Jewish swine, Weiss, comes in here provoking us with his presence." The session was abandoned, and Parliament adjourned until June.[122]

Groener resigned as defense minister the same day. Goebbels registered this as "a success for Schleicher," who had indeed put Groener

under enormous pressure.[123] The next day, after Helldorf had visited
Schleicher, he noted: "The crisis continues according to plan. That's
good!"[124]

THE FALL OF BRÜNING

On May 18 and 19, Werner von Alvensleben, a close confidant of
Schleicher's, provided Goebbels with further information about the
increasing isolation of Brüning engineered by Schleicher.[125] This is
how he learned on May 24 of the chancellor's imminent fall: "Schleicher is doing good work. Alvensleben has his list of ministers: Chancellor v. Papen, Foreign [Konstantin von] Neurath." However, there
were two points that meant more to Goebbels than these appointments: new elections and the prospect of forming a coalition with the
Center Party, the prize held out to the NSDAP in return for tolerating
the new government.[126]

Schleicher's candidate, Franz von Papen, was scarcely known to
the public at large. The conservative estate owner from Westphalia, a
diplomat and officer under the Kaiser, was a rather inconspicuous
Center Party backbencher who also chaired the board of the party
newspaper *Germania*. His combination of a highly conservative outlook, aristocratic origins, a career history appropriate to his class,
and membership in the Catholic Center Party all led Schleicher to
believe that von Papen was the right man to present to Hindenburg
as Brüning's successor.

In accordance with the calculations made by Schleicher, Hindenburg informed Brüning at this time, through his state secretary, Otto
Meissner, that he was aiming for a more right-wing government tolerated as much as possible by the National Socialists, whose participation in a Prussian government he thought desirable.[127]

While Schleicher continued to work for Brüning to be replaced,
on May 25 Goebbels participated in the inaugural meeting of the
newly elected Prussian Landtag. Thanks to Center Party abstentions,
the NSDAP managed to get its representative Hanns Kerrl elected
president of the Parliament; otherwise, however, no progress was
made toward brown (Nazi)–black (Center Party) cooperation in Parliament. On this day in the Prussian Landtag, there were violent disturbances as well. After a dispute with the communists, the NSDAP

members brawled, rapidly emptying the chamber. "Briefly but boldly, with inkwells and chairs," observed Goebbels, with barely suppressed pride: "The Party members were singing the Horst Wessel song. 8 badly injured from different parties. That was a warning example. Creates respect."[128]

The next day he left for a campaigning trip to Oldenburg, where on May 29 Landtag elections were likewise due to be held. En route, he met up with Hitler, who told him that Brüning's political fate was to be decided on the following Sunday.[129] Once again Hitler turned out to be extremely well informed: On Sunday May 29 the president received Brüning and told him, much to the chancellor's surprise, that he did not intend to issue any further emergency decrees on behalf of the Brüning government. Since this was tantamount to completely demolishing the legitimacy of his government, Brüning was left with no choice but to offer the resignation of his cabinet.[130]

The final spur for Hindenburg's decision to withdraw his support from Brüning completely was the chancellor's proposal to oblige owners of bankrupt estates in eastern Germany to auction them off for resettlement.[131] Spokesmen for the Reichslandbund and the DNVP had made forceful representations to Hindenburg over the previous few days, and as a landowner himself he had no taste whatsoever for his chancellor's "Bolshevist agrarian" line. "The bomb went off yesterday," noted Goebbels on Brüning's resignation.[132] His euphoria was understandably heightened by the fact that the day before the NSDAP had gained an absolute majority of seats in the Oldenburg elections.[133]

On May 30 Hitler was already in discussions with Hindenburg, the result of which Hitler passed on to leading Party comrades in Goebbels's apartment: "Ban on SA dropped. Uniforms permitted and Reichstag dissolved. That's the most important thing. Everything else will sort itself out. Von Papen is the man. That's not important either. Voting, voting! Get to the people!"[134] The next day, as Goebbels was informed by Hitler, von Papen confirmed the new arrangements.[135]

REICHSTAG ELECTIONS IN JULY 1932

The von Papen government, composed predominantly of aristocratic, ultra-conservative ministers, had the weakest conceivable power base in the Reichstag. On account of all the intrigue leading to Brüning's downfall, von Papen's own party, the Center Party, had withdrawn all cooperation from the chancellor, and von Papen— who had originally accepted the chancellorship with the full confidence that he would have the support of the Center Party—had resigned from the party. He could survive in Parliament only with the support of the NSDAP. Relying on a vague pledge of backing from Hitler, Hindenburg and von Papen accepted with equanimity the increased share of the vote the National Socialists were expected to gain in the new Reichstag elections.[136] But in the meantime, for the NSDAP the case was much altered. By breaking with the Center Party, the chancellor had in their eyes lost much of his value.

Meanwhile, Hitler and Goebbels were keeping election appointments in Mecklenburg, where voting was to take place on June 5. Both stayed for some days in secluded Severin, where on the first evening there was a heated debate about the form of a future state, which shows the extent to which Hitler—in keeping with his potential right-wing partners—was still toying with the idea of restoring the monarchy after seizing power: "Hitler is in favor of a reformed monarchy. I am too. But we don't have to select Auwi [August Wilhelm, the fourth son of the last German Kaiser] right away as protector of the Reich. [. . .] Hitler overestimates the people's promonarchy instincts. Thinks he would be defeated in a contest between Hitler and the Crown Prince. Impossible!"[137]

On Friday June 3 Hitler had a meeting with Schleicher. Immediately afterward, he came back to Severin and reported to Goebbels: "Reichstag is being dissolved immediately. SA ban lifted."[138] The next day the president proclaimed the dissolution and announced July 31, 1932, as the date for new elections.[139]

Negotiations were going on at the same time concerning the next steps in Prussia. At the top of the agenda was the possible participation of the NSDAP in a coalition government or at least a promise of parliamentary acquiescence. The previous autumn, Schleicher had already been contemplating an alternative solution, the appointment of a governor for Prussia by the Reich government, which now, with the Center Party having lost its old function of linking Prussia and the Reich by virtue of being the ruling party in both parliaments, was on the table again. Goebbels favored this solution.

On the evening of June 4 Hitler telephoned Schleicher from Severin. Goebbels noted: "Prussia question still not settled. Governor or prime minister from us." One thing was definite, however: "No Bavarian and no Protestant." This ruled out Gregor Strasser.[140] In the next few days, Goebbels found himself strengthened in his opinion that the chance of governing in Prussia should be turned down unless the same could be achieved in the Reich: "We're remaining in opposition until we have complete power, so that we have complete freedom of action. I talked to Hitler by phone: He fully agrees with me."[141] In the following days Goebbels published two articles in *Der Angriff* placing the von Papen cabinet firmly at arm's length.[142]

On June 9 the head of his propaganda staff in Munich, Heinz Franke, briefed Goebbels on the situation there, particularly on the imminent reorganization of the Party leadership by Gregor Strasser. Goebbels summarized his plans: "Strasser will give radio talks, Strasser will put together the list of candidates, Strasser appoints the Gau commissars. Strasser takes Hitler for a ride. And he doesn't put up any resistance."[143]

On June 14 he had a "good long personal talk" with Göring, whom he had so often criticized and disparaged. They agreed to bury their past differences; the background of this ceasefire was obviously the common interest they had in preventing Strasser from gaining influence.[144] On the evening of June 14 Goebbels listened to the speech his Party rival Strasser was allowed to give on behalf of the NSDAP on nationwide radio. For the first time, party political broadcast time had been allocated in this election campaign, and as Hitler would not agree to the conditions—speeches had to be submitted for vetting beforehand—Strasser stepped in. Above all Strasser emphasized state intervention to boost the feeble economy and reduce unemployment. Goebbels's verdict was: "Not aggressive enough. Too 'state-political.' That man will become a danger to Hitler one day."[145]

Despite his tireless contribution to the Party's propaganda work, Goebbels could not prevent Strasser, who had consolidated his position within the Party leadership, from putting his stamp on the campaign with his demand for job-creation measures. So, for example, Strasser distributed six hundred thousand copies of his booklet, *Urgent Economic Program of the NSDAP,* across the Party organization, setting out his agenda for job creation.[146]

In the instructions issued by the Reich propaganda office led by Goebbels, the stress was above all on distancing the Party from von

Papen's cabinet and the Party's commitment to fighting the KPD as much as the "system" and its parties, particularly the SPD and the Center Party.[147] Once again, great emphasis was laid on "individual propaganda": "Every comrade must select 2–3 fellow citizens and work on them very intensively until polling day."[148] The attention of the Party organization was drawn explicitly to the whole gamut of publicity methods available: from mass meetings, loudspeaker vehicles, sound films, flags, and banners to flyers, the campaign newspaper *Der Flammenwerfer*, leaflets, and posters.[149]

In mid-June, more or less as a prelude to the election campaign, Goebbels spent an evening with SA leaders in full uniform in the Haus Vaterland, the big amusement palace on Potsdamer Platz—a deliberate provocation in response to the ban on the SA. But the police did "not do the participants the favor of intervening," observed Goebbels. At this point he was not aware that the Reich government had lifted the ban.[150]

On June 27 he was at a meeting of Gauleiters in Munich to present his planning for the ongoing election campaign. There he found out that by means of "organizational changes," Strasser had been "rigging the Party to suit himself": "The General Secretary. Means to gradually displace Hitler. Honorary President. That's not what he wants. He must be primed. Str[asser] is giving all the jobs to his lackeys. That's how he's rigging the whole machine. The Party dictator!"[151]

On July 8 Hitler came to Berlin. Goebbels learned from Alvensleben that Hitler was talking to Schleicher and preparing their next joint move, which this time would be directed against von Papen: He had to "fall."[152] On July 9 Goebbels gave a speech in the Lustgarten in front of—according to the *Völkischer Beobachter*—a crowd of two hundred thousand; by Goebbels's highly exaggerated estimation "the biggest and most powerful rally Berlin has ever seen."[153] The next day he set out again on the election trail, starting in Rheydt and taking in several west German towns. Back in Berlin, he shared a platform with Goebbels in the Sportpalast.[154] But the main attraction of the campaign was another aerial tour by Hitler through Germany, spun by the Nazi press as a "freedom flight."[155]

On July 18 Goebbels gave his first broadcast talk, the von Papen government having enabled the parties for the first time to use the new medium for propaganda purposes.[156] He had to make substantial changes to the script—originally titled "National Socialism as a

State-Political Necessity"—after lengthy wrangling with the Reich minister of the interior, whose approval was required for this kind of party-political broadcast. In the end his talk was on "National Character as the Basis of National Culture." He for one was more than pleased with the result: "The speech makes a fabulous impression. I'm in top form. Brilliant press reaction today."[157]

Meanwhile, the von Papen government after its fashion was setting about resolving the stalemate in Prussia. The Prussian government under the Social Democrat prime minister Otto Braun had resigned after the Landtag elections in April, but was still acting as a caretaker administration. The coalition parties—the SPD, the DDP, the Center Party—no longer had a majority in Parliament. In terms of numbers, there was a possibility—while there was still a Brüning government, a politically feasible one—of forming a Center Party–NSDAP majority coalition. But under von Papen, who had severed all ties with the Center Party, the NSDAP no longer saw any chance of such a political arrangement at the Reich level. This was why in internal Party discussions since June Goebbels had been strongly opposed to compromising with the Center Party in Prussia.[158] In principle, his preferred option (but only if the Party was also participating in a Reich government) was to appoint a governor in Prussia. This option was something Schleicher had brought into play as early as autumn 1931. Since June he had been discussing it with the NSDAP leaders, and now, in July 1932, it was a solution the Reich government was seriously trying to put into effect—albeit without the participation of the National Socialists. At the same time, however, it was an advance concession to a future alliance with the NSDAP.

On July 20, 1932, von Papen made use of an emergency decree already signed by the president[159] giving him carte blanche powers and appointed himself state governor of Prussia. He called in Franz Bracht, mayor of Essen, to be his minister of the interior. The excuse for this step arose out of the events of the "Altona Bloody Sunday," a violent clash on July 17 involving the police, National Socialists, and communists that resulted in eighteen deaths.[160] All Social Democrat officeholders were relieved of their positions at this time, as were the top echelon of the Berlin police headquarters, including Goebbels's arch-enemy Bernhard Weiss.[161]

The Nazi leadership knew about the forthcoming "Prussian coup" by July 19, 1932, as Goebbels's diaries demonstrate.[162] When the action took place on July 20, Goebbels confirmed that everything was "going according to plan," and he recorded that the Nazi leadership was putting together a "wish list" for Bracht, together with a "list [. . .] of all those in Prussia due for the axe."[163]

Goebbels threw himself once more into campaigning, putting in appearances all over Germany.[164] On July 31, election day, he went to Munich to join in celebrating the anticipated victory. The National Socialists managed to win 37.4 percent of the vote, which gave them 230 seats, making them the largest party in the Reichstag.

Goebbels, whose result in Berlin was, at 28.7 percent, far below that of the average in the Reich as a whole,[165] drew his conclusion: "Now we have to gain power and eradicate Marxism. One way or the other! [. . .] We won't get an absolute majority this way. So take a different path."[166] But he did not mention what that path would be.

CHAPTER 9

"I Have a Blind Faith in Victory"

On the Way to Power

As head of Reich propaganda, Goebbels in 1932 was responsible for four country-wide election campaigns. But the permanent mobilization of Party comrades against the Weimar Republic did not lead to the expected political breakthrough. Despite making consistent election gains, at the end of the year the NSDAP experienced its stormiest internal crisis.

On August 2, two days after the elections, there was an outing to Lake Tegernsee: "Hitler deliberates. Difficult decisions ahead. Legally? With the Center Party? Makes me sick! [. . .] We consider, but come to no conclusion."[1]

A few days later, on August 6, Hitler informed Goebbels in Berchtesgaden of a discussion he had recently conducted with Schleicher in Fürstenberg, near Berlin. According to this report, the situation seemed to have changed radically. And Hitler's appointment as chancellor seemed imminent: "It will all be out in the open in a week's time. Boss becomes Reich chancellor and Prussian prime minister. Strasser interior minister for Prussia and Reich. Goebbels Prussian culture and Reich education. Darré agriculture in both places, Frick state secretary in the Reich Chancellery, Göring Air Ministry. We still have Justice Ministry. [. . .] If the Reichstag rejects the Enabling Act, it will be sent packing. Hindenburg wants to die with a nationalist cabinet. We'll never relinquish power; our dead bodies will have to be carried out first."[2] The next day he continued the discussion with Hitler until late into the night: "I get schools, universities, cinema, radio, theater, propaganda. A huge territory. Will fill a whole life. A historic task. [. . .] The national education of the German people is placed in my hands."[3]

Hitler had certainly painted a very optimistic picture for Goebbels—according to Meissner's report[4]—of his future sphere of government activity. In his talks with Schleicher he had not actually requested the Ministry of National Education on behalf of Goebbels. And in the following months, too, Hitler continued to conjure up for Goebbels a conception of his future ministerial activity that went far beyond the responsibilities he was actually to be given in spring 1933 as Reich minister for popular enlightenment and propaganda. Hitler did not share Goebbels's vision of himself as national educator of the German people. For him Goebbels was a competent and willing head of propaganda—and, as Hitler saw it, that was what he ought to remain after the "seizure of power."

But first of all, Hindenburg would need to agree to Hitler's appointment. The elite of the SA, which convened at Lake Chiemsee on August 11, was informed that Hindenburg was still relentlessly opposing such a step. The decision was made to go on negotiating with the Center Party in order to put von Papen and Schleicher under pressure to act.[5] In addition, the SA organized large-scale "maneuvers" in the Berlin area as a way of putting further pressure on the government.[6] The next day Goebbels—having meanwhile returned to Berlin—noted how eager the SA people were to march, which led him to worry that Helldorf might one day lose his grip on his units.[7]

The decision about Hitler's chancellorship came on August 13. He talked first to Schleicher and then to von Papen; they tried to persuade him to accept the position of vice chancellor, which he rejected.[8] He then went on to see the Reich president. After forty-five minutes he was back in Goebbels's apartment, reporting that it had been established all along that von Papen should remain chancellor. He had not even had a chance to speak but had really been "lured into a trap." For Goebbels, the idea that Hitler could be fobbed off with the vice chancellorship was "grotesque nonsense."[9] The official communiqué about the meeting was packed with lies, it was claimed, which is why von Papen and Schleicher were called on to produce a new version. When they failed to do so, the Nazi leadership produced their own report of the encounter.[10]

It now became ever more difficult to rein in an SA that considered itself already on the brink of power. In the evening the Berlin SA leaders met in Goebbels's apartment to confer: "Helldorf above all was overoptimistic. Now we'll have to break this news. A bitter task." A few days later the *Völkischer Beobachter* carried an appeal by Röhm to his "SA and SS comrades" announcing a "pause in the action."[11] To put pressure on the government, the Party leaders returned to the project of a parliamentary solution to the conflict in Prussia. Negotiations with the Center Party began but were soon broken off by the other side.[12]

Goebbels now found time for a week's vacation on the Baltic.[13]

BATTLE WITH VON PAPEN'S GOVERNMENT

When Goebbels resumed work in Berlin on August 22, the political situation was dominated by five death sentences pronounced by a special court in Beuthen against National Socialists for the brutal murder of a communist in the Potempa area of Upper Silesia. The accelerated sentencing of violent political aggressors, which was specifically aimed at combating Nazi terrorism, was an innovation that had gone into effect only a few days earlier.[14] At the beginning of August, the SA in East Prussia and Silesia had begun to subject its political opponents, mainly on the left, to a wave of terror, carrying out several bomb attacks and attempted assassinations that had resulted in injuries and one death—that of a communist local councilor.[15] The Potempa murder case thus represented the high point of a campaign of violence to which the state was now seeking to call a halt. But the reaction of the Nazi leadership left no doubt that they approved of the violence of their rank and file. Hitler sent the murderers a telegram of sympathy, which was published by the Party press on August 23,[16] while in an editorial in *Der Angriff* of August 24 Goebbels came up with the pithy formulation "It's the Jews' fault."

On August 24 Goebbels learned that the sentences would not be carried out. But the political repercussions were nonetheless considerable: "Schleicher of two minds. General mood against us. Schl. says Röhm has done the dirty on him. He didn't want to order anything illegal, but what about East Prussia."[17]

There remained the Center Party option. On August 25 Goebbels was with Hitler in Berchtesgaden. They were joined by Frick and Strasser, who had just met with Brüning in Tübingen: "The Center Party wants to go with us. Condition is a durable alliance and Prussian minister to be Goerdeler. [. . .] Strasser strongly in favor of Center Party solution. Hitler and I on other hand are for continuing with the presidential idea." Eventually the group agreed on three possible options: "1. Presidential. 2. Coalition. 3. Opposition. Work on them in that order."[18] The diary documents Goebbels's willingness to accept all conceivable tactical variations compatible with the "legal" course of the Party. He could see only too clearly that to continue with political terror methods as practiced in East Prussia and Silesia would only lead the Party into the wilderness.

The following weeks saw all sorts of complicated tactical maneuvering. The very next day Goebbels met Schleicher in Berlin, but the stance of the latter remained unclear. Goebbels thought he could apply pressure on him with the threat of a coalition with the Center Party and reported to Hitler accordingly.[19] The next day he traveled to Caputh. In this village near Potsdam, Goebbels had for the first time rented a vacation home, where Hitler appeared at 10 P.M. with a "large entourage": "We must get into power. If the government breaks constitutional law, that's an end to legality in general. Then there'll be tax refusal, sabotage etc."[20] This final step was, however, not a desirable option for Goebbels in August 1932. He had internalized the policy of obtaining power by means of negotiation.

The next day in the Hotel Kaiserhof he met with Hitler, who informed him about the talks he had held in the meantime with Brüning, von Papen, and Schleicher: "Always the same delaying tactics." There was a threat that the Parliament that had just been elected might be dissolved immediately: "And we're left in the lurch."[21]

On August 30 Goebbels attended the inaugural session of the Reichstag. The house elected Göring as its president, a decision to which Goebbels initially reacted with mixed feelings. But over the course of the session he found that Göring did "a good job."[22]

At a party in Göring's house on August 31, Hitler, Goebbels, Göring, and Röhm withdrew for a "secret conference" in which a "bold plan [. . .] for toppling the old man" was "hatched." Goebbels's diaries for the next few days reveal the strategy.[23] The idea was to make use of Article 43 of the Reich constitution, which stipulated that if two-thirds of the Reichstag supported a motion to depose the president, it could be taken to a referendum. The first thing was to make sure of Center Party support, which, together with the BVP and KPD, would constitute a large enough majority in Parliament.[24]

As the Party leaders conferred on this issue, Goebbels eagerly added to his list of criticisms of Strasser, who "as ever" was against the plan because, as Goebbels speculated, the fall of the president might interfere with his own machinations. He registered that both Göring and Röhm had a negative opinion of Strasser and that Hitler "spoke out sharply against him," even questioning Strasser's recently completed reorganization of the Munich headquarters: "Hitler is afraid of Strasser, but he's not fond of him."[25]

It was during these days of intrigue that Goebbels became a father for the first time. On September 1 at 2:20 P.M., Magda gave birth to a baby girl they would name Helga. "Only a girl, unfortunately," recorded a disappointed Goebbels. But Hitler was "thrilled": "Hr had always predicted a girl." "A girl is better," Hitler consoled him the next day, "because a boy was bound to fall short of his father." Hitler was also full of praise for Magda, "whom he very much admires and considers the loveliest, dearest, and cleverest of women."[26]

On September 8 and 10 Goebbels took part in talks at the Reichstag Presidential Palace that brought together delegations from the Center Party and the NSDAP. Here Hitler leaned heavily on the Center Party, calling for its support in toppling Hindenburg. Goebbels had the impression that the Center Party representatives were receptive to this demand. However, they asked for time to think it over.[27] It took a powerful intervention by the former chancellor, Brüning, to fend off this attack on the Reich president.[28] But both parties did agree on the basis of a new bill relating to the Reich president's deputy. They no longer wanted the Reich chancellor to deputize for the president when the head of state was not available but rather the president of the Reich Supreme Court. This move was motivated by the desire to prevent a concentration of power in the hands of Chancellor von Papen, in the reasonably likely event of Hindenburg's suffering a serious illness.[29]

On September 12 Goebbels was present in the chamber when the KPD brought in a surprise vote of no confidence against von Papen in the Reichstag. The NSDAP and the Center Party coordinated their response. In the ensuing vote, practically the whole house came out against von Papen.[30] Voting had actually been possible only because the Reichstag president, Hermann Göring, had carefully ignored the folder handed to him by von Papen as the session proceeded. It contained Hindenburg's order for the dissolution of Parliament.[31] However, in constitutional terms the situation was clear: The Reichstag had been dissolved, and new elections were set for November 6.

THE ELECTION CAMPAIGN AND THE BVG STRIKE

On September 13 Hitler gave the Party's Reichstag members the motto for the coming election: "Against Papen and the reactionaries." On the same day, Goebbels went about ensuring that the Berlin Party organization and the Reich propaganda office were committed to campaigning on this watchword.[32]

The rallying cry issued by Hitler indicated clearly that—in contrast to the campaign of June and July 1932—it was not the "system parties" but von Papen and his "reactionary henchmen," above all the DNVP, that the NSDAP propaganda machine had in its sights this time.[33] Thus the Party press actually went so far in the campaign as to call on its readers to boycott bourgeois-nationalist publications.[34] More forcefully than in the July campaign, in which Strasser had been allowed to showcase his sociopolitical demands, the person of the Party leader was held up in opposition to the "reactionaries" as "the last hope," as an election poster put it.[35]

During a visit to Munich at the beginning of October, Goebbels reorganized the Reich propaganda office. In this, he benefited from the fact that a few weeks earlier Strasser had ceded to him responsibility for film and radio.[36] This enabled Goebbels to create four main departments, with information service and propaganda alongside film and radio.[37]

Early in November the Berlin NSDAP became embroiled in a

labor dispute that had serious repercussions. In the Berlin transportation network (BVG, Transport for Berlin), a dispute with the companies involved had led to the formation of a strike committee dominated by the KPD but also containing representatives of the National Socialist industrial cell organization (NSBO), responsible for organizing workers at their place of work. On November 3 all buses, streetcars, and subway lines came to a standstill.

The National Socialists had placed themselves in a difficult position by taking part in the strike. On the one hand, if they wanted to maintain their claim to be a workers' party, they could not back out of the strike; at the same time, though, the Party leadership was aware that cooperating with the KPD would lose the Party votes among bourgeois voters. On November 3 the state arbitrator imposed a mandatory award, and the next day the unions called on their members to return to work. The KDP and the NSDAP jointly opposed this course of action; there were violent clashes, shootings, and several fatalities. "We are in a precarious position," Goebbels recorded on the second day of the strike.[38] The following day he perceived the upsurge of a "revolutionary mood," consequently urging: "Keep going!"[39] But by November 5 he had to admit that the strikers were in danger of being forced onto the defensive vis-à-vis the BVG, and on November 6, election day, he conceded that the strike was looking shaky, blaming this on the Social Democrats.

Collaborating with the KPD in a labor dispute that rapidly became hopeless was undoubtedly part of the reason the NSDAP vote dropped substantially in the November 6 Reichstag results. Its share of the vote fell by more than four points, to 33.1 percent. In Berlin the losses were less marked but also started from a lower base: The NSDAP received 26.0 percent (against 28.7 percent in July), which put them 5 points behind the KPD and only 3 points ahead of the SPD. There could be no talk of making inroads into the working-class vote, let alone of "conquering" solidly "red" Berlin. Only in a few arch-Catholic areas of the country did the NSDAP perform less well than in the capital.[40]

Goebbels acknowledged that this was a "bad setback." He attributed the losses to "August 13 and [the] negotiations with the Center Party": "The first was necessary, the second superfluous." He agreed with Hitler that a "tough fight" lay ahead: "The Party must be sustained, the mood lifted, the organization consolidated." He was not prepared to admit that his campaign plan of foregrounding Hitler personally had not been a conspicuous success. And in the subsequent analysis of the campaign, he was not willing to mention the BVG strike, which was abandoned by the KPD and the NSDAP on November 7.[41]

For the Berlin NSDAP, the discontinued strike was a resounding failure. The Party had allowed itself to be pushed into the strike by its anticapitalist NSBO wing and at the height of the election campaign had become entangled in cooperation with the arch-enemy, the KPD, inflicting serious damage on its own credibility—and didn't even achieve the aims of the strike. It is interesting to see how Goebbels dealt with the debacle after the fact. While the subject had not loomed very large in his diary in the days of the strike—it was only gradually that he became aroused on behalf of the strikers by late October—he wove into his book *Vom Kaiserhof zur Reichskanzlei* (published in 1933) long passages in which he expatiated on the strategy and strike tactics of the Berlin NSDAP, a post hoc vindication owing very little to the original diary entries. What he later presented as a cool calculation was in reality a chaotic situation in which he was completely out of his depth.[42]

THE WAR OF SUCCESSION TO VON PAPEN

Von Papen announced on November 17 that he was stepping down. Hitler hurried to Berlin, where two days later he had a conversation with Hindenburg. Goebbels advised Hitler the night before to "go to the old man as though to a father. Use quite uncomplicated language and try to gain his trust. Don't take anyone with you, and above all leave Röhm behind."[43]

In his discussion with Hindenburg, Hitler once again claimed the office of chancellor, together with presidential support on the basis of Article 48—in other words, the power to issue presidential decrees. However, Hindenburg made it clear to him that initially the NSDAP would not be offered more than a few ministerial positions in what would amount to a "non-party" government. If Hitler wanted to be chancellor, he would first have to take soundings of the parties to prove to Hindenburg that he had a majority.[44] Hindenburg reiterated this viewpoint in another conversation on November 21.[45] Goebbels, informed by Hitler about the ongoing talks, sensed they were heading for a repetition of August 13. As far as taking soundings was concerned, this would be pointless, since Hugenberg, whose DNVP had emerged strengthened by the election, would once more block the way. Goebbels's feeling was that the Center Party would tolerate Hitler as chancellor, but without DNVP backing he would not enjoy a parliamentary majority.[46] Moreover, Goebbels suspected a trap: The plan was to make Hitler chancellor of a government fettered by presidential caveats, then allow him to fail and destroy him politically.[47] Goebbels learned from Göring that Hindenburg had made it a condition of a government role for Hitler that he, Goebbels, and Röhm should not be appointed to any office. "Fine company I'm in," wrote Goebbels mordantly.[48] In the discussion that followed, Strasser argued in favor of negotiating with Hindenburg: "Hitler quite right: Implacably rules it out. [. . .] Later maybe. Eyes on presidential solution for now."[49]

On November 30, 1932, Goebbels met Hitler in Weimar: "Schleicher can't make up his mind. Wants acquiescence from us. Conditions for and against." Göring, Strasser, and Frick, who had also arrived in Weimar, discussed the situation: "Strasser wants us to participate. Paints a very bleak picture otherwise. Hitler sharply opposed to him. Sticks to his guns. Bravo! Göring and I back him solidly. Str. gives way. Hitler has the right view of the situation."[50]

The next day Lieutenant Colonel Eugen Ott came to Weimar to negotiate with Hitler, or "parley for Schleicher," as Goebbels put it. Goebbels held firmly to Hitler's position: "Suspending of Reichstag until January. Amnesty and streets clear and right to self-defense. Otherwise fight. Total chaos in Berlin. Our seed-corn is ripening."[51] The next day, December 1, Hitler delivered "a 3-hour lecture to Lt. Col. Ott": Schleicher should not accept the position of chancellor, otherwise the Reichswehr (army) would be "consumed" by an internal political struggle. Ott, according to Goebbels "deeply impressed," made a call "to Berlin" but learned from it that "there was no turning back" for Schleicher and that he was asking for toleration of his future government.[52]

In the meantime Schleicher had taken the decisive steps toward being appointed the next day, December 2, as von Papen's successor. On this day he allowed his colleague Ott, just back from Weimar, to give the cabinet a lecture asserting that if a state of emergency was declared, the Reichswehr would not be in a position to guarantee domestic security. In other words, the Reichswehr (Schleicher) was withdrawing its support from von Papen. Schleicher would now have to manage with only a feeble prospect of acquiescence from the National Socialists.[53]

STRASSER, SCHLEICHER

On December 5 the Party elite held a large consultation meeting to consider what attitude to take toward a Schleicher government: "Strasser and Frick do not have a firm grip. Hitler clashes sharply with them."

Goebbels learned here that Frick and Strasser "were with Schleicher. He wants to dissolve [Parliament] if we don't acquiesce." A real threat lurked behind these words, since the NSDAP had suffered some serious losses in local elections in Thuringia the day before.[54] The Party leaders then formulated, as they had done a few days earlier in Weimar, their list of conditions for tolerating a Schleicher government: "Amnesty, social improvements, the right to self-defense and to demonstrate." If Schleicher accepted them, they would vote for an adjournment of the Reichstag. Goebbels supported this course of action without reservation. In the meeting of NSDAP members of Parliament that followed, Hitler "spoke out sharply against compromising": "Strasser's features harden. Members unanimous about maintaining consistent course. If possible, no dissolution before Christmas."

Academic accounts of this period assume for the most part that by this point, to be precise from December 4 onward, Strasser was holding an offer from Schleicher to join his government as vice chancellor and minister of labor.[55] The general view is that Schleicher's move was an attempt to divide the NSDAP and—to avoid becoming bogged down in a party-political confrontation—to construct a "cross front" composed of "left-wing" National Socialists, trade union members, and representatives of professional associations.[56] This supposed offer of Schleicher's to Strasser is derived from a single source: the revised version of Goebbels's diary, published in 1934 as *Vom Kaiserhof zur Reichskanzlei*. But a comparison with the original diary published in 2006 demonstrates that the passage about Schleicher's alleged offer to Strasser and the latter's intention of running for election with his own list of candidates, in other words of "betraying" the Party, was inserted into the text at a later date. It was an act of vengeance against Goebbels's long-term Party opponent.[57] But that was not all: Comparing the original diary with the *Kaiserhof* text reveals that Goebbels later doctored many references to Strasser's attitude at this critical juncture in order to demonstrate how the "villain" Strasser consistently evolved his anti-Hitler policies over a long period.[58] This also accounts for the considerable annoyance aroused by the "revelations" of Goebbels's *Kaiserhof* book in Nazi Gauleiter circles when it was published in 1934.[59]

The original version of the diaries shows a completely different picture of those days. It is true that, as is made clear by the diary entries concerning NSDAP leadership consultations in Weimar in late November and early December, the "Strasser crisis" was all about the modalities of acquiescing in a Schleicher government. While Strasser was willing to compromise, Hitler (with Goebbels's eager support) on the other hand formulated tighter conditions for provisional acquiescence, which Schleicher, for his part, felt able to accept. The NSDAP leaders had painted themselves into a corner. For months, their demand to be given the office of chancellor with full presidential powers had consistently been turned down by the president. But they lacked the partners to form a coalition. What remained was the poorest option, the provisional arrangement with Schleicher. In December 1932 there were no moves to make Strasser vice chancellor, no serious efforts by Schleicher to split the NSDAP, and no attempt to form a cross-party front.[60]

In any case, from Goebbels's point of view the first few days of Schleicher's government were relatively relaxed. The Reichstag met from December 6 to 9. Things were fairly calm, apart from a "bloody brawl in the galleries and the lobby between the KPD and us" on December 7.[61] The Reichstag decided to reconvene in mid-January. There was certainly no talk of an immediate dissolution of Parliament. And it did in fact pass resolutions completely in accord with the National Socialists' demands, including an amnesty, as well as sociopolitical measures.[62] Later in December the government followed through with the expected relaxation of measures to curb internal-political terrorism (the third condition imposed by the NSDAP leaders), among other things winding up the special courts established in August.[63] Schleicher therefore had every reason to instill confidence in his cabinet that the NSDAP would go along with his administration.[64]

On December 5 Hitler, Göring, Epp, and Rosenberg came to an "artists' evening" at Goebbels's home; the next evening was again spent in a relaxed mood in his apartment, where Hitler, Hess, and Ernst Hanfstaengl, Hitler's "head of foreign press relations," were present; the evening after that, Leni Riefenstahl, of whom Goebbels had long been an ardent admirer, invited Goebbels, Hitler, and Hanfstaengl to her home.[65] Since 1932 she had leaned toward the NSDAP;[66] during these weeks she was to put in more frequent appearances at Nazi Party events, at the Goebbelses' apartment, and at parties given by leading National Socialists. The descriptions of these relaxed evening affairs do not convey the impression that the Nazi elite were confronting an immediate crisis with the potential to tear the Party apart.

On December 8, however, there was a sudden flurry of rumors that Strasser was planning a "palace revolution."[67] Eventually Hitler received a letter[68] in which Strasser—forever torn between loyalty to the Party and his commitment to what he thought was right, his job-creation policies—said he was resigning from all his Party positions. The reason he gave ("lead the Party to the State") hardly seemed valid to Goebbels: He thought Strasser's only objective was to become a government minister.[69] In the middle of the night Goebbels was summoned to an emergency meeting at the Kaiserhof, where Hitler, Röhm, and Himmler had already gathered. An article had just appeared in the newspaper *Tägliche Rundschau,* written by a close associate of Otto Strasser's named Herbert Blank: Hitler was to be pushed aside.[70] Strasser's letter to Hitler was therefore "the height of Jesuitical chicanery." That same night the organizational consequences were drawn from Strasser's resignation: The structure created by Strasser was to be broken up. (Goebbels was one of the beneficiaries of the new order.) The atmosphere was tense: "Hitler says: If the Party falls apart, I'm going to end it all in 3 minutes. Terrible!"[71]

In the course of the day Hitler addressed Gauleiters and inspectors and then the Reichstag members: "Devastating attack on Strasser. [. . .] They were all howling with rage and pain. Really great success for Hitler. At the end, spontaneous declaration of loyalty. They all shake

Hitler's hand. Strasser is isolated. Dead man!" Satisfied, Goebbels summed it all up: "I fought 6 years for this."[72] Outwardly, however, although gaining so much from it, he tried to suppress his triumphalism over Strasser's downfall. Thus, for example, he dismissed a sharp attack on Strasser in *Der Angriff* of December 9, a few days later, as "tactless remarks" that had been published without his consent.[73]

Strasser's departure necessitated a considerable reorganization at the top of the NSDAP, which Goebbels discussed with Hitler at lunch on December 13: "This is fun. I get Party training and popular education. They belong to my department anyway."[74] However, the difficult financial position of the NSDAP forced Goebbels to fire a third of the personnel in the Reich propaganda office. Franke, until now chief of staff, was replaced by Wilhelm Haegert.[75]

With Magda being ill—she was hospitalized, and her life was in danger—in the critical weeks leading to the formation of a Hitler-von Papen coalition, Goebbels was practically excluded. His diary shows that he was grateful for any information he received about the process, but also that in this decisive phase his advice was never really sought. Because of Magda's illness, on January 1 Goebbels broke off a trip to Bavaria—he had celebrated the New Year on the Obersalzberg with Hitler—to return to Berlin.[76] Extremely worried about her condition, he visited Magda daily in the hospital during the following weeks whenever he was not prevented by external commitments and was often accompanied by Hitler, who also visited her alone.[77]

In the meantime, the NSDAP was concentrating all of its energies on the election scheduled for January 15 in the tiny state of Lippe. Like other prominent Party members, Goebbels made various appearances at election campaign meetings there.[78] On one of his trips to Lippe, on January 9, he met up with Hitler and perceived that the latter was gradually emerging from his political isolation. Former chancellor von Papen was "sharply opposed to Schleicher": He wanted to "bring him down and get rid of him completely," in which regard he had "the ear of the old man."[79] Von Papen's offer consisted of either the chancellorship or the "ministries with power"—that is, the Defense and Interior ministries. Von Papen was indeed the man to persuade Hindenburg to depart from his previous demand and grant Hitler the position of chancellor even without a parliamentary majority initially, but "framed" by conservative politicians. It was only in small increments that Goebbels received information about the gov-

ernment that was shaping up. He met Hitler again on January 11 in
Bad Oeynhausen: "Everything still in the balance." Schleicher's side,
he now learned, was offering Strasser the position of vice chancellor:
"Just how I imagine a traitor."[80]

In the Lippe election the NSDAP received just 39.5 percent of the
vote, less than the record result of July but markedly better than in
the Reichstag election in November. In the event, the Party's propaganda declared this success an overwhelming victory. In an editorial
in *Der Angriff*, Goebbels announced that the "popular verdict of
Lippe" showed that the stagnation of the NSDAP was over.[81] Hitler
was so reinvigorated by this favorable election result that he even felt
able to tackle his relationship with Gregor Strasser, left unresolved
since December. At a Gauleiter conference on January 16 in Weimar,
he managed to set practically all of the Party elite against the dis-
senter: "Poor Gregor! Butchered by his best friends," wrote Goebbels.[82]

On January 24, over coffee in Munich, Hitler explained to Goebbels, who was not involved, the latest developments in the negotiations to form a government: "On Sunday he was together with Papen,
Meissner, and Hindenburg Junior. [. . .] All three sharply opposed to
Schleicher. He must go. Papen wants to be vice chancellor. That's all.
Schleicher's position very much endangered. He still seems unsuspecting. Poor naive creature!"[83]

Two days later, while Goebbels was on an election trip to Upper
Silesia, he learned that Schleicher was going to fall in a few days:
"Harzburger Front reappears. Frick and Göring negotiating."[84] He
made no comment on the sudden resurrection of the alliance with
the far right, the Stahlhelm, and the DNVP, to which he had objected
so strongly in earlier years. The following day, with Goebbels back in
Berlin, there was still no decision about Hitler's chancellorship: "The
old man doesn't want it. So: Keep at it!"[85] He registered varying items
of news about the negotiations,[86] until he heard of the final outcome
from Göring: "Hitler Chancellor, Papen Vice Chancellor, Frick Reich
Interior, Göring Pruss. Interior. Hugenberg Emergencies etc. And
above all: The Reichstag is to be dissolved." "The last time [i.e., the
last election]," wrote Goebbels: "We'll manage it." Finally, Hitler told
him that the promised Ministry of Popular Education was reserved
for him—but first there was an election to get through.[87]

INTERIM REVIEW:
GOEBBELS'S PATH TO THE "SEIZURE OF POWER"

Watching the negotiations about forming a government from the perspective of a mere onlooker, early in 1933, was not a new experience for Goebbels. He had never been directly involved in the various discussions and soundings undertaken by Hitler in the preceding years to move the NSDAP closer to power.

Surveying the deliberations, advice, and initiatives associated with Goebbels up to this point in the National Socialist quest for power, the inconsistency and at times even naïveté of his approach become apparent. Ever since Hitler had begun in 1929 to seek a closer liaison with the DNVP and the Stahlhelm, Goebbels had always been hostile to this alliance, afraid that the NSDAP would be too restricted politically by such a constellation. At the same time, he had presented himself as an uncompromising radical. Eventually, after many crises, when this partnership had finally shown itself in the presidential election of 1932 to be incapable of action, Goebbels, in an astonishing change of direction, became willing to entertain the other alternative, a coalition with the Center Party (in the Reich and in Prussia), in particular because he hoped in this way to be able to play a decisive role in Prussia. For a while, with the fall of Brüning and von Papen's accession to the chancellorship at the end of May 1932, it seemed that this dream was about to be fulfilled. But it ended when the Center Party broke with von Papen. Goebbels's comportment in these months indicates that he had finally realized that his ostentatious posturing as a radical was a hindrance both to the Party and to his own career. He now swung completely behind Hitler's tactical policy of negotiation. When the NSDAP emerged from the election of July 1932 as the strongest party, Goebbels—spurred on above all by the promise of an extensive Culture Ministry—naturally supported Hitler's project of becoming chancellor with full presidential powers. When Hitler's plan was frustrated by Hindenburg's resistance, Goebbels willingly followed his leader's policy of tolerating a Schleicher cabinet. When Hitler returned in January 1933 to his original approach of seeking a coalition with his old partners from the Harzburg days, the Stahlhelm and the DNVP, Goebbels noted this without commenting. In the last year before the "seizure of power," he simply went with the flow of NSDAP policy, determined by Hitler.

Goebbels's behavior makes superabundantly clear his total dependence on Hitler. Any doubts he might have had about the Party leader's policies—whether it was in relation to the Stahlhelm and the DNVP, the question of the Party's "socialism," Hitler's stalling over the Reich propaganda position, and other such occurrences—he always put aside in the end, submitting completely to Hitler's political genius. Correspondingly, his position within the Party was based entirely on Hitler's support. He was not tied to firm alliances with other leading Party comrades or to networks: In fact, he shied away from such ties in order to give himself maximum freedom to accommodate the Party leader. His total dependence on Hitler also explains why Goebbels relied completely on the nebulous ideas of the leader as far as future National Socialist policies for governing were concerned and why he made no significant effort to develop political concepts of his own: By 1931 he had dropped his vague "socialist" notions for good. After the end of the 1920s, when he gave up the idea of an alliance with Russia, he never had any thoughts about future foreign policy; equally unfathomable is his conception of the office of "National Educator" that Hitler dangled in front of him from time to time.

In his special area, Party propaganda, Goebbels had likewise done little to make himself stand out. In his first election, in summer 1930, when he had admittedly only just taken office, he did not diverge at all from the previous line of targeting the "fulfilment policy" of the Young Plan. It was in the presidential election campaign of spring 1932 that he first deployed the idea of placing Hitler squarely at the heart of Party propaganda, but the defeat of Hitler in this contest emphatically showed the risk of such a single-pronged propaganda ploy. For that reason the Reichstag election of July 1932 was dominated by other themes, above all the fight against the "system parties." It was not until the November election that the spotlight returned to the person of the Party leader, presented as an alternative to von Papen and "the reactionaries" but once again with only limited success. For all Goebbels's admiration for Hitler and his dependence on him as the central fixed point determining his political activities, it was only at a relatively late juncture, hesitantly and with dubious success, that he imposed his "Führer cult" on Nazi propaganda—and even then, primarily out of tactical considerations. Only under the conditions of dictatorship and within the constraints of public surveillance did he succeed in establishing the Führer myth, the notion of a far-reaching union of *Volk* and *Volksführer*, as a central element of his propaganda.

1933—1939

CONTROLLING THE PUBLIC SPHERE UNDER DICTATORSHIP

CHAPTER 10

"We're Here to Stay!"

Taking Power

Book burning in the Berlin Opernplatz on May 10, 1933, where Goebbels made an inflammatory speech. In the first months after his appointment as minister, Goebbels's reorientation of German cultural life was quite unmistakable.

After the appointment on January 30 of the Hitler–von Papen coalition government, combining National Socialists, German Nationalists, and the Stahlhelm, Goebbels was fully taken up with preparations for the next election campaign.[1] The president's order to dissolve the Reichstag, a precondition for calling new elections, was in Hitler's hands by February 2, 1933. At a cabinet meeting on January 31, Hitler's national-conservative coalition partners had reluctantly acceded to his demand for an election. He declared that this poll for the Reichstag would be the last.[2]

Goebbels was disappointed to discover that for the moment nothing came of Hitler's magnanimous promise of a grand-scale Ministry of Popular Education, one that would assume responsibility for schools and universities. He heard on February 2 that Bernhard Rust was to have the Ministry of Culture, and not simply—as he had still been thinking right up to that morning—as a "stand-in" for himself, but permanently.[3]

According to the diary, however, Goebbels had been given far-reaching promises of a future ministry in January 1932 and again the following August.[4] Significantly, in the *Kaiserhof* version of the diary he edited the relevant passages in order to conceal his setback. There was no longer any mention of the promised responsibility for schools and universities, just as he also omitted the "link" with the Prussian Ministry of Culture he had been promised in January, and he turned the assurance of a position as minister of popular education received in August into a "plan of popular education."[5] Magda, released from the hospital on February 1, was "very unhappy. Because I'm not getting ahead."[6] The rumor that reached him around this time was that he was going to be fobbed off with the subordinate role of "commissioner for radio" ("disgusting").[7]

He was then approached by Walther Funk, who a few days earlier had been appointed head of the government press agency (until then Funk had headed the economic policy unit of the NSDAP), with the request to be made "state secretary for press and propaganda." "That's all I needed," was Goebbels's furious reaction. In short, he concluded, "I'm being pushed out of the way. Hitler doesn't help much. I give up. The reactionaries are calling the tune."[8] Two days later he learned via a phone call from Hitler that the leader had already confirmed Funk in his future office. For Goebbels, this appointment meant that his most important collaborator would simultaneously be serving as Hitler's government spokesman, directly under him and continually on the receiving end of the leader's directives. Responsibility for press policy in the new government was therefore divided from the start, so that there were constraints on Goebbels's freedom of action as head of propaganda.[9] In the version of his diary published in 1934 he turned this painful defeat on its head: "The director of the Reich press office was my choice for state secretary."[10]

At the behest of the new government, on February 4 the president signed an emergency decree "for the protection of the German people," giving the regime the power to forbid strikes, meetings, and demonstrations. It also became easier to silence newspapers, a provision the new masters of Germany exploited to the full in the days that followed.[11]

The funeral of Hans Maikowski, the leader of an SA unit dubbed "Murder-Stormtroop 33" by his opponents, was a chance for the new regime to put on a lavish display. He had been killed on the evening of January 30 in an exchange of fire with the communists after the SA march through the Brandenburg Gate.[12] Following the ceremony in the cathedral and a slow march through the city, Goebbels gave a memorial address in the Invalidenfriedhof (Veterans' Cemetery) that was broadcast by all the German radio stations. "Perhaps we Germans do not know how to live—but we certainly know how to die fabulously": This rhetorical high point of his speech was borrowed from the U-boat movie *Morgenrot* (Dawn), whose premiere he had attended the day before.[13]

On February 6 Goebbels succumbed to the constant strain and disappointments he suffered in the early days of the Third Reich, going down with an influenza attack that kept him in bed for several days with a high temperature.[14] Barely recovered, a few days later he plunged energetically into the task of organizing the election campaign, both in the Berlin Gau and in the wider Reich.[15] Initially, however, the campaign was handicapped by an acute lack of funds.[16] For a while Goebbels was even forced to halt the printing of propaganda material.[17] This, together with his disappointment over government positions, led to a degree of resentment toward the headquarters in Munich, which he vented in his diary: "Munich=Mecca=murder of NS."[18] Eventually he was in danger of falling into a bout of depression.[19]

When Göring appointed the new Berlin Police Commissioner, Magnus von Levetzow, Goebbels's diary entry for February 16 records the fact with no great enthusiasm but also reveals that as Gauleiter of Berlin he was not consulted at all about filling this important position—one from which he had, after all, often been attacked over the years.

But at the same time there was a change of fortune: In the middle of the month, Frau von Schröder, the wife of the Cologne banker in whose house Hitler and von Papen had planned the formation of a new government, donated twenty thousand Reichsmarks to the Berlin Gau election campaign, and a few days later Goebbels heard from Göring that three million marks were available for the nationwide campaign: "Now we can really put some pep into it."[20]

The themes of the campaign centered on the slogan "Build with Hitler," and—reinforced after the Reichstag fire—on confrontation with left-wing parties, with "corrupt rule," and with communist "terror."[21] Goebbels appeared at a series of mass rallies throughout the Reich, sometimes together with Hitler, whose speeches were broadcast, introduced by a commentary from Goebbels. Broadcasting election campaign rallies was a novelty for German radio. Although von Papen had used the radio for government propaganda purposes, in principle broadcasting had been limited by party-political neutrality. As a result some regions that were not yet dominated by National Socialists took exception. According to the cabinet decision of February 8, a compromise was reached whereby Hitler would enjoy airtime only in his capacity as head of government (and not as leader of a party), and the introduction should be limited to no more than 10 minutes. However, Goebbels managed to stretch out his evocative commentaries to nearly 45 minutes.[22] In February and the beginning of March he appeared at mass rallies in, among other places, Stuttgart, Dortmund, Essen, Cologne, Hanover, Frankfurt, Breslau, and Hamburg, and of course he spoke in the Berlin Sportpalast.[23] At the end of the month Hitler expressed himself simply "delighted" with his commentaries.[24]

On one of these trips he visited his hometown, Rheydt; sat ensconced in the town's Palast Hotel with family and friends for long sessions; and obviously enjoyed being cheered in the streets as a celebrated son of the locality: "The whole town in uproar," he recorded.[25]

Even his relations with Hitler, troubled for a while, were now straightened out, with the Führer promising him that his ministry would be set up immediately after the election.[26] Together with Magda they attended a Wagner opera, and Hitler resumed his evening visits to the Goebbels apartment.[27]

A new acquisition seems to have contributed a good deal to improving Goebbels's mood. At the Berlin automobile exhibition, opened on February 12 by Hitler and visited twice by Goebbels, he admired a new Mercedes, a "top-class, highest-quality product."[28] A short while later in Stuttgart he had an opportunity to raise the matter with Jakob Werlin, a Mercedes dealer who had often been helpful to Hitler and the NSDAP.[29] Once again it turned out that Werlin was able to help, and a week later in Berlin Goebbels took delivery of his glamorous automobile, "on the most favorable terms."[30]

THE REICHSTAG FIRE

On the evening of February 28—Hitler and Prince Auwi were visiting—Hanfstaengl called Goebbels at home with the startling news that the Reichstag was on fire. It transpired that what was thought at first to be just some "crazy fantasy" was actually true. They drove quickly to Parliament: "The whole building is in flames. Inside. Göring already there. Papen, too, whom I meet here for the first time. Fire set in 30 places. Carried out by communists. Göring is furious. Hitler in a rage. [. . .] Now is the time to act!"

While Hitler and von Papen were conferring, Goebbels was at the Gau headquarters taking the first steps to quell a supposed communist uprising. Later they met up again in the Kaiserhof in high spirits: "Everybody's beaming. That's exactly what we needed. Now we're sitting pretty. Perpetrator caught. 24-year old Dutch communist."[31]

Goebbels's diary entries show that from the point of view of the Nazi elite, the Reichstag fire was a unique stroke of luck, presenting the National Socialists with the perfect excuse to proceed against the left, particularly the KPD, with the utmost brutality. All that we learn from the diary about the actual culprit is that it was the twenty-four-year old Dutch communist Marinus van der Lubbe, later condemned to death by the Reich Supreme Court for this act. In Goebbels's notes there is not the slightest hint that the Nazi leadership seriously thought that Lubbe's action was intended by the KPD as a signal for revolt. And the turn of events clearly caught communist leaders themselves completely unawares. The action taken by the new regime that night was prompted not by genuine fear of a communist uprising but by a sense that fate had played right into their hands.

Too good to be true? There is nothing whatsoever in Goebbels's diary to support the suspicion, still often mentioned to this day, that the Reichstag fire was staged by the Nazi leadership. But this omission is not conclusive; it is quite possible that the real perpetrators behind the arson attack (Hitler? Göring?) left Goebbels in the dark about their plans, and it is also conceivable that even if Goebbels had been initiated into these plans he might have feigned innocence in the diaries.[32]

After their nocturnal meeting in the Kaiserhof, Hitler and Goebbels went to the editorial office of the *Völkischer Beobachter,* where Hitler personally recast the next morning's edition. Goebbels then returned to the Gau headquarters, designed a poster, and wrote a "fabulous article" to appear in the next day's *Angriff*: "Time to make a radical end! What more are we waiting for? A twenty-four-year-old foreign communist acting for Russian and German agents of this world pestilence setting fire to the Reichstag!"[33]

That same night there was a wave of arrests of communist functionaries. The entire left-wing press was banned, and before the day was over a cabinet meeting chaired by Hitler passed a decree, endorsed by the president, "for the protection of people and state." The decree suspended the fundamental rights of the Weimar constitution, enabled the Reich government to seize the reins of power in the various states in the case of serious disturbance to public order and security, and imposed heavy penalties for contraventions.[34]

ELECTION DAY

The peak of the National Socialist election campaign was reached on March 4, which was designated "the day of national uprising." The great event was completely focused on Hitler personally, who was now presented with almost religious fervor as the savior of the nation. The radio transmitted a speech given by Hitler in Königsberg, once again introduced by Goebbels.[35] The plan for the spectacle had been announced to *Angriff* readers a week earlier: "From our suffering Eastern Frontier the gospel of a reawakened Germany will be proclaimed, and the whole German people will be aural witnesses to this unique, unprecedented mass event."[36]

The speech was not only broadcast but also conveyed by loudspeakers distributed throughout the Reich; they were placed in fourteen city squares in Berlin alone, to which the ranks of uniformed NSDAP members marched to take up their positions. The population had been exhorted to decorate their homes with flags. To "issue a wake-up call to the sluggish and the indecisive," as the *Völkischer Beobachter* described Nazi intimidation, "Hitler Youth and SA men" patrolled the streets. Bonfires were lit all over the Reich. After Hitler's speech his audience in Königsberg sang the famous "Niederländisches Dankgebet" (Dutch Thanksgiving Prayer), while the crowds listening to the broadcast transmitted over loudspeakers joined in with the singing.[37]

It is difficult to imagine anything more emotionally overblown than Goebbels's introduction to Hitler's appearance: "Throughout East Prussia the bells are ringing from church towers across the broad fields, over the great silent woods and the mysterious stillness of the Masurian Lakes. [...] From the Maas to the Memel, from the Etsch [Adige, South Tyrol] to the Great Belt, all of Germany is now bathed in the light of the fire of freedom. The day of national uprising has arrived. The people arise, the storm breaks forth."[38]*

After such all-out preparations, on election day Goebbels was full of confidence: "It will be a great victory."[39] Indeed, the NSDAP and the new government really had pulled out all the stops to ensure success—and not only with a massive propaganda effort. The liberal *Frankfurter Zeitung* described the situation in the capital as follows:

> Today there were hardly any black-red-gold flags to be seen in the Reich capital, no red ones, none with the symbol of the three arrows [flag of the antifascist organization Iron Front]. KPD and SPD flags were not allowed. [...] The intensive propaganda of the right had succeeded in creating a nervous, feverish atmosphere. Nonsensical rumors were flying around. Auxiliary police were deployed (a measure never before needed on election days), a signal to the population that danger must be in the air: Every policeman on watch on Sunday was armed with a carbine. The feeling of oppression among the population was great.[40]

With all these advantages, the National Socialists succeeded in gaining 43.9 percent of the ballot. Together with their allies, the DNVP,

---

* Translators' note: "Das Volk steht auf, der Sturm bricht los," a famous 1814 quotation from the patriotic poet Theodor Körner from the time of the War of Liberation, the "national uprising" against Napoleon.

campaigning as the "Black-White-Red Fighting Front," they formed a majority of nearly 52 percent.

The outcome was certainly a considerable success for the National Socialists, but taking into account the huge obstacles placed in the way of the left, the high level of support the Nazis enjoyed from powerful financiers, and the Nazis' hold on broadcasting, the increase of six and a half points over the previous record result of July 1931 was hardly sensational. The landslide expected and publicized in advance by the Party leadership did not materialize. In its triumphalist tone, Goebbels's diary entry on the evening of election day seems to betray a need to talk up the victory—especially given that in Berlin, with 34.6 percent, his performance was once again substantially below the Reich average.[41]

MINISTERIAL APPOINTMENT

After the election Goebbels was mainly preoccupied with the question of whether and in what way Hitler would keep his preelection promise of government office. At the beginning of March the difficulties involved in building up the promised ministry loomed so large that he felt like abandoning the whole project.[42]

On the day after the Reichstag election, when Hitler again talked over "his" ministry with him, he still "had his doubts," because he wanted "the whole thing. Press, radio, film, propaganda." With Funk, his future state secretary, he visited the Reich government press office on the Wilhelmsplatz, where he was soon to be installed: "Wonderful Schinkel building." In the days that followed, progress was made with planning for the new ministry, and in order to lighten his load as Gauleiter Goebbels appointed a deputy, the former Gau business manager Artur Görlitzer.[43] On March 11 the cabinet agreed to form a Reich ministry for popular enlightenment and propaganda.[44] "I'm so happy. What a [career] path! Minister at 35. Unimaginable."[45]

Meanwhile the new rulers were getting on with their "cold revolution," Goebbels's term for the coup d'état by which the regime was displacing other political institutions. As the new jargon had it, the latter were being "coordinated" or brought into line.[46] From the beginning, the Reichstag fire emergency decree was applied very widely; governors were dispatched to the different states, most crucially to the second-largest state, Bavaria.[47] There were local elections in Prussia on March 12. The NSDAP[48] in Berlin, with the benefit of massive state backing, achieved 38.2 percent of the vote and became the largest party, slightly ahead of the DNVP.

On the same day, in connection with National Remembrance Day, Goebbels took part in a memorial ceremony at the Linden Opera, where, he proudly remarked, he was already allowed to sit "among the ministers"—although he did not feel exactly positive about the event: "To me Hindenburg is like a mythical monument. Almost unreal. Next to him Hitler seems like a boy." He disliked the order of ceremony: "I'll do all this much better later on."[49]

On March 14 he received via the state secretary in the Reich Chancellery, Hans-Heinrich Lammers, the announcement of his appointment as a minister of the Reich. The next step was an appointment with the "Old Gentleman." The swearing-in ceremony was followed by a conversation with Hindenburg, who said "flattering things about my work."[50] He joined his first cabinet meeting the next day. "Everybody is very nice to me," he commented in his diary, but he did not have much of a clue about the content of the session.[51]

The following day he addressed the press in Berlin, explaining the duties of the new ministry. The creation of his department, he expounded, "was a revolutionary act of government, in that the new government intends no longer to leave people to their own devices. This government is a people's government in the truest sense of the word." The ministry would forge "active contact between the national government as the expression of the people's will and the people themselves," which for Goebbels clearly amounted to a "coordinating of the government and the people." He explained the title of his ministry as follows: "Popular education is essentially passive, while propaganda is active. We can't stop at telling the people what we want to do and informing them about how we're doing it. This information must be accompanied by active propaganda on the part of the government, propaganda aimed at winning people over." The plan was to "work on people until they accept our influence, until they begin to grasp in terms of ideas that what is taking place in Germany does not just *have* to be accepted but that they *can* accept it."[52]

POTSDAM DAY AND THE ENABLING LAW

The new government now proceeded to expand its power base in a relatively rapid series of steps, with the rank and file of the Party staging great spectacles and mass actions as an introduction to carefully targeted government measures. Goebbels was to play a central part in this gradual escalation of the regime's power and the process of "coordination."

His first great undertaking as head of propaganda for the regime was to make the arrangements for March 21, the ceremonial opening of the Reichstag. While the date of this event related to the anniversary of the opening of Parliament in 1871, the site of the ceremony, Potsdam, had special associations with Prussian monarchical and military traditions. In the Potsdam Garrison Church two Prussian kings, Frederick William I and Frederick II (the Great), were interred, and until the end of the First World War it was here that the flags and battle standards captured by the Prussian army from the Wars of Liberation onward were displayed. Here the alliance between National Socialists and national conservatives was to be valorized and celebrated. This was to be expressed above all by a solemn handshake between chancellor and president, where Hitler, in dark morning suit and top hat, would bow deeply to Hindenburg, wearing the uniform of a field marshal of the Kaiser's army. Accordingly, Goebbels's plan was that the formalities should be "grand and classical."[53]

One day before the event, however, Hitler and Goebbels decided not to attend the church service in Potsdam the next morning, opting instead to make a pointed statement by visiting the graves of SA members in the Luisenstadt cemetery in Berlin. The ostensible justification for this was that the two Catholics were both regarded by their church as "apostates." As a result, they arrived in Potsdam around half past eleven.[54]

Everything there was "hustle and bustle," Goebbels noted. Hindenburg seemed to him "almost like a stone monument." Goebbels was carried away by the show he himself had staged: "Then Hitler speaks. His best speech. At the end everybody very moved. I have tears in my eyes. This is how history is made. [. . .] Army, S.A., and Stahlhelm march. The old gentleman stands and salutes. Sheer ecstasy at the end."[55]

Immediately after the Potsdam ceremony, Hitler's ministers agreed on further emergency laws. They concerned the creation of special courts, prosecutions to deal with "treacherous" attacks on the new government, and a further penalty that Goebbels was particularly eager to see. Goebbels commented, "I act as a firebrand. String 'em up, string 'em up!"[56]

Two days later he attended the Reichstag session held in the Kroll Opera House, which had been turned into a temporary parliament and was now surrounded and sealed off by SA guards. The session opened with a speech by Hitler in which he gave a preview of the work of the government. But the main object was to force through the Enabling Law. The required two-thirds majority was achieved only because the Communist Party members had been arrested, and great pressure was put on members of the bourgeois centrist parties to vote in favor.

When the leader of the Social Democrats, Otto Wels, set out the reasons why his party had voted against the Enabling Law and voiced a challenge to this burgeoning dictatorship, Hitler made another speech, a direct response to Wels. By Goebbels's account, he "gave Wels a fierce lambasting. You don't often see such a slaughter. Hitler in full force. And a huge success."[57]

FIRST STEPS AS PROPAGANDA MINISTER

Later in March Goebbels took further preliminary steps as propaganda minister. He appeared at a series of press conferences, always presenting different angles: On the one hand he left no doubt about the Nazis' claim to power, not stopping at open threats; but on the other hand, by his apparent openness to unconventional ideas, he gave the impression that he was opposed to a stupid media dictatorship.

On March 25 he addressed three hundred broadcasting employees and then the directors of radio: "Some of them have got to go," was his diary comment on his audience.[58] Presenting himself as a "passionate lover of radio," he told the assembled mass media employees that their main task in future would be "intellectual mobilization." "The first rule" of their work must be "not to become boring." Radio must be close to the people, he said, and as an example of a successful impact on the people Goebbels "Potsdam Day." In short, those in charge of radio had to occupy "the same ideological ground" as the government.[59]

At an evening event he spoke to representatives of the film industry. Contrary to what is recorded in the diary, the text of his speech shows that he did not "develop a program" on this occasion. He did no more than issue a series of hints, warnings, and exhortations to the "film creators" concerning their future work.

Once again Goebbels introduced himself as someone who was "passionate"—this time about the cinematic arts. He himself had sat "with the Reich chancellor on many an evening in the cinema during the recent days of enervating struggle and found relaxation there." The present crisis of the cinema, said Goebbels, was an "intellectual one"; it could be overcome only by a "root and branch reform of German film." The film industry had better get used to the idea that the reign of the present rulers will be a good deal longer than those of the Weimar governments, because "we're here to stay!"

Goebbels then talked about some films that had made an "indelible impression" on him. The first movie mentioned was Sergei Eisenstein's revolutionary classic *Battleship Potemkin:* "Anyone without a solid ideology might be converted to Bolshevism by this film." Secondly, he praised Garbo's *Anna Karenina* as an example of "distinctly cinematic art." He moved on to Fritz Lang's *Die Nibelungen,* which was so "modern, so contemporary, so topical" that it had "profoundly moved those fighting for the National Socialist movement." Another positive example was Luis Trenker's film *The Rebel.* On the other hand, he criticized "colorless and shapeless works," and he wanted German film to have stronger "*völkisch* outlines." At the moment it lacked realism, it had "no connection with what was actually going on among the people." But dealing artistically with the current upheavals would only work if "you have put down roots in National Socialist soil."

An unambiguous warning followed: "We have absolutely no intention of allowing ideas that have been totally eradicated from the new Germany to be reintroduced by film, whether openly or in disguise." But he rejected "doctrinaire authoritarianism." And Goebbels acknowledged that there would still be room for pure entertainment in film: "Neither do we want to stop anyone [. . .] from making even the slightest little divertissement. You shouldn't live your principles from morning till night."[60]

Just a few hours before this meeting Goebbels had in fact made an example of the Fritz Lang film *Dr. Mabuse the Gambler*, banning it because, he said, it was a "practical guide to committing crime."[61] But his intention was not to exclude the director from making films; on the contrary, he picked him to make a film along lines laid down by himself.[62] However, Lang declined the offer, preferring instead to leave Germany. He did not do so instantly, as the director later claimed, but only after a few months. Lang may have heightened the drama in his encounter with Goebbels and the immediate aftermath, but the original version of the Goebbels diary does at least prove the meeting actually took place, something film historians have long doubted. It also shows that Goebbels was very accommodating toward the director. His Jewish origins were either unknown to Goebbels, or else Goebbels was prepared to turn a blind eye. In October, when Goebbels again refused to release a Lang film, *The Testament of Dr. Mabuse*, it was not because of reservations about Lang himself but on the grounds that this was another "guide to crime."[63] Goebbels simply disliked crime films.

On March 29 he held a reception for newspaper publishers and representatives of the German Press Association. In his address to them he declared that the press should "not only inform but also instruct." In particular, the "explicitly nationalist press" should surely "perceive that it was an ideal state of affairs" if "the press [. . .] is like a piano in the hands of the government, on which the government can play."[64]

On April 6 Goebbels appeared with Hitler before the Berlin correspondents of the German press. On this occasion Goebbels gave a talk on the topic of "The Press and National Discipline," which many have seen as the final swan song of press freedom. He stressed that "public opinion is made, and those who work at forming public opinion take upon themselves an enormous responsibility before the nation and the whole people." From this responsibility there arose for the press the requirement that any criticism should be kept "within the framework of a general intellectual national discipline."

And he threatened that those who set their minds against this requirement could expect "to be excluded from the community of those forces prepared to do the work of construction and to be considered unworthy to collaborate in forming the public opinion of the German people." Goebbels also announced there would be a new press law and came up with the motto that the future would be about "uniformity [. . .] of principles but multiformity [. . .] of nuances."[65]

ANTI-SEMITIC BOYCOTT

Between his two speeches to the press, the new propaganda minister was preoccupied mainly with the growing criticism from abroad, where there was concern about the increasing violence of the Nazis and signs of lawlessness under the new regime. The regime in its turn blamed international Jewish circles. It was not long after the election that Nazi activists in many towns were calling for a boycott of Jewish businesses. What was really happening was that potential customers were being deterred from entering Jewish shops by the threat of violence. Until the opening of the Reichstag, the regime had kept this wave of anti-Semitism under control. But now it seemed opportune to the Party leadership, backed by an anti-Semitic campaign authorized from "above," to let the Party's activist wing have its head, at the same time subjecting German Jews to great intimidation, with a view to silencing international Jewry's propaganda campaign against German "atrocities."

Thus the Jews became the target of a further "action" staged by the regime designed to consolidate its hold on power. It was one in which Goebbels figured prominently. On March 26, after visiting Hitler in Berchtesgaden, he was set on drawing up a proclamation calling for a boycott of German Jews.[66] At the same time Party headquarters formed a "central committee" to organize the boycott. Its membership included Robert Ley, Heinrich Himmler, and Hans Frank but no government representative: Nuremberg Gauleiter Julius Streicher presided. On March 29 the committee published in the *Völkischer Beobachter* a text composed by Goebbels[67] and explicitly authorized by Hitler.[68] From April 1 the population was urged to boycott all Jewish shops, doctors, and lawyers and all goods marketed by Jews.

The proclamation immediately had the desired effect: Various Jewish organizations issued declarations of loyalty to the regime and tried to exert a moderating influence on international criticism of the new government. On March 31, the eve of the action, after consulting Hitler and Göring, Goebbels called a press conference to announce that the measures would be confined to Saturday, April 1, and would only be resumed on the following Wednesday if the "atrocity propaganda abroad has not ceased completely."[69] This time limit was in deference to the reservations of their conservative coalition partners, who feared that the boycott would bring economic sanctions down upon Germany and have negative foreign policy repercussions. In addition, the deadline gave the Party leadership an early opportunity to declare the action an overwhelming success, which they duly did on the evening of April 3.[70]

Thus confined to a single day, the action—the first centrally directed anti-Semitic campaign under the new government—produced an unusual sight on German streets: In front of shop windows covered in anti-Semitic slogans stood SA and SS men on guard, preventing passersby from entering the shops.[71] On April 1 Goebbels checked out the effect of these measures for himself.[72] That evening he delivered a speech at a mass Nazi rally at the Berlin Lustgarten, in which he made it clear that the boycott could be resumed at any time.[73]

Shortly after the boycott—which was followed a few days later by the first special anti-Semitic legislation, including banning Jews from holding civil service positions—Goebbels addressed the subject of the future of Jewish artists in German cultural life. The occasion was provided by a letter from the conductor Wilhelm Furtwängler protesting the ousting of Jewish artists from German musical life and the disruption by Nazi activists of concerts under Jewish conductors such as Bruno Walter and Otto Klemperer. Goebbels sent a reply in which he suggested to Furtwängler that he should publish the correspondence in the press, which the conductor proceeded to do.

In his response, Goebbels said he could not follow Furtwängler's argument that he was only prepared to make one "distinction," that between good art and bad art. Goebbels retorted that only "art that drew fully upon *Volkstum* [the spirit of the people] could be good art and mean something to the *Volk* for whom it is created." The kind of "art in an absolute sense" that "liberal democracy" believed in did not exist. In this letter Goebbels also solemnly announced that there would be support for artists "of real ability whose activities outside their art do not offend against the basic norms of the state, politics, and society."

Furtwängler (whom Goebbels, shortly before the correspondence was published, made a point of visiting backstage on April 10 during a concert intermission) may have read this sentence as a guarantee that Jewish musicians could continue to perform. But such a guarantee was far from Goebbels's mind: He had no intention of letting Jewish artists continue appearing with German orchestras. For Goebbels, however, the correspondence was a great success. After all—coming as it did only a few days after the anti-Jewish boycott and the passage of the bill excluding Jews from the civil service—it gave him a welcome chance to demonstrate his generous approach to cultural policy. "That worked well," he noted in his diary.[74]

BEGINNING TO ENJOY POWER

By April the regime seemed to be so firmly in the saddle that Goebbels could afford to relax somewhat and bask in his newfound fame. To add to his sense of well-being, his relationship to Hitler, after the irksome early phase of the "seizure of power," was now fully restored. Whenever Hitler was in Berlin—and that was where he most often was during these months—Goebbels saw the leader almost daily, whether on official business or privately, with or without Magda.

In mid-April he permitted himself an "Easter trip." On Good Friday he flew from Berlin to Cologne, meeting Magda there. They went on to Koblenz, where they had a serious heart-to-heart talk. His diary shows that yet again they had differences to settle: "We felt that something wasn't quite right. The air needed to be cleared. Everything is straightened out now."[75] The next day they traveled to Freiburg via Heidelberg—towns that, of course, held many memories for Goebbels. Mentally at this time he was on an Anka nostalgia trip. So they continued via Konstanz, where he had spent time with Anka in 1918, to Meersburg, Lindau, Innsbruck, St. Johann, Bad Reichenhall, and finally to Berchtesgaden. "With Hitler by 9o'c. Like being at home."[76]

Goebbels and Magda stayed at Hitler's residence on the Obersalzberg, the Berghof, overnight. The next day Goebbels set out for Berlin with Hitler. Hitler was detained in Traunstein to pay his respects to a dying Party comrade, so Goebbels continued on his own to Mu-

nich, catching the night train to Berlin.[77] On April 19 he was surprised to find that Hitler had not yet returned to Berlin. In fact, he
was spending his birthday on April 20 in seclusion on the Tegernsee,
while, in his honor, meetings, torchlight processions, and marches
were taking place throughout the Reich.[78] He was not back in Berlin
until April 21.[79] Magda, who had remained on the Obersalzberg,
traveled directly from there to the Rhineland, where Goebbels indulged in one of the greatest triumphs of his life so far: an official
reception for this great son of Rheydt, recognized at last by his hometown.[80]

He saw this well-prepared visit as a "pure triumphal procession."
The townsfolk lined the street—now, of course, renamed in his
honor—where his parental house stood, and as his motorcade swept
into sight "the cheering became tempestuous," as the report in the
Rheydter Zeitung had it. His status as local hero was definitively confirmed when he announced the next day in front of the Town Hall
that the incorporation of Rheydt into the neighboring town of
Mönchengladbach in 1929, which had been an extremely painful
blow to local pride, was about to be reversed. Joy was unconfined;
Party formations staged a two-hour torchlight procession in honor of
the minister, and the National Socialist council showed its gratitude
by bestowing on him the Freedom of the City. Back in Berlin, he
gloated over the fact that the "Rheydt press was madly enthusiastic."[81]

When the law restoring the independence of Rheydt was proclaimed on June 24, Goebbels was back in the market square of his
hometown basking in the applause of the population, which did not
deter him from expressing his private aloofness from this small-town
population: "The petit bourgeois are going wild," he remarked in his
diary.[82]

NATIONAL LABOR DAY

As early as March 24—he had only just begun to construct his new
ministry—Goebbels had proposed in the cabinet the introduction of
three new national holidays: March 21, the "Day of the German Uprising"; May 1, "National Labor Day"; and the last Sunday in September, the "Day of National Honor."[83]

The most provocative of these suggestions was of course the idea of declaring May 1, then less than six weeks away, a national holiday. Since the end of the nineteenth century the First of May had been celebrated within the international socialist movement as the "day of the working-class struggle" and was observed in many countries with demonstrations and rallies. The socialist parties in Germany, since the end of World War I, had been pressing to have the date permanently recognized as a national paid holiday. Now this new government had adopted it. The other two proposals were deferred.[84]

Given the shortness of time, the preparations were bound to be somewhat hectic, but the Propaganda Ministry still managed to dress up "National Labor Day" as a day of bombastic national celebration.[85] On the morning of May 1 Goebbels and Hindenburg spoke in the Lustgarten, where "German youth" were drawn up. In the afternoon, according to official figures, a crowd of a million and a half assembled on Tempelhof Field, including workers' representatives from across the Reich. Goebbels opened the rally, and then Hitler spoke. The event was broadcast on the radio, of course, and included a commentary transmitted from a zeppelin circling above the grounds.[86]

Immediately after these pompous festivities had paid homage to the German worker, on May 2 the regime showed the other, authentic face of its labor policy: The unions were forcibly disbanded, an action Goebbels had discussed with Hitler at Berchtesgaden in mid-April. He noted its results in his diary on May 3: "Functionaries arrested. It all goes like clockwork. With Hitler. High spirits. The revolution continues."[87]

BUILDING THE PROPAGANDA MINISTRY

Goebbels was now making progress with constructing his ministry. The first structural features were beginning to emerge.

The directive to set up the ministry issued on March 13 had prescribed that its precise duties should be determined by the Reich chancellor, specifically including those that had previously been the responsibility of other ministries. This meant that Hitler was given carte blanche by the cabinet to reassign powers, even those central to the ministries in question; a control of controls that went far beyond previous practice. So Goebbels found himself in a favorable negotiating position vis-à-vis other departments, but he was dependent on Hitler's support. The new style of government was becoming apparent. Decisions geared to personalities were to replace responsibilities defined and fixed in advance.[88]

By March Goebbels had already taken over control of the radio from the Reich postal service and the Reich Ministry of the Interior.[89] He had also secured Göring's support for a transfer of authority over theaters to his new ministry's jurisdiction, out of the hands of the Reich Ministry of Education.[90] However, a few months later he was to find that Göring had arrogated to himself extensive powers over playhouses in Prussia.[91]

Early in April Goebbels procured assent in principle to the reallocating of the cultural section of the Reich Interior Ministry to his department.[92] But by the end of April it transpired that he was only going to be given responsibility for art. Overcoming further difficulties, he successfully negotiated more concessions in the end.[93] All in all, it is clear that his cabinet colleagues were not prepared to add to Goebbels's portfolio without a struggle, despite Hitler's solid support for him.

In May he succeeded against Foreign Office opposition in creating a foreign department of his own. The old press department of the Foreign Office remained in existence, but Goebbels would now take over "active propaganda" directed at foreign countries. It was a ruling that was to lead in later years to many tedious disputes between competing authorities.[94]

In May Goebbels took his first active steps in a variety of cultural areas. As with his speech to media representatives a few weeks earlier, on the one hand he flaunted the Nazis' claim to power, but on the other he tried to counter the impression that an era of cultural dictatorship was about to impose its own attitudes and tastes. He often took an implicit stand against the kind of one-sided, doctrinaire, völkisch traditionalism characterized by the activities of the National Socialist "Combat League for German Culture" under Alfred Rosenberg. Addressing theater managers and directors in the Kaiserhof on May 8, for example, Goebbels came across as relatively restrained: "Art is a matter of ability, not of will," he had no intention of "cramping artistic creativity." In his speech Goebbels tried to give the assem-

bled theater people a little artistic orientation. He acknowledged that
Expressionism had had "healthy beginnings" but had then degener-
ated into experimentation. But his prescription for the future direction of art was rather different: "German art in the next decade will
be heroic, steely but romantic, factual without sentimentality; it will
be nationalistic, with great depth of feeling; it will be binding and it
will unite, or it will cease to exist."[95]

His initial contribution to a new order of things in German literature was even more drastic. By way of an "intellectual" contribution
to the Nazi revolution, the German Students Association decided to
cleanse public libraries of "trashy and obscene" literature. The high
point was a public book burning, which took place on the Opernplatz in Berlin on May 10.[96] The official speaker at this barbaric event
was Joseph Goebbels, who declared that the "age of pretentious Jewish intellectualism" was over. He praised the book burning as "a
strong, great, and symbolic action—an action meant to put on record
for the whole world the collapse of the intellectual basis of the November Republic."[97] The books burned that evening included works
by Karl Marx, Leon Trotsky, Heinrich Mann, Erich Kästner, Sigmund
Freud, Emil Ludwig Cohn, Theodor Wolff, Erich Maria Remarque,
Alfred Kerr, Kurt Tucholsky, Carl von Ossietzky, and many more.[98]

On May 18 Goebbels spoke again, this time to members of the film
industry gathered in the tennis courts in Wilmersdorf. His speech
spelled out the fundamental message that "film cannot be immune to
these mighty intellectual and political upheavals." At the same time
he was at pains to stress that the "tendency" called for by the new
government did not imply any intention whatsoever of curbing artistic freedom.[99]

Goebbels also announced a new film credit bank, to be incorporated on June 1, 1933. Jointly underwritten by the Propaganda Ministry, the film industry, and several large banks, it made credit
available on favorable terms. If a project passed the scrutiny of state
agents, up to two thirds of production costs could be covered by this
credit. By 1935 70 percent of all feature films were being subsidized
by the bank. However, it was mainly the big film companies, Ufa and
Tobis, who benefited from the support.[100]

Two weeks later the cabinet passed a law creating an interim Reich
Film Chamber under the aegis of the Propaganda Ministry. From

now on, everyone involved in the film industry was obliged to join the Chamber, which was empowered to prescribe the framework for their financial operations. The Reich Film Chamber was the first step toward the "corporate" structuring of the entire cultural sector that was to make great strides in the following months.[101]

In the course of 1933 the Ufa and Bavaria film companies rushed out three films glorifying the Nazi "time of struggle." These projects did not by any means find whole-hearted favor with Goebbels. The first, *Brand of the SA,* he initially found "not as bad as I feared," but by the next day, after the premiere attended by Hitler, he changed his mind, deciding to "make massive cuts."[102]

His response to *Quex of the Hitler Youth* was mixed; here, too, he seems to have intervened, because after the premiere he declared proudly: "After the changes I made, it seems almost like a different film."[103] On the other hand, he would not allow the Horst Wessel film to be distributed to cinemas. When consulted, Hitler agreed with Goebbels's reaction. It was only after some reworking that the film was released, with the title *Hans Westmar.*[104] The fact was that the brash depiction of SA fighters no longer suited the regime's policy, which in the second half of 1933 was looking to bring the National Socialist revolution to an end. In a few public speeches, Goebbels made it clear that such films would not be welcome in future.

As minister for film, Goebbels came more and more into contact with directors and actors. Early in April he was already organizing a "film tea" at the Ministry that was attended by the most important film stars. Hitler dropped by and was delighted with the company.[105] In May Goebbels had a chance to discuss "film plans" with Luis Trenker ("a wild man").[106] He personally assisted the actress Maria Paudler, who was seeking work.[107] During a visit to the Ufa studios in Babelsberg he met the film star Willy Fritsch ("nice lad!"); a few weeks earlier at a party he had spent some time in the company of Hans Albers ("A good lad! Gutsy and decent.").[108]

Among the "film creators," there was one woman he was particularly taken by: The previous year Leni Riefenstahl had told him she was an ardent supporter of National Socialism, and she had now returned to Germany after a long spell of filming in Switzerland. In mid-May she reacted "enthusiastically" to his suggestion that she should make a "Hitler film," and at the end of the month she took part in his one-day outing to the Baltic, the diary making a laconic reference to another member of the party: "Boss with us."[109]

Goebbels thought that Riefenstahl was "the only star who understands us." After some discussion with Hitler she made an early start on the proposed film. The close contact between Goebbels and Riefenstahl was to last throughout the summer, culminating in the project of filming the Party rally.[110]

Meanwhile, the structure of the Propaganda Ministry was taking solid shape. At the end of June the department's responsibilities were set out in a new decree.[111] However, the desired "coordination" of radio—a key ambition of the new minister—faced an obstacle in the summer of 1933: The individual states still had a great deal of autonomy in this sphere. Göring in particular had no intention of giving up this independence for Prussia without a fight. But Goebbels managed to acquire Hitler's consent to annulling the remaining control of the regions over broadcasting.[112]

Ultimately, in July Hitler instructed the Reich governors in the various states about the central role of Goebbels's department in questions of culture and propaganda, especially with regard to broadcasting.[113] In the months that followed, the states ceded their interest in regional broadcasting stations to the Propaganda Ministry; regional broadcasting companies were liquidated and turned into "Reich broadcasting stations," all under the control of the Reich Broadcasting Corporation (Reichsrundfunkgesellschaft, RRG).[114]

Many staff in radio were fired from March onward,[115] and in the summer some broadcasting managers from the Weimar period were arrested.[116] Goebbels recorded that it was on his instructions that these "radio bigshots" had been sent to Oranienburg Concentration Camp.[117] But in the subsequent legal proceedings it transpired that the charges of corruption against these former radio bosses had been trumped up.[118]

The new ministry now consisted of seven sections. The core of the operation was the propaganda section, led by the current staff manager Wilhelm Haegert.[119] It was here that all of the planning and direction of the large-scale propaganda campaigns took place, with pride of place being taken by the desk responsible for mass rallies, managed by Leopold Gutterer,[120] a former Gau head of propaganda. The know-how acquired in the past by the Party's Reich propaganda office in organizing large-scale events and extensive campaigns was now applied within the propaganda section to the work of the new ministry.

The press section was led by the journalist Kurt Jahncke,[121] whose politics were nationalist rather than Nazi. The film section was under the command of Ernst Seeger (since 1924 head of the Board of Film Censors; Goebbels had acquired him from the Interior Ministry);[122] and actor and Nazi functionary Otto Laubinger was responsible for theater. The first head of the foreign section was Hermann Demann, followed in 1935 by Franz Hasenöhrl, the exporter and former head of the China country group of the NSDAP Auslands-Organisation, (Foreign Organization).[123]

After the dismissal of Gustav Krukenberg, head of radio, the radio section was taken over by Horst Dressler-Andress, previously broadcasting specialist in the Party's Reich propaganda office, and Eugen Hadamovsky (previously Gau radio supervisor in the Berlin Gau office) headed the Reich Broadcasting Corporation.[124] Erich Greiner became head of the Administrative Section of the Ministry: A nationalist-conservative civil servant who never joined the NSDAP, he had been a principal officer in the Finance Ministry.[125] Apart from State Secretary Walther Funk, Goebbels was assisted by his personal adviser Karl Hanke, the former organizing manager in the Berlin Gau office.

Goebbels's choice of important collaborators was therefore marked from the beginning by a high degree of pragmatism: Apart from Party propaganda specialists and Party functionaries, there was plenty of room for administrators and experts not selected on account of their NSDAP affiliation.

EXCURSION INTO FOREIGN AFFAIRS: GOEBBELS'S TRIP TO ROME

In late May Goebbels set out for Rome on his first journey abroad as a Reich minister. He was not the first member of the new government to visit the Italian capital. In April and May Göring and von Papen had both been there, and just before Goebbels's visit, Göring had returned to the Eternal City in connection with foreign policy negotiations. The immediate objects of Goebbels's trip were to promote personal connections with leading representatives of the fascist regime and to study some of its cultural institutions which he had long regarded as role models. Ultimately what concerned him was a series of practical questions arising out of ongoing projects in his domain. Beyond all this, in general the idea was for Goebbels to help break down the foreign affairs isolation in which the new German government found itself. However, Goebbels was not to play a major part in shaping the political relations between the two countries.

Crossing the border by train at the Brenner Pass on May 28, he noted with gratitude that Mussolini had sent a saloon car to meet him. In Bologna he encountered "effusive hospitality," and after a further overnight journey he arrived in Rome, where he was greeted with a "great fuss." For the next few days, it was a matter of getting through a crowded engagement schedule.

After some briefing by the German ambassador, Ulrich von Hassell ("an uninspired petit bourgeois," "completely incompetent," "has got to go"), Goebbels had initial discussions with Italian foreign minister Fulvio Suvich, a "wily native of Trieste" who was by no means well disposed toward Germany. They talked about the "global situation," dwelling briefly on Mussolini's "Four-Power Pact," which was nearing ratification at the time.

At the ensuing audience in the royal palace he gained a "good impression" of the Italian king. Afterward he was taken on a tour around the Italian capital: "Eternal Rome. [. . .] Just looking gives me a warm feeling. Such a fulfilment of long-felt yearning." There followed a reception given by Mussolini, his longstanding hero, whose aura he obviously found spell-binding: "He's short. But a huge head. Quite classical-looking. Is like a friend to me right away. 'Il dottore.' We hit it off immediately. And talk for an hour. About everything. He's quite delighted with my explanations."

The next morning he breakfasted with the president of the organization for artists and professionals, Emilio Bodrero, and met several prominent Italian intellectuals. In the evening he was invited by Mussolini to a dinner in the Grand Hotel. "Great gala event. Mussolini leads Magda in. She performs wonderfully well. He looks magnificent. Charming to Magda."

Other visits followed the next day, including one to the L'Unione Cinematografica Educativa (LUCE), the Italian propaganda organization, whose director he had met in April in Berlin,[126] as well as the head office of the fascist leisure organization Dopolavoro, which impressed Goebbels very much: "We must do something like that. The people at leisure. Sport, recreation, hospitals, tourism."

The next day's visits included the Fascist Revolution exhibition: "Fascism is modern and has close ties with the people. We should learn from it." After a visit to the German Academy and a speech to the Roman section of the NSDAP Foreign Organization and German expatriates ("In great form. [. . .] Rapturous success"), he left Rome the same day to head back north.[127]

Two points emerge from Goebbels's report on this varied program of visits: first, how easily impressed he was by the Italians' charm offensive. He was simply not capable of perceiving that all the carefully chosen visits and receptions, the many honors, presents, and gestures of political goodwill were not about Dr. Paul Joseph Goebbels, the brilliant propaganda expert and hero of the Nazi revolution, but part of the Italian regime's efforts to improve its relations with Germany. A second important point is that the significance of the role played by the German propaganda minister in shaping Italo-German relations stood in inverse proportion to the amount of ceremony surrounding Goebbels's reception in Rome—something that becomes clear from reading Goebbels's diary, where he indulges freely in self-satisfied reflections on his pompous welcome in Italy.

The fact is that while he was in Italy—behind his back—the German and Italian regimes were making decisive progress toward political agreement. The agreement in question was the Four-Power Pact, a project pursued by Mussolini since 1931, and to which he returned in March 1933. According to the pact, the four leading West European countries—Britain, France, Germany, and Italy—were to take the lead in ensuring the security of Europe and revise the Versailles Treaty. After many months of negotiation, however, the original draft had been reduced to a collection of declaratory compromise formulae that in no way reconciled the political interests of the participating nations. On the German side, Göring had conducted the concluding negotiations during his Rome visit on May 19 and 20. The decision to join the pact was made at the end of May, while Goebbels was in Italy. It was made in Berlin after intense consultations involving Hitler, Neurath, Göring, and Werner von Blomberg, and the treaty was finally signed on June 7 in Rome. Goebbels was not informed by Hitler until the day before—although he had been in the dictator's company almost without interruption since his return from Italy. Goebbels noted the news laconically in his diary, but it cannot have escaped his attention that his Italian visit had been first and foremost what would nowadays be called a public relations event.[128]

CONFLICTS WITHIN THE NATIONAL SOCIALIST REVOLUTION

The Reich conference of NSDAP leaders took place in Berlin in mid-July. Goebbels held forth on the need to "cleanse the Party" and to take action "against the arrivistes," a matter he had been pursuing for some weeks for Hitler's benefit, and very publicly.[129]

So, for example, in several speeches in May and June Goebbels had stressed that the Party must not be "distorted" by mass recruitment. On May 21 at a general parade of members of the Nazi industrial cell organization in the Grunewald Stadium, he had exclaimed: "Don't admit to this movement either communists in disguise or the covert petit bourgeois. This movement is revolutionary and will remain revolutionary. The revolution is not over yet." That the National Socialists were serious about their "revolution" and that they intended it to continue was another leitmotif of his speeches in those weeks; it united him with SA boss Röhm, who also never ceased to beat the revolutionary drum at the time.[130]

At the leaders' conference in mid-June, Goebbels proposed a concrete move: a decree to regulate the "incorporation of new Party comrades into the National Socialist organization," a suggestion that was taken up by Hitler.[131] It was with satisfaction that Goebbels listened to Hitler's speech that same day, in which he not only told the Party leaders about purifying the Party but also committed them to a slogan that was music to Goebbels's ears: "The revolution continues."[132]

Goebbels also used the leaders' conference to announce a social "relief drive" for the coming winter, which soon appeared in his notes under the motto "war against hunger and cold." All in all, at this conference he had succeeded in projecting himself as the exponent of a radical, "socialist" Party line.[133]

During this time the "coordination" of political life was making rapid progress. On June 22 the SPD was prohibited from all further activity. After the Stahlhelm had been incorporated into the SA on June 21 and the "Fighting Squads" of the Nationalists had been banned, the German Nationalist Party effectively disbanded itself at the end of June. At the same time, the head of the DNVP, Hugenberg, stepped down after causing some irritation at the London Economic Conference. Reporting on the cabinet meeting of June 27, at which Hitler announced this development, Goebbels simply noted laconically: "Hitler conveys Hugenberg case. No tears shed."[134] But something did come out of this for Goebbels, as Hitler told him the next day: "Hugenberg's official residence. Fabulous!"[135]

So by the time Magda came back from vacation Goebbels was able to surprise her with a present: the keys to Hermann Göring Strasse 20, where, however (under Albert Speer's direction), rebuilding was still going on. Goebbels enthused in his diary about his "fairy-tale palace," set in a "glorious park."[136] By the middle of the month it was ready for them to move in, and they gave a housewarming reception that was attended by Hitler.[137]

The NSDAP was also making progress with consolidating its power: On July 5 the Center Party dissolved itself. Three days later came the signing of the Concordat with the Vatican; Catholicism as a political factor was thereby neutralized. On July 14 the cabinet imposed a law forbidding the formation of new parties.

Meanwhile, Hitler had introduced a change in the process of taking over power. The phase that saw the regime gradually extending its power by means of carefully targeted "actions" by the Party rank and file, combined with legal measures, was, by the middle of 1933, slowly coming to an end. Goebbels grasped that Hitler had decided against any continuation of the National Socialist revolution, a deliberate challenge to Röhm, whose fast-growing SA threatened to become an unpredictable power factor.[138] Goebbels, now swiftly changing course, began to retreat from the emphatically "revolutionary" position he had been preaching in the previous weeks. In *Der Angriff* of July 11 he wrote an article expounding once more the need to "purify" the Nazi movement, which had expanded greatly in the previous few months. But this time his arguments were directed against the Nazi industrial cell organization, which he accused of "Marxist tendencies."[139] The press was instructed to syndicate this contribution.[140] He struck the same note in a radio broadcast a few days later, the text of which was also reproduced across the German press. "Fabulous response in the press," wrote the delighted propaganda minister. In any case, it was now on record that he had placed himself on the right side in any forthcoming conflict over the future of the "Nazi revolution."[141]

He rapidly abandoned the revolutionary rhetoric he had deployed in the previous weeks.

CHAPTER 11

"Only Those Who Deserve Victory Will Keep It!"

Consolidating the Regime

Goebbels appearing on an unaccustomed foreign political stage during the meeting of the League of Nations in Geneva, September 1933. Whereas he believed that he had impressed foreign critics and skeptics there, in fact his appearance was simply a maneuver staged by Hitler in order to distract the international public from his imminent spectacular break with the League of Nations.

Early in July 1933, Goebbels and his wife planned to add to their family. The way that Goebbels recorded this decision in his diary suggests that it was mainly his idea: "I have resolved with Magda that we want another baby. A boy this time." The wish soon came true: Magda was already pregnant before the end of July.[1]

On July 11, Magda went off alone on a three-week summer vacation in Heiligendamm; Goebbels stayed behind in Berlin. They saw each other only twice in that time: once when Goebbels made a little detour from Hamburg to the Baltic seaside resort and again toward the end of the month, when he went to the Derby in Hamburg and stopped off briefly to see Magda.[2] Goebbels's diary entry about his short trip to the Baltic shows that things were not altogether ideal in their marriage: "All this work and a certain sense of weariness had made us drift apart slightly. We've got to get back to the way we were. We've promised each other as much."[3] In mid-July, though, he and Magda had a serious argument: She wanted take on a role in public life by becoming the patron of an official Nazi fashion design office. "Magda must act in a more reserved manner. This won't do. In this respect she causes me nothing but trouble."[4]

The argument continued the next day, and Magda refused to go with him to the Bayreuth Festival as planned. So Goebbels went to Bayreuth alone. Hitler, whom he met there for lunch, was "appalled that Magda isn't with me" and arranged for a plane to bring her from Berlin. Late in the afternoon, just as the intermission following the first act of *Die Meistersinger von Nürnberg* began, Magda arrived at the Festival Theater. "She's more beautiful than all of them," observed Goebbels, but also: "Very depressed mood."

After the performance Hitler invited them in for coffee in the little house he used when in Bayreuth: "He makes peace between Magda and me. A true friend. He backs me up, too: There's no place for women in political life." The argument with Magda flared up again later, but eventually they reconciled. The question of Magda taking on a public function outside the Goebbels household, however, did not go away.[5]

At the beginning of August he went on vacation to Heiligendamm with Magda, but various engagements interrupted his time there. He used his stay to start writing a new book, with the working title "Path to Power"; this was probably the inception of *Vom Kaiserhof zur Reichskanzlei*. A few visitors came over to Heiligendamm. Leni Riefenstahl, for example, whom he had met with frequently in Berlin, dropped in for two days, no doubt to talk about filming the Party rally, and he met the actor Werner Krauss, by whom he was so deeply impressed that he instantly appointed him deputy head of the Reich Theater Chamber.[6]

On August 6 he attended a conference of Gau and Reich leaders on the Obersalzberg, where Hitler gave a three-hour speech. According to the text of the address printed the next day in the *Völkischer Beobachter,* Hitler's topics included the autobahn construction project and the establishment of a Senate. Goebbels added something that was passed over in the *Völkischer Beobachter* report: "Sharply attacked the churches"; "we ourselves will become a church."[7]

On August 20, while Goebbels was busy in Berlin, Magda went to Munich, where Hitler met her and then escorted her to Berchtesgaden. Goebbels arrived two days later. Goebbels had several important discussions lined up on the Obersalzberg, including one with Göring, "the old horror." Goebbels was annoyed by Göring's wish to become a general: "Why not go straight to field marshal?" But the three of them—Goebbels, Göring, and Hitler—were united in their negative view of Rosenberg and his Party Foreign Office, and in their criticism of conditions in the German Labor Front. Its director, Robert Ley, was "not up to it. Bad ambience. We are concerned about his Labor Front. A lot of Marxism."[8]

On the afternoon of August 24, Goebbels, Magda, and Hitler went to view a site above Walchenfeld House, where the Goebbelses planned to build a house.[9] Afterward he had a "thorough discussion with the boss" covering a series of essential points.

After agreeing that Goebbels would give a key speech at the next Party rally on the topic of "the race question and world propaganda," they went on to discuss the further consolidation of the regime. They agreed, for example, on the future of the individual German states: "Got to go. As soon as possible. We're not here to conserve them, but to liquidate them." All Gauleiters should become governors, and in addition there should be a "Senate of the N.S.D.A.P." to guarantee "the stability of the regime."[10] They also talked over the question of what to do about the presidency once the eighty-five-year-old Hindenburg left office, probably not too far away. In March, Hitler, still undecided about this, had considered appointing Prince Auwi as Hindenburg's successor, not least because he hesitated to take over the presidency himself if it meant making the obvious candidate, Göring, Reich chancellor.[11] Now though, in August, Hitler was saying that when the time came he wanted to be "proclaimed" president immediately; his assumption of office was then to be blessed retrospectively by a plebiscite.[12] He also announced to Goebbels his stamp of approval for two pieces of legislation, relating to the press and to the cultural chamber.

On August 25 Goebbels left Berchtesgaden for Munich: "Magda is staying on."[13] In the evening Hitler followed him to Munich, and they traveled to Berlin together. Around August 28 Hitler returned to Berchtesgaden, and Hitler and Goebbels met up again on August 31 in Nuremberg. Magda stayed on the Obersalzberg during this time.

PARTY RALLY

Goebbels took part in the Party rally as a visitor—although a very important one—and not as one of the organizers. The arrangements for the rally, the gigantic annual get-together of the NSDAP, were not in his hands but were the direct responsibility of Party headquarters. In the hubbub of the rally, this year completely dominated by the Führer cult, he spotted an unexpected visitor: "Dr. Mumme is sitting down below in the hotel. Intolerable." A confidant told him that Anka was "going completely to pieces." "Lost! What a decline! I'm very sorry to hear it."[14] But Goebbels was determined to surrender totally to the atmosphere of the event, this mixture of vast milling crowds, marching, roll calls, "solemn moments," and rousing speeches.

The rally was formally opened on September 1. Goebbels heard speeches by Hess, Streicher, Gross, and Göring as well as Hitler's proclamation, read out by Gauleiter Adolf Wagner. He particularly liked the "tough message to the states, especially Prussia," and noted that Hitler's speech worked in the phrase the Führer had used to himself a few days before: "Not to conserve but to liquidate."[15]

In the afternoon he took part in the cultural session. "Boss talks about cultural questions. Completely new perceptions. Hot on Dada-ists and the like"—for Goebbels an early warning not to make his openness to "modern" tendencies in art too public. The next day Goebbels gave his set-piece address to the rally. In his speech he con-centrated above all on the regime's anti-Jewish measures and an-nounced that he was going to launch a big propaganda campaign to counter international criticism of the government. He also stressed that the "settlement of the Jewish question along legal lines [had been] the most decent way to solve the problem," hypocritically adding the rhetorical question: "Or should the government have fol-lowed the democratic principle, complied with the sovereignty of the majority, and left it all to the people?" It was impossible to miss the veiled threat of violence to German Jews from the spontaneous forces of "popular anger."[16]

"The parade ground is a magnificent sight. 100,000 men marching up. The organization goes like clockwork. Hitler comes at 8 o'c. A stirring moment," reads Goebbels's diary entry the next day. The cer-emony in honor of the dead and the solemn "dedication" of SA stan-dards using the "blood flag" of 1923 seemed to him like a "religious service": "we don't need the dog collars any more." In the afternoon, another high point was a four-hour military review by Party forma-tions. Finally came the closing ceremony, at which Hitler gave the concluding speech: "Grand and fundamental. No compromises. Fan-tastic ovations at the end." That evening, back in Berlin, the shouts of "'Heil,' the marching steps, and the fanfares were still ringing in [his] ears."

Goebbels's report above all makes one thing clear: The chief orga-nizer of the ballyhoo of National Socialist propaganda was all too ready to be captivated by the "fine show" with which the regime cel-ebrated itself.

MOBILIZING NATIONAL COMRADES: CELEBRATIONS AND LARGE-SCALE EVENTS

Only a week after the rally ended, on September 13, Hitler and Goeb-bels jointly opened the Winter Relief drive Goebbels had been pre-paring for since July.[17] The concept of Winter Relief rested on the notion of supplementing the limited state assistance available by holding large-scale street collections, lotteries, and voluntary pay cuts as well as by offering voluntary work and services—all, of course, accompanied by more or less forceful pressure from the Party organs. While Propaganda Minister Goebbels was to remain nominally in charge of this plan in the years to come, its practical application was in the hands of the National Socialist People's Welfare organization (Nationalsozialistische Volkswohlfahrt, NSV). During the winter of 1933 more than 358 million Reichsmarks were raised, however, a sum that increased every year and was presented by the regime as an important indicator of the population's support for its policies.[18] The campaign against "hunger and cold" announced by Goebbels, meant to bring the German people together as "one great community,"[19] additionally gave him the chance to strike a different note from that of a certain prevalent "pompous style."[20] In this way he could put himself forward as a man of the people, as the champion of an egalitarian national community. In other words, he was trying—since "revolutionary" demands had been rejected by Hitler—to align the radical, "socialist" image he had cultivated in previous years with the conditions of the Third Reich as it was gradually being consolidated.

The Party rally and the opening of the Winter Relief drive in September were the overture to a further series of large events and propaganda actions that held the attention of the German population during the autumn and winter.

On September 13, at a Sportpalast event for Party functionaries, he explained his tactics for mobilizing public opinion:[21] "Of course, we know how to celebrate festivals. But we don't just celebrate festivals without a reason, and every celebration has a meaning, and after every celebration comes some kind of action which has only been made possible by the celebration." By way of example, Goebbels brought up Potsdam Day and the state opening of the Reichstag that followed it; the May 1 celebrations and the occupation of trade union headquarters that came immediately afterward; and the Party rally and the campaign against "hunger and cold." For years a "grand-scale plan" had been followed, and this was now being put into effect "bit by bit and move by move, and every great national day is only a milestone on the way to realizing this one grand plan."

Naturally, no such "grand plan" actually existed, but Goebbels was determined to use every opportunity to present to the German population and the international public a pyrotechnic display of festivities. While the first months after the "seizure of power" had been entirely about "revolutionary" changes, now in the second half of the year celebrations were meant to mark the internal consolidation of the regime and the solidarity of the "national community."

One of these grand events took place for the first time on October 1, just two weeks after the launching of the Winter Relief campaign: the harvest festival. Goebbels opened the proceedings that morning with a radio speech that was broadcast by all stations. Then, together with Agriculture Minister Richard Walther Darré, he welcomed a delegation of farmers at Tempelhof Airport; they were subsequently received by Hitler. There followed a "hot-pot" meal, intended to set in motion a new campaign: In future during the winter months all "national comrades" should go without their Sunday roast on the first Sunday in every month in favor of a stew and donate the money saved to the cause of Winter Relief. The leadership elite were setting a good example.

And then the whole government flew together to Hanover, where, as Goebbels recorded, they drove in a single "triumphal procession" the thirty miles to Bückeberg near Hamelin, where the main harvest festival event was being held. So many people had flocked to it that the specially constructed festival ground, built into a hillside, looked to Goebbels like a "living mountain." Once more he entered wholeheartedly into the great occasion: "Half a million. Fantastic teeming mass. After dusk the searchlights and beacons flare up. Then Darré speaks. Good. And Hitler very good. The moon above it all. The crowd sings: Now thank we all our God! Emotional moment."[22]

Further events followed in October. Overnight, from October 14 to 15, he traveled with Hitler to Munich, where the "Festival of German Art" was celebrated and the foundation stone for the House of German Art was laid.[23] From Munich he flew to Bonn. In the Siebengebirge mountains, on Mount Himmerich, a monument was to be erected celebrating the defeat of Rhineland separatism. He gave a speech there on the theme "We don't want war—we want peace with honor."[24]

With his new duties as propaganda minister and the increasing number and variety of festivities and mass meetings with which National Socialism celebrated its rule, Goebbels's repertoire as a speaker also expanded. Whereas before 1933 it was the inflammatory language of the agitator that had filled his rhetoric entirely, now he was moving on to other forms. Alongside his radio speeches—ever more frequent but mostly somewhat monotonous—he had hit on a form of expression much more congenial to him in his lively "commentaries" framing Hitler's appearances. His range also included the minister's rather affable, half-confidential chats to various people in his own line of work; the solemn and measured style of address whenever he appeared in a representative role; and finally, the high-flown speeches of allegiance to the Führer whom he so revered. All in all, as a rhetorician Goebbels developed an amazing virtuosity.[25]

REICH CULTURE CHAMBER AND PRESS LAW

When he visited the Obersalzberg on August 24, 1933, Goebbels had gained approval for two bills that were to be indispensable in buttressing his position of power as propaganda minister: the Press Law and the Cultural Chamber Law.

As early as July 1933 Goebbels had begun an initiative to introduce a Reich culture chamber, which was to include all those working in the cultural sphere. Goebbels was provoked into acting quickly to form this unitary organization because of Ley's plans to incorporate the whole of the working population into a system of "employment-related" organizations—which would also contain all cultural activity. In a letter to the head of the Reich Chancellery, Goebbels had expressed his opposition to this attempt at "representation by material interests" which would not do justice to the "individual organizational life enjoyed by the cultural professions." He also announced his intention of creating a Reich culture chamber.[26] Coming back later to his critique of Ley, he accused him of "reviving trade-union thinking"[27] and charged him with wanting to compel the integration of cultural interest groups into the German Labor Front by the use of force and the illegal requisitioning of the property of others.[28] By the middle of July he had succeeded in gaining Hitler's agreement in principle to the founding of an independent Culture Chamber.[29]

By August his ministry had drafted a Culture Chamber Bill, which got past the cabinet with some difficulty despite Hitler's approval.[30] The law, consisting of just a few sentences, entitled him to enroll in "public bodies" members of professions that fell within the purview of his ministry. The groups created, in addition to a Reich chamber of literature, were chambers for press, radio, theater, music, and fine art, all to be organized along the lines of the Reich Film Chamber established in July. This section of the law contained Goebbels's decisive lever on power, since his first decree establishing the Reich Film Chamber had stipulated that membership of the chamber was a precondition for working in the film industry and that, by means of directives, the chamber could regulate the economic conditions of the entire industry.

The same powers were now to apply to the new Culture Chamber as a whole.[31] By the end of the year he would have cultural workers in sixty-three professional associations organized into seven chambers.[32] What was truly crucial for Goebbels, however, was that "I've got the whole organization in my hands. Great intellectual authority."[33]

In parallel with constructing the Reich Culture Chamber, Goebbels set about perfecting his control of the German press. In the first few months of the regime the main ways to silence opposing and critical voices had been the prohibiting of newspapers and the use of all kinds of intimidation in order to force the press to toe the government line. Now, in the second half of 1933, a system of press direction came about by stages.

One important step was taking control of the Reich press conference, a gathering organized during the Weimar Republic by journalists based in Berlin. By March 24 it had been moved from the Palais Leopold, the location of the government press office, to the former Prussian Upper House of Parliament. The political composition of the select committee of journalists convening the conference was now purely Nazi or nationalist.

However, on July 1, 1933, the head of the press department in the Propaganda Ministry, Kurt Jahncke, abolished the old conference and convened a new one, to be presided over by him. This fundamentally altered the nature of the conference. From now on it was no longer an event organized by journalists to inform themselves but a conduit for Propaganda Ministry directives to the press, effectively a press briefing rather than a conference.[34]

After a few difficulties—overcoming the objections of publishers, reservations on the part of the vice chancellor—Goebbels succeeded in getting his press law passed by the cabinet.[35] The Press Law of October 4, 1933, imposed certain conditions on journalists: They had to be, among other things, of "Aryan extraction" and must not be married to "a person of non-Aryan extraction." Admission to the profession entailed registration in a professional directory, by which the journalist became a member of the Reich Press Association.[36]

The basic idea of the law was, in the words of the Propaganda Ministry's official explanation, the "transformation of the press into a public organ and its legal and intellectual incorporation into the State." As a result, from now on journalists were deemed to hold "public office";[37] it accorded with their new status that, for example, where a journalist was fired by his publisher because of a difference of opinion, such a dismissal could now be contested before an employment tribunal.

Having taken over responsibility in this way for the journalists, the Propaganda Ministry could then go on to extend the system of press directives. The "language regulations" issued at the daily press conference were formulated in written orders to the whole of the press. With the "coordination" of the news agencies, moreover, the Propaganda Ministry was in a position to channel the flow of information reaching editorial offices.[38] It was made abundantly clear to the accredited journalists at the press conference in October that they were "officeholders entrusted with serving the minister." It was announced that, in the case of any "transgressions," journalists, and particularly editors-in-chief, would "be held personally accountable."[39]

This warning related directly to a tirade against the press that Hitler had delivered on October 17 to Reich leaders and Gauleiters, which obviously prompted Goebbels to introduce certain measures for press restructuring. In his speech to the Gauleiters Hitler had been very critical of the Party press, deploring its uniformity and comparing the Party journalists unfavorably with, of all things, the bourgeois press. It was very evident that the measures Goebbels brought in to direct the press had gone too far even for the dictator himself.[40] As he nearly always did when his own work was the target of criticism, Goebbels sought to downplay the problem: "We've got a few small worries about the press," he noted in his diary.[41]

In connection with his diatribe about the press, Hitler a few days later, through Hess, forbade leading Party comrades to be newspaper publishers. This was aimed above all at Goebbels, who had himself been wondering whether he ought to pull out of *Der Angriff*; he did so at the end of October, having published the paper for six years.[42]

GOEBBELS'S APPEARANCE IN GENEVA

Meanwhile, in September Goebbels had undertaken another important step aimed at using an official appearance to give himself prominence in the field of foreign relations.

Goebbels could not help noticing at the beginning of the month that the Reich Party rally had played very badly abroad. The meeting of the League of Nations in October seemed a good opportunity to break out of the regime's still-prevalent isolation and especially to confront the international criticism provoked by the persecution of the Jews. It was also a chance to create a favorable climate for the imminent disarmament conference. When Foreign Minister Neurath suggested that Goebbels should accompany him to Geneva, he was all for it.[43]

So it was that on September 24 Goebbels arrived in Geneva to participate as a member of the German delegation in the annual assembly of the League of Nations. Joseph Goebbels, the Party agitator, the rabid anti-Semite, the choreographer of gigantic mass rallies, now took the floor as a diplomat. It is not surprising that the international press were very interested to see how he would perform in this unaccustomed role.[44]

Goebbels made a very self-confident entrance in Geneva, proving more than capable of dealing with diplomatic interchanges. He relied entirely on his ability instinctively to weigh the strengths and weaknesses of his interlocutors and convince them of his argument in direct exchanges. What counted was the "personal impression."

He found the League of Nations meeting, opened on September 25, "depressing. An assembly of the dead. Parliamentarianism of the nations." He penned little caricature sketches of the delegates of other nations: "Sir John Simon: Engl. Foreign [Minister]. Tall and imposing. But an old hand. Paul Boncour: vain poseur. Frenchman and writer. Not much of a man.[45] Dollfuss: a dwarf, a dandy, a rogue. Otherwise nothing out of the ordinary. Formalities this morning. I'm being looked over and appraised. How vastly superior we Germans are, though."

The next day he had a series of discussions. First of all he met the Polish foreign minister, Józef Beck, whom he sized up as "clever and natural": "Wants to move away from France, more toward Berlin. Has a series of concerns, but they're not major ones. We can deal with Poland." The Swiss Federal Council member Giuseppe Motta ("a politicizing petit bourgeois") was followed by the Italian foreign minister, Fulvio Suvich (whom he consistently called "Suvic"): "Suvic is opposed to us. He tries to cover it up. Talks about worldview and liberalism. But I'm not taken in!"

Significantly, the speech he gave the next day to about three hundred journalists was the high point of his excursion into diplomacy:

"Received quite coolly. I talk and have one of my best days. Striking success. In the discussion I'm the absolute winner. Tricky questions, but I'm never lost for an answer. It all goes well. I'm quite blissful." In his speech, Goebbels represented the reconstruction efforts of National Socialism in the most glowing colors. The new regime was being carried along by the popular will; in fact, it was actually a "noble kind of democracy," which wanted nothing but international parity and peace.[46]

After a few more discussions there was a return to Berlin which, according to Goebbels's subjective impression, was nothing less than a triumphant journey. For Goebbels there could be no doubt about the conclusion to draw from this trip to Geneva: "Hitler must negotiate with Daladier. In private. Direct and open. That's the solution. Legality in foreign affairs policy."[47] A few days later he was able to put this view to Hitler: "France, that's the alpha and omega. We must have breathing-space now. Otherwise another occupation of the Rhineland is on the cards."[48]

Hitler's fundamental re-think about the disarmament question— the Geneva Conference was due to resume in October—came as a relative surprise to him: From the diary it is clear that Hitler certainly did not ask for his opinion when he called Goebbels to the Reich Chancellery on October 11 to inform him of his "completely new ideas about the disarmament question."[49]

The fact was that even by this point Hitler was determined to take a drastic step with regard to disarmament, to which he had already agreed in principle on October 4 with Reich Defense Minister Werner von Blomberg and State Secretary Bernard von Bülow.[50] A week later, only one day after informing Goebbels about his "completely new idea," Hitler announced his new policy in the cabinet: Germany would withdraw from all international bodies that did not grant her parity, including, therefore, the League of Nations. He would announce this decision together with a message of peace and secure popular backing for it by seeking reelection to the Reichstag. Hitler had already developed this idea of a kind of "plebiscite" on his policies in a discussion with Goebbels in July.[51] Withdrawal from the League of Nations simply offered a suitable move to initiate a plan conceived long before.[52] The cabinet's approval of this plan on October 13 was a mere formality.[53]

For all his vigorous engagement with the disarmament question, as shown by his participation in Geneva, it is plain that Goebbels was not brought into the decision-making process in early autumn 1933. In fact, although they met often in this period, Hitler had left him in the dark for more than a week about his intention of making a policy volte-face. In view of Hitler's decision not only to back out of the Geneva negotiations but also to withdraw completely from the League of Nations, Goebbels's suggestion of a one-to-one discussion with Daladier, the French prime minister, in order to establish a basis of trust seems in retrospect positively naive.[54]

It was now apparent that Hitler sent his propaganda minister to Geneva in order to create the impression that the German government was as ready as ever to negotiate seriously on the disarmament question. In this way international criticism of the regime was to be deflected during the League of Nations meeting, thus avoiding a united international front against Germany. Goebbels's mission to Geneva had been a diversionary tactic. His self-confident appearance there, which he had thought so brilliant, was designed to pull the wool over the eyes of the international diplomatic fraternity. It had all been nothing but a charade. Naturally, Goebbels refused to acknowledge this quite obvious conclusion but instead threw himself immediately into the election campaign, boasting in the diary in the following days about his skill as the "architect" of the campaign.[55]

In November Hitler assembled an advisory "Foreign Policy Committee" over which he presided; it included Blomberg, Neurath, Schacht, Economics Minister Kurt Schmitt, and Goebbels (but not Göring, as Goebbels was pleased to note). At its opening meeting on November 16, the dictator expounded his foreign policy direction: "10 years of peace, even at the cost of sacrifices." It seems the committee never met again.[56]

GOEBBELS'S MODESTY VERSUS GÖRING'S POMPOSITY

Since the late summer Goebbels's relationship with Göring, never good, had deteriorated further. Goebbels agreed with Hitler about the need to break up the federal structure of the Reich and dispense with the individual states once and for all (he had a particular stake in transferring their cultural-political responsibilities to his own Ministry). Göring, on the other hand, wanted to cement in place the special arrangements for Prussia within the Reich. Goebbels's sustained attack on his rival took advantage of the many gaps in Göring's armor: his highly developed status consciousness, his obsession with collecting titles, and his fixation on uniforms.[57]

When Goebbels spoke out in the next few weeks about excessive "pomp," it was obvious whom he had in mind.[58] What Goebbels found particularly provocative was Göring's project of forming a new "Prussian State Council" consisting of leading personalities, to replace the identically named body that had previously represented the Prussian provinces but had been made redundant by "coordination" measures. When he learned that Hitler had no intention of attending the ceremonial opening of the State Council on September 15, he decided that he too would ignore the occasion.[59] When Göring complained to him some days later about his absence, Goebbels gave him "a very clear answer."[60]

In the following weeks there are numerous negative comments about Göring in the diaries, and he noted assiduously the poor opinion of him that Hitler and other leading National Socialists were disseminating.[61] In mid-October he worked on Hitler to issue a "popular decree" intended to abolish "detrimental and ostentatious behavior in the Party."[62] When Hitler spoke to leading Nazis in the Prussian Landtag on October 17, Goebbels noticed with great interest the "sharp words attacking ostentation and the obsession with uniforms": "The hall goes mad. Boss has mentally broken with Göring already. The poor show-off. He's nothing but a standing joke."[63]

However, Goebbels was cultivating his own image, too, but it was one of ostentatious austerity. For example, at a state banquet given in honor of his visit to the state government of Baden in Karlsruhe, he pointedly declined the food: "I protest, and don't eat anything. A touch of the old days."[64] On an official occasion in December at the Kaiserhof, he appeared without decorations: "Made something of a stir—especially with Göring. I'm sticking to it. I don't wear medals."[65]

He also declined Berlin's offer to make him an "Honorary Citizen" and to name a street after him on the occasion of his birthday.[66] But he was not consistent on this point: He had already accepted an honorary citizenship from his hometown of Rheydt in April, and he soon relented with respect to Berlin as well. He accepted the honor in February 1934, albeit in the name of the many Party comrades who "have suffered and bled."[67]

Although Goebbels did not show off in the manner of Göring, his lifestyle could hardly be called modest. At Christmas, for example, he bought himself a new car ("8 cylinder 200 hp. Wonderful piece of work!"),[68] and the following spring he acquired another luxurious Mercedes.[69] At the end of November the Goebbelses started to build their house in Göringstrasse, but not before Hitler had given his blessing to their plans and personally drawn a sketch for them.[70]

NOVEMBER: THE REICHSTAG FIRE TRIAL AND THE ELECTION

In November the election campaign ended its final phase. Goebbels was not only intensively involved in organizing it but also gave speeches in Frankfurt, Breslau, Stuttgart, Karlsruhe, Hamburg, Berlin, Cologne, and of course Rheydt.[71]

The Reichstag fire trial, beginning in the Leipzig High Court on September 21, gave Goebbels yet another opportunity to indulge his insatiable appetite for public appearances. On trial were van der Lubbe and his alleged communist backers, the former Reichstag member Ernst Torgler and his three Bulgarian comrades, Georgi Dimitroff, Blagoy Popov, and Vassil Tanev. Göring's testimony at the beginning of November caused a sensation. By clever questioning, Dimitroff managed to rattle Göring so badly that the latter began to react with monumental invective and threats. Dimitroff had thus succeeded in exposing the proceedings to the international public as a show trial. Goebbels, watching these outbursts of Göring's, registered them as counterproductive.[72]

On November 8 he had his chance as a witness to correct the bad impression made by Göring. "Dimitroff and Torgler take a terrible beating. [...] A complete victory. Fabulous press here and abroad. Best of all, I outclass Göring."[73] But all these efforts turned out to be in vain: Just before Christmas Goebbels was appalled to hear that the court had not been prepared to accept the version that the Reichstag fire had been the communist leadership's signal for an uprising. Van der Lubbe was sentenced to death, but the other accused were acquitted.[74]

Immediately after giving his evidence in the trial, Goebbels flew to Munich to give yet another election campaign speech and to attend the ceremonies commemorating the tenth anniversary of the failed putsch. Participation was not quite unproblematic for him, since there was no overlooking the fact that, unlike for example Göring, Rosenberg, or Röhm, at the time of the putsch he had had no connection with the Party whatsoever. Perhaps this explains his late arrival for the ceremony in the Feldherrnhalle.[75]

A few days before the election on November 12 he was dismayed to find that the general outlook was not exactly rosy: "A bad mood among many of the population because of too much pageantry, price rises, inheritance tax, etc." At last, he recorded, the Party had taken on board something for which he had been calling for months: "Hess issues a strong declaration against ostentation. Finally. Thank God!"[76]

The high point of the election campaign, on which Goebbels was now fully concentrating, was Hitler's address to workers in the electrical power plant of the Siemens factory in Berlin on November 10, which Goebbels once again introduced with a commentary.[77] The Propaganda Ministry was faced with the task of representing this speech as the reconciliation of Hitler with the industrial workers, the great majority of whom, particularly in Berlin, had voted for the left in every free election. The ministry rose to the occasion in exemplary fashion.

The election was not, of course, in any sense "free." On November 12—the Reichstag election was combined with a plebiscite vote of confidence in the government's policies in general—a good deal of rigging took place: Ballot papers were numbered; there were no voting booths; well-known opponents of the regime were turned away at the polling stations; ballot papers were altered after the vote; it was hardly possible to abstain from the plebiscite, given the friendly urging by local Party organizations; and the possibility of rejecting the only list of contestants—that of the NSDAP—was not envisaged.[78]

Even spoiled ballots—which often conveyed protests—were disregarded in the count. The official result of the plebiscite was that 91.5 percent of the electorate had voted "yes." In reality, 89.9 percent of those eligible to vote had done so in favor of the government. The approval rating of the solitary NSDAP list of candidates in the "election" was 2.1 points behind the triumphant plebiscite result.[79]

Goebbels was delighted by the results: "Unimaginable. I'm scared of the envy of the gods." Later that evening he met Hitler, who "put his hands on my shoulders, quite moved." Goebbels summed it all up: "We've made it. The German people are united. Now we can face the world."[80]

Did Goebbels really believe that in a year the German people—who in the last free elections, in November 1932, had only delivered 33.6 percent of the vote for the Nazis—had been won over to the extent of giving them almost 90 percent of the vote, this despite the massive repressive measures against large sections of the population, the international isolation, and an economic situation that was as bad as ever?

This is probably the wrong question to ask. The fact is that Goebbels was incapable of a reality check on the picture of national unity produced by his own propaganda in conjunction with the regime's repressive terror measures. The glossy appearance of things, largely produced by his propaganda—a personal success—was for him the only reality that mattered.

THE YEAR'S END, 1933

From Goebbels's point of view, the rest of 1933 was marked by a further series of successes and festivities. Together with Hitler on November 15, three days after the political triumph of the election, he opened the new Reich Culture Chamber in the Berlin Philharmonie. It was "a day in my honor," as he bluntly described the event in his diary.[81] Less than two weeks later came the official launch of the leisure organization created under Goebbels's aegis, dubbed "Kraft durch Freude" (Strength Through Joy). "It will be a great operation. Attached to my Ministry," noted Goebbels. In fact, though, the KdF organization was unambiguously assigned to the German Labor Front. After a discussion with Ley, Goebbels had merely secured the right, through a representative, to make appointments to the cultural office of the KdF.[82]

By the end of November the film made by Leni Riefenstahl at the Nuremberg Party rally was at last finished. The work had not gone entirely smoothly: Riefenstahl had complained frequently and vociferously about the film department of the Propaganda Ministry, which was responsible for producing the film.[83]

With the film completed, it was apparent that a conventional documentary record of the Nuremberg event had been far from Riefen-stahl's mind. She had conceived the film—titled *The Victory of Faith*—from the beginning as a propaganda stylization and height-ening of the Party rally as spectacle. However, the film was by no means technically perfect, and it also revealed at many points that the staging of Nuremberg had had its rough edges.

But when Hitler and Goebbels viewed a private screening of the film in November, they did not take offense: "Fabulous S.A. sym-phony. Riefenstahl's done well. She's completely shattered by the work. Hitler moved."[84] According to Goebbels's notes, the premiere on December 1 was a "smash hit."[85]

On December 24 he enjoyed his "best Christmas"; the Berlin NSDAP organized a big Christmas party in the Berlin working-class quarter of Moabit, where 1,400 children received presents from SA men. "When I arrive, tempestuous cheering breaks out," he added emotionally. There followed a "blessed Christmas" in the bosom of the family.[86]

On the evening of Christmas Day he went with his family to Rheydt for a few days. He met up with old schoolfriends, which he found "quite nice"; by contrast, he did not like the behavior of his brother Hans, who, exploiting the seizure of power to advance his own career, turned up in a "big fat limousine." On the train ride back to Berlin—Magda stayed on in Rheydt a bit longer—there was a sur-prise for him: In the sleeping car, Anka Mumme aroused him from his bed: "Chatted to her until Bielefeld, cool right down to my heart. Over, passé!"[87]

It stopped at that. In the course of 1935 he did meet Anka a few times, with lengthy intervals in between, and she complained repeat-edly about her "miserable marriage," but he saw no way to help "Frau Mumme," as he now called his former girlfriend. He seems to have seen her for the last time at the end of 1936.[88] The coolness with which he regarded Anka seems to be symptomatic of Goebbels's fur-ther personal development in the years after 1933. The more he stood at the center of public attention, bathing in the glow of his own suc-cess, the more distance he placed between himself and the people to whom he had once been close. The narcissistic formation of his per-sonality was a process that was not yet complete.

CHAPTER 12

"Whatever the Führer Does, He Does Completely"

The Establishment of the Führer State

Goebbels with Hitler after the latter had usurped the office of Reich president, August 19, 1934. The Führer State had been installed once and for all, but its popular base was altogether in doubt.

By the beginning of 1934, a year after the seizure of power, lunch with Hitler had become a regular feature of Goebbels's daily routine. But because of the fairly unstructured pattern of Hitler's day, these visits were very time-consuming. Hitler's guests—generally numbering around twenty to thirty—often had a long wait before he arrived for the meal. The conversation at table—the fare was usually modest—

always centered on the same topics and often ran on well into the afternoon.[1] According to Albert Speer's memoirs, among the regular guests it was Goebbels who perhaps did most to entertain the company. His speciality was the joke or anecdote used to caricature or ridicule his competitors and opponents in the leading ranks of the regime, disparaging them in a seemingly harmless way. Information flowing in the opposite direction was invaluable to him: Hitler's remarks about current affairs gave him the clues he needed to adjust his propaganda line to Hitler's thinking down to the last nuance.[2]

On a normal Berlin working day, therefore, these extended sessions in the Reich Chancellery meant that Goebbels's time was taken up for practically the whole afternoon. The hectic pace at which he worked and the overwork that he constantly describes in the diary—the "mountains of work" which he "rushed through" "at full pelt"—were partly due to the fact that on many days he had only the morning hours at his disposal.[3] In time he seems to have found these lengthy sessions with Hitler increasingly onerous, so that he was positively relieved on those occasions that lunch was canceled or he had a good excuse to miss it. Then he could for once "work right through without interruption."[4]

In the evenings he often found himself back in the Reich Chancellery, where Hitler liked to end the day by watching feature films. Hitler's comments on these were, of course, extremely important for Film Minister Goebbels. In the first half of 1934, therefore, Goebbels spent at least twenty-six evenings in Hitler's private cinema in the Reich Chancellery[5]—although Hitler's taste in films did not always agree with his own, and often it was only the presence of "lovely" or "nice" women that helped him get over "bad films."

Magda often accompanied him on these visits to the Reich Chancellery,[6] although she sometimes called on Hitler without her husband[7] or escorted the Führer to events.[8] Conversely, Hitler was in the habit of returning the honor by dropping in on the couple in their official Berlin apartment or at their summer residence.[9] Sometimes the Führer made such visits unannounced[10] or was already there when they returned from a journey. Often, he then stayed on late into the night.

In March Magda found "a little summer house on the Wannsee" in the village of Kladow, right on the edge of Berlin. By March, the

Goebbels family had already moved into their summer quarters, remaining there until September.[11] At the Berlin water sports exhibition, a particularly fine motorboat caught Goebbels's eye, and he bought it a few days later.[12] In the season that followed, Joseph Goebbels fancied himself as a Sunday skipper, although he left the steering to his driver, Albert Tonak.[13] Spending a day in Kladow in April—his first visit there—Hitler was enthusiastic about this summer retreat, and from then on during the summer months he made use of every opportunity to spend his leisure time there, scooting about on the Wannsee and nearby waterways with his propaganda minister. But other people too came to enjoy their spare time at the Goebbels place, for example the Helldorfs, the Blombergs, Party treasurer Franz Schwarz with his family, or Pfeffer.[14]

On April 13 Magda gave birth to her second child: "Once again, the Führer was the only one who got it right. It's a girl." They decided to call her Hilde.[15] Two days later, when Goebbels went to see Magda in the hospital, he found she had another visitor: "Führer already there" ran Goebbels's laconic remark in the diary. At this time Hitler helped with another piece of Goebbels family business. According to the divorce settlement between Magda and her first husband, on completing his fourteenth year their son Harald was supposed to move from his mother's household to that of his father. With this deadline approaching, Goebbels made every effort to annul the agreement. To this end, he applied massive pressure in his dealings with Quandt's lawyer. He prevailed without too much difficulty— after all, a few days after the birth of Hilde, Hitler had promised him his full support.[16] Shortly afterward, on the occasion of the first Reich Theater Festival Week in Dresden, Hitler opened up to him about his own private concerns. Goebbels's comment on the discussion was: "He is so nice, it's touching. He's so lonely. Must have a wife. It can't go on like this."[17]

His close, almost daily contact with Hitler had its down side. He was no longer master of his own spare time. Hitler and the Goebbels family—Magda had by now recovered from the birth—were supposed to be going on a trip together for Whitsun. But when it came to it, Hitler dithered about the arrangements, and as late as the Friday evening he had still not made up his mind. Goebbels was obviously annoyed: "It's sickening. I'm not waiting any longer. I'm pushing off.

To Cladow. I need to relax. I can't spend the whole of Whitsun waiting around, after all."[18] On Whitsunday he heard that Hitler intended
to fly to Munich. Goebbels could enjoy a quiet day off.[19]

During this time his relationship with Magda underwent various
crises. At the end of May Hitler had warned him of "nasty females
spreading gossip about Magda," and the next day there was a violent
argument with Magda that went on for days.[20] "I'm sick and tired of
all this," he commented on the situation at home at the beginning of
June.[21] His wife did her best to sort things out: "Magda has spoken to
Führer. I must have a vacation. As soon as possible." But the rest of
summer 1934 was so eventful that Goebbels was obliged to do without his vacation.

A few weeks later he heard "a terrible thing about Magda." He does
not say what this was, perhaps more evidence of her unfaithfulness.
In any case, there had been "dreadful scenes," which left him shattered. The next day the couple carried on with their bitter argument.
Surprisingly, though, Goebbels was prepared to come around in the
end, because Magda was "basically good": "I'm very much to blame
as well. I must make up for it." The next day they reached an
agreement—if only temporarily.[22]

HOW MUCH FREEDOM WILL THE DICTATORSHIP TOLERATE?

Politically, the year 1934 began on January 30 with the celebration of
the first anniversary of the "seizure of power."[23] In the Reichstag, Parliament passed the "Act for the Reconstruction of the Reich," which
among other things abolished the parliaments and sovereignty of the
federal states and gave the government the authority to bring in new
constitutional laws without consulting Parliament.[24] In the evening
Goebbels gave a speech in the Sportpalast on the topic of "Germany's
change of fortune: one year on."[25] There followed a two-day Gauleiter
conference, at which he expressed dissatisfaction with the Prussian
ministries and with those addicted to presenting themselves in
puffed-up, overweening style.[26]

With the title "No Pomp, but 22 Million for the Poor," on January 30 in *Der Angriff* Goebbels published his own contribution to the
anniversary. He proclaimed that January 30 was the "day of the national community" and announced that in honor of the occasion

Winter Relief would be distributing generous quantities of food and coal coupons. However, the festivities should not be too luxurious. He called on people "as befits the hardships and seriousness of the times, to abstain from all showy, pompous festivals, torchlight processions and the like [. . .] but to give visible expression on January 30 to their joy, confidence and heartfelt satisfaction by flying the flag of the Reich from 7 in the morning until 8 in the evening."[27]

Just a few days later he published in the *Völkischer Beobachter* another article, which attracted considerable attention.[28] Under the headline "More Morality, Less Moralizing," he took exception to "the vice-sniffing which [. . .] might just be all right for regulating the life of a convent community but is completely out of place in a modern civilized state." In the article, he particularly objected to the Party's stereotypical ideal image of the "German woman." In fact, there were "good and bad, hardworking and lazy, decent and less decent women, with or without bobbed hair; whether they powder their noses or not is not always a sign of their intrinsic worth, and if they smoke the occasional cigarette at home or in company, this does not mean they should be condemned and cast out." He ironically criticized the notion that a Nationalist Socialist must not enjoy life but live it in "pessimism" and "misanthropy": "So: more embracing of life, less sanctimoniousness! More morality, but less moralizing!"

He recorded that Hitler was "enthusiastic" about the article.[29] But two weeks later, asked to say something about the "woman question," he took a completely different approach. On February 11 he gave a talk to the National Socialist Women's Association of the Berlin Gau on the topic of "National Socialism and the Woman Question." The role he assigned to women in the Third Reich of the future clearly contradicted the "modern" image of women he had put forward in his "moralizing" essay at the end of January. Women, he explained, had "understood that it is a great calling, in no way inferior to the calling of men, to lend spirit, emotion, and—so to speak—'color' to men's decisions." But women would find fulfillment "precisely in their finest vocation, that of mother."[30]

Goebbels's contributions in January and February 1934 show how eager he was around this time to give the public image of the Third Reich some kind of face. They indicate that in many areas of life the regime had not yet succeeded in imposing truly binding norms of behavior.

This also applied to the question of how much public criticism the new regime could tolerate. On February 7 Goebbels gave a speech to the Presidium of the Reich Culture Chamber, in which he complained that the German press was either "anarchic, destroying and undermining everything, or it was as tame as a lapdog!" It was simply not capable of finding "a golden mean," "that is to say an independent, decent, well-intentioned critique of individual measures mixed with good, positive advice!"

The speech provoked contradiction. The old flagship of the German liberal press, the *Frankfurter Zeitung*, offered a direct response to Goebbels's speech a few days later in an editorial.[31] Wrapped up in polite language and deference to the minister, the message was that the press was no longer in a position "to echo public opinion," for "who is this public for whom the press would like to speak?" The article suggested that to call for more criticism from the press, as Goebbels had done, was rather simplistic. For the "desire to avoid fruitless criticism under any circumstances" had in reality led the press— under government tutelage—"for the time being to stop dealing with certain topics." Finally, the paper nailed its colors to the mast by defending the "principle of press freedom as a life element indispensable in the long run for the existence of the state."

In another article, bearing the byline of the newspaper's editor-in-chief, Rudolf Kircher, the newspaper returned to the theme a few weeks later, on March 24. It addressed openly the "crisis of the press," reflected not least in falling subscription figures.[32] "Germans," the article asserted, had certainly "been brought to recognize clearly their ties to the community," but within these ties they also wanted, "thanks to their unchanging German character, the open expression of their feelings and judgments, subject only to tact and decency." Under the article there was a very somber obituary for the *Vossische Zeitung*, that other great liberal newspaper, which had just ceased publication—after 230 years!

Finally, on April 19 another article by Rudolf Kircher appeared in the *Frankfurter Zeitung*, this one dealing with a decline in the standing of the German press abroad and diminishing sales at home, but not inclined to view this situation as irrevocable. This series of articles in the *Frankfurter Zeitung* represented a valiant attempt to defend at least the remnants of press freedom under dictatorship. It is remarkable that Goebbels was prompted by these comments to go on responding publicly, rather than simply resorting to repressive measures to silence the newspaper.

On April 19, the same day that Kircher's attack on the system of press control appeared, Goebbels was already hitting back. At an event to which the Reich Press Association had been invited, he felt obliged to take up the charge of the "monotony" of the press. He blamed the journalists, who were practicing "excessive compliance." They needed to be gradually replaced by "young blood [. . .]; we must have people raised in the spirit of National Socialism, who have it in their blood."[33]

Naturally, the speech received a mixed reception. While *Der Angriff* spoke of a well-founded critique, executed with "biting sarcasm," of this "limp-rag mentality," the Berlin correspondent of the press agency "Dienst aus Deutschland" (German Service), Georg Dertinger, wrote a letter to the editor deploring the "undifferentiated defamation of non–National Socialist journalists" and declaring himself incapable of writing any commentary that "might reflect our views and yet be compatible with present possibilities."[34]

But in an editorial in the next day's *Frankfurter Zeitung* Rudolf Kircher found a way of countering Goebbels's attack by using irony in response to his sarcasm. The journalists, stated Kircher, had sat in front of Goebbels like "school-leavers facing the school principal as he hands out the exam results. Needless to say—nobody passed." Kircher continued: "Of course, the easiest thing for us journalists would have been for the government to declare from the start that in such difficult times there must not be any criticism. But instead of that the cry goes up, 'Don't be shy, take a risk—but only where you should!' There's something almost cruel about this. Yet the minister left the podium amid storms of applause."

A further response appeared on April 29 in the Sunday paper *Grüne Post;* it was written by the editor-in-chief, the author Ehm Welk. In ironic form it shot Goebbels's accusation of the uniformity of the German press back at him: "Herr Reich Minister, I see what you're asking, but frankly—I'm not sure I'm with you." This disrespectful article earned the *Grüne Post* a three-month ban as well as banishment to a concentration camp for Welk.[35]

Less than three weeks later, at a "press convention" for Party journalists, Goebbels came back to his speech and the slogan "More courage!" He used the occasion to read out a new announcement "easing" press conditions, ostensibly giving journalists greater room to maneuver, as well as moderating the Propaganda Ministry's insistence that the press should publish official pronouncements.[36]

It was pure sarcasm when the conservative journalist Georg Dertinger reported to his editorial office a few days later that according to the propaganda minister the "partial restoration of press freedom" had now proven its value in practice. Dertinger was referring to an address given by Goebbels on May 11 in the Berlin Sportpalast. It was designed to overrule any possible criticism of the regime as the superfluous grumbling of people who "get themselves down" and "always object to everything."

Goebbels had no doubt about who was behind such criticism: "the Jews" and "small cliques within the churches."[37] In the space of a few days, therefore, the vaunted "easing" of pressure on the press had turned into an all-out campaign against critical voices.[38] When Goebbels proclaimed in the *Völkischer Beobachter* two weeks later that the purpose of his propaganda efforts was to instill "dedication to the high aims of the National Socialist state," the direction of the winds was clear.[39] There would be no public criticism of the press control system from now on.

Goebbels's launched a campaign in May 1934 against "grumblers and faultfinders." It was an impressive demonstration of how much distance there now was between subtle debates about the nuances of press freedom and the reality of the ruthlessly manipulated public sphere in the Third Reich. The campaign was aimed first and foremost at criticism of the regime from reactionary and ecclesiastical sources. The official publication of the Reich propaganda office printed a firsthand account by a Party functionary in Wiesbaden about the conduct of the campaign. It was held up as a model, and it made clear the extent to which everyday life just over a year after the "seizure of power" was already dominated by the detailed work of local Party organizations.

When the high point of the action was still two weeks away—it was to culminate in a wave of events—the whole of the local press was forced to report daily on the campaign. Among other things, the papers called on readers to acquire swastika badges—giving right of access to the planned rallies—and to wear them in public. A week before the series of events, four thousand posters went up around the city, and during the day before the action itself they bore stickers with the text "Tonight only moaners will stay at home." Banners were stretched across the street bearing messages such as "Moaners are traitors," "Don't whine, work!" and so forth. Twenty groups of painters were set to work applying the same slogans to the pavements.

In the course of the action, furthermore, fifty thousand leaflets were distributed to all households; sixteen trucks drove through the city, each carrying thirty or forty uniformed Party comrades chanting slogans; troops of speakers visited pubs according to a prearranged program to deliver short speeches; and in the cinemas public announcement slides were inserted into the scheduled screenings. The main meetings then took place simultaneously in one evening in twenty-four halls. To make up for any possible shortfall in audience numbers, Hitler youth members had been placed on standby to fill the gaps, but it turned out that the meetings were over-subscribed, so that on short notice—by resorting to a special "reserve pool" of speakers—further meetings were improvised in the open air. Would anybody have been able to resist "invitations" on this scale? Nothing was left to chance: At the end of the action all the inscriptions and posters instantly disappeared from the city scene.[40]

STRUGGLES WITH RIVALS FOR CONTROL

From the beginning of 1934, Goebbels made considerable efforts to consolidate and extend his control of propaganda and cultural areas, both at the state level and within the Party. Early in the year he started restructuring the Party propaganda office to align it more with the ministry.[41] Goebbels also took care to ensure that the newly created— on April 1—regional branches of his ministry, called *Landestellen* (federal state offices), known from 1937 onward as *Reichspropagandaämter* (Reich propaganda offices), were staffed by personnel who covered the same duties in the Gau propaganda departments. However, the Gau propaganda directors, now also working for the central state propaganda office, were in practice much closer to their individual Gauleiters than to Goebbels, so that he could not afford to rely on them as thoroughly as his own lieutenants.[42]

In 1934 Goebbels was at great pains to underline his central role in cultural politics. Among the steps he took to achieve this was the creation of national book and film prizes. In Hitler's presence, on

May 1, 1934, at a gala event of the Reich Culture Chamber in the Berlin State Opera House, Goebbels presented prizes to the Nazi writer Richard Euringer and to Gustav Ucicky for his anti-Soviet film *Flüchtlinge* (Refugees).

What Goebbels was counting on above all, however, was the reform of the Reich Hitler had repeatedly promised. With the federal states abolished, all cultural affairs would fall to him.[43] But at the end of 1933, this move had come up against fierce opposition from Göring, whose relations with Goebbels at that moment happened to be at their lowest ebb.[44] Even a visit shortly before Christmas by Goebbels and his wife to Göring's private apartment (for Goebbels, its opulent style made it a "chamber of horrors"), although it passed off in friendly enough fashion, had not solved the problem.[45]

When in 1934 the Prussian minister of culture, Bernhard Rust, was appointed to head a Reich ministry for science, education, and popular information,[46] Goebbels thought that he could take his place in Prussia. He arranged with Göring that he would be joining the Prussian cabinet, taking over the running of Prussian cultural affairs from Rust. Eventually, Goebbels decided to rename the sphere over which he would thus preside the "Culture Ministry" (it was to have been the "Reich and Prussian Culture Ministry").[47] But he still ran into difficulties with the name, and a few days later he thought he could win support for the designation "Ministry for Culture and Popular Enlightenment."[48] He had a mandate to this effect drafted and sent to Lammers on May 8.[49] But Hitler was opposed to the new name. He did not want Goebbels acquiring ministerial rank in Prussia, and he decided that Göring should simply hand over authority to Goebbels without further change.[50]

What Goebbels actually did acquire, after lengthy negotiations,[51] was what had long been his heart's desire—authority over the Prussian theaters, which the "theater pasha" Göring[52] had hitherto treated mainly as a prize possession enhancing his status-conscious lifestyle. Even after the new arrangements were in place, Goebbels agreed to leave Göring a few crown jewels, in the form of responsibility for the state theaters in Berlin (the Playhouse on the Gendarmenmarkt and the State Opera), in Kassel, and (albeit temporarily) in Wiesbaden. But in all other German theaters—including the non-Prussian states—Goebbels had ultimate control over all important appointments and could intervene in the repertoires of individual theaters.

What is more, the Propaganda Ministry provided the theaters with annual subsidies that increased every year, which further increased their dependence on Berlin.[53] While most theaters were owned by local authorities or individual Länder (states), the propaganda minister had direct responsibility for several playhouses, called "Reich theaters": These venues could always expect special attention from the propaganda minister.

The German theaters were now under the direction of the drama department of the Propaganda Ministry, initially headed by Otto Laubinger. After his death, he was replaced in October by Rainer Schlösser, who acted at the same time as Reich dramaturge, the person responsible for repertoires. With the annual Reich Theater Festival Week instituted in 1934, moreover, the Propaganda Ministry had given itself a regular opportunity to set the signals in the German theater landscape through programmatic speeches and productions.[54]

However, Goebbels was not to succeed in taking the German museums into his empire. "Reform of the Reich at a snail's pace," he sighed in June.[55] Thus his ministry continued to be saddled with the old title he so disliked, "Popular Enlightenment and Propaganda." The exasperation this caused him revealed itself in May, when he told the German press not to keep referring to "the Reich Culture Ministry and Culture Minister Rust," since the area of culture was divided among three authorities, those being Rust; the Ministry of the Interior, responsible for religious matters; and finally Goebbels himself, responsible for questions of art, among other topics.[56] But it was not only in the state sector that Goebbels found his claim to a role in cultural life endangered in 1934.

On January 24 Hitler had entrusted to Rosenberg—at Ley's suggestion—the "supervision of the whole intellectual and ideological training and education" of the National Socialist movement.[57] By thus commissioning Rosenberg, Hitler reinforced his position within Nazi cultural politics along with that of the dogmatically *völkisch* line he represented. Goebbels stood for a more flexible cultural-political course, not necessarily excluding elements of artistic modernism— after all, in the 1920s he had been an enthusiast for van Gogh, Nolde, and Barlach. Now, fearing that Rosenberg wanted to "erect a control organization over me," he complained to Hitler accordingly. He demanded that Rosenberg's Combat League for German Culture be dissolved. Early in March he had a discussion with Rosenberg and Hess, at which—according to Goebbels's notes—Rosenberg agreed to disband the Combat League.[58]

In reality Rosenberg had no intention of abolishing the League. Instead he contacted Robert Ley, chief organizer of the NSDAP in the Reich and head of the German Labor Front; merged the Combat League and the Deutsche Bühne (German Stage), responsible for organizing theater visits—also part of his purview—into a single "National Socialist Cultural Community"; and incorporated this new organization in its entirety into the Kraft durch Freude organization, which was run by Ley. In addition he tried to persuade Ley to integrate the federal state leaders of the Combat League as "ideological commissioners" into the headquarters of each Gau, thereby rendering redundant the Gau branches of the Reich Culture Chamber instigated by Goebbels.[59] Furthermore, Rosenberg ensured that Goebbels relieved Hans Weidemann, responsible in the Propaganda Ministry for matters to do with fine art, of his second position as head of the KdF culture office (since his agreement with Ley the previous autumn, the office had been under Goebbels's patronage).[60] Weidemann, a painter, had strongly advocated a symbiosis of National Socialism and modern art, especially Expressionism, something Goebbels had explicitly warned him not to do in February 1934.[61] Goebbels now started gradually removing Weidemann from cultural politics entirely.[62]

But for Goebbels the real confrontation with Rosenberg was not to come until the second half of 1934. Having blocked the "revolutionary forces" within the cultural activities of the Nazi movement, Rosenberg thought that the moment had come to set in motion a broad campaign against all aspects of cultural modernism within the NSDAP.

JUNE 30, 1934

The fundamental conflict between the National Socialist Party leadership and that of the SA, which had erupted spectacularly before 1933 in the two "Stennes revolts," had not disappeared with the "seizure of power" but in fact had become more critical. The SA had increased its numbers by massive recruiting as well as by incorporating other, "coordinated" paramilitary units: Its membership, 500,000 in 1933, had risen to four and a half million by the summer of 1934. With this mighty, miscellaneous, somewhat unruly force behind him, Röhm as SA chief of staff now tried to anchor the whole organization securely within the new National Socialist state.

With the help of SA commissioners, Röhm attempted to assert his influence on the state administration and to build up the SA into a people's militia in competition with the Reichswehr as a homeland defense force. But by spring 1934 at the latest, these efforts had plainly foundered. The fact was that Hitler's rearmament plans were based firmly on the Reichswehr. However, Röhm, showing no sign of giving up on his ambitions for his defense force, continued his efforts to militarize the SA and to arm at least some of his troops. It is true that there is no evidence that he was planning an armed insurrection, but within the top echelons of the regime and in Reichswehr circles, Röhm's self-confident pursuit of power was being followed with great anxiety.

Alongside the thwarted ambitions of the SA leadership, the millions of SA members represented a hotbed of growing unrest. The "veterans," often occupying a lower social status and still without jobs, saw themselves being cheated of their reward for years of tireless activism on behalf of the Party. New members could not fail to notice that their commitment was not being repaid. The SA leadership was increasingly subject to criticism by the mass of brownshirts and, with its repeated demand for a "second revolution," tried to create a kind of safety valve for this pent-up dissatisfaction. The frustration of the SA men was expressed from time to time in a spate of attacks and violent outbursts, often aimed—since the completion of the "seizure of power"—at the general population.[63]

The conflict between the Party and the SA was duly reflected in Goebbels's diary. In February 1934 he criticized the overblown ambitions of the SA, which was extending its grip at the expense of the Party.[64] In the weeks that followed, he noted repeatedly that there were "complaints" and "concerns" about the SA; the Reich governors were also expressing annoyance about it to Hitler.[65] When Hitler complained in private to Goebbels in May about Röhm's appointments policy, all Goebbels noted was: "§175. Revolting!"[66] Both Hitler and Goebbels increasingly distrusted the SA leadership, for example the head of the Berlin-Brandenburg SA Karl Ernst, and in

June Hitler observed that Röhm was "a captive of the people around him."[67]

On the other hand, Goebbels had not by any means broken with Röhm and the SA leadership. For example, he praised a speech by Röhm to the assembled diplomatic corps and foreign press in 1934 (part of the self-confident Röhm's drive to establish independent international contacts) and forced the press to feature it prominently. His praise was all the more noteworthy given that Röhm's talk had somewhat overshadowed his own speech to the same audience.[68] When Goebbels watched an hour-long military review by the SA in Dresden at the end of May, he found it simply "magnificent."[69]

During the first half of 1934, the confrontation between the Party and the SA developed into a comprehensive domestic political conflict. Hitler's conservative coalition partners, who had continuously lost ground since the start of 1933, thought they saw in the conflict a chance for themselves. In these circles there was a widespread notion that they might be able to use the increasing difficulties within the Nazi movement to strengthen their own position and perhaps even restore the monarchy as a stabilizing element. Thus Goebbels wrote in January that among his intimate circle Hitler had held forth about the "spread of monarchist propaganda":[70] The vice chancellor, von Papen, was now increasingly putting himself forward as the spokesman for the idea of a restoration. In the diary there are various complaints about the "reactionaries" and the "parsons." After the intensive criticism he had faced from bourgeois quarters about his press control system, the campaign against "grumblers and faultfinders" started by Goebbels in May had been aimed precisely at "reactionary" and "ecclesiastical" circles.[71]

A further irritant was the news von Papen broke in the middle of May, when he informed Hitler that Hindenburg had drawn up a political testament based on suggestions from him, von Papen. The contents of this document were unknown, but it was feared that it expressed the president's wish that the monarchy should be restored after his death.[72] However, it was Blomberg who was the source of the rumor that von Papen himself wished to succeed Hindenburg.[73]

The situation became more critical on June 17 when von Papen gave a speech at the University of Marburg in which he mounted a fierce attack on the despotic nature and terrorist tactics of Nazi rule.[74] On Hitler's orders, Goebbels banned the entire press from publishing the speech,[75] and von Papen reacted by offering his resignation to the president. Goebbels's relationship with the vice chancellor deteriorated still further in the days that followed: "Papen is sabotaging [us]."[76]

At the end of June Goebbels gave talks in several major cities, stoking up animosity toward von Papen.[77] He flew from Essen to Hamburg to watch the Great Derby horse race, where the public was, he said, "completely on his side" and openly gave von Papen, who was also present, a hostile reception. Goebbels had no doubt about who would win in the imminent domestic political confrontation: "I pity the poor Gentlemen's Club* once things come to a head."

Rudolf Hess played on the same theme in a speech on June 25 in Cologne with a warning against provoking a "second revolution."[78] According to Goebbels, the situation was becoming more serious all the time: "The Führer must act. Otherwise the reactionaries will get the better of us." Back in Berlin, on the morning of June 29 he received a call from Hitler asking him to fly to Bad Godesberg immediately. The reason for the meeting was clear to Goebbels: "So it's starting."[79]

At Hangelar Airport near Bonn he was met by the Cologne Gauleiter Josef Grohé. Later that afternoon, toward four o'clock, Hitler arrived from Essen and told him about the latest developments: "He's going to take action on Saturday. Against Röhm and his rebels. With blood. Got to know that price of rebellion is one's head." Allegedly, Hitler went on, there was evidence that Röhm had conspired with the French ambassador, André François-Poncet, together with Schleicher and Strasser. Goebbels immediately declared that he welcomed the forthcoming action wholeheartedly.

So it must have come as an almost total surprise to learn that the blow he was expecting was aimed at the SA and not at the forces of "reaction." His diary entries show that up to this point he had been expecting a reckoning with von Papen and his supporters, not an action against Röhm. But that was indeed what the Gestapo, the SS, and the army had been preparing intensively over the previous few days. Significantly, as late as June 20, Goebbels—who since the beginning of his time in Berlin had always set great stock in his good contacts with the SA and its leadership—had received the Silesian SA

---

* Translators' note: A reference to the Herrenklub, an exclusive club for aristocrats, leading officials, and industrialists.

leader Edmund Heines, who was within a few days to fall victim to the murderous action of June 30.[80]

Goebbels had failed to grasp the complexity of the domestic political crisis, and—as in so many other instances—he was left out of the decision-making process leading up to the dramatic events of June 30. The dubious privilege he now enjoyed, of being as surprised by the attack on the SA leadership as they were, was no doubt meant as a salutary lesson for him: Hitler made sure he was present at the "action" against Röhm's group in Bavaria. A second reason for ordering him to Bavaria was, however, that Hitler obviously wanted to keep him away from the secondary scene of the action: It was Göring who was to take charge in Berlin during the following days—a striking defeat for Goebbels. When it came to real questions of power politics, Hitler trusted another.

For the time being, however, Hitler carried out his program as normal in Bad Godesberg. In the evening they both attended the Labor Front military ceremony, while Goebbels unobtrusively made sure that his wife and children were moved from Kladow to Berlin and into police protection.[81] Goebbels flew overnight with Hitler from Bonn to Munich. Here Hitler learned that during the night members of an SA standard, about three thousand men, had been alerted and had gone on a noisy rampage through the streets. It is possible that they had gotten wind of the preparations for the anti-SA action.

Hitler now decided to speed up the pace of the planned action. He did not wait for SS reinforcements from Berlin and Dachau but moved with Goebbels, the SA leader Viktor Lutze, and a contingent of SS men to Bad Wiessee, Röhm's vacation resort, to which, on Hitler's instructions, he had summoned SA leaders for a conference to be held in the morning. The evening before there had been heavy drinking, and they were still sleeping it off when Hitler's motorcade drove into Bad Wiessee. Goebbels was now an eyewitness as Hitler had the members of the completely unsuspecting SA leadership arrested. Heines, to whom he had promised assistance just a few days before, he now thought "pitiful," especially as he had been discovered together with a "catamite," whereas Röhm, he judged, had maintained his dignity.

They returned to Munich, where the news of the action in Berlin was trickling through: "Strasser dead, Schleicher dead, Bose dead,

Clausener* [properly Klausener] dead. Munich 7 SA leaders shot." Back in Berlin he heard from Göring, who had led the butchery in the capital, that everything had gone according to plan. The only "slip" was that "Frau Schleicher died too": "Pity, but that's how it is."

The next day Goebbels joined Hitler, who had meanwhile arrived in Berlin.[82] After a report from Göring, Hitler decided on several further executions that he still deemed "necessary"—thereby downgrading his Berlin Gauleiter to a mere witness of these murderous resolutions. Goebbels estimated that about sixty "death sentences" in all had been handed down. Actually the number of murders was rather higher, somewhere between 150 and 200, and the action eliminated not only SA leaders but "reactionaries," known opponents of Nazism, and assorted enemies of Hitler. Röhm was finally numbered among the victims, shot in his prison cell when he failed to commit suicide as commanded.[83]

On the evening of July 1 Goebbels gave an eyewitness account on the radio of the events of the previous few days. He described in detail for his listeners the journey to Bavaria and the arrests in Bad Wiessee, hypocritically asking them to spare him from having to "describe the revolting, almost stomach-churning scenes" he had witnessed there.[84] He justified the murders by recapitulating the accusations Hitler had made against Röhm and his associates in a speech[85] to leading Party comrades in Munich. They were guilty of conspiring with a foreign power, "debauched living," and "ostentation and gluttony." They threatened to give the whole leadership of the Party a reputation for "disgraceful and disgusting sexual abnormality," and their entire activity had been dictated by a personal lust for power.

Goebbels's broadcast ended with one of his most florid hymns of praise to Hitler, one that contained a warning at the same time: "What the Führer does, he does completely. The same with this business. Nothing by halves. [...] But anyone who consciously and systematically rebels against the Führer and his movement should be in no doubt that he is playing a risky game with his own life."

For Goebbels, the next few days were filled with the direct repercussions of the purge: The impact abroad was disastrous, but the reaction of the German population was restrained. Relieved, Goebbels

* Translators' note: Erich Klausener (1885-1934) was the head of Catholic Action and a close associate of von Papen.

noted that Hindenburg had provided a convenient screen for the proceedings. Finally, he heard that Wolf-Heinrich von Helldorf had taken control of the Berlin SA again, in place of Karl Ernst, another victim of the purge. Goebbels had not been consulted about this appointment.

At the first cabinet meeting after the murders, on July 3, Hitler was giving a detailed report when von Papen suddenly appeared, looking "completely broken." To Goebbels, von Papen's resignation now seemed inevitable, given that many supporters of his were among the victims, such as Edgar Julius Jung, who had organized von Papen's address in Marburg, and von Papen's adviser Herbert Bose. Even Goebbels found it sheer mockery when the cabinet continued with "business as usual" in these circumstances, passing thirty-two new laws.[86]

PUTSCH IN AUSTRIA

On July 15, obviously acting on a spontaneous decision, Hitler, Goebbels, and Magda went off to Heiligendamm. Goebbels had to leave his vacation home again the next day for a trip to Mannheim and Heidelberg, leaving Magda and Hitler there alone.[87]

On July 22, during the Bayreuth Festival, Goebbels took part in a discussion with Hitler. Also in attendance were the NSDAP superintendent for Austria, Theodor Habicht, whom Goebbels regarded as a "bonehead";[88] the head of the Austrian SA, Hermann Reschny; and Pfeffer, the former SA chief of staff who was now employed on the liaison staff of the Berlin NSDAP. Goebbels noted: "Austrian question. Will it work? I'm very skeptical."[89]

Goebbels's brief note is clear proof (so far not provided by any other source) that the putsch mounted by the Austrian Nazis a few days later had the personal blessing of the Party's highest authority in Germany. Goebbels's note also shows that Superintendent Habicht and SA Chief of Staff Reschny had discussed the forthcoming putsch with Hitler. We can therefore absolutely refute the often-heard assumption that the distrust arising from the "Röhm affair" prevented any collusion with SA leaders over plans for the putsch. Goebbels's diary entry does shed light on the puzzle of the background to the putsch.[90] Goebbels's entry for July 24 also reveals that his old crony

Pfeffer, whose role in the Third Reich has previously remained rather shadowy, quite clearly played a key role in the backing given to the Austrian putsch conspiracy by German Party headquarters; as it happens, Goebbels had been for a spin in his boat with Pfeffer two weeks before the putsch.[91]

What is more, it also emerges from this short diary note of Goebbels's that on July 22 Hitler had received Major-General Walther von Reichenau, head of the Wehrmacht Office in the War Ministry. This visit had taken place immediately before his talks with Habicht, Reschny, and Pfeffer. So it would appear that the army service chiefs had been informed about the undertaking, at least in broad outline. This too was completely unknown until now.[92]

July 25 was the actual day of the putsch attempt. Members of an SS standard, mostly ex-Austrian army men, occupied the Austrian Radio transmitter building and the federal chancellor's office, murdering Federal Chancellor Engelbert Dollfuss, the head of government.[93] In the course of the day, Goebbels, still in Bayreuth and waiting nervously, began to hear the first optimistic reports of the putsch.[94] But the situation changed quickly: By the same evening the Austrian government managed to suppress the revolt in the capital.[95] The uprising, which had spread to many parts of Austria on July 25, was soon quickly and thoroughly crushed everywhere.[96]

The next day, Habicht and Pfeffer turned up in Bayreuth to report. Habicht was forced to resign, and a few days later the Austrian headquarters of the Party was closed down. Hitler also decided to make von Papen German ambassador in Vienna. An international crisis was in the offing. Even if only temporarily, Goebbels thought that there was a "danger that the great powers would step in."[97] The decisive factor in the failure of the putsch was that Mussolini had immediately lent his support to the Austrian government.[98] If Hitler had deduced from his discussions with Mussolini in Venice that the latter would approve of a German intervention against Dollfuss, then this was a miscalculation.[99] All that Mussolini had agreed to was the ousting of Dollfuss and Austrian Nazi participation in government, not a putsch and the cold-blooded murder of the head of state.

Goebbels was particularly angered by the sharply polemical stance of the Italian press toward the attempted putsch. Obviously seeking a scapegoat to blame for an undertaking about which he had completely miscalculated, Hitler declared to Goebbels that he had now "broken with Rome for good and all" and was looking for "stronger support from Yugoslavia."[100] In the following months he maintained his negative attitude toward the Italians; in October Goebbels learned that the dictator was now counting on a Berlin-Belgrade-Warsaw axis.[101]

DEATH OF HINDENBURG, AND ELECTIONS

His health deteriorating, Hindenburg had withdrawn to his Neudeck estate at the beginning of June, and by the end of July his condition had worsened further. The Nazi leadership were agreed on their course of action: Immediately after Hindenburg's death, the Führer was to be named as his successor.[102] When the bulletins from Neudeck became increasingly grave, Hitler left for East Prussia on August 1 and was in time to see Hindenburg alive. Meanwhile, in Berlin Goebbels was making preparations for the funeral.[103] On the evening of August 1, Goebbels attended a cabinet session in which an act was passed whereby, on the death of the Reich president, his office should be merged with that of the Reich chancellor. At this session, moreover, Blomberg announced that after Hindenburg's death, he would have members of the armed forces swear an oath of loyalty to Hitler personally.[104]

On Thursday, August 2, the president's death was reported: "At 9:45 I put out the report on all stations. Broadcasting silence for half an hour. Then new laws announced. The whole city covered in flags of mourning."[105] The cabinet reconvened in the evening to settle the details of the funeral ceremony. Hitler proposed a referendum for August 19 in order to confirm his succession, which had already been legislated for.[106] Hitler's position as the omnipotent Führer of Germany was to be further secured by a plebiscite.

Goebbels not only took part in the obsequies in the Reichstag, he also attended the ceremony at the Tannenberg memorial the following day. For him the meaning of this farewell had a much deeper import; it was a leave-taking from the old Germany. Impressed as he was by the ceremony, he found the funeral address of Dohrmann, Bishop to the Forces, insupportable: "I'm never going to have any parson talking at my graveside."[107]

There was some agitation around the subject of Hindenburg's political testament,[108] which had been inspired by von Papen, who had informed Hitler of its existence in May. The concern was exacerbated by the fact that its contents were unknown and the fact that the document could not immediately be located.[109] Hitler tasked von Papen with acquiring the ominous testament from Neudeck. When he received it, to his and Goebbels's relief it transpired that the dreaded recommendation to restore the monarchy, which von Papen had tried to persuade the president to make, was not contained in this document. It was only present in a letter dated July 14 and addressed by Hindenburg to Hitler. Hitler ordered the testament to be published in the daily press but of course kept the letter to himself.[110]

Immediately after the cabinet resolution, Goebbels began preparing for the August 19 referendum, which Hitler intended would confirm him in office as Reich president. Goebbels spoke at mass meetings in Berlin, Hamburg, Essen, and again in Berlin; finally he accompanied Hitler to the main rally of the campaign, which took place in Hamburg.[111]

Despite all these efforts, however, for the Nazis the result of the ballot was on the disappointing side. Only 89.9 percent of valid votes were for "yes"; taking into account all those who had not yielded to the pressure to vote, along with the invalid ballot papers, only 84.5 percent of those entitled to vote had submitted their approval, a little over five percentage points lower than in autumn 1933. This relative drop in positive votes—the numbers of which, as with all ballots in the Nazi period, were massaged upward in every possible way—was a clear indication that compared to the year before, the approval rating of the regime had plainly slipped.[112]

Disappointed, Goebbels wrote that he had expected more; Catholics had withheld their support. He also blamed his arch-rival Rosenberg and his neo-heathen masquerade: "Führer agrees with me it's time to get rid of this intellectual claptrap."[113] But it was not only Catholic areas that returned disappointing results. The same was true of many large cities, formerly bastions of the working-class movement, including Berlin. In the capital, only 81.2 percent of valid ballot papers recorded a "yes" vote; if invalid ballots were deducted, as well as the figures for those who had abstained from voting, the proportion of positive votes left was only 76.3 percent.[114] Goebbels called the Berlin result "very bad. Partly our own fault." First and foremost he blamed the deputy Gauleiter, Artur Görlitzer.[115]

At the usual lunchtime gathering of Hitler's court there was a post-mortem on this "failure." Goebbels ascribed it to the ongoing dispute with the religious denominations, the lack of contact with the people, corruption, and laxity toward "enemies of the state." Referring to the widely used sanction of concentration camp sentences, he added: "Konzi [concentration camp] no picnic."[116] But the propaganda minister was clear that terror and repression were not enough by themselves to get the regime out of this crisis. Through the purge of June 30 and his usurping of the presidential office, Hitler had certainly succeeded in consolidating his rule and installing a "Führer state," but none of this had made the regime any more popular.

CHAPTER 13

"Taking Firm Control of the Inner Discipline of a People"

Propaganda and Manipulation of the Public Sphere

By means of mass events, such as this harvest festival on the Bückeberg hill near Hamelin (September 1934), the regime found many effective ways of staging the solidarity of the "national community" for the public.

In the months following the evisceration of the SA, Hitler's assumption of the presidency in succession to Hindenburg, and the election, the regime consolidated its power in every way it could. One of the most important ways was a new series of mass meetings and campaigns designed to demonstrate unbridled self-confidence and the unity of the "national community." It was now up to Goebbels to show off the extent to which Party and state were able to dominate the public sphere of the Third Reich by means of National Socialist symbols, rituals, propaganda, and rhetoric.

Together with Hitler, Goebbels on August 26 opened a Saarland exhibition in Cologne, accompanying the leader afterward to a mass rally on the Ehrenbreitstein in Koblenz. After a short stay in Berlin, Magda and Goebbels flew with their daughter Helga to the Obersalzberg for a few days.[1] There they once again discussed with Hitler whether they should acquire a plot of land on the Obersalzberg in order to have a convenient second home there, like other top Nazis.[2]

Goebbels traveled on September 4 from the Obersalzberg to the annual Nuremberg Party rally, which featured parades, marching columns, roll calls, torchlight processions, military displays by the Wehrmacht, and endless speeches. Goebbels gave his usual address to the Reich propaganda chiefs and expressed his thanks to workers of the National Socialist People's Welfare organization involved in the Winter Relief effort.[3] However, the Reich propaganda minister essentially took no part in organizing the rally, nor in the media presentation of the Nuremberg spectacle after the event. Organization was the job of Nazi headquarters in Munich, while it was not Goebbels who became famous for making propaganda use of the rally but Leni Riefenstahl, for whom he had come to have no high regard.

It was in spring 1934 that Hitler once again asked Riefenstahl to film the rally in September. This time the film was financed from Party funds and not by the Propaganda Ministry, and an administrative strategy was devised whereby Riefenstahl would avoid interference from the Reich propaganda office. It is not surprising that Goebbels, thus circumvented, was lukewarm about the venture. Before filming began he predicted morosely: "Not much will come of it. She's too flighty."[4]

The result, under the title *The Triumph of the Will*, was to become the Nazi regime's best-known propaganda film, and it differed from conventional documentaries not only in its highly mobile use of the camera and unusual, even spectacular camera angles but also in its cutting technique, which was more like that of a feature film. The film was technically perfect but also presented to perfection the sequence of events at the rally. In contrast to Riefenstahl's first Nuremberg film, here the whole ceremonial of the rally appears orderly, centering on the figure of Hitler. The "ornamentation of the masses" under National Socialism was surely nowhere more impressively displayed than in Riefenstahl's film.

The premiere of the film, presented with much fanfare, was attended by Goebbels and Hitler on March 28, 1935, at the Ufa Picture Palace in Berlin, which had been specially refurbished by Albert Speer himself. Goebbels's comments on the screening were terse. He did acknowledge "Leni's great success" but thought the film had its longueurs. "Brilliant reviews, naturally."[5]

The rally in 1934 was rapidly followed by a series of other large-scale events. By the second year of Nazi rule, the "National Socialist calendar" was already firmly established, including the harvest festival on the Bückeberg,[6] the big collecting drives for Winter Relief,[7] the ceremony commemorating the ill-fated Nazi putsch in November,[8] and public gift exchange at Christmas.[9]

In the autumn and winter months the public arena of the Third Reich was again dominated by huge publicity around the Winter Relief drive and its many volunteers out on the streets with their collection boxes. Goebbels ordered the Reich propaganda office to support the efforts of Winter Relief with a series of meetings. It speaks volumes that the Reich propaganda office put out a warning to Party comrades not on any account to use "coercion or force" to make the public attend "any of the planned tens and hundreds of thousands of meetings."[10] Mild pressure was usually enough to ensure full houses, however. As with the intensive action against "grumblers and faultfinders," it was hard for the average citizen to evade the Party's gentle persuasion.[11]

Although it was likewise difficult to resist the eager street collectors' boxes—contributors were rewarded with various badges, making non-donors highly visible—the sums collected were claimed by propaganda as evidence of a functioning "national community" and of general agreement with the policies of the regime. Goebbels's diaries reveal, however, that these results—a few million more donated than in the previous year—were achieved only by sustained appeals for volunteers at the end of October to redouble the intensity of the collecting drive.[12]

On October 25 Goebbels took part in a Gauleiter conference in Munich. Reform of the Reich was the focus of the meeting this time, but Goebbels again found the debate quite unproductive: "They all go on warming up their stale ideas. [. . .] Theorizers and romantics! No élan, no enthusiasm. Plodders!"[13]

Goebbels's comments give the impression that these sessions, which Hitler had introduced to inform the Gauleiters about his policy initiatives, had set into a rigid routine: There seem to have been six such meetings in 1933, and this one was already the eighth of 1934. It was not as though the Gauleiters really learned anything about Hitler's political plans, and neither did the meetings have a direct influence on government policy: They were not even particularly useful for coordinating the policies of the Gauleiters and the Reich governors in the federal states. Their only point seems to have been the opportunity to pool information and experience. In October 1936 Hitler finally declared to Goebbels that the "Gauleiter parliaments have got to go."[14] The Führer appeared increasingly rarely at the meetings. All the same, they went on taking place.

Strangely enough, the Goebbels diaries are the only extant written source reflecting meetings of the Party elite—leaving aside independent meetings of the Reich leaders and the joint meetings of leaders and Gauleiters—from 1933 until the end of the Third Reich as a series of more or less regular events. All other relevant information is very fragmentary. It is almost exclusively thanks to Goebbels's account that we know the topics of the talks delivered there; the tone and content of Hitler's addresses to these gatherings; the mood of those assembled; and indeed in many cases that these meetings happened at all.

MANAGING THE PUBLIC SPHERE

The lavish festivities, mass meetings, and propaganda drives continuously staged by the regime were designed to demonstrate the high degree of enthusiasm allegedly felt by the great majority of the population for the regime's policies. Moreover, by its second year in power the regime had succeeded to a large extent in making the everyday scene in the Third Reich systematically conform to Nazi precepts.

In particular, the Nazis had very largely managed to impose their rituals and symbols on the public sphere. We might think of the ubiquitous posters and banners; the showcases in which were displayed the Party's "saying of the week" and copies of *Der Stürmer;* the decorating of entire streets for big events; the renaming of roads and squares; the infiltrating of stereotypical Nazi terms into everyday language, which was so acutely described by Victor Klemperer;[15] the "managing" of large masses of people into marching columns and serried ranks for roll calls and parades; but also the complete makeover of public spaces by means of imposing and dominating architecture, designed to form a suitable "thousand-year" backdrop for the molding of the masses.[16] This dominance over the public sphere can also be seen in relatively nonpolitical areas, for example in the Nazi motifs permeating advertising, ordinary window displays, and graphic art.[17] Efforts were also made—albeit relatively unsuccessfully—to promote a fashion for "aryanizing"—that is, removing all "un-German" influences.[18]

The great majority of the public had grown used to manifesting their support for the regime—as was expected of them—in their everyday behavior. This happened, for example, through the officially encouraged "Heil Hitler!" greeting;[19] the wearing of uniforms by a large part of the population, or at least the wearing of insignia to signal their support for the regime; the public display of flags at home; attendance at Party events and mass rallies; donations to street collectors; listening en masse to broadcasts in public squares; the gradual exclusion of Jews, labeled enemies of the state, from normal daily life; and many other ways.

However, it would be completely wrong to assume that between 1933 and 1945 the Germans lived in a kind of totalitarian uniformity. A mass of research has shown that there was plenty of dissatisfaction, divergent behavior, and dissent under National Socialism. Admittedly, critical sentiments were most likely to be heard in private or semi-public areas, for example among colleagues and friends, or in the pub: in the immediate neighborhood, in other words. It is true that criticism was also heard within the traditional social milieus still untouched by the Nazis, such as parish congregations, village communities, conservative elite circles, bourgeois groups, or the socialist underground. But the regime did its utmost to ensure that these deviant views were never given a public airing.

As a result of the regime's domination of the public sphere, German society under National Socialism was very largely atomized, lacking the sites of communication and discursive mechanisms needed to establish an alternative public opinion independent of the regime.

For Goebbels's propaganda it was an easy matter to represent as broad support for the regime two conditions it had itself created: on the one hand control of the public and widespread adjustment to Nazi norms of behavior, and on the other the silence of oppositional tendencies. The many reports on the public mood commissioned by the regime primarily served the same purpose: They recorded the success of its propaganda and were meant to further promote the unity of the "national community." In fact, however, this material often showed the limits of the conformity imposed by the regime, although it was not the intention of the reports' authors to calibrate precisely oppositional tendencies or dissatisfaction.[20]

Only against this background of far-reaching domination of the public sphere could Nazi control of the mass media become fully effective.

JOURNALISTS AS "CIVIL SERVANTS"

Once the top SA leadership had been removed and the Party's monopoly of political power established in the summer of 1934, the regime was poised to close some of the remaining gaps in its management of the media along National Socialist lines. Whereas before June 30 the regime had occasionally tolerated (or purported to tolerate) some alternative opinions, those days were now over.

After Goebbels's public altercation with the bourgeois press in the spring of 1934, he made another attempt that autumn to control news reporting. He sent out some general guidelines, containing fifteen points in all, to every German editorial office. On closer inspection, the point of the document was to let journalists know what areas were out of bounds for critical, or even just independent, reporting.[21]

There should never, for example (stated Point 1 on the list of guidelines), be any broad-brush description of "official ceremonial occasions": This took Goebbels back to one of his favorite themes, the avoidance of "pomp" in the Third Reich.[22] Another rule was that any controversial discussion of proposed legislation was incompatible with the idea of a "Führer state."[23] Likewise, to discuss the form of government was "intolerable."[24] When reporting political trials it was undesirable to "discuss in detail false assertions that are the subject of the trial."[25] One of Goebbels's guidelines stated succinctly: "Today, the church question has been settled." With regard to ecclesiastical affairs, in order to avoid confusion as well as adverse reactions from foreign propaganda, only reports from the German News Service should be used.[26] And as far as the much-lamented monotony of the German press was concerned, Goebbels forbade any discussion of press uniformity outright.[27]

Karl Silex, editor-in-chief of the conservative *Deutsche Allgemeine Zeitung*, brought this move to regulate the German press, communicated in confidence, a little more out into the open by presenting and commenting on it in an editorial. It was a rare instance of readers learning from a newspaper something about the mechanisms of press control under the Nazi dictatorship. When Silex stated that journalists had become "civil servants,"[28] he was summing up the emasculation of the press. Goebbels reacted directly to this provocation.

On November 18 he gave a talk to the Reich press managers in which, with profound irony, he characterized the attitude now taken by German journalists toward the Nazi regime as "neue Sachlichkeit."* As a positive example he mentioned the situation after the death of Hindenburg: "The merest hint sufficed to let the press know that 'we're not having any discussion at this point about constitutional law!' [. . .] When it comes to things that affect the national existence of a people and must therefore be solved by the government, the job of the press is just to take note. Discussion changes nothing, in any case."[29] Two days later he recorded cynically that his remarks had prompted "very decent editorials." "The press is now all mine."[30] There is no doubt he was right.

At a press convention in Cologne a year later, at the end of November 1935, Goebbels addressed once more—in conclusion, so to speak—the problem of press freedom. When and where, Goebbels asked his audience, had there ever been a right to freedom of expression in earlier times? Goebbels continued: "We have removed the journalist from his humiliating and demeaning dependence on par-

---

* Translators' note: An ironic reference to the "Neue Sachlichkeit" (New Objectivity) artistic movement of the 1920s, which, rejecting expressionism, practiced a new realism.

ties and business interests, thereby placing him in a position of honorable and loyal dependence on the state. For we see the freedom of Germans not in the opportunity to do or not do what one wants, but in the opportunity to integrate freely and responsibly into the higher laws and higher moral commandments of a state."[31] Although Goebbels's ministry possessed the powers necessary to make journalists comply, as far as the structure of the press estate was concerned he was obliged to leave the field to a rival. In April 1935 Max Amann, a Reich leader of the NSDAP and as such responsible for the press, issued, in his capacity as president of the Reich Press Chamber, several edicts that were to bring lasting changes. In future Amann would be entitled to close down newspaper publishers in order to "obviate unhealthy conditions of competition" or for sundry other reasons. In particular, Catholic papers and the "Generalanzeigerpresse" (popular commercial newspapers without religious or political affiliation) could now be shut down or their publishers forced to sell to holding companies controlled by the Party-owned Eher Verlag.[32] By the end of 1936 between 500 and 600 newspapers were closed, and by 1944 the number of papers overall had dropped from more than 3,000 in 1933 to 975. By then, 80 percent of papers in print came from the Eher Verlag.[33]

Not only was Goebbels not involved in formulating the edicts issued in 1935 by Amann, with their rationale for suppressing or acquiring newspapers; he was actually opposed to promulgating them. In his diary he held that Amann's decrees amounted to the "destruction of the bourgeois press." In subsequent negotiations with Amann, he thought he had at least secured the involvement of the Propaganda Ministry in applying the edicts.[34] From the diaries in following years it does seem that such participation (but nothing more) did indeed occur when he negotiated with Amann over the fate of individual newspapers; we will return to this in more detail later. There was a solid underlying reason for his relatively weak position as regards the press landscape. Because of various extremely lucrative publishing contracts, Goebbels was financially dependent on Amann.[35]

CULTURAL POLITICS TAKES A SHARPER TURN

In the second half of the year, with the "revolutionary" forces within the Nazi movement eliminated, Goebbels's political rival in the cultural field, Alfred Rosenberg, thought the time was right to use his role as "overseer" of Nazi ideology to launch an all-out campaign against the propaganda minister.

Having complained in July about Goebbels's "unsuitable" speech on the subject of June 30, 1934,[36] in August Rosenberg (in Goebbels's opinion an "unbending, obstinate dogmatist") had Goebbels in his sights because of his allegedly excessive cultural permissiveness.[37] Rosenberg sent Goebbels a letter sharply attacking Richard Strauss, probably the most renowned personality in German musical life, whom Goebbels had appointed president of the Reich Music Chamber, and for whose seventieth birthday lavish celebrations had been staged.[38] Rosenberg accused Strauss of having let the "Jew Zweig" write the libretto of his opera *Die schweigsame Frau* (The Silent Woman); "Zweig" was said to be in contact with émigrés.

In his response, which he himself described as "harsh," Goebbels pointed out that the Zweig in question was not the "émigré Arnold Zweig" (which Rosenberg had never asserted) but Stefan Zweig, who was living in Austria, and he condescendingly advised Rosenberg to be more careful about his information in future.[39] Incidentally, a performance of the opera, which Goebbels had initially wanted to prevent, took place in June 1935, now explicitly sanctioned by Goebbels.[40]

At the end of August, Rosenberg sent the propaganda minister another letter, accusing him of being too receptive to Jewish personalities such as Arnold Zweig, Bruno Walter, and Hugo von Hofmannsthal. He also attacked him on account of an exhibition of Italian Futurists that had taken place with Goebbels's support in Berlin in March 1934. Rosenberg alleged that under the cover of the Italians he had smuggled harmful modern elements into the German art scene through the back door.[41]

Rosenberg's attacks raised fundamental questions about the future direction of Nazi cultural politics. Hitler himself was to use the Party rally in September 1934 to state his views. Surprisingly, in his cultural address the dictator not only condemned the "vandals" of modern art but also spoke out against "backward-looking people" and their "old-world Teutonic art"—those of Rosenberg's persuasion, in other words.[42]

After Hitler had shown his hand, Goebbels found himself much better placed in his dispute with Rosenberg. The fact was that Rosenberg's influence on German cultural life was based on a dogmatism which Hitler clearly wanted to circumscribe, while Goebbels, who actually had no clear concept of art, needed only to refrain from his occasionally expressed support for "modern" artistic tendencies in order to assume a leading role in cultural politics. So it was that at the end of 1934 he felt able to spell out, once and for all, a zero-tolerance policy for the remnants of artistic "depravity" still extant in German cultural life. This unyielding policy immediately claimed an eminent victim in Germany's star conductor, Wilhelm Furtwängler. As recently as 1933 Goebbels—apparently prepared to make concessions— had engaged with him in public discussions about the freedom of art.

In an article of November 25, 1934, published in the *Deutsche Allgemeine Zeitung*, Furtwängler, who was among other things deputy director of the Reich Music Chamber, had come to the defense of the composer Paul Hindemith when he came under attack by Rosenberg's Nazi cultural organization. Hindemith was charged with having "non-Aryan relatives" as well as unacceptable politics. Furtwängler had conducted the premiere of Hindemith's latest work, *Mathis der Maler* (Matthew the Painter) in March and planned to stage the first performance of the composer's opera on the same subject—the life of the Renaissance painter Matthias Grünewald—at the Berlin State Opera, until he was informed that Hitler disapproved of the premiere.[43]

The Nazi press hit back hard at Furtwängler for his attempts to defend Hindemith. *Der Angriff*, for example, wanted to know why the "opportunist musician" Hindemith should be "praised prematurely."[44] According to the diaries, the affair kept Goebbels and the Nazi leadership very busy for some days, with Goebbels—who had initially been eager to retain Hindemith in German musical life[45]— advocating an uncompromising line. The affair ended with Furtwängler's resignation as deputy director of the Reich Music Chamber and as conductor of the Berlin Philharmonic Orchestra.[46] Goebbels now followed through with a sharp attack on the conductor (although without mentioning him by name) in a speech to the Reich Culture Chamber on December 16, 1934.[47]

At the end of February 1935 he had a meeting with Furtwängler at the latter's request.[48] After a lengthy discussion, they agreed on an explanation whereby Furtwängler's Hindemith article of the previous November would be presented as written "from the musical point of view": He had no intention of interfering in the "arts policy" of the Reich. This explanation, together with a few other gestures on Furtwängler's part toward the regime, was the prerequisite for Furtwängler's resumption of his conducting activities in April, all of which was accounted a "great moral success" by Goebbels.[49] Actually, however, Furtwängler's reinstatement amounted to an obvious admission by the regime that the gap created in German musical life by his enforced temporary absence could not be filled by anyone else.[50] On the other hand, Furtwängler's resignation gave the Propaganda Ministry the opportunity substantially to increase its influence over the Berlin Philharmonic Orchestra, which had been taken over by the Propaganda Ministry on behalf of the Reich in 1933. The "Reich orchestra" was supposed to demonstrate by its many guest appearances abroad that National Socialist Germany was as much the home of culture as ever.[51]

Furtwängler, whose concerts were conspicuously attended by Hitler, Göring, and Goebbels in the spring of 1935, agreed to conduct a performance of *Die Meistersinger von Nürnberg* in Nuremberg on the eve of the Party rally in September. But it was a step too far when he was asked to present Beethoven's Fifth during the NSDAP cultural conference at the rally.[52]

If Goebbels's intention was that Furtwängler's reinstatement should prepare the way for Hindemith's return to musical life in the Third Reich, then in this respect he was to be disappointed. Rosenberg successfully intervened with Rust to ensure that Hindemith was not allowed to resume his position as professor at the Berlin Music Academy—from which he had been suspended at the end of 1934—despite a positive recommendation to that effect from the Propaganda Ministry. The composer emigrated soon afterward.[53]

It was hard for Goebbels to gain any ground in the battle with Rosenberg. Alongside the altercation over the musicians, Rosenberg had written what Goebbels considered an "impudent article" for the *Völkischer Beobachter* in December 1934. Here Rosenberg self-confidently underlined his leading position in cultural politics and complained about "personalities" who previously had had little or nothing to do with National Socialist cultural politics and art, rendering more difficult the work of the "National Socialist Cultural Community" established by himself, Rosenberg.[54] Goebbels was particularly hard hit by the further negative comments in the *Völkischer Beobachter* about the cultural endeavors he was promoting; he suspected Rosenberg of being behind these comments.[55]

In June 1935, Rosenberg used the occasion of a Reich conference of his National Socialist Cultural Community to launch further attacks on Goebbels.[56] The latter responded a few days later with a speech to the Reich Theater Chamber, albeit "only to a specialist audience," where he criticized the influence (represented by Rosenberg as beneficial) of the Cultural Community on German theaters' repertoire for producing results that were not national-socialist enough.[57]

But then, in July 1935, he was forced to drop the second greatest figure—after Furtwängler—in German musical life, Richard Strauss, from the presidency of the Reich Music Chamber, after Rosenberg produced a letter addressed to the émigré Stefan Zweig, which had been intercepted by the Gestapo. Strauss's remark that he was just "acting the part" of president of the Music Chamber seemed to render him completely unsuitable.[58] After a handful of performances, Strauss's opera *Die schweigsame Frau* vanished from the stage of the Dresden Opera.

At the same time, Goebbels was setting a clear antimodern course in the visual arts as well. In April 1935 he gathered several prominent artists around him, including his old friend Hans Herbert Schweitzer, Albert Speer, the painter Adolf Ziegler, and the sculptor Kurt Schmidt-Ehm, exhorting them "to assert themselves against the Cubists."[59]

These examples show that in 1934–35 Goebbels was by no means the unconstrained sole master and expert helmsman of Germany's culture and media he liked to claim he was: He had to share control and management with others.

A further case will highlight this. In the spring of 1935, the Gestapo drew his attention to the Berlin cabaret venues "Katakombe" and "Tingel-tangel," where; behind a front of entertainment, "propaganda harmful and occasionally even hostile to the state was being put out."[60] With Goebbels's acquiesence, the venues were closed by the Gestapo, although Goebbels gives the impression in his diary that the shutdown had been on his orders.[61] For his part, Goebbels called on the Gestapo to send six members of the cabaret casts who in the meantime had been arrested to a concentration camp for an initial stint of six weeks.[62]

The *Völkischer Beobachter* made much of the shutdown on May 11, 1935, under the headline "Jewish Insolence at Berlin Cabarets": "As some of the participants [. . .] are only superficially informed, if at all, about important arrangements in the new state, against which they have vented their wrath, they will now have the opportunity through decent and solid work in a camp to catch up on what they have neglected for far too long."

As it turned out, the trial of five of the performers from the two theaters ended in October 1936 with an acquittal in all cases.[63] But the regime had demonstrated that it was serious when it came to open expressions of criticism of its policies. Goebbels was to keep to this line in subsequent years too, although he made sure the Gestapo never again got the better of him, as it had in this case.

Thus in spring 1936 he procured a Führer edict that strengthened his position enormously. The decree stipulated that the Ministry for Popular Enlightenment and Propaganda possessed full policing rights for all matters that fell within its jurisdiction, so that it could, for example, issue bans accompanied by threats of punishment.[64]

In addition, in June, the Propaganda Ministry produced at its regular press conference an internal directive prohibiting all authorities, organizations, and associations from giving the press any instructions or orders. Likewise, no one was entitled to exercise criticism of the press.[65] In April 1937 the Propaganda Ministry explicitly informed the press again that it possessed the sole right to control the press; all other attempts "to put pressure on the press by means of influence or threats" would be rejected.[66]

FILM POLICIES

In the area of film, too, Goebbels tried to exert a controlling influence in 1934 and 1935, although with only limited success.

Once Goebbels had made work in the film industry dependent on membership of the Reich Film Chamber, he made sure that his control over film was considerably enlarged by the Cinema Law of February 16, 1934.[67] Films could now be banned on account of offending

"national-socialist" or "artistic sensibilities,"[68] and the law of censorship had been tightened in such a way[69] that Goebbels could ban individual films by order, which he promptly did "on grounds of taste."[70]

The law also introduced the classification of films by the state
board of censors: The board was authorized to categorize films as "of
political value to the state," "artistic," "educational," or "culturally
valuable," thus exempting the films in question from the entertainment tax.[71] Additionally, the Cinema Law provided for a "Reich film
dramaturge" who—independently of the board of censors—was entitled to oversee all film projects at the planning and screenplay
stages.[72] The editor of Der Angriff, Willi Krause, took over the position of film dramaturge in February 1934.[73] He was followed in 1936
and 1937 by the writer Hans Jürgen Nierentz, who also came from
the editorial office of Der Angriff, but Goebbels soon became dissatisfied with him;[74] in 1937 Fritz Hippler was appointed to the job.

On February 9, 1934, Goebbels gave a lecture in the Kroll Opera
House to "film creators." He took a conciliatory approach, protesting
"against the imputation [. . .] that we intend to falsify films for National Socialist purposes." National Socialism should be "conveyed
not by the choice of subject matter, but the way the material is
treated."[75]

Just a few months after his Kroll Opera House talk, Goebbels let
leading representatives of the film world know that his demands actually went further. In the Propaganda Ministry on June 21, at a session for film administrators, leading lights of the film industry, and
famous film stars—including Heinrich George, Heinz Rühmann,
and Hans Albers—Goebbels stated that he did not demand "programmatic National Socialist films," but that "film subjects should be
imbued with national-socialist ideas and problems, and should acknowledge and represent the principle of the highest responsibility,
but also the highest authority." He was not against "entertainment
films" as such, just against "mindless entertainment films."[76]

There were several reasons that most entertainment films were
banal in the extreme (Goebbels's diaries fully attest to this)[77] and that
propaganda films were mainly limited to nationalist clichés. Above
all there was, of course, the difficult economic situation of the film
industry, aside from the somewhat impenetrable system of censorship and the lack of clear direction from the propaganda minister.
The film industry was not willing to take risks.[78] Goebbels tried to

change this unsatisfactory situation by having a law passed at the end of 1934 adjusting the film dramaturge's brief such that in future he would no longer be responsible for the majority of entertainment films.[79]

But from the end of 1934 onward, Goebbels himself pursued a few film projects he wanted to recommend to the film industry as models of the great "art film" of the future. Joseph Goebbels was determined to go down in German film history as a kind of inspirational force. In November 1934 he held a conference with film creators in which he presented three projects: a film about Oliver Cromwell; a movie based on the Wars of Liberation in the Napoleonic period; and an epic about the years 1918 to 1932. Two further projects were soon added: a Joan of Arc film and an "emigration film," with Luis Trenker to direct.[80]

In February 1935, in connection with the opening of the Berlin Reich Film Archive, Goebbels gave a speech singing his own praises as reformer of the German film. He declared that in current productions he felt the lack "of the artistically and ideologically assured film." Also lacking, however, was the "good, skillful, witty and spirited, or superior satirical, German entertainment film." The various measures instituted by the regime since 1933 to promote film (founding the Film Bank, introduction of the film dramaturge, the prospect of film prizes, and so on) had "not led to conspicuous success in the area of film."[81]

Only one of his big projects, mentioned once more by Goebbels in this speech, seems to have been realized. In 1935 the movie *Das Mädchen Johanna* (The Girl Joan) was released, dealing with the Joan of Arc theme. Goebbels had followed the project with great interest and enthusiasm,[82] but the finished product was a disappointment to him, and—more decisively—it disappointed Hitler too, ruling it out for the National Prize.[83] This put an end to Goebbels's efforts to exert his influence on "film creation" through the promotion of certain exemplary projects.

At an "international" film congress in April 1935—only Germany, Austria, and Czechoslovakia were represented, in point of fact—Goebbels set out seven "principles" for the future German film. He particularly complained about the stage-bound nature of the German film—which in terms of international comparisons was indeed one of its principal aesthetic shortcomings. He also called on the film industry to "liberate itself from the vulgar triviality of mere mass amusement." Film must, "like any other art, be topical in order to have a topical impact." In practice it was evident that such generalized, often complacent advice from the propaganda minister hardly offered the film industry any kind of guidance.[84]

The same was true of his efforts to regulate film criticism. In December, when he invited critics from the various cultural sectors to the Propaganda Ministry, all he had to offer was a series of platitudes, with one fact emerging for sure: The cultural activities subsidized and regulated by the dictatorship could not be reconciled with art criticism.[85]

On December 15, 1935, Goebbels gave another set-piece lecture at the Kroll Opera to "film creators."[86] Here he accepted in principle the justification for "entertainment films" but was critical of their "stupidity" and the "assembly-line production of those who followed the same formula." Almost three years after the "seizure of power," this was a fairly damning indictment of his own impact on filmmaking,[87] despite the fact that, by changing the Cinema Law and by virtue of orders given by Hitler in the course of 1935, he had succeeded in strengthening his censorship powers in film considerably.[88]

Since all his exhortations, principles, and guidelines had essentially failed to improve the quality of films, in 1936 he decided to take direct control of the big studios.

HITLER AND THE GOEBBELS FAMILY

In all his activities in the media and cultural fields, one thing above all was decisive for Goebbels: his close relationship with Hitler, with whom he regularly discussed individual measures within his sphere of operations and whose taste in art and personal preferences shaped his work. So it was devastating for him to see that in autumn 1934 the Goebbelses' personal relationship with Hitler was in a state of crisis.

In the middle of October he noticed with consternation that Hitler had suddenly become distant with him, although he could not identify the cause of this behavior. On October 15 he noted in his diary: "Führer does not call at suppertime. We have the feeling that somebody is influencing him against us. We are both very pained by it. Go to bed with a heavy heart." When he met Hitler the next day he observed that he was "somewhat reserved" toward him. They thought Magda might be able to help, but when she tried to arrange a meeting with him "to clear things up," Hitler could not spare the time. Her attempts over the next few days to get access to Hitler were, as Goebbels meticulously recorded, likewise "unsuccessful."[89] When she finally succeeded in reaching him a few days later, she learned from Hitler that he had been the victim of a "gossip" campaign instigated by Frau Schirach and had therefore decided to be more reserved in company from now on: "No more ladies in the Reich Chancellery." Eventually, Hitler repeated the story to Goebbels in private. When Goebbels asked whether he, too, should be more withdrawn in social terms, Hitler does not seem to have given him a direct answer but simply reassured Goebbels in a general way that he had "complete confidence in him." Goebbels found it "painful that there should be a shadow over our friendship. I'm quite depressed. Yet as innocent in the matter as a newborn child."[90] Although Goebbels soon resumed his old routine at the Reich Chancellery, he recorded that he was suffering from this tense situation. He was not alone: "Magda has become ill over it."[91]

The episode reveals clearly how profoundly dependent they both were on Hitler emotionally: The mere suspicion that they were losing favor with the Führer was enough to plunge both of them into a real depression.

Shortly afterward Goebbels had a serious argument with Magda that tested the strength of their marriage. The cause is not clear; from the relevant passage of the diary, which is scarcely legible, it seems that it had to do with the question of "her offspring"—with Harald, that is. In the spring there had been a heated argument between Goebbels and Harald's father, Günther Quandt, about which of his parents Harald should live with in future. It is possible that this argument, which Goebbels claimed in the diary was settled in his favor, had further consequences.[92] In any case, as Goebbels wrote on November 20, Magda wanted to "get away from me," but he also wrote that he was not giving in over the vexed question. She was already packing her bags; there was a "state of war" between them.[93]

On Perritence and Prayer Day the argument escalated into a "disaster": "Against my wishes, she left for Dresden after an abrupt goodbye. So the break has happened." After a long talk with Magda's sister-in-law Ello, from whom he learned some "quite unpalatable details," he came to the conclusion that the separation was unavoidable. In the diary he gave full rein to self-pity and the next morning compelled himself to make a final attempt to bring Magda to heel: "Order immediate return. She is cheeky, very unsure of herself. If she doesn't obey, I'll take steps."[94]

But Magda did submit, and returned from her Dresden exile. Then, however, there was another "serious confrontation": They were on the point of divorce when she finally gave way, and promised to make it "a better marriage." Goebbels, too, came around, admitting, "I've made mistakes as well. Everlasting conflict: marriage/Party."[95] His relationship with Magda became a good deal more harmonious in the New Year; one reason was that Magda was pregnant again.[96]

With the gradual entrenchment of the regime and the development of the Propaganda Ministry into an organization controlling and directing the German public sphere, Goebbels was inclined to accentuate more and more the importance of his position, no longer avoiding outward display. The conspicuous austerity he had made such an effort to maintain, even in 1933, was now gradually being discarded.

As head of the Propaganda Ministry, Goebbels placed great importance on an imposing style. The Hohenzollern palace that housed his ministry contained several grand and lavishly appointed historic rooms, which Goebbels used for big formal occasions and celebrations,[97] such as the reception in connection with the annual Berlin Automobile Exhibition,[98] or in November, when his Reich Cultural Senate had its conference.[99] Once the ministry's theater had been enlarged in 1938, regular performances took place there.[100]

In contrast to the years before 1933, when he cultivated his anti-bourgeois image by wearing a leather jacket or a worn trench coat, as a minister Goebbels thought it important to wear carefully chosen, elegant clothing. Photographs from the years between 1933 and 1939 mostly show him in impeccable suits of superior quality. He was always suitably attired for the occasion, whether at soirées or at leisure, as a boat owner for example.[101] The wardrobes in his various dwellings were neatly organized: In his official residence in Göringstrasse, aside from a variety of uniforms, he had 3 tailcoats, 4 tuxedos, 3 suits for afternoon wear, 1 frock coat, another 30 suits, 13 pairs of outdoor gloves, and 12 pairs of white dress gloves.[102] And Goebbels was intent that his staff be well dressed too: In autumn

1937 he gave his top officials an allowance of 1,000 Reichsmarks to buy "better clothes."[103]

The Goebbels couple became increasingly accustomed to the luxury that went with their exalted social position. Between March and June 1935 their home in Göringstrasse underwent structural alterations, following plans drawn up by Albert Speer.[104] As one of their first visitors after the rebuilding, Hitler was "enthusiastic" about the result.[105] Among the amenities enjoyed there was a television set, installed in February 1935; the propaganda minister loved watching it with his family, although broadcasting was limited to a few hours and was still at the test stage.[106] In October 1934 he took delivery of a new 5-liter limousine ("a noble, fiery beast");[107] in February 1935 he bought Magda a "wonderful new car," a Mercedes he had seen at the Automobile Exhibition; and for himself he acquired a new Horch in May.[108]

In other respects his lifestyle was less opulent. In culinary matters Goebbels continued to be undemanding;[109] in all of his diaries there is not a single mention of the quality of the food he consumed. He had avoided alcohol since embarking on his political career; only when he had a cold did he comsume a few glasses to put himself into a deep sleep. Smoking, on the other hand, was something he could never shake off, despite various attempts to give up.[110]

During spring and summer the Goebbels family stayed at their summer home in Kladow.[111] At the end of March a new boat arrived; what Goebbels called a "real recreation facility."[112] As in the previous year, Hitler was among the guests he entertained on the boat.[113]

His close relationship with Hitler, which in October had been temporarily threatened by a growing coolness, had now been restored. Since the end of 1934, Goebbels had been observing the state of Hitler's health with growing anxiety. In December Hitler was so gravely ill that Goebbels—who suspected poisoning—already feared the worst when Hitler settled the question of his successor by means of an emergency act passed by the cabinet but never subsequently published.[114] He repeatedly resolved to find a really good doctor for Hitler.[115] A few months later he was afraid that a serious throat problem indicated that Hitler had cancer. But in June it transpired that this was a benign growth.[116]

He also worried once more about Hitler's private life. At the end of January he stayed in his apartment in the Reich Chancellery until

3 A.M.:[117] "He tells me about his lonely, joyless private life. Without women, without love, always full of memories of Geli." A few days later Hitler came back to the topic: "Women, marriage, love, and loneliness." And with obvious pride Goebbels remarked: "It's only me he talks to like this."[118]

The restoration of the old harmony also had the result that Goebbels now continued to cater to all of Hitler's wishes, even when they made deep inroads into his private life. By way of example: In April 1935 Julius Schaub, Hitler's adjutant, called, telling Goebbels that he and his wife were to present themselves the next day in Munich. There Hitler, who had just undergone a turbulent flight, brought him together with the English fascist leader Oswald Mosley, chatted with Goebbels for a while about his foreign policy, and then released him to return to Berlin, where Goebbels arrived the same afternoon. He spent the night in a hotel—as his official residence was being rebuilt—working late into the evening. The diary does not reveal why Hitler summoned Magda to Munich.[119]

CHAPTER 14

"Never Tire!"

Foreign Policy Successes and Anti-Jewish Policies

During his summer vacation in July 1935 at the Baltic resort of Heiligendamm, Goebbels found himself obliged to curb the escalation of anti-Semitic thuggery in Berlin. The summertime relaxation shown in this press photo is intended to distract attention from the seriousness of the situation (from left to right, SA-Gruppenführer Ludwig Uhland, Artur Görlitzer, Wolf-Heinrich von Helldorf, Goebbels, Kurt Daluege, and Julius Lippert).

By concluding a non-aggression pact with Poland in the summer of 1934, the regime took a step forward in breaking out of its near-total diplomatic isolation. Goebbels played a very active role in this improvement in German-Polish relations. In February 1934 the two sides had signed up for a press truce, and in June Goebbels had visited Warsaw on a fact-finding tour, including talks about cultural questions of mutual interest.[1] Over the course of 1935, the regime brought in other policies that had even greater significance in leading

Germany out of its isolation. This development began with the removal of two important Versailles Treaty restrictions: the decision about annexing the Saarland to the Reich and the reintroduction of conscription. It was difficult to calculate where foreign policy developments would go from here and what their impact at home might be, but the propaganda minister's diary shows that, while the leadership of the regime was certainly experiencing insecurity and anxiety, it was also gaining in self-confidence, sometimes to the point of feeling triumphantly superior.

January 13, 1935, was the date set for a plebiscite in the Saar territory (mandated to the League of Nations by the Versailles Treaty) to decide its future: annexation by Germany, annexation by France, or an independent political entity? Naturally, the Propaganda Ministry had thrown everything into the campaign effort. While the Nazi "German Front," with huge support from the Propaganda Ministry and other German sources, almost completely dominated the campaign in this tiny area of just 800,000 inhabitants, in the southwest of the Reich, in Trier, Koblenz, and other places, mass rallies were held to back the annexation of the Saarland by Germany. Goebbels himself had spoken at several events.[2]

Ten days before the vote, a meeting of the "German leadership" was convened in the Berlin State Opera, to which cabinet members, Gauleiters and NSDAP Reich leaders, other top officials of the Party, and high-ranking military personnel were invited. This hastily summoned gathering was a response, on the part of a regime that was evidently rattled, to proliferating rumors of divisions within the government, indeed of an imminent domestic political settling of scores comparable to June 30, 1934.[3] After Hess had opened this memorable occasion with a "declaration of loyalty" on behalf of all present, Hitler gave an hour-long speech in which he called for unity, particularly in view of the forthcoming Saarland plebiscite. In conclusion, Göring read out a "loyal address," which, as its co-author Goebbels recorded, was "received with cheers."[4]

An entry the next day in Goebbels's diary, about a conversation with Hitler, bears witness to the regime's deep insecurity, which had motivated the dictator to stage such an overt demonstration of the alleged unity of his administration: "After the Saar we'll be facing extortion from Paris. 1935 another tough year. Keep nerve."[5]

On the morning of January 15, two days after the plebiscite ballot on January 13, the preliminary results were announced, indicating an overwhelming victory. Almost 91 percent of the population had voted for the Saar to join the German Reich. Goebbels then gave the signal for celebrations throughout Germany: "In a few minutes the entire country covered in flags. It's beyond description. Triumph of patriotism!"[6]

Goebbels had issued the call for flags everywhere that morning on the radio and in the press. In addition, between 12 and 1 o'clock the bells of every church in Germany were to be rung; by order of the education minister a school holiday was also declared. In his capacity as head of propaganda for the Reich, Goebbels ordered that "between about 19 and 21 hours today, Tuesday, January 15, the population will spontaneously [sic] attend mass rallies to celebrate victory in the Saar."[7]

In the days that followed, Goebbels had the opportunity to discuss the diplomatic situation with Hitler in depth, as for example on January 20: "Big project re: England. Protection of the Empire, therefore 30-year alliance. Still in progress. He's working hard on it." And on Hitler's view of the situation, he noted: "Poland will stand solidly with us. France and England are getting ready for extortion. But we will stay tough."

A few days later, during a train journey, Hitler informed him about a visit by the pacifist British politician Clifford Allen, which had just taken place: "The English are having political trouble domestically. That is to our advantage. The Führer hopes to have them in an alliance in 4 years' time: us superior on land, them at sea, parity in the air. This offer made an impression. Well, we can only wait and rearm."[8]

Goebbels was pleased at the outcome of Franco-British discussions at the beginning of February in London: There were proposals for an international air pact and for the replacement of the disarmament provisions of the Versailles Treaty by an international arms agreement. And in fact, in the middle of the month the Reich government reacted for the most part positively to the proposals.[9] Foreign Secretary Simon and Lord Privy Seal Anthony Eden were invited to talks in Berlin for March 7. But when in early March the British government published a "nasty white paper on German rearmament"—as Goebbels put it—"the Führer became hoarse and canceled the English visit."[10] On Goebbels's advice, Hitler abstained from all official business in the following weeks, went to Bavaria, and recovered from his sore throat in Wiesbaden. It had actually been more than a mere diplomatic indisposition.[11] In the end it was agreed that the British visit to Berlin should take place at the end of the month.

The self-assurance of the head of state was boosted not least by the "liberation festivities" that had celebrated the annexation of the Saar on March 1. Goebbels had insisted on personally overseeing the final preparations for the main rally in Saarbrücken. The annexation was officially completed with the ceremonial hoisting of the swastika flag in Saarbrücken; howling sirens throughout the Reich; and the official handover of authority in Saarbrücken Town Hall to the Reich governor, Gauleiter Josef Bürckel, who was responsible for incorporating the Saarland into the Reich. In Saarbrücken, Hess, Goebbels, Bürckel, and finally Hitler all gave speeches that were broadcast across Germany. In his address, Goebbels called the Saar population "soldiers of peace" and said that the vote gave Hitler the opportunity "to shape this declaration into the basis of a new European understanding and a better order in Europe."[12]

In an interview for the *Daily Mail* on March 10 Göring revealed, more or less in passing, the existence of a new German air force—another breach of the Versailles Treaty. Goebbels's reaction to this news was conspicuously relaxed. He had little choice, since Göring had obviously given him no opportunity in advance to devise a propaganda presentation of the move. So, on the afternoon of the day when Göring's interview appeared in the German press, Goebbels decided to take the day off and visit the Berlin Boat Show, where he viewed a motorboat he was thinking of buying.[13]

Equally unexpected for Goebbels was the announcement Hitler made to him three days later. The Führer had decided to introduce universal conscription. Hitler justified his decision by saying that he wanted to create a fait accompli before the visit by the British delegation later in March.[14] In an editorial in *Der Angriff*, titled "Clarity and Logic," Goebbels praised this violation of the Versailles Treaty—which became law on March 16[15]—as an "open and unrestrained presentation of German intentions," representing, as such, an "element of reassurance" meant to further the preservation of peace.[16]

No serious repercussions for the regime stemmed from this move.[17] On March 24 Simon and Eden arrived in Berlin as planned, to spend the next two days—though without managing to extract any promises from the German leadership—discussing with Hitler the topic of arms limitation and the possible inclusion of Germany in international treaty agreements. Goebbels was told retrospectively by Hitler about the most important results of these talks; he himself took no part in the visit except to arrange the accompanying social agenda.[18]

After the British visit, Goebbels went over various aspects of the foreign relations situation with Hitler. He thought Mussolini was bluffing when he said, as reported by Ambassador Ulrich von Hassell, that he believed war was inevitable, but in Goebbels's estimation there was a danger that "the ball might be set rolling by some sudden stupid action."[19] Hitler, stated Goebbels, did not believe in a war, either, but "if it should happen, it would be dreadful," because Germany had very limited stocks of raw materials.[20] When the Italian, French, and British heads of government declared in Stresa in the middle of April that they would "oppose with all appropriate means the unilateral cancellation of treaties," Goebbels was unconcerned: "We don't care, as long as they don't attack us. Just keep on rearming."[21] He was equally relaxed in his comment on a further reaction to Germany's remilitarizing policy, the signing of a Franco-Soviet military pact on May 2, 1935: In his view it was nothing more than a "legal anomaly."[22]

DISAPPOINTMENT

At the beginning of April Goebbels flew to the Danzig Free State to support the Danzig election campaign by attending a mass rally of the local Nazi Party, for which sixty thousand people turned out.[23]

But it was a great disappointment to find that the outcome of the Danzig election on April 7 was nowhere near the high level of approval the NSDAP now routinely expected in the Reich. The election target announced beforehand was a majority of two thirds, but the NSDAP gained only 59.3 percent of the vote. Only with some difficulty was Goebbels able to restrain Gauleiter Albert Forster from announcing a result of 67 percent on the radio. "We're all very disappointed. People have become quite sullen here and there. We've got to pull ourselves together. We've played too well and too often on the 'soul of the Volk.' Less pomp and speeches, more simplicity and work."

But things were to get even worse: The opposition contested the result. However, the League of Nations could not bring itself to revoke the election, despite the Danzig High Court's finding of wide-scale manipulation. While funding from the Reich had enabled the NSDAP to mount a comprehensive campaign, the opposition parties' campaigns—the Communist Party had been banned since 1934—had been largely suppressed. They had scarcely been able to hold public meetings; press bans were in place; and the authorities had massively favored the NSDAP in other ways. Finally, there was the outright falsification of results, particularly in rural areas. The court, under great pressure from the Nazi local government, did not propose that the election should be held again, but it did retroactively reduce the NSDAP's share of the vote. What is more, its sober findings brought to light the terror tactics and manipulation employed by the Danzig Nazis, thus giving a glimpse of the reality behind the facade of the supposedly irresistible and unstoppable process of mobilizing mass sentiments by National Socialism.[24]

It should be borne in mind that the NSDAP in the Danzig Free State, despite huge interference in the democratic voting process, had only managed an increase of nine points on its above-average result of 50.1 percent in 1933. Taking the manipulation into account, this means that the Party enjoyed scarcely more support from the voters than in 1933, arguably less. The judicial exposure of the extensive manipulations in Danzig also throws light on the state of affairs in the Reich. If we take Danzig as a model, it becomes clear that the much-vaunted solidarity of the "national community" was to a very large extent an illusion created by the regime, produced by the celebrations, orgies of flag-flying, and mass marches decreed by Goebbels and reinforced by the everyday use of intimidation and terror on the part of the regime. This is all the more evident when we take into account that both terror and propaganda were even less constrained in the Reich than in the "Free State" on the Baltic.

It is not really surprising that the NSDAP had not succeeded by 1935 in raising its standing with the public. For by that date the regime had not actually achieved any grand-scale successes. Internationally, despite some important progress, the Reich was as isolated as ever; the economic upturn had certainly had a beneficial effect on employment, but the financial circumstances of most Germans were just as modest as before. In addition, there were several negative factors: the anticlerical policy; the aggressive attitude toward "reactionaries," that is to say, that section of the population that voted for the nationalist parties; the terror tactics used against political opponents and other undesirables; and the arbitrary, self-important, and officious manner of many Party functionaries toward their fellow citizens. At the same time, the euphoric honeymoon period of the early days was a thing of the past.[25]

Goebbels had his eye on this uncertain public mood in spring 1935, when he became preoccupied with another great event. "Göring is marrying Frau Sonnemann on April 11," wrote Goebbels in his diary in March, adding with a sigh: "Why should he have it better than me."[26] Actually there had been a long-term relaxation in Goebbels's relationship with Göring. After Goebbels, on Hitler's recommendation, had included some praise of Göring in his *Kaiserhof* book, Göring approached him in June 1934 to make "a renewed offer of friendship."[27] Yet now, in April 1935, he took a somewhat jaundiced view of the ostentatious wedding planned by Göring and the actress Emmy Sonnemann: He feared that "this will do us no good at all among the little people."[28] The great day finally came: He and Magda took part in the solemnities in Berlin Cathedral as well as the banquet in the Kaiserhof to follow: "7 courses. Uplifting sight for the hungry. Best forget it."[29]

SPRING 1935: FIRST STEPS TO END INTERNATIONAL ISOLATION

When Marshal Józef Piłsudski—the man whose authoritarian regime had ruled Poland since 1926 and who was responsible for the rapprochement with Nazi Germany since 1934—died on May 12, 1935, Goebbels was highly alarmed: "Poland is losing its best man, and we're losing the most important figure in the great game."[30] On May 13 he talked to Hitler about the situation arising from Piłsudski's death,[31] and the two men continued the debate the next day, this time accompanied by Göring and by Hitler's foreign policy adviser Joachim von Ribbentrop (whom Goebbels did not rate highly):[32]

"Poland decisive. Year 1936 and especially 1937 dangerous. We prepare for all eventualities. For most extreme possibility, too. Rearm,
rearm!"[33] These remarks show how unstable Germany's foreign policy situation seemed to the leading figures of the regime in spring
1935. They were somewhat reassured when Göring returned from
the funeral ceremony in Warsaw to report that Józef Beck, now securely ensconced in office, had promised him that "Poland would
stand by its treaty with us."[34]

There was another glimmer of hope, too, as Goebbels discovered
from a conversation with Hitler on May 14: "Mussolini seems to be
getting entangled in Abyssinia. [...] Looking to us for friendship
again."[35] Mussolini's unmistakable preparations for war against Abyssinia led to increasing friction abroad and, eventually, to a huge international crisis in the summer.[36] The Nazi regime, of course, wanted
to exploit the situation to break out of the foreign policy isolation of
the Third Reich: To this end, the German press was repeatedly
warned as early as February 1935 not to criticize Italy's Abyssinian
policy.[37]

Noting the increasing divisions between Italy and the two other
big European powers, Hitler decided in May to take the foreign policy initiative. On May 21 he gave a speech in the Reichstag that German propaganda represented as a "speech for peace."[38] A significant
point in the address was Hitler's promise to preserve the territorial
integrity of Austria, which the Italians had long angled for. Mussolini
was quick to respond in a friendly manner to this gesture, broaching
with the German ambassador the possibility of a German-Italian understanding.[39] On May 25 Goebbels directed the press "in future and
in all areas to avoid any kind of friction with Italy."[40]

Aside from this, Hitler's speech contained in particular an offer to
Britain to negotiate. Among other things, Hitler declared that Germany would agree to limit its naval tonnage to 35 percent of British
capacity. At the same time, Hitler used the speech to launch an attack
on France, openly stating that his western neighbor was endangering
the future of the Locarno Treaties by its military alliance with the
Soviet Union. Furthermore, he did not hold back when questioning
the demilitarization of the Rhineland. The "speech for peace" was
therefore in reality an obvious attempt at splitting the "Stresa Front."
Among the audience, Reichstag member Joseph Goebbels listened

reverently to the words of his leader: "Our national destiny rests in good hands."

Goebbels's diary also establishes that he was not involved in preparations for the Anglo-German Naval Agreement, signed on June 18. On June 4, the day when Hitler's newly appointed ambassador-at-large, Joachim von Ribbentrop, opened the negotiations in London, there is a first, very brief mention of the pact.[41] However, in the preceding weeks, when Hitler frequently discussed the foreign affairs situation with him, and in particular Germany's relationship with Britain, he does not seem to have raised the naval question in his presence.[42] Hitler did not touch on the subject until the negotiations were completed: "As I arrive at the Führer's office, Naval Agreement just signed in London. Führer very happy. Big success for Ribbentrop and all of us."[43]

When Goebbels writes triumphantly about this conversation, "We move closer to the goal: friendship with England," he reveals a basic misreading on the part of the German leadership of the British negotiators' motives for signing the agreement. The goal of achieving a close bilateral alliance with Hitler's partner of choice, Great Britain, was in fact not any nearer. The British side saw the treaty with Germany not as a move away from a multilateral system of security but as a first step toward tying Germany once more into a collective European security nexus. Dividing the spheres of interest into a colonial British empire, on the one hand, and German hegemony over the European continent on the other, was not on the agenda as far as the British were concerned. Hitler was as deeply mired in this misconception as his ambassador-at-large and his propaganda minister, and they never tired of compounding one another's errors in this regard. "Within 5 years," held Goebbels with respect to Anglo-German relations, "an alliance must be in place."[44]

FROM RIOTS ON THE KURFÜRSTENDAMM TO THE NUREMBERG RACE LAWS

At the beginning of June, the Goebbels family left for a vacation, once more in the Baltic resort of Heiligendamm.[45] The break gave Goebbels the rare opportunity to become more intensively involved in

Helga's education as a father. When she occasionally became cheeky, he applied what he thought was the best possible corrective: "Sometimes she gets a spanking. But then she behaves herself again."[46] A few weeks later he records that after a few "strokes" Helga was "a model of charm and friendliness."[47]

Early in July he returned to Heiligendamm. Magda came a good two weeks later, but only for a three-day visit, after which she went back to Berlin.[48] Before Magda arrived he was twice visited by the actress Luise Ullrich; he had long been a fan of hers,[49] and he now discussed "film questions" with her. On her second visit she stayed for four days by the Baltic,[50] and toward the end of his vacation she visited Goebbels once more in Heiligendamm.[51]

When he finally returned to Berlin at the beginning of August, there was an awkward confrontation with his wife: "Magda gives me a grilling." But after a few days came the obligatory reconciliation.[52]

Hitler, too, made a surprise appearance in Heiligendamm. They talked over various issues of cultural and domestic politics, and otherwise Goebbels tried to make the visit as pleasant as possible for his leader: "Eating together. Then walks and a boat trip by moonlight. Wonderful atmosphere. I steer. Back and forth across the Baltic. Führer very happy."[53] But the moonlit idyll did not last. Back in Berlin, Jews were being subjected to violent attacks, actions for which Goebbels had prepared the ground and for which he had given the order—but not before securing Hitler's backing.

The so-called Kurfürstendamm riots had a long prehistory. Since the Christmas shopping season of 1934, Nazi activists had organized further boycotts of Jewish businesses and carried out excesses against Jews. Along with the SA, as in previous years the NS-Hago, the Nationalsozialistische Handelsorganisation (National Socialist Trade Organization) played a leading role. This new anti-Semitic wave continued after the turn of the year 1934–35 and gathered momentum from February 1935 onward—following the successful Saarland plebiscite—with the Nazi press and regional Party leaders playing a central part. Aside from the exclusion of Jews from business, Party activists were demanding above all an end to "racial disgrace"—that is, intimate relations between Jews and non-Jews.

However, since the end of April the Party leaders had started trying to curb anti-Semitic excesses. A decisive factor in this was the precarious international situation of the Reich, which led to a fear of sanctions, while there was some hope that negotiating a naval treaty with Britain represented the seed of Germany's eventual emergence from international isolation. With some difficulty, the Berlin Party leadership had largely succeeded, by June, in putting a stop to anti-Semitic disturbances.[54]

But Goebbels foresaw that this could only be a temporary halt to the "actions." He took every opportunity in conversation with Hitler to secure his agreement to "proceed more radically on the Jewish question," and he was determined to "sort things out" in Berlin before too long.[55] It seemed to him that intensifying attacks on Jews was the best way of diverting attention from the critical political situation at home and of sending a signal to Party activists that the regime was serious about fulfilling the core ideological demands of the National Socialist program. Not least, he wanted to be seen as taking the lead on this; in fact, his plan was to set an example in Berlin of what a thoroughgoing anti-Semitic policy ought to look like. The radicalism on which he prided himself was now concentrated entirely on "the Jews." He had given up his "revolutionary" rhetoric in the middle of 1933; the "reactionaries" had been much weakened since June 30, 1934, and were no longer a particularly worthwhile target, and the regime had become relatively cautious about confronting the churches. With his ruthless move against the Jews in Berlin, so Goebbels thought, he had instinctively grasped the main trend to which the Party's policy would be reverting in the next few months.

After the signing of the Anglo-German Naval Agreement on June 18, disturbances did in fact flare up again in many places across the Reich. Once again, Berlin was one of the main sites for these activities: Since the beginning of June, members of the Hitler Youth had been loitering outside Jewish shops and obstructing their trade. As Gauleiter of Berlin, Goebbels fueled this pogrom atmosphere in his speech to the Gau Party rally on June 30, objecting that "Jewry is once more trying to assert itself today on every street."

On July 13 news reached Goebbels, vacationing in Heiligendamm, of a Jewish "demonstration" in Berlin: A Swedish film with anti-Semitic tendencies had allegedly been hissed at and jeered at by Jews in the audience, and this had been interpreted by the Party press as a deliberate provocation. Goebbels used the opportunity to enlist his guest, Hitler, against his adversary, Magnus von Levetzow. The Führer immediately assured him that the Berlin chief of police would be removed from his position (an idea Goebbels had been pursuing since the year before):[56] "We're getting there at last."[57]

In Berlin the Party organized a "counterdemonstration," in which *Der Angriff* of July 15 openly invited readers to participate. The desired reaction soon followed: By the same evening "outraged national comrades" were terrorizing Jewish fellow-citizens on the Kurfürstendamm, which led to sharp clashes between Party comrades and the police, who were uncertain how to deal with this outburst of "popular anger." These events were reported in the international press as "the Kurfürstendamm riots."

Goebbels noted two days later: "Riot on Kurfürstendamm. Jews beaten up. Foreign press screaming 'pogrom.'" Just as he had hoped, the Berlin police chief, Levetzow, was blamed for the affair and replaced by Goebbels's friend Wolf-Heinrich von Helldorf, who had visited him in Heiligendamm just a week before the riots.[58] On July 19 Lippert, Görlitzer, and the head of the Berlin SA, Ludwig Uhland, arrived for discussions in Heiligendamm.[59] Their conclusions were reported in *Der Angriff* the same day: "Berlin to be cleansed of communists, reactionaries and Jews. Dr. Goebbels tidies up in his Gau." Goebbels was reaping praise for redeeming a precarious situation which his own behavior had, in fact, deplorably done so much to escalate.

In mid-August he went to Nuremberg to join Hitler in putting the finishing touches on preparations for the Party rally. The event was to be used this year above all to make clear who the main enemies of the regime were. To this end, the 1935 Party rally was held under an "Anti-Comintern" slogan. By contrast, Hitler wanted to "make his peace" with the churches (in July he had appointed Hanns Kerrl as minister for churches in an attempt to place the regime's relationship to the churches on a new footing); the Stahlhelm movement was to be disbanded, but he seems to have said nothing further about his next steps regarding the "Jewish question." Subsequently he and Goebbels went on to Munich, where they inspected the Party premises that were being built on the Königsplatz.[60]

During Goebbels's stay in Upper Bavaria—visiting NSDAP Reich leader Franz Schwarz by the Tegernsee—there was a dramatic news flash. Everything indicated that an attack by Italy on the Abyssinian Empire was imminent. This development suited Hitler perfectly, as

the forthcoming war fit well into his foreign policy plans. The dictator immediately gave his listeners an account of what these plans
were: "Permanent alliance [with] England. Good relations Poland.
Limited number of colonies. But expansion to east. Baltic area belongs to us. Dominate Baltic Sea. Conflicts Italy-Abyssinia-England,
then Japan-Russia around the corner. That's to say maybe in a few
years' time. Then our great historic hour will come."[61]

The Party rally in Nuremberg was opened on September 10. The
thrust of the mass event was made apparent by Hitler's "proclamation," which was read out by Hess and enthusiastically followed by
Goebbels: "Three enemies of the state, Marxists, clericalists, and reactionaries. Implacable war without compromise. Anti-Bolshevist
and anti-Jewish. My course justified a thousand times over."[62] But
during the rally one particular enemy of National Socialism was to
emerge as a clear priority.

Goebbels gave his speech on the third day, and naturally, as he
noted, it was a "tremendous success." As instructed by Hitler, his leitmotif was anti-Bolshevism. Germany, he explained, was fulfilling a
"global mission" by leading "all like-minded groups" in the "struggle
against the international Bolshevizing of the world." On the successful accomplishment of this mission depended "the fate of all civilized
nations."[63]

Late on the evening of the next day, Hitler called him in: Together
with Frick and Hess they considered several proposed legislative
bills. The first concerned making the swastika the sole national flag.
This innovation was prompted by an incident in New York in which
demonstrators protesting Nazi policies had torn down the swastika
flag on a German ship. This led Hitler to summon, on short notice,
a special session of the Reichstag in Nuremberg to pass an act elevat-
ing the status of the Nazi symbol. At the same time, the new law
was clearly aimed at the "reactionaries," as it now outlawed the
displaying—hitherto favored by nationalists—of the old black, white,
and red imperial flag as the national flag alongside the swastika.[64]

That evening, September 14, they also gave intensive consideration to two anti-Jewish laws, which ministry officials had prepared
months before, but which now, on a spontaneous decision of Hitler's,
were to be passed by the Reichstag, and change the direction of the
whole event. First, a new citizenship law was to deprive the Jews of

their status as German citizens on equal terms with others. And second, what was later called the Law for the Protection of German Blood and German Honor (Gesetz zum Schutze des deutschen Blutes und der deutschen Ehre) proscribed marriage or sexual relations between Jews and non-Jews. Hitler's political calculation was evident: Since radical action on the confrontation with the "reactionaries" and on the church question was ruled out for the time being, the "Jewish question" would have to satisfy the radical mood that had been whipped up among the Party comrades over the previous few months.[65]

The Reichstag session began on Sunday evening at nine o'clock. In a short statement Hitler explained the new laws, which were then read out by Göring, who also supplied the reasoning behind them.[66] Goebbels found his speech almost "unbearable," however—the diary does not reveal why—and so he had the radio broadcast interrupted at this point.[67]

When Hitler addressed the Gauleiters again at the end of the rally, specifically forbidding any further excesses in connection with the "Jewish question," Goebbels doubted whether the appeal would work.[68] But it was genuinely the case that, in view of the coming Olympic year, the regime had no desire for its international reputation to suffer further damage from anti-Jewish brutality. For the same reason, after the Nuremberg rally Goebbels's propaganda became more restrained where the "Jewish question" was concerned: For the time being, it was no longer a topic for discussion.

REARMING—AND CELEBRATING

On October 2, 1935, Magda gave birth to the son they had longed for. They intended to call him Helmut. When Goebbels visited Magda in the hospital, he was overjoyed: a "Goebbels face. I'm happy beyond words. I could smash the place up for joy. A boy! A boy!"[69]

The next day Goebbels heard the news that Italy had begun its long-anticipated assault on Abyssinia.[70] When the League of Nations then imposed sanctions on Italy, Goebbels ordered the press to take a more strongly pro-Italian line, a direction for which he had obtained Hitler's approval.[71] Some days later he attended a talk given by

Hitler in the Reich Chancellery to the assembled cabinet and top military men: "All this is coming three years too soon for us. [...] We can only rearm and prepare. Europe is on the move again. If we're clever, we can be the winners."[72]

The international sanctions[73] against Italy, which were to go into effect on November 18, had only a marginal impact on Italy's ability to make war on Abyssinia, and by May 1936 the country was taken. As far as the foreign policy of the Reich was concerned, however, the war was an opportunity to exploit the rupture between Italy and the Western powers to avoid attracting too much attention as it continued to rearm.

The forced pace of rearmament and the regime's measures to make Germany economically more self-sufficient resulted in, among other things, reduced food imports, leading to supply bottlenecks and forcing Goebbels, starting in autumn 1935, to deal with growing complaints from the public about the deteriorating food situation.[74] Incorrigible complainers, said Goebbels, were using the temporary butter shortage to sow discontent among the "national community."[75] When his appeals failed to achieve results, his tone became shriller: He contended that such shortages had to be accepted for the sake of Germany's striving for economic self-sufficiency. The "eternal gripers" were therefore sabotaging the policy of building "fortress Germany."[76] The propaganda arm was now increasingly forced to explain to the population the background to the critical shortage of foodstuffs and to try to steer consumption in the right direction.[77]

Useful in this respect, as well as supplying a distraction from everyday adversity, were the numerous celebrations and mass events that began with the Party rally in September and were continued by the Party throughout the autumn and winter. Much of public life had already taken on a ritualized complexion.

While the harvest festival on the Bückeberg at the beginning of October[78] offered the opportunity to spread a reassuring message about the food supply, the opening of the Winter Relief campaign in the Kroll Opera on October 10, where in the presence of Hitler Goebbels delivered the usual report, was about communicating "national solidarity."[79] At this point a new cycle of meetings began, which— with a break at Christmas—lasted until March 1936. The meetings, numbering probably more than a hundred thousand, not only served to extol Winter Relief as "socialism in action" but also ensured the continuous briefing of the public on the food situation while in general underlining the Party's closeness to the people.[80]

However, the newsletter of the Party propagandists clearly indicates that the willingness of the public to take up "invitations" to such events was on the wane.[81] The suggested remedy was to reinforce the appeal of advertising "by increasing the personal impact" on the individual citizen,[82] although at the same time there was a warning against open threats on campaign leaflets ("those who fail to attend the meeting will be putting themselves outside the national community")[83] and "overemphatic" propaganda.[84]

Soon after the launch of the collecting season, Goebbels took part in other large-scale central events such as the commemoration of the Munich putsch in November[85] and, a few days later, the anniversary of the Reich Culture Chamber. Goebbels enhanced the anniversary by publicly presenting the Reich Cultural Senate he had recently formed. This presentation had been preceded by another dispute with Rosenberg: To Goebbels's surprise, at the previous Party rally Rosenberg had announced that there was to be an NSDAP prize for "art and science" and that he was going to create a Reich Cultural Senate.[86] Since Goebbels had long been nursing the idea of setting up a committee with the same name, he appealed to Hitler and at the end of November got him to ban Rosenberg's Cultural Senate.[87] Thus Goebbels, in his speech on November 15 at the anniversary celebrations of the Reich Culture Chamber—attended by Hitler along with many other prominent figures—was able to ceremoniously proclaim the founding of "his" Reich Cultural Senate. He used the speech to come out in opposition to "mysticisms which seem designed only to confuse public opinion"—a sideswipe at Rosenberg, to whose "cultic nonsense" Hitler had clearly expressed his animus some months earlier in the presence of Goebbels.[88] "Leadership of culture definitely with me," wrote Goebbels as this day ended.[89]

The year went out on the note of the "Volk Christmas," an action carried out by the Party across the whole Reich, whereby over five million children received presents at thirty thousand ceremonies. Goebbels attended one such event, in the Berlin Friedrichshain hall. In his speech, broadcast to the nation, he described Christmas as a Christian festival but at the same time claimed it for National Socialism, which in the form of the "national community" had given the command to love your neighbor a "new and unexpected content" in the form of the national community.[90] He himself celebrated Christmas with his family.[91] Obviously, although he had just advocated an anti-Christian position, Goebbels did not have much time for the idea of turning Christmas into a Germanic "yuletide festival," as advocated by the anticlerical wing of the Party. For him in 1935, a traditional Christmas, "the most German of all festivals," was still indispensable.

CHAPTER 15

"The Tougher the Better!"

The Olympic Year, 1936

During a trip to Greece, in September 1936, the Goebbels and Hoffmann families admire the Zeus of Artemision statue in the National
Museum in Athens. By 1936, the Nazi regime seemed to be solidly established, both at home and abroad. For Goebbels, there were many
opportunities to enjoy the fruits of success.

On February 4, 1936, the eve of the opening of the Winter Olympics
in Garmisch, Goebbels was at an evening reception with Hitler when
some "sad news" reached them. Wilhelm Gustloff, leader of the Swiss
NSDAP, had been assassinated in his hometown of Davos. The perpetrator was a Jewish student named David Frankfurter. "The Jews

are going to pay a high price for this," wrote Goebbels.[1] Yet large-scale vengeance was ruled out because of the coming Olympic Games: For weeks the Propaganda Ministry had been commanding the mass media to exercise restraint over the "Jewish question" for the duration of the Games.[2] Thus the press reaction was—as per instructions—relatively muted.[3]

On the evening of February 5 Goebbels, Magda, and Hitler left by special train for Garmisch. Goebbels spent the next two days there, attending the opening ceremony (which he regarded as a "rather old-fashioned ritual") and was pleased to see that nearly all the participating nations "marched past the Führer giving the Hitler salute." He watched a few events and generally enjoyed the "glorious snow landscape."[4] On February 8 the Goebbels couple moved on to Munich, where there were a few social occasions to attend in the days that followed: the Press Ball, the Artists' Festival, and an Olympic reception given by the Reich government at which Goebbels made a speech about international understanding.[5]

On February 11, with other high-ranking Nazi officials, they boarded the special train bound for Schwerin, where Gustloff's funeral was taking place. Goebbels noted with enthusiasm that at the burial ceremony Hitler gave a "radical, trenchant speech against the Jews."[6]

The concurrence of prescribed state mourning, ongoing state business, and the Olympic Games imposed a complicated itinerary over the next few days that Goebbels was forced to undergo, to the point of physical exhaustion. They went via Berlin, where they stopped off briefly, back to Garmisch, where they arrived on the morning of February 13 and watched several sporting events together. But by the following night Goebbels was off again to Berlin by sleeping car. Magda stayed on in Munich for a while.[7]

On Saturday morning, February 15, together with Hitler Goebbels opened the International Automobile Exhibition in Berlin.[8] They both returned by sleeper car that evening to Garmisch, where they attended the closing of the Winter Olympic Games: "Fine victory ceremony. [. . .] Everybody is praising our organization. And it certainly was brilliant." There followed another overnight trip to Berlin, this time accompanied by Magda. Goebbels now became unwell: "I dose myself with alcohol because of the flu. Slept like a log."[9]

REMILITARIZATION OF THE RHINELAND, AND ELECTION

Some days after the end of the Winter Games, Hitler prepared to take the next step in his revision of the Versailles Treaty: the reoccupation of the Rhineland, demilitarized since 1919. This would be a breach not only of Versailles but also of the Locarno Pact. A first hint of Hitler's intention is found in Goebbels's diary as early as January 20, 1936, reporting that Hitler had announced over lunch that at some point he was going "suddenly to resolve the problem of the Rhineland zone."[10]

A month later, in conversation with Goebbels, Hitler came back to the subject: "He is pondering it. Should he remilitarize the Rhineland? Difficult question." Evidently Hitler no longer feared that the Western powers would seize on a German military incursion into the Rhineland as a welcome opportunity to switch their focus away from the Abyssinian conflict and onto the situation in Central Europe. And there would be a pretext for the occupation of the Rhineland: The Franco-Russian Pact concluded in May 1935 was about to be ratified. Goebbels commented after this conversation: "The situation is ripe just now. France won't do anything, much less England. But we'll wait and see, and keep calm."[11]

On the evening of February 28, when Goebbels and Magda were about to leave for home after an event in the Deutschlandhalle, "there's a call from the Führer, I've got to go with him to Munich. He wants me at his side while coming to his difficult decision about the Rhineland." Naturally, Goebbels complied instantly: "So, it's all change. Get packed, and off we go. Magda's coming with us."[12]

During the rail journey through the night and later in Munich the debate continued, until on Sunday, March 1, Hitler struggled through to a solitary decision—as usual in such critical situations. As he told Goebbels (and contrary to the latter's advice),[13] he was going to act in the next week without waiting for the decision of the French Senate, expected on March 12.[14]

In the afternoon Goebbels flew to Leipzig, where he gave a talk to the foreign and domestic press (not on the subject of the coming conflict, of course), while Magda took the overnight train to Berlin with Hitler.[15] On March 2 Hitler summoned to the Reich Chancellery Goebbels; Göring; the minister of war, General Werner von Blomberg;

the head of the army, General Werner von Fritsch; the head of the navy, Admiral Erich Raeder; and Ribbentrop to inform them that on the coming Saturday in the Reichstag he would announce the remilitarization of the Rhineland. At the same time, the Reichstag would be dissolved and new elections would take place under the watchword "foreign relations." To maintain the element of surprise, members of the house would be invited on the Friday evening to a "beer evening."[16] Only on that day, March 6, did Hitler officially tell his cabinet, who—apart from a few who were in the know—were "immensely astonished" by this latest decision of the "Führer."[17]

In the course of this week, which was highly charged with tension, Goebbels had already begun to prepare his Propaganda Ministry for the election campaign to come. Early in the morning he directed two planeloads of journalists to the Rhineland, their destination a secret until the last minute.[18]

On Saturday, March 7, in his speech to the Reichstag, Hitler announced—wrapped up in orotund assertions of his will to peace—the annulment of the Locarno Treaties, which he justified by reference to the Franco-Soviet military pact. The high point of the speech was his statement that the German government "has today resumed full and unrestricted sovereignty over the demilitarized zone of the Rhineland." At that same moment, German troops—numerically relatively weak—began their march into the territory on the left bank of the Rhine.[19]

Goebbels recorded a "frenzy of enthusiasm" after the speech, not only among Reichstag members but also in the "newly liberated" Rhineland. His mother, who called him from Rheydt, "went wild," and his old teacher Voss, who happened to be in Berlin, was "in raptures"; later in the evening, Goebbels took him along to meet Hitler. Goebbels learned from Hitler that there would be no serious international repercussions; France merely planned to raise the matter at the League of Nations.[20]

A few days later the election propaganda campaign began with a vengeance. Goebbels himself spoke in the weeks to come at mass events in, among other places, Potsdam, Berlin, Leipzig, Breslau, Nuremberg, Frankfurt, Düsseldorf, Koblenz, and Cologne.[21] Mobilizing the masses in centrally organized meetings throughout the Reich, partly characterized by peace declarations but also by a renewed sense of national self-confidence, was meant to strengthen the hand of the regime in the international negotiations that now followed.[22]

A hastily convened London meeting of the Council of the League of Nations on March 19 passed a resolution[23] condemning the German action as a clear breach of the Locarno Treaties. A compromise proposal by the Locarno powers based on this resolution—met by Goebbels with the response "They've gone mad"[24]—was rejected by the German side, which put forward its own "peace plan" instead, the draft of which Hitler had discussed on March 31 with Göring, Goebbels, and Hess.[25]

It was no accident that the confident rejection of the Locarno powers' offer of negotiation came on March 31: Two days earlier, the regime had staged the "election" as a huge spectacle expressing the solidarity of the "national community."[26]

The campaign had begun its final phase on the afternoon of March 27, a Friday. All newspapers had been instructed to foreground the mass meetings arranged over the next two days.[27] Hitler began the program with a visit to the Krupp Works in Essen, broadcast by all German stations and relayed in "community reception" over loudspeakers. The meeting in Essen was introduced by one of Goebbels's commentaries, and at 3:45 P.M. precisely he also gave the command over the loudspeakers to "hoist flags," whereupon, according to the *Völkischer Beobachter*, in an instant "the whole of Germany [. . .] was like a hurricane of swastika flags."[28] Hitler's speech, in which he among other things declaimed his desire for peace and called for solidarity in the nation, was followed by other events featuring the Party elite. There was a mass meeting in the Berlin Sportpalast at which Göring spoke, while Goebbels addressed an audience of several hundred thousand in Düsseldorf.[29]

Goebbels had named the day before the election "the People's Day of Honor, Peace, and Freedom." The high point was another evening speech by Hitler in Cologne, which was again broadcast in public places and was meant to end with a "gigantic chorus of 67 million Germans." The press had called on the public to gather in the large city squares and join in with the singing of the "Dutch Thanksgiving Prayer."[30]

The country went to the polls on the Sunday. "A Nation Privileged to Serve by Voting for the Führer," ran the headline in the *Völkischer Beobachter*.[31] Once again, the results of the vote were massively manipulated: "Terror, pressure on voters, falsifying of ballot papers reached unheard-of proportions this time," reported informants for the SPD in exile.[32]

The published result—a "yes" vote of 99 percent—did not record the numbers of "no" votes separately but merged them with the figure for spoiled ballot papers: Blank ballot papers were interpreted as approval, and observers working for SOPADE* reported that even those voting slips not explicitly marked with the word "No" were counted as a "Yes." Despite great pressure, more than four hundred thousand people had chosen not to vote at all.[33] However, the regime felt that the outcome of the vote had strengthened its position vis-à-vis the Locarno powers. Goebbels commented: "The Führer has united the nation. It's more than we could have hoped for in our wildest dreams."[34]

In the end, it transpired that Hitler's bluff had worked: No sanctions were imposed by the European powers, and there was no practical outcome from the talks between the British and French general staffs.[35] Tolerating the German march into the Rhineland underscored the decay of the security system established at Locarno.

PRIVATE AMENITIES

In March Magda and Joseph Goebbels planned to buy the summer residence they had been renting in Kladow. Goebbels turned to Hitler, who promised to speak to Amann about the funds they needed (and also to raise Goebbels's salary). Goebbels said of his private situation: "We have so many other worries that we can't sustain such money worries as well."[36]

In the end an alternative presented itself: Their eye fell upon a "summer house" in one of the most exclusive Berlin locales, on the island of Schwanenwerder in the Wannsee.[37] Some days later, in connection with a private invitation, Hitler gave Goebbels the agreeable news that he was going to raise his expenses allowance to 4,000 Reichsmarks. "It's a weight off all our minds. We're very happy. The Führer is so noble and generous."[38] He proceeded to buy the house the very next day, in the full expectation that Hitler would cover the

* Translators' note: The SPD in exile in Prague.

funding gap by "arranging for an advance from Amann," and indeed Hitler called from Munich a few days later: "Money for Schwanenwerder secured. Amann was generous again. I'm so grateful to the Führer."[39]

In the next few days Magda and Joseph wondered how they might recompense Hitler for his support: "If we could just create a little home for him here!"[40] As always in his diary when Goebbels was describing intimate moments with his idol, he lapsed into a fervent and quite maudlin tone. For Hitler's birthday, April 20, Magda did in fact prepare for him a little guesthouse on the grounds of the property. When the Führer paid a visit to Schwanenwerder on the eve of his birthday, he was "absolutely thrilled" with the place and promised to "come and visit often."[41] Later in the evening there was a chance for Goebbels to have a long private conversation with Hitler: "He is very happy that we are happy."[42] Magda, Hitler assured him some months later, was "charming, the best wife I could have found,"[43] and he loved their daughter Helga "like his own child."[44]

The moment the water sports season began, Goebbels acquired a new boat—the third since taking office—which he proudly showed off to Hitler at the beginning of May. They went on boat trips together again, and the opportunity of spending the early summer days in the company of his Führer helped Goebbels to forget his "money worries about the boat."[45] In July, he generously bought another, smaller motorboat for his wife and children, but it appealed to him so much that he commandeered it for outings himself.[46] In the summer he also indulged in a new car, a "5.4 l Mercedes sportscar,"[47] and a few weeks later he ordered in addition a "limusine [sic] for the winter," a vehicle that he liked for one particular reason above all: "One like the Führer's got."[48]

All of this of course consumed a large amount of money, but in autumn 1936 Goebbels was for the time being able to put his financial affairs on an even keel. He managed to sell his diaries on quite sensational terms to Max Amann, head of the Party's publishing house, the Eher Verlag: "To be published 20 years after my death. 250,000 marks now and 100,000 per year. That's very generous."[49] It is hardly conceivable that this extraordinary transaction could have taken place without Hitler's consent.

It might be thought that Goebbels would have been more than satisfied with his extremely comfortable home life, but the opposite was the case. His relationship with Magda was constantly marred by intense arguments, as for example in May 1936, when after a daylong argument Goebbels was contemplating moving out of the villa on Schwanenwerder, which Magda had just finished lavishly decorating.[50] Goebbels often noted long discussions with Magda in his diary but rarely conveyed anything about their content—in striking contrast to other entries, which largely consisted of records of conversations. While he often testified to her exemplary conduct of household affairs and social obligations, the unavoidable evening chats with her seem to have bored him.

A few weeks later, on June 2, 1936, Goebbels had a fateful encounter. During an evening walk on Schwanenwerder he met Lida Baarová, the Czech actress. She was the girlfriend of the actor Gustav Fröhlich, who had recently moved into a house very near to Goebbels. Since the previous year, Baarová, then just twenty-one, had been cast by the Berlin film company Ufa to play seductive "vamp" parts, roles that the prim and proper German film industry under the Nazis preferred to fill with foreign actresses. On that July evening, Goebbels fell into a conversation with the actress, and at his request she showed him the house she and Fröhlich were living in.[51]

A few weeks later, as Baarová reports in her memoirs, Goebbels invited her, along with Fröhlich and some other guests, for a trip in his boat. When Fröhlich had to go back to the studio for some evening filming, Goebbels insisted that she should stay on board with his other guests; it then turned into quite a late night.[52]

Around this time, in August 1936, it was from Rosenberg of all people that Goebbels learned of an "unpleasant business with Lüdecke." Quite evidently this was one of Magda's affairs, which she initially denied and then confessed to him.[53] Admittedly, this faux pas on Magda's part lay some time back in the past. Kurt Lüdecke had been an active Hitler supporter before 1933 but had then fled Germany in 1934 as an opponent of Nazism. It was in these circumstances that Goebbels arranged a further meeting with Baarová, to take place during the Nuremberg rally in September. He had taken care that her latest film, *Traitor*, a movie that glorified the work of military counterespionage and that the propaganda minister was sponsoring, should be premiered at the Nuremberg rally—in the presence, moreover, of Himmler, Justice Minister Franz Gürtner, and counterintelligence chief Admiral Wilhelm Canaris.[54] Goebbels was able to persuade Baarová to stay on and have a look around at the rally, and the next day, sharing a meal with Ufa personnel, the two became rather closer to each other: "A miracle has occurred," wrote Goebbels in his diary.[55]

Back in Berlin, at the end of September he invited Fröhlich and his girlfriend to his box at the opera, and a few days later he asked them over to his house on Schwanenwerder for a screening of Fröhlich's latest film.[56] After that he met the Czech film star not only in company[57] but more often alone, preferably at his house in Lanke. And at some point in the following winter, as she recalls, their relationship became intimate.

There was a major confrontation when, on a winter's day on Schwanenwerder, Fröhlich thought he had caught his girlfriend and the minister in a compromising situation.[58] The rumor—which was unfounded—that he slapped Goebbels's face during this showdown seems to have spread like wildfire. It is not surprising that after this Goebbels's attitude to the actor became less than positive.[59] During the war Fröhlich was one of the few top German actors to be called up for military service—if only temporarily.

FOREIGN POLICY IN SPRING AND SUMMER 1936

For all the attraction Goebbels felt to fascist Italy and however much he admired Mussolini's risky war-making in Africa,[60] he agreed with Hitler that Mussolini's Abyssinian adventure and the resulting Italian-British conflict ought first and foremost to improve the chances of an Anglo-German rapprochement. "Eventually there will be an alliance of the two Germanic peoples," was Goebbels's summary of Hitler's views in May 1936.[61] This hope seemed to be reinforced when Mussolini annexed Abyssinia in May and proclaimed the Italian king emperor of Ethiopia: "The Führer's alliance with England will now be almost automatic."[62] For Goebbels's benefit, at the end of May Hitler put a name to the prospect he visualized coming out of an alliance of this kind: the "United States of Europe under German leadership. That would be the solution."[63]

For his part, during the Abyssianian conflict Mussolini found it politic to try to improve his relations with Germany. A decisive factor was the need to remove the tensions that had arisen between the two states after the 1934 Nazi putsch attempt in Austria. Correspond-ingly, Mussolini let Hitler know in January 1936 that he would have no objection if Austria, while remaining formally an independent state, in fact became a satellite of the German Reich. At the end of May, via Ambassador Bernardo Attolico, Mussolini asked Goebbels whether "the German press could play down the English-Italian rift somewhat. I'm doing the same, because we've got to keep some irons in the fire."[64]

In June the Italian foreign minister, Suvich, who favored an under-standing with France and Britain, was replaced by Mussolini's son-in-law, Count Galeazzo Ciano. Ciano's successor as propaganda minister was Dino Alfieri; this was a changeover that Goebbels accu-rately assessed as favorable to Germany. It was a fortunate turn of events that Countess Ciano, Mussolini's daughter Edda, happened to be in Berlin while this reshuffle was taking place, and that the Goeb-belses were able to give her a good deal of attention.[65]

Weakened by the withdrawal of Mussolini's support, Chancellor Schuschnigg was forced to settle with Nazi Germany.[66] In what was called the July Agreement, there were negotiations, among other things, over improving press relations, to which both countries had assented by August 1935 in an exchange of communiqués.[67]

Goebbels, whose area of responsibility involved many parts of the July Agreement, had been following the negotiations conducted by Ambassador von Papen in Vienna[68] from the sidelines with a degree of skepticism, but he had no part in the final formulation of the ac-cord.[69] Nonetheless, he could not refrain from announcing the com-muniqué of July 11 to the regular press briefing as a "big sensation."[70] Naturally, as Goebbels and Hitler agreed, the accord should above all be a platform from which further to undermine the authority of the Austrian government. At the beginning of May Hitler had left with him the memorable sentiment: "We must maintain tension in Austria and Czechoslovakia. Never let things settle down."[71]

On July 19 Goebbels once again went to Bayreuth for the Wagner Festival. While he was following the performances (mainly with en-thusiasm), taking an interest in the personal details of top artists, and chatting for hours with Hitler about this and that, the latter—without bringing Goebbels into the actual decision-making process—was initiating a momentous change of direction in German foreign pol-icy.[72] For on July 25 Hitler granted an audience to an envoy from

General Francisco Franco, the leader of an officers' plot against the left-wing government in Madrid. Soon after that he gave orders to support the putsch, so that the revolt, based in Spanish North Africa, could be successfully transferred to metropolitan Spain.[73]

This significant foreign relations decision sprang from a mixture of ideological, strategic, anticommunist, and military-industrial motives and was highly significant in paving the way for the subsequent German-Italian alliance. Nonetheless, it was a decision that passed Goebbels by, even though he was on hand in Bayreuth at the time, preoccupied with a performance of *Siegfried*. It was not until the next day that Hitler and Göring informed him of the decision made the previous night, to which Goebbels pointedly attributed only minor significance in his diary entry: "So we're getting a bit involved in Spain. Planes etc. Not obvious. Who knows what the point is."[74]

All the same, Goebbels followed the developments in and around Spain very closely in the following weeks and months.[75] While the Luftwaffe continued to increase its covert support for the rebels, Hitler pursued far-reaching deceptive tactics at the diplomatic level. In August Germany joined an arms embargo initiated by France and starting in September took part in meetings of an international non-intervention committee.[76] In line with this new foreign policy orientation, the topic of "anti-Bolshevism" became more central to German propaganda in the months to come.

OLYMPIC GAMES AND *OLYMPIA*

When Goebbels returned from Bayreuth to Berlin at the end of July, he discovered a "proper festival city,"[77] abundantly decorated and comprehensively geared up for the imminent Olympics.[78] In the next two weeks he plunged completely into the Olympic proceedings, attending numerous sports events, taking an active part in the accompanying social and cultural program, and using the opportunity to mingle with high-ranking foreign guests such as the Bulgarian Tsar Boris III, the Italian crown prince, Dino Alfieri (Goebbels's Italian counterpart), and Sir Robert Vansittart, the longstanding undersecretary of state at the British Foreign Office. He registered German sporting successes as "the outcome of reawakened national ambition."[79] But it stuck in his craw that so many medals were won for the

United States "by negroes": "It's a disgrace. The white race should be ashamed of itself."[80]

At the end of the Games, Goebbels organized on the Pfaueninsel ("Peacock Island," on the River Havel) a magnificent party for some three thousand guests, meant to outshine all the other festivities and celebrations during the Berlin Olympics. Goebbels welcomed the Bulgarian tsar, the whole of the diplomatic corps, numerous representatives of the Reich government, and many Gauleiters and NSDAP Reich leaders. The Wehrmacht Pioneer Corps had erected a pontoon bridge—hung with festive lanterns and with the Berlin regional orchestra playing on it—across to the island for the occasion. Three more dance bands and the German Opera House Ballet provided the entertainment, and the midnight fireworks display was so colossal that it reminded the U.S. ambassador, William Dodd, of a battle scene.[81]

On August 16 Goebbels took part in the closing ceremony in the Berlin Olympic stadium, summing up: "With 33 gold medals, Germany easily tops the table. The leading sports nation. That's glorious."[82]

By summer 1935, Hitler had commissioned Leni Riefenstahl to make a permanent film record of the Olympics, a project Goebbels was happy to pursue and of which he was the official promoter.[83] In October 1935 the Propaganda Ministry awarded the project 1.5 million Reichsmarks, a fund to be administered by a specially created company, Olympia Film Ltd.[84]

Riefenstahl's energetic working style and her unstoppable determination led to unpleasant scenes here and there in sporting arenas with the supervisory staff. Goebbels found himself forced to intervene in one of these confrontations: "I chew Riefenstahl out. Her behavior is impossible. A hysterical woman. She's just not a man!"[85]

As a result of the enormous film footage, which Riefenstahl with her characteristic perfectionism finally assembled into two featurelength movies, completing the film cost a considerable amount of time and money. Accusations of profligate spending and negligent use of funding—Goebbels referred to "complete financial chaos"[86]— were later withdrawn.[87]

Despite resistance from Goebbels, in a personal audience with Hitler in November 1937 Riefenstahl succeeded in securing extra funding for the film. The Propaganda Ministry had to supply a further 300,000 marks.[88] Meanwhile, Goebbels was obliged to put out a press statement denying reports in the foreign press of a shouting match between Riefenstahl and himself at a social event. Hitler and Goebbels then visited Riefenstahl in her villa in Dahlem; the German press published photos of their visit.[89]

In November 1937 Goebbels had a chance to see some parts of Riefenstahl's opus—and he was utterly captivated.[90] The gala premiere planned by Hitler and Goebbels for both parts of the film, *Festival of Nations* and *Festival of Beauty*, finally took place—after many postponements[91]—on April 20, 1936, Hitler's forty-ninth birthday, in the presence of the entire Nazi elite.[92] On May 1, 1938, Leni Riefenstahl once again received the National Film Prize, from Goebbels himself.[93]

THE FRUITS OF SUCCESS:
TRAVEL, CELEBRATIONS, HONORS, GIFTS

For the regime, the Olympics represented a considerable increase in international reputation. This, as well as a few other factors, contributed to the sense that the regime was now by and large securely established. Political opposition had almost been eliminated; there was a ceasefire in the war against the churches; and mass unemployment had been considerably reduced by the rearmament buildup. Staged in the form of a celebration of national unity, the "election" and the Olympiad had provided plenty of opportunities to show off the supposed harmony between regime and people. Now, at the end of the summer, there began a period of some months when Goebbels could bask in the glory of success, collect rewards and approbation, and savor to the fullest the privileges that went with his status.

At the end of August he spent three days at the Venice Biennale with Magda. Goebbels was highly impressed by the city, which he found "absolutely stunning."[94] He noted with satisfaction the results emerging from the International Film Festival: Trenker's *The Emperor of California* was declared the best foreign film.[95] Flying back, he interrupted his journey to stay for a few days on the Obersalzberg. He discussed various political topics with Hitler, but there was also time for relaxation: "Bowling. But the Führer is the master of that, too."[96]

The Nuremberg Party rally of 1936—Goebbels had tried in vain to persuade Hitler to shorten the program, in view of the recent Olympic upheaval, or even cancel the rally altogether[97]—took the motto of "anti-Bolshevism." Goebbels made his main contribution on September 10 with a speech on "Bolshevism, the World Enemy." He had already belabored the theme in his address the year before, but now, against a background of ongoing international developments, the speech was the starting signal for a big anticommunist propaganda campaign.[98] Hitler found the speech "classically good," and as usual Goebbels could not get enough of the press response, which, being under the direction of the Propaganda Ministry, was outstanding.[99] During the Nuremberg show, with its usual parades, military displays, solemn ceremonial, torchlight processions, receptions, and endless speeches, he found time, as we have seen, to cultivate the first tender links with Baarová.

On September 20 Goebbels left on his long-planned trip to Greece.[100] In Athens on September 22, visiting the Acropolis, Goebbels experienced "one of the most profound and beautiful mornings of my life. [. . .] Spent hours strolling through the most noble site of Nordic art. The Propylaea, the Parthenon, and the Erechtheion. I'm quite stunned. Over everything this deep blue Attic sky. [. . .] How the Führer would love to be here with us!"[101]

The next day they went on via Thebes to Delphi: "That's antiquity, our blessing and our great saving grace." In the evening they boarded a little steamer in nearby Itea. Of the nighttime journey he noted that it had been sultry, almost unbearable, and Magda did not feel well. In fact, this is one of the very few entries in his detailed travel diary in which his wife gets even a brief mention. He does not seem to have shared with her the impressions that had moved him so deeply in the previous days but had quite deliberately chosen to enjoy these intense experiences alone. Significantly, it was Hitler he missed on his visit to the Acropolis.[102]

After a cruise of some days with the ship, during which he visited various excavations, he returned to Athens, from which he took his "melancholy" leave a few days later.[103]

Contrary to his principle of not accepting any pompous official honors,[104] he had not been able to refuse the highest Greek order, which Prime Minister Ioannis Metaxas bestowed on him in Athens. Goebbels had to "accept with a good grace." Hardly had he returned home when Alfieri gave him the Order of Mauritius. "Rather an embarrassing situation. But what can I do? Put a brave face on it and accept!"[105]

A month after his return, on October 29 and for the following three days Goebbels found himself at the center of numerous celebrations and honors. His thirty-ninth birthday coincided with the tenth anniversary of his tenure as Berlin Gauleiter, and this had to be celebrated in style. First he received a delegation of German artists, to whom he announced a donation of two million marks for the artists' old-age fund, and then the twenty-eight oldest Party comrades in the Gau, upon whom he bestowed the Party's Golden Badge of Honor. For Berliners who were not lucky enough to be able to congratulate the Gauleiter in person on his big day, lists were made available in the ministry to sign.

Finally, Hitler himself appeared at the ministry, and they both retired to Goebbels's private office. Deeply moved, Goebbels cherished the precious moments: "And then he talks to me very nicely and confidentially. About the old days, how we belong together, what he says to me is so moving. Gives me his portrait, with a wonderful dedication. And a painting of the Dutch School. It is a wonderful hour alone with him. He poured out his whole heart to me." There followed a torchlight procession in the Lustgarten, a military review of Hitler's SS bodyguard, the Leibstandarte, and then at home he gave a reception, at which Hitler was present once more.[106]

The next day, at a reception in the City Hall, Goebbels presented himself completely as a "socialist." He maintained in his speech of thanks that he felt "more closely connected to the poor of our own country than to the king of any other."[107] The City of Berlin turned over to him a "simple log cabin by one of the quiet lakes around Berlin," as *Der Angriff* reported in a special jubilee issue.[108] It was in fact a four-room timber house with various outbuildings, situated in the middle of a large forest plot on the Bogensee, about twenty-five miles north of the center of Berlin, directly on the newly completed Berlin-Stettin autobahn. He had the use of the house cost-free for life.[109]

After this, he visited an exhibition called "10 Years of Struggle for Berlin," laid the foundation stone of a "Goebbels housing estate" in Friedrichshain, and placed a wreath on Horst Wessel's grave. In the evening he made his way through a city decked out with flags in his honor to the Sportpalast, where he and Hitler spoke: "He presents me in a way I've never heard before. I hadn't expected that. I'm moved and touched. He finishes by calling for a 'Heil' for me. I'm so happy. Frenetic storms of applause."[110] The next day he made sure that Hitler's speech was given due prominence in the press.[111]

On October 31 there was an SA roll call in the Lustgarten, and in the evening a "Party festivity" was held in the Deutschlandhalle. "I'm being spoiled with love and devotion. It's so wonderful."[112] Gratefully he received "good wishes"[113] from all sides, "mountains of letters, flowers and presents,"[114] expressions of love "from the whole nation."[115] He was "completely stunned" and "deeply moved" by the many honors.[116]

There was still a "youth rally" to come, on November 1 in the Ufa-Palast am Zoo (Ufa cinema near the Zoo Station), where among other things Schirach "gave a lovely speech" in Goebbels's presence. A Hitler Youth read out his Wessel obituary from 1930: "What a poem of an essay." The festivities ended in the evening with a performance of *The Merry Widow*, which he attended in the company of old Party comrades at the Berlin Opera House.[117]

FOREIGN AFFAIRS IN AUTUMN 1936

In the months after Mussolini's victory in Ethiopia, and under the impact of the Spanish Civil War beginning in August, Hitler's foreign policy underwent a change of direction. Precisely because Goebbels was excluded from the actual process of foreign policy planning and decision-making, he was all the more eager to collect in his diary any hints of the Führer's intentions.

Until spring 1936, Hitler went on thinking that the chances of an Anglo-German alliance were improved by Italy's invasion of Abyssinia and the international crisis it created. But now, viewing international affairs from the perspective of a comprehensive bloc formation, he began to push things in that direction. In autumn 1936 Hitler frequently evoked for Goebbels the inevitability of confronting "Bolshevism." The topic had been the leitmotif of the Party rally and since then had been widely deployed by propaganda. In view of what Hitler saw as the distinct possibility that France would go communist and the fact that he did not expect German rearmament to be completed until 1941, he began to pin his hopes on an anticommunist bloc including—first and foremost—Italy, and then Japan, and eventually Great Britain.[118]

As far as the understanding with Italy was concerned, Goebbels was only too willing to act as go-between. The annual Farmers' Rally was a convenient occasion to bring together, through his mediation, Hitler and Goebbels's Italian counterpart, Alfieri.[119] Hitler wanted Italy to leave the League of Nations. "Then we'd have freedom of action. He doesn't intend to do anything against Italy. Wants an entente of minds. Mussolini invited to Germany. Direct talks."

On October 24 Ciano visited Hitler at the Berghof. During this conversation, according to Goebbels's record, Hitler opened up to his Italian guest much broader vistas of German-Italian cooperation, which was to grow into a European anti-Bolshevist front. Furthermore, Hitler declared unambiguously that Germany would be ready for war in three to five years and designated the Mediterranean and Eastern European areas, respectively, as Italian and German spheres of interest.[120] Mussolini picked up this clear signal a week later in a speech in Milan, where he talked of a "Rome-Berlin axis" around which "all those European states can move which have a will to cooperation and peace." Goebbels interpreted this speech immediately as an obvious message "to Germany, Austria, and Hungary."[121] In mid-December he met the new Italian consul-general, Major Giuseppe Renzetti, a close friend of Mussolini's whom he had already gotten to know in the 1920s as an important intermediary of "Il Duce"; he discussed with him possible ways of "supporting and promoting the German-Italian relationship."[122]

Along with the improvement in German-Italian relations, the alliance with Japan was also strategically significant. Hitler had already told Goebbels in June that he believed a clash between Japan and Russia was inevitable, and once the colossus to the east began to totter "we must supply our need for land for the next hundred years."[123]

On November 25 the Anti-Comintern Pact was signed with Japan in Berlin. The pact aimed to combat the Communist International by exchanging information. In a secret rider, both states agreed to remain neutral in the case of an attack by the Soviet Union and in addition pledged not to conclude any treaties contrary to the "spirit of this agreement."[124]

In a three-hour speech on December 1, Hitler explained his view

to contest, the claim to total power of National Socialism. One
[no]de, on January 30, shows how urgent a task the regime consid-
[ered] this. Still in shock, Goebbels reported that after Hitler's speech,
["]inconceivable" happened. Hitler, "deeply moved," had thanked
[the] cabinet for their work and solemnly declared that in honor of the
[ann]iversary all cabinet members who were not Party comrades were
[to] be accepted into the Party. But Reich Transport Minister Paul von
[El]tz-Rübenach flatly rejected this offer. He thought National Social-
[is]m would "suppress the Church"—and, what is more, he demanded
[a] statement of Hitler's proposed policy toward the Church.[10] Accord-
[in]g to Goebbels, Hitler ignored this intervention, while the other
[c]abinet members sat "as though paralyzed." The "mood is ruined."
Inevitably, the minister had to resign on the spot.

STRUGGLE WITH THE CHURCHES

After the ferment over Eltz-Rübenach, the struggle between National
Socialism and the churches entered a decisive phase. It had become
increasingly evident since the end of 1936 that the policy of Hanns
Kerrl, the Reich minister for church affairs, of uniting the Protestant
church had failed.[11] Within his inner circle, Hitler criticized Kerrl for
this[12] while at the same time taking an uncompromising stance
toward the churches.[13]

With the Reich Church Commission stepping down (this was the
body created by Kerrl to unite the Protestant church) on February 12,
1937, Kerrl announced that the churches would now be placed under
much tighter state control.[14] To discuss this question, on short notice
Hitler summoned Kerrl, Frick, Hess, Himmler, and Goebbels to talks
on the Obersalzberg.

Along with his fellow passengers, Himmler and a state secretary in
the Interior Ministry, Wilhelm Stuckart, Goebbels used the train
journey to prepare intensively for the top-level meeting. It is probably no coincidence that they were traveling on the same overnight
train, considering that they all—together with Hess's deputy, Martin
Bormann—subscribed to a rigorous approach to the church question. They were united in opposition to Kerrl's policy, which aimed to
reconcile the Protestant church with the National Socialist state
under the leadership of the pro-Nazi German Christians. In his notes

of things to the cabinet; aside from the account given in Goebbels's
diary, no other record of this talk appears to exist. Europe, said Hitler, was already divided into two camps. France and Spain were the
next victims of the communist drive for expansion. If communist
regimes were to come to power there, it would lead to a Europe-wide
crisis for which Europe was not yet militarily prepared.[125] In the long
run the "authoritarian states" (Poland, Austria, Yugoslavia, Hungary)
were not dependable either. The only "consciously anti-Bolshevist
states," apart from Germany, were Italy and Japan, and with them
"agreements" would be concluded. "England will come in if France
goes into crisis."

When addressing his closest followers, at least, Hitler persisted in
the notion that his increasingly aggressive foreign policy would still
lead to an alliance with Great Britain.

CHAPTER 16

"The Most Important Factors in Our Modern Cultural Life"

Consolidating Nazi Cultural Politics

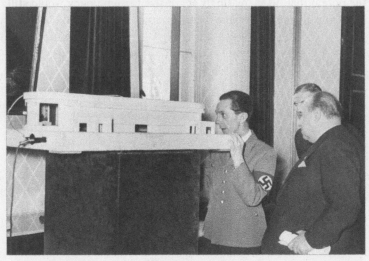

In 1937, Goebbels made considerable efforts to establish his absolute leadership of cultural politics. This picture shows him with the architect's model of an exhibition hall designed for the Berlin exhibition "Give Me Four Years." On the right is State Secretary Walther Funk.

On January 30, 1937, Goebbels was among Reichstag members when Hitler addressed the house on the fourth anniversary of the "seizure of power."[1] In his speech, Hitler, among other things, unilaterally rescinded the recognition of the war guilt clause of the Versailles Treaty that the German government had been forced to accept in 1919—a symbolic step toward annulling the peace settlement. At the same time, Hitler promised that "the time of so-called surprises is over"; however, his sharply polemical attacks on British Foreign Secretary

Anthony Eden made clear that he had certain [...] to pacifism.[2]

On the contrary: Just a few days earlier Hit[...] Goebbels that he hoped "to have another 6 years [...] portunity arose, he would not want to miss it.[3] S[...] added that he expected—as Goebbels has it—"a gr[...] in 5–6 years. In 15 years he would have wiped out th[...] phalia. [. . .] Germany would be the victor in the co[...] cease to live."[4] It is against the background of this long [...] tive that Hitler's foreign policy actions in the next few [...] be viewed.

In the following months, between the beginning o[...] spring 1938, Hitler conducted a reorientation of Germ[...] policy clearly documented in the propaganda minister's [...] tries. The Führer largely gave up his hopes of an alliance wi[...] and concentrated on his Italian ally.[5] The joint engagement o[...] states in the Spanish Civil War and the helpless efforts of Gre[...] ain to establish a policy of "non-intervention" by diplomatic [...] formed the background to this change of policy.[6] With regret, G[...] bels observed the widening rift with Britain but placed the blam[...] it on the German ambassador in London, Ribbentrop, and no[...] Hitler.[7] Hitler's calculation was that before too long the new allia[...] would allow him to subjugate Austria and Czechoslovakia. He w[...] already telling Goebbels on March 1, 1937, that it was necessary t[...] have these two states "to round off our territory,"[8] and it was in thi[...] light that Goebbels perceived the beginnings of Austria's gradual iso-lation.[9]

This period of largely silent reorientation had an effect on propaganda policy. Goebbels had now entered a phase in which propaganda was no longer concentrated primarily, as in earlier years, on the stability of the regime at home or dealing with foreign affairs crises. Matters of cultural policy were now central to his work. Between the autumn of 1936 and the spring of 1938, his objects were to assert the absolute grip of National Socialism on the central areas of cultural policy and to give the regime as a whole a rounded cultural policy profile. Naturally, this effort was also calculated to distract attention from the tinderbox situation building up internationally.

The first priority was to dispel the influence of the Church on public life, as it was the only institution that contested, or was in a posi-

CHAPTER 16

"The Most Important Factors in Our Modern Cultural Life"

Consolidating Nazi Cultural Politics

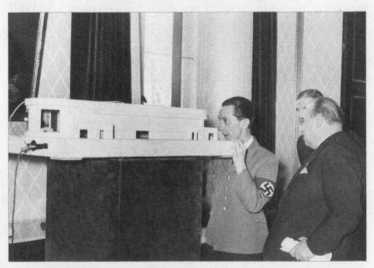

In 1937, Goebbels made considerable efforts to establish his absolute leadership of cultural politics. This picture shows him with the architect's model of an exhibition hall designed for the Berlin exhibition "Give Me Four Years." On the right is State Secretary Walther Funk.

On January 30, 1937, Goebbels was among Reichstag members when Hitler addressed the house on the fourth anniversary of the "seizure of power."[1] In his speech, Hitler, among other things, unilaterally rescinded the recognition of the war guilt clause of the Versailles Treaty that the German government had been forced to accept in 1919—a symbolic step toward annulling the peace settlement. At the same time, Hitler promised that "the time of so-called surprises is over"; however, his sharply polemical attacks on British Foreign Secretary of things to the cabinet; aside from the account given in Goebbels's diary, no other record of this talk appears to exist. Europe, said Hitler, was already divided into two camps. France and Spain were the next victims of the communist drive for expansion. If communist regimes were to come to power there, it would lead to a Europe-wide crisis for which Europe was not yet militarily prepared.[125] In the long run the "authoritarian states" (Poland, Austria, Yugoslavia, Hungary) were not dependable either. The only "consciously anti-Bolshevist states," apart from Germany, were Italy and Japan, and with them "agreements" would be concluded. "England will come in if France goes into crisis."

When addressing his closest followers, at least, Hitler persisted in the notion that his increasingly aggressive foreign policy would still lead to an alliance with Great Britain.

Anthony Eden made clear that he had certainly not been converted to pacifism.[2]

On the contrary: Just a few days earlier Hitler had remarked to Goebbels that he hoped "to have another 6 years," but if a good opportunity arose, he would not want to miss it.[3] Some weeks later he added that he expected—as Goebbels has it—"a great world conflict in 5–6 years. In 15 years he would have wiped out the Peace of Westphalia. [. . .] Germany would be the victor in the coming battle, or cease to live."[4] It is against the background of this long-term perspective that Hitler's foreign policy actions in the next few months must be viewed.

In the following months, between the beginning of 1937 and spring 1938, Hitler conducted a reorientation of German foreign policy clearly documented in the propaganda minister's diary entries. The Führer largely gave up his hopes of an alliance with Britain and concentrated on his Italian ally.[5] The joint engagement of the two states in the Spanish Civil War and the helpless efforts of Great Britain to establish a policy of "non-intervention" by diplomatic means formed the background to this change of policy.[6] With regret, Goebbels observed the widening rift with Britain but placed the blame for it on the German ambassador in London, Ribbentrop, and not on Hitler.[7] Hitler's calculation was that before too long the new alliance would allow him to subjugate Austria and Czechoslovakia. He was already telling Goebbels on March 1, 1937, that it was necessary to have these two states "to round off our territory,"[8] and it was in this light that Goebbels perceived the beginnings of Austria's gradual isolation.[9]

This period of largely silent reorientation had an effect on propaganda policy. Goebbels had now entered a phase in which propaganda was no longer concentrated primarily, as in earlier years, on the stability of the regime at home or dealing with foreign affairs crises. Matters of cultural policy were now central to his work. Between the autumn of 1936 and the spring of 1938, his objects were to assert the absolute grip of National Socialism on the central areas of cultural policy and to give the regime as a whole a rounded cultural policy profile. Naturally, this effort was also calculated to distract attention from the tinderbox situation building up internationally.

The first priority was to dispel the influence of the Church on public life, as it was the only institution that contested, or was in a position to contest, the claim to total power of National Socialism. One episode, on January 30, shows how urgent a task the regime considered this. Still in shock, Goebbels reported that after Hitler's speech, the "inconceivable" happened. Hitler, "deeply moved," had thanked the cabinet for their work and solemnly declared that in honor of the anniversary all cabinet members who were not Party comrades were to be accepted into the Party. But Reich Transport Minister Paul von Eltz-Rübenach flatly rejected this offer. He thought National Socialism would "suppress the Church"—and, what is more, he demanded a statement of Hitler's proposed policy toward the Church.[10] According to Goebbels, Hitler ignored this intervention, while the other cabinet members sat "as though paralyzed." The "mood is ruined." Inevitably, the minister had to resign on the spot.

STRUGGLE WITH THE CHURCHES

After the ferment over Eltz-Rübenach, the struggle between National Socialism and the churches entered a decisive phase. It had become increasingly evident since the end of 1936 that the policy of Hanns Kerrl, the Reich minister for church affairs, of uniting the Protestant church had failed.[11] Within his inner circle, Hitler criticized Kerrl for this[12] while at the same time taking an uncompromising stance toward the churches.[13]

With the Reich Church Commission stepping down (this was the body created by Kerrl to unite the Protestant church) on February 12, 1937, Kerrl announced that the churches would now be placed under much tighter state control.[14] To discuss this question, on short notice Hitler summoned Kerrl, Frick, Hess, Himmler, and Goebbels to talks on the Obersalzberg.

Along with his fellow passengers, Himmler and a state secretary in the Interior Ministry, Wilhelm Stuckart, Goebbels used the train journey to prepare intensively for the top-level meeting. It is probably no coincidence that they were traveling on the same overnight train, considering that they all—together with Hess's deputy, Martin Bormann—subscribed to a rigorous approach to the church question. They were united in opposition to Kerrl's policy, which aimed to reconcile the Protestant church with the National Socialist state under the leadership of the pro-Nazi German Christians. In his notes on the nighttime debate en route, Goebbels concisely summarized the anti-Kerrl position: "Kerrl wants to conserve the Church, while we want to liquidate it. Our differences are not just tactical but fundamental."[15]

After the session in Berchtesgaden, Goebbels summarized Hitler's thinking on church policy as follows: "He doesn't need a battle with the churches at the moment. He anticipates the great world struggle in a few years. If Germany were to lose yet another war, that would be the end." For this reason there was no question of accepting Kerrl's proposed measures, which would amount to making him a combined secular/religious ruler, a "summus episcopus" (as the minister for church affairs) and could only be imposed "by force." After Himmler had expressed himself "very forcibly against Kerrl and his see-saw policy" and the target of his attack had responded—as Goebbels saw it—with nothing but "empty phrases," the propaganda minister seized the opportunity: "I put forward the suggestion that we either separate church and state—which I think is premature—or elect a new synod to revise the constitution (keeping the Party and the State out of it), with the most liberal proportional representation, and then generous stipends for the synod delegates. In a year they'll be begging the State for help against themselves." His suggestion immediately met with a positive response, and a declaration to that effect was formulated. Goebbels called a press conference in Berlin on the theme of "Führer's step toward peace in the Church question." He gratefully acknowledged a directive from Hitler whereby all press contacts concerning the church question were to be channeled solely through his ministry.[16]

Two days later Goebbels discovered that his suspicions about Kerrl had been justified: "Kerrl wants to support the German Christians. That is out and out sabotage of the Führer's plans. Utterly scandalous." From the Obersalzberg he learned through the head of his Press Department, Alfred-Ingemar Berndt, that the Confessing Church, the ecclesiastical opponent of the German Christians, was unwilling to take part in the elections: "Kerrl is making things too easy for these parsons," he noted angrily. "He's incapable of carrying out his very delicate mission."[17] In contrast to Kerrl, Goebbels favored "absolute neutrality" with regard to the proposed church elections.[18]

Just a few days later, however, on February 27, he found that he was already out of step: Hitler had changed course. He was now fully

behind the German Christians, and after their victory in the ecclesiastical elections he intended to annul the Concordat with the Vatican. In the long term the dictator proposed to declare National
Socialists "the only true Christians." "Christianity means a call to destroy the priests, as Socialism once meant the destruction of Marxist
apparatchiks."[19]

Goebbels was so impressed with all this that he did not find it too
difficult to switch to the new course—supporting the German Christians. During discussions in April and May, he patiently acquiesced
by letting Kerrl and his state secretary, Hermann Muhs, explain the
new line to him. Finally, at the end of July, preparations for the church
elections were halted, never to be resumed. Goebbels's grand plan
had sunk without a trace.[20]

In the meantime, relations with the Catholic Church, too, had deteriorated.[21] In February Goebbels had already noted irately that Cardinal Michael von Faulhaber had "delivered a sharp sermon against
the Führer in Munich." It was time to "talk straight to these priests."[22]

But things very soon got worse. Late in the evening of March 20,
the head of the security police, Reinhard Heydrich, called on Goebbels to tell him about an impending message from the Pope to his
German bishops. He meant the encyclical *With Burning Concern,* in
which the Pope pronounced on the Nazi regime and its pseudo-
religious ideology, openly bringing up the many violations of the
1933 Concordat.[23] How should they react to this? Heydrich and
Goebbels were in agreement: "Act indifferent and ignore it," "economic pressure instead of arrests," "confiscation and banning" of
church publications, and in general "keep calm and wait for the right
moment to shake off these agitators."[24]

Two days later Goebbels was pained to see that the foreign press
had made a meal of the pastoral letter. And whereas restraint was
supposed to be the watchword—a view shared by Hitler—the situation was further exacerbated by "a very clumsy article" of Rosenberg's
in the *Völkischer Beobachter.*[25]

A few days later, however, Hitler told him on the telephone that he
now wanted "to take action against the Vatican." He proposed to reopen on a grand scale the pedophile abuse cases that had been put on
ice in summer 1936. They should start with a raft of charges already
filed with the public prosecutor in Koblenz. Hitler envisaged as a
"prelude" the "horrifying sexual murder of a boy in a Belgian monas-

tery"; Goebbels immediately dispatched a "special rapporteur" to Brussels.[26]

Shortly afterward, Hitler ordered the judicial authorities to reopen the trials.[27] There was no lack of suitable ammunition, as Goebbels wrote some days later: "We've still got 400 unresolved cases."[28] The series of trials in Koblenz began at the end of April. Goebbels was displeased by what he considered the inadequate reaction of the media, and he summoned a special press conference at which the papers were commanded to launch "a large-scale propaganda campaign against the Catholic Church." The results were so impressive that Goebbels was moved to express his appreciation of the journalists at the press conference the next day.[29]

In May, he recorded with satisfaction that Hitler was pleased with the new wave of propaganda. He also learned that Hitler did not want "the Party to be identified with any denomination," and neither did he want "to be given god-like status." Rather, the National Socialist movement should "make the churches bend to our will and become our servants." In concrete terms, celibacy should be abolished, the wealth of the churches seized, and no one under the age of twenty-four should be allowed to study theology. Moreover, the religious orders must be disbanded, and the churches must lose their license to teach. "That's the only way we'll break them down in a few decades."[30] Over the next few days Goebbels savored the press reports of the trials[31] and reacted hypocritically to the demagoguery persistently encouraged by his own ministry[32] by registering "disgust and outrage."[33]

On May 28 Goebbels gave a speech in the Berlin Deutschlandhalle condemning "the sex offenders and those behind them." The key sentences of this speech (which is generally regarded as the high point of the regime's campaign against the churches in 1937) were not his own, however, as the diary reveals: "Führer with me, dictating my declaration of war against the clergy today regarding the sexual abuse trials. Very stinging and drastic. I would not have gone that far."[34]

In his speech Goebbels made clear that the cases of sexual abuse by the clergy that had for some time been filling the courts of the National Socialist state were not "regrettable isolated incidents"; it was, rather, a matter of "general moral decay." Striking the pose of a disgusted paterfamilias, Goebbels did not shrink from giving details of this "hair-raising moral degeneration": "After confession, sexual offenses occurred with under-age young people in the sacristies; the victims who had been seduced were rewarded with pictures of the saints for their cooperation with the depraved desires of the sex offenders, and after the offense the violated youngster was given a benediction and a blessing."

Goebbels announced that "this sexual scourge must and would be wiped out at the root"; it might be necessary "to hold some very highly placed members of the clergy [. . .] to account in court under oath."[35] The next day he noted that the domestic press, whose attention since May 26 had repeatedly been drawn by the Propaganda Ministry to the fundamental importance of the speech, had printed it "whole and prominently, with powerful, outraged commentaries. It shows you how well I expressed everybody's feelings."[36]

On July 2 Goebbels was present at the Air Ministry when Hitler addressed the Gauleiters on the topic—among others—of church policy; he said that he declined the "role of religious reformer." Goebbels was pleased to hear it: "All this is grist to my mill. I've been proved 100% right."[37]

In the following weeks he continued to stoke the propaganda campaign against the Catholic Church.[38] At the beginning of July, though, he became angry about what he considered the lenient sentences handed down in the "priest trials."[39] The arrest of Pastor Martin Niemöller in early July—the leading representative of the Confessing Church was accused of "inflammatory remarks" about prominent National Socialists—suited Goebbels very well: Niemöller must be "put away until he can no longer see or hear."[40]

During the Bayreuth Festival he had further discussions with Hitler over the church question. On this occasion he advised the Führer to break off the trials for a couple of months "so that people don't become blunted to them."[41] Goebbels's advice clearly came after the event, however, because Hitler had already stopped the court cases by July 24 at the latest. Presumably the reasons why Hitler declared a truce with the churches had to do with foreign policy. The press was briefed accordingly at the end of July.[42]

It was in Bayreuth that Goebbels also heard that, to his surprise, Hanns Kerrl had now switched to a policy of separating church and state. He wanted a vote on this in the Protestant churches, which Goebbels initially thought "very questionable." But when he heard the next day that Hitler agreed with Kerrl, he found Kerrl's idea was "quite good": "This will be a total disaster for the churches."[43]

The struggle with the churches had Goebbels in its grip over the following months. He made several attempts to persuade Hitler to resume the "priest trials."[44] He also read Ludwig Thoma, and as he wrote in the diary: "I fill myself with hatred against the priests."[45]

But Hitler urged "restraint" over the church question. According to Goebbels, he was moving "more and more toward separation of church and state. But that will mean the end of Protestantism. And then we'll no longer have a counterweight to the Vatican."[46] However, in light of a huge rearmament drive and preparations for war, altering the status quo with regard to church policy was the last thing on Hitler's mind.[47] His caution concerning church questions shows that after more than four years of dictatorship, the regime was still insecure about its hold on the population.

When the trial of Pastor Niemöller began in 1938, such a high-profile action against one of the leading representatives of the Confessing Church no longer fit the political bill. This is why the case did not quite work out in the way radical enemies of the Church had hoped. Despite constant pressure on the judiciary from Goebbels to end the case quickly and "silently" with a severe sentence—Hitler assured him that in any case it was his wish that the pastor "should never be released"[48]—this was not the way things went. The courtroom gave Niemöller the opportunity to talk at length about himself and his motives, to call highly regarded witnesses for the defense, and to expand his closing statement into a wide-ranging lecture. Goebbels was not a little angered by the procedure.[49]

Eventually Niemöller was sentenced to seven months' imprisonment and a fine of two thousand Reichsmarks. The judge's reasoning read like a declaration by the pastor. However, instead of being set free immediately because of time already spent in custody, Niemöller, on Hitler's orders, was hauled off to a concentration camp,[50] where he was held until the end of the war as a "personal prisoner of the Führer."

"The foreign press will rage for a few days," concluded Goebbels. "But we can put up with that. The main thing is that the people are protected from the subversion and division [caused] by these irresponsible creatures."[51]

GOEBBELS'S ASSERTION OF HIS
LEADERSHIP IN MATTERS OF CULTURAL POLICY

Ousting the churches from public life was one side of National Socialist cultural policy and the main focus of Goebbels's work from
the end of 1936 onward, following the domestic and foreign affairs
stabilization of the regime. The other side consisted of the minister's
sustained attempt to bring individual cultural areas, as well as the
entire media landscape, as much as possible under his control and
imbue them with something like a National Socialist spirit. These
efforts can be observed in all of the central areas of cultural and
media policy.

At the end of 1936, the regime signaled clearly that it would exert
an even more decisive influence on cultural policy in the future. On
November 23, 1936, the Norwegian Nobel Committee announced
that the Peace Prize for the previous year would be awarded retrospectively to the German pacifist Carl von Ossietzky, who had been
in prison and a concentration camp since 1933. Hitler reacted to this
"impudent provocation," as Goebbels called it,[52] by decreeing that in
future no German citizen would be allowed to accept a Nobel Prize.
At the same time, he created the valuable German National Prize, to
be awarded annually to three outstanding figures from the worlds of
science and culture. This decision was announced at the beginning of
1937, in connection with the celebration of the January 30th anniversary.[53]

In the same week, at the third annual meeting of the Reich Culture
Chamber, Goebbels made a speech heavily publicized by the propaganda machine that was intended to underline his claim to leadership of the whole cultural domain. Among other things, he highlighted
the "creation of our great national-socialist celebrations" as one of
"the most important factors of our modern cultural life." This was
developing into "a very clear, modern, and simple rite, forming a
fixed tradition." But Goebbels also issued an unmistakable warning
against "devaluing the powerful feelings engendered [by this tradi-
tion] by trivializing it": "not every club social celebrates a cult." The
warning makes it clear that, after only a few years, the newly created
festive rituals were in danger of wearing thin in everyday life through

too much imitation and repetition, while behind the fervor of national-socialist festivals and solemn celebrations, the banality and kitsch threatened to show through all too visibly.

Goebbels also stressed his decisive influence on cultural policy by announcing the abolition of arts criticism,[54] a form of journalism he had often publicly attacked in the past.[55] By May 1936 Goebbels had already prohibited "evening criticism"—that is, short reviews of plays, concerts, and films appearing in the evening newspapers of the same day.[56] His reason was that this was a practice introduced by "the Jewish-owned press," which lacked "all respect for artistic achievement."[57] But all his attempts to regulate and limit arts criticism could not alter the basic dilemma, which was that the state-subsidized and controlled culture industry could not endure free criticism. The ban on arts criticism pronounced by Goebbels in November 1936 and then issued as an edict was only logical: It meant primarily no questioning of the fruits of the Propaganda Ministry and Goebbels's cultural policy.[58]

Goebbels's ability to impose himself more and more decisively on cultural life was due in no small measure to his success in 1936–37 in sidelining Rosenberg's cultural-policy ambitions. In the spring of 1936 Rosenberg had declined Goebbels's invitation to join the Cultural Senate. The offer from Goebbels had in any case been somewhat provocative, since in the previous year his intervention with Hitler had stopped Rosenberg from forming a cultural senate of his own.[59] When, in the course of his altercations with Goebbels, Rosenberg complained that the propaganda minister's stalling tactics had once more prevented one of his speeches from being broadcast, the Party's ideologue was simply confirming how much ground he had lost to the head of the propaganda machine.[60]

In the summer of 1936 it had appeared as if Goebbels and Rosenberg were close to settling their dispute over another bone of contention, the incorporation of the National Socialist Cultural Community into the Reich Culture Chamber, where it was to form an eighth chamber. Rosenberg had shelved earlier plans to place the association under the Kraft durch Freude (Strength Through Joy) organization and was now looking to link up once more with Goebbels.[61] But the negotiations on this score ran into the sands in November, not least because Goebbels had concluded in the meantime that Rosenberg's position at Hitler's "court" was not particularly strong, so that he could safely put a distance between himself and his cultural-policy rival, who had in recent years created one or two difficulties for him.[62] He found this assessment confirmed when he sat at Hitler's lunch table on November 14 while the leader held forth against exaggerated admiration for the ancient Teutons and the defaming of Charlemagne as "the butcher of the Saxons." "Rosenberg, at whom this is aimed, sits there silent and resentful."[63]

Rosenberg was also trying to negotiate with Ley, but now from a considerably weaker position: Eventually, in June 1937, the National Socialist Cultural Community was indeed absorbed into Kraft durch Freude, as envisaged in 1934, but now it was downgraded to a mere association for organizing cultural visits. This spelled the end of Rosenberg's attempt to set up an equally powerful organization in opposition to the Reich Culture Chamber.[64] Without his own power base, and in view of Hitler's lack of support for his "völkisch-Germanic" ambitions, Rosenberg's mission to "spiritually educate" the whole Nazi movement carried little weight. The central role in cultural life was played by Goebbels's ministry and the system of chambers he had created. In 1937 this became evident in individual areas of Nazi cultural policy and in the management of the mass media. However, it would transpire that the power of the key player in Nazi cultural policy was by no means unlimited in all departments.

FURTHER "COORDINATION" OF RADIO

In 1937 Goebbels achieved considerable progress with the further "bringing into line" of broadcasting. Since 1936 he had increasingly advocated more entertainment on the radio. Space for spoken-word programs was to be restricted, and airtime for light music further expanded.[65] In March 1936 he instructed directors to reserve the best evening broadcasting slot for entertainment programs.[66] He admonished the Reich director of radio programming, Eugen Hadamovsky, for the "pedagogical" content of broadcasting: "General tendency everywhere: Loosen up!"[67]

In order to put this directive into operation, the Reich Broadcasting Corporation was reorganized in 1937 in line with his concept, and new staff were appointed. The new office of Reich director was created, to be filled by Heinrich Glasmeier, who concurrently became director general of the Reich Broadcasting Corporation and thus Hadamovsky's superior. With this reorganization Goebbels ensured that the "executive control of broadcasting" could be exerted efficiently by his ministry, while the administrative work was in the hands of Eugen Hadamovsky and the various radio directors. Hans Kriegler replaced Horst Dressler-Andress as head of the radio department in the Propaganda Ministry.[68]

In his talk at the opening of the Radio Exhibition at the end of July, Goebbels confirmed that his call for more entertainment had already been heeded. In future he wanted no more broadcasting experiments. There was no need to "fill the ears of the broad masses with juvenile stammerings," particularly radio plays, which, "with their frenzies of shouting, had an irritating and off-putting effect on the listener."[69]

All the same, by 1938 he had come to the conclusion that more "serious music, opera, and symphonies" should be broadcast; there was "too much droning" on the radio. Entertainment was "good, but it must not become too primitive."[70] However, there was no echo of this change of direction when he opened that year's Radio Exhibition in August: Entertainment clearly still had priority.[71]

Apart from the aim of offering the public more relaxation and diversion, Goebbels had a solid motive for making programs as popular as possible. In 1933 the Postal Ministry had agreed to pass on a percentage of the radio license fee to the Propaganda Ministry. This income largely covered the Propaganda Ministry's budget; during the war, in fact, income considerably exceeded expenditure. The agreement with the Postal Ministry was modified a few times: In February 1935 it was established that the Propaganda Ministry should receive 55 percent of the radio fees; if listener numbers (4.5 million in 1933, 5.4 million in 1934) rose above seven million, the extra fees would be shared between Propaganda and Post at a ratio of 3 to 1. This figure was surpassed as early as 1936; in 1937 there was a radio audience of 8.5 million, and the addition of the annexed territories made the number even higher.[72] The Propaganda Ministry made every effort to increase listener numbers by promoting the spread of the People's Receiver, a cheap and robust radio set.

EFFORTS TO RESTRUCTURE THE PRESS

From 1936 to 1938, Goebbels once again put in a great deal of effort to build up his central role in the Nazi press policy. When the president of the Reich Press Chamber, Max Amann, proposed a new press law in October 1936, Goebbels signed on to the changes, subject to certain amendments; Hitler, too, was in agreement.[73] Goebbels's willingness to accept Amann's proposals may have had something to do with the fact that at this time, as we have seen, Goebbels was in the process of selling Amann the publication rights to his diary, on the most extraordinarily favorable conditions.[74]

But once that contract had been signed, the proposed legislation underwent drastic revision by the Propaganda Ministry.[75] Serious objections to the revised draft were raised not only by Amann, who now scarcely recognized his own bill, but also by Frick and Blomberg. They objected that Goebbels had written a key sentence into the bill giving the Propaganda Ministry the sole right to issue directives to the press. Both the Ministry of the Interior and the Defense Ministry saw this as encroaching on their authority, and the Reich press chief, Otto Dietrich, recalled an edict of Hitler's from February 28, 1934, by which he alone was entitled to give orders to the National Socialist papers.[76]

When there was no sign of agreement between ministries, Goebbels indicated that he was prepared to shelve the bill;[77] Hitler had it removed from the cabinet agenda, and it was filed away.[78] But what had clearly emerged was that Goebbels's claim to control of the press was by no means absolute.

At this time Goebbels was also trying to reshape the press landscape, although with doubtful success. In October 1936 he was determined to close down the *Frankfurter Zeitung* and the *Deutsche Allgemeine Zeitung*. A little later, however, Hitler told him that he wanted these two "bourgeois" papers to continue, provided there were changes to their management.[79] Goebbels did not succeed in imposing on the *Frankfurter Zeitung* his chosen appointees, Martin Schwaebe (editor-in-chief of the Nazi Gau newspaper *Westdeutscher Beobachter*), as head of publishing and the Nazi journalist Walter Trautmann (editor-in-chief of the *Mitteldeutsche Nationalzeitung*) as the new managing editor.[80] And when he called in Editor-in-Chief

Silex of the *Deutsche Allgemeine Zeitung* to charge him with "too much opposition," the eloquent Silex was able to impress Goebbels with an exhaustive account of his "difficulties."[81] Silex retained his position.

Goebbels went on vacillating in his approach to the *Frankfurter Zeitung*, the leading bourgeois paper; sometimes he wanted to close it, at other times to let it carry on.[82] But he did manage early in 1937 to replace Paul Scheffer, editor-in-chief of the *Berliner Tageblatt*—formerly the most important liberal paper in the capital—with Erich Schwarzer, who himself was relieved after fifteen months by Eugen Mündler.[83] The *Tageblatt* ceased publication in January 1939.

In June and July 1938, Goebbels was still rejecting Amann's attempt to take all the big newspapers into state ownership,[84] but he soon agreed with Amann on the principle that the latter would be allowed "gradually to take over all newspapers" as long as the "political leadership" remained in Goebbels's hands and he was consulted about all personnel changes on the main papers.[85]

Although Amann accepted these terms, in practice the agreement did not actually work in the way the Propaganda Ministry intended. So, for example, when the *Deutsche Allgemeine Zeitung* was sold at the end of 1938 to Amann's Deutscher Verlag (German Publishing House, the former House of Ullstein) and Secretary of State Otto Dietrich attempted to appoint Mündler in place of Silex as editor-in-chief, he was blocked by Amann's chief of staff, Rienhardt.[86] In April 1939, the *Frankfurter Zeitung*, too, was acquired—as a birthday present from Amann to Hitler—by the Eher Verlag, but for the time being there were no decisive changes of personnel on the paper, as Goebbels had in mind.[87] In 1938, when Dietrich tried to expand the conservative *Berliner Börsen-Zeitung* (Berlin Stock Exchange News) and turn it into an outlet for the Propaganda Ministry—a move supported not only by Goebbels[88] but also by the minister for economic affairs, Walther Funk—Amann was having none of it; this paper too was absorbed into his empire.[89]

Thus there is a mixed picture as far as Goebbels's position vis-à-vis Nazi press policy is concerned: While it is true that by 1933–34 he had built up a refined system of press control, when it came to the structure of the press landscape and to personnel matters, Amann's grip on publishing turned out to be stronger than Goebbels's claim to "political leadership."

He was, however, able to assert himself without reservation against another competitor in the press sector: Ernst "Putzi" Hanfstaengl, head of the Foreign Press Bureau in Berlin. To the propaganda minister, Hanfstaengel was an irritating survival from the "Time of Struggle," when the well-connected and cosmopolitan son of a well-known Munich art publisher had become a confidant of Hitler's. Goebbels's aim was to undermine and destroy Hanfstaengl's position.

By November 1934 Goebbels had already begun to intrigue against Hanfstaengl; in 1932 the latter had allegedly written a leaflet hostile to Hitler.[90] In August 1936 Goebbels called a halt to a film project of Hanfstaengl's before it could be completed and blackened his name with Hitler on account of supposedly excessive fee payments.[91]

At the beginning of 1937 the idea was thought up at Hitler's lunch table—according to Goebbels—of playing a practical joke on Hanfstaengl. The day before his fiftieth birthday he was sent on a fictional "special mission" to Spain. During the flight he was told that the plan was to drop him behind enemy lines. However, the pilot actually put the plane down on an emergency landing strip in Saxony.[92] Goebbels initially found this story "side-splittingly funny." But he had not anticipated that Hanfstaengl regarded this kind of humor as life-threatening, and he elected to leave Germany immediately.[93] Subsequently Goebbels made him some lucrative offers to lure him back to Germany, but to no effect.[94] In April Hanfstaengl moved to London. Goebbels feared "revelations," and after further efforts to bring him back had failed,[95] in July he and Hitler were agreed: "Hanfstängl [sic] must go, too."[96]

NATIONALIZATION OF THE FILM INDUSTRY

In the last months of 1936, criticism of German film's insufficient propaganda content runs like a thread through Goebbels's diaries.[97] What was most alarming for him was the dissatisfaction with German films that Hitler expressed to him; they were not "national socialist" enough.[98] Consequently Goebbels demanded that his producers and directors should make "more use of contemporary subject matter."[99] What he wanted, he wrote, was "the new political film," but the film industry brought forward no usable suggestions of appropriate topics.[100] He subjected the colleagues closest to him in the film sector to rebukes of varying severity.[101] Since all the instruments he had devised—film dramaturgy, the Film Chamber, a system of awards, and so on—had failed to produce the desired results, he decided to take the film industry directly under his control.

The idea of a "great new film company with the state as majority stake-holder" first appears in the diaries in June 1936.[102] In autumn 1936 the plan took concrete shape, and Goebbels initiated takeover negotiations with Ufa. Even during the negotiations he tried to impose an "artistic committee" on Ufa in order to have a body that could bypass the management and exert its influence on the content of productions.[103] At Tobis* he had already instituted just such a committee.[104]

In early March he received a "long letter" from Alfred Hugenberg, whose group of companies owned Ufa. Hugenberg wrote that "at least for the time being" (as Goebbels noted) he rejected "artistic boards." Goebbels was now determined to apply ruthless pressure. This letter, he asserted, would cost the "Hugenbergers" "at least 3 million marks." More effective was a "general attack" by the media on the insubordinate film company. The first target was the Ufa film *Menschen ohne Vaterland* (People Without a Fatherland), which was now savagely criticized throughout the press.[105] Just a few days after having "worn Ufa down," he exulted in the fact that the "biggest film, media, theater and radio concern in the world" was about to be born.[106] On March 20 it was all over: The Ufa company had "finally been bought out," and Goebbels wanted to get rid of the old supervisory board ("German Nationalist uncles") as quickly as possible.[107] It goes without saying that the press campaign against *Menschen ohne Vaterland* was now instantly dropped.[108]

Shortly after nationalizing the most important film companies, Goebbels gave another big speech in the Kroll Opera to the "film creators."[109] Hypocritically, Goebbels put himself forward as a "warm-hearted but ultimately neutral observer" of German film, and he asserted with regret that in contemporary German film "the purely commercial tendencies" had displaced "the artistic element," so that it was "more accurate today to speak of the film industry than of cin-

* Translators' note: A major film company.

ematic art." As a counterweight he praised the model already introduced at Tobis: placing artists on the supervisory boards of the film
industry.

As Goebbels went on with his speech, his message was clear: When
he talked of orientating the film along "artistic" lines, he meant "I
want [. . .] an art which expresses an attitude through its national-
socialist character and by taking up national-socialist problems." But
this orientation should not "appear deliberate"; propaganda only
worked when it "remains in the background as a tendency, as character, as attitude, and only becomes apparent in action, unfolding
events, processes, in the contrast between individuals."

Ewald von Demandowsky, who took over the office of film dramaturge in May 1937, became Goebbels's most important collaborator
in his bid to radically reorganize German film.[110] Ernst von Liechten-
stein, from the Reich propaganda office, took over management of
the film department from the beginning of 1938 and was followed by
Fritz Hippler in August 1939.[111]

Not only did Goebbels largely replace the supervisory boards of
Ufa and Tobis, he also involved himself directly in these companies'
productions:[112] He reserved the right to approve the acquisition of
individual artists;[113] made casting decisions;[114] assigned directing
contracts; imposed bans on filming[115] and directing;[116] and evaluated
screenplays.[117] In short, he was determined "to intervene more firmly
in film production by giving orders."[118] At the end of July 1937 he
forbade "this everlasting singsong in entertainment films," and he
tasked Demandowsky with "cutting out never-never settings from
films."[119]

A few days later, angry at the "lack of quality in film," Goebbels
pulled a few directors off various projects.[120] Obviously alarmed by
Hitler's "very stinging verdict" on these "bad films,"[121] he summoned
the heads of production and the artistic directors of the film companies and complained about "recent banal and uninspired kitsch
films."[122] He ordered that films from the Weimar period in which
"Jews are still to be seen" should be banned "lock, stock, and barrel."[123] He also set about the "de-jewification [*Entjudung*] of film exports": The Party's organization abroad ought to intervene in film
sales to foreign countries.[124] Together with Demandowsky he compiled a list of actors, directors, and screenwriters who were especially

worth backing.[125] He made a sustained effort (though clearly without striking success) to develop guidelines to limit salaries.[126] He also developed his own subject matter: He closely supervised the production of the "autobahn film" *Die Stimme aus dem Äther* (The Voice from the Ether).[127] In 1939 he developed an idea for a "press film"; the project, never realized, went under the working title "Die 7. Grossmacht" (The Seventh Great Power).[128]

Goebbels pronounced a mainly negative verdict on the "national-political" films that were made before the takeover of the big studios and reached the cinemas in the early months of 1937.[129] The anti-communist films made in 1936–37 were not biting enough for him either.[130] He was boundlessly enthusiastic—admittedly, after a good many improvements had been made to the screenplay[131]—about the film *Patrioten* (Patriots; his lover Lida Baarová starred in it), as he also was about Veit Harlan's *Der Herrscher* (The Ruler), a picture about a captain of industry with a social conscience who bequeaths his capital to the state.[132] Among the films appearing later in the year, he liked, up to a point, the satire *Mein Sohn der Herr Minister*[133] (My Son the Minister) and the First World War epic *Unternehmen Michael* (Operation Michael), but he had reservations about both films.[134] However, there was no end to his praise for *Urlaub auf Ehrenwort* (Leave on Parole).[135] On the other hand, the project of a film "about Spain" that he was promoting came to nothing,[136] as did an anticlerical Lola Montez film.[137]

In mid-1937 he managed to add the film company Terra to his stable.[138] He wanted originally to liquidate Bavaria Film in Munich, but—with Hitler's support and against Goebbels's will—Gauleiter Adolf Wagner pushed through a re-founding of the company early in 1938 in order to preserve filmmaking in Munich.[139]

Goebbels now continued to pursue his objective of steering the film companies' productions with the help of "artistic committees," designed as a counterweight to the supervisory boards, with their predominantly commercial interests. At Ufa, this role was taken on by the director Carl Froelich and the actors Mathias Wieman and Paul Hartmann;[140] at Tobis[141] there were Emil Jannings and Willi Forst (Gustave Gründgens once again declined on grounds of over-commitment);[142] and at Terra, most notably, Heinrich George.[143] Yet complaints soon proliferated in Goebbels's diary about the ineffectiveness of this system.[144] While the number of filmgoers continued to rise in 1937, production costs were spiraling out of control, and film exports continued the steep decline that had begun in 1933.[145]

By the end of 1937 Goebbels was becoming increasingly critical of film production,[146] and after a long discussion with Demandowsky he came to a terse and sobering conclusion: "Our films are just very bad."[147] At the end of November he gave a talk to leading film people to point out "mistakes and failings."[148] The comedies produced in the following few months he found particularly unappealing.[149]

In general it is striking that film production in 1938–39 was not primarily concerned with preparing for war: Only a handful of films from each year dealt with political themes. Neither do Goebbels's diary entries suggest that he wanted to use film purposefully and extensively as psychological preparation for war.[150]

Apart from his direct influence on the film companies, Goebbels was ambitious to secure the quality of filmmaking in the long run by nurturing talent. In March 1938 he established the cornerstone of a film academy in Babelsberg.[151] Within a two-year course of study, the training of future specialists in the artistic, technical, and financial aspects of cinema was to be carried out by three faculties.[152] But Goebbels was soon expressing doubts about the head of the academy, Wilhelm Müller-Scheldt. Most of all he objected to Müller-Scheldt's admissions policy,[153] so he issued "a clear directive to select candidates suited to our time and our taste, i.e. beautiful women and manly men."[154]

At the end of 1938 Goebbels concluded that the system of artistic committees he had been sponsoring so far was unproductive.[155] After lengthy consultations[156] he placed heads of production in all the film companies, to whom he issued instructions directly,[157] in order at last to achieve total control over the production companies.[158] In March 1937, in a further speech to filmmakers, Goebbels gave his reasons for appointing "independently responsible heads of production" and ending the experiment of artistic committees: The committees had not been able to prevail against the supervisory boards, representing as they did narrow financial concerns.[159]

Yet despite all his efforts, in June 1939 Hitler pronounced himself still "somewhat dissatisfied," and Goebbels decided to take the problem in hand by changing the heads of production where appropriate.[160] The propaganda minister continued to be skeptical about the

effectiveness of his far-reaching interference in the German film industry, but at the same time he was not prepared to admit to himself
the reasons for this. For all his general demand for improvements to
the quality of pictures and for all his hectic giving of "orders" to the
film industry and his personal intervention, Goebbels the film ty-
coon had not been able to give the huge conglomerate he had been
running for two years clear and practical guidelines for adapting
their film production in the medium term. An industry in which the
gestation of a film normally took a year, from conception to finished
product, could not be steered by "orders" and interventions à la
Goebbels.

"GERMAN" AND "DEGENERATE" ART

In summer 1937 Goebbels was completely taken up with the reorientation of German art. His diary entries show clearly how strenuously
he tried in these months to adjust to the dictator's taste in art. Hitler,
for his part, was evidently eager to put his propaganda minister (who
in the early phase of the regime had not entirely rejected "modern"
artistic tendencies as a matter of principle) on the right track by his
very own efforts.

Goebbels flew with Hitler in June to Munich to view the
almost-completed "Führer building" on the Königsplatz as well as
the recently finished House of German Art. Together with his propaganda minister, Hitler went on to inspect the works chosen by a jury
headed by the president of the Reich Chamber of Fine Art, Adolf
Ziegler, for display in the "Great German Art Exhibition" with which
the building was to be opened. Hitler was appalled, as Goebbels
noted: "They've hung works here that make your flesh creep. [. . .]
The Führer is seething with rage."[161]

The next day—they were both en route to Regensburg by now—
Hitler returned to the subject: He would rather postpone the exhibition for a year than "display such muck."[162] Eventually Hitler decided
to reduce the number of works to five hundred and left the selection
to his personal photographer, Heinrich Hoffmann.[163]

Alongside the Great German Art Exhibition intended to represent
art in the Third Reich, in 1937 Goebbels planned an "Exhibition of
Art from the Age of Decadence." Initially meant for Berlin, it was

moved to Munich. It was precisely the difficulties that had arisen over the selection of works for the Great German Art Exhibition that made it seem appropriate to define in a parallel exhibition exactly what art was *not* wanted in the Third Reich.[164]

At the end of June Goebbels gained Hitler's official approval for the plan. The exhibition was to be curated by Ziegler and Schweitzer, although Hitler forcibly expressed his reservations about the former *Angriff* caricaturist.[165] In order to requisition the relevant works, Goebbels gave Ziegler special permission, on the basis of "specially conferred Führer-powers," to "take custody" of works of art from any public museum in Germany that fit his description of "German decadent art since 1910."[166] In haste, the commission in July 1937 visited thirty-two collections in twenty-eight towns, and requisitioned seven hundred works of art.[167]

This looting of art museums represented an affront to Education Minister Rust, with whom Goebbels was on a war footing. The offense was compounded by the fact that on Goebbels's initiative artists shown in the Munich "Decadence Exhibition" were branded as "degenerate" even though they were teaching at state art schools or were members of the Prussian Academy of Fine Art.[168] Goebbels's strategy was clear: Rust was to be pushed into an untenable defensive position in the area of culture policy and his academy forced to close down, so that Goebbels could set up a "German Academy" under his own direction. Thus the threatened loss of prestige with Hitler over the business of the Munich art exhibition would be compensated for by a brilliant success.[169]

At the beginning of July the Goebbels family began their vacation preparations: They were off to Heiligendamm again. While Goebbels was supervising the packing in his Berlin house, he received a surprise call: "Führer's on the phone: Wants to visit us on Schwanenwerder." So the Goebbelses drove with their children back to Schwanenwerder to enjoy "a wonderful afternoon out there with the Führer."[170]

The next day, July 3, the Goebbels family flew to the Baltic: "Wonderful rest. And I certainly need it," confided Goebbels to his diary.[171] After the family had just gotten settled in at Heiligendamm, there was another change in their vacation plans. Hitler urged them by phone to spend their vacation with him on the Obersalzberg; an invitation to do so had already gone out a few weeks earlier.[172] So they packed up again and—with a short stop in Berlin—flew to Bavaria.[173]

The Goebbels family arrived on the Obersalzberg on July 9, where Hitler, as Goebbels recorded with pride, was "already waiting [for them] on the steps."[174] The following days were passed in all sorts of conversations, card games, and the obligatory home cinema. But the real reason for the pressing invitation was that Hitler wanted to instruct his propaganda minister thoroughly on the required direction of travel in cultural policy. On July 11 Hitler went with Goebbels to Munich; this time, Hitler was much happier about the works chosen for the Great German Art Exhibition.

On July 12 Goebbels left the Obersalzberg to fly to Berlin; Magda and the children stayed on in Berchtesgaden. On July 16 he flew back to Munich[175] to visit, together with Hitler, the "Exhibition of Degenerate Art," which opened a few days later in the Hofgarten Arcades, not far from the House of German Art. The show displayed six hundred works, including those by Emil Nolde, Max Beckmann, Marc Chagall, Max Ernst, Otto Dix, Paul Klee, George Grosz, Wassily Kandinsky, Ernst Ludwig Kirchner, Lyonel Feininger, and Franz Marc. In order to reduce the impact of the paintings, they were hung very close together, with an effect of randomness; titles of and commentaries to the pictures were written on the walls. By the end of November 1937, over two million people had seen this exhibition.[176]

After their joint visit to the exhibition, Goebbels spoke in Hitler's presence at the annual conference of the Reich Chamber of Fine Art, and took part the next day, July 18, in the grand opening of the House of German Art.[177] In the specially commissioned opening exhibition there were 1,200 predominantly conventional works of art on display, which, however, scarcely lived up to the exhibition's claim to be the artistic expression of National Socialism and, in terms of quality, to continue the tradition of nineteenth-century art. But how could this claim possibly have been fulfilled?

What was on display were overwhelmingly historical and genre pieces, monumental landscapes, various "blood and soil" motifs, heroic representations of an "awakening" Germany, and portraits of the Führer. In Hitler's and Goebbels's opening speeches, there were signs of dissatisfaction with what was on display,[178] which did not prevent Goebbels and Magda from acquiring pictures for the total value of 50,000 Reichsmarks on behalf of the Propaganda Ministry.[179]

Some months later, at the annual conference of the Reich Culture Chamber, Goebbels was even more open about the lack of quality in

Nazi art, with regard not only to pictorial art but also to literature. The "great ideological ideas" of the National Socialist revolution, he said, had "for the moment such a spontaneous and eruptive effect [. . .] that they are not yet ready for artistic treatment. The problems are too fresh and too new to lend themselves to artistic, dramatic, or fictional form. We must wait for the next generation to take on this task."[180]

Taking what we may call the "lack of maturity" of Nazi art into account, it is not hard to see why Goebbels and Hitler opened both exhibitions almost in parallel. Since official cultural policy had trouble providing examples of what the new "national-socialist" art was supposed to be, it had to fall back on help from an exhibition showing what "decadence" in art was.

At the end of July Hitler declared himself pleased with the success of the Degenerate Art exhibition and ordered a catalogue to be published.[181] The exhibition stayed in Munich until November and was then sent on tour around Germany: to Berlin first of all, where it could be seen for three months in 1938, after Goebbels himself had made a few changes.[182]

At the end of July, Hitler had given Ziegler the job of thoroughly "cleansing" the German art museums once and for all of these incriminating works of art. On his own initiative, Goebbels had already handed him the same assignment just a few days earlier.[183] Ziegler's commission then scoured the galleries, and presented the requisitioned works to Goebbels in November 1938.[184] What he had in mind for them became clear at the end of 1938: "The saleable pictures will be sold abroad, the others collected together in horror exhibitions or destroyed."[185] Goebbels had begun to put requisitioning on a legal footing by January 1938. The law on taking possession of "degenerate art" products gave the power to requisition to a commission headed by him; the selected works were subsequently sold on the international art market.[186]

One of his appointments indicates how determined Goebbels was to adhere rigidly to Hitler's taste in art: In autumn 1937 he made Franz Hofmann head of the Fine Art Department in the Propaganda Ministry. Hofmann was a hard-liner in artistic matters, who among other things had made a name for himself as art critic of the *Völkischer Beobachter* and had been a member of Ziegler's commission since

August 1937.[187] Ever since 1934, when Goebbels was obliged to withdraw his first appointee, Weidemann, the Fine Art Department of his ministry had been leading a shadowy existence.[188] In December 1937, furthermore, Goebbels ordered that foreign art exhibitions in Germany would in future require approval from him: Quite obviously, he wanted to close this kind of backdoor access for undesirable art.[189]

"DEGENERATE MUSIC"

In the early years of the regime, Rosenberg's doctrinaire policies had caused the propaganda minister several setbacks in the area of music. Rosenberg had managed to force Richard Strauss to resign as president of the Reich Music Chamber, and his uncompromising rejection of the composer Hindemith had not only induced the latter to emigrate but also led Goebbels to oppose Furtwängler and remove him from his position as deputy leader of the Reich Music Chamber. Moreover, Rosenberg's National Socialist Cultural Community had brought large parts of German musical life under its control. It functioned as concert organizer, coordinator of guest appearances and music congresses, and publisher of the most important musical journal; it also supported its own record-listening circle.[190]

It was not until 1936 that Goebbels set up a separate music department in his ministry and appointed the conductor Heinz Drewes to lead it.[191] Goebbels now attempted to strengthen his position in musical life. In autumn 1937, having assigned Drewes the task of "bringing the people to music," he sought to strengthen Drewes's position vis-à-vis the Reich Music Chamber, which since 1935 had been chaired by the conductor and musicologist Peter Raabe, a National Socialist.[192] At the end of 1937 Drewes founded a Reich music office as a central censorship authority for music publishing.[193]

In spring 1938 Goebbels made a public bid for a leading role in music policy. On May 28, 1938, he gave a talk at the opening of the "Degenerate Music" exhibition, a ceremony introduced by Richard Strauss's *Festive Prelude,* conducted by the composer in person.[194] The opening of the show, based like the "Degenerate Art" exhibition on an initiative of Ziegler's and reworked by Goebbels before the opening,[195] pertained to the first "Reich Music Days" organized by the Music Chamber. The exhibition denounced "atonality" in music as "degenerate" or "Jewish" and held up the composers Schönberg, Berg, Hindemith, Weill, and Stravinsky as particularly horrifying examples.

Goebbels began his opening speech[196] with a summary of achievements meant to demonstrate the upturn in German musical life since 1933. He emphasized that the precondition for this upswing was the "de-jewification" of the German music scene, especially the elimination of "Jewish music criticism."

He seized the opportunity to make a statement of intent, sketching out the future direction of German music under the heading of "Ten Principles of Music Creation." Initially, these consisted of a whole litany of clichés: "To be unmusical is the same for a musical person as being blind or deaf. [. . .] Music is the art that most profoundly moves the human soul. [. . .] The language of notes is sometimes more effective than the language of words," and so on. In general, what Goebbels's "principles" amounted to was a commitment to "popular music." Goebbels made the point, among others, that there was a place for "the kind of entertainment music that is acceptable to the broad masses." The equation of entertainment with popularity allowed Goebbels to spread an ideological fog. If music arose from "mysterious and profound forces rooted in the national character," then it could only be "formed and wielded by children of the people in accordance with the needs and the untamed musical drive of the nation." This naturally meant grasping that "Judaism and German music" were "opposites," which "by their nature contradict each other in the starkest manner." Inevitably, a reference to Richard Wagner's publication *Judaism in Music* followed from this. Goebbels's "principles" ended with a paean of praise for Hitler, who had "torn German music from the threat of decadence" and for whom music represented an "essential life element."

With this speech, Goebbels may have staked his claim to leadership in musical life, but there is every reason to doubt that he achieved a "reorientation" of German music. Goebbels, like the Nazi musicologists, was simply unable to define what "German music" actually was.[197] Marking it off against "atonal," "modern," "Jewish," and "degenerate music" served only to obscure this plain fact. So it is no accident that the "Ten Principles," Goebbels's main testimony to musical life under National Socialism, should have been proclaimed precisely in the context of a "degenerate music" exhibition.

Such conceptual failings aside, the German music scene may have been too varied to allow the Propaganda Ministry to give it a unified direction: Musical theater and orchestral music, entertainment and dance music, amateur music and choirs, Party bands and other musical activities did not lend themselves to the imposition of one musical policy "line."[198]

THEATER POLICY: PLAYHOUSES AS PLAYING FIELDS

The law of May 15, 1934, relating to theaters[199] had been used by the Propaganda Ministry, or to be more precise by its theater department (run from 1935 onward by Eugen Schlösser, who doubled as the "Reich dramaturge"), to secure a decisive influence on top theater appointments[200] and maintain effective censorship of programming.[201]

This influence of the Propaganda Ministry on theater practice showed up in a few key tendencies. The works of Jewish and politically undesirable playwrights were prohibited; this amounted, in effect, to a ban on practically all existing contemporary drama. Nationalist and *völkisch* authors stepped into the breach. Foreign works were out (with the exception of Shakespeare, classified as a "Nordic poet," and Shaw), and there was a heightened respect for the classics.[202]

Constituting 60 percent of productions, from 1934–35 onward contemporary German theater became the dominant genre, consisting mostly of comedies, "folk plays," and the like, but a third of plays were "serious drama," in other words more or less undisguised Nazi ideology onstage.[203] To these were added quite a few older *völkisch* dramatists from the first three decades of the twentieth century.[204]

By and large, these general tendencies in programming corresponded to Goebbels's personal taste in theater—with one significant exception. He was not fond of drama by *völkisch* and contemporary authors with close ties to National Socialism. His verdict on plays by Rudolf Billinger, highly regarded by Nazis as a "blood-and-soil" writer, was that they were "deadly dull" and "clumsy, stupid, and tasteless."[205] Goebbels was equally negative about Sigmund Graff's First World

War play *Die endlose Strasse* (The Endless Road; Graff, who had started out in the Stahlhelm, was actually a consultant for the theater department of the Propaganda Ministry): "Really endless. [...] Mind-numbing and pessimistic."[206] He characterized Erwin Guido Kolbenheyer's *Heroische Leidenschaften* (Heroic Passions) as "heroic boredom. Terrible! It makes me sick, all this philosophizing on the stage. Should make something happen, not just blather on."[207] *Herzog und Henker* (Duke and Executioner) by the *völkisch* poet Hermann Burte was "an unbearable jangle of words and verse without substance in problems or attitude. The whole thing a million miles from where we are."[208] This list of negative comments could go on.[209]

But there were exceptions: One play that appealed to him, for example, was Friedrich Bethge's *Marsch der Veteranen* (Veterans' March), a dramatization of the march by American ex-soldiers on Washington.[210] Similarly, he praised Hanns Johst's *Thomas Paine* (note that Johst was president of the Reich Chamber of Literature) as a "first-class revolutionary drama."[211] He particularly liked *Das Frankenburger Würfelspiel* (The Frankenburg Dice Game), written by the German Prize winner for 1935, Eberhard Wolfgang Möller; Goebbels became personally involved in directing the play when it was performed in the open-air theater in the Olympic Park during the Games.[212] But all in all, Goebbels seemed quite unconvinced by the idea that Nazi dramas could give the German stage an entirely new look.

Hence Goebbels preferred to promote established authors. This corresponded to his personal taste, as recorded in many comments on theater productions. Among great German writers it was Friedrich Schiller he loved best, the most-performed German classical author in the Third Reich.[213] "Great Schiller, what bunglers we have," wrote Goebbels after a performance of *Maria Stuart* at the Berlin Volksbühne (People's Theater).[214] He admired Shakespeare even more, and indeed after 1933 Shakespeare competed with Schiller for the title of most-performed author.[215] The English playwright, said the propaganda minister after seeing a production of *Coriolanus* in 1937, was "more relevant and modern than all the moderns. What a huge genius! How he towers over Schiller!"[216] He shared with Hitler[217] a strong predilection for George Bernard Shaw, possibly because he thought of the Irish dramatist as "more journalist than [creative] writer."[218] After a performance of *Saint Joan* in August 1936 he praised "Shaw's sparkling ideas and wit. Brilliant mockery! A man after my own heart."[219] On the other hand, Goebbels by no means despised light entertainment and robust folk comedies.[220]

When the Theater Law was passed in 1934, Göring obtained for himself the privilege of controlling the fate of several theaters under his jurisdiction. Thus the propaganda minister had no influence on the Prussian state theaters, as for example the Schauspielhaus am Gendarmenmarkt (a Berlin playhouse) and the State Opera. In 1934 Göring appointed Gustaf Gründgens director of the State Theater. Shortly after his appointment Gründgens showed that he was perfectly willing to cooperate with Goebbels. "I shall take him under my wing," wrote Goebbels patronizingly after a conversation with him, but in fact it turned out that for the most part Gründgens was quite capable of preserving "his" theater's independence from the Propaganda Ministry.[221]

From the mid-1930s onward, Goebbels began to set up several first-class "Reich theaters" in opposition to these top houses; the Reich theaters were run directly by the Propaganda Ministry, and Goebbels took a deep personal interest in them.[222] Not the least of his objectives was to convince Hitler—they often went to the theater together—of the superiority of Goebbels's taste in drama and to demonstrate his leading role in shaping the life of the German stage. The Reich theaters included the Städtische Oper (Metropolitan Opera) in Berlin, which passed into state ownership in March 1934 and then traded under the name Deutsche Oper (German Opera); the former Theater des Westens (Theater of the West), leased in 1934 by the Reich, after which it was the Volksoper (People's Opera); the Deutsches Theater (German Theater) after August 1934; the Volksbühne (People's Stage), which after 1933 gradually came under the direct influence of the Propaganda Ministry; and the former Grosses Schauspielhaus (Grand Playhouse), which the Propaganda Ministry ran jointly after 1933 as the Theater des Volkes (Theater of the People).

Goebbels stayed in close contact with the directors of the houses. He regularly discussed the situation of his theater with Eugen Erich Orthmann of the Volksoper without being particularly interested in his productions, which were standard opera repertoire.[223] He took more interest in the other theaters, however. With Hans Hilpert, whom he had moved in April 1934 from the Volksbühne to the Deutsches Theater,[224] he went over repertoires and the acquisition of new artists,[225] as he did with the director of the Volksbühne, Eugen Klöpfer[226] (the first director to follow Hilpert at the Volksbühne was the Nazi activist Count Bernhard Solms, but Goebbels soon came to regard his appointment as a mistake).[227] Klöpfer managed to cling to his position until 1944 and the demise of theater in the Third Reich, but Goebbels took an increasingly critical view of him.[228]

With Wilhelm Rode, head of the Deutsche Oper, Goebbels discussed not just appointments but also individual productions.[229] In January 1935, when he was dissatisfied with a performance of *Boccaccio* at the Deutsche Oper (and Hitler was "not very enthusiastic" either), he summoned Rode and gave him a severe dressing-down. Goebbels offered Rode a chance to redeem himself with the forthcoming production of *Tristan*, which he liked very much. Even so, a few days later he presented Rode with some "directing notes."[230] A week later he took in the production again, accompanied by Hitler this time: "My notes on direction have been put into effect. [...] Führer enthusiastic."[231] This was not the only direct intervention by the theater enthusiast Goebbels: In 1936, just before the performance was due, he made some changes to a review staged by the Kraft durch Freude organization in the Theater des Volkes to celebrate May 1. When he saw the premiere the next day, he was happy with the results of his intervention.[232]

In 1938 Goebbels obtained control of two more Berlin theaters. He nationalized the Nollendorftheater in Berlin and appointed the actor and director Harald Paulsen as director, mainly to put on operettas;[233] at the same time, he made Heinrich George director of the city-owned Schillertheater, thus gaining a powerful influence over that house too.[234] Furthermore, in the same year and the next, respectively, he acquired two further Berlin operetta theaters for the Reich: the Admiralspalast (Admiral's Palace) and the Metropoltheater (Metropole Theater).[235] In all, Goebbels presided over a considerable number of venues in Berlin that were directly under his influence, and this enabled him to showcase in all the important genres—operetta, opera, folk theater, and contemporary and classical drama—what he conceived as suitably representative theater in the National Socialist state.

"DE-JEWIFYING" CULTURAL LIFE

The complete removal of all Jews still active in his sphere of operations was an integral part of the enforced "reorientation" of the whole
of culture and media policy introduced by Goebbels in 1936–37.
From the autumn of 1935 onward, there are frequent diary entries
showing how concerned he was to thoroughly "de-jewify" the Reich
Culture Chamber. An edict from the Culture Chamber to this effect
was already in force by June 1935.[236] But excluding all Jews (including
"half-Jews," "quarter-Jews," and "those related to Jews") from German cultural life turned out not to be as easy as Goebbels had hoped.
The individual chambers, which by no means operated a unified exclusion procedure, were constantly making exceptions. Thus in 1937
the Reich Chamber of Fine Art still had 156 Jewish members, mostly
art dealers and art publicists. It was not until the end of 1937 that the
chambers coordinated their various "Aryan" provisions.[237]

Although Goebbels constantly gave instructions to accelerate the
"de-jewifying" process, reported "great progress,"[238] and by early February 1937 considered the Reich Culture Chamber to be "completely
de-jewified,"[239] he was forced to acknowledge soon afterward that the
"cleansing" was not yet complete.[240] In the first months of 1938,
Goebbels complained of considerable difficulty in "de-jewifying" the
Reich Music Chamber,[241] and in February 1939 he obtained Hitler's
permission to go on employing "21 non-fully-Aryan or Jewish-related
theater or film actors."[242] Various entries from the first half of 1939
show that the action was still not yet over[243]—and in fact it would
never be completed. Even by May 1943, he found himself stating
with consternation that "the Reich Culture Chamber is not yet as
de-jewified as I intended"; "a whole lot of quarter-Jews, even a few
half-Jews, and numbers of Jewish-related are hanging around there."
But during the war he was no longer so eager to come to grips with
the problem, considering that this would "kick up too much dust,"
especially in artistic circles.[244]

BIOGRAPHICAL STOCKTAKING: SUCCESS AND DISTANCE

While Goebbels was increasingly successful in bringing the whole cultural life of the Third Reich under his control and thereby strengthening his power base, one aspect of his personal development stands out: his increasing isolation from other people. The more lavish his external lifestyle, the more he craved solitude. In his narcissistic self-absorption, he obviously did not feel the need to share the rewards of fame and success with family or friends.

After 1933, he failed to sustain friendships he had made in his youth, as a student, or during his early Berlin years. Certainly, during his visits to Rheydt, which he went on making two or three times a year,[245] he met up with old friends, but these encounters mainly allowed him to measure the distance he had so gloriously put between himself and his small-town origins.[246] In January 1938, for example, he invited "boyhood friends" over to his hotel in Rheydt: "How unfamiliar and distant they have become to me now,"[247] he noted. And of another meeting a couple of evenings later where politics and the economy were discussed, he wrote: "You're so far from things out here in the country." In his circle of old friends, since he left town "so much had changed, a few were already dead, most simply petit bourgeois."[248] When old friends visited him, his verdict on them was similar in its condescension: Pille Kölsch was a "real philistine," and Fritz Prang "a grumbler," even if "not a bad type."[249]

Contact with his brothers was confined to a bare minimum of dutiful visits. In February 1935, Konrad became director of the Völkisch Verlag in Düsseldorf[250] but was forced to resign before long because of a conflict with the president of the Reich press chamber, Max Amann,[251] although he soon found employment again in the newspaper sector as business affairs manager of the Gau publishing house in Frankfurt.[252] After the seizure of power in 1933 Goebbels's brother Hans, like Konrad a Nazi activist, had found a relatively favorable position in the insurance business,[253] but relations with him were complicated by the fact that Joseph could not stand his sister-in-law Hertha.[254]

By contrast, he had a rather closer relationship with his sister Maria, who in 1936 stayed for some time as a guest in the Goebbels household and who often accompanied her brother and her sister-in-law on their visits to Hitler.[255] In 1937 a new visitor often showed up at Schwanenwerder: the screenplay writer Axel Kimmich, with whom Maria had fallen deeply in love.[256] Goebbels, who naturally suspected that Kimmich might be using this private relationship to further his career, immediately had him vetted by the police: The results were positive.[257] Having at first cast a skeptical eye at him,[258] the head of the household eventually decided he was "nice, but not over-bright."[259] Finally Kimmich, four years older than Goebbels, formally requested her brother's permission to marry Maria: Goebbels felt "a bit silly in the role of father-in-law."[260] He had further checks carried out on his potential brother-in-law; the answers were again positive. "So as far as I'm concerned they should get married. I don't want to stand in the way of their happiness."[261] He approved of a film script that Kimmich had shown him.[262] The engagement was celebrated on Schwanenwerder in August—Hitler was among the guests[263]—and the wedding took place in February 1938.[264] But it did not take long for Goebbels to change his mind about his brother-in-law: "Fathead," "numbskull," "a proper milksop."[265] What Goebbels had feared then duly happened: Kimmich, in his view not particularly talented, tried to enlist his brother-in-law's support in his disputes within the film business. For Goebbels this was another argument for keeping his distance from family affairs. Negative remarks about his sister Maria, too, now began to appear in the diary.[266]

However, Goebbels made one exception to his self-imposed rule about keeping his distance from relatives: his mother. As ever, he sought a close emotional relationship with her. She often came on visits to Berlin, where she eventually had her own apartment: "Mother is so kind and so wise. Such a refreshing time for me," he wrote after visiting her. "My best mother! If I didn't have you. My mainstay!"[267]

From about the end of 1936, Goebbels's attitude to Magda gradually changed. Various entries scattered throughout the year indicate this development. With the house on the Bogensee, Goebbels had a refuge all to himself, one that allowed him to avoid Magda, even after the family had moved back to Berlin from their summer residence on Schwanenwerder at the beginning of October 1936.[268] He often spent time there, in the solitude of his large wooded grounds.[269] Goebbels was far from open in his diary entries about his private life or his emotions; it is especially noticeable that his affair with Baa-rová, which began in the winter of 1936–37, left no trace there at first. Certainly, this relationship was an important factor in increasing his distance from his wife, but there are indications that Goebbels be-came ever more deeply caught up in the affair because he found his relationship with Magda, and his whole private situation, increas-ingly unsatisfactory and problematic. This is brought out by some entries at the turn of the year, 1936–37, which offer some hints about his state of mind.

Magda had arranged the festivities for Christmas 1936 on a lavish scale. But although Goebbels enjoyed being with the children, he could not get into the Christmas spirit, and he spent the whole day in "sorrow and melancholy." On Christmas Day he felt the pull of the Bogensee again, where he spent the next few days without his family: "Away from all this festive kitsch!" On December 27 Hitler, who had invited the Goebbels family to Berchtesgaden for Christmas, wanted to know why they had not yet arrived. They packed in great haste, but in the evening they heard that the journey was off, because Hitler suddenly had an important appointment in Berlin. On December 30 Hitler called the Goebbelses in to the Reich Chancellery to wish them a happy New Year; in the evening he traveled by train to Berch-tesgaden, where they joined him a few days later at his request.

At the Berghof Goebbels had a chance to discuss all kinds of polit-ical topics with Hitler.[270] Goebbels left the Obersalzberg for Berlin on January 8; Hitler followed the next day. Magda, however, stayed on in Hitler's residence a little longer for a rest. Hitler kept her company there again starting on January 18 and then traveled back with her to Berlin five days later.[271] During this separation from Magda, Goeb-bels remarked repeatedly in his diary how much he missed his wife in Berlin and hated being alone: He seemed to resent the fact that this time she was the one who had left hearth and home behind.[272] In these days, Goebbels sought opportunities to air personal matters: On January 18 he sat with Magda's sister-in-law Ello and the actress Erika Dannhoff (a frequent visitor to the house) talking "for a long time about love, marriage, jealousy, etc." The next day he had a long talk with his state secretary, Funk. "I tell him about my worries and fears. That I can never find peace and completely lack freedom."[273] During these days alone in Berlin, he seems to have become aware how much his marriage and his whole private life were interlinked with his political position in Hitler's regime. The more he allowed Hitler to take part in his life and that of his family, thus increasing his closeness to his idol, and the more his family life became a component of his existence as a public figure, the less his family could offer him something like a protected private space. When his wife and children finally returned from Obersalzberg to Berlin, he was quite relieved, and his diary entry suggests that there were emotions at play here that went beyond the pleasure of reunion after a fourteen-day separation: "It's wonderful. The Führer is very kind, Helga is crying with joy, and then Magda and Hilde. I'm so happy. At home Magda tells me all sorts of things about the Führer, life up there, we talk everything through."[274] He spent the next few days with Magda in their Berlin house.

Family life was overshadowed by serious concerns in the following months. At the beginning of February Magda, who was pregnant, suffered from heart problems and had to go back to hospital once more.[275] There, on February 19, she gave birth to her fourth child, a daughter.[276] But it was four weeks before she was allowed home.[277] Magda's doctor told Goebbels that she should not have another baby for two years, to give herself the chance of a complete cure.[278]

As Magda lay in hospital in March, they had planned with Hitler a "summer as a trio together,"[279] but Hitler's invitation to a trip down the Rhine had to be declined because of Magda's poor health.[280] Once Magda was feeling slightly better, though, they spent a good deal of leisure time together: In the spring the Goebbels family moved back into their summer residence on Schwanenwerder, where the dictator often visited.[281] When he did so, Hitler took an active part in the Goebbels family life. Among the children, it was Helga with whom he was most taken; at the beginning of February Hitler was "extremely" pleased with some photos showing Helga on the Obersalzberg: "Says that if Helga was 20 years older and he was 20 years younger, she would be the wife for him."[282] The Goebbels family made return visits to the Reich Chancellery, and it often happened that Magda spent time in the Reich Chancellery without her husband.[283]

In June Magda had to go off again for several weeks to undergo heart treatment in Dresden.[284] After her return, there followed a shared vacation in Upper Bavaria, as prescribed by Hitler, although only Magda was able to enjoy it without interruption. But her health was still so fragile that she elected not to go with her husband to Bayreuth.

Even after the family had moved out to Schwanenwerder, Goebbels stayed for the most part in his official house in Berlin or on the Bogensee and mainly went to the Wannsee to receive guests, whom he took for trips around the nearby lakes. Otherwise, he nearly always made just short visits there. Gradually he began to distance himself from the routine of life there. About one of his visits, Goebbels noted at the beginning of June: "To Schwanenwerder. Magda is expecting ladies for tea. I push off again right away."[285] In August he found his brother Hans with his family there as well as his sister Maria and her fiancé: "Family tittle-tattle. I can't take it anymore. I've grown completely away from that milieu."[286] Schwanenwerder seemed to him less and less like a genuine family refuge; for him it had become a place for display, with his family above all part of Goebbels's self-presentation.

It was in August that Magda—in spite of the doctor's warning—discovered that she was pregnant again. Magda now decided to follow the medical advice and largely withdraw from Berlin society. So she stayed on at Schwanenwerder even over the winter,[287] which suited Goebbels's tendency to gradually detach himself from the everyday life of his family. "I get a great reception, like a guest," he noted—somewhat surprised—on November 6, when he appeared at Schwanenwerder to join in Magda's birthday celebration.[288] In December he established himself in the "Gentleman's House" on the grounds so that he would no longer have to spend the night under the same roof as Magda when he visited.[289]

On Schwanenwerder, what he enjoyed most was time spent with the children. But the countless entries in his diary where he mentions romping around and horseplay with the "lovely," "sweet" children are remarkably stereotyped and superficial. Basically he had little interest in their development and education. From time to time, though, he found himself obliged to give them a "thrashing," to beat the "stubbornness" out of them—as Goebbels saw it, a tried and tested educational method.[290] The family happiness he constantly invoked in his diary meant one thing above all for him: It was an important accessory to demonstrate his personal success story.

As Goebbels isolated himself more and more from other people, he was at the same time set on making his lifestyle as lavish and prestigious as possible. It is almost as if he was doing so precisely in order to further emphasize his distance from others. From April 1937 onward Magda and Joseph Goebbels were preoccupied with plans for a new house to replace their old home in Berlin, which had become "much too small" for five children.[291] Goebbels's justification to the Finance Ministry for this new building (which at Hitler's specific behest was meant to conform to his plans for the "rebuilding of Berlin") was that it had to meet the high standards set by the Führer for his future capital. A "prestigious and spacious treatment" was therefore essential.[292] Speer was then called in to cooperate on the plans.[293] But when these were ready in the autumn, they did not meet with Hitler's approval, and the project was put on hold.[294]

In October Hitler raised Goebbels's salary "substantially."[295] This raise came at exactly the right time, as he was about to replace his Horch with a Maybach ("A magnificent car!").[296] For her birthday in November Magda too received "a beautiful new car."[297] But in January 1938 he decided to exchange his Maybach for another Horch, because he now found it "too clumsy."[298] Soon afterward his eye fell on two other luxury cars he wanted to add to his pool.[299] In 1939, there was further progress in the motorizing of the family: In April he gave his mother a car, and Magda received another new one in June.[300] When in August Ley let him try out one of the new Volkswagens, he saw immediately: "That's the car for our children."[301]

There was one reason above all for his family's extremely lavish lifestyle: It served to confirm his success and his unique greatness. First and foremost, however, it reflected recognition by his political idol, Hitler, to whose generosity he owed all this. And the more recognition and affirmation Goebbels received, the more he cut loose from the mundane ties binding him to the people around him.

Even after many years of activity as propaganda minister, the need for further recognition and success was the most important driving force behind Goebbels's restless work. He never tired of celebrating his unusual success as a politician, propagandist, journalist, and orator; carefully documenting this was a central motive for his regular diary entries. It did not bother him that the overwhelming response his work met with in the German media was imposed and carefully orchestrated by his own ministry: For him, the fine, staged illusion was the same as the real thing. It is true that the emotional thrill of success, which he wanted to feel always, was often disturbed by other moods, particularly when autumn was approaching or the weather was dismal. At these times he was overcome by a melancholy, brooding feeling.[302] But he knew the antidote: "Work. Medicine for melancholy."[303]

CHAPTER 17

"Don't Look Around, Keep Marching On!"

The Firebrand as Peacemaker

A rare snapshot: Goebbels's secret mistress, Lida Baarová, at the premiere of Leni Riefenstahl's film *Olympia*, April 20, 1938.

At the end of September 1937, the Third Reich reached the highest point so far in its efforts to achieve international recognition: a state visit by Benito Mussolini, which "Il Duce" began in Munich on September 25. The program opened with a tour of the new showcase state buildings in the Bavarian capital, and on the following days Mussolini dropped in on Wehrmacht maneuvers and visited the Krupp Works.[1] As on previous encounters, Goebbels positively melted under the impact of the Italian charm offensive: "You can't help really liking him. A great man! [. . .] Alfieri tells me that Mussolini is quite taken with me. And I am with him."

Il Duce's visit continued in Berlin, where he was to celebrate the German-Italian alliance at a gigantic rally. Goebbels had the honor of receiving Hitler and Mussolini at the entrance to the Maifeld, the great parade ground in front of the Olympic Stadium. His words of greeting were broadcast on all stations: "I report: on the Maifeld in Berlin, in the Olympic Stadium and the spaces around the Reich Sports Field, 1 million people; on the route from Wilhelmstrasse to the Reich Sports Field 2 million people, so in all 3 million people gathered for this historic mass meeting of the National Socialist movement."[2]

A glance at the newspapers around that time reveals that the appearance of the three million—a majority of Berlin's population—was not exactly a display of spontaneous popular enthusiasm. On September 26, for example, there was an article in the *Völkischer Beobachter* peremptorily commanding "the working Berlin population" to attend the rally en masse. The guarantee of "en masse" participation was achieved—to mention only one detail of the nearly perfect planning for this event—by the German Labor Front. After work ended early, they made the staff fall in and marched them en masse to their allocated sector of the approach roads. It was not easy to escape: If you felt ill, for example, you had to request special permission to leave from the works organizer.[3]

On the evening after the mass rally[4] at which Mussolini and Hitler had celebrated the friendship between their two countries, Goebbels noted Hitler's reaction to Mussolini's demeanor: "He will never forget our help for him. Acknowledged it openly. And will go all the way with us to the end as a friend. And there's nothing else he can do. England wants to destroy him. He has to stick with us. That's the best basis for friendship." But Goebbels added: "But let's hope he's not deceiving himself."[5]

TOUGHER LINE IN FOREIGN AFFAIRS
AND PERSECUTION OF JEWS

A choral festival attended by Hitler and Goebbels in Breslau at the end of July at which thirty thousand people took part;[6] the Party rally with its strong anticommunist message;[7] and the sealing of the partnership with Italy—all were part of the consolidation of the regime's new foreign policy turn, which Hitler had prepared in 1937 with his swing toward Italy. The Third Reich was now openly on the path of expansion. The objects of this policy were primarily Austria and Czechoslovakia.

The pretext for a contrived clash with Czechoslavakia was provided in autumn 1937 by an incident in Teplitz-Schönau, where Karl Hermann Frank, a leader of the National Socialist–oriented Sudetendeutsche Partei (SdP, Sudeten German Party), was arrested after a violent altercation with a Czech security agent. Thereupon Goebbels started a press campaign against what he called the "Prague rabble."[8]

The intense polemical pressure of the German media, coupled with the aggressive behavior of the SdP, led to a sharp reaction on the part of the Czechs: The Prague government postponed the local elections that were in the offing and banned all political meetings. Goebbels called off the campaign on November 3 after representations from Karl Henlein: The head of the SdP feared events might escalate out of control, something that would not suit the Reich government at this juncture.[9]

There was now an attempt by the Germans to prevail on the Czechoslovak government, by diplomatic means, to act against those German-speaking newspapers, the "émigré press" published by anti-Nazis who had fled the Reich to Prague. The threat to resume the anti-Czech press campaign lurked in the background. The Czechs then promised to put pressure on the newspapers in question.[10]

On November 5 Goebbels was at Hitler's lunch as usual: "We talk over the situation: restraint on the Czech question, because we're not yet in a position to follow through with any consequences." Goebbels then went home; his diary entry indicates that Hitler was "busy with General Staff discussions."[11] In fact, this was the afternoon when Hitler held the conference that paved the way for war, informing War Minister Blomberg, Foreign Minister Neurath, and the heads of the army, navy, and air force of his political and strategic plans. A summary is preserved in the well-known memorandum by his Wehrmacht adjutant Colonel Hossbach, who took notes for his own use.[12]

Hitler made clear at the beginning of his talk that this was by way of "a testament he was setting out in case of his death." He went on to cite the Germans' "lack of living space" as the central problem of the future; only "the way of force" could solve this problem, and that could "never be risk-free." Starting from this premise, it could only be a matter of deciding "when" and "how." The optimum time for a German war of conquest would be in the years 1943 to 1945, at a juncture, that is, when rearmament would be complete (scenario 1); after that point, time would be working against Germany. However, there were two possible circumstances that would make it necessary to strike earlier: If France was paralyzed by a civil war (scenario 2), or if there was a war against Italy (scenario 3). In both cases the "moment for action against Czechoslovakia would have come"; if France was embroiled in war, Austria should be "overthrown" at the same time. Hitler thought it possible that scenario 3 might come about as early as the summer of 1938. He was therefore reckoning with the possibility that the alliance with Italy might trigger concrete action quite soon.

The discussion demonstrates not only Hitler's grim, long-term determination to wage war but also shows that he was already thinking that solving the "problem cases" of Austria and Czechoslovakia in the medium term was possible only through conventional military surprise attacks in the context of a convenient European situation in which France was incapacitated. At this point he does not seem to have had in mind the mixture of internal and external pressure by which, in the coming year, he would "annex" Austria and carve off the Sudeten German territories from Czechoslovakia. And if he did have such ideas, he was leaving his most important collaborators in the dark about them. It is not surprising, therefore, that when Henlein wrote to him two weeks later asking him to annex the whole Bohemian-Moravian-Silesian area to the Reich and offering him the help of the Sudeten German Party in doing so, he did not consider this initiative at all. At the time, the idea of using the SdP as a fifth column was obviously beyond his intellectual horizon.[13]

Evidently Goebbels was completely oblivious to all of these deliberations on how to put a quick end to Czechoslavakia. During these weeks he was concentrating entirely on his contribution to a policy aimed at forcing the Czech government to capitulate on the "émigré press" question.[14] By the end of the year, the result of German-Czech negotiations was a "press truce" imposed by the Reich; it was to last into the first few months of 1938.[15] However, Goebbels declined to enter into a formal "press agreement" with Prague, although such an agreement would be concluded with Austria in the summer of 1937,[16] and deals with Yugoslavia[17] and Poland[18] followed the same pattern in January and April 1938, respectively. In this case he did not want to tie the German side down to any commitments.[19]

In parallel with its incipient policy of expansion, in autumn 1937 the regime entered a new, more radical phase of Jewish persecution. After setting the signals at the Party rally, Goebbels continued this course in November during the usual ceremonies around the anniversary of the 1923 Hitler putsch in Munich, where he and Julius Streicher opened the exhibition "Der ewige Jude" (The Eternal/Wandering Jew). The "Jewish question" was a "world problem," declared Goebbels in his opening address, which he used among other things to revive memories of his campaign against Police Commissioner Weiss.[20] In the evening, as was usual on these occasions, he was in the Bürgerbräu beer hall, where veteran Party comrades were treated to an hour-long speech by Hitler; the next day there was the customary march from the beer hall to the Königsplatz.

A few weeks later Hitler tasked him with drawing up a law forbidding Jews to visit theaters and cultural events.[21] Goebbels got to work immediately but learned from Hitler that this law was not the real aim: "The Jews have to get out of Germany, out of the whole of Europe, in fact. It will take time, but it must and will happen."[22] Then Hitler decided to ban Jews from cultural events simply by police ordinance, since a law would create too much of a stir, which he must have thought inopportune at that juncture in domestic politics.[23]

Goebbels had great hopes of the policy of Octavian Goga, elected prime minister of Romania in December, who during his short term in office was to try to introduce an authoritarian, pro-German, anti-Semitic line.[24] When this experiment failed—Goga resigned in February 1938—Goebbels naturally inferred "pressure from the Jews."[25] The propaganda minister took comfort from the thought:

"How good it is that we have the people behind us and we're tough with the Jews. First you have to knock their back teeth out, then negotiate."[26]

RESHUFFLING THE STAFF

As head of the Propaganda Ministry, Goebbels developed a leadership style entirely in keeping with his egomaniacal personality structure. The activities of the ministry were supposed to reflect his genius. His sudden brainwaves and changes of course, his direct interventions in departmental work, and his shifting allegiance to different senior colleagues all contributed to an atmosphere of unpredictability and constant turbulence in the building. This suited Goebbels. In a rare moment of self-criticism, he said about his own attitude in the autumn of 1937: "The same old trouble: If I don't do everything myself, I'm pleased when things go wrong."[27]

Goebbels was not only a dedicated and tireless worker, he was also a difficult and unpleasant boss to work for: He loved making coarse jokes at the expense of his underlings and humiliating them in the office;[28] hardly any of his senior colleagues escaped his biting and savage criticism, which often hit them completely out of the blue. His dissatisfaction with his colleagues reached its peak in March 1937; they should "spend a few months in the trenches, so as not to lose the smell of the masses in their nostrils."[29] For this purpose he dispatched a large number of senior staff to companies where they had to sign on as laborers, a move he made sure was reported in the press.[30] It is no surprise that his ministry—aside from the actual administration, where he depended on bureaucratically trained personnel—was not exactly known for the continuity of its staffing. "Geniuses consume people," as he wrote in his novel *Michael*.[31]

As the transition to an accelerated policy of rearmament and expansion in autumn 1937 kicked off an extensive reshuffle within the regime, Goebbels's sector took on a leading role. When Reich economics minister Schacht declined to go on accepting responsibility for the risky foreign exchange policy resulting from the breakneck speed of German rearmament, the question of his successor became urgent.[32] Goebbels recommended his state secretary, Walther Funk, for the job. He imagined that Funk "would still be available to him" where "economic matters" were concerned; in other words, he expected to be able to exercise a certain amount of influence over the new minister of economics.[33]

Having been reluctant at first to let Schacht go, Hitler took up Goebbels's recommendation in November, although the arrangements for the succession would not go into effect until the New Year.[34] Nonetheless, Goebbels set about reorganizing the top ranks of his ministry immediately. Funk left the Propaganda Ministry, to be replaced by Goebbels's personal adviser Karl Hanke. Otto Dietrich, Reich press chief of the NSDAP, became Goebbels's second state secretary.[35] Apart from the changes at the top of the organization, there were a few other new appointments: Werner Naumann, head of the Party's Reich propaganda office in Breslau, became his new personal adviser; Ernst Leichtenstern took over the film department; and Franz Hofmann, as noted earlier, became responsible for fine art.[36] There was a newly created Department for Special Cultural Affairs, whose duties included specifically the "de-jewifying" of German cultural life.[37] In the propaganda department, Leopold Gutterer replaced the incumbent head of the department, Wilhelm Haegert, with whom Goebbels had become increasingly dissatisfied.[38] Following a suggestion from Otto Dietrich, the press department, now directed by the latter, was divided into separate sections for home and abroad.[39]

All in all, the ministry now consisted of fourteen departments. In addition to the specializations already noted (propaganda, home and foreign press, film, fine art, literature, special cultural affairs), there were foreign propaganda (under Franz Hasenöhrl, as before), broadcasting (Hans Kriegler), theater (Rainer Schlösser), and music (Heinz Drewes). The relatively large number of departments suited Goebbels's leadership style: The "flat hierarchy" of the ministry allowed him to intervene at any time in individual areas. He rejected any consolidation into larger departments.[40] Apart from the various specializations, under its head of administration (the career bureaucrat Erich Greiner) the Propaganda Ministry possessed departments dealing with the budget and legal matters as well as a personnel department, run from 1937 onward by former Berlin police chief Erich Müller.[41]

Up until the outbreak of war, there was to be another important new arrangement in the Propaganda Ministry: Hermann Esser, one of the founding members of the NSDAP who had been dismissed as

Bavarian economics minister after his involvement in an intrigue, was appointed third state secretary, responsible for a new tourism department. Goebbels had been resisting Esser's appointment to his Propaganda Ministry since 1935,[42] but after much ado he was given his new position in January 1939.[43] Goebbels had not been in a position to prevent this senior appointment in his organization.

THE BLOMBERG-FRITSCH AFFAIR

By the time State Secretary Funk officially took up his new position early in February 1938, the political scene had changed completely.[44] At the beginning of the year the regime suffered one of its most serious internal crises since 1934, from which, however, Hitler was to escape with a sensational personnel-management coup.

In January 1938, Reich War Minister Blomberg had married a much younger woman. "Everyone's taken aback," was Goebbels's comment on the matter: He had arranged "as requested" that the newspapers should play down the wedding (at which Hitler and Göring had been witnesses).[45]

Just two weeks later, it emerged that Blomberg's wife had multiple convictions for "immoral conduct" and had been registered with the Berlin police since 1937 as a prostitute.[46] The matter was treated by the Nazi leadership as an affair of state: "The regime's worst crisis since the Röhm affair," wrote Goebbels, and—referring to Blomberg— he added: "There's no way out of this. Nothing for it but a revolver."[47]

What is more, at the end of January Göring, who fancied himself as Blomberg's successor and was the first to inform Hitler about the scandal, presented incriminating material against the head of the army, Werner von Fritsch—his most powerful rival for the succession to Blomberg. Gestapo documents shown by Göring to Hitler led to an accusation of homosexuality against Fritsch.

Goebbels was highly alarmed, even slightly confused, despite Fritsch's emphatic denials: "He swears on his honor that it's not true. But who can believe it now? Did Blomberg know? About his own wife? And how can he let the Führer down like this? The honor of an officer? Where is it now? All unresolved questions."[48] Hitler summoned Fritsch to the Reich Chancellery and confronted him with the sole witness for the prosecution, a young man with convictions for blackmailing his sexual partners. The witness claimed to identify Fritsch as a former client, which Fritsch strenuously denied. Further investigations were left to the Gestapo.[49]

Goebbels's notes from that time contradict any tendency to assume that Hitler immediately welcomed the Blomberg-Fritsch affair as a great opportunity to reshape the top echelons of the army in view of the coming war. On the contrary, Hitler was "very serious and almost sad" about the affair.[50] Goebbels, too, was depressed about the chaotic situation.[51]

On January 31 Hitler called Goebbels in for a private discussion: "He's a bit more composed, but still very pale, gray-faced and shattered. [. . .] Blomberg marries a hooker and sticks with her and doesn't give a damn about the state. The Führer thinks he knew all about this beforehand."[52] Fritsch, said Hitler, had "almost been unmasked as a 175er [a homosexual]." Hitler now wanted "to take over the armed forces himself."[53] "In order to cover the whole business with a smokescreen," Hitler continued, there should be a wholesale reorganization. "I'm hoping we'll get off fairly lightly," commented Goebbels. Over the following days he was obliged to look on while the crisis deepened and Hitler could not bring himself to make a decision. There was more and more speculation in the foreign press; rumors were spreading throughout the Reich.[54]

By February 4 Hitler had a plan: "Blomberg and Fritsch retired on 'health' grounds. Führer takes over command of the forces personally. Immediately beneath him Wilhelm Keitel as Supreme Commander of the armed forces with ministerial rank. Göring appointed field marshal. [Walter] Brauchitsch succeeds Fritsch." Hitler's foreign affairs adviser, Ribbentrop, replaced Neurath as foreign minister; Neurath was fobbed off with the presidency of a newly formed "Cabinet Privy Council," an international policy committee to which Goebbels was also supposed to belong but which never actually met.[55] Ribbentrop was appointed against Goebbels's advice; he had openly told Hitler on January 31 that he thought he was a "flop."[56] In addition, there were far-reaching changes of personnel in the officer corps, the Foreign Office, and the Economics Ministry.[57] In a single stroke, Hitler had succeeded in overcoming a grave internal crisis and turning the situation to his advantage by strengthening his own position. All the key positions that mattered for his transition to an aggressive foreign policy were now in the hands of reliable Party supporters. The preconditions for implementing the proposed expansionist policy were all in place.

Hitler called the cabinet together on February 5 to make a statement on the affair. Goebbels's report brings out the drama of the occasion: "As he speaks he sometimes chokes back tears. That he was too ashamed to step out onto the balcony on January 30." Hitler said they would all have to stand by a communiqué to be compiled by Goebbels after the meeting.[58] Incidentally, this was the last cabinet meeting in the history of the Third Reich.

Goebbels was told by Helldorf, who had already complained to him a week earlier about the Gestapo's "snooping methods," that the treatment of Fritsch had "not been very decent."[59] Fritsch's case was tried in March before a court martial chaired by Göring. The prosecution witness was forced to admit that he had mixed the general up with somebody else and Fritsch was acquitted.[60] "Very bad, especially for Himmler," commented Goebbels. "He's too hasty and too prejudiced. The Führer is quite angry."[61]

THE ANNEXATION OF AUSTRIA

Nazi Germany had been systematically increasing its political and economic pressure on Austria since the end of 1937. In German leadership circles, there was open talk of the imminent "annexation" of the country.[62] A further press agreement negotiated by Ambassador von Papen in the summer of 1937 (once again Goebbels had been taken completely by surprise on his very own territory) had somewhat eased the way for Nazi propaganda in the country.[63] It is a fair reflection of the deliberations going on at this time around Hitler that Goebbels records in December 1937 a lunchtime conversation in which von Papen mentioned a plan he had devised to bring down Schuschnigg.[64] The big reshuffle of personnel in February was about to have a direct impact on the regime's foreign policy.

On February 12, 1938, Federal Chancellor Schuschnigg was invited by Hitler to the Berghof. The dictator put immense pressure on him, threatening him with German troops marching into Austria, thus extorting from him his signature to an agreement stipulating freedom of operation for the Austrian NSDAP and the appointment of the National Socialist Arthur Seyss-Inquart as minister of the interior.[65]

As so often with foreign affairs initiatives taken by Hitler, it was only after the event that Goebbels was informed about these developments. Not until February 15 did Hitler, now back in Berlin, tell him about his discussion with Schuschnigg.[66] And according to Hitler, the discussion in Berchtesgaden constituted a threat of war.[67] "The world press is outraged," noted Goebbels, "talking about rape. And they're not wrong. But no one's lifting a finger to do anything about it."[68]

Goebbels's main preoccupation in these days was with shifting the German press, enjoined to exercise restraint over the Austrian question since the end of 1937, onto the footing of a "press feud with Austria."[69] On February 20 Hitler gave a three-hour speech to the Reichstag about the latest events. With reference to Austria and Czechoslovakia he declared, "Among the interests of the German Reich is the protection of those national comrades who [. . .] are not in a position along our borders to ensure their right to human, political, and ideological freedom!"[70]

Schuschnigg replied in a speech to the Austrian Federal Parliament on February 24, where he stressed the sovereignty of his country: *"Bis in den Tod Rot-Weiss-Rot"* (red, white, red until we're dead). He prohibited out of hand Nazi demonstrations intended as a prelude to annexation. Hitler was "furious" about Schuschnigg's speech.[71] When there was a "popular uprising" in Graz stage-managed by the Nazis and the government in Vienna sent in troops, Goebbels (who, like many, had hoped that Schuschnigg would gradually surrender power to the Austrian Nazis) dubbed the Austrian chancellor "schwarzes Schweinchen."*[72] But the German press were ordered to go on observing a degree of restraint toward Schuschnigg personally.[73]

A new situation arose when the Austrian cabinet, prompted by Schuschnigg, decided during the night of March 8 to 9 to hold a referendum on the issue of sovereignty. Seyss-Inquart was not present when this decision was made.[74] On the evening of March 9 Hitler called Goebbels in to discuss this "extremely low, sly trick" of Schusch-

---

* Translators' note: Literally, "black piglet," where "black" refers to Schuschnigg's Catholic-conservative politics.

nigg's: "We consider: either [Nazi] abstention from voting, or send 1,000 planes over Austria to drop leaflets, then actively intervene." Goebbels went off to his ministry to assemble a team to work on the propaganda angles of the coup. Later that evening Hitler summoned him again, and they deliberated until early morning: "Italy and England won't do anything. Maybe France, but probably not. Risk not as great as with the occupation of the Rhineland."[75]

The next day he again discussed the situation with Hitler, who had still not ruled out Nazi participation in Schuschnigg's referendum. The alternative was to demand a change in the terms of the plebiscite and march in if the Austrian government refused to comply. Toward midnight Goebbels was summoned once more by Hitler, who told him of his decision: The invasion would take place the day after next. Goebbels promptly busied himself making sure that from the following day onward the whole of the German press was focused on annexation.[76]

The next day Hitler and Goebbels worked together composing leaflets: "Terrific, inflammatory language." But in the course of the day the text had to be altered several times to keep up with the changing situation. Under enormous pressure from German threats and ultimatums, that afternoon Schuschnigg stood down, and later the Austrian president, Wilhelm Miklas, named Seyss-Inquart as the chancellor's successor. Although all German demands had now been met, Hitler refused to be deprived of his invasion. An Austrian "plea for help" was quickly put together: "We dictate a telegram to Seyss-Inquart[77] asking the German government for help. It arrives quickly. This gives us legitimation."[78]

The next day, March 12, Goebbels reveled in reports of the "revolution for Austria." During the late morning he read out a "proclamation" from Hitler, broadcast on all stations, justifying the invasion. Three days of flag-flying were decreed for the whole Reich territory.[79] The international reaction remained low-key, as Goebbels noted with some relief. Only the British government issued a sharp protest, but Goebbels thought "Chamberlain has to do that for the sake of the opposition."

On March 14 reports arrived in rapid succession from Austria: The Seyss-Inquart government decreed "reunification" with the Reich, Federal President Miklas resigned, and the Austrian armed forces had to swear allegiance to Hitler personally. He arrived in Vienna that evening. Goebbels had a Reich propaganda bureau set up in Vienna[80] and sent Otto Dietrich to the Austrian capital armed with instructions about "the reform of the Austrian press."[81] On March 15 Hitler gave a speech in the Heldenplatz [Heroes' Square] in which he celebrated before a crowd of 250,000 people "the greatest report of an aim accomplished" in his life: the "entry of my homeland into the German Reich."[82]

In Berlin Goebbels prepared a "triumphal reception" for Hitler that was to put "all earlier events of the kind in the shade." (The complication was that all "stocks of flags and bunting" had been lent to Austria in aid of the celebrations there.)[83] In the *Völkischer Beobachter* he urged the population forcefully:

> *Nobody must be absent from the streets when the Führer*
> *arrives.*
> *Berliners! Shut the factories, shut the shops.*
> *Be in place on time.*
> *March along the streets as commanded by Party and German Labor Front*
> *officials [. . .].*
> *All homes, buildings, shops to be decorated with flags and*
> *garlands.*[84]

On the morning of March 16, he "set the *Volk*-machine in motion," as he put it. After a telephone conversation with Hitler, he noted: "Exhilarating feeling of commanding the masses." Hitler's plane landed punctually at 5 P.M. at Tempelhof, where he was greeted by Göring and Goebbels, who were allowed to accompany him on his "triumphal drive" through the city.[85]

On March 18, the Reichstag having been convened on short notice, Hitler announced the dissolution of Parliament and new elections.[86] Goebbels commented that, with this ballot, "we'll throw off the last bits of democratic-parliamentary eggshell." It was definitely to be the last visit to the polls in the Third Reich, after which—as Hitler put it to his circle—there would be "unity, no more troublemaking, and no religious conflicts."[87]

Goebbels's diaries document the intensity of the regime's preoccupation in the next few days with incorporating Austria. At the usual lunchtime session in the Reich Chancellery, there was already debate about autobahn routing when the road system was extended to Austria: "Linz is going to be completely rebuilt." The reconstruction of Berlin was to be speeded up considerably, "because otherwise it will fall way behind Vienna."[88] Goebbels was invited to the Reich Chancellery the next evening to meet Austrian guests and discuss the Salzburg Festival, "which we're going to make a good deal of."[89] At Hitler's lunch table the next day the topic was the future of Vienna: "We've got to push the Jews and the Czechs out of Vienna quickly and make it a purely German city. That will also help to solve the housing problem."[90]

Goebbels visited Vienna at the end of March. He entered the city in a "triumphal drive"—his preferred mode of transportation—and stopped at the Imperial Hotel, from whose balcony he received "a terrific ovation," before moving on to the Town Hall to give a "short address" to "old campaigners." Then he spoke in the great hall of the former North West Station, naturally "on top form."

He held talks the next day in the Hofburg with Austrian artists, among others, and attended a performance at the Burgtheater in the evening: He found it good, even if not up to "Berlin standards."[91] At a reception in the Hofburg the next day, he took the actor Attila Hör-biger "seriously to task": He really must do something about his wife, Paula Wessely, and all her "Jewish friendships." In other discussions, he took soundings about the future directorships of the State Opera and the Burgtheater.

The election campaign concluded on April 9 with a big showpiece event, again in Vienna. At noon precisely, Goebbels proclaimed from the balcony of the Town Hall the commencement of the "Day of the Greater German Reich": "At a given signal flags are hoisted through-out the Reich. 30,000 homing pigeons flutter aloft. Airforce squad-rons appear. Sirens howl. Then the Führer steps on to the balcony."[92]

On the same day Hitler had another discussion with the Viennese Cardinal Theodor Innitzer at which he intended to speak "quite openly." Hitler's interest in this conversation was far-reaching, as he confided to Goebbels: "We need a prince of the church if we want to break away from Rome. And we must do so. There must be no authority outside Germany able to give orders to Germans." A few hours later, after the discussion, Hitler told him that Innitzer was "very depressed," but he was resolute in his "commitment to German-ness": "That's something to latch on to. Start a secession movement and undo the counter-reformation. Well, we'll see!" Goebbels's diary shows that, if only for a brief moment, the bizarre idea was raised of a wide-ranging restructuring of church policy: the project of a German Catholic Church without the Pope.

From the balcony of the hotel Goebbels introduced Hitler's concluding speech of the election campaign with a commentary broadcast over German radio.[93] Hitler expressed his conviction that "this too was the will of God, to send a boy from here to the Reich, let him grow up, and make him leader of the nation so that he could bring his homeland into the Reich." This self-bestowed aura of the One sent from God stirred deep emotions in Goebbels: He felt as if at a "religious service," while the ovation concluding the event was "almost like a prayer."[94]

They both left for Berlin by train. At breakfast the "Jewish question" came up: "The Führer wants to force them all out of Germany. To Madagascar or somewhere. Quite right!"[95]

In Berlin, where the Goebbels children greeted Hitler's arrival by handing him bouquets, they proceeded to the Reich Chancellery, where the early election results were coming in. Goebbels himself described them as "incredible, fantastic." In fact, with a turnout of 99.6 percent, 99 percent of valid votes were in favor.[96]

Studying a memorandum about the vote a few days later, he found that even to his mind they had gone a little too far this time in rigging the results. Munich had "cheated a bit," and Gauleiter Adolf Wagner had "done it very stupidly."[97]

THE SUDETENLAND CRISIS

After the Austrian Anschluss, the Nazi leadership cast their eyes on the Sudetenland as the next target of German annexation policy. As late as November 1937 Hitler had thought a move on Czechoslovakia impossible unless France was out of action, but now, buoyed by his Austrian triumph, he no longer considered this a precondition for aggression toward Czechoslovakia.

On March 19, in Hitler's study in the Reich Chancellery, Goebbels was informed about Hitler's further foreign policy plans: "Then we study the map: Czechoslovakia is next. We share it with Poland and Hungary. [Go in] relentlessly at the next opportunity." It emerges at this point that "we wanted to bag" the Memel area, administered by Lithuania, "if Kovno had gotten into a conflict with Warsaw," but the case had not arisen: "We are now a boa constrictor, digesting its prey." But it did not stop there: "Then the Baltic, and a chunk of Alsace and Lorraine. We need France to sink further and further into its crisis. No false sentimentality."[98]

Goebbels was not greatly impressed when, in the second half of March, the Czechs showed themselves increasingly prepared to concede more autonomy to the Sudeten Germans: "That won't help them much anymore. They've had it."[99] Thus the leader of the Sudeten German Party was instructed by Hitler on March 28 to become more aggressive toward the Czech government,[100] and Goebbels too was told "always to ask for more than can be given."[101]

Correspondingly, on April 24 in Karlsbad, Henlein announced an eight-point program still ostensibly based on notions of autonomy but in fact framed in such a way that its demands could only be met by incorporating the Sudetenland into the Reich.[102]

During May, as instructed, the German press exercised restraint (relatively speaking) with respect to the controversial question of minorities. Incidents in the Sudeten territories should certainly be reported, but not in "sensational style."[103] This restraint was motivated mainly by a state visit to Italy that Hitler undertook, accompanied by Goebbels, from May 3 to 10.[104] In his narcissistic quest for recognition, Goebbels was once more blinded by the lavishness of the social program, while merely noting the political results of the trip as a kind of side issue: "Mussolini completely agrees about Austria. [. . .] Mussolini gives us an absolutely free hand over the Czech question."[105]

While Goebbels was still in Italy, Magda gave birth to her fourth child, a daughter, to be called Hedwig. Goebbels heard the news from Hitler—they were on a warship in the Gulf of Naples at the time—who had received a telegram to that effect.[106]

After his return from Italy, on May 19 Goebbels set in motion a huge campaign against the Prague government. His pretext was an interview with Foreign Minister Kamil Krofta.[107] The newspapers were ordered to appoint "special correspondents for Sudeten German questions" and not just go on producing "small beer."[108]

By contrast, the Foreign Office continued to advise restraint on the Sudeten question.[109] Ribbentrop himself complained to Goebbels about the "fierce campaign against Prague," but knowing he had his leader's support in the matter, Goebbels was like a brick wall.[110] Hence on May 21 the German press made a great clamor about new incidents in Prague and Brno; this started a "hellish concert."[111] The Foreign Office now fell into line with Goebbels and did its best to inflame the anti-Czech polemic in the German press.[112] This began a press campaign against Prague which—with Goebbels raising or lowering the temperature according to political expediency—was to last four months.

In May, false reports of alleged German troop movements and further incidents along the German-Czech border led to a "weekend crisis" full of hectic activity in Prague, Berlin, London, and Paris.[113] Goebbels felt that the "pussyfooting" Ribbentrop was still putting the brakes on his campaign. He soon saw the German press engaged in "rearguard actions" so that the campaign had to be officially reined in by May 28.[114] And on May 29 Hitler expressed his concern that they were "not yet there in terms of rearmament." Hitler added that this in no way ruled out "more hell-raising" against Prague.[115] In this vein, the next day Hitler signed the "Führer directive concerning Operation Green," in which he asserted, "It is my irrevocable intention to smash Czechoslovakia by military action in the near future."[116]

In the weeks that followed, Goebbels constantly took the initiative in blasting noisy propaganda at the Czechs to intimidate the Prague government.[117] But he was also frequently forced to tone down his campaign,[118] and not only for reasons of foreign policy: Domestically, too, it was not easy to sustain a mood of crisis in the long term without offering the home population some possibility of a solution.

In mid-July he came to the following conclusion: "The public are getting a bit tired of our campaign against Prague. You can't keep a crisis on the boil for months on end." But Goebbels was also deterred by the medium- and long-term effect his aggressive propaganda was having at home, for there was a growing "war panic" in Germany that might become unmanageable: "People think war has become inevitable. Nobody likes it. This fatalism is the worst thing of all. This is how it was in July 1914. So we'll have to be more careful. Otherwise we'll slide into a catastrophe that nobody wants but that happens all the same."[119] Two days later he reports that he has had a "serious discussion with Hanke about the possibility of war." The press had made "mistakes," he writes, using "the sharp weapon of attack too often, so that it becomes chipped in the process."[120]

Despite these doubts and reservations on the part of the propaganda minister, the press campaign was continued into July, if only at a low level of intensity.[121] But Goebbels's entries for this month show how far he still was from taking the ultimate step and putting propaganda directly to work preparing for war. Given that the regime had avowed its peaceful intentions for years, such a complete U-turn would not have been unproblematic—and Goebbels himself was not yet ready for it.

A POGROM IN BERLIN?

Goebbels's other main preoccupation in the months after the Anschluss was a new, more intensive phase in the persecution of the Jews.

The widespread acts of anti-Semitic aggression committed by Austrian Nazis during and after the Anschluss[122] also aggravated Jewish persecution in the "Old Reich," a tendency that had been encouraged by the Party leadership since autumn 1937, in parallel with the change of direction toward an expansionary foreign policy.[123] Now, in March 1938, not only did Party activists in many places commit offenses against Jews but within the regime, too, efforts were stepped up to complete a process begun in 1933, expelling the Jews from economic and social life. In this, as in the waves of Jewish persecution of 1933 and 1935, Joseph Goebbels played a leading role. His ambition was to set an example in Berlin and thereby figure within the regime as the representative of a tough line on future "Jewish policy." As he wrote, "You've got to make a start somewhere."[124]

In April 1938 he began systematically to harass the Berlin Jews, aiming to isolate them from the rest of the population and drive them out of the city. This action was coordinated with Police Commissioner Helldorf, who ordered a comprehensive list of anti-Semitic measures for the capital to be drawn up.[125] However, Goebbels then obtained Hitler's agreement to postpone these measures until after his Italian journey.[126]

In fact, Party activists started in May to deface or smash in the shop fronts of Jewish businesses and to damage synagogues. Once again the propaganda minister interpreted these attacks as signs of "popular anger," taking them as legitimating his move—in conjunction with Helldorf—to carry out his plans for a "Jew-free" Berlin uto-pia. Again he took care to secure Hitler's agreement to his "Jewish program for Berlin" and then spurred Helldorf into action.[127]

In a big raid on the Kurfürstendamm—since 1931 at the latest, this stretch of road, so beloved of strollers in central Berlin, had been Helldorf's happy hunting ground for anti-Semitic operations—the police arrested three hundred people in a café, mostly Jews. The fol-lowing day, when, to Goebbels's chagrin, Helldorf released the ma-jority of them,[128] the propaganda minister put Helldorf under great pressure, addressing three hundred Berlin policemen: "What I'm doing is trying to incite you. Against any kind of sentimentality. The watchword is not the law but harassment. The Jews have got to get out of Berlin."[129]

Within the framework of a movement to apprehend "asocials" throughout the Reich, he did in fact bring about the arrest of increas-ing numbers of Jews—over a thousand in Berlin alone—mostly for minor transgressions. The message conveyed by propaganda con-cerning these arrests was clear: Jews were by nature criminals and asocials, and the power of the state must be used to exclude them. But in view of the great international tension around the Sudeten-land crisis, Hitler could not afford any more negative headlines in the foreign press, which was following events in Berlin very closely. Hence his personal order on June 22 to halt the action.[130]

Thanks to reports in the foreign press and Hitler's decision to backpedal, Goebbels appeared in a fairly dubious light as the origina-tor of the Berlin action, as he had in 1935 following the "Kurfürsten-damm riots." He was already trying, to some degree, around June 20, 1938, to rein in the activities of the Berlin Party organization.[131] He now tried to put the blame for the desecration of the Jewish shop fronts squarely on Helldorf, whose actions were, so Goebbels said, completely contrary to his own "orders."[132] Eventually Goebbels iden-tified "a Police Director and a District Leader" as the real perpetra-tors of the "Jewish action."[133] At the Solstice Ceremony of the Berlin Gau, he made another inflammatory anti-Semitic speech but an-nounced at the same time that the appropriate measures would be pursued within the law.

The Berlin "action" was followed in June, July, and August 1938 by further demonstrations and excesses carried out in other cities by Party adherents against Jews. In the case of Stuttgart at least, Goebbels's hand can be seen in these events. At the same time, the Party press stepped up its anti-Semitic propaganda once again.[134] Various entries in Goebbels's diaries show that over the summer the propaganda minister continued to be very busy with police and administrative measures designed to chase the Jews out of the city; he secured Hitler's backing for this.[135] It was not until September, when the Sudeten crisis was mounting to a new peak, that the regime eased off somewhat on its anti-Semitic campaign.[136]

CONTINUATION OF THE SUDETENLAND CRISIS

During the Bayreuth Festival in July Goebbels had a lengthy discussion with Hitler about the Sudeten question, which the latter wished to see "resolved by force." "The Führer wants to avoid war," noted Goebbels. "That's why he's preparing for it by all possible means."[137]

Starting in late July, German press policy toward Czechoslovakia was very much influenced by the Runciman mission, an unofficial British delegation under Lord Runciman due to begin an attempt at mediation in Czechoslovakia in early August.[138] In the following weeks, the German press veered between a degree of restraint on the one hand (not wanting to give the impression that the Sudeten German Party was merely a puppet of Berlin),[139] and on the other hand a combination of fiery polemics and demonstrations of German strength and determination, aimed at influencing the negotiations.[140]

Between August 22 and 26, Goebbels was completely taken up with the visit to Germany of the Hungarian "Regent" Miklós Horthy, whom he accompanied on trips to Kiel and Heligoland and during his subsequent stay in Berlin.[141] During this time there was a temporary lull in sharp attacks on Czechoslovakia, but then the press polemics started up again with full force. As instructed, the German press questioned the raison d'être of the "Czech state," while the Sudeten German Party was negotiating with Lord Runciman and Edvard Beneš.[142]

Meanwhile, Karl Hermann Frank, one of the Sudetenland's leading figures, was directed by Hitler to provoke the Czech government.[143] When the Prague government largely met the demands of the Sudeten German Party, coming up with its "Fourth Plan," the SdP in Mährisch-Ostrau provoked an incident—a violent confrontation with the police—to provide a pretext for breaking off the negotiations. For Goebbels, this came "at exactly the right time."[144] The German press was instructed to say as little as possible in concrete terms about the Czech government's proposals but make a splash with the events in Mährisch-Ostrau.[145]

The Nuremberg Party rally, taking place from September 6 to 13, gave the Nazi leadership another excellent opportunity to make further monumental threats against Czechoslovakia and the western powers. Hitler asserted in his closing speech that "Herr Benesch" was not in a position "to make any gifts to the Sudeten Germans"; they had the same rights as other peoples, and if the western powers "felt they must go all out to sponsor the repression of Germans," then this would have "grave consequences." In his diary, Goebbels gives a knowing interpretation of this passage, revealing the plain text behind this slyly phrased but in fact brazen message: "Herr Benesch must ensure justice. How he does so is his business. We're not telling him what justice is. But if he doesn't ensure it, which is something we will be the judges of, then we intervene." In short: "a diplomatic masterstroke."[146]

Immediately after the rally, events seemed to be about to peak. "The Sudeten Germans are driving the revolution onward," noted Goebbels. "Massive demonstrations everywhere, marching, sometimes states of emergency. Things are developing just as we wanted them to."[147] After his return from Nuremberg on September 13, Frank further exacerbated the situation by issuing an ultimatum to the Prague government: They must suspend the martial law they had imposed on Western Bohemia because of the Sudeten German unrest.[148] This obviously created a pretext that could have been used to justify intervention by the Reich.[149] Goebbels threw himself into the campaign on September 14 with an aggressive editorial (appearing under the pseudonym "sagax") in the *Völkischer Beobachter*.[150] He was enthusiastic about the latest "alarming news from Sudeten Germany" and was obviously completely indifferent to whether the reports of atrocities had any foundation in reality: "They have found over 50 dead in just one village. This will trigger the most terrific revolutionary outbreak imaginable."

But Hitler hesitated to react to Frank's maneuvering, and the unrest (which Goebbels was ready to see as the beginning of an uprising) collapsed for lack of support from the Reich and in the face of solid resistance from the Czechs.[151] Then, on the evening of September 14, came the great sensation: "Chamberlain asks the Führer for a meeting." Hitler immediately invited the British prime minister to visit the Obersalzberg the next day. Goebbels's commentary on the turn of events reveals the concerns of the German leadership: "These sly Englishmen are covering themselves in advance. Creating a moral excuse for themselves. And gradually devolving the war guilt on to us if it should come to a conflict."[152]

Goebbels was not involved in the September 15 discussions in Hitler's Berchtesgaden refuge. From Berlin, however, he ensured that they took place against a backdrop of threats, with press and radio reports of panic supposedly sweeping through Czechoslovakia and military measures taken by Prague to which the German side would not fail to respond.[153] By contrast, only the most uninformative communiqué was issued about the talks with Chamberlain. In fact, the British prime minister, agreeing in principle to the secession of the Sudeten German areas, suggested a plebiscite on the question.[154]

On September 17 Hitler finally called Goebbels to the Obersalzberg.[155] The solution the British prime minister had put into play "does not quite suit us," said Hitler. But "at the moment, there's not much we can do about it." Goebbels appeared convinced that Czechoslovakia would be "dissolved amicably": "London is extremely scared of a world war. The Führer has declared emphatically that he will not shrink from it if need be. But Prague remains intransigent for the time being."[156] They continued their discussion the next day. Meanwhile, Paris and London were proposing a plebiscite on the question of sovereignty in the Sudeten German areas. Would Prague bow to the pressure? "The Führer thinks not, but I say they will."[157]

The next day, still more positive news reached the Obersalzberg. At a Franco-British summit, the decision had been made to call on Czechoslovakia to cede the Sudeten territories. Furthermore, Chamberlain had asked Hitler for another meeting.[158] Triumph seemed within reach: "Complete change of direction in the London and Paris press. They're all furious with Prague. [. . .] The Führer is already redrawing the map. He's going to raise quite categorical demands with Chamberlain. [. . .] They will accept."[159]

Accordingly, the regime no longer assigned much importance to Prague's newfound willingness to make concessions, especially since a new situation had arisen with the territorial demands now being made by Poland and Hungary upon the Czech Republic.[160] There was one task left for the press, as Goebbels noted: "Our people have created enough incidents along the border. The press is taking them up. We're working on aggravating them."[161]

Goebbels had now been involved in running his intensive press campaign against the Czechs for months. It was the first instance of the whole German press being coopted for a long period in the service of a calculated diplomatic blackmail maneuver. But the campaign worked only in close conjunction with military threats, diplomatic moves, and the unrest generated by the Sudeten German Party. Moreover, as we have seen, Goebbels was more than once obliged to alter course drastically in response to a quickly changing situation. Above all it became clear, as Goebbels had perceived back in July, that the effect on domestic politics of his propaganda campaign—designed to accustom the population to the idea of war— was difficult to calculate; pro-peace propaganda had been too dominant in recent years.[162]

FROM GODESBERG TO MUNICH

But for the moment all efforts were bent toward resolving the conflict by a combination of diplomatic maneuvering and political pressure. The opening move was the meeting with Chamberlain, for which Hitler, Goebbels, and Göring traveled to Bad Godesberg together overnight from September 21 to 22.

At his first encounter with Chamberlain in the Dreesen Hotel, Hitler surprised the British prime minister, who thought he had come to work out the details of a referendum in the Sudeten territories, with an ultimatum demanding that Czech troops vacate the disputed territories. Hitler also announced that the Wehrmacht would move in there on October 1.[163] A memorandum in which these demands were only slightly modified was handed to Chamberlain for transmission to Prague.[164]

On September 24 Hitler and Goebbels flew back to Berlin together. Goebbels could not quite gauge the mood in the city: "Half war fever, half determination. Not really definable. But everybody thinks something is about to happen soon."[165] While the Godesberg talks were under way, the press had been told to hold back the speculation but to make even more of the atrocity stories from the disputed territories.[166] But Goebbels was still reluctant to switch his propaganda effort to an open and unrestrained pro-war message. He continued to put his faith in a resolution of the crisis through political pressure rather than war.

On September 25, according to Goebbels a "glorious Sunday" which "doesn't look at all like war," he conferred at length with Hitler: "Big question: Will Benesch give in? The Führer says no, I say yes."[167] They took a walk, and Hitler explained his strategy to him: The deployment plans allowed only a few days' breathing room. "Führer is a divinatory genius."

The next day Horace Wilson, Chamberlain's closest adviser, brought the news that the Prague government had rejected the ultimatum. Hitler abruptly turned down Chamberlain's proposal of further talks with Prague.[168] On September 26, Hitler spoke in the Berlin Sportpalast. "I have prepared the meeting down to the last detail," boasted Goebbels. "I just want the audience to represent the nation."[169] He issued a call to Berliners: "If there isn't room for you in the Sportpalast, then line the route so that the Führer is greeted by vast numbers as he drives to and from the Sportpalast, to convey to him the feelings this historic hour is stirring in all of us."[170] In his speech, Hitler insisted that the Sudeten problem must be solved but also promised that "this is the last territorial demand I have to make in Europe."[171] The press was now under orders to mount a sharp and personal attack on Edvard Beneš. The aim was "to sow discord between Benesch and his people."[172]

On the following day, September 27, Wilson brought further news from Chamberlain: France would honor its pledge of support for Czechoslovakia, and Great Britain would stand by France. Hitler remained completely unimpressed.[173] The same afternoon, he ordered a motorized division to parade through Berlin.[174] All extant reports of this demonstration of military strength convey the same impression: The reaction of the Berlin population was subdued rather than enthusiastic.[175] Nicolaus von Below, Hitler's Luftwaffe adjutant, wrote in his memoirs that Goebbels could have "done more to organize the cheering."[176] Remarkably, the next day at Hitler's lunch table, Goebbels observed—"loudly to the Führer, across all those present," as State Secretary Ernst von Weizsäcker noted—that the population was not in favor of war.[177] Goebbels himself noted meaningfully in

his diary that the division's military review had "left the most profound impression everywhere."[178] This entry suggests that von Below
was right: The noticeable lack of enthusiasm for war was due to
the fact that on this occasion Goebbels had not switched on the
"*Volk*-machine"—suggesting that this was a successful tactic.

For Hitler now adjusted his attitude, showing himself willing to
negotiate.[179] On September 28, when Chamberlain asked Mussolini
to mediate, in the course of the same day the heads of government in
Britain, France, Italy, and Germany agreed to a four-power conference to resolve the problem. This meant, in Goebbels's summary of
the situation, that "there was no jumping-off point for war," since you
cannot really go to war over mere "modalities."

The following day, Chamberlain, Daladier, Mussolini, and Hitler
agreed in Munich on a plan set out by Mussolini, according to which
the Wehrmacht would march into the disputed territories within ten
days. In other respects, Czechoslovakia would receive a guarantee of
its integrity from Britain and France.[180]

During the Munich conference, Goebbels remained in Berlin. The
day before the meeting, September 28, he organized throughout the
Reich a wave of events under the watchword "An end to Benesch." At
the central rally in the Berlin Lustgarten, Goebbels himself addressed
a crowd of five hundred thousand. Unfortunately, he wrote in his
diary, he could not yet say anything publicly about the Munich conference, because "the reactions would otherwise have been too positive." In other words, Goebbels wanted to avoid giving Berliners
another chance to demonstrate publicly their aversion to war.[181]

On the day after the Munich Agreement, Goebbels noted: "Everybody is relieved that this great, dangerous crisis is over. We've all
been crossing a dizzying abyss on a thin high-wire. . . . Now we really
are a world power once again. Now the motto is: Arm, arm, arm! It
was a victory achieved by pressure, nerves, and the press."[182]

Goebbels saw the Munich Agreement as a confirmation of his
stance. On October 1, preparing the usual bombastic reception for
Hitler in the city,[183] he wrote of the festive mood: "Everybody is delighted that peace has been preserved. We must be clear that this
applies to us too. That's how it is throughout the world. The nations
do not want another world war."[184] In this light, he ascribed the success very largely to himself, for he was the one who "in the hour of
decision had presented the situation to the Führer as it really was."

The military review of the motorized division had shed light on the mood of the population. "And it was not for war."

He spent the evening with Hitler on October 2: "His determination eventually to destroy Czechoslovakia is implacable. [...] This dead, amorphous state formation must go. He stresses again that if it had come to the crunch, London and Paris would not have acted." Goebbels did not entirely share this opinion: "Without really wanting to, both countries could have slipped into the thing." And almost defiantly he added, "And I'm sticking to this opinion."[185]

CHAPTER 18

"Maturity Is Only Achieved Through Suffering!"

Preparations for War—
from the Munich Agreement to the Attack on Poland

The official photo for the German press announcing the continuation of the marriage of Joseph and Magda Goebbels, October 1938.

In the summer of 1938, Goebbels seems to have made a serious effort with Magda to find a solution to their chronic marital problems. He gave her a "beautiful ring," and his diary entries indicate that they came to a carefully considered agreement.[1]

Goebbels's lover Lida Baarová described this arrangement in her memoirs: Over a weekend on Schwanenwerder to which she was invited along with other guests, Magda and Joseph Goebbels had tried to persuade her to enter into a ménage à trois. Magda was willing to go on playing the part of the resident matriarch at Schwanenwerder and to tolerate Baarová as her husband's official mistress.[2]

But right after this weekend, when everything seemed settled, Goebbels was to discover that Magda was not in the least prepared to share him with another woman. For on the evening of August 15 Magda had a long heart-to-heart with Hitler, who then summoned his propaganda minister to him. There developed "a very long and serious discussion" that "shook [Goebbels] to the core." Hitler demanded nothing less than a break with Baarová, and Goebbels promised to fulfill his leader's wish. "I come to very difficult decisions. But they are final. I drive around in the car for an hour. Quite a long way, without going anywhere in particular. I'm living almost as though in a dream. Life is so hard and cruel. [. . .] But duty comes before everything else."

He then had, as he wrote self-pityingly, "a very long and very sad telephone conversation" with his mistress. "But I remain firm, even though my heart threatens to break. And now a new life is beginning. A hard, tough life, dedicated to nothing but duty. My youth is over."[3] Goebbels had miscalculated Hitler's willingness to give up the arrangement he had entered into with the Goebbels couple in 1931. Hitler had become a kind of family member, and in particular it was only possible to maintain his close relationship with Magda as long as her reputation was protected by her marriage to Goebbels. But Goebbels had also underestimated how vital this agreement was to his special place in Hitler's court—and the extent to which his attempt to dissolve the 1931 arrangement placed a question mark over his position and his career.

Over the next few days, Goebbels, for whom this was "the hardest time in my life," had further discussions with Magda, whose behavior he found "hard and cruel."[4] He found solace with his mother, who was staying in Berlin at the time.[5] Finally, Magda and Joseph concluded a "truce" until the end of September.[6] In the following days Magda made a point of appearing at her husband's side on official occasions; they actually did seem to have arrived at some kind of ceasefire.[7]

When the armistice ran out at the end of September, at the height of the Sudeten crisis, Goebbels took his state secretary, Karl Hanke, into his confidence and asked him to mediate. Goebbels was glad that "at least now I've got someone I can talk to."[8] But the discussion with Magda on his behalf went badly: "It seems it's all over." Hanke spoke with Baarová too. Eventually, Goebbels asked him to put the matter to Hitler again: "After that everything depends on his decision."[9]

On October 12, Hanke did have a word with Hitler; the latter sent a message that he would come to a final decision after a personal discussion with Goebbels.[10] Goebbels meanwhile saw "only one way out, and I'm prepared to take it."[11] What he meant was obviously a separation from Magda. How would Hitler react to this unwelcome request? Goebbels knew from previous discussions that although the Führer was basically "modern and broad-minded" when it came to a marriage breakup, he took a highly critical view of a certain "divorce mania" in the ranks of the leadership.[12]

His uncertainty about Hitler's decision, upon which the future of his family and his career depended, plunged him into a profound personal crisis.[13] A couple of days later his chauffeur, Alfred Rach, drove him in the direction of Stettin until Goebbels made him turn around and stop at the Bogensee. He took to his bed with a high temperature, using alcohol to help him sleep. He did not come around again for twenty-four hours; his worried colleagues, taking care of him in his refuge, could not wake him any sooner. He developed "terrible heart pains" and thought his end was near. But somehow he got back on his feet, and came—once more!—to "a firm decision. This state of affairs must end, come what may. Otherwise it's going to destroy me."[14]

Desperate, he drove back to Berlin, where he saw the film *Preussische Liebesgeschichte* (Prussian Love Story), Baarová's latest movie, which was emotionally deeply painful for him. Eventually he confided in his old friend Helldorf, the Berlin chief of police. Helldorf conveyed to him some "terrible revelations," which profoundly shocked him; the diaries do not go into detail.[15] The next day he took Walther Funk into his confidence, giving him "a frank account of my situation"; Funk eventually arranged for him to have a talk with Göring. Funk, Helldorf, and he then sat together for a long time, a "real trio of friends."[16] The next day Göring received him at his house in Schorfheide. "He is deeply moved by it and touchingly human. I'll never forget this. He suggests radical solutions. He now wants to go to the Führer and tell him the plain truth. [. . .] We part as true friends."[17]

By this point, he had not a good word to say about Hanke, whom he had first drawn into his confidence as a mediator: "He is a dreadful disappointment to me." Was it the information from Helldorf that led to the break with Hanke?[18] It appears that he had traded upon his position of mediator to offer more than kind words of comfort. Several months later Magda was to confess to her husband that she had had an affair with Hanke.[19]

Goebbels's behavior during this crisis is barely comprehensible. He, who had systematically kept his private life free of friendly relationships and devoted himself to his career, now initiated Hanke, Funk, Helldorf, and Göring into his most intimate problems without a thought to the fact that he was giving this circle of people deep insights into his personal affairs. At this juncture he was instantly willing to embrace as a friend anyone who would listen to him. The need for consolation was paramount, displacing all other considerations.

On Sunday, October 23, at Hitler's invitation,[20] he arrived with Helldorf on the Obersalzberg to discuss the future of his family. "I put forward my standpoint, upholding my view vigorously and logically, until the Führer starts pleading solidarity, the state, and the great cause we share. I cannot and will not resist that appeal."[21]

Then Helldorf joined in, representing Goebbels's position with "great and impressive firmness," but without managing to talk Hitler around. Finally Magda was called in: "At first she's quite aggressive, but then we both have to submit to the Führer's wish. He puts it forward in such a decent, kind way that there is no choice. The matter is postponed for 3 months, and thus consigned to the future." Goebbels's "very firm decisions" of a few days earlier were rendered null and void by this conversation. Given Goebbels's fixation on Hitler, now vital to him in every sense, it was not for a moment conceivable that he would evade Hitler's "wish," insist on a divorce, and thus inevitably bring an end to his career. Or, in other words, there was no escaping the arrangement he had entered into with Magda and Hitler in 1931—marriage to Magda coupled with toleration of Hitler's special relationship with his wife, from which the two men in turn had evolved a special kind of closeness. The realization that his dependence on Hitler was total, leaving him no room to set an independent course in his private life, must have been as depressing for him at the time as the loss of his mistress.

Having gotten his way, Hitler used his old trick on Goebbels, confiding to him in a long conversation his "deepest and most human secrets." Needless to say, Goebbels took these confessions at face value: "His devotion to me is heartwarming." Hitler then treated him—at least, this is how Goebbels saw it—to a deep insight into his political and strategic thinking: "In the near future he foresees a very grave conflict. Probably with England, which is seriously preparing for it. We must face up to it, to decide the matter of European hegemony. [. . .] And in view of that, there is no place for any personal hopes or desires. What are we individuals compared to the great destiny of the state and the nation?"[22] Goebbels was only too willing to see the frustration of his private hopes justified in the name of service to a greater cause.

At Hitler's specific request, a few press photos were then taken, showing Hitler with the whole Goebbels family, to put this reconciliation on record.[23] Back in Berlin, Helldorf reported to him that he had carried out "the difficult task" Goebbels had requested him to undertake, "with distressing results." For the nature of Helldorf's mission we can turn once again to Lida Baarová's memoirs: He had called her in to tell her that she would no longer be allowed to perform.[24] Baarová had no choice but to accept the end of both her relationship and her career.

Goebbels spent the evening with Göring, to whom he could "pour out his whole heart."[25] The next day Goebbels set about "liquidating" the case, as he put it. Helldorf and Funk were under orders never to mention the business again.[26] On Schwanenwerder there followed a long discussion with Magda, stretching into the early hours. In the process, "terrible things came out," and only by dint of "enormous nervous strength" had he been able to keep going with the conversation.[27] In spite of much further discussion, in the next few weeks there was no improvement in his relationship with Magda.[28] Her constant reproaches got on his nerves: "No dog could live thus anymore!"*[29] On October 29 he spent the "saddest birthday of my life."[30] Not only did Magda give him a "very frosty" birthday greeting that

---

* Translators' note: A quotation from Goethe's *Faust*.

morning; Hitler was also very cool, sending him just a "short, frosty telegram." He did, however, derive some comfort from Göring's "extraordinarily kind and comradely telegram."

He noted with some relief at this time that the premiere of Baarová's film *Der Spieler* (The Gambler) "went off not too badly." In the preceding days he had thought about having the film withdrawn, then decided to let the screening go ahead; he had found the whole thing a "constant torment to his nerves." His affair with Baarová had become such common knowledge by then that he was afraid the premiere might be subject to disturbance by some elements wanting to cause him public humiliation.[31]

NOVEMBER POGROM

In the course of October, the anti-Semitic mood became more extreme among radical Party followers. It had been inflamed during the summer by Goebbels's Berlin "action," but then he had been obliged to tone it down because of the Sudeten crisis. It seems that Party activists now blamed "the Jews" for the depression that gripped the whole Reich during September because of the threat of war. There must be revenge: Immediately after the conclusion of the Munich Agreement, anti-Jewish activities were resumed. Jewish businesses and synagogues were attacked and damaged. According to the SD [*Sicherheitsdienst* (Security Service)], a real pogrom atmosphere was spreading. On October 26, Himmler ordered the expulsion of Polish Jews living in Germany, and in the following days eighteen thousand people were arrested and driven across the German-Polish border— the first mass deportation of the Nazi period. On November 7, the attempted assassination, in Paris, of the German diplomat Ernst vom Rath, by the seventeen-year-old Herschel Grynszpan, seeking revenge for his parents' deportation from Germany,[32] provided the regime with a pretext for unprecedented levels of violence against German Jews.

Goebbels, long one of the leading anti-Semitic rabble-rousers of the NSDAP, now saw his chance to seize a foreground role by displaying particular zeal over the "Jewish question." No doubt he was trying to repair relations with Hitler after the strain caused by his marital crisis, but his conduct should above all be seen in the context of the differences of opinion that had arisen between him and Hitler at the height of the Sudetenland crisis. Goebbels's objective now was to demonstrate the complicity of the German "Volk"—so obviously lukewarm about the prospects of war a few weeks earlier—in a barbaric, and allegedly collective, action against German Jews, thus making a public display of the solidarity and ideological radicalism of the "national community." Goebbels's line of violence against Jews as compensation for the public's lack of bellicose spirit resonated loudly with the radical wing of the Party.

The first entry in the diary concerning the impending pogrom occurs on November 9. As usual with Goebbels, it refers to the day before, and mentions Grynszpan's action: "Now's the time to talk straight. Big anti-Semitic rallies in Hesse. Synagogues are being burned down. If we could only unleash popular anger!" The Nazi media had followed instructions and given the "greatest possible prominence" to the assassination attempt, combined with threats against the German Jews. In response, Party activists in Hesse had already organized full-scale acts of violence against Jewish shops and synagogues during the night of November 7–8 and on the following day.[33]

Goebbels, who had traveled to Munich on November 7, was back in the Bürgerbräu on November 8 with the "old campaigners" who met there every year. He later attended a reception in the Führer Building, after which he accompanied Hitler and a few cronies to the Café Heck.[34]

By the next day—when the traditional march took place from the Bürgerbräu to the Feldherrnhalle, and from there to the Königsplatz—vom Rath's condition had not improved. The press continued with its anti-Jewish campaign.[35] Goebbels was pleased with the order issued by his police chief friend Helldorf for all Jews in the capital to hand over any weapons in their possession:[36] "They're going to have to put up with more than that."

During the day reports came in of big anti-Jewish demonstrations in Kassel and Dessau, where synagogues had been set on fire and shops demolished. In the afternoon came the announcement of vom Rath's death.

In the late afternoon, Goebbels met Hitler in the Munich City Hall. The following quotation from Goebbels's diary for November 10 is the most important evidence of Hitler's undeniable responsibility for the pogrom: "I tell the Führer about the business. He orders: Let demonstrations continue. Withdraw police. For once, the Jews should feel the anger of the people. That is right. I immediately instruct police and Party accordingly. Then I speak briefly in the same vein to the Party leadership. Wild applause. They all dash for the telephones immediately. Now the people will take action."

Goebbels gave an incendiary talk to the leading Party cadres in which he pointedly referred to the excesses already seen in Kassel and elsewhere and remarked that Hitler himself had told him that he had no objection to further "spontaneous" events. Later, in a report from the Supreme Court of the NSDAP investigating unauthorized assaults during the pogrom of February 1939, his speech was interpreted to mean that "the Party should not appear to be the originator of these demonstrations, though in fact it should organize them and carry them out."[37] That evening, Goebbels was in his element, as his diary entry attests: "One or two shilly-shallyers copped out. But I pulled everyone together again. We can't let this cowardly murder go unanswered." He then proceeded with Gauleiter Adolf Wagner to the Gau office to compose a "precise circular [. . .] setting out what can be done and what not." He phoned an order through to Berlin to "smash up the synagogue in Fasanenstrasse."[38]

The investigation by the Party's Supreme Court reported that the deputy Gauleiter of Munich/Upper Bavaria had testified that, toward two in the morning when news of the first death in the pogrom reached him, Goebbels said they should "not get worked up about a dead Jew; in the next few nights thousands of them will catch it."[39]

Toward midnight Goebbels took part in the swearing-in ceremony for new recruits to the SS that was staged outside the Feldherrnhalle every year. On his way back to his hotel he noted "a blood-red sky": "The synagogue is burning. [. . .] We only fire-fight as much as necessary to protect nearby buildings. Otherwise let it burn down. [. . .] Reports are now coming in from all over the Reich: 50, then 70 synagogues burning. The Führer has ordered the immediate arrest of 25–30,000 Jews." He received news from Berlin that the synagogues were burning there too: "The people's anger is raging now. There's no stopping it tonight. Not that I want to. Let it rip. [. . .] The synagogues are burning in every major city."[40]

Early the next morning Goebbels read the first reports: "The whole nation is in uproar. This death is going to cost Jewry dear."[41] It did not matter to him that the "people" were, in fact—in accordance with his own orders—well-instructed Party comrades: Stage-managed "popular rage" had now become a reality for him.

Goebbels then formulated a proclamation[42] "demanding in the strongest terms" that "all demonstrations and acts of revenge against Jewry [. . .] should cease immediately." The violence was threatening to get out of hand. He went to Hitler's habitual haunt, the Osteria in Schellingstrasse, to gain the Führer's approval for this draft. He was in agreement: "The Führer wants to take very sharp measures against the Jews. They'll have to put their shops back in order themselves. The insurance companies won't pay out. Then the Führer wants to gradually expropriate Jewish businesses and give the owners bonds for them which we can devalue anytime we like." Cooperating closely with Heydrich, Goebbels continued to work at dampening down and ending the "actions."

Subsequently, with Goebbels and other prominent Party members present, Hitler received four hundred representatives of the press in the Führer Building on Königsplatz in order, as reported in the papers, to thank them "for their commitment to the struggle for the German people's right to life."[43] In fact, though, Hitler went much further in his speech: He explained to the journalists how he had been forced by circumstances "for years to talk about almost nothing but peace." Only by "constantly stressing the German will to peace and peaceful intentions" had he been able to achieve his great foreign affairs successes. However, there was a questionable aspect to this "peace propaganda that had been pursued for decades"; it could give people the mistaken impression that he wanted to preserve "peace at any price." It was time to dispel this mistaken idea; over some months he had begun "gradually making clear [to the nation] that there are things which [. . .] must be accomplished by means of force." This propaganda line now needed to continue and be reinforced.[44]

On the one hand, Hitler was clearly expressing his dissatisfaction with the German people's lack of psychological preparation for war, manifested just a few weeks earlier; on the other hand, his speech contained an indirect acknowledgment and affirmation of the mobilizing of violence as practiced by Goebbels in the past few days. Goebbels's calculation had proved correct: With his unleashing of the "people's anger" on November 9 he had managed to signal that a more radical initiative in domestic politics could contribute fully to creating a pro-war mentality. Late that evening Goebbels returned to Berlin. In a laconic diary comment, he interpreted the speech simply, and absurdly, as general praise for his propaganda: "As regards Berlin, I'm going to take on the whole violence [thing] myself. In such times of crisis, one person has to be in charge."[45]

The next morning, he established to his satisfaction that in the capital and the rest of the Reich during the night "everything had been quiet": "My proclamation worked wonders. The Jews have reason to be grateful to me, into the bargain." He tried to dilute negative reports abroad with a statement to Berlin-based foreign correspondents. He also contributed a "spirited article" to the German press.[46] He wrote menacingly that "the place of Jews in public, private, and business life depends on the behavior of Jews in Germany and above all the behavior of Jews in the rest of the world." This was followed by a warning to "anti-Germans abroad," who would do well to leave "this problem and its solution to the Germans themselves. If they feel like supporting the Jews and adopting their cause, any number of them are available."[47]

On November 12 he participated in a "conference on the Jewish question" at Göring's ministry: "Heated conflict over the solution. My standpoint is a radical one." In fact, over one hundred representatives of the Party, the state, and business associations had gathered in the Air Ministry to deliberate on further measures regarding "Jewish policy." The substantive outcome was a legal "solution": The Jews must pay a contribution of a billion Reichsmarks; they were excluded from business life for good; and their insurance claims were to be taken over by the state. At this session various other anti-Jewish measures were raised, most of which were adopted in the following weeks and months.[48]

Göring expressed himself very negatively at the meeting about the damage caused and the destruction of "the people's property" ("I would prefer you to have killed 200 Jews rather than destroy such assets").[49] This was clearly a criticism of Goebbels, widely regarded as the instigator of the violence. But he gives the impression that this criticism went right over his head and that the session had been a great personal success for him: "I work fantastically well with Göring. He takes a tough line, too. The radical line carried the day."

Goebbels took an active part in the discussions, putting forward many ideas. One was a call for all synagogues that were not completely undamaged to be "demolished by the Jews," to make way for parking lots (for example). He also proposed banning Jews by edict from visiting "German theaters, cinemas, and circuses." He himself had introduced such an edict in relation to the Culture Chamber.[50] Furthermore, Jews should be "removed from all the public places where they give offense." It was impossible for a German to share a sleeping car compartment with a Jew. Jews must be banned by edict from visiting "German health spas, beach resorts, and recreation spots." Thought might also be given "to whether it might not be necessary to exclude Jews from German forests." Jews should not be permitted "to sit around in German parks"; special parks should be allocated to them—naturally "not the most attractive"—as well as separate park benches. Finally, he demanded that "Jews should absolutely be removed from German schools."[51]

The next day, at an *Eintopfessen* (a single-pot austerity meal) in Wedding, he issued a statement announcing that all Jewish businesses would soon become German and condemning attacks on such businesses as "damaging the property of the German people."[52] He gave an interview to Reuters, the British press agency, which was widely reproduced in the German press, and in which he made light of the whole development as "purely about separating Germans from Jews."[53]

With Hitler supporting the "Jewish campaign" incited by the Propaganda Ministry, Goebbels proceeded to order all propaganda media to "prepare a big anti-Semitic drive."[54] He perceived a general need for work to be done in the area of "informing" the public about anti-Semitism. The mass observation reports that reached him were mixed, however: "We must do more to inform the people about the Jewish question, above all the intellectuals."[55]

Consequently, in the following months the "Jewish question" did indeed become the dominant theme of propaganda. In the individual German papers, and not just the Party organs, contributions appeared daily on this topic. The Propaganda Ministry attached particular importance to anti-Semitic polemics in the area of cultural policy, where the bourgeois public in particular could be targeted—this being the sector of the population known to have held, both during and after the pogrom, the strongest reservations about the violent anti-Jewish policy of the regime.[56]

But despite the concentration of effort specifically on this area, up until 1939 the Propaganda Ministry remained dissatisfied with what the press had achieved.[57] Goebbels therefore deployed the Party's propaganda machine to strengthen the anti-Semitic campaign. A few days after the pogrom, Goebbels issued a directive, in his capacity as Reich head of propaganda, that the series of rallies already begun should be extended to March of the following year, for the purpose of "enlightening the whole population about Jewry." But he warned against going about this too crudely, because it had become apparent during the pogrom that "a large part of the bourgeoisie was not entirely in sympathy with the measures taken." "The mass of the population," said Goebbels, "did not regularly read national-socialist newspapers during the years of struggle or later, and therefore did not undergo the education that was a given for National Socialism in the struggle."[58]

The anti-Semitic propaganda campaign continued into the next year, despite recurrent signs of flagging. It reached its zenith on January 30, 1939, when Hitler's speech to the Reichstag—given great exposure by Goebbels's ministry—foretold "the destruction of the Jewish race in Europe" should another world war break out.[59]

MARITAL CRISIS: ROUND II

Despite their problems, in autumn 1938 Magda and Joseph Goebbels appeared together in public on multiple occasions, no doubt to demonstrate that their marriage was now back in order.[60] After one such evening—they had been with Hitler, fittingly enough, to a performance of Schiller's *Kabale und Liebe* (Intrigue and Love)—Hitler drove with the couple to Schwanenwerder. They chatted for some hours; Hitler eventually decided to spend the night in Schwanenwerder, which Goebbels found "very nice," and he stayed on the island the next day—a holiday—and even held military discussions there with his top Wehrmacht men.[61] There could have been no clearer demonstration of Hitler's faith in the restored Goebbels marriage.

In November and December 1938 Goebbels was working intensively on a book with the provisional title "Adolf Hitler—A Man Who Is Making History": an attempt to bring him closer to Hitler again and regain his favor.[62] He had the manuscript finished by the end of the year, but in January he learned from Amann, whose Eher Verlag was supposed to publish it, that it could not come out for the time being.[63] Goebbels does not indicate the reasons, but the negative reply clearly suggests that Hitler judged the time was not right for another fulsome homage from the pen of his propaganda minister. Goebbels immediately plunged into another book project, to which he gave the working title "The Better Society," but he seems to have given up on the project fairly soon. Neither of these two works has ever appeared.[64]

Goebbels also busied himself with preparations for the "supplementary elections" to the Reichstag, carried out on December 4 in the Sudeten territories now incorporated into the Reich.[65] He himself took part in the election campaign, appearing at various mass meetings.[66] At 98.9 percent, the election results returned what had by now become the anticipated success rate.[67]

In December he developed progressive symptoms of illness: He had severe stomach pains and suspected a tumor.[68] But hospital checks revealed no physical condition, and the diagnosis read "serious nervous disorders."[69] The recurrence of mood swings also point to the psychological nature of his problem: "The glorious weather," he noted, "makes me increasingly melancholy"; three days later, though, it was the "gray autumn" that plunged him into a melancholy mood.[70] By the middle of the month the pain had become so bad that when Professor Sauerbruch was called in he sent him straight to the Charité Hospital. Sauerbruch wanted to operate at once, but Goebbels postponed the intervention. Eventually he was taken back to Schwanenwerder. On the evening of Christmas Day he lay in his bed in the Gentleman's House with his family celebrating in the main house next door; they paid him a visit, but still he felt abandoned and neglected.[71]

At the end of December he started getting up for a few hours, which cost him considerable effort. "What else can I do?" he wrote. "Everything has become so absurd. I can't see any way out."[72] When he had to cancel his "Volk Christmas" talk, he feared that this would fuel "the most dreadful rumors."[73] So he gave the customary New Year's speech on the radio on the evening of December 31—with which he was quite pleased—before taking to his bed again.[74]

During this time Magda subjected him to icy silence,[75] but also to new "interrogations" and recriminations.[76] An invitation from Hitler to spend a few days on the Obersalzberg did represent a glimmer of light, however.[77] He was there from January 5 to 15.[78] On the day after his arrival there was a four-hour discussion with Hitler about his marital crisis, but no clear resolution emerged.[79] Goebbels sent for a few colleagues from Berlin and got through a certain amount of work, but in the end a kind of "tropical frenzy" came over him, he suffered from sleeplessness, was full of "burning agitation," and was finally "close to a nervous breakdown."[80] But there was some cheering news: Although Amann rejected his book project, as already noted, the head of the Party publishing house did offer him a "very generous contract" for weekly commentaries in the *Völkischer Beobachter.*[81]

When Goebbels returned to Berlin, he felt "nothing but grief and bitterness."[82] Most of all he suffered from the lack of opportunity to unburden his personal sorrows to Hitler, who had come back to the capital at the same time.[83] After Hitler's harsh intervention in his private life, Goebbels was more dependent on his emotional support than ever.

He only "partly" reached an understanding with Magda.[84] In the end the Goebbels couple signed a contract drawn up by Magda and approved by Hitler. Hitler also wrote a detailed letter to Magda, in which he stood surety for the agreement.[85] In the next few weeks, Goebbels occasionally put in an appearance with Magda at Hitler's court or in public,[86] but he loathed such social events more than ever.[87]

REAL ESTATE

Goebbels's troubled relations with Magda came at a time when the couple were in the throes of bringing their Berlin accommodation up to the highest standards, befitting their status. Since spring 1937 they had pursued a plan to replace their Berlin "official accommodation" in Hermann-Göring-Strasse with something a good deal more spacious, but initially this project fell through because, as has already been mentioned, Hitler did not approve of the plans.[88]

In February 1938 new plans were drawn up, once more presented to Hitler, and approved. During the rebuilding operations,[89] Goebbels set himself up in a small apartment and thus had a retreat in

Berlin where he could avoid Magda even after they had moved back into their main residence.[90]

The Göring-Strasse project encompassed a banqueting hall and other reception rooms on the ground floor and private accommodations for the family on the first and second floors, as well as business rooms, and accommodations in the cellar and attic rooms for domestic staff.[91] In February 1939 the cost of the whole project was estimated at 2.5 million Reichsmarks. The building costs amounted to 1.6 million marks, to which was added the expense of the extremely lavish furnishings.[92]

Later, during the war, Goebbels was to supplement the exquisite decor with purchases made in occupied Paris. He acquired valuable furniture, rugs, and artworks with a total value of 2.3 million marks, all at the expense of the Propaganda Ministry. However, these treasures embellished not only his main residence but also his other properties. An eighteenth-century Gobelin worth 800,000 Reichsmarks hung in Lanke (the Bogensee house), and a rug dating from around 1700, valued at 750,000 marks, graced Schwanenwerder.[93]

It would take a staff of eighteen, paid out of the Propaganda Ministry budget, to run the residence in Hermann-Göring-Strasse.[94] By August he was finally able to move in.[95]

Because of his private torment, however, the project soon "gave him no real pleasure" anymore.[96] Since early January 1938 he had been contemplating acquiring a bigger refuge for himself. He considered buying an estate but soon decided to build something bigger to replace the "block-house" on the Bogensee.[97] It appeared from the building plan, produced—under high pressure—by March, that the new "sanctuary" was shaping up to be "very commodious," although "unfortunately rather dear."[98] It is true that the district governor in Potsdam was unwilling to give building consent, because the plot was located on land belonging to a proposed conservation area. But this was no obstacle: Göring took care of the matter.[99]

The new building, which Goebbels moved into at the end of 1939,[100] consisted of an ample country house with about thirty rooms, a service building with about forty rooms, and a garage complex. The total building costs came to over 2.3 million Reichsmarks.[101] Goebbels himself contributed 1.3 million marks to this, with funding borrowed from the Bank der Deutschen Arbeit (German Labor Bank, which belonged to Robert Ley's German Labor Front empire).[102] He was, however, forced to give up his original plan to enclose 840 hectares of land; he had to be content with 210 hectares.[103]

The project landed him in considerable financial difficulties, causing him a good deal of anxiety.[104] But Goebbels found an elegant solution. In November 1940 he sold the house on the Bogensee to the state media holding company Cautio GmbH, although in point of fact he was not the owner, and therefore the property was not his to sell: The city of Berlin had merely granted him the right to use the estate. The Propaganda Ministry paid for the upkeep of the estate, to the tune of 70,000 Reichsmarks per year.[105] In 1943 the house became the property of Ufa—which continued to put it at Goebbels's disposal—officially for the "production of German newsreels."[106] Since he conducted official business in Lanke, the Propaganda Ministry paid out of its budget for him to employ other staff there.[107]

Schwanenwerder too was caught up in the momentum of Goebbels's real estate plans. Since the spring Magda and he had been thinking of enlarging the property: In 1938 they had already bought the neighboring plot with the villa that stood on it. Goebbels's friend Helldorf had put pressure on the Jewish vendor to reduce the selling price. Goebbels had thereby acquired his own villa on Schwanenwerder and was no longer dependent on the little Gentleman's House.[108] After starting to build in Lanke in the spring of 1939, he sold the second house on Schwanenwerder but rented it back in spring 1941, so that, in addition to the house for guests, the Goebbels family continued to have two villas on Schwanenwerder at their disposal.[109]

At the same time he planned, at least from February 1939, to build a house in Munich. The plans for it had already been drawn up, but the project, which he continued to pursue until at least the end of 1940, was eventually shelved—presumably because of financial difficulties.[110]

AGAINST COMEDIANS AND INTELLECTUALS

Goebbels used his function as the editorial writer for the *Völkischer Beobachter* first of all to conduct a campaign against the bourgeois "intellectuals" he hated so much, the circles most unsympathetic to the regime, particularly those in the capital. Basically this was the class at which he had directed his anti-Semitic campaign after the November pogrom. He would now, and in the following years, repeatedly target these circles.

By the end of 1937, by order of Hitler, he had already prohibited all political jokes at vaudeville performances and the like.[111] Naturally he suspected that this prohibition was being evaded and concentrated his attention particularly on the Berlin Kabarett der Komiker (Comedians' Cabaret).[112] When Hitler remarked to him during a stroll[113] at the end of January 1939 that it was necessary to "crack down hard on political jokes, but be all the more generous where erotic material was concerned," Goebbels struck to close down the Berlin troupe's current show. He had the artists concerned—including the cabaret star Werner Finck—ejected from the Reich Culture Chamber and publicized this measure (tantamount to a ban on working) in the press.[114]

He gave his reasons for this step in an editorial for the *Völkischer Beobachter* entitled "Have We Still Got Humor?" The choice of title— it was also used in an opinion poll for the *Berliner Tageblatt* in December 1938, to which Finck had given a scurrilous reply[115]—showed unmistakably that Goebbels was intending to bring down the iron fist and make an example of the comedians. In this piece he represented the "so-called political joke" as a Jewish invention, to which a clear answer had been found: "We have no wish to let useless intellectuals go on trashing our Party, our state, and our public institutions." We ourselves, continued Goebbels, have plenty of humor, but it tends to be of the "grim" variety.[116]

After the ban the theater stayed in business until 1944 but confined itself to innocuous material.[117] A few weeks after the ban, Goebbels himself attended a performance "to check it out" and to make sure the content was inoffensive.[118]

The ban seems to have caused something of a stir, for a week later Goebbels returned to the subject, albeit in a rather different form. In the *Völkischer Beobachter* of February 11 he embarked on a "detailed characterization of the intellectual type" in order to clarify his previous attacks on the "humorists" and on "intellectualism," since these had led to "misunderstandings and annoyance." He was on relatively safe ground here, in the sense that just three weeks earlier, in Hitler's presence, he had vehemently cursed "intellectualism" and had earned the Führer's approval.[119]

According to Goebbels's remarks in the *Völkischer Beobachter,* an "intellectual [is] a so-called educated person who wants to say that cowardice is cleverness, lack of discrimination is objectivity, arrogance is courage, and indulgence is higher wisdom." These people represented that "one percent of the electorate who voted 'no' to the Führer and the work of National Socialism in every election—even in those which accomplished real historical developments—and will no doubt forever say 'no.'" In all the crises of National Socialism so far, they had failed us miserably.[120]

With his critique of the intellectuals, Goebbels seemed to have identified on behalf of National Socialism still more enemies within who could be branded as outsiders and against whom the "national community" had to close ranks—in much the same way he had dealt with the "moaners and grumblers," "reactionaries," "parsons," and Jews. Another Goebbels article, called "Heads, Empty Heads," made it clear[121] that he was not in the least interested in a genuine debate with "intellectualism" but only with ruling out any criticism from bourgeois and educated circles on a wide range of topics. His frequent return to the subject suggests that this was not quite as easy as the propaganda minister had imagined.

On March 11 he published an article in the *Völkischer Beobachter* with the title "Coffee Aunties" that was mostly concerned with the temporary shortage of coffee.[122] Goebbels explained the causes of this situation, which had to do with "currency and export policy": In any case, "a thoroughgoing German rearmament [. . .] was right and proper [. . .] compared to supplying sufficient coffee for Auntie's coffee-afternoon." Most annoying for Goebbels, though, were the lines forming outside shops selling coffee, a blot on the urban scene. In fact, he suspected that "a certain kind of person who had never previously drunk coffee now suddenly felt compelled to register their need for coffee." It was "always the same kind of customer": "They are reluctant to contribute to Winter Relief, they moan about the national-socialist state and above all the national-socialist movement [. . .], the block warden of their building is a thorn in their flesh, they are convinced supporters of the Confessing Church, they enthuse about political [cabaret] compères and they get their news from foreign radio stations or foreign newspapers."

Goebbels held that pictures of coffee lines would be used by the foreign press to demonstrate that there were food shortages in Germany. That is why, the minister declared, "we have made sure that these coffee lines disappear from the German city scene." It is not hard to imagine how this was done: Those lining up will have been politely requested by SA men and Party activists to kindly move on. This example shows that trivial matters were enough to prompt joint action by the propaganda machine and the Party to iron out blemishes in the public image of the Nazi dictatorship. But it was rare for these mechanisms to be so openly exposed as in Goebbels's "Coffee Aunties" article.

Goebbels sometimes vented his anger at opponents of the regime—particularly if he saw them as "intellectuals"—in face-to-face confrontations, indicating that this was no mere propaganda posture. He frequently summoned opponents of the regime to his office in order to degrade and humiliate them. The first known instance took place in 1938: The writer Ernst Wiechert had informed local Party officials that he would not be contributing to any welfare institutions in the future but instead donating the equivalent sum to the wife of the imprisoned Pastor Martin Niemöller. This cost Wiechert three months in a concentration camp. Goebbels had Wiechert "brought before him" when he was about to be released and told him, according to Wiechert, that if he made the slightest slip again he would find himself back in the camp, but this time "for life and with the aim of destroying him physically." This threat of "physical destruction" is actually recorded verbatim in Goebbels's diary entry concerning the encounter.[123]

In autumn 1939 he personally berated "a certain Petermann," charged with having distributed leaflets against the regime over several years: "A piece of filth whose impudence is even greater than his stupidity. We'll see if he's got any backers. Then execution."[124] And in February he had a student "brought before him" who had "drivelled boastfully about assassinating the Führer." This "intellectual creature," wrote Goebbels scornfully, had broken down in tears when confronted with the propaganda minister.[125]

WAR IN SIGHT

Early in February Hitler told Goebbels that, as the latter recorded, he was going to "go up to the mountain and think about his next foreign policy steps. Perhaps it'll be Czechoslovakia again. Because that problem is only half solved. But he's not quite clear about it yet. Maybe the Ukraine, too."[126] Although Goebbels was no better informed about his master's next foreign policy moves, he now proceeded to shift his propaganda effort entirely toward preparing for war. In the following months Goebbels was the most consistently pro-war member of the regime's highest echelon, both within and outside its circle. Although he himself would have preferred to avoid full-scale war at this point, he did everything in his power to make up for the "failure" of his propaganda during the crisis of autumn 1938.

A first step in this direction was Goebbels's editorial "War in Sight" in the *Völkischer Beobachter* of February 25; the title was an allusion to a newspaper article, inspired by Bismarck, of April 1875, which had triggered an international crisis. He tried to pin the responsibility for international tensions on the "string-pullers" in the background who were "well known": "They are to be found in the circles of international Jewry, international Freemasonry, and international Marxism." By the next day the article had caused "a great sensation" both at home and abroad. And no wonder: "It's brilliantly written."[127]

His editorials for the *Völkischer Beobachter* evolved a style quite different from that of his earlier journalistic contributions. In *Der Angriff* he would write ironically, bitingly, casually, and flippantly. Now, however, his style was serious, statesmanlike, even pompous, meant to indicate that he was viewing current affairs from a certain distance, from a higher vantage point. In his editorials for the weekly *Das Reich,* which he wrote regularly from 1940 onward, he would develop this elevated attitude even further. Part of this was his penchant for advancing his arguments as eternally valid, irrefutable truths by pointing, for example, to supposed "great historical developments," which "followed their own laws," or by referring to the "nature of war"[128] or deploying the power of facts or incontestable life experiences. Characteristic were stiff generalizing phrases such as: "Once more we feel the need to hold up to ridicule a certain question of the day," or: "We were obliged some days ago to deal in this publi-

cation with the excesses of the Polish press," or: "In this connection
we have little need to refer back to the facts."[129] The "we" he liked to
use in these articles denoted not only the author Goebbels but often
also the Nazi leadership or simply the collective of the German "national community." This manipulative game with the collective pro-
noun characterizes the leadership's claim to identity with the nation.

In March he suffered from renal colic, which confined him to bed
for several days, suffering such "savage pain" and being so incapable
of working that he even put off writing his diary entries.[130] After
hours of agony he eventually passed the kidney stone. On the same
day, Magda left for a six-week recuperative vacation in Italy, a departure he registered with evident relief: "And now a bit of peace again at
last."[131]

While Goebbels was recovering, he learned that Hitler had come
to a decision: Czechoslovakia was in his sights. The pretext for his
move against the country was the conflict in March 1939 between
Prague and the government of Slovakia, which, immediately after the
Munich Agreement, had succeeded in asserting its autonomy within
Czechoslovakia. On March 9 the Prague government dismissed the
cabinet in Bratislava as a preventive measure to stop Slovakia from
giving way to German pressure and quitting the union completely.[132]
Goebbels noted: "Now the question we only half resolved in October
can be completely resolved."[133]

Around noon on March 10 he was summoned by Hitler: "Immediately afterward Ribbentrop and Keitel arrived. Decision: We go in
on Wednesday March 15 and smash the whole misbegotten Czechoslovakian construct." Goebbels immediately put his "Ministry on the
alert." The press was ordered to add fuel to the fire.[134] By late afternoon he was back with Hitler. They composed a report according to
which "before being arrested the Tiso government had appealed in a
note to the German Reich government." The precise content of the
fictional Slovakian cry for help could be "handed in later as required."
But during the night, sitting up until the small hours, the dictator
and his minister learned that Tiso was not willing to sign.[135]

From March 13, the Czechoslovakian crisis dominated the German press. At first Goebbels's instruction was to "squeeze the tube a
bit harder, but don't let the cat out of the bag yet,"[136]—in other words,
not to deploy as yet the threat of an invasion that had already been
decided upon.[137] On March 13, Goebbels and Hitler collaborated on

drafting leaflets for the invasion.[138] On the same day, Hitler received Slovakian Prime Minister Jozef Tiso to offer him help in forming an independent Slovakia. Should he decline, Hitler's threat—conveyed to Goebbels that same evening—was that "they'll be swallowed up by Hungary." Tiso, declining to be pinned down, returned to Bratislava. "Not a revolutionary," was Goebbels's verdict.[139]

Tiso was supplied with a telegram drafted in the German Foreign Office immediately after his discussion with Hitler: It contained an appeal to the Reich for help. At the same time Ribbentrop presented Tiso with an ultimatum: He must declare his country's autonomy by the very next day.[140] Accordingly, the next day the assembly in Bratislava proclaimed an independent Slovakian state, and under German pressure[141] the appeal for help was handed over on March 15. The new state was also forced to agree to a "protective treaty" formally acknowledging its dependence on the German Reich.[142]

Late on the evening of March 14 the Czech president, Dr. Emil Hácha, and his foreign minister, František Chvalkovský, arrived in Berlin. During a nighttime session, which according to Goebbels was conducted with "brutal bitterness," they were forced to surrender completely.[143] At six the next morning, German troops began their entry into Czech territory.[144] On the evening of March 15 Hitler arrived in Prague, took possession of Hradschin Castle, ancient residence of the Bohemian kings, and proclaimed from here the next day that he had formed a protectorate of the "Bohemian and Moravian lands."[145]

While the Party was organizing "spontaneous rallies" throughout the Reich for March 19,[146] Goebbels laid on another "triumphal reception" for Hitler in Berlin on the same day; a welcome, wrote the *Völkischer Beobachter,* such as "no head of state in world history has ever enjoyed." The paper reported the next day that searchlights formed a "canopy of light" above the broad, flag-bedecked avenue Unter den Linden, and fireworks completed the effect of a street clad in "a magic, fairyland mantle of swastika banners, pylons, and Bengal lights."[147]

Hitler's decision to occupy the Czech territories, thereby breaking the Munich Agreement, marked a turning point in the attitude of the western powers to the Third Reich. It was all too obvious not only that Hitler had reneged on a treaty but also that what supposedly legitimated his previous policy—bringing "home into the Reich" those Germans cut off from it by the Versailles Treaty—had now been unmasked as a duplicitous ploy. At a stroke, London and Paris realized that Hitler would not be satisfied with further concessions and that the only answer was deterrence. But as Hitler told Goebbels on his return to Berlin, he was not taking the protests from Britain and France seriously.[148] Goebbels talked about "stage thunder."[149]

The self-confidence of the regime is apparent from the fact that, totally unimpressed by western protests, it immediately set about its next foreign affairs "coup." Directly after his return from Prague, Hitler began preparing to enforce a solution to the "Memel question." The Memelland, predominantly inhabited by Germans, had been separated from the Reich by the Versailles Treaty, placed at first under French administration, then occupied in 1923 by Lithuania and subsequently administered by the Baltic State. In a directive dating from October 1938 Hitler was already calling for the early annexation of the territory by the Reich.[150]

On March 20, Foreign Minister Ribbentrop forced his Lithuanian counterpart, Juozas Urbšys, on a visit to Berlin, into agreeing to surrender the strip of land.[151] Goebbels was triumphant: "Either-or. These little Versailles thieves have now got to disgorge their stolen goods—or else!" By March 22, Goebbels was announcing the successful completion of the latest coup while prescribing the usual celebrations.[152]

Following the occupation of Prague and Memelland, the question of German-Polish relations moved to the center ground of German foreign policy. Via the Polish ambassador in Berlin, Ribbentrop had called upon his opposite number in Poland, Józef Beck, to come to Berlin for talks about the prospects for a joint policy. A precondition for this, however, would be the fulfillment of the well-known German demands concerning Danzig and the Polish Corridor.

Beck did not appear; the German proposals were unequivocally rejected. The Polish government, having temporarily mobilized its military forces, instead turned to Britain for help. The appeal was received positively by Chamberlain with a statement in the House of Commons, while the Polish foreign minister firmly informed the German ambassador at the end of the month that any attempt by Germany to impose a solution of the Danzig question by force would mean war. At the beginning of April, a visit to London by Beck, arranged on short notice, resulted in the announcement of a pact of mutual support.[153]

At this point, therefore, Goebbels's attention switched to Great Britain. He started an anti-British campaign, in keeping with the old adage "attack is the best form of defense," as he recorded on March 21. His opening salvo in the *Völkischer Beobachter* was an editorial entitled "Away with Moral Hypocrisy" in which he made short shrift of "humanity, civilization, international law, and international trust," asserting, "Our morality lies in our rights. Anyone suppressing these rights is dealing immorally with us, even if he envelops his action in a cloud of incense and murmurs a pious prayer. We are no longer impressed by that."[154] On the same day the newspapers were instructed to attack British global policy by casting historical aspersions.[155]

In another editorial in the *Völkischer Beobachter* Goebbels provided a "final reckoning with British arrogance." German actions in the past few weeks had not been taken out of overweening pride, only "because we want to live."[156] The "anti-England campaign" was short-lived; within a few days Goebbels declared it over for the time being.[157]

One result of the tense international situation was that Goebbels had to contend with increasing competition from ambitious rivals in the area of propaganda directed at foreign powers and, later, wartime propaganda. The outcome was that he was forced to pull in his horns, with his reputation within the Nazi leadership somewhat dented.

The previous autumn, a conflict had broken out with the Foreign Ministry. In 1933, it had relinquished to the Propaganda Ministry the press office responsible for analyzing the foreign press: Now the Foreign Office wanted to reclaim and develop it for itself. In the course of this dispute the fundamental question had arisen as to which party was responsible for dealing with the foreign press, a role claimed by both sides, each citing decisions by the Führer to back its claim.[158]

Goebbels and Hitler relied on a decree issued by Hitler on February 16, 1939, and orally confirmed by the Führer on February 28.[159] Ribbentrop, on the other hand, likewise referring to Hitler's intentions, gave orders in June 1939 for a foreign-language broadcasting service to be set up within the Foreign Office but could not push it through against the propaganda minister's opposition.[160] He had equally little success in June in retrieving the press attaché bureaus assigned to German overseas representations, which had likewise been reallocated to the Propaganda Ministry in 1933.[161]

Rivalry and mistrust also characterized relations between Goebbels and the propaganda arm of the Wehrmacht. Since about 1935 Goebbels's officials had been discussing with offices from the War Ministry questions of military and home-front propaganda in the case of a war;[162] jointly they had begun to devise a mobilization plan to cover the full portfolio of the Ministry of Popular Enlightenment and Propaganda.[163] During the maneuvers of autumn 1936 the Propaganda Ministry had deployed on a trial basis a "propaganda task force" consisting of civilian reporters.[164] Goebbels arranged with the War Ministry in 1937 that, should war break out, units from his ministry would be put in uniform and "embedded" with the Wehrmacht. The new organizational structure was tried out in the autumn maneuvers,[165] and Goebbels had the opportunity to hold a "maneuver discussion" in his ministry.[166]

And yet since the end of 1937 Goebbels had been pursuing the aim of disbanding the propaganda department within the Wehrmacht.[167] In December he thought he had reached an understanding with Wilhelm Keitel guaranteeing his ministry command of war propaganda.[168] However, in the years that followed, the military actually succeeded in strengthening the position of military propaganda. According to principles negotiated at the end of September 1938 between the Propaganda Ministry and the Wehrmacht High Command governing the control of propaganda in wartime,[169] the Wehrmacht set up its own propaganda companies and by means of "general instructions" to the Propaganda Ministry was supposed to enable the ministry to coordinate the "propaganda war" with the "war of weapons." Admittedly, the Propaganda Ministry had some influence over the appointment of specialists, and it was able to exert control of the use of propaganda material outside the military sphere. But when Goebbels in his diaries presented the propaganda companies as an extension of his ministry's operations in the case of war, he did so in order to conceal a defeat.[170]

On April 1, 1939, a department of Wehrmacht propaganda was created in the Wehrmacht High Command, concentrating military authority in this field.[171] Goebbels observed these activities with deep mistrust: "The Wehrmacht is meddling too much in my affairs. But I won't put up with it. The Wehrmacht can do the fighting, and I'll do the propaganda."[172]

VISIT TO THE BALKANS AND EGYPT

In view of the tense international situation it seemed questionable to Goebbels in spring 1939 whether he should really embark on his long-planned[173] trip to Greece and Egypt, but Hitler advised him to do so: He did not think Goebbels indispensable in Berlin.[174] Moreover, the fact that his propaganda minister, so prominent as a firebrand in recent weeks, was setting off on a fairly long journey would show the world how relaxed the regime was about the international protests. Goebbels on the other hand took Hitler's approval of his trip to be a clear confirmation that the signals were set for détente on the international scene. He could not imagine that hugely significant decisions would be maturing in Berlin during his absence, and he did not grasp that his trip was a political diversionary tactic.

So it was that on the evening of March 27 Goebbels set off on a journey of almost three weeks, predominantly private in nature.[175] At his first stop, Budapest, he stayed for a few days and used the opportunity to pay his respects to Regent Horthy and Prime Minister Pál Teleki.[176] From there he flew—with a brief stop in Belgrade—to Athens, where he was greeted by his old acquaintance, Minister Konstantinos Kotzias. In the Greek capital, as on his last stay there in 1936, he visited Prime Minister Ioannis Metaxas—now ruling with dictatorial powers—and the Greek king[177] as well as taking in the Acropolis and other famous ancient sites. Reverently he marveled at "the antique cultural soil across which so much history has swept."[178]

On April 1 he flew on to the island of Rhodes, occupied since 1912 by the Italians.[179] There he relaxed for two weeks, enjoying the "glorious sun."[180] What he did not hear on his vacation was that on April 3, in reaction to Chamberlain's speech, Hitler had drawn up instructions for "Case White." The Wehrmacht should gear itself for war against Poland from September 1, 1939; he was prepared to launch this war if the Poles maintained their intransigent attitude to German demands.[181]

On April 5 Goebbels interrupted his vacation on Rhodes to fly to

Egypt for two days. He had been planning a lengthy stay in Egypt since the end of 1938 but postponed it for reasons of personal security. On this short trip he explored, among other sites, Cairo and its National Museum, the pyramids at Saqqara, the pyramid of Cheops, and the Sphinx.[182] Far from his homeland, Goebbels could enthuse about the exotic: "Late in the evening a camel-ride into the desert. Under a heavy full moon. [. . .] Out in the desert colorful tents have been put up. There the Arabs perform a fantasia for us. Terrific, wild folk-plays that we find very fascinating." On the way home he became "quite melancholy: what a country and what a wide world! For a long time I can't sleep for excitement."[183]

On Rhodes, to which he had now returned, on April 9 he caught up with further international developments: On April 7 Mussolini had occupied Albania, and on April 6 Great Britain and Poland had concluded a mutual assistance pact. Goebbels commented: "So, Beck has fallen into the Lords' trap after all. Poland may have to pay a high price for this one day. That's how the Czechs started, too."[184] It obviously never occurred to him that the British pledge of support for Poland might be deadly serious—or else he suppressed the thought.

HITLER'S FIFTIETH BIRTHDAY

On returning from his vacation Goebbels was heavily involved in preparations for Hitler's fiftieth birthday. He was aware that in London war was being talked about "like you might mention supper," but he took these threats no more seriously than he ever had; for him they were primarily meant to be "panic inducers."[185] Occasionally, though, he did have doubts: Was the "agitation" in the press not bound "to lead to war in the long run"?[186]

Hitler's fiftieth birthday marked the ceremonial high point of 1939, a year in which the capital saw plenty of great occasions:[187] This self-confident display of the dictator's power was to set the scene for further aggression abroad.

On the day before the celebrations, in the Kroll Opera House, Goebbels gave his "Führer's birthday address," which, he proudly reported, was "broadcast practically throughout the world." The Party leadership formally congratulated their leader, and Hitler then proceeded to open Speer's east-west axis road, the first great artery to be built under the plan for reshaping Berlin. Some two million people had turned out to line the brightly lit route, the Berlin population having been notified in no uncertain terms: "On the eve of the Führer's birthday the whole of Berlin lines the east-west axis. [. . .] Flags out, decorate houses and streets!"[188] There followed a military tattoo and a "torchlight procession of the old guard from all over the Reich." Goebbels was among the small group of confidants who were allowed to congratulate Hitler on his birthday at midnight.

The next day, declared a holiday on short notice,[189] the celebrations proper began: In the morning, a parade of the Leibstandarte in front of the Reich Chancellery, followed by formal congratulations from the Reich government, and then—on the east-west axis road again—an almost five-hour parade by the Wehrmacht. The solemn induction of newly appointed political leaders of the Party rounded off the day's events.

Goebbels learned from Hitler a few days later that the Führer, too, regarded the British and French threats as a bluff and was counting on Poland to give way. "Will there be war?" Goebbels asked himself: "I don't think so. In any case, nobody really wants it at the moment. That's our best ally."[190]

Over the following few days he resumed his fierce anti-British polemic in the *Völkischer Beobachter*, which prepared the way for further aggressive moves by Hitler.[191] On April 28 the Führer gave a speech to the Reichstag which he used to conduct a foreign affairs tour d'horizon. First in the line of fire was President Franklin D. Roosevelt. Two weeks earlier, Roosevelt had called on Hitler to swear that he would not commit any aggressive act against thirty specifically named states. Hitler's answer, ridiculing Roosevelt, had his audience of parliamentary delegates—which included a completely spellbound Goebbels—roaring with laughter. Furthermore, Hitler canceled the naval agreement with Britain and the non-aggression pact with Poland.[192]

At the beginning of May German propaganda began to produce anti-Polish polemics, albeit kept low-key for the time being.[193] The idea was to reinforce the message contained in Hitler's speech about a break with Poland.[194] At the heart of the campaign were two articles by Goebbels in the *Völkischer Beobachter* complaining about alleged anti-German tendencies in Poland: Elsewhere, in an explanation directed at the rest of the press, the Propaganda Ministry spoke of a "trial shot."[195] The press was enjoined to publish a steady stream of reports about border incidents, although still in a restrained manner.[196]

The announcement of the military alliance between Germany and Italy on May 8 was what Goebbels called another "body blow"—a clear signal to the western powers, who were committing themselves more and more to the support of Poland.[197] Two weeks later Galeazzo Ciano came to Berlin for the formal signing of the pact.[198] Disappointment was mixed with triumph, however: Japan was not prepared to join the signatories.[199]

THE ATTACK TURNS ON BRITAIN

In May the regime received clear signals that the British intended to stand by their commitment to Poland.[200] This prompted Goebbels to start another anti-British campaign, continuing into July, under the banner of "inciting hatred for England."[201] On May 20 he published an attack on the "encirclers":[202] "Take a good look at them as they squat together in their clubs, Freemasons' lodges, and Jewish banks hatching new mischief to afflict Europe."[203]

The key term *encirclers,* referring to the "encircling" of Germany by coalition forces led by a grasping Great Britain, was meant to recall the situation in 1914, when Germany alleged that the Entente Powers had hemmed the country in. Goebbels was trying to provoke new fears of a threat to the Reich and to shift the blame in advance for any possible outbreak of war. The shrill tone of his propaganda warned the German population unequivocally that war was inevitable to ensure the survival of the nation. But there was no mood of pro-war enthusiasm comparable with that of summer 1914.

The focus of Goebbels's attacks varied. At some points he homed in on Britain's interference in German-Polish negotiations, said to have handed the Poles a "blank check" allowing them to decide on war or peace;[204] at other times he stressed that Germany did not want to number perennially among the "have-nots";[205] or he moved the Danzig question into the foreground in order to test "the international atmosphere" on this point.[206]

While Hitler remained convinced that the British were bluffing,[207] Goebbels increasingly turned his attention to the demand for access to resources and enlargement of *Lebensraum* ("living-space"). In his speech at the Solstice Festival in the Berlin Stadium, he declared that a "nation of 80 million could not be excluded from the riches of the earth": As long as this remained the case, "any peace program was just empty words."[208] Two days later, in the *Völkischer Beobachter,* he ventured to predict that "in a war with Germany Great Britain would lose its empire."[209]

In the *Völkischer Beobachter* in July Goebbels attacked the British politician and writer Stephen King-Hall, who had sent a leaflet addressed to Germans; however, the article did not appear until it had been thoroughly redacted by Hitler.[210]

BAD GASTEIN—BAYREUTH—SALZBURG—VENICE

On July 2 Goebbels went to Salzburg to check on preparations for the Festival. He had first visited the Festival the year before and had not been impressed by the building ("must be torn down") or by the productions: "beneath contempt in terms of singing, scenery, and decor. [. . .] This is real Viennese kitsch. But I'll get rid of it all."[211]

He used the journey to make a slight detour to meet up with his family in Bad Gastein, where Magda had been undergoing spa treatment since the end of June.[212] It was in the Austrian resort that she confessed to him her affair with Hanke, who thus stood unmasked for Goebbels as a "first-class rogue"—but had a touch of respect crept in there?[213]

From Bad Gastein they traveled together to Bayreuth. In the intermissions between the opera performances, the usual social obligations, and the hours of conversation with Hitler, Goebbels tried to put an end to the relationship between Magda and Hanke. He had the head of personnel at the Propaganda Ministry working on Hanke in Berlin on his behalf, while he talked for hours with Magda, who was "very disturbed and upset," frequently fainting; the confrontation placed him, too, under "the greatest nervous strain."[214] Eventually he discovered that Magda had changed the complexion of the matter by putting it to Hitler, as she always did when her marriage was at stake.[215] Hitler followed the same line as he had in the Baarová case; the couple must remain together under all circumstances. There followed a headlong departure from the town of Richard Wagner.[216]

Back in Berlin, the first thing he did was to send Hanke off on vacation. With the beginning of war he would go into the army; there could be no question of letting him return to the Propaganda Ministry.[217] Goebbels, the deceived husband, found himself in a "severe state of shock." It was "terrible to lose all faith in your fellow man." But perhaps this was "necessary and useful for the future"; you were then "free of illusions and can face life in a more open, freer and more mature way. You don't have friends anymore, just acquaintances and colleagues."[218]

After spending the first two weeks of August at the Salzburg Festival,[219] he went with a delegation from the Propaganda Ministry and numerous representatives of the German press to the Biennale in Venice, where he had talks with his Italian counterpart, Dino Alfieri, about further cooperation in various areas of propaganda but also found time to simply lounge around on the beach or in cafés.[220] On August 15 he flew back to Berlin, surely aware that with the "anti-Polish campaign" Hitler had signaled the beginning of the "final sprint."[221]

Following Hitler's lead, in the second half of August the press adopted an anti-Polish stance of almost unparalleled aggressiveness. The pressure on that country was to be stepped up, and at the same time the home population was to be attuned to the inevitability of a war.[222] On August 19 Goebbels received a call from the Obersalzberg: In two days the propaganda effort was to reach a "full crescendo. After that, we're off."[223]

Goebbels had concluded that the war "was anticipated with a certain fatalism. It would almost take a miracle to stop it. If it has become necessary, then the sooner the better."[224] The propaganda was framed accordingly. In the last prewar phase it concentrated on blaming the war on the attitude of Poland and the western powers. There was still no mention of enthusiasm for war, either from Goebbels or in the pronouncements of his propaganda machine.

NON-AGGRESSION PACT WITH
THE SOVIET UNION AND THE BEGINNING OF THE WAR

On August 21 there was further "news from the Obersalzberg": "Non-aggression pact with Moscow completed. Ribbentrop in Moscow on Wednesday." Once again the decision-making process had entirely bypassed the propaganda minister, as he was only informed post facto of highly significant developments.[225] On the day Goebbels received this message, he struggled to put this "global sensation" into words: "The whole scene of power in Europe has been transformed. London and Paris bewildered. [. . .] The Führer has pulled off a brilliant chess move."

At Hitler's request, he made his way early next morning to Berchtesgaden.[226] During the following two weeks he was to stay in close daily contact with Hitler, and although Goebbels was not involved in the actual decision-making process that was eventually to unleash the Second World War, his diary entries for this critical period contain extremely interesting insights into the individual steps and the motives of the German leadership.

A letter from Chamberlain delivered to Hitler by Ambassador Nevile Henderson reinforced the message of Britain's resolve in the event of an attack on Poland. Hitler replied to the letter with an equally clear counterthreat.[227] As Goebbels's notes have it, the Führer's general assessment of the situation is as follows: The situation of Poland was "desperate. We will attack them at the first opportunity. The Polish state must be smashed, just like the Czech." This would not be too difficult, but the question of whether the West would intervene was more complicated: It was not certain. "Italy is not enthusiastic, but will have to go along with us. It hardly has any choice."

Hitler then informed Goebbels of the details of the way the pact with Stalin had come about and its consequences: "Eastern Europe will be divided between Berlin and Moscow." Naturally, a surprise treaty with the Soviet arch-enemy was a risky business. But Goebbels noted: "Beggars can't be choosers."

Finally, at two in the morning, the long-awaited communiqué from Moscow arrived, sealing the alliance with Stalin: "Non-aggression and consultative pact for 10 years. [. . .] A world-historical event with vast implications."[228] The treaty, and a Secret Supplementary Protocol signed at the same time, did indeed provide for the division of Poland and the Baltic states into German and Soviet spheres of influence, respectively: Hitler now had the necessary rear cover for his planned war on Poland.[229]

The next day Hitler and his propaganda minister left Berchtesgaden for Berlin.[230] Here preparations were begun immediately for the invasion of Poland, scheduled for the night of August 25–26. At midday on August 25, Goebbels saw Hitler, who instructed him to draw up two proclamations, one to the German people and one to the Party. "Clarification of the need for an armed conflict with Poland, adjustment of the whole nation to war, if necessary for months and years."[231]

Later in the same day Hitler met the British and French ambassadors. He declared plainly to Henderson that "the German-Polish problem must be resolved and could be resolved." If Britain declared war because of a military move by Germany against Poland, then Germany would accept this challenge.[232] On the other hand, Hitler promised Britain extensive cooperation once "the resolution of this problem had been achieved." However, this step did not seem very promising even to Goebbels: "England will no longer believe we mean it." The encounter with the French ambassador did not offer the prospect of peace, either: Robert Coulondre assured Hitler "on his word of honor as an officer" that if Germany attacked Poland, France would be obliged to act.[233]

But events then took a turn that upset all of Hitler's calculations. Early in the evening Ambassador Attolico appeared in the Reich Chancellery with a surprising message: "He delivers Mussolini's declaration that Italy cannot participate in a war at present. Serves us right. It's what I've always feared and have really known all the time since Venice: Italy won't go along with us." In fact, Mussolini complained to Hitler that "in their encounters [. . .] war was envisaged for 1942," and in accordance with this understanding he would of course be ready by that juncture "on land, at sea, and in the air," but at the present moment he was insufficiently prepared for armed conflict with the western powers. Hitler immediately drew his conclusion: Mobilization was to continue, but the attack planned for that night was called off.[234]

What to do? "The Führer broods and ponders. It's a heavy blow for him." Goebbels was confident that Hitler would "find a way out, even from this damned situation." But all Hitler came up with was to go to war without his assiduously cultivated ally.[235]

The next day Ambassador Coulondre handed over a letter from Daladier,[236] the content of which, according to Goebbels's report of

Hitler's reaction, was of no consequence, obviously serving the purpose of avoiding "possible war-guilt."²³⁷ Although the French were promised confidentiality, two days later the German side broadcast the letter and Hitler's answer "in every language"; Goebbels thought this was "the best possible propaganda for us."²³⁸

When he met Hitler the following day, August 27, the leader was "in fine form and full of confidence." He had no intention of giving up his minimum demands regarding Danzig and Poland. That evening, Henderson brought the British note replying to Hitler's proposals of August 25. The British government took cognizance of Hitler's offer of extensive cooperation but stressed that the outstanding differences between Germany and Poland must be settled first—on the basis of Hitler's speech to the Reichstag of April 28. Attention was clearly drawn once more to the existing commitments of Great Britain to Poland.²³⁹

In addition, the Swedish industrialist Birger Dahlerus, whom Hitler had requested a few days earlier to present his ideas about a resolution of the crisis directly to the British government, brought a message from London. Goebbels noted: "England might possibly agree to ceding of Danzig and a corridor in the Corridor. But guarantee of Polish border in return. Later also to discuss question of colonies. Long peace with England. [. . .] Everything still hangs in the balance."²⁴⁰

The German reaction the next day was to describe the prospects for any further negotiations with Poland as no longer encouraging, but nonetheless the German side was ready to receive a Polish representative in Berlin for discussions, provided he arrived by the next day, meaning August 30.²⁴¹ On the morning of August 30 Goebbels summarized the thinking behind this reply: "The Führer wants a plebiscite in the Corridor under international control. That way, he still hopes to pry London loose from Warsaw and find an excuse for striking. London's attitude is not as rigid as previously."

It was clear that any negotiations would be a sham. The real aim was, on the one hand, to weaken the British guarantee to Warsaw and on the other to create a pretext for military action against Poland.

The extremely tight deadline set for a Polish representative to be sent to Berlin made a resumption of negotiations appear quite improbable. But if, against the odds, Beck should come to Berlin, Goebbels was worried above all that the unexpected chance of peace could lead to an "unstoppable wave of optimism here," which would "ruin our whole position."[242] Evidently, Goebbels was still assuming that the nation was not exactly enraptured by the prospect of war. Meanwhile, the press was instructed "to play up reports of Polish atrocities."[243]

Around midnight on August 30 Ribbentrop received the British ambassador to inform him that the German side had formulated some proposals to resolve the Polish issues. These had lapsed, however, since contrary to German wishes no Polish plenipotentiary had presented himself to the Reich government. Ribbentrop went on to read out the proposals to Henderson at top speed, without handing him a copy of the document. It was quite clear that the German side no longer had any interest whatsoever in negotiating.[244]

At about the same time, Hitler summoned Goebbels to tell him about the details of the "negotiating proposal" and the background of this tactic: "The Führer thinks there'll be war." Hitler had composed a memorandum which, among other things, stipulated the incorporation of Danzig into the Reich and a plebiscite in the Corridor. Hitler proposed to "launch this document into the global public sphere at the most favorable opportunity." He himself was making it apparent that the sixteen-point catalogue he had drawn up was never intended as the basis for negotiations but simply to demonstrate to the world the "good will" of his regime—for the time *after* the now inevitable war had begun.

"England's reply," added Goebbels in his account of the conversation with Hitler, "is playing for time. But also disrespectful and provocative. They think Germany is weak. They are deceiving themselves." These words of the dictator's to his propaganda minister were all part of the charade Hitler was acting out: Neither the Poles nor the British were going to be given any chance of reacting to the proposals.

When the Polish ambassador called on Ribbentrop the next day to present his government's response to the British proposal that direct talks should be arranged with Germany, Ribbentrop made an excuse to cut the conversation short. Soon afterward the German Foreign Office handed the German "proposals" to the ambassadors of Britain, France, Japan, the United States, and the USSR, declaring that the Polish side had not availed themselves of the chance to negotiate.[245] This communication and the sixteen-point document were announced on German radio at around nine o'clock.[246]

On the German side, the decision had been made long before: At midday on August 31 Hitler had given orders for the invasion of Poland to begin that night. Hitler did not believe that Britain would intervene, but whether this prediction would turn out to be accurate, wrote Goebbels, "nobody can say at the moment."[247]

1939—1945

WAR——TOTAL WAR——TOTAL DEFEAT

CHAPTER 19

"War Is the Father of All Things"

The First Months of the War

The government front bench in the Kroll Opera House during Hitler's speech after the attack on Poland, September 1, 1939. Goebbels's reaction to the outbreak of war was far from enthusiastic.

The Nazi regime represented the opening of hostilities on September 1, 1939, as a response to alleged provocation by the Poles on the frontier. Border incidents faked by the SS, especially the alleged "raid" on the Gleiwitz radio transmitter, were to supply the pretext for the German assault. The corresponding entry in Goebbels's diary reads: "The SS given special orders for the night," and a few paragraphs later comes the phrase "Polish attack on the Gleiwitz transmitter."[1] For him, the carefully contrived lie had transformed itself, all unawares, into a real event. The fiction was maintained by Hitler's speech in the Reichstag on the morning of September 1: "Fire has been returned since 5:45 A.M.!"[2]—although in fact the attack had begun an hour earlier. Hitler also announced the ratification of the German-Soviet Non-Aggression Pact and declared that he had no interest in changing Germany's western borders, the perfect lifeline for London and Paris, decided Goebbels, who was present in the Reichstag for the speech.[3]

But these maneuvers proved futile. That very evening, September 1, the ambassadors of Britain and France called on Foreign Minister Ribbentrop to assure him that their countries would stand by their pledges to Poland. At the same time the two countries declared general mobilization.[4] On September 3, the British ambassador handed over a last, short-term ultimatum from his government, which Hitler rejected. Whereupon Britain declared war. The French government followed suit, albeit after several hours' delay.[5]

By that morning, in parallel with his rejection of the British ultimatum, Hitler had already addressed separate appeals to the people, the Party, and members of the armed forces, which Goebbels immediately had broadcast over the radio. That same evening, Hitler left Berlin on his special train, "in order," as Goebbels dramatically phrased it, "to make his way to the Eastern Front." In fact, during the following weeks, Hitler was to move around at a relatively safe distance from the fighting.[6]

Exploiting the propaganda value of the Polish "campaign," already victorious after only five weeks, was one of the chief tasks falling to Goebbels's propaganda machine at this time. As before, during the Sudeten crisis, and as in the days before the beginning of hostilities, Goebbels's office made strenuous efforts to disseminate reports of alleged Polish atrocities, inflicted first and foremost on the German minority population, although in most cases these horror stories were either invented or highly exaggerated.[7] In point of fact, during the course of the war, many thousands of "ethnic Germans" lost their lives, some as a result of combat action, others executed by the Polish military, or killed by civilians. The civilian attacks peaked at the beginning of September in Bromberg (in Polish: Bydgoszcz), and while it is true that some hundreds of "ethnic Germans" were killed as alleged "saboteurs," Nazi propaganda described the "Bromberg Bloody Sunday" in terms of a massacre of thousands.[8] After the Polish action, German propaganda was to assert that over fifty thousand "ethnic Germans" had fallen victim to such atrocities at this time. In reality, the total number of people of German origin who had died was multiplied by a factor of ten.[9]

The Germans used this atrocity propaganda to justify "retribution." During the Polish campaign and in the following months, German units (including task forces, police, the ethnic German self-defense force newly formed by the SS, and also regular German troops) shot tens of thousands of Polish civilians, members of the intelligentsia, the clergy, and the aristocracy and thousands of Jews.[10] German actions were systematically planned from the beginning to carry forward the wishes of the political leadership. By September 7, Heydrich had already given orders at a conference of leading officials that "as much as possible the Polish elites are to be rendered harmless."[11] Action was taken accordingly.

During these weeks, while creating suitable atrocity propaganda around the mass shootings of "ethnic Germans," Goebbels also directed propaganda efforts at the Western powers. At a meeting with Hitler on September 3, guidelines were set for wartime propaganda. The byword for the coming weeks ran: "Against Chamberlain and his associates. Divide leadership from people. Leave France unmolested for the present."[12]

CONFLICTS OVER THE DISTRIBUTION OF RESPONSIBILITIES

An immediate result of the opening of hostilities was that Goebbels had to fight off increased competition for command of the propaganda effort. In fact, arguments over responsibility for this area were to continue until the end of the war; indeed, it is quite clear that Hitler deliberately left unresolved certain questions of authority so that, if necessary, he would have the opportunity to intervene personally. These conflicts over authority, often fought out in bitter personal arguments between the leading figures, typified the Nazi state.

By August 1939, a new dispute had already flared up between the Foreign Ministry and the Propaganda Ministry, when State Secretary Ernst von Weizsäcker, once again citing an oral command from the Führer, requested permission from the Wehrmacht High Command for his ministry, instead of that overseen by Goebbels, to be allowed to convey to the press certain directives, which had been drawn up in readiness for mobilization.[13] When State Secretary Dietrich proved obstructive, Ribbentrop again brought in Hitler and rapidly demonstrated that his recent diplomatic successes in Moscow had reinforced his position at Hitler's court. On September 3, Hitler placed all overseas German representatives, whether of State or Party, under the command of the respective Heads of Mission.[14]

When Goebbels resisted this ruling, Hitler summoned him to his headquarters, where Goebbels arrived on the same day, aboard a bomber. Hitler forced the two opponents to come together and settle their differences in a compartment of his special train, which served as his headquarters at this time. The two emerged and reported to Hitler three hours later, as Dietrich tells us in his memoirs, both of them "red in the face," to tell him that a compromise could not be found. The next day, Hitler penned a written "Führer decree," which stated that, "in the sphere of foreign policy propaganda [. . .], the foreign minister will issue guidelines and instructions [. . .]. For the purpose of putting these instructions into effect, the foreign minister will have the entire apparatus of the Propaganda Ministry at his disposal."[15] Hitler, angered by this territorial dispute, insisted that Goebbels and Ribbentrop immediately "agree to carry out his order," whereupon they agreed on a division of labor. Essentially, what was agreed on was the exchange of liaison personnel.[16]

On his return to Berlin, Goebbels carried out a substantial reorganization of his ministry. He introduced a daily meeting of his most important staff members, fixed for 11 A.M. His aims were to coordinate the work better and to maintain control of it. This measure was meant to counteract competition not only from the Foreign Ministry but also from Dietrich, whom Goebbels, in any case, saw as a dimwit, lacking in imagination and reasoning power. Goebbels took the view that Dietrich all too frequently acted independently and cherished ambitions to become press minister.[17]

In the months that followed, Goebbels went on the offensive, particularly against the placement of liaison personnel in his ministry,[18] while, at the same time, he was building up his Foreign Department. This took place against a background of constant complaints from him about what he perceived as the incompetence of the Foreign Ministry in matters of propaganda.[19]

Goebbels was also unhappy about the performance of Armed

Forces propagandists who had been removed from his immediate control. He always found the reports and film footage delivered to him by the propaganda companies completely inadequate, obviously the work of soldiers, not propagandists.[20] After Hitler, too, had severely criticized the quality of the newsreels, in December Goebbels attempted, in long discussions with his liaison officer in the Armed Forces High Command, Bruno Wentscher,[21] to make it clear that the work of the propaganda staff required more than just military discipline and drill.[22] He complained to Wilhelm Keitel and discussed the matter with Hitler's Wehrmacht adjutant, Rudolf Schmundt.[23] In January 1940, Wentscher was replaced by Major Leo Martin.[24]

WAR WEARS DOWN THE NERVES

Goebbels's enthusiasm for war was by no means boundless. At the beginning of September he agreed with Göring that a full-scale war was not desirable. After only a few days he was beginning to find the war very strenuous; as he put it in an emotional diary entry on September 24, it "takes a toll on the nerves:[25] War consumes everything, even our own egos!" A few days later, in view of the glorious autumn weather, he could not "imagine that a world war was about to begin."[26]

In the following weeks, Goebbels strove above all to discover more about Hitler's further intentions. On a lightning visit to Hitler's headquarters at the troop training ground of Gross-Born on September 27, Hitler explained to him that first of all he wanted to smash Poland and then make peace in the West. "He doesn't need a long war," was Goebbels's summary of his impressions a few days later. "If it must be war, then short and all-out. We cannot allow London to force us to our knees once more through attrition (time and hunger)."[27]

A few days after the war began, the Italian culture minister, Dino Alfieri, had tried to involve Goebbels in the mediation efforts pursued by the Italian government to bring Germany and the Western powers together, even to negotiate. Goebbels put the matter to Hitler and, in accordance with Hitler's wishes, gave Alfieri an evasive reply.[28] In early October he was still hoping that Italian soundings in Paris might bring results in some way.[29] What he did not know was that

Hitler had just informed Foreign Minister Ciano quite clearly that he did not want the services of the Italians as mediators.[30]

By means of the reports available to him, which in the early weeks of the war were constantly being compiled by his own propaganda machine, by the Party, and by government agencies, Goebbels carefully observed the "mood" of the population, which seemed to him "calm and composed," "quiet and confident": The hope of an early peace must have played an important part in creating this mood.[31] It is not surprising that the tendency of all these reports was so uniform. After all, in a speech on September 1 to Reichstag members, Hitler had declared that he didn't want anyone reporting to him that the mood in his Gau, district, or Party cell might sometimes be bad. "You are the bearers, the responsible bearers of the public mood!"[32]

Right at the beginning of the war, the propaganda minister took an important step to protect "public opinion" from harmful outside influences. On September 2, the press announced an order issued by the Council of Ministers concerning extraordinary measures governing the radio. It proclaimed that listening to foreign radio stations would be a punishable offense and that the disseminating of news obtained from these stations was even punishable by a death sentence.[33]

This decree, initiated by Goebbels, had not in fact been a product of the Council of Ministers. Indeed, it had been strongly rejected there. Rudolf Hess later explained that it had nonetheless been published as the result of a misunderstanding. Until the order was set out in an official version in the Reich legal bulletin a few days later, there continued to be hectic negotiations among the various ministries, which led to considerable changes to the order as it appeared in its final form. In particular, what was now missing was the decree permitting the Propaganda Ministry to order that radio sets should be confiscated.[34]

Even in its revised form, the order turned out to be an effective instrument. Naturally, it could not prevent a significant portion of the public from listening to foreign broadcasts. But for the individual citizen it was practically impossible to refer, in a public conversation, to a foreign radio station as the source of information departing from the official propaganda line. Thus the order represented an important measure in the hands of the Nazis for sealing off the public. The regular press reports about sentences passed for "radio crimes," of which there were three dozen by the end of 1939 and 830 in 1940, ensured that the desired deterrent effect was achieved.[35]

What the reports of the public mood actually signified in these first few weeks was that the German population, among whom there was scarcely a trace of enthusiasm for war to be detected (in contrast to the mood of 1914), was complying with the orders of the regime; hardly anyone dared show recalcitrance in public. This compliance was ensured not least by the punitive measures introduced at the beginning of the war: Aside from Goebbels's radio law there was the war-economy legislation of September 4, with its long catalogue of punishments, as well as the so-called Edict on National Vermin of September 5. In addition, sentences based on these new laws, which frequently included the death sentence, were announced in the press in the same way as the executions carried out, by way of example, by the Gestapo, without any corresponding sentence having been pronounced. The aim in both cases was a particular kind of deterrent effect through terror.[36]

What did threaten to have a negative effect on the public mood in the early weeks were the rigorous measures taken to bring about mobilization for war: They cut deep into economic and social life. For this purpose Goebbels was regularly summoned, from September 19 onward, to the sessions of the Ministerial Council for the Defense of the Reich, newly created as the war began, as a kind of war cabinet presided over by Göring to carry out the essential measures needed to place the administration and the economy on a war footing.[37]

Goebbels was among those members of the Nazi leadership elite who felt that the schematic execution of civilian war-related measures in the early weeks of the war had gone too far. Thus in his diary he criticized the laying off of workers, which took place immediately after the war began and rapidly led to considerable unemployment, and he also opposed plans, originating from the Reich economics minister, Funk, to reorganize industrial pay at a lower level.[38] Finally in mid-November the Council of Ministers decided, much to Goebbels's approval, to reverse several social policy steps introduced at the beginning of the war.[39]

But when the SD (Security Service) reports about the mood of the public continued in November to yield what Goebbels perceived as an unsatisfactory picture, Goebbels stepped in to correct it with other means. He declared the methods used by the SD to be increasingly unreliable and at a ministerial meeting warned those reporting on the mood of the country against "exaggeration."[40]

CONTINUATION OF WAR?

Nearly three weeks after his speech in the Reichstag, on September 19 Hitler once again addressed the public. In his speech in the historic Artus Hof in Danzig, which was broadcast by all German stations, he again proclaimed his supposed love of peace but also his determination to continue the war if need be.[41]

A few days later Goebbels learned from Dietrich, who had just returned from Hitler's headquarters, that after his victory over Poland, now clearly in sight, Hitler wanted to drive a wedge between France and Britain—that is to say, to make a separate peace with France. But it wasn't only Goebbels who asked himself, "How can that be done?" He also heard from Dietrich that Ribbentrop lacked the proper connections to enable him to make approaches to Paris.

During the following weeks, Goebbels took every opportunity to find out the dictator's further plans for the war, avidly noting down every hint that war on a larger scale might still be avoided. These entries demonstrate yet again how cut off Goebbels was from decision-making in central political matters, however hard he might try to maintain the impression that he enjoyed Hitler's full confidence. At the end of the month, Hitler, who had returned to Berlin for a few days, realized the possibility that there could still be a "Potato War" (a war of attrition) in the West, since there was no threat of a serious and long-lasting military conflict because the Western powers were unwilling to go to war.[42] Two days later, Goebbels noted Hitler's view that if London and Paris accept the peace proposals that he was about to offer them, "then order would soon be restored in Europe. If they don't, then it is clear where war-guilt will lie, and the battle begins."[43]

On the same occasion, Hitler explained his ideas for the future treatment of the occupied Polish territories: Poland should be divided into "three zones"—that is, into a strip to be, once more, completely "germanized"; a "Protectorate" for the "good Polish elements";

and finally, east of the Vistula, a territory for the "bad Polish elements" and the Jews, including Jews from the Reich.[44] In fact, the *Reichssicherheitshauptamt* (Reich Security Main Office) would start, as early as Autumn 1939, to send thousands of Jews from Reich territory to the planned reservation in eastern Poland. But the plan to "cleanse" the Reich of Jews in this way had to be deferred for the time being.[45]

They were now acquiring, as Hitler explained to Goebbels in the same conversation, a huge expansion of territory, but at the same time they had to accept that "Moscow's influence in the Baltic had been strengthened. But he personally was convinced of Russia's good faith. After all, Stalin had made enormous gains."[46] Hitler's remarks were informed by the Border and Friendship Agreement signed on September 28 in Moscow by his foreign minister, which laid down the division of spheres of influence in Poland and the Baltic and reinforced the alliance of the two states.[47]

Talking to Ribbentrop, just back from Moscow, on September 30, Goebbels criticized what he felt to be Ribbentrop's all-too-positive assessment of the Soviet Union, something he carefully avoided doing with Hitler, "as though Bolshevism was just a kind of National Socialism."[48] On October 3, he met Hitler again: "The Führer still believes he will manage to restore peace. I have very strong doubts right now; the enemy governments are not yet exhausted enough."[49]

Hitler, fresh from the victory parade in Warsaw, spoke again in the Reichstag on October 6 to make an offer of peace to the western powers. Hitler's reasoning was as simple as it was astonishing: War in the west should be avoided, since now that the Polish state had been dissolved the original reason for the French and British declaration of war, the German attack on Poland, was null and void. The final shape of this territory could only be resolved by Germany and the Soviet Union. If the western powers accepted the German-Soviet actions as a fait accompli, the future could be glorious. It would be possible to create a comprehensive European security system and introduce arms limitation. Germany had no interest in any further revision of its borders.[50]

Goebbels was so impressed by this speech—"a masterpiece of diplomacy"—that he assumed France and England would not be able to resist its powerful emotional appeal.[51] By October 12 he was still asking himself, "Are we truly heading for real world war? Even now nobody can tell." Notes of his lengthy discussion with Hitler the day before reveal how hard he was trying, in this critical situation, to reinforce his own confidence in victory. "With the Führer we will always win; he combines in himself all of the virtues of the great soldiers: courage, smartness, circumspection, and a complete disregard for a life of ease."[52]

When Chamberlain rejected Hitler's proposals in a speech on October 12, Hitler, despite his supposed hopes for peace, expressed his satisfaction to Goebbels that "we can now make a start against England."[53] Hitler didn't even take the time to examine the details of Chamberlain's reply, so set was he on going ahead with the imminent offensive in the West he had decided on a few days earlier.[54] It seemed the moment had finally arrived for even Goebbels to adjust to the idea of a lengthy war.

WAR PROPAGANDA AGAINST THE WEST

During the following months, the phase of phony war on the Western Front, Goebbels basically continued his previous propaganda line: The main attack should be directed at Great Britain; Paris must be spared.[55] For domestic consumption his watchword was to warn against illusions as much as against pessimism.[56] in German propaganda there was to be no more mention of neutral or enemy voices in favor of peace. In general, Goebbels was concerned to make the propaganda attack on France and England somewhat more realistic: "After all, war is not child's play."[57]

In the meantime there was little to report from the Western Front. In the conflict with Britain it was mainly maritime themes that preoccupied German war propaganda in these early weeks of the war. The sinking of the British passenger liner *Athenia* on September 3, 1939, by a German U-boat, in which more than one hundred passengers were drowned, was denied by the German side and written off as a British propaganda lie. From the point of view of the Nazi regime this affair was seen as particularly critical, as the victims had included American passengers, and the sinking had caused a corresponding furor in the United States.[58]

Goebbels had gone on the offensive right from the beginning and had accused the British First Sea Lord Winston Churchill of having ordered the sinking of the ship after the German submarine fleet had pulled off an important coup by sinking the British battleship *Royal Oak* within what had been assumed to be the absolutely secure naval base of Scapa Flow in Scotland on October 14. Goebbels now took up the *Athenia* case again in a widespread press and radio campaign. No doubt he had agreed with Hitler that every effort should now be made to topple the supposedly weakened Churchill.[59]

On October 21, under the pseudonym Sagax, Goebbels himself contributed an editorial to the *Völkischer Beobachter* and followed it up the next day with a radio address. The latter was given great prominence in the press: "A biting reckoning with an arch-liar," as Churchill was called, who was placed in the role of "the accused."[60]

POLAND

Occupied Poland played a completely secondary role in German propaganda at this stage. After extensive territories had been annexed, the remainder of the country was now combined into a General Government under Hans Frank. The thinking behind this arrangement was heavily influenced on the one hand by the deep contempt Hitler felt for the Poles, expressed to his propaganda minister as "more animals than human beings," and on the other hand by the fact that the violent application of the race laws[61] in the occupied territories was associated, even in this first phase of occupation policy, with the murder of tens of thousands of Poles and Jews, which made it seem inadvisable to draw attention to this territory. In addition, there was a certain lack of clarity about a solution to the self-created "Polish problem" and the "Jewish question." Hence, the German press was instructed, in connection with the imminent setting up of the General Government, that not much was to be said about this area, as much for domestic as for external reasons.[62]

On October 31, Goebbels embarked on a journey to Łodz, where he met Governor General Hans Frank and his deputy, Arthur Seyss-Inquart, and realized that Frank was installing his own propaganda office and that his own powers in this case were limited to giving professional advice.[63] It was made clear once again to Goebbels that he was by no means the omnipotent master of the propaganda machine. Goebbels also took a tour of the Jewish quarter:

"These are no longer people, they are animals. So our task is not a humanitarian one but a surgical one. Incisions will have to be made, and quite radical ones at that. Otherwise Europe will be destroyed by the Jewish sickness." On the same day he traveled on by car to Warsaw, where he arrived after an endless journey "across battlefields and past completely shattered villages and towns." "Warsaw is hell. A demolished city. Our bombs and shells have done their work well. Not a single house is left intact. The population is stunned and shadowy. People creep through the streets like insects. It is repulsive and almost indescribable." Standing on the destroyed fortress, Goebbels, who a few years earlier had prided himself on having contributed much to the improvement of German-Polish relations, was convinced that "Polish nationalism must be totally eradicated, otherwise it will arise again one day."[64]

On the very next day, Goebbels had a chance to give Hitler an oral account of his journey. "Above all, he was in complete agreement with my presentation of the Jewish problem. The Jews are a waste by-product. More a hygiene than a social matter."[65]

THE MUNICH ASSASSINATION ATTEMPT

On November 8, Goebbels joined in the annual Party ceremonies in Munich, sitting in the Bürgerbräukeller with "old campaigners" that night, listening to Hitler's incisive verbal reckoning with Britain. Immediately afterward, he took the night train back to Berlin with the dictator.

Passing Nuremberg, they were sitting chatting in the saloon of Hitler's special coach, when dire news was brought to them. Goebbels had to tell Hitler that "shortly after their departure from the beer cellar there had been an explosion, leaving 8 dead and 60 wounded." For Goebbels, the background was immediately obvious: "an assassination attempt, doubtless conceived in London and probably committed by Bavarian monarchists." Both immediately realized that Hitler would have fallen victim if he had not left the event earlier than originally planned. Goebbels was convinced: "The Almighty is guarding him. He will not die until his mission is complete."[66]

Goebbels's diaries document that in the next few days the Party leadership remained completely in the dark about the background of the attack.[67] However, this did not inhibit German propaganda from linking the attack to the British Secret Service.[68] After a few days the would-be assassin, a political loner, was arrested trying to cross the border into Switzerland, and it was established beyond doubt that he was the culprit. Hitler and Goebbels perceived him as a tool of Otto Strasser, who had emigrated to Switzerland and was then regarded as an instrument of the British Secret Service.[69] This impression was to be communicated to the public.[70] However, just a few days later, the propaganda effort reverted to its chief focus, the war that had begun but had now come to a standstill.

CHAPTER 20

"There Is Only One Sin: Cowardice!"

The Expansion of the War

Reception of troops in Berlin on July 18, 1940, following the French campaign (Goebbels with arm raised). During the war Goebbels was sometimes obliged to take part in public events that he was unable to organize according to his own ideas.

The last months of 1939 and the first months of 1940 passed without any spectacular political or major military events occurring. Following their declarations of war, the western powers had been unable to decide to mount an attack on the Reich, so there was hardly any movement or fighting on the Western Front. Goebbels used his proximity to Hitler to gather assiduously any information that might illuminate his views of the international situation and his future political and military plans. The remarkable diplomatic arrangements in which Germany found itself currently involved—the alliance with Stalin, who until recently had been regarded as the arch-enemy, and with Mussolini, who did not want to join in the war—posed additional problems for German propaganda.

Goebbels noted that while attending a small soirée in January—Magda was also among the guests—Hitler had indicated that he was "determined on a major war with England": "England must be swept out of Europe and France must be deposed as a great power. Then Germany will be dominant and Europe will have peace. That is our great, our eternal goal." After that, Hitler continued, he wanted "to stay in office for a few more years, carry out social reforms and his building projects and then withdraw."[1] A few days later Hitler talked about the "old Holy Empire," whose imperial traditions he intended to continue: "Given our organizational talents and our exceptional qualities it will be automatic that we eventually acquire world domination."[2]

But as yet this was a long way off. Hitler and Goebbels were particularly concerned about their awkward Italian ally.[3] At his meeting with Mussolini at the Brenner Pass on March 18, 1940—the first meeting of the two dictators since Munich—Hitler pursued the goal of trying to persuade Mussolini to enter the war without initiating him into his plans for an attack in the West in any concrete way.

On his return Hitler told Goebbels he had been "deeply impressed" by the "strong personality" of Il Duce: "Mussolini will be with us right to the end." However, Hitler appears to have concealed from Goebbels that, while the Italian dictator had responded positively in principle, he had not made any definite promise to enter the war.[4] Moreover, Goebbels was concerned not to make too much of the meeting in German propaganda reports in order not to feed rumors that Mussolini might be acting as a peace envoy.[5]

The alliance with the Soviet communists was an increasing pain for Hitler and his propaganda minister. The basic principle adopted for propaganda was "be cautious"; ideological topics should not be addressed either in a positive or in a negative sense.[6] In January Goebbels commented on a report he had received: "Terrible report from Lemberg [Lviv] about what the Soviet Russians are getting up to. They have no compassion. What's more, the Jews are still on top.

The troops are untrained and poorly equipped. It's unadulterated Bolshevism."[7]

The same issue came up at midday on the same day when Hitler told him that the evident backwardness of the Soviet Union under Stalin had significant advantages: "It's good for us. It's better to have a weak partner as one's neighbor than an alliance, however good it may be." In any case, as Hitler pointed out around two weeks later, the Russians were behaving in an "increasingly loyal way. And they have good reasons for doing so."[8] Two months later the Führer opined that it was good that "the Russians no longer have any Germanic leaders, so they can never be a threat to us. And if Stalin shoots his generals, then we won't have to do it ourselves. Is Stalin gradually also liquidating the Jews? Perhaps he's just bandying the word around in order to deceive the world. Trotskyists. Who knows?"[9]

Shortly afterward Goebbels read a book by the Soviet satirist Michail Sostschenko with the title, *Sleep Faster, Comrade!* He considered the stories to be above all "a terrible portrait of the Bolshevist lack of culture, social misery, and organizational incompetence." Disgusted, he continued: "We've really picked the best possible ally. If only we hadn't been up to our neck in it." On the other hand: "We are only having to fight on one front. And, when it comes to it, what have the social and cultural standards of Moscow Bolshevism got to do with us."[10]

In March, shortly after reading the book, he banned all "Russian books, positive and negative ones," because "at the moment they [can] only cause trouble."[11] Hitler adopted the same position when, in April, he objected to all attempts by the Foreign Ministry to start a German-Russian cultural exchange; Goebbels noted that that kind of thing must not go "beyond its political usefulness."[12]

At that time, the Propaganda Ministry's foreign propaganda operation was very much engaged in a rivalry with the Foreign Ministry. During the first months of 1940 the Propaganda Ministry objected strongly to the sending of liaison officers by the Foreign Ministry that had been agreed to in September 1939.[13] On the other hand, it was building up their own organization, "massively" according to Goebbels, in particular the Foreign Propaganda department and the radio broadcasts designed for foreign listeners.[14] Although this rivalry was intense, in fact the two ministries hardly differed from one another in terms of their ideas on what the propaganda should contain. This was because on all politically important matters they tried as much as possible to keep a low profile. They were not allowed to give concrete information about German war aims and postwar plans, so what remained were stereotypical phrases and accusations.[15]

In winter 1939–40 Britain was the main target of German propaganda, although France was no longer being "protected."[16] Comments by Hitler such as that he was determined to completely destroy the "Peace of Westphalia" and that he wanted to "beat England whatever it cost" confirmed Goebbels in his strongly anti-British attitude.[17]

Shortly before Christmas—the festival was on no account to be allowed to encourage a sentimental mood to develop[18]—Goebbels ordered the anti-British propaganda to be more geared to the slogan "Fight Against Plutocracy,"[19] and in fact, during the following months this topic very much came to the fore.[20] The fight against the "moneybags democracies" was to be augmented with anti-Semitic undertones, although despite all the anti-Semitic attacks, particularly in the Party press, this topic had not yet become a leitmotif in the German press.[21]

Goebbels was only informed about the preparations for the Western offensive, if at all, after some delay. At the end of January he learned from the Düsseldorf Gauleiter, Friedrich Karl Florian, that in fact the western offensive should have begun already but had been postponed because the relevant German plans had fallen into the hands of the Belgian authorities.[22]

There is an entry in the diary for March 13 that shows that Goebbels had been initiated into the preparations for the western offensive. The Army High Command's campaign plan had already been finalized more than two weeks earlier, and the attack was scheduled to begin in the middle of April. Goebbels noted: "It will be a tremendous blow. A fortnight until M[arne]. Then we'll have a breather. And then a second blow."[23] But the attack was postponed several times, as the German war plans were focusing on northern Europe.

WAR IN SCANDINAVIA

On April 7 there is the first mention in Goebbels's diary of an imminent "extension of the war" by Britain. It refers to the British plan—

the Norwegian government had been put in the picture by London—
to lay mines in Norwegian waters in order to disrupt German ship-
ping.[24] The British action appeared to play into the hands of German
policymakers, as Goebbels pointed out: "That's the excuse we were
looking for." In fact, however, at this point he was not yet aware of
how far German plans for extending the war to Scandinavia had already proceeded.[25]

In fact, from the end of 1939 onward, the Germans had been pursuing a plan to invade Norway and Denmark and thereby secure
control over the iron ore transportations that went via the Norwegian port of Narvik and use the Norwegian coast as a strategic base
for continuing the war against Britain.[26] It was only on April 8, the
day before the invasion of Norway and Denmark, that Hitler considered it fit to inform his propaganda minister about the impending
operation. When the German invasion troops had already left their
harbors he summoned Goebbels in order to explain his plans to him
during a walk. Impressed, the latter noted: "Everything has been prepared down to the last detail. The action will involve around 250,000
men. Most of the guns and ammunition have already been transported concealed in ships." Hitler appeared to be confident of victory.
Resistance "was inconceivable." But would the operation not have
repercussions in terms of America's attitude? According to Goebbels
he was "not interested in that at the moment. Its material aid would
only have an impact in around 8 months and, as far as people were
concerned"—a revealing utterance, that—"in around 1½ years." But,
Hitler explained to his propaganda minister, "we must achieve victory this year. Otherwise the other side's superiority in terms of
matériel would become too great. Also a long war would be difficult
to cope with psychologically."

Goebbels improvised—he had to. "Secretly and unnoticed got the
radio mobilized. Prepared quarters in the ministry. It's very difficult
to do because I can't talk to anyone. The main thing now is to keep it
secret, then afterward we can do things properly." The following day
he had his staff get "out of their beds" and explained the operation to
them, issuing guidelines as to how it was to be treated.[27]

The invasion of the two Scandinavian countries began in the early
morning. While the German troops succeeded in getting control of
Denmark on the same day, the operations in Norway came up against
much greater difficulties. The plan for a rapid takeover of Oslo by a

combined air and sea operation failed, giving the Norwegian government time to organize military resistance and escape from the Wehrmacht. The landings in the other Norwegian ports were largely
successful, but this success came at the cost of heavy losses by the
German navy. All in all, the surprise attack had failed: The expeditionary force found itself caught up in fighting that was to last until
June; it probably ended in victory only because of the successful campaign in western Europe. In addition, looked at over the medium and
longer term, because of the significant weakening of the navy as a
result of the operation, the bases could not be strategically exploited
and the extensive Norwegian merchant fleet had gone over to the
enemy camp.[28]

On the morning of April 9 Goebbels had the task of reading out
the German memoranda communicated to the Danish and Norwegian governments: "Our well-known position: protection for Copen-
hagen and Oslo. Oslo is still resisting."[29] On the same day Goebbels
issued detailed guidelines for the "protective custody of Scandinavia"; that these contained, to put it mildly, certain flaws in their arguments is clear from the directive that he issued to his staff at the same
time, namely that "this line about protective custody should not be
questioned by you, let alone be ridiculed."[30]

On the following day Hitler outlined to Goebbels his thoughts on
the future of the two occupied countries. He did not want a "protectorate, more an alliance. Uniform foreign, economic, and customs
policies. We shall acquire the most important military bases as our
own property, take over their protection, and the two states will cease
having any armed forces. The aim: a north-Germanic confedera-
tion."[31]

On the same day—it was the third day of the invasion—in view of
the losses Goebbels felt obliged to instruct German propaganda to be
less defensive about the question of Norway: Success was what
counted; losses would have to be accepted.[32] "Propaganda: with Denmark tact, discretion, no pushiness, emphasis on the particular character of the Danes and its legitimacy; no talk of a protectorate etc.
Whereas with Norway: senselessness of resistance. Example of Poland. We want peace. Nothing can alter the facts. This will get us
through for the time being."[33]

It soon became apparent, however, that the invasion of Norway
was not going as smoothly as Hitler and his propaganda minister had

anticipated.[34] On April 13 a unit of the Royal Navy succeeded in pen-etrating the Narvik fjord and sinking eight German destroyers or forcing them to scuttle.[35] The Germans were forced to the defensive both militarily and in terms of their propaganda.[36]

On April 16, when Goebbels made his midday visit to Hitler, he found him looking "very serious."[37] He was very hesitant in mention-ing the news of the loss of the destroyers: "We praise the heroism of our navy that will go down in German history." He admitted, how-ever, that "people were getting a bit worried about our secrecy."[38]

On April 20 the Reich Chancellery celebrated Hitler's birthday. After the congratulations and a big meal, Goebbels took part in a discussion in a small group in which Hitler outlined his next goals: "Italy seems to want to intervene. It can't avoid it." England, on the other hand, appeared not "to have any idea of the seriousness of its situation. The Führer intends to give it a knock-out blow. And never-theless he would make peace this very day. Condition: England must leave Europe and return our colonies, but rounded up. [. . .] He doesn't want to crush England at all or destroy its empire."[39]

In addition to the lack of clarity about the military situation in the north of the country, Goebbels was also concerned about political developments in Oslo. On April 24 his old comrade Josef Terboven, the longtime Gauleiter of Essen, had been appointed Reich commis-sioner in Norway. Terboven's main problem turned out to be the ap-pointment of a new government in Norway. Vidkun Quisling, the leader of the small Norwegian Nazi party who had peremptorily ap-pointed himself prime minister on April 9 but then resigned a few days later, considered himself the right candidate for the job, a view supported by Alfred Rosenberg.[40]

Whereas Terboven was working for a political solution without Quisling, Goebbels wanted at least to hold him in reserve; on the occasion of a short visit to Berlin on April 25 Terboven agreed to this.[41] Goebbels also spoke to Rosenberg in favor of Quisling: He was "a greater German patriot,"[42] they should not drop him completely. During the coming months Goebbels's view of Quisling would fluc-tuate.[43]

Toward the end of the month, the military situation appeared to be gradually improving from the German point of view. German troops succeeded in advancing from the Oslo area toward Trond-heim, where in the meantime a German expeditionary force had been cornered by British and French troops; these were now forced to re-embark.[44] The situation in Narvik in the north of Norway, where British and French troops had landed at the end of April and were soon to be reinforced, was still giving cause for concern.[45] Gobbels was already assuming that the three thousand men based there would inevitably be interned in Sweden.[46] Thus the official propaganda line was: "Narvik should never be mentioned and on no account be turned into a matter of prestige."[47]

WAR IN THE WEST

A few days before the start of the war in the west, Hitler once again explained his policy to Goebbels: "England must be given a major blow but not destroyed. For we can't and don't want to take over its empire. So much wealth wouldn't even make one happy."[48]

Goebbels spent May 9 largely in the company of his Italian colleague, Alessandro Pavolini, who had come to Berlin in order to coordinate Italian and German propaganda. The day was taken up with meetings and sightseeing, followed by a visit to the State Theater for a performance of Mussolini's play Cavour; afterward there was a reception at the Haus der Flieger (Pilots' House). Goebbels spent the following night in the ministry, since nothing much new was happening: "The Führer is determined to launch the attack in the west. It is taking place in great secrecy."[49] During the night he and Dietrich decided on "how our publications will handle it."[50]

The following morning Goebbels read out on the radio the text of the memoranda the Reich government had sent to the governments in Brussels and The Hague a few hours earlier. They accused the Netherlands and Luxembourg of breaching neutrality and demanded that all three governments offer no resistance to the German troops.[51] Meanwhile, his high-ranking Italian visitor had to cool his heels: "I ditch the whole program with Pavolini. He'll have to look after himself for a bit. I entrust him to Esser."

The war began on May 10 with a series of spectacular and generally successful German commando raids against Belgian and Dutch bridges and fortresses; other paratroop operations, such as the attempt to capture the Dutch government quarters in The Hague, proved unsuccessful.[52]

On the first day of the war the city of Freiburg had already suffered an air raid that killed twenty-four people. After initial hesitation, Hitler decided to use the raid for a big propaganda campaign, threatening the western powers with massive retaliation. Goebbels, who made occasional references in his diary to the "terrible consequences" of the raid, wanted to go on "exploiting" the incident, but the Luftwaffe was wary of doing so because it wanted to secure air superiority before making any threats of retaliation. Although Goebbels was certainly aware of it, he did not make any mention in his diary of the fact that the bombs had been dropped by German planes by mistake. As far as he was concerned, the official lie that was being put out was inviolable fact.[53]

Right at the start Goebbels used a ministerial briefing to lay down certain basic ground rules for the way propaganda should deal with the campaign. Thus, on May 10 he instructed that "during the conflict in the west the press [should] neither go in for exaggerated optimism nor indulge in panic mongering."[54] On the following day he ordered that all usable material should be put together for foreign news outlets; in the current situation "news [is] more important than polemics." Moreover, "any enemy reports that are not accurate or can be at all dangerous for us" should be immediately and decisively denied; there was no need to check "whether or not the details of the report [are] true."[55] He was pleased at Churchill's appointment as British prime minister: "Clear battle lines: That's what we like."[56] During the following weeks he devoted considerable attention to studying Churchill's personality, read some of his speeches, and concluded that the man was "a strange mixture of heroism and triviality. If he had come to power in 1933 we wouldn't be where we are today. Moreover, I believe that he will be a hard nut to crack."[57] The rest of the war would give him little reason to alter this assessment.[58]

Meanwhile the German invasion had been making progress. While on May 15 the 18th Army forced the Dutch armed forces to capitulate, on May 13 and 14 the tanks of the 4th and 12th Armies had crossed the Meuse and now were making major advances toward the west in a sickle cut formation. On May 20 they reached the mouth of the Somme and thereby prevented the British and French forces in Belgium from retreating back into France.[59]

Goebbels followed the announcements of these victories with great enthusiasm; he informed himself of the current situation through daily telephone conversations with Dietrich at the Führer's headquarters. The basic propaganda line during the war was "quite clear: At home celebrate victory [. . .] abroad create panic and confusion."[60] The "secret stations" broadcasting from German radio stations played a special role: They claimed to represent opposition groups in the enemy countries and were intended to create confusion and cause demoralization. During the first days of the campaign they broadcast "subversive propaganda to the Netherlands and Belgium";[61] a few days later the emphasis was on "panic propaganda" aimed at Britain and, in particular, France.[62] Goebbels noted that he wrote "most of the commentaries" for the radio propaganda himself, and "I very carefully supervise the others."[63]

At the end of May, after Belgium's capitulation and with Hitler's encouragement, he increased the output of the secret stations targeted at France and unleashed a wave of anti-French propaganda within Germany.[64] At the beginning of June Dunkirk fell after more than three hundred thousand British and French troops had managed to escape over the Channel to Britain. After this came the second phase of the war in the west. Goebbels noted: "The aim is for France's total defeat."[65]

Goebbels now concentrated on the secret radio station "Humanité," which claimed to be staffed by French communists. He hoped that it would produce revolutionary unrest, particularly in Paris, which was now within striking distance of the Wehrmacht. Goebbels had compelled several communists, including the former head of the KPD Reichstag parliamentary group, Ernst Torgler, who had already been given a few jobs by the regime,[66] to write scripts for the station.[67] His decision to do this was evidently influenced by a sense of triumph over his former opponents. On June 8 he noted: "I have a funny feeling about instructing our former dangerous opponents in how to write our propaganda."

Paris fell on June 14.[68] Hitler ordered "3 days of putting out the flags and bell ringing."[69] On June 17 Marshal Philippe Pétain took over the French government and on the same day Hitler informed Goebbels on the telephone of France's capitulation.[70] Goebbels's interpretation of the French request for an armistice on June 17 as a "capitulation" was naturally not a misunderstanding but the official line. On June 18 he instructed the media "to nip in the bud" all attempts by the French "to turn what had been a capitulation into some kind of amiable surrender arrangement."[71] Two days earlier he had ordered that France must "once and for all [be excluded] from Europe as a power that has to be taken seriously. [. . .] For this reason we must deal a lethal blow to France's national honor and pride."[72] For the time being, however, the military operations in France were continuing, so Goebbels geared his propaganda to deal with that.[73]

Finally, Hitler ordered that negotiations should take place at Compiègne in Marshal Ferdinand Foch's historic railway coach in which, on November 11, 1918, a German delegation had signed the armistice. Goebbels issued the following instructions for the ceremony: "No demonstrative humiliation, but the disgrace of November 1918 must be erased."[74] The negotiations in Compiègne began on June 21; to begin with, Hitler attended in person but left Keitel to lead the discussions. The negotiations continued until the following evening, with the propaganda minister nervously following the proceedings.[75] The treaty that finally emerged established the German occupation of the majority of French territory and the substantial demobilization and disarming of the French armed forces, with the exception of the navy.[76] On June 22 Goebbels ordered an announcement that the war had ended to be broadcast on all radio stations: "With a prayer of thanksgiving. Very grand and solemn. Then the final report from Compiègne. So much historical greatness comes as quite a shock."[77]

AFTER THE VICTORY OVER FRANCE

At the end of June Goebbels went on a trip through the conquered territories in the west. To begin with he flew—"over fat Dutch soil"— to The Hague, "a clean, attractive, and cozy city," and was briefed about the situation in the country by his staff who had been deployed to the occupied Netherlands.[78] He then traveled on to Brussels via Antwerp and Louvain. Belgium, he noted, was "not quite as clean as Holland," but here too, as in the Netherlands, he claimed to find a "positive" mood on the part of the population.

On the early morning of the following day he visited various First World War battlefields ("sites of heroic struggles"), including Ypres, Langemarck, and Arras. He looked around Dunkirk and visited Compiègne, "a site of disgrace and of national resurrection." In the evening he arrived in Paris. His first impression: "A marvelous city. What a lot we've still got to do to Berlin!"[79] On the following day he took time out for an extensive sightseeing tour of the city: "It's like a dream. Place de la Concorde, the Étoile. Very generously laid out. The Invalides. Napoleon's tomb. Very moved. In spite of everything a great man. Notre Dame. Rather absurd architecture for a church, like the Madeleine." He was rather disappointed by Sacré-Cœur, but he very much liked the view from Montmartre: "I'd like to live here for a few weeks." He set aside the afternoon for a visit to Versailles, which for him was above all a place "where Germany [had been] condemned to death."

During his visit he received a telegram summoning him to Hitler's headquarters near Freudenstadt in the Black Forest. When he arrived there the next day, the dictator outlined to him his plan to address the Reichstag and "to give England a last chance." Britain, according to Hitler, could be "defeated in 4 weeks," but it was not his intention to destroy the empire, for "what it will lose in the process is likely to end up not in our hands but in those of foreign great powers." Hitler assumed that by making a peace offer he would be putting "England in a difficult psychological situation, but it [might] also bring about peace." There was "much to be said for and against both."[80]

The first thing to do was to provide Hitler with a terrific reception in Berlin. The greeting of the "victorious Führer" in the Reich capital was one of the most spectacular mass demonstrations that Goebbels had ever orchestrated. Nothing was left to chance in order to convey to the German people and the world at large the impression that the people of Berlin were standing behind the regime as one man and were full of confidence in victory and genuine enthusiasm for the war. The impression made by this demonstration was so strong that even skeptical and critical observers in Germany could not escape its attraction; even decades later historians interpreted it as proof that there had been "genuine enthusiasm" for the war in the country: Hitler had allegedly appeared to the Germans as a "super figure."[81]

In fact, however, the mass enthusiasm was perfectly choreographed, for which the Propaganda Ministry had worked out an elaborate "working plan."[82] In an announcement that appeared in the press on July 6, was distributed by the Party organization, and then reinforced by appeals through "house propaganda,"[83] Goebbels called on the population to greet Hitler "in our million strong city" with "unparalleled enthusiasm." "In a few hours the city will be a sea of flags. [. . .] At 12 o'clock midday factories and shops will close. [. . .] The workers of Berlin will march in closed ranks to the road along which the Führer will drive from the Anhalt Railway Station [. . .] to the Reich Chancellery. No one will want to stay at home, everybody will want to be swept along by the terrific enthusiasm that this afternoon will fill our beloved Reich capital."[84]

The *Völkischer Beobachter*'s report on this spectacle reveals further details of how it was organized: During the night, eight thousand people worked to decorate the streets that Hitler was going to drive down the following day. The walls of the houses were garlanded, flag poles erected, and additional poles fixed to the roofs. In the early morning the Party units that were being deployed to control the crowds marched into the city center and were followed at 10 o'clock by the Hitler Youth and League of German Girls (Bund Deutscher Mädel, BDM), who were assigned to fill the front rows of the spectators.

The fact that factories and shops closed at 12 o'clock did not mean that employees had a free afternoon; on the contrary, they were shepherded en masse to particular points: The *Völkischer Beobachter* described how in the early afternoon the workers marched out of their work places in long processions. But it was not only the workers who were being dragooned: The Propaganda Ministry's instructions stated that "the population will assemble along the road designated for the celebration in accordance with a special plan; the celebratory stretch is to be divided into assembly sections and sub-sections, which will invariably be filled via a side street."[85] Anyone who thought they could escape the celebration was informed by the press that on that day the transportation company had canceled schedules to local vacation destinations and the swimming pools would be closed until the evening.

Photos of the event show flower-bedecked streets, indeed a carpet of flowers on which Hitler's Mercedes drove to the Reich Chancellery. But this sea of flowers was not a product of the spontaneous enthusiasm of the "national comrades" but rather was the result of good organization. The flowers had been ordered from the Berlin Allotments' Association.[86] The *Völkischer Beobachter* reported on their distribution as follows: "Large trucks arrive at every street corner full to the brim with the most magnificent flowers. Crowds of

BDM girls and Hitler Youth stand ready to spread these flowers over the road minutes before the Führer's arrival providing him with a unique kilometer-long carpet of flowers."[87]

Hitler was expected around 3 o'clock in the afternoon at the Anhalt Station. Goebbels described the scene in his diary, absolutely carried away by the spectacle organized by his department: "Within an hour of my announcement Berlin is on the move. When I arrive at the Wilhelmstrasse in the morning it is already full of people. So they are going to wait six hours for the Führer. [. . .] Then the Führer arrives. A storm of applause fills the station. The Führer is very moved. He has tears in his eyes. Our Führer! Ride through the streets to the Chancellery. It is impossible to describe the huge enthusiasm of a happy people. The Führer rides over nothing but flowers. Our people, our wonderful people!"[88]

CHAPTER 21

"Our Banners Lead Us on to Victory!"

Between the War in the West and the War in the East

On October 21, 1940, Goebbels inspects houses destroyed in the air war. The first air raids on Berlin in 1940, which caused comparatively little damage, were used as the pretext for the Blitz on London.

After Hitler's July 19 "peace offer" to Britain—his "appeal that even Britain should come to its senses"[1]—was rejected, there was a lengthy phase when Goebbels received little information about Hitler's political and military ambitions. He was only on the periphery of the soundings taken by Hitler as to whether it might be possible to form a European alliance aimed against Britain. By contrast he learned nothing about the alternative plan that was increasingly taking shape in Hitler's mind of attacking the Soviet Union in order not only to eliminate the Bolshevist arch-enemy but also to crush Britain's last potential ally on the continent.

During the remaining summer months, unburdened by such far-reaching strategic calculations going on behind his back, Goebbels concentrated entirely on the main task assigned to him by Hitler: Providing the accompanying propaganda for the air offensive that was designed to force Britain to surrender. The watchword that Goebbels gave to his staff in this new round of the conflict with Britain was: "Don't attack the people, attack the plutocracy. [. . .] In the process spread panic, suspicion, and horror."[2]

On July 24 Hitler told Goebbels that he was planning to launch massive air raids on Britain.[3] But at first the dictator hesitated. Final attempts to put out "feelers" to Britain via third-party states failed.[4] On August 4 Hitler summoned Goebbels to the Reich Chancellery: "He has decided to get tougher. Large-scale air raids on England impending. Accompanied by a barrage of propaganda to the English people that I'm to prepare and carry out."[5]

British air defenses were to be tested by major air raids combined with long-range guns based on the Channel coast. If the losses proved too much, the raids would be broken off and "new approaches would be tried." But the dictator made it quite clear to his propaganda minister: "No invasion planned," although propaganda should encourage fears of invasion by dropping hints "in order to confuse the enemy."[6]

The dictator's continued hesitation and poor weather ensured that the attack would once again be postponed.[7] Goebbels recorded the events of the next few days in minute detail: After the first major air battles over the Channel, from August 11 onward the Luftwaffe increasingly focused on targets in Britain. On August 13 the first big raid, which had been long in planning, was launched with almost 1,500 aircraft sorties and, over the following days, it was continued on a massive scale.[8] However, the German plans were increasingly hampered by fog and poor weather; large-scale raids could be resumed only toward the end of the month.[9]

The flip side of the coin was the advent of increased British raids on the Reich. After German squadrons had bombed residential areas in the East End of London, according to Goebbels an air raid warning lasting four hours on August 24 had put "the whole of Berlin in a state of turmoil" without the bombs causing significant damage.[10]

Two days later, twelve British planes turned up over the city and dropped several bombs, causing ten fatalities.[11] On September 5, after further British raids, he learned from Hitler: "The Führer is fed up and has now permitted London to be bombed at will."[12] In the meantime, a ring of antiaircraft batteries had been established around Berlin that promised to provide improved protection from further retaliatory attacks.[13]

In September, in response to the reports from London ("frightful," "an inconceivably huge inferno"), Goebbels had reached the conclusion that Britain would soon capitulate: "A city with 8 million people can't cope with that for long."[14] He was already busy setting up a propaganda unit for London.[15]

Goebbels now gave instructions for propaganda to make more of the attacks on Berlin: "Make a huge thing of it in order to provide us with moral alibis for our massive raids on London."[16] Now German newspapers increasingly carried pictures of and reports on the destruction of civilian targets. On September 12, for example, the *Völkischer Beobachter* reported that "national monuments, hospitals, and residential areas" were the targets of the British air pirates. "We shall take revenge for that," the paper reassured its readers.[17]

On September 23, during his midday visit to Hitler, Goebbels learned that an invasion was impossible without "absolute command of the air," and "at the moment there was no question of that."[18] In fact, a few days earlier Hitler had postponed Operation Sea Lion, as the ambitious plan to invade Britain was called, indefinitely.[19]

On September 26 or 27 Hitler instructed Bormann to see to the evacuation of children from cities under threat from air raids. This directive launched the Extended Children's Evacuation Program. What was in reality an evacuation to prepare for air war was portrayed as merely an extension of the program already in operation for improving children's health by sending city children to the countryside.[20]

In Berlin an early announcement by the National Socialist Welfare Organization responsible for the program caused concern: The population gained the impression that the children were to be compulsorily removed from their parents, which was not in fact intended. Goebbels was concerned about the alarm provoked in the population. Initially he tried to reassure people by launching a big campaign by the Party and then made an announcement in the press. The whole affair showed how worried the population was about the air war, which was only just beginning.[21]

The unrest among the Berlin population was also due to the fact that the city administration had been in a bad state for a long time. Goebbels, as its power-hungry Gauleiter, was not prepared to tolerate a strong personality at the head of the city government. In 1933 he had appointed his old colleague on *Der Angriff,* Julius Lippert, as "state commissioner" to control the city administration. Despite his considerable doubts about Lippert's capabilities[22] (among other things, he called him "old sleepyhead," "puppet")[23] in 1936 Goebbels had agreed to appoint him to succeed Heinrich Sahm, Berlin's German nationalist Oberbürgermeister (mayor), who had stepped down the previous year. A law of December 1936 had combined Lippert's position—in the meantime he called himself "City President"—with the office of Oberbürgermeister. The law permitted Goebbels as Gauleiter of Berlin to be consulted before decisions of "fundamental importance" were made, in other words a right to intervene that was not defined in concrete terms.[24]

However, even with his increased authority, Goebbels was still not content with Lippert. In August 1938 the tension between them reached a high point: In a long conversation Goebbels endeavored to make clear to him "all the mistakes and omissions that had been made in Berlin," but Lippert, "a real numbskull with the stature of a Mecklenburg village mayor," simply would not listen. Goebbels pondered whether he ought to appoint a commissioner with special powers above Lippert.[25] During the following months he continued to express dissatisfaction with Lippert as well as with his deputy Gauleiter, Artur Görlitzer.[26] But he did not want to dismiss them; he was presumably happy with the fact that the city and Gau administrations were both headed by relatively weak figures.

During the course of 1940, however, his criticism of Lippert increased. In May 1940 he issued "severe reproaches" to Lippert for "Berlin's disorganization." Above all, Goebbels was annoyed with the "unpleasant lines in front of shops," which had to be avoided at all costs.[27] The public image of the capital must on no account be marred by the shortages caused by the war. Finally, after a long period of in-fighting[28] Hitler accepted Lippert's resignation.[29] Goebbels and Hitler now considered whether once again to separate the two combined functions of City President and Oberbürgermeister. But what "significant figure" could stay the course with Goebbels as Gauleiter? For the time being Goebbels and Hitler were unable to find a solution to this problem.[30] And so for several years Bürgermeister Ludwig Steeg, Lippert's deputy, officiated as acting Oberbürgermeister and City President.

DIPLOMATIC INTERMEZZO

By the end of July 1940 Hitler had already told his military commanders to prepare plans for war with the Soviet Union. This was prompted by the belief that quickly crushing the Soviet Union, whose military was generally considered to be weak, would cause Britain to lose its last potential ally on the continent and thereby be forced to make peace. These were not, however, the only strategic considerations that underpinned this decision: The "Bolshevist" Soviet Union was Hitler's real arch-enemy; in his view the pact with the Soviet Union could not last forever. Hitler would have preferred to start the war in the autumn of 1940 but had to take account of the concerns of his military leaders and postpone it to the following spring.[31]

Hitler evidently did not inform his propaganda minister at all about these plans. For Goebbels, who after his conversations with Hitler always conscientiously recorded all the Führer's comments about his foreign policy and military plans, does not report anything in his 1940 diaries about concrete plans for an attack on the Soviet Union. Rather, Goebbels's entries in his diary for August 1940 show that Hitler intentionally left him in the dark about his war plans. Thus on August 9 their conversation touched on the "terror regime" that the Soviet occupation forces had imposed on the Baltic states. Goebbels noted: "Bolshevism is world enemy No. 1. One day we shall clash with it. The Führer thinks so too."[32] But the dictator did not initiate Goebbels into his war plans: When it came to devising strategies for the continuation of the war, he was not Hitler's trusted adviser but his propaganda minister.

Even when some days later Goebbels learned of substantial troop deployments to the east, he did not connect them with an impending military operation: "Reason: insecurity in the west because of air raids. In reality on the principle: better to be safe than sorry."[33] A few days later when he banned his department from making "any over-tures to Russia" he did so knowing that conflict with the Soviet Union was inevitable, but the date for it seemed to him uncertain, a long way off: "One day we must settle accounts with Russia. When, I don't know, but I do know it will happen."[34]

Hitler's plans for war with the Soviet Union were, however, only one of several options. At first he had, as we have seen, tried to defeat Britain militarily through massive air raids and even, conceivably, through an invasion. In September, however, this project had proved impossible for the foreseeable future. Before Hitler committed himself definitively in December 1940 to an attack on the Soviet Union, between September and December he had toyed with a third option, an alternative scenario through which to defeat Britain: This was Foreign Minister Ribbentrop's idea of constructing a "continental bloc" against Britain—if necessary including the Soviet Union.[35] The Tripartite Pact, the military alliance between Germany, Italy, and Japan, initiated by Hitler and signed at the end of September, offered a basis for this. German policy initially focused on trying to reduce tensions in the Balkans and on bringing a few nations in southeastern Europe into the pact: Following the Vienna Award, which forced Romania to cede territory to Hungary at the end of August 1940, Romania, Hungary, and Slovakia were admitted into the Tripartite Pact in November and, during the following months, Bulgaria and Yugoslavia were courted.

In order to expand the "bloc" still further, between September and December 1940 Hitler and his foreign minister met representatives of states that might be possible partners in the alliance against Britain: It was intended that Spain should join the Axis (and enable the Reich to conquer Gibraltar from the land side), that France should become actively involved in the war with Britain, and that arrangements would be made with their ally, Italy, as to what role the "new" partners, France and Spain, would play in the Mediterranean. Finally, the main problem facing the future "continental bloc" was the demarcation of interests with the Soviet Union.

Goebbels's diary entries show that while during these months he was informed of particular diplomatic steps by Hitler, as far as the major lines of foreign policy were concerned he remained in the dark. He was neither given the full picture of the overall diplomatic project that lay behind the negotiations of these months, nor was he aware that the idea of a continental bloc that was gradually taking shape was just one option that Hitler was simply trying out, whereas the fact that the continental bloc proved not to be feasible relatively quickly strengthened Hitler in his determination to seek a final show-down with the Soviet Union. Goebbels remained to a large extent unaware of Hitler's return to his original fundamental goals.

But let us return to the late summer of 1940, in other words to the point when Hitler began his foreign policy experiment. Goebbels was informed relatively early about Italy's plans to extend the war in the Balkans, as is shown by his diary entry for August 24: "Italy wanted to intervene in Yugoslavia and Greece," he wrote, but Hitler "expressed the wish that they not do that. We must defeat England. That is the first and most important task." The Italians acceded to Hitler's wish, but only for two months.[36]

At the beginning of September Goebbels noted mysteriously in his diary that Hitler still had "a few irons in the fire, which at the moment cannot be spoken or written about. Herr Churchill will have a surprise."[37] But he does not appear to have been informed about what these "irons" were. Thus, he was not told about the conclusion of the Tripartite Pact, which established the "axis" uniting Germany, Italy, and Japan until September 27, the evening before it was signed.[38]

Goebbels did not learn any details about the conversations Hitler had with Mussolini at the Brenner Pass on October 4 apart from the fact that the result had been "good, as I was told by telephone."[39] On the other hand, since the visit of the Spanish interior minister, Ramón Serrano Suñer, in the middle of September,[40] Goebbels had been in-formed about the German-Spanish plans for a military coup against Gibraltar on which the Wehrmacht had been working since July.[41] On October 23 Hitler met the Spanish dictator at the Franco-Spanish border in Hendaye in order to negotiate the planned alliance.[42] On his return Hitler told Goebbels only that he had "not formed a good opinion [of Franco]. A lot of talk, but little will. No substance."[43] On December 4 he noted that the attack was "to go ahead in about 3 weeks."[44] But three days later Franco canceled it,[45] which Goebbels did not note in his diary until nearly two weeks after the fact.[46]

During his journey to Spain in October, Hitler had stopped off twice in the town of Montoire in southern France in order to negoti-ate with the French government. On October 22 he met Pierre Laval, and after his meeting with Franco on October 24 he met Pétain and

Laval.[47] "This is the start of the new major development," he commented meaningfully on the negotiations.[48] He was not informed of the details of the conversations,[49] but after a few days he was convinced that Vichy had "accepted": "That means France is in the continental bloc. London is absolutely isolated."[50]

In fact the results of Montoire were exceedingly meager: There could be no question of France's having agreed to join in a war against Britain as part of a continental bloc led by Germany. That Goebbels had gained this impression shows the extent to which he was excluded from the actual diplomatic negotiations that were going on during these weeks.[51]

At the end of October 1940, during the return journey from the south of France Hitler had met Mussolini in Florence. During this meeting he learned that, despite his express wishes, the Italians had decided to attack Greece. As a result, the Balkans threatened to become a trouble spot directly contradicting the idea of a united continental bloc.[52]

The Italian action had been prompted by the fact that, responding to a Romanian request, the Germans had sent a military mission to Romania in October 1940. Their main aim had been to secure the Romanian oil fields. Feeling surprised and somewhat duped by this German action, the Italians now decided to push ahead with the Balkan plans that had long been in preparation and to attack Greece from Albania. Goebbels commented laconically on the surprising move by Il Duce: "He too is trying to get what he can."[53] The advance soon came to a halt, however, and the Italian forces had to retreat back into Albania. The German leadership now believed that they had to intervene if they were to prevent Britain from becoming involved in the conflict and establishing itself in the Balkans.[54] It is clear from various entries in the diaries that from December 1940 onward Goebbels was informed about the German military intervention in Greece.[55]

Foreign Minister Vyacheslav Molotov's visit to Berlin in the middle of November represented the high point of the diplomatic negotiations in autumn 1940. Goebbels, who ensured that the visit went ahead without much participation by the Berlin population, had resolved to "keep somewhat in the background" during the visit.[56] However, this unusual display of modesty on the part of the propaganda minister did not derive from his own decision to keep a low profile; it was simply that Goebbels was excluded from the decisive conversations.

He took part only in a midday diplomatic "breakfast" in the Reich Chancellery on November 13 and used the opportunity to make some psychological observations about the Soviet visitors. Above all he noted "mutual fear and inferiority complexes": "The GPU is keeping an eye on them." He concluded that cooperation with Moscow must "in the future as well be [governed] solely by considerations of expediency": "The more we move closer together politically, the more alien we shall become spiritually and ideologically. And that's a good thing!"[57]

The German government was disappointed by the visit: Molotov responded to the German invitation to join the anti-British pact and to participate in the destruction of the British Empire by taking over territory in Asia by asking pointed questions and making requests concerning the future demarcation of German and Soviet interests in Europe. Hitler concluded from all of this that the German-Soviet alliance would inevitably collapse sooner or later as a result of the insuperable clash of interests and reverted to his plan for a war against the Soviet Union.[58]

Goebbels knew nothing about any of this. After a conversation with Hitler at the beginning of December he established that the Führer agreed with him that Russia would "never undertake anything against us"—"out of fear," he added.[59] Goebbels was, however, not aware of the consequences that Hitler was drawing from the purported Soviet weakness: Two days after this conversation with Goebbels Hitler was discussing the plans for the eastern campaign with his military leaders.[60]

PLANS FOR THE DEPORTATION OF THE GERMAN JEWS

After the victory over France, German "Jewish policy" acquired a new momentum, not least owing to Goebbels's initiative. For Goebbels saw the opportunity at last to begin the forcible expulsion of the Jews from Berlin, a goal that he had been pursuing since 1935. Now that the Third Reich controlled most of the European continent, the time seemed ripe for the final "de-jewification" (Entjudung) of Berlin.

Such a radical step would have a marked effect on Jewish policy throughout the Reich. In any case Goebbels was determined to play a pioneering role in the radicalization of Jewish policy during the war as well.

On July 19, 1940, he discussed with Hitler among other things the fact that the Jews were numbered among the "habitual criminals" and that they should "make short work" of them. A few hours earlier Leopold Gutterer, a department head in the Propaganda Ministry, had reported at a ministerial meeting that on the previous day, during the ceremonial entry of the Berlin division returning from France, "the same riff raff could be seen as always strolling" along the Kurfürstendamm. Goebbels seized on this remark and announced, "Immediately after the end of the war all the 62,000 Jews still living in Berlin [are] to be deported to Poland within a time span of a maximum of eight weeks"; as long as they were still living in Berlin, they would have a negative impact on morale in the capital. Berlin, according to Goebbels, should be the first German city to be made "free of Jews" (judenfrei). Hans Hinkel, the person in the ministry who was most involved with the "de-jewification" of German cultural life, was able to report that they had already worked out a "removal plan" with the police.[61]

Five days later Goebbels brought up the topic with Hitler, who approved his comments.[62] On the following day Goebbels was already noting that he had "approved a large-scale plan for the evacuation of the Jews from Berlin. Moreover, after the war all the Jews are going to be deported to Madagascar. It will then become a German protectorate under a German police governor."[63]

At the beginning of September 1940 Hinkel once again reported to the ministerial meeting on the deportation plans for the Berlin and Viennese Jews. The plan now was to send "ca. 500 Jews to the southeast" each month, immediately after the end of the war a further sixty thousand within four weeks.[64] It is clear that these deportation plans were based on the Madagascar project,[65] which in the meantime had begun to take on a clearer shape as a result of further planning in the Foreign Ministry and the Reich Security Main Office.

In October Gauleiters Baldur von Schirach (Vienna) and Erich Koch (East Prussia) demanded further deportations to the General

Government.*[66] At the beginning of November Hitler decided to deport 150,000 to 160,000 Jews and Poles from the annexed territories to the General Government in order to make room for the settlement of ethnic Germans, called *Volksdeutsche*.[67] On the same day the functionaries who were affected—Gauleiters Koch and Wilhelm Forster (West Prussia) and the Governor General, Hans Frank—argued about the deportation quotas at a meeting with Hitler. "The Führer, laughing, makes peace" between them, Goebbels noted in his diary. "They all want to get rid of their rubbish into the General Government. Jews, the sick, the idle, etc. And Frank objects to this." Poland, according to Goebbels's report of Hitler's statements, was to "become a big reservoir of labor: Frank doesn't like it, but he'll have to put up with it. And one day we'll shove the Jews out of this area too."

During the end of 1940 and the beginning of 1941, Hitler gave Heydrich the task of drawing up an overall plan for the deportation of all the Jews in the territories controlled by the Germans after the war, and a few weeks later Heydrich produced a plan (it has not survived), which, according to a few important pieces of evidence, envisaged ultimately deporting the Jews living in the German sphere of influence to the Soviet Union.[68] In the middle of March 1941 Goebbels, who presumably had not been informed about the details of these plans, received the impression during one of his lunchtime visits to Hitler that the deportations from Berlin were about to begin.[69] Adolf Eichmann, the "Jewish expert" of the Reich Security Main Office, was invited to speak at the ministerial conference about the practical problems created by the deportations and then requested to work out further details.[70] Soon afterward, however, Goebbels discovered that the deportations could not be carried out quickly because the Berlin armaments industry was in urgent need of labor.[71] He had to get used to the idea that a significant number of Jews would continue to live in Berlin for quite some time.

On the other hand, on the basis of reports from occupied Poland, Goebbels had acquired a very good idea of what "Jewish policy" really involved at this juncture. He knew that thousands of Polish Jews had been the victims of German murder squads. In March 1941 he felt compelled to do something to prevent the morale of his propaganda experts from being damaged: "I am forbidding our people

---

* Translators' note: The General Government (Generalgouvernement) was the part of Poland that was not annexed to Germany or (until 1941) to the Soviet Union.

to view Jewish executions. The person who makes the laws and supervises their implementation should not witness them being actually carried out. That will weaken their mental powers of resistance."[72]

THE PROPAGANDA MACHINE DURING THE WAR

The start of the war had brought about several personnel changes in the radio and film branches of the mass media. Shortly before the beginning of the war Goebbels had appointed a new head of the radio department within the Propaganda Ministry in the shape of Alfred-Ingemar Berndt, the previous head of the press department. However, in February 1940 he had to resign after a major dispute with the head of Reich radio and of the Reich Broadcasting Corporation (RRG), Heinrich Glasmeier. His successor was one of the directors of the RRG, Reich Chief of Broadcasting Eugen Hadamovsky, who continued to hold his previous position.[73] At the same time, Goebbels reduced Glasmeier's responsibilities against the latter's strong opposition, calling him "stubborn as a mule."[74]

The new distribution of responsibilities was designed above all to increase the direct influence of the ministry on the radio programs: A new sub-department created by Berndt within the ministry at the start of the war was given the revealing title of Radio Command Center.[75] Above all Goebbels was concerned to reduce the number of talk programs, which had increased since the beginning of the war. He demanded a more "relaxed approach and entertainment."[76] In July 1940 the Propaganda Ministry's ability to control the programming was increased through the introduction of a single program for all German radio stations,[77] and now Goebbels pressed even more strongly for more entertainment and dance music.[78]

The propaganda minister was relieved that the start of the war had brought about an increase in cinema receipts: The number of cinemagoers had increased, and the proportion of foreign films had declined.[79] The program alterations necessitated by the war—for example the withdrawal of anticommunist films—had resulted in heavy losses for the film industry, which, however, could be made up for in the production year 1939–40.[80] Goebbels streamlined production: In November 1939 he reduced the number of films to be shot each year to around a hundred; in fact, during the production year 1940–41 considerably fewer were produced.[81] Also in November 1939 he introduced pre-censorship for all films for which he was responsible.[82]

Goebbels's main problem, however, was the lack of subject matter for films relevant to the war. On December 11, 1939, while lunching with Hitler, he was obliged to sit through a twenty-minute tirade from the Führer "sharply criticizing the cinema, above all the weekly newsreels." Rosenberg, who was also present, recorded the details of the occasion. According to Hitler, the cinema was paying no attention to the "national mobilization" that was in progress, the National Socialist revolution had not occurred in cinema. Responding to Goebbels's objection that there were some "good nationalist films," Hitler replied, "Our cinema has not dared to touch the Jewish Bolsheviks," which was rather unjust since they had just withdrawn the anti-Bolshevik films from circulation. Goebbels had been simply reduced to silence in the face of this criticism, made in front of a large number of lunch guests.[83]

Goebbels himself noted the humiliation in his diary: He considered the criticism to have been "not fully justified." Naturally he was aware that Hitler had criticized him so publicly "in front of all the officers and adjutants," but added, in order to swallow his irritation, "he has the right to do so; he's a genius."[84]

In any case, shortly afterward Goebbels began vigorously to demand more propaganda films from the film industry. During the first months of 1940 a large number of such films were conceived, but Goebbels was only partially content with the results.[85] He shelved "problem films," which dealt with marriage crises and the world of work, as well as pure entertainment films, which completely disappeared from cinemas during the campaign in the west.[86] He demanded that 50 percent of the total number of films in production should be propaganda films even if it risked incurring financial losses.[87]

The propaganda films included, in particular, a series of shoddy anti-Semitic films:[88] the feature films *The Rothschilds*[89] and *Jud Süss*[90] as well as the compilation film *The Eternal Jew*. All three films were conceived in autumn 1939 and were shown in cinemas between July and November 1940. Goebbels devoted most of his attention to *The Eternal Jew*. From October 1939 onward he reviewed the raw film several times—among other things he had had film shot in the Warsaw ghetto—commenting, "These Jews must be annihilated."[91]

The film was re-edited several times with Hitler's views being taken into account in the process.[92] As far as the general public was concerned, however, despite the large-scale propaganda for it,[93] the film proved a flop. The SD reported that the film, which among other things compared Polish ghettos to rats' nests, was only seen by the "more politically active sections of the population," while "typical film audiences" to some extent avoided it; in some places "there was word-of-mouth propaganda against the film and its starkly realistic portrayal of the Jews."[94] By contrast, what was probably the best known of these films, the feature film *Jud Süss*, was a hit, while *The Rothschilds* achieved only moderate success with the public.[95]

The anti-Semitic films initiated a wave of propaganda films arriving in cinemas from the end of 1940 onward.[96] Among them were "grand films," involving historical topics such as *Bismarck*,[97] *Ohm Krüger* (on which Goebbels himself worked),[98] and *Carl Peters*,[99] for example, but also "contemporary" films dealing with people's individual fates in the context of the war, such as *Above Everything in the World*[100] (about the fate of Germans abroad at the start of the war) or the films *Goodbye, Franziska*[101] and *Request Concert*,[102] in which partings and separation were dealt with. Goebbels was only partially satisfied with the results. In February 1941 he (once again) demanded: "We must film stuff that is true to life, portraying real people."[103]

From February 1941 onward he worked on material for a film that was probably prompted by the Führer's Chancellery in which "euthanasia" was advocated; Goebbels considered it a "real discussion film."[104] After the halt to "euthanasia" in autumn 1941, however, the film *I Accuse*, directed by Wolfgang Liebeneiner, was shown in cinemas only in a toned-down version.[105]

Numerous films that celebrated German military successes, such as *Stukas, U-Boat Going Westwards*, or *The Lützow Squadron* also came under the category of propaganda film. They arrived in cinemas at a time when preparations for war against the Soviet Union were moving ahead at full steam. They were often initiated and partially produced by the Wehrmacht, and some of them were very much disparaged by Goebbels.[106]

Apart from having to gear the mass media film and radio for war, during its first months Goebbels made a considerable effort to underline his responsibility for war propaganda. In the meantime, in order to emphasize his central role in this sphere he had developed an important mouthpiece of his own. From the end of May 1940 he regularly published editorials in the prestigious weekly journal *Das Reich*, published by Deutsche Verlag, which was controlled by Max Amann. Clearly aimed at the German intelligentsia, *Das Reich* was also intended to make an impact abroad. The fact that Goebbels wrote editorials for it almost every week not only provided him with a useful source of income and satisfied his journalistic ambitions,[107] it also provided him with an organ that underlined his claim to dominate the public sphere. From autumn 1941 onward his editorials were read on the radio on a regular basis.[108] Goebbels ensured that the Propaganda Ministry gave the journal exclusives, which emphasized its privileged position within the German press.[109] By the beginning of July the new journal's circulation had climbed to almost five hundred thousand copies[110] and by December 1940 to almost nine hundred thousand.[111]

In autumn 1940 German domestic propaganda was showing signs of fatigue. Despite the triumphal successes of the Wehrmacht and various German diplomatic maneuvers, there was no end to the war in sight and the air raids were getting on people's nerves.[112] Goebbels tried to get on top of the rather flat mood and prepare the population for another winter of war with the usual winter propaganda campaign covering the whole of the Reich with a wave of rallies and meetings, which this year was fought under the motto "Our Banners Lead Us on to Victory."[113] As far as press guidance was concerned, however, it was not Goebbels but Dietrich who took the initiative. By introducing the so-called daily official line at the beginning of November, Dietrich tried to concentrate the propaganda lines, which during the previous weeks had been somewhat indecisive, and, over the longer term, to secure for himself more influence over the direction of the press. From now on, at the start of the press conference a list of numbered instructions was read out, which contained all the official lines for the press. If other agencies wished to issue instructions to the press, they had to submit them beforehand to the head of the German Press department. Then, at the "official line conference" (*Tagesparolenkonferenz*), which took place at 11:30, Dietrich, or his Berlin representative, would decide what would be contained in the daily official lines. This new regulation affected Goebbels in particular, who from now on was obliged to coordinate his press instructions more closely with Dietrich. In his diary, however, he portrayed this new regulation as a move against the Foreign Ministry, which, starting immediately, could only "deliver the material" for the daily guidance of the press.[114]

The relationship with the Foreign Ministry was, as in the past, extremely cool. Goebbels continued to resist the agreement of September 1939 that his ministry should receive liaison officers from the Foreign Ministry. He had also been unable to prevent the Foreign Ministry from sending in February 1940 its own press officers to German foreign missions, although for years the press work there had been carried out by desk officers provided by the Propaganda Ministry.[115] When in November 1940 the Foreign Ministry once again established a liaison office in the Charlottenburg radio station, its furniture was forcibly removed by the head of the studio; the Foreign Ministry then tried to reoccupy the rooms with the help of the SS. Goebbels engaged in the negotiations over the question of the responsibility for foreign propaganda, which began again in November 1940, without much enthusiasm.[116] He aimed rather gradually to defeat the Foreign Ministry by building up his own propaganda agencies.[117] He carefully collected negative comments by Hitler about Ribbentrop and his ministry.[118]

Even if Goebbels sometimes worked together with Dietrich in his conflicts with the Foreign Ministry, he could not prevent the latter from emphasizing his relatively independent position in the press field in a way that was clearly embarrassing for the propaganda minister. In February 1941, for example, Goebbels gave the press a massive scolding. He told the head of the press department, Hans Fritzsche to take steps against the *Berliner Börsenzeitung* and the *Deutsche Allgemeine Zeitung* since they "contravene my instructions."[119] "At the press conference," he wrote in his diary, "the journalists are not encouraged to show initiative. There it's simply a matter of: banned, blocked, undesirable. If this goes on then during the war the nation will fall asleep."[120] It was clear to all those involved who was the target of his criticism.

After Goebbels had expressed strong criticism of the German press at the ministerial conference of February 10 and afterward, among a smaller group, had gone on to upbraid Fritzsche and Karl Börner,[121] at the press conference on the following day the Reich press chief issued a "special commendation" to the German press for its work,[122] to which Goebbels objected as an "underhand edict to the

press": "a soft, puffed-up individual, a born mediocrity."[123] These conflicts with Dietrich and Ribbentrop had, however, shown that Goebbels could by no means call himself the unchallenged ruler of the
German press.

Thus Goebbels had good grounds to do what he could to consolidate the organization of his propaganda machine and secure it against
the influence of competitors. He had still not named a successor to
his state secretary, Karl Hanke, who was on leave and in the meantime serving in the Wehrmacht. The most promising candidate was
the head of the propaganda department, Leopold Gutterer, to whom,
in August 1940, Goebbels subordinated all the ministerial departments involved in specialized functions with the exception of the two
departments responsible for press matters, in other words Dietrich's
area of responsibility.[124]

In October 1940 he discussed a reorganization of the ministry
with Gutterer. The first idea was to put a stop to the rampant prolif-
eration of, at the time, fifteen departments (a new department for
journals was established as number sixteen in July 1941),[125] by subor-
dinating them to five main departments and so provide for greater
clarity. The departments responsible for cultural and political matters would be combined into two groups, headed by Hinkel and Berndt. State Secretary Hermann Esser, however, had concerns about
the prominence given to Berndt's role and put forward plans of his
own for the ministry's reorganization. But these were so far-reaching
that Goebbels decided to abandon the whole reorganization project
in order to avoid causing disquiet within the ministry.[126] Finally, in
May 1941 he appointed Gutterer state secretary; he was convinced
that he would "be a loyal follower."[127] Given the strong competition
within the propaganda sector, loyalty to the minister was evidently
the most important criterion for Gutterer's appointment.

RESTORING HIS RELATIONSHIP WITH HITLER

In the autumn of 1940 it appeared as if Goebbels's hard work in the
field of war propaganda was going to be rewarded in another fashion.
It seemed as if the Goebbels family would succeed in restoring their
close relationship with Hitler. When Goebbels was staying in Kraków
at the beginning of September, he had a telephone call from Magda

in which she told him that the day before, Hitler had called while they were celebrating Helga's birthday at Schwanenwerder and had given her a very generous present. "I find that sweet of him."[128] A few days later, now in Berlin, Goebbels received Hitler for tea at home. "The Führer played with the children as if the outside world no longer existed," noted the proud father.[129]

When in October Goebbels was suffering from "stress because of overwork," Hitler expressed concern: "The Führer orders me to make sure I get more sleep." Goebbels responded obediently: "I must try to get some in the afternoons."[130] When, on October 29, his birthday, Magda produced another girl—they decided to call her Heide—Hitler shared the Goebbels family's joy.[131]

On November 11, Magda's birthday, Hitler surprisingly arrived in the afternoon to offer his congratulations. The Goebbelses used the opportunity to show him their new house in the Göringstrasse, which he liked "very much." In the evening they had a small soirée there to which Hitler came, staying until four o'clock in the morning. He was "quite confident and relaxed, just like in the old days," and talked about the political situation and vegetarianism, which he saw as a "coming religion." Goebbels's account of the evening reads just like a near-perfect idyll. "Apart from that, he is longing for peace, happiness, and the joys of life. We all dream of what we're going to do when the war is over."[132] A few months later, in February 1941, Magda traveled to Obersalzberg with the children for a week, staying in the Görings' house.[133] On the telephone she told Goebbels "of her visit to Hitler: It was all very nice."[134]

THE BALKAN WAR AND THE HESS AFFAIR

On March 25, 1941, Hitler, the Italian foreign minister, Galeazzo Ciano, and the Yugoslav prime minister, Dragiša Cvetković, signed an agreement for Yugoslavia to join the Tripartite Pact. Yugoslavia's decision to join the Axis provoked considerable opposition, however, and two days later Cvetković's government was overthrown by a pro-British military coup with the regent, Prince Paul, replaced by the underage King Peter II.[135] The situation was unclear; for the moment, Goebbels ordered German propaganda to adopt a moderate line.[136] This line was retained even after Hitler had decided, on

March 27, to rapidly remove the new Yugoslav government. In December 1940 he had prepared for the intervention of German troops in Greece and, at the beginning of March, German troops had already been moved into Bulgaria from Romania; the lack of clarity in the Yugoslav situation now gave him the opportunity to move against both states.[137]

Goebbels noted, however, that "public opinion in the Reich is already running far ahead of events," in other words that war against Yugoslavia was now anticipated.[138] Goebbels's diary entry for March 29 makes it clear that he had been initiated into the secret of the forthcoming war. But, at the same time, he noted that "later a major operation is being mounted—against R." This is the first reference in his diaries to the forthcoming war against the Soviet Union. Goebbels continued: "The whole thing poses certain psychological problems. Parallels with Napoleon etc. But we'll easily get over them with anti-Bolshevism." Moreover, he appears to have had no difficulty in coming to terms with the surprising change in German policy—at the end of 1940 he was still assuming the Soviet Union would remain neutral. Here too he was simply going along with the brilliant decisions of his Führer, despite his not having been involved in the decision-making process.

At his ministerial briefing Goebbels issued detailed instructions for the propaganda campaign against Yugoslavia—the German attack had begun on April 6—which he summed up in his diary as follows: "Propaganda line: tough against the clique of Serbian generals. Don't attack the people. Cosset the Croats! Suggest autonomy. Focus against Serbia. Slovenia in the middle between Serbia and Croatia." As far as the Greeks were concerned, "For the time being we should treat them gently and with consideration. Until they start becoming uppity."[139]

The war in the Balkans made rapid progress. On April 12 Yugoslavia capitulated;[140] the war in Greece went on for a few more days,[141] but already on April 28, Goebbels could note the march into Athens.[142] Propaganda during these weeks was marked by the same triumphal confidence in victory that had been displayed in 1940.[143]

Two weeks after the German entry into Athens, on the evening of May 12, Goebbels received some "frightful news": "Contrary to the Führer's instructions Hess has taken off in a plane and has been missing since Saturday. We must assume he's been killed. [. . .] According to the Führer's communiqué he had insane notions of making illusory peace overtures. [. . .] The Führer is completely shattered. What a spectacle for the world: a mentally deranged second man after the Führer. Dreadful and unimaginable."[144] Goebbels's shock is understandable given the fact that only a few months before, after meeting with Hess, he had come to the conclusion that he was "a reliable man in whom" Hitler could "have total confidence."[145]

But it got worse. The explanation for the flight that Hitler had attempted in his communiqué of May 12 could only be maintained for a day. On May 13 a clearer picture had emerged: "Hess landed by parachute in Scotland, let his plane crash and sprained his foot. Then he was nabbed by a peasant and later arrested by the Home Guard. A tragicomedy. One wants to laugh and weep simultaneously."[146]

On the same day Goebbels flew to Berchtesgaden, not without having warned those attending his ministerial briefing on no account to show "a hint of pessimism or any weakness or depression."[147] The press was instructed "not to give [the matter] undue prominence beyond what is necessary for informing the nation."[148] In Berchtesgaden Hitler showed him the letters that Hess had left behind for him, in Goebbels's opinion "a chaotic confusion of primary school dilettantism."

Hitler decided to abolish the position of the Führer's deputy, to rename Hess's office the Party Chancellery, and to appoint Hess's deputy, Martin Bormann, to head it. Hitler then informed the Gau and Reich leadership, who had been summoned to Berchtesgaden, about the situation. This prompted, as Goebbels noted, "first astonishment" and then "huge outrage."[149]

Back in Berlin, on May 14 Goebbels explained the situation at his ministerial briefing: "Watchword: at home be composed with provisional news embargo, abroad rejection of the lies, and hint at the facts of the case."[150] He quickly came to the conclusion that the whole affair would have to be "systematically kept quiet" and, on May 19, he finally told those attending his ministerial briefing that the Hess case was over.[151] This tactic seemed to work. He noted that the excitement about Hess was slowly subsiding, "nothing more than a half-week wonder."[152] He was pleased that they had been able to overcome the "blow to morale" caused by the flight of the Führer's deputy relatively quickly.[153] Initially he expressed skepticism about Hess's successor, Bormann, with whose work he had previously not always been happy:[154] He had secured "his position more by intrigue than by work." But soon he noted that he was getting on "quite well" with him. "He does everything I want."[155]

PREPARATIONS FOR THE WAR AGAINST THE SOVIET UNION

From May 1941 onward there are an increasing number of references in Goebbels's diaries to the forthcoming war with the Soviet Union. At the beginning of the month he noted: "Russia is increasingly becoming the focus of interest. Stalin and his people are remaining completely inactive. Like a rabbit in front of a snake."[156] A little later he learned: "It's going to begin in the east on May 22."[157] But the attack was postponed several times.

He appointed Eberhard Taubert, his longstanding specialist for anticommunist and anti-Semitic propaganda, as his contact man to Rosenberg, whom on April 20 Hitler had appointed his "Representative for the Central Coordination of Issues Concerning the Eastern Territories."[158] He was informed by the Wehrmacht that thirteen propaganda units were going to be established.[159] On May 22 the Gauleiter of East Prussia, Erich Koch, informed him about the "Eastern Question" and told him who was to be appointed Reich commissioner in Moscow, the Ukraine, and the Baltic states: "He is to go to Moscow, [Arno] Schickedanz to the Ukraine, [Hinrich] Lohse to the Baltic. R will fall to pieces like tinder. And our propaganda will be a masterpiece."[160]

Goebbels, who until the end of March had remained completely in the dark about the preparations for the war against the Soviet Union, now tried ostentatiously to place himself completely at the service of the new task. The aim was above all to focus propaganda on diverting attention from their own aggressive attentions. Thus, on Hitler's orders, at the end of May Goebbels published in the *Völkischer Beobachter,* though not under his own name, an anti-Roosevelt article describing the latter's most recent fireside chat as the "typical product of a Jewish windbag."[161] He found it particularly embarrassing, however, that his deception policy was counteracted by a security lapse in, of all places, his own ministry. In May 1941 Hitler ordered a Gestapo investigation of the head of Goebbels's foreign press department, Karl Bömer. Bömer was suspected of having made remarks at a reception, probably under the influence of alcohol, which could be interpreted as referring to German preparations for war against the Soviet Union. Goebbels became heavily involved in the affair, which he blamed partly on Bömer's careless behavior ("It comes from his being drunk") and partly on an intrigue launched by his rival, Ribbentrop.[162] Although Goebbels strongly supported him, he could not prevent Bömer from being sent to prison.[163] This had the effect of poisoning the relationship with the Foreign Ministry over the long term.

The embarrassment of the Bömer case was an additional incentive for Goebbels to try to perform exceptional propaganda feats during the weeks before Operation Barbarossa, the code name for the Russian invasion. The main emphasis was, in the first place, on feigning an impending invasion of Britain: "I am having an invasion song written, new fanfares composed, arranging English broadcasts, organizing English propaganda units, etc."[164] On the other hand, at the beginning of June he produced the first directives for propaganda "to R": "No anti-socialism, no return to Tsarism, don't refer openly to the breakup of Russia because otherwise we shall alienate the Army, which has designs on expanding Mother Russia, against Stalin and the Jews behind him, land for the peasantry, but maintain the collective farms for the time being so that at least the harvest can be rescued, strong attacks on Bolshevism, denounce its failure in every sphere. And otherwise wait and see how things develop."[165]

The deception strategy appeared to be working. "Our deception strategy," Goebbels noted proudly, "is functioning perfectly. The whole world is talking of an impending military pact between Berlin and Moscow."[166] On June 12, as a further diversionary tactic, Goebbels wrote an editorial for the *Völkischer Beobachter* with the title "The Example of Crete," in which clear hints were dropped of an impending invasion of Britain; he had it approved by Hitler personally. Some of the edition was distributed and then, as part of the deception tactic, confiscated. "London will hear about this within 24 hours through the American embassy. That's the point of the exercise."[167] Also, the "relaxing" of the radio program for the coming summer, with which Goebbels was heavily involved in May and June and which he publicly announced, was intended, as was the lifting of the ban on dancing in June, to divert attention from the preparations to attack the Soviet Union.[168]

On June 15 Hitler ordered Goebbels to come to the Reich Chancellery and told him that the attack would begin in about a week's time. Hitler estimated the "action" would take approximately four months. Goebbels thought it would be significantly shorter: "Bolshevism will collapse like a house of cards."[169]

Hitler once again gave Goebbels a detailed explanation of the reasons for the war: "We must act. Moscow wants to keep out of the war until Europe is exhausted and bled dry. At that point Stalin is aiming to act, to Bolshevize Europe and begin his reign." But the war was also necessary from the point of view of their ally Japan: "Tokyo would never act against the USA if Russia was still intact in its rear. Thus Russia must be destroyed for this reason as well. England wants to maintain Russia as its hope for the future. [. . .] But Russia would attack us if we became weak and then we would have a two-front war, which we shall avoid through this preventive action. Only then shall we have our backs free."

Finally, there was another reason for the attack: "We must also attack Russia in order to free up manpower. So long as the Soviet Union exists Germany is compelled to maintain 150 divisions, whose personnel is urgently needed for our war economy, for our weapons, U-Boat, and airplane programs [. . .] so that the USA can no longer threaten us."

Goebbels summed up: "Bolshevism must be destroyed, and England will then have its last conceivable continental sword struck from its hand." He was in full agreement with Hitler: "And when we're victorious who will question our methods. We have done so many things that we must win because otherwise our whole nation, with us at the forefront with everything that is dear to us, would be eradicated." In this way Goebbels and Hitler had referred with remarkable clarity to the real reason for the continuation of the war. The regime had become so involved in its criminal policy that it had to continue the war to the bitter end.

CHAPTER 22

"A Great, a Wonderful Time, in Which a New Reich Will Be Born"

The Attack on the Soviet Union

Goebbels and Hitler at the Berghof around 1941. Every few weeks during the war, Goebbels had lengthy conversations with Hitler in which the latter conveyed the impression that Goebbels was an intimate adviser to whom he was revealing the closest secrets of his policies and ideology.

BOLSHEVISM AS THE ENEMY

Despite his doubts, Goebbels saw his main task as being to go on making "careful preparations." He prided himself on the fact that he had "flooded the world with so many rumors that one hardly knows what to make of it oneself. Between peace and war there is a huge range of options from which everyone can choose what they want."[1] A few days before the start of the attack he ordered the production of two hundred thousand leaflets for the troops. The workers involved were simply confined to the print works under Gestapo supervision.[2] Goebbels was convinced: "The whole thing has been marvelously prepared. We shall have a good start."[3]

On the eve of the attack on the Soviet Union, Goebbels received an Italian delegation led, as had happened before the start of the war in the west the previous year, by his Italian counterpart, Pavolini. There was a "naive, unsuspecting atmosphere"; they watched *Gone with the Wind.* Goebbels, who was continually called out to answer the telephone, finally left his guests in order to go to the Reich Chancellery. There he and Hitler made final changes to the proclamations that the latter intended to make to the German people and to the Wehrmacht on the following day. Hitler gave Goebbels further details of the impending invasion. At 4:30 A.M. 160 divisions were going to attack on a front nearly two thousand miles long.

Goebbels left at 2:30 A.M. and returned to his ministry, where the most important members of his staff, whom he had instructed to be present during the night, were awaiting him. And now he put them in the picture: "Everyone was absolutely astonished, even though most had guessed half of what was going on, some all of it. Feverish activity begins. Radio, press, and newsreels are mobilized." In the early morning his reading of Hitler's proclamation to the German people was carried by all radio stations to the sound of the fanfare from *Les Préludes,* the symphonic poem by Franz Liszt, which he and Hitler had chosen to accompany special announcements concerning the new theater of war.[4]

During the following days Goebbels noted the first promising reports of military successes[5] and the reactions of enemy and neutral states, which above all indicated their astonishment. To his surprise the anticipated increase in British air raids did not occur.[6] He had sent his children to the Salzkammergut until a "large bunker" in the Göringstrasse could be completed in August.[7]

At his propaganda briefing on June 23 Goebbels gave his staff three reasons for the war against the Soviet Union, which should figure prominently in propaganda. These were, first, the fact that "the possibility of mounting a major attack on England [. . .] did not exist so long as Russia remained a potential enemy" because they had to keep a large proportion of their own military potential on the Eastern Front in order to have a counterweight to the Soviet military machine. Second, the attack would provide an enormous "increase in gasoline, petroleum, and grain supplies," an argument that, however, because of its utilitarian bluntness, was more appropriate for person-to-person propaganda than for the media. Third, the "conflict with Russia" was basically unavoidable—that is to say, "For Europe to remain at peace for several decades Bolshevism and National Socialism could not exist side by side." In short: "It's better for the conflict to happen now than when Russia has got its act together internally and has rearmed."[8]

On June 24 he noted in his diary: "Once again we are setting the anti-Bolshevist propaganda steamroller in motion," but gradually, in order not to make the transition appear too obvious. He outlined what the new propaganda line should be in an editorial in the *Völkischer Beobachter* of June 26. He called it "the old line of attack" and referred to the "plutocratic-Bolshevist plot," the "united front of capitalism and Bolshevism, which is so familiar to us and which has now reemerged in terms of foreign policy."[9]

At the start of the war, however, Goebbels the propagandist found himself in a serious dilemma: The German people had been completely unprepared for the outbreak of war. Moreover, German propaganda suffered above all from the fact that, for reasons of security, during the first days of the war the report from the Oberkommando der Wehrmacht (OKW) did not provide concrete details about military events.[10] Thus Goebbels was concerned about the German people's response. While he characterized the nation's mood at the start of the war as "slightly depressed" (people, he wrote, "want peace"),[11] soon "illusions" started spreading about the course of the war. It was only after strong pressure from Goebbels that Hitler finally agreed to end the silence about the military situation.[12] In the meantime Goebbels had decided to write an editorial explaining the cautious news policy.[13]

On Sunday, June 29, in other words a week after the outbreak of war, Hitler ordered a string of special radio announcements to be broadcast. Thus, among other things, the German public learned that, after a series of victorious frontier battles, the Wehrmacht was pushing forward toward Lemberg [Lviv] and Minsk.[14] The effect, however, did not meet expectations: "People can see through our news policy too easily. The intention behind it was too obvious. I gave due warning but in vain."[15]

At the start of the war Goebbels placed great hopes in three secret radio stations aimed at the Soviet Union: "the first Trotskyist, the second separatist, and the third Russian nationalist. All strongly opposed to the Stalin regime."[16] He ordered that the aim of the secret and other radio stations and the other propaganda material targeted at the Soviet Union, such as leaflets, should be to spread defeatism and panic.[17]

On July 5, after having given appropriate instructions to his staff,[18] Goebbels gave the press the "starting signal for a really major campaign." Now "the main focus must [. . .] be on denouncing the criminal, Jewish, Bolshevik regime." German propaganda appeared to have found its theme for the coming weeks. This major campaign against "Jewish Bolshevism" had been prompted by a massacre of political prisoners and Ukrainian rebels carried out by the Soviets in the prison in Lemberg prior to their departure. According to the press instructions, "Lemberg is more or less the Jewish-Bolshevist norm, which proves the bloodthirstiness of the Jewish-Soviet rulers."[19] And in their reporting of these events in the Ukraine the Party press placed particular emphasis on the alleged guilt of "the Jews."[20] On July 7, in a commentary in the *Völkischer Beobachter* entitled "The Mask Has Dropped," Goebbels set the tone in which the campaign was to be conducted. He foretold "a terrible end for the Jewish-terrorist Bolshevik leadership."[21]

It was only in July, after he had been clearly instructed by Hitler to do so, that Goebbels adopted the latter's propaganda line that the invasion had been a preventive action necessary to forestall an imminent attack by Stalin. During the weeks before the invasion and in the first days of the war, as we have seen, Goebbels concentrated on emphasizing the advantages of the German attack for the future conduct of the war without referring to an alleged impending attack by the Red Army. Goebbels adopted this U-turn in his argumentation even though the major military successes during the early days by no means justified the thesis of an impending Soviet attack. They had met an opponent who was not remotely anticipating the imminent outbreak of war and was not yet prepared for it.[22]

On July 8, for the first time since the beginning of the war, Goebbels had the chance of a tête-à-tête with Hitler on the occasion of a visit to headquarters, when the latter made a "really optimistic and confident impression" on him. Hitler instructed him to continue to conduct the anti-Bolshevist struggle with increased force. Goebbels noted with satisfaction that the "policy of reconciliation with the Kremlin" that had been launched in autumn 1939 had "not even penetrated our people's skin." The attack on the Soviet Union, for which there had been no "propaganda or psychological preparations whatever, had for a short time produced a certain shock effect on the German population," but this inadequate preparation of the nation had had to be accepted in view of the need for military surprise.

"Nothing must be left of Bolshevism. The Führer intends to have cities like Moscow and Leningrad wiped off the map." Hitler also said that he was "completely convinced" that Japan would join in the war with the Soviet Union. Whether or not Britain would succeed in dragging the United States into the war would depend in the first instance on the way in which the Soviet Union was defeated. He predicted "England's fall [. . .] with the confidence of a sleepwalker." "The empire is a pyramid that stands on its apex." Goebbels summed up the lesson of his visit as "the war in the East has basically been won. [. . .] We must continue to expose the cooperation between Bolshevism and plutocracy and increasingly emphasize the Jewish character of this combination."

At his ministerial briefing on July 9 Goebbels ordered that the sentence "the Jews are to blame" should be the main theme of the German press.[23] In response to instructions,[24] during the following days the whole of the German press[25] and the newsreels[26] produced a flood of anti-Semitic tirades. In accordance with Hitler's comments to Goebbels, the alleged symbiosis between Bolshevism and the Jews was a prominent theme, as well as the claim that western capitalism and the governments in London and Washington were puppets of the Jewish world conspiracy.[27] Goebbels himself made a personal contribution to this campaign. On July 20 his article entitled "Mimicry" appeared in *Das Reich*, in which he threatened the Jews with "punitive justice," which would be "fearful": "The enemy of the world shall fall, and Europe shall have peace."[28]

In his propaganda Goebbels endeavored as much as possible to avoid another ideological motif. When, at the end of June, the Reich press chief, Otto Dietrich, issued the slogan "Crusade against Bolshevism" to the press, Goebbels successfully opposed using this Christian motif in German propaganda. In his view, the use of religious symbols represented an unnecessary gesture of respect to the Chris-

tian churches, which were systematically to be ignored during the
war in the east and their importance reduced.[29]

PROPAGANDA

In the meantime the Wehrmacht had been achieving major successes, which were communicated to an anxiously waiting public in
the form of individual announcements. On July 22 German propaganda announced that for the first time the "Stalin line" had been
breached and that they were now just outside Kiev.[30] Goebbels hoped
that this would produce a "noticeable improvement in the popular
mood."[31] A few days later German propaganda could report the taking of the city of Smolensk after a hard fight.[32]

In view of the improvement in the news situation, Goebbels considered the mood in July to be relatively balanced and "calm."[33]
Among the problem areas were certain difficulties in the provision of
food supplies,[34] the British air raids on west German cities,[35] the "vacation evacuees" (better-off people who were escaping from the cities
to vacation resorts)[36] as well as, on occasion, the behavior of the
Catholic Church.[37]

Toward the end of the month, however, Goebbels, regarding the
situation as "rather tense," attempted to adopt a "tougher" line in propaganda.[38] He was clear about the reasons for this, concluding, "Any
information policy that is too optimistic in tone will in the end lead
to disappointment." "The advantages of being optimistic are out-
weighed by the disadvantages that arise when the optimism proves
false. Moreover, the nation is generally used to having to bite the bullet. It does not shrink from the truth and simply becomes grumpy if
it gains the impression that promises cannot be kept."[39] Assessing the
mood initially as "calm and composed,"[40] two days later, on July 29,
he was referring to a "crisis" as far as the "psychological situation"
was concerned because the enemy propaganda had moved onto the
offensive.[41] At the beginning of August the SD report on the nation's
morale also referred to a "certain pessimism";[42] Goebbels even claimed
to perceive a "depression."[43] Apart from the existing negative factors
affecting morale, now it was above all the growing concern of church-
goers about the arbitrary confiscation of church property[44] that was

having a negative impact on morale, as well as the spreading of information and rumors about the "euthanasia" program.[45]

At the beginning of August, however, German propaganda completely dispensed with the reserve that had governed its reporting of the military situation during the previous weeks. On August 6 the radio broadcast a series of dramatic special announcements concerning the situation on the Eastern Front, which, taken together, provided a very optimistic picture.[46] In this way the German public learned that the Wehrmacht had taken almost nine hundred thousand prisoners, the Stalin line had been overrun, and the Battle of Smolensk had been comprehensively won. After these fanfares, Goebbels, who now requested the propaganda services "to be very bold and brazen," considered the mood to be "extremely stable."[47] Thus, by releasing positive news about the military situation in stages, Goebbels was able to respond to the public mood as it appeared in the official reports: Each positive report produced the reflex of an improvement in morale on the home front.

At the end of August Goebbels took the opportunity to visit one of the numerous camps in which the Soviet prisoners of war, whom his propaganda had written off as "sub-humans,"[48] were interned. For this purpose he went to Zeithaim, near Riesa. Evidently impressed, he wrote that "the camp looks awful. Some of the Bolsheviks have to sleep on the bare earth. It was pouring rain. Some of them have no roof over their heads and, insofar as they have one, the sides of the huts are not yet covered. In short, it's not a very pretty picture. Some of the types are not as bad as I had imagined. Among the Bolsheviks there are quite a few fresh, good-natured peasant boys." In talking to them he got the impression that the prisoners were "not as dull and animal-like as one would assume from the pictures in the newsreels." Furthermore, he notes in a remarkably humane manner: "We trudge through this camp for a few hours in the pouring rain and see around thirty prisoners standing behind barbed wire in a cage. They have done something wrong and are being brought to their senses through harsher punishment. Visiting such a POW camp can give one very odd ideas about human dignity in war."[49] Following the visit and evidently still somewhat affected by it, he told a small group that the war must not become "the normal state of affairs." He could not agree with the view that peace serves only to prepare for war but rather

believed that war was justified only if it "later on secures a long period of peace."[50] His direct contact with Soviet POWs—during the
following months the majority were to succumb to the appalling
conditions in the camps—appears momentarily once again to have
aroused in Goebbels reservations about war and fear of its horrors,
which he had expressed in particular in 1938–39 but had then carefully suppressed.

THE HALT TO "EUTHANASIA"
AND THE IDENTIFICATION OF JEWS

As a result of the positive depiction of military developments Goebbels noted that morale within Germany during the second half
of August was good.[51] He now began, however, to arm himself for
the next crisis of morale. First, he ordered the replacement of Ernst
Braeckow, hitherto head of the propaganda department, with whose
work he was not satisfied, by the previous head of the radio department, Alfred-Ingemar Berndt, whom he fetched home from the
North African theater of war and to whom he assigned the reorganization of propaganda for the coming winter.[52]

He wanted to strengthen morale above all by emphasizing the
contribution required from the Party's work on the ground and ordered it to ensure that it had an appropriate public presence in his
Gau. At the beginning of August Goebbels instructed the Berlin SA
"to establish a propaganda organization. [. . .] We can't simply leave
the field open to the grumblers. [. . .] There ought really to be a Party
comrade standing in every line in front of shops, who can intervene
and sort things out the moment disagreements occur or grumbling
starts."[53]

In the autumn when, as a result of a shortage of tobacco, lines
started forming outside the tobacconists in Berlin, he was concerned
about the damage to the official image of Berlin, which must not be
allowed to be affected by shortages. Thus, as in 1939 when he ordered
that lines in front of cafés should be dispersed, Goebbels gave orders
that this should be stopped. In November, however, Berliners were
still lining up for cigarettes.[54]

Above all, however, he developed the idea of extending the
anti-Semitic campaign, which he had launched in the propaganda

aimed at the Soviet Union and in his raving against the plutocratic-Bolshevist world conspiracy, to German domestic policy. The German Jews were to be stigmatized as the enemy within, in order to support the assertion of the existence of an international world conspiracy. Moreover, on August 12, he referred in his diary to the idea that he had been pursuing since the spring,[55] "to identify the Jews by a badge," because they act as "grumblers and killjoys." The Jews were "to be excluded from the German nation" by being given a visible mark of identification. His initiative coincided with efforts by the security police and the Party that tended in the same direction.[56] On August 14 an inter-ministerial conference took place in the Propaganda Ministry at which, among other things, this plan to visibly identify the Jews was discussed.[57]

As well as the "Jewish question" Goebbels addressed another problem that threatened to damage morale: the conflict with the churches. When, at the beginning of July 1941, the feared British air raids, particularly against targets in northwestern Germany, had begun,[58] it was soon clear to Goebbels that the air raids were aimed specifically at "Catholic" cities such as Aachen, Münster, and Cologne because the British believed that they could damage morale the most there.[59] This was a further reason for Goebbels not to get involved in confessional issues during the war as a matter of principle. In this he was largely at one with Hitler,[60] even if in the spring he had been reluctant to obey Hitler's order not to leave the church. "And that's the rubbish I've been paying my church tax for over a decade for. That's what really gets me."[61] In general, however, the watchword was not to respond to criticism by the churches during the war. This proved particularly difficult when information about "euthanasia" became increasingly widespread.

As is clear from his diary,[62] Goebbels himself was informed about the "T4 action," the systematic murder of many patients in institutions for the mentally handicapped ordered by Hitler at the beginning of the war, at the latest from early 1940. When, at the beginning of July 1941, a pastoral letter was read aloud in Catholic churches protesting against the killing of innocent people, in other words "euthanasia," he gave instructions to ignore the incident.[63] On August 3, 1941, the Bishop of Münster, Clemens August von Galen, who had already protested the confiscation of church property in two sermons, now publicly condemned the systematic murder of such patients in a sermon. During the following days news of his protest spread rapidly throughout the Reich.[64] Goebbels only noted this "outrageous and provocative address" in his diary on August 14, while at the same time expressing his regret that "at the moment [it was] probably not really psychologically feasible" to make an "example" of von Galen, as really ought to happen.[65] On the following day he wrote that he must "ask the Führer whether he wants a public debate about the euthanasia problem at the moment"; he himself in any case was against the idea at the present time.[66]

A few days later he heard about a letter from the chairman of the German Catholic bishops' forum, the Cardinal of Breslau, Adolf Bertram, in which he requested that the minister for churches, Hans Kerrl, comment on the "euthanasia issue." According to Goebbels, Bertram "brings up a lot of stuff that can't simply be rejected"; thus he was confirmed in his view that "the church question should be put on ice," and, continuing in the same vein, "it's different with the Jewish question. At the moment all Germans are hostile to the Jews. The Jews must be put in their place. It seems grotesque that that there are still 75,000 Jews in Berlin, of whom only 23,000 are employed."[67]

On the occasion of his visit to Führer headquarters on August 18, Goebbels had the opportunity to bring up both issues. Even before his interview with Hitler he came to an agreement with Bormann that for tactical reasons it would now be more prudent to exercise restraint in the church question. When, shortly afterward, he met the dictator, the latter was in complete agreement with this line.

As Goebbels had previously assumed, Hitler too adopted an uncompromising position on the "Jewish question." "He agrees that we should introduce a large visible Jewish badge for all Jews in the Reich" so that "the danger of Jews being grumblers and malcontents without people recognizing them as Jews is removed." Moreover, Hitler had promised "to deport the Berlin Jews as quickly as possible to the east as soon as the first transportation becomes available. There they will be subjected to a harsher climate." Later Hitler once more returned to the topic and expressed his conviction that "the prophecy that he had made to the Reichstag back then that, if the Jews succeeded once again in provoking a world war, the final annihilation of the Jews would be assured. During these weeks and months, that was coming true with a certainty that was almost uncanny. The Jews must pay the bill in the east; in Germany they had almost paid it and would have to pay still more in the future."

Hitler was referring to the increasing number of mass shootings of Jewish civilians by SS and police units, sometimes with the support of indigenous forces, that had been carried out in the east since the beginning of the war. Based on the diaries, it can be shown that at this point Goebbels was already aware of the massacres and during the coming weeks discovered concrete details about them.[68]

On August 22 Goebbels discussed the "church question" with the Westphalian Gauleiter, Dr. Alfred Meyer.[69] He advised moderation: "The church question can be solved after the war with a stroke of the pen. During the war it's better not to touch it; it can only become a hot potato. [. . .] Whether it was a good idea to set the euthanasia ball rolling in such a major way as has been done in recent months is an open question." At the time of this conversation Goebbels already knew that the mass murder of patients in the context of the "T4 action" was coming to an end.[70] On August 24 the "euthanasia program" was then officially ended by an order from Hitler. This was partly because of the discontent and the protests on the part of the churches and partly because at this point those responsible for the "euthanasia" considered that they had achieved the goal they had set themselves at the start of the war, namely the murder of seventy thousand people.[71] The murder of patients in mental institutions was to continue during the coming years but in a decentralized and more carefully disguised manner.

Goebbels attempted to avoid unnecessary attacks on the churches in other spheres as well. Around this time he told Gauleiter Albert Forster that he was opposed to further interference with church life. All "the hard-liners who just at this critical time want to take up all these tricky problems should be brought to heel."[72] In this connection he was not at all happy about an edict issued by the Gauleiter of Munich/Upper Bavaria and Bavarian Interior Minister Adolf Wagner ordering the removal of crucifixes from all school buildings in Bavaria. "Whether or not crucifixes hang in schools is probably unlikely to have much impact on the outcome of the war. But the fact that the removal of the crucifixes is likely to produce conflict and discord among our people is of very considerable importance." According to Goebbels he succeeded in securing the withdrawal of Wagner's edict in August after it had led to protests and even to public demonstrations.[73]

In the coming months Goebbels continued to stick to this cautious, but always tactically determined, line on church issues. Typical of his real opinion was the malicious way in which he continued to gather material against von Galen, who in his opinion was an "impudent liar and agitator" whom they should "deal with at the next favorable opportunity." Goebbels kept bemoaning the fact that nothing could be done about the bishop so long as the war in the east was continuing.[74] On the other hand, when in October, through the mediation of Ambassador Attolico, his sister Maria managed to secure a private audience with the Pope, and Pius used the opportunity to "pass on his blessing to him personally," Goebbels noted this gesture with obvious satisfaction and a certain pride, even if he added that he could "not buy much with it."[75]

Whereas he was anxious to maintain a trouble-free relationship with the churches, his views on the "Jewish question" were quite different. Two days after Hitler promised him the introduction of the "Jewish badge" on August 20, 1941, Goebbels expressed his opinion in another diary entry that "with the help of this identification of the Jews [he would] very quickly be able to carry out the necessary reforms without [the need for] legal documents." Thus the introduction of the badge served in the first instance to enable him to push through further restrictions on the life of the Jews, who had now been made "visible," through simple administrative regulations instead of having to get involved in laborious legislative procedures. In fact, between July and September 1941 the regulations for Jewish forced labor in Berlin were toughened and the movement of Jews to the capital was completely stopped.[76] "Even if it is at the moment impossible to make Berlin a completely Jew-free city," Goebbels further noted on August 20, "in any case Jews will no longer be allowed to appear in public." In the medium term, however, the Jewish "problem" would be solved in an even more radical way, for Hitler had promised him that "I can deport the Jews to the east immediately the eastern campaign is over."[77]

While he was dealing with the practical aspects of introducing the badge,[78] Goebbels launched a new anti-Semitic campaign in order to prepare the population for it. He gave the starting signal at the ministerial briefing in the Propaganda Ministry on August 21.[79] A central role in this campaign was played by a pamphlet published in the United States in which a certain Theodore N. Kaufman had among other things demanded that the German people be sterilized.[80] After this pamphlet had been attacked by the German press in July,[81] Goebbels ordered a pamphlet to be printed in which Kaufman's piece was extensively quoted and commented on, with an afterword written by though not specifically attributed to Goebbels. He had sought Hitler's express permission for this action.[82] In this pamphlet, of which millions of copies were produced,[83] Kaufman, who was in fact a private individual completely unconnected to American government circles, was described as a Roosevelt adviser and his pamphlet, which had appeared early in 1941, was linked to the Atlantic Charter. Kaufman was described as "one of the intellectual originators of the meeting between Roosevelt and Churchill."[84] In fact, the communiqué that Roosevelt and Churchill signed on August 14 after their meeting on a British battleship off of Newfoundland defined the Allied goals for the postwar world.

On September 12 Goebbels issued a short press announcement about the impending introduction of the Jewish badge.[85] The *Völkischer Beobachter* of September 13 contained, in addition, a commentary directly inspired by Goebbels[86] that made a direct link between the badge and the war in the east: "During the eastern campaign the German soldier has got to know the Jew in all his repulsiveness and cruelty. [. . .] This experience has prompted German soldiers and the German people as a whole to demand that the possibility of Jews disguising their identity at home and so of breaking the regulations that enable German national comrades to avoid coming into contact with them be removed."[87] There were similar commentaries, particularly in the Party press.[88] Finally, the Propaganda Ministry had a leaflet[89] printed specifically dealing with the badge that was distributed to all German households along with their food ration cards.

The introduction of the "Yellow Star" was thus accompanied by a comprehensive program of propaganda. According to the general line, German Jews were part of a worldwide conspiracy for the destruction of the German people. By visibly identifying Jews living in Germany, this internal enemy would be marked. And, above all, it was intended that the population would express its acceptance of the anti-Jewish policy through its overtly reserved behavior toward this publicly identified minority.

While the badge decree was accompanied by a considerable amount of propaganda, at the end of August a new crisis of morale occurred, which was to last for two or three weeks.[90] In Goebbels's view it was once again caused mainly by a lack of news from the front. He endeavored to clarify this situation in an article with the title "About Silence in War" that was broadcast by all radio stations.[91]

During the following days he advocated a fundamental change in news policy. They had been "rather too boastful during the first weeks of the eastern campaign." They should be more open in their news policy, he concluded, and "excessive secrecy" should be avoided.[92] In fact the way in which the military situation was developing suggested that, despite all the military successes, the war was not going to end soon.[93] Goebbels was already expressing the view that "we must now get the nation gradually used to the idea that the war will go on for some time."[94]

REPRESSION AND PROPAGANDA IN THE OCCUPIED TERRITORIES

Apart from the propaganda linked to the war in the east, Goebbels was continually compelled to deal with the situation in the occupied territories. For after the attack on the Soviet Union, resistance movements began increasingly to emerge everywhere in occupied Europe. Goebbels tried to use propaganda to get on top of this phenomenon. He attempted to take over a propaganda campaign in the occupied territories initiated by the British scheduled to start on July 20. Its aim was to display the V sign for "victory" (or "victoire") everywhere. Goebbels, however, launched a countercampaign of "V for Victoria," claiming success for his campaign from the fact that the V could be seen "on all Wehrmacht vehicles;[95] it is in all the newspapers in the occupied territories; cinemas, cafés, and restaurants are being renamed 'Viktoria'; huge banners carrying the V sign are already hanging from the Eiffel Tower; in short I hope that in a few days, through the massive adoption of this fateful letter, we shall succeed in completely crushing the enemy's propaganda."[96]

What Goebbels claimed as a great success was evidently distinctly counterproductive for domestic propaganda. Thus the deputy Gauleiter for Magdeburg-Anhalt reported that "at home the campaign [must be] described as a complete failure." Millions of people received information concerning it from acquaintances and colleagues in the occupied territories and would "lose faith in German propaganda's truth and honesty."[97] Significantly, after July 1941 Goebbels never again referred to his V-propaganda.

In the occupied territories the regime did not limit itself to propaganda slogans. During the course of the summer attacks on German soldiers occurred in several countries under German occupation. From the very beginning Goebbels responded to these acts of resistance by advocating that the "enemy [be shown] the armored fist."[98] In response to reports that in the Netherlands the population was waving at British bombers, he threatened that the streets in question should be bombed by the German Luftwaffe.[99] From August onward he pressed for assassinations in Paris to be countered with the shooting of hostages and above all advocated publishing the names of those who were liable to be shot beforehand.[100] In fact, from September onward, the German authorities in France, Belgium, and Norway carried out shootings of hostages; this had already been going on in Serbia since July, which Goebbels considered exemplary.[101]

The tough measures immediately adopted by Heydrich after his appointment as deputy protector of the Reich in Prague naturally met with Goebbels's full approval.[102] By the end of November 1931 Heydrich had had 404 men and women shot on the basis of verdicts by drumhead courts martial.[103] In addition, the Propaganda Ministry ruthlessly exploited the situation in the protectorate to take "almost all the cultural institutions into the hands of the Reich." Prague film production was concentrated into a "Prague Film Company," and the cinemas and bookshops were also taken over by the Reich.[104]

However, Goebbels was, as so often, flexible in his approach, if this reflected the views of the supreme leadership. In October in occupied France he advocated the shooting of hostages in the proportion announced by the occupation authorities of 50 to 1 and pressed the military authorities to actually carry out the executions they had announced.[105] But when Hitler suspended the shooting of fifty hostages in Nantes, initially for a few days and then indefinitely, Goebbels supported the decision unreservedly.[106]

CONTINUING CONFLICT WITH THE FOREIGN MINISTRY

Even after the invasion of the Soviet Union Goebbels continued to spend a not inconsiderable amount of his time maintaining and trying to expand his responsibilities in the fields of propaganda and information, particularly in conflict with the Foreign Ministry.

In June 1941, shortly before the start of the war in the east, Goebbels made a new approach to the head of the Reich Chancellery, Hans-Heinrich Lammers, in order to try to clarify the vexed question of the responsibility for foreign propaganda. He failed, however, to gain the "Führer decision" he was seeking; instead, Lammers requested that Goebbels seek agreement with Ribbentrop through negotiation.[107] The negotiations began in August; Goebbels had great hopes, since he believed that the Foreign Ministry had gone "weak at the knees" in the confrontation with his ministry.[108] The core of the agreement reached on October 22 was the combination of all foreign broadcasting stations, including the Seehaus radio listening service established by the Foreign Ministry, into a holding company, the Interradio AG, as well as the establishment of other jointly controlled holding companies to direct publishing houses and marketing companies. Moreover, the Propaganda Ministry was to be permitted to send "experts" to German missions abroad. The agreement was a success for Goebbels insofar as the Foreign Ministry's right to give instructions to the Propaganda Ministry in matters concerning foreign propaganda, contained in the Führer order of September 8, 1939, was not included. The particularly controversial issue of responsibility for foreign press policy was not, however, resolved.[109]

At the end of September Goebbels requested Hitler to restrict the right of the Party and state leadership to listen to foreign broadcasts. The foreign radio stations were after all, he argued, "the only source of news that is outside our official news service. The defeatist effect of this news source, he argued, then comes to predominate and in the long run can inflict serious damage."[110]

In other words Goebbels wanted to prevent members of the Nazi leadership from being able to refer to other information than that controlled by the Propaganda Ministry; he wanted to establish a monopoly of information for his ministry. Hitler agreed to this proposal in principle.[111] Lammers then drafted a "Führer instruction" restricting the right to listen to foreign broadcasts to a few prominent ministers.[112] These ministers were permitted to delegate this authority to individual members of their staff, but only with the express approval of the Propaganda Ministry. The Foreign Ministry, however, immediately raised an objection to this interference in its sphere of responsibility and finally, in January, got its way.[113]

Now Goebbels concentrated on substantially restricting the reports of the Seehaus service, of which hundreds of copies circulated in the ministries. Anyone who did not have permission to listen should also not have the right to read these reports.[114] This action, which Goebbels specifically justified by referring to a "Führer command,"[115] produced massive objections from the Reich agencies affected, some of which then tried to destroy the Seehaus service by withdrawing its funds or to set up their own listening service.[116] Finally, in the middle of February a compromise was reached by which the information was subjected to greater filtering and the distribution list was shortened, although not as much as Goebbels had envisaged.[117]

HIGH MORALE AND DEPORTATIONS

In the second half of September German propaganda, which was able to announce the capture of Kiev,[118] once more succeeded in raising morale. But Goebbels was not looking for a mood of triumphalism but rather "a calm middle position."[119] It was with this in mind that he organized the Party's big annual winter aid campaign, which this time went under the relatively bland slogan "Germany's Victory— Bread and Freedom for Our Nation and for Europe."[120] Toward the end of the month, however, "the national mood [was] far in excess of what was really feasible." Goebbels observed that people were hoping that "the war will come to an end this winter," but he would "have a lot to do in the next few weeks to prevent the mood from going to the other extreme and to bring it back to a normal level."[121]

Hitler too, Goebbels noted, was "in an excellent mood" and very confident when he met him at headquarters on September 21. During this visit Goebbels learned of Hitler's decision, in view of the successes in the east, to begin deporting the German Jews. Before the end of the year they were to be taken off to ghettos in east European cities and the following spring transported to Soviet territory, which by then would be under German occupation, a project that Hitler had been contemplating since the start of the planning for Barbarossa.

During his visit to headquarters Goebbels met Heydrich, whom Hitler had just appointed deputy protector of the Reich in Prague, to "sort out" the rather unstable situation there.[122] Heydrich assured Goebbels that he would soon begin deporting the Berlin Jews. They would be "transported [. . .] to the camps established by the Soviets." Hitler, whom Goebbels met later, confirmed this information: "The first cities that are going to be made Jew-free are Berlin, Vienna, and Prague. Berlin is going to be the first, and I'm hoping that in the course of this year we shall succeed in transporting a substantial number of Berlin Jews to the east."[123]

Hitler's motives for making this decision were complex. They can, however, be summed up in a main motive, namely to conduct the war, which was now expanding into a worldwide conflict, as a "war against the Jews," a struggle against an alleged world conspiracy that embraced the Anglo-Saxon powers and the weakened but not yet defeated Soviet Union and that was also behind the resistance movements that were springing up all over the occupied territories. In this context the German Jews, as part of this conspiracy, were to be treated as enemies.

With the decision to begin the deportations, Goebbels's policy of making the Jews visible in order to ban them from the public sphere was, as far as propaganda was concerned, redundant. For, as much as possible, the deportations were intended to be carried out without creating too much of a stir. In fact it turned out that the population's response to the introduction of the badge was much less positive than Goebbels was expecting. Although morale was high because the war situation was perceived as positive, there was little enthusiasm for the introduction of the Jewish star.

According to the minutes of the propaganda briefing of September 25, the ministry had been informed that "the Jewish badge had produced expressions of sympathy from a section of the population, particularly from the better off," an impression that is confirmed by other sources.[124] Goebbels expressed his disappointment at the negative reactions in bourgeois circles to his staff: "The German educated classes are filthy swine."[125]

The press was given appropriate instructions[126] but in fact the "campaign to enlighten people about the Jews" initiated by the Propaganda Ministry did not happen.[127] For the badge was evidently not a topic that lent itself to further intensive propaganda treatment; this was clear from the population's negative reactions and, above all, from the fact that the deportations were not to be a subject for propaganda and thus it was not advisable to draw too much attention to the Jews who were being forced to wear a badge.

Goebbels, however, found another way to prevent unwanted contacts between Jews and non-Jews. On the basis of a suggestion that he made at the ministerial briefing on October 6,[128] the Reich Security Main Office issued a police regulation in October ordering that persons who conducted "friendly relations with Jews in public" were to be taken into "protective custody" and sent to a concentration camp for up to three months.[129] Following Goebbels's suggestion, the decree was not, however, published as such; instead, the propaganda minister took it upon himself to refer to its contents in an editorial, which was effectively a public announcement and to which we shall return.

On October 2 the Wehrmacht began its autumn offensive on the Eastern Front.[130] On October 3 Hitler arrived in Berlin and, "bubbling over with optimism," told Goebbels that he was convinced that the Red Army would be "effectively destroyed within fourteen days," provided that the weather cooperated. In the afternoon Hitler spoke at the opening of the Winter Aid program at the Sportpalast. It was his first public appearance since the beginning of the war in the east and had been longed for by Goebbels as a desperately needed appeal to the population.[131]

The speech, in which Hitler spoke above all about the military successes as well as about the continuing reports of the progress of the German offensive, produced a distinctly optimistic tone in the propaganda media and the usual positive reports about morale. Goebbels had difficulty in "dampening down somewhat the excessive optimism aroused in the broad mass of the population." He saw himself in the role of "the German people's general practitioner who is continually concerned to keep the nation at the normal temperature."[132]

Reich Press Chief Dietrich, on the other hand, gave a further boost to the positive mood. At a press conference held on October 9 in

Berlin he announced in all seriousness that the war in the east had been won.[133] Goebbels by contrast was skeptical, indeed alarmed. "The mood," he noted on the following day, "had turned around and was almost illusionistic." Goebbels now began cautiously to counteract this trend and instructed the press to adopt a somewhat more realistic course.[134] But now something began happening that on no account ought to have been allowed to happen, namely "a certain divergence between the Führer's view and the view that was being given to the press here." Goebbels responded by requesting that General Alfred Jodl adapt the Wehrmacht report to the "mood that was developing in the Führer's headquarters on the basis of indisputable facts."[135] But this then resulted in the Wehrmacht report of October 16 announcing that the first defense line in front of Moscow had been breached. But whatever the advantages of a uniform news policy, such a report went too far for Goebbels, for he suspected, not unreasonably, that "given the actual situation the mood is somewhat too optimistic."[136]

In this critical situation the deportation of the Berlin Jews, which had been ordered by Hitler four weeks earlier, began on October 15. At the ministerial briefing on October 23 Goebbels ordered that, as far as the "deportation of the first 20,000 Jews" was concerned, "nothing [was] to be said on this topic." The foreign correspondents should simply be told that "it is a matter of economic warfare that is not going to be reported. [. . .] The Jews are not going to a camp, neither to a concentration camp nor to a prison. They will be treated as individuals. We cannot say where they are going for reasons of economic warfare." By contrast, domestic propaganda "should not comment at all" on the issue of deportations.[137]

At the same time—that is, on October 24—Goebbels wrote about the deportations: "The Jews are writing anonymous letters to the foreign press appealing for help and in fact some news is leaking abroad. I forbid any further information about it being given to foreign correspondents. Nevertheless, it won't be possible to prevent the topic being taken up during the following days. That can't be helped. Even if at the moment it's rather unpleasant to have this issue being discussed in front of an international public, we have to put up with it. The main thing is for the Reich capital to be made Jew-free."

In the propaganda briefing of October 25, apart from the reporting of the foreign press, Goebbels dealt with the question of how they could secure the complete isolation of the Jews from the German people: It was "impractical to issue a general regulation that Jews have to give up their seats in public transportation vehicles; it's the Party's task to educate individuals to exercise tact and to have empathy. In addition posters are to be put up in the subway and other transportation vehicles in which, without referring to the issue of seats, it will be stated: 'The Jews are our misfortune. They wanted this war in order to destroy Germany. German national comrades, never forget that!' This will create a basis for possible incidents which can be referred to if necessary."

At the ministerial briefing on October 26 Goebbels ordered the intensification of anti-Jewish propaganda.[138] In his diary entry of October 28, 1941, he also commented on the impending deportations. Unlike in the propaganda briefing, he made it clear that, according to the reports on morale, the population had relatively strong reservations about the deportations, which is confirmed by other sources.

Thus in October 1941 Goebbels the propagandist was confronted by an almost insoluble dilemma. On the one hand, the deportations were not to figure in German propaganda; on the other hand, the topic was discussed abroad to such an extent that the ministry had to respond. Moreover, knowledge of the deportations was widespread among the German population, produced generally negative reactions, and threatened to add to the difficulties of what in terms of general morale was an already critical situation.

Goebbels's solution was to launch another anti-Semitic campaign at the end of October without referring to the deportations from Germany. This campaign once more targeted the alleged dominant influence of the Jews in the Soviet Union, in the United States, and in Great Britain and was intended to prove the existence of the Jewish world conspiracy.[139] Another event, however, formed the prelude: A letter written by the Romanian head of state, Ion Antonescu, to Wilhelm Filderman, the leading Jewish representative in that country, in which he strongly rejected the latter's complaints about the deportation of the Bessarabian Jews to Transnistria, was given widespread coverage in the press. The press was instructed to give this letter and the deportations from Bessarabia prominence and to recall Hitler's prophecy of January 1939 in which he had predicted "the annihilation of the Jewish race in Europe" in the event of a world war.[140] The *Völkischer Beobachter* reported on October 27 under the headline

"They Dug Their Own Grave! Jewish Warmongers Sealed Jewry's Fate." As instructed by the propaganda minister, the article included the quotation from Hitler's speech of January 30, 1939, in full and added: "What the Führer announced prophetically then has now become reality. The war of revenge against Germany stirred up by the Jews has now turned on the Jews themselves. The Jews must follow the path that they prepared for themselves."[141]

While this campaign was running, however, Goebbels had to deal with another, even more important factor influencing morale: At the end of October 1941 the whole military situation altered fundamentally. The change in the weather made major operations impossible. The "major offensive that had been planned," Goebbels noted on October 31, "has for the time being ground to a halt."[142] As a result Goebbels had to make a major change in the war propaganda. From the beginning of the war until late summer 1941 it had operated in the context of the Wehrmacht's great military successes; the burdens imposed on the population had been limited by the short "Blitzkriegs." But now it was clear that the planned march to victory against the Soviet Union was turning into a lengthy war. In consequence propaganda was forced to undergo a fundamental reorientation.

CHAPTER 23

"Getting the Nation to Accept Tough Policies"

The Winter Crisis of 1941–42

The more Hitler withdrew from the public following the winter crisis of 1941–42, the more Goebbels acquired the role of the regime's most important communicator. The propaganda minister speaks at Heldenplatz in Vienna on the occasion of the fourth anniversary of the Anschluss, March 13, 1942.

During his visit to the headquarters of the Army High Command in Mauerwald near the Führer's headquarters, the "Wolf's Lair," at which he met the commander-in-chief, Walter Brauchitsch, and the quartermaster general, Eduard Wagner, Goebbels made extensive inquiries about the reasons for the army's failure in the east and was particularly impressed by an exhibition of the army's winter clothing and equipment: "Everything has been thought of and nothing missed. If the enemy are pinning their hopes on General Winter and think that our troops will freeze or starve to death, then they're barking up the wrong tree."[1]

Immediately after this visit Goebbels had his own experience of the Russian winter. Attempting to fly from East Prussia to Smolensk, he was held up in Vilnius because of poor weather.[2] During an improvised sightseeing tour of the city, he also visited the ghetto: "There were frightful characters hanging around the streets, whom I wouldn't want to come across in the dark. The Jews are lice that live on civilized humanity. They must somehow be exterminated, otherwise they will keep on tormenting and oppressing us." On the following day it turned out that because his aircraft had iced up, it was impossible for him to fly back to East Prussia. He had a time-consuming journey by road in a convoy of cars through Lithuania and East Prussia, which made an impression on Goebbels: "It's rather worrying seeing these piles of snow now even in East Prussia: What will it be like on the Eastern Front?!"[3]

Back in Berlin, as expected he had to deal with sinking morale: "As I anticipated, following Dr. Dietrich's forecast, people have gotten the wrong idea about what's going on and we are having to pay the price."[4] But two days later he considered that the mood had "stabilized." Although there were "a lot of complaints everywhere about this or that shortage or this or that problem that hasn't been solved," what seemed vital to him was that "the German people are gradually getting used to the idea of the war going on for some time and are putting up with it with stoicism and dignity."[5]

As this example shows, right from the start of the war in the east Goebbels was preoccupied with the fact that, as he could gather from the relevant reports, the mood of the population was fluctuating greatly. The reports on morale were largely intended to capture the immediate response of the population to military successes or to negative reports or the absence of reports from the front whereby the official propaganda line prevailing at the time provided the context within which the assessment was made. Inevitably he found the rapid "changes in mood" that regularly occurred extremely irritating when it came to planning a propaganda line.

Goebbels had repeatedly attempted to keep morale steady at a moderate level, in other words to avoid excessive swings as much as possible. And now that they were faced with a hard winter at war—

a war that was threatening to become a world war and that would continue for an incalculable length of time—he was forced to make increasing efforts to achieve this moderate level. Goebbels used various methods. First, he attempted to block optimistic reports, particularly those that were forecasting a rapid end to the war. If the propaganda was not too effusive but instead was more restrained, albeit still positive, then there would not be any euphoric reports. During the coming months, when dealing with this issue he kept returning to Dietrich's October comments about the war in the east having been won, which in his view represented "the biggest psychological mistake of the whole war."[6]

Second, Goebbels began to introduce different criteria for assessing morale. During the autumn he changed the propaganda emphasis from promises of victory to a lengthy and tough war in which the Reich's very existence was at stake, with the home front having to bear greater burdens.

Third, comments that were too pessimistic and negative were removed from the reports. In the meantime, Goebbels had come to the conclusion that there were far too many reports on morale, most of them unreliable. The lower-level agencies "feel obliged to express their opinions in weekly or half-weekly reports on morale. If they haven't got anything to say, then they invent something." The reports that came about in this way tended to "provoke agitation in government offices" and thus had to be reduced.[7] In particular the SD reports were in many cases unreliable and indulged in "hysterical and frightened descriptions of the situation."[8]

In all these measures to control morale, it was not of course a question of finding out what people were really feeling; on the contrary, Goebbels used all the means at his disposal through his control of the propaganda apparatus and the information services to establish guidelines for an officially approved state of morale, a model according to which people were expected to orient their daily behavior.

Two editorials that appeared in *Das Reich* in November 1941 were responsible for setting out the guidelines for this change in approach. Goebbels had come to the conclusion that his *Reich* articles, which were regularly read on the radio and in some cases distributed by the Party in special editions,[9] represented an indispensable "collection of arguments" for the ordinary Party member. They gave the "political fighter" the down-to-earth examples and proofs with which he could confront grumblers and malcontents.[10]

The first article, for which Goebbels obtained Hitler's approval before its publication on November 9,[11] dealt with the tricky question of victory in the east, which kept being announced but now appeared to have been postponed to the distant future; he responded by asserting that it did not matter *when* the war came to an end, it mattered *how* it came to an end. In the case of the current war, according to Goebbels, it was a struggle for Germany's existence. If the war was lost, then "our national life would be completely and totally" destroyed. Any further discussion of how long the war would last was unproductive and damaging; all effort had to concentrate on achieving victory: "Don't ask when it's going to come, let's make sure that it comes."[12] That represented a clear ban on any further discussion about how long the war was going to last and a clear reprimand of Dietrich for his excessive optimism. On the day the article appeared, Hitler made a speech to the Reich Party leaders and Gauleiters on the occasion of the usual November celebrations in Munich in which he made the same point using virtually the identical words. Goebbels considered this "a marvelous confirmation of the propaganda line that I have been requesting for so long in vain."[13]

Goebbels's article was not only read aloud over the radio; its publication was also made compulsory for the press,[14] and a million copies of it were distributed to the soldiers at the front in accordance with an instruction from Führer's headquarters.[15] It appeared widely in the press of Germany's Axis allies,[16] and Goebbels considered the fact that it was printed word for word by *The New York Times* a particular honor.[17] He was convinced that within the Reich the majority of people would gradually get used to "the idea of a long war."[18]

In the meantime Goebbels had written another major article, which appeared in *Das Reich* on November 16 with the title "The Jews Are to Blame!"[19] In it Goebbels referred to Hitler's prophecy of January 30, 1939: "We are now experiencing the realization of that prophecy and the Jews are experiencing a fate which, while hard, is more than deserved. Sympathy with them or regret about it are completely inappropriate." "World Jewry," Goebbels continued, was now suffering a "a gradual process of annihilation," a phrase that left little doubt about the fate of those who had been deported.

The article ended with a true edict from on high: detailed instructions for behavior toward the Jews remaining in Germany. This was not simply an appeal; the article represented the public announcement of the unpublished police regulation that had been issued in October on Goebbels's initiative and that had threatened those who had contact with Jews with a stint in a concentration camp. This ban is contained in Goebbels's article in the form of an ominous threat: "If someone is wearing the Jewish star, this means that he has been identified as an enemy of the people. Anyone who has private contact with him belongs with him and must be considered and treated as a Jew."[20]

With his statement, which was spread widely by German propaganda, Goebbels was making it clear that the regime was not prepared to tolerate expressions of disapproval of its official "Jewish policy" or gestures of solidarity. There were now definite rules governing the population's behavior toward Jews, rules that had to be obeyed. Moreover, Goebbels also used an intensive anti-Semitic propaganda campaign by the Party to ensure that these instructions for behavior toward Jews spread to the furthest corners of the Reich and were effectively carried out in everyday life.[21]

As had been arranged during his visit to the Army High Command in October, exhibitions of winter clothing and equipment for the army were hurriedly prepared for five major cities to win the population's support for the winter war. The opening was, however, initially postponed; in the end they were canceled altogether.[22] During November it became clear that further mention of the topic was inopportune: The troops had not yet received the winter clothing.

At the beginning of December the German offensive in Russia came to a halt. Under the most extreme climatic conditions without adequate winter clothing and equipment, the German troops had to suspend their attack on Moscow and, in particular, withdraw their front line in the south. At the beginning of December Goebbels learned that while winter clothing for the troops existed, due to transportation difficulties it could not be delivered to the troops until the end of January.[23] He was compelled "in view of the military situation" to order "our propaganda agencies to exercise restraint."[24] On the other hand, Goebbels saw in these negative military developments confirmation of the line he had been taking for months on the need to follow a "tougher" domestic policy.[25] Hence his recommendations at the ministerial briefing that they should "tell it as it is and [...] say: 'We didn't want this war; don't talk so much and get used to it!'"[26]

THE DECLARATION OF WAR ON THE UNITED STATES

On December 8 the developing crisis was overshadowed by an event that came as a complete surprise to the German government: the Japanese attack on the American fleet in Pearl Harbor and the resulting extension of the war to the Pacific.[27]

Goebbels considered that "a complete shift in the world situation had occurred." The United States would "now hardly be in a position to transport significant amounts of matériel to England or the Soviet Union; during the following months they will have need of it themselves." As far as domestic politics was concerned, here too he only saw advantages: "The whole nation breathes a sigh of relief. The psychological fear of a possible outbreak of war between the USA and Germany has gone."[28]

On December 9 Goebbels had the opportunity to discuss the new situation with Hitler.[29] Although Hitler had told him at least two weeks earlier that he believed that Japan would become actively involved in the war in the foreseeable future (Goebbels did not agree),[30] now, he told Goebbels, he had been "completely surprised" by the outbreak of hostilities "and at first, like me, had not wanted to believe it." On this occasion Hitler informed him that he wanted to use his Reichstag speech, planned for December 11, to announce Germany's declaration of war on the United States.

Goebbels also attended this session of the Reichstag.[31] When, during the course of his speech, Hitler reminded the "homeland" emphatically of its wartime duties, Goebbels was pleased to note that this fit in "very much with the line that I have been following in German propaganda for weeks, if not months."[32]

On the afternoon of the following day Hitler then spoke to the Reich leaders and Gauleiters who had gathered in the Reich Chancellery. Goebbels's diary entry covering this speech, for which there is no other source, is six pages long.[33] Hitler began by speaking about the situation created by the war with the United States. Goebbels's report shows how on this occasion Hitler succeeded in putting a positive gloss on the extension of the war, which, in hindsight, appears to have been a decisive step on the path to his downfall: "Now the conflict in East Asia is a piece of luck for us. [. . .] If we had declared war on the United States without the conflict in East Asia to compensate, the German people would have found it difficult to take. Now everyone takes this development for granted."

Hitler dealt with the situation on the Eastern Front and, as he had done before with Goebbels, he tried to make light of it. The Wehrmacht was in the process of "carrying out a realignment of the front." It was his "firm decision [. . .] next year to finish off the Soviet Union at least as far as the Urals." Finally, Hitler talked about the "Jewish question": "As far as the Jewish question is concerned the Führer is determined to make a clean sweep of it. He had prophesied to the Jews that if they brought about another world war, they would experience their annihilation. That was not empty talk. The world war has happened. The annihilation of Jewry must be the inevitable consequence. This question must be regarded without any sentimentality. It's not our business to have sympathy with the Jews, but only sympathy with our German people. If the German people have once again sacrificed 160,000 dead in the eastern campaign, the originators of this bloody conflict will have to pay for it with their own lives." This clear statement by Hitler must have confirmed Goebbels in his conviction that his radical view of the "Jewish question" was very much in line with that of the Führer. Hitler had announced the "annihilation" of the Jews several times during the preceding months, and in his article "The Jews Are to Blame" of November 16, Goebbels had used the same phrase and significantly had referred to Hitler's prophecy of January 30, 1939, just as Hitler himself had now done in front of the Reich leaders and Gauleiters.

The German declaration of war on the United States did not result in any fundamental change in the regime's anti-U.S. propaganda. As before, it continued to concentrate on the American president and his "war guilt." Above all, Goebbels assumed that by emphasizing the "Jewish question" he would make a big impact in the United States, since "all Americans are anti-Semites"—American anti-Semitism just needed to be organized. "The line must be: Roosevelt is to blame, and the Jews are to blame. Whenever the Americans have a defeat or a setback, we must point out: You can thank Roosevelt and your Jews for that."[34]

THE COLLECTION OF WINTER CLOTHING

In the next few days Goebbels acquired a new task that was very much in line with his demand that domestic propaganda adopt a tougher approach. On December 17 Hitler made him responsible for a campaign to "collect wool clothing for the troops on the Eastern Front," which had been requested by the Army High Command.

In view of objections from Oberkommando der Wehrmacht (OKW), which claimed that the clothing was actually available but just could not yet be transported to the front, on December 20 Goebbels secured Hitler's agreement to announce the collection drive on the radio the very same evening.[35]

Goebbels used his authorization in order once again to dominate the Third Reich's public sphere with one of his major campaigns, using all the media to project an image of the solidarity of the "national community." "Domestic politics is completely dominated by my collection campaign. Our dramatic reporting of it has made a huge impression on the German people."[36] Moreover, in his view it offered him the opportunity to counteract what he considered the "melancholy" mood, which during the Christmas period must not be allowed to spread too far.[37]

Immediately after Christmas, however, there were an increasing number of negative reports from the various fronts. The British captured Benghazi and, according to Goebbels, various reports from the Eastern Front concurred in asserting that "our forces' resistance has been reduced to an alarming extent."[38] For this reason it was excellent that "the clothing collection has started. For now at least people have a useful task, and the Party too has something to do and needn't spend its time making clever assessments of the situation. In fact, all in all, it's best if people get on with their daily lives and apart from that have faith in the Führer."[39] He made it clear in an article to which he gave the title "What Is a Sacrifice?" that the current "restrictions" were nothing compared with what people at the front had to put up with.[40]

During this period the clothing collection came up constantly in the ministerial briefing.[41] "The more people at home have to do," Goebbels concluded, "the better their morale will be; the more people believe that they are carrying out essential war work, the more they will be committed to the war and feel responsible for ensuring its success."[42] On January 21 he announced that over fifty-six million pieces of winter and woollen clothing had been donated; the final result was sixty-seven million items. As Goebbels recorded, the whole operation had proved a "real blessing [. . .] for our domestic situation."[43]

The parallel action to collect ski equipment, however, proved to be rather a debacle.[44] Pressed by the propaganda minister, hundreds of thousands of Germans delivered up their winter sports equipment, and at the same time all winter sports events were canceled.[45] But when the campaign was already under way, the Wehrmacht suddenly declared that instead of a million pairs of skis it needed only four hundred thousand, considerably fewer than had been collected by that point.[46] Goebbels, who found this change of plan "extremely embarrassing," responded by ordering that the action should simply be dropped.[47] Moreover, the Wehrmacht could not do much with the four hundred thousand skis it had collected because for the most part these were alpine skis designed for going downhill and not cross-country skis, which were what were required for winter warfare. In addition, the vast majority of soldiers were not able to ski and proved an easy target for enemy snipers.[48] During 1942 Goebbels and the Propaganda Ministry then had to deal with the question of how, in accordance with a decision of Hitler's, they were to return the skis that were left over to their owners.[49]

DOMESTIC PROPAGANDA:
MORE TOUGHNESS AND CONTINUING HIGH MORALE

During the following winter months Goebbels was preoccupied above all with ensuring that, through a combination of increased efforts on the "home front" and the carefully controlled release of news, German propaganda could cope with the military crisis on the Eastern Front and in North Africa.

During the first months of 1942 Goebbels's propaganda directives and public comments are replete with demands for greater "tough-

ness," both in information policy and more generally as far as the civilian war effort was concerned: "If we really get a grip on the nation,
give it jobs to do and lead it, then it will certainly be willing to follow
us through thick and thin. Also, such a nation can't be defeated," he
wrote on January 8 in connection with Hitler's New Year message.[50]

As far as he was concerned, the collection of wool clothing was a
successful pilot project for a "tougher" domestic war policy.[51] At the
end of January he published an editorial in *Das Reich* in which he
noted with satisfaction that there was hardly anybody left "who
within their domestic circle allowed themselves the luxury of pre-
tending that peace was reigning, while the furies of war were ram-
paging over Europe."[52] He praised Hitler's speech of January 30 not
least because of its attempt to "get the nation to accept tough policies."[53] He now believed that he could sense "a general firming up of
attitudes."[54] As so often, he tried to find out more about the real mood
through a long conversation with his mother: "She knows the popular mood better than most experts, who judge it only from an exalted
academic standpoint, whereas with her one hears the true voice of
the people. Once more I can learn a lot, above all that the people are
much more primitive than we imagine." He considered his basic
views confirmed: "Thus, the essence of propaganda is to keep it simple and use constant repetition."[55]

Apart from his dogged attempts to force the population to make
greater efforts in support of the war, in winter 1941–42 Goebbels as
propaganda minister followed a kind of compensation strategy by
introducing a more relaxed policy for the mass media of radio and
film, which were expected to deliver more entertainment and to put
people in a "good mood." These attempts can be traced back to autumn 1941 and reached their high point in February 1942.

Since Goebbels had concluded that radio was still not broadcasting enough "good and entertaining material,"[56] as early as mid-October
1941 he had assigned the desk officer responsible for matters concerning the Chamber of Culture within the ministry, Hans Hinkel,
the task of "contacting our best light orchestras, our best light music
conductors and light music composers" and making sure they produced "a decent evening program."[57]

After Hinkel had introduced the requested reforms, which soon
covered the whole of the entertainment programming,[58] Goebbels
noted a generally very positive response from listeners. In January,

however, he once again had some complaints about the radio programming. Hinkel was on vacation, so Goebbels mainly blamed the Reich head of broadcasting, Glasmeier, who was also head of the Reich Broadcasting Corporation.[59] In February Goebbels became heavily involved in reforming the programming[60] and in the end carried out a comprehensive reassignment of responsibilities.[61] He gave Hinkel "overall responsibility for the artistic and entertainment programming of the Greater German Radio" and appointed Wolfgang Diewerge, who for years had been one of the most prominent propagandists in the ministry, to head its radio department and at the same time gave him "overall responsibility for the political and propaganda broadcasts of the Greater German Radio."

Following Goebbels's instructions Hinkel established an editorial staff consisting of ten groups, each of which was responsible for a particular branch of entertainment. Goebbels now had an organization that enabled him to issue direct instructions for the programming.[62] He even made detailed comments on programming during his ministerial briefings. Thus, on March 9 he decided on the exact wording of the introduction to a Schumann Lieder recital.[63]

Simultaneously with the reorganization Goebbels reduced the authority of the director general of the Reich Broadcasting Corporation, restricting him to a largely administrative role.[64] In an article published in the *Völkischer Beobachter* on March 1 he announced a reorganization of the radio program. While it was obvious that jazz music was unacceptable, at the same time "it was not right to insist that musical development came to an end with our grandparents' waltzes and everything after that is bad."[65] He noted in his diary how pleased he was with the new program. It was "a pleasure to listen to a broadcast for half or quarter of an hour in the evening."[66]

From autumn 1941 onward Goebbels also introduced a change in film policy;[67] once again it would focus on light entertainment. "During this coming winter," he had noted in September, "we must do all we can to keep the nation in a good mood."[68] This was "really vital for the war effort."[69] When the Rühmann film *The Gasman* was criticized by Party officials because it contained a reference to Party bigwigs, Goebbels, significantly, mocked those Gauleiters who thought that "morale would suffer because of harmless jokes, which once in a while may target state or Party institutions."[70]

During the winter, cinemas were once again showing more entertainment films, which began to replace the political propaganda ones, although at the end of the year Goebbels was still undecided what line to take: "At the moment the situation is so uncertain that one hardly knows what to show: political, military, musical, or entertainment films." In any case, it was a good idea to provide the nation with "the relaxation it needs through art, theater, film, and radio."[71] At the beginning of 1942 the preference for entertainment films was clearly established: "What we need is a domestic form of patriotism," he wrote in January after visiting a cinema.[72]

An important reason for the change was the fact that "big films" were often opulently staged epics that were simply becoming too expensive,[73] and for this reason alone Goebbels preferred relatively cheap comedies staged in studios: "What we need is good quality, good value entertainment films."[74] At the end of 1942 the Propaganda Ministry issued an edict to "improve the quality" of films, which brought together the whole of the film industry in an umbrella organization. All the existing film studios were brought together in Ufa-Film GmbH, with separate companies established for the old cinemas belonging to Ufa and for film distribution. At the same time, within the management of Ufa-Film, Goebbels created the new position of director of Reich film, to which he appointed Fritz Hippler, the head of the film department, who was specifically authorized to intervene directly in film production. The edict specifically established the priority of films "with entertaining content" for the period of the war.[75] The parallels with the reform of radio were clearly more control and more entertainment. On the day the edict appeared Goebbels made a speech to "film creators" in which he explained his new line: In general more films were to be produced, fewer grandiose and expensive "national-political" films, instead more "good, solid entertainment films." The proportions of the two categories were to be around 20 to 80.[76] The change produced, as Goebbels noted, "some astonishment" among his audience, indeed a certain discontent, for he was prompted to make the harsh comment: "If there's anyone here who doesn't want to cooperate of their own free will, he will simply have to be forced to do so."

During 1942 Goebbels considered a whole series of films that fulfilled the criteria "cheap, entertaining, witty"—his comment on the film *Meine Frau Theresa* (My Wife Theresa)[77]—as the successful result of his changes.[78] Summing up the reforms he had introduced at the beginning of March, he noted, "During this period of extreme tension film and radio must enable the people to relax. [. . .] We must keep them in a good mood."[79]

"FINAL SOLUTION OF THE JEWISH QUESTION"

In February Hitler had told Goebbels in connection with the impending destruction of Bolshevism that he was determined "ruthlessly to sort out the Jews in Europe": "The Jews have deserved the catastrophe that they are now experiencing. Along with the destruction of our enemies they will now experience their own destruction." The gradual improvement in the military situation in the spring, in particular on the Eastern Front, offered the prospect of the realization of this aim in the very near future.

On March 1 Goebbels discussed the impending further "evacuation" of the Berlin Jews at his ministerial briefing. He gave Hinkel the task of getting in touch with the agencies responsible and in fact, at the end of March, the deportations from Berlin, which had been interrupted because of the winter weather, started again. At the same time, Goebbels had lengthy discussions with his staff about how those Jews who were capable of work could be given special permits to allow them to use Berlin streetcars. They must be prevented at all costs from "standing around in the streetcars looking for sympathy."[80] Goebbels's particular interest in such details demonstrates how much he was concerned to make sure that the Jews still living in Germany should disappear from the Third Reich's public sphere as much as possible.

On March 6 Goebbels read a "detailed memorandum prepared by the SD and the police about the final solution of the Jewish question." This was clearly one of the thirty copies of the minutes of the meeting that was held on January 20 at the guest house of the SS on the Grosser Wannsee; Goebbels's state secretary, Leopold Gutterer, had been invited to the meeting but had been prevented from going. Goebbels noted a few points that seemed to him vital: "The Jewish question must be solved in a Europe-wide context. There are still more than 11 million Jews. Later on they must first be concentrated in the east, and then after the war they might be able to be sent to an island, possibly Madagascar. In any case, there won't be any peace in Europe until the Jews have been excluded from European territory." But what was to happen "with the half-Jews [. . .] with those related to Jews, related to Jews by marriage, or married to Jews?" "In settling this problem" there would "undoubtedly be quite a lot of personal tragedies," but this was "inevitable." And, as if to counteract any remaining qualms raised by the consequences of the "final solution," he continued, "Later generations won't have the drive and the instinct for this, so it's good that we are being radical and decisive."[81]

In fact the systematic murder being carried out in occupied Poland had already begun by this point in time. At the beginning of December a base for gas vans had been established at Chelmno, in the annexed territory of the Warthegau, which was used to murder the Jews of the surrounding region. In the autumn the district SS and police leader, Odilo Globocnik, had begun to construct an extermination camp with gas chambers in Bełżec, in the Lublin district of the General Government; from March 17 onward Jews from the district were being murdered there.[82]

Goebbels was made aware of this action, which was carried out in strict secrecy, just a few days after it had begun. On March 27 there is a detailed entry in his diary referring to it: "The Jews are now being deported to the east from the General Government, beginning with Lublin. A fairly barbaric procedure, not to be described in any detail, is being used here, and not much is left of the Jews themselves. In general it can probably be established that 60 percent of them will have to be liquidated, while only 40 percent can be put to work." The entry continues with a justification of the program of murder; it is clear that Goebbels was indulging in these thoughts in order to overcome certain qualms: "A judgment is being carried out on the Jews that is barbaric but thoroughly deserved. The prophecy that the Führer gave them along the way for bringing about a new world war is beginning to come true in the most terrible fashion. There must be no sentimentality about these matters. If we didn't ward them off, the Jews would annihilate us. [. . .] No other government and no other regime could produce the strength to solve this question generally. Here too the Führer is the unswerving champion and advocate of a radical solution that the situation requires and therefore appears unavoidable." The ghettos in the General Government that "became free" were "filled with Jews deported from the Reich"; in this way "after a certain length of time the process will start all over again."[83]

On April 26 Goebbels had the opportunity to discuss "the Jewish question in detail" with Hitler. He noted that Hitler remained "pitiless": "He wants to force the Jews to get out of Europe completely. And that's right. The Jews have caused so much suffering in our part of the world that the toughest punishment we can impose is still too mild for them."[84]

In May 1942 a left-wing resistance group in Berlin carried out an arson attack on the propaganda exhibition "The Soviet Paradise," which the Propaganda Ministry had organized in the Berlin Lustgarten. The police investigation into the act, which caused little damage, was completed relatively quickly. Goebbels, however, was very shocked that almost all the members of the group led by Herbert Baum were Jews or Jewish "mongrels" (Mischlinge). He urged Hitler "to arrest around 500 Jewish hostages and respond to any future attacks by shooting them." In fact on May 27 the Berlin Gestapo arrested a large number of Berlin Jews: 154 were taken to Sachsenhausen concentration camp and shot, together with 96 Jews who had been there for some considerable time. Moreover, a further 250 Jews were taken to Sachsenhausen and held there. The leaders of the Jewish community in Berlin were informed that these were hostages who would be shot in the event of any "further acts of sabotage."[85]

Goebbels used the opportunity to press Hitler for a more rapid deportation of the Berlin Jews, as the approximately forty thousand who remained were "in reality hardened criminals who had been released" and who had "nothing more to lose"; instead of deporting them, it would be even better to "liquidate" them. When Albert Speer objected to the "evacuation" of the Jews employed in the Berlin armaments industry, Goebbels found it "funny" that "we now think we can't do without the Jews as skilled workers, when not so long ago we were claiming that the Jews weren't working at all and didn't know how to work." He does not seem to have been bothered by the fact that his comment reveals the absurdity of the regime's anti-Semitic policies.[86]

UNINVITED PROPAGANDA CAMPAIGNS

After the end of the winter clothing collection Goebbels looked for new topics with which the "home front" could be geared to the seriousness of the war situation and through which the "mood" could be controlled. One issue that seemed to fit the bill was a "major campaign" in January against the increasing problem of the "black market,"[87] which had already been preoccupying him during the second half of 1941.[88]

Before this campaign could begin, however, elaborate preparations had to be made, for it became clear that it was necessary "to cleanse the Party organization from this evil,"[89] and the laws dealing with this problem, which contained wide discrepancies, had to be made uniform.[90] Moreover, Hitler warned him not to engage in "cold Calvinism."[91] In the following weeks he was warned not to overdo the campaign. Göring considered that they should "not be mean-spirited about this." Hitler said that the campaign should not be allowed to descend to mere eavesdropping and snooping,[92] and Bormann wanted the main emphasis placed on "educating people."[93]

Although the various obstacles that Goebbels was encountering made it clear that he was stirring up a hornet's nest, he did not allow himself to be discouraged from preparing the campaign in detail.[94] It took almost three months before it could start, albeit in a considerably watered-down version. Thus the decree issued by the Ministerial Council for the Defense of the Reich dealing with black market activities merely imposed imprisonment or a fine instead of the draconian penalty demanded by Goebbels.[95]

A few days earlier Hitler had signed his edict on "the lifestyle of leading personalities."[96] He announced that he had instructed Goebbels "to launch a comprehensive propaganda campaign against black marketeering." Such a campaign could not be successful, however, without "exemplary adherence to the wartime laws and decrees by leading personalities of the state, the Party, and the Wehrmacht." In the event of transgressions, "ruthless action would be taken irrespective of the person involved."

While this decree was not published,[97] Goebbels ordered that half a dozen of the "harshest sentences imposed on black marketeers," in other words death sentences or long sentences of penal servitude, should be published.[98] He was well aware of the danger of creating the impression that during the war the problem had developed into "a huge epidemic."[99] To launch the campaign, on March 29 Goebbels published an article in *Das Reich* with the title "An Open Discussion," which contained a clear declaration of war on "black marketeering."[100] Three weeks later, however, he was obliged to defend his campaign in a further article. For, as Goebbels had feared, British propaganda had used it as proof that Nazi Germany was riven with widespread corruption.[101]

Apart from the fight against corruption, "unnecessary private trips" were a particular target. After getting Hitler's permission,[102] he had the press publish a "sharp warning against pleasure trips"; serious cases would result in confinement in a concentration camp.[103] However, this measure also provoked objections, for example from Göring and the Transport Ministry.[104] Moreover, it was impossible to implement such a regulation effectively. Goebbels wanted above all to create the impression that those in public life were taking account of the seriousness of the situation. A few weeks later, however, he was complaining that once again the trains during the Easter vacation were overcrowded because the Reich railways had gone out of their way "tacitly to annul [my] decree. [. . .] Above all, word has quickly gotten around that the sentences that I threatened were not actually being passed and this has had a negative effect."[105]

Goebbels saw the appointment of the Thuringian Gauleiter, Fritz Sauckel, to the position of Reich director of labor mobilization on March 21, 1942, as at last offering the prospect that the measures required for labor mobilization would be introduced; for him this was the key problem for the home front. A few days after Sauckel's appointment Goebbels received him with great expectations,[106] and in the course of their conversation he felt "bitter satisfaction" that "all the ideas and proposals that I have been putting forward for almost a year and a half are at last going to be taken up and put into practice."[107] Sauckel, however, told him that, to begin with, he wanted "to bring as many people as at all possible from the east"; if the labor problem could not be solved in this way, then he would "take up the question of female labor conscription." Four weeks later Goebbels read a memorandum by Sauckel from which, to his disappointment, he was forced to conclude that Sauckel had put the question of female labor service on ice.[108]

None of the initiatives started by Goebbels in spring 1942 to improve domestic morale—the introduction of labor conscription for women, the fight against the black market, and the threat of concentration camp for pleasure trips—met with success. Goebbels would have sensed that he might have gone somewhat too far with his continual appeals for a tougher line in domestic affairs. That would probably have been why, in April 1942, he introduced a "campaign for more politeness in public life,"[109] for he had noticed that "a very boorish tone has become prevalent in the streets, on public transportation, in restaurants, and theaters, which gets on one's nerves and which in the long run is intolerable."[110] Evidently he wanted to use this flanking initiative to demonstrate that the toughness which he was so vigorously propagating should not be confused with uncouth behavior in everyday life.

UNDER THE BRITISH AIR OFFENSIVE: CONFIDENCE IN VICTORY BEGINS TO FALTER

While the military situation in the east eased during the spring, the general war situation was being increasingly influenced by the major air raids on German cities that were getting under way. It was this new threat that gave Goebbels the opportunity to continue to assert his demand for greater "toughness" in the conduct of the war; in dealing with the effects of the air war, he was able to secure a new role, one that went far beyond his core duty as propagandist.

On Sunday, March 29, one of the first spring-like days of the year, Goebbels received the first reports of an "extraordinarily heavy air raid that the English have carried out on Lübeck." In fact, the previous night the Royal Air Force had attacked the city on the Trave with over two hundred bombers and in the process had set fire to and almost completely destroyed the heavily populated old part of the city, with its intricate streets of timber-framed houses. It was the worst raid on a German city so far, causing more than three hundred deaths.[111]

Goebbels noted that, in view of the evident lack of support for the affected population, following a telephone conversation with Hitler the latter had removed the "responsibility for looking after areas damaged by air raids from the Interior Ministry and gave me unlimited powers in this matter." Goebbels immediately convened a meeting of state secretaries, in which it was decided to send large amounts of aid to Lübeck.[112]

However, the very generous distribution of aid within the city by the Nazi welfare organization (Nationalsozialistische Volkswohlfahrt, NSV) was exploited by its local functionaries to enrich themselves substantially in the process. As a result, in August 1942 three death sentences were passed, one of which was actually carried out. Goebbels, who took a great interest in the scandal, maintained that all three should have been executed.[113]

In April, despite the raid on Lübeck, despite the news that meat rations were about to be cut[114] and all of the other concerns of the population, Goebbels claimed to note a gradual improvement in the national mood.[115] He dismissed anonymous critical letters without more ado as Jewish ("one can tell from the style") and continued to do so during the following months. In general he attributed the improvement in mood to the fact that "the line adopted in my articles has produced a new attitude toward the war on the part of our people and a realistic assessment of the overall situation."[116] Thus the mood had not improved; instead, the criteria against which it was measured had been adjusted to suit the changed circumstances.

Hitler's fifty-third birthday was celebrated by a ceremony in the Philharmonie on April 19; he did not in fact attend. Goebbels made the speech, which had been approved by Hitler beforehand.[117] In it he referred to the film *Der große König*, which had been recently finished, claiming to observe remarkable parallels between the life of the Prussian king Frederick II (Frederick the Great) and the present day.[118] Goebbels praised the king as someone who "again and again under the pressure of shattering blows, which sometimes brought him to the brink of collapse, found the strength to raise himself triumphantly above trials and defeats and to provide his people, his soldiers, the doubting generals, wavering ministers, conspiring relatives, and rebellious officials with a shining example of steadfastness in adversity," while as far as Hitler was concerned Goebbels emphasized "the heavy burden of responsibility" and spoke of a "titanic struggle" that the Führer was carrying on for "the life of our people."

Thus the birthday speech also used the leitmotif of a tougher conduct of the war. Above all, it introduced a change in the previous Führer propaganda. Hitler's successes were no longer at the core of

Führer admiration but rather his leadership potential. The speech was nothing more than a request for an advance of trust, although the comparison with the prematurely aged Prussian king bent under the weight of his troubles was not very flattering to Hitler.

On April 25 Hitler came to Berlin in order, after a long pause, to speak in the Reichstag. Before his speech the dictator reassured Goebbels once more, as the latter gratefully noted, that he was in favor of a "radical conduct of the war and radical policies." In his speech the following day Hitler commented on the difficulties of the previous winter and promised to learn the lessons from these experiences for a possible second winter of war in the east. He sharply criticized sections of the civil service and demanded from the Reichstag wide-ranging powers in order to correct shortcomings in the administration and the judicial system.[119] Such powers were very much along the lines of what Goebbels had already been proposing in March. The judiciary was to be effectively emasculated and irksome provisions in civil service law suspended.[120]

The Reichstag unanimously approved Hitler's demands, according to which he was entitled to hold "every German," whether officer, civil servant, judge or Party functionary, to account in the performance of his duty and, if necessary, "irrespective of any rights he might possess," to dismiss him from his position, a clear attack by the leadership of the regime on the privileges of public officials.[121]

Although Goebbels heaped praise on the speech and its brilliant effect on the population, he could not ignore the fact that Hitler's address had also provoked concern and some lack of understanding. The passage about preparations for war during the coming winter produced great disappointment, since it was interpreted as a denial of the possibility of a victory in the coming summer and questions were raised about why, in view of Hitler's absolute authority, a further legal authorization had been necessary at all.[122] The press was therefore instructed to play down the Reichstag declaration in its reporting.[123]

Goebbels returned to this criticism several times until well into May,[124] and, somewhat irritated, he noted that the speech had "to some extent provoked uncertainty. Above all, people want to know what the Führer is intending to do in order to deal with the shortcomings that he criticized and to bring to account the people responsible."[125] Thus he was obliged to recognize that one of the central propaganda themes, the repeated emphasis on the unity of Führer and people, had lost its credibility to a significant extent and this was despite or even because of his own efforts to reinforce the Führer myth. It was an example of where his propaganda, with its attempt to create a uniform German public opinion, had run up against clear limits.

On April 23, barely four weeks after the British air raid on Lübeck, the Royal Air Force had begun bombing Rostock, a raid that involved more than one hundred bombers over four consecutive nights. Above all, during the third night they succeeded in setting fire to a large part of the old part of the city. Over six thousand dwellings were destroyed and more than two hundred people killed.[126] Goebbels expressed his conviction that "we must deal the English similar blows until they see reason."[127]

In conversation with Goebbels during his stay in Berlin, Hitler too was "annoyed about the recent English raid on Rostock." He had already ordered "retaliation." Since air raids had little impact on the enemy's armaments industry, he had ordered that they should "now attack cultural centers, seaside resorts, and non-industrial cities, for the psychological effect would be much greater there and at the moment the psychological effect is what it's all about." The first raids were on Exeter (April 23 and 24) and above all Bath (April 25). When the RAF continued its raids on Rostock, the Luftwaffe attacked Bath again on April 26.[128] Bath was followed by Norwich (April 27 and 29) and York (April 28) and then Exeter again (May 3). In the future British propaganda would refer to such raids, aimed primarily at targets of cultural significance, as "Baedeker" raids, an expression that was invented for the first time—"stupidly," according to Goebbels—by a Foreign Ministry official at a press conference.[129] Goebbels told his staff that they should not "boast about the destruction of cultural objects."[130]

The raid on Rostock prompted Goebbels to return to the task that Hitler had given him after Lübeck. Thus, on April 28, he informed the Gauleiters (writing to them in their dual capacities as Reich governors and Reich defense commissioners) that the "Führer" had assigned him "responsibility for introducing immediate and uniform measures to aid localities suffering from bomb damage" if the damage could not be dealt with using the Gau's own resources. He had established a help line in his ministry for this purpose that would be permanently staffed.[131]

However, when Goebbels tried to turn this message into a formal instruction to be issued jointly by Frick, Göring, and Bormann he encountered opposition from several ministers.[132] Nevertheless, he had succeeded in acquiring a degree of authority enabling him to intervene in the event of major raids on cities in the future. He was quite correct in assuming that repeated air raids would provoke considerable anxiety among the population and was therefore intent on acquiring control over morale through direct and rapid intervention in the cities affected by the air war.

GOEBBELS'S WAY OF LIFE DURING THE WAR

In response to the increasing seriousness of the situation Goebbels appeared more and more often in public wearing his Party uniform, although this only emphasized his unattractive appearance. In the meantime he had more or less geared his routine to wartime requirements. As a rule his working day began at nine o'clock. To start with, his military adjutant briefed him on the contents of the Wehrmacht report, which, from the middle of 1941 onward, as was the case with his diary, was recorded by a stenographer. The "diary" now became quite large, as Goebbels included not only personal observations but also letters that he had received, reports, notes about conversations, press statements, and other matters. After that the minister left for the "conference" at eleven o'clock (the time was postponed several times during the war) in order to brief the senior officials of his ministry and the officials of the (Party's) Reich Propaganda Headquarters, the Party Chancellery, the Foreign Ministry and so on, who were liaising with the ministry about the current propaganda line. The whole thing was not a conference in the normal sense but rather a detailed briefing by Goebbels in which he often dictated the key phrases of the daily propaganda line himself.

Goebbels kept his distance from his staff; indeed he had developed a certain air of unapproachability. Thus he repeatedly gave orders that he was not to be spoken to on his way from his office to the daily ministerial briefing; he also reprimanded staff for hanging around in his anteroom without an official reason for doing so and disturbing him with their conversations.[133]

He ruthlessly exploited his powerful position to bring insubordinate personnel in his sphere of operations to account. When, in October 1940, a desk officer from the Vienna Party propaganda headquarters wrote a "stupid but very aggressive article against Berlin" in a local newspaper, he gave instructions for "the man to be relieved of his position immediately and to have him locked up for a few days."[134] In May 1940 he ordered Wilhelm Fritzsche "to issue a very tough warning to the editor of a newspaper in Lippe" for daring to raise the question as to "whether it was as important to broadcast the program 'Request Concert' in the afternoon as broadcasting a football match." The journalist was "to be informed that if he repeats such an incredibly impertinent intervention in political matters in the future he can expect to be sent to a concentration camp."[135] When, in February 1942, the cultural section of the *Westdeutscher Beobachter* dared to write a "really mean article against Berliners," he ordered the journalist responsible, who was its Berlin correspondent, to leave the city "by 10:00 this evening," threatening him that otherwise he would send some Berlin stormtroopers to set him straight.[136]

Goebbels's maintenance of personal distance in his official life mirrored the almost total isolation of his personal life. During the 1930s he had no longer been keeping up with friends from his school and student days or from his early years in Berlin; during his occasional visits to Rheydt he sometimes invited old mates and acquaintances, but this was probably above all in order to reassure himself how far he had come from his petit bourgeois and provincial background.[137]

On several occasions in 1942–43 he met Schweitzer/Mjölnir, who had failed in the tasks he had been given by the Propaganda Ministry and, in the meantime, had found employment as a graphic artist with the propaganda troops. But in the remarks in his diary Goebbels was pointedly concerned merely to comment on his former friend's professional and political development; he was pleased to be able to "recruit him once again for my work."[138] In June 1943 he received a letter from Fritz Prang, by now "with a propaganda unit on the southern front," and Goebbels was pleased that "his remarks reflect strong political commitment"; once again in his view there was no need for any comment of a personal nature.[139]

After having been forcibly kept intact by Hitler in 1938–39, Goebbel's relationship with Magda appears to have developed above all into a marriage of convenience that worked. The diaries endeavor to create the impression of a harmonious family routine marked by affection and mutual respect. There are no further references to arguments with Magda or infidelities on the part of either of them; above all he is concerned about her continuing rather delicate health.

The only person who was really close to him appears to have been his mother, who after 1942 was living mainly in Berlin.[140] Goebbels valued his mother as a woman from the people who allegedly had a real insight into the state of the population and its mood.[141] "For me, with her primitive character and peasant cunning, she represents the voice of the people. I idolize her," he noted in April 1941.[142] Sometimes, for example at family celebrations, he met his other relatives, above all his sister Maria.[143]

During the war his constitution continued to cope with the heavy workload and extreme stress from which he suffered almost permanently. He was, however, susceptible to kidney complaints, which sometimes prevented him from leaving his bed.[144] In addition he suffered from a skin ailment. In February 1942, shortly before the end of the winter crisis a "nervous rash," which he had had for some time, became worse. He could no longer sleep properly and hoped to get relief from X-ray treatment.[145] During the spring his eczema caused him so much trouble that in May he was forced to spend a few days in Lanke receiving special treatment.[146] When the rash returned in the autumn "like a rose garden," he felt that it was because "this is such a tense and stressful time."[147] In April 1943 the rash came up again so severely that for several days he was incapable of working.[148] Moreover, he evidently suffered from periodic bouts of slight depression. In the autumn, and especially during the war, he was regularly prone to attacks of melancholy, which he tried to suppress with increasing activity, but to a certain degree he also indulged in them.[149]

Even if, in view of the seriousness of the war situation, Goebbels never tired of exhorting the German people to make ever more sacrifices and tried gradually to gear them to an acceptance of "total war," these efforts had little effect on his own opulent lifestyle. With his family he continued to inhabit three large properties: one in the Göringstrasse, one on the Bogensee, and one on Schwanenwerder; however, he evacuated the "summerhouse" in the summer of 1943 because of the threat of air raids. In 1940 he had acquired a new Mercedes: "a magnificent car." But, he added regretfully—even he had to make some concessions to the wartime situation—it was "only suitable for peacetime."[150] His financial situation, which in the past had often been precarious, had now been put fully in order. Thus, in the year 1943, for example, Goebbels's income was over 424,000 Reichmarks, of which only 38,000 came from his ministerial income, while 375,000 came from his literary and journalistic activities, the majority, around 300,000 Reichmarks, from his editorials in *Das Reich*.[151]

Although Goebbels had succeeded, during the course of 1940, in repairing his somewhat damaged relationship with Hitler and managed to get close to him again, the future course of the war was to cause complications. The fact that after the outbreak of the war with the Soviet Union Hitler spent most of his time in various headquarters provided, on the one hand, a certain relief for Goebbels, who was now spared the hours spent visiting him at midday and watching films in the evening in the Reich Chancellery. On the other hand Goebbels was vitally dependent on direct personal contact with Hitler in order to be able to establish what propaganda line was to be taken and, above all, to secure the continuing flow of praise from his Führer, so necessary to his self-esteem. Apart from frequent telephone calls to Hitler or Dietrich, who informed him of the latest propaganda line from Führer headquarters, after the start of the Russian campaign Goebbels made a habit of visiting Hitler in his headquarters every few weeks and carrying out intensive conversations with him, a habit that he continued until the end of the war. He also used Hitler's presence in Berlin to have detailed conversations with the Führer. The exceptionally long entries in his diaries concerning these conversations indicate how important they were for Goebbels, and not just from a political point of view. Given his fixation on Hitler, they were also a source of strength and inspiration for him. However depressed and doubting he was when he arrived at headquarters, he invariably departed mentally fortified and full of confidence.

Goebbels's account of these conversations was always structured in the same way. First he noted his impression of Hitler's appearance, state of health, and mental vigor. Then he gave a detailed account of the conversations, which often lasted a whole day or longer. They usually began with the military and international situation and then the domestic situation was discussed. Usually they took the form of

monologues by the dictator to which Goebbels contributed inter-
jections, questions, and comments. The conversation then became
somewhat more intimate. They discussed personalities (in this way
Goebbels was able to discover who was in the Führer's favor and who
was in the firing line). Toward evening cultural matters were discussed, with Hitler seldom failing to declare how much he missed
peacetime with its cultural delights and the society of artists. Finally,
the dictator almost always made attentive inquiries about Goebbels's
family and indulged in almost wistful reminiscences of the "days and
evenings he had spent with our family in the Reichskanzlerplatz." For
example, on October 27, 1943, he assured Goebbels that "our life together then" seemed to him "the happiest time of his life."[152] The
whole thing very quickly became a ritual, which Goebbels eagerly
recorded in order to reassure himself about the extent to which he
was in the Führer's favor and had his trust.[153] His accounts of these
conversations featuring an astute, benevolent, indeed humane dictator show how naive he was and, inhibited by his personal dependence on Hitler, how he allowed himself to be captivated by the
latter's conversational tactics and skill in personal relations. Moreover, by discussing a combination of political, cultural, and personal
topics, Hitler used the conversations in a psychologically skillful way
to convey the impression to his propaganda minister that he held a
special position in the esteem of the Führer.

CHAPTER 24

"We Can See in Our Mind's Eye a Happy People"

Offensives and Setbacks

Constant activity on the home front meticulously recorded by the media. Reich Minister Goebbels visits the National Socialist German College in Feldafing on July 8, 1942.

In spring 1942 the military situation began to improve from the regime's point of view, both on the Eastern Front, in particular in the Crimea,[1] and later, albeit briefly, in North Africa. Goebbels immediately saw the danger of the population becoming too optimistic. In view of the "good news at Whitsun"[2]—on May 23 the OKW report mentioned for the first time a major German offensive on the Eastern Front[3]—Goebbels at once went about "ensuring that our news policy does not become too effusive."[4] The really great summer offensive in the south of the Eastern Front, however, was still to come. Goebbels made his own contribution to the success of the operation by using propaganda to employ diversionary tactics and spread disinformation.[5]

With the aim of winning the population's support for the forthcoming military efforts, at the end of May he published an editorial in *Das Reich* with the title "What's It All For?" In it, while not outlining actual political war aims, he nevertheless tried to give "the ordinary man" a foretaste of life in a future Greater German Reich. Concerned to persuade his readers of the rosy prospects that lay ahead, he produced a kitsch vision of the postwar world: "We are dreaming of a happy people in a country blossoming with beauty, traversed by wide roads like bands of silver which are also open to the modest car of the ordinary man. Beside them lie pretty villages and well laid-out cities with clean and roomy houses inhabited by large families for whom they provide sufficient space. In the limitless fields of the east yellow corn is waving, enough and more than enough to feed our people and the whole of Europe. Work will once more be a pleasure and it will be marked by a joy in life which will find expression in brilliant parties and contemplative peace."[6]

THE ASSASSINATION OF HEYDRICH

On May 27, 1942, Goebbels received "alarming" news: An assassination attempt had been made on Reinhard Heydrich in Prague. Although there was no immediate threat to Heydrich's life, his condition was "giving cause for concern." Significantly, Goebbels continued with his diary entry by announcing an even tougher "fight against the Berlin Jews." "I have no desire to have a 22-year-old eastern Jew— the saboteurs of the anti-Soviet exhibition included types like that— putting a bullet in my guts. I prefer ten Jews in a concentration camp or under the earth than having one in freedom."[7]

Heydrich's condition, which at first had appeared to stabilize, deteriorated after a few days. To start with, Goebbels speculated as to whether the attack on Heydrich had been carried out by British or Soviet agents; it became clear later that Czech resistance fighters, who had been trained by the British Special Operations Executive (SOE) and parachuted in, were responsible.[8]

Goebbels was clear about who was behind the assassination: "As planned, I have 500 Jews in Berlin arrested and inform the leaders of the Jewish community that for every Jewish assassination attempt or every Jewish attempt to revolt 100 or 150 of the Jews in our hands will be shot."[9] The arrests had in fact already been carried out by the Gestapo at the end of May. Once again Goebbels had exaggerated his own role. He applauded the tough repressive measures, the death sentences, and mass arrests carried out by the German occupiers in Prague.[10]

On May 29 he met Hitler for a lengthy conversation.[11] It was naturally concerned above all with the assassination and what lay behind it. Hitler advocated taking "very energetic and ruthless measures against those groups who are likely to carry out assassinations." In this context Goebbels brought the conversation around to his intention "to evacuate all the Jews from Berlin," since "there are 40,000 Jews free to go around the capital who have nothing more to lose"; this was "simply an invitation for assassinations." Hitler agreed at once; where Jews were still employed in the armaments industry, Speer should replace them with foreign workers.

Then the conversation turned to the "eradication of criminals." If, during the war, "a really dangerous development occurred," then, both men were agreed, "the prisons should be cleared through liquidations." Hitler stated "once more his demand for the loss of idealists to be balanced by the loss of negativists," a line of argument that Goebbels found "absolutely convincing."

In any case they had to "liquidate the Jewish threat, whatever it costs to do so." What he would like to do most, Hitler said, would be to "settle them in central Africa," because then they would have to live in a climate "that would certainly not make them strong and hardy." In any case, Hitler's aim was "to make western Europe completely free of Jews." Hitler's statements indicate that, while the mass murder of Jews had already been under way since the summer of the previous year, the final decision over how and where the remaining Jews would be murdered had still not been made. This was, however, to change radically during the coming weeks.

On the morning of June 4 Goebbels learned that Heydrich had just died. "The loss of Heydrich is irreplaceable," he commented, still very much in shock over the events. Heydrich, who apart from his position in Prague had remained head of the Reich Security Main

Office and thus had held a key position for the systematic mass murder of the Jews, "was the most radical and successful fighter against enemies of the state."[12]

A few days later there was an elaborate state memorial ceremony for Heydrich in Berlin.[13] Hitler, who used the occasion for a lengthy conversation with Goebbels, appeared rather depressed: "The Führer is seriously concerned about the large number of deaths being suffered by the Party. The Party and state leadership now hardly ever get together except for state memorial ceremonies."[14]

The occupying authorities in the protectorate continued to take "revenge" for the Heydrich assassination. On June 10 the security police murdered all the men of the village of Lidice near Kladno, 199 people in all, deported the women to Ravensbrück concentration camp, and the children, after the most "racially valuable" ones had been removed, to the Chelmno extermination camp.[15] On June 11 the Germans announced the Lidice act of retaliation on the radio: Its population had been supporting the enemy parachutist agents, and so they had to make an example of them.[16]

Goebbels was unimpressed by the fact that enemy propaganda attacked the mass murder as a barbaric act: "We must do what we consider necessary and what the vital interests of the German Reich and the German people require."[17] The press, however, was instructed not to report anything about the "punishment measures" in the protectorate.[18]

One of these "retaliation measures" was directed against the Prague Jews. On June 10, 1942, a thousand of them were deported to Majdanek and locked up there as well as in surrounding camps.[19] Under the impression of the assassination attempt on Heydrich and his subsequent death, however, the Nazi leadership decided to accelerate the preparations, in which Heydrich had played a leading role and which were already under way, for extending the mass murder of the Jews to the whole of Europe. Thus, with his proposal of May 29 to deport the Berlin Jews Goebbels was fully in line with the radicalization of the regime's Jewish policy. In July the trains began to arrive at the Auschwitz extermination camp from all over Europe.[20]

During 1942, leading representatives of the regime, including Hitler, made repeated public statements about the extermination and annihilation of the Jews, thereby sending clear signals about the fate of the people who were being deported to the extermination camps. Goebbels participated in this intentional breach of the secrecy surrounding Jewish policy when, for example, in June 1942, in connection with the air war, he wrote of the impending "extermination" of the Jews and kept forcing the press to take up anti-Semitic topics. In general, however, during 1942 propaganda responded to the "final solution" with silence, a silence that, in view of the bits of information and rumors about the mass murder that were going around, was eloquent and uncanny. The fact that in this way many people acquired a rough idea that the regime was perpetrating a crime on the Jews of unimaginable dimensions was one of the factors that facilitated Goebbels's "direction of morale," by underlining the seriousness of the situation in the third year of the war; they had burned their bridges behind them.[21]

THE AIR WAR: THE FIRST THOUSAND-BOMBER RAID

A few days before Heydrich's death, on the morning of May 31, Goebbels received the first news reports "of a massive air raid by the English on Cologne."[22] In fact, the night before, the RAF had attacked Cologne in unprecedented numbers. It was the first thousand-bomber raid in military history, an exceptional effort by RAF Bomber Command, which anticipated that the raid would completely destroy one of the most important German cities, a devastation that was intended to have a strong demoralizing effect on the whole of Germany's civilian population. As a result, British propaganda made much of the fact that one thousand bombers were involved and announced there would be more devastating raids.

Goebbels considered that such a large number of enemy planes was "quite out of the question" and assumed that three hundred bombers at most had participated in the raid. The press was therefore instructed not to discuss the number of enemy planes.[23] Apart from that he agreed with Hitler that German propaganda should not gloss over the damage, not least in order to have arguments with which to justify "retaliation."[24] During the night of May 31 the Luftwaffe responded with a "retaliatory attack" on Canterbury, with Goebbels ordering it to be given prominent propaganda coverage.[25]

Despite the enormous number of planes that appeared over Co-logne, however, the city was not destroyed, and the demoralizing effect that the British had anticipated did not occur. Almost five hundred people were killed during the bombing of Cologne, more than in any other raid up to that point, and over 250,000 dwellings were destroyed; the cathedral city with its 750,000 inhabitants had been badly hit but by no means completely destroyed.[26]

After the raid on Cologne Goebbels published an article in *Das Reich* in which he wrote that the air war was above all a "war of nerves." He gave the number of victims of the raid on Cologne as 305 and estimated the number of all air raid victims at 7,430.[27] Following the raid on Cologne at the end of May, there were over fifty further major raids by the RAF on German cities during the next seven months of 1942, with more than one hundred bombers involved on each occasion.[28]

GERMAN OFFENSIVES IN AFRICA AND IN THE EAST

In June 1942 Goebbels judged the nation's mood as being somewhere between "not particularly positive" and "relatively depressed."[29] He blamed this state of affairs on the continuing air raids and worries over how long the war would last but also on the precarious food situation,[30] with which he was obliged to get involved throughout the summer.[31] The military situation in the east, however, in other words the impending summer offensive, and surprisingly positive news from the North African theater promised to bring about an improvement in the nation's mood.

While Field Marshal Rommel's offensive had come to a halt relatively quickly—in the so-called First Battle of El Alamein, which lasted throughout July, Rommel had not succeeded in breaking through the British defenses[32]—at the end of June it appeared as if there was going to be a triumphant military success on the Eastern Front. On June 28 the Wehrmacht began its real summer offensive in the southern sector of the front, by the end of July achieving its operational goal of reaching the River Don on a broad front.[33] In a second phase of the offensive Army Group B marched toward Stalingrad, reaching it in August; Army Group A advanced toward the Caucasus and the Caspian Sea until the offensive came to a halt at the beginning of September.[34] In view of the not particularly positive news from North Africa, at the beginning of July Goebbels's propaganda began to focus on the successes in the east.[35]

In this situation Goebbels took umbrage at a radio talk by Colonel Dietrich von Choltitz, who as a regimental commander had played an important role in the taking of Sebastapol at the beginning of July. Choltitz reported his experience of battle in a way that contradicted Goebbels's line: "It's intolerable the way he praises the Bolsheviks' fighting spirit."[36]

Goebbels gave his opinion of the talk at his ministerial briefing. On May 7 he stated, "The German people [have been] freed from the ba-cillus of communism and Bolshevism only after a long cure. But they're still susceptible to Bolshevism." Two days later he used his briefing to give his staff what amounted to a speech on this issue, the minutes of which ran to ten pages. Objecting to a "Dostoyevsky philosophy of war" and "salon Bolshevism" tendencies, he warned his staff that he would "ruthlessly crush any further example of the tendencies that I have outlined here."[37] Moreover, in an editorial in *Das Reich* with the title "The So-Called Russian Soul" Goebbels inveighed against the danger of creating myths. The Russians had "a kind of primitive tenac-ity" that did not "deserve the honor of being called courage."[38]

Assessing the impact of his article, he reckoned that the majority of his arguments had had an effect, but there was "still a remnant of suspicion that Bolshevism had done more for the Russian people than we were now prepared to accept."[39] He gained a similar impres-sion from a conversation with Sepp Dietrich, the commander of the SS Leibstandarte division deployed in the east, who was visiting him. It was clear that "in the end lengthy stays in the Soviet Union have a fascinating effect on National Socialists as well."[40] These were the fears of a man who in the mid-1920s had admired Lenin, had read Dostoyevsky with enthusiasm, had called himself a "German com-munist," and had seen Russia as a natural ally. His continuing at-tempts to eliminate any remnant of the German people's admiration and respect for Russia and Soviet communism can also be seen as an obsessive attempt to kill off the last germ of this dangerous sickness in himself.

FURTHER SETBACKS IN THE AIR WAR

Successes in the east were counterbalanced by further setbacks in the air war. Goebbels normally noted the increase in British raids, which were mainly on west German targets, in the military section of his diary entries,[41] rarely commenting on them, however. He was only too well aware that there was a direct link between the eastern offensive and Germany's relative inability to fend off the air raids. At the beginning of August he took part in a meeting of Gauleiters hosted by Göring at which the Reich marshal told him that during the next few months they were expecting an increase in Allied air raids and that, because of its heavy involvement in the east, the Luftwaffe had few resources with which to confront them. Various practical questions affecting civilian air raid defense were also discussed.[42] In particular, however, it was necessary to come to grips with the possibility of growing disquiet, and this was the main reason that after the meeting Goebbels embarked on a tour of inspection of the western areas that had been particularly affected.

On the morning of August 7 he arrived in Cologne accompanied by the Gauleiters Josef Grohé (Cologne) and Friedrich Karl Florian (Düsseldorf). Goebbels was pleasantly surprised by the "healthy optimism" that he found among the city's population.[43] He made detailed inquiries of the various agencies involved in the provision of aid and then toured the heavily damaged city.

In the afternoon he gave a speech in the Cologne-Deutz engine factory. He emphasized that "we must accept the wounds that the British air force is now inflicting on us in the west in the interests of pressing ahead with our victorious offensive in the east." Goebbels made sure that not only this speech but also his whole trip was prominently reported in the press. He was quoted in *Das Reich,* for example, saying that "children have become heroes here."[44]

That evening he traveled to his beloved home city of Rheydt, which he found "completely undamaged." He naturally found being accommodated in Schloss Rheydt, a Renaissance palace, which had hitherto been used as a museum and had recently been extensively renovated, particularly "pleasing." It had been placed at his disposal by the city authorities.[45]

On the following day he visited the cities of Neuss and Düsseldorf, which had been damaged in air raids.[46] The Gau capital, Düsseldorf, was still suffering from a kind of "shock effect," for it had suffered its first major raid only a few weeks earlier. He spent that night and the next day once more in Rheydt. At midday he met his schoolfriends Beines and Grünewald, who gave him the latest "city gossip," and in the evening he spoke at another rally in the city.[47]

A few days later he discussed the situation with Hitler, whom he had provided with a fifty-page report of his tour[48] and whom he was now visiting at his headquarters in Vinnytsia in the Ukraine. As far as the propaganda treatment of air raids was concerned, the dictator agreed with him that he did not want any "sensational treatment of the damage that had been caused" but a "vivid depiction of the steadfast bearing of the population under the air raids."[49] On this occasion Hitler told him "in confidence" that "the English raids on certain cities, however cruel they may have been, have a positive side." Looking at the city plan of Cologne he had come to the conclusion that "to a large extent streets that had been flattened would have needed to be flattened in order to open up the city, but flattening them would have imposed a serious psychological burden on the population. So the enemy has done the work for us."

PROPAGANDA STRUGGLES

In the summer and autumn of 1942 Goebbels once again found himself involved in struggles with his main rivals for control over the conduct of propaganda. As in previous years, in these conflicts Goebbels was less concerned with pushing through a particular propaganda line than with asserting or enforcing his claim to direct propaganda. All these conflicts were inextricably linked with personal feuds with his opponents within the leadership of the regime.

Various entries in his diaries show that the appointment of Propaganda Ministry press officers in German foreign missions that had been planned in the agreement with the Foreign Ministry of October 1941 was not going at all smoothly.[50] Moreover, a further argument with the Foreign Ministry occurred in summer 1942. Goebbels wanted to introduce censorship for foreign correspondents[51] after Scandinavian correspondents in Berlin had reported peace overtures from the German government.[52] In view of the doubts expressed by the Foreign Ministry,[53] a series of measures imposing substantial restrictions on the work of correspondents was finally agreed upon without, however, introducing a general censorship.[54]

In July Goebbels also tried to gain ground in his permanent conflict with Dietrich. At the beginning of July he gave instructions to his staff that in the future they should "coolly reject" requests from Führer's headquarters to issue special announcements over the radio on short notice. This was a measure clearly aimed at Dietrich, whom Goebbels still blamed for the premature announcement of victory in the east the previous autumn. Goebbels told his staff that generally "in such cases the Führer headquarters was not identical with the Führer."[55]

Goebbels was, however, completely surprised by Dietrich's announcement that Helmut Sündermann, his "chief of staff" in his Party role as Reich press chief, would in the future also act as his deputy in his state role as Reich press chief.[56] Goebbels, who suspected that Dietrich wanted to establish an independent press ministry, protested to Hitler about this high-handed decision,[57] whereupon the Führer issued a "Basic Instruction for Securing Cooperation between the Reich propaganda minister and the Reich press chief."[58] Goebbels then entered negotiations with Dietrich, which produced a formal "Working Agreement" containing thirteen points and defining responsibilities in detail.[59]

At the same time that he was fixing the boundaries of his turf with respect to Dietrich, Goebbels brought back the former head of the ministry's press department, Hans Fritzsche, who, no doubt worn out by the continuing disagreements between his two bosses, had applied to join the army in the spring of 1942.[60] Goebbels wanted to remove Fritzsche from the "endless personal arguments in the press department" and assign him a new task: overseeing radio news. In reality, however, this only opened up a new front in the war with Dietrich, as the latter was claiming responsibility for the radio's news agency, the Wireless Service.[61]

At the ministry briefing of September 27, prompted by a conversation with Fritzsche the previous day, Goebbels complained that the day-to-day propaganda often used trite jargon and a clichéd style, which "was getting on the nerves" of the German public, while in the neutral countries it was considered "boring and stupid."[62] Goebbels resolved "fundamentally to change the whole tone of our public announcements" during the coming weeks.[63] Fritzsche was to be mainly responsible for pushing through this change. At the beginning of October, Goebbels decided to transfer not only the radio news service to him but also the whole of the radio department, whose responsibilities he had substantially increased in February 1942 at the expense of the Reich Radio Corporation,[64] thereby facilitating effective control over programming. This increase in Fritzsche's responsibilities found expression in his appointment as "the official responsible for the Political and Propaganda Direction of Radio."[65]

After the winter crisis of 1941–42 Goebbels had become convinced that it was necessary to "reorient our policies and propaganda" with respect to the occupied territories in the east. In agreement with numerous experts, he had identified the following points as important: an announcement that *kolkhoz* (collective farm) land would be distributed to farmers; religious tolerance; elevation in the "cultural level"; improvement in social conditions (at least "here and there"), as well as—and here he had strong reservations—the appointment of "pseudo-governments" composed of indigenous personnel.[66] He had naturally concluded that the Reich Ministry for the Occupied Eastern Territories was the most important opponent of such a pragmatic policy.[67] In May, however, he saw Rosenberg adopt a "new course."[68] For during that month Hitler and Rosenberg decided to grant religious toleration in the occupied eastern territories,[69] and in the same month Hitler ordered that in future, if Soviet commissars switched sides, they were no longer to be executed.[70] Although Goebbels saw "signs of a general change of course as regards the Russian mentality,"[71] in neither case was Hitler prepared to make much of the change of direction in propaganda terms, as he was afraid of the threat posed to the authority of German rule in the east.[72] Thus Goebbels had every reason to go on complaining in July about the propaganda situation in the occupied eastern territories and to accuse the Ministry for the East of failure.[73] A lengthy study trip to the east by a delegation of propaganda experts from his ministry gave him additional material with which to make his point.[74] Goebbels concluded from this assessment that he needed to establish his own propaganda apparatus in the east independent of the Ministry for the East (Goebbels referred to it as the "ministry of chaos")[75] and against the will of Rosenberg.[76] At the end of October 1942 negotiations began between the two ministries concerning this issue, without them coming to an

agreement.[77] To put Rosenberg under pressure, Goebbels demanded—
along the same lines as ideas being proposed within the general staff—
that Hitler issue a "Proclamation to the East" containing promises of
a better future for the indigenous population.[78] In January 1943 Hitler did indeed order Goebbels to prepare a draft of such a proclamation.[79] However, in view of the relaxation in the war situation in
spring 1943, Hitler considered that the timing was no longer suitable
for such a declaration. Goebbels naturally blamed Rosenberg for the
proclamation's never being issued.[80]

As far as the Reich's cultural propaganda was concerned, from
1941 onward Goebbels carried on a vigorous feud with the Gauleiter
of Vienna, Baldur von Schirach. Having at first welcomed his appointment in 1940,[81] Goebbels now accused him of pursuing an active cultural policy in Vienna and so of trying to usurp Berlin's
leading role. Thus, during the years 1941–42 Goebbels increasingly
determined to place Berlin more at the forefront of the cultural life of
the nation and to systematically marginalize Vienna.[82]

Goebbels began his demonstrative punishment of Vienna at the
end of 1942. Although he traveled to the Austrian capital in December to attend the celebrations of the 150th anniversary of Mozart's
death and gave a speech there,[83] the following day at the official state
ceremony "the whole affair" seemed to him "so stupid that I considered it better to have my wreath placed by an adjutant."[84] Schirach's
cultural policy was "pubescent, Hitler Youth culture completely unsuitable for the Reich."[85] Shortly afterward he was annoyed that in a
speech in December 1941 Schirach had adopted "to some extent the
Viennese population's objections to the old [i.e., pre-1938] Reich and
above all to the north Germans."[86] In January 1942 he noted that after
"a long struggle" he had at last succeeded in securing the production
of propaganda films of Berlin so that "a true and effective propaganda
for Berlin can counterbalance the excessive glorification of Vienna,
which happens in the production of feature films as well."[87]

During his next trip to Vienna in March 1942, while impressed by
the cultural life of the city,[88] he was strengthened in his view that, as
the capital of the Reich, Berlin must continue "to fulfill its cultural
mission."[89] In May 1942 he ordered the press "to play down Vienna's
cultural ambitions somewhat."[90]

He was encouraged in his efforts by the fact that Hitler kept emphasizing to him the need to marginalize Vienna culturally.[91] That

Hitler had his own axe to grind emerged very clearly during these conversations when he justified his antipathy to Vienna by saying that the city had neglected its great artists so much that they had been forced to live in poverty.[92] During these conversations Hitler kept returning to his far-reaching plans for Linz,[93] which was to replace Budapest as the most beautiful city on the Danube[94] and so "be a major competitor" to Vienna.[95] Goebbels's plan to establish a center near Linz to foster the works of Hitler's favorite composer, Bruckner, including the formation of a first-class orchestra, held particular appeal for the dictator.[96]

During his conversations about Hitler's favorite topic of Linz versus Vienna, Goebbels attempted to systematically undermine Schirach's reputation with the Führer.[97] "His attitude toward Vienna," he noted in November 1941, "is particularly useful to me in my current dispute with von Schirach about cultural policy."[98] And in August 1942 he was content to note that Hitler now "recognizes the problems that have developed because of Schirach's intellectual failure in dealing with Viennese artistic and cultural affairs and is going to give me substantial support in coping with these problems."[99] Thus Goebbels understood how to exploit for his own purposes these nighttime chats with the dictator in which, exhausted by his efforts in running the war, Hitler fantasized about his cultural plans for the postwar era.

CHAPTER 25

"Do You Want Total War?"

The Second Winter Crisis

Following Goebbels's instructions, the Sportpalast, the Nazi movement's "battleground" as he called it, is filled with "true old Party comrades" during a "plebiscite" for total war there, February 18, 1943.

During Goebbels's visit to Führer headquarters on August 19, 1942, Hitler appeared extremely optimistic: He not only wanted to advance as far as Krasny and Baku during the summer and autumn in order to secure German oil supplies, but in addition he intended "to push forward to the Near East, occupy Asia Minor, take Iraq, Iran, Palestine by surprise and thereby, given the loss of its East Asian sources, cut off Britain's remaining oil supply." Meanwhile, he already envisaged Rommel "advancing to Cairo." On this occasion he also opposed taking any propaganda initiatives "to counter the increasing optimism of the German people," which had been disturbing Goebbels for some weeks.[1] Contrary to Goebbels, Hitler took the view that "it will balance itself out on its own." During the coming weeks this differing assessment of the situation was to cause considerable irritation for those in charge of propaganda.

The Battle of Stalingrad began at the end of August 1942. German forces reached the outskirts of Stalingrad and during the following weeks fought their way street by street and house by house toward the Volga, where by the end the Red Army held only a small strip of land.[2] Goebbels was clear about the fact that "to a large extent the fate of this year's summer and autumn offensive" depended on the city.[3] In this critical situation Goebbels was concerned above all to pursue a course whereby excessive expectations of victory were avoided and the population was gradually geared to accepting another winter at war.

In the middle of September it looked as though the fall of Stalingrad was imminent. At the ministerial briefing on September 15, as a precaution, Goebbels was already issuing instructions on how the special announcements about the capture of the city were to be delivered.[4]

At the same time, Dietrich went one step further: Evidently caught up in the very optimistic mood at Führer headquarters, he issued an announcement that the "struggle for Stalingrad" was nearing "its successful conclusion." "Important announcements by OKW" on this were to be expected on the same day or the day after. The press was advised to prepare special editions, a recommendation that some papers did indeed follow.[5]

On the same day, however, Goebbels advised Führer's headquarters not to make such a premature announcement,[6] and on the following day the press was informed that several "limited operations" had to be carried out before the final announcement of victory could be made.[7] During the following days Goebbels kept warning those attending the ministerial briefing to be cautious in their comments on the topic of Stalingrad.[8] Thus, on September 26 he referred once again to Dietrich's premature announcement, which he called "incredible and stupid."[9] On the same day he took Dietrich to task, criticizing his "incompetent news policy" while at the same time complaining to the Wehrmacht High Command about the, in his view, inappropriate way they were releasing information.[10] Evidently he used the incident to put Dietrich, whose self-confidence had considerably increased as a result of their agreement, in his place.[11] For this reason, a few days later he brought the dispute to the attention of Hitler, who agreed with him, albeit in general terms, that "it was inconceivable to have a Propaganda Ministry without uniform control of the press."[12]

DISILLUSIONMENT

On September 30 Hitler spoke for the first time in more than five months, once again at a large public rally broadcast over the radio. Celebrating the opening of the Winter Aid program at the Sportpalast he praised the regime's successes and appeared confident of victory without, however, referring in detail to the situation in Stalingrad, which was being watched with general concern. Goebbels noted with relief that Hitler had been prepared to take on the speech on short notice. During the summer rumors about his state of health had begun to spread because of his absence from the media.[13] On the following day Goebbels took part in a meeting of Reich leaders and Gauleiters at which Hitler made a three-hour speech in order to convince this small group of elite functionaries of his own confidence in victory; the alternative to "total victory" was "total destruction."[14] The aims of this war, Hitler concluded, were very wide-ranging and would require many more sacrifices; however, these would be justified since the war "would make possible the lives of millions of German children."[15]

In the middle of October Goebbels published an article in *Das Reich* in which, along the same lines as Hitler's remarks, rather than focusing on ideological differences he commented in a relatively pragmatic way on the "war aims" for which this continuing conflict was being fought: "This time it's not about throne and altar but about grain and oil, about space for our growing numbers, who cannot live and cannot be fed in the restricted territory in which they have had to stay up until now."[16] The relatively cautious tone of this article indicated that Goebbels was intending to introduce a reorientation affecting not only propaganda but the whole of domestic policy. Winter was coming, and Goebbels saw the opportunity to press once again for a tougher line to be taken in the civilian war effort, and he met with a very positive response in his conversations with leading members of the Party and the Wehrmacht.[17]

In October he determined to use the coming winter with its anticipated difficulties to move more and more toward "a total and radical way of conducting the war both domestically and abroad."[18] That the October reports on the public mood were now once again showing an awareness of the seriousness of the war situation—after a series of speeches by prominent figures earlier reports had temporarily revealed what he regarded as dangerous illusions[19]—was considered by Goebbels to be "a remarkable success for the new form of propaganda that I introduced a year ago with my article 'When or How?'"[20] To set the scene for the campaign he was planning at the beginning of November, he published an editorial in *Das Reich* with the title "War as Social Revolution," in which he emphasized how different the Germans were from "their plutocratic enemy," which was fighting the war in the first instance "against our revolution and particularly against its socialist aspect."[21]

He was concerned that Hitler was becoming largely isolated in his headquarters as a result of his tense relations with his generals and so was becoming increasingly lonely.[22] But the dictator's physical condition was also giving cause for concern. When, on October 29, Goebbels received a personal letter from Hitler on the occasion of his birthday—the "first handwritten letter by the Führer for three years," as Bormann assured him—he read that Hitler hoped that he could decipher his handwriting because his hands were "gradually beginning to shake."[23] Hitler's increasing physical frailty was a growing problem in terms of the deployment of the Führer for propaganda purposes. Thus Goebbels was obliged to note that Hitler "is very unwilling to appear in the weekly newsreels" and kept removing clips in which he was shown, but the people did not understand this.[24] In October 1942 there was a danger that the most important weapon in the propaganda minister's arsenal was no longer going to be usable—this at a time when the regime was confronting its greatest military crisis yet.

VISIBLE SIGNS OF A TURN IN THE WAR

In October 1942 the 6th Army continued to fight its way through the city of Stalingrad toward the banks of the Volga. Toward the end of the month, however, the German offensive began to lose momentum.[25] More serious were the negative reports arriving simultaneously from North Africa. At the end of October the British army launched a counteroffensive against Rommel near El Alamein[26] and on November 2 achieved a breakthrough. Some of Rommel's forces were surrounded and destroyed; the majority had to retreat to the west.[27]

It was high time that Goebbels prepared the German population for another winter crisis. At the beginning of November he published an editorial in *Das Reich* in which he developed two central ideas. On the one hand, he came back to a notion that had already preoccupied him during 1941 and that he had used in an editorial written for January 30, 1942, and on other occasions.[28] Once again he drew a parallel between the Party's position in the months before the "seizure of power" on January 30, 1933, and the current situation. At that time, as now, they had also been involved in a struggle with the alliance between "plutocrats and communists." Although the situation had sometimes seemed hopeless, they had kept their nerve and finally won.[29] Goebbels kept returning to this line of thought during the future crises that the war had in store. He did so both in public statements[30] and above all in conversations with Hitler,[31] whom he tried to encourage in this way, while at the same time reminding him that in those days he, Joseph Goebbels, had been loyal to his Führer.

The article contained a second idea that Goebbels, no doubt intentionally, preceded with a *ceterum censeo:* "Apart from that, we believe that in future our enemies should spend less time talking about our mood [*Stimmung*] and more about our bearing [*Haltung*]. Mood is usually a temporary phenomenon, whereas bearing is something that lasts."

This distinction between "mood" and "bearing" introduced by Goebbels undoubtedly made sense semantically. In view of the harsh conditions of the war, "mood" had frivolous connotations; "bearing" seemed somehow more appropriate to the situation. By distinguishing between them, Goebbels was marking a change of course, which he had been introducing in stages since the beginning of the war. Up until 1940, the year in which the regime achieved its greatest successes, he had pursued a policy that had helped to ensure that the population's approval of the policies of Party and state had been expressed in numerous collective gestures that were publicly documented. However, the days in which the regime could mobilize millions of people in order to carry out pompous parades or to cheer triumphant entries by the Führer or the reception of friendly heads of state had been over for at least two years. Mass events now tended to be held indoors in halls; on the occasion of major Nazi public holidays there were no elaborate street decorations or calls for everyone to put out flags. The more the war penetrated everyday life, the more the regime avoided documenting the population's support for the regime through grandiose gestures and behavior. Now it sufficed if the population went about its daily activities and performed its duties without grumbling or becoming apathetic. That showed a good bearing *(Haltung)*.

By distinguishing between mood and bearing Goebbels also possessed an instrument with which to counter increasingly annoying references to negative tendencies within the population. If bearing and not mood was the decisive criterion, then it could be considered defeatist to refer to mere fluctuations in mood in order to justify particular political measures. Phases in which, as was now frequently the case, the mood was described as "calm," "composed," "serious," could be maintained over a lengthy period, whereas an excessively optimistic mood was not at all appropriate for the seriousness of the situation.

On November 8, as every year, the Nazi leadership met in Munich to commemorate the anniversary of the failed 1923 putsch. Their conversations were dominated by the dramatic developments on the Egyptian front, when suddenly an entirely new situation emerged: British and American forces had landed at various points on the Moroccan and Algerian coasts.[32] Goebbels met Hitler, who three days earlier had been convinced after Montgomery's breakthrough that Egypt would be regarded as the real "second front" and was now rather baffled.[33] Would the Vichy government be in a position, or be willing, to get the French troops in their North African colonies to resist? Hitler was waiting for a reply from the Vichy government, to which he had offered a military alliance against the Allies.[34] Goebbels was already contemplating the prospects for an effective European propaganda initiative offered by such a step. He was dreaming of a "Charter for the Reordering of Europe," although he conceded that such prospects were "too attractive" to be achieved in reality. Finally, Hitler stated that he was willing to dispense with a formal declaration of war by Vichy, provided the French troops offered military resistance. If they did not do this, then he would occupy the unoccupied part of France "in the shortest time." In his speech that evening in the Löwenbräukeller, which was broadcast on the radio, he gave the "old fighters" from the Party the impression that he was confident of victory but made only a brief mention of the situation in North Africa.[35]

During the night of November 9–10—the usual celebrations of the 1923 putsch had taken place during the day—the French prime minister, Pierre Laval, arrived in Munich to discuss the new situation with the Nazi leadership; it was becoming clear that the French resistance in North Africa was at most symbolic.[36] Hitler retaliated in the way that he had already announced. The German invasion of the hitherto unoccupied part of France began on November 11 and after three days was essentially concluded.[37]

While the German forces in the west of the African theater tried to build a new bridgehead[38] and, as Goebbels dramatically put it, were in a race with the American army to Tunis,[39] at the same time in the east Rommel was marching rapidly toward the Tunisian border; they had been forced to give up Tobruk on November 13.[40] Goebbels learned from the SD report that the events in North Africa had "deeply shocked the German public."[41] In fact they were to initiate the turn in the war.

In the middle of November Goebbels once again made a trip to western areas affected by bombing. He inspected the damage in Duisburg, where he was informed about the situation by the local authorities and spoke to representatives of the Gau agencies and the state authorities. He then visited Elberfeld where, during his visit to the town hall, the "streets [were] packed with masses of people. [. . .] A triumphal journey like in peacetime." In his speech he thanked the people of Elberfeld, describing their damaged city as a "West wall of German fighting spirit."[42]

Goebbels's private arrangements for this trip were in marked contrast to this heroic spirit. He stayed in the Rheydt Schloss, which "has been made exceptionally comfortable for our stay." He had invited "a few old schoolfriends" for the evening, among them Beines and Grünewald, but also a senior teacher, Voss. "We sat together until late in the evening, telling stories and exchanging memories." On the afternoon of the following day he gave theater fans in his hometown a special treat: "On my instructions," as he noted, there was a guest performance in the city theater by the Berlin Schiller Theater with Heinrich George and other famous actors. In the evening he again invited some of the theater people and "various acquaintances and friends from my school days" to the Rheydt Schloss.[43] Even after ten years as propaganda minister his need to show off on his home turf was still unsatisfied.

Back in Berlin, however, Goebbels soon adjusted to the seriousness of the situation. He was encouraged in his aim of supporting "a radicalization of our war efforts toward total war in all spheres" by the fact that in the middle of November, like all the Gauleiters, he had been appointed a Reich defense commissioner. This authorized him to give instructions to the authorities in all matters concerned with the civilian war effort.[44]

Understandably, the "general propaganda situation" was giving him cause for concern: "In general we are rather on the defensive. We have little to offer foreign countries, particularly as far as plans for the future of Europe are concerned." At home they lacked "an overarching idea for war propaganda over the longer term," a situation that had been caused by the "stupidities of subordinate agencies."[45]

It was no surprise that this time his seasonal depression[46] affected him very badly: "November is National Socialism's unlucky month. The revolt* broke out in November 1918; the putsch failed in November 1923; in November 1932 we lost 32 [Reichstag] seats; in November last year we had the Rostov catastrophe; in November this year we are experiencing North Africa and the Bolshevist success at Stalingrad."[47]

THE MURDER OF THE JEWS: NO DENIAL

In December 1942 a growing number of reports about the mass murder of Jews in German-occupied Europe began to appear in the in-

---

* Translators' note: Significantly, Goebbels uses the pejorative term *revolt* rather than *revolution*.

ternational media. On December 17 the Allies published a statement about the systematic murder of the Jews by the Nazi regime; accusations about this formed a central theme of Allied propaganda, albeit only for a relatively brief period.[48]

Goebbels followed this development with interest. On December 5, 1942, he took note in his diary of the worldwide protests against the "alleged atrocities committed by the German government against the European Jews." In the following days Goebbels issued repeated instructions at his ministerial briefings to ignore the Allied accusations without, however, denying them to his staff.[49] The statement that he gave to his subordinates on December 12 was disarmingly frank: "Since the enemy reports about the alleged German atrocities committed on Jews and Poles are becoming increasingly extensive and yet we have not much evidence with which to counter them," he gave instructions "to start an atrocity propaganda campaign ourselves and report with the greatest possible emphasis on English atrocities in India, in the Near East, in Iran, Egypt etc., everywhere where the English are based."[50]

Goebbels returned to the subject on December 14: "We can't respond to these things. If the Jews say that we've shot 2.5 million Jews in Poland or deported them to the east, naturally we can't say that it was actually only 2.3 million. So we're not in a position to get involved in a dispute, at least not in front of world opinion." At the same briefing Goebbels gave further instructions for the "exoneration campaign": All reports about alleged atrocities by the enemy had to be "given big coverage"; every day "something new [must] be found."[51]

There were in fact several articles in the press[52] that reflected these instructions, but within a few days the campaign died down,[53] to Goebbels's annoyance.[54] However, repeated admonishments, issued both in the internal ministerial briefings and to the press, show that this campaign never really got going, and in fact that German propaganda was on the defensive.[55] German propaganda had no reply to the Allied accusations that they were murdering Jews.

GEARING UP FOR "TOTAL WAR"

On November 22 Goebbels learned that, as a result of a Soviet pincer movement, the German troops in Stalingrad were surrounded.[56] On November 24 Hitler gave the order to hold the pocket at all costs; supplies would arrive via the air.[57] During the coming weeks Goebbels followed the fate of the 6th Army in Stalingrad, although to begin with his diaries give no inkling that he expected a military catastrophe.[58] Shortly before Christmas, however, he came to the conclusion that the general situation in the east was "critical."[59] He considered the Christmas festivities, which encouraged reflection, to be psychologically problematic.[60]

During these days of Christmas sentimentality he attempted to give death at the front a kind of metaphysical significance. At the end of the year he published an article in *Das Reich* in which, as he put it in his diary, he "wanted to see the problem of our dead [. . .] from a more profound perspective." Thus, referring to those who had died young in the war: "At the moment when they gave up their lives, life itself surrounded them with a heroic rhythm. [. . .] Our dead are standing on the other side of life with its light shining upon them. We are the seekers, they have found fulfillment. They have fulfilled their time early, time which still lies before us with a thousand riddles and tasks."[61]

On December 28 Martin Bormann arrived in Lanke on Hitler's behalf[62] to discuss with Goebbels the planned celebration of the tenth anniversary of January 30, 1933. According to Bormann, the day should "not be used for talking about the future but rather for weighing up what has happened since then." This was a proposal that went directly counter to Robert Ley's plans. He had been trying to persuade Goebbels that the anniversary should be used to announce far-reaching social legislation.[63] Moreover, Bormann had been told by Hitler "to discuss with me the question of total war in all its aspects." This represented a "real triumph" for Goebbels, as it appeared that "all the ideas and wishes that I have kept putting forward for a year and a half are now suddenly going to be acted upon."

Goebbels now energetically pursued his plans to introduce measures that would produce "total war." His main objectives were the introduction of labor conscription for women, closing down companies that were not essential for the war effort, and shutting down expensive restaurants and luxury shops.[64] He had his ministry produce a "memorandum on the conduct of total war," which he then sent to the head of the Reich Chancellery, Hans-Heinrich Lammers.[65]

After speaking to several individuals,[66] preaching to those attending his ministerial briefings,[67] and reassuring himself in daily entries in his diary that introducing measures for "total war" was the decisive key to victory,[68] on January 8 Goebbels chaired a meeting attended by Lammers, Bormann, Keitel, Funk, Sauckel, and Speer.[69] Here he demanded that "in a relatively short space of time we should place at the Führer's disposal 500,000 people who have hitherto been excused military service"; in addition, there were another 200,000 people whom Hitler had ordered Speer to remove from the armaments industry. Sauckel made some objections on the grounds that the problem could be solved with the existing arrangements, but in the end they agreed on the text of a Führer edict that was submitted to Hitler.[70]

To reinforce his position Goebbels began a propaganda campaign, aiming to put pressure on colleagues who were still hesitating and to fill the propaganda vacuum that was threatening to develop in view of Hitler's continuing silence in the face of the growing crisis. On January 17 he published an important article in *Das Reich* to which he gave the title "Total War." His main thesis was: "The more radically and the more totally we fight the war, the quicker we shall come to a victorious conclusion." "A certain small section of our people" did not seem to be concerned, so he duly attacked "do-nothings," "idlers," and "parasites."[71]

The following week he kept up the pressure and made the point in another article with the title "The Appearance of War." "Looked at from the outside, the way the war is being waged on the home front does not at first glance give one the impression that it is a matter of life or death." So what was to be done? Naturally it was the right thing to do "to maintain our cultural life." But shops in which there was nothing left to buy, bars, gourmet restaurants, and so on had to be shut.[72]

The Führer edict concerning the Comprehensive Deployment of Men and Women for Reich Defense Tasks finally signed by Hitler on January 13 envisaged, as Goebbels had wished, purging the labor market in order to free up as much labor as possible for deployment in the armaments industry and the Wehrmacht. To achieve this, all dispensations from military service were to be reexamined, all those who were not yet at work were to be registered, and all businesses not engaged in essential war work were to be shut down.[73]

Hitler assigned the coordination of these measures to a "Committee of Three." To begin with Goebbels assumed that he was going to be a member of this committee but then had to accept that Keitel would be its third member, in addition to Bormann and Lammers.[74] However, the edict stated that the three should maintain "close contact" with him. Immediately after the decree had been signed, Goebbels was already noting negative reactions: "Certain circles are doing everything they can to exclude me from the inner group of advisers. [. . .] I'm very worried that Lammers and Keitel in particular will try to water down radical decisions."[75]

On January 2 a meeting of the "Committee of Four," as Goebbels now called it, took place, to which some experts, as well as Sauckel and Funk, were also summoned. Goebbels used the opportunity to clarify his position vis-à-vis the committee: "I am seen and recognized as the driving force in the whole thing, and in any case all the proposals that I make for new decrees or alterations to old ones are accepted without demur." At the end of the meeting, as far as labor conscription for women was concerned, he believed that he had gotten his way against "every bureaucratic obstacle and objection," though this soon proved to be an illusion.[76]

The more the public mood was affected by the deteriorating military situation, the more urgent Goebbels believed it was to introduce radical measures to boost the war effort.[77] Concern was focused on the situation on the Eastern Front and specifically the fate of the 6th Army. On January 16 the regime felt obliged to announce that it was surrounded in Stalingrad, but after that propaganda said remarkably little about the fate of those involved.[78]

Goebbels now hoped that a massive public campaign for "total war" launched in this situation would secure relief, provide a diversion and a kind of work therapy, and at the same time expand the regime's room for maneuver. The mobilization for "total war" was intended to strengthen the authority of Party and state and increase their powers of control over the population. His model was the wool clothing collection of the previous year, but this time the campaign would be on an even larger scale.[79] It was hoped that a population that was totally involved in dealing with the harsh realities of the home front would demonstrate a firm "bearing," rendering crises in the public "mood" of secondary significance.

"We must gradually come to terms," Goebbels noted on January 21 in reference to Stalingrad, "with having to inform the German people about the situation there." In reality this should have happened long before, but Hitler had always been against it. Goebbels, however, believed that by giving the people a frank account of the situation in Stalingrad, they could bind them even more closely to the regime. He wanted to use the Stalingrad defeat to push through his policy of total war.

Goebbels had the decisive conversation with Hitler on January 22, 1943, in his East Prussian headquarters, where a "somewhat depressed and extremely serious mood" prevailed.[80] Before meeting Hitler Goebbels had reassured himself through various conversations that "my preparatory work on the question of the move to 'total war' has already struck deep roots." Rudolf Schmundt, Hitler's Wehrmacht adjutant, encouraged him in his intention "to be ruthless in getting everything off my chest with Hitler," and Hitler's adjutant, Albert Bormann, and his physician, Karl Brandt, encouraged him in this, as did the new army chief of the general staff, Kurt Zeitzler. Karl Wolff, Himmler's liaison to Hitler, assured him of the Reichsführer's full support.

Goebbels also used the opportunity of his visit to Führer headquarters to have a detailed discussion with Dietrich. "The press must adopt a completely different tone than hitherto [. . .] now, instead of pursing our lips, we must start to whistle." Dietrich took the point and immediately produced a slogan with which the press was inducted into its new tasks. The "great, moving, and heroic sacrifice that the German troops who are surrounded in Stalingrad are making for the German nation, together with the impending labor conscription for women and other drastic measures for the conduct of 'total war' will provide the moral incentive for a truly heroic bearing on the part of the whole of the German nation and the starting point for a new phase of a German will to victory and for mobilizing all our energies."[81]

Finally, Goebbels met Hitler around midday for a tête-à-tête, having been allowed to accompany him on a walk during the morning and to listen to his worries about Stalingrad. Then, during their detailed discussions, Hitler began by expressing his concern about the crisis in the east: Their allies had failed, and the Luftwaffe leadership had not fulfilled its promises. In the middle of the conversation, as if it had been orchestrated by Goebbels, there was a telephone call from Zeitzler reporting a major breakthrough by the Red Army into the German defenses in Stalingrad.

Goebbels exploited the situation to put his "plan for reorganizing the home front" to Hitler: the introduction of female labor conscription, the "closing of all institutions and companies not essential to the war effort," and the "gearing of the whole of the organization of civilian life to the needs of the war." And he was successful; indeed, he noted that Hitler "is going in some points even further than I suggested." Hitler told Goebbels, however, that he did not want "me personally to join the Committee of Three so that I wouldn't be burdened by the administrative work of this great program." Instead, Goebbels should "take on the role of the continually running engine in this whole operation" and keep an eye on the work of the committee. However, in the case of one decisive point Hitler watered down his edict of January 13, a fact of which Goebbels took only marginal note: The maximum age for female labor conscription was reduced from fifty to forty-five.

After a lengthy interruption there was a final conversation, which lasted from ten o'clock at night until three-thirty in the morning. Goebbels had finally succeeded in achieving his aims: "There will be a sort of dictatorship of the four men concerned, of whom I am to be the psychological dictator and the engine driving the whole thing." In the middle of the night Goebbels drove back to his quarters in Rastenburg: "I believe that the resolutions made on this decisive Friday may give the war a decisive change in direction." On the following day, in order to make a record of it all, he prepared a ninety-page set of minutes of his conversations with Hitler.[82]

Soon, however, strong resistance to the "introduction of total war measures on the home front" began to make itself felt from various quarters, particularly in respect of both the closing down of businesses and the systematic implementation of female labor conscription.[83] For example, Goebbels was surprised that Göring urgently requested that gourmet restaurants in Berlin such as Horchers and other exclusive restaurants and shops should be allowed to remain open.[84] By intervening with Hitler Lammers too succeeded in ensuring that women with children should be free from labor conscription, even if the care of their children was being provided for. Goebbels considered this "a serious breach" of the "uniform approach" that he was advocating. He began to regard Lammers as the center of opposition. He was considering "the whole thing from a bourgeois-*gemütlich* perspective."[85] The changes watering down the Führer edict of January 12, which were then contained in the decree on labor conscription issued on January 27,[86] represented a clear signal to the bureaucracy that it was possible to resist Goebbels's radicalism successfully.

On January 28 a further meeting of the Committee of Four took place, which in Goebbels's view was "extraordinarily ill-tempered." It concerned the planned closure of businesses. While he, Funk, and Speer demanded "radical decisions," Lammers, who was supported by Bormann and Sauckel, tried to "torpedo" this line. What Goebbels did not mention in his diary was that in the meeting Lammers and Bormann referred to a decision by Hitler that the closing of businesses should not cause unnecessary unemployment. Despite this intervention, at the end of the meeting Goebbels believed that measures had been taken to make 300,000 people available for the armaments industry. In fact the actual results of the action were to be far more modest than expected.[87] His diary entry, which provided a very shortened account of the debate, shows that he was simply unwilling to admit that, as with the case of female labor conscription, Hitler's support for radical measures was only halfhearted. The Führer was not eager to take up a position on such matters; he certainly did not want to appear as the person behind unpopular measures.

On the day before the meeting Goebbels had written another editorial on the topic of "total war." He described his tactics: "If I have more problems with the 'Committee of Four' I intend to take my message more to the public."[88] "Many of us do not show sufficient understanding for this change of approach," he asserted in an article entitled "The Hard Lesson." These people consider that "for a civilized life certain things cannot be done without, things that were unknown twenty years ago, let alone a hundred years ago. If we lacked the strength to bring this war to a victorious conclusion, they would very quickly be compelled to do without not only these things but several others as well."[89]

On January 30 the tenth anniversary of the "seizure of power" was celebrated, although, in view of the military situation, the elaborate program that was originally envisaged had been considerably reduced by Hitler on Goebbels's advice.[90] Goebbels now had the honor of reading out a proclamation from Hitler in the Berlin Sportpalast, introducing it with a trend-setting speech.[91] Since Hitler was avoiding a public appearance at the high point of the crisis, it more or less automatically fell to Goebbels to take on the role of being the regime's main state orator.

Goebbels used this opportunity to put forward his own agenda. "From the depths of our nation we are hearing the cry for total commitment to the war effort in the broadest sense of the word," he proclaimed to the Sportpalast audience.[92] Goebbels considered that his speech had had an "enormous" effect. He regarded the "waves of applause" and the "enthusiastic interruptions" as a plebiscite for his demands for "total war." "So I'm not only not too radical in my views on total war, in the people's eyes I'm not radical enough. Now there's no limit to what we can do to move things along." He was particularly impressed that "within five minutes" a few of the top Nazi functionaries in the hall, including Hierl, Ley, and Himmler, were "at one with the rest of the audience." The final part of the rally reminded him of the best days of the "time of struggle"—that is, pre-1933. That night, Hitler, who had heard the speech on the radio, called to applaud his propaganda minister's success.[93]

Goebbels learned from the reports on the public mood that his speech had relieved the negative mood to a considerable extent. "Above all, the huge applause that followed my announcement of radical and total measures has caused quite a stir."[94] According to these reports the people wanted "total war [. . .] as quickly as possible," for it was the case that "they considered the measures taken hitherto as too weak, that trust in the leadership, even in the Führer himself, had been shaken because the conclusions that should have been drawn from the setbacks that have happened have not in fact been drawn."[95]

In Goebbels's view Hitler's silence in the face of the crisis—his last radio broadcast was in November—was having far-reaching consequences. The political system of the "Führer state" depended on producing continuing public support for the dictator's policies. If he stayed out of sight for several months, then the system lost its corner-stone and must inevitably be coasting. There was a dearth of opportunities to organize the usual public demonstrations of mass support for Hitler's policies, and the lack of publicly documented support was inevitably going to be perceived by those reporting on the public mood in terms of a leadership crisis. For the Führer state to be maintained in the absence of the Führer was going to require extraordinary efforts.

THE DEFEAT AT STALINGRAD: GOEBBELS'S CHANCE

After Goebbels's conversation with Hitler on January 22, propaganda had begun to prepare the population to receive the news of the catastrophe engulfing the 6th Army. During the last week in January, for example, the *Völkischer Beobachter* daily carried headlines about the "heroic" resistance in Stalingrad, which would be to the "immortal honor" of the 6th Army.[96] The southern sector of the pocket that had now been cut in half surrendered on January 31, and two days later resistance ceased in the northern sector.[97] Goebbels regarded the fact that the commander of the 6th Army, General Friedrich Paulus, who had been promoted to field marshal on January 31, was taken prisoner, together with some other generals, as "deeply regrettable"; he had assumed, as indeed had Hitler, that, in view of the defeat, Paulus had "no alternative but an honorable soldier's death."[98]

From the beginning of February Goebbels had been preoccupied with the special announcement of the fall of Stalingrad. He decided on a tone that should be "kept very realistic, very matter-of-fact, and entirely unemotional." He managed to persuade Hitler to have only three days of remembrance instead of the seven originally planned.[99] On February 3, at four o'clock in the afternoon, the radio announced the fall of the city. The announcement had "a kind of shock effect on the German people," according to Goebbels.[100]

An editorial written by him on the same day established the line that was to be taken in the propaganda campaign that followed. The aim was to relieve the nation's depression through the measures for "total war" that he had been preparing during the preceding weeks. The people know "the hard reality and are now enthusiastically demanding that equally tough conclusions should be drawn from it. [. . .] In one word: Total war in all areas is the order of the day."[101]

On February 5 and 6, directly after the fall of the city, he took part in a meeting of Gauleiters in Posen, where his talk on "the issues involved in the conduct of total war was received with unreserved approval and unanimous applause."[102] Whereas Goebbels approved of the speeches of Speer, Funk, and the head of agriculture, Herbert Backe, he objected to Sauckel's talk, not only for being boring but also for failing to provide any advice for the Gauleiters. In fact Sauckel had made clear that the priority for labor mobilization continued to lie with the recruitment of foreign labor, whereas the reserves of female labor had been largely exhausted and they would have to show maximum consideration when it came to recruiting further women.[103] In fact the majority of Gauleiters supported this line of not expecting too much from the home front rather than Goebbels's radicalism. Thus when Sauckel had finished Goebbels felt obliged to return to the podium "to make up for what had been left out."

On the afternoon of February 7 the Gau and Reich leaders gathered in the Führer's headquarters to listen to a speech by Hitler about the current situation that was almost two hours long.[104] Hitler pointed out to his old comrades that they must now use "the means and the methods with which we used to master Party crises in the old days." He blamed their allies, the Romanians, the Italians, and the Hungarians, for the catastrophe in the east. He admitted, however, they had not had "a clear idea of the numbers of people involved in the east." "The problem," Goebbels noted later, was that "the Bolsheviks had mobilized their people's energies far more than we did." This comparison was of course grist to his mill.

Hitler did not forget to emphasize an important "enemy advantage": "The Jews operate in all the enemy states as a driving force, and we have nothing comparable with which to counter it. This means that we must eliminate the Jews not only from Reich territory but from the whole of Europe." And Goebbels noted: "Here too the Führer adopts my point of view that Berlin must come first and that in the foreseeable future not a single Jew shall be permitted to remain in Berlin."

THE SPORTPALAST SPEECH

In the middle of February Goebbels complained to Bormann[105] and to the Reich Chancellery that the "so-called Committee of Three" was making decisions in which he had not been involved. Since, however, the relevant Führer decree did not envisage his participation in measures taken by the Committee of Three, his complaint fell on deaf ears, and in the end he decided against making a direct appeal to Hitler.[106]

This made him all the more determined to mobilize "public opinion" for the implementation of his demand for "total war." On February 9 he had already noted that the "inadequate legal bases" for "total war [. . .] can be replaced only by the Party adopting a sort of terrorist approach, which will enable us to deal with those who have hitherto tried in some way to avoid taking part in the war." He was strengthened in this view by his interpretation of the reports he was receiving on the public mood.[107] The worse the reports from the Eastern Front, the more "vigorously the broad masses are asking for the adoption of total war";[108] indeed, they were now demanding "urgently from the government the introduction not of total but of the most total war. I have been increasingly recognized as the spiritus rector of this movement."[109]

The entry for February 13 in Goebbels's diary contains the first reference to his plan for a speech, which he had scheduled for the 18th. According to Goebbels, in view of the "measures necessary for total war," it was vital to continue to agitate and press on with it and "for this purpose I am organizing [. . .] a new mass rally in the Sportpalast, which once again I'm going to fill with real old Party comrades." As many prominent people as possible were to be invited so that they would experience a rally, which "in its radicalism will surpass anything that has gone before."

"This meeting [will] once again be broadcast on all radio stations in order to put pressure on public opinion in the individual Gaus, so that if any Gauleiter has hitherto resisted implementing a tough measure, he will perhaps now feel obliged to make up for it." Two days later, describing his own role in relation to this speech, he stated that he was "still the driving force, and I shall go on making use of the whip until I've woken up the lazy sleepers."[110] Hitler's public silence had created a vacuum, which the propaganda minister was now entering with a vengeance.

On the day of the rally the press was instructed to publish "impressions of the mood" of the meeting that "express the fighting spirit of the whole German nation." Particular emphasis should be given to "the two central points of the speech [. . .], first, the theme of anti-Bolshevism and secondly the theme of the commitment to total war." The "greatest emphasis, however, should be given to the ten questions that Dr. Goebbels will ask the German people."[111] They could use "the language of the time of struggle."[112]

On February 18 Goebbels finally made his speech on "total war," which is generally regarded as his most important and at the same time his most repulsive rhetorical performance. He had intentionally chosen the Sportpalast, the Nazi Party's preferred venue for its mass rallies since the end of the 1920s. This sports arena was considered to be the traditional "battleground" of the Berlin Nazis, who had used the particular aura of this popular venue, where usually it was six-day races and ice hockey and boxing matches that aroused the emotions of the masses, for their political rallies. This time too the hall was decorated with large swastika flags; at the front of the hall hung a huge banner with the motto of the evening: "Total War—Shortest War."

The central message of Goebbels's speech of February 18 was that only the Wehrmacht and the German people were in a position to stop the Bolshevik onslaught, but that they must act "quickly and thoroughly."[113] Once again the speech contained a tough anti-Semitic passage, which was intended to make it clear against whom the "total war" was in essence directed: "We see in Jewry an immediate danger for every nation. [. . .] Germany, in any case, does not intend to submit to this threat but instead to oppose it in a timely manner and if necessary with the most radical countermeasures." Total war, Goebbels continued, "is the order of the day. We must put an end to the bourgeois scruples of people, who even in this fight for our existence want to operate on the principle of: 'make me an omelette, but don't break any eggs.'"

Goebbels referred to his speech of January 30 and to the "gales of applause" that had greeted his announcement of total war: "So I can say that the leadership's actions have the complete support of the whole of the German nation, both at home and at the front. [. . .] So it's now time to get those who are not pulling their weight to buck up." To document this consensus Goebbels simply declared his audience to be a representative "sample of the whole German nation," which now collectively—"as part of the people"—had assembled to carry out a plebiscite for total war.

The high point of his speech consisted of the ten questions, to which the audience responded with waves of applause and which had everything: ecstatic professions of faith, a demonstration of determination and loyalty, as well as enthusiastic personal commitment. This inclusion of the audience, which replied to the speaker each time like a chorus, is certainly reminiscent of liturgical forms. The number of questions and the phrase with which Goebbels introduced each question, "I ask you," must have aroused biblical associations.[114] The following provides a sample: "Are you determined to follow the Führer through thick and thin in the struggle for victory and to put up with even the heaviest burdens? [. . .] Do you want total war? If necessary, do you want it to be more total and more radical than we can imagine it today? [. . .] Do you swear a solemn oath to the fighting front that the country is behind it with its morale high and that it will give everything necessary to achieve victory?" While in previous years he had carefully avoided such religious associations, now, with the regime in it up to its neck, it seemed to him once again appropriate to use religious imagery, albeit in judicious doses.[115]

When Goebbels posed the question as to whether they trusted the Führer, he received the longest applause of all. The *Völkischer Beobachter*'s reporter had already used so many superlatives in describing the audience's enthusiasm that evening that he had difficulty in finding a way of doing justice to the applause that followed it: "The crowd rises as one. They erupt in an unprecedented storm of applause. The hall echoes to the sound of tens of thousands of people chanting: 'Führer command us; we'll follow!,' a never-ending wave of shouts of Heil to the Führer."

Goebbels described his impressions of the meeting as follows: "The audience is composed of all sections of the nation, from the government at the top to the unknown munitions worker." He seems to have forgotten that he himself had ordered a mass rally with old Party comrades. "My speech makes a very deep impression. From the start it was continually interrupted with terrific applause. [. . .] The Sportpalast has never seen such turbulent scenes as when at the end

I put my ten questions to the audience. The response was massive approval."[116]

Magda, who to his delight had just decided to begin war work in the Telefunken plant (in fact this plan came to nothing because she had a hospital stay lasting several weeks),[117] was in the audience, as were his daughters Helge and Hilde, who were attending such a mass rally for the first time: "It made a strong impression on Helga, in particular, even though she didn't understand everything I said in my speech. I'm pleased that our children are already being introduced to politics at such a young age."

In the evening he entertained some prominent figures, including Luftwaffe field marshal Erhard Milch; Speer; Stuckart; the future Reich minister of justice, Otto Thierack; and many others: "During the evening many people were saying that this meeting represented a sort of quiet coup. [. . .] Total war is now no longer a matter for a few perceptive men; it's now supported by the whole nation."

His response to the reactions to his speech at home and abroad was typically over the top:[118] "During the whole war there surely hasn't been a speech made in Germany that has been quoted and commented on so much throughout the world as this Sportpalast speech of February 18."[119] And finally, there was news from the Führer: "He describes this speech as a psychological and propaganda masterpiece of the first order."[120]

The only thing he was annoyed about was the SD report, which, in his view, was simply interested in taking note of "all those who were grumbling" and which did not fit in with the "get up and go" mood that he had wanted to create.[121] In fact, during this period, as in December,[122] Goebbels was thoroughly discontented with the SD reporting: "Grumbling by groups that are permanently discontented" was falsely being portrayed as "the opinion of the German people."[123] A few days later, however, he was revising his opinion: "The new SD report is entirely focused on my Sportpalast speech, stating that it has made a very deep impression on the German public."[124] However, a perusal of the reports of February 24, 1943, which formed the basis for his self-praise, presents a more mixed picture of the speech's impact. In particular, large numbers of people were all too aware of "the propaganda motive" of the ten questions he had posed.[125]

The discontent within the Propaganda Ministry, however, was directed not only at the SD reports. A few days later the ministry sent a circular to the Party's Reich propaganda offices complaining about the fact that recently reports had been submitted "in which for no good reason or on the basis of insignificant incidents conclusions have been drawn about the poor morale of certain groups. It would be better to deal with these matters yourselves using the methods of the time of struggle rather than reporting them to us."[126]

The proclamation issued by Hitler in Munich on February 24 on the occasion of the anniversary of the Party's foundation—Goebbels, pleading the excuse of flu, remained in Berlin[127]—was "very much along the lines of my Sportpalast speech," Goebbels noted with satisfaction. "So there's no danger that I might in some way be repudiated." It was always best to create a "fait accompli." "If the nation comes to terms with these facts, then that means we've achieved our goal."[128] A few days later, however, he learned from Ley that "there have been complaints about my Sportpalast speech from various people in Munich"; Goebbels concluded that the critics had been "consumed with envy."[129]

THE COMMITTEE OF THREE: TOTAL WAR ON THE CHEAP

In the meantime Goebbels had been becoming more involved in the work of the Committee of Three. In February and March it dealt, among other things, with the standardization of wage reductions and the simplification of taxes, with cuts to universities and various administrative reforms, including restrictions on the appointment and promotion of civil servants.[130]

During the committee's sessions Goebbels took on the role of activist and hard-liner. On February 27 he demanded from the representatives of the Wehrmacht "more energetic measures" in order to achieve the recruitment figures that had been envisaged and told Keitel, when he tried to respond, how much his agencies were "in need of reform." During the discussion of cuts to the universities on March 16, he pointed out that "the daughters of wealthy families are studying in order to avoid labor service." At the same session, during the discussion of a decree against the sabotaging of total war measures, he demanded that the death penalty be introduced for the most serious offenders.[131]

In several instances, however, it can be shown that Goebbels played up his role in the sessions in his diary entries and exaggerated the "successes" that he claimed. Although he acted as the vigorous proponent of a radical course in the committee, many of the changes that he sought or believed to have pushed through were simply not implemented, or only to a very limited extent.

Thus, on March 16, for example, he saw the "reform of the judicial system [...] now being carried out in exact accordance with my views"; in particular the right of appeal in civil cases was to be abolished; in fact, however, there was merely a simplification of the appeal process.[132] Concerning the same session he wrote in his diary that he had strongly criticized the way in which recruitment to the Wehrmacht was being carried out, but there is no record of his contribution in the minutes because, at Keitel's request, the item had been removed from the agenda. Similarly, he praised his role in getting the Reich Headquarters for Regional Planning abolished; in fact, however, the decision was simply to reduce the scope of its activities.[133] Having banned horse riding in the Berlin Tiergarten, Goebbels did not succeed in persuading Hitler to put an end to horse racing altogether. The latter took the view that "during wartime" they must "continue to maintain [...] entertainment for the general public."[134]

Above all, Goebbels was aware that the most important obstacle to a rationalization of the administration—the unsolved and "difficult problem of the division of responsibilities between the various ministries"—could not be removed so long as Hitler could not be "persuaded to make clear and tough decisions." But Hitler was precisely not prepared to do that, as his power depended not least on the carefully balanced rivalry and tension that existed among the individual members of the leadership corps. Goebbels could do nothing but comment with a certain resignation that it was "completely absurd that individual ministries and important agencies are fighting each other while the enemy is achieving one success after another."[135]

In the meantime, however, Goebbels had begun to assess the possibilities of undermining the power of the Committee of Three. One evening at home in February he discussed with Speer, Ley, and Funk the possibility "of neutralizing the Committee of Three by reviving the Ministerial Council for the Defense of the Reich." For this purpose, Göring, the chairman of the Ministerial Council, was to be provided with "a suitable deputy." Right away Speer and Funk came up with the appropriate candidate: Joseph Goebbels. "I would be very happy to do it." Goebbels then continued: "I would assemble a group of around ten men, who are all excellent people, and I would then rule with them, i.e. establish a domestic political leadership."[136]

Speer contacted Göring and two days later met the Reich marshal in Berchtesgaden.[137] During a long conversation in which the "minor disagreements" of the past apparently no longer played a part, Göring agreed with Speer's suggestion that the "leadership role carried out by the Committee of Three be transferred to the Ministerial Committee for the Defense of the Reich." Moreover, both were agreed on "what would threaten us all if we became weak in this war"; they had committed themselves so far in the "Jewish question" that "there is no possible chance of escape. And that's a good thing." For "experience shows that a movement and a nation which has burned its bridges fights with far fewer reservations than one that still has the possibility of withdrawal."

During his next visit to Führer's headquarters in Vinnytsia on March 8, however, Goebbels learned that "Göring's prestige with the Führer had declined hugely"; indeed the Führer told him during a tête-à-tête that he wanted to dismiss Göring.[138] Thus the plan to reactivate the Ministerial Council had to be postponed. At the decisive meeting on March 18, attended by, in addition to Goebbels, Speer, Ley, and Funk,[139] it was agreed in principle to revive the council and for this purpose initially to add to it "a few strong men"; this meant in the first instance Speer, Himmler, and Goebbels. Funk was already a member of the council in his capacity as economics minister. Goebbels had to put up with the fact, as he put it, that "nolens volens" (like it or not), Frick was also a member.

According to the plan, Göring was to propose the changes to Hitler, and then the work of the Committee of Three would be transferred to the reactivated Ministerial Council and dealt with there. In the event that Göring was not in a position to attend weekly meetings of the Ministerial Council, Goebbels would represent him. "It is intended that over time this will develop into a permanent deputization." This would have had a not insignificant impact on the whole leadership structure. "Lammers would thereby lose his role as Göring's deputy without much of a to-do, and he would be pushed back into the position of secretary, for which he was intended in the first place. In their spheres of operation Bormann and Keitel are also effectively secretaries of the Führer and have not the right to exercise power on their own authority." The reactivation of Göring, which Goebbels energetically pursued during the following weeks, would thus have had far-reaching consequences for the regime's whole leadership structure.

However, as long as this had not yet happened and as long as the proposals for "total war" were blocked in the Committee of Three, Goebbels's attempts to secure radical measures for the pursuit of the war were more or less ineffectual, indeed from his point of view were becoming counterproductive. Having appeared in the Sportpalast as the leading advocate of "total war," he was now in danger of being blamed for its halfhearted implementation. He gathered from the SD reports that there was support for the planned measures but also growing criticism that the steps that had been taken were not radical enough. After reading the SD report he commented: "The point is: No storm has burst forth, as I promised in my Sportpalast speech."[140] When he read in the SD report that, on the contrary, sections of the population had reservations about class conflict tendencies in the "total war" campaign,[141] he responded immediately. It was inevitable, he declared in an article in *Das Reich*, that total war would bring about a "certain amount of egalitarianism." But this did not happen "out of envy or class prejudice" but rather "from absolute necessity, as a result of the goal being pursued."[142] A week later he followed this up with a further article in *Das Reich* objecting to the fact that "for example, a few hotheads are trying to exploit the favorable opportunity to indulge their unadulterated class prejudices."[143]

Clearly Goebbels, who had been so eager to appear as the advocate of a "socialist course" in the Nazi Party and who, the previous November, had referred to "war as social revolution" in *Das Reich*, was afraid that he could come under the not unjustified suspicion of wanting to introduce a kind of war communism. All this may have prompted him to gradually withdraw from excessive commitment to total war. There were other fields in which his radicalism could find expression.

THE FACTORY ACTION

In February he learned that the deportation of the Berlin Jews was to begin in March "in stages"; he set himself the target of ensuring that the city would be "completely free of Jews" by the middle or, at the latest, the end of March, from which he hoped for "a great relief of the psychological situation."[144]

On February 27 the "factory action" began in Berlin, the sudden arrest of more than eight thousand Jews, the majority at their places of work. "Unfortunately," Goebbels noted a few days later, "the upper classes, in particular the intellectuals, don't understand our Jewish policy, and some of them support the Jews." Four thousand people had managed to escape because they had been warned in time.[145] Moreover, a few days later he noted that "there have been some rather unpleasant scenes in front of a Jewish old people's home where large numbers of people gathered, some of whom even took the side of the Jews." And on March 11: "Unfortunately, initially the male and female Jews in privileged marriages were arrested as well, which has produced a lot of fear and confusion." Goebbels was referring to silent protests, above all by non-Jews who were in "mixed marriages" with Jews who had been arrested during the action. Since a major air raid on Berlin had occurred on March 1, to which we shall return, Goebbels tried to persuade the SD to halt the deportations in order not to add to the tension that already existed in the city. However, the deportations continued. Around two thousand Jews married to non-Jews, who were incarcerated in the Jewish community offices in the Rosenstrasse, were released after a few days. This was not, however, the result of Goebbels's intervention, nor was it the result of the protests; the SD had not intended to deport this group from the start.[146]

On March 8 and 14, Hitler once again told Goebbels that he was entirely correct in his policy of "getting rid of the Jews from Berlin as quickly as possible."[147] A few days later Hitler was "extremely shocked" by the fact that seventeen thousand Jews were still living in so-called mixed marriages in Berlin and gave Frick instructions, as Goebbels discovered, "to facilitate the divorce of such marriages and to terminate them even when a mere wish has been expressed." Goebbels backed this initiative to the hilt[148] and, furthermore, noted that he was convinced that "by liberating Berlin from Jews I have carried out one of my greatest political acts."[149] At the ministerial briefing he ordered that the number of "Jewish apartments" that had become vacant should be revealed via word of mouth propaganda.[150] Furthermore, he asked to be regularly informed about the number of Jews still living in Berlin. He blamed them for "most of the subversive rumors" and did his best to have them "moved out" as soon as possible.[151]

AIR RAIDS ON BERLIN AND THE RUHR

At the beginning of 1943 Goebbels succeeded in formalizing the responsibilities that Hitler had given him the previous spring for combating air raid damage across the nation. On January 15 the Air Raid Damage Committee met for the first time under his chairmanship, after Frick had declined to chair it.[152]

To begin with, however, Goebbels had to deal with the bomb damage on his own doorstep. In the middle of January, for the first time since the air raids of 1941, there had been a significant British raid on Berlin. It had been carried out by around thirty-five planes and caused relatively little damage but cost the lives of thirty people.[153] Goebbels had complained in January that the civilian air defenses were very inadequate: "The whole apparatus has become completely rusty during the past few months because of the lack of air raids." So he had made a "huge fuss" and boasted that he had "gotten the whole operation moving again within a very short time."[154]

The test came on the evening of March 1, 1943. Over 250 planes attacked the city, killing more than seven hundred people.[155] Goebbels, who had been staying in Munich, arrived in the morning and inspected the damage. He considered the population to have demonstrated "a magnificent bearing" and he gave instructions to a hastily arranged meeting of the Berlin Party functionaries to ensure that this was sustained.[156] Goebbels's behavior is characteristic of the way in which he dealt with air raids. He was concerned above all to ensure that the population affected by bombing should maintain the "right bearing" (Haltung). This was the theme of the propaganda concerning the air war. In fact, by rapidly deploying Party agencies to the affected areas Goebbels aimed to prevent any indications of poor morale—apathy, war weariness, let alone discontent or protests. But he went even further: He kept visiting the affected areas, as in March 1943 in Berlin, in order to reassure himself that the "population is extremely nice and friendly to me."[157] The propaganda minister chatting with the victims of bombing became a central topos of propaganda during the second half of the war. Goebbels continued to be concerned with making absolutely sure that a certain image of the Third Reich be maintained in the propaganda media rather than finding out what the survivors of the bombing really felt. In a proclamation, which appeared in the Berlin press, he expressed "to the population of the Reich capital his acknowledgment of and gratitude" for the superb "bearing" they had demonstrated.[158]

Given the continuing Allied air raids, people feared the worst when, on March 21, for the first time in four months, Hitler gave a ten-minute address in Berlin on the occasion of the Heroes Memorial Day, which was broadcast on all the radio stations. But, to Goebbels's relief, the anticipated air raid did not occur. Goebbels considered the "construction and style of the speech marvelous,"[159] but a few days later he was worried that the number of those killed in the war, given by Hitler in his speech as 542,000, which was probably more or less correct,[160] was "generally considered by the German people to be too low."[161] There could hardly have been a clearer indication of the decline in the Führer's aura and in the loss of the political leadership's credibility.

At the end of March a further British air raid on Berlin, this time with over three hundred aircraft, arrived punctually, as Goebbels had feared, to coincide with Wehrmacht Day.[162] Two nights later the Royal Air Force appeared once again with three hundred bombers over Berlin. This time the raid resulted in over two hundred deaths, and the material damage was considerable. Among other things, the German Opera was hit. Goebbels, who sent all available fire engines to deal with it, credited the saving of the building to his own personal intervention.[163]

But it was not only Berlin that was being affected by the air war. Between March and June the RAF carried out multiple raids on Essen, above all hitting the Krupp factories.[164] Goebbels was extremely concerned about the damage.[165] In April, in his role as chairman of the Air Raid Damage Committee, he visited the city, which had been so badly hit and which, he concluded, "to a large extent would have to be written off." In Essen he had a meeting with Ley, the West German Gauleiters, and several Oberbürgermeisters. They discussed giving preference to the areas affected by the air war in the provision of necessities, the evacuation of the population, the construction of air raid shelters, and other matters.

On the following day, at his ministerial briefing back in Berlin, he gave his impressions of the trip. The Party was gradually coming to be seen as "responsible for the population's pastoral care,"[166] and he gave instructions to the press to give more prominence to the provision of air raid shelters. Reporting the "Essen meeting" and the speech he had given at it would provide a "good opportunity" to do this.[167]

MORE RELAXATION IN RADIO AND FILM

The more the Reich was threatened by Allied bombers and the more the situation at the various fronts became critical, the more Goebbels endeavored to provide the population with relaxation through the most important mass media of the time: radio and film.

Goebbels's demand, which he had been making increasingly urgently since 1941, for more entertaining and reasonably priced films was largely being fulfilled by the film industry right up until the end of the war.[168] The diaries show clearly that he was also prepared to admit—more or less unwillingly—that his demand for quality and good taste was increasingly being left on the cutting room floor and also that his ideas of "contemporary" topics and "homely patriotism" could not be realized. In his analysis of Goebbels's film policy, the film historian Felix Moeller suggests that the "Film Minister" was unhappy with almost half the films produced during the second half of the war. In 1944 he banned more films on the grounds of their poor quality than ever before, and yet the majority of films were shown.[169]

In September 1943, Goebbels noted that "a few entertainment films are being strongly criticized as no longer appropriate for the present time." In fact he was finding himself confronted with an insoluble dilemma. For, as he continued, how "can one gear an entertainment film that was shot a year ago to the situation that exists 12 months later?"[170] In December 1943 he noted that "the current standard of films is beneath contempt."[171] In 1944 he was particularly displeased with several productions set in the pre-1914 period.[172] In December he wrote that he was going to deal "ruthlessly" with the tendency to avoid the tough conflicts of the present day by seeking escape in the Biedermeier period. He no longer wanted to view films that took place in a "blatantly luxurious milieu."[173]

There were, however, exceptions among the run-of-the-mill films, for example, the color film *Münchhausen,* produced in 1943, which Goebbels described as "an extraordinarily colorful and lively fairytale picture."[174] Goebbels also enjoyed the films *Romanze in Moll* (Romance in a Minor Key, 1943) and *Unter den Brücken* (Under the Bridges, 1944), both directed by Helmut Käutner. Käutner was "the avant-gardist among German film directors."[175]

Goebbels focused mainly on the films remaining in the production program, some of which were elaborate propaganda films. The majority of projects, however, were victims of the times and therefore were rejected by Goebbels before shooting started or else displeased him when they had been completed. He judged that the film *Besatzung Dora* (The Crew of the Dora, 1943) would have been better suited to "the second year rather than the fourth year of the war," and the film was not shown in cinemas.[176] He also blocked various other film projects dealing with military triumphs of the Wehrmacht from the past. Also, films of catastrophes, that had already been completed, such as *Titanic,* or *Panik* (in which animals break out of a zoo after an air raid), or the Käutner film *Grosse Freiheit Nummer 7,* which is set in a Hamburg that had not yet been bombed, no longer reflected the reality of the war and so were also not shown in German cinemas.[177]

He was impressed, however, by the film *Die Degenhardts* (The Degenhardts), completed in 1944, which deals with the topic of the air war by using the example of the destruction of Lübeck.[178] He also liked the film *Junge Adler* (Young Eagles), directed by Alfred Weidenmann and based on the book by Herbert Reinecker, which was aimed at young people. This was the first production of the team that was to create a successful postwar television crime series. It was the story of a group of apprentices, who, with great enthusiasm, were helping in a factory building bombers. It was one of the few films of this period that showed swastika flags and Hitler Youth uniforms. The young main characters were played by the successful postwar actors Hardy Krüger, Gunnar Möller, and Dietmar Schönherr.[179] To Goebbels's disappointment, however, the film was not popular with the public; he suspected the reason was that people "don't want to watch any political films at the moment."[180]

His favorite project was the history of the successful defense of the Prussian fortress of Kolberg by the Prussian army and the local militia against an overwhelmingly superior force of Napoleonic troops in 1807. The Kolberg project, he wrote in May 1943, will suit "to a tee the political and military situation that we shall probably be facing at the time when the film comes out."[181] He intervened frequently in the conception and production of this extraordinarily lavish film.[182] He finally viewed the film in December 1944 on two occasions, one shortly after the other and, while recognizing that it was a "masterpiece of direction," he demanded that its director, Veit Harlan, make some cuts.[183]

He was not, however, at all pleased with Harlan's changes: "He has treated the scenes of destruction and despair in the city so crudely that I'm afraid that in the current situation large sections of the public will simply refuse to watch it."[184] The film, which had been altered once again, was shown in cinemas in January 1945, but only a few copies were made available. The audiences in the bombed-out cities could watch the gradual destruction of an East German small town in 1807 whose inhabitants defied Napoleon but at the same time naturally could not prevent the defeat of the Prussian state. Goebbels, however, was pleased that Hitler "has been very enthusiastic about the effect of the Kolberg film," which, in particular, "made a huge impression when shown to the general staff."[185]

When the real Kolberg had to be evacuated in March 1945 in the face of the Soviet advance, he did not want any reference to it in the OKW report. They "could do without" such reports "at the moment, in view of the powerful psychological implications for the Kolberg film."[186] Goebbels could not accept that reality had overtaken propaganda.

Typically, he blamed all the difficulties that arose for German film during these years on other people and withdrew into the stance of a disgusted spectator. Initially, the head of production at Ufa, Otto Heinz Jahn,[187] acted as his scapegoat, until in April 1943 he was finally replaced by the director Wolfgang Liebeneiner.[188] Fritz Hippler's reputation soon declined in Goebbels's eyes, and on July 1, 1943, he was dismissed as Reich superintendent of film, although initially he was not replaced.[189]

In July 1943, having secured Hitler's approval, Goebbels relaxed his control over film production. He ordered that production companies should in future provide only short content reports for each film being proposed: "I only want to get involved in the script and the casting in the case of particularly important projects."[190] Hans Hinkel was appointed as the new Reich superintendant of film in April 1944, and he also took over the ministry's film department.[191] Shortly afterward, Gutterer, who was leaving his position as state secretary in the Propaganda Ministry, was given the sinecure of chairman of the Ufa board, although he soon ran into criticism from the propaganda minister in this job as well.[192] Hinkel's "strict regime" soon brought him into conflict with Goebbels's Reich commissioner for the film industry, Max Winkler, who was continually complaining about the constant interventions in the current production and with the individual production companies, interventions that were contrary to Goebbels's instruction of July 1943. Goebbels supported Winkler, who, "apart from anything else ensures that the film industry operates along commercial lines."[193] This was a clear admission by Goebbels of the failure of his film policy. For a long time he had opposed the existence of an independent film industry working along commercial lines and instead had attempted to subordinate film production to the political control of his ministry. Now he had given this up, as well as his ideas about how to reform the content of German film.

As far as radio was concerned, during the second half of the war Goebbels continued to pursue his policy of a far-reaching "relaxation" of the program. In May 1943, for example, he complained to Karl Cerff, the head of the Main Cultural Office of the Hitler Youth leadership, that on the question of scheduling he was adopting "a rather too National Socialist standpoint." It would not do for "radio music to be made exclusively with lurs."*[194] Above all he pressed for a further reduction in the spoken word. With the exception of the first weeks after Stalingrad, in which the scheduling adopted a more serious tone, right up until the end of the war German radio broad-

---

* Translators' note: A lur is an ancient Germanic musical instrument, a blowing horn without finger holes that is played by embouchure.

casts were dominated by entertainment and the attempt to create a good mood.[195]

Apart from his assignment to take charge of the political and propaganda content of the radio schedule, in April 1944 Fritzsche was also made responsible for musical entertainment.[196] He was supposed to achieve the right balance between "music" and "words."[197] Nevertheless, Goebbels kept intervening directly in the scheduling, attempting to achieve a balance between the modern entertainment music, which was so much in demand among the public, and the seriousness of the war situation. In August, for example, he objected to "a few excesses, particularly in the case of the dance and entertainment music."[198] As so often, it seemed to him that here too a middle way was required. They should "not have a mournful program or a program of marching bands" but "moderate entertainment."[199]

CHAPTER 26

"The Masses Have Become Somewhat Skeptical or ... Are in the Grip of a Sense of Hopelessness"

Crisis as a Permanent State

During the war, personal contact with Hitler continued to remain critical for Goebbels's position in the Third Reich. The dictator and his propaganda minister on the Obersalzberg, 1943.

At the end of February, as the first thaw set in, the Soviet winter offensive came to a halt and from the middle of March 1943 the situation on the Eastern Front had more or less stabilized; indeed, with its recapture of Kharkov the Wehrmacht had even achieved a prestige success.[1] This development gradually had a positive effect on the nation's mood; in March it increasingly appeared to have "stabilized," and in April it continued to improve, at least according to the reports produced by the Party's Reich propaganda offices and letters sent to the ministry.[2] However, these reports did not so much reflect an improvement in the population's mood as the fact that Goebbels had been continuing to alter the criteria for the assessment of its mood. On April 11 he expatiated once more on his preferred distinction between "mood" and "bearing," the latter allegedly playing "a decisive role [. . .] in modern war."[3]

In his view, however, the SD reports continued to be much more negative than those from his own area of responsibility.[4] The SD reports, he noted in the middle of March, were recording "more grumbling" and "in general have recently been annoying me." The reports recorded "too many details. The leadership of the Reich has no interest in knowing that somewhere in a small country town there is someone who is sounding off about something." Thus he gave the head of the Ministry's propaganda department, Berndt, the task of improving the harmonization of the reporting by the SD and by the Party's Reich propaganda offices.[5]

However, this did not happen. Instead, the SD's "Reich Reports" were stopped in June 1943 and replaced by the Reports on Domestic Issues, which were geared to recipients responsible for particular spheres of responsibility.[6] However, even in their new version Goebbels found the reports "completely useless for practical work" for, as before, they continued to record "what some anonymous person in some town or village or other has thought fit to express as his opinion."[7]

"TOTAL WAR" IS NOT HAPPENING

In spring 1943 Goebbels had to face the fact that, as a result of the "slowly recurring spring or summer illusions," his ideas of "total war" were being further undermined by every conceivable agency. Hitler, in particular, was all too prone to respond positively to such initiatives. Goebbels noted that these included such widely varying things as the reappearance of entertainment magazines, the reopening of casinos, the inadequate enforcement of labor conscription for women, the suspension of travel restrictions, and other issues.[8] This situation was also reflected in the fact that Hitler was not prepared to discipline leading members of the regime whose personal conduct was grossly at odds with the requirements of total warfare.

At the beginning of 1943 the Berlin criminal police uncovered a crime in which the Berlin food purveyor August Nöthling had delivered expensive foodstuffs to numerous prominent figures without the requisite ration coupons having been provided. Among those implicated were Reich Interior Minister Frick, Foreign Minister Ribbentrop, Minister of Education Rust, Agriculture Minister Darré, and others, in other words figures who did not necessarily enjoy the propaganda minister's approval.[9]

In March, Goebbels, who had detailed information on the matter via the Berlin police chief, Helldorf, informed Hitler.[10] He was "fairly shocked," but did not want to make it a "matter of state." Goebbels should contact the Reich minister of justice, Thierack, and get him to deal with the issue without too much fuss. "Sometimes the Führer is rather too generous in these decisions," Goebbels commented.[11]

He discussed the matter with Thierack the following day[12] and a few weeks later learned that Hitler had at least ordered that those involved should be interrogated by Thierack.[13] However, most of them had responded to the latter's questions insolently, as Goebbels soon discovered.[14] Apart from that, the case against Nöthling was soon closed following his suicide while on remand. As far as the prominent figures involved were concerned, in July Hitler finally decided that they were not to be prosecuted, which Goebbels was not entirely happy with.[15] Hitler, however, was prepared to sign an "Instruction Concerning the Exemplary Behavior of Persons in Leading Positions." But Goebbels was not surprised that the head of the Reich Chancellery, Lammers, had watered down the instruction, as he too had been one of Nöthling's customers.[16]

In the middle of April Goebbels's idea of mobilizing Göring for his plans for making the war more total ended, for the time being in any case, in a fiasco. Goebbels's health let him down in a decisive situation. His skin condition, a rapidly spreading eczema, had affected him so much that he had had to spend a few days at home convalescing.[17] Then, on April 12, on the way to Berchtesgaden, where Göring had summoned a meeting intended to give a new impetus to the mobilization of labor resources, Goebbels suffered a "terrible pain in the kidneys" shortly before arriving. The pain was so "barbaric" that he was unable to leave his sleeping car.[18]

Later he learned that Sauckel had largely gotten his way at the meeting. He had succeeded in portraying the situation in relation to labor deployment in such a way that neither Göring nor Speer nor Milch could put forward effective counterarguments in favor of further decisive measures for total war. For, according to Goebbels, they had naturally been depending entirely on his "knowledge and expertise" but had had to do without it because of his illness.[19] After he had once again discussed the situation with Speer and Funk at the beginning of May, he came to the conclusion that at that point it was not possible to "persuade Göring to take over the domestic conduct of the war. At the moment he is rather weary and is on leave for four weeks."[20]

Although Goebbels noted that the dictator was "unreservedly" in favor of the principle of total war,[21] a conviction in which he was encouraged by Speer,[22] the reality was rather different. On May 9, for example, Hitler told him categorically that "total war" must "not involve a war against women [. . .] as soon as you interfere with their beauty treatment you become their enemy." Casinos and betting on horses were also to remain in order to soak up consumer spending.[23] A few days later he was told that Hitler was opposed to all plans to use the measures for rationalizing the administration, which were being undertaken as part of "total war," for bringing in a "reform of the Reich" through the back door, in other words to carry out far-reaching alterations in the structure of the Reich and the states (Länder) while the war was going on.[24]

On the other hand, Goebbels felt duty bound: "The nation associates the notion and the conception of total war with me personally. I am, therefore, to a certain extent publicly responsible for carrying on total war."[25] Now the strategy he had adopted at the start of the year began to come home to roost. At the beginning of the year he, Goebbels, had attempted to fill the vacuum that had developed because of Hitler's absence from the public sphere. He had announced "total war" in the latter's name, and now, since he had been unsuccessful in pushing the responsibility on to Göring, he had to cope with the consequences of the unsuccessful mobilization measures. Goebbels's solution to this dilemma was to play down the theme of "total war" somewhat during the following months. In the meantime he had discovered another topic, which he was to make the leitmotif of German propaganda during the coming weeks.

KATYN

At the end of March and the beginning of April 1943 Goebbels had ordered an increase in the existing anti-Bolshevik and anti-Semitic propaganda,[26] and so the discovery of the mass graves of Polish officers at Katyn at the beginning of April—they had been shot by the Soviet occupation forces in 1940—offered an unexpected opportunity to make these topics the overwhelmingly dominant theme of German propaganda.[27] Having secured Hitler's approval, on April 14 Goebbels noted that the discovery of the corpses would "now be exploited in a major way for anti-Bolshevik propaganda"; using the available material would enable them "to keep going for several weeks."[28]

German propaganda crudely assumed that the murders were the work of Jewish communists. With Katyn the stereotypical image of Jewish Bolshevism had now acquired a human face. On April 16 Goebbels noted in his diary: "We shall stoke up anti-Semitic propaganda to such an extent that, as in the 'time of struggle' [i.e. pre-1933], the word 'Jew' will once again have the devastating impact that it should have."

The start of the uprising in the Warsaw Ghetto on April 19 fit into the scenario of a threat from the Jews that propaganda had already been painting in broad strokes. Goebbels commented: "It's high time that we removed the Jews from the General Government as quickly as possible."[29] The extent to which he coordinated the Katyn campaign with Hitler is clear from his diary entries during these days.[30] By increasing anti-Jewish propaganda Goebbels was very much hoping to strengthen anti-Semitic sentiment in the enemy states, particularly in Britain.[31] Moreover, the aim was to use the mass murders in Katyn to drive a wedge into the enemy coalition.

Urged on by the Propaganda Ministry,[32] under the motto "Katyn" the German press carried out what was probably the most vigorous anti-Semitic campaign since the start of the regime. On April 14 the whole of the press gave coverage, often sensationalist, to the opening of the mass graves of Katyn under banner headlines. Within a few days the whole of the press had adopted the slogan of "Jewish mass murder" (*Der Angriff* of April 16). For weeks this remained the main topic.[33] In Goebbels's view the breach between the Polish government

in exile and the Soviet Union at the end of April represented the first
success of his campaign.[34]

It is clear from the internal documents of the Propaganda Ministry, however, that it was by no means satisfied with the way in which
the press was conducting the campaign. Thus Goebbels expressed his
disappointment at the ministerial press briefing on April 30. There
were some editors who were past it, who were only carrying out
anti-Semitic propaganda "by the book" and who were not engendering "any fury or hatred" because they "did not share these feelings
themselves."[35] Thus the ministerial spokesman complained at the
press conference that the press was "much too reserved" on this issue.
The "authorities" had the impression that the "Jewish topic was felt to
be unpleasant."[36]

The Katyn propaganda was now embodied in a key statement: The
Jews must be destroyed in order not to be destroyed by them. This
thesis can be found in numerous variations in the German press.
Thus, referring to the Jews, *Der Angriff* of May 4, for example, states:
"Their aim is the destruction of Germany"; the May 6 issue of the
same paper stated that "the Jews" will continue the war "with all
available means until either Germany is destroyed or they themselves
lie shattered on the ground."

Goebbels's article "The War and the Jews," which appeared on
May 9, 1943, in the journal *Das Reich*, represented a high point in the
propaganda campaign and summed up Germany's lethal objectives
by taking the line that "Jewry" was the real guilty party in this war
and that the Jews represented the "cement that is holding the enemy
coalition together." Goebbels's further statements leave little room for
doubt concerning the regime's intentions regarding this enemy. "It is
thus necessary for the security of the state that we take the necessary
measures within our own country that appear appropriate to protect
the German national community at war from this threat. That may
lead here and there to serious decisions having to be made, but that
is unimportant compared with this threat. For this war is a racial war.
It was begun by Jewry, and its purpose and the plan behind it are
nothing less than the destruction and the extermination of our people."

In the end, according to Goebbels, "the Führer's prophecy will be
fulfilled, the one that, when it was made in 1939, world Jewry simply
laughed off. The Jews in Germany also laughed when we began op-

posing them for the first time. But they're certainly not laughing now. [. . .] When they devised the plan for the total destruction of the German people, they were signing their own death warrant. Here too world history will be a world court."

On May 7, two days before the appearance of this article, Goebbels joined the Reich leaders and Gauleiters whom Hitler had assembled in the Reich Chancellery in order to address them. Hitler argued that, as far as the "intellectual basis of our fight against the Soviet Union" is concerned, "anti-Semitism, as previously cultivated in and propagated by the Party, must once again be at the core of our intellectual confrontation." Using the example of the Hungarian dictator, Miklós Horthy, who "with his family [has] very strong Jewish connections" and was refusing to support Germany's persecution of the Jews, Hitler made it clear that in the future he would regard an uncompromising attitude on the "Jewish question" as an essential criterion in assessing the reliability of his allies. Horthy's soft attitude had strengthened Hitler in his view that "the junk of small states which still exists in Europe must be liquidated as quickly as possible." Hitler endeavored to drum into the Party leadership the central importance of his Jewish policy: "Given that eastern Bolshevism is nowadays largely led by Jews and the Jews are also prominent in western plutocracies, this must form the starting point for our anti-Semitic propaganda. The Jews must get out of Europe."[37]

During these days Goebbels commented with some annoyance on news from the Warsaw Ghetto uprising. On May 1 he noted: "The Jews have actually managed to mount a defense of the ghetto"; during the following days he was equally astonished by the fact that the uprising had "still" not been crushed.[38]

DEFEAT IN TUNIS

On May 13 the German and Italian forces in North Africa, which had been pushed back to Tunis, capitulated; over a quarter of a million men were captured by the British and the Americans. After the catastrophe of Stalingrad it was the second major defeat of the Wehrmacht within the space of only a few months. This was the turning point of the war.[39] Newspaper reports of the "heroic struggle" in Tunisia, of the "struggle to the bitter end" that had been fought there, had prepared German readers for the impending defeat.[40]

Goebbels tried to console himself with the thought that the German soldiers in Africa had taken part in "an epic struggle that will go down in the annals of German history." Nevertheless, he had to admit that they were experiencing a "kind of second Stalingrad" in Africa.[41] Goebbels prescribed the line to be taken by German propaganda by noting in an article in *Das Reich* that the losses in Tunis would not impair Germany's chances of victory.[42] His diaries, however, contain passages that cast doubt on such optimism: "Sometimes one has the feeling that we lack the necessary initiative in our conduct of the war. [. . .] It is high time that we—as indeed can be expected—achieved a tangible result in the east."[43]

What was above all embarrassing for German propaganda was the fact that, instead of the war hero Rommel going down with flying colors in Tunisia, for the previous few months he had been back in Germany. Goebbels and Hitler decided to inform the German public of this. The press published a two-month-old photograph of Rommel and Hitler, commenting that the field marshal had been recalled in March for health reasons and had been awarded the Knight's Cross, with its oak leaves, swords, and diamonds, by the Führer. Now he was well again and awaiting new tasks.[44]

In the middle of May, on top of the military defeats, Germany was faced with a serious domestic political problem. The regime was compelled to announce a reduction in the meat ration. It had long been clear that this step would be necessary, but Hitler had resisted it, a stance that Goebbels had considered a "short-sighted policy," indeed a "catastrophic policy."[45] On May 9 Goebbels spoke to Hitler about the now unavoidable cut. It was to be "somewhat sweetened" by an increase in the rations for fats, sugar, and bread.[46] However, Goebbels was by no means happy with the way in which the press announced the cuts in the middle of the month. They had been "minimized" and as a result had appeared "provocative."[47]

At the end of the month Goebbels noted that the Party's Reich propaganda offices were reporting that the whole nation was "generally in a severe depression." What was particularly alarming was his discovery that "not only a deterioration in mood but also a collapse in people's firmness of purpose" was detectable. This was "mainly attributable to the fact that at the moment the nation cannot see a way out of the dilemma. The war has become a great enigma."[48] At the beginning of June the bad mood continued.[49] The system of carefully leading and controlling public opinion established by Goebbels was evidently coming up against its limits. The reports indicate that people were expressing their discontent and despair about the war situation in a way that contravened what was officially considered the appropriate "bearing" in public.

In Goebbels's view the lack of domestic political leadership was one of the main factors contributing to the current crisis and mood of resignation in the Reich.[50] At a small evening get-together with Speer, Ley, and Funk he discussed the urgent domestic political problems under the motto of the "Göring crisis." "Göring is showing a certain lethargy in letting the whole situation pass by him, without trying to resist the decline in his prestige."[51] It was time, he continued, that "the Führer created order and stability here by making a decision of far-reaching importance affecting personnel. But such a decision is probably a long way off." Joseph Goebbels, in any case, was ready to accept such a decision.

Goebbels tried to calm the serious concerns about the war situation that were emerging on a large scale through an article in *Das Reich*. He explained that the military conquests of recent years were entirely sufficient to "ensure us an absolutely secure position from which we can move with virtual certainty toward victory." Without mentioning Stalingrad or Tunis directly he commented that it was in the "nature of such a wide-ranging conduct of the war that it is bound to be vulnerable at the margins, leading to signs of crisis from time to time, which cannot affect the core of our political and military position but produce certain problems, particularly of a psychological nature."[52]

THE CONTINUATION OF ANTI-SEMITIC PROPAGANDA

However, as far as propaganda was concerned another avenue seemed to him more promising: to continue and expand the anti-Semitic propaganda campaign initiated in connection with the Katyn incident. On May 12 he carefully studied the propaganda work *The Protocols of the Elders of Zion* and was pleased to discover that he could make excellent use of it. "If the Zionist protocols aren't genuine, then they have been invented by a brilliant contemporary critic." During his midday visit to the Reich Chancellery he spoke to Hitler about the topic. The latter, he noted, did not share his cautious view about their authenticity at all. Hitler considered that the protocols could "claim absolute authenticity. [...] No one could describe so brilliantly the pursuit of world domination by the Jews as they have done themselves."

In any case Goebbels was convinced that he had a trump in his hands with this topic: "As after Stalingrad anti-Bolshevik propaganda, now after Tunis anti-Jewish propaganda forms the core of all our journalism."[53] In the middle of May Berndt presented him with a memorandum with the title "For Boosting Anti-Jewish Propaganda." Goebbels approved it and gave instructions to republish the "standard anti-Semitic literature" that had become somewhat forgotten.[54] He wanted "a few anti-Semitic novels to be written and by respected writers. [...] I'm thinking here of [Hans] Fallada, Norbert Jacques, and others."[55] He was aiming to make "anti-Semitism once again the standard topic of our whole propaganda."

And that is what happened. The German press faithfully implemented the instructions of the Propaganda Ministry, which continually fed it with relevant material.[56] From the beginning of May until the beginning of June, in some papers there was at least one anti-Semitic article in almost every issue, in others about half that number.[57]

At the end of May Goebbels regarded the dissolution of the Comintern as an important victory and as the opportunity for a "new stage in the anti-Bolshevik and anti-Jewish campaign."[58] He carefully noted any signs of an increase in anti-Semitism among the enemy.[59] The topic of Katyn was now used less and less in propaganda,[60] being replaced by other anti-Semitic diatribes.

Thus the Propaganda Ministry announced that the bombing of the Möhne and Eder dams on the night of May 16–17 had been prompted by a Jewish scientist;[61] the North African territories conquered by the Allies were now being subjected to a Jewish "regime of terror"; the American intention of establishing a World Food Bank was portrayed as a "plan for the Jewish exploitation of the world."[62] Moreover, the German press seized on reports of Allied postwar plans and attacked them as proof of the—Jewish-inspired—intention to "destroy" Germany; in view of this threat the annihilation of the Jews was nothing more than an act of self-defense.[63]

However, the effect of the anti-Semitic campaign on the population was highly ambivalent, as is clear from the surviving reports on the public mood. Apart from positive reactions it also produced irritation and opposition. On the one hand, there was astonishment and unease about the fact that, in view of the widely known atrocities that it had itself committed, the Nazi regime should now attack the enemy's conduct of the war as inhumane; on the other, there was concern for the prisoners of war in the Soviet Union, while the idea that in the event of defeat they would themselves become victims of the methods of the Soviet secret police that were being given so much publicity induced a sense of horror.[64]

Also, the propaganda assertion that the Allied air attacks were the work of Jewish instigators proved at least partly counterproductive, because among some sections of the population it led to undesirable discussions about Jewish persecution and its consequences for people's own fates. Moreover, in many cases the population rejected the propaganda assertion that "the Jews" were entirely responsible for the war. Goebbels's anti-Jewish propaganda campaign, in which he threatened that in the event of defeat they would be faced with "Jewish reprisals," did not, therefore, produce the expected mobilization of the last reserves but rather encouraged skepticism about official policy and a sense of fatalism, as people believed that in view of enemy superiority they would be defenseless in the face of the threatened annihilation. The deep depression among the population that Goebbels detected at the end of May had to a significant extent been caused by the excessive use of anti-Semitism.

On May 18, while he was fully occupied with dealing with the crisis and with anti-Semitic propaganda, Goebbels met his favorite poet, Knut Hamsun, who had arrived in Germany on a visit. The Norwegian poet visited him together with his wife at home in the Göringstrasse.[65] Goebbels was "deeply moved," indeed "shaken" by this meeting with the eighty-four-year-old. Conversation with Hamsun proved extremely difficult because of his deafness; Frau Hamsun "has to translate what I said into Norwegian and then shout it into the ears" of the elderly poet. According to Goebbels, however, Hamsun's brief comments "radiated the experience of old age and of a rich, varied, and combative life." Above all Goebbels liked the fact that his "faith in a German victory [was] completely unshaken."

Five weeks later he received a letter from Hamsun honoring him with his Nobel Prize medal and certificate. Goebbels, "deeply moved by this extraordinarily fine gesture," wrote Hamsun a thank-you letter in which he described the gift "as an expression of your support for our struggle for a new Europe and a happier humanity." In this situation he was happy to ignore the fact that ever since it had been awarded to Carl von Ossietzky the Nobel Prize was frowned upon in Germany.[66] However, the elderly poet's visit to the Führer a few weeks later became something of a fiasco, as Goebbels learned from a handful of informants. For "egged on by Norwegian journalists," as Goebbels assumed, Hamsun dared to pose serious questions about the political future of Norway and to criticize the policies of Reich Commissioner Josef Terboven. It was reported to Goebbels that Hitler had responded impatiently and broken off the conversation. "In future it will be more difficult to introduce 'lyric and epic poets,' as he puts it, to the Führer."[67]

ANOTHER SPORTPALAST SPEECH

On June 5 Goebbels gave a "major political speech" in the Sportpalast in order to improve what was generally considered to be a bad mood in the country. Originally it had been envisaged that Göring would carry out this task, but the Reich marshal balked at the last minute. Since Hitler's public speeches were becoming increasingly infrequent—at that point he had only spoken once in 1943, namely for the Heroes Memorial Day on March 21[68]—Goebbels increasingly had to assume the role of chief orator for the regime.[69] Hitler, however, censored the speech himself; to Goebbels's great regret, a section dealing with Tunis fell victim to this revision as well as a passage in which Goebbels had wanted to make a few points about a future Europe under German leadership.[70]

Speer spoke first at the mass rally about German success in armaments production. In his speech Goebbels, on the other hand, declaring himself the "son of my West German homeland," concentrated on the situation in the areas affected by the air war and on the fact that the winter crisis had been overcome.[71] Unlike his Sportpalast speech in February, this time he focused not on winning massive applause but on being "realistic,"[72] above all as far as the regions affected by the air war were concerned, where people "certainly have no sympathy for the fact that people in Berlin are applauding while in the West the population has to bear the brunt of the bombing."

The speech concluded with a section on the "Jewish question," which in terms of "realism" could hardly have been surpassed: "The total exclusion of Jewry from Europe is not a question of morality but a question of the security of states. [. . .] Just as the potato beetle destroys potato fields, indeed has to destroy them, so the Jews destroy states and nations. For that there is only one remedy: radical removal of the threat."

Goebbels considered his speech to have once again had a marvelous effect; the "psychological crisis of recent weeks" had been completely overcome.[73] Abroad too the effect had been "incredibly great," even in London, where they were "deeply impressed."[74] He paid no attention to the fact that, according to SD reports, at home the speech had also provoked negative responses, for example criticism as to why he had not mentioned "retaliation."[75] Goebbels's tactics were transparent. After his speech German propaganda began a wave of praise designed to obscure the negative aspects of the popular mood. Thus Goebbels believed that if his speech were to have any negative repercussions they would be very different, namely he feared that the population's optimism might go too far. But after only a week the mood deteriorated once again, which Goebbels attributed to the declining impact of his speech.[76]

The entries in Goebbels's diary show once again how selective he was in his interpretation of the reports on the effects of his propaganda. This applies particularly to his anti-Semitic campaign, which reached its zenith with his diatribe of June 5; he had indeed gone too far. In view of the increasing skepticism that was spreading among the population because of the excessive exploitation of anti-Semitism, the campaign had been gradually toned down from the end of May onward. The negative repercussions were so serious that Goebbels even felt obliged to counter criticism of the campaign from within the Party. In a circular of June 12, 1943, sent to the Gauleiters[77] he wrote that after the conclusion of the "Katyn campaign [. . .] various Gaus had referred to the lack of understanding shown by non-Party circles for the breadth and frequency of the coverage given it in the press and on the radio." Goebbels defended himself by claiming that the frequent repetition of a topic had been "a method proved and tested in the time of struggle"; this was "the only way of drumming it in to large numbers of people." And he emphasized: "The struggle against Bolshevism and Jewry is at the forefront of our propaganda. It must be carried out on the broadest possible basis."[78] He did not, however, refer to this evident failure of his propaganda in his diaries.

THE CONTINUATION OF THE AIR WAR AGAINST WESTERN GERMANY

The raid on the dams in the middle of May was followed at the end of the month by the next major attack by the RAF. The raid on Wuppertal on the night of May 29–30, carried out by over seven hundred bombers, resulted, as Goebbels noted, in "a real catastrophe"; around three thousand people died, up until that point the highest number of casualties of any British air raid.[79] Barely two weeks later, on the night of June 11–12, the RAF attacked Düsseldorf, once more with more than seven hundred bombers, and over 1,200 people died; on the following night it was Bochum's turn.[80]

Responding to the raids on the Rhine-Ruhr district, Goebbels had increasingly begun to focus on the question of evacuating the areas affected by the air war. He drafted an evacuation program, which he got Hitler to approve in the middle of June. He informed the Gauleiters of the details in a circular while inviting them to Berlin on short notice. In this way he initiated a significant increase in his responsibilities in the sphere of civil defense, as had already been suggested to him by Field Marshal Milch in April.[81]

The Gauleiter meeting in Berlin was entirely devoted to the problems arising from the air war. Speer's lecture, in which he pointed out that in practice Ruhr production could not be transferred elsewhere, had a sobering effect. They might possibly have to resort to a partial compulsory evacuation, which Goebbels, however, doubted, since he did "not believe that people would leave the area without being forced to do so."[82] The audience was disappointed to learn from Milch that they would have to wait a bit longer for the expected retaliation raids to be launched.

In the evening Goebbels invited the Gauleiters and ministers to his home. He concluded his diary entry by noting that "if I had the authority to play at least a coordinating role in other spheres of domestic policy as I do in the issues arising from the air war, then the general situation of the Reich would be better than is unfortunately the case at the moment. We are suffering from a chronic lack of demarcation of responsibilities. If only the Führer would make some decisions over this! But they affect questions of personnel to such an extent that he finds it difficult to make up his mind to act. But I fear that in the long run he won't be able to avoid doing so." But Goebbels knew only too well that to achieve the desired domestic political reforms and to secure the central role that he was seeking would require a further and more far-reaching overall crisis of the regime, which (as was clear from the continuing setbacks) would not be long in coming.

At the beginning of July Goebbels felt compelled to play down the topic of "retaliation" in German propaganda: "I'm afraid that if this slogan is used too often it will gradually lose its potency, particularly since we shall have to wait a few more months before we can reply to the English terror raids on a large scale."[83] The reports on the nation's mood during the following days were to show that his assessment was correct.[84]

As chairman of the Air Raid Damage Committee he was now increasingly obliged to deal with evacuation issues and other consequences of the air raids.[85] Naturally he was not shy in promoting his role in this through propaganda, as an editorial in *Das Reich* of July 4 makes clear: "There is not a single event in the areas affected by the air war of which we are unaware; where there is the slightest possibility of providing help, we move heaven and earth to protect and provide support for the hard-pressed and tormented victims of enemy terror."[86]

On July 8 he flew to Cologne in order to observe the consequences of the air raid that had taken place a few days earlier. As far as the "bearing" of the population of Cologne was concerned he reached a more positive assessment than in the case of Düsseldorf, which he had visited a few weeks earlier. Using his local knowledge as a Rhinelander, he put it down to the fact that "the Düsseldorf population is more saturated with intellectualism than the Cologne one is, whereas the people of Cologne have more humor and optimism." Nevertheless, he found the overall picture of the city depressing: The center was "a scene of general destruction. All this destruction could make one cry."[87]

Goebbels's engagement in civil defense matters, made much of by propaganda, inevitably resulted, through a kind of reflex, in the propaganda apparatus subordinate to him reporting an increase in his popularity. At the end of June Goebbels was delighted to note that the Party's Reich propaganda offices were unanimously reporting that "my reputation among the German people has increased enormously." His work was "being regarded by the public with the greatest respect and admiration" and "in many cases [was being] contrasted in drastic fashion with the work or rather the lack of work by other prominent figures [!], who as the domestic crisis continues and gets worse are increasingly disappearing from public view."[88] This dig referred in particular to Göring, whose air defenses, despite boastful announcements by the Reich marshal, had failed, and also to Interior Minister Frick, whom Goebbels had for a long time considered totally inactive.

A DAY ON THE OBERSALZBERG

That Goebbels could now make a reputation for himself in the field of civil defense meant that his already minimal interest in the work of the Committee of Three now more or less disappeared completely. On June 24 he once again took part in a meeting of the committee on the Obersalzberg. Goebbels considered the tasks of the committee as essentially concluded: "I don't care at all about whether or not a regional post office headquarters in Kassel or Potsdam should be closed down or who should then move into the vacated building." On the other hand, in recent months nearly a million soldiers had been mobilized: "Total war, which involved such a fight, has achieved its goal."[89]

After the meeting he met with Hitler. The core of the conversation this time was a discussion of various aspects of the air war. He discovered that Hitler did not consider the effects of the air raids particularly dramatic. It was naturally "terrible to think that artworks that we can't replace are being destroyed in the west. [. . .] That churches are being wrecked is not so bad. Insofar as they have cultural value they can be rebuilt, and if they don't we shall have to do without them. Apart from that, the majority of industrial cities are badly planned, fusty, and wretchedly built. Thanks to the British air raids we shall get some space."

As was usual in such conversations, apart from surveying the military situation, they discussed some personnel matters. Once again[90] Hitler expressed very negative opinions about Interior Minister Frick, whom he had not dismissed only because he could not think of a suitable replacement. Goebbels shared Hitler's poor opinion of Frick, but, as he had noted a few weeks earlier, he was pleased that the Interior Ministry had such a weak occupant, since as a result Frick was not standing in the way of his political ambitions.[91]

Among the questions Goebbels discussed with Hitler on June 24 was the troublesome issue of responsibilities for "eastern propaganda." As a result of the discussions concerning the Eastern Proclamation that had taken place in February 1943 the conflict with Rosenberg over the responsibility for "eastern propaganda" had broken out again with great intensity. Since then Rosenberg and Goebbels had carried on a bitter dispute without managing to clarify the situation.[92] Now Goebbels saw the opportunity for a fait accompli. When Hitler made negative comments about Rosenberg's leadership qualities as Reich minister for the occupied eastern territories, Goebbels brought up the question of eastern propaganda. Hitler supported him 100 percent and promised that he would issue a Führer edict along the lines he wanted.[93] But Goebbels's attempt to force Hitler's hand on this issue was in the end unsuccessful. For as became clear during the following days Goebbels and Rosenberg could not agree on the text of a Führer edict. Once again the matter had to be brought before Hitler for his decision.[94]

When, during the course of the day, Hitler received the chief of the general staff, Kurt Zeitzler, for a briefing, Goebbels used the opportunity to have a long talk with Eva Braun, Hitler's mistress. "She makes a very positive impression on me, is very well read, exceptionally clear and mature in her judgments on artistic matters and will certainly be a valuable support for the Führer." They talked mainly about literature, and Goebbels was able greatly to impress Eva Braun with an account of his meeting with Knut Hamsun, of whom she turned out to be a great admirer.

At the end of the day Goebbels sat with Hitler and other guests for the usual evening chat. During the course of the evening an incident occurred for which Goebbels shared some of the blame. One of Hitler's favorite topics on such evenings was Vienna. His dislike of Vienna and his attempts to reduce the city's status in the cultural life of the Reich had in recent months acquired a particular target: It increasingly took the form of criticism of the Vienna Gauleiter, Baldur von Schirach.[95] Thus a few months earlier Hitler had shut down an exhibition of "Young Art" put on by Schirach in Vienna.[96]

During the following weeks Hitler had repeatedly commented in negative terms about the cultural policy in Vienna and had repeatedly singled Schirach out for criticism,[97] complaining that the latter had "gone native" in Vienna *(verwienert).*[98] On the evening of June 24 Schirach, who was also staying on the Obersalzberg, found himself the target of a tirade. Among other things Hitler claimed that Vienna's reputation as a cultural metropolis was partly undeserved, its population treated "great achievements very unfairly," in the past it had tried to overshadow the provinces, and so on. By contrast, Goebbels was delighted to note, "Berliners were most suited [...] to populating the capital of the Reich." Hitler wanted, Goebbels noted, "one day to make Berlin if not the biggest then the most beautiful city in the world. He will not tolerate any substantial building work in Vienna that might once again put it in competition with Berlin."

According to Goebbels, Schirach and his wife had then tried to claim that Vienna was "very enthusiastic about Nazism" but had met with a brick wall as far as Hitler was concerned. In the course of the evening Hitler became more and more annoyed with the Schirachs. Evidently Hitler was giving full expression to his feelings of resentment about the failure of his artistic career, which he blamed on Vienna. Finally, the situation escalated, and Frau Schirach requested that Hitler allow her and her husband to leave Vienna, which he brusquely refused. According to Goebbels the dispute continued into the small hours.

In his memoirs Schirach described the episode rather differently. He attributed the escalation of the situation to clever interventions by Goebbels, who had egged Hitler on to his tirade against Vienna. This seems entirely plausible. Goebbels also mentions in his diary his "witty remarks," with which he allegedly tried to rescue the situation. In any event the banning of the Schirachs from Hitler's court was not inopportune for Goebbels.[99] He now knew, as is clear from his diary entries during the following months, that he was in full agreement with Hitler that Schirach would have to be replaced in Vienna.[100]

Schirach, however, remained in Vienna, which also suited Goebbels, since he now found it easy to outdo the discredited Gauleiter in what he called the "cultural competition" with Vienna.[101] When, for example, in June 1944 Hitler once again criticized Schirach, Goebbels noted: "I shall exploit this criticism of Schirach by the Führer to impose various conditions on him in relation to Viennese cultural policy."[102]

The meeting of June 24 demonstrates that Goebbels's visits to Hitler's headquarters enabled him not only to acquaint himself with the general political line that was being taken (as well as numerous nuances) but also to exploit them in order to find out, either through tête-à-têtes or in social conversation, who was rising or falling in the Führer's favor, to hinder opponents and to launch intrigues. Goebbels was fully aware that when practical issues were being dealt with at Hitler's court, they were always simultaneously treated as personnel matters.

On the following day, on June 25, Göring requested an interview with Goebbels. He found the Reich marshal less resigned than at the previous meeting, and he appeared "much fresher and more flexible in terms of his health." Göring complained bitterly to Goebbels about the many unjustified complaints being made against him. It was true that the Luftwaffe had made many mistakes in the past, but people ought to recognize its current achievements.

According to Goebbels, during the course of the conversation Göring had been "exceptionally intimate, warm, and friendly to me." If it were possible, he conjectured, "to get the Führer on the same wavelength as me and Göring, it would be the saving of German politics and of the conduct of the war." But he realized that he was a long way off from realizing this idea, which he had already been contemplating in the spring. Göring's lethargy was standing in the way.[103]

THE SUMMER CRISIS

As in the previous year, in 1943 the German leadership once more planned to win back the initiative in the eastern theater of war. On July 5 "Operation Citadel" was launched. Two German armies with a total of 1.3 million men and over three thousand tanks endeavored to cut off the bulge in the Soviet front in the Kursk area through attacks launched from both north and south.

Goebbels began his diary entries dealing with the matter on July 6, a day after the beginning of the battle. Writing on July 7 that the "offensive in the Bjelgorod-Orel-Kursk region came as great surprise to the enemy," he was evidently not aware that the Red Army (having been forewarned of the German battle plan), through the use of well-prepared defensive measures, had inflicted heavy losses on the attackers. Thus, although the two Wehrmacht spearheads had penetrated deep into the Soviet defenses, they were too far apart to join together in an encirclement and, on July 9, the German attack stalled.[104]

In the meantime, Goebbels was on the move. After visiting badly damaged Cologne he traveled to Heidelberg where, on July 9, a reception mainly intended to celebrate the renewal of his doctoral diploma was held at the university. Afterward he met some students, went sightseeing around the city, ate lunch in the student dining hall, and reminisced about his old student days.[105] In the afternoon he spoke in the city hall to an audience of academics and students at a large rally; the speech was broadcast on the radio. In his speech he addressed a topic that he often dealt with during these months, criticizing "intellectualism" as "a symptom of the degeneration of healthy common sense" and attempting in this way to attribute discontent and criticism among the population to a small minority who were separating themselves off from the "national community."[106] "Intellectual life," Goebbels insisted, "also has its roots among the people." He declared himself in favor of freedom of research and of the traditions of the German university system and explained—in Heidelberg, of all places—why the old student fraternities, which the regime had abolished in the 1930s, were no longer in keeping with the times. His statement that he had never participated in the "superficialities" of the old student life was an opportunistic lie that must have surprised his old comrades in the Unitas Sigfrida fraternity. Finally, Goebbels referred to the wartime tasks facing academics and in his conclusion tried to sum up the intellectual heroism that was required through a quotation from Nietzsche's *Thus Spoke Zarathustra*.[107]

Back in Berlin he had to devote himself once again to the less agreeable realities of the war. "At last the invasion that has long been awaited and often talked about has happened," wrote Goebbels on

July 11, 1943, in his diary. He was referring to the landing of Allied troops in Sicily, Operation Husky, which had occurred the day before. In fact during the following days the troops managed to consolidate their bridgeheads and push back the Italian and German troops on Sicily relatively quickly.[108] By July 15 Goebbels was noting pessimistically that "in the long run" they were "in no position to stop" the enemy.[109] On July 13, faced with the landing in Sicily and the strengthening of Soviet resistance—on July 12 the Red Army had begun an offensive north of Kursk[110]—Hitler made the decision to break off the Kursk battle.[111] Goebbels was not informed of this decision. It was only on July 15 that he noted in his diary the deteriorating military situation in the Kursk area and for the first time contemplated the possibility that they might have to abandon the operation. But by then the decision had long been made.

On July 17 he noted: "The question increasingly arises of how on earth we are supposed to cope with a two-front war," particularly as such a constellation had always "been Germany's misfortune." There was "nothing for it but to try to use political means to achieve a certain amelioration." The diary entry is a remarkable indication that Goebbels was coming to the conclusion that the war was lost and recognizing the need to begin seeking alternative solutions.

After breaking off the Kursk battle, the German army in the east was increasingly forced onto the defensive. Goebbels was compelled to recognize that the "situation [is] becoming critical" because "for the first time since the beginning of the war our summer offensive has not only not achieved any successes but we are having to fight tooth and nail to prevent the enemy from achieving its objectives."[112] He was already seeing the impending military reverse as a "second Stalingrad." He noted that people in "leading circles, particularly in the military, are beginning to ask whether the Soviet Union can be beaten militarily at all."[113]

The situation was looking no better in the southern theater. Under the impression of the military situation in Sicily Goebbels was confronted with suggestions, particularly from General Alfred Jodl and the Reich press chief, Dietrich, for "propaganda gradually to prepare the population for a withdrawal from Sicily," an idea that Goebbels considered "completely stupid and short-sighted." Thus he opposed a pessimistic statement by Dietrich along those lines and substituted it with an optimistic portrayal of events.[114]

On July 18 Hitler traveled to Italy to meet Mussolini near the town of Feltre in the Veneto in order to give him "a blood transfusion," as Goebbels put it.[115] While Hitler spoke to an exhausted Mussolini for hours on end in order to persuade him of the future viability of the Axis, the Allies bombed Rome for the first time, a clear warning of the sacrifices that the Italian people would have to suffer if the war continued.[116] Goebbels was convinced of the success of this visit: "So long as this man has the Italian tiller in his hand, we need have no concerns about Italy's solidarity."[117]

On July 24, however, Goebbels received "confidential news [...] that change is in the offing in Italian domestic politics." Under the leadership of Roberto Farinacci the old Fascists had requested "Il Duce to summon a meeting of the Grand Fascist Council" in order to get him "to pursue a more energetic policy." They wanted to persuade Mussolini to "free himself from being overburdened by his offices in order once again to have the initiative and energy for directing overall policy and the conduct of the war." Goebbels was in favor of the move, for Farinacci was "an energetic man" and a "definite friend of Germany."[118]

In fact the meeting of the Grand Council took place on the evening of the same day. After a long and lively debate Dino Grandi, the chairman of the Chamber of Corporations, the Italian pseudo-parliament, pushed through a resolution in which the king was requested once more to take over the supreme command of the Italian armed forces in place of Mussolini. On the following day the king received Mussolini to dismiss him as head of the government and appoint Marshal Pietro Badoglio as his replacement. On leaving the palace Mussolini was arrested and taken to a closely guarded location.[119]

To begin with, Goebbels was unaware of these dramatic events, although since November 1942 he had possessed information indicating that a plot was brewing in Italy.[120] On July 25 in a phone call from Führer's headquarters he heard only that "Il Duce [has] resigned" and that Badoglio had taken over the government. Goebbels assumed, however, that the "Roman camarilla intends to find some elegant means of wriggling out of the war."[121]

Early the following day he flew to East Prussia to discuss the situation with Hitler's innermost circle.[122] At first, still not having any concrete information, he went over with Bormann and Himmler all the possible permutations that might lie behind the change of regime in Italy. Goebbels already understood that Farinacci's criticism of Mussolini had been used by the group around Badoglio in order to force through a real regime change. He brooded to himself: "It's really shocking to think that a revolution that has after all been in power for 21 years can be liquidated in such a way."

At ten o'clock, together with Göring, he had a first meeting with Hitler, which Ribbentrop joined half an hour later. In the meantime, Hitler too had reached the conclusion that Mussolini had probably not resigned voluntarily. Hitler believed that "Italian freemasonry" was "behind the whole thing," for although it had been banned he claimed it was still active. He also announced his intention of "carrying out a great coup," namely to use a parachute division to surround Rome, take control of the city, and arrest "the king together with his family, as well as Badoglio and comrades" and then bring them to Germany. Ribbentrop and Goebbels had difficulty persuading him not to use the opportunity to occupy the Vatican.

At midday, as Goebbels had anticipated, the first news came in that "the mob is beginning to make itself felt." Fascist symbols were being removed from public view and streets renamed. Goebbels welcomed the development: "The more things in Italy go topsy-turvy, the better for the measures we're planning." Experienced in staging "spontaneous demonstrations" himself, he noted: "That there are demonstrations in favor of Badolgio is a sign that they were probably staged by him."

During the course of the day Farinacci appeared at Führer's headquarters. He made an extremely unfavorable impression on Hitler and Goebbels, as he made it clear that he did not support Mussolini. Goebbels concluded that "we can hardly make much use of Farinacci."[123]

The situation was made more difficult for Goebbels by the fact that he could not explain to the German people the background to the changes in Italy, although he could already see the danger that in Germany too "some subversive elements" believed that "they could bring about the same thing here that Badoglio and his comrades engineered in Rome."[124] In terms of propaganda Goebbels was confronted with a real dilemma. He had had to abandon the anti-Semitic campaign in June; the anticipated military successes on the Eastern Front had not occurred; in July he had had to play down the theme of retaliation. Initially the regime was at a loss as to how to respond to the new situation in Italy. They could see from correspondence that the population was feeling the lack of a speech by Hitler to clarify the situation. "We can't neglect the nation for too long," noted Goebbels. But then in this already difficult situation a new catastrophe occurred.

THE AIR WAR: HAMBURG AND BERLIN

After the series of air raids on the Rhine-Ruhr area, which the RAF had begun in March 1943, Bomber Command found a new target for a spectacular raid: Hamburg, the second-largest city in Germany, which was largely destroyed in Operation Gomorrah between July 24 and August 3. For the first time American bombers participated in a joint raid by both air forces, mounting daylight raids on Hamburg's industrial districts. In a new tactic, masses of reflective aluminium strips were dropped to block German radar and so limit the number of Allied losses.

Operation Gomorrah was the most devastating air raid carried out on a German city during the Second World War. As a result of the massive bombardment, for the first time firestorms were created covering wide areas and preventing people from leaving the air raid shelters; many suffocated to death in the shelters. The total number of deaths was more than forty thousand. Over 40 percent of the housing stock was destroyed, and nine hundred thousand inhabitants were made homeless. The public life of the city effectively came to a halt.[125] "At the moment I don't quite know how we are going to deal with these problems," wrote Goebbels after the first nighttime raid.[126] The air war was "the Reich's bleeding wound, so to speak."[127]

Goebbels was now worried above all that Berlin could be hit in the same catastrophic way as Hamburg. He considered the preparations made by the Reich Air Defense League, which was responsible for civil defense in the capital, to be inadequate. The Party, he ordered, should become more involved.[128] The press prepared the population in unmistakable terms for heavy air raids. It not only appealed to the Berliners' determination to stick it out but also gave practical tips, for example for the construction of slit trenches and for combating incendiaries.[129]

Although these measures "made the inhabitants of the capital extremely nervous," Goebbels believed he had to put up with that.[130] Finally, he published an article in the *Völkischer Beobachter* in which he advocated the evacuation of children from Berlin and appealed to people to maintain their morale: "The watchword of the hour [is] discipline, a steadfast spirit, and a heart of iron."[131] The Goebbels family also took precautions. Artworks and valuable pieces of furniture from the two houses on Schwanenwerder were transported to Lanke and, with the transfer of his daughters Helge and Hilde and his mother, who like them had hitherto lived on the Wannsee island, all the family members had now moved to the Bogensee.[132]

Goebbels began preparations to move less important departments of his ministry out of the city.[133] Above all, however, the evacuation of some eight hundred thousand people was set in motion. Long lines formed in railway stations and post offices, as people wanted to send valuable household goods. "Crowds gathered," and "somewhat panic-like behavior" occurred. Goebbels, who was now concerned about the city's image, deployed Hitler Youth and Party members on a large scale to sort it out.[134]

In an appeal, which for once was made in a sober tone, Goebbels requested that Berliners who were not forced to remain in the city for professional or other reasons leave Berlin.[135] Because of his heavy involvement in Berlin matters for three weeks in succession he did not write an editorial for *Das Reich,* which, he was proud to note, "caused something of a sensation among the German public."[136]

While the partial evacuation of Berlin was under way,[137] Goebbels visited the Hansa city of Hamburg two weeks after Operation Gomorrah.[138] It presented him with a "picture of the most appalling devastation." Goebbels spoke in the Party's Gau headquarters to around 150 Party functionaries and citizens who had made a name for themselves during the nights of bombing. He tried to set "the air war in the overall context of the problems of the war as a whole, and I believe I succeeded in giving people some encouragement and support." He would have very much liked to use the theme of retaliation, which he hoped would provide relief and a diversion. But in August he learned from Hitler that the massive retaliation against London using bombers and rockets could not, as originally planned, be carried out at the end of 1943 but only in the following year.[139]

In view of this timetable any further emphasis on retaliation in propaganda media would prove counterproductive. Goebbels, however, ensured that the topic was taken up in word-of-mouth propaganda and that a very concrete impression of what would be involved was conveyed by spreading rumors of wonder weapons, which in the coming months were in fact to fuel the fantasy of many Germans.[140] However, at least in the short term, this was evidently unlikely to produce much in the way of success; the topic of retaliation was a hot potato. Goebbels, therefore, instructed that it could be spoken about in public only in the most exceptional circumstances.[141]

In August he established "a small organization of activists" who were to "use force in dealing with defeatists in public life." The Party, according to Goebbels, "has been pushed somewhat onto the defensive by the endless criticism of malcontents, although it now "has much more power and influence than during the years 1931 and 1932, for example, when we would never have put up with things that we are now having to put up with all the time." They should get back to the methods used in the "time of struggle": This was once again the message that Goebbels was sending out, one that he was fond of using when there was a crisis.[142]

In the middle of August, after a visit to a Hamburg that had now been largely destroyed, Goebbels noted that there were "shady characters on the evacuation trains exploiting the depressed mood of the victims of the bombing in order to agitate against the state. However, all these attempts have failed. But I conclude that we must increase the involvement of the Party not only in Berlin but also in other Gaus and use force."[143]

At the ministerial briefing Goebbels announced that he would not use the police against "grumblers" in Berlin but would deploy roughly three thousand Party activists, who would confront anyone who opposes the government, if necessary using force.[144] During the following heavy raids on Berlin Goebbels used these bands of thugs on several occasions to control the "mood." His diaries document that these actions were carried out repeatedly at other times and always with the same satisfactory results.[145] After more than ten years of Nazi rule the public image of the Third Reich was under control to such an extent that hardly anyone dared to criticize the regime in front of someone they did not know.

If it proved successful in Berlin Goebbels contemplated introducing this organization throughout the Reich.[146] In fact there are a series of indications that gangs of Party activists were deployed in other Gaus in order to suppress public criticism of the regime by force. A separate organization proved unnecessary. Such activities could be linked to the Reich-wide network established by the Nazi Party for word-of-mouth propaganda and on the extensive organization the Party maintained for keeping tabs on the public "mood." Thus Goebbels's liaison officer at the Party Chancellery, Walter Tiessler, had already drafted a circular in May, on behalf of Goebbels, which stated: "It is not acceptable for us magnanimously to ignore negative rumors and jokes and even join in without contradicting them. On the contrary, in this situation we must recall the methods of the time of struggle when we responded to such insults with force."[147] Responding to unwelcome "manifestations of people's mood" with the "methods of the time of struggle" was something that the Reich Propaganda Ministry had been recommending to the Party's Reich propaganda offices for months.

A message from the head of the Posen Reich propaganda office to the Party's propaganda headquarters shows that such combative arguments were routine, although in observing the public mood they "consider it important that now and then people should be allowed to speak their mind without us cracking down on them right away so that we can see whether or not they are going to go on doing so. If it really proves necessary we shall ruthlessly gag the person involved."[148] These documents from people associated with Goebbels, together with his relevant diary entries, make it clear that the violent suppression of rash "grumblers" was practiced systematically.

After the raids on the Rhine-Ruhr area and the destruction of Hamburg in the late summer of 1943 the RAF began its third great wave of air raids during that year. Three heavy raids on the capital between August 23 and September 4 began the air battle for Berlin, which Bomber Command was to begin in earnest from November 1943 onward.[149]

Goebbels watched the first raid on the night of August 23–24 with a degree of optimism because the air defenses, at least as far as he could see, appeared to be functioning. But when he entered the city after the all-clear had been given, he was forced to recognize that a good deal of damage had been done: "The whole of Charlottenburg

Station is on fire, there are a large number of roof fires on the Kurfürstendamm, in the Leibnizstrasse, and in Steglitz, and since there is often a lack of water they turn into major house fires." Goebbels did not hesitate to intervene himself. "I make various interventions, encourage the fire brigade to speed up their work and to go about it more carefully."[150]

He devoted the whole of the following day to dealing with the aftermath of the raid. The city was covered by a thick pall of smoke, and in the evening numerous fires were still burning. He visited the parts of the city that had been particularly badly affected: "The population is generally willing, and if one looks after them a bit they are easily satisfied."

To his regret he noted that the Party agencies had "not really done their job properly." He now intervened "extremely energetically," organized food supplies and the collection of furniture that had been removed from houses, and prepared emergency accommodations. In Steglitz he appointed the Party's district leader as a sort of special commissioner, making him responsible for all Party organizations and municipal agencies.[151] Exceptional situations required exceptional measures. He blamed Oberbürgermeister Ludwig Steeg for the inactivity of the municipal authorities and threatened to dismiss him if matters failed to improve. He sent "researchers" to the various districts to acquire a firsthand impression of what was going on. He gave Heinz Jetter, a member of his staff, "dictatorial powers to sort out the provision of food supplies for the affected districts" and the right to issue instructions to Party and municipal agencies. He appointed twelve Reich Party speakers as "inspectors" to be responsible for inspecting the accommodation of evacuees from the bombing in the Gaus where they had been quartered. Thus Goebbels actively exploited the situation in order to expand the Party's responsibilities.[152]

During his various trips around the affected areas he had unsurprisingly acquired "only the very best impressions" of the population's behavior: "Berliners treat me with a love and affection that could hardly be bettered." Goebbels had in fact not been idle in taking steps to ensure that the "mood" remained good. On the previous evening he had deployed " 'Organization B' [. . .] in groups of three in the working-class districts." "It unobtrusively inspected 35 pubs with the aim of beating up anyone who criticized the Führer or the general conduct of the war." But the mere appearance of these gangs of thugs was evidently sufficient: "It's significant that during this first 'raid' Organization B didn't have to intervene once."[153]

In spite of all these organizational successes, when, during the night of September 1, his home city of Rheydt was severely damaged by a British air raid, Goebbels's mood was bleak. "My home was spared as if by a miracle."[154] On the following day he learned further details: "My old grammar school is no longer standing, my old elementary school has been destroyed [. . .] the family grave in the cemetery has been quite severely damaged. [. . .] As a result the city of Rheydt, at least as far as its core is concerned, has effectively ceased to exist." At least when he telephoned the mayor he could comfort him with "the reassurance that when the war is over one of my first tasks will be to start rebuilding the city."[155]

The continual air raids had a negative impact on people's mood: "The masses have become somewhat skeptical or, one could even say, are in the grip of a sense of hopelessness. Above all people are complaining that there is no word from the Führer to explain matters, particularly as far as the air war is concerned. [. . .] Hardly anyone believes in retaliation anymore. We have prophesied it too many times." Because of the rather "unclear and uncertain, not to say critical situation," there is "a lot of irritation with our propaganda and information policy."[156] "Allegedly we say too much in public, and that's what annoys people. In reality people are horrified by the air war and are looking for a scapegoat."[157] The only cure-all for this trend that he could think of was a speech by Hitler.[158]

Contrary to his expectation that because of their heavy losses the British would not mount any further raids on Berlin, there was another major raid on the evening of September 3. After the all-clear had been given he made a "tour of the affected districts." Despite the serious amount of destruction, he was happy to note: "At least the Berlin organization has begun to work after the two previous air raids, and at the moment I have no reason to complain."[159] Once again he sought reassurance that his popularity had not suffered through immediate contact with those affected. Thus, on the following day, he was "stopped by a large crowd who greeted me and hosted me with great warmth, questioning me about lots of things and in the process displaying an attitude that's very moving. I have to go upstairs to the workers' apartments, go into details, and am able here and there to give help and advice and sort out minor problems for them. In the afternoon I send them cigarettes and a few other luxury foods." His staffer, Jette, who was responsible for this, reported that evening that "these gifts to the Wedding district were received with absolute delight."[160]

For the time being, however, the situation in Berlin settled down again and during the following weeks Berlin was spared further raids.

FURTHER REVERSES ON THE
EASTERN AND SOUTHERN FRONTS

In the meantime, after a period of relative calm,[161] the military situation in the east had deteriorated. The Soviet offensive that had developed out of the battle to defend Kursk was achieving its initial successes. Orel, north of Kursk, had to be evacuated on August 5, which Goebbels considered a "great blow to prestige."[162] On the same day, to the south of the Kursk battlefield Belgorod was reconquered, and the Red Army then moved on to attack Kharkov.[163] Moreover, on August 7 it launched another major offensive around 250 miles further north in the Smolensk area.[164]

"We must now start using politics," wrote Goebbels on August 8. "For there are very obvious contradictions between the plutocratic west and the Bolshevist east," and they would become very strong in the event of communist successes. But unfortunately "for obvious reasons"—Goebbels meant the negative military situation—they were unable to start seeking a political solution to the war. However, given that he was more and more doubtful about pure military success in the war, he became increasingly preoccupied by the notion of a "political solution."

On August 9, on a visit to Führer's headquarters Goebbels learned further details about the situation in Italy. During the course of the conversation Hitler announced that he had no intention of "surrendering [Italy] as a battle zone." He even wanted to defend Sicily for as long as possible against the superior Allied forces. Goebbels learned that Hitler regarded Badoglio as "nothing but a traitor." The official explanation for Mussolini's resignation was completely implausible. Hitler then informed Goebbels "in absolute confidence" that he wanted to arrest the king, "take Badoglio and all his gang into custody, liberate Il Duce, and then give him and Fascism the opportunity of once more climbing into the saddle and establishing a solid regime."[165]

During the further course of the conversation Goebbels made several suggestions for far-reaching changes of personnel. Wilhelm Frick, who was "too old and worn out," should be replaced by Wilhelm Stuckart as interior minister and Himmler as police minister. Furthermore, the education minister, Bernhard Rust, should be dismissed and the labor minister, Franz Seldte ("the old slacker") be replaced by Robert Ley, the head of the German Labor Front. Hitler was "somewhat taken aback" by these "categorical suggestions," but in general accepted them in a good spirit. On this occasion Goebbels asked Hitler "whom the Führer would replace me with if I was no longer there." According to Goebbels, the Führer replied that "I was a unique phenomenon of National Socialism, who would be completely irreplaceable"; he did not know "anyone who could take over a fraction of the responsibility that I am now having to carry." Goebbels was "naturally very proud of this assessment," although he would have wanted "the organization in which I am working to remain after my own work has finished." Hitler agreed in principle. Although Goebbels was glad that the offices which he had accumulated over the course of time would remain together over the longer term, he was also concerned, as is clear from his diaries, that a weaker successor would not in fact be able to hold these offices together. In his view his "uniqueness," which Hitler had once again confirmed to him, made the question of a suitable successor a problem that was virtually insoluble.[166]

In the middle of August the Wehrmacht's situation in Sicily had become so precarious that the troops had to be evacuated over the Strait of Messina. It was successful in transporting over one hundred thousand German and Italian troops with much of their heavy equipment onto the Italian mainland within a week.[167]

In the east the Soviet offensive was continuing. A Red Army spearhead deployed against Army Group Center in the Smolensk area succeeded in conquering Spas-Demensk; on August 23 Kharkov was lost to the Red Army's southern offensive. In his assessments of the military situation on the Eastern Front, Goebbels's comments during these weeks alternated between being quite pessimistic and cautiously optimistic. As far as his propaganda instructions went, he recommended "muted optimism."[168]

Thus it is clear that in the meantime Goebbels had acquired serious doubts about whether the war could still be won by military means. In recent months there had been an uninterrupted series of defeats and setbacks. He had given up the attempt at "total" mobilization, and his efforts to mobilize the last reserves of the German population through the propaganda motif of an allegedly lethal Jewish threat had failed. He lacked any other promising propaganda themes. The "political solution" to the war was indeed the only way out, and during the coming months he was to pursue this more vigorously.

CHAPTER 27

"I Have No Idea What the Führer's Going to Do in the End"

The Search for a Way Out

A public display of confidence in victory: The propaganda minister receives a group of soldiers from the Cherkasy pocket on March 1, 1944, among them soldiers of the Waffen-SS and the army. From the summer of 1943 onward, Goebbels recognized that Germany could no longer win the war militarily and began to raise with Hitler the possibility of making a separate peace.

On September 3, 1943, British troops landed in Calabria.[1] At first Hitler believed the operation was a diversion and that the real invasion was still to come and would be in western Europe.[2] On September 9 Goebbels noted a "sensational development" that he had learned about the previous day: Badolgio's signing of the armistice, which had happened on September 3 and initially had been kept secret. On the same evening Goebbels was summoned by Hitler to his east Prussian headquarters.

When he arrived in the Wolf's Lair the following morning, he learned that the measures that had been prepared since July for the eventuality of an Italian defection had already been set in motion the previous evening. German troops had moved into north and central Italy as well as into the Italian-occupied territories in Croatia, Greece, and southern France, disarming their former allies. On September 10 a German paratroop division managed to occupy Rome.[3] On the other hand, on the early morning of September 9 American and British forces had begun to land at Salerno with the aim of taking Naples.[4]

In view of the situation in the Mediterranean but also on the Eastern Front, Goebbels now decided—as far as can be seen it was his first initiative in this direction—to speak to Hitler about the possibility of ending the war through a political solution. He asked bluntly "whether in the short or the long term something could be arranged with Stalin." Hitler's response was negative, in view of the current military situation: "Hitler thinks it's more likely something could be done with the English than with the Soviets." Hitler believed that with the permanent seizure of Sicily, Calabria, Sardinia, and Corsica, Britain had already achieved important war aims and would then "possibly be more open to an arrangement." Goebbels had a different view: "I tend rather to think that Stalin is more approachable, for Stalin is more of an adherent of *Realpolitik* than Churchill."

Once again Goebbels "strongly" advocated that Hitler should speak to the German people and Hitler finally agreed, although he would have preferred to wait until the situation in Italy had been sorted out. On the following day both of them read through the speech that had been drafted in the meantime, essentially dealing with the situation after Italy's defection, and it was then broadcast that evening,[5] the first radio address by the dictator in almost six months.

However, as Goebbels well knew, a speech by the dictator was hardly sufficient to repair the damage that had already been done to the Führer's image. And, what was worse from Goebbels's point of view, he was not in a position to offer any propaganda alternatives. The military situation and the air raids were depressing; the campaigns with whose help he had tried, in view of the threat of defeat, to mobilize the last reserves of energy, namely "total war" and Katyn, had failed and the preconditions were lacking for a massive propaganda campaign promising retaliation.

On the evening of September 12 Goebbels learned that in a spectacular operation German commandos had succeeded in freeing Mussolini from the mountain hotel on the Gran Sasso where he had been interned by the Badoglio government. He regarded the new situation with a certain amount of skepticism, however. "So long as Il Duce was not there we had the opportunity of creating a tabula rasa in Italy. [. . .] I had thought that, quite apart from South Tyrol, we might possibly have extended our frontier to the Veneto. If Il Duce once again takes on a political function that will hardly be possible [any longer]."[6]

Two days later Mussolini met Hitler in his headquarters. "It is a scene that represents a moving example of loyalty among men and between comrades," commented Goebbels.[7] But secretly he continued to fear that this male friendship, so impressively demonstrated, could give rise to new difficulties.

In the meantime, the situation around the bridgehead at Salerno had changed completely in favor of the Allies. A German counterattack, from which Goebbels and German propaganda had been expecting great things,[8] had collapsed after only a few days.[9] Goebbels blamed the military's information policy for the fact that propaganda had been too optimistic about Germany's chances of success in the Salerno area.[10] "Now the enemy propaganda mob are attacking me and blaming me for this failure in our news policy."[11] He made comparisons with the similarly overoptimistic news policy pursued in the autumn of 1941 during the initial battles at Stalingrad, as well as over the Battle of El Alamein.[12] According to Goebbels, the incident provoked "a very serious confrontation" with Dietrich and Jodl, whose staff blamed each other.[13] After all, Dietrich had assured him that "such reports would no longer be issued without my express confirmation and approval."[14]

On the following day Goebbels had the opportunity of speaking to Hitler about Dietrich and was convinced that he would immediately be able "to neutralize Dietrich as Reich press chief if I had a position for which I could recommend him. But unfortunately the Führer doesn't think him capable of taking on any significant role."[15]

On September 22 Goebbels visited Hitler once more in his head-quarters. The conversation gave Goebbels completely new insights into the background of the Italian crisis. "I hear from the Führer for the first time that Edda Mussolini isn't the daughter of his wife Rachele but an illegitimate child of Il Duce whom he adopted during his marriage." Hitler did not know who the mother of Edda, the wife of Foreign Minister Galeazzo Ciano, was but believed that "she is the result of a liaison between Il Duce and a Russian Jewess." The idea had an electrifying effect on Goebbels. "That would explain every-thing," he wrote, for Edda had succeeded in achieving a reconcilia-tion between Mussolini and Ciano. "That means that once again the poisonous mushroom is sitting in the middle of the revived Fascist Republican Party."[16]

During dinner, which he ate alone with Hitler, Goebbels returned to the topic he had broached barely a fortnight before: the question of a separate peace. This time he did not mention Stalin as a possible interlocutor but made another suggestion. "I asked the Führer whether he would possibly be prepared to negotiate with Churchill or whether he rejected that idea out of hand." Hitler replied that as a matter of principle politics should never be determined by "personal issues," but he did not believe that "negotiations with Churchill could ever lead to a result, because his views are too fixed and opposed to ours and, moreover, he is governed by hatred rather than reason." He was more inclined to negotiations with Stalin, Goebbels learned, but "he didn't believe that that would lead to a result because Stalin couldn't cede what he is demanding in the east." Goebbels did not give up, arguing that "we must deal with one side or the other. The Reich has never won a two-front war."

Thus Goebbels was clear about the fact that, with the defection of Italy, the continuing setbacks on the Eastern Front, the anticipated landing in the west and the continual air raids, the gradual dissolu-tion of the Nazi empire was imminent. During the year and a half that were still to go before the end of the Third Reich, the search for a political means of avoiding defeat was one of the questions with which he was most preoccupied.

THE BEGINNING OF AUTUMN:
ATTEMPTS TO CONSOLIDATE THE HOME FRONT

The situation on the Eastern Front, which in view of the dramatic events in Italy had taken something of a back seat, now at the start of the autumn once more became the focus of Goebbels's concern. On August 16 the Red Army had begun its operation to re-conquer the Donets Basin in the far south of the front and, on August 26, 1943, it had also begun a big offensive farther north, level with Kursk. In addition, from the beginning of September, there were further attacks in the whole of the Ukraine. As a result Army Group South was forced to retreat to the Dnieper, but the advancing Red Army was able to establish bridgeheads on the west bank.[17] In the middle of September the Red Army began a further offensive against Army Group Center and captured Smolensk on September 25.[18]

To prevent a mood of depression from developing during the autumn, in the middle of September the Party carried out a major propaganda campaign organized by Goebbels and Bormann that was to last for two months. It comprised a "wave of meetings," the establishment of "discussion squads" and "air raid shelter-discussion squads," whose job it was to oppose negative rumors and assert the public presence of the Party with demonstrations and marches and similar activities.[19] Goebbels, however, regarded with a degree of unease the fact that in the autumn of 1943 in many German cities there would be processions of well-nourished Party functionaries apparently in the best of health and in the prime of life. He spoke of "noncombatant marches" but then suppressed his concerns. In the end he considered the campaign had been a complete success. He was particularly pleased by the "report that everywhere there was a shortage of Party badges. Once again Party comrades are wanting to wear their Party badges in public." But there was one problem: "Unfortunately at the moment we're not in a position to produce more of them."[20]

On October 6 Goebbels went to another meeting of Reich leaders and Gauleiters in Posen.[21] The main item on the agenda was problems connected with the armaments industry. Goebbels was particularly impressed by a speech by Speer, who announced in grand style that he wanted to transfer civilian plants with a total of a million employees to armaments production. This would enable him to withdraw sufficient young men to form twenty new divisions. "Actually the Speer program will implement the 'total war' that I was calling for in my Sportpalast speech in February [!]. Unfortunately at the time this Sportpalast speech did not produce any action." Goebbels blamed the economics minister, Walther Funk, in particular for this lack of action. Shortly afterward the latter's position was considerably weakened when SS functionaries took over responsible positions in his ministry.[22]

After further speeches Himmler spoke at the end about his new tasks. On August 25, as Goebbels had advocated, he had been made Reich interior minister. Goebbels approved of Himmler's attacks on the Soviet general Andrey Andreyevich Vlasov and on "the attempts by various German agencies to cultivate the Slav race." Goebbels agreed with Himmler that the Wehrmacht's efforts to establish volunteer units under Vlasov composed of Soviet POWs was a disastrous idea.[23]

Finally, Himmler discussed the "Jewish question," of which, according to Goebbels, he provided "a completely unvarnished and frank picture." Goebbels's diary entry covering the Reichsführer's comments was marked by the same frankness with which Himmler had spoken about the "final solution": "He is convinced that by the end of the year we can solve the Jewish question for the whole of Europe. He advocates the most radical and toughest solution, namely to exterminate the Jews, the whole lot of them. That is certainly a consistent, albeit brutal solution. For we must take on the responsibility for ensuring that this issue is resolved in our time. Later generations will certainly not have the courage and obsession to tackle this problem in the way we can now."[24]

Late in the evening they went to the headquarters, where on the following day as usual Hitler spoke to his senior functionaries. Goebbels ensured that the text of his address was given to the press in the form of a long communiqué. It stated that the dictator had spoken "frankly" and in "unvarnished" terms: The whole German nation knew that it was a matter of life and death. They had burned their bridges behind them. Their only alternative was to go forward. Ever since Himmler's speech of the previous day, that was clear to every leading functionary.[25]

A SEPARATE PEACE?

On October 27 Goebbels once again visited Hitler at his headquarters. After Hitler had explained the military situation to him, as always in a very optimistic way, he broached the "key question," namely: "How do we get out of the two-front war, and is it better to reach a deal with England or with the Soviets?"

In general Hitler believed that it would be possible "to do a deal" with the Soviets "roughly on the basis of 1939 after the Polish campaign. Then we would have the opportunity to sort out the west thoroughly and destroy England, using the Atlantic coast as our base." Goebbels, on the other hand, argued that it would be more feasible to do a deal with Great Britain and "create space in the east, which is vital for our survival." Goebbels recognized that they had to "get used to the idea that the big gains that we anticipated from this war can't be achieved for the time being." But now was "not the time to begin negotiations," because they must wait and see "how things develop politically and militarily. [. . .] I have no idea what the Führer's going to do in the end."

He told Hitler that he thought that "really we must speak to anybody who wants to talk to us. In fact the Führer is not totally averse to this idea." In any event "soon" they would be "at a crossroads" and would then be forced to decide to go "one way or the other." Although, Goebbels concluded, Hitler was "still very skeptical about all these options," as far as he was concerned what was vital was that the dictator had talked through the problems "openly and frankly" and had brought him into his "confidence as a trusted adviser."

During his stay at headquarters and over the following days and weeks Goebbels followed up the issue of peace that he had raised with Hitler. On October 27 he learned from Walther Hewel, Hitler's liaison with the Foreign Ministry, that "in reality Ribbentrop could be won over for either option." Two days later he discovered from Werner Naumann, who had been talking to Gustav Adolf Steengracht, the state secretary at the Foreign Ministry, that Ribbentrop wanted to contact the Pope, who had himself indicated an urgent willingness to talk because he feared that "Bolshevism was going to spread throughout Europe."[26] A few days later Goebbels also concurred with Himmler that "in this war we must use not only military but also political means." Himmler complained about the "complete lack of flexibility in foreign policy and strongly criticized Ribbentrop." Goebbels was aiming to win a new ally.[27] At the end of November he also learned that Bormann was very concerned about German foreign policy but evidently did not believe that Hitler "could be persuaded to part with his foreign minister." In any case "if that happens" Ribbentrop would "not be in a position to negotiate with either London or Moscow."[28] However, after all these soundings Goebbels was no further forward. It appears that it was not until June 1944 that Goebbels had the opportunity of raising the issue of a separate peace with Hitler. The dictator was well aware of the fact that, in view of the military situation, neither the western Allies nor the Soviet Union would be in the least bit interested in negotiating an end to the war with him.

THE WINTER OF 1943–44:
THE EASTERN FRONT AND THE AIR BATTLE OF BERLIN

After Operation Citadel had been abandoned, the military situation on the Eastern Front was dominated by the Wehrmacht's retreat in all sectors; during the autumn and winter of 1943 German troops had to fight a series of defensive battles against the advancing Red Army.[29]

Goebbels believed that the depressing reports continually arriving from the Eastern Front offered him the opportunity of getting people used to the situation. He did not consider that the public mood was in permanent decline but interpreted the reports he received as indicating that the mood was stabilizing at a low level; above all, he detected a "great seriousness" and a "very firm and manly spirit."[30] His diary entry of November 12, 1943, is particularly revealing of the way in which the negative mood was prevented from having an impact: "The continual grumbling has been sharply reduced since we have been passing death sentences on defeatists, which we have carried out and publicized."

After all, there was not an immediate threat of military defeat. The battles were continuing to take place hundreds of miles from the German borders, and the Red Army was not succeeding in cutting off and encircling German troops in large numbers. The argument widely used in German propaganda that they had won so much territory in the east that they could afford to give up large amounts of it for operational reasons appeared to make a certain sense.

The main concern in the winter of 1943–44 was a different one: the unprecedented extent to which Berlin was being bombed. The British air offensive against the capital began at the end of 1943. Between November 1943 and March 1944 the RAF took part in a total of sixteen major raids on Berlin. On November 18, during the first of these raids, 143 people died and over 500 houses were destroyed. "If the English continue carrying them out in the same way, they won't be able to achieve much," noted Goebbels.[31] But during the following days three more raids occurred with far more devastating consequences. On November 22, 23, and 26 over 3,700 people were killed, and 8,700 buildings were destroyed.[32]

On the evening of November 22 Goebbels was surprised by an air raid as he was attending a Party meeting in Steglitz. He immediately went to the "command bunker" at Wilhelmplatz that he had established only a few days before[33] as a base from which to direct "our defensive battles for the Reich capital." The journey there turned out to be quite dramatic: "There are fires burning everywhere; the streets are blocked, bombs and mines keep falling, in fact it really feels like being in a war zone."[34] Among the buildings hit during this night were the Foreign Ministry, the Reich Chancellery, and the ministries of transportation, finance, and agriculture. Goebbels's house in the Göringstrasse was also on fire. Numerous theaters had been hit, and many large cinemas had burned down.[35]

On the following evening, the city was, in Goebbels's words, still "on fire" and the sky "blood red" when there was a further "major first-class raid."[36] Goebbels experienced it in his "command bunker" in Wilhelmstrasse. "A truly hellish noise is going on above us. Mines and explosives are continually raining down on the government quarter. The most important buildings are starting to burn one after the other." The Propaganda Ministry was also hit, and it took hours to bring the fire under control.

Goebbels responded with tireless activity, just as he had to the series of raids in August and the beginning of September. His report creates the impression that he was entirely responsible for the measures being taken to limit the damage. Writing about the situation in heavily populated housing districts, he noted: "I quickly organize the evacuation of the population from the area and deploy large num-

bers of fire engines."[37] In another section of the same entry he reports: "I have to go to great lengths to get the traffic moving again."
"The Wehrmacht willingly adopts my plans and within 24 hours is
prepared to put 2½ divisions, the equivalent of 50,000 men, at my
disposal." And: "I dictate a message to the population of Berlin in
which I give expression to the feelings which are now in the hearts of
everyone. [. . .] The message is to be distributed in millions of leaflets
to the welfare centers and will appear in the Berlin press."

In fact Goebbels was responsible neither for the actual air defense
measures nor for the reestablishment of public life after air raids.
Firefighting, rescue, and recovery work were the responsibility of the
police, the Reich Air Defense League, and the fire service; the reinstatement of essential services and transportation was the task of the
municipal authorities and the Reich railways. By contrast, Goebbels's
task was to use the Party organization to help provide immediate assistance for the civilian population and, crucially as far as he was
concerned, to subject those affected to propaganda. By intervening
everywhere, tirelessly encouraging people to act, putting pressure on
the authorities, and pushing the Party into the foreground on top of
that, in the hectic atmosphere of these days he perceived himself to
be omnipotent.

On November 26 the third raid in the series occurred, which this
time focused mainly on the northern suburbs. During this period he
reiterated that in his encounters with those who had been affected by
bombing he had found "the attitude of the Berlin population toward
me beyond praise." He noted various experiences which confirmed
this impression: "I take some of the women from the aid centers with
me and have them brought to the east, which they can't reach on
normal public transportation. They're delighted. By making a few
small friendly gestures to these people one can wrap them around
one's little finger."[38] By continuing to try to convince himself that the
population admired him and was maintaining its morale, he was not
only satisfying his insatiable hunger for recognition but at the same
time providing propaganda with a leitmotif: The nation, which Nazism had welded together into a community of struggle, was discov-
ering that its sense of solidarity was increasing as a result of the efforts
involved in fighting the war.

All these measures had the effect of raising the Party's profile. It
dominated the scene in the parts of the city that had been affected.

Goebbels insisted that it must appear more "in uniform in public because many people believe that what's being done for them is being carried out by the city administration."[39] Goebbels had two hundred Party functionaries who were proven good speakers brought to Berlin so that they could speak in the aid centers and in the provisional mass accommodation that had been created.[40] At the beginning of December he brought around a thousand full-time Party functionaries from the neighboring Gaus to the city to support the Party's aid and propaganda measures.[41]

Goebbels placed great emphasis on propaganda, continuing to stress the unbroken morale of the population that had been badly affected by the air war. On November 28 Goebbels spoke at a rally organized by the Hitler Youth in the Titania Palace, which had survived the bombing: "The speech is surrounded with a solemn, heroic ceremonial that will undoubtedly be very impressive for the radio broadcast. My speech is just right. When I get to the key sentences the audience breaks into loud applause. It almost looks as if we had devised this whole scenario in order to impress the English."[42] Goebbels was of course fully aware that this was the whole point of the occasion. On the following day the *Völkischer Beobachter* report carried the headline "The Whole of Germany Is Calling for Revenge!" on its front page.[43]

Goebbels's vigorous activity in Berlin and the fact that he had kept approaching Hitler about matters to do with the air war now began to pay off. On November 25 Goebbels noted that "based on my Berlin experiences" Hitler had given him the task of establishing an "Inspectorate for Air War Damage" under his command. "This inspectorate has the task of visiting all areas in which air raids have not yet occurred and checking the measures that have been taken to deal with them."[44]

Four weeks later Hitler signed a Führer edict ordering the inspection of "all measures that have been taken at local level to prepare for, prevent, and assist with aerial war damage" and to involve the relevant agencies.[45] Since the air war was increasingly becoming the main issue in domestic policy, Goebbels had thereby acquired an instrument enabling him to intervene in matters affecting a whole range of aspects of life in the individual Gaus.

Hitler appointed Albert Hoffmann, the Gauleiter of Westphalia-South, as his deputy rather than, as Goebbels had wanted, the Cologne Gauleiter, Josef Grohé, whom Hitler envisaged for other tasks. Instead, Goebbels appointed Berndt (alongside his function as coordinator of the Air Raid Damage Committee) to be "secretary" of the new inspectorate. At the beginning of January 1944 three expert committees were created, which were to visit the Gaus.[46]

In December four more air raids on Berlin occurred, which together resulted in over a thousand deaths.[47] Toward the end of the year Goebbels summarized the effects of the air war on the Reich: Up until then there had been ninety-eight thousand deaths, and around one million homes had been destroyed, about 4 percent of the total. "If the English carry on the air war in the same way they will have to go on for years if they really want to hurt us."[48] He spent Christmas Eve alone in Schwanenwerder: "This year it's a sad Christmas, which I don't want to spend outside the city with the family in Lanke."[49]

The RAF continued its raids on Berlin over the New Year vacation. On January 2 and 3, 1944, the city was attacked once more, although losses and damage were limited.[50] On January 20 there was a further raid that resulted in over three hundred deaths.[51] At the end of January the British launched heavy raids on Berlin over three nights—it was not by chance that they coincided with the eleventh anniversary of the "seizure of power"—and more than 1,500 people died.[52]

On January 30, 1944, a "gray Sunday" as Goebbels noted, he reminisced "wistfully" about the "happy day" eleven years earlier.[53] The prospect of having to experience another heavy raid seriously depressed him. In the middle of the broadcast of Hitler's speech to mark the January 30 anniversary the air raid warning once again sounded, as a large force of American bombers was on its way. While the Americans peeled off just before reaching the city, there was a further British raid that evening, in Goebbels's view "one of the heaviest we've experienced so far." Among other buildings the Philharmonie burned down, as well as several theaters, but Goebbels was particularly upset by, on this day of all days, the "loss of our old battleground in the Potsdamer Strasse, the Sportpalast."

For about a week Goebbels was preoccupied with reestablishing seminormal life in the Reich capital.[54] On February 4 he undertook an extensive tour of inspection through the city, mingled with people at an aid center in order once again to note "how friendly and nice," indeed "extraordinarily grateful" people were to him.[55]

He wrote an editorial in *Das Reich* on the theme of "The Battle of

Berlin" in which he succeeded in praising the badly hit capital as a "truly socialist community." He was once more proving that the expression "socialist utopia" that he had used in the 1920s could be applied to anything.[56]

ACTIVATING THE PARTY

In the middle of February Goebbels carried out one of his inspection tours of the city and convinced himself, as always, that the Party was engaged in dealing with all the trouble spots. "What would happen to the population of a bombed city," he pondered, "if we didn't have a Party!"[57] In view of the very precarious general situation, Goebbels considered the Party to be the decisive instrument for stabilizing the Reich's internal position. In order to counteract the population's low morale,[58] at the beginning of 1944 the Party's Reich propaganda directorate began a new campaign to "mobilize the Party," which after careful preparation culminated in a whole series of public meetings.[59] The aim was to raise the Party's public profile in order to demonstrate that the population was solidly behind the regime.

The Allied bombing campaign was also at the top of the agenda of a meeting of Gauleiters that took place on February 23 and 24 in Munich. After various contributions by, among others, Ley, Grohé, Backe, and Jodl, the first day concluded with a two-hour speech by Goebbels. According to him, its "middle and concluding passages were positively dramatic," listened to "with rapt attention," received with "huge applause," and celebrated as "the sensation" of the meeting; there were spontaneous calls for its publication.[60]

On the afternoon of the following day in the Hofbräuhaus there was the usual celebration of the founding of the Party, suffused with the "old Munich atmosphere," which "we Berliners don't have much taste for but is nevertheless full of good cheer." Hitler then spoke to the "Old Fighters." He concentrated above all on the vital task of trying to convey confidence in victory. Goebbels noted down one of the key sentences in the speech: "Our enemies are now going to have to face everything that we went through in the struggle for power, but, the Führer emphasized, the Jews in Britain and America are still going to have to face what the Jews in Germany have already been through."

Originally Hitler wanted his speech to be broadcast but then, after some hesitation, recognized that "because of an array of psychological issues"—his way of making light of them—it was not suitable for a general audience. Two months later Hitler admitted to Goebbels that "because of his health he does not feel he is up to speaking at a rally. He is afraid that in certain circumstances he might not be able to get through it and that would be a big risk."⁶¹ Goebbels had to put up with the fact that the Nazi Party's main rhetorical weapon was out of action. During 1944, apart from his addresses on January 30 and after the July 20 assassination attempt, Hitler made no speeches that were broadcast and did not speak at any major events.⁶² Goebbels was thus faced with the increasingly urgent problem of trying to compensate for the loss of the Führer's authority with a substantial change in the public portrayal of the regime. It was now necessary to raise the profile of other figures engaged in public affairs without damaging the position of the Führer.

Goebbels was already thinking of several suitable people. After the Munich meeting he invited Himmler to give a talk on the "Internal Security Situation" at a meeting of the heads of the Party's Reich propaganda offices. He considered Himmler one of the "strong personalities involved in the conduct of the war."⁶³ Goebbels found the talk very informative: "The concentration camp inmates are treated pretty roughly. They are all deployed in war production." The production of the new A4, or V-2, rockets had been largely transferred underground, and Himmler was trying to do the same with aircraft production.

Afterward he joined the Reichsführer for "a cup of tea" and discovered that "Himmler has a very clear and penetrating sense of judgment." Goebbels noted that he had an "excellent personal and comradely relationship" with Himmler.⁶⁴ He was, however, forced to agree with Bormann, who had often complained to him that Himmler was "taking over too many things." According to Goebbels, it was "not good if one of the NS leaders gets too big; then the others must make sure that he is brought back into line."⁶⁵ In the meantime Goebbels had developed a "good personal and businesslike relationship" with Bormann; he respected him above all because "he has been extremely useful in dealing with a whole number of things through his direct contact with the Führer."⁶⁶ Despite the rivalry between them, as representatives of the Party organization and the SS, Himmler and

Bormann seemed to him to be important potential allies within the power structure.[67] Goebbels envisaged a new coalition emerging with which he could attempt to transform the domestic conduct of the war. This would also include Speer, with whom he was in regular contact during these months,[68] as well as the Gauleiters, in whom he placed great hopes following the Munich meeting, whereas in the meantime he had written off Robert Ley, whom he had regarded as an ally in his attempts to introduce "total war" during 1943, as well as Funk.[69]

STRUGGLES OVER RESPONSIBILITIES

Between autumn 1943 and spring 1944, while the air war was raging over Berlin, Goebbels's disputes with his main competitors in the field of propaganda were continuing with undiminished ferocity. Thus, despite the continually shrinking area of the occupied eastern territories, neither he nor Rosenberg saw any reason to moderate their conflict over the responsibility for "eastern propaganda." Goebbels had been extremely discontented with the Führer edict of August 15, 1943, which regulated the dispute between him and Rosenberg over the responsibility for "eastern propaganda." The edict decreed that the minister for the east should issue the "political guidelines," while the actual propaganda would be carried out by the Propaganda Ministry with the aid of its own offices in the east.[70] Goebbels considered the guidelines for eastern propaganda, which he eventually received from the Ministry for the East after a long delay,[71] to be basically "anachronistic."[72] Goebbels once again contacted Hitler, who was very unsympathetic, insisting that the two ministers should sort the matter out themselves; he no longer wished to be consulted on the matter.[73] Finally, in December 1943, after laborious negotiations,[74] the two ministries reached an agreement.[75] On the basis of this, during 1944 the Propaganda Ministry could establish its own offices in the eastern territories insofar as these were still occupied.[76]

Apart from the dispute with Rosenberg, there was the ongoing conflict with Dietrich. In September 1943 Goebbels had attempted to integrate the press offices Dietrich had established in the various occupied territories into his propaganda apparatus. However, although

Hitler had agreed to this in principle and he thought he had Dietrich's approval, Goebbels's initiative came to nothing.[77] When, in February and March 1944, Goebbels tried to transfer the press offices in Kraków and The Hague to his own organization, Dietrich (described by Goebbels as "a little man suffering from an inferiority complex") dug in his heels and blocked the move.[78]

In autumn 1943 Goebbels renewed his attempt to get Hitler to agree to transfer Wehrmacht propaganda to his ministry. He had first tried in May 1943 and had been supported by Speer.[79] Hitler had promised to do this on several occasions but had never fulfilled the promise.[80] In October 1943 Goebbels broached the subject once more with Hitler, who replied that he "still believed" that the transfer "should happen as soon as possible," but he did not want "to pick up this hot potato while there is a crisis in the east," a reply that evidently satisfied Goebbels.[81]

There continued to be violent disputes with the Foreign Ministry. Apart from various other matters,[82] the main focus was on propaganda in occupied France. Goebbels intervened after the Wehrmacht High Command had ordered the transfer of a substantial number of responsibilities of the Wehrmacht's propaganda department in France to the Foreign Ministry in November 1943. He sent the former Reich broadcasting chief, Glasmeier, to Paris as his special representative, who managed for the time being to prevent the transfer from happening.[83]

After Hitler had told Goebbels that he wanted to transfer propaganda in France to the Foreign Ministry, in November 1943 Goebbels protested vigorously "against the destruction of a proven instrument of propaganda" and naturally also against Ribbentrop's action in approaching Hitler without previously informing him.[84] Goebbels noted in his diary that Hitler had been "absolutely furious" with Ribbentrop and had forbidden similar interventions by his foreign minister in the future.[85] According to the evidence, however, the question of which department was responsible for propaganda in occupied France remained unresolved until the Allied landings.

Thus Goebbels failed to secure Hitler's actual support in any of the disputes in which he was engaged, even though in two of them (with Dietrich and with the Wehrmacht) he had explicitly—so Goebbels in any case believed—promised it. Not being able to rely on Hitler's promises was, however, by no means a new experience for Goebbels.

He had had numerous similar disappointments since he had committed himself to his Führer in the mid-1920s. But his loyalty to his idol still appeared to be unshaken.

In 1944 Goebbels instituted several changes of personnel within the Propaganda Ministry. These were prompted not least by the need to counter his rivals in the field of propaganda. He replaced his state secretary, Gutterer, with whose performance he had been unsatisfied for some time,[86] with his old office chief, Naumann, who returned to the ministry from service in the Wehrmacht. He compensated Gutterer by appointing him director general of Ufa with "a huge salary."[87] In September Naumann also became chief of staff of the Party's Reich propaganda directorate; his predecessor Hadamovsky joined the Wehrmacht.[88]

In fact for a long time Goebbels had been accusing Hadamovsky of neglecting his work in the Reich propaganda directorate in favor of his literary ambitions.[89] In June Draeger took over the foreign department in place of Heinrich Hunke. At his induction to the position Goebbels informed him that the "Foreign Ministry" was at the moment "in rather a weak position" and that he must try to make use of this.[90] In June Goebbels also had to dismiss Berndt as head of the propaganda department because he had spoken in public about the defensive preparations in the west.[91]

At the end of 1943 the question of the political leadership in Berlin, which had been open for so long, required a decision. In December Hitler asked Goebbels to take on the office of city president (which Oberbürgermeister Ludwig Steeg had provisionally taken over in 1940) "at least during the war and preferably in peacetime as well," which Goebbels agreed to do.[92] "In this way I have direct control of the municipal authorities, which I have lacked in terms of my control of the Reich capital." The new regime meant that the offices of city president and Oberbürgermeister, which since the Berlin law of 1936 had been united in one person, were now separated, and the office of city president was now made dominant. Typically, during the coming months Goebbels resisted transferring the full powers of his office as Oberbürgermeister to Steeg, who had only been appointed acting Oberbürgermeister in 1940.[93] When Steeg was "finally" appointed at the beginning of 1945 Goebbels managed to ensure that the appointment was not for a fixed term of twelve years but for an indefinite period, because he considered the position of

Oberbürgermeister of Berlin to be "a political office whose incumbent can be replaced as required."[94]

Goebbels aimed to reduce the staff of the city president's office from 250 to 50 and with the help of this small leadership cadre to exercise "real control over Berlin's municipal affairs."[95] In the medium term he intended to expand the position to that of a Reich governor.[96] Part of this arrangement involved the dismissal of Görlitzer, whom he had long wanted to get rid of, as deputy Gauleiter, among other things because he suspected Görlitzer of wanting to replace him as Gauleiter. Görlitzer was replaced by Gerhard Schach, a long-term colleague in the Berlin Gau headquarters.[97]

Hitler formally appointed Goebbels as city president only at the beginning of April 1944.[98] During the first days Goebbels was preoccupied with reorganizing the office;[99] he had the ambition of creating "an urban leadership cadre that could be a model for other cities and Gaus."[100] In fact Goebbels interpreted the term *leadership* to mean a situation in which neither at the municipal nor at the Gau level was there anybody who could form a counterweight to his autocratic exercise of power. The position of city president was thus a de facto extension of the power of the Gauleiter, who during the final phase of the regime found it all the more easy to intervene in the administration of Berlin at will. It does not, however, appear as if during the year that remained Goebbels did in fact use the office of city president in this way. In his diary, in any case, he barely mentions the office. But Goebbels advocated making the combination of the offices of Gauleiter and city president in one person permanent by law.[101]

THE FURTHER DISINTEGRATION OF THE WARTIME ALLIANCES

During the first months of 1944 the Reich was threatened not just from the air. The Battle of Monte Cassino had begun in the middle of January 1944; the Allied offensive was supported by a landing behind the German front at Anzio. This landing, only twenty-five miles from Rome, came as a complete surprise to the Germans, a fact that Goebbels found difficult to grasp: "We should have known that two to three enemy divisions were embarking in Sicily."[102]

But Italy was more of a sideshow. The German leadership was most concerned about the increasingly desperate situation on the

Eastern Front. In the meantime it had developed in such a dramatic way that the Germans began to become anxious about the loyalty of their allies.

Since February Goebbels had been carefully watching the attempt by the Finnish government to explore the conditions for a possible ceasefire.[103] On March 3 he discussed the matter with Hitler. Following Hitler's instructions, he drafted a "statement" publicly exposing the Finnish maneuvers and threatening them with what might happen "in the event that they change sides, in frank terms as far as the Bolsheviks are concerned and somewhat obliquely as far as we are concerned." Hitler looked through the text again and instructed Goebbels to begin by publishing articles in the *Völkischer Beobachter* and the *Berliner Börsenzeitung* on the same theme.[104] Hitler had told Goebbels in connection with the Finnish activities that he was now "absolutely determined to deal with the Hungarian question." This was prompted by the fact that Horthy, whom Hitler and Goebbels had long distrusted,[105] had announced the withdrawal of the Hungarian troops remaining on the Eastern Front. According to Hitler, the Hungarians were "continually committing treason," so he wanted to depose the government, take Horthy into custody, and attempt to install a regime under Béla Imrédy. Once he had disarmed the army, he could also "come to grips with the question of the Hungarian aristocracy and above all with Budapest Jewry." So long as "the Jews are sitting in Budapest we can't do anything with this city, nor with the country, in particular with its public opinion." They could use the Hungarian army's weapons, as well as Hungary's oil supplies, "quite apart from the food reserves."

During another conversation on March 14 Hitler returned to the question of the two unwilling allies. Were the Finns to "break away" from the alliance, he would withdraw German troops from the current front line to north Finland.[106] However, this did not yet happen, because in April the Finnish-Soviet negotiations collapsed because the Soviet conditions for ending the war appeared unacceptable to the Finns. Meanwhile, Goebbels was carefully following the individual stages of this intermezzo.[107]

In the meantime, during the spring of 1944, a catastrophic situation was increasingly developing on the Eastern Front. In March the 1st Panzer Army, encircled around Kamenez-Podolsk, succeeded in escaping destruction only through a daring breakout,[108] while in April the besieged garrison of the "fortress" of Tarnopol was almost completely wiped out.[109] In addition, Odessa had to be evacuated on April 9.[110]

Under the impression of these developments Hitler had told Goebbels during their conversation on March 14 that he was bringing forward the action against Hungary ("because the Hungarians had smelled a rat"); it was to begin in a few days' time. "Hungary has 700,000 Jews; we shall make sure that they don't slip through our fingers."[111]

On March 18 Goebbels heard about the conference, which had taken place on the same day at Schloss Klessheim. Hitler had given Horthy a dressing-down, informing him of the occupation of his country, which had already begun the night before. Horthy finally gave way, promising not to resist. In view of this "amicable" solution Goebbels was obliged to withdraw leaflets that had already been printed and that "had used quite tough language."[112] He anxiously followed the occupation of the country, which in fact went off smoothly, and also the measures that were taken there during the following days: the appointment of Edmund Veesenmayer as the new ambassador and plenipotentiary of the Greater German Reich in Hungary, in other words as German governor, and the establishment of a new Hungarian government under the Hungarian ambassador in Berlin, Döme Sztójay.[113]

During the next few weeks Goebbels's diaries reflect the German government's attempts to get the Hungarian government to introduce tougher measures against the indigenous Jews.[114] Goebbels and Hitler saw the new Hungarian government's treatment of the Jews, namely the degree of its radicalism, as an indicator of its loyalty.[115] By the end of April Hitler had achieved his goal. Horthy had not only fulfilled the German demands, but he was now "absolutely furious with the Jews and has no objections whatever to our using them as hostages; he has even proposed it himself." Through its involvement in Germany's Jewish policy the Hungarian government had compromised itself to such an extent that it could not escape the alliance. "In any case the Hungarians will not be able to escape from the rhythm of the Jewish question," went Goebbels's summary of Hitler's comments. "Anyone who says A must say B, and now that the Hungarians have begun implementing our Jewish policy they can no longer back out of it. After a certain point the Jewish policy gains its own momentum."[116]

In the middle of April the Hungarian Jews had begun to be concentrated in camps in the provinces and on May 3 the SS began deporting them to Auschwitz. Up to the time the deportations were stopped at the beginning of July, a total of 437,000 people were deported to the extermination camps, where the overwhelming majority were murdered immediately after their arrival. But even after this point Goebbels regarded any sign of a concession by the Hungarian government toward the surviving Jews as an indication of possible disloyalty toward the alliance with Germany.[117]

During 1944, as in Hungary, the Nazi regime tried to involve the governments of its other allies in its radical Jewish policy in order to bind them to the German Reich until the bitter end. While their efforts in Romania proved unavailing, they succeeded in enforcing deportations to the death camps in both northern Italy and Slovakia.

The near-total annihilation of European Jews required, as Goebbels was soon to discover, a reorientation of German propaganda, which had hitherto focused very much on the Jews as enemies. From the summer of 1941 onward, the Third Reich had fought the war above all as a "war against the Jews," in other words against an imaginary enemy that was allegedly holding the enemy alliance together and at the same time trying to sabotage the attempt to establish a new European regime from within. During the previous years Goebbels had orchestrated German propaganda along those lines. But now that the Third Reich had finally gone on the defensive, Hitler considered it no longer advisable to put the image of the Jews as enemies of the world at the center of propaganda. It was not by chance that Hitler introduced this change in the spring of 1944 for, in view of the impending destruction of the remaining Jewish communities in German-occupied Europe, the image of the Jews as an internal enemy that must be fought by Germany and her allies in order to create the basis for the "New Europe" had inevitably ceased to serve its purpose.

On April 26, 1944, Goebbels learned from Hitler, who had invited him to dinner, that he believed that "Stalin isn't as popular with international Jewry as everybody thinks. In some respects he's quite tough with the Jews." This laconic comment by Goebbels in fact refers to a remarkable line taken by Hitler that was to introduce a fundamental change in the direction of propaganda. While hitherto German propaganda had put forward the thesis that "the Jews," either as plutocrats or as communists, were the "glue" holding the enemy coalition together (an assertion that Goebbels frequently made both in public and in private), now, in view of the threat of military defeat, it was necessary to emphasize the contradictions within the enemy camp. For this purpose and contrary to the previously predominant image of Jewish communists, the anticommunist theme was distinguished from the anti-Semitic propaganda line, and the notion of a Jewish "world conspiracy" was played down. Anti-Semitism continued to play a major role in German propaganda, but principally in relation to American Jews; this was juxtaposed with the threat of "Bolshevism" with all its horrors.

THE CONTINUATION OF THE AIR WAR AND RETALIATION

At the beginning of March 1944 for the first time the Americans launched a series of daylight air raids on Berlin, primarily aimed at industrial targets but causing limited damage.[118] Goebbels's propaganda tactic was to not refer to the "extremely stupid and contemptible boasts" of the Americans about the alleged success of the raids "because it's in our interest that the Americans should be satisfied with their raids on Berlin."[119] The last raid on Berlin for the time being occurred on March 24. During the following months the Allied air forces concentrated on preparing for the landing in France.[120]

In view of the air raids the German authorities began to concentrate more of their efforts on retaliation. In January the Luftwaffe had launched a counteroffensive against London (described by the British as the "Baby Blitz"), of which Goebbels had great expectations.[121] But the raids remained largely ineffective; only a few bombers actually managed to reach the British capital. In January there were two, in March six raids with a decreasing number of aircraft.[122]

Despite this comparatively limited offensive potential, Goebbels claimed that these air raids had had "an enormous impact"; he believed they had caused "substantial damage throughout the London area" and gave credence to absurdly exaggerated reports stating that the raids had caused more casualties than all the Allied raids on Berlin put together.[123] On the other hand, his notes also contain doubts about the devastating effect of the bombing—for example, when he writes that the raids might have been launched more for "psychological than material reasons."[124] But even as far as this aspect was concerned, he tended to gross exaggeration. He believed that the "hysterical reactions" of the London press showed "how low morale in England has sunk."[125]

The last of these raids occurred on April 18. After that the ever smaller fleet concentrated on other targets until the raids were broken off at the end of May.[126] Now the regime's hopes were focused on the new weapons of retaliation, which were expected to produce a powerfully demoralizing effect that would decide the outcome of the war. The deployment of these weapons, however, kept being postponed.[127]

On April 17 Hitler argued that they should postpone the retaliation for a time even though the weapons were ready for action. If they succeeded in defeating an Allied invasion, that would be the moment to deploy the weapons in order to bring about a catastrophic blow to morale in Great Britain.[128] State secretary Walter Schieber informed him at the beginning of May that, although the flying bomb was ready, the A4 (V-2) could not yet be deployed, as improvements were necessary that could take between two and four months. A third weapon, the Millipede, could be ready for deployment in June or July. (This referred to the project for a long-range gun, also called a high pressure pump, that in fact was never used against Great Britain.)[129] The news about the A4 in particular came as a "great disappointment" to Goebbels, and he wondered whether Hitler, who had told him something different a few days before, was actually informed about the state of affairs. He evidently did not consider whether Hitler might have given him rather too optimistic a picture.[130]

In the meantime, in spring 1944 the Allies were continuing their air raids on German territory. In April Goebbels had to deal with the raid on Cologne on April 20[131] and the raid on Munich on April 24. He objected to the fact that Gauleiter Paul Giesler was making what he considered exorbitant demands for the provisioning of the Munich population: "Hardly have they experienced a major raid, and they behave as if they were bearing the whole burden of the air war."[132]

Apart from bombing cities, however, during the spring the Allies developed a further strategy that very soon placed the German war machine in serious difficulties. The raids by the Allied air forces in May concentrating on the German hydrogenation plants soon led, as is clear from the Goebbels diaries, to an alarming shortage of fuel. It was only the fact that from June 1944 onward the main task of the Allied air forces was to provide support for the landing in Normandy that prevented the German war machine from grinding to a halt.[133] Understandably, this aspect of the Allied air war was not referred to by German propaganda.

The raids on the German civilian population were handled differently. On May 24 Goebbels noted in his dairy that up until then the air war had resulted in a total of 131,000 deaths in the Reich as a whole, a figure that was undoubtedly "worrying." On the same day he wrote an article whose contents he had discussed in detail with Hitler and which appeared the following day in the *Völkischer Beobachter* under the title "A Word About the Air War." According to Goebbels the enemy's air war was aiming to "break the German civilian population's morale." In his article Goebbels expressed sympathy for the fact that the rage and hatred of the population that was directly affected was finding expression in acts of revenge on Allied pilots who had been shot down, and he made it clear that they could no longer claim the protection of the German security forces. "It does not seem to us possible and tolerable to deploy the German police and Wehrmacht against the German people when they are treating child murderers in the way they deserve."[134]

After the article had appeared, he hoped that "very soon a big pilot hunt would begin in Germany."[135] By launching—fictitious—reports of actual instances of vigilantism committed against pilots, he hoped to make an impact in the enemy countries.[136] He returned to the topic in a speech made in Nuremberg on June 3 announcing that nobody would be "put in prison [. . .] for speaking German" with a pilot who had been shot down.[137] In fact there were probably around 350 lynchings of Allied pilots, which were usually carried out by local Party functionaries, SS members, soldiers, and police, almost all of them after the publication of this article.[138]

The increasing number of Allied air raids in the west suggested that the enemy was trying to cut off links to the Atlantic Wall,[139] a clear indication of the Allied landing that was to come. From April onward Goebbels was expecting an invasion "in the very near future."[140] Hitler told him that "the invasion will fail, indeed even that he can repel it with a vengeance." Hitler was convinced that with its failure, the crisis in Britain would "accelerate" and that this would then lead to an increase in the communist movement, as had happened in Germany in November 1918.[141] But if he succeeded in defeating the invasion then "we would have an entirely new war situation."[142]

The reports on the public mood prepared by the Party's Reich propaganda offices were in line with this assessment. They interpreted the fact that large sections of the population were expecting the invasion to decide the outcome of the war "for good or ill" as an anticipation of victory.[143] On several occasions in May Goebbels read into these reports that people were "longing for"[144] the invasion; indeed on June 3 he noted that the population was really "afraid" that the invasion might not happen. This fear was very soon shown to be completely unjustified.

CHAPTER 28

"Virtually a Wartime Dictatorship on the Home Front"

Between an Apocalyptic Mood and Total War

Accomplices and rivals: In summer 1944, Goebbels, together with Himmler and Bormann, succeeded in establishing a "wartime internal dictatorship," as he called it, and in reducing the inactive Göring to a largely ceremonial role. From left to right, the main protagonists: Göring, Goebbels, Himmler, and Bormann.

On June 5, 1944, Goebbels visited Hitler on the Obersalzberg. The meeting took place against the rather gloomy background created by a German announcement on the same day of the fall of Rome.[1] But Hitler wanted to read something positive into the increasing number of failures, since every "military defeat provides us with a political opportunity" and, in particular, "further military successes by the Soviets would have a devastating effect on the western enemies."

During the following months Goebbels was to cling to this peculiar logic like a drowning man clutching at straws.

During a walk to the Tea House, Hitler then outlined his further plans, which, according to Goebbels, demonstrated "an extraordinarily profound imagination." "The Führer is now convinced that we can't do a deal with England. He considers England a lost cause and is thus determined to strike it a lethal blow if there is the slightest opportunity of doing so." Goebbels, however, was somewhat irritated by this announcement: "At the moment I'm rather puzzled by how he is actually going to do this, but the Führer has so often made plans that at the time appeared absurd but he was then able to carry out." In fact, however, Goebbels must have been very disappointed with Hitler's statement. The last time Goebbels raised with Hitler the question of a separate peace with Britain appears to have been in October 1943, and now he was forced to face the fact that since then he had made no progress whatsoever.

Goebbels used the conversation to strongly criticize Ribbentrop, whose diplomatic abilities Hitler "greatly overestimated." Goebbels disputed the claim that Ribbentrop had a "very effective and constructive policy." And he was "horrified" when Hitler suggested Rosenberg as a possible successor to Ribbentrop as foreign minister. "Rosenberg instead of Ribbentrop would be going from the frying pan into the fire."

After this meeting—it was already late at night—Goebbels had been invited to visit the Bormanns. At four o'clock in the morning after an entertaining evening, he headed for Berchtesgaden. There he was informed that the Allied landing in France had begun in the early hours. This did not come as a total surprise to Goebbels because on June 2 he had learned from Göring's intelligence service (Forschungsamt) that the French resistance had received instructions from Britain that indicated that it must "be going to happen in the next few days."[2]

Hitler, who was receiving the Hungarian prime minister, Döme Sztójay, at Schloss Klessheim on that day, asked Goebbels to meet him there. Goebbels found the Führer "full of vim and vigor" since, Hitler reassured him, the invasion had occurred "exactly at the spot" where they had thought it would come, moreover "using precisely the means and methods" that they had prepared for. Both these statements were obviously white lies designed to perk up his propaganda minister. Hitler made it clear he was convinced that the troops that had landed could be wiped out by the available Panzer reserves.[3]

The Allies were able to link their bridgeheads together relatively quickly and to land considerable numbers of troops and amounts of equipment, but during the following weeks they did not succeed in breaching the German lines, manned by units that had been hurriedly brought together, or to penetrate into the French interior. Thus until the middle of July Goebbels's diaries contain varying reports of the Normandy battles, as there still seemed to be a chance that the Allied bridgehead could be crushed.

RETALIATION—AND NO ALTERNATIVE

Although Goebbels had banned the use of the term *retaliation* at the end of 1943,[4] during the first months of 1944 propaganda had continually hinted that a massive counterblow was impending, most recently Goebbels on June 4 in a speech at Nuremberg, where he said that they were hoping that the retaliation would have a "decisive impact on the war."[5] During the past months his word-of-mouth propaganda had further strengthened this expectation.[6] But Goebbels had to take account of the fact that the longer the retaliation failed to happen, the less credible it became.[7] When there was no response to the Allied invasion in the form of huge "retaliatory attacks," there was a danger that the continual disappointment of people's expectations would become a problem for domestic propaganda.[8]

It was not until the night of June 15–16 that London began to be targeted by flying bombs.[9] Goebbels's response to the news was almost euphoric: "The German people are ecstatic. Without our having to use the word 'retaliation,' news of the retaliation is spreading like wildfire among the public."[10] However, he warned against excessive optimism about the new weapon. At his ministerial conference on June 16 he urged restraint on his staff.[11] On the same day, however, Dietrich ignored this approach by instructing the press to comment on the attacks in such a way that the reader was left to draw the conclusion that this was the start of the anticipated "retaliation."[12]

The following day Goebbels noted that he considered that "this development represented a tremendous danger for us, for if these hopes and illusions are not fulfilled then in the end [. . .] the government will be held responsible."[13] By the word *government* he meant above all himself, for he was the public figure who had recently been most associated with the topic of retaliation. Goebbels then gave the "strictest instructions effectively to put the brakes on the retaliation propaganda and revert to normal reporting."[14] However, it is clear from the diary that it was not Dietrich but Hitler himself who had instructed that "the German press should make the most of the question of the retaliation weapon." When Goebbels pointed out "the difficulties that might be anticipated," the "Führer" agreed with him that "the deployment of the retaliation weapon should be given very thorough coverage in the press but without raising any hopes among the German people that, given the situation, cannot be fulfilled for the time being."

That the British described it as purely a terror weapon persuaded Goebbels that it would be inadvisable to retain its original name of "hell hound."[15] Hitler finally decided—Goebbels claimed to have been the originator[16]—to call it the V-1 (for *Vergeltung*, "retaliation") in order to make it clear that it was the first in a series of weapons of retaliation, each of which would be more effective than its predecessor.[17]

In the meantime, the impact of the V-1 propaganda was in danger of getting out of control. On June 20 Goebbels noted: "Some people still believe that retaliation will play a decisive role in a very short time. Naturally there's no question of that."[18] The "hangover"[19] that he had been afraid of soon kicked in. He learned from the reports of the Party's Reich propaganda offices that "after the sudden improvement brought about by the deployment of the retaliation weapon the mood has significantly deteriorated."[20]

Meanwhile, Goebbels tried to collect all the information he could about the impact of the bombs, which, given the British ban on news reports, was extremely difficult. His diary entries were thus inevitably speculation.[21] He was completely wrong about their accuracy, believing that 80 to 90 percent of the bombs reached their target; in fact just over 20 percent reached the Greater London area.[22]

He reached the provisional conclusion that "our retaliation weapon is not having the huge success that some of our hard-liners assumed it would, but it has had a fairly devastating effect on English morale and strength of purpose as well as on English military potential."[23] But despite such supposed "successes" of retaliation, he had no doubt that the "overall picture of military developments" was extremely negative. As he wrote on June 21, if he "bore this in mind, both as regards the west, the south, as well as the Karelia front, and in the air, then it makes me feel rather dizzy. One only needs to consider where such a development, if it went on for a year, might lead in order to see how critical the situation currently is." Then once again he tried to reassure himself. There was a whole series of positive factors in the current situation and, above all, one should not forget that "every military crisis is extraordinarily beneficial for political developments because they increasingly sharpen the differences in the enemy camp, which can only work to our advantage." In other words, Goebbels had completely adopted Hitler's logic.

In fact he saw another way of at least prolonging the war. On June 21 he outlined to Hitler on the Obersalzberg his view that so far "total war" had just been "a slogan." It was vital to "reform the Wehrmacht from top to bottom." He told Hitler that "by using drastic measures" he was "prepared and in a position to provide him with a million soldiers and this would be done by ruthlessly screening the Wehrmacht's organization as well as the civilian sector."

As he told his propaganda minister, however, Hitler believed that the moment for "a big appeal for total war in the real sense of the word" had not yet come. Goebbels took the opposite view but failed to get his way, concluding that Hitler wanted "to follow the evolutionary rather than the revolutionary path," which he could "not quite see the point of."

As far as further political developments were concerned, he was obliged to recognize that Hitler was "further away than ever from believing or hoping that he could come to an arrangement with England." England, according to Hitler, "would be totally destroyed in this war." He preferred to leave aside the question of whether, on the other hand, "at some time in the future we shall be able to reach a deal with the Soviet Union." He thought that in view of the current military situation he was unable to answer this question. Once again Goebbels's attempt to raise the issue of a separate peace had come to nothing. "This conversation," he concluded, "was one of the most serious that I have ever had with the Führer. But it was completely harmonious. I believe that the Führer has inscribed in his memory many of the things I have said to him. Sooner or later he will undoubtedly return to them."

On June 22, the day after this conversation, the major Soviet sum-mer offensive against Army Group Center was launched and soon produced important advances leading to large German units being outmaneuvered, surrounded, and then destroyed.[24] Goebbels, who in contrast to Hitler had not reckoned with a Russian offensive on the third anniversary of the German attack on the Soviet Union,[25] noted on June 27 that "a real crisis has developed."[26]

At the end of June the 3rd Panzer Army was largely wiped out near Witebsk, as was the 9th Army, which had been surrounded near Bo-bruisk. On July 3 the Red Army succeeded in taking Minsk.[27] During the following days the 4th Army, which was surrounded east of Minsk, was also, bit by bit, almost completely destroyed.[28] But the Soviet advance went farther: Vilnius was surrounded on July 8 and had to be surrendered on the 14th.[29]

Goebbels's diary entries reflect his increasing helplessness, indeed despair at this situation. "It must after all be possible to hold the front at some point," he noted on July 9. "If things go on like this the Sovi-ets will very soon be on our East Prussian border. I keep asking my-self in despair what the Führer is doing about it." At the same time, in view of these events, he was preoccupied with a somewhat macabre idea: "I can only hope that if the Soviets really do reach our Reich frontier, then at last total war will be realized. Why it isn't happening already is completely beyond my comprehension." Sometimes he even began to doubt Hitler's leadership skills. "At the moment the Führer's playing a very risky game. It would be wonderful if he won it because then we would rescue the Baltic states and the Baltic Sea, but equally it would be terrible if he lost the game."[30] Goebbels was somewhat relieved when, in the middle of July, he learned that after almost four months Hitler had returned from the Obersalzberg to the Wolf's Lair in East Prussia.[31]

In view of the bad news coming from every front as well as Hitler's unwillingness either to declare total war or to seek a political conclu-sion to the war, Goebbels decided to concentrate propaganda entirely on the theme of retaliation. Although he had had to accept the fact that so far this had been rather counterproductive as far as the Ger-man population was concerned, he now hoped that a new V weapon campaign could bridge the gap until the arrival of the V-2 weapon. At the meeting on June 22 Hitler had told him that the V-2 would be deployed starting in August, and while it would "not achieve an immediately decisive impact on the war," it would bring "a decision closer."[32] Moreover, in writing "retaliation is our number one weapon,"[33] he was making the point that at that moment there were no other alternatives either in terms of propaganda or in terms of politics.

Thus at the beginning of July Goebbels instructed the media "to emphasize even more than before the retaliatory character of our weapon."[34] He considered the speech that Churchill made to the British Parliament on July 6, 1944, concerning the effects of the V weapons as simply an attempt to play them down, and he was pleased to note that the evacuation of women and children from London was being restarted.[35]

On July 23 in an article in *Das Reich* dealing with "The Question of Retaliation," Goebbels stated that it "was not coming to an end but had only just begun." But he emphasized that in the end technological superiority was decisive only when linked to superior "morale."[36] In his speech broadcast on July 26, Goebbels attempted to sustain people's hopes about the decisive effects of the new technology by announcing further V weapons. They had "not only caught up with the enemy but overtaken them." And to emphasize the point he added a personal experience: "Recently, I saw some German weapons, and looking at them not only made my heart beat faster but for a moment it stopped altogether."[37]

PREPARATIONS FOR "TOTAL WAR"

Goebbels, however, knew only too well that retaliation propaganda would be insufficient on its own to transform the popular mood. As in the previous year, by renewing the proclamation of "total war" he was banking on sending out a signal to try to mobilize the whole population and thereby gear the public sphere in the Third Reich to the grave wartime conditions. In the middle of July he interpreted the generally very pessimistic reports on the public mood as a "cry for total war," which he ascribed above all to a speech he had made in Breslau on July 7 as well as to his most recent newspaper articles.[38] As in the previous year, in his struggle for the introduction of tougher measures for "total war" Goebbels turned for support to the armaments minister, Speer. On the evening of July 10 he had a long conversation with Speer. Afterward he noted that the armaments minister also thought that "the German people were capable of providing another few million workers and soldiers."[39] Speer and Goebbels agreed that each would send a memorandum to Hitler.

On the following day Speer gave Goebbels a memorandum, which he had already submitted to Hitler on June 30 and in which he had described the catastrophic effects of the Allied air raids on the German hydrogenation plants.[40] On July 12 Speer showed Goebbels another memorandum, which he sent to Hitler on the same day. In it he requested that Hitler "carry out the total mobilization of the German people for our struggle." This was to be achieved through the closure of businesses, the mobilization of female labor, the reduction of administrative staff, as well as the screening of the Wehrmacht's home bases for surplus personnel. The implementation of these measures should not be left to the administration, business, or the Wehrmacht but must be entrusted to "personalities."[41] On July 20 Speer went further and by using concrete figures pointed out that there was "a complete mismatch between the numbers of people who are working productively for the home front and those who are unproductive in that they are simply needed to maintain living standards and the administration." In order to rectify this mismatch Speer once again recommended a "new personality equipped with full powers."[42] Goebbels thoroughly approved of these ideas.[43]

Goebbels was also delighted with the film of the launch of an A4 (V-2) rocket shown him by Speer. "One has the impression of being there at the birth of a new world. I can imagine that the A4 will bring about a complete revolution in weapons technology and that future wars will look completely different. [. . .] The A4 as it soars upward is not only an imposing but also an aesthetic sight."[44]

Goebbels now set about composing a memorandum of his own in which he tried to acquaint Hitler with his "Ideas for the Total Mobilization of Our National Resources for the Purpose of Achieving Victory through our Weapons." He concentrated on trying to supplement Speer's figures with arguments based on mass psychology. Goebbels made the assumption that, because of their unbridgeable differences the enemy coalition was bound to break up. Thus in his view it was vital to get through the next few months. As so often, Goebbels argued that the Reich still possessed "huge resources in men and in her economy" that still had to be exploited.

Goebbels proposed having the Wehrmacht thoroughly investigated by an "outsider" and, in addition, getting the Party to eliminate the "slack" in the administration through a ruthless process of inspection, restricting it to work that was absolutely essential. "For every task that needed to be undertaken" Hitler should grant "the widest possible powers to a man whom he could trust and to one of these men the job of coordinating these plans and then, with all those involved, bringing them to you for approval."

Goebbels did not forget to include a few examples in his memorandum illustrating in a particularly graphic way the "slack in the administration," and it is not surprising that he used the behavior of his archenemies, Rosenberg and Ribbentrop, whom he accused of providing entirely superfluous competition for his Propaganda Ministry.

The memorandum concluded with a lengthy section that could be headed "personal matters" and which was a kind of résumé of his almost twenty-year-long relationship with Hitler. He had been loyal to Hitler during the critical situation in 1932. He was well aware that during the past two decades, particularly during 1938–39, he had "caused Hitler some concern" about his private life, and he now wanted to repay his "generosity and kindheartedness." It was not "personal ambition" that was motivating him, and his "political ambition" was focused "entirely on the practical issues at stake." Toward the end of the memorandum he wrote that when he was with his family in Lanke it was entirely clear to him that "not only I but also all my family could never live in a time that was not our time."[45]

A few days before he sent off the memorandum a meeting of state secretaries had taken place at which Speer's proposals had been discussed. Naumann informed Goebbels about the upshot of the meeting, reporting that it had basically amounted to an attempt to continue the work of the Committee of Three. "The same gentlemen who during the discussions of the Committee of Three criticized and torpedoed my proposals will have no right to decide anything on the question of total war; they must resign and make way for more tough-minded people."[46]

In July Goebbels was so busy with the conduct of the domestic side of the war that he even considered the heavy air raid on Munich during this month, which caused two thousand deaths,[47] primarily as a positive indication of the movement toward total war. On July 14 he

wrote that it was "perhaps necessary for the capital of the movement
to make this sacrifice so that every single member of the Party leadership comes to his senses." He was not too upset by the destruction
of the Party court and its organization department since "the war
could be won without these two offices." The Artists' House, one of
Hitler's favorite haunts in Munich, was burned out. This was "sad, but
as far as the attitude prevalent in this house is concerned it isn't in the
least sad."

THE 20TH OF JULY

According to his own account, Goebbels received news of the assassination attempt on Hitler by Colonel Claus von Stauffenberg on
July 20, 1944, at midday on the same day. He was working in his
Berlin office when the Reich press chief, Otto Dietrich, brought him
the news and told him that Hitler had received only minor injuries.
At this time, however, it was not clear what lay behind the attack.[48] In
particular, Goebbels had no idea that it represented the start of an
attempted coup.

That afternoon Lieutenant Hans Wilhelm Hagen, a ministerial official who was serving with the Grossdeutschland regiment, contacted Goebbels to say that his battalion was in the process of sealing
off the government district; Hitler was dead and the Wehrmacht had
received the order to take over full powers. Hagen and the officer in
command of the regiment, Major Otto Ernst Remer, were suspicious
of this order and, to make sure, had therefore decided to contact
Goebbels.[49] The suspicions of Remer and Hagen were justified. In
fact, after the bomb attack in the Führer headquarters by Colonel
Stauffenberg, the military conspiracy planned to set in motion Operation Valkyrie, which had been designed to deal with emergencies.
The Reserve Army was to take over power in the Reich in order to
prevent potential unrest. Only a small group of senior officers within
the Reserve Army was privy to the plot; the majority of officers and
men were to be used by the plotters without being aware of the political background to the events in which they were involved.

Hagen was admitted to see Goebbels around 5:30 P.M. It was only
then that Goebbels became aware that the assassination attempt in
the Wolf's Lair was part of a comprehensive coup. He asked Hagen to

fetch his commander, Remer; in the meantime, having spoken to Hitler on the telephone, he had discovered that the assassination attempt had been carried out by Stauffenberg, the chief of staff of the Reserve Army.

When Remer arrived at the Propaganda Ministry after 7:00 P.M., he was still unaware what role he and his troops were playing in the dramatic events that were taking place that day. For in the meantime he had learned that Goebbels's arrest had been ordered as part of the purge going on in the government district. Was Goebbels part of a coup that was in progress, or was the action also directed against him as one of the most important representatives of the regime? His encounter with Goebbels soon clarified matters. Goebbels agreed to arrange for him to speak to Hitler on the telephone; Hitler then informed him about the background to the assassination attempt and ordered him to crush the coup in Berlin. Remer thereupon ordered his battalion to assemble in the garden of Goebbels's official villa, where Goebbels addressed the soldiers. After that some of these troops took part in the occupation of the Bendlerblock (War Ministry), the headquarters of the plot. The plotters were arrested, and four officers, including Stauffenberg, were shot on the spot.

However, at this point the coup had already failed, even if Goebbels later tried to dramatize his own role in the affair.[50] What was decisive was the fact that Hitler had not been killed. An additional factor was the hesitation of the conspirators. By waiting for Stauffenberg to arrive in Berlin in the afternoon and only then issuing the order for Operation Valkyrie, they gave the Führer's headquarters the opportunity to launch countermeasures.[51]

THE IMPLEMENTATION OF "TOTAL WAR"

From Goebbels's point of view the attempted coup had occurred at a very opportune moment. Who after July 20 could now seriously oppose the measures for "total war" that he and Speer were demanding? Thus he was convinced that "the general crisis will lead rather to a strengthening than a weakening of German resistance,"[52] and in this he was proved right. The winners from the July 20 crisis were those who had been advocating a radical course in the conduct of the war: Himmler, Bormann, Speer, and Goebbels himself. Himmler had already been appointed commander of the Reserve Army on July 20 and had been given the task of surveying the Wehrmacht in order to assign as many men as possible to frontline duty. Bormann had also been instructed by Hitler on July 20 to "issue the necessary orders [. . .] to ensure total engagement in the war" by the Party.[53]

In Goebbels's view, the meeting that set the agenda for this issue, which took place in the Reich Chancellery on July 22, went "exactly along the lines that I wanted." Lammers began by acknowledging the work of the Committee of Three, whose effectiveness had nevertheless been limited by the personal interventions of individual ministers with Hitler. Goebbels was somewhat surprised that Lammers then proposed that "now substantial powers should be granted to individuals": to Himmler to "reform the Wehrmacht" and to Goebbels "to reform the state and to reform our public life."[54]

Goebbels then spoke for an hour about his program for "total war." At the end of his speech he announced that he was willing "to take on the responsibility if I am given the necessary powers." Once again he was surprised when Keitel gave him unqualified support, declaring that he was prepared to transfer responsibilities in the military sphere to Himmler. He was also supported by Bormann but with certain qualifications. Finally, Goebbels got his way with his proposal that they should go and see Hitler on the following day and propose that "he must grant wide-ranging powers covering, on the one hand, the Wehrmacht and on the other the state and public life." The obvious candidates for these comprehensive powers were: "Himmler for the Wehrmacht and me for the state and public life." Bormann was to have comparable powers for the Party, while Speer already had sufficient powers in the armaments sector. According to Goebbels, these decisions had created what was "virtually a wartime dictatorship on the home front."

Goebbels then met Hitler; it was the first time since the coup attempt. He was "deeply moved" by the greeting he received: "I have the feeling that I'm standing in front of someone who is working under the protection of the hand of God." To begin with Hitler showed him the damaged barracks in which the assassination attempt had taken place and explained that he was determined "to exterminate the whole clan of generals who have been working against us root and branch." Goebbels was delighted. He saw a purge coming such as the Party had gone through during the "time of struggle" because of Strasser and Stennes. He was "concerned," however, about the fact that "the Führer has gotten very old" and is making "a really frail impression." On the other hand, he was the "greatest historical genius of our time. With him we shall be victorious or with him we shall die as heroes."

On July 23 the decisive meeting with Hitler, to which Goebbels attributed "historical significance," took place in the Führer's headquarters. To begin with, Hitler dismissed some misgivings from Göring, who, conscious of his status as Reich marshal, felt marginalized in view of the far-reaching reforms proposed. Then Hitler addressed the basic issues raised by "total war." Goebbels was pleased to note that Hitler's line of argument was very similar to that contained in his memorandum of July 18, 1944, which, according to Goebbels, the "Führer" had evidently "studied [. . .] diligently."

After Hitler's statement Goebbels in a long presentation once more outlined his ideas on "making the war a total war." Hitler then supported the points he had made and, Goebbels noted, shook him "very warmly" by the hand. Hitler then left the meeting. When it came to approving the final draft, Göring dug in his heels. He declared that if the draft was signed off in its present form, he would be "more or less forced to resign." Goebbels, who continued to believe that Göring's authority must be sustained at all costs because he realized that Hitler did not yet want to dismiss him, proposed a compromise. The "Führer's Edict for Total War" that was signed two days later stated that Göring would recommend to Hitler a "Reich Plenipotentiary for Total War," a pure formality since it was clear that there was only one candidate for the position: Joseph Goebbels. This Reich Plenipotentiary was assigned the task of examining "the whole of the state apparatus [. . .] with the aim of freeing up the maximum amount of manpower for the Wehrmacht and the armaments industry through a completely rational deployment of men and equipment, by closing down or restricting activities that are of marginal importance for the war effort and through a rationalization of organization and procedures." He was authorized to request information from the responsible supreme Reich authorities and issue them with instructions.

A careful perusal of the edict, however, shows that the powers of the Reich Plenipotentiary to direct the authorities were by no means total. The edict even included the right of appeal against his "instructions"; the issuing of "legal provisions and fundamental administrative regulations" in the sphere of total war was reserved to the supreme Reich authorities and the formula stating that Bormann would support these measures "by deploying the Party" made it clear that Goebbels's powers did not apply to the Party.[55] Lammers then subsequently issued a list of those agencies to which the instructions of the Plenipotentiary did not apply.[56]

Goebbels, however, tended to ignore such niceties. On the evening of July 23 he believed he had reached his goal. "I can leave the Führer's headquarters having achieved what is probably the greatest success of my life."[57] The fact that he had achieved this "success" in a situation in which, by means of a final effort, the Nazi leadership was seeking to avert a catastrophic defeat was, characteristically for Goebbels, of secondary importance.

"TOTAL WAR": INITIAL MEASURES

During the next few days the military situation became critical. By the end of July 1944, in the final phase of the major Soviet operation against Army Group Center, the Red Army had advanced to the outskirts of Warsaw and, on August 1, it succeeded in building a bridgehead on the west bank of the Vistula to the south of the city, while farther north it had arrived at the borders of East Prussia.[58] Meanwhile, in the sector of Army Group Northern Ukraine the front temporarily collapsed in the area around Lemberg, which was captured by the Red Army on July 22, and it was only with difficulty that a new defensive front could be established during August.[59] On July 26 the Americans launched an offensive in the west that led in August to the strategically important breakthrough near Avranches, giving the Allies the opportunity to encircle the German army in Normandy from the south. Goebbels had every reason to view the situation in the west during August as "worse than bad."[60]

This was all the more reason for him to plunge into his new task on the home front. To carry it out he established a small planning staff under Naumann as well as an executive committee under the Oldenburg Gauleiter, Paul Wegener, with a proven administrator in the form of Hans Faust, a district governor, as secretary.[61] On July 26 he spoke on the radio detailing the events of July 20 and emphasizing his own role in suppressing the coup in Berlin. He then went on to outline the "conclusions" to be drawn from these events, namely the need to completely "exhaust" the huge "potential reserves of strength" that were still available. Goebbels then announced that Hitler had assigned him "comprehensive powers" to achieve this goal.[62]

In the evening he listened to the broadcast of his speech with Magda, who had just returned from Dresden. "I think the style and presentation were a model of how it should be done." Of course the speech "made a very deep impression on the nation." On the following day, he claimed that the speech had even been "the center of attention of world opinion."[63] On July 26 the press, which had been given detailed instructions on how to go about it the day before, announced his appointment, and Goebbels was pleased to note the big splash and "favorable commentaries."[64] On July 28 the Reich Plenipotentiary issued a decree concerning the "Reporting of Bogus Employment," which, however, was so vacuous that, according to a minute by the Reich Chancellery, it was a perfect example of the truth that "overhasty legislation is a bad idea."[65]

At the beginning of August Goebbels proudly presented Hitler with a final report on the work of the Reich Air War Inspectorate, of which he was in charge. All Gaus had been inspected, and Hitler's instructions had largely been carried out. "That's the way an assignment from the Führer should really be carried out."[66]

In implementing the concept of "total war," to which he was now enthusiastically committed, Goebbels was heavily dependent on the cooperation of the Gauleiters. Thus at a meeting of Party leaders on August 3, which was once again held in Posen, he appealed to them for support. After again describing the events of July 20, in the second section of his speech Goebbels outlined the measures that were planned for "total war."[67] He thought his speech, which he considered "exemplary in form and content," had "convinced" the Gauleiters that "total war is now developing along the right lines and above all that total war is now in the right hands." Sauckel was the only one who was going to "make serious difficulties." He was "vain and stupid and is particularly annoyed that a large number of the tasks that he hasn't completed are now being done by me."

In August Goebbels sent the supreme Reich authorities two circulars exhorting them to adapt their operations to the seriousness of the situation. Everybody should work until their task had been completed, at a minimum of sixty hours a week.[68] Moreover, in a further circular he urged that they should cultivate a "style appropriate to wartime" that demonstrated that "we are fighting for our lives." To achieve this, there should be no more events such as receptions, official appointment ceremonies, commemorations, and the like.[69]

Goebbels wanted his right to request information from the state authorities to be conferred on the Gauleiters but had to be reminded by Bormann that they already possessed this right.[70] Finally, following a proposal from Bormann, a directive for the implementation of total war created Gau and district commissions to inspect public authorities and agencies to see whether they contained personnel who could be called up into the Wehrmacht. The Gauleiter was to take the chair in the Gau commissions, and he was to appoint the chairmen of the district commissions within the Gau. These commissions contained representatives of the various state authorities as well as other "suitable men from the Party and the state."[71]

By the end of the year Goebbels aimed to have replaced 1.5 million of the workers in the armaments industry who had a dispensation from service in the armed forces with other personnel. To achieve this, against opposition from Sauckel, he raised the upper age limit for the conscription of women for work from forty-five to fifty;[72] he set about finding alternative work for the two hundred thousand foreign women employed as maids; and, finally, he endeavored to secure men from the administration, from industries not vital to the war effort, and from the service sector by carrying out closures, cuts, and rationalization on a large scale. During the following weeks he was fully engaged in this work. Among other things he secured a reduction in postal deliveries, the simplification of ticket inspection on the railways, the closing down of newspapers and journals, the closure of technical schools, the abolition of "excessive questionnaires," the cancelation of all congresses and conferences as well as the simplification of the tax and social security systems.[73]

Soon, however, Goebbels found obstacles being put in his path, which he could only partially overcome, especially since Hitler, typically, objected to measures that he considered too radical. Goebbels noted, for example, that Hitler had been "very strongly opposed" to the closure of all theaters and music halls. Once the theaters had been closed they could never be reopened during the war, and "once people had gotten used to the lack of theaters then that could become permanent." In the end the Führer bowed to the exigencies of "total war." Theaters, orchestras, cabarets, and other cultural institutions were shut, "initially" for six months.[74] Goebbels himself considered closing the theaters to be "the most visible measure indicating a commitment to total war," which "for psychological reasons must be maintained at all costs," which is why during the following weeks he fought any attempt to reopen them tooth and nail.[75]

Hitler succeeded in preventing Goebbels's attempt to stop people sending packages and private telegrams.[76] He also opposed stopping the production of beer and candy. Soldiers needed candy on route marches, and a ban on brewing beer would have "a bad psychological effect in Bavaria." Goebbels went along with this reluctantly. "The Führer sees this in terms of the Bavarian mentality, which is rather a closed book to me."[77] Goebbels was also unable to prevent art journals from continuing to be published until January 1, blaming it on an intervention with Hitler by his photographer, Heinrich Hoffmann.[78] And although on August 28 Hitler agreed to raise the age of female conscription yet again, to fifty-five, in fact this was never put into effect.[79]

Above all, Goebbels was gradually forced to recognize that his original intention of using the excuse of "total war" to introduce a broader reform of the Reich's administrative structures ("the major reform of the Reich") could not be carried out.[80] He had already failed the previous year. Although he had succeeded in closing down the Prussian Finance Ministry, Lammers and Bormann succeeded in convincing Hitler that Goebbels's plan to abolish the office of Prussian prime minister would constitute the removal of an indispensable part of the administration.[81] He also failed in his attempt to close down the Economics Ministry and several other government bodies.[82]

When in October State Secretary Wilhelm Stuckart presented a memorandum on reform of the Reich administration, Goebbels described his proposals as "logical and correct" but considered them "impossible to implement at the present time." "The Führer will never be able to bring himself to undertake such a far-reaching reform of our Reich administration and Reich government, and who knows whether that would be the right thing to do in wartime."[83]

DEALING WITH THE CONSPIRATORS

Goebbels responded to the attempt on Hitler's life on July 20 by ordering the Party's Reich propaganda department to organize a "series of loyal rallies" in every Gau representing "our nation's spontaneous response to the heinous assassination attempt." The "national comrades" were "to be invited to participate in the rallies by the Block Wardens."[84] The SD reports duly referred to the population's rejection of the assassination attempt.[85]

During the following days, apart from "total war," Goebbels spent much time discussing with Hitler the sentencing of the July 20 conspirators, as up and down the land "the people" were demanding that they be severely punished. Hitler told Goebbels that they should make a clean sweep of them at the coming trials. They should all be hanged, as "bullets would be wasted on these criminals." The question of Rommel came up during these discussions, since according to the investigations he had known about the preparations for the assassination. Goebbels commented disparagingly on this national hero whom he had created: "He's very useful when things are going well, but the moment there's a serious crisis Rommel lacks any powers of resistance."[86]

The first trial against eight key members of the conspiracy, which took place in the People's Court on August 7 and 8, was discussed in detail by Hitler and Goebbels beforehand. Goebbels decided to "receive" the chairman of the judges, Roland Freisler, before the start of the trial and to "spell out in detail how the trial is to proceed." The reckoning with the conspirators should, as Hitler instructed him, "on no account lead to attacks on the officer corps as a whole, on the generals, on the Army or on the aristocracy." They would, however, "sort out" the aristocracy, according to Hitler "a cancerous growth on the German people," "sometime later on."[87]

The eight death sentences that had been anticipated were given much publicity and according to Goebbels had "a tremendous impact on the German people."[88] There were further trials in the People's Court lasting until April 1945 with more than 150 people accused of participating in the conspiracy, of whom over a hundred were sentenced to death and hanged.[89]

At the end of July Goebbels learned from the head of the Security

Police and SD, Ernst Kaltenbrunner, that allegedly his old friend, the police president of Berlin, Count Wolf-Heinrich von Helldorf, had been involved in the coup attempt.[90] By the middle of August Helldorf was standing before the People's Court where, as it was reported to Goebbels, he had "performed reasonably well." He had openly confessed to his participation in the affair.[91] A week later, however, Goebbels saw a film of the trial in which it was clear that during the interrogation Helldorf had appeared a broken man whose responses had been "tearful."[92] Two hours after the end of the trial he and five other defendants were executed. Goebbels noted that "on Hitler's orders" before his own execution Helldorf had been forced to watch the executions of two others. Goebbels's summation of someone whose career he had actively sponsored from the very beginning (although he continued to spell his name incorrectly, despite having known him since 1931) showed relief but no real satisfaction: "That's the end of the unpleasant story of Helldorff. It's probably the worst in the history of the Berlin party."[93]

SETBACKS

On August 15 American and French forces landed in southern France.[94] On August 21 in the north of France the Allies succeeded in surrounding the bulk of the German Normandy army in the Falaise pocket and subsequently destroying it. Paris was liberated on August 25, and German forces began hurriedly retreating from France, Belgium, and Luxembourg. In the central sector of the front, Allied forces had reached the borders of Germany.[95] Summing up the situation at the beginning of September, Goebbels commented: "The situation on the Western Front has now become more than dramatic."

Goebbels had learned that, in view of the encroaching fronts, Speer had requested that Hitler designate the area "he could reckon on being defended at all costs for the whole length of the war in Europe." Hitler had then described this area "as running along the Somme in the west, ending in the foothills of the Alps in the south, including parts of Hungary in the southeast and in the east running more or less along the current front line. In the north we shall hold onto southern Norway at all costs." Goebbels responded to this piece of news by commenting that "in view of the growing crisis in the general war situation" they must "come to terms with a reduced set of war aims" and say "goodbye to the fantasies of 1940 and 1941." If they could succeed in holding on to the area designated by Hitler, then "we would nevertheless have achieved the greatest victory in German history."[96]

On August 23 King Michael of Romania dismissed the prime minister, Ion Antonescu, and announced that he wanted to agree to an armistice with the Allies. The decision to leave the alliance with Germany was supported by a large majority of the army and the population. Goebbels's contemptuous comment that the king had "undoubtedly" been persuaded to make this decision by his "entourage of fawning courtiers" was a complete misreading of the situation.[97] When German forces then tried to occupy Bucharest and the Luftwaffe bombed the capital, Romania declared war on Germany on August 25.[98]

According to Goebbels the armistice between Finland and the Soviet Union at the beginning of September was "not taken too badly in Führer headquarters." The military consequences were bearable as the German forces succeeded in pulling back to northern Norway. But he considered that politically the loss of their last ally but one was liable "to reduce our chances in the war."[99]

The Goebbels family did not remain unaffected by the large German losses on all fronts. On September 9 Goebbels learned that in central Italy Magda's son, Harald, had "been wounded and was missing in fighting on the Adriatic and there was no news yet of his having been taken prisoner."[100] He told Magda about it only a fortnight later, and she, despite her poor health, took the news "very calmly." Perhaps, he thought, Harald had been captured by the British, but only if he had been seriously wounded. For "Harald is not a lad to let himself be taken by the enemy through cowardice."[101] Finally, in the middle of November, Goebbels received the news that Harald had been found in a North African POW camp, in recovery after having been seriously wounded. Magda was greatly relieved, and Goebbels admitted in his diary that he "had already given Harald up for dead."[102]

"TOTAL WAR": "THE BALANCE
BETWEEN MILITARY AND CIVILIAN MANPOWER"

In the meantime Goebbels was continuing with his efforts to make the war "total." Shortly after his appointment as Reich Plenipotentiary Goebbels had begun to address the "balance between military and civilian manpower." He wanted to "squeeze" 1.2 million men from the civilian sector to be deployed "on the front line." An initial quota of three hundred thousand men was established for the month of August, with each Gau being given a target to meet.[103] By the beginning of September, apart from a few thousand, the August quota of three hundred thousand had allegedly been met. However, a comparison with the Wehrmacht statistics shows that once again Goebbels was giving rather an overoptimistic assessment of what he had achieved. At the end of September there was still a shortfall of around 30 percent.[104]

The mobilization of three hundred thousand men, mainly from the armaments industry, led almost inevitably to a conflict with Speer.[105] On September 2 the two adversaries put their cases to Hitler, who, according to Goebbels, supported him and declared that it was not a question of "providing weapons or soldiers but weapons and soldiers." It was essential to take men from the armaments industry in order to provide new divisions.[106]

The aim in September was to recruit 450,000 men from the civilian sector.[107] A few days later, Goebbels gave a figure of only 250,000[108] and for October only 240,000 men.[109] Later these quotas appear to have been reduced even further.[110] Goebbels has little to say in his diaries about the fulfillment of these quotas. However, there is a reference to the fact that at the beginning of October he was still pressing the Gauleiters to fulfill their September quotas.[111] It is clear from a calculation at the end of the year that there was a considerable "shortfall" in the September and October quotas, which had to be "made up" during the coming year.[112] According to Wehrmacht statistics, with 500,000 men having been recruited by the end of the year, the aim of securing 700,000 men during the months of August, September, and October had not been nearly reached.[113]

Also, the provision of substitutes, which Goebbels had wanted to achieve through various measures such as the conscription of older women and administrative rationalization, was, according to his own figures, far less successful than he had anticipated. In the middle of September he noted that a total of 1.3 million people had signed on at the labor exchanges but only 125,000 had as yet been placed in employment.[114] The recruitment of the armaments workers who had been released from their plants into the Wehrmacht was also happening slowly. Of the 300,000 released in August, only 191,000 had joined the Wehrmacht by the end of October.[115]

It is typical of Goebbels's diary entries that rows of such figures can never be followed over long periods. Instead, he keeps introducing new aspects of "total war." His notes reveal far more about his volatile work methods than about the concrete results of "total war." They provide a good impression of how he threw himself with great enthusiasm into carrying out parts of a project, putting maximum pressure on his staff, whom he then blamed for the failure to achieve the overall goal, while he himself preened in the glory of apparent successes. Then the topic would fade into the background of his diary entries, to be replaced by a new task, to which he then devoted the same enthusiasm. In implementing "total war" Goebbels was primarily concerned to ensure that the daily life of citizens and thus the image of the Third Reich as a whole was geared to an overall goal, namely total mobilization for war. In a daily life governed by "total war" there was simply to be no place for disruptive debates about the military situation, the possibilities for peace and talk of the postwar era, discussions about who was politically responsible for the disaster, or complaints about the effects of the war. Moreover, as a result of "total war" the existing structures were being eroded and a radicalizing trend unleashed, enabling him, as the general Plenipotentiary, to intervene in almost every sphere. The more the Third Reich moved toward its downfall, the more powerful Joseph Goebbels became.

THE THREAT FROM THE WEST

In September the bombing campaign against the Reich began again with full force, after the main raids during the previous three months had been directed at targets in France. During the four months between September and December 1944 the RAF dropped more bombs on Germany than in the years 1942 and 1943 combined, and the U.S.

Air Force exceeded its total of bombs dropped during 1943 six times over.[116] The German hydrogenation plants were a key focus of the Allied bombing offensive, particularly in November, and "transportation targets" were also subjected to heavy raids, especially in the west. However, cities continued to be the main target of the raids during autumn 1944.[117] On September 10 Mönchengladbach was badly affected.[118] On September 11 the RAF succeeded in creating a firestorm in Darmstadt that killed 12,000 people.[119] After that the raids focused particularly on Duisburg on October 14 and 15 (causing more than 2,000 deaths), on Essen between October 23 and 25 (over 1,600 victims), on Bochum and Solingen (both raids during the night of October 4–5, each causing more than 2,000 deaths). There were also 2,000 deaths in Freiburg, which was bombed on the night of November 27–28. Heilbronn was hit by a devastating raid on the night of December 4–5, during which 5,000 people died and the old part of the city was almost completely destroyed.[120] During the autumn Berlin was also subjected to several daylight air raids by the Americans. By far the worst of these occurred on October 6 and December 5.[121]

Moreover, the western Allies were also operating close to the German border. On September 17 the largest airborne operation of the war began in the area around Arnhem, although the Germans succeeded in preventing Allied troops from seizing the bridge over the Rhine.[122] However, in the meantime the Allied forces had advanced into the area around Aachen, posing a much bigger threat and forcing the partial evacuation of the city.[123]

Under the impression of this direct threat to the western borders of the Reich, Goebbels began advocating a "scorched earth" policy, an idea which had been mentioned in his diaries since the early summer[124] and for which he now believed he was sure of Hitler's support. For "now it's a matter of all or nothing, and if the nation is fighting for its life, then we mustn't shrink from the ultimate."[125] But by the following day, after a conversation with Speer, he was beginning to have second thoughts. There was no point in their letting the enemy conquer territory that had been devastated if they were planning soon to re-conquer it.[126]

In the meantime the reports that he was receiving described a further decline in the national mood. In his view this was due not least to people's sense that the measures of "total war" were insufficiently comprehensive or radical.[127] He faced serious problems in writing his editorials: "I can't deal with the issues on which I could provide interesting information, and the issues I can write about have been dealt with so often that nobody's interested in them anymore."[128] Writing them gave him a "real headache," but he thought he could not possibly stop doing so because for the nation waiting for his articles to be read out on the radio every Friday it was "like its daily bread ration."[129]

At this point, thanks to an Allied indiscretion, he learned of the plan by the American treasury secretary, Hans Morgenthau, to deindustrialize Germany, turning it into a largely agricultural country. In this desperate situation the news came "as a godsend."[130] Goebbels gave instructions "to do everything possible to make the German people aware of this plan for our annihilation." Accordingly, on the following day the press carried big headlines attacking "the Jewish financier Morgenthau" and his "threat of annihilation."[131]

GOEBBELS'S INITIATIVE FOR A SEPARATE PEACE

Goebbels, however, was aware that while a further intensification of "total war" might gain time, defeat could be averted only through political action. Thus his fevered search for a way out of the disastrous situation in which the Reich found itself in the late summer of 1944 focused above all on one option: the possibility of making a separate peace, an idea that he had repeatedly put to Hitler since 1943. In August he had tried to convince Bormann of his plans. They must make the attempt somehow "to get out of the two-front war," though this would be impossible so long as the Foreign Ministry was headed by "a stubborn, obstinate boss."[132] At the beginning of September he noted that "attempts had been made from every conceivable quarter to achieve a political dialogue about the war. We are receiving news from England that influential circles would like to reach a compromise with the Reich," since they wanted to get out of the alliance with the Soviet Union.[133] On the other hand, the Japanese were trying "to get us into talks with the Soviets." Ambassador Hiroshi Ōshima, under instructions from his government, had already approached Hitler concerning this matter; his response had been noncommittal.[134] Moreover, the Foreign Ministry had initiated contacts with "influential Soviet Russians" in Stockholm.

On September 10 Goebbels noted that "Spanish diplomatic circles are making great efforts to mediate between us and the West. On the other hand, Japan is making feverish attempts to mediate between us and the Russians. [. . .] It looks as if the Soviets are much more open to the possibility of a separate peace than our enemies in the west."[135] A few days later he learned that the Foreign Ministry was very actively engaged in this matter.[136]

Goebbels did not believe that Ribbentrop was capable of conducting such a set of negotiations; they needed a new foreign minister. During this period he found himself urged from various quarters to play a leading role in foreign affairs in place of Ribbentrop. The state secretary in the Interior Ministry, Wilhelm Stuckart, wanted him to take over the Foreign Ministry; his own state secretary, Naumann, reported that Himmler, Bormann, and General Heinz Guderian were of the same opinion, while Speer believed that Hitler should grant Goebbels special powers in foreign policy in place of Ribbentrop.[137]

After his conversation with Naumann Goebbels thought through the whole situation and concluded that if he replaced Ribbentrop he would be able to achieve "quite a lot" as far as the "political side" of running the war was concerned, as foreign policy needed to be "in the hands of a man with intelligence, energy, and the requisite flexibility." At the same time he was quite skeptical about the possibility that Hitler could "decide to carry out such a far-reaching reshuffle of the German government at such a critical time."[138]

Goebbels paid great attention to the Quebec Conference attended by Churchill and Roosevelt on September 16. He suspected that it represented an attempt by the two western allies to improve the coordination of their positions vis-à-vis the Soviet Union that might presage the start of a serious conflict within the enemy coalition. However, he attributed reports in the neutral press, according to which the Soviet Union was planning separate peace negotiations with the Reich, to a tactical move on Russia's part. It wanted "to put strong diplomatic pressure on the Anglo-Americans." This was, of course, wild speculation. In fact the main issue discussed in Quebec was the future policy to be pursued in occupied Germany.[139]

On September 19 Goebbels passed on an important piece of information to Himmler and Bormann so that they could give it to Hitler. He had learned from his state secretary, Naumann, that the Japanese ambassador, Ōshima, had renewed the offer of his services for negotiating a separate peace with the Soviet Union.[140] But Ōshima's initiative was not news to government circles in Berlin. Goebbels learned that Ley had spoken "to a group of intimates" maintaining that "negotiations with the Soviet Union were under way via Ōshima and that they would soon be making peace with Moscow." Goebbels considered that this way of proceeding was "absolutely criminal," and took Ley to task.[141]

In fact the incident showed that Ōshima's initiative was hardly suitable as the basis for a secret diplomatic démarche. Indeed there is some indication that Hitler had made sure that rumors about Ōshima's activities were spread in order to sow mistrust among the enemy coalition and to lead his own officials to believe in the prospect of a political conclusion to the war. But Goebbels, who was completely incapable of seeing through such maneuvers,[142] did not give up so easily. On September 20 he prepared a memorandum for Hitler proposing that they should follow up Ōshima's initiative and attempt to begin peace negotiations with the Soviet Union through the mediation of Japan.[143]

His proposal began with the point that they could "neither make peace with both sides simultaneously nor in the long term successfully make war with both sides simultaneously." Goebbels stated bluntly that "we have never in our history won [. . .] a two-front war and, based on the power relationships as reflected in terms of numbers, it is impossible for us to win the current war by military means either." To win Hitler over to the idea, Goebbels made an analogy with the situation at the end of 1932. In those days they had also been confronted by an enemy coalition that they had eventually smashed by taking the initiative themselves. Goebbels then outlined to Hitler his view of the Quebec Conference and suggested that the contradictions that were allegedly emerging in the enemy coalition should be "seized on and exploited with every trick and cunning move possible."

A separate peace with the Soviet Union, Goebbels continued, "would open up marvelous perspectives. We would have room to breathe in the west and under the impact of such events the English and Americans would hardly be in a position to continue the war in the long term. We would not have achieved victory as we had dreamt of it in 1940, but it would nevertheless be the greatest victory in German history."

However, he made it clear that he did not consider Ribbentrop "capable" of carrying out such a step. He must be replaced by a foreign minister with the "requisite clarity of vision and toughness combined with a high degree of intelligence and flexibility." It was only too clear whom he envisaged for this task.

Goebbels anxiously awaited Hitler's response. He learned via Hitler's adjutant, Julius Schaub, that the Führer had carefully read his memorandum but had not commented on its contents.[144] During this period Goebbels's views were reinforced by reports from Britain, according to which "there is not the slightest willingness to negotiate with us. They want to carry through the experiment with Europe whatever the cost."[145]

But despite waiting anxiously for a response, he was to be disappointed. As Hitler fell ill at the end of September and was out of action for a week, Goebbels did not get the chance to speak to him personally about his proposals. Even after Hitler's recovery there are no entries in his diaries about Hitler's response, and he does not seem to have taken any further initiatives in this direction.[146] Goebbels had thrown all his political and personal weight onto the scales to persuade Hitler to undertake a peace initiative toward the Soviet Union. It appears that Hitler completely ignored his proposal. Goebbels, however, knew only too well that the continuation of the two-front war would inevitably lead to defeat. In reality he might as well have shot himself at this point.

CHAPTER 29

"But When Will There Be Some Action?"

Downfall

Day trip to the front: Goebbels speaks to troops on March 7,
1945, in the marketplace in Lauban, Silesia, which had just
been recaptured.

On September 7 the army had begun to launch the first V-2 rockets
at enemy territory. To begin with they were launched at London and
Paris; then at other cities in Belgium, the Netherlands, and Britain;
and from October 12 exclusively at London and Antwerp, the most
important Allied supply harbor.

The Wehrmacht did not report the deployment of the second "retaliation weapon" until November 8. The way in which the report was phrased, namely that the new weapon had already been deployed for weeks, was sufficient to remove any remaining illusions people may have harbored that the wonder weapon would produce a rapid change in the war. Repeated German propaganda reports of the rockets' allegedly devastating effects on the population of London could not disguise the fact that this weapon was not going to decide the outcome of the war.[1]

A few days before the launching of the rockets Goebbels had discussed the presumed effects of the new weapon with its designer, Wernher von Braun, and a fortnight after the deployment of the V-2 had begun Goebbels was briefed on the program by the man in charge of the operation, SS-Obergruppenführer Hans Kammler.[2] The news blackout that the British initially imposed on the effects of the new weapon prevented Goebbels from acquiring even a vague notion of the impact it was having. Thus he considered plausible reports that in London alone nine hundred thousand houses had been rendered uninhabitable, in other words that the city had been completely devastated; this was far from the truth. That the rockets were widely scattered and distributed over a long time meant that they were incapable of bringing such a vast city to a halt.[3] When in November Churchill commented on the rockets publicly for the first time Goebbels gained the impression that the weapon had had a "fateful" effect. And he organized word-of-mouth propaganda to "pass this on to the German public."[4]

At the beginning of October the Americans launched an attack on Aachen; by the 16th they had surrounded it, and on the 19th the old imperial city capitulated, the first large German city to surrender to the Allies.[5] On October 10 the Soviet offensive on the Baltic cut Army Group North off from the rest of the German forces, pushing it back toward Latvian Courland, where it continued to defend its position until the German capitulation in May 1945.[6]

When in October 1944 Soviet forces advanced for the first time into East Prussian territory and German civilians in the village of Nemmersdorf were murdered in the most brutal fashion Goebbels decided to exploit this with a big propaganda campaign.[7] But while on the one hand this atrocity propaganda met with disbelief, on the other hand people criticized that this strip of territory had not been evacuated.[8] Thus a few days later Goebbels noted that at the moment he was disinclined to "inform the public" of further "terrible atrocities" by the Bolsheviks of which he had learned "because I don't anticipate it having the effect of spurring on our troops."[9]

"TOTAL WAR": "COMBING THROUGH" THE CIVILIAN SECTOR

In the meantime, during the last months of 1944 and the beginning of 1945 Goebbels was continuing his tireless efforts to implement "total war." However, the precipitate measures to draft labor into the Wehrmacht led to temporary unemployment, as the armaments industry was not in a position to employ a large number of unskilled workers as substitutes.[10] Thus in October the Reich Plenipotentiary announced that those workers who had been earmarked for employment in jobs essential for "total war" and who "could not yet be assigned" to the armaments industry could also be employed in other spheres such as in workshops carrying out repairs or in the construction industry.[11] As for those for whom there was no prospect of employment, in November the Reich Plenipotentiary announced euphemistically that they would provide the labor exchanges with a "labor reserve" that was "urgently required."[12] He was also forced to accept that a large number of the women liable to conscription could be employed only in part-time work.[13] Moreover, in January he was complaining that the Wehrmacht's preparations for processing the recruits remained inadequate, which "meant that the men who had been withdrawn from vital war work at home were sometimes sitting around in barracks for weeks on end with nothing to do."[14] It had become clear that to mobilize additional labor and soldiers was a highly complex task, one that was impossible to perform adequately with the kinds of impromptu initiatives carried out by Goebbels. He was also unsuccessful in gaining acceptance for his idea of a Military Auxiliaries Law subjecting all women under thirty to military conscription and thereby recruiting two hundred thousand women as "military auxiliaries." It was blocked by Bormann and Himmler.[15] Thus at the end of November he had the impression that "Bormann in particular is rather envious of the title I have been given as the person responsible for implementing total war measures," and he was thus increasingly making difficulties for him.[16]

At the end of October Göring delegated to Goebbels the authority to examine the whole of the Luftwaffe, starting with the Air Ministry itself, to facilitate mobilization for total war. Goebbels's staff began the task at once. Goebbels bemoaned the ministry's opaque bureaucratic structures, but he did not record what results, if any, were achieved by this investigation; his diary entries referring to it cease in November 1944.[17] At the beginning of December he had a conversation with Göring at the latter's country house, Karinhall, in which the Reich marshal sounded quite confident that "with a certain amount of difficulty and with a great deal of effort he would slowly succeed in recovering his position," but in the New Year Goebbels was to give him up for good.[18]

At the beginning of November he appointed inspectors to the individual ministries to examine what measures each had hitherto undertaken to implement "total war."[19] In this way for the first time Goebbels gained an insight into the internal workings of other ministries and rapidly came to the conclusion that "at the start of the total mobilization" his colleagues had "pulled the wool over his eyes by promising the earth."[20] It was not surprising that pruning those ministries that were headed by his archenemies Rosenberg and Ribbentrop afforded him particular pleasure. Rosenberg, he noted, "is desperately hanging on to a ministerial organization that has completely lost any raison d'être."[21] Ribbentrop's resistance was equally vigorous when Goebbels set about abolishing those departments in the Foreign Ministry that in his eyes were in competition with the Propaganda Ministry.[22] That the investigation of the Foreign Ministry was still going on in April 1945 and that at the same time Rosenberg was still defending his phantom ministry (the eastern territories) shows that their delaying tactics had been quite successful.[23]

During the last months of the Third Reich Goebbels did everything he could to undermine Ribbentrop's position. At the end of September, he prepared a memorandum for Hitler, based on information that he had received from Ernst Wilhelm Bohle, with the title "Defeatists and Turncoats," which, according to Goebbels, the Führer read "with great interest" and which had awakened his "mistrust of German foreign policy." Goebbels considered it his "national duty" to provoke this mistrust still further, as it was necessary "to remove" Ribbentrop and his "damaging influence on our foreign policy as quickly as possible."[24]

He aimed to use the investigation of the Wehrmacht High Command, which he had been authorized to carry out by Hitler at the end of the year (we shall return to this), in order to significantly reduce the size of the Wehrmacht's propaganda department, transferring its responsibilities to the Propaganda Ministry; here too he was unsuccessful.[25]

The mobilization measures introduced by Goebbels had increased his differences with Speer, which had already emerged in August and also resulted in personal confrontations.[26] As has already been mentioned, Goebbels had summed up the conflict by saying it was not a question of "weapons instead of soldiers" (as Speer maintained) but rather of "weapons and soldiers."[27] However, according to Goebbels, it gradually became apparent that "under constant attack from the Party" Speer had "become somewhat weak at the knees" and had started trying to repair fences with him.[28] At the end of November they "sorted out their differences" during a long conversation because both had concluded that it "did not make sense for either of them to continue in this way."[29]

On January 3 Speer and Goebbels put their differences concerning priorities for the deployment of manpower to Hitler, and after a long discussion he insisted on a compromise between the claims of the Wehrmacht and the armaments industry. On this occasion Hitler announced that, during the coming summer, thanks to the fifty divisions that he would form from the 1928 cohort of recruits, in other words a "totally committed group of young men," he would secure "the crucial breakthrough in this war."[30]

Goebbels's figures outlining the success of the "combing through process," to which the armaments industry and the state administration had been subjected and which he insisted had been completed by mid-January, were contradictory. He claimed that by the end of December 1944 "thanks to my efforts" around "700,000 men had been sent to barracks," and a few days later he even gave a figure of 1.2 million, shortly afterward referring to a million men, who by the end of January had been transferred from the civilian sector to the Wehrmacht through the program of "total war." Since the total number of those recruited into the Wehrmacht during 1944 was 1.308 million and Goebbels had only taken up his position as general plenipotentiary at the end of July 1944, his figures are obviously totally exaggerated. More realistically it can be assumed that through the work of the Gau commissions, which were at the heart of the

Reich Plenipotentiary's efforts in the sphere of recruitment, by the end of March 1945 slightly more than four hundred thousand men had been recruited into the Wehrmacht.[31]

As Gauleiter of Berlin since September 1944 Goebbels had also been actively involved in the regime's efforts to organize a last stand against the enemy. On September 26 Hitler signed the "Decree Concerning the Establishment of a German Volkssturm [Home Guard]" according to which all men aged between sixteen and sixty capable of bearing arms were required to become members of this new organization. The Gauleiters and Himmler shared the responsibility for organizing and running it.[32] Goebbels was determined to "establish it on a grand scale in Berlin." He was primarily interested in the propaganda aspects of mobilizing this last reserve and believed that it would have a particularly positive effect as far as "raising morale in the country" was concerned.[33]

On November 12, 1944, oath-taking ceremonies for the Volkssturm were held throughout the Reich. In Berlin the ceremony took place in ten squares simultaneously, on which around a hundred thousand Volkssturm men had gathered. Goebbels administered the oath from the balcony of the Propaganda Ministry, with his speech relayed to the other squares. He summoned up the "spirit of 1813,"* but they would fight with the weapons of 1944. "The rally gives a decidedly combative impression," he noted. "Wilhelmsplatz with its singed and burned ruins forms a background to this rally very much in keeping with the times."[34]

HITLER—A "MEMBER OF THE FAMILY" TO THE END

On November 20 Hitler left his no longer secure headquarters in East Prussia and went to Berlin in order to undergo a further operation on his vocal chords.[35] After a few days he had recovered from the operation and once again could speak normally; during the previous months he had been plagued by a "chronic hoarseness."[36] His health problems, which included a bout of jaundice at the end of September and the beginning of October,[37] were a significant reason why Hitler had made no further attempts to speak in public. Goebbels was par-

* Translators' note: The War of Liberation against Napoleon.

ticularly put out by this long silence because there were evidently rumors in circulation to the effect that the Führer was either seriously ill or even dead.[38]

On December 1 Hitler had recovered sufficiently from the operation to summon Goebbels to the Reich Chancellery. During their conversation, which began in the afternoon and after a break was resumed during the night, Hitler, whom Goebbels found to be in "excellent" shape, outlined his plans for a major offensive in the west. Hitler told Goebbels that he would be able to "destroy [...] all the enemy forces," mount a "massive" attack on London with V-2s, and thereby once again secure a change in the direction of the war.[39]

As was almost always the case during such meetings, at the end of this long conversation, according to Goebbels one of the "most interesting and most reassuring" that he had ever had with Hitler, they discussed cultural issues and reminisced about the "time of struggle" they had shared. Hitler inquired after the family and in particular Magda and the children. In fact she had visited Hitler the day before and had told him "about the family."

In recent months Hitler's concern for Magda's well-being had gone far beyond simply taking a friendly interest in her welfare. During a visit to Führer headquarters in September 1943 Hitler had shown a "detailed" knowledge—Goebbels does not recount where he got it—of an illness from which Magda had long been suffering: severe pains in her face caused by the trigeminal nerve. At the time Hitler had told Goebbels that he did not want a planned "operation to take place because he is afraid that it would have bad effects on her face." Goebbels had agreed to persuade Magda not to go ahead with it, and the operation was postponed.[40] In May 1944 Magda had traveled to Berchtesgaden in order for her "annoying trigeminal neuralgia" to be examined by Hitler's personal physician, Professor Theo Morell.[41] After that Magda had joined Hitler for dinner and, as she reported to Goebbels, she had spent a nice evening with the Führer.[42] The operation, which had become unavoidable and was carried out by a specialist in Breslau, was successful. Goebbels had used his visit to Magda in Breslau to sort out his relationship with Karl Hanke, now the Gauleiter and provincial governor, who during their marital troubles had acted as a shoulder for Magda to cry on.[43]

Two days after his meeting with Goebbels on December 1, Hitler visited the Goebbels family at home for the first time in a long while, this time in Lanke: "He's received like a member of the family, and the children assembled in their long dresses to greet him." Hitler had not seen the children for almost four years. The proud father noted that Hitler had admired Helga and Hilde, who in the meantime had become "little ladies," and was particularly interested in and approving of Hedda and Hilde, while he had also taken to Helmut, who had become a "fine boy"; "the Führer stays for tea with us for two hours and we pass the time chatting and reminiscing." Among other things Hitler talked at length about the problems of "degenerate art [. . .] in connection with some superior pictures we had hung in the rooms in his honor"; the Goebbelses had evidently gone to some lengths to prepare for the visit.

"Our family," concluded Goebbels, "will never forget this afternoon."[44] It was to be the last private visit that Hitler made to the family, and the emotional intensity with which Goebbels described it indicates that there was something of a farewell atmosphere hanging over it.

THE ARDENNES OFFENSIVE
AND THE ALLIED COUNTEROFFENSIVE

While the American troops in the Aachen area initially failed to make much progress in advancing farther into German territory, they were more successful in the southern sector of the front. By the end of November 1944 the American forces, together with French units, had advanced to the Upper Rhine, and in the Saar they had even succeeded in capturing a strip of German territory.[45]

On the morning of December 16 the last great German offensive of the Second World War, on which Hitler had pinned such hopes in his conversation with Goebbels at the beginning of December, was launched. Three German armies made a surprise attack through the snow-covered Ardennes, which were only thinly manned by American troops, with the aim of rapidly advancing toward Antwerp, the most important Allied supply port. Initially the offensive seemed to be going well—the weather conditions prevented the Allies from deploying their air power. The spearheads advanced up to sixty miles into Belgian territory. To begin with, Hitler and Goebbels imposed a total blackout on the German media.[46] But even after it was lifted they were very cautious about providing details of the operation.[47]

After two days Goebbels noted that "our military action has put the English and Americans completely off their stroke."[48] The following day he received a phone call from Hitler reassuring him that "the effect of our attacks" had been "colossal." Although the first news of the offensive quickly produced a "complete change of mood,"[49] this only posed the old problem for Goebbels of a total overestimation of what had been achieved, for during the days after Christmas the Americans began a major counteroffensive,[50] and during January the Allies gradually forced the German troops back to their starting lines.[51]

During the last quarter of 1944 the situation on the Eastern Front had been relatively stable. But from January 12, 1945, the Red Army launched its major offensive from the bridgeheads over the Vistula. That large numbers of troops had been moved to the west for the Ardennes offensive now had fatal consequences. After only a few days Goebbels was forced to admit: "The crisis in the east is becoming increasingly catastrophic."[52] In January in the northern sector of the front the Red Army succeeded in cutting off the troops in Pomerania and East Prussia. At the end of the month Soviet forces managed to establish bridgeheads over the River Oder near Küstrin; they were now only about forty miles from Berlin. Goebbels considered the situation so critical that he moved his family from Lanke to his official apartment in Berlin.[53]

In addition there was the problem of the air war, against which there was effectively no defense. The Allied squadrons were now rapidly destroying in turn those cities that had hitherto been unaffected or only partially damaged. After Nuremberg and Munich had been badly hit at the beginning of January[54] Berlin was targeted on February 3 by an American daylight raid, causing over 2,500 deaths.[55]

In January Goebbels's Gauleiter colleague, Karl Kaufmann of Hamburg, reported to him on the investigations in Saxony that he had carried out as part of his role in the Air War Inspectorate. Kaufmann, Goebbels noted, had "discovered that the situation was generally satisfactory," and that only in Dresden were "things still in a bad way," which Goebbels attributed to the conflict that existed between Gauleiter Martin Mutschmann and Oberbürgermeister Hans Nieland. Goebbels did not think much of Nieland and thought that "if Dresden were hit by massive air raids he would be useless." During the night of February 13–14 such raids did indeed take place; the city, which was full of refugees, was bombed by the RAF. As a result of a double raid the whole of the historic center of the city was transformed into a sea of flames, and around 35,000 people were killed, almost as many as in the destructive raid on Hamburg in 1943.[56] Goebbels appears to have come to appreciate the sheer scope of this catastrophe only gradually. On March 7, after visiting the head of the SS and police in Dresden, Ludolf-Hermann von Alvensleben, he referred to a "tragedy [. . .] such as has seldom occurred in the history of humanity and almost certainly won't occur again during the course of this war."

"TOTAL WAR": "COMBING THROUGH" THE WEHRMACHT

In December 1944 new perspectives opened up for Goebbels in his role as Reich Plenipotentiary for the mobilization for total war. Hitler signed a decree that had been long and impatiently awaited by Goebbels[57] extending his responsibilities to cover the Wehrmacht. The decree ordered the inspection of all Wehrmacht organizations based in the homeland in order to free up soldiers for frontline duty. The inspection was to be carried out by Gau commissions of which half the members would be from the Party and half from the Wehrmacht. Goebbels was responsible for setting the guidelines for the inspection.[58] At the end of 1944 Goebbels had set himself the target of securing two hundred thousand men per month from the military and civilian sectors. That was the number of reserves that the Wehrmacht calculated were necessary to replace the losses that were occurring.[59]

However, the Wehrmacht's losses in terms of deaths amounted to 450,000 men in January alone and in the following months to nearly 300,000 each month, not to mention soldiers who were no longer deployable because of injury or because they had been taken prisoner.[60] After a few weeks, therefore, Goebbels made his target more specific. He thought that during the next period he could secure between 800,000 and one million men from the Wehrmacht alone,[61] and at the end of January he claimed that as a result of the measures he was taking in the military and civilian sectors he would be able to provide 300,000 men per month for frontline duty.[62]

In February he desperately tried to secure authority from Hitler to "comb through" the whole of the Wehrmacht (in other words not just the homeland bases) in order to fulfill the requirements of the military, which looking ahead to the beginning of August had reached 768,000 men.[63] If Hitler refused to authorize him to do this, he was determined "to resign my position."[64] It appears, however, that he failed to receive this authorization but did not resign as Reich Plenipotentiary. It is very difficult to provide details of his further activities as Reich Plenipotentiary. There is only fragmentary documentation on the Wehrmacht's "personnel budget" during the final months of the war (indeed it is conceivable that this form of planning was simply abandoned),[65] and the series of announcements of his successes as Reich Plenipotentiary contained in his diaries cease in February. Although he was not relieved of this position, it appears that his attempts to achieve the complete "combing through" of the country in search of soldiers were pushed into the background by other ad hoc measures. He was naturally not prepared to admit that they had ended in complete failure.

ONCE AGAIN: A SEPARATE PEACE?

During this last phase of the war Hitler was not prepared to permit the possibility of a military defeat's being discussed among the people around him. Instead, as before, he was banking on the enemy coalition breaking up. He reckoned that this could happen if the Third Reich succeeded in achieving a military success or at least in bringing the enemy offensives to a standstill for a lengthy period. That would be the moment to agree to a separate peace either with the western Allies or with the Soviet Union and then to fall upon the remaining enemy and finish the war once and for all. However, so long as the Wehrmacht was in retreat on all fronts, in Hitler's view it made no sense to start peace negotiations; on the contrary, in his opinion such initiatives would only be interpreted as signs of weakness.

Hitler's position should not be confused with that of a fantasist.

His view was to a certain extent realistic. The possibility of a breakup of the enemy coalition, though very small, was not out of the question, and it remained the only chance of preventing the downfall of his regime. Hitler concentrated his thoughts on this one remaining possibility and (this is very characteristic of him) in the event of its failing to transpire had no alternative plan. At the beginning of February he told Goebbels: "The best thing to do is to burn one's bridges, not only professionally but also personally. The person who no longer cares whether or not he lives is usually the one who wins in the end."[66] In any event the dream of a collapse of the enemy coalition recurs in almost all the conversations that Hitler had with Goebbels between January and April 1945 that the latter recorded in his diaries. And now even Goebbels's hopes were focused on this final way out that Hitler was suggesting as a realistic option.[67]

Goebbels, whose September 1944 proposals for a separate peace had not been taken up, once again broached the topic in his conversation with Hitler on January 22, but was told that there were no signs that the western Allies were interested in dialogue.[68] "Ribbentrop would very much like to put out feelers, at least to the British," but Hitler had "for the time being vetoed it completely" because the current military situation offered no prospects for it. However, in principle Hitler was in favor of peace negotiations with the western powers when it was the right moment to do so. On January 25 he told Goebbels that the Soviet Union's military successes were precisely the thing that could be used for establishing contact with the western powers. Stalin's intention "of Bolshevizing Europe under all circumstances," he told him, was "our big opportunity, for England and America couldn't allow that to happen. But if they wanted to resist it then they would have to seek German assistance."[69]

Two days later, on January 27, Goebbels had a long conversation with Göring,[70] who was extremely concerned about the general situation but also completely confused about the intentions of the Führer, a result of his rapidly sinking prestige with Hitler, which had been going on for months. Goebbels noted: "If we don't succeed in stopping the Soviets he doesn't see much chance of our being able to continue fighting the war." Göring was very doubtful that "we shall succeed in persuading the Führer to negotiate in time"; indeed, the Reich marshal had asked him "urgently" whether "I was convinced that the Führer really wanted a political solution," to which Goebbels responded that he was. Göring, he continued, "would be very willing to establish contact with the English via his friends in Sweden, but naturally he can't do that without the Führer's permission, and the Führer won't give him permission." Göring and Goebbels were at least agreed on one thing: It would be possible to pursue an "an active wartime foreign policy" only if Ribbentrop was dismissed.

Immediately after this conversation Goebbels again met with Hitler, who told him that "at the moment" he considered that "there was no possibility of a dialogue with the western powers." Goebbels believed that Hitler was basically prepared "to become politically engaged," but who was to advise him with regard to this? "Ribbentrop is too undiplomatic and at the moment Göring is not sufficiently in with the Führer to be able to approach him on such a delicate matter." So he was the only one left. This task was undoubtedly "the most glorious [. . .] one that has to be carried out during this decade." He was ready to do it but "at the moment I don't believe that the Führer will let me do it."

On January 29 he met Speer, who informed him that with the loss of the Upper Silesian industrial area, Germany would probably be reduced to 30 percent of its armaments production. That would be "insufficient for her to win the war militarily," so they must now focus on getting a political solution. This view provided the basis for the memorandum that Speer submitted to Hitler shortly afterward and which he gave to Goebbels to read.[71]

On January 28 Hitler once again reassured him that they would "slowly manage to reestablish strong lines of defense in the east." Goebbels noted that it would "naturally be a fatal mistake if we clung to fantasies about our defensive capabilities." He "sometimes [had] the impression that that is the case with the Führer." Now he was having increasing doubts. Naturally "it [is] right that we must stop the enemy somewhere. But whether that's possible with the limited means currently at our disposal will only become clear in the next few days." Basically he agreed with Hitler that the enemy coalition would collapse, but at the moment there was little sign of its happening.[72]

Thus at the end of January Goebbels became preoccupied with the question of how to defend Berlin against a Soviet breakthrough.[73] His defense of Berlin would, he wrote at the end of January, be a "masterpiece."[74] He organized the building of barricades and tank traps and studied the Soviet preparations for the defense of Leningrad and Moscow.[75] He planned the formation of four divisions for Berlin composed of Wehrmacht, police, and Volkssturm,[76] but had to put up with the fact that the moment they had been established, at least in rudimentary form, they were dispatched to the Eastern Front. Hitler explained that he wanted the city defended "in the forward area."[77] Lacking strong forces, he contemplated the formation of women's battalions and units made up of prisoners.[78]

Using word-of-mouth propaganda he encouraged the Berlin population to leave the city—with relatively little success, which he interpreted as "real trust in our defensive capabilities."[79] As ever he was not slow in publicizing his efforts in the media. On March 18, for example, reporting on the defensive preparations in the capital, *Das Reich* noted: "Reich Minister Dr. Goebbels is the soul of our defensive operations."[80]

At the end of January and the beginning of February Goebbels undertook repeated attempts to persuade Hitler to embark on a foreign policy initiative, preferably toward the west. But Hitler responded negatively: They must "go on waiting until a favorable opportunity" occurred. "I'm only afraid that in the end going on waiting will rob us of our most valuable and perhaps last opportunity," Goebbels commented critically.[81]

On February 11 Hitler told Goebbels that he was convinced that Churchill "would like to jump ship if he had the opportunity," but for domestic and foreign policy reasons he was probably unable to do so. Goebbels then urged Hitler "at least to provide the English with a board from which to spring, but the Führer doesn't think the time is yet right." Hitler continued to insist that "during the course of this year the enemy coalition will break up. We must hold on, defend ourselves, and stand our ground waiting for this moment." Goebbels thought that Hitler was now pinning his hopes more on Great Britain rather than, as had still been the case shortly before, the United States. "But I keep telling the Führer in response to all his arguments that we must take advantage of our political opportunities, which I don't think is really happening, particularly given the current phase of the war."[82]

On February 12, following the Yalta Conference, Hitler once again discussed with Goebbels the prospects for a separate peace. Now it was mainly up to Stalin whether he wanted to cause a breach in the

coalition, but in view of his military successes this was highly unlikely. Goebbels believed that Hitler was now "much more receptive
to such political considerations." He felt bound to admit that Hitler
was right in thinking that "a political solution" was possible only if
they had had some military successes. On the other hand, he reached
the logical conclusion: "If we no longer have a military presence at
all, then we can no longer exploit a change in the war situation." But
however clear-sighted his conclusion and however much he doubted
Hitler's willingness to end the war and despite all his criticism, Goebbels was not in a position to oppose Hitler's policy, which amounted
to a total catastrophe for the German Reich.

Nevertheless, Goebbels seized the initiative. The following day he
discussed matters with the head of the Reich Security Main Office,
Ernst Kaltenbrunner. They aimed to use a planned trip to Switzerland by the former Polish ambassador to the United States, Count
Jerzy Józef Potocki, who was living in Vienna, to point out to the
western powers that Germany was the only power that could prevent
the Bolshevization of Europe.[83] In fact, of course the whole idea was
a nonstarter, and there is no further mention of it in Goebbels's diaries.

FINAL PROPAGANDA EFFORTS

In their conversations during these weeks Goebbels and Hitler tried
to find historical precedents for nations being saved at the last minute as proof that hanging on at all costs was the right strategy. The
history of their own party in 1932 was brought up again[84] but also the
example of Frederick the Great, who in the end won the Seven Years'
War despite his prospects having appeared hopeless.[85] Goebbels
based this argument on Thomas Carlyle's biography of the Prussian
king, which he passed on to Hitler.[86]

At the end of January he referred Hitler to the example of the Second Punic War, in which the Romans had finally succeeded in defeating Hannibal despite major setbacks.[87] A few weeks later the
Führer instructed him to publish lengthy accounts of it in the German press. It was the "great example on which we can and must
model our actions."[88] Goebbels, however, believed that another propaganda theme would be more effective than such excursions into

history. At the beginning of January, after a long gap—"We mustn't let the topic be forgotten"[89]—he once again published an article on the "Jewish question," in which he revived his old line that the Jews were the "glue that binds the coalition together, despite its major ideological differences and clashes of interest."[90] He could not, however, make the topic of anti-Semitism once again the main leitmotif of German propaganda. That was blocked by Hitler's statement of April 1944 that anti-Bolshevik and anti-Semitic propaganda should remain distinct.

Goebbels now placed more emphasis on the topic of Bolshevik atrocities than on "Jewish revenge." In January he had still been wary about releasing "reports on Bolshevik atrocities" in eastern Germany for domestic propaganda.[91] But in February he changed his mind. He dismissed fears that using atrocity propaganda might cause a panic; on the contrary, they must commit themselves "unconditionally" to the "final struggle" against Bolshevism.[92] On February 7 he wrote that, having secured the requisite authorization from Hitler, "I'm ratcheting up atrocity propaganda against the Soviets throughout the Reich." However, there was an obstacle in the way of his campaign in the form of the Reich press chief, Otto Dietrich, who believed that "the German people would be shocked" by details of Soviet brutality.[93]

On February 28 Goebbels made a radio broadcast in which he acknowledged the "military crisis." They were facing "the hardest test," and only by maintaining "an iron will to carry on" could they stave off the threat of defeat. He made a fairly brief reference to "horrific reports" from eastern Germany without going into detail about the atrocities. He concluded the broadcast with a lengthy quotation from a letter Frederick the Great wrote to his sister in 1757 at a particularly critical moment during the Seven Years' War ("We are faced with either death or victory").[94] He described the reception of this address in his diary in unusually guarded terms as "mixed."[95]

As Hitler had repeatedly reassured him that he approved of the attack on Soviet atrocities,[96] Goebbels endeavored to give the topic greater prominence in propaganda, as for example on March 8, when he undertook a day trip to Silesia, which the front line had now reached. He visited Lauban, which had been reconquered that very morning, although it was largely destroyed. He made a speech in the city hall in Görlitz in front of soldiers, members of the Volkssturm, and civilians, in fact his last public speech, which was shown in the weekly newsreel. In this speech Goebbels emphasized the themes of atrocity and revenge by proclaiming that "those divisions [. . .] which during the coming weeks and months will be taking part in major offensives" would be taking part in this struggle "as if in a religious service" with "their murdered children and raped wives before their eyes."[97] In general, however, he was unable to achieve his aim of making the Red Army's atrocities a propaganda leitmotif with which to mobilize the nation's last reserves.[98]

Goebbels tried to persude Hitler to give another speech. He unwillingly agreed to do so,[99] but it never happened. "The Führer now has a fear of the microphone that's incomprehensible to me."[100] Now, lacking resources, he had to switch the focus of propaganda to "small-scale activity": word-of-mouth propaganda, stickers, chain letters, and the like—of necessity propaganda had to return to the methods of the Party's "time of struggle."[101]

GROWING CRITICISM OF HITLER

After his conversations with Hitler Goebbels eagerly took note of the Führer's criticism of Göring, of his lack of interest in the political and military situation, his "pompous lifestyle," his lack of "steadfastness."[102] He had, he told Goebbels on January 31, "serious doubts" about whether Göring was suitable as his successor.[103] Goebbels decided to urge Hitler strongly that he must either "get Göring to change both his attitude and his behavior or kick him out."[104] But Hitler kept saying that he did not see any possibility of dismissing the Reich marshal; there was no suitable successor.[105]

Hitler's stubborn retention of the Reich marshal was partly responsible for Goebbels increasingly including the Führer in his criticisms. For even when Goebbels finally asked him whether the "German people were going to be destroyed because of the failure of their Luftwaffe," Hitler continued to hang on to Göring for lack of an alternative.[106] "But it's always the same story when one talks to the Führer about this. He explains the reasons for the Luftwaffe's failure, but he can't make up his mind to draw the necessary conclusions."[107] "I'm furious," he wrote a few days later, "when I think that despite all the good reasons for it and arguments in favor of it, it's impossible to get the Führer to make the change."[108]

The topic of Göring was not the only issue that prompted Goebbels to become increasingly critical of Hitler during these weeks. In March Goebbels's diaries became full of entries expressing growing doubts about Hitler's leadership qualities. When Hitler repeatedly complained to him about the generals having given him false prognoses or not having obeyed his orders, he noted that it was "incomprehensible how the Führer, given his clear view of things, could not get his way with the general staff, for after all he is the Führer and is the one who gives the orders."[109] During the following days he kept trying to get Hitler to show greater "decisiveness."[110]

On March 15 he wrote in an aggrieved tone that "instead of giving long speeches to his military staff [Hitler] would do better to give them brief orders and then brutally ensure that these orders are carried out. Thus the numerous wrong moves that we have made at the front are attributable not to a faulty assessment of what should be done but rather to flawed methods of leadership."[111] He could tell from the reports on the public mood that Hitler was now quite evidently included in the criticism of the regime's policies that was now prevalent among the population.[112]

Goebbels could not understand the decision Hitler made in the middle of the month to continue to evacuate people in the west, even though the population was refusing to leave their homes. "The Führer's decision is based on the wrong premises."[113] Toward the end of the month he came to the conclusion that "in some respects we are fighting the war in a vacuum. We in Berlin are giving out orders that lower down the line are effectively not even received, let alone carried out. I can see the danger of a massive loss of authority."[114] After a lengthy discussion with Hitler on the same day he noted resignedly: "When talking to Hitler one feels 'Yes, you're right. Everything you say is true. But when will there be some action?'"

It was not by chance that he kept commenting on Hitler's physical frailty. Thus at the beginning of March he was "horrified" to note that "the nervous shaking in Hitler's left hand [...] [had] gotten a lot worse"; at the end of the month he noted "sadly that his gait is much more bent."[115] Although the entries indicate that he was concerned about whether Hitler was physically and psychologically in a fit state

to lead the country, he kept convincing himself that Hitler was indeed fully capable of doing so.[116] Goebbels could not free himself
from his total psychological dependence on his Führer.

PEACE IN THE EAST?

Goebbels was increasingly concerned about whether it would still be
possible to find the right moment to undertake a peace initiative with
one side or the other. Having repeatedly discussed this question with
Hitler in January and February, at the beginning of March Goebbels
discovered to his surprise that Hitler no longer considered the best
prospects for a separate peace to be in the west but rather in the east,
as Stalin was having "very serious difficulties" with the Anglo-
Americans. After having reached a deal with the Soviet Union, Hitler
then wanted "to continue the fight against Britain with the most brutal energy."[117]

On the same day, on March 4, Goebbels learned from Ribbentrop's
liaison at Führer headquarters, Walther Hewel, that the foreign minister's attempts "to put out feelers to the western countries [. . .] have
no prospect of success at the moment." Goebbels was now finally prepared to put all his efforts into seeking an arrangement with the Soviet Union. On March 7 he met Himmler in Hohenlychen, the SS
sanatorium north of Berlin, where the Reichsführer was recuperat-
ing from a nervous breakdown following the failure of the Army
Group Vistula, which he was commanding, to halt the Red Army
offensive in Pomerania. This defeat also marked the start of the final
break between Hitler and his "loyal Heinrich." For Hitler told Goebbels some days later that he blamed Himmler personally for this defeat and was accusing him of disobedience. Hitler had already
dropped plans, which Goebbels had supported, to make Himmler
commander-in-chief of the army.[118] Thus the Himmler Goebbels met
on March 7 was not only in poor health but was also someone whose
aura as the second most powerful man in the Third Reich was in decline. Himmler told Goebbels that "reason tells him that we have little hope of winning the war militarily, but his instinct tells him that
sooner or later a political opportunity will occur to secure a change
in our favor. Himmler sees this as being more likely to occur in the
west than in the east. [. . .] I believe that we have a better chance in

the east, as Stalin seems to me more of a realist than the English-American lunatics."[119]

However, he did not express these views to Himmler on March 7. He now knew that Himmler's idea that they could establish contact with the west had completely isolated him politically and that any further attempts to put out feelers to the west would inevitably lead to a final breach with Hitler. On leaving the sanatorium Goebbels was quite cheerful: "I felt that Himmler was surrounded by a very nice, modest and absolutely National Socialist atmosphere, which was extremely agreeable."

A few days later Goebbels learned that the idea of a "western option" had finally been abandoned. Ribbentrop had had to admit that his attempts to establish contacts with Britain via Stockholm had proved a complete fiasco.[120] The almost triumphant tone in which Goebbels recorded this and other pieces of news shows that, in the face of the catastrophic situation, he took comfort from one thought: Whereas Göring, Himmler, and Ribbentrop were setting their hopes on contacts with the west, he knew that at this moment Hitler was looking only to the east.

Four days after his visit to Himmler, Hitler confirmed Goebbels in his approach. "A separate peace with the Soviet Union would not of course fulfill our 1941 aims, but the Führer hopes that nevertheless there will be a division of Poland and that Germany will acquire sovereignty over Hungary and Croatia and secure a free hand in the west." Goebbels considered this "program [. . .] terrific and convincing." The only problem was that "for the time being [!] . . . there is no possibility of achieving it."[121]

On March 21 Hitler, who made a very tired and worn-out impression and was "somewhat in despair" about the military situation, told Goebbels that the enemy coalition would "inevitably break up, so it is only a question of whether it breaks up before we are knocked out or when we have already been knocked out." Once again Hitler was assuming that the breakup of the enemy coalition would be "more likely to be caused by Stalin than by Churchill and Roosevelt."

After Goebbels had once again tried in vain to persuade Hitler of the need to appoint a new commander-in-chief of the Luftwaffe, he was on the edge of despair. "How can I do what I know is the right thing to do? I feel a great moral and national sense of duty toward the German people, since I'm one of the few people who now still have the ear of the Führer. Such an opportunity must be exploited in every sphere. But I can't do more than I am doing."

On March 22 he saw a real chance to intervene in the course of events. He urged Hitler to put out feelers to the Soviet Union via Sweden. "But the Führer doesn't want to. The Führer thinks that at the moment making an approach to the enemy would be a sign of weakness." Goebbels took a very different view. "I take the view that the enemy already knows we're weak and that we are not proving it to him through our willingness to negotiate. But the Führer won't budge. He thinks that speaking to a leading Soviet representative would simply encourage the English and Americans to make further concessions to Stalin and the negotiations would end in complete failure." Despite having serious doubts, Goebbels was obliged to settle for this response.

At the beginning of April he learned that the Foreign Ministry had put out feelers in Switzerland, Sweden, and Spain in order to assess the enemy's willingness to make peace, but this had yielded completely negative results. The feelers to the Soviet Union had proved the most productive, although it was demanding East Prussia, which "naturally" was out of the question. Goebbels put the main blame for the failure of these contacts on the Foreign Ministry's incompetence.[122]

SCORCHED EARTH

In the meantime the military situation had deteriorated dramatically. At the beginning of March an offensive had been launched in Hungary under Waffen-SS General Sepp Dietrich through which Hitler aimed to regain control of the Hungarian oil fields. By the middle of March, however, it had come to a halt; under pressure from a Soviet counteroffensive the German troops had to withdraw to Austria.[123]

At the beginning of February the British and American offensive in the northern sector of the Western Front had begun and succeeded in driving the Wehrmacht back over the Rhine. On March 7 the Americans were unexpectedly able to cross the Rhine at Remagen, news that surprised Goebbels so much that at first he considered it "more or less out of the question." But during the following days it became clear that, while the Americans had succeeded in consolidating the bridgehead, it did not provide a suitable strategic basis for continuing Allied operations in the German interior.[124] It was only two weeks later that Goebbels received the next terrible news from the Western Front: the Americans' success in crossing the Rhine near Darmstadt on March 22 and the British advance over the Rhine near Wesel on March 24.[125] It was now, he noted despondently "a question of whether we can hold the Rhine"; the war in the west had "entered its decisive phase."[126] But the following day he was already confidently predicting that "we shall succeed once again in placing a barrier somewhere in the way of the eastward march of the English and Americans."[127]

In the meantime the air war, which according to Goebbels's information had already cost 253,000 deaths,[128] was continuing relentlessly. The final raids on Berlin in February and March caused another thousand deaths.[129] On March 13 the Propaganda Ministry was at last destroyed in a Mosquito raid.[130] Goebbels noted in short diary entries the total destruction of the cities of Würzburg on March 15 and Hildesheim on March 22, both of which had hitherto been spared raids, commenting resignedly: "The consequences of the air war can no longer be recorded in detail."[131]

On March 14 Speer, who had just returned from a trip to western Germany, had already informed him on the basis of his impressions there that "economically speaking the war was more or less lost."[132] On the following day Speer was to express this negative view in a memorandum he presented to Hitler on March 18. Goebbels agreed with Speer on March 14 that a policy of "scorched earth" should be rejected, for "if the food supplies and economic lifeline of the German people are to be cut off, then that can't be our job; that must be the enemy's job."[133]

Hitler responded to Speer's memorandum with the "Nero order" of March 19 in which he ordered that all "military, transportation, communications, industrial, and supply facilities as well as all material resources within the territory of the Reich that the enemy can use for the continuation of their struggle, either now or in the foreseeable future," should be destroyed.[134] A few days later Hitler informed Goebbels of his intention to replace Speer with his state secretary, Karl-Otto Saur. Hitler explained: "Speer is more of an artist type. He's very good at organization, but he's politically inexperienced and too untrained to be absolutely reliable during this critical period." He could not accept Speer's statement that he was "not prepared to lend a hand in cutting off the German people's lifeline."

As so often in the past, Goebbels immediately adopted Hitler's line and opposed Speer's standpoint: "It's absolute nonsense to claim that we ought not to accept responsibility for destroying our war potential. [. . .] We must take the responsibility for it and must prove ourselves worthy of it."[135]

Speer protested vehemently against this course of action, and Goebbels learned that, at the end of the month, during "a very dramatic confrontation" and with his dismissal appearing imminent, he succeeded in persuading Hitler decisively to modify the Nero order of March 19 by issuing an additional order. Now it was no longer a question of destroying but rather of temporarily paralyzing infrastructure and industry, and Speer was now made responsible for implementing all of these measures.[136]

The conflict led to an irreparable breach between Hitler and his armaments minister. Goebbels had used the conflict to make it clear to Hitler that, in contrast to Speer, he unreservedly supported his policy of either/or. In one of his frequent conversations with Hitler, he also made clear in a similar manner that he had differences with Bormann. For "as far as the radicalization of our conduct of the war is concerned, [Bormann] has not done what I expected of him." Both Bormann and Speer were "too bourgeois.[. . .] But now the revolutionaries must take over. I make this point to the Führer, but the Führer tells me that he's got very few of those at his disposal."[137]

Moreover, in the course of several tête-à-têtes with Hitler, Goebbels had learned that Himmler, who for a few weeks had taken over command of Army Group Vistula, which in fact existed largely on paper, had been discredited by his military failure. Hitler accused him of "blatant disobedience," and Goebbels appears to have done nothing to try to defend the Reichsführer.[138] On the contrary, after a further conversation with Hitler on March 31 he noted what was for him the decisive point. Hitler had told him that he had "allowed himself to be talked into it by Keitel, Bormann, and Himmler, and he hadn't done what was necessary, and I am the only one who has been right all along, which the Führer freely admits."

During this last phase of the war Goebbels evidently placed great stock in distancing himself in Hitler's eyes from his former allies, Speer, Himmler, and Bormann, the men with whose help Hitler had established the "wartime dictatorship on the home front." As far as he was concerned, Göring was already finished.

Finally, his old rival for control of the press was also removed. At the end of March Hitler decided to suspend the Reich press chief, Dietrich, according to Goebbels because of his complaint about the former's work. He recorded the deposing of his rival with grim satisfaction: "Dr. Dietrich is an absolute weakling who's not up to the present crisis." And he determined to "rapidly purge the press department of obstructive and defeatist elements." When Dietrich's longtime colleague Helmut Sündermann tried to court him, he was shown the door. Goebbels issued a slogan for the press instructing it to focus all of its energies on increasing the war effort and strengthening morale.[139]

WERWOLF

At this time the situation on the Western Front was developing very rapidly. On March 27 Goebbels noted a surprising advance by the Americans in the direction of Aschaffenburg; on March 30 they had reached Fulda, and two days later they were close to Kassel and were getting ready to advance into Thuringia. From the end of March 1945, Goebbels, who had long been calling for partisan warfare in the event of the Allies occupying German territory, began to get actively involved in practical aspects of guerrilla warfare. "I'm now," he wrote, "in the process of organizing the so-called 'Werwolf Action' on a grand scale." This was in fact one of Goebbels's usual exaggerations. The Werwolf organization that had been established in September 1944 was in fact firmly controlled by Himmler and the SS. Although it did not succeed in producing a guerrilla war behind the Allied lines, it was responsible for a considerable number of assassinations of Allied soldiers and German "collaborators." Thus, at the end of March members of the Werwolf murdered Franz Oppenhoff, who had been appointed Oberbürgermeister of Aachen by the Allies, and, with the help of some Berlin Party comrades, Goebbels hoped to inflict the same fate on the mayor of Rheydt—the town had been occupied by the Americans on March 1—though without success.[140] He was particularly annoyed that the inhabitants of his hometown were cooperating with their new overlords.[141]

However, his ambitions for an underground struggle went further. At the end of March 1945 he announced that he wanted to get Hitler to transfer the leadership of the Werwolf to him because the SS was not sufficiently systematic and too slow.[142] As he was unsuccessful he tried at least to support the Werwolf through propaganda. He personally drafted "an extraordinary revolutionary appeal" for the first program of a Werwolf radio station on the old wavelength of the Deutschlandsender (German Station), which according to his diary was actually broadcast.[143] He intended his Werwolf propaganda to unleash once again the old "fighting spirit" that had characterized the first years of *Der Angriff.*[144]

During this period Goebbels kept trying to boost his morale with memories of that period. One evening he rummaged in old papers and found "a whole lot of reminiscences of the movement's time of struggle, which gave me hope." In those days they had kept managing "to turn around even the most difficult situations," and it will "be the same this time as well."[145]

THE END IN BERLIN

Goebbels had given considerable thought to his decision to stay in Berlin with his family, whatever happened. He had already told Hitler at the end of January that Magda was also determined to stay in Berlin and wanted to have the children with her. Hitler thought this decision was "not right but admirable."[146] A few days later Hitler, who had moved into the Reich Chancellery's air raid shelter after his living quarters had been destroyed in the air raid of February 3, told Goebbels that he had decided to stay in the capital.[147]

In his broadcast address of February 28 Goebbels had announced quite frankly that in the event of a defeat he would put an end to his life and that of his close family. If the enemy is victorious he would consider his life "no longer worth [. . .] living, neither for me nor for my children." What he meant by this strange way of expressing himself was that in that case he, Joseph Goebbels, did not think his children's lives would be worth living.[148]

However, as in all important matters affecting the Goebbels family during the past fourteen years, putting this decision into effect required Hitler's express approval. At the beginning of March Goebbels once again told Hitler about his plan to stay in Berlin with his family. He noted that "after a certain amount of hesitation" the latter had approved his proposal.[149] In the middle of April Goebbels once again publicly confirmed his decision to put an end to his life and that of his family. In an article in *Das Reich* of April 15, "Committing One's Own Life," he had posed the rhetorical question: Who after a defeat "could imagine wanting to continue to live in such a situation."[150]

The last of the surviving diary entries was on April 10 and contains only a report on the military situation, on which Goebbels did not comment. The report contained the information that in Vienna the Red Army had penetrated as far as the Danube Canal, that the garrison under siege in Königsberg had been reduced to holding a small pocket, while the British were close to Hanover and the Americans were occupying Göttingen. The entry for April 10 was in any case the last that was microfilmed for security purposes, which Goebbels had begun doing in November 1944.[151] In March 1941 he had deposited the existing volumes in the vaults of the Reichsbank.[152]

His last article in *Das Reich* appeared on April 22. He chose the title "Resistance at All Costs." This war will be decided, he told his readers, "in the very last minute"; apart from that he called for a "people's war" against the Allied armies, even if this were to result in "heavy casualties."[153]

The death of the American president, Franklin D. Roosevelt, on April 15 seemed once again to give Goebbels grounds for great optimism. This might, he speculated, be the event that would lead to the breakup of the enemy coalition.[154] But such illusions were soon shattered. On April 16 the Red Army began its attack on Berlin, and the scratch German forces that remained had to prepare to defend the capital.[155]

On April 19, for the last time, Goebbels gave a radio address to mark Hitler's fifty-sixth birthday, which was the following day. To begin with, Goebbels used the opportunity to talk about himself and his relationship with the Führer: "For over twenty years I've been at the Führer's side, I've participated in his rise and that of his movement from the smallest and most obscure beginnings until the seizure of power and I've done my best to give it my support. Sharing joy and sadness with the Führer, I've lived through the years 1939 to today, years that have been so rich in victories that were historically unique as well as in terrible setbacks, and I'm still standing by him since fate is now confronting him and his people with the final and most difficult challenge and will then, and of this I'm sure, present both of us with the laurels." Goebbels then praised Hitler as the "man of this century," "the heart of the resistance against world decline"; he was "Germany's bravest son and the one among us with the strongest will." He will "follow his path to the end" and lead his people into a "period in which ethnic Germans will blossom as never before." The address ended with an emotional declaration of loyalty: "Never will history be able to report of this time that a people abandoned its Führer or a Führer abandoned his people."[156]

Numerous prominent Nazis assembled in the Reich Chancellery once again to celebrate Hitler's birthday, but after the celebration major figures such as Göring, Ley, Rosenberg, and Himmler left Berlin.[157]

On April 21 Soviet artillery began to shell Berlin from Marzahn on the outskirts of the city.[158] On this day Goebbels held his last ministerial conference; according to the notes of his personal assistant, he conducted it "in a routine manner."[159]

At the military conference on the same day Hitler became very agitated, blaming the failure of his generals and announcing that he had decided to remain in Berlin in order to take over personal direction of the defense of the city.[160] Goebbels and others succeeded in calming him down. On the same day Goebbels and his family moved from his Berlin apartment into Hitler's bunker, taking over a total of five rooms.[161]

On the following day, April 22, Hitler announced how he envisaged organizing the defense of the city. He ordered the armies of Walther Wenck and Theodor Busse, together with Steiner's corps, to relieve the city by mounting counterattacks. In fact these were units that had been thrown together, units that no longer possessed any combat strength and had no chance of mounting a successful counterattack against the Red Army.[162]

On April 22 and 23 Goebbels addressed two appeals to the German people. In the first one he announced that Lieutenant-General Hellmuth Reymann had been appointed to conduct the military defense of Berlin. Goebbels also announced that he, together with his staff, was "of course remaining in Berlin" and his wife and children "are here and will stay here." In his appeal of April 23 he announced that Hitler too was staying in Berlin and had taken over supreme command of the defense of the city. The Führer had deployed all available forces "against Bolshevism."[163]

On April 23 a radio message came from Göring, who, in the meantime, had arrived in Berchtesgaden. He announced that, unless he received instructions to the contrary, he would in a few hours take over the "overall leadership of the Reich" since this would presumably mean that Hitler had lost his freedom of action. The "Führer" responded with a fit of rage, dismissing Göring from his position as commander-in-chief of the Luftwaffe.[164]

During the last military conferences Hitler, who still believed that Wenck and the others would succeed in breaking through to him, was clinging to a fantasy: "If I can keep going and hold the capital then perhaps there's a chance that the English and Americans may decide that in certain circumstances and with the help of Nazi Germany they could still cope with this threat. And I'm the only man capable of doing it." Goebbels encouraged him in his decision: "If such an idea is at all feasible, then you're the only one who could bring it off, and you could only do it here. If you leave this city then you will lose everything else."[165] Two days later Hitler returned to this idea. "There are signs of an anti-Russian mood developing, so if we can successfully defend Berlin, then you'll see that the people who have the necessary broad vision will gain courage in the face of this colossus. These people will then say to themselves: If we work together with Nazi Germany, then we may be able to cope with this colossus." Goebbels agreed with him: "It would also encourage the other side to do a deal. If Stalin sees the way things are developing among the western states as a result of our successful defense of Berlin, then he'll say to himself: I'm not going to get the Europe I'm looking for. I'm only uniting the Germans and the English. So I'll get together with the Germans and reach some sort of deal with them."[166] He added: "If it works, it's fine. If it doesn't work and if the Führer were to suffer an honorable death in Berlin and Europe were to become Bolshevik, at the latest within five years the Führer would have become a legend and Nazism a legendary movement because he would have been immortalized by his final magnificent actions and all the human failings for which he is now criticized would be swept away at a stroke."[167]

On April 28 Hitler and the bunker community finally realized that they could no longer rely on being relieved from the outside.[168] On the same day the BBC broadcast the news that a few days earlier Himmler had met the Swedish Count Folke Bernadotte in Lübeck and offered to surrender to the western Allies. Hitler was furious about this betrayal by his "loyal Heinrich," whom he later dismissed from all his offices in his will. Evidently this contributed to his decision to have Himmler's liaison officer at Führer headquarters, Hermann Fegelein, shot for defeatism.

On the same day Hitler decided to marry his long-standing partner, Eva Braun (she was related to Hermann Fegelein by marriage). The simple ceremony in the bunker took place during the night of April 29 in the presence of a registrar summoned for the purpose. Goebbels and Bormann were witnesses, and afterward there was even a small celebration.[169] Goebbels and Bormann were both among the witnesses who signed the two wills that Hitler wrote after the wedding. Among other things they contained Hitler's appointment of his successors. He named Grand Admiral Dönitz as Reich president and Joseph Goebbels as Reich chancellor.

Goebbels added a postscript to the will stating that he would not follow Hitler's instructions to leave the capital if Berlin's defenses collapsed. "For the first time in my life I must categorically refuse to obey an order of the Führer's. My wife and children join with me in refusing to do so." "For reasons of humanity and personal loyalty" he could "never bring himself to abandon the Führer in his greatest hour of need." Moreover, he believed that in doing this he was "acting for the best as far as the future of the German people is concerned for in the difficult times that are approaching models to live up to will be more important than men." He and his wife were determined not to leave Berlin "and rather to end our lives side by side with the Führer, a life which in any case is of no more value for me if I cannot live it in the Führer's service and by his side." This "decision" he was also making for his children, "who are too young to be able to express themselves, but if they were old enough would entirely agree with this decision."[170]

It took more than a day, until the afternoon of April 30, before Hitler finally decided to take his own life. He had been forced to face the fact that the reserves he had requested had not managed to break through to Berlin. After saying goodbye to Joseph and Magda Goebbels and the other occupants of the bunker, he withdrew into his private apartment. A few days earlier he had presented Magda with a golden Party badge.[171] Otto Günsche, Hitler's servant, reported after the war that at this point Magda had wanted to speak to Hitler and urged him to leave Berlin, but the Führer had categorically rejected her request.[172]

After a few minutes Günsche told those who were waiting that the Führer and Eva Braun had committed suicide. Goebbels, together with some other occupants of the bunker, now entered Hitler's private room in order to establish that Hitler had in fact died. Shortly afterward he was one of the small group who, standing at the entrance to the bunker, watched Günsche burning the bodies of the recently married couple.[173]

That sealed the fate of Joseph Goebbels and his family. Twenty-four hours later, after his attempt to start peace negotiations with the Soviet Union had been rejected, Joseph and Magda Goebbels murdered their six children and followed Hitler's example by committing suicide.[174]

CONCLUSION

In this biography we have gotten to know Goebbels primarily in three roles. In the first part we saw his development from a failed writer and intellectual to a Nazi agitator; in the second part his efforts as propaganda minister to introduce uniformity into the media, cultural life, and the public sphere; and in the third part we concentrated on his role as a wartime propagandist and advocate of "total war." Or, to express it in visual terms, we have described the life of a person who initially preferred to wear a proletarian leather jacket or a worn trench coat, then once in power appeared in carefully selected suits or in exclusive leisure clothing, and finally, during the war, normally wore his Party uniform, however unflattering it was to his figure. But however Goebbels presented himself, the most important driving force in his life was a deeply narcissistic personality, which fed a desire for recognition that was never satisfied.

I

Goebbels's ambition and narcissism cannot be attributed to an attempt to compensate for his disability and his origins in a depressing lower-middle-class milieu. His tendency toward narcissism had developed before his disability, which occurred during his primary school years. It originated in his failure to develop independence at the ages of two and three; his dependence on his mother, the model for his future girlfriends and his wife, lasted throughout his life. The image of a joyless youth and an unrecognized loner derives mainly from Goebbels's own literary fantasy during the manic-productive phase of the years 1923–24. In fact he definitely experienced recognition and affection during his childhood and youth in Rheydt, had friends and love affairs, and, finally, in 1917, was free to choose the life he wanted to lead.

The year 1923, which we have chosen for the start of this biography, sees Goebbels as a failure and as someone in despair. Despite having studied and acquired a doctorate, his plans to play a leading role in the reordering of the intellectual landscape of his fatherland had failed as a consequence of his own lack of ability; of his social background, which meant that he lacked an entrée into the middle-class intelligentsia; and of the times in which he was living. He was at odds with the Catholic faith in which he had been raised and was seeking "redemption" or rather a "redeemer" figure, which, after several detours, he finally found in Adolf Hitler. Goebbels's development from being a seeker after Christ to the follower of a political Messiah, Hitler, can be traced in great detail. This phase of his life could function as a textbook for the phenomenon of political religion.

He was inspired by the idea of finding a place in the *völkisch* movement as a political and cultural journalist, the prospect of which lifted him from his depression. He still had little time for ordinary politics, but his ambition and his passionate fixation on his idol, Hitler, and also his low regard for the political program of the Party's "left wing," with which he had at first been associated, all contributed to his winning a place in the leadership of the Nazi Party, albeit not yet in its innermost circle. His appointment as Gauleiter of Berlin in 1926 occurred in the context of Hitler's seeking to achieve a balance among various Party groups. Goebbels developed his own style of agitation appropriate to this city, with its hectic way of life and penchant for sensation, a combination of rowdy propaganda and violence, aiming to focus attention on the Party at all costs, challenge the left for control of the public sphere, and provoke the authorities. During the 1920s he was already making propaganda for himself by publishing "Fight for Berlin" as the story of his success. In fact his provocative tactics resulted in bans, prosecutions, and opposition from within the Party, while the election results were below the Reich average. Without the support of the Party headquarters in Munich, his Berlin career would soon have come to an end. The overtly proletarian orientation of the Berlin Nazi Party and its Gauleiter could not disguise the fact that the Party's main support came above all from middle-class districts.

Early in 1930, after his appointment as head of the Party's Reich propaganda department, over which Hitler had hesitated for a long time, Goebbels began to centralize the Party's propaganda organization and took increasing control of the big election campaigns, which during the early 1930s turned the Nazi Party into a mass movement. However, it wasn't until 1932 that he was able to establish a uniform approach during election campaigns. In 1930 the campaign's main theme was rather conventional, with Goebbels concentrating on attacking the Young Plan.

Under Goebbels's guiding hand, Hitler appeared for the first time as the central figure in the Party's propaganda during the Reich presidential elections of 1932, in which he was portrayed as the "leader of young Germany" and as the man to rescue Germany from the crisis. After Hitler had clearly lost the presidential elections Goebbels concentrated the election campaign for the July 1932 Reichstag elections more on practical issues, and it was only during the months after the election that he could bring himself to focus Nazi propaganda on the image of Hitler as a popular leader. The increasing prominence given to Hitler and the personalizing of the political struggle was not a brilliant invention by Goebbels but rather the result of the Nazi Party's structure as a "Führer party" and was supported by a broad consensus within the Party leadership. After 1933, however, Goebbels had the chance of using the Führer propaganda that was already in full swing to establish a full-blown Führer cult through a campaign involving all the media.

From 1931 onward, apart from leading the Party in Berlin, Goebbels had been increasingly involved in the politics of the Party as a whole. His diaries document in detail the influence of the Party leadership on the presidential cabinets and its attempts to position itself to take over the government. It is clear that while Goebbels was well informed, he did not belong to the small inner circle of Nazi leaders whom Hitler allowed to participate in his discussions and negotiations.

That Hitler distanced himself somewhat from Goebbels may also be attributable to differences in their respective political strategies. Whereas from the end of the 1920s Hitler concentrated on coming to power through a coalition with conservative elements, Goebbels wanted to get the Party into power without assistance and thus adopted a more uncompromising and radical stance, one that brought him into frequent conflict with the "policy of legality" being pursued by the Party leader.

Given his strong antibourgeois prejudices, Goebbels's overt radicalism appears logical, but in fact it was largely inspired by tactical considerations. Goebbels was especially dependent on the Berlin SA as the people who had to carry out the Party's propaganda. The Party troops had to be kept happy with organized violence and constantly whipped up with extreme rhetoric. Although he always supported Hitler in the conflicts between the Party leadership and the SA, he tried to do so without alienating the SA. When in the spring of 1932 Hitler's attempts to come to power with the aid of right-wing elements initially failed—he had not succeeded in winning the support of the "Harzburg front" for his candidacy in the presidential elections—Goebbels was remarkably quick in coming to terms with Hitler's alternative strategy of seeking power in the Reich and in Prussia with the help of the Center Party, in other words a party associated with the hated Weimar "system." Goebbels now downplayed his radicalism and went over completely to Hitler's policy of negotiation.

The conflict in which the Party was involved at the end of 1932 and which ended with the resignation of Gregor Strasser from all his offices turns out, on the basis of a detailed analysis of the originals of Goebbels's diaries, which have only recently become available, to have been far less serious than has generally been thought until now. The alliance between Strasser and Schleicher, the core of a "cross front" that was designed to split the Party and that allegedly collapsed at the last minute, turns out to have been a propaganda myth. Goebbels propagated it after the "seizure of power" in the heavily edited version of his diaries, which he published under the title "My Part in Germany's Fight" in order to get his revenge on his old political mentor and rival.

In fact Hitler was concerned to use the Strasser crisis to impose stricter conditions for his willingness to tolerate the Schleicher government, contrary to the views of his Party opponents. Goebbels was prepared to go along with this line adopted by the Party leader, just as a few weeks later he was willing to accept the latter's decision to come to power with the aid of right-wing conservative partners. During the last decisive year of the Weimar Republic Goebbels did not have his own plan for how to secure power.

II

In 1933 Goebbels received only part of the Ministry for Popular Education with extensive responsibilities for the whole of German culture that had long been promised him by Hitler. Essentially he was confined to the role of Reich minister for popular enlightenment and propaganda. During the following twelve years he was not even successful at getting control of the whole of the propaganda machine in a way that could match his ambition as Reich minister and head of the Party's Reich propaganda department or that corresponded to the very effective myth that he had propagated of a virtuoso master of an all-powerful propaganda machine.

As far as control of the press was concerned, the Reich press chief, Otto Dietrich, retained considerable powers to shape press reporting, while the structure of the press was largely determined by Max Amann, who was in charge of the publishing side. The Wehrmacht possessed its own elaborate propaganda organization, and from 1938 onward Goebbels had to share foreign propaganda with the Foreign Ministry and from 1941 propaganda in the occupied eastern territories with Rosenberg.

Apart from such problems concerning the division of responsibilities, it is clear that Goebbels's "successes" in directing the media were very dubious. By 1934 he had effectively achieved complete success in imposing Nazi norms on the press and silencing opposition views. He had to put up with the uniformity and boring quality of the German press, about which, particularly during the early years, he frequently complained. In the Third Reich there was no conceivable alternative to the rigid system of instructions and restrictions on what and how events and issues could be reported.

The political and propaganda broadcasts of German radio were marked by the same uniformity. However, by the mid-1930s Goebbels had abandoned the idea of turning this modern medium into an instrument of political leadership. That every listener could easily evade the broadcasts of German radio by turning the dial to a foreign radio station convinced him that it was advisable to respond increasingly to the desire of the people for light entertainment, and he proved flexible in terms of the level of quality he demanded.

As far as film production was concerned, Goebbels made multiple attempts over the years to extract from the film industry both high-quality entertainment and relevant political propaganda. But although he increased his control of film production to the extent of imposing his personal views on casts, scripts, and editing, neither he nor—which was more serious—Hitler was content with the films that were produced. It became clear that, as a result of the complexity of the conditions involved in the production and distribution of films, the minister's frequently changing requests could not be met at all or, apart from a few exceptions, not to his satisfaction. In the end here too Goebbels had to make do with cheap mass entertainment, which was far beneath his original ambitions, both aesthetically and in terms of political propaganda.

Cultural policy presented a similar picture. Between the end of 1936 and the beginning of 1938 Goebbels made serious effort to establish himself as the dominant figure in cultural policy but failed in his attempt to shape the arts in accordance with Nazi ideology. The Nazis launched a campaign against the artistic avant-garde in order to cover up the fact that their attempts to impose Nazism on the visual arts had, in the view of both Goebbels and Hitler, met with only modest success. After initial attempts Goebbels did not make much effort to continue trying to introduce Nazism into the theater or musical life on a large scale. On the other hand, Goebbels claimed that his propaganda had played a major part in ensuring that the German people were united and totally committed, indeed enthusiastic in supporting the regime's policies, a claim that is apparently supported by a large amount of contemporary material and is still believed as part of the myth of the oppressive Goebbels propaganda to which the German people fell victim.

In fact Goebbels was not concerned with securing support for

Nazi policy from a majority of the population or convincing or se-
ducing them through more or less intensive propaganda. He saw
himself rather as the brilliant controller of an elaborate and highly
complex propaganda machine who, in intuitive harmony with his
political idol, Hitler, and possessing an intimate awareness of mass
psychology, had brought about a near-perfect understanding between the nation and its political leadership. This image developed
by Goebbels, one that reflected his narcissistic personality, is in a
sense his historical legacy; it represents the main challenge facing
historical study of the "public sphere" during the Nazi period.

In order to decipher this mythmaking initiated by Goebbels himself, it is necessary to remember that his propaganda was not confined to control of the media and the "coordination" of cultural life
but operated as a closed system.

In this system, first of all, alternative views were not tolerated. As
early as 1933–34 Goebbels ensured that even criticism from within
the system made on the basis of Nazi principles disappeared from the
media. If it occurred, he responded angrily. This aversion to criticism
led him to ban artistic criticism in 1936 and to a systematic attack on
political references in cabarets, on satirists and comedians, and on
critical comment in literary journalism. He tried as much as he could
to prevent disruptive influences from outside. Foreign films were
subjected to the same careful censorship as German ones, the sale of
foreign newspapers was controlled and in the end largely banned,
listening to foreign broadcasts was disapproved of and after the outbreak of war could be harshly punished.

Second, a central feature of this system, its sounding board so to
speak, was its substantial control over the public sphere, which appeared to function in accordance with Nazi norms. People were expected to demonstrate their loyalty to the regime's policies through
their public behavior.

The claim that the nation and its leadership were in tune with one
another was expressed in a variety of forms of behavior. They included mundane things such as the Nazi salute or wearing the Party
badge but also the everyday response to those sections of the population that had been excluded, such as the Jews, as well as participation
in the various national celebrations, mass rallies, and plebiscites,
whose results were not left to chance. If the population behaved as

the regime wished, and in general it did so, it became propaganda's task to document this behavior and thereby to strengthen the desired impression of the national community's solidarity.

Third, Goebbels's system provided its own proof of its success in the form of pictures and recordings, in press reports, and in internal reports on the popular mood, which were specifically designed to convey the positive resonance of the propaganda and to present negative reactions as departures from the norm. When negative reactions went beyond what was considered acceptable, the reports were altered, the criteria for judging positive responses were changed, or the critics and complainants were silenced. Finally, Goebbels's own diaries, which were to be published posthumously, were also intended to form part of the documentation of his success.

III

The preparation of the German people for war during the years 1938–39 and the war itself placed heavy demands on Goebbels's system. People's behavior and the regime's public image had to be repeatedly adjusted to fit in with the changing conditions.

In 1938 Goebbels carried out a propaganda campaign over a period of several months, which for the first time was devoted to foreign policy and aimed at wearing down Czechoslovakia and mobilizing the German population against Prague. But Goebbels neither wanted nor was he in a position to allow the mood of crisis that had been created with the help of this propaganda to turn into enthusiasm for war. During the previous years German propaganda had emphasized the theme of peace to such an extent that it was impossible to change course suddenly, and in any case neither Goebbels nor the majority of the population was prepared for war. In short, the Goebbels system did not deliver the required results.

Goebbels's involvement in the launching of the November pogrom can, therefore, be seen as having an additional function. By claiming the pogrom carried out by Party activists was a manifestation of "popular anger," he was attempting to publicly demonstrate the radical commitment of the "national community," which a few weeks earlier had been so little in evidence at the height of the Sudeten crisis.

It was not by chance that immediately after the pogrom Hitler ordered German propaganda to switch to preparing for war. Goebbels implemented this change in his speeches and articles from the beginning of 1939 and became a leading advocate for war. But while the propaganda that was now preparing the German population for a confrontation with Poland justified the use of military means, it also led to this war, which allegedly had been forced on Germany, being seen as an exceptional situation. The result was that after its rapid conclusion the vast majority of the population wanted to return to peacetime conditions.

Thus in September 1939 there was little evidence of enthusiasm for war in Germany. Goebbels, who himself responded to the outbreak of war without much enthusiasm and for weeks afterward was hoping for a rapid end to it, nevertheless during its initial phase succeeded by various means in creating a mood appropriate to the requirements of war. According to the Propaganda Ministry, by calmly performing its wartime duties the population was demonstrating its support for the regime's policies.

From the start of the war until the late summer of 1941, Goebbels's propaganda was entirely focused on celebrating Germany's military successes. Every victory aroused people's hopes that the war would soon be over, and Goebbels found it relatively easy to convert this longing for peace into euphoric celebrations of victory. The war against the Soviet Union, for which propaganda had not prepared the public, and the targeted release of information during its initial phase upset the public, although this agitation could be soothed relatively quickly by reports of victories.

While the regime suspended its program of systematically murdering patients in institutions for the mentally ill in August 1941, not least in order not to damage its relationship with the churches any further, it responded harshly to a certain amount of criticism of its decision to introduce badges for Jews in September. Goebbels himself took on the task of advocating and enforcing the exclusion of the Jews who had been singled out in this way, and his public comments on the deportations, which began in October 1941, made it clear that the program involved extermination. The open advocacy of a radical "final solution" of the Jewish question thus became an integral part of the regime's war policy. In the course of the expansion of the war the Jews were declared to be internal enemies who had to be annihilated.

The situation changed radically in the autumn of 1941, when the German advance into the Soviet Union stalled. Now Goebbels set about trying to adapt the "national mood" to the seriousness of the situation: In the future, propaganda was to avoid excessive euphoria, and the population had to get used to the idea of the war lasting a long time and involving considerable personal hardships while at the same time avoiding too much negativity. The collection of winter clothing, which had begun during the Christmas holidays, gave him the chance to mobilize the population in a major campaign and adapt the public image of the Third Reich to the existing wartime conditions. The collection acted as occupational therapy, providing a distraction from the military situation in the east and demonstrating the solidarity of the "national community." The campaign appeared to him a suitable means of requiring the home front to get more involved in the war effort. At the same time he reprogrammed the mass media of film and radio to provide more relaxation and entertainment.

However, Goebbels's further attempts to demand more "toughness" from the home front even after the end of the winter crisis by, among other things, making a big fuss about the fight against the black market and the introduction of female labor conscription proved counterproductive. Indeed, it became clear that his attempt during spring 1942 to reinforce the Führer myth, which had been undermined by the reverses on the Eastern Front, had more or less proved to be a failure.

At the end of March 1942 the series of major night air raids on German cities began, and Goebbels recognized at once that in the medium term they represented the biggest threat to popular support for the regime. By immediately offering to coordinate the initial measures taken to aid the affected cities, a role that, as part of his duties as inspector of war damage, he then expanded to include preventive measures, he was attempting to acquire control over the public image of the areas under air attack. The Party became involved in these aid measures, thereby taking on the leading role in dealing with the issues that posed a particular threat to popular morale. Goebbels used every available means to try to demonstrate that morale in the areas that had been bombed had not been affected by the air raids.

His attempts to introduce "total war," which he began in 1943 in response to the impending defeat at Stalingrad, were also largely determined by his conviction of the need to gear people's everyday behavior to the seriousness of the war situation. The continuing commitment of the whole nation to "total war" was designed to distract people from their concerns about the war situation and make expressions of discontent appear defeatist. Total mobilization increased the regime's authority and created new possibilities for social control. At the same time, with his spectacular announcements of "total war," Goebbels was filling a vacuum that had been created by Hitler's failure to appear in public at the height of the crisis. As far as propaganda was concerned, right up until the end of the war Goebbels was faced with the problem that the public demonstration of the permanent support of the majority of the population for the policies of the Führer, which was constitutive for the Führer state and which until then he had been able to guarantee through his control over the public sphere, now began to lose its impact.

After a few months he ceased his active support for the work of the Committee of Three (which was supposed to coordinate the measures for carrying out "total war") after he had reached the conclusion that Hitler was not sufficiently committed to this project and that he, Joseph Goebbels, as its original guiding spirit, could be made to bear the responsibility for the inadequate way in which "total war" was being implemented. Thus, in the final analysis, his attempt, in view of Hitler's absence, to deputize for him in this sphere had failed.

As an alternative, in spring 1943 Goebbels found a new topic with which he could commit the population to unconditional support for the regime. The discovery of the mass graves of the Polish officers who had been shot by the Soviet Union's People's Commissariat for Internal Affairs (NKVD) near Katyn provided him with the opportunity to exploit the theme of the threat of Jewish-Bolshevik atrocities in the event of a German defeat in the starkest form. His propaganda now went so far as to state publicly that the murder of the Jews (who had, it was stated, hatched a plan to exterminate the Germans) was now a German war aim. However, this campaign soon had to be stopped because the Germans realized that its aim was to make them accessories to the murder of the Jews, which resulted in negative comment.

Up until the end of the war Goebbels tried to sustain the resistance of the German people with two new propaganda topics. From 1943 onward, as a result of the increasingly devastating Allied air raids on

German cities, propaganda made cautious references to impending retaliatory attacks on Great Britain. These would produce a major change in the war, so people must keep going until then. But the longer they were delayed, the trickier the issue of retaliation became from the point of view of sustaining morale. In dealing with this topic, Goebbels wavered between banning discussion of it and giving the public hints that the attacks were soon to occur. When the V weapons were actually deployed, from the summer of 1944 onward, it soon became clear that they were not going to bring about the change that had been anticipated, and the resultant frustration on the part of the public was correspondingly great.

Goebbels used another topic to try to mobilize the German people's last reserves of energy: the atrocities the Red Army had been committing since its first incursion into the Reich in October 1944. However, he was unable to achieve his aim of turning this into a systematic campaign to arouse fear during 1945.

Thus in the course of 1944 he endeavored once again to make total war a central theme of propaganda, indeed to use it to transform the whole domestic governance of the Third Reich. However, it was only after the Allied landings in Normandy, after the major Soviet summer offensive, and under the immediate impression created by the assassination attempt of July 20 that Goebbels, together with Speer, Himmler, and Bormann, succeeded in playing a key role in the mobilization of the last reserves. Hitler appointed him Reich Plenipotentiary for total war mobilization.

During the following months Goebbels was fully preoccupied with trying to shift hundreds of thousands of people from economic sectors not vital to the war effort into the armaments industry and armaments workers who had hitherto been exempt from the Wehrmacht into the armed forces, and to deploy more men within the Wehrmacht to front-line duty. It is highly questionable whether Goebbels's efforts amounted to much more than playing with numbers, for neither the armaments industry nor the Wehrmacht could within a short time absorb large numbers of untrained or poorly trained people. Goebbels was in fact primarily concerned with the psychological effects of these measures. All efforts on the home front were to be devoted to the overriding aim of mobilization for total war, which was to determine the public image of the Third Reich during the last months of the war. Thus discussion and complaints were taboo. In addition, the dissolution of established bureaucratic structures strengthened the influence of the Party still further and not least the position of the Plenipotentiary for total war mobilization, who vigorously used his new responsibilities to close down the offices of his main competitors and opponents.

IV

Even after a careful perusal of his extensive writings, the reader remains unclear as to what Joseph Goebbels's political agenda was and what political maxims he was advocating.

Certainly nationalism, which had been considerably strengthened by his experience of the Allied occupation of the Rhineland following the First World War, played a significant role in his thinking, as did a preference for an authoritarian system with a strong leader figure at its head. In addition, there was his lifelong anti-Semitism. Since 1923 and his temporary employment as an employee of a Cologne bank he appears to have become increasingly hostile toward the Jews. In the spring of 1924 he gave public expression to his hatred of everything having to do with the Jews. His anti-Semitism did not, however, form a fixed part of a fully formed racist "world view," as was the case with other members of the *völkisch* movement, and he did not systematically pursue any kind of anti-Semitic "program." The origins of his hostility toward "the Jews" were very simple: He was looking for a scapegoat for the serious economic, political, and cultural crises of the times. Anti-Semitism provided him with a convenient substitute for a social analysis of which he was incapable. The Jews represented for him the opposite of his idea of what was "German," which remained indistinct and idealistic. His hatred of the Jews expressed much of the resentment he felt toward the bourgeois intellectual establishment, which during the 1920s had in his view blocked his richly deserved rise in the world. In later years the negative image of the Jew could be deployed almost in any way he liked. "The Jews" were not only responsible for the crisis of the Weimar Republic but also represented for him a synonym for all the cultural trends that annoyed him during the first years of the Third Reich:

They were behind the international criticism of the Nazi regime; they were to blame for the poor mood in the Reich; finally, they were behind the enemy coalition. Goebbels repeatedly seized the initiative to play a pioneering role in Nazi "Jewish policy": in 1933 at the time of the Jewish "boycott," in 1935 with the Kurfürstendamm riots, in 1938 when in the summer he tried to unleash a pogrom and a few months later when he played an active role in the November pogrom, and finally during the war with his continuing efforts to make Berlin "free of Jews."

By the beginning of the 1930s Goebbels had abandoned his "Socialist" ideas of the 1920s, which in any case consisted largely of antibourgeois sentiments, in favor of a rhetoric of "national community." His diaries and the hundreds of articles he wrote provide the reader with no clue as to what form of economic or social order Joseph Goebbels was trying to achieve for the Third Reich.

The same was true of foreign policy. After Goebbels gave up his idea of an alliance with a future "nationalist" Russia at the end of the 1920s, it is extremely difficult to discern any further independent foreign policy ideas of his. In 1933, as his main proposal for his trip to the League of Nations assembly, Goebbels recommended to Hitler an agreement with France, immediately before the latter left the League of Nations, initially leading Germany into a further period of diplomatic isolation. Goebbels's later contributions to the foreign policy of the Third Reich were restricted to following each of Hitler's next steps with admiration, indeed wonder.

V

Goebbels's lack of systematic political ideas and programs matches his personality, which was entirely geared to achieving personal recognition and success at any price. If he was the center of attention, if his cause was successful, the substance of that success was of secondary importance to him. Thus he interpreted the increase in his power on the home front from 1942 onward above all as a series of great personal successes, ignoring entirely that he owed this second career primarily to the catastrophic course of the war.

His narcissism could be satisfied, however, only if the fruits of his labors were recognized and confirmed by a person whom he respected. After a desperate search he had found this person in 1924; it was his relationship with Hitler that gave his life a measure of stability.

Goebbels's deeply rooted psychological dependence on Hitler—he repeatedly attested to his love for him, particularly in the early years of the relationship—was the strongest impulse in his career. Goebbels attributed superhuman qualities to Hitler, indeed considered that he had been sent by God. He was deeply impressed by the way in which Hitler showed great strength of nerve in coping with crises or radiated confidence in difficult situations, and he admired his ability to develop far-reaching political visions, abilities that Goebbels himself lacked.

Hitler, who had quickly recognized Goebbels's psychological dependence on him, systematically exploited it during the two decades of their relationship. He knew that through praise he could inspire Goebbels to make exceptional efforts and that the slightest snub could plunge him into the deepest despair. During the war, when Goebbels visited Hitler in his headquarters for lengthy conversations at regular intervals of a few weeks, Hitler was almost invariably able to overcome Goebbels's doubts and concerns by developing grand political and military plans.

Hitler kept testing Goebbels's excessive loyalty to the limit as, for example, in 1929–30, when for a long time he failed to support him in his dispute with Otto Strasser, disappointed him through his alliance policy with the Conservatives, and delayed his promised appointment as head of the Party's propaganda department. The same thing occurred in 1933 when he failed to grant Goebbels the extensive responsibilities for his new ministry that he had promised and then in the autumn gave him a high profile at the League of Nations assembly in Geneva without informing him of his real intentions concerning the disarmament question. This list of humiliations and deceptions can be continued until the end of the Third Reich. In September 1944 Goebbels was duped by Hitler's hints about being ready to make a separate peace into presenting him with a detailed memorandum on peace with the Soviet Union; Hitler evidently failed even to respond to it. Even as late as March 1945 the dictator managed to sustain his propaganda minister's illusion that there was still the prospect of making a successful bid for peace with one side or the other.

Goebbels's diary also does not contain any serious consideration of the fact that he was not involved in most of the major domestic and foreign policy decisions and was only informed about them shortly beforehand or even after they had been made. The point is that he was Hitler's propaganda chief and not his closest political adviser. It was only during the second half of the war that Hitler discussed domestic and foreign policy issues with Goebbels in more detail and at least gave him the impression of being consulted before important decisions were made.

Goebbels was not involved in the negotiations concerning the formation of the Hitler–von Papen government, nor was he informed in good time about the ending of the "Nazi revolution" in July 1933. At the time of the Night of the Long Knives action against the SA on June 30, 1934, Goebbels was left in the dark right until the end. In 1936 he was only casually informed of German intervention in the Spanish Civil War, and he was not present when, in November 1937, Hitler outlined his long-term strategic goals to his foreign minister and to the heads of the armed forces. Goebbels was totally surprised by the conclusion of the Nazi-Soviet pact in August 1939 (which created the precondition for the attack on Poland). He learned of the German plans for offensives against Scandinavia, western Europe, and the Soviet Union relatively late, and Hitler also left him in the dark about the background to his diplomatic initiatives in the second half of 1940. When total war was declared in 1943, for which he had long been pressing, he was not appointed to the new key decision-making body, the Committee of Three.

Goebbels sometimes criticized Hitler's behavior, as for example at the time of the Party crises of 1929–30; in 1933, when it looked as if he was not going to get the ministry he had been promised; in 1942–43, when Hitler blocked his attempts to introduce total war; and most strongly in 1945, when he began to have serious doubts about Hitler's leadership qualities. But he never made a serious attempt to oppose Hitler and indeed ultimately forgave him all his mistakes and weaknesses.

Goebbels's narcissism manifested itself in particular in his attempts to persuade his contemporaries (but also posterity) of his complete success as propaganda minister. That he, Joseph Goebbels, had succeeded in uniting the German people behind his idol, Adolf Hitler, not only represented the completion of a political task for him, it was also the fulfillment of a key aim of his life. He regarded even the slightest doubt raised about this as a personal attack to which he responded implacably. His attempt to meticulously document the perfect operation of the system that he had created provides a good example of this need for success and recognition in his professional work, which was at the core of his personality.

Goebbels's narcissistic dependence on Hitler also particularly affected his private and family life. His marriage to Magda in 1931 was based on an arrangement that he and his bride had together made with Hitler. Hitler, who had fallen in love with Magda, gave up his aspirations and—in a formal sense—approved the marriage. From then onward Hitler was treated as a member of the family. Not only did Goebbels see Hitler, when he was in Berlin, almost every day, the Führer also spent a considerable amount of his leisure time with the Goebbels family, either in their apartment or in their summer residence, on boat trips, visits to the theater, or film evenings in the Reich Chancellery, and they even went on vacation together. By making generous grants Hitler ensured that the Goebbelses could maintain their extravagant lifestyle. He also took part in the planning of their various residences, and there was even a plan to provide Hitler with a kind of informal sanctuary on the grounds of the Goebbelses' villa on Schwanenwerder. Finally, Hitler developed, insofar as he was able to do so, a relationship with the Goebbelses' children, whose first names all began with H. Goebbels's diaries show—unintentionally— the extent to which his everyday activities were burdened by having to be continuously on call for Hitler and how much Goebbels and his wife were upset by even the slightest indications that he might withdraw his friendship from them. He noted, in the laconic tone to which he always resorted when he was describing unpleasant but unavoidable events, that Magda often spent days, sometimes weeks, alone with Hitler as his guest.

Initially this triangular relationship brought a considerable amount of stability into Goebbels's life and brought him considerable advantages. To a significant extent, indeed, it provided the basis for his professional success. But when, in the second half of the 1930s, he began to grow apart from Magda, he placed, perhaps unconsciously, the triangular relationship in jeopardy and thereby the basis of his position within the regime. When he wanted to abandon the marriage in 1938, Hitler, as the third person involved, intervened and dictated to the married couple the terms for the continuation of their marriage. From this point onward their marriage was likely one of convenience.

As a result of these disputes, Goebbels's emotional life seems to have become more or less numbed, and he became rather isolated. As propaganda minister he had ceased to cultivate friends from his youth and student days, and in his personal relations he had adopted a distant attitude, which was emphasized by his exclusive lifestyle. His behavior was determined by his narcissism, which, particularly in times of crisis, required a large amount of confirmation and recognition. He could achieve this only if, through his activities as propaganda minister, he succeeded in completely winning back Hitler's approval, which to some extent had been withdrawn during his marital crisis. After the outbreak of war he did indeed manage to do this.

During the war the contact between Goebbels and Hitler remained intact, even if they met less often. Hitler was particularly concerned about Magda's delicate health. His concern went so far that in 1943 he told her not to have a facial operation that was planned because of his fear that it might affect her appearance. Goebbels naturally acted as a witness at Hitler's wedding to Eva Braun in April 1945, as the latter had done at his wedding in 1931. In the meantime Goebbels had obtained Hitler's express approval for his family to remain in Berlin.

The decision of Magda and Joseph Goebbels to follow Hitler in committing suicide and to murder their children appears logical when one considers their relationship to Hitler from 1931 onward. They had tried to provide Hitler with a substitute family, and both felt in their different ways closely linked to Hitler, which led to the premise that in view of his death, no member of this family should remain alive.

Goebbels was also concerned, as he wrote in a farewell letter to Magda's son Harald, that his suicide should send a signal. From his perspective, at the end of the war he had finally succeeded in turning his relationship with Hitler into one of real trust and in establishing his position as that of a unique favorite. The old competitors for Hitler's favor, the Görings, Speers, and Himmlers, were, not without his connivance, confined to the political margins, and Bormann seemed to have been reduced to the role of a mere secretary. Thus Goebbels had indulged his narcissistic needs to the limit. By following Hitler's example and committing suicide with his family, he had confirmed for all time the special relationship he believed he had with his idol.

In the end, his self-delusion had won out.

ACKNOWLEDGMENTS

I would like to thank all those who have helped me to write this book and prepare it for publication. Foremost are my colleagues and students at Royal Holloway College of the University of London, who once again provided me with time for my research, without which this book could not have been written. The staff of the archive and library of the Institut für Zeitgeschichte in Munich have, as always, been extremely helpful in providing me with assistance, as have the staff of the Bundesarchiv, the Landesarchiv in Berlin, and the other archives that I was able to use. I would particularly like to acknowledge the exceptional assistance provided by Herr Gerd Lamers of the Stadtarchiv in Mönchengladbach and the friendly cooperation of Andreas Kunz and Michael Weins of the Freiburg Bundesarchiv/Militärarchiv. I have also been assisted in writing this biography by a group of Hamburg psychoanalysts who gave me the opportunity for extensive discussions about the personality of its main subject. I would like to thank Christiane Adam, Sabine Brückner-Jungjohann, Gundula Fromm, Rüdiger Kurz, Astrid Rutetski, and Dirk Sieveking for important suggestions that helped me to understand certain character traits of Goebbels. I am also indebted to the staff of the Siedler Verlag, in particular Antje Korsmeier, Jan Schleusener, Andreas Wirthensohn, and Elke Posselt for their painstaking work on the manuscript.

Munich and London
October 2013

SOURCES

As already mentioned in the prologue, the main problem of a Goebbels biography is the fact that by far the majority of documents about the propaganda minister were written by himself or by people close to him with the clear purpose of enhancing his historical significance, indeed of portraying him as a great man. In addition to critical analysis of the texts written by Goebbels himself, for which the author's unrestrained compulsion to communicate provides a variety of starting points, it is important to explore as wide a range as possible of other sources that can contribute to penetrating Goebbels's self-presentation and self-projection.

For the period up to 1923—that is to say, before the diaries begin—we have practically no sources that do *not* come from Goebbels himself. Apart from the "memoirs" composed in 1924, what we have, aside from a few journalistic articles, is above all his early correspondence and his literary efforts, which, together with a few other documents, are preserved among his private papers in the Bundesarchiv (Federal Archive) in Koblenz. The Goebbels collection in the Mönchengladbach City Archive contains further important information, especially about his years in Rheydt. But the various texts Goebbels composed about himself at this time record above all his inner insecurity and conflicts: They show a young person playing with invented variations on his life story and with fantasy projections that gave him psychological support. Precisely because of their contradictory nature, these texts provide plenty of scope for interpretation.

For the period from October 1923 onward, the chief source of this biography are the Goebbels diaries, published in full for the first time in 2006.[1] These diaries, published without a commentary, represent, as the prologue makes clear, a particular challenge to the historian, amounting as they do to a conscious attempt by Goebbels the propagandist to create a main source for a future history of Nazism and in the process to exert a powerful influence on the future interpretation of his own historical role, if not to control it. Their sheer length, their countless details, and the prominent position of their author within the Nazi system have ensured that the diaries are now, in fact, among the original sources most often cited by historians of Nazism.

The diaries demonstrate that from 1925 onward, when he became involved in politics, first as a full-time employee of the NSDAP in the Rhineland and then in his role as Gauleiter in Berlin, Goebbels worked increasingly to project himself as a successful, radical, early fighter for the Nazi cause and its leader. This self-projection also left its mark on his copious journalistic output. Other sources, however, allocate to him a much less impressive role in the "time of struggle." We have at our disposal both a series of papers from various Party collections and, increasingly, documents deriving from state institutions of the Weimar Republic, among them, and particularly valuable, the court records of Goebbels's numerous lawsuits from this time, which are available at the Berlin Landesarchiv. In addition, there are the reports from the non-Nazi press, which gradually began to take notice of him and provide a critical assessment of his role.

There are far more sources available for Goebbels's period as Reich propaganda minister. Useful here were the records of the Propaganda Ministry, incomplete as they are, and those of the Reichskulturkammer (Reich Culture Chamber) as well as those of the Party's Reich propaganda headquarters. For the period from the end of October 1939 to the end of 1942 we have the minutes of the "ministerial conferences," briefings for which Goebbels daily assembled his closest colleagues. While these have been comprehensively edited through the end of May 1941, the subsequent incomplete edition (covering the time until March 1943) can be augmented by copies of the original minutes from the Moscow Special Archive covering the years 1941 and 1942 and for April 1943 by a single file in the Bundesarchiv.[2] The Propaganda Ministry's instructions to the press during the peacetime years are available in an edited form,[3] and for the wartime period there are extensive collections in the Bundesarchiv Koblenz.[4] Contemporary media sources give us an idea of the way these guidelines were put into effect; here Goebbels's own journalistic writing (especially in the *Völkischer Beobachter* and in the weekly *Das Reich*) frequently provided guidance. In addition, there are the contrasting records of other ministries and Party agencies (most of them are in the Berlin Bundesarchiv), which illuminate the influence of the propaganda minister from the perspective of his competitors and partners. All in all, therefore, it is to a large extent possible today to reconstruct the process of producing Nazi propaganda and to make a critical assessment of the version provided by Goebbels in his diaries. By the same token, the self-image Goebbels conveys of being a close confidant of Hitler, consulted on all important decisions, is revealed to a high degree to be self-propaganda, and the same is true of his self-assigned role as the pioneer of "total war."

Naturally, any biography of Goebbels must be stimulated and influenced by earlier work. This is, however, less true of the purported diaries or memoirs of his former colleagues, some of which appeared shortly after the end of the war. These are of limited value simply because of their apologetic purpose and are therefore only occasionally quoted in this book.[5]

The serious biographies provide two contrasting images of Goebbels: On the one hand there is the Machiavellian propaganda specialist, the intelligent cynic, the ice-cold, evil genius who was too intelligent to believe his own propaganda, and on the other the believer, weighed down by numerous complexes and highly dependent on Hitler. The following contributions were particularly significant in the development of this Janus-faced image of Goebbels.

After a critical biography by Curt Riess, published in 1950, developed the image of an unscrupulous cynic,[6] Heinrich Fraenkel and Roger Manvell, using a wider source base, undertook a more nuanced portrait of the propaganda minister's personality in 1960, in which some of his personal difficulties are evident.[7]

In 1962, Helmut Heiber produced an intellectually ambitious and well-written biography that settles very personal scores with the subject, being mainly concerned to unmask and demolish the propaganda minister's personal character. Goebbels is presented here not only as a consummate liar but also as a windbag, a ham, and a thug, who fell victim to his compulsion to project his own self-image.[8] Viktor Reimann's 1971 biography places the emphasis on Goebbels's role as a propagandist, among other things crediting him with being the architect of the "Führer myth."[9]

Ralf Georg Reuth's 1990 Goebbels biography is a serious and reliable piece of work that also has the virtue of being based on a considerably broader range of sources. A slight weakness of the book, however, is that the image of the "believer," which Reuth eventually succeeds in establishing, is not always consistently sustained.[10] Claus Ekkehard Bärsch's study of the young Goebbels is an unconventional and extremely stimulating book, which has to be regarded as an essential contribution, even though when his book was published Bärsch lacked access to important parts of the early diaries.[11] It brings out Goebbels's fundamental narcissism and his search for a god (including his attempt at "self-deification") as well as his image of mothers and women. The book by the psychoanalyst Peter Gathmann and the writer Martina Paul about Goebbels the narcissist might have offered the opportunity of pursuing Bärsch's insights further but is undermined as a biography because it is based on completely inadequate sources; what is inexplicable, above all, is why the authors did not use the edition of the diaries completed in 2006 and almost entirely ignored the relevant historical research literature, while at the same time relying heavily on the dubious memoirs of Goebbels's former colleagues and on earlier publications of poor quality. Its countless banal mistakes, incorrect dates, muddled information, and erratic source references (for example, "ZDF") make the book an irritating read.[12]

The first Goebbels biography based on the full version of the diaries is the book by Toby Thacker, which was published in 2009.[13] Thacker succeeds in providing a more nuanced assessment of Goebbels's importance for Nazi propaganda. He rightly states that Goebbels was not the inventor of the Hitler myth, that he had no monopoly on Nazi propaganda, and that his propaganda enjoyed limited success with the German population. Although he is aware of Goebbels's histrionic qualities and his role as the liar *par excellence,* Thacker convincingly resists the notion of the propaganda minister as an unprincipled cynic and emphasizes four central convictions that were essential to Goebbels: nationalism, anti-Semitism, his sense of the need for social solidarity, and his total devotion to Hitler. However, in point of detail, Thacker is only partially successful in balancing the self-image projected by Goebbels in the diaries with material from other sources and in anchoring his findings within existing scholarship, as he fails to make use of important source materials and research literature.

In addition, there is a series of studies that deal with particular aspects of Goebbels's life.

Dietz Bering's exceptional study has analyzed Goebbels's campaign to defame the Berlin Police Chief Weiss by giving him the Jewish name Isidor.[14] In a study based on a wide range of sources, Ulrich Höver[15] portrays Goebbels as a "National Socialist," though the present author cannot share his conclusions. Christian T. Barth has thoroughly researched Goebbels's anti-Semitism,[16] and Helmut Michels has convincingly demonstrated Goebbels's lack of a coherent foreign policy agenda; in the final analysis the propaganda minister played only a minor role in foreign policy.[17]

Finally, this biography was able to draw on the extensive literature, too extensive to be listed here in full, on the various aspects of Third Reich propaganda containing material concerning Goebbels's role.

BIBLIOGRAPHY

NEWSPAPERS AND PERIODICALS

12 Uhr Blatt
Der Angriff
Berliner Adressbuch
Berliner Arbeiterzeitung
Berliner Börsen-Zeitung
Berliner Lokal-Anzeiger
Berliner Morgenpost
Berliner Tageblatt (BT)
Berliner Zeitung am Mittag
Deutsche Allgemeine Zeitung (DAZ)
Einwohnerbuch Rheydt
Film-Kurier
Frankfurter Zeitung (FZ)
Die Grüne Post
Hamburger Nachrichten
Der Kinematograph
Kölner Tageblatt
Lichtbild-Bühne
Münchner Neueste Nachrichten (MNN)
Münchner Post
Der Nationale Sozialist

Neue Zürcher Zeitung
The New York Times
Nationalsozialistische Briefe (NS-Briefe)
Das Reich
Reichsgesetzblatt (RGBl.)
Reichswart
Rheydter Jahrbuch
Rheydter Zeitung
Die Rote Fahne
Spandauer Zeitung
Der Spiegel
Stadtverordneten-Versammlung der Stadt Berlin 1930
Statistisches Jahrbuch der Stadt Berlin
Tägliche Rundschau
The Times
Unitas, Organ des Verbandes der wissenschaftlichen katholischen Studentenvereine
Unser Wille und Weg (UWW)
Völkische Freiheit (VF)
Völkischer Beobachter, in various editions:
   Berlin edition *(B)*
   Munich edition *(M)*
   Nuremberg edition *(N)*
   Reich edition *(R)*
Vossische Zeitung (VZ)
Westdeutscher Beobachter
Westdeutsche Landeszeitung (WLZ)

UNPUBLISHED SOURCES

BUNDESARCHIV, ABT. BERLIN (BAB)

NS 1: Reichsschatzmeister der NSDAP
NS 6: Partei-Kanzlei der NSDAP
NS 8: Kanzlei Rosenberg
NS 10: Persönliche Adjutantur des Führers und Reichskanzlers
NS 18: Reichspropagandaleitung
NS 22: Reichsorganisationsleiter der NSDAP

NS 26: Hauptarchiv der NSDAP
OPG: Oberstes Parteigericht der NSDAP
R 2: Reichsfinanzministerium
R 6: Reichsministerium für die besetzten Ostgebiete
R 43 II: Neue Reichskanzlei
R 55: Reichministerium für Volksaufklärung und Propaganda
R 56 V: Reichschrifttumskammer
R 58: Reichssicherheitshauptamt
R 78: Reichsrundfunkgesellschaft
R 109 I: Universum Film AG
R 1501: Reichministerium des Innern
R 8150: Reichsvereinigung der Juden in Deutschland

BUNDESARCHIV, ABT. KOBLENZ (BAK)
NL 1118: Nachlaß Goebbels
NL 1548: Nachlaß Rüdiger Graf von der Goltz
ZSg 101: Sammlung Brammer on the press policy of the Nazi state
ZSg 102: Sammlung Sänger on the press policy of the Nazi state
ZSg 109: Sammlung Oberweitmann on the press policy of the Nazi
state
ZSg 158/40: Erich Bandekow on cases of corruption

BUNDESARCHIV/MILITÄRARCHIV, FREIBURG (BAM)
RH 2: OKH/Generalstab des Heeres
RH 5: OKH/Chef des Kriegskartenwesens und Vermessungswesens
RH 15: OKH/Allgemeines Heeresamt (AHA)

INSTITUT FÜR ZEITGESCHICHTE, MUNICH (IFZ)
ZS: Zeugenschriften

LANDESARCHIV BERLIN
LA Berlin A Pr. Br. A Rep 057: Der Stadtpräsident der Reichshaupt-
stadt Berlin
LA Berlin A Rep 358-01: Generalstaatsanwaltschaft bei dem Land-
gericht Berlin
LA Berlin B Rep 058: Staatsanwaltschaft bei dem Landgericht Berlin

OSOBY-ARCHIV MOSKVA/MOSKAUER SONDERARCHIV (OA MOSKAU)
Bestand 500: Sicherheitspolizei
Bestand 1363-3: Reichsministerium für Volksaufklärung und Propaganda (Goebbels's ministerial briefings, here shorted to MK)

POLITISCHES ARCHIV DES AUSWÄRTIGEN AMTES BERLIN (PAA)
Files from various departments

STADTARCHIV MÖNCHENGLADBACH (STA MG)
Various documents concerning the Goebbels family
Nachlaß Goebbels

CONTEMPORARY PUBLICATIONS

15 Entwürfe für Schriftplakate oder Flugblätter zur Ankündigung von Vorträgen für die NSDAP (Manuscript). Elberfeld, n.d.

Berber, Friedrich, ed. *Locarno. Eine Dokumentensammlung*. Berlin, 1936.

Diewerge, Wolfgang. *Das Kriegsziel der Weltplutokratie. Dokumentarische Veröffentlichung zu dem Buch des Präsidenten der amerikanischen Friedensgesellschaft Theodore Nathan Kaufman "Deutschland muss sterben" ("Germany must perish")*. Berlin, 1941.

Dodd, William Edward. *Diary*. New York, 1941.

Engelbrechten, Julius K. *Eine braune Armee entsteht. Die Geschichte der Berlin-Brandenburger SA*. Munich/Berlin, 1937.

Führer durch die Ausstellung Entartete Kunst. Munich, 1935.

Gundolf, Friedrich. *Caesar in der deutschen Literatur*. Berlin, 1904.

———. *Caesar. Geschichte seines Ruhms*. Berlin, 1924.

Hadamovsky, Eugen. "Großkampftage der Rundfunkpropaganda. Vom 30. Januar bis zum 'Tag der erwachenden Nation,'" in idem, *Dein Rundfunk. Das Rundfunkbuch für alle Volksgenossen*. Munich, 1934: 82–90.

Hartungen, Christof von. *Psychologie der Reklame*. Stuttgart, 1921.

Henderson, Nevile. *Fehlschlag einer Mission. Berlin 1937 bis 1939*. Zurich, 1939.

Hillebrand, Wilhelm. *Herunter mit der Maske. Erlebnisse hinter den Kulissen der N.S.D.A.P.* Berlin, 1928. Pamphlet.

Hitler, Adolf. *Mein Kampf*, 2 vols. in one, 286th–290th eds. Munich, 1938.

Kaufman, Theodore N. *Germany Must Perish*. Newark, n.d. [early 1941].

König, Theodor. *Reklame-Psychologie. Ihr gegenwärtiger Stand—ihre praktische Bedeutung*. Munich, 1924.

Lösener, Bernhard. "Als Rassenreferent im Reichsministerium des Innern," Walter Strauss, ed., *VfZ* 9 (1961): 262–313.

Lysinski, Edmund. *Psychologie des Betriebs. Beiträge zur Betriebsorganisation*. Berlin, 1923.

Parteitag der Freiheit vom 10.–16. September 1935. Offizieller Bericht über den Verlauf des Reichsparteitages mit sämtlichen Kongreßreden. Munich, 1935.

Das Recht der Reichskulturkammer. Sammlung der für den Kulturstand geltenden Gesetze und Verordnungen, der amtlichen Anordnungen und Bekanntmachungen der Reichskulturkammer und ihrer Einzelkammern. Im Einvernehmen mit der Hauptgeschäftsführung der Reichskulturkammer. Karl-Dietrich Schrieber, Alfred Metten, and Herbert Collatz, eds., 2 vols. Berlin, 1943.

Reichstags-Handbuch 1933, Bureau des Reichstages, ed. Berlin, 1934.

Reichstagung in Nürnberg 1934, Julius Streicher, ed. Berlin, 1934.

Reupke, Hans. *Der Nationalsozialismus und die Wirtschaft*. Berlin, 1931.

Schwendemann, Karl. *Handbuch der Sicherheitsfrage und der Abrüstungskonferenz, mit einer Sammlung der wichtigsten Dokumente*, 2 vols. Leipzig, 1932–33.

Shirer, William L. *The Journal of a Foreign Correspondent, 1934–1941*. New York, 1942.

Stark, Georg. *Moderne politische Propaganda*. Munich, 1930. Volume 1 of the RPL series edited by Goebbels.

Strasser, Otto. *Ministersessel oder Revolution. Eine wahrheitsgemäße Darstellung meiner Trennung von der NSDAP*. Berlin, 1933.

Weinbrenner, Joachim. *Handbuch des Deutschen Rundfunks 1938*. Heidelberg, 1938.

———. *Handbuch des Deutschen Rundfunks 1939*. Heidelberg, 1939.

DOCUMENT COLLECTIONS

Akten der Partei-Kanzlei, 2 parts, Helmuth Heiber and Peter Longerich, eds. Munich, 1983 and 1991. Microfiches, vol. 4.

Akten der Reichskanzlei, Das Kabinett von Papen (1932), Karl-Heinz Minuth, ed. Munich, 1989.

Akten der Reichskanzlei, Das Kabinett von Schleicher 1932/33, Anton Golecki, ed. Munich, 1986.

Akten der Reichskanzlei, Regierung Hitler 1933–1945, vol. 1 (2 parts), Karl-Heinz Minuth, ed. Munich, 1983.

Akten der Reichskanzlei, Regierung Hitler 1933–1945, vol. 2, Friedrich Hartmannsgruber, ed. Munich, 1999.

Akten der Reichskanzlei, Regierung Hitler 1933–1945, vol. 3, Friedrich Hartmannsgruber, ed. Munich, 2002.

Akten der Reichskanzlei, Regierung Hitler 1933–1945, vol. 5, Friedrich Hartmannsgruber, ed. Munich, 2008.

Akten der Reichskanzlei. Das Kabinett von Papen, Karl-Heinz Minuth, ed. Munich, 1989.

Akten der Reichskanzlei. Die Kabinette Brüning I und II, 3 vols., Tilman Koops, ed. Boppard a. Rh., 1982–1990.

Akten der Reichskanzlei. Die Kabinette Marx I und II, vol. 1, Günter Abramowski, ed. Munich, 1973.

Akten zur deutschen Außenpolitik 1938–1945. Aus dem Archiv des Auswärtigen Amtes, Series C: 1933–1937, 6 vols. Göttingen, 1973–1981); Series D: 1937–1941, 13 vols. Göttingen, 1950–1961); Series E: 1941–1945, 8 vols. Göttingen, 1969–1979.

Alfred Rosenberg. Das politische Tagebuch 1934/35 und 1939/40, Hans-Günther Seraphim, ed. Munich, 1964.

Arnberger, Heinz, et al., eds. *"Anschluß" 1938. Eine Dokumentation,* Dokumentationsarchiv des österreichischen Widerstandes. Vienna, 1988.

Bischof Clemens August Graf von Galen. Akten, Briefe und Predigten, vol. 1: *1933–1946,* vol. 2: *1939–1946,* Peter Löffler, ed. Mainz, 1988.

Boelcke, Willi A., ed. *Deutschlands Rüstung im Zweiten Weltkrieg. Hitlers Konferenzen mit Albert Speer, 1942–1945.* Frankfurt a. M., 1969.

———, ed. *Wollt Ihr den totalen Krieg? Die geheimen Goebbels-Konferenzen 1939–1943.* Stuttgart, 1967.

———, ed. *Kriegspropaganda 1939–1941. Geheime Ministerkonferenzen im Reichspropagandaministerium.* Stuttgart, 1966.

British and Foreign State Papers, vol. 139, 14 April 1935.

Dabel, Gerhard. *KLV. Die erweiterte Kinder-Land-Verschickung. KLV-Lager 1940–1945. Dokumentation über den "Größten Soziologischen Versuch aller Zeiten."* Freiburg, 1981.

Deutschland-Berichte der Sozialdemokratischen Partei Deutschlands (SOPADE) 1934–1940, Klaus Behnken, ed., 7 annual volumes as a reprint. Salzhausen/Frankfurt a. M., 1980.

Dussel, Konrad, and Edgar Lersch, eds. *Quellen zur Programmgeschichte des deutschen Hörfunks und Fernsehens.* Göttingen/Zurich, 1999.

Frank, Hans. *Das Diensttagebuch des deutschen Generalgouverneurs in Polen,* Werner Präg and Wolfgang Jacobmeyer, eds. Stuttgart, 1975.

"Führer-Erlasse" 1939–1945, Edition sämtlicher überlieferter, nicht im Reichsgesetzblatt abgedruckter, von Hitler während des Zweiten Weltkriegs schriftlich erteilter Direktiven aus den Bereichen Staat, Partei, Wirtschaft, Besatzungspolitik und Militärverwaltung, Martin Moll (ed. and introd.). Stuttgart, 1997.

Halder, Franz. *Kriegstagebuch. Tägliche Aufzeichnungen des Chefs des Generalstabes des Heeres, 1939–1942,* Hans Adolf Jacobsen, ed., 3 vols. Stuttgart, 1962–1964.

Hill, Leonidas E., ed. *Die Weizsäcker-Papiere 1933–1950.* Frankfurt a. M./Berlin/Vienna, 1974.

Hitler, Adolf. *Reden und Proklamationen 1932–1945. Kommentiert von einem deutschen Zeitgenossen,* Max Domarus, ed. 2 vols. Neustadt a. d. Aisch, 1963.

Hitler, Adolf. *Reden, Schriften, Anordnungen. Februar 1925 bis Januar 1933,* Institut für Zeitgeschichte, ed. Munich, 1991–2000.

Hoch, Anton, and Hermann Weiss. "Die Erinnerungen des Generalobersten Wilhelm Adam," in Wolfgang Benz, ed., *Miscellanea. Festschrift für Helmut Krausnick zum 75. Geburtstag.* Stuttgart, 1975: 32–62.

Hubatsch, Walther, ed. *Hitlers Weisungen für die Kriegsführung 1939–1945. Dokumente des Oberkommandos der Wehrmacht.* Koblenz, 1983.

International Military Tribunal: Der Prozess gegen die Hauptkriegsver-

brecher vor dem InternationalenMilitärgerichtshof, 14. Oktober
1945 bis 1. Oktober 1946, 42 vols. Nuremberg, 1947–1949.

Jacobsen, Hans-Adolf, ed. "Spiegelbild einer Verschwörung." Die Op-
position gegen Hitler und der Staatsstreich vom 20. Juli 1944 in der
SD-Berichterstattung. Geheime Dokumente aus dem ehemaligen
Reichssicherheitshauptamt, 2 vols. Stuttgart, 1984.

———, ed. Misstrauische Nachbarn. Deutsche Ostpolitik 1919/70. Dokumentation und Analyse. Düsseldorf, 1970.

Jäckel, Eberhard, and Otto Dov Kulka, eds. Die Juden in den geheimen NS-Stimmungsberichten, 1933–1945. Düsseldorf, 2004.

Jedrzejewicz, Waclaf, ed. Papers and Memoirs of Jozef Lipski, Ambassador of Poland, Diplomat in Berlin 1933–1939. New York/Lon-
don, 1968.

Jochmann, Werner, ed. Nationalsozialismus und Revolution. Ursprung und Geschichte der NSDAP in Hamburg, 1922–1933. Dokumente. Mannheim, 1963.

Keiper, Gerhard, and Martin Kröger, eds. Biographisches Handbuch
des deutschen Auswärtigen Dienstes, 1871–1945. Paderborn, 2005.

Kriegstagebuch des Oberkommandos der Wehrmacht 1940–1945, kept
by Helmuth Greiner and Percy E. Schramm, vol. 1: 1. August
1940–31. Dezember 1941. Frankfurt a. M., 1965; vol. 4: 1. Januar
1944–22. Mai 1945. Frankfurt a. M., 1961.

Kropat, Wolf-Arno. Kristallnacht in Hessen. Der Judenpogrom vom
November 1938. Eine Dokumentation. Wiesbaden, 1988.

Longerich, Peter. "Joseph Goebbels und der Totale Krieg. Eine unbekannte Denkschrift des Propagandaministers vom 18. Juli
1944," VfZ 35 (1987): 289–314.

Meldungen aus dem Reich 1938–1945. Die geheimen Lageberichte des
Sicherheitsdienstes der SS, Heinz Boberach (ed. and introd.), vols.
1–17. Herrsching, 1984.

Die Okkupationspolitik des deutschen Faschismus in Dänemark und
Norwegen (1940–1945). Dokumentenauswahl, Fritz Petrick (ed.
and introd.). Berlin/Heidelberg, 1992.

Politik und Wirtschaft in der Krise, 1930–1932. Quellen zur Ära
Brüning, Ilse Maurer and Udo Wengst, eds., 2 parts. Düsseldorf,
1980.

Schneider, Hans. Neues vom Reichstagsbrand—Eine Dokumentation.
Ein Versäumnis der deutschen Geschichtsschreibung, with a preface

by Iring Fetscher and contributions from Dieter Deiseroth, Hersch Fischler, Wolf-Dieter Narr. Berlin, 2004.

Smith, Bradley F., ed. *Heinrich Himmler. Geheimreden 1933 bis 1945 und andere Ansprachen*. Frankfurt a. M., et al., 1974.

Die geheimen Tagesberichte der Deutschen Wehrmachtführung im Zweiten Weltkrieg 1939–1945. Die gegenseitige Lageunterrichtung der Wehrmacht-, Heeres- und Luftwaffenführung über alle Haupt- und Nebenkriegsschauplätze: "Lage West" (OKW-Kriegsschauplätze Nord, West, Italien, Balkan), "Lage Ost" (OKH) und "Luftlage Reich." Kurt Mehner, ed. 12 vols. Osnabrück, 1984–1995.

Tyrell, Albrecht. *Führer befiehl [. . .] Selbstzeugnisse aus der "Kampfzeit" der NSDAP. Dokumentation und Analyse*. Düsseldorf, 1969.

Ursachen und Folgen. Vom deutschen Zusammenbruch 1918 und 1945 bis zur staatlichen Neuordnung Deutschlands in der Gegenwart. Eine Urkunden- und Dokumentensammlung zur Zeitgeschichte. Herbert Michaelis and Ernst Schraepler, eds. 27 vols. Berlin, 1958–1979.

Verhandlungen des Reichstags. Stenographische Berichte, vol. 423 (4th Legislative Period); vol. 446 (5th LP); vol. 457 (8th LP). Berlin, 1929–1933; reprint Bad Feilnbach n.d.

Walk, Joseph, ed. *Das Sonderrecht für die Juden im NS-Staat. Eine Sammlung der gesetzlichen Maßnahmen und Richtlinien-Inhalt und Bedeutung*, 2d ed. Heidelberg, 1996.

Die Wehrmachtberichte 1939–1945, 3 vols. Munich, 1985.

"Wirtschaftliche Grundanschauungen und Ziele der N.S.D.A.P. Ein unveröffentlichtes Dokument aus dem Jahre 1931," *Jahrbuch des Instituts für Deutsche Geschichte* 7 (1978): 355–85.

Wulf, Joseph, ed. *Die bildenden Künste im Dritten Reich*. Gütersloh, 1963.

———, ed. *Musik im Dritten Reich. Eine Dokumentation*. Frankfurt a. M., 1989.

———, ed. *Presse und Funk im Dritten Reich. Eine Dokumentation*. Frankfurt a. M., 1989.

———, ed. *Theater und Film im Dritten Reich. Eine Dokumentation*. Frankfurt a. M., 1989.

WORKS BY JOSEPH GOEBBELS

Goebbels, Joseph. *Tagebücher 1945. Die letzten Aufzeichnungen.* Hamburg, 1980.

Goebbels Reden 1932–1945. Helmut Heiber, ed. Düsseldorf, 1971–72.

Goebbels, Joseph. *Der steile Aufstieg. Reden und Aufsätze aus den Jahren 1942/43.* Munich, 1943.

———. *Das eherne Herz. Reden und Aufsätze aus den Jahren 1941/42.* Munich, 1943.

———. *Der Angriff. Aufsätze aus der Kampfzeit.* Munich, 1935.

———. *Michael. Ein deutsches Schicksal in Tagebuchblättern,* 7th ed. Munich, 1935.

———. *Vom Kaiserhof zur Reichskanzlei. Eine historische Darstellung in Tagebuchblättern* (1 January 1932–1 May 1933). Berlin, 1934.

———. *Signale der neuen Zeit. 25 ausgewählte Reden.* Munich, 1934.

———. *Revolution der Deutschen. 14 Jahre Nationalsozialismus. Goebbelsreden.* Oldenburg i. O., 1933.

———. *Kampf um Berlin. Der Anfang.* Munich, 1931.

———. *Knorke. Ein neues Buch Isidor für Zeitgenossen,* 2d ed. Munich, 1931.

———. *"Der Nazi-Sozi." Fragen und Antworten für den Nationalsozialisten,* various editions. Munich, 1930–.

Goebbels, Joseph, and Hans Schweitzer. *Das Buch Isidor. Ein Zeitbild voll Lachen und Haß.* Munich, 1929.

Goebbels, Joseph. *Wege ins Dritte Reich. Briefe und Aufsätze für Zeitgenossen.* Munich, 1927.

———. *Lenin oder Hitler? Eine Rede. Gehalten am 19. Februar 1926 im Opernhaus in Königsberg i. Pr.* Zwickau, 1926.

———. *Die Zeit ohne Beispiel. Reden und Aufsätze aus den Jahren 1939/40/41.* Munich, 1941.

———. *Zweite Revolution. Briefe an Zeitgenossen.* Zwickau, 1926.

———. *Das kleine ABC des Nationalsozialisten.* Greifswald, 1925.

———. *Wilhelm von Schütz als Dramatiker. Ein Beitrag zur Geschichte des Dramas der romantischen Schule,* MS. diss. Heidelberg, 1922.

Joseph Goebbels, Das Tagebuch 1925/26. Helmut Heiber, ed. Stuttgart, 1960.

Die Tagebücher von Joseph Goebbels. Elke Fröhlich, ed. 32 vols. Munich, 1993–2008.

Die Tagebücher von Joseph Goebbels. Sämtliche Fragmente. Elke Fröhlich, ed. 4 vols. Munich et al., 1987.

SECONDARY LITERATURE AFTER 1945

Abel, Karl-Dietrich. *Presselenkung im NS-Staat. Eine Studie zur Geschichte der Publizistik in der nationalsozialistischen Zeit.* Berlin, 1968.

Abendroth, Hans-Henning. *Hitler in der spanischen Arena.* Paderborn, 1973.

Adam, Uwe Dietrich. *Judenpolitik im Dritten Reich.* Düsseldorf, 1972.

Adler, Hans-Günther. *Der verwaltete Mensch. Studien zur Deportation der Juden aus Deutschland.* Tübingen, 1974.

Ahrens, Yizhak, Stig Hornshoj-Moller, and Christoph B. Melchers. *"Der ewige Jude." Wie Goebbels hetzte. Untersuchungen zum nationalsozialistischen Propagandafilm.* Aachen, 1990.

Albrecht, Dieter, ed. *Politik und Konfession. Festschrift für Konrad Repgen zum 60. Geburtstag.* Berlin, 1983.

Albrecht, Gerd. *Nationalsozialistische Filmpolitik. Eine soziologische Untersuchung über die Spielfilme des Dritten Reichs.* Stuttgart, 1969.

Andreas-Friedrich, Ruth. *Schauplatz Berlin. Ein deutsches Tagebuch.* Munich, 1962.

Anschluß 1938. Protokoll des Symposiums in Wien am 14. und 15. März 1978. Vienna, 1981.

Arendes, Cord. "Schrecken aus dem Untergrund. Endphaseverbrechen des 'Werwolf,'" in idem, ed., *Terror nach innen. Verbrechen am Ende des Zweiten Weltkrieges.* Göttingen, 2006.

Aster, Misha. *"Das Reichsorchester." Die Berliner Philharmoniker und der Nationalsozialismus.* Munich, 2007.

Baarová, Lida. *Die süße Bitterkeit meines Lebens.* Koblenz, 2001.

Bach, Steven. *Leni: The Life and Work of Leni Riefenstahl.* New York, 2007.

Bachrach, Susan D. *The Nazi Olympics: Berlin 1936.* Boston, 2000.

Backes, Uwe, Karl-Heinz Janssen, Eckhard Jesse, Henning Köhler, Hans Mommsen, and Fritz Tobias. *Reichstagsbrand–Aufklärung einer historischen Legende.* Munich, 1986.

Baird, Jay W. *The Mythical World of Nazi War Propaganda 1939–1945*. Minneapolis, 1974.

Bajohr, Frank. "Hamburgs 'Führer.' Zur Person und Tätigkeit des Hamburger NSDAP-Gauleiters Karl Kaufmann," in *Hamburg in der NS-Zeit*. Hamburg, 1995: 59–91.

———. *Parvenüs und Profiteure. Korruption in der NS-Zeit*. Frankfurt a. M., 2001.

Baranowski, Shelley. *Strength Through Joy: Consumerism and Mass Tourism in the Third Reich*. Cambridge, 2004.

Barkai, Avraham. *Vom Boykott zur "Entjudung." Der wirtschaftliche Existenzkampf der Juden im Dritten Reich, 1933–1943*. Frankfurt a. M., 1983.

———. "Wirtschaftliche Grundanschauungen und Ziele der N.S.D.A.P. Ein unveröffentliches Dokument aus dem Jahre 1931," *Jahrbuch des Instituts für Deutsche Geschichte* 7 (1978): 355–85.

Bärsch, Claus-Ekkehard. *Der junge Goebbels. Erlösung und Vernichtung*. Munich, 1995.

Barth, Christian T. *Goebbels und die Juden*. Paderborn/Munich, 2003.

Bauer, Kurt. *Elementar-Ereignis. Die österreichischen Nationalsozialisten und der Juliputsch 1934*. Vienna, 2003.

Becker, Wolfgang. *Film und Herrschaft. Organisationsprinzipien und Organisationsstrukturen der nationalsozialistischen Filmpropaganda*. Berlin, 1973.

Behn, Manfred. "Gleichschritt in die 'neue Zeit.' Filmpolitik zwischen SPIO und NS," in Hans-Michael Bock und Michael Töteberg, eds., *Das Ufa-Buch. Kunst und Krisen, Stars und Regisseure, Wirtschaft und Politik*. Frankfurt a. M., 1992: 340–42.

Behrenbeck, Sabine. "Der Führer. Einführung eines politischen Markenartikels," in Gerald Diesener und Rainer Gries, eds., *Propaganda in Deutschland. Zur Geschichte der politischen Massenbeeinflussung im 20. Jahrhundert*. Darmstadt, 1996: 51–78.

———. *Der Kult um die toten Helden. Nationalsozialistische Mythen, Riten und Symbole, 1923–1945*. Vierow bei Greifswald, 1996.

Below, Nicolaus von. *Als Hitlers Adjutant 1937–1945*. Mainz, 1980.

Bentley, James. *Martin Niemöller. Eine Biographie*. Munich, 1985.

Benz, Wigbert. *Der Rußlandfeldzug des Dritten Reiches: Ursachen, Ziele, Wirkungen. Zur Bewältigung eines Völkermordes unter Berücksichtigung des Geschichtsunterrichts*. Frankfurt a. M., 1986.

Benz, Wolfgang. "Judenvernichtung aus Notwehr? Die Legende um Theodore N. Kaufman," *VfZ* 29 (1981): 615–30.

Berghahn, Volker R. *Der Stahlhelm. Bund der Frontsoldaten 1918–1935.* Düsseldorf, 1966.

Bering, Dietz. *Kampf um Namen. Bernhard Weiss gegen Joseph Goebbels.* Stuttgart, 1991.

Berkholz, Stefan. *Goebbels' Waldhof am Bogensee. Vom Liebesnest zur DDR-Propagandastätte.* Berlin, 2004.

Bezymenskij, Lev A. *Der Tod des Adolf Hitler. Der sowjetische Beitrag über das Ende des Dritten Reiches und seines Diktators,* 2nd ed. Munich/Berlin, 1982.

———. *Der Tod des Adolf Hitler. Unbekannte Dokumente aus Moskauer Archiven.* Hamburg, 1968.

Biddiscombe, Perry. *Werwolf! The History of the National Socialist Guerrilla Movement, 1944–1946.* Toronto, 1998.

Blank, Ralf. "Albert Hoffmann als Reichsverteidigungskommissar im Gau Westfalen-Süd 1943–1945. Eine biographische Skizze," in Wolf Gruner, ed., *"Bürokratien." Beiträge zur Geschichte des Nationalsozialismus.* Berlin, 2001: 189–210.

———. "Kriegsalltag und Luftkrieg an der 'Heimatfront,'" in Jörg Echternkamp, ed., *Die deutsche Kriegsgesellschaft 1939–1945,* vol. 1: *Politisierung, Vernichtung, Überleben.* Munich, 2004: 357–461.

Bleyer, Wolfgang. "Pläne der faschistischen Führung zum totalen Krieg im Sommer 1944," *ZfG* 17 (1969): 1313–29.

Boelcke, Willi A. "Das 'Seehaus' in Berlin-Wannsee. Zur Geschichte des deutschen 'Monitoring-Service' während des Zweiten Weltkrieges," *Jahrbuch für die Geschichte Mittel- und Ostdeutschlands* 23 (1974): 231–64.

———. *Die Macht des Radios. Weltpolitik und Auslandsrundfunk 1924–1976.* Frankfurt a. M./Berlin/Vienna, 1970.

———. "Goebbels und die Kundgebung im Berliner Sportpalast vom 18. Februar 1943," *Jahrbuch für die Geschichte Mittel- und Ostdeutschlands* 19 (1970): 234–55.

Bohn, Robert. *Reichskommissariat Norwegen. "Nationalsozialistische Neuordnung" und Kriegswirtschaft.* Munich, 2000.

Böhler, Jochen. *Auftakt zum Vernichtungskrieg. Die Wehrmacht in Polen.* Frankfurt a. M., 2007.

———. *Der Überfall. Deutschlands Krieg gegen Polen.* Frankfurt a. M., 2009.

Böhnke, Wilfried. *Die NSDAP im Ruhrgebiet*. Bonn/Bad Godesberg, 1974.

Bohse, Jörg. *Inszenierte Kriegsbegeisterung und ohnmächtiger Friedenswille. Meinungslenkung und Propaganda im Nationalsozialismus*. Stuttgart, 1988: 97–136.

Bollmus, Reinhard. *Das Amt Rosenberg und seine Gegner. Zum Machtkampf im nationalsozialistischen Herrschaftssystem*. Stuttgart, 1970.

Bonacker, Max. *Goebbels' Mann beim Radio. Der NS-Propagandist Hans Fritzsche (1900–1953)*. Munich, 2007.

Boog, Horst. "Strategischer Luftkrieg in Europa 1943–1944/45," in Horst Boog, Detlef Vogel, and Gerhard Krebs, *Das Deutsche Reich in der Defensive. Strategischer Luftkrieg in Europa, Krieg im Westen und in Ostasien 1943–1944/45*. Munich, 2001: 3–414.

Borresholm, Boris von, ed. *Dr. Goebbels. Nach Aufzeichnungen aus seiner Umgebung*. Berlin, 1949.

Bosworth, Richard J. B. *Mussolini*. London, 2002.

Botz, Gerhard. *Die Eingliederung Österreichs in das Deutsche Reich. Planung und Verwirklichung des politisch-administrativen Anschlusses (1938–1940)*, 3rd ed. Vienna, 1988.

———. *Nationalsozialismus in Wien. Machtübernahme und Herrschaftssicherung 1938/39*, 3rd ed. Buchloe, 1988.

Boveri, Margret. *Wir lügen alle. Eine Hauptstadtzeitung unter Hitler*. Olten, 1965.

Bracher, Karl Dietrich. *Die Auflösung der Weimarer Republik. Ein Studie zum Problem des Machtverfalls in der Demokratie*. Königstein i. Ts., 1978.

———. "Stufen der Machtergreifung," in Karl Dietrich Bracher, Gerhard Schulz, and Wolfgang Sauer, *Die nationalsozialistische Machtergreifung. Studien zur Errichtung des totalitären Herrschaftssystems in Deutschland*. Frankfurt a. M./Berlin/Vienna, 1960: 31–368.

Braham, Randolph L. *The Politics of Genocide. The Holocaust in Hungary*, 2 vols. New York, 1994.

Brandes, Detlev. *Die Tschechen unter deutschem Protektorat*, 2 vols. Munich/Vienna, 1969.

Braun, Christian A., Michael Mayer, and Sebastian Weitkamp, ed. *Deformation der Gesellschaft? Neue Forschungen zum Nationalsozialismus*. Berlin, 2008.

Brenner, Hildegard. "Die Kunst im politischen Machtkampf der Jahre 1933/34," *VfZ* 10 (1962): 17–42.

Broszat, Martin. *Nationalsozialistische Polenpolitik 1939–1945.* Stuttgart, 1961.

———. "Die Anfänge der Berliner NSDAP 1926/27," *VfZ* 8 (1960): 85–118.

———. "Zur Perversion der Strafjustiz im Dritten Reich," with a documentary appendix, *VfZ* 6 (1958): 390–443.

Brüning, Heinrich. *Memoiren 1918–1934.* Munich, 1972.

Brunswig, Hans. *Feuersturm über Hamburg.* Stuttgart, 1978.

Buchbender, Ortwin. *Das tönende Erz. Deutsche Propaganda gegen die Rote Armee im Zweiten Weltkrieg.* Stuttgart, 1978.

Bucher, Peter. *Der Reichswehrprozeß. Der Hochverrat der Ulmer Reichswehroffiziere 1929/30.* Boppard a. Rh., 1967.

———. "Die Bedeutung des Films als historische Quelle: 'Der ewige Jude' (1940)," in Heinz Durchhardt and Manfred Schlenke, eds., *Festschrift für Eberhard Kessel zum 75. Geburtstag.* Munich, 1982: 300–29.

———. "Hitlers 50. Geburtstag. Zur Quellenvielfalt im Bundesarchiv," in Heinz Boberach and Hans Bohms, eds., *Aus der Arbeit des Bundesarchivs. Beiträge zum Archivwesen, zur Quellenkunde und Zeitgeschichte.* Boppard a. Rh., 1977: 423–46.

Bücherverbrennung Deutschland 1933: Voraussetzungen und Folgen. Exhibition of the Akademie der Künste, 8 May–3 July 1983. Berlin/Vienna, 1983.

Buchholz, Wolfhard. *Die nationalsozialistische Gemeinschaft "Kraft durch Freude." Freizeitgestaltung und Arbeiterschaft im Dritten Reich,* diss. Munich, 1976.

Budzinski, Klaus, and Reinhard Hippen. *Metzler Kabarett Lexikon.* Stuttgart/Weimar, 1996.

Burleigh, Michael. *Tod und Erlösung. Euthanasie in Deutschland 1900–1945.* Zurich/Munich, 2002.

Büsch, Otto, and Wolfgang Haus. *Berlin als Hauptstadt der Weimarer Republik, 1919–1933.* Berlin/New York, 1987.

Bussemer, Thymian. *Propanganda. Konzepte und Theorien.* Wiesbaden, 2005.

Bussmann, Walter. "Zur Entstehung und Überlieferung der Hoßbach-Niederschrift," *VfZ* 16 (1968): 373–84.

Calic, Edouard. *Reinhard Heydrich. Schlüsselfigur des Dritten Reiches.* Düsseldorf, 1982.

Carmon, Arye. "The Impact of the Nazi Racial Decrees on the University of Heidelberg. A Case Study," *Yad Vashem Studies* 11 (1976): 131–63.

Ciolek-Kümper, Jutta. *Wahlkampf in Lippe. Die Wahlkampfpropaganda der NSDAP zur Landtagswahl am 15. Januar 1933.* Munich, 1976.

Collier, Basil. *The Defence of the United Kingdom.* London, 1957.

Conradi, Peter. *Hitlers Klavierspieler. Ernst Hanfstaengl. Vertrauter Hitlers, Verbündeter Roosevelts.* Frankfurt a. M., 2004.

Coulondre, Robert. *Von Moskau nach Berlin: 1936–1939. Erinnerungen des französischen Botschafters.* Bonn, 1950.

Curth, Roland. "Insel Schwanenwerder," in Helmut Engel, Stefi Jersch-Wenzel, and Wilhelm Treue, eds., *Zehlendorf.* Berlin, 1992: 412–28.

Czapla, Ralf Georg. "Erlösung im Zeichen des Hakenkreuzes. Bibel-Usurpation in der Lyrik Joseph Goebbels' und Baldur von Schirachs," in Ralf Georg Czapla and Ulrike Rembold, eds., *Gotteswort und Menschenrede. Die Bibel im Dialog mit Wissenschaften, Künsten und Medien. Vorträge der interdisziplinären Ringvorlesung des Tübinger Graduiertenkollegs "Die Bibel–ihre Entstehung und ihre Wirkung" 2003–2004.* Frankfurt a. M., et al., 2006: 283–326.

——. "Die Entfesselung des Prometheus. Erlösungssehnsucht und Geschichtseschatologie in Gedichtentwürfen des jungen Joseph Goebbels," *Internationales Archiv für Sozialgeschichte der Literatur* 29 (2004): 55–83.

Dahlerus, Birger. *Der letzte Versuch. London–Berlin, Sommer 1939.* Munich, 1948.

Dahm, Volker. "Anfänge und Ideologie der Reichskulturkammer. Die 'Berufsgemeinschaft' als Instrument kulturpolitischer Steuerung und sozialer Reglementierung," *VfZ* 34 (1986): 53–84.

Dallin, Alexander. *Deutsche Herrschaft in Rußland 1941–1945. Eine Studie über Besatzungspolitik.* Düsseldorf, 1958.

Deiseroth, Dieter, ed. *Der Reichstagsbrand und der Prozess vor dem Reichsgericht.* Berlin, 2006.

Demps, Laurenz. "Die Luftangriffe auf Berlin. Ein dokumentarischer Bericht," *Jahrbuch des Märkischen Museums* 4 (1978): 27–69.

Dengg, Sören. *Deutschlands Austritt aus dem Völkerbund und Schachts "Neuer Plan." Zum Verhältnis von Außen- und Außenwirtschaftspolitik in der Übergangsphase von der Weimarer Republik zum Dritten Reich (1929–1934).* Frankfurt a. M., 1986.

Deschner, Guenter. *Reinhard Heydrich. Statthalter der totalen Macht.* Esslingen, 1977.

Detwiler, Donald S. *Hitler, Franco und Gibraltar. Die Frage des spanischen Eintritts in den Zweiten Weltkrieg.* Wiesbaden, 1962.

Deuerlein, Ernst, ed. *Der Aufstieg der NSDAP in Augenzeugenberichten.* Düsseldorf, 1968.

Dietrich, Otto. *Zwölf Jahre mit Hitler.* Cologne, 1955.

Diller, Ansgar. *Rundfunkpolitik im Dritten Reich.* Munich, 1980.

Dillmann, Michael. *Heinz Hilpert. Leben und Werk.* Berlin, 1980.

Dobroszycki, Lucjan. *Die legale polnische Presse im Generalgouvernement 1939–1945.* Munich, 1977.

Dörp, Peter. "Goebbels' Kampf gegen Remarque. Eine Untersuchung über die Hintergründe des Hasses und der Agitation Goebbels' gegen den Roman *Im Westen nichts Neues* von Erich Maria Remarque," *Erich Maria Remarque Jahrbuch* 1 (1991): 48–64.

Döscher, Hans-Jürgen. *"Reichskristallnacht." Die Novemberpogrome 1938.* Berlin, 1988.

Drewniak, Boguslav. *Das Theater im NS-Staat.* Düsseldorf, 1983.

Dümling, Albrecht, and Peter Girth, eds. *Entartete Musik. Zur Düsseldorfer Ausstellung von 1938. Eine kommentierte Rekonstruktion.* Düsseldorf, 1988.

Dussel, Konrad. *Hörfunk in Deutschland. Politik, Programm, Publikum (1923–1960).* Potsdam, 2002.

Ehls, Marie-Luise. *Protest und Propaganda. Demonstrationen in Berlin zur Zeit der Weimarer Republik.* Berlin, 1954.

Eicher, Thomas, Barbara Panse, and Henning Rischbieter, eds. *Theater im "Dritten Reich." Theaterpolitik, Spielplanstruktur, NS-Dramatik.* Seelze-Velber, 2000.

Eicher, Thomas. "Theater im 'Dritten Reich.' Eine Spielplananalyse des deutschsprachigen Schauspieltheaters 1929–1944," in Thomas Eicher et al., eds., *Theater im "Dritten Reich." Theaterpolitik, Spielplanstruktur, NS-Dramatik.* Seelze-Velber, 2000.

Engele, Christian, and Wolfgang Ribbe. "Berlin in der NS-Zeit (1933–1945)," in *Geschichte Berlins. vol. 2: Von der Märzrevolution bis zur Gegenwart.* Berlin, 1987: 927–1024.

Engelhardt, Katrin. "Die Ausstellung 'Entartete Kunst' in Berlin 1938. Rekonstruktion und Analyse," in Uwe Fleckner, ed., *Angriff auf die Avantgarde. Kunst und Kunstpolitik im Nationalsozialismus.* Berlin, 2007: 89–187.

Essner, Cornelia. *Die "Nürnberger Gesetze" oder die Verwaltung des Rassenwahns, 1933–1945.* Paderborn/Munich, 2002.

Faber, David. *Munich: The 1938 Appeasement Crisis.* London et al., 2008.

Faustmann, Uwe Julius. *Die Reichskulturkammer. Aufbau, Funktion und Grundlagen einer Körperschaft des öffentlichen Rechts im nationalsozialistischen Regime.* Aachen, 1995.

Fest, Joachim. *Staatsstreich. Der lange Weg zum 20. Juli.* Berlin, 1994.

Fetscher, Iring. *Joseph Goebbels im Berliner Sportpalast 1943: "Wollt ihr den totalen Krieg?"* Hamburg, 1998.

Fiederlein, Friedrich Martin. *Der deutsche Osten und die Regierungen Brüning, Papen, Schleicher.* Würzburg, 1966.

Finck, Werner. *Alter Narr—was nun? Die Geschichte meiner Zeit.* Munich/Berlin, 1982.

Fraenkel, Heinrich, and Roger Manvell. *Goebbels. Eine Biographie.* Cologne/Berlin, 1960.

Frauenfeld, Alfred. *Und trage keine Reu'. Vom Wiener Gauleiter zum Generalkommissar der Krim. Erinnerungen und Aufzeichnungen.* Leoni am Starnberger See, 1978.

Friedlander, Henry. *Der Weg zum NS-Genozid. Von der Euthanasie zur Endlösung.* Berlin, 2002.

Friedländer, Saul. *Das Dritte Reich und die Juden. Die Jahre der Verfolgung, 1933–1939.* Munich, 1998.

Friedrich, Thomas. *Die missbrauchte Hauptstadt. Hitler und Berlin.* Berlin, 2007.

Frieser, Karl-Heinz, ed. *Die Ostfront 1943/44. Der Krieg im Osten und an den Nebenfronten.* Munich, 2007.

——. "Die Schlacht am Kursker Bogen," in idem, ed., *Ostfront,* 83–208.

——. "Das Ausweichen der Heeresgruppe Nord von Leningrad ins Baltikum," in idem, ed., *Ostfront,* 278–96.

——. "Der Rückzug der Heeresgruppe Mitte nach Weißrußland," in idem, ed., *Ostfront,* 297–338.

——. "Die Rückzugsoperationen der Heeresgruppe Süd in der Ukraine," in idem, ed., *Ostfront,* 339–490.

———. "Der Zusammenbruch der Heeresgruppe Mitte im Sommer 1944," in idem, ed., *Ostfront*, 526–603.

———. "Die Rückzugskämpfe der Heeresgruppe Nord bis Kurland," in idem, ed., *Ostfront*, 623–79.

Fröhlich, Gustav. *Waren das Zeiten. Mein Film-Heldenleben.* Munich, 1983.

Fuchs, Friedrich. *Die Beziehungen zwischen der Freien Stadt Danzig und dem Deutschen Reich in der Zeit von 1920 bis 1939. Unter besonderer Berücksichtigung der Judenfrage in beiden Staaten.* Freiburg, 1999.

Gathmann, Peter, and Martina Paul. *Narziss Goebbels. Eine psychohistorische Biographie.* Vienna/Cologne/Weimar, 2009.

Gebel, Ralf. *"Heim ins Reich!" Konrad Henlein und der Reichsgau Sudetenland (1938–1945),* 2d ed. Munich, 2000.

Gelderblom, Bernhard. "Die Reichserntedankfeste auf dem Bückeberg 1933–1937. Ein Volk dankt seinem Verführer," in Gerd Biegel and Wulf Otte, eds., *Ein Volk dankt seinem (Ver)führer: Die Reichserntedankfeste auf dem Bückeberg 1933–1937. Vorträge zur Ausstellung.* Brunswick, 2002: 19–62.

Gemzell, Carl-Axel. *Raeder, Hitler und Skandinavien. Der Kampf für einen maritimen Operationsplan.* Lund, 1965.

Gerlach, Christian, and Götz Aly. *Das letzte Kapitel. Realpolitik, Ideologie und der Mord an den ungarischen Juden 1944/1945.* Stuttgart/Zurich, 2002.

Gerlach, Christian. "Die Wannsee-Konferenz, das Schicksal der deutschen Juden und Hitlers politische Grundsatzentscheidung, alle Juden Europas zu ermorden," in idem, *Krieg, Ernährung, Völkermord. Deutsche Vernichtungspolitik im Zweiten Weltkrieg.* Zurich/Munich, 2001: 79–152.

Gillessen, Günther. *Auf verlorenem Posten. Die Frankfurter Zeitung im Dritten Reich.* Berlin, 1983.

Girbig, Werner, . . . *im Anflug auf die Reichshauptstadt. Die Dokumentation der Bombenangriffe auf Berlin–stellvertretend für alle deutschen Städte.* Stuttgart, 1971.

Giro, Helmut-Dieter. *Frankreich und die Remilitarisierung des Rheinlandes,* MS diss., Düsseldorf, 2005.

Gottwaldt, Alfred B., and Diana Schulle. *Die "Judendeportationen" aus dem Deutschen Reich 1941–1945. Eine kommentierte Chronologie.* Wiesbaden, 2005.

Graham, Cooper C. *Leni Riefenstahl and Olympia*. Metuchen/London, 1986.

Grimm, Barbara. *Lynchmorde an alliierten Fliegern im Zweiten Weltkrieg*. MS diss., Munich University, 2006.

Gröhler, Olaf. *Bombenkrieg gegen Deutschland*. Berlin, 1990.

Groscurth, Helmuth. *Tagebücher eines Abwehroffiziers 1938–1940. Mit weiteren Dokumenten zur Militäropposition gegen Hitler*. Helmut Krausnick, ed. Stuttgart, 1970.

Gruchmann, Lothar. *Justiz im Dritten Reich. Anpassung und Unterwerfung in der Ära Gürtner*. Munich, 1988.

———. "Korruption im Dritten Reich. Zur Lebensmittelversorgung der NS-Führerschaft," *VfZ* 42 (1994): 571–93.

Gruner, Wolf. "Lesen brauchen sie nicht zu können. Die 'Denkschrift über die Behandlung der Juden in der Reichshauptstadt auf allen Gebieten des öffentlichen Lebens' vom Mai 1938," *Jahrbuch für Antisemitismusforschung* 4 (1995): 305–41.

———. *Widerstand in der Rosenstraße. Die Fabrik-Aktion und die Verfolgung der "Mischehen" 1943*. Frankfurt a. M., 2005.

Haasis, Hellmut G. *Tod in Prag. Das Attentat auf Reinhard Heydrich*. Reinbek bei Hamburg, 2002.

Hachmeister, Lutz, and Michael Kloft, eds. *Das Goebbels-Experiment*. Munich, 2005.

Hacket, David Andrew. *The Nazi Party in the Reichstag Election of 1930*. Ph.D. diss., University of Wisconsin, 1971.

Hagemann, Jürgen. *Die Presselenkung im Dritten Reich*. Bonn, 1970.

Hale, Oron J. *Presse in der Zwangsjacke 1933–1945*. Düsseldorf, 1965.

Hanfstaengl, Ernst. *Zwischen Weißem und Braunem Haus. Memoiren eines politischen Außenseiters*. Munich, 1970.

Hansen, Thorkild. *Knut Hamsun. Seine Zeit–sein Prozess*. Munich/Vienna, 1978.

Hecht, Cornelia. *Deutsche Juden und Antisemitismus in der Weimarer Republik*. Bonn, 2003.

Hehl, Ulrich von. "Die Kontroverse um den Reichstagsbrand," *VfZ* 36 (1988): 259–80.

Heiber, Helmut. *Die Katakombe wird geschlossen*. Munich/Berlin/Vienna, 1966.

———. *Joseph Goebbels*. Berlin, 1965.

———, ed. *Lagebesprechungen im Führerhauptquartier. Protokollfrag-*

mente aus Hitlers militärischen Konferenzen 1942–1945. Hamburg, 1963.

Heinen, Armin. *Die Legion "Erzengel Michael" in Rumänien. Soziale Bewegung und politische Organisation. Ein Beitrag zum Problem des internationalen Faschismus*. Munich, 1986.

Heller, Renate. "Kunst-Ausschuss. Emil Jannings als Schauspieler und Produzent," in Jan Distelmeier, ed., *Tonfilmfrieden/Tonfilmkrieg. Die Geschichte der Tobis vom Technik-Syndikat zum Staatskonzern*. Munich, 2003: 150–58.

Henke, Klaus-Dietmar. *Die amerikanische Besetzung Deutschlands*. Munich, 1996.

Hensle, Michael P. *Rundfunkverbrechen, Das Hören von "Feindsendern" im Nationalsozialismus*. Berlin, 2003.

Herbst, Ludolf. *Der Totale Krieg und die Ordnung der Wirtschaft. Die Kriegswirtschaft im Spannungsfeld von Politik, Ideologie und Propaganda 1939–1945*. Stuttgart, 1982.

Hermann, Angela. "Hitler und sein Stoßtrupp in der 'Reichskristallnacht,'" *VfZ* 56 (2008): 603–19.

Hetzer, Gerhard. "Die Industriestadt Augsburg. Eine Sozialgeschichte der Arbeiteropposition," in Martin Broszat and Hartmut Mehringer, eds., *Bayern in der NS-Zeit*. Munich, 1977: 1–234.

Hildebrand, Klaus. *Das vergangene Reich. Deutsche Außenpolitik von Bismarck bis Hitler, 1871–1914*. Stuttgart, 1996.

Hillgruber, Andreas. *Hitlers Strategie. Politik und Kriegführung 1940–1941*. Marburg. 1965.

Hilton, Christopher. *Hitler's Olympics: The 1936 Berlin Olympic Games*. Stroud, 2006.

Hockerts, Hans Günter. "Die Goebbels-Tagebücher 1932–1941. Eine neue Hauptquelle zur Erforschung der nationalsozialistischen Kirchenpolitik," in Dieter Albrecht, ed., *Politik und Konfession. Festschrift für Konrad Repgen zum 60. Geburtstag*. Berlin, 1983: 359–92.

———. *Die Sittlichkeitsprozesse gegen katholische Ordensangehörige und Priester 1936/1937. Eine Studie zur nationalsozialistischen Herrschaftstechnik und zum Kirchenkampf*. Mainz, 1971.

———. "Kreuzzugsrhetorik, Vorsehungsglaube, Kriegstheologie. Spuren religiöser Deutung in Hitlers "Weltanschauungskrieg," in Klaus Schreiner, ed., *Heilige Kriege. Religiöse Begründungen mi-*

litärischer Gewaltanwendung: Judentum, Christentum und Islam im Vergleich. Munich, 2008: 229–50.

Hoensch, Jörg K. Die Slowakei und Hitlers Ostpolitik. Hlinkas Slowakische Volkspartei zwischen Autonomie und Separation 1938/1939. Cologne/Graz, 1965.

Hofer, Walther. Die Entfesselung des Zweiten Weltkrieges. Darstellung und Dokumente. Berlin, 2007.

Hofer, Walther, Edouard Calic, Christoph Graf, and Friedrich Zipfel. Der Reichstagsbrand—Eine wissenschaftliche Dokumentation. Freiburg i. Br., 1992.

Hoffmann, Gabriele. NS-Propaganda in den Niederlanden. Organisation und Lenkung der Publizistik unter deutscher Besatzung 1940–1945. Munich-Pullach, 1972.

Hoffmann, Heinrich. Hitler, wie ich ihn sah. Aufzeichnungen seines Leibfotografen. Munich, 1974.

Hoffmann, Hilmar. Mythos Olympia–Autonomie und Unterwerfung von Sport und Kultur: Hitlers Olympiade, olympische Kultur und Riefenstahls Olympia-Film. Berlin et al., 1993.

Hoffmann, Peter. Widerstand–Staatsstreich–Attentat. Der Kampf der Opposition gegen Hitler, 4th ed. Munich, 1985.

Höhne, Heinz. Mordsache Röhm. Hitlers Durchbruch zur Alleinherrschaft 1933–1934. Reinbek bei Hamburg, 1984.

Hollstein, Dorothea. Jud Süß und die Deutschen. Antisemitische Vorurteile im nationalsozialistischen Spielfilm. Frankfurt a. M., 1983.

Hölsken, Dieter. Die V-Waffen. Entstehung, Propaganda, Kriegseinsatz. Stuttgart, 1984: 98.

Horn, Wolfgang. Der Marsch zur Machtergreifung. Die NSDAP bis 1933. Königstein i. Ts./Düsseldorf, 1980.

Hornshoj-Moller, Stig. "Der ewige Jude." Quellenkritische Analyse eines antisemitischen Propagandafilms. Göttingen, 1995.

Hörster-Philipps, Ulrike. Konservative Politik in der Endphase der Weimarer Republik. Die Regierung Franz von Papen. Cologne, 1982.

Höver, Ulrich. Joseph Goebbels. Ein nationaler Sozialist. Bonn, 1992.

Hubatsch, Walther. "Weserübung." Die deutsche Besetzung von Dänemark und Norwegen 1940, 2nd ed. Göttingen, 1960.

Hunt, Richard M. Joseph Goebbels: A Study of the Formation of His National Socialist Consciousness. Cambridge, 1960.

Hüttenberger, Peter. *Die Gauleiter.* Stuttgart, 1969.

Jablonsky, David. *The Nazi Party in Dissolution: Hitler and the Verbotzeit, 1923–1925.* London/Totowa, 1989.

Jäckel, Eberhard. *Frankreich in Hitlers Europa. Die deutsche Frankreichpolitik im Zweiten Weltkrieg.* Stuttgart, 1966.

Jäger, Wolfgang. *Es begann am 30. Januar.* Munich, 1958.

Jagschitz, Gerhard. *Der Putsch. Die Nationalsozialisten 1934 in Österreich.* Graz, 1976.

Jansen, Christian, and Arno Weckbecker. *Der "Volksdeutsche Selbstschutz" in Polen 1939/40.* Munich, 1992.

Janssen, Gregor. *Das Ministerium Speer. Deutschlands Rüstung im Krieg,* 2nd ed. Berlin, 1969.

Janssen, Karl-Heinz, and Fritz Tobias. *Der Sturz der Generäle. Hitler und die Blomberg-Fritsch-Krise.* Munich, 1994.

Jastrzebski, Włodzimierz. *Der Bromberger Blutsonntag. Legende und Wirklichkeit.* Pozna, 1990.

Joachimsthaler, Anton. *Hitlers Ende. Legende und Dokumente,* 2nd ed. Munich, 2004.

Jochmann, Werner, ed. *Nationalsozialismus und Revolution. Ursprung und Geschichte der NSDAP in Hamburg, 1922–1933. Dokumente.* Mannheim, 1963.

Jones, Larry Eugene. "The Harzburg Rally of October 1931," *German Studies Review* 29 (2006): 483–94.

Das Juliabkommen von 1936. Vorgeschichte, Hintergründe und Folgen. Protokoll des Symposiums in Wien am 10. und 11. Juni 1976. Munich, 1977.

Jung, Otmar. *Direkte Demokratie in der Weimarer Republik.* Frankfurt a. M., et al., 1989.

———. *Plebiszit und Diktatur. Die Volksabstimmungen der Nationalsozialisten.* Tübingen, 1995.

Jungbluth, Rüdiger. *Die Quandts. Ihr leiser Aufstieg zur mächtigsten Wirtschaftsdynastie Deutschlands.* Frankfurt a. M., 2002.

Kaiser, Gerd. *Katyn. Das Staatsverbrechen–das Staatsgeheimnis.* Berlin, 2002.

Kallis, Aristotle A. *National Socialist Propaganda in the Second World War.* Basingstoke, 2005.

Kater, Michael H. *Die mißbrauchte Muse. Musiker im Dritten Reich.* Munich, 1998.

Kegel, Jens. *"Wollt Ihr den totalen Krieg?" Eine semiotische und linguistische Gesamtanalyse der Rede Goebbels' im Berliner Sportpalast am 18. Februar 1943.* Tübingen, 2006.

Kellerhoff, Sven Felix. *Der Reichstagsbrand. Die Karriere eines Kriminalfalls.* Berlin, 2008.

Kempka, Erich. *Die letzten Tage mit Adolf Hitler.* Preussisch Oldendorf, 1975.

Kernberg, Otto F. *Borderline-Störungen und pathologischer Narzissmus,* 14th ed. Frankfurt a. M., 2007.

———. *Narzisstische Persönlichkeitsstörungen.* Stuttgart/New York, 1998.

Kershaw, Ian. *Der Hitler-Mythos. Führerkult und Volksmeinung.* Stuttgart, 2002.

———. *Hitler. 1889–1936.* Stuttgart, 1994.

———. *Hitler. 1936–1945.* Stuttgart, 2000.

Kessemeier, Karin. *Der Leitartikler Goebbels in den NS-Organen "Der Angriff" und "Das Reich."* Münster, 1967.

Kindermann, Gottfried-Karl. *Hitlers Niederlage in Österreich. Bewaffneter NS-Putsch, Kanzler-Mord und Österreichs Abwehrsieg 1934.* Hamburg, 1984.

Kinkel, Lutz. *Die Scheinwerferin. Leni Riefenstahl und das "Dritte Reich."* Hamburg/Vienna, 2002.

Kissenkoetter, Udo. *Gregor Straßer und die NSDAP.* Stuttgart, 1978.

Kivelitz, Christoph. *Die Propagandaausstellungen in europäischen Diktaturen. Konfrontation und Vergleich. Nationalsozialismus in Deutschland, Faschismus in Italien und die UdSSR der Stalinzeit.* Bochum, 1999.

Klabunde, Anja. *Magda Goebbels—Annäherung an ein Leben.* Munich, 1999.

Klee, Ernst. *"Euthanasie" im NS-Staat. Die "Vernichtung lebensunwerten Lebens."* Frankfurt a. M., 1983.

Klee, Karl. *Das Unternehmen "Seelöwe." Die geplante deutsche Landung in England 1940.* Göttingen, 1958.

Klein, Ulrich. "'Mekka des deutschen Sozialismus' oder 'Kloake der Bewegung'? Der Aufstieg der NSDAP in Wuppertal 1920 bis 193," in Klaus Goebel, ed., *Über allem die Partei.* Oberhausen, 1987.

Klemperer, Victor. *Ich will Zeugnis ablegen bis zum letzten. Tagebücher 1933–1945,* 2 vols. Walter Nowojski, ed. 7th ed. Berlin, 1997.

————. *LTI. Notizbuch eines Philologen.* Leipzig, 1996.

Klink, Ernst. "Heer und Kriegsmarine," in Horst Boog et al., *Der Angriff auf die Sowjetunion.* Frankfurt a. M., 1991: 541–736.

Knilli, Friedrich. *Jud Süß. Filmprotokoll, Programmheft und Einzelanalysen.* Berlin, 1983.

Knox, MacGregor. *Mussolini Unleashed, 1939–1941. Politics and Strategy in Fascist Italy's Last War.* Cambridge, 1982.

Koch, Hans-Jörg. *Das Wunschkonzert im NS-Rundfunk.* Cologne/Weimar/Vienna, 2003.

Kock, Gerhard. *"Der Führer sorgt für unsere Kinder." Die Kinderlandverschickung im Zweiten Weltkrieg.* Paderborn, et al. 1997.

Koerner, Ralf Richard. *So haben sie es damals gemacht. Die Propagandavorbereitungen zum Österreichanschluß durch das Hitlerregime 1933–1938.* Vienna, 1958.

Kohut, Heinz. *Narzißmus. Eine Theorie der psychoanalytischen Behandlung narzißtischer Persönlichkeitsstörungen.* Frankfurt a. M., 1973; new ed., 2007.

Kolb, Eberhard. *Die Weimarer Republik,* 2nd ed. Munich, 1988.

Koller, Karl. *Der letzte Monat, 14. April bis 27. Mai 1945. Tagebuchaufzeichnung des ehemaligen Chefs des Generalstabs der deutschen Luftwaffe.* Munich, 1985.

König, Malte. *Kooperation als Machtkampf. Das faschistische Achsenbündnis Berlin–Rom im Krieg 1940/41.* Cologne, 2007.

Kopper, Christoph. *Hjalmar Schacht. Aufstieg und Fall von Hitlers mächtigstem Bankier.* Munich, 2006.

Krausnick, Helmut. "Die Einsatzgruppen vom Anschluß Österreichs bis zum Feldzug gegen die Sowjetunion. Entwicklung und Verhältnis zur Wehrmacht," in Helmut Krausnick and Hans-Heinrich Wilhelm, *Die Truppe des Weltanschauungskriegs. Die Einsatzgruppen der Sicherheitspolizei und des SD 1938–1942.* Stuttgart, 1981: 13–276.

Krebs, Albrecht. *Tendenzen und Gestalten der NSDAP.* Stuttgart, 1959.

Krebs, Gerhard. "Von Hitlers Machtübernahme zum Pazifischen Krieg (1933–1941)" in Gerhard Krebs and Bernd Marin, eds., *Formierung und Fall der Achse Berlin–Tokyo.* Munich, 1994: 11–26.

Kroener, Bernhard R. "'Menschenbewirtschaftung,' Bevölkerungsverteilung und personelle Rüstung in der zweiten Kriegshälfte

(1942–1944)," in Bernhard R. Kroener et al., eds., *Organisation und Mobilmachung des deutschen Machtbereichs*, 2nd half-volume: *Kriegsverwaltung, Wirtschaft und personelle Ressourcen 1942– 1944/45*. Stuttgart, 1999: 777–1003.

Kroener, Bernhard R., Rolf-Dieter Müller, and Hans Umbreit, eds. *Organisation und Mobilmachung des deutschen Machtbereichs*. 2nd half-volume: *Kriegsverwaltung, Wirtschaft und personelle Ressourcen 1942–1944/45*. Stuttgart, 1999.

Kruppa, Bernd. *Rechtsradikalismus in Berlin 1918–1928*. Berlin/New York, 1988.

Kühnl, Reinhard. *Die nationalsozialistische Linke, 1925–1930*. Meisenheim a. Glan, 1966.

———. "Zur Programmatik der nationalsozialistischen Linken: Das Strasser-Programm von 1925/26," *VfZ* 14 (1966): 317–33.

Kunz, Andreas. *Wehrmacht und Niederlage. Die bewaffnete Macht in der Endphase der nationalsozialistischen Herrschaft, 1944 bis 1945*. Munich, 2005.

Lakowski, Richard. "Der Zusammenbruch der deutschen Verteidigung zwischen Ostsee und Karpaten," in Rolf-Dieter Müller, ed., *Der Zusammenbruch des Deutschen Reiches 1945*. Munich, 2008: 491–679.

Large, David Clay. *Nazi Games: The Olympics of 1936*. London/New York, 2007.

Latour, Conrad F. "Goebbels' 'Außerordentliche Rundfunkmaßnahmen' 1939–1942," *VfZ* 11 (1963): 418–35.

Lau, Dirk. *Wahlkämpfe der Weimarer Republik. Propaganda und Programme der politischen Parteien bei den Wahlen zum Deutschen Reichstag von 1924 bis 1930*, MS. diss. Mainz, 1995.

Leitz, Christian. *Economic Relations Between Nazi Germany and Franco's Spain, 1936–1945*. Oxford, 1996.

Lemmons, Russel. *Goebbels and Der Angriff*. Lexington, 1994.

Lerg, Winfried B. *Rundfunkpolitik in der Weimarer Republik*. Munich, 1980.

———. "Richtlinien für die Gesamthaltung der deutschen Presse," *Gazette. International Journal for Mass Communication Studies* 8 (1962): 228–45.

Lochner, Louis P., ed. *Goebbels Tagebücher*. Zurich, 1948.

Löhr, Wolfgang. "Mönchengladbach im 19./20. Jahrhundert," in

Loca Desiderata. Mönchengladbacher Stadtgeschichte, vol. 3/1. Mönchengladbach, 2003: 9–240.

Loiperdinger, Martin, ed. *Märtyrerlegenden im NS Film.* Opladen, 1991.

——. *Der Parteitagsfilm "Triumph des Willens' von Leni Riefenstahl. Rituale der Mobilmachung."* Opladen, 1987.

Longerich, Peter. *"Davon haben wir nichts gewusst!" Die Deutschen und die Judenverfolgung 1933–1945.* Munich, 2006.

——. *Deutschland 1918–1933. Die Weimarer Republik. Handbuch zur Geschichte.* Hanover, 1995.

——. *Die Wannsee-Konferenz vom 20. Januar 1942. Planung und Beginn des Genozids an den europäischen Juden.* Berlin, 1998.

——. *Heinrich Himmler. Biographie.* Munich, 2008.

——. *Geschichte der SA.* Munich, 2003.

——. *Politik der Vernichtung. Eine Gesamtdarstellung der national-sozialistischen Judenverfolgung.* Zurich/Munich, 1998. Revised English edition: *Holocaust: The Nazi Persecution and Murder of the Jews.* Oxford, 2010.

——. *Propagandisten im Krieg. Die Presseabteilung des Auswärtigen Amtes unter Ribbentrop.* Munich, 1987.

Loock, Hans-Dietrich. *Quisling, Rosenberg und Terboven. Zur Vorgeschichte und Geschichte der nationalsozialistischen Revolution in Norwegen.* Stuttgart, 1970.

Lukes, Igor. "The Czechoslovak Partial Mobilization in May 1938: A Mystery (Almost) Solved," *JCH* 31 (1996): 699–720.

Lüttichau, Mario-Andreas von. "'Deutsche Kunst.' Der Katalog," in *Die "Kunststadt" München 1937. Nationalsozialismus und "Entartete Kunst,"* Peter-Klaus Schuster, ed. Munich, 1987.

Maier, Klaus A. "Die Luftschlacht um England," in Klaus A. Maier et al., *Die Errichtung der Hegemonie auf dem europäischen Kontinent.* Stuttgart, 1979: 375–408.

Maier, Klaus A., and Bernd Stegemann. "Die Sicherung der europäischen Nordflanke," in Klaus A. Maier et al., *Die Errichtung der Hegemonie auf dem europäischen Kontinent.* Stuttgart, 1979: 187–231.

Maiwald, Klaus Jürgen. *Filmzensur im NS-Staat.* Dortmund, 1983.

Mallmann, Klaus-Michael, and Bogdan Musial, eds. *Genesis des Genozids. Polen 1939–1941.* Darmstadt, 2004.

Mallmann, Klaus-Michael, and Martin Cüppers. "Die Rolle der Ord-
nungspolizei und der Waffen-SS," in idem, eds. *Genesis des Genozids. Polen 1939–1941*. Darmstadt, 2004.

Mannes, Stefan. *Antisemitismus im nationalsozialistischen Spielfilm.
"Jud Süß" und "Der ewige Jude."* Cologne, 1999.

Manoschek, Walter. *"Serbien ist judenfrei." Militärische Besatzungspolitik und Judenvernichtung in Serbien 1941/42*. Munich, 1993.

Martens, Erika. *Zum Beispiel "Das Reich." Zur Phänomenologie der
Presse im totalitären Regime*. Cologne, 1972.

Martin, Bernd. *Deutschland und Japan im Zweiten Weltkrieg, Vom
Angriff auf Pearl Harbor bis zur deutschen Kapitulation*. Göttingen,
1969.

Marwell, David George. *Unwanted Exile. A Biography of Ernst "Putzi"
Hanfstaengl*. MS diss., State University of New York of Bingham-
ton 1968.

Matic, Igor-Philip. *Edmund Veesenmayer. Agent und Diplomat der
nationalsozialistischen Expansionspolitik*. Munich, 2002.

Mattioli, Aram. *Experimentierfeld der Gewalt. Der Abessinienkrieg
und seine internationale Bedeutung 1935–1941*. Zurich, 2005.

McGilligan, Patrick. *Fritz Lang: The Nature of the Beast*. New York,
1997.

Meier, Kurt. *Der evangelische Kirchenkampf*, vol. 2: *Gescheiterte Neu-
ordnungsversuche im Zeichen staatlicher "Rechtshilfe."* Göttingen,
1976.

Meissner, Hans-Otto. *Magda Goebbels. Ein Lebensbild*. Munich, 1978.

Meissner, Karl-Heinz. "'Deutsches Volk, gib uns vier Jahre Zeit ...'
Nationalsozialistische Kunstpolitik 1933–37. Große Deutsche
Kunstausstellung–Ausstellung 'Entartete Kunst' Munich 1937," in
*"Die Axt hat geblüht ..." Europäische Konflikte der 30er Jahre in
Erinnerung an die frühe Avantgarde, 11. Oktober–6. Dezember
1987*, Jürgen Harten, Hans-Werner Schmidt, and Marie Luise Sy-
ring, eds. Düsseldorf, 1987: 368–77.

———. "Große Deutsche Kunstausstellung," in *Stationen der Moderne. Die bedeutenden Kunstausstellungen des 20. Jahrhunderts in
Deutschland*. Berlin, 1988: 276–84. Exhibition catalogue.

Meissner, Otto. *Staatssekretär unter Ebert, Hindenburg, Hitler. Der
Schicksalsweg des deutschen Volkes von 1918–1945, wie ich ihn erlebte*. Hamburg, 1950.

Mendelssohn, Peter de. *Zeitungsstadt Berlin. Menschen und Mächte in der Geschichte der deutschen Presse Berlin,* 2nd revised and extended ed. Frankfurt a. M., 1982.

Merkes, Manfred. *Die deutsche Politik im spanischen Bürgerkrieg 1936–1939,* 2nd revised and extended ed. Bonn, 1969.

Meyer, Ahlrich. " '[. . .] dass französische Verhältnisse anders sind als polnische.' Die Bekämpfung des Widerstands durch die deutsche Militärverwaltung in Frankreich 1941," in Guus Meershoeck et al., *Repression und Kriegsverbrechen. Die Bekämpfung von Widerstands- und Partisanenbewegungen gegen die deutsche Besatzung in West- und Südosteuropa.* Berlin, 1997: 43–91.

Michalka, Wolfgang. *Ribbentrop und die deutsche Weltpolitik. Außenpolitische Konzeptionen und Entscheidungsprozesse im Dritten Reich.* Munich, 1980.

Michel, Kai. *Vom Poeten zum Demagogen. Die schriftstellerischen Versuche Joseph Goebbels.* Cologne/Weimar/Vienna, 1999.

Michels, Helmut. *Ideologie und Propaganda. Die Rolle von Joseph Goebbels in der nationalsozialistischen Außenpolitik bis 1939.* Frankfurt a. M., 1992.

Middlebrook, Martin. *Arnheim 1944: The Airborne Battle, 17.–26. September.* Harmondsworth, 1994.

———. *Hamburg Juli 43. Alliierte Luftstreitkräfte gegen eine deutsche Stadt.* Berlin, 1983.

Moeller, Felix. *Filmminister. Goebbels und der Film im Dritten Reich.* Berlin, 1998.

Moll, Martin. "Steuerungsinstrument im 'Ämterchaos'? Die Tagungen der Reichs- und Gauleiter der NSDAP," *VfZ* 49 (2001): 215–73.

———. "Die Abteilung Wehrmachtpropaganda im Oberkommando der Wehrmacht: Militärische Bürokratie oder Medienkonzern?" *Beiträge zur Geschichte des Nationalsozialismus* 17 (2001): 111–50.

Moltmann, Günter. "Goebbels' Rede zum totalen Krieg am 18. Februar 1943," *VfZ* 12 (1964): 13–43.

Morsey, Rudolf. *Die Protokolle der Reichstagsfraktion der deutschen Zentrumspartei 1926–1933.* Mainz, 1969.

———. *Der Untergang des politischen Katholizismus. Die Zentrumspartei zwischen christlichem Selbstverständnis und "Nationaler Erhebung" 1932/33.* Stuttgart, 1967.

Mühleisen, Horst. "Das Testament Hindenburgs vom 11. Mai 1934," *VfZ* 44 (1996): 356–71.

Mühlen, Patrick von zur. *"Schlagt Hitler an der Saar!" Abstimmungs-kampf, Emigration und Widerstand im Saargebiet 1933–1935.* Bonn, 1979.

Mühlenfeld, Daniel. "Joseph Goebbels und die Grundlagen der NS-Rundfunkpolitik," *ZfG* 54 (2006): 442–67.

———. "Zur Bedeutung der NS-Propaganda für die Eroberung staatlicher Macht und die Sicherung politischer Loyalität," in Christian A. Braun, Michael Mayer, and Sebastian Weitkamp, eds., *Deformation der Gesellschaft? Neue Forschungen zum Nationalsozialismus.* Berlin, 2008: 93–117.

Müller, Manfred. *Im Schatten des "Grandgoschiers." Generaldirektor Hans Goebbels, Bruder des Reichspropagandaministers.* Aschau, 1994.

Müller, Rolf-Dieter et al., eds. *Organisation und Mobilisierung des deutschen Machtbereichs.* Stuttgart, 1999.

Münk, Dieter. *Die Organisation des Raumes im Nationalsozialismus. Eine soziologische Untersuchung ideologisch fundierter Leitbilder in Architektur, Städtebau und Raumplanung des Dritten Reiches.* Bonn, 1993.

Nadolny, Rudolf. *Mein Beitrag.* Wiesbaden, 1955.

Neuber, Gerhard. *Faschismus in Berlin. Entwicklung und Wirken der NSDAP und ihrer Organisationen in der Reichshauptstadt 1920–1934.* MS diss., Berlin, 1976.

Nolzen, Armin. "Die NSDAP, der Krieg und die deutsche Gesellschaft," in Jörg Echternkamp, ed., *Die deutsche Kriegsgesellschaft 1939–1945,* vol. 1: *Politisierung, Vernichtung und Überleben.* Munich, 2004: 95–193.

Nowak, Kurt. *"Euthanasie" und Sterilisierung im "Dritten Reich." Die Konfrontation der evangelischen und katholischen Kirche mit dem Gesetz zur Verhütung erbkranken Nachwuchses und der "Euthanasie"-Aktion.* Göttingen, 1978.

O'Donnel, James P., and Uwe Bahnsen. *Die Katakombe. Das Ende in der Reichskanzlei.* Stuttgart, 1975.

Obenaus, Herbert. "'The Germans: 'An Antisemitic People.' The Press Campaign after 9 November 1938," in David Bankier, ed., *Probing the Depths of German Antisemitism: German Society and the Persecution of the Jews, 1933–1941.* New York et al., 2000: 147–80.

Oberwallney, Stefan. *SA in Berlin. Die Realität des Straßenkampfes 1926–1933.* MS diss., Free University Berlin 1993.

Obst, Dieter. *"Reichskristallnacht." Ursachen und Verlauf des antisemitischen Pogroms vom November 1938.* Frankfurt a. M., et al., 1991.

Oertel, Thomas. *Horst Wessel. Untersuchung einer Legende.* Cologne, 1988.

Ottmer, Hans-Martin. *"Weserübung." Der deutsche Angriff auf Dänemark und Norwegen im April 1940.* Munich, 1994.

Oven, Wilfried von. *Mit Goebbels bis zum Ende,* 2 vols. Buenos Aires, 1949–50.

Overmans, Rüdiger. *Deutsche militärische Verluste im Zweiten Weltkrieg.* Munich, 1999.

Pätzold, Kurt, and Manfred Weissbecker. *Rudolf Heß. Der Mann an Hitlers Seite.* Leipzig, 1999.

Pätzold, Kurt. "Hitlers fünfzigster Geburtstag am 20. April 1939," in Dietrich Eichholtz and Kurt Pätzold, eds., *Der Weg in den Krieg. Studien zur Geschichte der Vorkriegsjahre (1935/36 bis 1939).* Cologne, 1989: 309–46.

Panse, Barbara. "Zeitgenössische Dramatik," in Thomas Eicher et al., *Theater im "Dritten Reich." Theaterpolitik, Spielplanstruktur, NS-Dramatik.* Seelze-Velber, 2000: 489–720.

Paul, Gerhard. *Aufstand der Bilder. Die NS-Propaganda vor 1933.* Bonn, 1990.

———. *"Deutsche Mutter–heim zu Dir!" Warum es mißlang, Hitler an der Saar zu schlagen. Der Saarkampf 1933–1935.* Cologne, 1984.

Pauley, Bruce F. *Der Weg in den Nationalsozialismus. Ursprünge und Entwicklung in Österreich.* Vienna, 1988.

Permooser, Irmtraut. *Der Luftkrieg über München. Bomben auf die Hauptstadt der Bewegung.* Oberhaching, 1997.

Petersen, Jens. *Hitler–Mussolini. Die Entstehung der Achse Berlin–Rom 1933–1936.* Tübingen, 1973.

Petzold, Joachim. *Franz von Papen. Ein deutsches Verhängnis.* Munich/Berlin, 1995.

Pietrow-Ennker, Bianka, ed. *Präventivkrieg? Der deutsche Angriff auf die Sowjetunion.* Frankfurt a. M., 2000.

Piper, Ernst. *Alfred Rosenberg. Hitlers Chefideologe.* Munich, 2005.

Plehwe, Friedrich-Karl von. *Reichskanzler Kurt von Schleicher. Weimars letzte Chance gegen Hitler.* Berlin, 1990.

Podewin, Norbert, and Lutz Heuer. *Ernst Torgler. Ein Leben im Schatten des Reichstagsbrandes: 25. April 1893 Berlin–19. Januar 1963 Hannover.* Hanover/Berlin, 2006.

Poetsch-Heffter, Fritz. "Vom Staatsleben unter der Weimarer Verfassung," in *Jahrbuch des öffentlichen Rechts der Gegenwart*, vol. 21 (1933–34): 102ff.

Portmann, Heinrich. *Der Bischof von Münster*. Münster, 1947.

Presse in Fesseln. Eine Schilderung des NS-Pressetrusts. Berlin, 1947.

Prieberg, Fred K. *Kraftprobe. Wilhelm Furtwängler im Dritten Reich.* Wiesbaden, 1986.

———. *Musik im NS-Staat*. Frankfurt a. M., 1982.

Pünder, Hermann. *Politik in der Reichskanzlei. Aufzeichnungen aus den Jahren 1929–1932.* Thilo Vogelsang, ed. Stuttgart, 1961.

Pyta, Wolfram. *Hindenburg. Herrschaft zwischen Hohenzollern und Hitler.* Munich, 2007.

Raem, Heinz-Albert. *Pius XI. und der Nationalsozialismus–die Enzyklika "Mit brennender Sorge" vom 14. März 1937.* Paderborn/Munich/Vienna/Zurich, 1979.

Ramm, Arnim. *Der 20. Juli 1944 vor dem Volksgerichtshof.* Berlin, 2007.

Rave, Paul Ortwin. *Kunstdiktatur im Dritten Reich.* Hamburg, 1949.

Rebentisch, Dieter. *Führerstaat und Verwaltung im Zweiten Weltkrieg. Verfassungsentwicklung und Verfassungspolitik, 1939–1945.* Stuttgart, 1989.

Reif, Janin, Horst Schumacher, and Lothar Uebel. *Schwanenwerder. Ein Inselparadies in Berlin.* Berlin, 2000.

Reimann, Viktor. *Dr. Joseph Goebbels.* Vienna, 1971. 2nd ed., Vienna/Munich, 1978.

Reimer, Klaus. *Rheinlandfrage und Rheinlandbewegung (1918–1933). Ein Beitrag zur Geschichte der regionalistischen Bestrebungen in Deutschland.* Frankfurt a. M., et al. 1979.

Reinhardt, Dirk. *Von der Reklame zum Marketing. Geschichte der Wirtschaftswerbung in Deutschland.* Berlin, 1993.

Reschke, Oliver. *Der Kampf der Nationalsozialisten um den roten Friedrichshain 1925–1933.* Berlin, 2004.

Reuband, Karl-Heinz. " 'Jud Süß' und 'Der Ewige Jude' als Prototypen antisemitischer Filmpropaganda im Dritten Reich. Entstehungsbedingungen, Zuschauerstrukturen und Wirkungspotential," in Michal Anděl et al., eds., *Propaganda, (Selbst-) Zensur, Sensation. Grenzen von Presse-und Wissenschaftsfreiheit in Deutschland und Tschechien seit 1871.* Essen, 2005: 89–148.

Reuth, Ralf Georg. *Goebbels.* Munich/Zurich, 1990.

———. *Joseph Goebbels, Tagebücher 1924–1945.* Munich/Zurich, 1992.

Richardi, Hans-Günter. *Bomber über München. Der Luftkrieg von 1939 bis 1945, dargestellt am Beispiel der "Hauptstadt der Bewegung."* Munich, 1992.

Riefenstahl, Leni. *Memoiren.* Munich/Hamburg, 1987.

Riess, Curt. *Goebbels. Eine Biographie.* Baden-Baden, 1950.

Rischbieter, Henning. "NS-Theaterpolitik," in Thomas Eicher et al., *Theater im "Dritten Reich." Theaterpolitik, Spielplanstruktur, NS-Dramatik.* Seelze-Velber, 2000.

Römer, Felix. *Der Kommissarbefehl. Wehrmacht und NS-Verbrechen an der Ostfront 1941/42.* Paderborn et al., 2008.

Rönnefarth, Helmuth. *Auswirkung.* Wiesbaden, 1961.

Roseman, Mark. *Die Wannsee-Konferenz. Wie die Bürokratie den Holocaust organisierte.* Munich/Berlin, 2002.

Rosenkranz, Herbert. *Verfolgung und Selbstbehauptung. Die Juden in Österreich, 1938–1945.* Vienna, 1978.

Rossino, Alexander B. *Hitler Strikes Poland: Blitzkrieg, Ideology, and Atrocity.* Lawrence, Kan., 2003.

———. "Nazi Anti-Jewish Policy During the Polish Campaign: The Case of the Einsatzgruppe von Woyrisch," *GSR* 24 (2001): 35–54.

Roth, Karl Heinz. "Filmpropaganda für die Vernichtung der Geisteskranken und Behinderten im 'Dritten Reich,'" in *Reform und Gewissen. "Euthanasie" im Dienst des Fortschritts.* Berlin, 1985: 125–93.

Rother, Rainer. *Leni Riefenstahl. Die Verführung des Talents.* Berlin, 2000.

Rühle, Günther. *Theater in Deutschland 1887–1945. Seine Ereignisse, seine Menschen.* Frankfurt a. M., 2007.

Sabrow, Martin. "Der 'Tag von Potsdam'—Zur Karriere eines politischen Symbols," in *Der Tag von Potsdam. Bildungsforum und Schülerprojekt.* Landtag Brandenburg, ed. Potsdam, 2003: 91–104.

Sänger, Fritz. *Politik der Täuschungen. Missbrauch der Presse im Dritten Reich. Weisungen, Informationen, Notizen, 1933–1939.* Vienna, 1975.

Sauer, Wolfgang. "Die Mobilmachung der Gewalt," in Wolfgang Sauer, Gerhard Schulz, and Karl-Dietrich Bracher, *Die nationalso-*

zialistische Machtergreifung. Studien zur Errichtung des totalitären Herrschaftssystems in Deutschland. Frankfurt a. M./Berlin/Vienna, 1960: 685–972.

Schaeffers, Willi. Tingel Tangel. Ein Leben für die Kleinkunst. Hamburg, 1959.

Schaumburg-Lippe, Friedrich Cristian Prinz zu. Dr. G. Ein Porträt des Propagandaministers. Wiesbaden, 1963.

Schausberger, Norbert. Nationalsozialismus in Wien. Machtübernahme, Herrschaftssicherung, Radikalisierung 1938/39. Vienna, 2008.

———. Der Griff nach Österreich. Der Anschluß. Vienna/Munich, 1978.

Scheel, Klaus. Der Tag von Potsdam. Berlin, 1996.

Scheer, Regina. Im Schatten der Sterne. Eine jüdische Widerstandsgruppe. Berlin, 2004.

Scheffler, Wolfgang. "Der Brandanschlag im Berliner Lustgarten im Mai 1942 und seine Folgen," in Berlin in Geschichte und Gegenwart, Jahrbuch des Landesarchivs. Berlin, 1984: 91–118.

Scheil, Stefan. Churchill, Hitler und der Antisemitismus. Die deutsche Diktatur, ihre politischen Gegner und die europäische Krise der Jahre 1938/39. Berlin, 2008.

Schieder, Wolfgang. "Faschismus im politischen Transfer. Giuseppe Renzetti als faschistischer Propagandist und Geheimagent in Berlin 1922–1941," in Sven Reinhardt and Armin Nolzen, eds., Faschismus in Italien und Deutschland. Studien zu Transfer und Vergleich. Göttingen, 2005: 28–58.

———. "Spanischer Bürgerkrieg und Vierjahresplan. Zur Struktur nationalsozialistischer Außenpolitik," in Wolfgang Michalka, ed., Nationalsozialistische Außenpolitik. Darmstadt, 1978: 325–59.

Schildt, Axel. Militärdiktatur mit Massenbasis? Die Querfrontkonzeption der Reichswehrführung um General von Schleicher am Ende der Weimarer Republik. Frankfurt a. M., et al., 1981.

Schildt, Gerhard. Die Arbeitsgemeinschaft Nord-West. Untersuchungen zur Geschichte der NSDAP 1925/26. MS diss., Freiburg, 1964.

Schirach, Baldur von. Ich glaubte an Hitler. Hamburg/Zurich, 1967.

Schirach, Henriette von. Der Preis der Herrlichkeit. Erinnerungen. Munich, 1978.

Schirmann, Léon. Altonaer Blutsonntag 17. Juli 1932. Dichtungen und Wahrheit. Hamburg, 1994.

Schlafranek, Hans. *Sommerfest und Preisschießen. Die unbekannte Geschichte des NS-Putsches im Jahre 1934.* Vienna, 2006.

Schlemmer, Martin. *"Los von Berlin": Die Rheinstaatbestrebungen nach dem Ersten Weltkrieg.* Cologne, 2007.

Schlenker, Ines. *Hitlers Salon. The Große Deutsche Kunstausstellung at the Haus der Deutschen Kunst in Munich 1937–1944.* Oxford et al., 2007.

Schmidt, Dietmar. *Martin Niemöller. Eine Biographie.* Stuttgart, 1983.

Schmidt, Klaus. *Die Brandnacht. Dokumente von der Zerstörung Darmstadts am 11. September 1944,* 6th ed. Darmstadt, 1964.

Schmidt, Paul. *Statist auf diplomatischer Bühne. Erlebnisse des Chefdolmetschers im Auswärtigen Amt mit den Staatsmännern Europas.* Bonn, 1953.

Schmidt, Rainer F. *Rudolf Heß. "Botengang eines Toren"? Der Flug nach Großbritannien vom 10. Mai 1941,* 2nd ed. Munich, 2000.

Schmitz, Hubert. *Die Bewirtschaftung der Nahrungsmittel und Verbrauchsgüter 1939–1950, dargestellt am Beispiel der Stadt Essen.* Essen, 1956.

Schmuhl, Hans-Walter. *Rassenhygiene, Nationalsozialismus, Euthanasie. Von der Verhütung zur Vernichtung "lebensunwerten Lebens," 1890–1945.* Göttingen, 1987.

Schönherr, Klaus. "Der Rückzug der Heeresgruppe A über die Krim bis Rumänien," in Karl-Heinz Frieser, ed., *Die Ostfront 1943/44. Der Krieg im Osten und an den Nebenfronten.* Munich, 2007: 451–90.

Schramm, Percy Ernst, ed. *Kriegstagebuch des Oberkommandos der Wehrmacht (Wehrmachtführungsstab),* 4 vols. Frankfurt a. M., 1961–1965.

Schreiber, Gerhard. "Das Ende des nordafrikanischen Feldzugs und der Krieg in Italien," in Karl-Heinz Frieser, ed., *Die Ostfront 1943/44. Der Krieg im Osten und an den Nebenfronten.* Munich, 2007: 1101–62.

Schreiner, Klaus. "'Wann kommt der Retter Deutschlands?' Formen und Funktionen von politischem Messianismus in der Weimarer Republik," *Saeculum* 49 (1998): 107–60.

Schröder, Josef. *Italiens Kriegsaustritt 1943. Die deutschen Gegenmaßnahmen im italienischen Raum: Fall "Alarich" und "Achse."* Göttingen, 1969.

Schug, Alexander. "Hitler als Designobjekt und Marke. Die Rezeption des Werbegedankens durch die NSDAP bis 1933/34," in Hartmut Berghoff, ed., *Marketinggeschichte. Die Genese einer modernen Sozialtechnik.* Frankfurt a. M./New York, 2007: 325–45.

Schulz, Gerhard. *Von Brüning zu Hitler. Der Wandel des politischen Systems in Deutschland 1930–1933.* Berlin/New York, 1992.

Schulze, Hagen. *Weimar. Deutschland 1917–1933.* Berlin, 1982.

Schüren, Ulrich. *Der Volksentscheid zur Fürstenenteignung 1926. Die Vermögensauseinandersetzung mit den depossedierten Landesherren als Problem der deutschen Innenpolitik unter besonderer Berücksichtigung der Verhältnisse in Preußen.* Düsseldorf, 1978.

Schwarzenbeck, Engelbert. *Nationalsozialistische Pressepolitik und die Sudetenkrise 1938.* Munich, 1979.

Semmler, Rudolf. *Goebbels: The Man Next to Hitler.* London, 1947.

Siemens, Daniel. *Horst Wessel. Tod und Verklärung eines Nationalsozialisten.* Munich, 2009.

Silex, Karl. *Mit Kommentar. Lebensbericht eines Journalisten.* Frankfurt a. M., 1968.

Smelser, Ronald. *Das Sudetenproblem und das Dritte Reich (1933–1938). Von der Volkstumspolitik zur nationalsozialistischen Außenpolitik.* Munich et al., 1980.

Smith, Bradley F. "Die Überlieferung der Hoßbach-Niederschrift im Lichte neuer Quellen," *VfZ* 38 (1990): 329–36.

Sodeikat, Ernst. "Der Nationalsoialismus und die Danziger Opposition," *VfZ* 14 (1966): 139–74.

Sontheimer, Kurt. *Antidemokratisches Denken in der Weimarer Republik. Die politischen Ideen des deutschen Nationalismus zwischen 1918 und 1933.* Munich, 1968.

Speer, Albert. *Inside the Third Reich: Memoirs.* New York, 1970.

Springer, Hildegard. *Es sprach Hans Fritzsche. Nach Gesprächen, Briefen und Dokumenten.* Stuttgart, 1949.

Steinert, Marlis G. *Hitlers Krieg und die Deutschen. Stimmung und Haltung der deutschen Bevölkerung im Zweiten Weltkrieg.* Düsseldorf/Vienna, 1970.

Steinweis, Alan. *Art, Ideology, and Economics in Nazi Germany: The Reich Chamber of Music, Theater, and the Visual Arts.* Chapel Hill/London, 1993.

Stephan, Werner. *Joseph Goebbels. Dämon einer Diktatur.* Stuttgart, 1949.

Sternburg, Wilhelm von. "Es ist eine unheimliche Stimmung in Deutschland." *Karl von Ossietzky und seine Zeit.* Berlin, 1996.

Stourzh, Gerhard, and Brigitta Zaar, eds. *Österreich, Deutschland und die Mächte. Internationale und österreichische Aspekte des "Anschlusses" vom März 1936*. Vienna, 1990.

Strauss, Richard, and Stefan Zweig. *Briefwechsel*. Willi Schuh, ed. Frankfurt a. M., 1957.

Strenge, Irene. *Kurt von Schleicher. Politik im Reichswehrministerium am Ende der Weimarer Republik*. Berlin, 2006.

Stumpf, Reinhard. "Die alliierte Landung in Nordwestafrika und der Rückzug der Deutsch-italienischen Panzerarmee nach Tunesien," in Horst Boog et al., *Der globale Krieg. Die Ausweitung zum Weltkrieg und der Wechsel der Initiative 1941 bis 1943*. Stuttgart, 1990: 710–57.

Süss, Winfried. *Der "Volkskörper" im Krieg. Gesundheitspolitik, Gesundheitsverhältnisse und Krankenmord im nationalsozialistischen Deutschland 1939–1945*. Munich, 2003.

Sywottek, Jutta. *Mobilmachung für den totalen Krieg. Die propagandistische Vorbereitung der deutschen Bevölkerung auf den Zweiten Weltkrieg*. Opladen, 1976.

Tegel, Susan. *Jew Süss/Jud Süss*. Trowbridge, 1996.

Teppe, Karl. *Massenmord auf dem Dienstweg. Hitlers "Euthanasie"-Erlass und seine Durchführung in den Westfälischen Provinzialanstalten*. Münster, 1989.

Thacker, Toby. *Joseph Goebbels: Life and Death*. Houndmills, 2009.

Thamer, Hans Ulrich. *Verführung und Gewalt. Deutschland 1933–1945*. Berlin, 1986.

Thielenhaus, Marion. *Zwischen Anpassung und Widerstand: Deutsche Diplomaten 1938–1941. Die politischen Aktivitäten der Beamtengruppe um Ernst von Weizsäcker im Auswärtigen Amt*. Paderborn, 1985.

Tobias, Fritz. *Der Reichstagsbrand—Legende und Wirklichkeit*. Rastatt, 1962.

Trimborn, Jürgen. *Riefenstahl. Eine deutsche Karriere*. Berlin, 2002.

Turner, Henry Ashby. "The Myth of Chancellor von Schleicher's Querfront Strategy," *CEH* 41 (2008): 673–81.

———. *Die Großunternehmer und der Aufstieg Hitlers*. Berlin, 1985.

Tyrell, Albrecht. "Führergedanke und Gauleiterwechsel. Die Teilung des Gaues Rheinland der NSDAP 1931," *VfZ* 23 (1975): 341–74.

Ueberschär, Gerd R. *Freiburg im Luftkrieg, 1939–1945. Mit einer*

Photodokumentation zur Zerstörung der Altstadt am 27. November 1944. Freiburg/Würzburg, 1990.

Umbreit, Hans. "Der Kampf um die Vormachtstellung in Westeuropa," in Klaus A. Maier et al., *Die Errichtung der Hegemonie auf dem europäischen Kontinent.* Stuttgart, 1979: 235–327.

Ungváry, Krisztián. "Kriegsschauplatz Ungarn," in Karl-Heinz Frieser, ed., *Die Ostfront 1943/44. Der Krieg im Osten und an den Nebenfronten.* Munich, 2007: 849–958.

Uziel, Daniel. *The Propaganda Warriors: The Wehrmacht and the Consolidation of the German Home Front.* Bern, 2008.

Vogel, Detlef. "Das Eingreifen Deutschlands auf dem Balkan," in Gerhard Schreiber, Bernd Stegemann, and Detlef Vogel, *Der Mittelmeerraum und Südosteuropa. Von der "non-belligeranza" Italiens bis zum Kriegseintritt der Vereinigten Staaten.* Stuttgart, 1984: 417–511.

Vogelsang, Thilo. *Reichswehr, Staat und NSDAP.* Stuttgart, 1962.

Voigt, Gerhard. "Goebbels als Markentechniker," in Wolfgang Fritz Haug, ed., *Warenästhetik. Beiträge zur Diskussion, Weiterentwicklung und Vermittlung ihrer Kritik.* Frankfurt a. M., 1975: 231–60.

Voigt, Hans-Gunter. *Jüdisches Leben und Holocaust im Filmdokument 1930 bis 1945,* MS diss., Koblenz, 2000.

Völker, Karl-Heinz. *Die deutsche Luftwaffe 1933–1939. Aufbau, Führung und Rüstung der Luftwaffe sowie die Entwicklung der deutschen Luftkriegstheorie.* Stuttgart, 1967.

Volsansky, Gabriele. *Pakt auf Zeit. Das Deutsch-Österreichische Juli-Abkommen 1936.* Vienna/Cologne/Weimar, 2001.

Vorländer, Herwart. *Die NSV. Darstellung und Dokumentation einer nationalsozialistischen Organisation.* Boppard a. Rh., 1988.

Vysny, Paul. *The Runciman Mission to Czechoslovakia, 1938: Prelude to Munich.* Houndmills/New York, 2003.

Wagener, Otto. *Hitler aus nächster Nähe. Aufzeichnungen eines Vertrauten 1929–1932.* Henry Ashby Turner, ed. 2nd ed. Kiel, 1978.

Waldecker, Christoph. "Rheydt 1815–1974," *Loca Desiderata,* vol. 3/1. Cologne, 2003: 241–372.

Walter, Dirk. *Antisemitische Kriminalität und Gewalt. Judenfeindschaft in der Weimarer Republik.* Bonn, 1999.

Wambach, Lovis Maxim. *"Es ist gleichgültig woran wir glauben, nur daß wir glauben." Bemerkungen zu Joseph Goebbels' Drama "Judas Iscariot" und zu seinen "Michael-Romanen."* Bremen, n.d.

Warlimont, Walter. *Im Hauptquartier der deutschen Wehmacht 1939–1945. Grundlagen–Formen–Gestalten*, vol. 1. Augsburg, 1990.

Weber, Wolfram. *Die Innere Sicherheit im besetzten Belgien und Nordfrankreich, 1940–1944. Ein Beitrag zur Geschichte der Besatzungsverwaltungen*. Düsseldorf, 1978: 59ff.

Wedel, Hasso von. *Die Propagandatruppen der Deutschen Wehrmacht*. Neckargemünd, 1962.

Wegner, Bernd. "Das Kriegsende in Skandinavien," in Karl-Heinz Frieser et al., eds., *Die Ostfront 1943/44. Der Krieg im Osten und an den Nebenfronten*. Munich, 2007: 961–1008.

Wegner, Bernd. "Der Krieg gegen die Sowjetunion 1942/43," in Horst Boog et al., eds., *Der globale Krieg. Die Ausweitung zum Weltkrieg und der Wechsel der Initiative 1941 bis 1943*. Stuttgart, 1990: 761–1102.

Weinberg, Gerhard. "Die deutsche Außenpolitik und Österreich 1937/38," in Gerald Stourzh and Brigitta Zaar, eds., *Österreich, Deutschland und die Mächte. Internationale und österreichische Aspekte des "Anschlusses' vom März 1938."* Vienna, 1990: 61–74.

Weiss, Hermann, and Paul Hoser, eds. *Die Deutschnationalen und die Zerstörung der Weimarer Republik. Aus dem Tagebuch von Reinhold Quaatz 1928–1933*. Munich, 1989. Monograph series for *Vierteljahrshefte für Zeitgeschichte* 59.

Welch, David. *Propaganda and the German Cinema, 1933–1945*. London, 2001.

Westphal, Uwe. *Berliner Konfektion und Mode, 1836–1939. Die Zerstörung einer Tradition*. Berlin, 1986.

———. *Werbung im Dritten Reich*. Berlin, 1989.

Wiechert, Ernst. *"Der Totenwald." Ein Bericht*, in *Sämtliche Werke*, vol. 9. Vienna/Munich/Basel, 1957.

Wiggershaus, Norbert Theodor. *Der deutsch-englische Flottenvertrag vom 18. Juni 1935. England und die geheime deutsche Aufrüstung 1933–1935*. MS diss., Bonn, 1972.

Winker, Klaus. *Fernsehen unterm Hakenkreuz. Organisation, Programm, Personal*. Cologne/Weimar/Vienna, 1994.

Winkler, Heinrich August. *Weimar 1918–1933. Die Geschichte der ersten deutschen Demokratie*. Munich, 1993.

———. *Der Weg in die Katastrophe. Arbeiter und Arbeiterbewegung in der Weimarer Republik 1930 bis 1933*. Berlin/Bonn, 1987.

Wittmann, Manfred. "Das 'Gästehaus'—eine Episode in der Geschichte von Schloß Rheydt 1917–1945," *Rheydter Jahrbuch für Geschichte, Kunst und Heimatkunde* 21 (1994): 27–68.

Woller, Hans. *Die Abrechnung mit dem Faschismus in Italien 1943 bis 1948.* Munich, 1996.

Wörtz, Ulrich. *Programmatik und Führerprinzip: Das Problem des Strasser-Kreises in der NSDAP. Eine historisch-politische Studie zum Verhältnis von sachlichem Programm und persönlicher Führung in einer totalitären Bewegung,* diss. Erlangen, 1966.

Ziegler, Walter, ed. *Die kirchliche Lage in Bayern nach den Regierungspräsidentenberichten 1933–1943,* vol. 4: *Regierungsbezirk Niederbayern und Oberpfalz.* Mainz, 1973.

Ziegler, Walter. "Der Kampf um die Schulkreuze im Dritten Reich," in *Das Kreuz im Widerspruch. Der Kruzifix-Beschluss des Bundesverfassungsgerichts in der Kontroverse.* Hans Maier, ed. Freiburg/Basel/Vienna, 1996: 40–51.

Zuschlag, Christoph. *"Entartete Kunst." Ausstellungsstrategien im Nazi-Deutschland.* Worms, 1995.

Zweite, Armin. "Franz Hoffmann und die Städtische Galerie," in *Die "Kunststadt" München 1937. Nationalsozialismus und "Entartete Kunst."* Peter-Klaus Schuster, ed. Munich, 1987: 261–88.

NOTES

A (with newspapers): *Abendausgabe,* evening edition

A (with BAK, ZSg): evening briefing

AA: Auswärtiges Amt (foreign office)

ADAP: *Akten zur deutschen Außenpolitik 1938–1945. Aus dem Archiv des Auswärtigen Amtes.* Series C: 1933–1937, 6 vols. (Göttingen, 1973–1981). Series D: 1937–1941, 13 vols. (Göttingen, 1950–1961). Series E: 1941–1945, 8 vols. (Göttingen, 1969–1979).

BAB: Bundesarchiv, Berlin

BAK: Bundesarchiv, Koblenz

BAM: Bundesarchiv/Militärarchiv, Freiburg

BHStA: Bayerisches Hauptstaatsarchiv, Munich

BK: Boelcke, Willi A. (ed.), *Kriegspropaganda 1939–1941. Geheime Ministerkonferenzen im Reichspropagandaministerium* (Stuttgart, 1966).

BT: *Berliner Tageblatt*

BW: Boelcke, Willi A. (ed.), *Wollt Ihr den totalen Krieg? Die geheimen Goebbels-Konferenzen 1939–1943* (Stuttgart, 1967).

DAZ: *Deutsche Allgemeine Zeitung*

Domarus: Hitler, Adolf, *Reden und Proklamationen 1932–1945. Kommentiert von einem deutschen Zeitgenossen,* ed. Max Domarus, 2 vols., Neustadt a. d. Aisch 1963

E (with BAK, ZSg): Supplement

FZ: *Frankfurter Zeitung*

hs: *handschriftlich* (manuscript)

IMT: *International Military Tribunal: Der Prozess gegen die Hauptkriegsverbrecher vor dem Internationalen Militärgerichtshof, 14. Oktober 1945 bis 1. Oktober 1946,* 42 vols. (Nuremberg, 1947–1949)

LA Berlin: Landesarchiv Berlin

M (with newspapers): *Morgenausgabe* (morning edition).

M (with BAK, ZSg): midday briefing

MK: Osobyi Archive, Moscow/Moskauer Sonderarchiv (OA Moskau), Bestand 1363-3: Die geheimen Goebbels-Konferenzen 1939–1943.

MNN: *Münchner Neueste Nachrichten*

NS-Briefe: *Nationalsozialistische Briefe*

NSDAP: Nationalsozialistische Deutsche Arbeiterpartei

OKH: Oberkommando des Heeres (army high command)

OKW: Oberkommando der Wehrmacht (armed forces high command)

OKW: *KTB Kriegstagebuch des Oberkommandos der Wehrmacht 1940–1945,* kept by Helmuth Greiner and Percy E. Schramm. Vol. 1: *1. August 1940–31. Dezember 1941* (Frankfurt a. M., 1965); vol. 4: *1. Januar 1944–22. Mai 1945* (Frankfurt a. M., 1961.)

*PA: Presseanweisung des Reichsministeriums für Volksaufklärung und
Propaganda*

PAA: Politisches Archiv des Auswärtigen Amtes

RGBl: Reichsgesetzblatt

Recht RKK: *Das Recht der Reichskulturkammer. Sammlung der für den
Kulturstand geltenden Gesetze und Verordnungen, der amtlichen
Anordnungen und Bekanntmachungen der Reichskulturkammer
und ihrer Einzelkammern.* Im Einvernehmen mit der Hauptges-
chäftsführung der Reichskulturkammer, Karl-Dietrich Schrieber,
Alfred Metten, and Herbert Collatz (eds.), 2 vols. (Berlin, 1943).

RKK: Reichskulturkammer

RPL: Reichpropagandaleitung

RSA: Hitler, Adolf, *Reden, Schriften, Anordnungen. Februar 1925 bis
Januar 1933,* ed. Institut für Zeitgeschichte (Munich, 1991–2000).

RSHA: Reichsicherheitshauptamt

SD: Sicherheitsdienst der SS

SOPADE: *Deutschland-Berichte der Sozialdemokratischen Partei
Deutschlands (SOPADE) 1934–1940,* ed. Klaus Behnken, 7 annual
volumes as a reprint (Salzhausen/Frankfurt a. M., 1980).

TB: *Die Tagebücher von Joseph Goebbels* (Goebbels' diaries), ed. Elke
Fröhlich, 32 vols. (Munich, 1993–2008).

TP: *Tagesparole* (daily slogan)

UWW: Unser Wille und Weg

VB: *Völkischer Beobachter,* with various editions: Berlin (B),
Munich (M) Nuremberg (N), Reich (R)

VF: *Völkische Freiheit*

VfZ: Vierteljahrshefte für Zeitgeschichte

VI: *Vertrauliche Information* (confidential information)

VZ: *Vossische Zeitung*

WLZ: *Westdeutsche Landeszeitung*

ZfG: *Zeitschrift für Geschichtswissenschaft*

PROLOGUE

1. Bezymenskij, *Der Tod des Adolf Hitler* (1982), 128ff. (Dolmatowski statement, 129ff.).
2. O'Donnell and Bahnsen, *Die Katakombe*, 229.
3. *OKW KTB*, 2, 1468f.
4. Heiber (ed.), *Goebbels Reden 1932–1945*, no. 30, 435.
5. *Das Reich*, 15 April 1945.
6. Bezymenskij, *Der Tod des Adolf Hitler* (1982), 209ff.; Kunz interrogation of 7 May 1945 and p. 212f. of 19 May 1945.
7. Goebbels, *Tagebücher 1945*, 547f.; Farewell letter to Harald, 28 April 1945.
8. Ibid., 549f.
9. Bezymenskij, *Der Tod des Adolf Hitler* (1968), 111ff., 116ff. Postmortem reports for Joseph and Magda Goebbels, 9 May 1945. According to these, both corpses showed signs of poisoning from capsules.
10. LA Berlin, B Rep. 058, Nr. 6012, Statement by Günther Schwägermann, Hanover, 16 February 1948. According to the Soviet postmortem report, there were no bullet wounds in their bodies, but this may be attributed to the condition of the corpses following their incineration.
11. See in particular Bärsch, *Der junge Goebbels*, and recently also Gathmann and Paul, *Narziss Goebbels*. For an assessment of these books, see "Comments on Sources and Research Literature" in the appendix; on the phenomenon of narcissism, see 30ff.
12. Elke Fröhlich (ed.), *Die Tagebücher von Joseph Goebbels*, 32 vols. in three parts (Munich 1993–2008). The last volume of text appeared in 2006. Hereafter referred to as TB.
13. Goebbels was planning a two-volume book on Hitler. He wrote the first volume in November and December 1938, in other words at the height of his marital crisis, and gave it the working title "Adolf Hitler: A Man Who Is Making History." But in January 1939 Amann informed him that the work—according to Goebbels it was already finished—could not appear in the publisher Eher's list in the near future. TB, 13–30 November, numerous entries about his work on the manuscript, and on 17 January 1938. He was doing preparatory work on the second volume, the war period, in August 1941. He intended to work on it during the war and hoped to be able to "put it in the hands of the public" shortly after the end of the war. TB, 31 August 1941.

1. "RINGS A SONG ETERNALLY / FROM YOUTH'S HAPPY HOURS"

1. "Erinnerungsblätter," in *Die Tagebücher von Joseph Goebbels. Sämtliche Fragmente,* Elke Fröhlich (ed.), 1, 29. On its origins, see 60; on the edition, see note 5.
2. "Erinnerungsblätter," 26–28.
3. "Erinnerungsblätter," 27. On the crisis of 1923, see Winkler, *Weimar 1918–1933,* 186ff.; Longerich, *Deutschland 1918–1933,* 131ff.
4. "Erinnerungsblätter," 27.
5. Published in *Die Tagebücher von Joseph Goebbels. Sämtliche Fragmente,* Elke Fröhlich (ed.), vol. 1, 1–29.
6. "Erinnerungsblätter," 1. For details on the family history, see Reuth, *Goebbels,* 12f.
7. Compilation of the dates of the members of the Goebbels family by the Stadtarchiv Mönchengladbach on the basis of registration documents.
8. "Erinnerungsblätter," 1. According to the Mönchengladbach city archive (StA MG), Goebbels was born at Odenkirchener Strasse 186 (now 202). About two years after Goebbels's birth they moved to an apartment in Dahlener Strasse. Shortly afterward Fritz Goebbels bought Dahlener Strasse 140 (later 156). StA MG, *Hausbuch 25c/8752.* See also "Dr. Joseph Goebbels, 1897–1945," *Rheydter Jahrbuch* 10 (1973): 86–93.
9. "Erinnerungsblätter," 2. On his childhood and youth, see Reuth, *Goebbels,* 14ff.; Thacker, *Joseph Goebbels,* 10ff.
10. Bezymenskij, *Der Tod des Adolf Hitler,* 33f. According to the Soviet postmortem report of 9 May 1945, his right foot was bent so sharply inward that it was almost at a right angle to the bone of his lower calf. The right foot was swollen and 3.5 cm shorter than the left one, the right lower calf 4.5 cm shorter.
11. "Erinnerungsblätter," 2.
12. "Erinnerungsblätter," 3.
13. "Erinnerungsblätter," 4; BAK, NL 1118/113, school reports from the years 1912–1916. Goebbels received the mark "very good" on three occasions in these subjects.
14. NL 1118/126, Bl. 148–201, "Michael Voormanns Jugendjahre I. Teil." A Part III has also survived. See Michel, *Vom Poeten zum Demagogen.*
15. At the beginning of 1929, in some of the few entries in his diary he complains about his foot. He had been suffering for weeks, his handicap was simply "disgusting"; they must fit a new caliper; on the fitting of a new caliper, see TB, 26 and 29 January, 5 February 1929. In November 1931 he noted that he had had a new "apparatus" constructed by a Berlin orthopedic workshop; TB, 12 and 27 November 1931. It was the Franz Gstattenbauer workshop at Kurfürstenstrasse 45 *(Berliner Adreßbuch 1931).* 18 August 1934: "Thursday: a lot of pain in my foot. Didn't go out." 13 September 1935: "My foot is swollen. Have to lie in bed. The days here are very tiring."
16. Kernberg, *Narzisstische Persönlichkeitsstörungen* and *Borderline-Störungen und pathologischer Narzissmus;* Kohut, *Narzißmus.*
17. Fritz Prang, Herbert Beines, Hubert Hompesch, Willy Zille. Herbert Lennartz, however, died in 1912. Goebbels dedicated his first (surviving) poem to him. Another friend, Ernst Heynen, who had joined the Army, died in 1918. StA MG, NL Goebbels 54, 49.
18. "Erinnerungsblätter," 4. Voss was evidently the model for the teacher, Förder, in "Michael Voormann."

19. "Erinnerungsblätter," 4.

20. BAK, NL 1118/129 contains postcards from the front to Goebbels from, among others, Willy Zilles, Hubert Offergeld, and Brother Konrad.

21. 2 December 1915, StA MG, register of burials in the Catholic parish of St. Mary's in Rheydt.

22. BAK, NL 1118/117, "How can the noncombatant serve his fatherland during this period" (1914); Goebbels, *Das Lied im Kriege* (1915); "Erinnerungsblätter," 4.

23. BAK, NL 1118/120, In Memory of Hans Richter, Gerhard Bartels, including J. G., *Gerhardi Bartels manibus*, Munich, 6 December 1919.

24. BAK, NL 1118/126.

25. "Erinnerungsblätter," 5; letters from Lene Krage from the years 1916 to 1920 are in BAK, NL 1118/112.

26. "Erinnerungsblätter," 5. He took an apartment in Koblenzerstrasse: StA MG, NL Goebbels/16, Kollegienheft. On his semesters in Bonn, see Reuth, *Goebbels*, 29ff. On his student years in general, see Thacker, *Goebbels*, 17ff.

27. "Erinnerungsblätter," 5. Thus it is mentioned in reports on the fraternity written by Pilli Kölsch that Goebbels was "initiated" at the beginning of the semester. *Unitas, Organ des Verbandes der wissenschaftlichen katholischen Studentenvereine,* vol. 57, no. 5, June 1917, p. 227, available in BAK, NL 1118/119.

28. Raabe-Abend, *Unitas,* 57/6, August 1917, Kölsch report. StA MG, NL Goebbels/56, "Wilhelm Raabe and Us," speech, 24 June 1917. The speech was based on preliminary studies from 1916: StA MG, NL Goebbels/55: Raabe had "been misjudged by the whole of Germany." He had worked for a "later generation." "Are we that generation? I don't think so." Also 56, later version. On 26 July 1916 he also expressed his admiration for Raabe in a letter to his friend Willy Zilles, who was in a military hospital: StA MG, NL Goebbels/41. See also Reuth, *Goebbels,* 24.

29. *Unitas,* 57/6, August 1917, Kölsch report; 58/2, December 1917, p. 68, Goebbels report and 58/3, February 1918, p. 120, Goebbels report.

30. He informed the Magnus-Verein that he "was called up for military office services at the end of June" but had now been released (BAK, NL 1118/113, letter of 14 September 1917), also published in Fraenkel and Manvell, *Goebbels,* 32. "Erinnerungsblätter," 5: "Von der Einziehung nochmal frei," *Unitas,* 57/6, August 1917: "Also Goebbels [. . .] told my Leibfuchs Ulex to take part in the auxiliary service."

31. "Erinnerungsblätter," 5.

32. Documents and further correspondence concerning the application of 15 December 1917 in BAK, NL 1118/113.

33. "Erinnerungsblätter," 5; manuscripts in BAK, NL 1118/117, 127.

34. "Erinnerungsblätter," 5; he lived at Poststrasse 18 II. BAK, NL 1118/113, scholarship documents of the Albertus-Magnus-Verein.

35. "Erinnerungsblätter," 5f.

36. "Erinnerungsblätter," 6.

37. StA MG, NL Goebbels/3, Student documents (copies from Bonn University archive). Notes on the Heine lecture in StA MG, NL Goebbels/15, further notes from the Bonn period in StA MG, NL Goebbels/14, 15, 16, 19.

38. *Unitas,* 58/4, April 1918, Backus report. Berlin is mentioned as the future place of study.

39. "Erinnerungsblätter," 6. On the stay in Freiburg, see Reuth, *Goebbels,* 33f.; see also StA MG, NL Goebbels/3, Freiburg student documents.

40. That is clear from a later letter to her. BAK, NL 1118/126, letter of 29 June 1920.

41. "Erinnerungsblätter," 7f.
42. "Erinnerungsblätter," 9; BAK, NL 1118/112, letters from Agnes 7, 13, 15 August 1918.
43. "Erinnerungsblätter," 9.
44. BAK, NL 1118/127, J.G. to A.S., 21 August 1918 on the completion of the text which is in the same file. Wambach, "Es ist gleichgültig."
45. BAK, NL 1118/109, J.G. to A.S., 26 August 1918, J.G. to A.S., 30 August 1918; NL 1118/127, J.G. to A.S., 11 August 1918 (quotation); Reuth, Goebbels, 35.
46. "Erinnerungsblätter," 9f.
47. "Erinnerungsblätter," 10f. (on the stay in Würzburg). Reuth, Goebbels, 35ff.
48. Kollegienbuch, NL 1118/113. Lecture notes from Würzburg in StA MG, NL Goebbels/20.
49. Unitas, 59, 1918/19, p. 209, Unitas Würzburg report.
50. "Erinnerungsblätter," 10f.
51. Fraenkel, Goebbels, 38f.
52. BAK, NL 1118/113, 3 October, 14 November, 31 December 1918, 3 January 1919. BAK, NL 1118/112, 21 December 1919.
53. Czapla, "Erlösung im Zeichen des Hakenkreuzes." On the poems, see Michel, Vom Poeten, 35ff.
54. "Gesang in der Nacht," in "Aus meinem Tagebuch," BAK, NL 1118/126. On these more serious topics, see Czapla, "Erlösung im Zeichen des Hakenkreuzes," 292ff.
55. "Ein Nachtgebet," in "Aus meinem Tagebuch."
56. In TB, 12 December 1923; see also "Sommerabend im Schwarzwald," in "Aus meinem Tagebuch."
57. BAK, NL 1118/109, letter to Anka, 26 January 1919.
58. "Erinnerungsblätter," 27 January 1919.
59. "Erinnerungsblätter," 30 January 1919.
60. "Erinnerungsblätter," 11.
61. "Erinnerungsblätter," 13.
62. BAK, NL 1118/109, J.G. to A.S., 16 March 1919.
63. BAK, NL 1118/13, Vertrags-Entwurf; see Reuth, Goebbels, 41.
64. "Erinnerungsblätter," 14.
65. BAK, NL 1118/115; Michel, Vom Poeten, 60ff.
66. "Erinnerungsblätter," 14f.
67. "Erinnerungsblätter," 15. It concerns Frau Morkramer, presumably the widow of the former owner of the wick factory in which Fritz Goebbels worked. StA MG, Hausbuch Reydt, Odenkirchener Str. 63; StA MG, NL Goebbels/49; receipt from Frau Morkramer for the payments of RM 700, 4 June 1922.
68. "Erinnerungsblätter," 15f. On the stay in Munich, see Reuth, Goebbels, 42ff.
69. Kershaw, Hitler. 1889–1936, 140ff.
70. "Erinnerungsblätter," 17.
71. "Erinnerungsblätter," 15f.
72. "Erinnerungsblätter," 16.
73. "Erinnerungsblätter," 16f.; BAK, NL 1118/109, J.G. to A.S., 31 January 1919.
74. "Erinnerungsblätter," 16.
75. BAK, NL 1118/113, letter of 9 November 1919. "Erinnerungsblätter," 15, a "good" letter from father.
76. "Erinnerungsblätter," 17.
77. BAK, NL 1118/126, 6 September 1919.
78. "Erinnerungsblätter," 17; later he called the play "Die Arbeit" ("Work"); see Reuth, Goebbels, 42; fragment in StA MG, NL Goebbels/69.

79. On the stay in Rheydt, see "Erinnerungsblätter," 17f. Reuth, *Goebbels*, 45f.; on Hans, see letters to A.S., BAK, NL 1118/109, 29 and 31 January 1920, also 31 January, 6 February 1920; BAK, NL 1118/110, 2 March 1920.
80. BAK, NL 1118/110, letter to Anka, 14 April 1920.
81. BAK, NL 1118/110, letter to Anka, 4 March 1920.
82. BAK, NL 1118/117; on the contents, see Reuth, *Goebbels*, 47.
83. BAK, NL 1118/126, J.G. to A.S., 14 April 1920; lengthy quotation in Reuth, *Goebbels*, 48.
84. "Erinnerungsblätter," 18f.
85. "Erinnerungsblätter," 17.
86. "Erinnerungsblätter," 18: "Theo is making me suspicious," but then concerning a conversation with Anka: "Theo Gleitmann is finished."
87. BAK, NL 1118/126, letter of 29 June 1920.
88. "Erinnerungsblätter," 19; Reuth, *Goebbels*, 48f.
89. BAK, NL 1118/118.
90. Will of 1 October 1920, NL 1118/113 and 118.
91. BAK, NL 1118/126, A.S. to J.G., 24 November 1920; J.G. to A.S., 27 November 1920 with poem entitled "Ein Abschied" (A Farewell). Then there is a final undated farewell letter in the file.
92. "Erinnerungsblätter," 20f.; BAK, NL 1118/110, letter from Mumme, 20 November, 5 December; reply to Mumme, 6 December 1920, declining to accept any more letters. Here also letters from a Münster lawyer of 6 June 1921 and 14 March 1921, who had received the same brief from Anka Stahlherm.
93. "Erinnerungsblätter," 21.
94. BAK, NL 1118/110, 6 June 1920.
95. Gundolf's study was published in 1924 under the title *Cäsar. Geschichte seines Ruhms* (Berlin 1924). Caesar's greatness was a lifelong preoccupation of the Germanist, who had already written a doctorate on him: *Caesar in der deutschen Literatur* (Berlin 1904).
96. Lecture: "Ausschnitte aus der deutschen Literatur der Gegenwart" (Selections from contemporary German literature), 30 October 1922, see note 106.
97. "Goethes Antheil an den Recensionen der *Frankfurter Gelehrten Anzeigen*, aus dem Jahre 1782" (actually 1772), StA MG, NL Goebbels/24.
98. *Wilhelm von Schütz als Dramatiker. Ein Beitrag zur Geschichte des Dramas der romantischen Schule*, 1922; on the dissertation, see Reuth, *Goebbels*, 53f.
99. Doctoral diploma, 21 April 1922, NL 1118/128, *rite superato*.
100. Carmon, "Impact of the Nazi Racial Decrees," 138; on the celebrations in Heidelberg in 1942, see chapter 26.
101. "Erinnerungsblätter," 23. On these contributions, see Reuth, *Goebbels*, 56ff.
102. *WLZ*, "Vom Geiste unserer Zeit," 24 January 1922.
103. *WLZ*, 6 February 1922.
104. *WLZ*, 8 February 1922. On 11 February "Kritik und Kunst" appeared as his fifth article.
105. This polemic was published in two parts: "Zur Erziehung eines neuen Publikums," 21 and 27 February 1922. He also criticized the public in "Sursum Corda," which concluded the series on 7 March 1922.
106. "Sursum Corda."
107. "Vom Geiste unserer Zeit"; also "Publikum I."
108. *WLZ*, 13 October 1922. See also *WLZ*, 30 September 1922, "Schauspielhaus Rheydt, Flachsmann als Erzieher" (concerning a play about a school that was

published in 1900). BAK, NL 1118/113, newspaper's dismissal note, 16 October 1922.

109. BAK, NL 1118/133, Lecture: "Ausschnitte aus der deutschen Literatur der Gegenwart," 30 October 1922.

110. *WLZ,* 24 November 1922, "Der Bühnenvolksbund in Rheydt."

111. "Erinnerungsblätter," 23f.

112. "Erinnerungsblätter," 25.

113. BAK, NL 1118/126, 17 February 1919 to Anka.

114. Thus in his 1924 memoirs referring to a short stay in Frankfurt am Main he used the phrase "Jewish city."

115. On anti-Semitism after the First World War, see Walter, *Antisemitische Kriminalität und Gewalt;* Hecht, *Deutsche Juden und Antisemitismus in der Weimarer Republik.*

116. BAK, NL 1118/110, 22 December 1922, E.J. to J.G.; StA MG, NL Goebbels/45, E.J. to J.G., 24 December 1922.

117. BAK, NL 1118/110, E.J. to J.G., 11 February 1923 and 31 January 1923; her letter of 23 April 1923 (ibid.) reflects his depression.

118. "Erinnerungsblätter," 25f.

119. "Erinnerungsblätter," 25.

120. "Erinnerungsblätter," 27.

121. See Thacker, *Goebbels,* 312f.

122. "Erinnerungsblätter," 25.

123. *Kölner Tageblatt,* 24 June 1923. See also "Erinnerungsblätter," 27. There he refers to a second article in the *Kölner Tageblatt,* which could not, however, be found. The fiasco article was published again in an amended version in the *Völkische Freiheit* of 4 November 1924.

124. NL 1118/126; Reuth, *Goebbels,* 62f.

125. NL Goebbels/45, no. 45.

126. "Erinnerungsblätter," 26.

127. "Erinnerungsblätter," 27f.

128. *Rheydter Zeitung,* 22 December 1923, "Schöpferische Kräfte. Richard Flisges, dem toten Freunde."

129. BAK, NL 1118/110, E.J., 22 September 1923 on his search for work; H.G. to J.G., 18 September 1923.

130. StA MG, NL Goebbels/45, E.J. to J.G., 23 September 1923. Here there is also a copy of a letter from Goebbels in which he told Else that he was not going to return to the bank (22 September 1923). BAK, NL 1118/113 contains concerned letters from his father of 23 and 27 September 1923.

131. "Erinnerungsblätter," 28.

2. "SPARE THE ROD AND SPOIL THE CHILD"

1. TB, 25 January 1924.

2. Reimer, *Rheinlandfrage und Rheinlandbewegung (1918–1933),* 296ff.; Schlemmer, *"Los von Berlin,"* 161ff.

3. Löhr, "Mönchengladbach im 19./20. Jahrhundert," 174.

4. Waldecker, "Rheydt 1815–1974," 289ff.

5. TB, 23 October 1923.

6. TB, 24 October 1923.

7. TB, 22 October 1923.

8. StA MG, NL Goebbels/45, no. 59a, 4 November 1923.

9. TB, 18 and 27 October, 4, 5, and 7 November 1923. On the separation, see TB, 9 November; the entries of 14 and 20 November and 5 December 1923 point to the reconciliation that followed.

10. TB, 27 October 1923.

11. TB, 31 December; 27 December (Dream).

12. TB, 21 January 1924.

13. TB, 27 October 1923.

14. TB, 5 and 31 December 1923, 5 January 1924.

15. TB, 2 November 1923; the project was already mentioned in 17 October 1923. On the summer of 1920 (my "Prometheus problem"), see also "Erinnerungsblätter," 18; on the beginning of 1923 ("the problem of Prometheus"), see "Erinnerungsblätter," 25.

16. TB, 4, 5, 7, 8, and 10 November 1923.

17. TB, 12 November 1923.

18. TB, 18 November 1923.

19. Czapla, "Die Entfesselung des Prometheus."

20. TB, 10 November 1923.

21. TB, 7 November 1923.

22. TB, 14, 15, 16, 17, 20, 23, 27, and 28 November 1923. The idea emerges for the first time on 5 November.

23. TB, 5 November 1923.

24. TB, 5 December 1923.

25. TB, 12 December 1923; see also 5 December 1923.

26. TB, 9, 10, and 18 January 1924, 10 March 1924.

27. TB, 13 December 1923.

28. TB, 27 December 1923.

29. TB, 18 January 1924: "Artists can be compared with God. God is greater because he created new things from nothing. Artists make new things from material that already exists."

30. TB, 6 February 1924. See also the same formulation in the "Michael" manuscript (1 June).

31. For more on this, see Bärsch, Goebbels, 248ff.

32. See Czapla, "Entfesselung," which quotes the poem "God": "God is in me / and I in him." NL 1118/126, "Aus meinem Tagebuch."

33. TB, 14 January 1924.

34. TB, 18 January 1924.

35. TB, 10 and 23 November, 17 December 1923, 25 and 31 January, 16 February, 29 March 1924; on these musical experiences, see Thacker, Goebbels, 31, 37, 51, 60.

36. TB, 14 February 1924; see also TB, 18 January 1924 (The Idiot), TB, 13 and 20 February 1924 (The Devils) and 27 June 1924; 15 and 17 July 1924 (Netochka Nezvanova), 22 September 1924 (Humiliated and Insulted) and 21 and 26 February 1925 (The Brothers Karamazov).

37. TB, 30 January, 7 and 9 February 1924; by contrast he found What Is to Be Done? too West European (9 January 1925).

38. TB, 27 November, 5 December 1923.

39. TB, 20 and 19 December 1923.

40. TB, 15, 22, and 24 March 1924.

41. On the novel *Black Banners*, see TB, 1 November 1923. His *Getting Married* put him off (14 January 1924); on the novel *Inferno*, see also 25 February, 11 March 1924; on a performance of *Dance of Death*, see 7 April 1925.
42. TB, 5 November, und 5 December 1923.
43. TB, 23 October 1923.
44. TB, 23 July 1924.
45. TB, 25 May 1924.
46. TB, 10 and 14 November 1924.
47. TB, 29 August 1924 (about a visit to the Richartz-Museum in Cologne); 25 June 1925 (Düsseldorf Art Exhibition).
48. TB, 29 December 1923.
49. TB, 1 February 1924.
50. TB, 10 and 13 February 1924.
51. TB, 27 February–7 March 1924.
52. He had already determined to establish "the nicest possible monument" to his friend. TB, 11 December 1923.
53. Michael Voormann, Ein Menschenschicksal, BAK, NL 1118/127. See Hunt, *Joseph Goebbels*; Michel, *Vom Poeten*, 69ff.
54. BAK, NL 1118/127, entry of 15 September 1919. See also the phrases "His life, a sacrifice for humanity" (15 November 1919) and "He sacrificed himself for the idea of humanity!" (29 April 1920).
55. TB, 15 March 1924.
56. TB, 17 March 1924.
57. TB, 20 March 1924.
58. TB, 22 March 1924.
59. TB, 4 April 1924. On 10 June 1923 he had already written in "Michael" about the "fatherland": "I rooted myself in your soil; you are the mother of my thoughts and dreams." On 27 September he wrote of the "liberation of the maternal soil of Germany."
60. TB, 3 April 1924.
61. TB, 24 and 26 March 1924.
62. TB, 26 March 1924.
63. TB, 29 March 1924.
64. TB, 31 March 1924.
65. TB, 3 April 1924; also 5, 16 ("No bastards as children"), and 21 April 1924, about his ambivalent attitude toward her.
66. BAK, NL 1118/113, letter to Rudolf Mosse, 22 February 1924.
67. TB, 26 March, 3 April 1924.
68. TB, 22 and 23 September 1924, mentions applications for editorial positions.
69. TB, 29 March 1924.
70. TB, 31 March 1924.
71. TB, 5 April 1924. A report of a Nazi functionary, Kreisamtsleiter, W. v. Ameln, provides information about its founding: "Die Stadt Rheydt und die Nationalsozialistische Deutsche Arbeiterpartei," in *Einwohnerbuch Rheydt 1936*, 11f. See also Thacker, *Goebbels*, 35.
72. TB, 5 April 1924.
73. TB, 8 April 1924. On the origins of Goebbels's anti-Semitism, see in particular Barth, *Goebbels und die Juden*, 36ff. However, Barth was not yet able to use the passages of the TB quoted here from spring 1924 for his study.
74. TB, 9 April 1924.

75. TB, 10 April 1924.

76. TB, 10 April 1924; it is clear from the entries for 11 and 12 April that for the time being he had finished with the topic of anti-Semitism.

77. TB, 20 June 1924.

78. *Rheydter Zeitung,* 24 April 1924, Announcement of the election candidates of the Völkisch-Sozial-Block for the local government election in Rheydt.

79. TB, 29 April 1924, 1 May 1924.

80. TB, 29 April 1924; *Rheydter Zeitung,* 30 April 1924.

81. TB, 29 April 1924.

82. TB, 3 May 1924.

83. *Rheydter Zeitung,* 5 May 1924; on the election results, see also TB, 5 and 7 May 1924.

84. TB, 7 May 1924.

85. TB, 28 May 1924. In a leaflet of the Schillergemeinde ("Empor zu Schiller!") there is a reference to the Deutsche Schillergemeinde Verlags-Gemeinschaft Duisburg. See also Deutsche Schillergemeinde, *Satzungen* (both in the Staatsbibliothek in Munich). Later, however, he tried unsuccesssfully to give talks under the auspices of the Schillergemeinde: TB, 23 May, 7 June 1924; also TB, 10, 12, 14, and 16 June 1924.

86. TB, 30 May 1924; see also 19 May 1924.

87. TB, 12 May 1924.

88. TB, 6 June 1924.

89. TB, 16 and 19 May (only for the quotation about the Center Party people).

90. TB, 6 June 1924.

91. TB, 14, 16, and 23 June (house search) 1924.

92. TB, 14 June 1924.

93. TB, 30 June, 4 July 1924. See 1 May 1924: "We are looking for a Bismarck, who will be able to implement our ideas in the real world."

94. Sontheimer, *Antidemokratisches Denken in der Weimarer Republik,* 214ff.; Schreiner, "'Wann kommt der Retter Deutschlands?'"

95. TB, 25 July 1923; Bärsch, *Goebbels,* 221.

96. TB, 26 May 1924, see also 7 June 1924.

97. TB, 2 and 4 July 1924.

98. TB, 4 July 1924.

99. TB, 7 and 9 July 1924.

100. TB, 7 July 1924.

101. TB, 14 July 1924.

102. TB, 30 July, 13 and 14 August 1924.

103. TB, 28 July 1924.

104. TB, 25 May 1924.

105. TB, 10 June 1924.

106. TB, 23 July 1924.

107. TB, in particular 9 May, 18 June (dream), 9, 14, and 21 July (dream) 1924.

108. TB, 23 July 1924.

109. TB, 17 July 1924.

110. TB, 30 July 1924. On his depression, see also 31 July 1924.

111. TB, 11 August 1924.

112. TB, 7 August 1924.

113. TB, 13 August 1924.

114. TB, various entries between 1 and 11 August 1924. On 11 August he writes that

the "Erinnerungen aus der Jugendzeit" are to go up to "17 October 1923, the start of my diary."

115. TB, 8 August 1924.
116. TB, 1 and 2 August 1924.
117. Repeated in TB, 1 August 1924.
118. TB, 2 August 1924; see also 4 and 7 August 1924.
119. TB, 11 August 1924, see also 13, 14, and 15 August 1924.
120. TB, 1 August 1924.
121. TB, 8 August 1924. On his relationship with his mother and the transfer of the image of his mother to his girlfriends, see Bärsch, Goebbels, 230ff.
122. TB, 8 August 1924.
123. TB, 1 August 1924.
124. TB, 12, 13, and 15 August 1924.
125. TB, 13 August 1924; see also 14 August 1924.
126. TB, 11 and 13 August 1924.
127. TB, 1, 11, and 13 August 1924.
128. Reuth, Goebbels, 78ff.; Jablonsky, The Nazi Party in Dissolution, 118ff.
129. TB, 13, 14, and 15 August 1924.
130. TB, 19 August 1924.
131. TB, 31 August 1924.
132. Bärsch, Goebbels, 226.
133. TB, 19 August 1924.
134. TB, 20 August 1924.
135. TB, 22 August 1924; Reuth, Goebbels, 81.
136. TB, 4, 10, 17, 18, 19, 25, 27, and 28 September 1924; see also 11 August 1924: "Yesterday in Rheindahlen. Völkisch propaganda."
137. TB, 27 September 1924.
138. TB, 11 July 1924.
139. TB, 30 August 1924. During the following weeks there are almost daily entries concerning his journalism for the Völkische Freiheit. On this activity, see also Thacker, Goebbels, 42ff.
140. TB, 4 September 1924.
141. TB, 22 September 1924.
142. TB, 27 September 1924.
143. 13 September 1924, "National und sozial."
144. 4 October 1924, "Industrie und Börse." Similarly: "An alle schaffenden Stände," 15 November 1924: "Socialism is only possible at all within a nation state. National and social are not only not opposed to each other but are one and the same thing."
145. On the debate concerning the future economic system, see Kühnl, Die national-sozialistische Linke, 1925–1930, esp. 57ff. The debate was also conducted in the NS-Briefe in particular, e.g. Rud. Jung, "Nationaler oder internationaler Sozialismus," 15 September 1926; Rosikat, "Die Frage der Führungs- und Besitzbeteiligung" and W.W., "Werksgemeinschaft," both 15 December 1926; Gregor Strasser, "Nationaler Sozialismus!" 15 February 1927; W. v. Corswani-Cuntzow, "Die Frage der Führungs- und Besitzbeteiligung," 15 February 1927; "Privateigentum?" 1 March 1927; Willi Hess, "Gewinnbeteiligung," 1 August 1927; Gregor Strasser, "Ziele und Wege," 1 July 1927.
146. TB, 7 April 1925.
147. VF, 18 October 1924, "Völkische Kulturfragen."
148. VF, 25 October 1924.

149. TB, 15 September 1924.
150. TB. 27 September 1924.
151. TB, 3 October 1924; *VF,* 4 October 1924, Notiz.

3. "WORKING WITH THE MIND IS THE GREATEST SACRIFICE"

1. TB, 25 October 1924. The diary entries for 11 October 1924 to 14 March 1925 have been available only since 2004 in the Fröhlich edition and were first used by Thacker, *Goebbels,* 44ff.
2. Goebbels wrongly has it as Neuhöfer.
3. TB, 4 November 1924.
4. TB, 12 November 1924, also already in 11 October 1924.
5. TB, 22 November about events in Mönchengladbach and in Rheydt, 27 November Hamborn, 6 December Velbert.
6. TB, 22 and 29 November, 4 December 1924.
7. TB, 4, 9, 12 (quotation), and 19 December 1924, 2 February 1925. On Kaufmann, see Bajohr, "Hamburgs 'Führer.'" See also the portrait of Kaufmann that Goebbels published in the *NS-Briefe,* 15 June 1926.
8. TB, 9, 12, and 19 December, 6 January 1925 (quotation).
9. TB, 12 January, 9 February 1925.
10. TB, 9 December 1924.
11. *VF,* 20 December 1924, "Das Gebot der Stunde: Sammeln!"; see also Reuth, *Goebbels,* 85.
12. TB, 12 and 15 December 1924
13. TB, 12 December 1924.
14. TB, 19 December 1924.
15. TB, 23 December 1924.
16. TB, 30 December 1924, 2 January 1925.
17. TB, 30 December 1924.
18. *VF,* 8 November 1925, "Gebt Adolf Hitler dem deutschen Volke wieder" and hero worship ("Der Persönlichkeitsgedanke ist die innere Triebkraft jeder großen völkischen und nationalen Bewegung").
19. TB, 23 December 1924.
20. "Opfergang," 10 January 1925.
21. *VB* (B), 20 April 1935. On Goebbels's relationship to Hitler, see Bärsch, *Goebbels,* 193ff.
22. TB, 8 January 1925.
23. "Der Geist des Westens," in *VF,* 17 January 1925. On the origins, see also TB, 8 January 1925; partial reprint in *VB,* 24 May 1925. Goebbels read the article "Arbeiterpartei?" in the *Reichswart* of 17 January 1925 as the "best response to his attack on Reventlow"; 19 January 1925. However, this article was not a direct reply.
24. TB, 23 December 1924.
25. TB, 23 December 1924.
26. TB, 14 January 1925; also 17 and 26 January 1925.
27. TB, 29 January, 3 (quotation), 5, and 9 February 1925.
28. TB, 12 February 25; also 14 and 21 February 1925.
29. TB, 26 February 1925.
30. TB, 2 and 6 March 1925.

31. Jablonsky, *The Nazi Party,* 158.
32. TB, 14 February 1925.
33. Kershaw, *Hitler. 1889–1936,* 339.
34. TB, 23 February 1925. Albrecht Tyrell, *Führer befiehl,* no. 39: Presseerklärung der NSDAP, Gau Hannover, 23. Februar 1925 betr. die auf der Tagung in Hamm verabschiedete Entschließung (quotation).
35. TB, 26 February 1925.
36. TB, 23 February 1925.
37. TB, 3 March 1925. The announcement was published in the *VB* of 26 February 1925: Aufruf an die ehemaligen Angehörigen der Nationalsozialistischen Deutschen Arbeiterpartei. *Adolf Hitler, Reden, Schriften, Anordnungen,* vol. 1, doc. 3.
38. *15 Entwürfe für Schriftplakate oder Flugblätter zur Ankündigung von Vorträgen für die NSDAP (Schrift).*
39. TB, 28 March 1925. On his activities, see Reuth, *Goebbels,* 88f.
40. Goebbels, *Das kleine ABC des Nationalsozialisten* (Greifswald 1925).
41. TB, 21 October 1925.
42. TB, 2 and 6 May 1925. The organization was finally founded on 7 May in Hattingen: TB, 8 May 1925; also 11 and 12 May, 18 June 1925.
43. TB, 20 March 1943: "Reich presidential election. We should elect Ludendorff. Is it worth it?" 12 March 1925: "We're going to elect Ludendorff as Reich President. Hitler's a really good chap." See also Kershaw, *Hitler. 1889–1936,* 346.
44. TB, 18 March 1925.
45. TB, 7 April 1925.
46. TB, 16 April 1925; on the struggle with Ripke, see also 30 March, 14 and 28 April 1925.
47. TB, 4 April 1925.
48. *Deutsche Wochenschau, Nachrichtendienst der nationalsozialistischen Freiheits-Bewegung Großdeutschlands,* 21 June 1925, "Der Nationalsozialismus im Westen."
49. TB, 27 April 1925; see also 28 April 1925, where he was rather more skeptical about Hindenburg's future role. On the election meetings, see TB, 22 to 27 April 1925.
50. TB, 8 May 1925.
51. TB, 22 May 1925 (Relaxation); TB, 23, 27, and 28 May, 9 and 15 June 1925 suggest a relationship that was once again becoming critical.
52. TB, 15 June 1925.
53. See the speeches that Hitler made in June 1925 in Plauen and Stuttgart: *RSA,* vol. 1, docs. 48–51, e.g. doc. 48, Speech in Plauen, 11 June 1925: "National and social are two identical concepts. No socialism without ardent love of our nation, no National Socialism without a desire for real social justice."
54. On 24/25 May the *VB* published a long quotation from the article embedded in an article signed by Willi Hess, an acquaintance of Goebbels, entitled "National Socialism on the Rhine and Ruhr."
55. "Idee und Opfer," 14/15 June 1925, also in *Deutsche Wochenschau* of 23 August 1925, and in Goebbels, *Zweite Revolution,* 17–21. The reprints have slight variations from the original.
56. "Verkalkte Intelligenz," 21/22 June 1925, also in *Zweite Revolution,* 21–25.
57. "Volksgemeinschaft und Klassenkampf," 26/27 July, also in *Deutsche Wochenschau,* 11 October 1925 as "Volksgemeinschaft oder Klassenkampf," also (as "Klassenkampf und Volksgemeinschaft") in Goebbels, *Zweite Revolution,* 13–16. The article was written after a visit by Goebbels to the national conference of the

Völkische Freiheitsbewegung in Elberfeld (TB, 20 June 1925); on the article, see also TB, 1 July 1925: "Another blow at the rotten bourgeoisie."

58. "Der Freiheitsgedanke," 17 October 1925, also in Goebbels, *Zweite Revolution*, 48–51; "Weihnachtsbrief an einen Zuchthäusler," *VB*, 25/26 December, also as "Zuchthaus" in Joseph Goebbels, *Wege ins Dritte Reich. Briefe und Aufsätze für Zeitgenossen*, 56–60.

59. TB, 23 June 1925; see also 10 July 1925.

60. TB, 18 and 29 June, Ripke was shocked by the article "Verkalkte Intelligenz." On Ripke, see also 1, 6, and 8 July 1925.

61. TB, 2 April 1925. On financial worries, see among others 30 March, 4, 7, 11, and 28 April, 6 May 1925.

62. TB, 16 April 1925.

63. TB, 22 April 1925.

64. TB, 18 April 1925.

65. TB, 18, 20, and 22 April 1925; see also 23 June 1925: "Elisabeth Gensicke writes me a despairing letter. How can I help the poor thing?"

66. TB, 7, 18, and 25 April, 22 and 29 May 1925; Whitsun vacation with Else: 4 June 1925.

67. TB, 8 June 1925.

68. TB, 14 July 1925. Ulrich Höver claims that Goebbels first met Hitler in the second week in June 1925, which can be ruled out in the light of the complete edition of the diary. Höver, *Joseph Goebbels. Ein nationaler Sozialist*, 279. It confirms the assumption already made by Reuth that their first meeting occurred on 12 July. Reuth, *Goebbels*, 90; see also Thacker, *Goebbels*, 53.

69. TB, 10 July 1925, "No money in the kitty. That's what they're saying. We're prevented from checking." On Ripke's fall, see also Reuth, *Goebbels*, 90f., TB entries between 15 and 25 July 1925.

70. TB, 27 July 1925.

71. TB, 3 August 1925.

72. Klein, "'Mekka des deutschen Sozialismus' oder 'Kloake der Bewegung'?" 120.

73. TB, 29 July 1925.

74. TB, 31 July 1925.

75. TB, 29 July 1925.

76. TB, 15 August 1925.

77. TB, 21 August 1925. BAB, NS 1/340, Strasser to J.G. 29 August 1925, reply 31 August 1925. On the role of Goebbels in the "West block," see Reuth, *Goebbels*, 91ff.; Thacker, *Goebbels*, 56ff.

78. TB, 31 August, 7 September 1925.

79. TB, 29 August 1925, see also 10 August: "I'm reading Hitler's book, *Mein Kampf*, and I'm shaken by this political message."

80. TB, 11 September 1925; Reuth, *Goebbels*, 92; Schildt, *Die Arbeitsgemeinschaft Nord-West*, 105f. On Hagen, see BAB, NS 1/340, Strasser telegram, 9 September 1925, Goebbels to Strasser, 1 September 1925 (with a report on the meeting), also MS in Schildt, *Die Arbeitsgemeinschaft Nord-West*, viii and after; Hermann Fobke, "Aus der nationalsozialistischen Bewegung. Bericht über die Gründung der Arbeitsgemeinschaft der nord- und westdeutschen Gaue der NSDAP," 11 September 1925, published in Jochmann (ed.), *Nationalsozialismus und Revolution*, no. 66.

81. TB, 11 September 1925.

82. TB, 28 September 1925; Reuth, *Goebbels*, 92.

83. TB, 30 September, 2 October 1926.

84. BAB, NS 1/340, 9 October 1925, published in Jochmann, *Nationalsozialismus*, no. 67.

85. TB, 16, 25, 26, and 28 September, 12, 15, and 21 October 1925.

86. On the letters, see Schildt, *Arbeitsgemeinschaft*, 115ff.

87. "Das russische Problem," in *NS-Briefe*, 15 November 1925. The article is in the form of a letter to the imaginary Iwan Wienurowski, with Goebbels using parts of the "Michael" manuscript. Similar ideas are contained in the article "National-sozialismus oder Bolschewismus," in *NS-Briefe*, 15 October 1925. See also Höver, *Goebbels*, 184ff.

88. *VB*, 14 November 1925, "Rede und Gegenrede über das russische Problem." Originally the article was intended to have already appeared in the *VB* in August. TB, 10 August 1925.

89. TB, 12 October 1925.

90. TB, 14 October 1925.

91. Adolf Hitler, *Mein Kampf*, 358, 154; see also Reuth, *Goebbels*, 92f.

92. TB, 6 November 1925 concerning the meeting that took place on the 4th; see Reuth, *Goebbels*, 93f.

93. BAB, NS 1/340, 5 November 1925.

94. TB, 23 November 1925. Hitler's speech is documented in *RSA*, doc. 82, 4 November 1925.

95. Goebbels, "Die Führerfrage," *Zweite Revolution*, 5–8.

96. Kershaw, *Der Hitler-Mythos*, 40ff.

97. TB, 23 November 1925, see also Reuth, *Goebbels*, 94. On the discussion of the program at the start of the year, see Wörtz, *Programmatik und Führerprinzip*, 86ff.; on the Hanover meeting, see Schildt, *Arbeitsgemeinschaft*, 118ff.; report on the meeting by Goebbels in the *NS-Briefe*, 1 December 1925.

98. TB, 18 and 23 December 1925, 4 January 1926. On Strasser's draft program, see Schildt, *Arbeitsgemeinschaft*, 127ff. The draft is discussed in Reinhard Kühnl, "Zur Programmatik der nationalsozialistischen Linken." The original, together with various comments by Party members, is in BAB, NS 26/896.

99. TB, 29 December 1925.

100. TB, 16 and 29 December 1925.

101. TB, 11 and 16 January 1926. On the agreement with Pfeffer, see TB, 29 December 1925.

102. *NS-Briefe*, 15 January 1926; see also TB, 20 January 1926: "I have a long think about the foreign policy problem. We can't avoid Russia. Russia is the beginning and the end of any serious foreign policy."

103. *Deutsche Wochenschau*, 29 December 1925.

104. Work on the speech: TB, 24 and 30 December 1925, 4 and 6 January 1926.

105. NS 1/339II, manuscript sent to the publishers on 3 April.

106. Goebbels, *Lenin oder Hitler?*; Schildt, *Arbeitsgemeinschaft*, 174f.

107. Schildt, *Arbeitsgemeinschaft*, 140ff.

108. Feder to Goebbels, 23 December 1925, BAB, NS 1/341I.

109. TB, 25 January 1926; see also Reuth, *Goebbels*, 96; BAB, NS 1/340, Resolution (appendix to a letter from O. Strasser to Goebbels, 26 January 1925), both published in Jochmann, *Nationalsozialismus*, no. 72.

110. TB, 20 January, 6 and 11 February 1926.

111. Otto Strasser had opposed the compensation for the princes in the *NS-Briefe* under the pseudonym "Ulrich von Hutten" (15 December 1925), which Goebbels considered "terrific." Goebbels to Strasser, 11 December 1925, BAB, NS 1/340.

On the compensation for the princes, see Jung, *Demokratie*, 49ff.; Schüren, *Der Volksentscheid zur Fürstenenteignung 1926*.

112. TB, 15 February 1926. On Bamberg, see Reuth, *Goebbels*, 98f.; Horn, *Der Marsch zur Machtergreifung*, 240ff.; Schildt, *Arbeitsgemeinschaft*, 155ff. Hitler's speech is documented in *RSA*, doc. 101.

113. Only a short entry in the TB, 7 March 1926. See *NS-Briefe*, 1 March 1926, "Essen, eine Etappe" (announcement signed by Goebbels for the unity party conference in Essen on 6 and 7 March). See Schildt, *Arbeitsgemeinschaft*, 169ff.

114. Feder to Hitler and to Heinemann, chairman of the Mediation Committee, 2 May 1926, published in Tyrell, *Führer*, no. 52. Feder referred to Goebbels's article "Ost- oder Westorientierung" directly.

115. TB, 13 March 1926.

116. "Der Apfelsinenkrieg," in *NS-Briefe*, 15 March 1926, also in Goebbels, *Wege*, 40–44.

117. BAB, NS 1/340, Strasser to Goebbels, 1 April and reply of 6 April 1926.

118. TB, 13 April 1926 concerning the visit to Munich. See Reuth, *Goebbels*, 100f.

119. *VB*, 10 April 1926.

120. See the letter from Kaufmann to Heinemann in OPG-Verfahren Karl Kaufmann, 24 June 1926 in which Kaufmann complained specifically about the lack of "Socialist" ideas in the speech. Tyrell, *Führer*, 128f.

121. Joseph Goebbels, *"Der Nazi-Sozi,"* 18.

122. TB, 13 April 1926.

123. TB, 15 and 16 (quotation) April 1926.

124. On Hitler's visit to Stuttgart, see *RSA*, docs. 128–31, 17 and 18 April 1926.

125. TB, 19 April 1926.

126. BAB, NS 1/340, Goebbels to Gregor Strasser, 19 April 1926.

127. *NS-Briefe*, 15 May 1926; see also Reuth, *Goebbels*, 102.

128. TB, 24 May 1926; *RSA*, doc. 144, 22 May 1926, Minutes of the general membership meeting, 444. See also Horn, *Machtergreifung*, 278f.

129. TB, 3 and 8 May 1926; on the provisional sorting out of the "tricky issues," see 10 May 1926; Reuth, *Goebbels*, 102f.

130. TB, 12 and 14 June 1926. Given his psychological vulnerability his qualities as a political leader appeared dubious. See TB, 2 January 1926, concerning a New Year's celebration during which Kaufmann had "one of his most fearful attacks of nerves and threatened suicide"; also TB, 6 and 20 January 1926.

131. TB, 31 January 1926; 1 February 1926: "Kaufmann is not treating me in the way a friend should be treated. Elbrechter is behind it." Ibid., 29 March 1926: "Long conversation with Karl Kaufmann. About Elbrechter. Am I really the one to blame for everything? Am I personally opposed to Elbrechter?"

132. TB, 14 June 1926.

133. Kaufmann accused Pfeffer of running up debts of several thousand marks and not declaring them at the time when the parties amalgamated. This resulted in a case before the Party court in which Goebbels spoke in favor of Pfeffer. As a result Kaufmann complained to Himmler about Goebbels's "untruths": BAB, OPG Karl Kaufmann, 7 June 1927; Hüttenberger, *Gauleiter*, 47.

134. TB, 7 June 1926; see also the entries in the TB since 31 May 1926. On the change of Gauleiters, see Böhnke, *Die NSDAP im Ruhrgebiet*, 117f.

135. TB, 16 June 1926; also 17, 19, and 21 June 1926. On Hitler's appearances during these days, see *RSA*, doc. 152, 14 June, Speech in Elberfeld; doc. 153, 15 June (Hattingen); doc. 155, 16 June, 26 (Essen); doc. 157, 18 June (Essen); doc. 158, 20 June 1925 (Essen).

136. TB, 10 and 12 June, 6 July 1926. On the preparations for the takeover of the Berlin Gau, see Reuth, *Goebbels*, 104f.; Tyrell, "Führergedanke und Gauleiterwechsel," 352.

137. TB, 6 July 1926. On what happened, see the reports in the *VB*, 3–8 July 1926.

138. *VB*, 8 July 1926, Goebbels's speech "Arbeiter und Student."

139. TB, 6 July 1926.

140. TB, 12 July 1926.

141. TB, 18 July–11 August 1926.

142. TB, 23 July 1926.

143. TB, 24 July 1926.

144. TB, 25 July 1926, also 26 July 1926.

145. TB, 31 July–1 August 1926.

146. TB, 30 July 1926: "12 o'clock with the boss. Serious discussion. Pfeffer is becoming Reich SA leader."

147. TB, 4 August 1926.

148. *NS-Briefe*, 15 September 1926, "Die Revolution als Ding an sich"; also published in Goebbels, *Wege*, 44–51.

149. TB, 27 and 28 August 1926.

150. TB, 17 September 1926.

151. TB, 23–27 September 1926. The "farewell letter" that she wrote him was, however, not the first; see 12 June 1926.

152. TB, 16 October 1926. On his final decision, see also 18 October 1926. Heiber (ed.), *Joseph Goebbels, Das Tagebuch 1925/26*, doc. 2 (hereafter Heiber (ed.), *Tagebuch.*) See also the letter from Schmiedicke to Goebbels, 16 October 1926, according to which the Berlin Party leadership had requested the appointment of Goebbels. Heiber (ed.), *Tagebuch*, doc. 2.

153. TB, 1 and 6 November 1926.

154. *NS-Briefe*, 1 October 1926, Gregor Strasser, "Rückblick und Ausblick."

4. "FAITH MOVES MOUNTAINS"

1. Literature on the early history of the NSDAP in Berlin: Neuber, *Faschismus in Berlin*, 52ff.; Oberwallney, *SA in Berlin*; Kruppa, *Rechtsradikalismus in Berlin 1918–1928*; Friedrich, *Die missbrauchte Hauptstadt*, 72ff. On the membership figures and election results, see Oberwallney, *SA in Berlin*, 4; Engelbrechten, *Eine braune Armee entsteht*, 39; Büsch and Haus, *Berlin als Hauptstadt der Weimarer Republik, 1919–1933*, 408.

2. Kruppa, *Rechtsradikalismus*, 335f. There is a series of monthly reports covering the history of the Berlin NSDAP during this period, which the head of propaganda and organization of the Neukölln section, Reinhold Muchow, produced for internal party purposes. They appear in Broszat, "Die Anfänge der Berliner NSDAP 1926/27"; on the condition of the Berlin party organization before Goebbels's arrival, see the situation report of October 1926 on 101ff. On the meeting of 25 August 1926, see Abteilung I A Außendienst, Nachtrag zum Lagebericht der NSDAP, 26 August 1926, published in Heiber (ed.), *Tagebuch*, doc. 1 and Engelbrechten, *Armee*, 45f.

3. Heiber, *Joseph Goebbels*, 57ff.; Reuth, *Goebbels*, 108ff.; Longerich, *Geschichte der SA*, 60ff.; Kruppa, *Rechtsradikalismus*, 337ff.; Neuber, *Faschismus*, 62ff.; Friedrich, *Hauptstadt*, 123ff. (with a critical appreciation of Goebbels's descriptions).

4. Goebbels, *Kampf um Berlin. Der Anfang.*

5. This refers to the entries from 1 November 1926–13 April 1928, edited in volume II of the Fröhlich edition. The entries were first used in Thacker, *Goebbels*, 78ff.

6. TB, 11 November 1926.

7. Schmiedicke to Goebbels, 28 October 1926. Heiber (ed.), *Tagebuch,* doc. 3.

8. *RSA,* II/1 doc. 40, Hitler instruction of 26 October 1926 quoted from *VB,* 28 October 1926.

9. TB, 11 November 1926. On the lodgings with Steiger, see G. Strasser, Zusammenstellung der in der Funktionärssitzung vom Freitag, dem 10. Juni 1927, erhobenen Angriffe und deren Erwiderung. Heiber (ed.), *Tagebuch,* doc. 14.

10. TB, 11 and 13 November 1926: a "nice boy, a good sort, hard working, reliable." There are negative comments on 8, 15, and 17 December 1926. On Gutsmiedl, see *Reichstags-Handbuch 1933,* Berlin 1934. There, with reference to Gutsmiedl's leaving the Party's service, it is stated that in 1927 he returned to his original profession as a farm administrator "for health reasons" until August 1932. From September 1932 onward he was once again working full time for the Party, this time in the NSBO.

11. TB, 11 November 1926.

12. TB, 11 November 1926; *BT,* 10 November 1926. On the meeting, see Situationsbericht Oktober 1926, in Broszat, "Anfänge," 101ff.; Reuth, *Goebbels,* 111.

13. TB, 11 November 1926; see also the entry for 15 November 1926 about another meeting with Hitler, who had left the city on the 10th.

14. TB, 11, 12, 15, and 18 November 1926.

15. TB, 11 November 1926; see also 13, 15, and 18 November 1926.

16. TB, 1 December 1926 and 25 July 1927.

17. Friedrich, *Hauptstadt,* 119ff.

18. Circular of 9 November 1926, in Heiber (ed.), *Tagebuch,* doc. 4; see Reuth, *Goebbels,* 111.

19. TB, 12 November 1926; on Hauenstein already being derogatory, see 16 October 1926.

20. TB, 15 November 1926.

21. TB, 18 November 1926: "1600 Marks were donated"; Muchow, "Situationsbericht Oktober 1926" in Broszat, "Anfänge," 101ff., 104; Goebbels, *Kampf,* 26; Engelbrechten, *Armee,* 48; Goebbels, "Opfergang" (about its establishment), in *NS-Briefe,* 1 January 1927. On the speech to the Freedom League on the previous day, see also TB, 21 December 1926.

22. TB, 15 November 1926; *Spandauer Zeitung,* 15 November 1926; *Die Rote Fahne,* 16 November 1926; Engelbrechten, *Armee,* 48f.; see also Reuth, *Goebbels,* 113.

23. TB, 21 November 1926; Goebbels, *Kampf,* 43; Muchow, "Situationsbericht Oktober 1926," in Broszat, "Anfänge," 101ff., 104.

24. TB, 1 December 1926.

25. TB, 8 December 1926.

26. TB, 17 and 18 December 1926; see also 10 January 1927.

27. TB, 1, 12, and 17 December 1926; Situationsbericht Dezember 1926, in Broszat, "Anfänge," 105ff., 106; see also Reuth, *Goebbels,* 113.

28. TB, 17 December 1926; see also Goebbels, *Kampf,* 46, where it states that in Berlin he developed "an entirely new style of political rhetoric." Nazi propaganda in the capital "used a new and modern language that had nothing in common with the old-fashioned so-called *völkisch* forms of expression."

29. TB, entries for 18 November, 4, 15, 17, and 18 December 1926, among others; see

also his comments in *Kampf,* 45f. on Mjölnir and his article "Propaganda in Wort und Bild" in the *NS-Briefe* of 25 March 1927, also in Goebbels, *Wege,* 23–25.

30. TB, 18 November 1926.

31. TB, 21 November, and 3 and 18 December 1926: Goebbels continued his visits during the New Year; see, e.g., 3, 13, and 17 January 1927.

32. TB, 30 December 1926 and 1 January 1927.

33. TB, 15 December 1926, 4 January 1927; Goebbels, *Kampf,* 24f. (quotation) and 52; Muchow, "Situationsbericht Dezember 1926," in Broszat, "Anfänge," 105ff., 106; see also Reuth, *Goebbels,* 114.

34. Muchow, "Situationsbericht Dezember 1926," in Broszat, "Anfänge," 105ff., 106 (Musik); Engelbrechten, *Armee,* 48; TB, 29 January 1926 (Car); see Reuth, *Goebbels,* 114f.

35. TB, 28 November 1926, on his trip to West Germany and 6 December 1926 on his trip to Dessau and Weimar.

36. TB, 12 December 1926. On his reading of it, see also 30 December 1926: "I finished reading Hitler's book and am tremendously happy."

37. *Mein Kampf,* 726ff.

38. *VB,* 24 August 1927, "Dr. Goebbels über Propagandafragen."

39. *NS-Briefe,* 15 March 1927, "Propaganda in Wort und Bild."

40. Goebbels, *Kampf,* 28.

41. Goebbels, *Kampf,* 44.

42. 15 August 1926, "Neue Methoden der Propaganda," also in Goebbels, *Wege,* 15–18.

43. "Kleinarbeit," 15 December 1926, also in Goebbels, *Wege,* 19–23.

44. "Sprechabend," ibid., 15 April 1927.

45. "Massenversammlung," 1 April 1927.

46. Ibid.; his snide encouragement to use force against anyone who tore down posters in "Das Plakat," 15 May 1927. "Lecture him until he sees the error of his ways but make sure he doesn't get hurt."

47. Especially in the satirical contribution "Wenn ein Redner kommt," in ibid., 1 August 1926.

48. 15 May 1927, "Das Plakat."

49. Goebbels, *Kampf,* 18.

50. "Erkenntnis und Propaganda" in Goebbels, *Signale der neuen Zeit,* 28–52 (speech of 9 January 1928): *VB,* 24 August 1927, "Dr. Goebbels über Propagandafragen."

51. *Berliner Arbeiterzeitung,* 11 August 1929, Paper "Propaganda und praktische Politik," 2 August 1929.

52. Reinhardt, *Von der Reklame zum Marketing,* 87ff.; Schug, "Hitler als Designobjekt und Marke"; Voigt, "Goebbels als Markentechniker,"; Behrenbeck, "Der Führer"; Bussemer, *Propaganda.*

53. See, for example, Hartungen, *Psychologie der Reklame;* Lysinski, *Psychologie des Betriebs;* König, *Reklame-Psychologie.*

54. TB, 14 August 1929.

55. Stark, *Moderne politische Propaganda,* 4.

56. Ernst Hanfstaengl remembered his "smooth baritone voice." *Zwischen Weißem und Braunem Haus,* 198.

57. See, for example, the observations of such varied observers as the correspondent of the *Neue Zürcher Zeitung,* 29 September 1933, "Dr. Goebbels vor der internationalen Presse," and the old Nazi functionary Albert Krebs, *Tendenzen und Gestalten der NSDAP,* 160.

58. Victor Klemperer, *Ich will Zeugnis ablegen bis zum letzten. Tagebücher 1933–1945*, 2 vols., ed. Walter Nowojski, 7th edn, Berlin 1997, 30 July 1936. On Goebbels as a speaker, see also Heiber, *Joseph Goebbels*, 46f., and Heiber's introduction to his *Goebbels Reden 1932–1945*; Lochner (ed.), *Goebbels Tagebücher*, 25f.; Stephan, *Joseph Goebbels*, 108f.

59. Goebbels, *Kampf*, 59.

60. "Die Straße," in *NS-Briefe*, 1 June 1926.

61. TB, 26 January 1927; Engelbrechten, *Armee*, 52f.; Goebbels, *Kampf*, 61f.; Situationsbericht Januar 1927, in Broszat, "Anfänge," 107ff., 108; *Spandauer Zeitung*, 26 January 1927, "Schlägerei nach einer politischen Versammlung."

62. TB, 1 February 1927. "Situationsbericht Januar 1927," in Broszat, "Anfänge," 107ff., 109; Engelbrechten, *Armee*, 53.

63. TB, 12 February 1927; Muchow, "Situationsbericht Februar 1927" in Broszat, "Anfänge," 110ff., 111 (quotation); Engelbrechten, *Armee*, 54ff.; Goebbels, *Kampf*, 63ff.; *Berliner Morgenpost*, 12 February 1926, "Politische Schlägerei in der Müllerstraße"; *Die Rote Fahne*, 13 February 1927, considered the "fascist attack" as a "warning for all the working people of Berlin"; see also Reuth, *Goebbels*, 115f.

64. Goebbels, *Kampf*, p. 75.

65. TB, 16 February 1927; Muchow, "Situationsbericht Februar 1927," in Broszat, "Anfänge," 110ff., 112; Goebbels, *Kampf*, 78f.; Engelbrechten, *Armee*, 56.

66. "Parlamentarismus?" in *NS-Briefe*, 1 February 1927. The contribution is taken from an open letter to an unnamed Reichstag deputy, but the reference to Frick emerges in the text. Frick responded with a "crude letter," TB, 5 February 1927; on the improvement in his relationship with Frick, see 8 March 1927.

67. TB, 25 February 1927.

68. Special report on the events in the Lichterfelde-East station on 20 March 1927, in Broszat, "Anfänge," 115ff.; numerous witness statements in LA Berlin A Rep 358-01/302, vol. 1 (including Goebbels, 21 March 1927), vol. 2 and vol. 4 (here, in particular, Abt. I A Außendienst, 21 March 1927, Report on the march of the Nazi SA to Trebbin on the 19 and 20 March 1927); Report Abt IA of 28 March 1927 published in Heiber (ed.), *Tagebuch*, no. 5: Engelbrechten, *Armee*, 57ff.; Goebbels, *Kampf*, 100; *Vossische Zeitung*, 22 March "Schüsse auf Bahnhof Lichterfelde-Ost"; *BZ am Mittag*, 21 March 1927, "Feuergefecht zwischen Rechtsradikalen und Kommunisten"; 22 March 1927, "Schärfstes Vorgehen gegen die Hakenkreuzler von Lichterfelde"; *BT*, 21 March 1927, "Schwere Zusammenstöße auf dem Bahnhof Lichterfelde Ost"; see also Reuth, *Goebbels*, 116f.

69. TB, 21 March 1927.

70. *VZ*, 21 March 1927; see also Goebbels, *Kampf*, 102: "Late in the evening a few cheeky Hebrews who couldn't keep their gobs shut received a few clips."

71. *BT*, 22 March 1927.

72. *VZ*, 23 February 1927; *BZ am Mittag*, 22 March 1927; TB, 24 March 1927.

73. TB, 24 March 1927.

74. Report of 28 March 1927, Abteilung IA, 28 March 1927; Heiber (ed.), *Tagebuch*, doc. 5.

75. TB, 5 May 1927.

76. *VZ*, 6 May 1927, "Blutiger Terror der Nationalsozialisten"; LA Berlin, A Rep. 358-01/27, Charge of 23 November 1927.

77. *Vossische Zeitung*, 6 May 1927 and 7 May 1927 with a detailed justification of the ban; Goebbels, *Kampf*, 152; see also Reuth, *Goebbels*, 121f.; Friedrich, *Hauptstadt*, 160ff.

78. TB, 6 and 11 May 1927.

79. *Berliner Arbeiterzeitung*, 24 April 1927, Erich Koch, "Folgen der Rassenvermischung." Also in *Der nationale Sozialist*, no. 17; Heiber (ed.), *Tagebuch*, doc. 6.

80. TB, 27 April 1927.

81. Koch to Goebbels, 26 April 1927; Heiber (ed.), *Tagebuch*, doc. 7 and the statement of 17 June 1927, doc. 11. A year later (TB, 22 June 1928) Goebbels learned from Kaufmann that Koch had in fact written that "infamous article [. . .] against me" which he was pleased that he "had immediately recognized thanks to my reliable intuition," despite all assurances to the contrary.

82. Goebbels to Hitler; 5 June 1927; Heiber (ed.), *Tagebuch*, doc. 8; see also TB, 7 June 1927. On the growing conflict with the Strassers, see also 23 and 24 May 1927. Further letters from Goebbels to Hess, 9 June 1927, Heiber (ed.), *Tagebuch*, doc. 9.

83. Thus Holtz in his letter to Hitler, 17 June 1927; see also Heiber (ed.), *Tagebuch*, doc. 169.

84. TB, 16 June 1927.

85. TB, 18 May 1927: "The N.S. Briefe are appearing today without me. Revenge is a dish that is best served cold."

86. Reuth, *Goebbels*, 124 (based on a report by the Munich political police about the Party's evening meeting of 20 June 1927, in the BDC).

87. Statement by Hitler of 25 June 1927 in the *VB*, also in Heiber (ed.), *Tagebuch*, doc. 18: "Der Wunsch ist der Vater des Gedankens." Also report by the Uschla of 19/21 June 1927. On the previous conversation, see Heiber (ed.), *Tagebuch*, doc. 17. *Welt am Abend*, 4 June 1927, "Bruderzwist im Hause Hitler."

88. TB, 6 and 7 September 1927.

89. TB, 8 and 10 September 1927.

90. TB, 27 November 1927; also 14 October 1927.

91. TB, 12 December 1927.

92. TB, 23 and 19 June, 4 and 21 July, 24 August 1927.

93. TB, 25 August, 16 (quotation) and 17 September 1927.

94. TB, 30 October 1927.

95. TB, 28 November, 30 December 1926, 19 September 1927.

96. That is Josefine v. Behr, whom Goebbels had known since February 1926 (TB, 22 February 1926). Following an encounter at the Party rally in Weimar in July 1926 he noted: "I love her a bit!" (6 July 1926). For the number in Berlin who were involved, see in particular 28 February, 1 and 21 March 1927.

97. He had already noticed her in December 1926 (see 6, 8, 15, and 20 December 1926). On the affair, see in particular 17 January 1927, 19 ("Do I love Dora Hentschel?") and 28 February, 1, 2, 5, and 28 March, 7 and 11 April 1927 ("Dora Hentschel loves me").

98. TB, 12 April 1927.

99. TB, 20 April 1927.

100. TB, 29 April, 2 May, 1, 17, 18, and 26 June, 5 September, 1 October 1927.

101. TB, 1 December 1927, also 5 and 10 December 1927; 12 December 1927: "Do I love her?"; 10 January 1928: "I love Tamara v. Heede. Does she love me too? I can't really believe it!"

102. TB, 4 and 5 February; until the end of the month frequent entries about Tamara.

103. TB, 1 June 1927.

104. Lemmons, *Goebbels and Der Angriff*, 24f. On the founding of *Der Angriff*, see also Friedrich, *Hauptstadt*, 177ff.

105. TB, 4 July 1927 (on the preparations also 21 and 25 May, 1, 13, and 15 June 1927).
106. TB, 9, 17, and 23 July, but 10 August 1927: "The most recent issue of *Angriff* is pathetic"; 28 August 1927: "New issue of *Angriff* is the best yet."
107. Kessemeier, *Der Leitartikler Goebbels*, 86ff.
108. *Der Angriff*, 30 January 1928, "Durch die Blume"; 27 February 1928, "Eine Mücke hat gehustet"; 19 September 1927, "Justav"; 2 February 1930, "Politisches Tagebuch."
109. *Der Angriff*, 7 November 1927 (Politisches Tagebuch). The exclusion of Trotsky and Zinoviev provided the point of reference. See also 6 February 1928, "Stalin-Trotzki" editorial; see also his retrospective comments on reading Trotsky's *The Real Situation in Russia*, 21 March 1929.
110. 3 November 1927.
111. 14 November 1927, "Das Geheimnis von Konitz"; 28 November 1927, "Ein Ritualmord im Jahre 1926."
112. Bering, *Kampf um Namen*, esp. 241ff.
113. Bering, *Kampf*, 251; Goebbels and Schweitzer, *Das Buch Isidor;* Goebbels, *Knorke*.
114. Goebbels did not invent the rude name. Not only had the Nazis tried to denigrate Bernhard Weiss in this way before Goebbels's arrival, the Communists have been proved to have called the police president "Isidor" in 1923. Bering, *Kampf*, 242.
115. *Der Kampf gegen Young. Eine Sache des deutschen Arbeiters, Rede von Dr. Joseph Goebbels, M.d.R., gehalten am 26. September 1929 im Kriegervereinshaus Berlin.* Published as a manuscript.
116. LA Berlin, A Rep. 358-01/2; his appeal was, however, rejected.
117. Article of 9 April 1928, "Angenommen"; see Bering, *Kampf*, 245f.
118. On the trials, see Bering, *Kampf*, 283ff.
119. *Der Angriff*, 9 September 1929.
120. Engelbrechten, *Armee*, 61ff.
121. *BZ am Mittag*, 13 May 1927, "Macht Schluß mit den Kurfürstendamm-Krawallen!"
122. *Der Angriff*, 4 July 1927, "Das Schreckensurteil von Moabit." Also TB, 12 and 13 May 1927 on these incidents.
123. *Der Angriff*, 11 July 1927, "Trials."
124. *Der Angriff*, 28 November 1927, "Menschen, seid menschlich."
125. Goebbels, *Kampf*, 180.
126. VZ, 23 August 1927, "450 Nationalsozialisten festgenommen"; TB, 22 and 24 August 1927.
127. 29 August 1927; see further articles in the same issue and in particular 5 September 1927 on the subsequent fate of those arrested: "Das Polizeipräsidium verordnet Hungerkuren. 74 Arbeiter brotlos gemacht."
128. TB, 19 May, 18 and 30 June also 4 July. Engelbrechten, *Armee*, 65.
129. TB, 1–24 August 1927.
130. TB, 25 August 1927; on the lifting of the ban, see 30 November 1927.
131. *Der Angriff*, 14 November; TB, 8 November 1927.
132. TB, 14 and 28 January 1928.; *Der Angriff*, 16 and 30 January 1928, reports on the meetings under the heading "Kampf um Berlin."
133. TB, 11 March 1928; *Der Angriff*, 19 March 1928, "Bernau im Zeichen Hitlers"; Engelbrechten, *Armee*, 70.
134. At the beginning of November 1927 a court in Elberfeld condemned him to a fine of 100 RM because he had urged the SA to commit acts of violence in early writings: TB, 4 November 1927; *Der Angriff*, 14 November 1927, "Eine Ohrfeige für Bernhard Weiß."
135. On the trial, see LA Berlin, A Rep. 358-01/385, Bericht der Staatsanwaltschaft an

das Reichsjustizministerium, 2 March 1928, as well as further correspondence. Goebbels was indicted in particular for the content of his contribution "Massenversammlung" in the *NS-Briefe* of 1 April 1927: *Berliner Morgenpost,* 28 February 1928, "Völkische Hetzer zu Gefängnis verurteilt."

136. *Der Angriff,* 27 February 1928 and 5 March 1928 (quotation); see also TB, 28 and 29 February 1928.

137. TB, 30 March 1928: "München. Gleich zum Gericht. [. . .] 1500 Geldstrafe für Weiß"

138. TB, 21, 22, and 23 March, 2, 4, and 5 April 1927.

139. *VZ,* 17 April 1928, "Das Urteil im Nationalsozialisten-Prozeß"; see also *Der Angriff,* 14 April 1928; TB, 17 April 1928.

140. LA Berlin, A Rep. 358-01/24, vol. 4, Urteil Schöffengericht Berlin vom 28. April 1928 gegen Dürr und Goebbels, BM, 29 April 1928, "Völkische Frechheit vor Gericht"; TB, 29 April 1928.

141. TB, 18 and 30 December 1925, 6 January 1926, 3 August 1928, 4 October 1928.

142. TB, 13 January 1926.

143. TB, 1 December 1926 and 25 February 1927.

144. TB, 31 March 1927.

145. TB, 10 October 1928.

146. TB, 10 and 14 November 1929.

147. TB, 1 October 1930.

148. TB, 9 June 1927. Text in BAK, NL 1118/98.

149. TB, 21 October, 6 and 8 November 1927.

150. StA MG, NL Goebbels/79, newspaper review from 1933 (place of publication is unclear).

151. TB, 11 December 1927.

152. TB, 18 November 1927.

153. *NS-Briefe,* 15 November 1927, Aquino, "Der neue Stil? Grundsätzliches zur Nationalsozialistischen Versuchsbühne."

154. TB, 16 November 1927.

155. *Berliner Arbeiterzeitung,* 13 November 1927.

156. TB, 2 January 1928.

157. TB, 18 December 1928.

158. *Michael. Ein deutsches Schicksal in Tagebuchblättern* (7th edn, Munich 1935, used here). On the revising of *Michael,* see Michel, *Vom Poeten,* 126ff. The second edition of the book was published in 1931; TB, 1, 5, 6, 9, and 14 June, 23 July, 12–17 August 1928 and 19 and 21 September.

159. *Michael* (1928), 57f.; see also, among other references, p. 82: "Christ is the first Jewish opponent of substance," and so on.

160. Entry of 27 October 1919.

161. *Michael* (1924), entry of 27 October 1919.

162. *Michael* (1928), 78f.

163. *Michael* (1928), 101f. Also 149f. concerning a further encounter.

164. *Michael* (1928), 41.

165. *Michael* (1924), entry of 15 September 1919; *Michael* (1928), 68.

166. *Michael,* entry of 15 November 1919; *Michael* (1928), 81f.

167. *Michael* (1924), entry of 15 June 1919.

168. *Michael* (1928), 34f.

169. *Michael* (1924), entry of 8 July 1920.

170. *Michael* (1928), 121.

171. TB, 8 November 1928, 5 and 7 February 1929.

172. TB, 8–10 March 1929.
173. TB, 10 and 11 March 1929.
174. TB, 13 March 1929.

5. "STRUGGLE IS THE FATHER OF ALL THINGS"

1. TB, 24 November 1927.
2. TB, 18 February, 13 March 1928.
3. TB, 3 May 1928.
4. TB, 1 April 1928.
5. Der Angriff, 23 April 1928; Engelbrechten, Armee, 75; and TB, 14 April 1928.
6. TB, 28 June, 7 July 1928.
7. Engelbrechten, Armee, 71ff.; see also Daluege's "Gau order" of 3 April 1928, ibid., 74f.
8. TB, 5 and 14 April.
9. TB, 14 May 1928; Der Angriff, 21 May 1928; Engelbrechten, Armee, 77.
10. TB, 17 May 1928; Der Angriff, 21 May 1928; Engelbrechten, Armee, 77f.
11. Statistisches Jahrbuch der Stadt Berlin 1928, 308f.
12. TB, 22 May 1928.
13. Der Angriff, 28 May 1928, "I.D.I."
14. Otto Strasser, "Gedanken zum Wahlergebnis," in NS-Briefe, 1 June 1928; Gregor Strasser, "Ergebnisse und Lehren," in Berliner Arbeiterzeitung, 27 May 1928.
15. LA Berlin, A Rep 358-01/24 vol. 4, Verdict of the Berlin-Schöneberg Magistrates' Court of 28 April 1928, TB, 29 April 1928.
16. LAB, A Rep 358-01/27, Verdict of the Schöneberg Magistrates' Court of 6 June 1928; TB, 6 June 1928.
17. TB, 9 June 1928; Der Angriff, 11 June 1928.
18. TB, 20 June 1928.
19. TB, 14 July 1928; Law on Amnesty, RGBl. 1928 I, 195f.
20. TB, 10 July 1928, also 11 July 1928; Verhandlungen des Reichstags, vol. 423, 149ff.
21. TB, 29 June 1928; Tyrell, Führer, 313 (Kaufmann reports to the Uschla that Otto Strasser had repeatedly requested him to participate in the establishment of a new party); see also TB, 15 September 1928.
22. TB, 22 June 1928. On the project of a newspaper, see also 16 February 1928; and 30 June, 10 July 1928 on its publication.
23. TB, 1 July 1928 and 15 July 1928. In the TB there are numerous entries on the conflict with the Strassers, for example especially 10, 13, and 30 June, 12, 13, and 14 July 1928.
24. TB, 23 July–4 August 1928.
25. TB, 24 July 1928.
26. TB, 4 August 1928.
27. TB, 14 April 1928; also 31 May, 16 June, 17 and 20 July 1928.
28. TB, 7 and 8 August.
29. On the background to this conflict, see Longerich, Geschichte der SA, Parts I and II. On the conflicts during 1928, see also Reuth, Goebbels, 141f. and the booklet written by the NSDAP's former Reich Music Director, Wilhelm Hillebrand, Herunter mit der Maske. Goebbels was very interested in the inside information it contained; see TB, 10–13, 16, 17, and 25 November 1928.
30. TB, 7 and 8 August 1928.

31. TB, 12–20 August 1928.
32. TB, 13 August 1928.
33. TB, 24 August 1928.
34. TB, 24 August 1928.
35. TB, 25 August–1 September 1928.
36. TB, 14 September 1928.
37. TB, 1 and 4 September 1928. It concerned a general membership meeting and a subsequent meeting of leaders.
38. TB, 23 and 25 September 1928.
39. Announcement in *Der Angriff,* 3 September 1928, Berichterstattung 8 October 1928; *12 Uhr Blatt,* 1 October 1928, "Die Zusammenstöße am gestrigen Sonntag"; LA Berlin A Rep 358-01/697, Versammlungsbericht der Abteilung IA des Polizeipräsidiums, 2 November 1928; Engelbrechten, *Armee,* 80f.; TB, 1 October 1928. See also Friedrich, *Hauptstadt,* 198f.
40. TB, 4 October 1928.
41. TB, 14 October 1928.
42. TB, 5 November 1928; *Der Angriff,* 12 November 1928.
43. TB, 17 November 1928; see also his rhapsodic editorial "Adolf Hitler" in *Der Angriff* of 19 November 1928 and "Hitler spricht im Sportpalast" (ibid.); *Berliner Morgenpost,* November 1928, "Hitler in Berlin"; *RSA* III/1, doc. 50; Engelbrechten, *Armee,* 82; Friedrich, *Hauptstadt,* 200ff.
44. *Der Angriff,* 18 November 1928.
45. See also his birthday article "Der Führer" in *Der Angriff* of 22 April 1929.
46. See his contributions in *Der Angriff,* partly published in the volumes *Der Angriff* (1935) and *Wetterleuchten* (1939). Also the Party leader does not play a prominent role in the two propaganda pamphlets published by Goebbels, *Das kleine ABC des Nationalsozialisten* (Greifswald 1925) and *Der Nazi-Sozi* (1929).
47. TB, 17 November 1928; *Berliner Morgenpost,* 18 November 1928, "Mysteriöser Tod eines Hitler-Mannes"; Engelbrechten, *Armee,* 82; Reuth, *Goebbels,* 146.
48. TB, 18 November 1928 (Jewish press).
49. TB, 19 and 20 November 1928. Cancellation of the reward also in *Der Angriff,* 26 November 1928. On Kütemeyer, see also TB, 21 and 23 November 1928.
50. See the reports in *Der Angriff,* in particular 26 November and 3 December.
51. TB, 13 and 14 September, 12 October 1928.
52. TB, 25 November 1928.
53. TB, 5 November 1928: "Osaf is a crafty chap. I must watch out with him because he seldom says what he means."
54. TB, 6 December 1928, also 20 December.
55. TB, 20 and 21 January 1929.
56. TB, 16 January 1929.
57. TB, 6 June 1929.
58. Friedrich, *Hauptstadt,* 187f.
59. TB, 7 December 1928, also 7 February 1929 on "good sub-leader material." On the Gau Day rallies during this period, see also 10 January 1929, 12 April 1930.
60. See the contributions of Muchow in *Der Angriff,* 9 February 1930, "Die Vollendung der Straßenzellen-Organisation" and in the *VB,* 11 March 1930, "Die Straßenzellen-Organisation des Gaues Berlin."
61. *Der Angriff,* 2 January 1930, "Ein Jahr Kampf um die Betriebe"; 1 June 1930, "Betriebszellen"; Reuth, *Goebbels,* 143; TB, 30 July 1929 and 28 May 1930.
62. TB, 21 and 26 October, 21 November 1928, and 8 December 1929.
63. TB, 12 August 1931.

64. TB, 7 and 8 March 1928.
65. TB, 21 March 1928.
66. TB, 30 March 1928, 23 March 1928.
67. TB, 24 March 1928.
68. TB, 22 April 1928, on Tamara. Further entries on brief contacts with Tamara, 8 June, 8 August, 23 September 1928, 22 January 1929.
69. TB, 6 August 1928.
70. TB, 12 August 1928.
71. TB, 25 and 27 August, 1 and 4 September 1928.
72. TB, 29 and 30 August 1928.
73. TB, 11 September 1928; he mentions her already on 7 August 1928. Further entries on Hannah Schneider in September and the beginning of October. See also 7 October 1928.
74. TB, 26 September 1928.
75. TB, 2 October 1928.
76. TB, 8, 14, and 15 October 1928.
77. TB, 17 October 1928; on the separation, see also 21 October 1928.
78. TB, 30 July, also 2 August, 15 September 1928.
79. TB, 27 October 1928.
80. TB, 28 and 30 October 1928; 11 and 18 November 1928.
81. TB, 18 and 18 December 1928.
82. TB, 20 December 1928.
83. TB, 30 December 1928, also numerous entries from December to February.
84. TB, 24 February 1929.
85. TB, 13 and 27 March, 1 and 6 April 1929.
86. TB, 14, 15, and 16 December 1928, 19 and 20 January 1929, 7 March 1929.
87. TB, 10 March 1929.
88. TB, 11 March 1929.
89. On the meeting with Anka, see TB, 20 and 23 March 1929.
90. TB, 24 March 1929.
91. TB, 1 April 1929 (on the whole trip).
92. TB, 3 April 1929; numerous entries also in March and April, and then again on 8 May, 1 July 1930.
93. TB, 19 and 28 April 1929; first mention 18 April, numerous entries between 22 April and the end of June.
94. TB, 25 May, 21 July 1929.
95. TB, 23 July 1929, on the stay in Weimar, also 25 July 1929.
96. TB, 26 July 1929.
97. TB, 6 December 1929 and 10–12 January 1930.
98. TB, 26, 28, and 30 July, 5, 10, 14, and 15 August 1929.
99. TB, 13 July 1929, also 15 and 21 July.
100. TB, 17 July 1929, also 29 July 1929.
101. TB, 4–6 August 1929.
102. TB, 6 August 1929.
103. TB, 10 August 1929; also 11 August 1929: "Yes, I musn't let love penetrate my heart."
104. Various entries, August to January.
105. TB, 14 August 1929.
106. TB, 13 October 1929, numerous entries from November to January.
107. TB, 12 December 1929.
108. TB, 19 February 1930.

109. TB, 24 February 1930. Also 24 March 1930: "She loves me like mad." 17 April 1930: "She's crazy about me."
110. TB, 23 March 1930. On their meetings, see numerous entries from 27 February to the end of March.
111. TB, 6 March 1930.
112. TB, 23 March 1930.
113. TB, 6 March 1930.

6. "A LIFE FULL OF WORK AND STRUGGLE"

1. Berghahn, *Der Stahlhelm,* 118ff.; Jung, *Demokratie,* 109ff. On Goebbels's position, see Reuth, *Goebbels,* 147ff.
2. TB, 17 March 1929.
3. TB, 28 March 1929.
4. TB, 5 April 1929. On his uncertainty regarding Hitler's policy, see also 6 and 9 April 1929.
5. TB, 12 April 1929; on the beneficial effects of the conversation, see also 13 April 1929.
6. TB, 16 April 1929.
7. TB, 30 April 1929. It referred to Hitler's memorandum to the Stahlhelm executive of April 1929. Berghahn, *Stahlhelm,* 126f.
8. *Der Angriff,* 13 May 1929, "Gegen die Reaktion" and 27 May 1929, "Einheitsfront."
9. TB, 16 May 1929; see also 17 May 1929. On Hitler's assurances that he was going to distance himself from the Stahlhelm, see 29 and 31 May 1929.
10. TB, 28 June 1929.
11. He said this in a speech on 28 June, according to a diary entry the following day.
12. TB, 5 July 1929.
13. Jung, *Demokratie,* 110.
14. TB, 12 July 1929.
15. TB, 6 July 1929.
16. TB, 2 March 1929.
17. TB, 1 March 1929. On the criticism of the Party leadership, see also 6 April 1929 (with Robert Rohde); on a conversation with Baldur von Schirach, the "Reichsführer of students," see 18 April 1929.
18. TB, 30 April 1929. However, Goebbels added that he had been "very reserved" during the conversation.
19. TB, 13 June 1929; *NS-Briefe,* 3 August 1929.
20. TB, 29 May, 5 July 1929.
21. TB, 30 July 1929.
22. On the establishment of the department, see 14 and 28 May and 4 June 1929. On the intensification of propaganda, see 30 July, 29 August, 18 October 1929. However, he soon thought Stark's work "too theoretical" (8 October 1929).
23. TB, 1 August 1929.
24. TB, 4 August 1929.
25. TB, 13 and 14 August 1929.
26. TB, 20 October 1929.
27. TB, 20 and 22 November 1929.
28. *Der Angriff,* 16 September 1929, under the heading "Kampf um Berlin."

29. *Der Angriff,* 9 September 1929.
30. TB, 8 September 1929; Engelbrechten, *Armee,* 101.
31. TB, 16 September 1929; Engelbrechten, *Armee,* 101.
32. TB, 23 September 1929; *Der Angriff,* 23 and 30 September 1929 ("Auf den Schanzen") and 20 October ("Neukölln ist nicht rot"); Engelbrechten, *Armee,* 102f.
33. *Der Angriff,* 16 September 1929.
34. *Der Angriff,* 3 and 6 October 1929, under the heading "Kampf um Berlin."
35. *Der Angriff,* 13 October 1929 with a detailed program (17–25 October); 20 October (on the ban), 24 October (under the heading "Kampf um Berlin": on developments): TB, 19 October 1929 (on the ban); see also Ehls, *Protest und Propaganda,* 154.
36. TB, 11 September 1929.
37. TB, 12–14 September 1929.
38. *Der Kampf gegen Young. Eine Sache des deutschen Arbeiters. Rede von Dr. Joseph Goebbels, M.d.R., gehalten am 26. September 1929 im Kriegervereinshaus Berlin.*
39. Jung, *Demokratie,* 116f.
40. Jung, *Demokratie,* 128ff.; Turner, *Die Großunternehmer und der Aufstieg Hitlers,* 141.
41. TB, 20, 21, and 23 October 1929.
42. TB, 28 October 1929.
43. TB, 31 October, 1 November 1929.
44. TB, 3 December 1929.
45. *Der Angriff,* 3 November 1939
46. *Der Angriff,* 24 November 1929 (Kampf um Berlin, about the Standarte IV's propaganda trip to Wedding); Engelbrechten, *Armee,* 107: On 17 November for the first time the whole of the SA was deployed in house-to-house propaganda.
47. *Statistisches Jahrbuch der Stadt Berlin 1930,* 347ff.
48. *Stadtverordneten-Versammlung der Stadt Berlin 1930,* 54f.; Reuth, *Goebbels,* 156.
49. Jung, *Demokratie,* 122ff.
50. TB, 8 January 1930.
51. TB, 14 March 1930.
52. LA Berlin, A Rep. 358-01/6015, Bericht der Abt. I A des Pol.Präs. of 2 April 1930; TB, 15 March 1930.
53. *Der Angriff,* 16 March 1931.
54. LA Berlin, A Rep 358-01/ 6015, verdict of 31 May 1930 and the indictment of 8 May 1930 and the institution of legal proceedings by the president on 31 December 1929; *VZ,* 1 June 1930, "Die Klage des Reichspräsidenten. Klamauk um Goebbels."
55. TB, 1 June 1930; see also 30 and 31 May 1930.
56. *Der Angriff,* 14 November 1929, reported on the funeral service carried out under the auspices of the Berlin NSDAP (Kampf um Berlin).
57. *Der Angriff,* 14 November 1929.
58. TB, 11 November 1929.
59. TB, 29 May, 4 June 1928.
60. TB, 24 and 29 November, 7 December 1929; on the death of his father, see also 8 December 1929.
61. TB, 11 December 1929.
62. TB, 8 and 11 December (quotation) 1929.
63. TB, 17 December 1929; see also Reuth, *Goebbels,* 148.
64. TB, 19, 23, and 30 December; Reuth, *Goebbels,* 157ff.

65. TB, 29 September 1929; also 16 January, 15 March, 5 April, also 28 April, 14 May 1929.
66. Siemens, *Horst Wessel;* Oertel, *Horst Wessel.*
67. TB, 15 January 1930.
68. TB, 19 January 1930.
69. On the cult of death and heroism associated with Wessel, see Siemens, *Wessel,* 131ff.
70. *Der Angriff,* 3 March 1930; on the riotous scenes surrounding the funeral, see Oertel, *Wessel,* 106ff. On the cult around Wessel and the other Nazi party deaths in Berlin, see Behrenbeck, *Der Tod um die toten Helden,* esp. 119ff.
71. As at the funeral and in an article in *Der Angriff* of 25 February 1930. Oertel, *Wessel,* 106ff.
72. *Der Angriff,* 6 March 1930, "Bis zur Neige."
73. On his plans, see TB, 2 May, 5 July, 12 September 1929; Reuth, *Goebbels,* 164.
74. TB, 20 October 1929.
75. TB, 6 December 1929.
76. TB, 13 January 1930; see also 17 January 1930.
77. TB, 24 and 25 January 1930.
78. TB, 29 and 30 January 1930.
79. TB, 31 January 1930.
80. TB, 5 and 6 February 1930; *VB,* 5 February 1930, Hitler's announcement of a Berlin edition of the *VB.*
81. TB, 15 February 1930, also 8 February.
82. TB, 16 February 1930.
83. *VB,* 16/17 February 1930. Hitler was emphasizing here the preeminence of the Party's central publishing house "in contrast to private publishers who publish Nazi newspapers or literature"; TB, 18 February 1930.
84. TB, 20 February 1930.
85. TB, 22 February 1930.
86. TB, 2 March 1930.
87. On Göring's and Lippert's negotiations in Munich, see TB, 5 March 1930. See also 8 March 1930.
88. TB, 16 March 1930; on his disappointment, see also 20 and 28 March 1930 (quotation).
89. TB, 5 March 1930.
90. TB, 23 March 1930.
91. TB, 1, 4, 5, and 14 April 1930.
92. TB, 25 April 1930.
93. Winkler, *Weimar,* 359ff.
94. TB, 1 April 1930.
95. TB, 4 April 1930.
96. *Der Angriff,* 6 April 1930, "Hugenberg" (editorial).
97. Winkler, *Weimar,* 378.
98. TB, 13 April 1930.
99. TB, 28 April 1930. On Hitler's speech, see *RSA* III/3, doc. 38.
100. TB, 2, 12, and 24 May 1930.
101. TB, 2 and 24 May 1930: "Himmler is still too preoccupied with detail. He has no wider vision."
102. TB, 27 May 1930.
103. TB, 24 May 1930; Paul, *Aufstand,* 70. This refers to Fritz Reinhardt, who had opened a speakers' school for the NSDAP in 1928.

104. TB, 2 and 3 May 1930; BAB, NS 26/133, NS-Führerbriefe July 1930, Hans-Severus Ziegler, *Ein Besuch beim Berliner Gau;* Reuth, *Goebbels,* p 163.

105. TB, 3 and 4 May 1930. On the Strasser crisis, see also Kershaw, *Hitler. 1889–1936,* 412ff.; Reuth, *Goebbels,* 163ff.

106. TB, 20, 22, and 24 May 1930.

107. TB, 22 May 1930: "Yesterday and today he had long talks with Dr. Strasser. The latter gives the impression of being completely rootless and inorganic, an intellectual white Jew, totally incapable of organization, a Marxist of the first order"; Strasser, *Ministersessel oder Revolution;* Tyrell, *Führer,* 314.

108. TB, 29 May 1930.

109. TB, 12, 14, and 23 June 1930.

110. *Der Angriff,* 3 July 1930, printed Hitler's letter to Goebbels of 30 June 1930, in which the Party leader authorized him to carry out a "ruthless purge" of the Berlin Party organization.

111. TB, 26 June 1930; on the exclusions, see 27 and 28 June 1930.

112. TB, 26 June 1930.

113. TB, 1 July 1930; Kissenkoetter, *Gregor Straßer und die NSDAP,* 44f.

114. TB, 1 and 3 July 1930; *Der Angriff,* 3 July 1930.

115. TB, 3 July 1930.

116. TB, 6 July 1930; on the crisis, see also 5 July 1930; *Der Angriff,* 6 July 1930, with a statement by Hitler of 4 July, according to which the newspapers of the Kampfverlag should be regarded as "opposition newspapers"; Wörtz, *Programmatik,* 34ff.

7. "DARE TO LIVE DANGEROUSLY!"

1. TB, 18 July 1930.

2. TB, 18 and 20 July 1930. On the dissolution of the Reichstag and its background, see Winkler, *Weimar,* 378ff.

3. TB, 20 July 1930.

4. TB, 23 July 1930.

5. TB, 28 and 29 July 1930. See also Goebbels's report on the meeting in *Der Angriff* of 2 August 1930: "Es kann losgehen." On the dissolution of parliament and the election campaign, see also Reuth, *Goebbels,* 168f.; Paul, *Aufstand der Bilder,* 73.

6. TB, 29 July, 2 August 1930.

7. This is revealed by the replies to a questionnaire that Goebbels sent to the Gaus in May 1930; NS 18/5010; see Mühlenfeld, "Zur Bedeutung der NS-Propaganda," 98. Goebbels undertook serious attempts to reorganize the propaganda machine only at the beginning of 1931; see 158f.

8. On the election campaign, see Lau, *Wahlkämpfe der Weimarer Republik,* 420ff.; Hacket, *The Nazi Party in the Reichstag Election of 1930;* Paul, *Aufstand,* 90f., which also includes reproductions of the posters, nos. 51 and 48; Goebbels's circular of 23 July 1930 (long quotations in Paul, *Aufstand,* 90f., former NL Streicher in the BAK); circular of 15 August 1930 in BHStA Varia, 1425.

9. TB, 13 August 1930; *Der Angriff,* 14 August 1930, "Dr. Goebbels freigesprochen" (headline); BAK, NL 1548/2, Lebenserinnerungen des Rechtsanwalts Rüdiger Graf v. d. Goltz, vol. 2, 171ff.

10. TB, 1 August 1930; the speech of 20 June 1927 is commented on in a report of the Reich Commissioner for the Supervision of Public Order of autumn 1927 pub-

lished in Deuerlein (ed.), *Der Aufstieg der NSDAP in Augenzeugenberichten,* 286ff.; BAB, NS 26/2512, correspondence of the Reich Court with Munich police headquarters; Thacker, *Goebbels,* 111f., gives further details.

11. TB, 5 and 6 July 1930; BAK, NL 1548/2, 168ff.
12. TB, 17 July 1930.
13. TB, 9 August 1930.
14. *VZ,* 15 August 1930, "Goebbels freigesprochen." See also Reuth, *Goebbels,* 170.
15. TB, 15 July 1930.
16. TB, 17 August 1930; *Der Angriff,* 29 December 1930, Politisches Tagebuch; LA Berlin, A Rep 358-01/25, indictment of 16 May 1930, verdict of 16 August 1930. On the reporting of the trial, see *Der Angriff,* 17 August 1930.
17. TB, 8 August 1930.
18. TB, 12 August 1930.
19. TB, 17 August 1930.
20. TB, 30 August 1930. On the Stennes rebellion of summer 1930, see Reuth, *Goebbels,* 171ff.
21. *Der Angriff,* 31 August 1930, "Der Sieg wird unser sein!" (headline).
22. LA Berlin, A Rep. 358-01/47, verdict of the Magistrate's court of 1 September 1930.
23. *RSA* III/3, doc. 99, telegram to von Pfeffer, 1 September 1930 and docs. 101 and 102, instructions of 2 September 1930.
24. *RSA* III/3, doc. 100.
25. TB, 8 September 1930 on the previous day. See also Engelbrechten, *Armee,* 139, and *Der Angriff,* 11 September 1930, "Riesenpropaganda der 'meuternden' S.A." The article reported that the SA had been driven through Berlin on 26 trucks, of which 24 had trailers.
26. TB, 11 September 1930; *VB* (B), 12 September 1930, "Adolf Hitler im Sportpalast," Reuth, *Goebbels,* 173f.
27. TB, 11 September 1930.
28. TB, 12 September 1930.
29. TB, 14 September 1930: "I'm expecting a big victory."
30. *Statistisches Jahrbuch der Stadt Berlin* 7 (1931), 339ff.
31. TB, 15 September 1930.
32. *Der Angriff,* 18 September 1930, "Unser der Sieg"; on the election victory, see also Reuth, *Goebbels,* 174.
33. TB, 18 September 1930.
34. TB, 21 Sepember 1930.
35. TB, 2 October 1930; see also 9 October 1930 about a Gauleiter meeting at which there was a very "hostile mood" toward the SA leadership.
36. TB, 26 September 1930; Bucher, *Der Reichswehrprozeß.*
37. TB, 23 September 1930.
38. On the meeting, see Pünder, *Politik in der Reichskanzlei,* 64f.; Brüning, *Memoiren 1918–1934,* 200ff.; Krebs, *Tendenzen und Gestalten,* 140f., on the background to the meeting. See also Reuth, *Goebbels,* 177.
39. TB, 6 October 1930. On 5 October in *Der Angriff* Goebbels had demanded the NSDAP's participation in the Prussian government as a precondition for the NSDAP taking part in government.
40. TB, 12 October 1930.
41. TB, 11 October 1930; *VZ,* 14 October 1930.
42. *Der Angriff,* 16 October 1930, "Wie Goebbels in den Reichstag kam."
43. TB, 14 October 1930.

44. TB, 23 September 1930, also 21 September 1930.
45. TB, 27 September 1930; see also 28 September 1930. On the reorganization of *Der Angriff* as a daily, see Reuth, *Goebbels,* 181.
46. TB, 9 October 1930.
47. *Der Angriff,* 1 November 1930; TB, 2 November 1930.
48. TB, 12 November 1930.
49. TB, 27 November 1930.
50. Longerich, *Geschichte der SA,* 45ff.
51. Longerich, *Geschichte der SA,* 108; TB, 28 November, 2 December 1931 (on the appointment).
52. TB, 6 December 1930; *VZ,* 7 December 1930, "Stinkbomben gegen den Remarque-Film" (a review of the film had appeared the day before). On the campaign, see Engelbrechten, *Armee,* 145; Reuth, *Goebbels,* 182f.; Dörp, "Goebbels' Kampf gegen Remarque." Goebbels had read the book the previous year and had loathed it; see TB, 21 and 23 July 1929.
53. *Der Angriff,* 8 December 1930, "Heraus zum Protest!"
54. TB, 9 December 1930; *VZ,* 9 December 1930, "Die Krawalle beim Remarque-Film"; see also the report in the *Berliner Lokalanzeiger,* 9 December 1930.
55. TB, 10 December 1930; *VZ,* 10 December 1930, "Herrschaft der Straße."
56. *VZ,* 12 December 1930, "Remarque-Film verboten"; TB, 12 December 1930.
57. TB, 14 December 1930, also 13 December.
58. TB, 18 January 1931. On the increased activism at the beginning of 1931, see Reuth, *Goebbels,* 187.
59. TB, 23 January 1931; Engelbrechten, *Armee,* 148; Reschke, *Der Kampf der Nationalsozialisten,* 92ff.
60. *VZ,* 24 January 1931.
61. *Der Angriff,* 23, 24 (quotation), 26, 27 (quotation), 31 January, 2 February 1931.
62. *VZ,* 3 February 1931, "Die Waffen nieder! Blutiges Wochenende."
63. TB, 11 January 1931. See also Reuth, *Goebbels,* 188.
64. TB, 20 January 1931.
65. TB, 11, 20, and 23 January 1931.
66. TB, 23 February 1931.
67. The TB entries in 1930 often include invitations to the Görings or visits together to the theater and the like, e.g., 8, 20, and 30 January, 8 and 12 February, 2, 13, 19, and 21 March, 1 and 7 April, 3 and 26 May, 1, 15–17, and 25 June, 2 and 16 July, 18 and 24 August, 11, 15, 22, 23, 29, and 30 September, 1 and 30 October, 17 and 19 November, 4 and 25 December.
68. TB, 18–24 April 1930.
69. TB, 4 January 1931; on the dispute with Göring, see also 3 January 1931.
70. TB, 20 February 1931.
71. TB, 18 January 1931.
72. TB, 12 and 28 January, 21 (conversation with Kaufmann) and 23 February, 1 March 1931.
73. TB, 13 and 22 January, 20 February 1931.
74. TB, 21 February 1931.
75. TB, 16 March 1931
76. TB, 26 February 1931.
77. TB, 15 January 1931.
78. TB, 27 February 1931.
79. TB, 4 March 1931.

80. TB, 6 March 1931.

81. TB, 6 March 1931.

82. TB, 25 March 1931. See also 26 February 1931. "Poor old Hitler! He must escape from the Munich Milieu."

83. "Wirtschaftsprogramm," *Der Angriff,* 12 October 1930, also already in "Weiter arbeiten!," 28 September 1930.

84. TB, 17 December 1930.

85. TB, 13 and 16 March 1931; Höver, *Goebbels,* 335ff.; the paper is published in Barkai, "Wirtschaftliche Grundanschauungen und Ziele der N.S.D.A.P.," 373ff.

86. TB, 17 March 1931; Reupke, *Der Nationalsozialismus und die Wirtschaft;* against Reupke, also TB, 23 and 28 March 1931.

87. TB, 25 March 1931.

88. TB, 14 March 1931.

89. *Der Angriff,* 14 March 1931, "Attentat auf Dr. Goebbels."

90. LA Berlin, A Rep 358-01/509, police interviews with former Party workers Weiss and Francke, 8 and 12 May 1931; Abteilung IA, report of 27 March 1931: "Thus all in all there is the suspicion that the attack on Dr. Goebbels was carried out by the NSDAP as a propaganda exercise"; *VZ,* 5 May 1931, "Die Bombe für Goebbels. Ein plumper Reklametrick. Wie 'Attentate' gemacht werden"; Reuth, *Goebbels,* 189f. and 195.

91. TB, 19 and 21 March 1931; *Der Angriff,* 20 March: "Dr. Goebbels darf sprechen—aber nur vor fünf Männern" (headline), here too an editorial by Goebbels: "Wie sollen wir's machen?"; 21 March 1931, "Gummiknüppel auf Dr. Goebbels—Unerhörte Vorgänge in Königsberg" (headline); see also Goebbels's editorial "Die Freiheit des Wortes"; 24 March 1931, "Allgemeines Redeverbot für Dr. Goebbels"; 25 March 1931, "Die Versammlungswelle steigt: Polizei besteht auf rechtswidrigem Redeverbot" (headline).

92. *RGBl.* 1931 I, 79ff., Reich Presidential Decree Against Political Disorder; *Der Angriff,* 31 March 1931, editorial in which Goebbels writes of a "Brüning dictatorship"; see also Reuth, *Goebbels,* 191.

93. TB, 28 March 1931, and 29 March 1931.

94. TB, 29 March 1931.

95. TB, 31 March 1931.

96. *Der Angriff,* 1 April 1931, "Hauptmann Stennes nicht abgesetzt! Eine Erklärung an die Presse" (headline); *VZ,* 2 April 1931, "Führerkrise im Hitler-Lager" (headline).

97. TB, 2 April 1931. On the conflict, see also Reuth, *Goebbels,* 192ff.

98. *Der Angriff,* 2 April 1931, "Kampf um den Nationalsozialismus" (headline). The full wording of this assignment of authority was published in the *VB* (Bavaria), in the form of a letter from Hitler to Goebbels, 3 April 1931.

99. TB, 4 April 1931. On the course of the coup, see also the detailed reports of the *VZ* during these days. The *VB* began its reporting of these events on 3 April and was already announcing that the coup had collapsed on 5 April (Bavarian edition).

100. This behavior prompted the *VZ* to publish an ironic article on 11 April, ("Goebbels meldet sich").

101. TB, 4, 6, 9, 10, 11, and 12 April 1931.

102. *VZ,* 8 April 1931, "Goebbels läßt Stennes pfänden."

103. *Der Angriff,* 7 April 1931, "Alles steht fest hinter dem Führer Adolf Hitler" (headline), see also "Der S.A. Konflikt" editorial.

104. TB, 16 also 15 April 1931.
105. TB, 17 April 1931; *Der Angriff,* 20 April 1931, "Die S.A. marschiert im Sportpalast."
106. LA Berlin, A Rep. 358-01/2, Minister of Justice to the General Prosecutor at the Supreme Court, 23 February 1931.
107. Reuth, *Goebbels,* 198ff.; TB, 10 February 1930.
108. A Rep 358-01/2, verdict of the Berlin-Mitte Magistrates' Court of 14 April 1931 and A Rep 358-01/2517, verdict of the Berlin-Mitte Magistrates' Court of 14 April 1931; *Der Angriff,* 15 April 1931; TB, 15 April 1931.
109. TB, 18 April 1931.
110. A Rep 358-01/23, vol. 2, verdict of the Berlin Provincial Court, 17 April 1931.
111. TB, 28 April 1931; A Rep 358-01/3, Prosecutor at the LG III, 27 April 1931 to the Police President Abt IA; report of the Berlin detective of 12 May 1931.
112. LA Berlin, A Rep 358-01/39, vol. 4, verdict of 29 April, after the proceedings of 27, 28, and 29 and A Rep 358-01/39, vol. 12, verdict of 27 April 1931. TB, 30 April 1931: Departing from the sentences imposed, Goebbels mentions here a second fine of 1000 RM. See Reuth, *Goebbels,* 200ff. His appeal against the fine of 1,500 RM was rejected: TB, 3 June 1931; A Rep. 358-01/2 appeal proceedings on 2 June 1931.
113. TB, 2 May 1931.
114. *Der Angriff,* 20 April 1931, "Prozesse" editorial.
115. Paul, *Aufstand,* 69ff.; TB, 12 November 1930.
116. BAB, NS 18/882, 15 January 1931; see Paul, *Aufstand,* 78.
117. TB, 28 April 1931.
118. *Unser Wille und Weg,* 2, May 1931, "Organisatorisches, Richtlinien der Reichspropagandaleitung," 43–63.
119. TB, 28 April 1931.
120. A few days before his trip to Munich he had contemplated resignation as Gauleiter; he wasn't the Party's "drain cleaner": TB, 22 and 25 April 1931.
121. TB, 10 and 20 May 1931.
122. TB, 9 May 1931.
123. Joseph Goebbels, *"Der Nazi-Sozi,"* 18f.
124. *VZ,* 9 May 1931, "Adolf Legalité. Hitlers Bekenntnis."
125. TB, 9 May 1931. Joseph Goebbels, *"Der Nazi-Sozi"* second edition (Munich 1931).
126. TB, 20 June 1931, on the conversation with Karin Göring, 18 June 1931.
127. TB, 27 June 1931, also 28 June 1931.
128. *Der Angriff,* 30 June 1931; TB, 30 June 1931.
129. TB, 30 June 1931.
130. TB, 3 July 1931, see also 4 July 1931, where he expressed his determination to kill off the "agency."
131. See also TB, 19 February 1931 concerning a further visit from Magda. On Magda's previous life, see Jungbluth, *Die Quandts,* 196ff. On Magda Quandt/Goebbels, see also Klabunde, *Magda Goebbels;* Meissner, *Magda Goebbels.*
132. Jungbluth, *Die Quandts,* 46ff.
133. On the marriage, see Jungbluth, *Die Quandts,* 67ff.
134. On the divorce, see Jungbluth, *Die Quandts,* 90ff.
135. TB, 23 February 1931.
136. TB, 26 and 27 February 1931.
137. TB, various entries in March 1931, especially 10, 15, and 22.
138. TB, 26 March 1931.

139. TB, 17 June 1931.
140. TB, 12 March, 4 and 9 April 1931.
141. TB, 12 April 1931.
142. TB, 13 and 14 April 1931.
143. TB, 17 April 1931.
144. TB, 18–22, 25, and 30 April, 8, 10, 11, and 15 May 1931.
145. TB, 22–31 May 1931.
146. TB, 31 May 1931.
147. TB, 11 June 1931.

8. "NOW WE MUST GAIN POWER . . . ONE WAY OR ANOTHER!"

1. TB, 6 July–5 August 1931. The diaries from 20 August 1931 to 21 May 1932 have been accessible only from 2004 and have already been used in Thacker, *Goebbels*, 121ff.
2. TB, 12 July 1931.
3. TB, 26 July 1931.
4. TB, 26 July 1931.
5. TB, 13, 24, and 31 July 1931.
6. TB, 17 July 1931.
7. TB, 27 July 1931.
8. TB, 5 and 7 July 1931.
9. Berghahn, *Stahlhelm*, 169, 172f.; Schulz, *Von Brüning zu Hitler*, 433ff.
10. TB, 10 August 1931.
11. *Der Angriff*, 15 August 1931, "Lachen links."
12. TB, 19 and 21 August 1931.
13. TB, 24 August 1931.
14. Schulz, *Brüning*, 554.
15. TB, 12, 16, and 22 August 1931.
16. TB, 24 August 1931.
17. TB, 25 August 1931.
18. TB, 26 August 1931.
19. TB, 27 August 1931.
20. TB, 4 September 1931.
21. TB, 4 September 1931.
22. TB, 14 September 1931.
23. TB, 16 September 1931.
24. Wagener, *Hitler aus nächster Nähe*, 375f.
25. Ibid., 392ff.
26. According to Wagner, Hitler had contemplated a partnership with Magda only after the death of Geli Raubal (who died in September) and his conversation with Magda took place on the way to the big SA demonstration in Braunschweig, which, however, occurred only in October 1931. Wagener, *Hitler*, 392ff. However, the Goebbels diaries make it clear that the Hitler-Goebbels arrangement was reached before Geli's suicide. There had been speculation about a triangular Hitler-Goebbels-Magda relationship in the secondary literature before the publication of the complete version of the Goebbels diaries, for example in Klabunde, *Goebbels*, 238ff., and in Reimann, *Dr. Joseph Goebbels*.
27. TB, 5, 10, 15, and 26 October 1931.

28. TB, 20 September 1931.
29. Reuth, *Goebbels,* 206; Longerich, *Geschichte der SA,* 121f. Friedrich, *Hauptstadt,* 318ff.
30. TB, 18 September 1931.
31. See the reports of the *VZ,* 19–24 September 1931; TB, 18–26 September.
32. TB, 25 September 1931.
33. In the text, Helldorff.
34. TB, 27 September 1931.
35. TB, 30 September 1931.
36. TB, 8 and 9 November 1931; on the trial, see *VZ,* 8 and 9 October, 8 November 1931; Reuth, *Goebbels,* 207.
37. LA Berlin A Rep 358-01/20, vol. 3, Verdict, 9:2.32 LG III Berlin; TB, 23 January 1932; Goebbels, *Vom Kaiserhof zur Reichskanzlei,* 22 January 1932, where Goebbels made rather more of the scene; *VZ,* 17 and 24 December 1931, 23 and 26 January 1932; see also Reuth, *Goebbels,* 207.
38. The first mention of the planned meeting is in the 3 October 1931 entry in the TB.
39. TB, 5 October 1931.
40. TB, 12 October 1931; Pyta, *Hindenburg,* 631; Brüning, *Memoiren,* 391f.
41. Jones, "The Harzburg Rally of October 1931."
42. *Ursachen und Folgen,* Michaelis and Schraepler (eds.), vol. 8, nos. 1784a and c; *Politik und Wirtschaft in der Krise, 1930–1932,* Maurer and Wengst (eds.), no. 341, report by Blank to Reusch, 12 October 1931 and *VZ,* 13 October 1931, "Die Front der Fronde, mit weiteren Einzelheiten zum Tagungsverlauf."
43. Kopper, *Hjalmar Schacht,* 191ff.
44. TB, 19 October 1931.
45. TB, 19 October 1931; *VZ,* 19 October 1931 (E=Evening edition), "Braunschweiger Treffen."
46. *Der Angriff,* 21 October 1931, also in Goebbels, *Der Angriff,* 211–12; TB, 20 October 1931.
47. TB, 25 October 1931.
48. TB, 30 and 31 October 1931.
49. TB, 1 November 1931.
50. TB, 8 November 1931.
51. TB, 1, 3, 23 and 26 October, 3 and 5 November 1931.
52. TB, 13 December 1931: "My sitting room and bedroom are very nice and have been prepared with a lot of loving care." See also 16, 17, and 21 November 1931.
53. TB, 22 November 1931
54. TB, 29 November 1931.
55. TB, 11 December 1931.
56. TB, 14 December 1931.
57. TB, 18 and 19 December 1931; *Die Rote Fahne,* 18 December 1931, "Wir gratulieren Herr Goebbels!"
58. TB, 20 December 1931; Reuth, *Goebbels,* 210f.; Meissner, *First Lady,* 110f.; Jungbluth, *Die Quandts,* 116ff. According to the privately published memoirs of Günther Quandt, which Jungbluth was able to look at, Quandt had known nothing about the wedding preparations of his ex-wife.
59. TB, 1 September 1931, concerning a conversation with Helldorf. The hitherto autonomous sub-group Greater-Berlin was amalgamated with the Gau storm Brandenburg. See also Engelbrechten, *Armee,* 190f.
60. TB, 9 December 1931.
61. Schulz, *Brüning,* 610ff.

62. TB, 9 December 1931.

63. TB, 1, 10, and 13 December 1931. The second ban was somewhat reduced: *Der Angriff* did not in fact come out between 10 and 14 December.

64. Reuth, *Goebbels,* 212f.; Schulz, *Brüning,* 704ff.

65. The exploratory discussions were undertaken by Groener, Schleicher, and Meissner. Pyta, *Hindenburg,* 649f.; there are numerous details in the Brüning memoirs, 468f., 495ff. Meissner had already been putting out feelers to Göring in December. *Akten der Reichskanzlei. Die Kabinette Brüning I und II,* Koops (ed.), no. 599, Vermerk Meissner über den Empfang Görings beim Reichspräsidenten am 11. Dezember 1931; see Pyta, *Hindenburg,* 649.

66. *Kabinette Brüning I und II,* no. 617: Vermerk Pünder über Besprechung des Reichspräsidenten mit dem Reichskanzler, 5 January 1932.

67. *Kabinette Brüning I und II,* no. 626, Vermerk StSekr Pünder über die Wahl des Reichspräsidenten: 8, 10, and 13 January 1932. Brüning, *Memoiren,* 501, on 6 January 1932. See also Pyta, *Hindenburg,* 653f.

68. *Kabinette Brüning I und II,* no. 623, Hitler to reich chancellor, 12 January 1932 concerning a conversation with Groener on 6 January 1932 as well as a memorandum for the president, published in Poetsch-Heffter, "Vom Staatsleben unter der Weimarer Verfassung," 102ff. (*VB,* 19 January 1932) and in: *RSA* IV/3, doc. 8, 15 January 1932; statement by Brüning of 22 January 1932 (*Kabinette Brüning I und II,* no. 642); Hitler's reply, 25 January 1932, published in Poetsch-Heffter, "Vom Staatsleben," 108ff. (*VB,* 29 January 1932).

69. TB, 6–11 January 1932.

70. See Goebbels, TB, 13 January 1932. The German Nationalist politician, Reinhold Quaatz, who was well-informed about the conversation, noted in his diary on 14 January about Hitler: "Driven by growing discontent in his party, he wanted to get out of Brüning's clutches and on Monday evening suddenly, using very inadequate means, tried to force Hindenburg to dismiss Brüning. At the same time, he wanted to appear to the outside world as the one at the center of events and to discredit Hugenberg. Result: complete failure." Weiss and Hoser (eds.), *Die Deutschnationalen und die Zerstörung der Weimarer Republik,* 168ff.

71. TB, 20 January 1932.

72. See also TB, 20 January 1932.

73. TB, 20 January 1932.

74. TB, 23 January 1932.

75. TB, 28 January 1932.

76. Goebbels discussed the matter intensively with Hitler during a visit to Munich and during a visit by Hitler to Berlin: TB, 3 and 10 February 1932.

77. TB, 23 February 1932; *Der Angriff,* 23 February 1932, "Schluß jetzt! Deutschland wählt Hitler!" (headline); *VZ,* 23 February 1932 (M=Morning edition), "Hitler und Duesterberg proklamiert."

78. TB, 22 February 1932.

79. *Verhandlungen Reichstag,* V. LP, vol. 446, 2252.

80. *Verhandlungen Reichstag,* V. LP, vol. 446, 2254.

81. *Verhandlungen Reichstag,* V. LP, vol. 446, 2346ff., 2353. See also TB, 26 February 1926.

82. TB, 20 January 1931; Paul, *Aufstand,* 74.

83. TB, 1 March 1932.

84. TB, 1 and 5 March; see Reuth, *Goebbels,* 215f.

85. BAB, NS 26/287, NSDAP Reich propaganda headquarters memorandum of 13 March 1932.

86. Paul, *Aufstand,* 95ff., 248ff.

87. TB, 27 February 1932; Engelbrechten, *Armee,* 207.

88. *Der Angriff,* 31 March, 1 and 4 April (quotation) 1932.

89. TB, 2–5 March 1932.

90. Excerpts from it appeared in the *Münchner Post* of 9 March 1932, which was also a Social Democratic paper; TB, 6 March 1932.

91. TB, 7 March 1932.

92. TB, 8 and 10 March 1932.

93. TB, 17 March 1932; Hitler expressed the same view a few days later to Goebbels (28 March 1932).

94. TB, 14 March 1932; see also Reuth, *Goebbels,* 216f.

95. TB, 16 March 1932.

96. TB, 16 March 1932.

97. TB, 16 and 17 March 1932; VZ, 16 March 1932, "Hitler also had to make a statement to the Investigating Committee of the Thuringian parliament, which was investigating Frick's failed attempt to gain German citizenship for Hitler by appointing him as a civil servant."

98. TB, 19 March 1932. Also 23 March 1932: "It's difficult to work with him. Too unpredictable. Big plans but can be implemented only with difficulty and against opposition."

99. TB, 20 March 1932.

100. TB, 29 March 1932.

101. However, Hitler's "flight over Germany" received barely a mention in Goebbels's diaries (there was only the entry for 6 April 1932), while in his 1933 "Kaiserfhof" edition he emphasizes it as a "decisive innovation": 18 March, 5 and 7 April 1932. On the "flight over Germany," see also Reuth, *Goebbels,* 217f. On the flight, see the reports in *Der Angriff,* which reported it between 2 and 7 April as headline news.

102. TB, 5 April 1932. On the lifting of the ban on demonstrations, see 2 April 1932.

103. TB, 6, 7, 9, and 10 April 1932.

104. Pamphlet *"Wenn Hindenburg gewählt wird, dann [. . .]. Ja, was dann?."* On the election campaign, see BAB, NS 26/290, in particular the guidelines signed by Goebbels and issued to the Gau headquarters for the second campaign as well as the draft leaflets (sent on the same day) and the circular of 7 April 1932.

105. Schulz, *Brüning,* 758.

106. TB, 16 and 18 March 1932; VZ, 18 March 1932, "Goebbels bei einer anständigen Handlung ertappt"; *Der Angriff,* 17 March 1932, interview with Dr. Goebbels.

107. Engelbrechten, *Armee,* 212.

108. TB, 24 March 1932.

109. TB, 8 April 1932.

110. TB, 11 April 1932; see Reuth, *Goebbels,* 218.

111. Thus for the "Kaiserhof" version of his diary, which he published in 1933, he cut the passages in which he had criticized Hitler's irregular working methods, replacing sections dealing with the situation before Hitler's decision to run, when he was still uncertain about his candidature, with various passages praising Hitler's leadership qualities. TB, 19 and 23 March; *Kaiserhof,* 4 and 10 February, 18 and 22 March 1931. He omitted Hitler's surprise at his defeat in the first round (TB, 14 March, *Kaiserhof,* 13 March 1931), and turned the criticism expressed by leading Party members of his own propaganda into "enthusiasm" (*Kaiserhof,* 19 March 1931) and gave great weight to the "flight over Germany" (see note 101).

112. TB, 15 April 1932. There are already references to the impending ban on 12 and 13 April 1932. For examples of disguise in the form of associations, underground

organizations, and continuation of SA duties, see Engelbrechten, *Armee,* 216ff.;
Reuth, *Goebbels,* 218.

113. TB, 25 April 1932; see also Reuth, *Goebbels,* 220f.

114. TB, 15 April 1932, concerning a conversation with Hitler: "Personnel issues relating to Prussia: Strasser Prime Minister, Göring Interior and Darré Agriculture. Strasser? Göring? Him to compensate him for not getting the Reichswehr. I'm getting indoctrination [Volkserziehung] for the Reich. That's my field and I'm looking forward to it. Helldorff [correct spelling: Helldorf] Berlin Police President. Schultz [correct spelling: Schulz] Minister for Labor Service." TB, 24 April 1943 (concerning 20 April.): "Helldorff: He's been to see Schl. [. . .] Is only acceptable for us for the R, if the Prussian IM has an incumbent who knows what he's doing. Str. and Gör. are completely out of the running. Helld.'s very eager to have me. I object. That's not my kind of position. They'll have to drag me to do it if they want me." TB, 24 April 1932 (concerning 22 April): "Röhm and Helldorf come and see me. Röhm moans a lot about Strasser and Schultz [correct spelling: Schulz]. [. . .] Göring too crude and boastful [. . .] Göring is to be Prime Minister, me IM. I agree. But the others will have to manage it." TB, 24 April 1932 (concerning 23 April): "Röhm and Helldorf. [. . .] Strasser's ruled out."

115. *Statistisches Jahrbuch der Stadt Berlin 1932,* 259f.

116. TB, 27 April 1932.

117. TB, 29 April 1932.

118. Pyta, *Hindenburg,* 691; Brüning, *Memoiren,* 575ff.

119. TB, 7 May 1932.

120. TB, 9 May 1932. See Reuth, *Goebbels,* 222.

121. TB, 9 May 1932.

122. LAB, A Rep 358-01/721, Generalstaatsanwalt, 6 June 1932 to Prussian Ministry of Justice; TB, 13 May 1932; *VZ,* 13 May 1932, "Polizei im Reichstagssaal"; *Verhandlungen Reichstag,* vol. 446, 2686ff.; Reuth, *Goebbels,* 224.

123. TB, 13 May 1932. On Groener's resignation, see Schulz, *Brüning,* 820f.

124. TB, 14 May 1932.

125. TB, 19 May 1932.

126. TB, 25 May 1932.

127. Pünder, *Reichskanzlei,* 126; Brüning, *Memoiren,* 593ff.; *Staatssekretär unter Ebert, Hindenburg, Hitler,* 224ff. See also Schulz, *Brüning,* 853.

128. TB, 28 May 1932; *VZ,* 26 May 1932, "Blutige Saalschlacht im Landtag" (headline).

129. TB, 28 May 1932.

130. On this conversation, see Schulz, *Brüning,* 843ff; *Kabinett Brüning I und II,* no. 773, Niederschrift des Staatssekretärs Pünder über die letzte Ministerbesprechung des Reichskabinetts Brüning am 30. Mai 1932; Brüning, *Memoiren,* 597ff.; Pünder, *Politik,* 128f., Brüning's report on the conversation immediately after the meeting with Hindenburg.

131. On the background, see Fiederlein, *Der deutsche Osten und die Regierungen Brüning, Papen, Schleicher;* Schulz, *Brüning,* 800ff.

132. TB, 31 May 1932.

133. TB, 30 May 1932.

134. TB, 31 May 1932.

135. TB, 1 June 1932.

136. On the von Papen government, see Hörster-Philipps, *Konservative Politik in der Endphase der Weimarer Republik;* Petzold, *Franz von Papen.*

137. TB, 1 June 1932; on the continuation of this "dispute," see 3 June 1932.

138. TB, 5 June 1932.

139. Schulz, *Brüning*, 879f.
140. TB, 5 June 1932.
141. TB, 7 June 1932.
142. *Der Angriff*, 6 June 1932, "Was müssen wir tun?" and 14 June 1932, "Papen, werde hart!" See also Reuth, *Goebbels*, 226.
143. TB, 10 June 1932; on reform, see Kissenkoetter, *Straßer*, 68ff.; *VB* (Bavaria), 15 June 1931, Hitler's instruction as well as Strasser's (extensive) regulations for implementing it.
144. TB, 15 June 1932.
145. TB, 15 June 1932; Reuth, *Goebbels*, 226, on the reaction to the speech; Kissenkoetter, *Straßer*, 139f.
146. Kissenkoetter, *Gregor Straßer*, 137ff.
147. BAB, NS 22/2, letter from Goebbels/Dietrich to all Party offices, 4 June 1932; letter from Goebbels/Dietrich to all Gauleiters and Gau propaganda directors, 27 June 1932; further detailed instructions of 5 July 1932; BAB, NS 26/289, undated memorandum on the Reichstag election and various circulars from the Party's Reich propaganda headquarters to the Gauleiters and Gau propaganda directors; see also Paul, *Aufstand*, 100ff.
148. BAB, NS 26/289, circulars from the Party's Reich propaganda headquarters to all Gau propaganda and press offices, 19 July 1932.
149. BAB, NS 26/289, memorandum by the Reich propaganda headquarters on the Reichstag election of 1932.
150. TB, 15 June 1932; the scenario described in the Kaiserhof version is much more detailed than in the original TB version. See also Reuth, *Goebbels*, 226f. Decree of the Reich President against Political Unrest of 14 June 1932, *RGBl*. 1932 I, 297; Goebbels learned about it on 16 June; TB, 17 June 1932.
151. TB, 28 June 1932.
152. TB, 9 July 1932.
153. TB, 10 July 1932; Heiber (ed.), *Goebbels Reden*, no. 4; *VB* (Bavaria), "200,000 im Berliner Lustgarten."
154. TB, 11–16 July 1932.
155. *VB* (Bavaria), 13 July 1932, "Des Führers Freiheitsflug über Deutschland beginnt" (headline); see also 17/18–31 July 1932: continued reporting on the flight.
156. Lerg, *Rundfunkpolitik in der Weimarer Republik*, 448. Text republished in Heiber (ed.), *Goebbels Reden*, no. 5.
157. TB, 19 July 1932; text in Heiber (ed.), *Goebbels Reden*, no. 5.
158. TB, 22 (quotation) and 24 June 1932; see also 10 June 1932.
159. Decree of the Reich President concerning the Re-establishment of Public Security and Order in the Territory of the State of Prussia of 20 July 1932, *RGBl*. 1932 I, 377; *Akten der Reichskanzlei, Das Kabinett von Papen (1932)*, Karl-Heinz Minuth (ed.), nos. 57 and 59, Ministerbesprechungen vom 11. Juli und 12. Juli 1932, 16:30 Uhr.
160. Schirmann, *Altonaer Blutsonntag 17. Juli 1932*.
161. Schulz, *Brüning*, 920ff.
162. TB, 20 July 1932 concerning the events of the previous day and on 20 July itself.
163. TB, 21–23 July 1932.
164. TB, 21–29 July 1932.
165. *Statistisches Jahrbuch der Stadt Berlin 1933*, 262ff.
166. TB, 1 August 1932.

9. "I HAVE A BLIND FAITH IN VICTORY"

1. TB, 3 August 1932; Reuth, *Goebbels*, 230.
2. TB, 7 August 1932.
3. TB, 9 August 1932.
4. On Meissner's report, see note 9.
5. TB, 12 August 1932.
6. TB, 11 August 1932: "S.A. concentrated around Berlin. Makes the honorable gentlemen very nervous. That's the point."
7. TB, 12 August 1932. The *VB* (R) of 12 August denied the rumors: "Judenschwindel über eine Berliner S.A.-'Aktion'" (headline). See also Reuth, *Goebbels*, 332.
8. TB, 14 August 1932; Pyta, *Hindenburg*, 718f.; Pünder, *Politik*, 141.
9. TB, 14 August 1932; *Kabinett von Papen*, p. 399, no. 101, Note by state secretary Meissner about a conversation between the Reich president and Adolf Hitler on 13 August 1932, at 16:15; see also Reuth, *Goebbels*, 232f.
10. What was being referred to was above all the communiqué's formulation that Hitler had demanded "the power of the state to its fullest extent," which Hitler had not in fact done. *Kabinett von Papen*, doc. 101n5. No. 102, Adolf Hitler an den Reichswehrminister, Staatssekretär Meissner und Staatssekretär Planck, 13 August 1932 (The Nazi leadership's account of the events).
11. *VB* (R), 17 August 1932.
12. TB, 14 August 1932: "Kerrl is given the task of negotiating with the Center Party. That's now the biggest threat we can make." Morsey, *Der Untergang des politischen Katholizismus*, 59f.
13. TB, 15–22 August 1932.
14. Reich Presidential Decree Against Political Terror; Decree of the Reich Government Concerning the Creation of Special Courts; Reich Presidential Decree Concerning the Securing of Domestic Peace; all of 9 August 1932, *RGBl.* 1932 I, 403ff. On their passage, see *Kabinett von Papen*, no. 98, Ministerbesprechung vom 9. August 1932.
15. On the wave of violence at the beginning of the month, see Longerich, *Geschichte der SA*, 156f.; see details in the daily reports of the *VZ* from 2 August 1932.
16. *RSA*, vol. 5, doc. 174, Hitler telegram to the five condemned SA men published in *Der Angriff* of 23 August 1932 and elsewhere.
17. TB, 26 August 1932.
18. TB, 26 August 1932. While the coalition with the Center Party was seriously considered as a second best solution, Goebbels, in revising the text for the Kaiserhof version, was to portray this solution as merely a feigned option (and thereby to emphasize that in this instance Strasser, who was no longer referred to by name, was advocating a maverick policy): "We set up contacts with the Center Party, if only as a means of putting pressure on the other side. It's naturally not really an option. A certain section of the Party strongly supports the Center Party solution. The Führer is in favor of continuing with the old line. I fully support him in this." On the meeting between Brüning and Strasser, see Brüning, *Memoiren*, 623; Morsey, *Untergang*, 61.
19. TB, 27 and 28 August 1932.
20. TB, 29 August 1932.
21. TB, 30 August 1932. Thus, according to this, the meeting between Brüning and Hitler took place on 2 August. Brüning confirmed in his memoirs that during this conversation he had offered to mediate between the NSDAP and the Center Par-

ty's central committee (p. 623f.). Schulz, *Brüning,* 968; Morsey gives 28 August as the date of the conversation. *Untergang,* 61.

22. TB, 31 August 1932. See also 30 August 1932: "Göring's going to be president of the Reichstag. That too!"
23. TB, 1 and 2 September 1932.
24. TB, 8 and 9 September. On the negotiations between the NSDAP and the Center Party, see Morsey, *Untergang,* 61ff.; on the subsequent "covering up of their tracks" by the Center, see 65ff.; on the plan to get rid of Hindenburg, see Pyta, *Hindenburg,* 736.
25. TB, 1–4 September 1932; see also 9 September 1932.
26. TB, 2 and 3 September 1932.
27. TB, 9 and 11 September 1932. In the published version of the diary (Kaiserhof) Goebbels omitted the demand for Hindenburg's resignation and maintained that Hitler had gone into the meeting convinced that it would not be possible to "bring [the Center] around" (10 September).
28. Brüning, *Memoiren,* 625f. According to Brüning he told the Center Party's Reichstag group that he would resign from the Party if any of its members entered negotiations with the NSDAP to bring "a charge" against Hindenburg for a breach of the Constitution.
29. Pyta, *Hindenburg,* 737. The law that was originally envisaged as implementing Article 51 in the end, under the changed circumstances of December 1932, was given the status of a law altering the Constitution. *RGBl.* 1932 I, 547.
30. TB, 13 August 1932; on the session, see Reuth, *Goebbels,* 235f.; *Verhandlungen Reichstag,* 6. Wahlperiode, 13ff. In view of the NSDAP/KPD majority in the Reichstag the Center Party's parliamentary group considered it foolish to continue sticking to this position. Morsey, *Die Protokolle der Reichstagsfraktion der deuschen Zentrumspartei,* no. 711, Vorstand, 2 September 1932. Bericht des Abg. Perlitius.
31. Schulz, *Brüning,* 973 and 993f.
32. TB, 14 September 1932.
33. Reuth, *Goebbels,* 236; Paul, *Aufstand,* 104ff.; BAB, NS 26/263, Streng vertrauliche Informationen der RPL, 20, 25, and 27 October 1932.
34. *Der Angriff,* 24 and 25 September 1932; TB, 22, 24, 27, and 30 September 1932.
35. Paul, *Aufstand,* 249f.
36. TB, 8 September 1932.
37. TB, 7 October 1932; *VB* (R), 27 October 1932, "Neuordnung der Reichspropagandaleitung"; BAB, NS 22/1 Anordnung no. 11, signed by Strasser and Goebbels, 4 October 1932; Paul, *Aufstand,* 74.
38. TB, 4 November 1932. On the BVG strike, see Winkler, *Der Weg in die Katastrophe,* 765ff.; on Goebbels's role, see Reuth, *Goebbels,* 238f.
39. TB, 5 November 1932.
40. *Statistisches Jahrbuch der Stadt Berlin,* 1933, 264f.
41. TB, 7 November 1932; on the breaking off of the strike, see 8 November 1932; Winkler, *Der Weg,* 771.
42. The first entry on the strike is in TB, 3 November 1932; see in contrast the Kaiserhof version, 2–5 November 1932.
43. TB, 19 November 1932.
44. *Kabinett von Papen,* no. 222, Note by Meissner concerning the Reich president's meeting with Hitler, 19 November 1932; Pyta, *Hindenburg,* 753ff.; on the conversations between Hindenburg and Hitler in November, see Meissner, *Staatssekretär,* 247ff.

45. TB, 22 November 1933; on this second meeting, Pyta, *Hindenburg,* 756f., *Kabinett von Papen,* no. 224, Aufz. Meissner, 21 November 1932.

46. TB, 21 November 1932.

47. TB, 22 November 1932.

48. TB, 21 November 1932.

49. TB, 22 November 1932. There followed an exchange of letters between Hitler and the president's office which did not, however, alter the positions. TB, 23 and 24 November 1932; *Kabinett von Papen,* no. 225, Meissner to Hitler, 22 November 1932; no. 226, Hitler's reply, 23 November 1932.

50. TB, 1 December 1932. In the Kaiserhof book Goebbels expanded his description of this scenario in which Strasser had been "pessimistic" to a degree that they "would not have thought possible" (1 December 1932). In the published version he does not mention the fact that Strasser had given way in the end.

51. TB, 1 December 1932. In this entry Ott is wrongly referred to as Otte.

52. TB, 2 December 1932. In the Kaiserhof version Goebbels added to the word "toleration" the half sentence "but there can no longer be any question of that." In fact, at the beginning of December 1932 this was a feasible option from the point of view of the Nazi leadership.

53. *Kabinett von Papen,* no. 239 b, Tagebuchaufzeichnung des Reichsfinanzministers über den Verlauf der Ministerbesprechung vom 2. Dezember 1932, 9 Uhr; IfZ, ZS 279, Ott note of 1946, concerning the war game. On Schleicher's soundings, see Bracher, *Die Auflösung der Weimarer Republik,* 667ff.; Vogelsang, *Reichswehr, Staat und NSDAP,* 318ff.; Kissenkoetter, *Gregor Straßer und die NSDAP,* 162ff.; Plehwe, *Reichskanzler Kurt von Schleicher,* 234ff.; Strenge, *Kurt von Schleicher,* 182ff.

54. The *Tägliche Rundschau* of 8 December estimated on the basis of the total number of votes that the Nazi party in Thuringia had lost 37.7 percent of the vote compared with the election of July 1932.

55. Vogelsang, *Reichswehr,* 340f.; Schulz, *Brüning,* 1040f.; Strenge, *Schleicher,* 205; Winkler, *Weimar,* 561.

56. On the notion of a "cross-front" and its continuing use in the literature, see above all Schildt, *Militärdiktatur mit Massenbasis?;* Schulz, *Brüning,* 1034ff. (with some reservations); Schulze, *Weimar,* 393ff.; Kolb, *Die Weimarer Republik,* 137, 205.

57. In the *Kaiserhof* version Goebbels added a paragraph according to which the Nazi leadership had already been informed about Schleicher's offer to Strasser on 5 December. "By chance we heard about the real reason for Strasser's sabotage policy: He had a meeting with General Schleicher on the Sunday evening in the course of which the general offered him the position of vice chancellor. Strasser not only did not reject this offer but informed him of his intention, in the event of new elections, to put forward his own list of candidates." Goebbels then added a devastating assessment: "That is the worst kind of betrayal of the Führer and the Party. I was not surprised. I never believed anything else of him. We are now simply waiting for the moment when he carries out his betrayal in public."

58. TB, 9 November 1932 on Hitler: "He's furious about Strasser. I can believe it. Strasser's always carrying out sabotage." *Kaiserhof,* 8 November 1932: "When I'm alone with the Führer he talks about how angry he is with Strasser and his undermining and sabotage activities. Much of our failure can be attributed to the unfair behavior of his clique. I also believe that this failure [he meant the BVG] was not unwelcome to him because this means that at least it looks as though he's been proved right and can blame us to the Party for our radical course." 21 November 1932: "Strasser is sticking with it. So are Frick and Göring." *Kaiserhof,* 20 Novem-

ber 1932: "All the sub-leaders are sticking with it, it's only Strasser who as usual is doing his own thing."

59. In June 1934 Goebbels noted that his "exposing of Strasser" had been heavily criticized by some Gauleiters. Goebbels believed that naturally the "old Strasser clique" had been behind this criticism (TB, 3 and 7 June 1934.) A few weeks later Alfred Rosenberg noted criticism from Gauleiters; that the things Goebbels was writing about Strasser were like "someone who now felt he was safe triumphantly kicking a rival when he was down." *Alfred Rosenberg,* Seraphim (ed.), 36.

60. Although such ideas may have been contemplated by Schleicher's entourage during the previous months, they did not play a decisive role in his policy at the end of 1932, which was influenced above all by his attempt somehow to survive the next few months through an arrangement with the NSDAP. See Turner, "The Myth of Chancellor von Schleicher's Querfront Strategy." Turner had already expressed previous doubts about Schleicher's offers. Ibid.; Winkler, *Der Weg,* 116.

61. TB, 8 December 1932.

62. The social policy section of the emergency decree of 4 September (through which the system of wage agreements had been largely abolished) was suspended, an amnesty law was passed, motions for the introduction of winter aid for the unemployed and for the suspension of the whole of the emergency decree of 4 September 1932 were sent to the committees, all with the support of the NSDAP; Winkler, *Weimar,* 560.

63. As early as 3 December the Schleicher cabinet was dealing with the question whether, as the chancellor formulated it, the "domestic emergency decrees" might be relaxed to a certain extent. *Akten der Reichskanzlei, Das Kabinett von Schleicher* 1932/33, Golecki (ed.), doc. 1. These efforts led to the Reich president's emergency decree for the Maintenance of Domestic peace of 19 December 1932, through which, among other things, the emergency decrees of 14 and 28 June, of 9 August, and of 2 November 1932 were suspended (*RGBl.* 1932 I, 548) and the Reich government's decree concerning the suspension of the special courts of the same day (*RGBl.* 1932 I, 550).

64. *Kabinett von Schleicher,* no. 5, Ministerbesprechung vom 7 December 1932.

65. At the beginning of 1927 he had already watched a dance presentation by Riefenstahl with great enthusiasm (TB, 13 January 1927: "A delightful and delicate creature."). On 1 December 1929, after seeing the film *Piz Palü* he wrote about Riefenstahl, that she was "a marvelous child." After seeing the Riefenstahl film "The Blue Light" he noted: "Sweet Riefenstahl" (TB, 1 April 1932).

66. Riefenstahl had written a letter to Hitler in May 1932 and then later met him personally. Kinkel, *Die Scheinwerferin,* 40f. The account of this meeting is based on Riefenstahl, *Memoiren,* 154ff. During the following months she was filming abroad.

67. On the Strasser crisis, see Reuth, *Goebbels,* 244ff.; Schulz, *Brüning,* 1040f.; and the reports in *Der Angriff,* 9–12 December 1932, and in the *VZ,* 12 December 1932.

68. Kissenkoetter discusses the contents of the letter in *Strasser,* 172, on the basis of a surviving draft. On these events, see also *VZ,* 9 December 1932, "Konflikt Hitler-Strasser"; *VZ,* 10 December 1932, Konrad Heiden: "Schach oder matt? Gregor Strassers Rebellion" (editorial).

69. TB, 9 December 1932.

70. *Tägliche Rundschau,* 10 December 1932, "Die Vorgänge in der NSDAP" (headline).

71. TB, 9 December 1932.

72. TB, 10 December 1932.

73. TB, 11 and 13 December 1932; *Der Angriff,* 9 and 12 December 1932.
74. On the reorganization after Strasser's departure, see Paul, *Aufstand,* 76f.
75. TB, 14 December 1932, also 13 December.
76. TB, 24 December 1932–1 February 1933. See also Reuth, *Goebbels,* 246f.
77. TB, 13 January (Hitler was with Magda) and 20 and 23 January 1933 (with Hitler in the Clinic).
78. Salzuflen (4 January 1933), various places on 9 January and (after a short trip to Berlin) between 10 and 14 January in Detmold and in various other places. On the election campaign in Lippe, see also Reuth, *Goebbels,* 248f.; Ciolek-Kümper, *Wahlkampf in Lippe.*
79. TB, 10 January 1933. 21 December 1932 was the first diary entry in which Goebbels indicated that he was no longer tolerating the Schleicher government.
80. TB, 13 January (quotation) 1933, 14 and 15 January 1932.
81. *Der Angriff,* 16 January 1933.
82. TB, 17 January 1933. On Hitler's negative comments on Strasser, see TB, 20 December 1932 and 1 January 1933; see also 22 January 1933.
83. TB, 25 January 1933.
84. TB, 26 January 1933.
85. TB, 28 January 1933.
86. TB, 28 and 29 January 1933.
87. TB, 30 January 1933.

10. "WE'RE HERE TO STAY!"

1. TB, 1–5 February 1933.
2. *Akten der Reichskanzlei, Regierung Hitler,* Karl-Heinz Minuth (ed.), no. 21; Bracher, "Stufen der Machtergreifung," 45ff.; Kershaw, *Hitler 1936–1945,* vol. 2, 555ff.
3. TB, 1 February 1933.
4. TB, 23 January, 9 August 1932.
5. *Kaiserhof,* 22 January 1932 and 8 August 1932; Reuth, *Goebbels,* 269f., already made this point.
6. TB, 3 February 1933.
7. TB, 2 February 1933. Such rumors can be confirmed for February from other sources: Diller, *Rundfunkpolitik im Dritten Reich,* 76; *FZ,* 2 February 1933, 2nd ed. (M), "Gerüchte über Dr. Göbbels *[sic]*": According to this the Berlin evening newspapers had spread the rumor that he would be appointed radio commissar and also it was said that he would be made police president of Berlin. Both rumors were, however, officially denied.
8. TB, 6 February 1933.
9. TB, 10 February 1933.
10. *Kaiserhof,* 7 March 1933.
11. On the newspaper bans above all of communist and Social Democratic papers, see the reports in the *FZ* in February 1933; TB, 16 February 1933: "Newspaper bans are coming thick and fast. *Vorwärts* and *8 Uhr.* Terrific!"
12. TB, 6 February 1933; *Der Angriff,* 6 February 1933, "Berlin trauert um Sturmführer Maikowski und Schupowachtmeister Zauritz"; Reuth, *Goebbels,* 256.
13. TB, 5 February 1933; the funeral oration is published in Heiber (ed.), *Goebbels Reden,* no. 10.

14. TB, 10 February 1933.

15. TB, 11–24 February 1933.

16. TB, 10, 11, 14, 15, 16, 18, and 21 February 1933.

17. TB, 16 February 1933.

18. TB, 14 February 1933.

19. TB, 15 February 1933.

20. TB, 21 February 1933. According to this, financial difficulties recurred because the flow of money took time to get under way: 26 and 28 February 1933.

21. Paul, *Aufstand*, 111ff.

22. See Diller, *Rundfunkpolitik*, 65ff.; *Regierung Hitler*, vol. 1, no. 17, Niederschrift über die Ministerbesprechung vom 8. Februar 1933; Hadamovsky, "Großkampftage der Rundfunkpropaganda"; this was already mentioned in Reuth, *Goebbels*, 259.

23. Heiber (ed.), *Goebbels Reden*, no. 11; TB, 10 February 1933.

24. TB, 11–25 February, 2, 3, and 5 March 1933. His appearances can be followed through the reports in *Der Angriff* during this period.

25. TB, 20 February 1933.

26. TB, 16 and 18 February 1933.

27. E.g. TB, 17, 22, and 28 February.

28. TB, 15 February; on the opening, see *FZ*, 12 February 1933 (M), "Die Berliner Internationale Automobil- und Motorrad-Ausstellung."

29. TB, 16 February 1933.

30. TB, 24 February 1933.

31. TB, 28 February 1933. The telephone conversation is confirmed in Hanfstaengl, *Zwischen Weißem und Braunem Haus*, 294f.

32. The question of who was responsible for the Reichstag fire has been the subject of a long controversy that has by no means been resolved in favor of the theory of a sole culprit. The most important works are Tobias, *Der Reichstagsbrand*; Backes et al., *Reichstagsbrand*; Hans Schneider, *Neues vom Reichstagsbrand—Eine Dokumentation. Ein Versäumnis der deutschen Geschichtsschreibung*, with a preface by Iring Fetscher and contributions from Dieter Deiseroth, Hersch Fischler, Wolf-Dieter Narr (Berlin 2004); Deiseroth (ed.), *Der Reichstagsbrand und der Prozess vor dem Reichsgericht*; Kellerhoff, *Der Reichstagsbrand*; Hofer et al., *Der Reichstagsbrand*; Hehl, "Die Kontroverse um den Reichstagsbrand"; on Goebbels's role, see Reuth, *Goebbels*, 262ff.

33. *Der Angriff*, 28 February 1933, "Der Reichstag brennt."

34. *Reichsgesetzblatt* 1933 I, p. 83.

35. TB, 5 March 1933.

36. *Der Angriff*, 25 February 1933, with Goebbels's editorial "Der Tag der erwachenden Nation."

37. See the reports in *Der Angriff* of 4 and 6 March 1933; *VB* (B), 5/6 March 1933, "Der Freiheitstag der erwachten Nation." The quotation refers to Hamburg.

38. "Hitler über Deuschland. Rundfunkreportage aus Königsberg zum Tage der erwachenden Nation am 4. März 1933," published in Goebbels, *Signale der neuen Zeit*, 109–117, quotations 109f., 116f.

39. TB, 5 March 1933.

40. *FZ*, 6 March 1933 (M). The election slogan in the *VZ* of 4 March 1933 (E) conveys the same image.

41. *Statistisches Jahrbuch der Stadt Berlin 1933*, 385.

42. TB, 3 March 1933.

43. TB, 7 March 1933; *VB* (B), 14 March 1933, "Dr. Goebbels an die Berliner Partei-genossen."

44. TB, 7–12 March; *Regierung Hitler,* vol. 1, no. 56; see also no. 46, Denkschrift über die Errichtung eines Reichskommissariats für Volksaufklärung und Propaganda, 7 March 1933. Erlaß über die Errichtung des Reichsministeriums für Volks-aufklärung und Propaganda, *RGBl.* 1933 I, 104.

45. TB, 12 March 1933.

46. TB, 9 March 1933.

47. TB, 9–11 March 1933; Bracher, *Machtergreifung,* 136ff.; Kershaw, *Hitler. 1936–1945,* 585ff.

48. *Statistisches Jahrbuch Berlin 1933,* 268ff.

49. TB, 13 March 1933.

50. TB, 15 March 1933; on his appointment, see also 14 March 1933. The document of appointment of Goebbels, "writer," as propaganda minister is in BAB, R 43 II/1149 (13 March 1933).

51. TB, 16 March 1933; *Regierung Hitler,* vol. 1, no. 61, 15 March 1933.

52. Speech to the press in Berlin on 16 March 1933, published in Goebbels, *Revolu-tion der Deutschen,* 135–51.

53. TB, 18 March 1933, see also 17 and 20 March 1933.

54. *Der Angriff,* 21 and 22 March 1933; *VB* (B), 22 March 1933.

55. TB, 23 March 1933; Scheel, *Der Tag von Potsdam;* Sabrow, "Der 'Tag von Pots-dam' "; Reuth, *Goebbels,* 277ff.

56. TB, 21 March (quotation) concerning the preliminary meeting on the previous day and 23 March 1923 concerning the cabinet meeting on 21 March; Verord-nung des Reichspräsidenten zur Abwehr heimtückischer Angriffe gegen die Re-gierung der nationalen Erhebung, 21 March 1933, *RGBl.* 1933 I, 135. The law imposed the death penalty in particularly serious cases: *Regierung Hitler,* vol. 1, no. 70, Sitzung vom 21 March (the session of 20 March is not documented).

57. TB, 25 March 1933; Gesetz zur Behebung der Not von Volk und Reich, 24 March 1933, *RGBl.* 1933 I, 141. On the speeches, see *Verhandlungen Reichstag,* 8. Legis-laturperiode, vol. 457, 23ff.

58. TB, 27 March 1933.

59. *VB* (B), 26/27 March 1933 "Minister Goebbels über das Ziel des deutschen Rund-funks. Das vornehmste Instrument in der Hand der Regierung." The speech is also printed in Heiber (ed.), *Goebbels Reden,* no. 13, quotations 87, 89, 78.

60. A shorter version in *Der Angriff,* 30 March 1933, complete in Albrecht, *National-sozialistische Filmpolitik,* 439ff., which also contains commentary (13ff.). See also Moeller, *Filmminister,* 152.

61. TB, 29 March 1933.

62. TB, 4 April 1933.

63. Lang himself reported that during this conversation Goebbels had offered him a leading position in the German film industry, whereupon he had decided to leave Germany immediately. However, in fact there is evidence that Lang was still in Germany during June and July. Moeller, *Filmminister,* 161. See also McGilligan, *Fritz Lang,* 173ff. Goebbels did not refer to the meeting with Lang in the *Kaiserhof* version, with the result that Lang's account was considered dubious. On "The Testament of Dr. Mabuse," see TB, 30 October 1933 ("Very exciting").

64. Published in Wulf, *Presse und Funk im Dritten Reich,* 64f. (excerpt); TB, 30 March 1933.

65. *VB* (B), 7 April 1933, "Adolf Hitler vor der auswärtigen Presse" (headline), and

"Unsere Revolution macht nirgends halt! Minister Goebbels über das kommende neue Pressegesetz," published in Goebbels, *Signale der neuen Zeit,* 127–35. *FZ,* 7 April 1933 (2nd M), "Der Reichskanzler vor der Auswärtigen Presse"; *FZ,* 8 April (2nd M), "Kommentar 'Pressefreiheit,'" which criticized the speeches; *VZ,* 7 April 1933 (M), "Der Kanzler an die Presse" (headline), including "Dr. Goebbels über Pressefreiheit."

66. TB, 27 March 1933.

67. TB, 28 March 1933; according to this, on 27 March Goebbels was engaged in preparing the announcement, which he then sent to Munich on the same day by telex for Hitler's authorization, which it received. (TB, 29 March 1933).

68. Statement by Hitler in the cabinet meeting of 29 March, *Regierung Hitler,* vol. 1, no. 78.

69. TB, 1 April 1933; *FZ,* 1 April 1933.

70. *VB* (B), 4 April 1933. See also the cabinet meeting on 31 March 1933, at which economic and foreign policy concerns were expressed and Hitler explained the "pause." *Regierung Hitler,* vol. 1, no. 80. On the whole issue, see Longerich, *Politik der Vernichtung* 34ff. On the anti-Jewish "action" see also *VB* (B), e.g. 25, 28 (headline), 29 (headline), 30 (headline), and 31 March and 1 (headline) and 2 April 1933 (headline).

71. On the Jewish boycott of March 1933, see Adam, *Judenpolitik im Dritten Reich,* 46ff.; Barkai, *Vom Boykott zur "Entjudung,"* 23ff.; Friedländer, *Nazi Germany and the Jews,* 19ff.; Longerich, *Holocaust,* 35ff.

72. TB, 2 April 1933.

73. *VB* (B), 2/3 April 1933, "Riesenkundgebung der N.S.D.A.P."

74. TB, 11 April 1933; see also 2, 6, and 10 April 1933. Publication of the correspondence in e.g. the *Vossische Zeitung* of 11 April, republished in Wulf, *Musik im Dritten Reich,* 86ff.; see also Prieberg, *Kraftprobe,* 78ff.

75. TB, 14 April 1933.

76. TB, 17 April 1933.

77. TB, 18 April 1933.

78. See *VB* (B), 19–21 April; Kershaw, *Hitler Myth,* 57ff.

79. *VB* (B), 19–21 April 1933.

80. TB, 19 and 20 April 1933.

81. TB, 26 and 27 April; reports in the *Rheydter Zeitung:* 6, 13, and 21 April and the headlines of 22, 24, and 25 April; the award of honorary citizenship of the city of Rheydt: StA MG, NL Goebbels/143. On the cancellation of the municipal incorporation, see Waldecker, "Rheydt," 304f.; on this visit, see also Reuth, *Goebbels,* 282f.

82. TB, 25 June 1933.

83. TB, 25 March 1933.

84. *Regierung Hitler,* vol. 1, no. 93, Ministerbesprechung vom 7. April 1933; Gesetz über die Einführung eines Feiertags der nationalen Arbeit, 10. April 1933, *RGBl.* 1933 I, 191.

85. On the preparations, see TB, 18 April–1 May 1933.

86. TB, 2 May 1933; *Der Angriff,* 1 May 1933, "Ehret die Arbeit und achtet den Arbeiter! Der Aufruf des Ministers für Volksaufklärung und Propaganda"; 2 May 1933, "Der 1. Mai: Deutschlands gewaltigster Bekenntnistag" (headline).

87. TB, 18 April 1933.

88. Erlaß über die Errichtung des Ministeriums für Volksaufklärung und Propaganda, 13 March 1933, *RGBl.* 1933 I, 104. The decree suspended the regulations in the standing orders of the Reich government of 3 May 1924, according to

which the Reich chancellor could transfer responsibilities only provided this did not "fundamentally" affect the competencies of the ministries. Published in *Akten der Reichskanzlei. Die Kabinette Marx I und II,* Abramowski (ed.), no. 192.

89. TB, 16, 21, and 23 March 1933.

90. TB, 25 March 1933.

91. Rischbieter, "NS-Theaterpolitik," 11ff.

92. TB, 8 and 20 April 1933.

93. TB, 28 April 1933, and 29 April 1933.

94. TB, 29 April, 5, 10, 11, 14, and 24 May, 8 June 1933. BAB, R 55/414, Protokoll vom Promi und AA über die Ressortbesprechung vom 12. Mai 1933. *Regierung Hitler,* vol. 1, no. 138, Chefbesprechung vom 24. Mai 1933. The press department of the Foreign Ministry was to restrict itself to the collection of information from abroad and basic information policy.

95. TB, 9 May 1933. Speech on "Die Aufgaben des deutschen Theaters im Hotel Kaiserhof zu Berlin" on 8 May 1933, in: *Der Angriff,* 9 May 1933, and in Goebbels, *Revolution der Deutschen,* 175–201. See also *FZ,* 10 May 1933 (M), "Die Aufgaben des deutschen Theaters. Eine Rede des Ministers Dr. Goebbels."

96. On the burning of the books, see Reuth, *Goebbels,* 285; "*Das war ein Vorspiel nur*." *Bücherverbrennung Deutschland 1933: Voraussetzungen und Folgen.* Ausstellung der Akademie der Künste vom 8. Mai bis 3. Juli 1983, Berlin/Vienna 1983, in particular: "Die Hochschulen und der 'undeutsche Geist.' Die Bücherverbrennungen am 10. Mai 1933 und ihre Vorgeschichte," 31–50. According to this the initiative definitely came from the Deutsche Studentenschaft.

97. Heiber (ed.), *Goebbels Reden,* no. 14, quotations 108, 110; TB, 11 May 1933.

98. Jäger, *Es begann am 30. Januar,* 47f. (based on the radio reports of the time).

99. TB, 19 May 1933. The speech is published in Albrecht, *Filmpolitik,* 442ff., comments 15ff. See also the report in *Der Angriff* of 19 May 1933. A few days earlier the Propaganda Ministry had issued an official statement with the aim of allaying fears that the new government was intending to restrict film. A law for the "Corporate Construction of the Film Industry" was announced (the later Reich Chamber of Film): *Der Kinematograph,* 9 May 1933; see the long quotation in Albrecht, *Filmpolitik,* 16.

100. TB, 7, 14, 21, and 27 May, 8 June 1933. Albrecht, *Filmpolitik,* 18f.; Behn, "Gleichschritt in die 'neue Zeit.'"

101. Gesetz über die Errichtung einer vorläufigen Reichsfilmkammer of 14 July 1933, *RGBl.* 1933 I, 483; Verordnung über die Errichtung einer vorläufigen Reichsfilmkammer of 22 July 1933, *RGBl.* 1933 I, 531; Official justification of the law in the *Reichsanzeiger,* 18 July 1933; Albrecht, *Filmpolitik,* 19ff.

102. TB, 14 and 15 June 1933.

103. TB, 6, 7, and 20 September 1933.

104. TB, in particular 7, 8, and 10 October; Loiperdinger (ed.), *Märtyrerlegenden im NS Film,* in particular the contributions of Loiperdinger on "Hans Westmar" and Schröter on "Hitlerjunge Quex."

105. TB, 2 April 1933, on another film tea on 9 May 1933.

106. TB, 20 May 1933, on an earlier meeting 9 April 1933.

107. TB, 10 April, 26 April, 21 May, 11 June 1933.

108. TB, 27 April 1933, 29 March 1933.

109. TB, 17 and 26 May 1933.

110. TB, 12, 14, 16, and 20 June. On these contacts, see Moeller, *Filmminister,* 160f.; Kinkel, *Scheinwerferin,* 47; Bach, *Leni,* 110ff. The account of her relations with Hitler and Goebbels during these months in Riefenstahl's *Memoiren* (194ff.) is

clearly misleading; she claims that she was forced into doing the project against her will by Hitler and Goebbels (who in addition had also tried to seduce her) and under pressure had agreed to do it only three days before the start of the Party rally. For criticism of this version that does not bear close examination, see also Trimborn, *Riefenstahl*, 168ff.; Rother, *Leni Riefenstahl*, 53ff.

111. Verordnung über die Aufgaben des Reichsministeriums für Volksaufklärung und Propaganda, 30 June 1933, *RGBl.* 1933 I, 446. According to this, apart from the responsibilities of the Foreign Ministry (AA) already referred to, the new ministry acquired the responsibility for: commercial advertising etc. from the Reich Economics Ministry, communications and transport advertising from the Reich Postal Ministry and the Reich Transport Ministry, and all technical radio matters from the Reich Postal Ministry insofar as they did "not affect the technical administration within the Reich Radio Association and the Radio Associations." The following responsibilities were transferred from the Reich Interior Ministry to the Propaganda Ministry:

- General domestic political enlightenment
- Hochschule für Politik
- National celebrations and state celebrations
- Press
- Radio
- The National anthem
- Deutsche Bücherei Leipzig
- Art
- Music
- Theater
- Cinema
- Combating pornography

112. TB, 17 June 1933; see also 12 May, 20 June, 24 June, 1, 7, and 9 July 1933. On the background, see Diller, *Rundfunkpolitik,* 84ff.; Reuth, *Goebbels,* 289.
113. *Regierung Hitler,* vol. 1, no. 196, letter from Hitler to the Reichsstatthalters of 15 July 1933 after the meeting with the Reichsstatthalters on 6 July, at which he defined the central role of the Goebbels ministry vis-à-vis the federal states in the fields of propaganda and culture. See also TB, 19 July 1933, in which Goebbels expressed great relief about the letter.
114. Diller, *Rundfunkpolitik,* 93ff.
115. Diller, *Rundfunkpolitik,* 108ff.
116. Diller, *Rundfunkpolitik,* 128.
117. TB, 9 August 1933.
118. Diller, *Rundfunkpolitik,* 130ff.
119. Haegert had replaced Franke in December 1932 (14 December 1932).
120. Gutterer's career data in his personal file of March 1938; BAB, R 43 II/1150c. Gutterer was originally envisaged as Franke's successor (TB, 28 November 1932).
121. Entry in Keiper and Kröger (eds.), *Biographisches Handbuch des deutschen Auswärtigen Dienstes,* 1871–1945.
122. Moeller, *Filmminister,* 118.
123. TB, 22 November 1934.
124. Boelcke (ed.), *Kriegspropaganda 1939–1941* (henceforth *BK*), 80f.
125. *BK,* 60.
126. TB, 9 April 1933.

127. The report on the whole Italian trip is in TB, 4 June 1933. There were frequent and extensive reports on the trip in the German press. See, for example, *Der Angriff,* 29 May–2 June. On the trip, see Michels, *Ideologie und Propaganda,* 144. PAA Bts Rom no. 692a, vol. 11: Embassy correspondence on the preparations for the trip, detailed program of visits: press statement by Goebbels about his impressions during the visit; report by ambassador von Hassell of 13 June 1933 about the visit, which makes clear in a thinly disguised way the minimal political importance of the visit.

128. TB, 7–9 June 1933. On the Four-Power Pact, see Petersen, *Hitler-Mussolini,* 137ff.

129. TB, 15 June 1933. He had already advocated a "purging of the Party" to Hitler on 17 May 1933, and had been promised one (TB, 18 May 1933).

130. *Der Angriff,* 22 May 1933, "Aufmarsch der 150,000 im Grunewald-Stadion"; brief mention in TB, 22 May 1933. On these speeches, see *Der Angriff,* 15 May, "Kundgebung in Leipzig am 14. Mai"; see also TB, 15 May 1933; on the speech in the Oberpräsidium, see *Der Angriff,* 13 June 1933, "Pg. Dr. Goebbels in Ostpreußen"; on Röhm, see Longerich, *Geschichte der SA,* 179ff.

131. TB, 15 June 1933; *Der Angriff,* 16 May 1933, "Der zweite Tag der Führertagung der NSDAP. Die Partei als Rückgrat des Staates."

132. TB, 15 June 1933.

133. *Der Angriff,* 15 June 1933, "Reichsführertagung der NSDAP." TB, 15 June 1933: "Discussion with the Propaganda Department. Discussed big aid program for the winter"; TB, 4 July 1933, "Big plan: 'War against hunger and cold.'"

134. TB, 28 June 1933; *Regierung Hitler,* vol. 1, no. 170, Ministerbesprechung vom 27 June 1933.

135. TB, 29 June 1933.

136. TB, 1, 3, and 4 July 1933. Albert Speer carried out the alterations. Speer, *Inside the Third Reich,* 21ff.

137. TB, 16 July 1933.

138. TB, 4 July 1933: "Hitler with the SA leaders in Reichenhall. Gave a good speech. Against the 'second revolution.'" See also *VB* (B), 4 July 1933: "Begeisterter Empfang des Führers im Chiemgau." According to that report Hitler called the SA leaders' meeting there a "landmark" on the way "to the completion of the German revolution." This rejection of a continuation of the revolution is confirmed by *VB* (B), 8 July 1933, official statement about a declaration by Hitler to the Reichsstatthalters on 6 July 1933: "The revolution is not a permanent condition. It must not develop into a permanent condition."

139. TB, 11 July 1933. *Der Angriff,* 11 July 1933, "Unsere nächsten Aufgaben": "Of the many hundreds of thousands who have joined us since the take-over of power the usable ones will gradually be merged into the Party; the others, insofar as they are useless, will be excluded from it."

140. *PA* 1933, p. 69 (11 July): "The article must be written early tomorrow morning"; *VZ,* 12 July 1933 (M); *DAZ,* 12 July 1933 (M); TB, 12 July 1933: "My big article is appearing in all the German newspapers."

141. TB, 18 and 19 July 1933. *PA* 1933, 73f. (17 July); *FZ,* 18 July 1933 (2nd M), *DAZ,* 18 July 1933 (M).

11. "ONLY THOSE WHO DESERVE VICTORY WILL KEEP IT!"

1. TB, 6 July 1933.
2. TB, 11 June–1 July 1933.
3. TB, 18 June 1933.
4. TB, 19 July 1933; see Reuth, *Goebbels,* 291f.
5. TB, 21 July 1933.
6. TB, 2–17 August; Riefenstahl and Krauss: 14–17 August; on Riefenstahl, see also 4, 9, 14, 18, and 19 July 1933. Goebbels had also met Leni Riefenstahl on 13 August during a brief visit she made to Berlin. (TB, 14 August 1933), then he saw her again on 26 August 1933 at Hitler's regular lunch (TB, 27 August 1933).
7. Statement by the Reich Press Office of the NSDAP, published in the *VB* (B), 7 August 1933.
8. TB, 20 and 23 August 1933.
9. TB, 25 August 1933.
10. Also in a previous conversation with Hitler from which Goebbels retained the quotations "The federal states must disappear" and "In three years nothing more will be left of them," TB, 28 July 1933.
11. TB, 27 March 1933.
12. TB, 25 August 1932. Goebbels had already discussed this solution with Lammers in July, TB, 19 July 1933.
13. TB, 25 August 1933.
14. TB, 1 September 1933.
15. TB, 2 September 1933. *VB* (B), "Die Proklamation des Führers: Die Eckpfeiler des Reiches: Das deutsche Volk—die N.S.D.A.P." (headline).
16. TB, 4 September 1933 (for a description of the whole of the Party rally); *Der Angriff,* 4 September 1933.
17. TB, 4, 6, and 8 July 1933.
18. TB, 14 September 1933; *Der Angriff,* 13 September 1933, "Sozialismus der Tat. Dr. Goebbels verkündet Aufbau und Durchführung des großen Winter-Hilfswerks" (headline). On the winter aid program, see Vorländer, *Die NSV,* esp. 44ff.
19. See his speech of 12 September *(Der Angriff)*.
20. See, for example, the Sports Palace rally on 13 September: *Der Angriff,* 14 September 1933, "Neuer Propagandafeldzug der Partei"; also TB, 14 September 1933.
21. *Der Angriff,* 14 September 1933.
22. TB, 2 October 1933; Bernhard Gelderblom, "Die Reichserntedankfeste auf dem Bückeberg 1933–1937."
23. TB, 16 October 1933; *Der Angriff,* 16 October 1933, on the laying of the foundation stone.
24. TB, 16 October 1933; *Der Angriff,* 16 October 1933. The monument was never finished.
25. See Helmut Heiber's introduction to his *Goebbels Reden.*
26. BAB, R 43 II/1244, 13 July 1933. On the establishment of the Reich Chamber of Culture, see Faustmann, *Die Reichskulturkammer,* 34ff.; Dahm, "Anfänge und Ideologie der Reichskulturkammer."
27. Grundgedanken für die Errichtung einer Reichskulturkammer, R 43 II/1241.
28. BAB, R 43 II/1244, Goebbels's letter to Ley, 28 July 1933. He also complained in a letter to Lammers of 12 August 1933 about continuing attempts by the DAF to undermine his organizations: ibid.

29. *Regierung Hitler,* vol. 1, no. 196, Hitler's letter to the Reichsstatthalters, 15 July 1933, announced the plan to establish the Reich Chamber of Culture.
30. BAB, R 2/4870, submission of the draft and justification to the Reich Chancellery on 18 August 1933; Minute of 2 September of the inter-ministerial meeting in the Propaganda Ministry, in which various objections were made by other ministries. R 43 II/1241, renewed submission of the draft on 15 September 1933. *Regierung Hitler,* vol. 1, no. 215, Kabinettssitzung of 22 September 1933. See also TB, 14 August 1933, on the preparation of the law; 25 August 1933, approval by Hitler; 20 September 1933, reference to the Cabinet meeting; 23 September 1933, approval by the Cabinet.
31. Kulturkammergesetz of 21 September 1933, *RGBl.* 1933 I, 661f. The legal regulations following from it are in: *Das Recht der Reichskulturkammer,* Schrieber, Metten, and Collatz (eds.).
32. Dahm, "Anfänge," 73.
33. TB, 23 September 1933.
34. *PA* 1933, p. 32f. Pressekonferenz: Hagemann, *Die Presselenkung im Dritten Reich,* 32ff.; Abel, *Presselenkung im NS-Staat,* 37ff.
35. TB, 5 and 8 August, 22 and 23 September 1933. A draft Editors' Law had in fact been produced by 20 September (R 43 II/1241). TB, 5 October: "Cabinet: Press law approved after a tough struggle." See *Regierung Hitler,* vol. 1, no. 224, Kabinettssitzung vom 4 October 1933.
36. Abel, *Presselenkung,* 29ff.; Hale, *Presse in der Zwangsjacke 1933–1945,* 90ff.
37. BAB, R 43 II/1241, Goebbels submits the Editors' and Reich Chamber of Culture laws with a letter of 15 September 1933.
38. Abel, *Presselenkung,* 50ff.; Hagemann, *Presselenkung,* 36ff.
39. *PA* 1933, 163, 170 (19 and 20 October).
40. *PA* 1933, 20 October 1933, Background report by the representative of the *Hamburger Nachrichten.VB* (B), 18 October, "Führertagung der N.S.D.A.P. in Berlin"; 19 October 1933, "Entscheidendes Stadium im Kampf um die Gleichberechtigung. Adolf Hitler auf der Führertagung der N.S.D.A.P." (SZ).
41. TB, 21 October 1933.
42. Instruction of 20 October 1933 (BAB, NS 6/215); TB, 29 October 1933; he had considered doing it on 11 October 1933, because there was "a lot wrong" with the newspaper. From 28 October his name no longer appeared on the front page of *Der Angriff* as editor but as founder. In 1934 *Der Angriff* was taken over by the Eher-Verlag. TB, 6 February 1934.
43. TB, 6, 7, and 9 September 1933.
44. *Regierung Hitler,* vol. 1, no. 208, Ministerbesprechung vom 12 September 1933. TB, 13 September 1933. On the prehistory, see Michels, *Ideologie,* 167ff. On Goebbels in Geneva, see Reuth, *Goebbels,* 296ff.; Schmidt describes how Goebbels behaved "naturally" and made a "cultured and calm impression," but his word was doubted by his interlocutors. Schmidt, *Statist auf diplomatischer Bühne,* 282ff.; Nadolny, *Mein Beitrag,* 113ff. The *Neue Zürcher Zeitung* wrote of "the small and unprepossessing Dr. Goebbels, whose appearance provides the sensation at this meeting," 25 September 1933, and 27 September 1933: "Goebbels in Genf" (editorial). On Goebbels, see also *New York Times,* 29 September 1933, "Reich Needs Peace Goebbels Asserts," and *The Times,* 29 September 1933, "German 'Desire for Peace.'"
45. His correct name was Joseph Paul-Boncour.
46. "Das nationalsozialistische Deutschland und seine Aufgabe für den Frieden, Rede vor der internationalen Presse in Genf am 28 September 1933," in Goebbels,

Signale der neuen Zeit, 233–49, quotation 236. *PA* 1933, 29 September: "The Propaganda Ministry attaches great importance to the foreign press giving detailed coverage to Dr. Goebbels's major speech in Geneva."

47. TB, 30 September 1933.
48. TB, 6 September, on the previous day's conversation.
49. TB, 12 October 1933. See also 11 October 1933: "Boss is wrestling with the most difficult decisions."
50. Dengg, *Deutschlands Austritt aus dem Völkerbund und Schachts "Neuer Plan,"* 292ff.; *Akten zur deutschen Außenpolitik 1938–1945. Aus dem Archiv des Auswärtigen Amtes* (henceforth *ADAP*) C I, no. 479, Aufzeichnung v. Bülow, 4 October 1939.
51. TB, 28 July 1933.
52. TB, 13 October 1933, concerning Cabinet meeting (possibly an informal ministerial meeting) on 12 October. This meeting is not mentioned in the edition of *Regierung Hitler.*
53. TB, 14 October 1933; *Regierung Hitler,* vol. 1, no. 230, Protokoll der Ministerbesprechung on 13 and 14 October 1933.
54. After Hitler's decision of 4 December, he met the dictator on 5, 9, and 10 December. TB, 5, 10, and 11 December 1933.
55. TB, 16, 17, and 18 October (on his speech at the meeting of leaders on 17 October).
56. TB, 17 November 1933.
57. TB, 6, 8, 9, and 13 September 1933.
58. TB, 10 September 1933 (in a conversation with Berlin SA leaders).
59. TB, 12, 13, 15, and 16 September 1933.
60. TB, 20 September 1933.
61. TB, 7, 16, 18, 19, and 20 October 1933. Further complaints about Göring: 24 and 26 November 1933. At the beginning of October they had both ostentatiously made peace overtures to one another but the relaxation in tension was only temporary (ibid. 5 and 6 October 1933).
62. TB, 14 October 1933, also 13, 17, and 24 October.
63. TB, 18 October 1933.
64. TB, 3 November 1933.
65. TB, 13 December 1933.
66. TB, 29 October 1933.
67. TB, 24 February 1934.
68. TB, 17 December 1933
69. TB, 30 April 1934.
70. TB, 27 November 1933, and 28 November 1933.
71. TB, 20 October–7 November 1933. The speech of 20 October was published in Goebbels, *Signale der neuen Zeit,* 250–77, and (with the same title) also as a separate pamphlet (Berlin 1933). On the elections, see also Goebbels's interview with a representative of Wolffs Telegraphen-Büro, 8 November 1933, published in *Ursachen und Folgen* 10, no. 2330, and in Reuth, *Goebbels,* 300.
72. TB, 4, 5, and 7 November 1933. On the Reichstag Fire trial, see the contributions in Deiseroth (ed.), *Reichstagsbrand;* on Goebbels's role, see also Reuth, *Goebbels,* 301f.
73. TB, 9 November 1933. *Der Angriff,* 8 November 1933, "Dr. Goebbels fertigt Dimitroff ab. Eine wohlverdiente Abfuhr" (headline).
74. TB, 23 December 1933.
75. TB, 9 November 1933. *VB* (B), 10 November 1933, "Der 9. November 1933 in München—der Tag der Bewegung."

76. TB, 8 November 1933. It referred to the circular of 7 November 1933, in which Hess was reminding people of an earlier circular (27 June 1933) about the need for "modesty in behavior and lifestyle" (BAB, NS 6/215).

77. TB, 11 November 1933; see also 1 and 8 November 1933.

78. Bracher, *Machtergreifung*, 481ff.; see also the examples in Hetzer, "Die Industriestadt Augsburg," 137ff. A review of complaints about the election produced by the Reich Interior Ministry contains objections from those who dared to query the results (BAB, R 1501/5350).

79. Jung, *Plebiszit*, 35ff.; on the result, see 50ff. (according to the Reich statistics office).

80. TB, 13 November 1933.

81. *Der Angriff*, 16 November 1933, "Feierliche Gründung der Reichskulturkammer durch Dr. Goebbels" (SZ). The speech was published in Goebbels, *Signale der neuen Zeit*, 323–36 with the title "Die deutsche Kultur vor neuen Aufgaben. Gründung der Reichskulturkammer am 15." November 1933 in der Berliner Philharmonie; on the event, see Reuth, *Goebbels*, 302f.

82. TB, 28 November 1933, on the preparations, see also 16 November 1933. *Der Angriff*, 28 November 1933. "Das große Feierabend-Werk gegründet." Buchholz, *Die nationalsozialistische Gemeinschaft "Kraft durch Freude,"* 7ff. (its establishment); on the KdF, see Baranowski, *Strength Through Joy*.

83. TB, 19 September 1933: "With Hitler. Riefenstahl was there. Complained about Raether. Goes on nagging. Raether's quite innocent." See also 21 September 1933. On the film, see Kinkel, *Scheinwerferin*, 45ff.; Trimborn, *Karriere*, 176ff.; Rother, *Verführung*, 55ff., Bach, *Leni*, 113ff.

84. TB, 29 November 1933. On meetings with Riefenstahl during the previous weeks in which problems with the film's production emerged, see 23 September, 9, 10, and 16 October 1933. On the production of the film, see Kinkel, *Scheinwerferin*, 52ff.

85. TB, 2 December 1933; Kinkel, *Scheinwerferin*, 56f. The *VB* (N) contained reports of the premiere for three days (1–3 December 1933).

86. TB, 23 and 25 December 1933.

87. TB, 29 December 1933. See also 8 December 1933, following an encounter in Berlin: "Anka Mumme: How old she's become. She's in a bad way. I'll try and help her."

88. 12 February, 6 and 30 March, 22 and 23 June, 15 October 1935; 11 December 1936.

12. "WHATEVER THE FÜHRER DOES, HE DOES COMPLETELY"

1. Below, *Als Hitlers Adjutant 1937–1945*, 20; Hanfstaengl, *Zwischen Weißem und Braunem Haus*, 309ff.; Reichspressechef Dietrich remembered that the lunches were so long that they were "almost unbearable" for the participants who had work to do. *Zwölf Jahre mit Hitler*, 152.

2. Speer, *Erinnnerungen*, 131ff. On Goebbels's needling to advance his intrigues, see also Hanfstaengl, *Zwischen Weißem und Braunem Haus*, 199ff.

3. E.g. 4 July, 24 November 1934, 25 January 1935, 31 January 1936, 13 January 1938.

4. TB, 24 February 1940.

5. Goebbels noted his participation in film evenings for the first months of the year

on the following dates: 28 January, 8, 14, and 21 February, 2, 13, 16 ("With the Führer. As always a film. [...] We soon slip away") and 24 March, 9, 11, and 26 April, 4, 13, 15, 17, 19, 21, 26, and 28 May, 7, 11, 20, and 27 June 1934.

6. Examples from the first half of 1934: 3 February, 7, 9, 11, and 13 March, 28 April, 4 and 10 May, 9 June.

7. TB, 27 January: "Magda was [...] with him in the evening." 8 June 1934: "Magda has spoken to the Führer. I must take a vacation. As soon as possible." 19 October 1934: "Magda is received by the Führer." See also 23 January 1936: "Call Magda. Everything's fine in Berlin. She was with the Führer."

8. TB, 23 September 1933: "Magda with the Führer in 'Krach um Jolanthe.'" TB, 6 December 1935, about a conversation with Funk: "Führer was with him and Magda on Wednesday evening at the Artists' Club." See also TB, 10 February 1934: "Führer with Magda at the Eltz-Rübenachs."

9. TB, 20 January 1934. "Führer at home with us." Similarly 21 and 24 January, 10 and 13 February 1934, 10 April 1934, 1, 6, 7, and 17 May 1934, and so on.

10. TB, 4 February 1934: "The Führer arrives unexpectedly late in the evening."

11. TB, 11, 13, 17 (about the move) and 19 March 1934 and 26 September (move to Berlin).

12. TB, 13, 17, and 25 March 1934.

13. Boat trips: 27 and 31 March, 25 May, 11 and 29 June, 13 July, 22 August, 17 September 1934.

14. TB, 21 May (Blomberg), 31 March (Helldorf), 13 July (v. Pfeffer), 13 May (Schwarz).

15. TB, 14 April 1934.

16. TB, 18 April 1934. On the dispute about Harald, see also 13 April, 5 and 9 May.

17. TB, 30 May 1934.

18. TB, 19 May 1934.

19. TB, 21 May 1934.

20. TB, 27 and 28 May 1934, 5 and 13 June 1934.

21. TB, 3 June 1934.

22. TB, 22 and 23 June 1934.

23. TB, 31 January 1934.

24. *RGBl.* 1934 I, 75; for Hitler's Reichstag speech, see *Adolf Hitler, Reden und Proklamationen 1933–1945*, 352ff. (hereafter *Domarus I and Domarus II*); on his participation in the session, see TB, 31 January 1933; on the preparation of the law, see 11 January 1933 (conversation with Frick).

25. TB, 31 January 1934: "A terrific ovation. I'm really happy." *Der Angriff,* 31 January 1934.

26. TB, 2 and 4 February 1934.

27. *Der Angriff,* 25 January 1934; TB, 26 January 1934.

28. *VB* (B), 28/29 January 1934.

29. TB, 28 January 1934. Here too: "Everybody is enthusiastic about my article."

30. *Der Angriff,* 12 February 1934; TB, 12 February 1934.

31. *FZ,* 11 February 1934, (2nd M), "Das empfindliche Instrument." See also Gillesen, *Auf verlorenem Posten,* 203f.; TB, 8 February 1934.

32. *FZ,* 24 March 1934, "Sind wir langweilig? Über die Krisis der Presse."

33. *Der Angriff,* 20 April 1934, "Gegen die Gesinnungslumpen. Minister Dr. Goebbels und Pg. Weiß vor der deutschen Presse."

34. *PA* 1934, 195 (20 April), letter from Dertinger.

35. *Die Grüne Post,* 29 April 1923, "Herr Reichsminister—Ein Wort bitte!" Welk signed the article as Thomas Trimm. The article is published in Mendelssohn,

Zeitungsstadt Berlin, 437ff., which also contains an account of the background to the affair. TB, 30 April 1934: "'Grüne Post' is offensive to me. It will be banned today. I'll show these impudent Jews that I can behave very differently." The comment referred to the fact that the *Grüne Post* was published by the Ullstein-Verlag. On the ban, see TB, 2 and 11 May 1934.

36. *VB* (N), 10 May 1934, "Bericht über die Reichspressetagung der NSDAP," reproduces the decree word for word.

37. *VB* (N), 13/14 May 1934, "Die Bewegung appelliert an die Nation-'Schluß mit ihnen!'-Offensive gegen Miesmacher, Kritikaster und Konfessionshetzer" (headline).

38. TB, 13 May 1934.

39. *VB* (B), 1 June 1934, "Reichsminister Dr. Goebbels: Wesen und Aufbau der nationalsozialistischen Propaganda" (headline).

40. K. Pfeil, "Wie wir unsere Aktion gegen Miesmacher und Kritikaster organisierten," in *Unser Wille und Weg,* 1934, 226–30.

41. TB, 3 January 1934.

42. TB, 11 January 1934. See also *BK,* 184ff.

43. Hitler had assured him of this once more in December: TB, 15 December 1933.

44. TB, 16 and 20 December 1933.

45. There was a press statement on this: *VB* (B), 23 December 1933, "Vereinheitlichung der deutschen Kulturpolitik. Besprechung Göring–Goebbels-Richtlinien für die zukünftige Arbeit."

46. Erlaß über die Errichtung des Reichsministeriums für Wissenschaft, Erziehung und Volksbildung vom 1. Mai 1934, *RGBl.* 1934 I, 365.

47. TB, 7 May 1935; see also 5 May 1935.

48. TB, 9 May 1935.

49. BAB, R 43 II/1149: Reichsministerium für Kultur und Volksaufklärung.

50. TB, 11 May 1933; BAB, R 43 II/1149, Vortragsvermerk Lammers and message to Funk, 9 May 1934.

51. The negotiations concerning this matter had been going on for several months: TB, 6, 16/18 and 21 February 1934, 21, 22, 24, and 27 March 1934.

52. TB, 13 January 1934.

53. TB, 17 May 1934: "Afternoon. Cabinet. My theater law gets through. All German theaters are subordinated to me. That means I have a free rein. I'm well in with Göring." Theater Law of 15 May 1934, *RGBl.* 1934 I, 411f.; see Rischbieter, "NS-Theaterpolitik," 20ff.

54. Rischbieter, "NS-Theaterpolitik," 23.

55. TB, 20 June 1934.

56. *PA* 1934, p. 221 (25 May).

57. Bollmus, *Das Amt Rosenberg und seine Gegner,* 54f., Piper, *Alfred Rosenberg,* 323f.

58. TB, 16 February, 9 March 1934.

59. TB, 18 June 1934; Bollmus, *Das Amt Rosenberg,* 63ff., also on various other aspects of the dispute.

60. Bollmus, *Das Amt Rosenberg,* 52.

61. Piper, *Alfred Rosenberg,* 373. TB, 6 February 1934: "Weidemann gets a bloody nose. Does 'modern art.' Ruins many possibilities for me and only helps the reactionaries in the process." 8 February 1934: "[. . .] Discussion about modern art with Weidemann. He now knows what it's all about. He'll exercise restraint."

62. Rave, *Kunstdiktatur im Dritten Reich,* 43; in 1935 he assigned Weidemann other tasks in the ministry: TB, 7, 9, and 31 May 1935.

63. On the SA after the "seizure of power," see Longerich, *Geschichte der SA,* 179ff.; on

the prehistory of 30 June, see, in particular, Sauer, "Die Mobilmachung der Gewalt," 897ff.; Höhne, *Mordsache Röhm*.

64. TB, 2 February 1934.
65. TB, 21 February, 2 and 24 March (on the Reichsstatthalters) and 5 and 23 May 1934.
66. TB, 15 May 1934.
67. TB, 26 May, 3 June 1934.
68. TB, 20 April 1934: "Röhm makes an excellent speech about the S.A." *PA* 1934, p. 190f. (18 April); *FZ*, 20 April 1934.
69. TB, 30 May 1934.
70. TB, 24 January 1934, also 9 and 31 January 1934.
71. On this campaign, see *VB* (N), 15 May 1934, "SA-Feindliches Treiben im N.S.D.F.B. (Stahlhelm)" (headline); *VB* (N), 18 May 1934, "Gegen Miesmacher und Nörgler. Gauleiter-Stellvertreter Dr. Görlitzer auf der Massenversammlung des Kreises VI"; *Der Angriff*, 7 June 1933, "Dr. Goebbels unter schlesischen Kumpels. Gegen Kritikaster und Nörgler"; 9 June 1934, "Goebbels im Meer der Begeisterung" (about an event in Bremen); 19 June, "Schluß mit ihnen!" (Poem).
72. TB, 16 May 1934: "I warn about monarchists. R.W. still very strong. Hindenburg has made a will. Contents unknown. Papen has it and informed the Führer. Won't be published without the Führer's approval."
73. TB, 21 May 1934.
74. Text in *Ursachen und Folgen X*, no. 2375.
75. TB, 18 June 1933; *PA* 1934 (18 June), ban on reporting Papen's speech. *PA* 1934 (18 June), Dertinger to editor.
76. TB, 20 and 23 June 1934.
77. TB, 25 June 1934; *Der Angriff*, 25 June 1934, "Achtung, Mauselöcher. Dr. Goebbels vor dem großen Gaukongreß der NSDAP in Essen."
78. Text in *VB* (N), 26 June 1934; TB, 27 June 1934. In the same edition the VB reported on the continuation of the campaign in Pomerania under the heading "Gegen Miesmacher und Kritiker."
79. TB, 29 June 1934.
80. TB, 20 June 1934.
81. TB, 1 July 1934.
82. These and the other entries about the immediate consequences of the action are in TB, 4 July 1934.
83. On the course of the 30th of June, see Longerich, *Geschichte der SA*, 216ff.; Höhne, *Mordsache*, 247ff.
84. *Der Angriff*, 2 July 1934, "Die Niederschlagung der Hochverräter. Wortlaut der Rede, die Dr. Goebbels am Sonntag an das deutsche Volk richtete"; TB, 4 July 1934: "I give a twenty-minute report on the radio in the evening."
85. Höhne, *Mordsache*, 271f.; *Domarus I*, p. 398.
86. TB, 4 July 1934; *Regierung Hitler*, vol. 1, no. 376, Kabinettssitzung vom 3. Juli 1934.
87. TB, 16 and 18 July 1934.
88. TB, 17 March 1934, negative assessments also in entries for 11 and 28 April 1934.
89. TB, 24 July 1934.
90. Gerhard Jagschitz assumed that the coup was caused by the competition between Reschny and Habicht. Jagschitz, *Der Putsch, 82ff.* A similar approach is taken by Norbert Schausberger, who doubts Hitler's involement. Schausberger, *Der Griff nach Österreich*, 289. However, Gerhard Weinberg and Gottfried-Karl Kindermann argued that it was improbable that the coup occurred without Hitler's

knowledge. Weinberg, "Die deutsche Außenpolitik und Österreich 1937/38"; Kindermann, *Hitlers Niederlage in Österreich,* esp. 151f. They could base this view among other things on the memoirs of the Gauleiter of Vienna, Alfred Frauenfeld. See Frauenfeld, *Und trage keine Reu',* 113. Hitherto this debate has been considered undecided; see Schlafranek, *Sommerfest und Preisschießen,* 214; Kurt Bauer assumes that Hitler had "simply let [things] take their course." Bauer, *Elementar-Ereignis,* 120.

91. TB, 13 July 1934.

92. What was known was simply that on the morning of 25 July the commander of Military District VII, Colonel-General Adam, was informed by Hitler of an imminent coup by the Austrian army. Hoch and Weiss, "Die Erinnerungen des Generalobersten Wilhelm Adam." Jagschitz maintained that Habicht had misled Hitler about the prospects for the coup by claiming that the Austrian federal army was planning a coup. Jagschitz, *Putsch,* 78f. At the beginning of June von Reichenau had already taken part in a meeting in Hitler's private apartment at which Reschny was also present. Schausberger, *Griff,* 287f.

93. Jagschitz, *Putsch,* 99ff.; Bauer, *Elementar-Ereignis.*

94. TB, 26 July 1934.

95. TB, 26 July 1934; here too: "Pfeffer and Habicht very subdued."

96. On this, see above all Bauer, *Elementar-Ereignis,* which provides a detailed account of the uprising.

97. TB, 28 July 1934; on the immediate consequences, see Jagschitz, *Putsch,* 182.

98. Bauer, *Elementar-Ereignis,* 120.

99. Hitler to Goebbels according to TB, 18 June 1934. On the Hitler-Mussolini conversation on 14 June in Venice, see *ADAP* C III 1, no. 5, Aufzeichnung Neuraths, 15 June 1934 and no. 7, nicht unterzeichnete Aufzeichnung, 15 June 1934.

100. TB, 28–31 July 1934.

101. TB, 23 October 1934.

102. TB, 31 July 1934; on the death of Hindenburg, see also Reuth, *Goebbels,* 319ff.

103. TB, 2 August 1934.

104. *Regierung Hitler,* vol. 1, no. 382, Ministerbesprechung on 1 August 1934; *RGBl.* 1934 I, 747, Law concerning the Head of State of the German Reich; TB, 2 August 1934.

105. TB, 2 August 1934.

106. *Regierung Hitler,* vol. 1, no. 383, Ministerbesprechung on 2 August 1934.

107. TB, 8 August 1934; *VB* (B), 8 August 1934.

108. TB, 31 July, 4 August 1934.

109. TB, 8 August 1934.

110. TB, 16 August 1934: "Hindenburg's will is being published. Papen's ideas aren't a threat. It can go out!" *VB* (B), 16 August 1934; Mühleisen, "Das Testament Hindenburgs vom 11. Mai 1934"; Pyta, *Hindenburg,* 865f.

111. TB, 4–8, 14, 16, and 18 August 1934.

112. On the plebiscite, see Jung, *Plebiszit,* 61ff.; results, 68.

113. TB, 20 August 1934.

114. *Statistisches Jahrbuch der Stadt Berlin 1934,* 317.

115. TB, 22 August 1934.

116. TB, 22 August 1934.

13. "TAKING FIRM CONTROL OF THE INNER DISCIPLINE OF A PEOPLE"

1. TB, 29 August 1934.
2. TB, 31 August 1934, on the stay from 29 August to 6 September 1934.
3. TB, 6, 8, 10, 11 September; *VB* (B), 7 September 1934, "Die Propaganda als Mittlerin zwischen Volk und Führung"; *VB* (B), 10 September 1934, "Die Kraft des Nationalsozialismus liegt in der persönlichen Vebindung mit dem Volke. Dr. Goebbels vor den Propagandaleitern und Rednern der N.S.D.A.P."
4. TB, 26 August 1934; he had already discussed the Party rally film with her at the beginning of May (TB, 4 May 1934). Later he referred to the result and its director in more positive terms (17 and 23 October), albeit still with an important qualification: "Leni is able. If only she were a man." TB, 22 November 1934. On the film, see Kinkel, *Scheinwerferin*, 62ff.; Trimborn, *Karriere*, 198ff.; Rother, *Verführung*, 67ff.; Bach, *Leni*, 123ff.; Martin Loiperdinger, *Der Parteitagsfilm "Triumph des Willens" von Leni Riefenstahl. Rituale der Mobilmachung*, Opladen 1987. BAB R 109 I/1029b, Protokoll der Ufa-Vorstandssitzung, 28 August 1934 (no. 1021).
5. TB, 30 March 1933, see also 28 March concerning the meeting with Riefenstahl.
6. TB, 1 October 1934; *Der Angriff*, 1 October, published Goebbels's speech at the opening ceremony, also published in Heiber (ed.), *Goebbels Reden*, no. 21.
7. On the opening ceremony, see TB, 11 October 1934; *Der Angriff*, 9 October 1934, "Ein Winter ohne Repräsentation—Aber der entschlossenen Hilfe aller. Der Führer und Dr. Goebbels eröffnen das soziale Werk der Winterhilfe" (headline). On 9 December politicians, actors, and sportsmen went onto the streets with collecting boxes and, according to Goebbels, collected "a huge amount." TB, 10 December 1934; *Der Angriff*, 10 December 1934, "Die Millionen Groschen haben's gemacht. Unbekannte und Prominente erzählen."
8. TB, 10 November 1934.
9. *VB* (B), 25/26 December 1934 "Volksweihnacht auf der Straße"; TB, 25 December 1934.
10. Hugo Ringler, "Und wieder rollt die Versammlungslawine," in *UWW*, 1934, 335–38, quotation 338.
11. Dietrich Thurner, "Werbemaßnahmen in bäuerlichen und kleinstädtischen Gebieten," *UWW*, January 1935, 18–19.
12. TB, 25–27 October 1934.
13. TB, 27 October 1934.
14. TB, 22 October 1936. See Moll, "Steuerungsinstrument im 'Ämterchaos'?"
15. Klemperer, *LTI*.
16. Münk, *Die Organisation des Raumes im Nationalsozialismus*, esp. 122ff.
17. Westphal, *Werbung im Dritten Reich*.
18. Westphal, *Berliner Konfektion und Mode, 1836–1939*.
19. Kershaw, *Der Hitler-Mythos*, 81.
20. I refer to the detailed analysis of the reliability of the regime's reports on the public's attitude toward the persecution of the Jews contained in my book "*Davon haben wir nichts gewusst!*"
21. Lerg, "Richtlinien für die Gesamthaltung der deutschen Presse."
22. Lerg, "Richtlinien," 239.
23. Lerg, "Richtlinien," Point 5, 240.
24. Lerg, "Richtlinien," Point 6, 240.
25. Lerg, "Richtlinien," Point 7, 240.
26. Lerg, "Richtlinien," Point 8, 240f.

27. Lerg, "Richtlinien," Point 15, 242.

28. *DAZ*, 29 October 1934 (E), "Unser öffentliches Amt" (editorial).

29. *Der Angriff*, 19 November 1934, "Die Presse Mitarbeiter der Regierung," also published in Heiber (ed.), *Goebbels Reden*, no. 23, quotations 178, 185; TB, 20 November 1934.

30. TB, 20 November 1934.

31. *VB* (B), 1 December 1935, "Reichsminister Dr. Goebbels vor den deutschen Schriftleitern" (headline).

32. Erste Anordnung des Präsidenten der Reichspressekammer aufgrund der 1. VO zur Durchführung des Reichskulturkammergesetzes vom 13. Dezember 1933 *(Handbuch Dt. Tagespresse*, 1934, p. 325); Anordnung über die Schließung von Zeitungsverlagen zwecks Beseitigung ungesunder Wettbewerbsverhältnisse vom 24. April 1935 *(Recht RKK*, RPK III, 13); Anordnung zur Wahrung der Unabhängigkeit des Zeitungsverlagswesens: *Recht RKK*, RPK III, no. 11); Hale, *Presse*, 153ff.

33. Hale, *Presse*, 157, 304f.

34. On his hesitant assessment of Amann's intentions, see TB, 30 March 1935; on his rejection of them, see 27 April 1935; on their agreement, 9 May 1935.

35. See p. 316.

36. Rosenberg, *Tagebuch*, 13 July, 2 August 1934.

37. TB, 11 and 22 July, 24 August (quotation), 13 and 28 September, 5 October, 2, 4, 14, and 28 November as well as 13 and 15 December 1934.

38. On the celebration of Strauss's 70th birthday, see Wulf, *Musik*, 195f.

39. BAB, NS 8/171, Letter of 20 August (on this TB, 26 August 1934).

40. TB, 24 July 1934: "Monday: Conversation with Strauss (!). He must withdraw his new opera with the Jewish libretto." 31 August 1934: "Strauss opera can be performed." On the production of "Die Schweigsame Frau," see Wulf, *Musik*, p. 196f.

41. Discussed in Brenner, "Die Kunst im politischen Machtkampf der Jahre 1933/34," 33f.; original in the YiVO Institute in New York.

42. Hitler's speech of 5 September, published in *Reichstagung in Nürnberg 1934*, Streicher (ed.).

43. *DAZ*, 25 November 1934, "Der Fall Hindemith"; abbreviated in Wulf, *Musik*, 373ff.; Prieberg, *Kraftprobe*, 168ff. (on the premiere) and 185ff. (on the Hindemith dispute).

44. *Der Angriff*, 28 November 1934, "Warum Vorschuß-Lorbeeren für Konjunktur-Musiker Hindemith? Musik ohne Resonanz im Volke" (headline); see also *VB*, 29 November 1934, Fritz Stege: "Und abermals Paul Hindemith."

45. Prieberg, *Musik im NS-Staat*, 61ff.

46. TB, 30 November, 2, 4, and 6 December; see also 19 and 25 December 1934.

47. Published in Wulf, *Musik*, 376ff., according to the reports of the *Berliner Lokal-Anzeiger* of 7 December 1934.

48. TB, 18 February 1935.

49. TB, 28 February 1935; *VB* (B), 1 March 1935, "Reichsminister Dr. Goebbels empfing Furtwängler"; Prieberg, *Kraftprobe*, 227ff. Furtwängler met Rosenberg on 9 April, Rosenberg and Hitler on 10 April 1935; TB, 11 April 1935.

50. Prieberg, *Kraftprobe*, 195ff.

51. Aster, *"Das Reichsorchester."*

52. TB, 5 May, 23 June, 11 September 1935; Prieberg, *Kraftprobe*, 232ff., 244f.

53. Bollmus, *Das Amt Rosenberg*, 77.

54. *VB* (M), 10 December 1934; TB, 13 December 1934.

55. TB, 28 November, 15 and 23 December 1934.

56. A letter from Dressler-Andress of 8 June 1935 reports on the Reich conference of the NS-Kulturgemeinde in Düsseldorf on 7 June being dominated by a real sense of victory vis-à-vis the RKK. Wulf, *Theater und Film im Dritten Reich*, 71f.

57. *VB* (N), 19 June 1935, "Wie steht der Nationalsozialismus zur Kunst"; see also the reply in ibid., 20 June 1935, Alfred Rosenberg, "Rückblick auf Düsseldorf." TB, 19 June 1935, 9 and 13 June 1935. On 3 June 1935 Rosenberg sent a 26-page memorandum to Hitler, in which he used the cases of Strauss, Hindemith, and Furtwängler to demonstrate that because its priority was representation and not ideology the Reich Chamber of Culture was not fit for the purpose. Piper, *Alfred Rosenberg*, 381.

58. Wulf, *Musik*, 194ff.; Strauss to Zweig, 17 June 1935, published in Strauss and Zweig, *Briefwechsel*, 142; Bollmus, *Das Amt Rosenberg*, 78.

59. TB, 13 April 1935.

60. Gestapo an die Verbindungsführer bei der Adjutantur des RfSS, 16 April 1935; published in Heiber, *Die Katakombe wird geschlossen*, 18ff. As is the case with the other official documents published in this book, the report is in the file BAB, R 58/739.

61. On the closure, see Gestapo report, 10 May 1935, published in ibid., 36f.; TB, 9 May 1935: "The closing of the 'Katakombe' and 'Tingeltangel' agreed with Heydrich. We'll do it very cleverly." TB, 13 May 1935.

62. Goebbels's minute on the Gestapo report of 14 May 1935, published in Heiber, *Die Katakombe wird geschlossen*, 49ff. One of those affected, Werner Finck reported on his imprisonment in a concentration camp in his memoirs. *Alter Narr—was nun?* 68ff.

63. Gestapo report, 29 October 1936, Heiber, *Die Katakombe wird geschlossen*, 65.

64. TB, 18 April 1936; *PA* 1936, 408 (16 April, referring to the official announcement of the previous day; see also *FZ*, 16 April 1936). Reference to the use of this responsibility also in TB, 8 May 1936: "We issue our first police order re: newspaper and book bans."

65. *PA* 1936, 674 (25 June).

66. *PA* 1937, no. 846 (12 April) and no. 923 (22 April), reminder of this directive.

67. *RGBl.* 1933 I, 95ff.

68. Maiwald, *Filmzensur im NS-Staat*, 88ff.

69. Maiwald, *Filmzensur*, 100ff.

70. TB, 30 November 1934.

71. Maiwald, *Filmzensur*, 112ff. Exemption was already possible according to a legal regulation of June 1933 but now it occurred not through special assessment panels but through the state censorship office itself.

72. On the law, see Maiwald, *Filmzensur*, 81ff. References to the preparation of the law: TB, 28 January, 6 and 18 February 1934. Goebbels had already established a "dramaturgical office" within the Reich Chamber of Film in November 1933, to carry out a form of pre-censorship of film projects, albeit on a voluntary basis. Originally this dramaturgical office had been established by the German film industry in April 1933. Maiwald, *Filmzensur*, 130.

73. TB, 6 February 1934.

74. TB, 19 May 1936: "He must not be allowed to make his own films. Must provide inspiration. Be involved in everything. And always keeping an eye on things." But evidently that's exactly what Nierenz did not do: 9 and 18 December 1936.

75. *Der Angriff*, 10 February 1934; TB, 10 February 1934; Moeller, *Filmminister*, 153; Albrecht, *Filmpolitik*, 21f. Text in *Film-Kurier* of 10 February 1934.

76. *Film-Kurier*, 22 June 1934.

77. The TB entries for 1934/35 are full of complaints about entertainment films of poor quality: "Cheeky rubbish" (*Wenn ich König wär,* 28 January 1934); "Stupid film" (*Freut Euch des Lebens,* 17 May 1934); "Fearful dilettantism" (*Susanne,* 28 September 1934); "sentimental trash" (*So endet die Liebe,* 19 October 1934); "Remarkably stupid nonsense" (*Mach mich glücklich,* 2 June 1935); "Kitsch" (*Amphitryon,* 13 July 1935); "Junk films" (*Königstiger und Klosterjäger,* 25 November 1935); "stupid films" (*Herbstmanöver und Teufelskerl,* 3 December 1935); "stupid kitsch. Intolerable" (*Weißes Rössl,* 6 December 1935).

78. Moeller, *Filmminister,* 156ff.

79. *RGBl.* 1934 I, 1236. See also the statements in the official justification of the amendment law, 15 December 1934, quoted by Albrecht, *Filmpolitik,* 26.

80. TB, 24 November, 19 December 1934.

81. *Film-Kurier,* 5 February 1935; TB, 6 February 1935.

82. TB, 26 February, 15 April 1935.

83. In fact his assessment was initially inconsistent: TB, 19 and 27 April, 1 May 1935.

84. *VB* (B), 1 May 1935. From 26 April the *VB* reported in detail on the congress. See also TB, 1 May 1935. The "Fundamentals" were also published in abbreviated form in the *Film-Kurier* vom 22–30 July 1935.

85. *VB* (B), 17 December 1935, "Wesen und Aufgaben der Kritik. Reichsminister Dr. Goebbels vor dem in der deutschen Presse tätigen Kritiker." In the inside pages of the newspaper there is a report on the "Kritikertagung in Berlin."

86. *Film-Kurier,* 16 December 1935; TB, 16 December 1935.

87. *Lichtbild-Bühne,* 16 December 1935. Goebbels also used the speech to give the production companies a set of concrete instructions for their work.

88. *RGBl.* 1935 I, 811, Zweites Gesetz zur Änderung des Lichtspielgesetzes; Maiwald, *Filmzensur,* 155ff. From October 1935 film bans could be decided on and issued only by Goebbels: BAB, NS 6/221, Rundschreiben 221/31 vom 21. November 1935 with the Führererlaß of 17 October 1935; published in Albrecht, *Filmpolitik,* 523; TB, 13 October 1935.

89. TB, 15 and 17 October 1934.

90. TB, 19 October 1934.

91. TB, 29 October 1934.

92. TB, 13 April, 5 and 9 May 1934.

93. TB, 20 and 22 November 1934.

94. TB, 22 November 1934.

95. TB, 24 November 1934.

96. TB, 12 January 1935.

97. See, for example, 21 April 1938, after the premiere of the Olympia film, 16 June 1937, and 15 June 1938, reception for the Berlin "Old Guard." See also Stephan, *Goebbels,* 73ff.

98. TB, 14 February 1935, 23 February 1937, 20 February 1938.

99. TB, 29 November 1936 and 28 November 1937

100. TB, 17 March 1937 (planning) and 27 November 1938, 1 March 1939.

101. His colleagues are also unanimous on this: Schaumburg-Lippe, *Dr. G.,* 207; Oven, *Mit Goebbels bis zum Ende,* vol. 1, p. 45; Stephan, *Goebbels,* 73f.; Semmler, *Goebbels,* 16.

102. BAB, R 55/23474, undated list.

103. TB, 30 October, 12 November 1937.

104. TB, 24 March, 28 June 1935 (concerning temporary accommodation in the Kaiserhof); on his preoccupation with plans, see also 6 January, 12 and 22 February 1935.

105. TB, 28 June 1935.
106. TB, 8 and 16 February 1935, 7 and 13 May 1935. See Winker, *Fernsehen unterm Hakenkreuz.*
107. TB, 29 October 1934.
108. TB, 16 February, 17 May 1935.
109. Semmler, *Goebbels,* 77; Oven, *Mit Goebbels bis zum Ende, vol. 1,* p. 56.
110. TB, 16 August 1926 and 4 January 1926 (quotation); on his continuing abstinence, see also 1 December 1926; Oven, *Mit Goebbels bis zum Ende,* vol. 1, p. 277f.; TB, 6 June 1944.
111. TB, 24 March, 11 September on the removals.
112. TB, 1 April 1935.
113. Boat trips: 7, 11 (Berlin SA leaders and Hitler) and 13 May, 17 (Jenny Jugo and Countess Helldorf) and 21 April (Helldorfs), 21 May (Blombergs), 5 June (Helldorfs), 28 June (Hitler), 25 and 26 August, 3 September 1935.
114. *Akten der Reichskanzlei, Regierung Hitler,* vol. 2, Hartmannsgruber (ed.), no. 63, Ministerbesprechung vom 13. Dezember 1934, agreed on the Gesetz über den Nachfolger des Führers und Reichskanzlers of the same date. This provided the subsequent legal basis for Hitler's decision of 7 December to appoint Göring as his successor (ibid., no. 58); TB, 15 December 1934.
115. TB, 15 December 1934 and 4 January 1935.
116. TB, 23 and 27 May 1935 on his throat problems. TB, 21 June 1935 on the diagnosis.
117. TB, 31 January 1935.
118. TB, 4 January 1935. See also the very similar entry of 14 April 1934.
119. TB, 27 April 1935.

14. "NEVER TIRE!"

1. In December 1933 Goebbels had already told the Polish ambassador, Lipski, of Hitler's intention to sign a non-aggression pact with Poland; see TB, 19 December 1933, and Lipski's note of 18 December 1933, published in Jedrzejewicz (ed.), *Papers and Memoirs of Jozef Lipski,* 112–15. On further meetings with Lipski on which Goebbels made positive comments, see TB, 2 February, 29 March 1934. On the press agreement, see Michels, *Ideologie,* 202f., 208f., 211f. PAA, Geheimakten 1920–1936, Polen, vol. 1, R 122848, letter to Aschmann, German Embassy Warsaw, 26 February 1934, concerning negotiations which took place on 23/24 February in Berlin between Aschman/Jahncke and the press chief of the Polish Foreign Ministry. They resulted in the press communiqué of 24 February. See also Michels, *Ideologie,* 214. Goebbels's speech of 13 June in Warsaw, "Das nationalsozialistische Deutschland als Faktor des Europäischen Friedens," PAA, Büro Reichsminister, R 28815. On the course of the Warsaw visit, see TB, 16 June 1934.
2. TB, 7 May (Zweibrücken), 29 August 1935 (opening of the Saar exhibition in Cologne and speech in Koblenz), 13 December 1934 (Trier). On the activities of the Deutsche Front, see Paul, *"Deutsche Mutter—heim zu Dir!"* 62ff.; on the mass meetings outside the Saar, see 114ff.; see also Mühlen, *"Schlagt Hitler an der Saar!"*
3. This was revealed by the journalist Joachim von Leers, who was close to Goebbels, in the February edition of the RPL journal *Unser Wille und Weg* ("Die Lage," 40–42). The event had been arranged under "pressure from a malicious propa-

ganda trying to create panic: "The craziest rumors about internal problems were being spread and it's difficult for people to get to the truth; they were widely believed and passed on" (p. 40).

4. TB, 4 January 1935 (here also the expression "declaration of loyalty").
5. TB, 6 January 1935.
6. TB, 16 January 1935.
7. *VB* (B), 15 January 1935, "Der Dank des Führers an die Saar" (headline). On the day of celebration Goebbels spoke at the Königsplatz in Berlin in front of, he estimated, 600,000 people. *VB* (B), 16 January 1935, "Aufmarsch der 500,000. Dr. Goebbels zur Saar-Feier der Nation."
8. TB, 22 and 27 January 1935; *ADAP* C III, no. 463 Aufzeichnung Lammers, 19 January 1935 concerning the conversation of 25 January.
9. Wiggershaus, *Der deutsch-englische Flottenvertrag vom 18. Juni 1935,* 261ff.; London communiqué of 3 February 1935 and German reply of 13 February 1935: Schwendemann, *Handbuch der Sicherheitsfrage und der Abrüstungskonferenz,* vol. 2, 787ff., 791ff.; TB, 2, 4, and 16 February 1935: "Reply to Paris and London: Willingness to negotiate. All doors are open. But nothing final. Now the others must do something."
10. TB, 6 March 1935 concerning 5 March. It referred to the *British White Paper on Defence* of 4 March 1935.
11. TB, 8, 10, 22, and 24 March 1935.
12. TB, 2 March 1935; *VB* (B), 2 March 1935, "Reichsminister Frick an die Deutschen der Saar" (repeating the points made in Goebbels's speech); Hitler's address: *Domarus I,* 484ff.; on the celebrations, see Reuth, *Goebbels,* 327.
13. TB, 14 March 1935. *VB* (B), 12 March 1935, General Göring on the German air defenses (report on the *Daily Mail* interview). On the "uncovering" of the German Luftwaffe in March 1935, see Völker, *Die deutsche Luftwaffe 1933–1939,* 68ff.
14. TB, 16 March 1935.
15. TB, 18 March 1935.
16. *Der Angriff,* 19 March 1935.
17. TB, 20 March 1935, and 22 March 1935.
18. TB, 26 and 28 March 1935; *ADAP* C III, no. 555, Aufzeichnung über Gespräch des Führers und Reichskanzlers mit dem englischen Außenminister Simon am 25. März 1935 (including its continuation on 26 March 1935); Wiggershaus, *Flottenvertrag,* 292ff.
19. TB, 1 April 1935.
20. TB, 5 April 1935, and 7 April 1935: "It's very serious. Raw materials crisis."
21. Petersen, *Mussolini,* 399ff. Stresa communiqué, *British and Foreign State Papers,* vol. 139, 756ff., 14 April 1935.
22. TB, 5 May 1935. He already had concerns about the military pact on 17 April.
23. TB, 7 April 1935.
24. The cuts amounted to 3 percent in urban districts and 10 percent in rural districts. Further details in Sodeikat, "Der Nationalsozialismus und die Danziger Opposition." See also Fuchs, *Die Beziehungen zwischen der Freien Stadt Danzig und dem Deutschen Reich,* 44ff.
25. See observations in Longerich, *Politik der Vernichtung,* 70ff.; Kershaw, *Der Hitler-Mythos,* 96ff.
26. TB, 12 March 1935.
27. TB, 11 April, 11 and 17 May as well as 3 June 1934. On the further improvement in the relationship, see TB, 31 August, 25 October 1934, 4 and 25 January, 4, 8, and 16 February 1935.

28. TB, 3 and 5 April 1935, and 9 April 1935.
29. TB, 10 April 1933; *Der Angriff*, 10 April 1935, "Flugzeuggeschwader über Berlin begleiten Görings Hochzeitszug" (headline); further contributions on the wedding in the inside pages and in the edition of 11 April 1935.
30. TB, 13 May 1935.
31. TB, 15 May 1935.
32. TB, 20 January 1934: "A conceited gossip. Can't understand why Hitler values him. Possibly suitable for using in minor intrigues."
33. TB, 15 May 1935.
34. TB, 21 May 1935.
35. TB, 15 May 1935. See also 5 May 1935: "Mussolini requests Neurath via Cerutti [the Italian ambassador in Berlin, whose name was actually spelled Cerruti] to provide good weather. The German sword is once again casting its shadow."
36. Mattioli, *Experimentierfeld der Gewalt.*, esp. 55ff.; Petersen, *Mussolini*, 385.
37. *PA* 1935, 74 (12 February): "Der abbessinisch-italienische Streitfall soll 'mit brutaler Desinteressiertheit' und völligster Objektivität behandelt werden." Further bans on criticism: *PA* 1935, p. 94 (19 February), p. 113 (27 February); p. 245 (29 April), p. 320 (25 May). See also Petersen, *Mussolini*, 391.
38. Petersen, *Mussolini*, 112; Kershaw, *Hitler. 1889–1936*, 555f.; *Domarus I*, 505ff.
39. TB, 25 and 27 May 1935. *ADAP* C IV, no. 109, Rome embassy to the AA, 26 May 1935; Nos 120 and 121; Ambassador v. Hassel to the AA, 30 and 31 May 1935.
40. *PA* 1935, p. 320.
41. TB, 4 June 1935. On the Anglo-German Naval Agreement, see Hildebrand, *Das vergangene Reich*, 600ff.; Wiggershaus, *Flottenvertrag*, esp. 313ff.
42. And also during the following two weeks, while the negotiations were proceeding in London, he was only superficially informed about their progress. TB, 13 and 15 June 1935.
43. TB, 19 June 1935.
44. TB, 21 June 1935.
45. TB, 5 June 1935.
46. TB, 11 June, also 1 August 1935: "Spent a sweet hour with Helga. Practiced obedience."
47. TB, 27 July 1935; see also 7 November 1935, "Afternoon, worked at home. 'Disciplined' Hilde."
48. TB, 3, 5, 21, and 23 July.
49. TB, 6 April 1935, during a visit to the Deutsches Theater.
50. TB, 11 July 1935, concerning her arrival on the previous day; TB, 13 July 1935, about a conversation on 12 July; TB, 15 July 1935, about 13 July: "Frau Ullrich is leaving. She is very sad that she now has to."
51. TB, 29 July 1935, and 27 July 1935.
52. TB, 3 August 1935; TB, 3 and 5 August about the trip; TB, 7 August 1935 about the reconciliation.
53. TB, 13 and 15 July 1935.
54. Details of the "Kurfürstendamm riot" in Longerich, *Politik der Vernichtung*, 78ff., and Longerich, *"Davon haben wir nichts gewusst!"* 79f.
55. TB, 29 April 1933 and 9 May 1933 (on the conversation with Hitler). TB, 29 May 1935: "Went shopping with Magda in the Kurfürstendamm. Once again quite a crowd of Jews. We'll have to sort that out again." Also 5 June 1935.
56. TB, 10, 12, 14, and 28 November 1934.
57. TB, 15 July 1935.

58. TB, 7 July 1935. Also on friendly relations with Helldorf: 9 and 21 April 1935, 17 May 1935, 5 June 1935, 9–17 June 1935.

59. TB, 21 July 1935.

60. TB, 19 August 1935.

61. TB, 19 August 1935.

62. TB, 13 September 1935; *Parteitag der Freiheit, vom 10.–16. September 1935,* Hitler speech 110ff.

63. TB, 15 September 1934; *VB* (B), 13 September 1935, "Goebbels reißt dem Kommunismus die Maske ab."

64. TB, 15 September 1935.

65. On the Nuremberg laws, see Essner, *Die "Nürnberger Gesetze,"* esp. 113ff.; Friedländer, *Das Dritte Reich,* vol. 1, 158ff.; Longerich, *Politik der Vernichtung,* 102ff.

66. *Parteitag der Freiheit,* 254ff. (Hitler's speech to the Reichstag).

67. TB, 17 September 1935. Hitler too, he discovered two days later, had "suffered" under Göring's speech.

68. TB, 19 September 1935.

69. TB, 3 October 1935, also entries for the following days.

70. TB, 5 October 1935. Entries from 20 August 1935, 2, 9, 22, 23, 25 September 1935. Mattioli, *Experimentierfeld,* 125ff.

71. TB, 13 October 1935, see also 9 and 11 October 1935 and 17 October (speech to the chief editors). This new course is only marginally evident in the press instructions. *PA* 1935, 665f., 671f. (12 October 1935).

72. TB, 19 October 1935. See also on the same day further down: "Is war going to break out in Europe? If so then 3–4 years too soon for us." *Akten der Reichskanzlei, Regierung Hitler,* vol. 2, Hartmannsgruber (ed.), no. 25. On 18 October a ministerial meeting (Chefbesprechung) had taken place at which the currency situation was discussed. The speech is not dealt with here.

73. Mattioli, *Experimentierfeld,* 125ff.

74. Speech on Wehrmacht Day in Karlshorst, 29 September 1935, *FZ,* 30 September 1935; speech on 3 October 1935 in Halle, *FZ,* 5 October 1935.

75. Speech on 4 December 1935, published in Heiber (ed.), *Goebbels Reden,* 269ff., esp. 271; see Sywottek, *Mobilmachung für den totalen Krieg,* 95.

76. New Year's Eve address 1935, in *Der Angriff,* 1 January 1936; *VB* (N), 19 January 1936, about Goebbels's speech at the Berlin Gau day.

77. *UWW,* November 1936, Erwin Schmidt, "Von Hamsterern und anderen Schweinen. Wirtschaftspolitische Aufgaben der Propaganda," 351–55.

78. TB, 7 October 1935; *VB* (N), 7 October 1935: "'Wir wollen das Rechte tun und niemanden scheuen.' Der Dank des Führers an den deutschen Bauern."

79. TB, 11 October 1935; *VB* (N), 11 October 1935, "Der Ruf des Führers an das deutsche Volk."

80. *UWW,* February 1936, Hans Riess, "Der erste Abschnitt des Winterfeldzuges 1935/36—ein voller Erfolg," 47–51. The report of the RPA Stuttgart noted for Gau Württemberg alone 4900 meetings up until the Christmas vacation. Ibid., June 1936, Walter Tiessler (Head of the Reichsring für NS-Propaganda), "Winter campaign 1935/36," p. 203f.

81. *UWW,* November 1935, Hermann Krüger, district culture warden *(Kreiskulturwart)* for the district of Gifhorn, "Aus der kulturellen Arbeit in einer Kleinstadt," 380–85, complained of a "real lassitude and indifference" in the Party meetings.

82. *UWW,* February 1937, Max Cronauer, Gau speaker, "Die öffentliche politische

Versammlung, wie sie der Redner sieht," 54–59. This report also refers to very poor attendance at meetings.

83. *UWW,* September 1935, Julius Krafft, district departmental head *(Kreisabteilungsleiter)* Frankfurt a. M., "Die öffentliche Versammlung," 305–9.

84. *UWW,* March 1937, Julius Krafft, "Keine Propaganda mit 'Nachdruck,'" 92f.

85. TB, 9 and 11 November 1935.

86. TB, 13 September 1935; Piper, *Alfred Rosenberg,* 392ff.; Reuth, *Goebbels,* 334ff.; Bollmus, *Das Amt Rosenberg,* 80f.; Faustmann, *Reichskulturkammer,* 63ff.

87. See BAB, NS 8/171, Goebbels to Rosenberg, 7 November 1935; and Goebbels to Rosenberg, 20 March 1936; and Rosenberg to Goebbels, 31 March, 22 April 1936. On the dispute and the ban, see also TB, 3, 5, 11, and 13 October, 9 November 1935. On the preparations for the Cultural Senate, see 19 and 24 October 1935.

88. TB, 17 November 1935; *VB* (N), 16 November 1935, "Die Jahrestagung der Reichskulturkammer—Der Reichskultursenat eingesetzt." For the Hitler quotation, see TB, 21 August 1935.

89. TB, 17 November 1935. The first session of the senate took place on 16th (ibid.).

90. *VB* (B), 23 December 1935; TB, 23 December 1935, and 24 December.

91. TB, 23 and 24 December 1937.

15. "THE TOUGHER THE BETTER!"

1. TB, 6 February 1936.

2. Longerich, *Davon,* 101.

3. *PA* 1936, 6 February 1936: The Propaganda Ministry warned the press, which had given prominence to the assassination, to exercise caution; see, for instance, *VB* (B), 5 February; *VB* (N), 6 February; *Der Angriff,* 6 February 1936. The following day, on which the newspapers were dominated by the opening ceremony of the Winter Olympics, the Gustloff topic was confined to the inside pages (*VB* (B) and *MNN,* which had already led with the Olympic Games on 6 February, did the same on 7 February, as did *VB* (N) and *Der Angriff*).

4. TB, 8 February 1936.

5. TB, 11 February 1936; *MNN,* 11 February 1936, Olympic reception for the Reich and state governments; *Der Angriff,* 11 February 1936 (photo), The Reich Propaganda Minister at the Munich press gala.

6. TB, 14 December 1936; *VB* (B), 13 February 1936, "Adolf Hitlers Abschied von Wilhelm Gustloff."

7. TB, 14 February 1936, 17 February 1936, telephone call to Magda (for the 14th).

8. TB, 17 February; on Hitler's itinerary, see *VB,* 14–16 March 1936.

9. TB, 17 February 1936.

10. TB, 21 January 1936.

11. TB, 21 February 1936, for 19 February. See also 20 February 1936: "Lunch with the Führer. He ponders and contemplates. To act or not to act? In the end he will act."

12. TB, 29 February 1936.

13. TB, 29 February 1936, according to which on 28 February he had recommended a postponement to the Führer.

14. TB, 29 February, 2 March 1936.

15. On the speech, whose text Hitler had modified in view of the impending crisis, see TB, 1 and 2 March; *PA* 1936, 228f., 231f. (28 and 29 February): instructions to

give extensive coverage to the speech. In the speech Goebbels extolled the Reich's success in producing new materials. *FZ*, 2 February 1936.

16. TB, 4 March 1936; *PA* 1936: On 4 March the press was confidentially informed that the deputies were being summoned to an evening get together on 6 March in Berlin that had long been planned and were being requested to stay in Berlin for a few days, as a Reichstag session was planned for the start of the following week; it was intended "as a diplomatic demonstration against the Franco-Soviet pact" (246f.).

17. TB, 8 March 1936. Kabinett: *Akten der Reichskanzlei, Regierung Hitler,* vol. 3, Hartmannsgruber (ed.), no. 39, Ministerbesprechung, 6 March 1936.

18. TB, 6 and 8 March 1936.

19. *Domarus I,* 583ff.; on the occupation, see Giro, Frankreich und die Remilitarisierung des Rheinlandes, 67ff.; Reuth, *Goebbels,* 337ff.

20. TB, 8 March 1936.

21. TB, 17–28 March 1936.

22. On election propaganda, see TB, 10–31 March 1936; *PA* 1936, 253f. (7 March).

23. Berber (ed.), *Locarno,* no. 62, Sitzung des Völkerbundrates in London am Nachmittag des 19. März; on the international reactions, see TB, 13, 15, 17, and 19 March 1936; Giro, *Frankreich,* 336ff.

24. No. 63, Vorschläge der Locarno-Mächte, 19 March 1936; TB, 21 March 1936.

25. Berber, *Locarno,* no. 68, Vorläufige Antwort der Reichsregierung, 24 March 1936; no. 74, Friedensplan der Deutschen Regierung vom 31. März 1936 (auch *ADAP* V/1, no. 242); TB, 2 April 1936, and 26 and 28 March 1936 concerning the ongoing negotiations.

26. *PA* 1936, 24–28 March 1936, documents the careful preparation of the campaign, which reached its climax on the election Sunday.

27. *PA* 1936, 345f. (26 March).

28. *VB* (B), 28 March 1936, "Kommando an die Nation. Hisst Flagge! Ganz Deutschland unter dem Hakenkreuzbanner zum 29. März angetreten" (headline). See also *VB* (B) of 27 March, "Der Führer spricht zu den Arbeitern und Soldaten des neuen Reiches. Noch nie erlebter Gemeinschaftsempfang eines ganzen Volkes— Allgemeine Verkehrs- und Arbeitsruhe" (headline).

29. *VB* (B), 28 March 1936, "Das ganze deutsche Volk hörte seinen Führer!" (with reports about companies granting holidays throughout the Reich); "Jubel um Hermann Göring. Der Preußische Ministerpräsident beschloß die Wahlkundgebungen in Berlin mit einem begeistert aufgenommenen Appell; weitere Berichte über diverse Veranstaltungen."

30. See the detailed instructions in the *VB* (B) of 27 March 1936 and the headline of 28 March, "Letzter Appell des Führers am freien Rhein. Der Volkstag für Ehre, Freiheit und Frieden."

31. *VB* (B), 29 March 1936.

32. Behnken (ed.), *Deutschland-Berichte der Sozialdemokratischen Partei Deutschlands 1934–1940* (henceforth *SOPADE*), April 1936, 407ff., quotation 407.

33. Ibid. p. 407; *VB* (B), 31 March 1936, with the provisional official election results. *PA* 1936, p. 362: On 30 March the press received instructions to calculate the percentages from the number of votes cast and not from the number of those entitled to vote. TB, 31 March 1936: "I correct a stupid legal quibble from Frick: 'valid and invalid votes!' What nonsense."

34. TB, 31 March 1936.

35. Giro, *Frankreich,* 339ff.

36. TB, 15 March 1936, and 17 March 1936.

37. TB, 22 and 29 March 1936: "Our house purchase on Schwanenwerder seems to be going through." On the house purchase, see Reuth, *Goebbels,* 340f.
38. TB, 2 April 1936.
39. TB, 2 and 8 April 1936; also 4 April 1936 (about viewing the house); 6 April 1936 (about the impending move) and 9 April 1936 (move); 7 May, 15 August 1936.
40. TB, 19 April 1936.
41. TB, 20 April 1936.
42. TB, 20 April 1936.
43. TB, 7 August 1936.
44. TB, 21 July 1936.
45. TB, 16 April, 2 May 1936 on the boat purchase. Also 13 May (Hitler's reaction), 4 and 9 May (boat trips), and 20 May 1936 (money worries).
46. TB, 9 July 1936, and 12 and 28 August 1936 about further trips.
47. TB, 27 June 1936.
48. TB, 30 July 1936. On the first trip with the new car, see 29 September 1936.
49. TB, 22 October 1936.
50. TB, 2, 3, 8, 9, 10, and 11 May 1936.
51. TB, 3 June 1936: "In the evening a stroll with Helga. Looked at their house with Gustav Fröhlich and Lida Baarová. It's very nice." On this, their first encounter, see also TB, 10 June 1936; Lida Baarová, *Die süße Bitterkeit meines Lebens,* 81f.
52. Baarová, *Die süße Bitterkeit,* 83ff. This must have referred to the boat trip, in which, as Goebbels noted on 19 August, Fröhlich und Baarová had taken part.
53. TB, 1–5 August.
54. TB, 10 September 1936.
55. TB, 11 September 1936, also 12 September 1936. On the Party rally, see Baarová, *Bitterkeit,* 88ff. *Film-Kurier,* 10 September 1936, "Erfolgreicher Filmstart in Nürnberg. 'Verräter'-Premiere in der Stadt der Reichsparteitage."
56. TB, 30 September, 2 October 1936; Baarová, *Bitterkeit,* 97f.
57. On social contacts with Baarová (whose name he kept spelling incorrectly until the spring of 1937), see 30 November, 10 and 21 December 1936, 14 February, 30 March, 21 April 1937.
58. Fröhlich, *Waren das Zeiten,* 156ff.; Baarová, *Bitterkeit,* 112f.
59. Fröhlich, he noted in his diary on 16 May 1937, was "really stupid." The incident on Schwanenwerder is not in fact mentioned in the diary.
60. TB, 15, 16, 18, and 19 April, 3, 7, and 8 May 1936.
61. TB, 11 May 1936.
62. TB, 11 May 1936, and 15 May 1936: "Führer is stirring up England against Italy. That's how we must get where we want to be. England feels very bitter and humiliated. One day Mussolini will get to feel it."
63. TB, 29 May 1936.
64. TB, 28 May 1936.
65. TB, 10 June 1936, and 11 June 1936; on Edda Ciano's visit, see TB, 3, 7–18 June 1936.
66. On the background, see *Das Juliabkommen von 1936;* Volsansky, *Pakt auf Zeit;* Pauley, *Der Weg in den Nationalsozialismus,* 161ff.; Schausberger, *Griff,* 349ff. On Mussolini's message, see Hassell to A. A., 6 January 1936 in *ADAP* C IV/2, no. 485.
67. *ADAP* C IV, no. 203, 11 July 1935, Aktennotiz mit anliegendem Entwurf; ibid., 578ff., editor's note re: Goebbels's participation in the formulation of the Austrian press agreement of 27 August 1935; see also Volsansky, *Pakt,* 20.
68. TB, 29 February 1936: "Discussed the Austrian question with Papen. He is still

dreaming of his 'arrangement.' But that's just naive. The Vienna government are traitors to Germanness." 4 July 1936: "Führer believes that Papen will bring about peace with Austria. I'm still doubtful."

69. Hitler only told him subsequently about his intentions, TB, 17 July 1936.

70. TB, 12 July 1936 and the entries for the previous and following days; *PA* 1936, p. 736f. (11 July) and p. 738 (13 July).

71. TB, 7 May 1936.

72. On his stay in Bayreuth, see TB, 20–28 July 1936.

73. Literature on the German intervention in Spain: Abendroth, *Hitler in der spanischen Arena;* Merkes, *Die deutsche Politik im spanischen Bürgerkrieg 1936–1939;* Leitz, *Economic Relations between Nazi Germany and Franco's Spain, 1936–1945,* esp. 8ff.; Schieder, "Spanischer Bürgerkrieg und Vierjahresplan. Zur Struktur nationalsozialistischer Außenpolitik."

74. TB, 27 July 1936.

75. TB, 29 and 30 July as well as numerous entries between 5 and 25 August; there are also several entries about Spain during the following months.

76. Abendroth, *Hitler,* 40ff., 95ff.

77. TB, 29 July 1936. The Olympic Games dominate the TB entries until 17 August 1936. On the Olympics, see Large, *Nazi Games;* Bachrach, *The Nazi Olympics: Berlin 1936;* Hilton, *Hitler's Olympics.*

78. On Goebbels's involvement in the preparations for the Olympics, see among others TB, 15, 25, 29, and 31 January, 2 and 21 February, 23 April, 14 May 1936.

79. TB, 3 August 1936.

80. TB, 5 August 1936.

81. Dodd, *Diary,* 343: TB, 16 and 17 August 1936; *Der Angriff,* 17 August 1936, "Märchen auf der Pfaueninsel. Dr. Goebbels lud zum Sommerfest der Reichsregierung."

82. TB, 17 August 1936. In fact Germany won 33 gold medals, ahead of the USA (24) and Hungary (10).

83. See, for example, *FZ,* 10 December 1935.

84. On the preliminary work, see TB, 17 August, 5 and 17 October 1935, 7 November 1935; on social contacts with Riefenstahl, see TB, 9 October 1936. On the *Olympia* film, see Kinkel, *Scheinwerferin,* 107ff.; Trimborn, *Riefenstahl,* 238ff.; Rother, *Verführung,* 87ff.; Bach, *Leni,* 141ff.; Graham, *Leni Riefenstahl and Olympia;* Hoffmann, *Mythos Olympia—Autonomie und Unterwerfung von Sport und Kultur.*

85. TB, 6 August 1936; also 31 July 1936 on Leni Riefenstahl, directly before the Olympic games; see also Kinkel, *Scheinwerferin,* 129f. Disputes between Riefenstahl and Weidemann, the head of the film department of the Party's Reich propaganda headquarters, who had directed the film of the Garmisch winter games, prompted Goebbels to make another critical comment about Hitler's favorite film director: "very hysterical" (TB, 18 September 1936); Kinkel, *Scheinwerferin,* 137f.

86. TB, 25 October 1936. BAB, R 55/503, Bericht über die in der Zeit vom 3. bis 8. Oktober 1936 stattgefundene Kassen- und Rechnungsprüfung bei der Olympia-Film G.m.b.H., 16 October 1936. See also Graham, *Riefenstahl,* 147ff.; Kinkel, *Scheinwerferin,* 139ff.

87. BAB, R 55/503, Präsident Reichsfilmkammer to Goebbels, 6 March 1937.

88. TB, 6 November 1936; Riefenstahl, *Memoiren,* 279. BAB, R 2/4754, letter from the Propaganda Ministry to the Reich Finance Ministry, 25 January 1937; Riefenstahl, *Memoiren,* 279f.; Graham, *Riefenstahl,* 152.

89. On "the mean attacks," see TB, 16 June 1937; on the visit to Riefenstahl, see TB, 1

July 1937; on the denial, see *FZ*, 16 June 1937; see also Kinkel, *Scheinwerferin*, 144ff.

90. TB, 24 and 26 November; Kinkel, *Scheinwerferin*, 148f.

91. TB, 21 December 1937 and 19 March 1938.

92. Kinkel, *Scheinwerferin*, 149f.; TB, 21 April 1938, also 22 April.

93. TB, 2 May 1938.

94. TB, 30 August 1936. On the stay, see also the reports in the *VB* (B), 30 August–2 September 1936.

95. TB, 1 and 4 September 1936.

96. TB, 1 September 1936.

97. TB, 7–9 August 1936.

98. See "Vertrauliche Anweisungen des Promi für den antikommunistischen Propagandafeldzug im Innern," n.d., published in Jacobsen (ed.), *Misstrauische Nachbarn*, 102–5, BAB, NS Misch 1594; on the propaganda exhibitions put on in autumn 1936 in connection with this, see Kivelitz, *Die Propagandaausstellungen in europäischen Diktaturen*, 214ff.; for the continuation of the anti-Communist propaganda in 1937: *PA* 1937, no. 501 (26 February), announcement of a propaganda campaign, Bolshevism and Jewry (see also no. 529, 1 March); no. 1432 (14 June): "Auf besonderen Wunsch der höchsten Reichsstelle" (instruction for anti-Soviet propaganda); see Sywottek, *Mobilmachung*, 104ff.

99. On the press response, see TB, 1, 12, and 13 September; *VB* (B), 11 September 1939, "Dr. Goebbels: 'Der Bolschewismus muss vernichtet werden, wenn Europa wieder gesunden soll'"; *PA* 1936, p. 1028f. (10 September): The Goebbels speech was to be published in full; see also Reuth, *Goebbels*, 354ff.

100. Already referred to in TB, 27 July 1936, during the Bayreuth festival.

101. TB, 23 September 1936.

102. TB, 24 September 1936. Otherwise Magda referred to only on 21 September ("Magda being very nice again"), on 2 September ("bit of a fight with Magda") and the short note quoted in the text.

103. TB, 27–29 September 1936.

104. TB, 22 September 1936.

105. TB, 4 October 1936.

106. TB, 30 October 1936; on the anniversary, see also Reuth, *Goebbels*, 351ff.

107. *Der Angriff*, 31 October 1936, "Die Partei des Arbeiters. Dr. Goebbels im Berliner Rathaus."

108. Goebbels knew about the gift beforehand: TB, 17 September 1936, and 18 September.

109. *Der Angriff*, 31 October 1936; Berkholz, *Goebbels' Waldhof am Bogensee*, 11ff.; Reuth, *Goebbels*, 352.

110. TB, 31 October 1936.

111. TB, 1 and 2 November 1936; *VB* (B), 1 November 1936, "Die Jubiläumskundgebung im Berliner Sportpalast. Die erfolgreiche Arbeit der Berliner Gauleitung findet die besondere Anerkennung des Führers."

112. TB, 1 November 1936.

113. TB, 1 November 1936.

114. TB, 30 October 1936.

115. TB, 31 October 1936.

116. TB, 31 October, 1 and 2 November 1936.

117. TB, 2 November 1936. On the youth rally, see *Der Angriff*, 3 November 1936.

118. TB, 21 October and 15 November 1936.

119. TB, 1 October 1936.

120. Ciano note, 24 October 1936, in *I Documenti Diplomatici Italiani,* Ottava Series: 1935–1939, vol. 5, Rome 1994, no. 277.
121. TB, 3 November 1936.
122. TB, 17 November 1936. On Renzetti, see Schieder, "Faschismus im politischen Transfer."
123. TB, 9 June 1936.
124. TB, 21 October 1936; *RGBl.* 1936 II, 28ff., Abkommen gegen die kommunistische Internationale; *ADAP* D I, no. 463, note 1, Geheimes Zusatzabkommen. See Krebs, "Von Hitlers Machtübernahme zum Pazifischen Krieg (1933–1941)."
125. TB, 2 December 1936; see also 7 December 1936.

16. "THE MOST IMPORTANT FACTORS IN OUR MODERN CULTURAL LIFE"

1. TB, 31 January 1937.
2. *Domarus I,* 664ff.
3. TB, 28 January 1937.
4. TB, 23 February 1937.
5. TB, 23 February: British rearmament was primarily "directed against Italy," but Germany could remain "neutral in any dispute." TB, 13 July: Hitler saw England's position thereafter as "seriously weakened."
6. On the attack on the battleship *Deutschland* and the subsequent bombing of Almeria, see TB, 31 May–2 June and 6 June 1937. On the German delaying tactics in the Non-Intervention Committee, see also 20, 23, 24, 30 June, 3 July, 1 and 8 August 1937.
7. Cautious criticism of Ribbentrop's performance in London in the entry for 7 February, increased in the entries for 3 and 6 March, and 4 April. 27 October 1937: "We evidently made a bad appointment in his case." Also 16 November 1937.
8. TB, 14 March 1937.
9. TB, 23–25 April 1937: Goebbels considered the meeting between Schuschnigg and Mussolini in Venice as a success for Germany's Austrian policy and as a defeat for the "Prague-Vienna-Paris Axis."
10. *Akten der Reichskanzlei, Regierung Hitler,* vol. 4, Hartmannsgruber (ed.), no. 23, Ministerbesprechung vom 30. Januar 1937 and no. 24, Eltz to Hitler, 30 January 1937.
11. On Kerrl's policy, see Meier, *Der evangelische Kirchenkampf,* vol. 2, 78ff.
12. TB, 14 January 1937.
13. TB, 5 January, 6 and 9 February, 1937; see also Hockerts, "Die Goebbels-Tagebücher 1932–1941," 371ff.
14. Meier, *Der evangelische Kirchenkampf, vol. 2,* 147f.
15. TB, 15 February 1937.
16. *PA* 1937, no. 424 (16 February), information on the Church elections; *VB* (B), "Befriedungswerk des Führers für die evangelische Kirche" (headline); Hockerts, "Die Goebbels-Tagebücher," 372f.
17. TB, 18 February 1937; Hockerts, "Die Goebbels-Tagebücher," 373.
18. TB, 20 February 1937.
19. TB, 23 February 1937.
20. TB, 21 April, 12 May 1936. See also Hockerts, "Die Goebbels-Tagebücher," 374.
21. On the action taken against the Catholic press in 1936, see 280.
22. TB, 18 February 1937.

23. Raem, *Pius XI. und der Nationalsozialismus.*
24. TB, 21 March 1937; Hockerts, "Die Goebbels-Tagebücher," 377.
25. TB, 23 and 24 March 1937.
26. TB, 2 April 1937.
27. This happened on 6 April 1937. Hockerts, *Die Sittlichkeitsprozesse,* 73.
28. TB, 7 April 1937.
29. TB, 2 and 30 April 1937; *PA* 1937, nos 985 and 991 (28 and 29 April). *VB* (B), "Kirchen und Klöster zu Lasterstätten erniedrigt" (headline).
30. TB, 12 May 1937.
31. TB, 13 May 1937.
32. *PA* 1937, no. 1119 (13 May), Vertrauliche Bestellung: Runderlaß des Promi an die Landesstellen über Berichterstattung zu den "Katholikenprozessen"; on the control of the reporting, see nos. 1170f. (20 May), 1189 and 1195 (22 May), 1201 and 1204 (24 May). See also TB, 16, 17, 21, and 23 May 1937.
33. TB, 14 May 1937.
34. TB, 25, 26, and 28 May 1937.
35. VB, 29 May 1937.
36. TB, 30 May 1937, on the reception of the speech also 31 May, 1 June 1937. On the instructions to the press, see *PA* 1937, no. 1221 of 26 May and no. 1245 of 28 May and 1256 of 29 May. On the speech, see also Reuth, *Goebbels,* 360f.; Hockerts, *Die Sittlichkeitsprozesse,* 112ff.
37. TB, 3 June 1937.
38. TB, 4, 10, 11, 12, 14, 15, 16, 23, and 26 June 1937.
39. TB, 4 July 1937. More on the trials in entries for 10, 18, 22, and 23 July.
40. TB, 3 and 4 July 1937. Further entries on the arrest of the pastor and on the preparations for the trial: 6 July, 1, 4, 12, and 15 August 1937 and 22 December 1937. See also Bentley, *Martin Niemöller,* 162ff.; Schmidt, *Martin Niemöller,* 133ff.
41. TB, 26 July 1937, and 27, 28, and 29 July 1937.
42. Hockerts refers in this connection to a telegram from the AA to the German ambassador at the Vatican, 24 July 1937, *ADAP* D I, no. 670. *Die Sittlichkeitsprozesse,* 74. Hockerts believes 21 July was the date of Hitler's decision; on the announcement of a pause in the trials: *PA* 1937, Nr. 1848 (29 July).
43. TB, 28 and 29 July 1937; Hockerts, "Die Goebbels-Tagebücher," 374.
44. TB, 5–16 August, 1 and 15 September 1937.
45. TB, 26 August 1937.
46. TB, 7 December 1937.
47. TB, 22 December 1937.
48. TB, 21 January 1938.
49. Numerous entries in the TB between 29 January and 1 March 1938. On the trial, see Schmidt, *Niemöller,* 133ff.; Bentley, *Niemöller,* 171f.
50. TB, 3 March 1938; *PA* 1938, no. 629 (3 March), concludes the reporting of the trial and confidentially informs the journalists of the imposition of protective custody.
51. TB, 3 March 1938.
52. TB, 25 November 1936.
53. On Hitler's reaction to the award of the Nobel Prize, see TB, 25, 26, 27, and 28 November 1936. See also Sternburg, *"Es ist eine unheimliche Stimmung in Deutschland."* On the announcement of the National Prize, see TB, 31 January 1937; *VB* (B), 31 January 1937; *Domarus I,* 664ff. The German National Prize should not be confused with the National Book and Film Prize, established in 1934.

54. *VB* (B), 28 November 1936, "Die dritte Jahrestagung der Reichskulturkammer" (headline); TB, 28–30 November 1936 on the Cultural Senate. See also Reuth, *Goebbels,* 357.

55. See chapter 13.

56. *PA* 1936, 492f., 496, 503f. (12, 13, and 15 May).

57. *Film-Kurier,* 13 May 1936.

58. Decree of 27 November 1936 in Wulf, *Die bildenden Künste im Dritten Reich,* 127ff., also *VB* (B), 28 November 1936. In October he had discussed the problem of "criticism" with Hitler: "In the end it must be gotten rid of completely." See also TB, 26 and 29 October, with similar entries. On the preparation of the decree, see TB, 18, 24, 27, and 28 November 1936.

59. See p. 308.

60. TB, 31 March 1936. BAB, NS 8/171, Rosenberg to Goebbels, 9 March 1936, Goebbels to Rosenberg, 31 March 1936, and Rosenberg's reply from the same day.

61. TB, 15 July, 1 August 1936; Bollmus, *Das Amt Rosenberg,* 84.

62. TB, 1 September, 6 (on his conversation with Hess) and 11 October 1936; see Bollmus, *Das Amt Rosenberg,* 84.

63. TB, 15 November 1936.

64. Piper, *Alfred Rosenberg,* 396; Bollmus, *Das Amt Rosenberg,* 99ff.; see also the comments in TB, 16 June 1937.

65. Diller, *Rundfunkpolitik,* 198ff.; Dussel, *Hörfunk in Deutschland.* This corresponded to the existing programming policy. See Weinbrenner, *Handbuch des Deutschen Rundfunks 1938,* 293, and *Handbuch 1939,* 317.

66. BAB, R 78/910, 4 March 1936. See also the speech at the radio exhibition of August 1936. TB, 29 August 1936. See Dussel and Lersch (eds.), *Quellen zur Programmgeschichte des deutschen Hörfunks und Fernsehens,* no. 33, esp. p. 136.

67. TB, 16 January 1937.

68. On the change of personnel, see 8, 11, and 20 March, 24 April 1937.

69. *VB* (B), 31 July 1937, "Die Eröffnung der großen Rundfunkschau. Dr. Goebbels über Leistung und Aufgaben des deutschen Rundfunks"; Text of the speech published in Dussel/Lersch, *Quellen,* no. 34. TB, 31 July, 1 August 1937.

70. TB, 8 June 1938, also 25 June: "I'm deciding on a new policy for radio: more serious, less light music. Broadcasts of operas and symphonies. Serious programs."

71. *VB* (B), 6 August 1938, "Rundfunkausstellung durch Dr. Goebbels eröffnet." Also TB, 6 August 1938.

72. See Mühlenfeld, "Joseph Goebbels und die Grundlagen der NS-Rundfunkpolitik," 442–67.

73. TB, 17, 18, 20, and 22 October 1936.

74. TB, 22 October 1936.

75. TB, 4, 9, 11, and 12 November 1936.

76. TB, 21 November 1936; *Akten Regierung Hitler,* vol. 3, no. 183, ministerial meeting at the Promi on 19 November 1936, Vermerk des Oberregierungsrats Brenner, Reichserziehungsministerium; no. 186, Begründung des Promi, 25 November 1936; no. 187 Funk to Lammers, 25 November 1936, BAB, R 43 II/467, bill and Dietrich's objection; here also further objections from other ministries.

77. TB, 23 and 30 November 1936; the entries for 13 December 1936 and 12 January 1937 show Goebbels's lack of interest in the project.

78. *Akten der Reichskanzlei, Regierung Hitler,* vol. 5, Hartmannsgruber (ed.), 718; BAB, R 43 II/467, Vermerke Lammers vom 28. November 1936 and 4. Februar 1937.

79. TB, 23 October, 14, 15, and 25 November 1937.

80. TB, 21 and 25 November 1936, 12 February 1937; Gillessen, *Auf verlorenem Posten,* 277ff.

81. TB, 18 March 1937.

82. TB, 26 January, 7 February 1938, TB, 12 April 1938, TB, 16 June 1938.

83. TB, 21 November 1936, 3 January 1937. Silex, *Mit Kommentar,* 127f.; Boveri, *Wir lügen alle,* 603f.

84. TB, 24 June 1938 and 11 July 1938.

85. TB, 14 July 1938.

86. Hale, *Presse,* 259; Silex, *Kommentar,* 203ff. Also the *Berliner Börsen-Zeitung* was acquired at that time by Amann. Hale, *Presse,* 259f.

87. TB, 26 April 1939; Gillessen, *Posten,* 389ff., on the sale of the newspaper by the Amann company.

88. TB, 17 June, 1 July, 28 September 1938.

89. *Presse in Fesseln. Eine Schilderung des NS-Pressetrusts,* Berlin, p. 68f. The well-informed book published in 1947 contained internal information about the Amann concern.

90. TB, 14, 16, 28 November 1934.

91. TB, 13–16 August 1936; see also 8 August 1937. Marwell, *Unwanted Exile,* 149ff. On Hanfstaengl, see also Conradi, *Hitlers Klavierspieler.*

92. Hanfstaengl, *Zwischen Weißem und Braunem Haus,* 362ff.; Speer, *Erinnerungen,* 141. According to him, Hitler and Goebbels had come up with this practical joke. Marwell, *Unwanted Exile,* 1ff.

93. TB, 11, 12, 19 February 1937.

94. TB, 12, 13, 16, and 20 March 1937.

95. TB, 13 and 16 April, 3 June 1937.

96. TB, 24 July 1937.

97. TB, 18 and 22 October 1936.

98. TB, 22 October, and 10 November 1936.

99. TB, 27 October 1936.

100. TB, 14 November 1936; he describes Weidemann, the deputy head of the film department, as on the lookout for material. On the lack of political films, see also 14 November 1936.

101. TB, 16 and 18 December 1936.

102. TB, 12 June 1936.

103. TB, 6 January, 20 February 1937.

104. TB, 22 January, 24 February 1937.

105. TB, 5, 9, 10, and 11 March 1937; *PA* 1937, no. 603 (9 March): "The film *People without a Fatherland* may and shall be given negative reviews." *VB* (N), 10 March 1937, Ewald von Demandowsky: "Versagen der Dramaturgie. Gedanken um den Film *Menschen ohne Vaterland.*" See also *UWW,* April 1937, Hein Schlecht, "Am Wendepunkt der deutschen Filmkunst," 106: "The conspicuous flop of *People without a Fatherland* is clear proof that Dr. Goebbels's ideas about the nature and purpose of film are right, not only in theory but also in practice."

106. TB, 17 March, also 13 and 16 March 1937. On the negotiations, see Moeller, *Filmminister,* 87ff.; Becker, *Film und Herrschaft,* 159f.

107. TB, 20 March 1937.

108. *PA* 1937, no. 709 (23 March).

109. Speech on the first anniversary of the Reich Chamber of Film on 5 March 1937 in the Krolloper, Albrecht, *Filmpolitik,* 447ff.; *PA* 1937, no. 589 (6 March): The speech "pointed the way forward," indeed it was "a great encouragement for all

those involved in making films." On the speech's impact, see TB, 6, 7, and 8 March 1937.

110. Introduction: TB, 4 May 1937. Goebbels praised Demandowsky particularly during the early months of his period in office: 6, 8, 13, and 26 May ("I'm doubling his salary"), 5 June, 14 and 23 July 1937.

111. Moeller, *Filmminister,* 141.

112. TB, 21 and 26 March, 1, 6, 13, and 17 April 1937; Moeller, *Filmminister,* 139; *PA* 1937, nos. 1051 and 1054, (5 and 7 May): "Nothing to be published about the Ufa general meeting."

113. Moeller, *Filmminister,* 101f.

114. TB, 3 April, 31 July 1937.

115. TB, 25 September 1937.

116. TB, 7 January 1938: "Film has the wrong casting. Ritter is supposed to be making a Harvey-, Boese Rühmann film. I'll stop that." Also 25 September 1937.

117. TB, 3 June 1937, 2 and 4 August.

118. TB, 1 July 1937.

119. TB, 31 July 1937, 1 August 1937.

120. TB, 3 August, also 6 August 1937.

121. TB, 5 August 1937.

122. TB, 12 August 1937.

123. TB, 11 September 1937.

124. TB, 11 and 30 September 1937, 7, 14, and 23 October, 9 December 1937.

125. TB, 9 June 1937, also 10 and 23 June also 25, 27, 28, and 31 August 1937.

126. TB, 18 and 30 June 1937, 14 August, 1 and 8 September 1937, 14 and 22 December 1937, 6 January, 1 and 28 July, 3 August 1938; also 9 May 1939.

127. TB, 27 October 1936: "following an idea of mine"; TB, 5 and 12 August, 17 September, 7 December 1937, 25 May, 8 June, 14 September 1938.

128. TB, 3 January 1939; see also 11 July, 1 August 1939.

129. Negative: *Fridericus* (23 January 1937), *Der Etappenhase* (24 February 1937), *Condottieri* (12 and 18 March 1937); mixed feelings: *Togger,* 12 February 1937.

130. TB, 24 June 1937, on *Starke Herzen* and *Weisse Sklaven.*

131. TB, 17 and 20 January, 14 February 1937.

132. TB, 12 and 15 March 1937.

133. TB, 18 June 1937.

134. TB, 23 July 1937.

135. TB, 1 December 1937.

136. TB, 30 September 1937; Moeller, *Filmminister,* 174.

137. TB, 20 June 1937.

138. Moeller, *Filmminister,* 91.

139. TB, 17 and 27 April 1937, 30 July, 12 August, 17 September 1937 and 14 January 1938. The press were not permitted to report on the collapse of the Bavaria film company: *PA* 1937, nos. 893 and 1015 (17 April and 3 May).

140. Moeller, *Filmminister,* 114f.

141. Renate Heller, "Kunst-Ausschuss," 150–58.

142. TB, 29 April 1937.

143. TB, 14 December 1937.

144. TB, 29 May, 2 and 3 June, 14 October, 19 November 1937, and 4 March 1938.

145. Welch, *Nazi Cinema,* 23ff. Concerns about the economic development of the film industry expressed above all in TB, 10 and 14 October, 24 November 1937.

146. TB, 14 October, 25 November 1937.

147. TB, 6 November 1937.

148. TB, 1 December 1937.

149. On *Capriccio,* see TB, 1, 3, and 12 March 1938; on *Der Tiger von Eschnapur,* see TB, 10 January 1938, on *Die Prinzessin kehrt heim,* see TB, 4 February 1938; very negative also about *Frühlingsluft,* 25 March 1938.

150. Moeller, *Filmminister,* 192ff.

151. TB, 5 March 1938. On the preparations, see TB, 7 and 27 October, 24 November 1937, 4 and 5 February; also 2 and 3 March 1938.

152. *Film-Kurier,* 5 March 1938. TB, 28 May, 11 June 1938, on the staffing of the art faculty. On the further development of the Academy, see 4 March, 3 and 18 May 1938.

153. TB, 20 and 29 July, 15 November 1938.

154. TB, 15 June 1939.

155. TB, 7 and 10 December 1938, 28 January 1939.

156. TB, 8, 9, and 12 February 1939; see also 16 February 1939.

157. TB, 16 and 28 February, 29 June 1939.

158. TB, 7 and 10 December 1938, 28 January 1939. As part of this reorganization he also let his most important assistant in film propaganda, Reich film dramaturge Demandowsky, move to Tobis as head of production, despite considerable reservations. The head of Terra production, Greven, took over the equivalent position at Ufa; in fact Goebbels had previously earmarked Emil Jannings for this job. The other film companies also had heads of production appointed, who were often replaced after a relatively short time. Greven was soon replaced by v. Leichtenstern, the head of the film department, who was then himself replaced by Otto Heinz Jahn the following year. Peter Brauer took over production at Terra. He was replaced in November 1940 by Alf Teichs. Schweikart's appointment to the Bavaria company (TB, 26 April, 25 July 1939) and Karl Hartl's appointment to the new Vienna film company (TB, 21 March 1939) also formed part of the reorganization of February 1939.

159. *Film-Kurier,* 11 March 1939, "Dr. Goebbels in der Krolloper. Im Film soll die Persönlichkeit führen." On the impact of the speech, see TB, 11 and 12 March 1939.

160. TB, 20 June 1939, and 21 June.

161. TB, 6 June 1937.

162. TB, 7 June 1937.

163. TB, 19 June 1937; Hoffmann, *Hitler, wie ich ihn sah,* 143ff. Further literature on the Große Deutsche Kunstausstellung: Meissner, "'Deutsches Volk, gib uns vier Jahre Zeit . . .'"; Meissner, "Große Deutsche Kunstausstellung"; Schlenker, *Hitlers Salon.*

164. TB, 5 and 19 June 1937; on opposition from Speer, among others, see 12 June 1937. Compare Lüttichau, "'Deutsche Kunst.' Der Katalog," which provides a reconstruction of the exhibition "Entartete Kunst" (120–83); Meissner, "Deutsches Volk"; Katrin Engelhardt, "Die Ausstellung 'Entartete Kunst' in Berlin 1938"; Zuschlag, *"Entartete Kunst."*

165. TB, 30 June 1937.

166. TB, 1 July 1937. The decree of 30 June is published in Engelhardt, "Ausstellung," 94. On the preparations for the exhibition, see in particular Zuschlag, *"Entartete Kunst,"* 169ff.

167. Engelhardt, "Ausstellung," 94.

168. TB, 17 and 18 July 1937; Brenner, *Ende,* 25f.; Lüttichau, "Deutsche Kunst," docu-

ments that the rooms with paintings by members of the Academy and lecturers were shut a few days after the opening of the exhibition (p. 109). In one case, that of the sculptor Gerhard Marcks, there is evidence that Goebbels personally insisted on his inclusion in the "exhibition of degenerate art" despite being aware that he was a member of the Academy. Brenner, *Ende,* 155.

169. 16, 24 (quotation), 25 (quotation), 27, and 29 July 1937.
170. TB, 3 July 1937.
171. TB, 4 July 1937.
172. TB, 6 and 8 August 1937; TB, 20 June 1937.
173. TB, 9 and 10 July 1937.
174. TB, 10 July 1937.
175. TB, 11–17 July 1937.
176. Literature in note 164.
177. TB, 19 July; *VB* (N), 18 and 19 July 1937.
178. Thus Hitler emphasized "a tremendous flourishing of German art" as a task for the future and it is clear from Goebbels's speech that his high expectations for German art were focused more on the future. *Domarus I,* 705ff., 708, and the reports in the *VB* (N), 18 July 1937.
179. TB, 18 July 1937.
180. *VB* (B), 27 November 1937, "Die Führung des deutschen Geisteslebens in deutschen Händen."
181. TB, 1 August 1937.
182. Berlin exhibition: TB, 28 February 1938: "Visit to the Reichstag 'Degenerate Art' exhibition. What filth! Now it's much more effectively arranged. I order a few changes to be made." 1 March 1938: "I have the 'Degenerate Art' rearranged. It's not sufficiently educational." See also 2 March 1938.
183. TB, 25 and 28 July 1937. Brenner, *Ende,* 26.
184. TB, 5 November 1938; on this second wave of confiscations and the valuation of the works that followed, see Zuschlag, *"Entartete Kunst,"* 205ff.
185. TB, 13 December 1938.
186. Through the Law for the Withdrawal of Degenerate Art Products of 31 May 1938, *RGBl.* 1938 I, 612. TB, 13, 14, 15 January, 12 February, 4 March, 18 and 26 May, 29 July 1938. Zuschlag, *"Entartete Kunst,"* 212ff.
187. TB, 29 October, 3, 12, and 18 November 1938; Zweite, "Franz Hofmann und die Städtische Galerie," 261–88.
188. In the list of departmental responsibilities of November 1936 the position of head of department was registered as unoccupied; BAB, R 55/21061.
189. TB, 30 December 1938.
190. Prieberg, *Musik,* 133ff.
191. TB, 24 October, 4 November 1936, 25 February 1937.
192. TB, 21 September, 9 October 1937.
193. Kater, *Die mißbrauchte Muse,* 32ff.
194. Prieberg, *Musik,* 275ff.; Dümling and Girth (eds.), *Entartete Musik.*
195. TB, 17 May 1938.
196. TB, 29 May 1937; *DAZ,* 29 May 1938 (M), "Zehn Grundsätze für das Musik-schafffen. Dr. Goebbels auf der Reichsmusikfestwoche."
197. Prieberg, *Musik,* 107ff.
198. Kater writes of music as the "most autonomous of all the arts" in the Nazi period. Kater, *Muse,* 363.
199. *RGBl.* 1934 I, 411f.

200. Rischbieter, "NS-Theaterpolitik," 23. On the theater under Nazism, see also Drewniak, *Das Theater im NS-Staat,* and Rühle, *Theater in Deutschland 1887–1945,* 734ff.

201. Panse, "Zeitgenössische Dramatik," 489–720.

202. Thomas Eicher, "Spielplanstrukturen" in *Theater im "Dritten Reich,"* 279–486.

203. Eicher, "Spielplanstrukturen," 596f.

204. Eicher, "Spielplanstrukturen," 478.

205. TB, 23 March 1933, on "Rosse" and 6 April 1934 on "Stille Gäste."

206. TB, 18 November 1933.

207. TB, 24 January 1935.

208. TB, 21 September 1937.

209. He is equally negative about Dietrich Eckart's *Heinrich der Hohenstaufe,* TB, 19 June 1935, Franz Sondinger's *Uta von Naumburg,* TB, 22 November 1935, or the play *Thors Gast* by the *völkisch* poet Otto Erler, TB, 31 October 1937.

210. TB, 26 June 1935.

211. TB, 17 November 1935.

212. TB, 15 April 1936 and 23 June 1936.

213. Eicher, "Spielplanstrukturen," 324ff.

214. TB, 2 November 1933. See also his positive criticism of *Die Räuber* (20 January 1934, 2 October 1936), *Don Carlos* (28 February 1937), and *Kabale und Liebe* (14 October 1937, 17 November 1938).

215. Eicher, "Spielplanstrukturen," 297ff.

216. TB, 27 March 1937. See also his extremely positive criticism of *The Taming of the Shrew* (7 October 1933, 15 June 1937), *Twelfth Night* (13 September 1934), and *King Lear* (23 January 1935).

217. Thus he noted Hitler's lavish praise of Shaw: "He lifts the veil from English hypocrisy."

218. TB, 7 October 1934, after a performance of *Saint Joan.*

219. TB, 6 August 1936. Equally positive *Pygmalion* (16 January 1935), *Saint Joan* (6 August 1936), *Androcles and the Lion* (17 December 1936), *The Apple Cart* (29 January 1938), *Man and Superman* (6 November 1939), *Caesar and Cleopatra* (12 December 1939). While he praised *Androcles and the Lion,* he did not see it as a "major work."

220. TB, 20 December 1935 (*Sprung aus dem Alltag* by Heinrich Zerkaulen); 7 January 1936 (*Krach im Hinterhaus*). 5 December 1936 (*Moral* by Ludwig Thoma), 2 March 1934 (*Dr. Prätorius* by Curt Goetz).

221. TB, 11 April 1934.

222. Rischbieter, "NS-Theaterpolitik," 70ff.

223. Rischbieter, "NS-Theaterpolitk," 72; on the meetings, see TB, 27 September 1935, 20 June 1936, 20 October 1937, 19 November 1938, 18 March 1939. Based on his diaries he only visited the theater twice: 6 June 1936 and 4 December 1937.

224. Goebbels had already noticed Hilpert in December 1933 on a visit to the Volksbühne: TB, 26 December 1933: "I'll get ahold of him some time when I've got control of the theater." On Hilpert, see Rischbieter, "NS-Theaterpolitik," 73ff.; Dillmann, *Heinz Hilpert.*

225. TB, 1 September 1937 and 17 February 1938.

226. TB, 21 August 1936, 19 December 1936, 18 May, 1 July 1937, 30 April 1938. On Klöpfer, see Rischbieter, "NS-Theaterpolitik," 80f.; TB, 17 June, 3 July 1936.

227. Rischbieter, "NS-Theaterpolitik," 79f.; criticism in TB, 25 October 1934, 8 March 1935, and 8 May 1935

228. TB, 21 November, 24 December 1937, 21 February 1940.

229. He also intervened in the new production of *The Merry Widow*, TB, 8 February, 3 March 1939.

230. TB, 6, 8, 21, and 24 January 1935.

231. TB, 31 May 1935.

232. TB, 30 April, 1 May 1936.

233. On the takeover of the theater on the Nollendorfplatz, see TB, 18 and 23 February, 2 and 9 March 1938.

234. On his disagreement with Lippert over the Schillertheater, see TB, 19 and 22 February 1937. TB, 27 January 1938: "With George Schillertheater repertoire and cast"; see also 24 February, 2 March 1938.

235. Rischbieter, "NS-Theaterpolitk," 81ff. On the takeover of the Metropoltheater, see TB, 24 July, 5 and 24 August, 5 and 6 October, 4 and 17 December 1937, and 5 January 1938.

236. TB, 5 October 1935, according to which he was hoping soon to have finished with the "dejewification" of the RKK; see also 19 October 1935; BAB, R 56 V 102, 27 June 1935: According to that the Chamber of Culture was to be gradually purged of Jews, non-Aryans and those related to Jews; in individual cases consideration should be given to negative domestic, diplomatic, and economic repercussions. On the "dejewification" of the RKK, see Steinweis, *Art, Ideology, and Economics in Nazi Germany*, 103ff.; Reuth, *Goebbels*, 333, 336f., 342f.

237. Steinweis, *Art*, 112, 115.

238. TB, 30 April 1936; Hinkel instruction of 29 April 1936, BAB, R 56 V 102; also TB, 11 December 1936.

239. TB, 3 February 1937, and 3 March 1937.

240. TB, 5 May 1937, 5 and 30 June 1937, 24 November, 3 December 1937.

241. TB, 13 January, 9 and 16 February, 16 March 1938, and 18 May 1938.

242. BAB, R 58/992, Gestapo Tagesmeldung, 25 May 1939; see also Steinweis, *Art*, 117.

243. TB, 16 March, 26 April, 23 June 1939.

244. TB, 4 May 1943.

245. For instance: TB, 24 February, 2–4 June 1935, 7, 26, and 27 January, 8 and 9 October 1936, 15 June, 27 September 1937, 3–6 January 1938; he does not appear to have been in Rheydt in 1939.

246. TB, 27 December 1934 and 5 and 6 January 1938.

247. TB, 3 January 1938.

248. TB, 3 and 6 January; on the meeting with friends, see 7 January, 8 and 9 October 1936, 15 June 1937.

249. TB, 27 December 1934 (on Kölsch), TB, 5 January 1938 (on Prang).

250. TB, 2 February 1935; see also 10 February 1935.

251. TB, 21 and 24 October 1935.

252. TB, 24 March 1936.

253. On Hans, see in particular TB, 6 April 1937; on his conflict with Gauleiter Florian, see 15 February, 3 and 11 March, 1 May 1939; see also Müller, *Im Schatten des "Grandgoschiers."*

254. TB, 22 May 1939: "Brief visit to Hans and Hertha. The ambience is terrible. Hertha has completely mucked up Hans."

255. TB, 1936, numerous entries.

256. TB, 18 February 1937.

257. TB, 27 February 1937.

258. TB, 27 and 30 March, 28 and 30 April 1937.

259. TB, 17 June 1937.

260. TB, 6 July 1937.

261. TB, 9 July 1937.
262. TB, 15 July, also 16 and 17 July 1937.
263. TB, 3 August 1937.
264. TB, 3 February 1938.
265. TB, 24 April, 22 July, 7 August 1938.
266. TB, 17 October, 22 November 1937, 6 January 1938.
267. TB, 27 September 1937 and 31 January 1938.
268. TB, 6 October 1936.
269. See in particular the numerous entries in his diary, especially in a second book that he was writing up on the Bogensee from 29 October onward.
270. TB, 5–8 January 1937.
271. TB, 1–22 January 1937.
272. TB, 10 January 1937: "I feel rather lonely in Berlin in the big house." 17 January 1937: "I'm longing to see both of them, Magda and Helga." 18 January 1937 (concerning his decision to stay overnight on the Bogensee: "No one's expecting me in Berlin"). 23 January 1937: "Being so alone is no fun at all."
273. TB, 19 and 20 January 1937.
274. TB, 24 January 1937.
275. TB, 3 and 6 February and the following days on contact with Magda.
276. TB, 20 February 1937.
277. TB, 24 March: "Magda arrives back after eight weeks' absence in the clinic."
278. TB, 25 February.
279. TB, 14 March 1937.
280. TB, 31 March 1937.
281. Thus, for example, on 3, 26, and 28 May, 2 June, 3 July, 30 August 1937.
282. TB, 2 February 1937; see also 3 July, 2 September 1937.
283. TB, 31 January 1937: "Still with the Führer among a large crowd. Magda stays on. I leave when the film starts." 2 May 1937 (following the 1 May celebrations): "Still a lot of work to do at home. Magda and Maria go to the Reich Chancellery on their own." Also at the end of Mussolini's state visit Magda spent time in the Reich Chancellery without her husband, TB, 26 October 1937.
284. TB, 5–30 June 1937.
285. TB, 4 June 1937.
286. TB, 22 August 1937.
287. TB, 24 September 1937.
288. TB, 7 November 1937.
289. TB, 11 and 19 December 1937.
290. TB, 25 April 1937 (Hannah), 16 May 1937 (Helmut), 12 August 1937 (Helga), 27 October 1937 (Helmut).
291. TB, 18 April 1937; see also 17, 19, 25, and 30 April, 24 August 1937.
292. BAB, R 55/421, letter from Goebbels to the Reich Finance Ministry, June 1937.
293. TB, 7 October 1937.
294. TB, 4 November 1937.
295. TB, 6 October 1937.
296. TB, 31 July, 26 October 1937.
297. TB, 7 and 12 November 1937.
298. TB, 8 January, 13 February 1938.
299. TB, 19 February 1938. "Mercedes. 200 hp. I'll buy it. Terrific sports convertible from Horch. Something for connoisseurs." On the plan to buy the Horch, see TB, 3 May 1938.
300. TB, 19 April and 22 June 1939.

301. TB, 18 August 1939.
302. See the corresponding entries for 1936/37: on 10 July, 21 and 26 August, 4, 9, 16, and 30 September, 4, 23, and 29 October, 23 November and 29 December 1936, 10 February, 26 March, 6 April, 17 June, 24, 27, and 28 August, 16 September, 5 and 18 October, 20 November 1937.
303. TB, 4 September 1936 and 18 October 1937: "If I don't have any work to do I become depressed."

17. "DON'T LOOK AROUND, KEEP MARCHING ON!"

1. TB, 27 September 1937. On the actual visit, see the reports in the *VB* (B), 25–29 September 1937.
2. *VB* (B), 29 September 1937, "Dr. Goebbels meldet den Aufmarsch von drei Millionen Menschen."
3. *SOPADE* 9/1937, 1219, Report from Berlin.
4. *VB* (B), 29 September 1939, "Ein geschichtliches Ereignis. Die Völkerkundgebung der 115 Millionen."
5. TB, 29 September 1937.
6. TB, 2 August 1937, and 1 August 1937; *VB* (B), 2 August 1937, "Überwältigende Manifestation des deutschen Volkstums. 30,000 Auslandsdeutsche marschieren am Führer vorbei—nie erlebte Stürme der Begeisterung" (headline).
7. TB, 10 September 1937; *PA* 1937, no. 2219 (9 September). Goebbels's belligerent speech attacking the "threat from 'Jewish Bolshevism'" was published in the *VB* (B) on 10 September 1937: "Dr. Goebbels enthüllt die dunklen Pläne des Bolschewismus—Nürnberg warnt Europa."
8. TB, 19 October 1937, and 20, 22, 24, 27, and 29 October 1937. On the event that provided the pretext, see Smelser, *Das Sudetenproblem und das Dritte Reich (1933–1938)*, 183, and Helmuth K. G. Rönnefarth, *Die Sudetenkrise in der internationalen Politik. Entstehung, Verlauf, Auswirkung*, 171ff.; on the press campaign, see Schwarzenbeck, *Nationalsozialistische Pressepolitik und die Sudetenkrise 1938*, 239f., and *PA* 1937, nos. 2502, 2506, 2512, 2523, 2530 (18–21 October).
9. TB, 4 November 1937: "Henlein requests us to moderate our campaign against Prague a bit, otherwise he won't be able to control his people properly. Also he doesn't know what he wants. But that's fine!" When the German envoy in Prague made the same request of him the day before, Goebbels had been much less willing to moderate the campaign (ibid., 3 November 1937, and then ending with the provisional conclusion of the press attacks 6 November 1937). On the halt to the campaign, see *ADAP* D II, no. 11, Aufzeichnung Mackensen, 3 November; *PA* 1937, nos. 2687 and 2702 (5 November).
10. Schwarzenbeck, *Pressepolitik*, 247ff. *ADAP* D II, no. 12, Bericht des deutschen Gesandten in Prag, Eisenlohr, über Gespräch mit Außenminister Krofta, 4 March 1938; no. 15, Bericht Eisenlohrs vom 9. November 1937 über Gespräch mit Staatspräsident Beneš; II 18, long version of this report 10 and 11 November 1937; no. 16, Aufzeichnung Leiter Presseabteilung des AA über Gespräch mit tschechischem Gesandten, 9 November 1937; no. 17, Aufzeichnung Staatssekretär über Gespräch mit tschechischem Gesandten, 9 November 1937.
11. TB, 6 November 1937.
12. Nuremberg document PS-386, published in *IMT*, vol. 25, 402–13. On the history of the document, see Bussmann, "Zur Entstehung und Überlieferung der

Hoßbach-Niederschrift"; Smith, "Die Überlieferung der Hoßbach-Niederschrift im Lichte neuer Quellen." TB, 6 November 1937.

13. Smelser, *Sudetenproblem,* 184f.; Henlein to Hitler, 19 November 1937, in *ADAP* D II, no. 23.

14. TB, 24 November, 14 December 1937.

15. *ADAP* D II, no. 29, Vermerk Leiter der Politischen Abteilung, v. Weizsäcker, über entsprechende Zusagen des tschechoslowakischen Gesandten, 10 December 1937; at the beginning of 1938 the German envoy in Prague reported that the authorities were beginning to "restrict or ban the émigré press" (ibid., *ADAP* D II, no. 47, 12 January 1938). On the "press peace," see Schwarzenbeck, *Pressepolitik,* 247ff.

16. See p. 369.

17. *PA* 1938, no. 159 (18 January); *VB* (B), 19 January 1938, German-Yugoslav press agreement.

18. TB, 9 and 22 April 1938.

19. TB, 21 December 1937.

20. TB, 9 and 10 November 1937; *VB* (B), 9 November 1937, "Eröffnung der Ausstellung 'Der ewige Jude.'"

21. TB, 26 November 1937.

22. TB, 30 November 1937.

23. TB, 3 December 1937; on the drafting of the law, see 2 December 1937.

24. TB, 30 and 31 December 1937, numerous entries in January and through mid-February. On the Goga government, see Heinen, *Die Legion "Erzengel Michael" in Rumänien,* 357ff.

25. TB, 13 February 1937, and 14 February.

26. TB, 12 February 1937.

27. TB, 15 October 1937.

28. Examples in Stephan, *Goebbels,* 95ff.

29. TB, 17 March 1937.

30. TB, 5 May 1937; *PA* 1937, no. 1640 (1 July).

31. *Michael* (book version). The quotation is also in TB, 2 February, 13 August 1924.

32. The "Schacht crisis" had been going on since March 1937. See TB, 19 March 1937 as well as 21 March 1937, 12 and 14 August, 5, 9, and 10 September, 27 October 1937; Kopper, *Schacht,* 312ff.

33. TB, 29 October 1937; see also 2 November 1937, conversation with Hitler about the same subject and 3 November 1937, conversation with Funk, 4 November 1937 about further negotiations. 6 November 1937: "Hitler wants to delay Schacht's dismissal until 11/9."

34. TB, 26 November 1937.

35. TB, 27 November 1937; also 28 November 1936 about Dietrich's and Hanke's visits on taking up their positions.

36. TB, 2, 4, 7, 9, 18 December 1937; on Naumann, see 8, 9, 12, and 31 December 1937.

37. *BK,* 182; TB, 24 February 1938, on Hinkel's impending appointment. He had already been doing the same job but in a special capacity.

38. TB, 18 February, 2 March 1938.

39. TB, 5 February 1938; and 2 March 1938; *PA* 1938, no. 585 (26 March), information about the creation of a foreign press department. While the newspaper academic, Professor Karl Bömer, took over the foreign section, the previous head of the department, Alfred-Ingemar Berndt (the experienced Nazi journalist had replaced Jahncke in 1936) was now responsible for domestic issues; however, at

the turn of the year 1938/39 he was already being replaced by the radio journalist, Hans Fritzsche, and took over the ministry's literature department founded in 1934. On Berndt, see *BK*, 75ff., on Bömer, see *BK*, 69ff.; on Fritsche, see TB, 20 January 1939; Bonacker, *Goebbels' Mann beim Radio*, 47; on the literature department, see BAB, R 55/432, Nachrichtenblatt des Promi, 5 September 1934.

40. TB, 20 January 1937.
41. TB, 25 August 1937; on the administration, see *BK*, 60f.; there are personal files for Ott and Müller: R 55/30326 and 30122.
42. TB, 30 March, 5 April, 21 and 25 August, 19 October, 21 November 1935.
43. It was initially unclear whether Esser was to become a departmental head, general inspector, Reich commissar or state secretary. Goebbels tried to make Esser's position as insignificant as possible: 16 December 1937, 20 and 22 January, 11 and 25 February, 4, 19, and 22 March, 3 June 1938, 20, 28, and 29 January 1939, 17 February, 21 June 1939.
44. TB, 5 February 1938.
45. TB, 13 January 1938. Blomberg had "blushingly" confessed the forthcoming marriage to him in December: TB, 15 December 1937.
46. TB, 26 and 27 January 1938.
47. TB, 27 January 1938. On the Blomberg-Fritsch affair, see Müller et al. (eds.), *Organisation und Mobilisierung des deuschen Machtbereichs*, 255ff.; Janssen and Tobias, *Der Sturz der Generäle*.
48. TB, 27 January 1938.
49. TB, 28 and 31 January on Gestapo investigations.
50. TB, 26, 28, and 30 January 1938.
51. TB, 29 January 1938; see also 30 January 1938.
52. TB, 1 January 1938.
53. On 27 January 1938, according to TB, 28 January 1938.
54. TB, 3–5 February 1938.
55. TB, 5 Febuary 1938.
56. TB, 1 February 1938.
57. See Janssen and Tobias, *Sturz*, 148ff.; TB, 5 and 6 February 1938; *PA* 1938, no. 359, Sonderpressekonferenz (4 February); no. 361, (5 February, Statement by Berndt).
58. TB, 6 February 1938. *Regierung Hitler*, vol. 5, no. 35, notes the address without adding further details. The communiqué that was issued that evening concerning the session is in BAB, R 43 II/1477.
59. TB, 23 February, 2 March 1938.
60. Janssen and Tobias, *Sturz*, 173ff.
61. TB, 18 March 1938.
62. On the "Anschluß" with Austria, see Heinz Arnberger et al. (eds.), *"Anschluß" 1938; Anschluß 1938. Protokoll des Symposiums in Wien am 14. und 15. März 1978*; Botz, *Die Eingliederung Österreichs in das Deutsche Reich*; Schausberger, *Griff nach Österreich*; Stourzh and Zaar (eds.), *Österreich, Deutschland und die Mächte*.
63. TB, 13 July 1937; *PA* 1937, no. 1729 (13 July), announcement of the text of the agreement.
64. TB, 15 December 1937.
65. *ADAP* D I, nos. 294 and 295, Protokoll über die Besprechung vom 12. Februar (including draft); Schausberger, *Griff*, 519ff.
66. TB, 16 February 1938, and 17 February 1938; 18 February 1938: "The Führer speaks with Seyss-Inquart, who's briefly in Berlin. I shall only hear more today."
67. TB, 21 February 1938.

68. TB, 17 February 1938.
69. TB, 18, 19, and 20 February 1938; *PA* 1938, no. 444 (16 February), detailed instruction concerning the reporting of changes to the Austrian government. See Koerner, *So haben sie es damals gemacht,* 68ff.
70. *Domarus I,* 792ff., quotations 802, 803; see also TB, 21 February 1938.
71. TB, 26 February 1938.
72. TB, 1 March 1938, and 2 and 4 March 1938; Schausberger, *Griff,* 542f.
73. *PA* 1939, no. 557 (24 February), no. 564 (25 February); no. 618 (1 March 1938): "restraint" and "care"; TB, 1 March 1938; Koerner, *So haben sie es,* 75ff.
74. Schausberger, *Griff,* 552f.
75. TB, 10 March 1938.
76. TB, 11 March 1938; *PA* 1938, no. 724 and 727 (11 March). *VB* (B), 11 March 1938, "Schuschniggs 'Volksentscheid'" (editorial); *DAZ,* 11 March 1938 (E), "Feuerüberfall auf Linzer Nationalsozialisten" (headline); Koerner, *So haben sie es,* 78f.
77. Correct spelling: Seyß-Inquart.
78. TB, 12 March 1938; Schausberger, *Griff,* 556ff.
79. TB, 13 March 1938; Text in: *Domarus I,* 815ff. On this and on the further propaganda handling of this action, see *PA* 1938, nos. 728f. and 733f. (12 March); *VB* (B), 12 March 1938, "Deutsch-Österreich aus dem Chaos gerettet. Provisorische Wiener Regierung Seyß-Inquart bittet den Führer um Entsendung reichsdeutscher Truppen" (headline); *DAZ,* 12 March 1938 (M), "Nationalsozialismus Österreichs an der Macht."
80. TB, 14, 15, and 16 March (there still Reichspropagandahauptamt) and 17, 19, and 20 March 1938.
81. TB, 14 March 1938.
82. *Domarus I,* 824f.; TB, 16 March 1938.
83. TB, 16 March 1938.
84. *VB* (B), 16 March 1938, "Heute Freudentag in Berlin" (headline) and Goebbels's announcement.
85. TB, 17 March 1938; *VB* (B), 17 March 1938, "Triumphaler Einzug des Führers in die Hauptstadt des Großdeutschen Reiches. 2,5 Millionen dankten jubelnd ihrem Führer."
86. *Domarus I,* 826ff.; TB, 18 and 19 March 1938.
87. TB, 20 March 1938.
88. TB, 18 March 1938.
89. TB, 19 March 1938.
90. TB, 20 March 1938.
91. TB, 31 March 1938; *VB* (B), 30 March, "Festlicher Empfang des Reichsministers Dr. Goebbels in Wien"; 31 March 1939 (headline), "Kundgebung der Hunderttausend in Wien"; *PA* 1938, no. 955 and nos. 956 and 958 (29 March), no. 965 (30 March).
92. TB, 10 April 1938; Heiber (ed.), *Goebbels Reden,* no. 33.
93. Heiber (ed.), *Goebbels Reden,* 299.
94. *Domarus I,* 848ff.; TB, 10 April 1938.
95. TB, 11 April 1938.
96. Jung, *Plebiszit,* 109ff.
97. TB, 26 April 1938.
98. TB, 20 March 1938. See also 7 March 1938, when Hitler told Goebbels that the ČSR would "one day be destroyed."
99. TB, quotations 21 and 28 March 1938; see also the corresponding entries of 25 and 30 March 1938.

100. *ADAP* D II, no. 107, Vortragsnotiz über meine Besprechung mit dem Führer der Sudetendeutschen Partei, Konrad Henlein, und seinem Stellvertreter Karl Hermann Frank; see Smelser, *Sudetenproblem,* 193f.; Rönnefarth, *Sudetenkrise,* 218f.

101. TB, 25 April 1938. See also Henlein's note after his conversation with Hitler (previous note): "In other words we must always demand so much that we can never be satisfied."

102. Smelser, *Sudetenproblem,* 198; see *PA* 1937, no. 1197 (25 April), ordering the German press to continue to exercise restraint. On the speech, see TB, 25 April 1938.

103. *PA* 1938, nos. 1272 (2 May), 1311 (7 May), 1340 and 1366 (11 May), 1425 and 1433 (18 May).

104. TB, 4–11 May 1938; *VB,* 4–11 May 1938.

105. TB, 7 May 1938. The "liquidation" of Austria and the promise of Italy not to intervene in the event of a conflict between Germany and Czechoslovakia were in fact the main results of the visit: *ADAP* D I, no. 761, Ribbentrop's circulars to embassies, and no. 762, Aufzeichnung Weizsäckers, 12 May 1938.

106. TB, 6 May 1938.

107. TB, 20 May 1938.

108. *PA* 1938, no. 1435 (19 May). On the continuation of the campaign, see *PA* 1938, no. 1445 (20 May 1938). For the implementation of these instructions see, for example, the reports in the *DAZ,* which, as ordered, changed the approach with the evening edition of 19 May, launching a series of attacks; the *FZ* followed suit by publishing an editorial on the 19th about the economic discrimination being allegedly practiced against the Sudeten Germans and on 21 May began to report "incidents." The *VB*'s anti-Czech campaign was launched in a big way on 21 May. On this change, of course, see Schwarzenbeck, *Pressepolitik,* 293ff.

109. *PA* 1938, no. 1440 (20 May).

110. TB, 23 May 1938.

111. TB, 22 May 1938; see *DAZ, FZ,* and *VB* of 21 May 1938.

112. *PA* 1938, no. 1467 (23 May).

113. On the weekend crisis, see Rönnefarth, *Sudetenkrise,* 277ff.; Scheil, *Churchill, Hitler und der Antisemitismus,* 193ff. It is still unclear where the false reports came from. See also Lukes, "The Czechoslovak Partial Mobilization in May 1938," which rather unconvincingly attributes it to Soviet intelligence. On the German propaganda, see *DAZ,* 22–25 May 1938; *FZ,* 22–27 May 1938; *VB,* 22–26 May 1938. See *PA* 1938, no. 1467 (23 May), nos. 1476, (24 May), 1487 and 1488 (25 May), no. 1504 (27 May).

114. *PA* 1938, no. 1510 (28 May); in its editorial of 30 May 1938, the *FZ* saw "signs of an easing of tension"; in their editions of 26–31 May *(DAZ),* and 29 and 30 May *(VB)* both papers dispensed with big spreads about alleged border violations.

115. TB, 23 (Pussyfooter quotation), 25, 26, and 27 May 1938; 29 May 1938. Goebbels hurried to include these instructions in a speech he gave in Dessau on 30 May, after Hitler had thoroughly vetted the text (TB, 30 May 1938). On the speech, see *VB* (B), 30 May 1938, "Scharfe Abrechnung mit den Friedensstörern."

116. *ADAP* D II, no. 221, 30 May 1938, Anlage: Führerweisung betr. Aufmarsch Grün; Rönnefarth, *Sudetenkrise,* 310; Smelser, *Sudetenproblem,* 201.

117. TB, 1, 2, and 3 June 1938. *PA* 1938, no. 1551 (2 June), no. 1565 (3 June); *VB* (B), 3 June 1938; *MNN,* 2 and 3 June 1938; *DAZ,* 2 June (M and E): Schwarzenbeck, *Pressepolitik,* 313f. His Königsberg speech of 17 June represented a particularly strong attack. TB, 17 and 18 June 1938, *FZ,* 19 June 1938, "Reichsminister Goebbels in Königsberg."

118. In his diary entries for 4, 5, and 8–12 June, Goebbels boasted of having continued

to mobilize the press against Prague. However, this is not reflected in his instructions to the press and only partially in the reporting of the press; *PA* 1938, no. 1601, no. 1613, no. 1620. The *FZ* carried an editorial on 3 June 1938 dealing with the "problem of Czechoslovakia"; in the same edition and on 7 June there were articles about "incidents." Up until 11 June the *DAZ* reported such events regularly on its front page, the *VB* (B) carried headlines on the issue from 2–9 and 11–13 June and on 18 June. There are entries on propaganda against Czechoslovakia in the TB for 15 and 21 June, 1 and 2 July 1938. During the second half of the month attacks by the *VB* and the *FZ* against Prague once again declined, as did those of the *DAZ* between 18 and 29 June. See also Schwarzenbeck, *Pressepolitik*, 314ff.

119. TB, 17 July 1938.
120. TB, 19 July 1938.
121. *PA* 1939, no. 1974 (18 July), nos. 1981 and 1988 (19 July), no. 2008 (22 July). On the reduced continuation of the campaign in July, see *DAZ, FZ, VB*.
122. On the start of the persecution of the Jews in Austria, see Gerhard Botz, *Nationalsozialismus in Wien,* 93ff.; Longerich, *Politik der Vernichtung,* 162ff.; Rosenkranz, *Verfolgung und Selbstbehauptung,* 20ff.
123. Adam, *Judenpolitik,* 172ff.; Barkai, *Vom Boykott zur "Entjudung,"* 233ff.; Friedländer, *Das Dritte Reich,* vol. 1, 262ff.; Longerich, *Politik der Vernichtung,* 155ff.
124. TB, 25 May 1938.
125. OA Moskau, 500-1-603, Wolf Gruner (ed.), "'Lesen brauchen sie nicht zu können.'"
126. TB, 21 April 1938.
127. TB, 25 May (Helldorf), 30 May (Hitler's agreement), 31 May 1938 (Helldorf).
128. TB, 2, 3, and 4 June 1938.
129. TB, 11 June 1938.
130. Longerich, *Politik der Vernichtung,* 178ff.
131. TB, 21 June 1938.
132. TB, 22 June 1938.
133. TB, 24 June; see also 26 June 1938.
134. Longerich, *Davon,* 114; TB, 9 July 1938 (on Stuttgart).
135. TB, 1 and 27 July, 31 August 1938.
136. Longerich, *Davon,* 114.
137. TB, 25 July 1938.
138. On the Runciman mission, see Rönnefarth, *Sudetenkrise,* 407ff.; Vysny, *The Runciman Mission to Czechoslovakia;* TB, 28 July 1938: They were adopting a "neutral stance" toward the mission. This corresponded to the attitude adopted by the AA in the press conference: *PA* 1938, no 2031 (26 July); no. 2039 (26/27 July), no. 2067 (30 July).
139. On the reporting of the Runciman mission, see, for example, *VB* (B), 4, 6, and 21 August (editorial) and *DAZ*: 2 August (E), 10 August (M); 11 August (M); 14 August (M) and 17–19 August 1938.
140. At the beginning of August the so-called Glatz incident received widespread coverage in all the papers: *DAZ,* 3 August (E), 4 August (M and E), 5 August (M and E) 1938; *VB* (B), 4 and 5 August 1938. Further examples of aggressive reporting: *DAZ,* 9 August (M), "Sudetendeutscher von Tschechen ermordet" (headline); 9 August (E), "Der Mörder vom Glaserwald verhaftet" (headline); VB (B), 9 August, "Wieder ein Todesopfer tschechischer Mordhetze" (headline); also similar articles on the front pages of 11, 12, 13, 16, 18, and 19 August. On this campaign, see the following instructions to the press: *PA* 1939, nos. 2112 and 2114 (3 Au-

gust), nos. 2118 and 2121 (4 August), nos 2125, 2138, and 2141 (5 August), nos. 2144 and 2150 (6 August), nos. 176 (9 August) and 2240, (16 August); Schwarzenbeck, *Pressepolitik,* 334f.; TB, 5 and 6, 10 August 1938.

141. TB, 23–27 August 1938.

142. Schwarzenbeck, *Pressepolitik,* 340ff. PA 1938, no. 2353 (27 August), no. 2372 (29 August), no. 2382 (31 August). See also VB (B), 26–30 August; MNN, 29 and 30 August, DAZ, 26–30 August.

143. On 27 August 1938 the *Abwehr* officer, Helmuth Groscurth, noted concerning a visit from Karl Hermann Frank, who informed him about his conversation with Hitler on 26 August: "Orders the creation of incidents in Czechoslovakia!" Groscurth, *Tagebücher eines Abwehroffiziers 1938–1940,* 104.

144. TB, 9 September 1938.

145. PA 1938, nos. 2455, 2458, 2459 (7 September), no. 2460 (8 September); TB, 8 and 9 September; VB (B), 8 September 1938, "Prager Regierung nicht mehr Herr ihrer Polizei" (SZ); "Prags verbrecherisches Spiel mit dem Feuer" (domestic); 9 September, "Prag spielt mit dem Feuer"; see also Smelser, *Sudetenproblem,* 210f., Schwarzenbeck, *Pressepolitik,* 350, Rönnefarth, *Sudetenkise,* 478ff.

146. *Domarus I,* 897ff., quotation 904; TB, 13 September 1938; Schwarzenbeck, *Pressepolitik,* 354ff.; Rönnefarth, *Sudetenkrise,* 497ff.

147. TB, 14 September 1938.

148. Rönnefarth, *Sudetenkrise,* 493f.

149. PA 1938, nos. 2524 and 2533, 14 September; VB (B), 14 September, "Feuerüberfälle, Morde, Standrecht" (headline); 15 September 1938, "30 neue Opfer tschechischer Mordschützen."

150. VB (B), 14 September, "Wie lange noch?" See TB, 15 September 1938: "My article in the VB makes a very aggressive impression. That was my intention."

151. Smelser, *Sudetenproblem,* 212f.; TB, 15 September 1938.

152. TB, 15 September 1939.

153. PA 1939, nos. 2533, 2549–2553 (15 September), nos. 2558–2562, 2569, 2570f. (16 September), nos. 2572, 2574, 2575, 2580–2582 (17 September), no. 2583f. (18 September). According to the TB of 17 September, these attacks were intended to go on until the start of the Bad Godesberg meeting. 18 September 1938: "We make a big thing of [. . .] Czech terror. The atmosphere must be built up to boiling point." See also Schwarzenbeck, *Pressepolitik,* 359f.

154. VB (B), 16 September 1938, "Die Besprechungen zwischen dem Führer und dem britischen Premierminister"; ADAP D II, Nr. 487, Aufzeichnung über Unterredung Hitler-Chamberlain, 15 September 1938; Rönnefarth, *Sudetenkrise,* 523ff.

155. "He wants to have me near him during these days," TB, 18 September 1938.

156. TB, 18 September 1938.

157. TB, 19 September 1938.

158. TB, 20 September 1938; Rönnefarth, *Sudetenkrise,* 540ff.; ADAP D II, no. 523, Text of the joint message of the British and French governments to Beneš on the basis of the conversations of 18 September.

159. TB, 20 September 1938; see also 21 September 1938.

160. PA 1938, nos. 2613, 2614, 2615, 2623, 2627, 2628, and 2632 (21 September).

161. TB, 21 September 1938; see also PA 1938, no. 2596 (19 September), nos. 2606, 2607, 2608 (20 September); VB (B), 20 September, "Tschechenstaat kracht in allen Fugen" (headline); 21 September, "Offene tschechische Angriffe auf das Reich" (headline); 22 September, "Fort mit dem Benesch-Staat" (headline).

162. Kershaw, *Der Hitler-Mythos,* 155ff.

163. He had discussed it with Goebbels and Ribbentrop the night before: TB, 22 and

23 September 1938; *ADAP* D II, no. 562, Aufzeichnung Schmidt über Unterredung Chamberlain-Hitler, 22 September 1938; Rönnefarth, *Sudetenkrise,* 581ff.; Kershaw, *Hitler. 1936–1945,* 169ff.; Schmidt, *Statist,* 407ff.

164. *ADAP* D II, nos. 572–74 (23 September 1938) and no. 583 (23 September Evening); TB, 24 September 1938; Rönnefarth, *Sudetenkrise,* 585ff.

165. TB, 25 September 1938.

166. *PA* 1938, no. 2633 (21 September), nos. 2636–2640, 2646f. (22 September), nos. 2648–2650, 2657, 2660f. (23 September), no. 2665 (24 September): "Die deutsche Presse muss die Ruhe und Sicherheit der Staatsmänner in Godesberg den Panikmachern in Prag gegenüberstellen und den schreienden Gegensatz zwischen dem Verhalten der Prager Regierung und den Bemühungen Chamberlains und des Führers um den Frieden deutlich machen." Also nos. 2663f., 2666f. (24 September). *VB* (B), 23 September, "Heute Fortsetzung der Besprechungen in Godesberg— Rote Militärdiktatur in Prag beginnt mit blutigen Verbrechen" (headline); 24 September, "Abschluß in Godesberg—Tschechische Armee besetzt die Grenzen" (headline).

167. TB, 26 September 1938.

168. Rönnefarth, *Sudetenkrise,* 615; TB, 27 September 1938.

169. TB, 26 September 1938.

170. *VB* (B), 26 September 1938.

171. *Domarus I,* 923ff., quotation 927.

172. TB, 28 September 1938. *PA* 1938, no. 2683f. (26 September) and nos. 2686f. (27 September); *DAZ,* 27 September 1938 (E), Kommentar: "Der Spieler"; *VB* (B), 27 September 1938, "Wir sind entschlossen. Herr Benesch mag jetzt wählen!" (headline); Schwarzenbeck, *Pressepolitik,* 380f.

173. TB, 28 September 1938; Kershaw, *Hitler. 1936–1945,* 174; Rönnefarth, *Sudetenkrise,* 618f.

174. 1780-PS, *IMT* XXVII, 345ff., Jodl, Official Diary, entry for 27 September 1938, 20:30 (p. 388).

175. Andreas-Friedrich, *Schauplatz Berlin,* 5f.; Schmidt, *Statist,* 417; Shirer, *The Journal of a Foreign Correspondent 1934–1941,* 114f.: "It has been the most striking demonstration against war I've ever seen"; on the lack of enthusiasm for war, see also *SOPADE* 1938, 913ff. (September 1938).

176. Below, *Als Hitlers Adjutant,* 127.

177. Hill, *Weizsäcker Papers,* 145, 171.

178. TB, 29 September 1938.

179. Kershaw, *Hitler. 1936–1945,* 175.

180. TB, 29 September: Goebbels, who was in the Reich Chancellery that morning, attributed the initiative for the conference to Hitler. "Then he suddenly thought of the idea of a four-power conference with Mussolini, Chamberlain and Daladier. In Munich. Within the hour Mussolini had agreed to it. On the Munich conference and its immediate background," see Rönnefarth, *Sudetenkrise,* 623ff.; Faber, *Munich,* 391ff.

181. TB, 29 September 1938; *PA* 1938, no. 2704 (28 September): "The huge demonstrations throughout Germany in support of the rights of the Sudeten Germans must be put on the front page with very big headlines and comment." Similarly no. 2706 (28 September). *VB* (B), 28 September, "Massenkundgebung der NSDAP im Lustgarten" (announcement); 29 September 1938, "Millionen-Kundgebungen im ganzen Reich. Die Nation will Freiheit der Sudetendeutschen"; *FZ* (M), 29 September 1938, "Das Treuebekenntnis zum Führer."

182. TB, 1 October 1938.

183. *VB* (B), 1 October 1938, "Berlin empfängt den Führer" (headline). The edition contains an appeal from Goebbels to the population, a further appeal from the deputy Gauleiter, Görlitzer, to companies to give their employees the day off, and an order from City President, Lippert, who not only granted schoolchildren a day off school but ordered that they should be brought by their teachers en bloc to the streets through which Hitler would be passing.

184. TB, 2 October 1938; *VB* (B), 2 October, "Erhebende Kundgebungen grüßten den Führer bei seiner Ankunft in der Reichshauptstadt" (page 1).

185. TB, 3 October 1938; see also 10 October. In fact shortly afterward Hitler signed a fundamental directive to the Wehrmacht in which, among other things, he declared the "elimination" of the "remainder of Czechoslovakia" as a military-political goal for the foreseeable future. *ADAP* D IV, no. 81, Weisung vom 21. October.

18. "MATURITY IS ONLY ACHIEVED THROUGH SUFFERING!"

1. TB, 3 and 4 August 1938; 5 August 1938: "At home Magda and I had an important conversation. It's very important for me. I'm glad that we've reached this stage." 6 August: "Not everything's been sorted out yet, but much is clear. I hope that we'll soon be able to turn over a new leaf. I need to. The last few months have been very wearing for me." 10 August 1938: "We're now seeing eye to eye. Let's hope it's for the long term."

2. Baarová, *Bitterkeit,* 134ff. The weekend referred to was 13 and 14 August (TB, 14 August 1938: "A large group of people arrives for lunch"). According to Baarová's report they viewed her most recent film, *Der Spieler,* which is confirmed by Goebbels's diaries. He had already seen the film twice (TB, 16 and 28 July 1938).

3. TB, 16 August 1938, and 17 August 1938: "Seeing the Führer. I have another long discussion with him. I'm very moved. I can no longer really see my way out of this." Baarová, *Bitterkeit,* 137ff., writes that Goebbels was sending out contradictory messages at this time. To begin with he told her they would have to part, but then later reassured her that he would find a means by which they could continue their relationship.

4. TB, 18 and 20 August 1938. Further conversations with Magda: 21 and 31 August, 2 September 1938.

5. TB, 19 and 20 August 1938.

6. TB, 21 August 1938.

7. TB, 25, 26, and 27 August 1938.

8. TB, 9 October, and 4 October 1938.

9. TB, 10 and 11 October 1938.

10. TB, 13 October, and 12 October 1938.

11. TB, 14 October 1938.

12. TB, 3 (quotation), 4 and 11 February, 14 March, 1 April 1937.

13. TB, 15 October 1938.

14. TB, 18 October 1938.

15. TB, 20 October 1938.

16. TB, 21 October 1938.

17. TB, 22 October 1938.

18. TB, 22 October 1938.

19. See TB, 23 July 1939; Speer, *Erinnerungen,* 161ff.

20. TB, 22 October 1938.

21. TB, 24 October 1938.

22. TB, 24 October 1938.

23. *VB* (B), 25 October 1938, "Adolf Hitler wieder auf dem Obersalzberg. Der Führer bei einem Besuch auf dem Kehlstein am Sonntag, 23. Oktober, mit seinen Gästen, Reichsminister Dr. Goebbels und Frau und ihren Kindern Hega, Hilde und Helmut."

24. Baarová, *Bitterkeit,* 142ff.

25. TB, 25 October 1938; Baarová, *Bitterkeit,* 145: Goebbels rang her from Göring's house.

26. TB, 26 October 1938.

27. TB, 26 October 1938.

28. TB, 27, 29, 30, and 31 October, 4, 5, and 7 November 1938.

29. TB, 29 October 1938.

30. TB, 30 October 1938.

31. TB, 27 and 29 October 1938.

32. On the November 1938 pogrom, see Obst, *"Reichskristallnacht";* Döscher, *"Reichskristallnacht";* for more detail, see Longerich, *Politik der Vernichtung,* 190ff.

33. On the events in Kurhessen, see Obst, *"Reichskristallnacht,"* 67ff.; Kropat, *Kristallnacht in Hessen,* 21ff. On Goebbels's role during the pogrom, see Reuth, *Goebbels,* 394ff.; Thacker, *Goebbels,* 206ff.

34. TB, 9 November 1938.

35. TB, 10 November 1938.

36. *Der Angriff,* 10 November 1938, "Razzia auf Judenwaffen. Aktion der Berliner Polizei."

37. Report of the Party's supreme court: 3063-PS, *IMT 32,* 21ff. Hitler's clear responsibility for launching the pogrom, which is incontrovertibly shown by the diaries, has long been emphasized in the historical literature. Longerich, *Politik der Vernichtung,* 198f.; Kershaw, *Hitler. 1936–1945,* 195f.; Friedländer, *Das Dritte Reich,* vol. 1, 293f.

38. TB, 10 November 1938.

39. 3063-PS, p. 29.

40. On the participation of the SS in the destruction, see Hermann, "Hitler und sein Stoßtrupp in der 'Reichskristallnacht.'"

41. TB, 11 November 1938.

42. *VB* (N), 11 November 1938.

43. *Der Angriff,* 12 November 1938, "Empfang im Führerbau"; TB, 11 November 1938.

44. *Domarus I,* 973ff., 974.

45. TB, 11 November 1938.

46. TB, 12 November 1938.

47. *VB* (N), 12 November 1938, "Der Fall Grünspan."

48. 1816-PS, *IMT 28,* 499ff.

49. Ibid., p. 518.

50. Ibid., p. 508f.; Walk (ed.), *Das Sonderrecht für die Juden im NS-Staat,* Part III 12, directive of 12 November 1938.

51. 1816 PS-PS, 508–11.

52. *VB* (N), 14 November 1938, "Alle jüdischen Geschäfte in kürzester Frist deutsch! Dr. Goebbels über die endgültige Lösung der Judenfrage" (headline); TB, 14 November 1938.

53. *VB* (N), 16 November 1938, "Reinliche Scheidung zwischen Deutschen und

Juden. Unterredung des Reichsministers Dr. Goebbels mit dem Sonderkorrespondenten des Reuterbüros"; TB, 13 and 15 November 1938.

54. TB, 17–25 November 1938. *PA* 1938, no. 3275 (Kommentierung vom 15. November). *VB* (N), 24 November 1938, "Keine Kompromisse in der Judenfrage! Reichsminister Dr. Goebbels über den Abwehrkampf gegen die internationale Judenhetze."

55. TB, 26 November 1938.

56. Details in Longerich, *Davon,* 136ff.; Herbert Obenaus, "The Germans: 'An Antisemitic People.' The Press Campaign after 9 November 1938," in David Bankier (ed.), *Probing the Depths of German Antisemitism,* 147–80. See also *PA* 1938, no. 3287 (17 November).

57. *PA* 1938, no. 3310 (19 November). Goebbels made it clear at the press conference of 22 November that he was by no means "content," the press should kindly put more effort in (*PA* 1938, no. 3336). See also *PA* 1938, no. 3378 (24 November), no. 3418 (28 November), nos. 3334 and 3337 (22 November), no 3388, (25 November), no. 3398 (26 November), nos. 3450 and 3455 (30 November), no. 3483 (2 December), no. 3612 (14 December); *PA* 1939, no. 68 (7 January). Sänger, *Politik der Täuschungen,* 64.

58. Nur für Redner. Sonderlieferung 3/1938 des Aufklärungs- und Redner-Informationsmaterials der Reichspropagandaleitung der NSDAP und des Reichspropagandaamtes der DAF, o.D., quoted in Barth, *Goebbels und die Juden,* 267.

59. Speech of 30 January, published in *Domarus II,* 1047ff., the relevant passage 1055–58; on the propaganda preparations for the speech, see Longerich, *Davon,* 142.

60. TB, 27 October 1938, theater visit; Magda accompanied him at the end of October on a trip to Erfurt, where he spoke to "producers of literature" (30 October 1938); see also 6 November 1938 on their visit to the theater together.

61. TB, 17 November 1938.

62. TB, 13–30 November (numerous entries) as well as 7, 12, and 30 December 1938.

63. TB, 17 January 1939.

64. TB, 6 and 8 February 1939.

65. On the preparation and carrying out of the election campaign, see TB, 6 and 8 October 1938, 5, 9, 12, 19, and 24 November 1938. On the election in detail, see Ralf Gebel, *"Heim ins Reich!"* 136ff.

66. TB, 20 November 1938 and 2 December 1938 on the two previous days.

67. TB, 5 and 6 December 1938.

68. TB, 8 and 9 December 1938.

69. TB, 10 December 1938.

70. TB, 13 and 16 December 1938.

71. TB, 30 December 1938. Between 18 and 29 December 1938 he had to interrupt the entries in his diary, one of the few substantial gaps in his diaries.

72. TB, 1 January 1939.

73. TB, 30 December 1938.

74. TB, 1 January 1939.

75. TB, 3 January 1939.

76. TB, 4 January 1939 and 30 December 1938.

77. TB, 4 January 1939.

78. TB, 8–18 January 1939.

79. TB, 8 January 1939.

80. TB, 15 and 17 January 1939.

81. TB, 17 and 20 January 1939.
82. TB, 18 January 1939.
83. TB, 18 January 1939.
84. TB, 19 and 20 January 1939.
85. The agreement and Hitler's letter have not survived; TB, 20–25 January 1939; Reuth, *Goebbels*, 404.
86. TB, 29 January, 27 February 1939.
87. TB, 17 February 1939: "A long chat with Magda. She tells me about her balls, social events and goodness knows what. But I'm not interested."
88. See p. 358.
89. On the building works, see BAB, R 55/421, and TB, 12 October, 17 and 18 November 1938 as well as 3, 4, and 10 February, 16 March, 25 April, 2 May, 2 June 1939.
90. TB, 12 January, 20 (apartment ready), 22 March, 15, 20, 21, and 28 April 1938 (moved in).
91. BAB, R 55/421, description of the new building, 26 August 1939.
92. R 55/421, Notiz betr. Neubau Dienstwohngebäude für den Reichsminister, 28 February 1939.
93. BAB, R 55/423, Aufstellung der von Herrn Brandl in Paris gekauften und von dem Propagandaministerium übernommenen Gegenstände.
94. R 55/421, Vorlage Ott für Goebbels, 2 March 1939.
95. TB, 29 July, 16–19 August 1939.
96. TB, 10 February 1939.
97. TB, 22, 24, and 29 January 1939; see also Berkholz, *Waldhof,* 28ff.
98. Entries 4, 7 (sanctuary quotation), and 12 February; also 2 and 18 March (quotation), 28 April 1939. On the progress of construction, see TB, 2, 5, and 7 May 1939.
99. BAB, R 55/422, Stellungnahme des Regierungspräsidenten Potsdam, 21 April 1939; Staatssekretär im Reichsforstamt to Staatssekretär Hanke, 31 May 1939.
100. TB, 13 and 26 November 1939.
101. BAB, R 55/422, Kostenaufstellung durch den Architekten Bartels, 1 November 1940. Berkholz, *Waldhof,* 29, 43.
102. BAK, ZSg 158/40, Erich Bandekow, "Über steuerliche Korruptionsfälle von Reichsministern, Reichsleitern usw.," 1948, p. 5.
103. Berkholz, *Waldhof,* 32ff.; TB, 17 January 1940, "Area somewhat reduced in size." LA Berlin A Rep 057, no. 2181, agreement according to which the city of Berlin would transfer to Goebbels for life a plot of 210 hectares on the Bogensee with grounds, a log cabin, a house for guests, 2 garages, a house for a caretaker, a shooting range, and a boathouse with equipment, 1 April 1940.
104. TB, 19 and 20 August, 7 November 1939.
105. BAB, R 55/759, Vermerk Promi, 30 March 1943; TB, 3 and 5 November, 5 December 1940.
106. BAB, R 55/675, Niederschrift über Besprechung vom 17. März 1943 mit Direktor von Manteuffel, Bürgermeister Winkler sowie Vertretern des RFM, des Propagandaministeriums und der Ufa; Berkholz, *Waldhof,* 44ff.
107. BAB, R 55/430, Aktenvermerk über Besprechung mit Leiter H., 1. Juli 1943 betr. den Diener Ludwig.
108. TB, 9, 22, 29, and 30 March 1938. Reif, Schumacher, and Uebel, *Schwanenwerder,* 116ff., 209ff.; Curth, "Insel Schwanenwerder," 420ff.
109. TB, 25 April, 14 and 17 June 1939; on the renting of the second house, see 24 and 30 March 1941; on the official house, see 7 June 1941; F Rep. 270 A, no. 9860, plan

to fix the lines of escape for the island road on Schwanenwerder, 26 June 1937; Reif, Schumacher, and Uebel, *Schwanenwerder,* 209f. In addition there was an official house that the Propaganda Ministry had bought.

110. TB, 26 February, 26 April, 4 May 1939, 19 December 1940.

111. TB, 2, 4, 7, 8, 9, and 17 December 1937. Goebbels also refused the request by the Bavarian comic, Weiss Ferdl, to give him an exemption from "the ban on political jokes" as he made clear in a private conversation: TB, 9 and 11 January 1938; 24 February 1939.

112. He had already issued a warning not to make political jokes in April 1937: TB, 13, 16, and 20 April 1937. Critical comment on the theater also on 10 March 1938.

113. TB, 30 January 1939.

114. *VB* (B), 4 February 1939; 1 and 3 February. Willi Schaeffers, the director of the cabaret, wrote about the conversation, which took place on 2 February in his memoirs. See *Tingel Tangel,* 186f.; Finck, *Alter Narr,* 112ff.

115. *BT,* 25 December 1938. Among other things Finck had used the play on words "whether we also have humor above us."

116. See TB, 5 February 1939.

117. "Kabarett der Komiker," article in Budzinski and Hippen, *Metzler Kabarett Lexikon.*

118. TB, 19 March 1939.

119. TB, 23 January 1939.

120. *VB* (B), 11 February 1939; *PA* 1939, no. 440 (10 February), he allowed the newspapers to reprint the article; also TB, 10 February 1939; on the preparation of the article, see 24 January 1939.

121. *VB* (B), 19 February 1939; once again the press conference was alerted to this article: PA 1939, no. 507 (17 February).

122. TB, 5 February 1939 on the article, which initially remained unpublished for a few days because of a veto by Funk on the grounds of "commercial policy." The article was recommended to the whole press (*PA* 1939, no. 742).

123. Wiechert came to terms with his experience of being under arrest in the text, written in 1939, *Der Totenwald,* quotation 327. TB, 30 August 1938, where, too, the word "vorführen" appears ("bring before me"). See 4 August 1938.

124. TB, 19 November 1939.

125. TB, 20 February 1940.

126. TB, 1 February 1939; on Hitler's intensive engagement on foreign problems, see also 3 February.

127. TB, 26 February 1939; see also 21 and 22 February 1939. The article was recommended to the rest of the press by the Propaganda Ministry (*PA* 1939, no. 597, 24 February).

128. *Das Reich,* 20 September 1942, "Der steile Aufstieg," and 5 September 1943, "Das große Drama."

129. *VB,* 11 March 1939, "Kaffeetanten," and 13 May 1939, "Bajonette als Wegweiser"; *Das Reich,* 12 December 1943, "Seifenblase."

130. TB, 10 March 1939. The gap in the diary went from 7 to 9 March.

131. TB, 10 March 1939.

132. Kershaw, *Hitler. 1936–1945,* 230ff.; Hoensch, Die Slowakei und Hitlers Ostpolitik, 210ff.

133. TB, 11 March 1939.

134. The press was instructed on 10 March to report on the conflict: *PA* 1939, no. 737 and 757 (10 March). On the 11th the press was instructed openly to support the Tiso government: *PA* 1939, no. 762 (11 March).

135. TB, 11 March 1939.

136. TB, 12 and 13 March 1939.

137. *PA* 1939, no. 770 (12 March), no. 772, special press conference and no. 776 (13 March.): "The front page must be entirely devoted to the Czech issue." Also no. 787 and no. 788 (14 March).

138. TB, 14 March 1939.

139. TB, 14 March 1939.

140. *ADAP* D IV, no. 202, Aufzeichnung Hewel über Gespräch Hitler-Tiso, 13. März 1939; no. 209, draft of a telegram from Tiso to Hitler, in which he requests aid from the Germans, n.d. See also Hoensch, *Slowakei,* 290ff.

141. TB, 15 March 1939.

142. TB, 17 March 1939; *ADAP* D VI, no. 40.

143. TB, 16 March 1939; *ADAP* D IV, no. 228, Besprechung zwischen Hitler und Ribbentrop sowie Hacha und Chvalkovsky am 15. März 1939. Protokoll Hewel 15. März 1939; no. 229, Erklärung der Deutschen und der Tschechoslowakischen Regierung, 15. März 1939.

144. TB, 15 March 1939.

145. *RGBl.* 1939 I, 485ff., Erlaß des Führers und Reichskanzlers über das Protektorat Böhmen und Mähren vom 16. März 1939.

146. *PA* 1939, no. 856 (18 March): "Im ganzen Reich wird es morgen spontane Kundgebungen geben. Keine Vorankündigungen, wohl aber gute Berichte über die Kundgebungen selbst."

147. TB, 20 March 1939; *VB* (B), 20 March 1939, "Der triumphale Empfang Adolf Hitlers in Berlin—eine stolze Dankes-Kundgebung des ganzen deutschen Volkes."

148. TB, 20 March 1939.

149. TB, 19 March 1939.

150. Kershaw, *Hitler. 1936–1945,* 238ff.; directive of 21 October 1938: *ADAP* D IV, no. 81.

151. TB, 21 and 23 March 1939. *ADAP* D V, no. 399, Aufzeichnung über die Unterredung zwischen dem Reichsminister des Auswärtigen und dem litauischen Außenminister Urbsys am 20. März 1939.

152. TB, 23 March 1939.

153. *ADAP* D VI, no. 61, Aufzeichnung Ribbentrop, 21 March 1939; no. 101, Gespräch zwischen Lipski und Ribbentrop, 26 March; no. 101, Aufzeichnung Ribbentrop, 26 March 1939; Anlage: Note der polnischen Regierung; no. 118, Bericht Botschafter Warschau, 29 March 1939 über das Gespräch Becks mit dem Botschafter vom Vortag; Kershaw, *Hitler. 1936–1945,* 240ff.

154. TB, 20 and 23 March 1939. Advance announceent in *PA* 1939, no. 870 (20 March). On the anti-British *VB* articles, see Michels, *Ideologie,* 395ff.

155. *PA* 1939, no. 885 (21 March). On the articles by Fritzsche covering this prescribed topic, see among others *FZ,* 22 March 1939, "Englands Hand in Indien," and *Der Angriff,* which began the series "Todeskampf der Buren" on 23 March.

156. *VB* (B), 25 March 1939, "Moral der Reichen"; see also *PA* 1939, no. 924 (24 March): Reference to the article for the whole of the press. TB, 24 March 1939.

157. TB, 26 March 1939; corresponding directive in *PA* 1939, no. 967 (29 March).

158. Details in Longerich, *Propagandisten,* 128ff.

159. TB, 24 February, 1 and 2 March 1939.

160. TB, 16 June 1939.

161. TB, 16 and 18 May, and 1 May, 12 June, 20 and 21 June 1939.

162. Uziel, *Propaganda Warriors,* 69ff.

163. TB, 10 January, 2, 8 March, 31 May, 27 September, 3 and 17 October 1935; on the drafting of the mobilization plan, see in particular 12 June 1936; on the preparations for war, see 15 April, 28 May, 6 October, 25 November 1936.

164. Buchbender, *Das tönende Erz*, 16; Uziel, *Propaganda Warriors*, 73ff.; Wedel, *Die Propagandatruppen*, 18f.

165. TB, 16 Sepember 1937; Uziel, *Propaganda Warriors*, 79ff.; see also Buchbender, *Erz*, 16, which refers to initial differences of opinion about the command structure; Wedel, *Propagandatruppen*, 19f.; TB, 1 September 1937.

166. TB, 22 September 1937, and 23, 24 September 1937.

167. TB, 3 November 1937; see also 7 October, 6 November 1937.

168. TB, 4 December 1937.

169. An agreement had already been reached in July: TB, 30 July 1938, entry concerning the conversation with Wentscher, the new head of the Reich defense desk in the Propaganda Ministry; Uziel, *Propaganda Warriors*, 84ff.; Buchbender, *Erz*, 17f.; Wedel, *Propagandatruppen*, 28ff.; Moll, "Die Abteilung Wehrmachtspropaganda im Oberkommando der Wehrmacht," 115f.

170. TB, 13 and 21 August 1939. Buchbender, *Erz*, 19; Uziel, *Propaganda Warriors*, 92ff.; Wedel, *Propagandatruppen*, 20ff. Five propaganda companies were already deployed during the occupation of the Sudetenland.

171. Buchbender, *Erz*, 22; Uziel, *Propaganda Warriors*, 97ff.

172. TB, 21 June 1939, also 21 February 1939.

173. He had already been planning an Egypt trip at the end of 1937 (26 November, 2, 16, 21, 22, 23, 24, 27, 28, and 29 December 1938), but had then given up the idea mainly because of concerns about his personal security.

174. TB, 26–28 March 1939. He had had the trip approved by Hitler in principle; 23 March 1939.

175. TB, 28 March 1939. On the preparations for the trip, see correspondence in PAA, Ref. Partei 44/2, R 99006.

176. TB, 29 and 30 March 1939.

177. TB, 1 April 1939.

178. TB, 31 March, 1 April 1939.

179. TB, 2 April 1939. On the stay in Rhodes, see 3–7, 9–12 April 1939.

180. TB, 3 April 1939.

181. Hubatsch (ed.), *Hitlers Weisungen für die Kriegsführung 1939–1945*, 19ff.

182. TB, 7 April 1939.

183. TB, 7 April 1939.

184. TB, 10 April 1939.

185. TB, 15 and 19 April 1939.

186. TB, 20 April 1939.

187. On the festivities, see TB, 20 and 21 April 1939; Bucher, "Hitlers 50. Geburtstag"; Pätzold, "Hitlers fünfzigster Geburtstag am 20. April 1939"; Kershaw, *Hitler. 1936–1945*, 247ff.; BAB, NS 10/127; Arbeitsplan zur Durchführung der Veranstaltung zum 50. Geburtstag des Führers, 12 April 1939, and detailed program for the event, 16 April 1939; *VB* (B), special edition for 20 April (with a contribution from Goebbels: "Die neue Zeit") and edition of 21 April 1939.

188. *VB* (B), 19 April 1939.

189. Gesetz über einmalige Sonderfeiertage vom 17. April 1939, *RGBl.* 1939 I, 763; Verordnung zum Gesetz über einmalige Sonderfeiertage (ibid., p. 764).

190. TB, 24 April 1939.

191. *VB* (B), 22 April 1939, "Lord Halifax macht Witze" (editorial), and 27 April, "Ein paar Worte über politischen Takt (editorial); see also instruction for the press in

PA 1939, no. 1234 (26 April). The article is a reply to the attacks of the British press on Ribbentrop's failure to receive the British ambassador. See also Henderson, *Fehlschlag einer Mission,* 255.

192. TB, 29 April 1939; *Domarus,* 1148ff. On the speech, see also Kershaw, *Hitler. 1936–1945,* 254f. On the abrogation of the pacts with Poland and Britain, see *ADAP* D VI, no. 276 and 277, Noten der Deutschen Regierung vom 27. April 1939. Goebbels had ensured that the *12 Uhr Blatt* published a "tough article against Roosevelt": TB, 18 April 1939; *12 Uhr Blatt,* 17 April 1939, "Was sagen Sie nun, Herr Roosevelt?"

193. *PA* 1939, no. 1338, (5 May), Sonderpressekonferenz, no. 1343 (6 May); TB, 7 May 1939: "The German press is taking the lead. A bit too much for my feeling. I tell them to put the brakes on a bit for the time being." No. 1363 (8 May 1939): "For tactical reasons the German press is to exercise some restraint with regard to the many news items from Poland, as the big Polish campaign has not been given the go-ahead yet."

194. *ADAP* D V, no. 334, note of 5 May 1939; see also TB, 6 May 1939.

195. *VB* (B), 5 May 1939, "Quo Vadis, Polonia?" and 13 May 1939, "Bajonette als Wegweiser"; TB, 5, 6, 11, and 12 May 1939; *PA* 1939, no. 1458 (12 May).

196. PA 1939, no. 1343 (6 May), no. 1363 (8 May), no. 1819 (13 June), no. 1951 (21 June), no. 1960 (21 June), no. 1993 (23 June), and no. 2015 (24 June).

197. *VB* (B), "Militärbündnis Deutschland-Italien" (headline); TB, 9 May 1939, and 10 May 1939. *ADAP* D V, no. 426 (22 May 1939): Freundschafts- und Bündnispakt zwischen Deuschland und Italien.

198. *VB* (B), 22 May 1939, "Berlin begrüßt Graf Ciano mit stürmischem Beifall" (headline); *VB* (B), 23 May 1939, "Bund Berlin-Rom besiegelt" (headline); TB, 22, 23, 24 May 1939.

199. TB, 24 April 1939.

200. *ADAP* D VI, report of the ambassador in Rome to AA, 13 May 1939, with the text of an intercepted instruction from the British Foreign Office to the embassy in Rome, 11 May 1939; no. 377 Aufzeichnung Staatssekretär über Gespräch mit britischem Botschafter, no. 385, 15 May 1939.

201. TB, 5 July 1939.

202. *VB* (B), 20 May 1939, "Die Einkreiser"; TB, 18 May 1939.

203. *VB* (B), 27 May 1939, "Nochmals: Die Einkreiser"; *VB* (B), 3 June 1939, "Klassenkampf der Völker?" and *VB* (B), 30 June 1939, "Das schreckliche Wort von der Einkreisung."

204. *VB* (B), 19 June 1939, "Erkläre mir, Graf Oerindur . . ."

205. Speech at the Essen Gau Day on 25 June 1939; see the report in *Der Angriff* of 26 June 1939.

206. *PA* 1939, no. 1890 (16 June); *VB* (B), 19 June 1939, "Danzig—Pflegestätte unserer Kultur. Große Kundgebung mit Reichsminister Dr. Goebbels im Danziger Staatstheater." See also TB, 19 June 1939.

207. TB, 21 June 1939. And even if it came to war, Hitler believed that within a fortnight it would be over.

208. *VB* (B), 22 June 1939, "Die Sonnwendfeier des Gaues Berlin" (SZ); TB, 23 June 1939 on the propaganda treatment. On the following day he took the same line in a speech to fifteen thousand Berlin streetcar workers; *VB* (B), 24 June 1939, "Dr. Goebbels sprach vor Berliner Arbeitern"; TB, 24 June 1939.

209. *VB* (B), 24 June 1939, "Die abgehackten Kinderhände." In his article Goebbels compared the British propaganda in the First World War with the current "swin-

dle of the British propaganda campaign against Germany"; see also TB, 22 June 1939.

210. *VB* (B), 14 July 1939, "So sieht Englands Propaganda aus"; TB, 5, 8, 9, and 12 July; *PA* 1939, no. 2237 (8 July 1939), no. 2296 (13 July 1939), no. 2310 (14 July 1939). See. *VB* (B), 19 July 1939, "Neue Enthüllungen über King-Hall. Schon 1938 forderte er ein Kriegskabinett mit Churchill und Eden" (headline).

211. TB, 24 July 1938.

212. TB, 29 June 1939, on Magda's departure.

213. TB, 23 July 1939. This was not the only meeting during her spa stay. He had already visited the family there in the middle of July, from 9 to 12 July 1939. On 17 July he met Magda in Munich; see 18 July 1939. Speer wrote in his memoirs that Magda told him that Goebbels had turned up unexpectedly in Gastein and put her under pressure because of her affair with Hanke. Speer, *Erinnerungen,* 165.

214. TB, 26 and 27 July 1939.

215. TB, 27 July 1939.

216. TB, 28 July 1939. According to Speer, Hitler had sent the Goebbelses back to Berlin. Speer, *Erinnerungen,* 165.

217. TB, 1 August 1939.

218. TB, 4 August 1939.

219. TB, 2–8 August 1939.

220. TB, 9–14 August 1939. The press carried daily reports of the visit. See, for example, the *VB* during these days.

221. TB, 16 August 1939, also 12 August 1939.

222. *PA* 1939, no. 2836 (special press conference, 20 August): "The newspapers must continue to focus on Poland; no. 2843, (21 August), "The press must go on focusing on Polish terror." See, for example, the reporting of the *VB* and the *DAZ* during these days, which from 16 August onward was dominated by anti-Polish propaganda.

223. TB, 20 August 1939. On the propaganda campaign, see also 22 August 1939.

224. TB, 17 August 1939.

225. TB, 22 August 1939. The only reference to a possible rapprochement with Moscow is in the TB for 9 July. During a visit to Obersalzberg Hitler had informed him that he "no longer [believed] that London and Moscow will come to an agreement. Then the way will be clear for us." Now, after the conclusion of the negotiations he judged that the agreement "had taken long enough to sort out." The fact that he was not actually informed about the negotiations is clear not only from the complete lack of references to them in the diaries but also from his total surprise at the diplomatic coup which Hitler was to tell him about on 23 August (TB, 24 August 1939).

226. TB, 23 August 1939.

227. TB, 24 August 1939, *ADAP* D VII, no. 200, note of 24 August 1939 concerning the conversation between Hitler and Henderson; *ADAP* D VII, no. 201, Hitler's reply, 23 August 1939.

228. TB, 24 August 1939.

229. *ADAP* D VII, no. 228, non-aggression pact 23 August 1939; no. 229 Secret Supplementary Protocol from the same day.

230. TB, 25 August 1939.

231. TB, 26 August 1939.

232. *ADAP* D VII, no. 265, Erklärung Hitler an Henderson, 25 August 1939 (quotation); Henderson, *Fehlschlag,* 298ff.

233. *ADAP* D VII, p. 237, editors' note about the conversation of 25 August, of which there is no German record. But see Robert Coulondre, *Von Moskau nach Berlin,* 422f.

234. *ADAP* D VII, no. 271, 25 August 1939, Mussolini to Hitler; Schmidt, *Statist,* 461f.; Halder, *Kriegstagebuch,* 25 August 1939; Hofer, *Die Entfesselung des Zweiten Weltkrieges.*

235. TB, 26 August 1939.

236. *ADAP* D VII, no. 324, 26 August 1939.

237. TB, 27 August 1939, also 28 August 1939 concerning the letter.

238. TB, 29 August 1939; *ADAP* D VII, no. 324, 26 August 1939, on this note p. 277 concerning confidentiality; no. 354, Hitler's reply, 27 August 1939.

239. British reply of 28 August, *ADAP* D VII, no. 384, Schmidt note of 29 August concerning the conversation between Hitler and Henderson at 22:30; the note is in the appendix; Henderson, *Fehlschlag,* 302f.

240. TB, 29 August 1939; on Dahlerus's attempt to mediate, see Kershaw, *Hitler. 1936–1945,* 304f.; Dahlerus, *Der letzte Versuch,* 75ff.

241. *ADAP* D VII, no. 421, note of 29 August 1939. TB, 29 August 1939.

242. TB, 30 August 1939.

243. *PA* 1939, no. 2986 (28 August), no. 3006 (29 August), no. 3019 (29 August), no. 3047 (30 August).

244. *ADAP* D VII, no. 461, Schmidt note of 31 August about the conversation between Ribbentrop and Henderson on 30 August at midnight.

245. *ADAP* D VII, no. 476, note of 1 September 1939 concerning the conversation between Lipski and Ribbentrop on 31 August 1939; ibid., no. 482, 31 August 1939, Weizsäcker note with appendix; TB, 1 September 1939.

246. TB, 1 September 1939; *ADAP* D VII, p. 390 (note on the radio).

247. *ADAP* D VII, no. 493, 31 August, Hitler's war directive, start of the offensive 1 September, 4:45.

19. "WAR IS THE FATHER OF ALL THINGS"

1. TB, 1 September 1939.

2. *Domarus II,* 1312ff., 1315.

3. TB, 2 September 1939.

4. *ADAP* D VII, no. 513, Schmidt note about the conversation between Henderson and Ribbentrop on 1 and 2 September 1939, no. 515, Schmidt note of 2 September about the conversation between Ribbentrop and Coulondre of 1 September 1939; on these conversations, see TB, 2 September 1939.

5. *ADAP,* D VII, no. 560, British ultimatum of 3 September 1939, no. 561. German reply from the same day, *ADAP* D VII, no. 563, note about the conversation between Ribbentrop and Coulondre of 3 September; TB, 4 September 1939.

6. TB, 4 September 1939; these appeals were published in *VB* (B) of 4 September.

7. BAK, ZSg 109/3, V. I., in particular 6 September, no. 3, 7 September, no. 4, 8 September, 2. E., no. 2, 9 September, no. 4, 10 September, no. 3, 11 September, no. 1, 12 September, no. 3, and 14 September 1939, no. 1; *VB* (B), 8 September 1939, "Grauenhafte polnische Verbrechen an Volksdeutschen" (headline), 9 September, 1939, "Das Blut der Gemordeten in Bromberg fordert London vor das Weltgericht" (headline), and a page of photos, 10 September 1939, "Ganz Wirsitz sollte in die Luft gesprengt werden!" (headline), 13 September 1939, "Polens

schmutzige Waffen: Heckenschützenkrieg und Greuelpropaganda," 14 September 1939, "Schärfste Maßnahmen gegen das polnische Heckenschützentum—Von jetzt ab mit allen Mitteln!" (headline), 15 September 1939, "Posen ein zweites Bromberg" (headline).

8. Jansen and Weckbecker, Der "Volksdeutsche Selbstschutz" in Polen 1939/40, 27ff.; Jastrzebski, Der Bromberger Blutsonntag; Böhler, Der Überfall, 112ff.

9. Broszat, Nationalsozialistische Polenpolitik 1939–1945, 48; Böhler, Überfall, 116.

10. Jansen and Weckbecker, Der "Volksdeutsche Selbstschutz," 111ff.; Böhler, Auftakt zum Vernichtungskrieg. On the Einsatzgruppen, see Rossino, Hitler Strikes Poland, 88ff.; Rossino, "Nazi Anti-Jewish Policy During the Polish Campaign"; Krausnick, "Die Einsatzgruppen vom Anschluß Österreichs bis zum Feldzug gegen die Sowjetunion. Entwicklung und Verhältnis zur Wehrmacht," 33ff.; Klaus-Michael Mallmann and Martin Cüppers investigate the role of the order police and the Waffen SS in an edited volume, Genesis des Genozids.

11. BAB, R 58/825, 8 September 1939.

12. TB, 4 September 1939. TB, 5 September 1939: "Vigorously attack England's government but leave the people alone. Don't touch France." A similar line appears in TB, 6, 7, 10, 13, and 15 September 1939; BAK, ZSg 109/4, 4 September, no. 1, 5 September, no. 7, and 15 September 1939, no. 2.

13. Longerich, Propagandisten, 134ff.; TB, 18 August 1939.

14. ADAP D VII, no. 574.

15. ADAP D VIII, no. 31, Führerbefehl vom 8 September 1939; Otto Dietrich, 12 Jahre, 129f.; TB, 7 and 9 September 1939.

16. TB, 9 September 1939, and 14 September 1939.

17. TB, 5 November 1939. Negative about Dietrich also in 13 January, 16 March, 18 April 1940. Some of the minutes of the ministerial briefings are edited in BK and in Boelcke (ed.), Wollt Ihr den totalen Krieg? (henceforth BW); a complete series for the years 1939–43 is in the Special archive in Moscow, Bestand 1363-3 (henceforth MK).

18. Longerich, Propagandisten, 137.

19. BK, 140ff.; on his further disputes with the AA, see also TB, 28 October, 18, 19, 21, 23, and 24 November, 21 December 1939.

20. TB, 6 October 1939.

21. TB, 12 and 13 December 1939.

22. Criticism also in TB, 16 September, and 5, 6 (quotation), 15 and 27 October, 17 and 26 November, 13, 15, and 22 December 1939 and 9–11 January 1940.

23. TB, 29 and 30 December 1939; Uziel, Propaganda Warriors, 184ff.

24. Uziel, Propaganda Warriors, 188.

25. TB, 6, 12, and 18 September 1939.

26. TB, 6 October 1939.

27. TB, 9 and 15 September 1939.

28. TB, 10, 11, and 13, also 3 September 1939; on the Italian initiative, see Thielenhaus, Zwischen Anpassung und Widerstand, 196ff.; and Knox, Mussolini Unleashed, 1939–1941, 49ff.

29. TB, 3 and 4 October 1939.

30. ADAP D VIII, no. 176, Schmidt note concerning the conversation between Hitler and Ciano on 2 October 1939; no. 222, Weizsäcker note, 9 October 1939.

31. TB, 4 and 22 September 1939; also 21, 24, 25, and 26 September.

32. Domarus II, p. 1317.

33. RGBl. 1939 II, 1683.

34. Various documents in BAB, R 43 II/669, to some extent published and discussed

in detail in Latour, "Goebbels' 'Außerordentliche Rundfunkmaßnahmen' 1939–1942"; here also the letter from Hess of 3 September (p. 420f.); *VB* (B), 2 September 1939, "Das Abhören ausländischer Sender ist verboten!"; TB, 2, 3, and 5 September 1939. On the origins of the decree, see most recently Hensle, *Rundfunkverbrechen,* 26ff., which emphasizes above all the role of Hess.

35. On the legal proceedings, see Gruchmann, *Justiz im Dritten Reich,* 905. Only a few death sentences were actually carried out. TB, 14 December 1939: "A lot of people are listening to foreign broadcasts. I get a few draconian sentences passed and published. Maybe that will help."

36. Gruchmann, *Justiz,* 901ff.; on the Gestapo executions, see Broszat, "Zur Perversion der Strafjustiz im Dritten Reich." On the publication of the sentences, see BAK, ZSg 109/4, VI, 4 October 1939, 8. This shows that the Reich propaganda offices decided which cases should be given publicity.

37. Minutes in 2852-PS, *IMT* 31, 224ff.

38. TB, 13, 19, 20, 21, and 23 September, 8 and 10 October 1939. On the population's concern, see the clear evidence in *Meldungen aus dem Reich 1938–1945,* Bericht zur innenpolitischen Lage, 11 October 1939, 339ff., esp. 345f.; 13 October 1939, 347ff., esp. 355f., 20 October 1939, 372ff., esp. 377.

39. TB, 16 November 1939; Session of 15 November, *IMT* 31, 236ff.; Müller, *Organisation und Mobilisierung,* 364ff.

40. TB, 8 November 1939; *BK,* 20 November 1939, 3.

41. *Domarus II,* 1354ff. TB, 20 September 1939: "A terrific speech." Also 21 September 1939 on the speech's impact. Because of this speech Goebbels had to cancel a planned broadcast speech (18 September 1939).

42. TB, 28 September 1939.

43. TB, 28 and 30 September 1939.

44. TB, 30 September 1939. The notes made on the same day by Rosenberg about Hitler's plans for Poland are very similar. Rosenberg, *Tagebuch,* 81. When Goebbels writes in his diary "The Führer explains the situation to me," he appears to be somewhat exaggerating the intimacy of this meeting.

45. Details in Longerich, *Politik der Vernichtung,* 251ff.

46. TB, 1 October 1939.

47. *ADAP* D VIII, no. 157.

48. TB, 1 October 1939.

49. TB, 4 October 1939.

50. *Domarus II,* 1377ff., quotation 1390; Kershaw, *Hitler. 1936–1945,* 364f.

51. TB, 6 October 1939, and 7 October.

52. TB, 12 October 1939.

53. TB, 14 Otober 1939.

54. Kershaw, *Hitler. 1936–1945,* 365.

55. TB, 13 October 1939 (see also 14 and 18 October on his agreement with Hitler's anti-British attitude).

56. TB, 11 October 1939; see also the corresponding press directives: BAK, ZSg 102/19, 24 October 1939; BAK, ZSg 109/4 VI of 24 October 1939, and 25 October 1939.

57. TB, 8 November 1939.

58. TB, 5 and 7 September 1939; BAK, ZSg 102/19, 4–7 September 1939; Reuth, *Goebbels,* 431f.

59. TB, 14, 15, and 19 October 1939; BAK, ZSg 102/19, 14 October 1939.

60. *VB* (B), 21 October 1939, "Churchill am Pranger"; 23 October 1939, "Schneidende Abrechnung mit einem Erzlügner. 'Jetzt hat der Angeklagte Winston

Churchill das Wort'"; 24 October 1939, "Wann antwortet Winston Churchill? Erste faule Ausflüchte des Angeklagten nach der Rundfunkrede von Dr. Goebbels" (headline); TB, 20 October, 23 October, 24, 25, 26, 27 October; BAK, ZSg 102/109, 22 October 1939 (broadcast speech recommended to the press). On the *Athenia* incident, see ibid., VI, 19 October 1939, 1. E., no. 1, 20 October 1939, no. 6; 23 October 1939, no. 3. 912-D, published in *IMT* 36, 3ff. (British minute of the broadcast speech). The *Athenia* incident continued to be used by German propaganda into the following year.

61. TB, 10 October 1939.

62. BAK, ZSg 102/19, 20 October 1939; see also 24 October: "Eine Berichterstattung in Polen ist im allgemeinen unerwünscht."

63. Dobroszycki, *Die legale polnische Presse im Generalgouvernement 1939–1945*, 66ff.; Frank, *Das Diensttagebuch des deutschen Generalgouverneurs in Polen*, 52.

64. TB, 2 November 1939; see also Reuth, *Goebbels*, 434f.

65. TB, 3 November 1939.

66. TB, 9 November 1939.

67. TB, 10–15 November 1939.

68. TB, 13 and 14 November 1939; *BK*, 11 November, 1; 13 November, 1, emphasizes England's responsibility; *DAZ*, 10 November 1939 (E), "Hintergründe und Vorbereitungen"; *Der Angriff*, 11 November 1939, "Mit Pfund und Höllenmaschine."

69. TB, 16 and 17 November 1939.

70. *VB* (B), 22 November 1939, "Der Attentäter gefaßt" (headline); 23 November 1939, "Otto Straßer das Werkzeug des englischen Geheimdienstes: Wiederholte Anschläge auf den Führer" (headline); 24 November 1939, "Captain Stevens sagt aus: Intelligence Service organisierte 1937–1938 Schiffs-Sabotageakte" (headline); 25 November 1939, "So wurde Straßers Werkzeug Elser zur Strecke gebracht." Similar line in the *DAZ* from 22 November and in *Der Angriff* on 22 November 1939.

20. "THERE IS ONLY ONE SIN: COWARDICE!"

1. TB, 22 January 1940.

2. TB, 6 February 1940.

3. TB, 28 January 1940. See also 4, 5, 7, and 8 March 1940.

4. TB, 20 March 1940. *ADAP* D IX, no. 1, Aufzeichnung des Gesandten Schmidt über die Unterredung; Kershaw, *Hitler. 1936–1945*, 396ff.

5. TB, 19/20 March 1940; *BK*, 18 March 1940, 1: They were not going to respond to rumors about the meeting; also 19 March 1940, 2.

6. TB, 29 December 1939; *BK*, 28 December 1939, 3.

7. TB, 13 January 1940.

8. TB, 25 January 1940.

9. TB, 15 March 1940. At the end of December Hitler had already referred to the removal of a class of "west European" leaders by the Bolsheviks (TB, 29 December 1939).

10. TB, 16 March 1940.

11. TB, 21 March 1940. See also *BK*, 9 January 1940 as well as 5 and 16 January 1940, according to which Goebbels had adopted a more benign attitude toward the anticommunist literature. However, see BAK, ZSg 101/15, 1 February 1940, Anweisung no. 224: "Representations of Russian life must not be allowed to create

the impression among the German public that we want a kind of ideological amalgamation and that it is as if we were simply adopting and imitating Bolshevist ideology."

12. TB, 12 April 1940.

13. Longerich, *Propagandisten,* 139. During this period there are repeated complaints in the diaries about the relationship with the Foreign Ministry: 23 January 1940: The AA was trying to "lure [editors] away" by offering higher salaries; see also 1 February 1940; 12 March 1940: The AA was wanting to "tempt [his able officials] away" also: 12, 16, and 19 January, 6, 7, 8, 13, 16, and 17 February, 3, 22, and 30 March, also 3, 5, and 6 April 1940.

14. TB, 9 January 1940; and 5, 12, 23, 25, and 28 January 1940.

15. *BK,* 18 March 1940, 10: "Der Minister betont nochmals, daß über deutsche Kriegsziele in der deutschen Presse überhaupt nichts erscheinen darf." Ibid. 6 May, 1 and 10 June 1940, 6; BAK, ZSg 102/29, TB of 5 November 1940: Reflections on the "future organization of Europe and the world" were "inappropriate"; see also Longerich, *Propagandisten,* 69ff.

16. TB, 14, 15, and 18 November 1939.

17. TB, 17 November, 12 December 1939; see also 7 November 1939.

18. TB, 13 December 1939; *BK,* 12 December 1939, 1, corresponding instruction to Fritzsche; see also TB, 21 and 24 December 1939.

19. TB, 21 and 22 December 1939; BAK, ZSg 102/19, 20 December 1939, Verstärkung der Plutokratiepropaganda; ibid.: BAK, ZSg 109/6, VI 5 December 1939, 2. E, no. 1, 7 December 1939, 1. E, no. 2, 20 December 1939, no. 1; *BK,* 23 December 1939, 3.

20. TB, 21 and 23 December 1939; *BK,* 2 February 1940, 3; BAK, ZSg 109/8,VI, 2 February 1940, no. 6: "Alle kommentarfähigen Zeitungen haben bis spätestens Dienstag einen Aufklärungsartikel über den Begriff 'Plutokratie' zu bringen." Also BAK, ZSg 109/9VI, 27 March 1940, no. 2.; *VB* (B), 3 February 1940: "Was ist Plutokratie? Eine deutliche Antwort geschichtlicher Tatsachen."

21. BAK, ZSg 109/7, VI, 13 January 1940; Longerich, *Davon,* 154.

22. TB, 26 January 1940; Umbreit, "Der Kampf um die Vormachtstellung in Westeuropa," 251. The incident had occurred on 10 January. When, as a result, the Belgian and Dutch armed forces were placed on alert Hitler did not consider it necessary to inform Goebbels of the reasons for the postponement (TB, 16 January 1940). Apart from the intelligence leak, weather conditions also played a part in the decision to postpone the offensive. See also Reuth, *Goebbels,* 439f.

23. OKH had worked out the final plan for "Sickle Cut" by 24 February; Umbreit, "Kampf," 254ff. Originally the attack was planned for mid-April (ibid., 283).

24. Maier and Stegemann, "Die Sicherung der europäischen Nordflanke," 203ff.

25. TB, 7, also 8 and 9 May 1940 (quotation).

26. Maier and Stegemann, "Die Sicherung," 197. In December 1939 Hitler agreed to an investigation by OKW of the possibility of an invasion of Norway in December 1939, in February 1940 appointed General Falkenhorst to head a special staff that had been formed in the meantime and on 1 March 1940 signed the directive "Weserübung" (Weser Excercise). On the background, see Bohn, *Reichskommissariat Norwegen,* 15ff.; Gemzell, *Raeder, Hitler und Skandinavien;* Loock, *Quisling, Rosenberg und Terboven,* 518ff.

27. TB, 9 and 10 April 1940.

28. On the military details of the operation, see Hubatsch, *"Weserübung";* Ottmer, *"Weserübung."*

29. TB, 10 April 1940; *VB* (B), 10 April 1940, "Memorandum der Reichsregierung."
30. *BK,* 10 April 1940, 1; TB, 10 April 1940.
31. TB, 11 April 1940.
32. TB, 12 and 13 April 1940; *BK,* 11 April 1940, 1.
33. TB, 14 April 1940; *BK,* 13 April 1940, 2 and 3.
34. On the first problems, see TB, 11 and 12 April 1940, but optimistic on 13 and 14 April 1940.
35. TB, 14 and 15 April 1940; Hubatsch, *"Weserübung,"* 110ff.
36. *BK,* 16 April 1940, 1, 17 April 1940, 19 April 1940, 1; TB, 16 and 17 April 1940.
37. TB, 17 April 1940.
38. TB, 19 April 1940. *VB* (B), 15 April 1940, reports on the battle near Narvik, but does not mention the German casualties; *VB* (B), 19 April, "Heldenhafter Kampf vor Narvik" (headline).
39. TB, 21 April 1940.
40. Loock, *Quisling,* 366ff.
41. TB, 26 April 1940. See also 25 April 1940: "In the ministerial briefing I speak up again for Quisling. We mustn't oppose him so long as the Führer supports him. I don't want any member of the Ministry to do that." *BK,* 26 April 1940, 1: "The Quisling issue has to be put on the back burner for the time being [. . .]."
42. TB, 28 April 1940.
43. "But we want to give him another chance" (TB, 9 May 1940); "he should be dropped" (25 May 1940). Goebbels received Quisling at the beginning of July: "A *völkisch*-Germanic dreamer, more of a professor than a political fighter. I don't really believe he can lead a country. But his heart's in the right place and ideologically he's OK" (6 July 1940). "He should remain in Norway and lead the party. That's OK. If he can get his way then fine, if he can't then it's his own fault" (22 July 1940). "Quisling will now secure the influence he deserves after all." (24 September 1940).
44. Maier and Stegemann, "Die Sicherung," 219. TB, 26, 27, 28, and 30 April, 1 and 5 May; *BK,* 29 April 1940, 1, Propaganda should emphasize the "hardships and difficulties" of the German troops, similarly 30 April 1940, 2, and 30 May 1940, 1.
45. Maier and Stegemann, "Die Sicherung," 219.
46. TB, 5 May 1940: "That really annoys the Führer."
47. *BK,* 7 May 1940, 1.
48. TB, 7 May 1940.
49. TB, 10 May 1940.
50. TB, 11 May 1940.
51. *ADAP* D IX, no. 214 (Belgium and the Netherlands) and no. 215 (Luxemburg). On Goebbels's role in the war in the West, see Reuth, *Goebbels,* 445ff.
52. TB, 11 May 1940; Umbreit, "Kampf," 285.
53. TB, 11, 12, and 13 May 1940; Ueberschär, *Freiburg im Luftkrieg, 1939–1945,* 88ff.
54. *BK,* 10 May 1940, 2.
55. *BK,* 11 May 1940, 3.
56. TB, 11 May 1940.
57. TB, 3 May, very similar on 18 June 1940.
58. See, for example, TB, 15 September 1940 and 19 November 1941.
59. On the military course of the war in the West, see Umbreit, "Kampf," 284ff.
60. TB, 22 May 1940.
61. TB, 14, 15 May 1940; *BK,* 12 May 1940, 3.
62. TB, from 18 May onward almost daily entries on the work of the radio stations.

From 17 May onward every day the minutes of the ministerial briefings contain detailed instructions for the work of the secret radio stations. On the secret radio stations, see Boelcke, *Die Macht des Radios*, 171ff.

63. TB, 21 and 22 May 1940.

64. TB, 30 May 1940 as well as 1 and 2 June 1940; *BK*, 30 May 1940, 1, and 7; BAK, ZSg 109/11, VI of 29 May 1940, 8, as well as 30 May 1940, 1, and 31 May 1940, 6. On the implementation, see *VB* (N), 29 May 1940, "Feige Mörder als 'Ankläger' "; 30 May 1940, "Deutscher Fliegeroberst schändlich von Franzosen mißhandelt"; 31 May 1940, "Gefangene grausam gequält und ermordet"; 1 June 1940, "Französische Tobsucht"; 2 June 1940, "Der Zusammenbruch des französischen Nationalismus."

65. TB, 5 June 1940.

66. TB, 21 August 1935: "Torgler has written a book attacking communism. Führer is interested in it"; 25 January 1937: "Torgler is given a salary of 800 Mk per month by the Führer. He is to work on academic matters but not appear in public." In spring 1941, however, Hitler told Goebbels surprisingly that he believed that Torgler had organized the Reichstag fire, which Goebbels refused to believe (TB, 9 April 1941).

67. TB, 3, 6, 7, 8, 9 June 1940; *BK*, 2 and 8 June 1940, 2 (on the employment of the communists); during June there are repeated references to the secret radio stations in the minutes of the ministerial briefings *(BK)*. There is no further information on this activity in Podewin and Heuer, *Ernst Torgler*.

68. Umbreit, "Kampf," 302ff.

69. TB, 15 June 1940.

70. TB, 18 June 1940.

71. *BK*, 18 June 1940, 1.

72. *BK*, 16 June 1940, 1.

73. TB, 20 June 1940; *BK*, 19 June 1940, 1, and 20 June 1940, 1 and 3.

74. TB, 22 June 1940.

75. TB, 22 and 23 June 1940; *BK*, 21 June 1940, 1 and 22 June, 1.

76. Umbreit, "Kampf," 316ff.

77. TB, 23 June 1940; *BK*, 22 June 1940, 1.

78. TB, 30 June 1940; the conversation took place in Scheveningen.

79. TB, 1 July 1940.

80. TB, 2 and 3 July 1940.

81. Reuth, *Goebbels*, 454. See Kershaw, *Hitler. 1936–1945*, 407; Thamer, *Verführung und Gewalt*, 647f.; Steinert, *Hitlers Krieg und die Deutschen*, 136f. But see also Below, *Als Hitlers Adjutant*, 237: "In Berlin following the successful campaign I noted, particularly among so-called educated circles, a very pessimistic mood. The campaign in the West left behind a mixture of fear, incomprehension and reluctant admiration."

82. Discussion of the program with Hitler: TB, 3 and 4 July 1940; on the preparations, see in general also the entries for 5 and 6 July. BAB, R 55/20007, Arbeitsplan betr. Rückkehr des Führers aus dem Felde und Reichstagssitzung, 3 July 1940.

83. BAB, R 55/20007, Arbeitsplan.

84. *VB* (B), 6 July 1940.

85. BAB, R 55/20007, Arbeitsplan.

86. *UWW*, August 1940, Alfred Günther (Berlin), "Die Reichshauptstadt empfängt den Führer," 90f.

87. *VB* (B), 7 June 1940 (also for the previous paragraphs); see also the plan "Ab-

schnittsweise eingeteilt Blumenstreuen von Fahrzeugen aus in der Zeit von 14:45 bis 15:00 Uhr."

88. TB, 7 July 1940.

21. "OUR BANNERS LEAD US ON TO VICTORY"

1. *VB* (B), 20 July 1940, "Die monumentale Rede Adolf Hitlers." On the preparation for and impact of the Reichstag speech, see TB, 9, 10, and 20–24 July 1940.
2. TB, 25 July 1940.
3. TB, 25 July 1940.
4. TB, 26 July, 1 August 1940.
5. TB, 5 August 1940. Führer directive no. 17 of 1 August 1940 for the command of the air and sea wars against England, in Hubatsch, *Hitlers Weisungen*, no. 17. On Goebbels and the air war against Great Britain, see Reuth, *Goebbels*, 457ff.
6. TB, 7 August 1940.
7. TB, 7–10 August 1940. From the entry for 8 August it is clear that the raid was planned for the following day.
8. TB, 12–15, 17, and 19 August 1940; Collier, *The Defence of the United Kingdom*, 183ff., 456f.
9. TB, 16–25 August 1940; on the continuation of the raids, see 26, 29, and 30 August, 1, 3, 4, and 5 September; Collier, *Defence*, 203ff., 458ff.
10. TB, 27 August 1940; Mehner (ed.), *Die geheimen Tagesberichte der Deutschen Wehrmachtführung im Zweiten Weltkrieg 1939–1945*, 26 August 1940 for Berlin: "No bombing of built-up areas." On the (unauthorized) raid on London, see Maier, "Die Luftschlacht um England," 386.
11. TB, 29 August 1940. Further raid or air raid warning: 31 August, 1 September; Daily reports, 29 August–1 September.
12. TB, 6 September 1940. On the background, see daily reports, 4 September 1940, notes on particular raids on hydrogenation plants near Stettin, a total of 105 enemy incursions and 17 deaths. See also 8 September 1940: "The Führer gives orders: Code word: Lodge. That means the most massive raid." On the first raids on London, see also TB, 7, 9, and 10 September 1940. On the command situation, see Führer directive for attacks on the population and the air defenses on large English cities including London of 5 September. Quoted in Maier, "Luftschlacht," 386.
13. TB, 4 and 5 September 1940.
14. TB, 11 September (all quotations). On the catastrophic effects of the bombing, see also entries from the days that followed.
15. TB, 5–7 September 1940.
16. TB, 10 September 1940. See also 12, 13, 18, 19, and 25 September. BAK, ZSg 102/27, 10 September 1940: "The raids on Berlin are to be more strongly emphasized than hitherto." 18 September 1940: "The continued British raids on Germany may be dealt with again and again in the German press." TB, 20 September: "The press is instructed to take a much tougher line than hitherto. We must dramatize the whole thing much more."
17. *VB* (B), 11 September 1940, headline over a page of photos; also 14 September, "Englands Schuldkonto wächst weiter."
18. TB, 24 June 1940.

19. Maier, "Luftschlacht," 389. On 14 September Hitler had told the commanders-in-chief that the preconditions for Sealion did not yet exist. On 17 September Hitler had ordered the postponement of Sealion "until further notice." Klee, *Das Unternehmen "Seelöwe,"* 205; Schramm (ed.), *Kriegstagebuch des Oberkommandos der Wehrmacht (Wehrmachtführungsstab),* vol. 1, 19 September 1940, Hitler's directive for the disbanding of the concentrations of ships in the "jumping off harbors."

20. Bormann circular of 27 September 1940, published in Dabel, *KLV,* 7; on the KLV, see also Kock, *"Der Führer sorgt für unsere Kinder,"* 76ff.

21. TB, 28 September, 1, 2, and 4 October 1940.

22. TB, 29 November 1935 and 26 May, 4, 10, 19, and 22 June, 2–4, 8 July, 22 October 1936. Goebbels soon gave up his original idea of initially leaving Lippert in his position of City President and putting in a "representative figure" as Oberbürgermeister alongside him; see in particular 22 June.

23. TB, 22 May, 27 June 1936.

24. Engele and Ribbe, "Berlin in der NS-Zeit (1933–1945)," 974ff.; Gesetz über die Verfassung und Verwaltung der Reichshauptstadt Berlin vom 1. Dezember 1936, *RGBl.* 1936 I, 957; see also TB, 13 and 15 December 1935, 27 November, 2 December 1936; *Regierung Hitler,* vol. 3, no. 194, Kabinettssitzung vom 1. Dezember 1936.

25. TB, 6 August 1938. Soon afterward a festival in the stadium organized by Lippert appeared to him "absolute rubbish," and he considered a report submitted by Lippert on future construction in Berlin as "completely inadequate" (19 and 28 August 1938).

26. TB, 7 October, 3 December 1938, 16 and 22 June 1939.

27. TB, 8 May 1940; on the countermeasures that were initiated, see *BK,* 6 May 1940, 5, and 7 May 1940, 6.

28. TB, 8 and 14 March, 30 April, 8 May, 21 June 1940.

29. TB, 19, 20, and 27 July 1940.

30. TB, 31 August 1940; 6 September 1940: According to this Speer wanted Goebbels to become City President. In November 1941 Goebbels brought the unresolved problem once again to Hitler's attention (TB, 22 November 1941). In October 1942 he briefly thought of the Oberbürgermeister of Wiesbaden, Mix (TB, 4 and 6 October 1942).

31. Kershaw, *Hitler. 1936–1945,* 415; Halder, *Kriegstagebuch,* vol. 2, 31 July 1942, 46ff.; Warlimont, *Im Hauptquartier der deutschen Wehrmacht 1939–1945,* 126ff.; Hillgruber, *Hitlers Strategie,* 223ff.

32. TB, 9 August 1940.

33. TB, 15 August 1940.

34. TB, 24 August 1940; *BK,* 22 August 1940, 9, and 23 August 1940, 10; BAK, 7.Sg 102/26, 22 August 1940: "The press must in all circumstances exercise restraint when it comes to discussing the Soviet Union. It would be completely wrong to have a cultural exchange between Germany and Soviet Russia in the daily papers." "No relations [between] the two systems."

35. See Michalka, *Ribbentrop und die deutsche Weltpolitik.*

36. *ADAP* D XI, no. 252, Bericht Militärattaché Rom, 28 October 1940. According to this Marshall Badoglio had told him on 23 August that Italy would take no action against Greece unless it was compelled to do so by actions taken by the Greeks or by Britain.

37. TB, 5 September 1940.

38. TB, 27 September 1940: "Discussed Ciano's visit with the Führer. The pact is

going to be signed." Thus the propaganda media were geared to the great event only on short notice: *BK*, 27 September 1940, 1; BAK, ZSg 109/15, VI, 27 September 1940, 1; *ADAP* D XI, no. 118, Tripartite Pact of 27 September 1940.

39. TB, 6 October 1940. *ADAP* D XI, no. 249. Hitler's conversation with Mussolini at the Brenner pass on 4 October 1940, Schmidt note from the same day.

40. *ADAP* D XI, Nr. 63, Ribbentrop's conversation with Súñer on 16 September 1940, Note of 17 September 1940; no. 66, Hitler's conversation with Súñer on 17 September, Note from the same day; no. 67, Ribbentrop's conversation with Súñer 17 September. Note from the same day; no. 97, Schmidt note, 26 September, concerning the conversation between Ribbentrop and Súner on the same day; no. 117, Hitler's conversation with Súner on 27 September, note of 28 September 1940. Detwiler, *Hitler*, 37ff.

41. TB, 19 September 1940; Detwiler, *Hitler, Franco und Gibraltar*, 30ff.

42. *ADAP* D XI, no. 220, Hitler's meeting with Franco, 23 October 1940 in Hendaye, undated note; no. 221, Ambassador Schmidt, note of 23 October 1940 concerning the conversation between Súñer and the RAM in Hendaye on the same day Tag. Detwiler, *Hitler*, 56ff.

43. TB, 31 October 1940.

44. TB, 4 December 1940; see also 15 November 1940, on the occasion of a further visit to Germany by Súñer.

45. Detwiler, *Hitler*, 85; *OKW KTB*, 1, 8 December 1940, Report of the Abwehr chief.

46. TB, 19 December 1940.

47. *ADAP* D XI, no. 212, Schmidt note, 22 October 1941 concerning the conversation between Hitler and Laval on the same day; no. 227, Schmidt, note of 24 October 1941 concerning Hitler's conversation with Pétain on the same day.

48. TB, 24 October 1940.

49. TB, 25 October 1940. After his return Hitler gave him a general account of his impression of Pétain (TB, 31 October 1940).

50. TB, 29 October 1940.

51. Jäckel, *Frankreich in Hitlers Europa*, 105ff.

52. *ADAP* D XI, no. 246, Schmidt note on the conversation between Hitler and Mussolini in Florence, 28 October 1940.

53. TB, 29 October 1940.

54. On the background, see TB, 10 and 17 July (first information concerning the plan to send troops to Romania), 9 October (concerning troop movements), 14 October 1940 (military mission). See also König, *Kooperation als Machtkampf*, 32.

55. TB, 20 and 23 December 1940 and 15 January 1941. By repeatedly giving the date of the impending intervention as January 1941—in fact it was planned for March—he was able to refer to the provision of German units in Romania. On the preparations for the war in the Balkans, see in particular *OKW KTB* I, p. 204, Briefing of Hitler by the Commander-in-Chief of the Army and by the Chief of the Army General Staff, 5 December 1940; I, p. 224: Deployment directive for the 12th Army, Operation Marita and Directive no. 18, 12 November 1940, also no. 20, 13 December 1940 (Hubatsch, *Hitlers Weisungen*); Vogel, "Das Eingreifen Deutschlands auf dem Balkan," 422ff.

56. TB, 11 and 12 November 1940.

57. TB, 14 November 1940.

58. Kershaw, *Hitler. 1936–1945*, 447f.; *ADAP* D XI, nos. 325–329 concerning the conversations on 12 and 13 November.

59. TB, 4 December 1940.

60. *OKW KTB* I, p. 208f., 5 December 1940.

61. TB, 20 July 1940.

62. TB, 25 July 1940.

63. TB, 26 July 1940. Also 17 August 1940: "Later on we want to pack the Jews off to Madagascar. There they can create their own state." See also Reuth, *Goebbels*, 455.

64. *BK*, 6 September 1940, 6.

65. Longerich, *Politik der Vernichtung*, 278ff.

66. Bormann minute of a conversation with Hitler on 2 October: docs. 172-USSR, in *IMT* 39, 425ff.

67. *Halder KTB*, vol. 2, 4 November 1940.

68. Longerich, *Politik der Vernichtung*, 285ff.

69. TB, 18 March 1941.

70. Published in Adler, *Der verwaltete Mensch*, 152.

71. TB, 22 March 1941.

72. TB, 21 March 1941.

73. TB, 10, 12, 13, 16, and 28 January, 1 February 1940; see *BK*, 78.

74. TB, 16 January, 21 February, 28 March 1940 (quotation); Diller, *Rundfunkpolitik*, 352f.

75. Diller, *Rundfunkpolitik*, 351.

76. Dussel, *Hörfunk*, 199ff.; TB, 23 and 28 April 1940, also 9 and 18 May 1940.

77. Dussel, *Hörfunk*, 199.

78. TB, 5 December 1940; *BK*, 20 December 1940, 4.

79. TB, 30 September, 21 October 1939, 2 and 25 January 1940, 22 March, 23 April 1940; Moeller, *Filmminister*, 93f.

80. TB, 29 October 1939, 21 November 1939. BAB, R 55/495, "Aufstellung Einnahmen."

81. TB, 7 and 14 November 1939; Moeller, *Filmminister*, 95; BAB, R 55/1352, Table for "Income," notes only 67 films for 1940/41.

82. Decree of 23 November 1939 (Albrecht, *Filmpolitik*, p. 526), which envisaged the submission of a treatment for every film: TB, 14 and 18 November 1939; *BK*, 3 November 1939, 12.

83. Rosenberg, *Tagebuch*, 11 December 1939 (and 30 December 1939); see Reuth, *Goebbels*, 436.

84. TB, 12 December 1939.

85. TB, 19, 24, and 31 January, 28 February, 13 March 1941; Moeller, *Filmminister*, 227ff.

86. TB, 23 and 25 April 1940; *BK*, 22 April 1940, 10, and 27 June 1940, 3.

87. Minute, presumably of 23 April 1940, quoted by Albrecht, *Filmpolitik*, 143.

88. Moeller, *Filmminister*, 238ff., and Barth, *Goebbels und die Juden*, 160ff.; Hollstein, *Jud Süß und die Deutschen;* Mannes, *Antisemitismus im nationalsozialistischen Spielfilm*.

89. "Die Rothschilds": TB, 13 March, 26 April, 7 and 23 July, 10 September 1940.

90. Literature on *Jud Süss:* Tegel, *Jew Süss/Jud Süss;* Knilli, *Jud Süß*. TB, 5 and 18 January, 2 and 15 February, 26 April, 18 August ("Harlan-Film 'Jud Süss.' [...] A really great and brilliant film. Just the kind of anti-Semitic film that we needed"), 6, 7, 10, and 25 September 1940 (on the premiere).

91. Hornshoj-Moller, *"Der ewige Jude.";* Mannes, *Antisemitismus*, 51ff.; Reuband, "'Jud Süß' and 'Der Ewige Jude'"; *BK*, 3 September 1940, 8 (instructions for the preparation of the premiere); TB, 17 October 1939, also 5 and 6 October 1939.

92. TB, 24, 28, and 29 October, 2, 11, and 28 November 1939, 9 and 12 January "Hitler demands changes," 2 April, 8 May, 9 June, 11 October 1940.

93. Vertrauliche Information, 28 November 1940 and 12 December 1940, BAK, ZSg 109/16 and 17.

94. Bericht RSHA, Amt III (SD), 20 January 1941, published in *Meldungen aus dem Reich*, vol. 6, 1914f., 1917ff. On the poor audiences for the film, see also Jäckel and Kulka (eds.), *Die Juden in den geheimen NS-Stimmungsberichten, 1933–1945*, no. 3215, SD-Außenstelle Höxter, 7 February 1941 and no. 3243, NSDAP-Kreisleitung Aachen-Land, 28 April 1941. On *Der Ewige Jude*, see Ahrens, Hornshoj-Moller, and Melchers, *"Der ewige Jude"*; Bucher, "Die Bedeutung des Films als historische Quelle."

95. Jäckel and Kulka, *Die Juden*, no. 3287 and 3306, SD-Außenstelle Bielefeld, reports of 11 August and 30 September 1941.

96. Moeller, *Filmminister*, 237.

97. TB, 7 December 1940 about the premiere, and 16 November with a very positive opinion.

98. TB, 16 and 26 March 1941 ("3 conclusions to 'Ohm Krüger.' The one composed by me is the best and will be chosen); first screening (at Goebbels's home): 2 April, and 5 April 1941 (in the cinema).

99. TB, 15 May 1941: "The line taken is too exaggerated; the sections attacking the previous regime don't work."

100. TB, 22 March, 28 August 1941 (critical assessment).

101. TB, 30 March 1941 ("mediocre stuff").

102. TB, 31 December 1940 (premiere) and 16 December (very positive critique).

103. TB, 7 February 1941.

104. TB, 14 February, 21 June 1941.

105. Roth, "Filmpropaganda für die Vernichtung der Geisteskranken und Behinderten im 'Dritten Reich'"; Moeller, *Filmminister*, 245ff.

106. Moeller, *Filmminister*, 253ff.

107. TB, 21 May 1940 (on the first article). On the preparations for the journal, see TB, 26 November, 6 and 14 December 1939, 13 January, 5 March, 4 April, 5 May 1940. Reuth, *Goebbels*, 447ff.; Martens, *Zum Beispiel "Das Reich"*; Kessemeier, *Der Leitartikler Goebbels*, 137ff.

108. According to Kessemeier, from 7 November on a regular basis; Goebbels, however, mentions in the TB of 18 September 1941 that an article was already being read out. Kessemeier, *Leitartikler*, 200.

109. *BK*, 21 May 1940, 5. *Das Reich* must be provided with privileged access to special material, so that the journal "can make an impact abroad right from the start." See also *BK*, 28 May 1940, 3, and 1 June 1940, 10.

110. TB, 2 and 7 June 1940.

111. TB, 6 December 1940.

112. Kallis, *National Socialist Propaganda in the Second World War*. See *Meldungen aus dem Reich*, October 1940, 1643ff.

113. BAB, NS 18/199, Rundschreiben des Reichspropagandaleiters Goebbels, 10 October 1940.

114. TB, 1 and 4 November 1940; *BK*, 147.

115. Longerich, *Propagandisten*, 193ff.

116. Longerich, *Propagandisten*, 138ff.; TB, 2, 5, 6, 7, 10, and 22 December 1940, 22 and 30 January, 18 March 1941.

117. The new appointment to head the foreign department served the same purpose: Helmut Hunke followed Ernst Brauweiler in December 1940. TB, 22 November, 5, 6, 10, and 14 December 1940. On 4 June 1941: "Hunke's department A must be

considerably increased. Otherwise he won't be able to get his way against the
A.A."

118. TB, 16 January, 17 February, 31 March, 1 June 1941.

119. TB, 8 February 1941, and 9 February 1941.

120. TB, 10 February 1941.

121. TB, 11 February 1941; the minutes of the meeting have not survived.

122. BAK, ZSg 109/18, 11 February 1941, TP 1.

123. TB, 13 February, and 12 and 14 February 1941. On the dispute with Dietrich, see
also 2 April 1941.

124. *BK,* 58; TB, 14, 16, 22, and 29 June 1940.

125. BAB, R 55/437, Nachrichtenblatt des Propagandaministeriums vom 18. Juli 1941.

126. TB, 3, 11, 12, 17, 22, 23, and 24 October 1940.

127. TB, 24 May 1940; on his intention to appoint Gutterer, see also 17 October 1940.

128. TB, 2 September; on the trip, see 1 September 1940.

129. TB, 9 September 1940.

130. TB, 2 and 16 October 1940.

131. TB, 30 October, 1 November 1940.

132. TB, 12 November 1940.

133. TB, 13 and 15 February 1941.

134. TB, 18 February 1941.

135. On the coup, see Vogel, "Eingreifen," 442ff.

136. On the coup, see TB, 28 and 29 March 1941; *BK,* 27 March 1941, 1.

137. On the decision, see Vogel, "Eingreifen," 445; on restraint in propaganda, see *BK,*
28 March 1941 1, 31 March 1941, 1, and 1 April 1941, 1.

138. *BK,* 3 April 1941, 1.

139. TB, 7 April 1941; *BK,* 6 June 1941.

140. TB, 18 April 1941.

141. TB, 19–27 April 1941.

142. TB, 28 April 1941.

143. *Meldungen aus dem Reich,* 10 April 1941, 2192f., 17 April 1941, 2203, 22 April
1941, 2217, 25 April 1941, 2227f.

144. TB, 13 May 1941; the official Party communiqué is, for example, published in the
VB (B) of 13 May 1941. On the Hess flight, see Schmidt, *Rudolf Heß;* Pätzold and
Weissbecker, *Rudolf Heß,* 261ff.; Reuth, *Goebbels,* 472ff.

145. TB, 16 October 1940.

146. TB, 14 May 1941.

147. *BK,* 13 May 1941, 1.

148. BAK, ZSg 102, 13 May 1941 (midday), TP 1.

149. TB, 14 May 1941.

150. TB, 15 May 1941; *BK,* 14 May 1941, 1. See also *BK,* 15 May 1941.

151. TB, 16 May 1941; see also 17 and 18 May 1941; *BK,* 19 May 1941, 1.

152. TB, 19 May 1941.

153. TB, 20 and 22 May 1941; *Meldungen aus dem Reich,* no. 186, 15 May 1941, 2302;
no. 187, 19 May, 2313; 188, 22 May, 2329f.

154. TB, 22, 25, and 26 March 1941.

155. TB, 20 and 29 May 1941.

156. TB, 7 May 1941.

157. TB, 9 May 1941.

158. TB, 24 May 1941, and TB, 9 May 1941, on Rosenberg's appointment.

159. TB, 25 May 1941.

160. TB, 23 May 1941 and 1 June 1941.

161. TB, 29 May, *VB* (B), 29 May 1941, "Roosevelts Kaminrede."
162. TB, 23 May (drunkenness quotation), 27 May (AA intrigue), also: 24, 26, and 31 May 1941. Ribbentrop had "behaved abominably" (14 June); for accusations against the AA in this context, see also 28 May, 1, 13, and 27 June, 15, 17, and 29 July 1941; Longerich, *Propagandisten,* 140f.
163. TB, 1 and 13 August 1941. On the trial, see also 26 September, 7, 15, 18, and 19 October 1941, also 15 November 1941. When in spring 1942 Goebbels finally succeeded in persuading Hitler to free Bömer he learned that, having been sent to the front to redeem himself, the latter shortly afterward died of his wounds. TB, 20 and 21 March 1942, also 26 March (about Bömer's reception in the Ministry). He still managed to have Bömer posthumously rehabilitated: TB, 24 June, 24 August 1942.
164. TB, 31 May 1941.
165. TB, 5 June 1941.
166. MK, 13 June 1941 (on the "most contradictory rumors about future military operations"); 16 June 1941: "The topic of 'Russia' must not however be touched on either in the domestic or in the foreign services." On the camouflage measures in general, see Reuth, *Goebbels,* 476ff.
167. TB, 11 June 1941, and 12, 13, 14, 15, and 16 June 1941; BAK, ZSg 102/32, 13 June 1941, no. 5, instruction from Fritzsche not to quote the article.
168. TB, 20 and 22 May 1941 and 11, 12, and 14 June, on the "lightening" of the Radio programming; see also Goebbels's editorial in the *Reich* of 15 June 1941, "Der Rundfunk im Kriege"; MK, 16 June 1941.
169. TB, 16 June 1941.

22. "A GREAT, A WONDERFUL TIME, IN WHICH A NEW REICH WILL BE BORN"

1. TB, 18 June 1941, also 17 June 1941.
2. TB, 19 June 1941.
3. TB, 21 June 1941.
4. TB, 22 June 1941; text in *Domarus II,* 1726ff.; see also Reuth, *Goebbels,* 481ff.
5. TB, 23, 24, and 25 June 1941.
6. TB, 24, 25, and 27 June 1941.
7. TB, 5 July, 3 and 29 August 1941; 5 June 1941: reference to the construction of the bunker.
8. MK, 23 June 1941; see also TB, 24 June 1941.
9. *VB* (B), 26 June 1941, also in *Die Zeit ohne Beispiel,* 508–13; TB, 25 June 1941, and 26 June 1941.
10. *Die Wehrmachtberichte 1939–1945,* 3 vols., vol. 1, 23–28 June; TB, 27 June 1941.
11. TB, 23 June 1941.
12. TB, 29 June 1941.
13. *Das Reich,* 6 July 1941, "Nachrichtenpolitik," also in *Zeit ohne Beispiel,* 514–19; see TB, 29 June 1941.
14. *Wehrmachtberichte,* vol. 1, 29 June 1941.
15. TB, 30 June 1941; MK, 30 June 1941. See also TB, 1, 3, and 5 July 1941; *Meldungen aus dem Reich,* no. 198 of 30 June 1941, 2458.
16. TB, 30 June 1941.
17. TB, 12 July 1941.

18. *BW,* 5 July 1941.
19. BAK, ZSg 102/33, 5 July 1941, Tagesparole. See also the addition in the Vertrauliche Information of 5 July 1941 (ibid.) and Tagesparole, BAK, ZSg 102/35, 7 July 1941.
20. See *VB* (B), 6 July 1941, which was very much in the light of this propaganda action. See also *Der Angriff,* 6 July 1941, "Viehische Bluttaten der GPU-Kommissare."
21. *VB* (B), 7 July 1941, "Der Schleier fällt." Also already in *Das Reich,* 6 July 1941, and in *Zeit,* 520–25.
22. His conversation with Hitler on 8 July was decisive for his change of stance (TB, 9 July); but see also already TB, 3 July 1941: "It's now clear beyond a doubt that Moscow intended to attack Germany and central Europe. The Führer acted at the very last moment." On the "preventive war thesis," see Benz, *Der Rußlandfeldzug des Dritten Reiches;* Pietrow-Ennker (ed.), *Präventivkrieg?*
23. The Party Chancellery's liaison official in the Propaganda Ministry, Tiessler, informed his office that at the briefing instructions had been given that the "on-going anti-Bolshevik campaign" was to have "a very specific anti-Semitic character." BAB, NS 18 alt/768, Telex Tiessler to Party Chancellery, 9 July 1941.
24. See BAK, ZSg 102/33, 9 July 1941, Kommentaranweisung.
25. Details in Longerich, *Davon,* 160f.
26. Deutsche Wochenschau no. 566 of 10 July 1941. Voigt, *Jüdisches Leben und Holocaust im Filmdokument 1930 bis 1945.*
27. The article in the *VB* of 13 July 1941, "Churchill–Roosevelt–Stalin. Das alljüdische Dreigestirn," in which once again all the "arguments" for this perspective were summarized, was typical of this campaign.
28. *Das Reich,* 20 July 1941, and *Zeit,* 526–31; TB, 13 July 1941.
29. BAK, ZSg 109/22, TP, 23, 27, and 30 June 1941; TB, 30 June 1941 (the idea of a crusade was "not appropriate"). See Hockerts, "Kreuzzugsrhetorik, Vorsehungsglaube, Kriegstheologie."
30. TB, 13 July 1941.
31. TB, 14 July 1941.
32. *Wehrmachtberichte,* 18 July 1941; TB, 19 July 1941.
33. TB, 10 and 14 July 1941; also 16, 17, 19, 23 July 1941.
34. TB, 10, 14, 17, 19, and 23 July 1941; *Meldungen aus dem Reich* no. 200 of 7 July 1941, 2487, no. 201 of 10 July 1941, 2502f., 2511ff.
35. TB, 14, 15, 16, and 19 July 1941; *Meldungen aus dem Reich* no. 201 of 17 July 1941, 2529f.
36. TB, 3, 6, 7, and 24 July 1941.
37. TB, 23 July 1941.
38. TB, 24 July 1941. There is a first hint of this new line in the entry for 15 July 1941. Here the demand for a tougher news policy is contrasted with the very optimistic mood, which, according to a report of Dietrich's, was prevailing at Führer's headquarters at this time.
39. TB, 24 July 1941. On the necessity to "toughen up" propaganda, see also 26 and 28 July 1941.
40. TB, 27 July 1941.
41. TB, 29 July 1941.
42. TB, 7 August 1941; the *Meldungen aus dem Reich* no. 208 (n.d.), 2608, wrote of a "decline in the mood of expectation."
43. TB, 9 and 10 August 1941 (in retrospect). On the change in mood, see *Meldungen aus dem Reich* of 28 July 1941, 2578, 31 July 1941, 2591.

44. See the files in BAB, R 43 II/1271, 1271a, 1271b, and 1272. On the treatment of this delicate question in Berlin, see TB, 6 August 1941.

45. *Meldungen aus dem Reich,* 17 July 1941, 2529f., and 28 July 1941, 2590; TB, 20 July 1941, from which it is clear that he left a letter of complaint from Cardinal Bertram, the chairman of the Bishops' Conference, about obstacles placed in the way of the work of the Church unanswered.

46. TB, 6 and 7 August 1941; *Wehrmachtberichte,* vol. 1, 6 August 1941.

47. TB, 8 August 1941. See also TB, 9, 10, and 11 August 1941; *Meldungen aus dem Reich,* 11 August 1941, 2631.

48. Examples of Goebbels's instructions for propaganda about POWs in MK, 23 July 1941, Order to publish more photos of POWs ("shocking types").

49. TB, 27 August 1941.

50. Tiessler report (he was a member of the visiting party), 28 August 1941; *Akten der Partei-Kanzlei,* 76209f. (from BAB, NS 18 alt/845).

51. On 14 August 1941 he observed "public opinion becoming more tense," but then the mood became positive (15 and 17 August 1941).

52. TB, 10, 12, and 29 August 1941. On the preparation of initial propaganda proposals by the department for "brightening up the mood within Germany" see, for example, TB, 9 and 11 September 1941. On Braeckow and Berndt, see *BK,* 59, 75ff.

53. TB, 2 August 1941. On 27 August he discussed with a senior Berlin SA leader the possibility of "using the SA and Party for our plan to spread positive rumors." TB, 28 August 1941.

54. TB, 1 October, and 11 November: "The increasing number of lines in front of tobacco shops is becoming an unwelcome sight in the streets of our major cities." He had already been concerned about the phenomenon of crowds of people lining up for tobacco—"hotbeds of grumbling"—in May: TB, 20 May 1941.

55. Goebbels had already been pursuing the idea of marking out Jews since April 1941; on 21 April he had ordered his state secretary, Gutterer, to prepare the marking out of Berlin's Jews: *Kriegspropaganda* (Boelcke) and *Akten der Parteikanzlei,* Mikrofiches, vol. 4, 76074, Vorlage Tiessler, 21 July 1941. At the beginning of July 1941 Goebbels urged Bormann to get Hitler to approve the marking out of Jews (ibid., 74650f., from BAB, NS 18 alt/808, Vermerk Tießler für die Parteikanzlei, 3 July 1941).

56. Longerich, *Davon,* 165, 393.

57. Lösener, "Als Rassenreferent im Reichsministerium des Innern."

58. TB, entries from 4–19 July 1941.

59. TB, 11 July 1941.

60. TB, 28 December 1939 (with Hitler): "The best way of getting rid of the Churches is to claim to be a more positive Christian than they are. Thus, as far as these issues are concerned for the time being it's best to be cautious and if the Churches become impudent and interfere in matters of state to coldly squash them." See also TB, 17 January 1940.

61. TB, 29 April 1941.

62. TB, 1 May 1940: "With the Führer. Bouhler reports on the process of liquidating the insane, that's so necessary and is now being carried out. Still secret. It's causing a lot of difficulties." TB, 31 January 1941: "Discussed with Bouhler the discreet liquidation of the mentally ill. 40,000 have gone, 60,000 have still to go. It's a tough but necessary job. And it has to be done. Bouhler is the right man to do it." On the "Euthanasia" program, see Klee, *"Euthanasie" im NS-Staat;* Friedlander,

Der Weg zum NS-Genozid; Burleigh, *Tod und Erlösung;* Süss, *Der "Volkskörper" im Krieg.*

63. TB, 9 July 1941. Also 11 and 19 July 1941; 23 July 1941: "Don't get involved in confessional matters." A lengthy statement on this in the entry of 7 July 1941. On the pastoral letter, see Nowak, *"Euthanasie" und Sterilisierung im "Dritten Reich,"* 112.

64. Nowak, *"Euthanasie,"* 161ff.; Portmann, *Der Bischof von Münster,* 143ff. The texts of the sermons of 12 and 20 July and 3 August 1941 are documented in *Bischof Clement August Graf von Galen. Akten, Briefe und Predigten, 1933–1946,* vol. 2, 1939–1946, nos. 333, 336, 341. On the "euthanasia" program becoming public knowledge in the Reich and the resulting protests, see Steinert, *Hitlers Krieg und die Deutschen,* 152ff.; Schmuhl, *Rassenhygiene, Nationalsozialismus, Euthanasie,* 312ff.; Longerich, *Davon,* 162ff.

65. TB, 14 August 1941.

66. TB, 15 August 1941.

67. TB, 18 August 1941. On Bertram's letter, see Nowak, *"Euthanasie,"* 160.

68. TB, 11 August 1941: "In the major cities the Jews are receiving their just deserts. Masses of them are being beaten to death by the self-defense organizations of the Baltic peoples. What the Führer prophesied is coming true: that if Jewry succeeded in once again provoking a war it would cease to exist." On the shooting of Jews by Romania in Bessarabia, see TB, 5 September 1941; he was informed about the "massive shooting of Jews in the Ukraine" at the latest in October: TB, 19 October 1941.

69. TB, 23 August 1941.

70. "At least we can be pleased if the operation involved with it is finished. It was necessary."

71. This is how it was put by the Westphalian Landeshauptmann, Kolbow, in a note of 31 July 1941: The "action in Westphalia was going full steam ahead and would be finished in around 2 to 3 weeks." Facsimile in Teppe, *Massenmord auf dem Dienstweg,* 21. Details in Longerich, *Davon,* 170.

72. TB, 24 August 1941.

73. TB, 29 August 1941, and 4 September 1941, on his attempts to sort out the matter through increased propaganda measures. Ziegler, "Der Kampf um die Schulkreuze im Dritten Reich"; on the protests and demonstrations, see Ziegler (ed.), *Die kirchliche Lage in Bayern,* no. 122, 283ff., Monatsbericht der Regierung Oberpfalz, 8 June 1941, no. 123, 8 July 1941, no. 124, 8 August 1941, no. 125, 7 September 1941, no. 126, 8 October 1941.

74. TB, 27 and 29 September 1941, 1 and 2 October (quotation), 18 October (death penalty would be appropriate); 22 November 1941, concerning a conversation with Hitler, who intended to act against the "traitor" von Galen, but not at the moment; 30 November 1941, about von Galen: "We must let the abscess get bigger until we can lance it"; 30 November 1941, Hitler assures him "that he will be watching bishop Count von Galen's activities from his lookout post." On other political issues affecting the Churches, see, for example, TB, 21 November 1941, about pro-Church passages in his son's school primer; 28 November 1941 concerning the confiscation of an SS anti-Christian pamphlet; on 29 November 1941 he noted that Hitler wanted "if possible to avoid a public conflict with the Church during the war. He's waiting for the right moment. But is then determined to take a tough line." In 1943 he still made an attempt to get Hitler to proceed against von Galen (TB, 11 and 18 July 1943).

75. TB, 26 October 1941.
76. Details in Longerich, *Davon*, 167.
77. TB, 20 August 1941, and 22 August 1941.
78. TB, 22 August 1941.
79. MK, 21 August 1941.
80. Kaufman, *Germany Must Perish;* Benz, "Judenvernichtung aus Notwehr?"
81. BAK, ZSg 102/33, 23 July 1941.
82. TB, 19 August 1941. On the production of the pamphlet, see 13, 29, and 30 August 1941.
83. On this campaign, see Longerich, *Davon*, 168f.
84. Diewerge, *Das Kriegsziel der Weltplutokratie*, 6. On Nazi propaganda against the "Atlantic-Charta," see TB, 16 August; *VB* (B), 17 August 1941; see also MK, 16–20 August 1941. BAK, ZSg 102/33, 15 August 1941 (M), TP 1: "Churchill–Roosevelt–Redebluff," "Propagandaschwindel"; BAK, ZSg 109/24, VI of 18 August 1941, Roosevelt was "rather the agent of international Jewry."
85. BAK, ZSg 102/34, 12 September, midday; TB, 13 September 1941.
86. TB, 13 September 1941.
87. *VB* (B), 13 September 1941.
88. Particular examples in Longerich, *Davon*, 169.
89. BAB, R 8150/18.
90. *Meldungen aus dem Reich*, 21 August, 2671, 25 August, 2684ff., 1 September, 2712f., and 8 September 1941, 2737f.; TB, 18, 25 August 1941 (SD report), 28 August 1941 (SD report), 5 September 1941 (SD report).
91. *Das Reich*, 31 August 1941; TB, 26, 28, and 30 August 1941.
92. TB, 5 September 1941.
93. Klink, "Heer und Kriegsmarine," 594f.
94. TB, 10 September 1941, also 12, 18, and 20 September 1941. *Meldungen aus dem Reich*, no. 218, 8 September 1941, expressed the conviction of many people that the war would not come to an end that year.
95. TB, 8, 14, 15, 16, and 17 July 1941.
96. TB, 18 July 1941; see also the to some extent triumphant entries between the 19 and 24 July 1941; NS 18/194, Tiessler note for Bormann about Goebbels's comments on the V Propaganda, 20 July 1941.
97. BAB, NS 18/195.
98. TB, 22 August 1941.
99. MK, 28 August 1941; see also TB, 29 September 1941.
100. TB, 23, 24, 28, and 29 August, 6, 7, 9, 19, 20, 21, and 24 September 1941.
101. MK, 28 August 1941 (on Serbia). Manoschek, *"Serbien ist judenfrei,"* 43ff.; Meyer, "'[. . .] dass französische Verhältnisse anders sind als polnische'"; Weber, *Die Innere Sicherheit im besetzten Belgien und Nordfrankreich, 1940–1944*, 59ff.; *Die Okkupationspolitik des deutschen Faschismus in Dänemark und Norwegen (1940–1945). Dokumentenauswahl*, 33.
102. TB, 24 September 1941 and entries between 29 September and 4 October 1941.
103. Detlev Brandes, *Die Tschechen unter deutschem Protektorat*, vol. 1: *Besatzungspolitik, Kollaboration und Widerstand im Protektorat Böhmen und Mähren bis Heydrichs Tod*, vol. 1, 207ff.
104. TB, 17 October 1941; already 3 October, and 11, 22 October, 5 and 18 November 1941.
105. TB, 21, 23, and 24 October 1941.
106. TB, 26, 29, and 30 October 1941; and 1 November 1941.

107. Longerich, *Propagandisten*, 141f.
108. TB, 12 August 1941. On the negotiations, see 13 and 24 August, 20, 23, and 28 September, 3, 4, 12, 18, 23, and 24 October 1941.
109. Text in PAA, Kult. Gen. Geh. 11, vol. 4; see Longerich, *Propagandisten*, 143ff.; Reuth, *Goebbels*, 485. TB, 25 October 1941, on the conclusion of the agreement as well as 18, 22, and 27 November, 4 December on the further development of the relationship to the Foreign Ministry and his personal relationship to Ribbentrop.
110. TB, 1 October 1941.
111. Latour, "Goebbels' 'Außerordentliche Rundfunkmaßnahmen,'" 424; also TB, 21 October 1941.
112. Latour, "Goebbels' 'Außerordentliche Rundfunkmaßnahmen,'" 427f. Significantly, after a conversation with Hitler, Goebbels claimed this draft as a Führer directive authorized by him: TB, 22 November 1941, and 27 November 1941.
113. Latour, "Goebbels' 'Außerordentliche Rundfunkmaßnahmen,'" 428; on this whole issue, see Longerich, *Propagandisten*, 178ff.
114. TB, 20–29 January 1942. See Longerich, *Propagandisten*, 177ff. On the Seehaus-Dienst, see, in particular, also Boelcke, "Das 'Seehaus' in Berlin-Wannsee"; Latour, "Goebbels' 'Außerordentliche Rundfunkmaßnahmen.'"
115. As in his announcement at the Ministerial briefing of 24 January 1942. At the meeting with Hitler on 29 January he had this measure approved once more by the highest authority and to secure a "blank check" for his further actions, TB, 30 January 1942; he also referred his colleagues to the blank check, MK, 30 January 1942.
116. Details in Longerich, *Propagandisten*, 181f.
117. Directive from the Propaganda Minister with regard to the Seehaus, "on the orders of the Führer and with the consent of the Foreign Minister," R 55/634. The decree was preceded by intensive negotiations (material ibid.); details in Longerich, *Propagandisten*, 182.
118. *Wehrmachtberichte*, vol. 1, 20 September 1941.
119. TB, 20, 21, and 23 (middle position quotation) September 1941.
120. BAB, NS 18/242, Goebbels's instruction 12 September 1941.
121. TB, 27 September 1941; on the very positive mood, see 25, 26, 27, and 28 September 1941.
122. Brandes, *Tschechen*, vol. 1, p. 207.
123. TB, 23 September 1941.
124. Longerich, *Davon*, 171ff.
125. Mitschrift der Reichspropagandaleitung, 25 September 1941, BAB, NS 18/188.
126. BAK, ZSg 102/34.
127. Longerich, *Davon*, 173ff.
128. MK, 6 October 1941; TB, 7 October 1941.
129. BAB, R 58/276, 24 October 1941, Runderlass des RSHA (published in Walk [ed.], *Das Sonderrecht für die Juden im NS-Staat*, Abschnitt IV, no. 257), is also available as Nuremberg Document L 152. "The Jewish party is in any case to be taken into protective custody in a concentration camp until further notice."
130. Klink, "Heer und Kriegsmarine," 677ff.
131. *Domarus II*, 1758ff.; TB, 4 October 1941.
132. TB, 5 and 9 October 1941.
133. BAK, ZSg 109/26, VI of 9 October 1941; TB, 10 October 1941.
134. TB, 11 October 1941, and 12 October 1941.
135. TB, 15 October 1941.

136. TB, 17 and 19 October 1941. Further on the positive mood: 26 October 1941.
137. Ministerkonferenz, Mitschrift des Verbindungsmanns zur Parteikanzlei, Tiessler, 23 October 1941, BAB, NS 18 alt/622.
138. MK, 27 October 1941.
139. BAK, ZSg 109/26, 28, and 29 October 1941 (Roosevelt). On the carrying out of the campaign in the German press, see Longerich, *Davon*, 185.
140. BAK, ZSg 109/26, VI of 26 October 1941.
141. Details in Longerich, *Davon*, 187ff; TB, 31 October 1941.

23. "GETTING THE NATION TO ACCEPT TOUGH POLICIES"

1. TB, 1 November 1941.
2. TB, 2 November 1941.
3. TB, 3 November 1941.
4. TB, 4 November 1941. See *Meldungen aus dem Reich*, 30 October 1941, 2927f.
5. TB, 6 November 1941.
6. TB, 11 January 1942; see also 24 November, 7 December 1941, 3 January 1942.
7. TB, 7 November 1941. On two reports on the situation on the Eastern Front, see 7 January 1942: "Such snapshots of morale emerge under the impression of a temporary situation or an actual event and if put down on paper would certainly no longer be taken seriously a year later by the people who are now composing them. [. . .]."
8. TB, 11 April 1942.
9. Kessemeier, *Leitartikler*, 200f., on the further distribution of the articles. Goebbels even advocated special editions for the Party offices: TB, 26 October, 5 November 1941. There are special copies of his articles in, for example, the Institut für Zeitgeschichte, Munich.
10. TB, 26 October 1941; also 15 November 1941.
11. TB, 4 November 1941.
12. *VB* (B), 9 November 1941, "Wann oder Wie," in Goebbels, *Das eherne Herz*, 78–84; TB, 30 October 1941 on the composition of his article.
13. TB, 10 and 22 November 1941: "The Führer approves my view that we should gear our propaganda entirely to the need to take a tough line in our conduct of the war. My article 'Wann oder wie?' shows the way." BAK, ZSg 102/35, 10 November 1941 (Fritzsche): "In our treatment of the Führer's speech we should stick to the line taken by Dr. Goebbels in his recent article, the line of being determined and ready to fight at any price."
14. BAK, ZSg 102/35, 6 November 1941, 13; MK, 10 November 1941. Goebbels wrote of the "change of course" in propaganda initiated by his article.
15. TB, 22 November 1941.
16. TB, 5, 8, and 9 November 1941.
17. TB, 11 November 1941.
18. TB, 13 November. The entries over the coming days were similar in tone: 15, 16, 17, 20, and 21 November 1941.
19. TB, 4 November 1941; "The Jews Are to Blame," 16 November 1941, also in Joseph Goebbels, *Das eherne Herz*, 85–91.
20. Goebbels, *Herz*. The passage on the "extermination" of the Jews is on p. 35.
21. Details in Longerich, *Davon*, 192. *Meldungen aus dem Reich* reported the article

had met with a "strong response," in particular the ten points at the end were considered "a clear call to action": *Meldungen aus dem Reich,* 20 November 1941, 3005ff.

22. TB, 11 and 13 November 1941.
23. TB, 2 December 1941.
24. TB, 7 December 1941, and MK, 7 December 1941.
25. TB, 8 December 1941; see also 7 December 1941.
26. MK, 7 December 1941. On the development of morale, see TB, 4, 7, 8, and 12 December 1941. *Meldungen aus dem Reich,* 1 December 1941, 3042f., 4 December 1942, 3059f., 8 December 1941, 3069f.
27. TB, 9 December 1941.
28. TB, 9 December 1941.
29. TB, 10 December 1941.
30. TB, 22 November 1941.
31. *Domarus II,* 1794ff.; Kershaw, *Hitler. 1936–1945,* 599ff.
32. TB, 12 December 1941; *Meldungen aus dem Reich,* 15 December 1941, 3089.
33. TB, 13 December 1941.
34. MK, 12 December 1941.
35. "Ruf zur Gemeinschaftshilfe. Aufruf zur Sammlung von Wintersachen für unsere Front," 21 October 1942, in *Herz,* 131–37; TB, 21 December, and 20 December 1941. On the collection of winter clothing, see also MK, 20–22 December 1941.
36. TB, 22 December 1941, and 25 and 27 December 1941.
37. TB, 24 and 25 December 1941. On Christmas festivities, see TB, 2 and 4 December 1942, also 23 November 1942; MK, 4 December 1941.
38. TB, 27 and 28 December (quotation), and 29 December on the poor situation on the Eastern Front.
39. TB, 28 December 1941.
40. *Das Reich,* 28 December 1941, also in *Herz,* 145–51.
41. MK, 1–15 January 1942.
42. TB, 2 January 1942. This is also reflected in the *Meldungen aus dem Reich,* which, just as Goebbels had intended, subordinated critical questions from the population to the effects of the action: 5 January 1942, 3120, 8 January 1942, 3133, 12 January 1942, 3151f., 15 January 1942, 3163.
43. TB, 11 (quotation), 12, and 15 January 1942.
44. TB, 29 December 1941, on the special Ski campaign.
45. MK, 2 January 1942.
46. TB, 3 and 6 January 1942.
47. MK, 5 January 1942: "The minister has ordered that the propaganda for the Ski campaign should be stopped without this change of policy, which is extremely embarrassing, being allowed to become apparent."
48. BAB, NS 18/463, Aktenvermerk des Gauwirtschaftsberaters des Gaus Tirol, 16 February 1942.
49. See correspondence in BAB, NS 18/462 and 463.
50. TB, 8 January 1942.
51. TB, 20 January 1942.
52. "Wandlung der Seelen," 25 January 1942, and in *Herz,* 187–94; TB, 17 January 1942, also TB, 25 January: "My ideal too would be a tougher new policy." MK, 12 January 1942: "The minister said it was necessary in future to take a rather tougher line toward the nation."
53. TB, 31 January 1942.
54. TB, 29–31 January 1942.

55. TB, 29 January 1942.

56. TB, 25 September 1941.

57. TB, 15 October 1941, and 16 October 1941.

58. See the regular reports by Hinkel in BAB, R 55/1254, from 20 October 1941 onward.

59. The programming was "now entirely geared to light entertainment and boosting morale," which the public "are all in favor of." TB, 7 November 1942, also 4 and 14 November 1942.

60. TB, 14 January, 1, 2, and 3 February; also 4 February 1942, the radio was not popular enough; 8 and 9 February 1942: substantially reduces Glasmeier's authority. A few months later Goebbels received Glasmeier and warned him to keep out of radio programming (TB, 27 June, and 31 July 1942 concerning a further conversation).

61. TB, numerous entries between 13 and 22 February 1942.

62. On 19 February he gave a two-hour speech to those responsible for devising the programs (BAB, R 55/695, TB, 20 February 1942). During the following weeks he gave instructions such as that "in the sphere of serious music no works should be performed that have not already proved themselves" or that the program "The German People's Concert" should be made lighter by introducing well-known soloists, popular overtures, and so forth, or that "old classical religious music (organ music by Bach, Handel, etc.) should once again be" broadcast on Sunday mornings: BAB, R 55/695, 25 March 1942, 2 April 1942, 6 May 1942 and 696 (from June 1942).

63. MK, 9 March 1942; see also 2 March 1942.

64. TB, 13 February 1942.

65. "Der treue Helfer," also in *Herz,* 229ff.; the *VB* (B) of 1 March announced the reform in the report about a speech to the "film creators" (editorial); on the preparation of his article, see TB, 20 February; on the positive effects of the announced reform, see 3, 6, 11, and 12 March.

66. TB, 3 March 1942; on the positive effects of the announced reform, see also 6, 11, and 12 March 1942.

67. During the first weeks of the war against the Soviet Union Goebbels had still been looking at a number "of new great national film projects that are about to go into production" and the anti-Soviet films that had been withdrawn were once again allowed to be shown. TB, 15, 29, and 31 July 1941.

68. TB, 7 September 1941, referring to the withdrawal of the film "Leichte Muse"; as also on 11 September 1941, when he saw the film "Das andere Ich." See Moeller, *Filmminister,* 260ff.

69. TB, 7 August 1941, and 17 November 1941.

70. TB, 28 September 1941. Heß had already criticized it: 18 February 1941.

71. TB, 30 December 1941.

72. TB, 27 February 1942, and 13 February 1942.

73. TB, 8 August 1941.

74. TB, 9 January 1942.

75. Decree of 28 February 1928, published in Albrecht, *Filmpolitik,* 529ff. On its drafting, see TB, 3, 8, 12, and 27 February 1942.

76. Albrecht, *Filmpolitik,* 484ff., quotation 495. See TB, 1 March 1942.

77. TB, 16 September 1942.

78. TB, 13 January ("Zwei in einer großen Stadt"), 31 March ("Nacht in Venedig"), 2 May 1942 ("Die Kleine Residenz"), 1 July 1942 ("Weiße Wäsche"), 13 September 1942 ("Ein Zug fährt ab"), 9 October 1942 ("Wir machen Musik"), 30 November 1942 ("Wen die Götter lieben").

79. TB, 3 March 1942.

80. MK, 1 March 1942. A week later he was discussing in similar detail the problem of how one could best control Jewish passengers who possessed the new special ID card, MK, 9 March 1942.

81. TB, 7 March 1942. Literature on the Wannsee Conference: Gerlach, "Die Wannsee-Konferenz"; Longerich, *Die Wannsee-Konferenz vom 20. Januar 1942*; Roseman, *Die Wannsee-Konferenz*.

82. Longerich, *Politik der Vernichtung,* 450ff., 504ff.

83. TB, 27 March 1942. Only a week before he had spoken to Hitler about the "Jewish question" and discovered that the Jews "must be gotten out of Europe, if necessary by using the most brutal means" (TB, 20 March 1942).

84. TB, 27 April 1942.

85. Scheffler, "Der Brandanschlag im Berliner Lustgarten im Mai 1942 und seine Folgen," 111. It is not clear, however, whether, as Goebbels claimed, he was responsible for these measures (TB, 25 May) or whether Hitler himself gave the order directly to Himmler or Heydrich (ibid., p. 106).

86. TB, 24 May 1942; the attack is already referred to in the entry of 19 May, and the exhibition on 13 May 1942. See Scheffler, "Brandanschlag." Apart from the Baum group the group around Joachim Franke and Werner Steinbrink were also involved in the attack. Scheer, *Im Schatten der Sterne.*

87. TB, 13 January 1942.

88. TB, 18 August, 28 October, 8 November; also 4 and 25 December 1942.

89. That was to be done through a letter from the Party Chancellery and, as far as the Reich authorities were concerned, through a letter from Reich Minister Lammers: TB, 13 January 1942, and MK, 12 January 1942.

90. MK, 22 January 1942.

91. TB, 19 January 1942.

92. TB, 11 and 16 February 1942.

93. TB, 11 March 1942.

94. TB, 23 January 1942, with a detailed plan. On the preparations for the action, see 24 and 28 January 1942. Material on the preparations for the action in BAB, R 43 II/371b: According to this, inter-ministerial meetings on the matter took place in the Propaganda Ministry on 9, 22, and 26 January 1942.

95. Verordnung zur Ergänzung der Kriegswirtschaftsordnung vom 25. März 1942, *RGBl.* 1942 I, 147ff.; TB, 19 March 1942. The first draft of a "war decree" against price rigging and barter prepared by the Economics Ministry had by contrast satisfied his expectations (8 February 1942).

96. *"Führer-Erlasse" 1939–1945,* Moll (ed.), no. 151, decree of 21 March. On the drafting and initial responses, see TB, 27 and 28 March 1942. The decree had already been approved by Hitler on 15 February 1942 (R 43 II/371b, Hadamovsky to Lammers, 16 February 1942).

97. MK, 27 March 1942.

98. TB, 31 March 1942; BAK, ZSg 102/37, 30 March 1942.

99. MK, 14 February 1942; see also 26 March 1942: "If we push too hard here it may do more harm than good."

100. Also published in *Herz,* 257–64. On the background, see TB, 22, 23, 24 (quotation), and 27 March 1942; on the positive response to his article (which "came as a real relief"), see TB, 1 and 2 April 1942.

101. TB, 30 and 31 March 1942.

102. TB, 20 March 1942; for his own observations during a train journey, see 19 March 1942.

103. TB, 23 March 1942. *VB* (B), 23 March 1942, "Wer zum Vergnügen reist, wird bestraft." This warning was passed on by the press: BAK, ZSg 102/37, 22 March 1942: "DNB will carry a piece on the topic of 'using the railways.' It will make the point very clearly. [. . .] Put it only on the inside pages but make it clearly visible."

104. TB, 24, 25, and 27 March 1942.

105. TB, 16 and 24 April 1942. His anger was directed at Dorpmüller, the head of the Reich railways. On his dispute with Dorpmüller, see also TB, 27 April 1942.

106. TB, 28 March 1942, on the appointment that was already scheduled for 13 March and which followed in the form of a Führer decree concerning a General Plenipotentiary for labor deployment of 21 March 1942, *RGBl.* 1942 I, 179.

107. TB, 1 April 1942.

108. TB, 27 April 1942.

109. TB, 9 April 1942.

110. TB, 11 April 1942.

111. TB, 30 March 1942; on the bombing of Lübeck, see Gröhler, *Bombenkrieg gegen Deutschland,* 36ff.

112. TB, 30 March 1942, and 31 March to 4 April 1942.

113. TB, 29 August 1942; also 3, 10, and 24 July, 22 and 28 August, 11 September, 14 October 1942; Bajohr, *Parvenüs und Profiteure,* 166ff.

114. TB, 21, 22, 23, 24, and 26 March, 2 April 1942. On 6 April the meat ration was reduced from 1600 to 1200 grams. Schmitz, *Die Bewirtschaftung der Nahrungsmittel und Verbrauchsgüter 1939–1950,* 466 (table).

115. TB, 13, 16, 18, 19, 23, 25, and 26 April 1942.

116. TB, 25 April 1942.

117. TB, 13 April 1942.

118. *VB* (B), 20 April 1942, "In Dankbarkeit und Treue."

119. *Domarus II,* 1865ff.

120. TB, 20 March 1942. On the background, see Kershaw, *Hitler. 1936–1945,* 669ff.

121. *RGBl.* 1942 I, 247.

122. TB, 27 and 28 April 1942. This is clearly noticeable in the *Meldungen aus dem Reich* of 27 and 30 April, 3673f., 3685f.

123. BAK, ZSg 102/37, 26 April 1942 (E), 1.

124. TB, 29 and 30 April 1942. On the impact of the Hitler speech, above all on lawyers, see 6, 8, and 13 May 1942. On the effects, see also Kershaw, *Der Hitler-Mythos,* 224ff.

125. TB, 29 April 1942. On the continuing irritation among the population caused by the speech, see *Meldungen aus dem Reich,* 4 May 1942, 3696, 7 May 1942, 3708.

126. Gröhler, *Bombenkrieg,* 48ff.; TB, 25 and 26 April 1942.

127. TB, 30 April, 1 and 4 May 1942; on Rostock, see 2 and 29 April 1942.

128. TB, 26–29 April 1942. On these attacks, see Collier, *Defence,* 303ff., 514f. (table).

129. TB, 1 May 1942, and 2 May 1942.

130. *BW,* 30 April 1942, and TB, 3 May 1942.

131. BAB, R 43 II/667.

132. Concern was expressed by among others Göring, Speer, Frick and Lammers: Letter from Frick to Lammers, 16 May 1942; Frick to Goebbels, 16 May 1942 (R 43 II/667); see also TB, 9 May 1942.

133. BAK, NL 1118/138, 17 April 1943; BAB, NS 18/422, Rundschreiben des Staatssekretärs, 18 February 1943.

134. TB, 6 October 1940.

135. *BK,* 16 April 1940, 5.

136. MK, 27 February 1942; TB, 28 February 1942.

137. For example his teachers Voß, Beines, and others (TB, 18 and 19 November 1942).

138. TB, 6 November 1942, 11 January, 24 February, 13 August 1943.

139. TB, 10 June 1943.

140. On the meeting with his mother, see TB, 23 February 1940, 12 January 1942, 19 April 1943.

141. TB, 19 April, 15 June 1940, 11 April, 15 June 1943.

142. TB, 19 April 1941.

143. TB, 13 January 1941, 26 October, 5 November, and 10 December 1942, 2 and 3 January; also 22 February 1943, 19 and 23 April 1944.

144. TB, 10 January 1940, 13 April 1943, 27 and 28 September 1944.

145. TB, 10 and 11 February 1942.

146. TB, 20 and 30 April, 6–8, 17, and 23 May.

147. TB, 29 November 1942.

148. TB, 1, 2, 3, and 8 April 1943.

149. TB, 16 December 1939, 6 and 7 October 1940, 14 November 1941, 12 and 16 October 1942, 27 September 1943, 25 November 1944.

150. TB, 23 October 1940.

151. BAK, ZSg 158/40, Erich Bandekow: on cases of tax corruption involving Reich ministers, Reich Party leaders etc. 1948.

152. TB, 28 October 1943.

153. See, in particular, TB, 20 January, 20 March, 26 April, 24 May, 9 and 24 June, 20 August, 29 September, 1 October 1942, 20 and 21 March, 7 and 11 May, 25 June, 9, 21, and 23 August, 23 September 1943, 6 and 22 June, 1 December 1944.

24. "WE CAN SEE IN OUR MIND'S EYE A HAPPY PEOPLE"

1. Wegner, "Der Krieg gegen die Sowjetunion 1942/43," 841ff.; VB (B), 20 May 1943.

2. TB, 25 May 1942.

3. Wehrmachtberichte, vol. 2, 23 May 1942.

4. TB, 26 May 1942.

5. See TB, 20, 21, and 30 May; also 6 June 1942.

6. Das Reich, 31 May 1941. See TB, 21 May 1942: "I make that clear in a leader with the title 'What's it all for?' in which for the first time I set out our war aims in general terms for the German people."

7. TB, 28 May 1942.

8. TB, 2 June 1942; On Heydrich's state of health, see 29 and 31 May, also 1 June 1942. On Heydrich's assassination, see Brandes, Tschechen, 251ff.; Deschner, Reinhard Heydrich, 273ff.; Haasis, Tod in Prag; Calic, Reinhard Heydrich, 476ff.

9. TB, 2 June 1942, also 4 June 1942.

10. TB, 30 May 1942.

11. TB, 30 May 1942.

12. TB, 5 June 1942.

13. VB (N), 10 June 1942, "Der Führer am Sarge Heydrichs."

14. TB, 10 June 1942.

15. Brandes, Tschechen, vol. 1, 262ff.

16. TB, 12 June 1942; BAK, ZSg 102/38, 11 June 1942 (M), TP 2: "The punitive measures being taken in the Protectorate against those supporting the murderers of

Heydrich are not to be referred to in the Reich press." Unfortunately they had already been announced on the radio.

17. TB, 12 June 1942, and 14 June 1942.

18. BAK, ZSg 102/38, 11 June (M) TP 2. On further German retaliatory measures, see TB, 20, 21, 22, 23, 25, and 26 June.

19. Gottwaldt and Schulle, *Die "Judendeportationen" aus dem Deutschen Reich 1941–1945*, 213.

20. Longerich, *Heinrich Himmler,* 587ff.

21. Longerich, *Davon,* 201ff.; *Das Reich,* 14 June 1942, "Der Luft- und Nervenkrieg."

22. TB, 1 June 1942.

23. BAK, ZSg 102/38 (E), 12.

24. TB, 1–4 June 1943; *Wehrmachtberichte,* 31 May 1942; for press reports, see *VB* (B), 1 June 1942, "44 Flugzeuge kostete der Terrorangriff auf Köln," 1; 2 June 1942, "Reuter zum Angriff auf Canterbury: 'Ein Vergeltungsschlag von besonderer Wildheit'" (headline) and 3 June 1942, "Teuer bezahlter Terrorangriff" (headline).

25. TB, 2 June 1942; *BW,* 1 June 1942.

26. Gröhler, *Bombenkrieg,* 60ff.

27. *Das Reich,* 14 June 1942; see also TB, 3 June 1942.

28. See the overview in Gröhler, *Bombenkrieg,* 76f.

29. TB, 9 and 13 June 1942; also 11, 17, 20, 21, 27, and 29 June 1942. See also *Meldungen aus dem Reich,* 4 June 1942, 3787ff., 11 June 1942, 3802ff., 15 June 1942, 3823f., 18 June 1942, 3836ff., 22 June 1942, 3852, 25 June 1942, 3872f. The last two reports reflect the relaxation in the mood as a result of positive reports from North Africa.

30. TB, 30 May, 6, 18, 26, and 27 June, 2, 10, 11, 18, 23, and 31 July 1942.

31. TB, 29 May 1942 (on the conversation with Backe), 28 May, 4, 5, and 6 June (on the potato situation in Berlin), 22 June (conversation with Backe), 24 June (on the conversation with Hitler) and 25, 27 also 28 June, 4, 8, and 26 July, 1 August 1942.

32. Stumpf, "Krieg," 648ff.

33. Wegner, "Krieg," 868ff.

34. Wegner, "Krieg," 861ff., 927ff. (Caucasus operations), 962ff. (advance on Stalingrad).

35. TB, 7 July 1942; the minutes of the MK show that Goebbels partially modified the instruction to play down the situation in the East, which was still operative on 17 and 19 September; BAK, ZSg 102/39, 8 July (M), TP 1, (E), TP 1; 13 July (M), TP 1; 20 July (M), TP 1; see the *VB* (B) and the *DAZ,* which on 1 and 3 July and 1 July, respectively, were publishing reports of successes on the North African front, but during the rest of the month were full of headlines about the war in the East.

36. TB, 7 July 1942, also 8 and 9 July 1942.

37. MK, 9 July 1942; see also TB, 10 July 1942.

38. *Das Reich,* 19 July 1942; TB, 10 July 1942.

39. TB, 28 July 1942.

40. TB, 15 July 1942.

41. Examples: TB, 2, 3, and 4 August, also 27 October (Düsseldorf) 1942; 3, 4, and 7 June, 15, 20, 21, 23, 27, 28, 31 July, 2, 3, and 8 August, 8 and 18 September 1942 (Duisburg); 3 and 7 June, 25 and 30 July, 8 August, 20 October 1942 (Bremen); 15 October 1942 (Hamburg).

42. TB, 7 August 1942.

43. TB, 8 August 1942.

44. *Das Reich,* 16 August 1942; *Westdeutscher Beobachter,* 8 August 1942 (M), "Es gibt nur eines: Sieg um jeden Preis!" (headline).

45. The first reference to the planned conversion is in Goebbels's diaries of February 1940. At that time Gauleiter Florian (whom he had met shortly before while visiting Rheydt, TB, 26 January 1940) visited him and discussed with him and his architects, Fahrenkamp and Gebauer, the conversion of the Rheydt palace into a guest house, which in future would be at his disposal on his visits to his home town. It was evidently Florian who had taken the initiative in providing this accommodation (TB, 17 February 1940). The palace was to be provided with a large number of costly art works and a library. R 55/766. Wittmann, "Das 'Gästehaus.'"

46. TB, 9 August 1942.

47. TB, 11 August 1942.

48. TB, 12 August 1942.

49. TB, 20 August 1942.

50. TB, 23, 25, and 28 June 1942.

51. PAA, HA Schmidt 12 Amt Ausl. Abwehr to Propaganda Ministry, 6 May 1942 (copy); Longerich, *Propagandisten,* 293ff.

52. Already in TB, 3 and 28 May, 2 June, 9 and 11 July 1942. See also *BW,* 16 July 1942, where he advocated pre-censorship; see also PAA, HA Schmidt 12, Krümmer report on the ministerial briefing of 16 July 1942.

53. TB, 16 July 1942; also 18 and 24 July 1942. On 22 July the head of the Foreign Press Department, Brauweiler, had sent the Foreign Ministry a set of working directives for correspondents, which amounted to the introduction of pre-censorship. (The document has not survived, but there is a response to it from Schmidt, HA Schmidt 12, 30 July 1942.) The press department of the Foreign Ministry responded with a lengthy memorandum: HA Schmidt 12, Denkschrift zur Frage der Einführung einer Vorzensur für Auslandskorrespondenten, 31 June 1942. In fact the Foreign Ministry feared that by introducing pre-censorship the Propaganda Ministry would secure control of the foreign correspondents (ibid., Notiz Schmidts für Ribbentrop, 14 September 1942; see also TB, 5 August 1942).

54. PAA, HA Schmidt 12, Bekanntmachung an die Auslandspresse über die Verstärkung der Sicherungen über den Telefon- und Telegrammverkehr, 7 September 1942.

55. MK, 2 July 1942.

56. TB, 17 July 1942; and 23 July, also 14 and 20 August 1942; see Longerich, *Propagandisten,* 114.

57. TB, 20 and 22 August 1942.

58. TB, 23 and 24 August 1942, on the drafting, see 25 August 1942. Also 27 August (with Amann concerning the dispute), 28 August (with Schaub), and 29 August 1942 (unable to receive Dietrich because of a prior engagement).

59. TB, 29 August, 3, 9, 10, 16, and, in particular, 17 September 1942 (on final conversation with Dietrich); R 55/969, Vereinbarung zur Durchführung der Verfügung des Führers zur Sicherung der Zusammenarbeit zwischen Reichspropagandaminister und Reichspressechef of 23 August 1942, 15 October 1942.

60. Bonacker, *Goebbels' Mann beim Radio,* 144.

61. On this continuing dispute, see TB, 22 and 28 April 1941, and BAB, R 55/1254, Fritzsche to Dietrich, 21 August 1944, from which it is clear that Dietrich was still claiming responsibility for the "Wireless Service."

62. MK, 27 September 1942; *BW,* 27 September 1942.

63. TB, 28 September 1942. The lengthy passage in his diary largely corresponds to the minutes of the MK from the previous day.

64. Bonacker, *Goebbels' Mann beim Radio*, 153.

65. BAB, R 55/20617, Nachrichtenblatt no. 27/42: TB, 5 and 6 October, also 4 November 1942; Bonacker, *Goebbels' Mann beim Radio*, 150f.

66. TB, 24 February 1942.

67. TB, 25April 1942.

68. TB, 10 May 1942.

69. TB, 22 May 1942; this occurred during the meeting with Rosenberg, Hitler, and Bormann on 8 May 1942, to which Goebbels's entry of 10 May 1942 presumably refers. 1520-PS, *IMT 27,* 286ff.

70. TB, 11 May 1942.

71. TB, 11 May 1942.

72. Dallin, *Deutsche Herrschaft in Rußland 1941–1945,* 492ff., and Römer, *Der Kommissarbefehl,* 535ff.

73. TB, 17 July (quotation) and 26 July 1942.

74. TB, 13 August, 3, 15, 20, 21, and 22 September 1942.

75. TB, 23 October 1942.

76. TB, 25 and 27 September 1942.

77. TB, 18 October, 1 December 1942. On 6 December Goebbels concluded that he must bring the matter to Hitler's attention once more, which he duly did in March 1943.

78. TB, 14 January 1943; he had already received a memorandum from the General Staff in which such ideas were discussed in December 1942 (TB, 10 December 1942).

79. TB, 23 January 1943; Goebbels produced the requisite document: TB, 31 January, 1, 5, 6, and 8 February 1943.

80. TB, 11 February 1943; see also TB, 9 and 16 February 1943. Rosenberg naturally objected to such criticism and demanded that Goebbels instruct his staff "to refrain from any further activity in the field of Eastern policy" (Rosenberg to Goebbels, NS 6/1435, 9 [?], February 1943). Complaints about the failure to issue the Eastern Proclamation also in the entries of 26 and 27 February, 5 May 1943; for further unsuccessful approaches to Hitler in this matter, see 9 and 21 March 1943.

81. TB, 27 September, 6 October 1940.

82. TB, 3 March 1942, and 26, 29, and 30 March, also already 20 December 1941.

83. "Im Herzen seines Volkes. Rede zum 150. Todestag Wolfgang Amadeus Mozarts," published in *Herz,* 105–10.

84. TB, 6 December 1942, and 5 December.

85. TB, 5 December 1941.

86. TB, 28 December 1941.

87. TB, 27 January 1942.

88. TB, 14–16 March 1942.

89. TB, 14 March 1942.

90. TB, 27 March, 23 May 1942.

91. TB, 23 and 30 May, also 1 and 23 June 1942.

92. TB, 1 June 1942.

93. TB, 30 May, 10 June 1942.

94. TB, 22 November 1941.

95. TB, 24 May 1942.

96. TB, 22 November 1941. On the preparations, see TB, 13 March, 14 August, 9 October 1941, also 20 August, 29 September 1942.

97. TB, 1 and 2 December 1941, 24 and 30 May, also 23 June 1942.

98. TB, 22 November 1941.

99. TB, 20 August 1942; also 17 November, 9 December 1942.

25. "DO YOU WANT TOTAL WAR?"

1. TB, 15 August 1942; also 16 and 19 August 1942: "The excessive optimism of the German people about the situation at the front, which is growing grotesquely day by day, is positively disastrous." See also 22 and 25 August 1942.

2. Wegner, "Krieg," 976ff.

3. TB, 15 September 1942. On the start of the battle, see 28 August, 5, 6, 7, and 14 September 1942.

4. MK, 15 September 1942.

5. Press directives BAK, ZSg 109/37, 15 September 1942, TP 1; *BW,* 369, gives as an example a special edition of the Stuttgart *NS-Kurier.*

6. TB, 16 September 1942; see also MK, 16 and 17 September 1942.

7. BAK, ZSg 102/40, 16 September 1942 (M), 1 TP 1.

8. MK, 19–21, also 23, 24, and 26 September 1942.

9. MK, 26 September 1942.

10. TB, 1 October 1942.

11. TB, 27 September 1942, and 1 October 1942 (reproaches about Dietrich's staff). For his remarks to Colonel Martin, see TB, 1 October 1942.

12. TB, 4 October 1942.

13. TB, 29 September 1942; *Meldungen aus dem Reich,* 5 October 1942, 4279; Kershaw, *Der Hitler-Mythos,* 230.

14. TB, 2 October 1942; and 4 October 1942, on a meeting with Hitler in which the latter once again reiterated his goals.

15. TB, 2 October 1942.

16. *Das Reich,* 18 October 1942, "Der Segen der Erde"; TB, 8 October 1942.

17. TB, 27 and 29 September 1942 (about a conversation with Luftwaffe officers) and 30 September 1942 (about conversations with Hewel und Schaub).

18. TB, 12 October 1942.

19. TB, 8, 11, 15, 16, and 23 October 1942. See *Meldungen aus dem Reich,* 8 October 1942, 4291f., 12 October 1942, 4309ff., 15 October 1942, 4329ff.; reflecting on the seriousness of the situation on the Eastern Front, ibid., 19 October 1942, p. 4342f.

20. TB, 26 October 1942.

21. *Das Reich,* 1 November; see also TB, 23 October 1942.

22. TB, 15 and 21 October 1942.

23. TB, 30 October 1942.

24. TB, 6 October 1942, also 8 and 20 October 1942.

25. Wegner, "Krieg," 994ff. The deteriorating situation is clearly reflected in the diary entries between 21 and 24 October.

26. Stumpf, "Die alliierte Landung in Nordwestafrika," 702ff.; TB, 25 October 1942, also 26 and 27 October 1942.

27. Stumpf, "Landung," p. 704; TB, 2–4 November 1942.

28. *Das Reich,* 30 January 1942, "Der 30. Januar"; examples from the year 1941: TB, 1 and 11 January, 9 and 16 July 1941; also TB, 13 January 1942 (in a speech to Berlin Party functionaries); 30 May 1942 (to Hitler).

29. *Das Reich,* 8 November 1942, "Vor die Probe gestellt"; see also TB, 26 October 1942.

30. Thus, for example, in his article "Der Totale Krieg" (*Das Reich*, 17 January 1943), in his speech on the tenth anniversary of the "seizure of power" on 30 January 1943, published in Goebbels, *Der steile Aufstieg. Reden und Aufsätze aus den Jahren 1942/43*, 138–50, and in his article "Damals und heute," *Das Reich*, 7 March 1943.

31. TB, 23 January, 10 September, 27 October 1943 (with Hitler).

32. TB, 8 November 1942; Stumpf, "Landung," 710ff.

33. TB, 9 November 1942. "The Führer is not yet quite clear about what he should do."

34. This offer, which Abetz was supposed to submit to the French government on Hitler's behalf, is published in *ADAP* E IV, no. 151, Weizsäcker to Ribbentrop, 8 November 1942.

35. TB, 9 November 1942; text of the speech in *Domarus II*, 1933ff.

36. TB, 10 and 11 November 1942.

37. Stumpf, "Landung," 743ff.; TB, 11, 12, and 13 November 1942.

38. Stumpf, "Landung," 721.

39. TB, 15 November 1942.

40. Stumpf, "Landung," 725ff.; TB, 14–19 November 1942.

41. TB, 16 November 1942.

42. *Westdeutscher Beobachter*, 18 November 1942 (E), "Der Feind zerbricht an unserer Härte!"

43. TB, 18 and 19 November 1942.

44. TB, 26 November 1942, and 27 November. Eighteen Gauleiters had already been appointed Reich Defense Commissioners on 1 September 1939; on 16 November this arrangement was extended by declaring all the Party Gaus to be Reich defense districts. Up until then the Brandenburg Gauleiter, Sturz, had been responsible for the Defense District III (Berlin).

45. TB, 28 November 1942.

46. TB, 24 October, 30 November 1942.

47. TB, 24 November 1942.

48. Longerich, *Davon*, 240ff., 255ff.

49. MK, 8 December 1942; the press was informed: BAK, ZSg 102/41; MK, 9 December 1942 (betr. Kundgebungen schwedischer Studenten gegen die deutsche Judenverfolgung). See the ministerial briefings of 12, 14, and 16 December and also the excerpts from the minutes published in *Wollt Ihr den totalen Krieg?*

50. MK, 12 December 1942; see TB, 13 and 14 December 1942.

51. MK, 14 December 1942, also 16 December; see also TB, 17 and 18 September 1942.

52. BAK, ZSg 102/41, 17 December 1942 (daily slogan); ibid., 18 December 1942 (daily slogan).

53. Details in Longerich, *Davon*, 260.

54. MK, 18 December 1942.

55. MK, 19 and 29 December 1942; BAK, ZSg 109/40, 17 and 19 December 1942; Longerich, *Davon*, pp 260f.

56. TB, 23 November 1942.

57. Wegner, "Krieg," 1026ff.

58. E.g. TB, 27 November, 4 and 18 December 1942.

59. TB, 22 and 23 December 1942.

60. TB, 18 and 23 December 1942.

61. *Das Reich*, 27 December 1942, "Die Vollendeten"; TB, 16 December 1942.

62. TB, 29 December 1942.

63. He spoke to Ley about this on 28 November and 17 December: TB, 29 November, 18 December 1942.
64. TB, 5 January 1943.
65. TB, 3 January 1943; BAB, R 43 II/655; see Herbst, *Der Totale Krieg und die Ordnung der Wirtschaft*, 199ff.
66. TB, 5 January 1943, with Unruh and with Lammers.
67. *BW*, 4, 5, and 6 January 1943.
68. TB, 5, 7, and 8 January 1943.
69. BAB, R 43 II/655 (invitation); on this and the following measures, see also Rebentisch, *Führerstaat und Verwaltung im Zweiten Weltkrieg*, 474ff.; Herbst, *Der Totale Krieg*, 199ff.; Kroener, "'Menschenbewirtschaftung,'" 847ff.; Reuth, *Goebbels*, 511ff.
70. TB, 10 and 13 January 1943 concerning conversations with Bormann and Speer; the diaries during these days are full of further statements by Goebbels on the need for "total war."
71. On the background to the article, see TB, 3 January 1943. See also "Die Heimat im Kriege," 3 January 1943, also in *Zeit ohne Beispiel*, 113–20, in which he had written generally in positive terms about the home front's performance.
72. *Das Reich*, 24 January 1943; TB, 13 January 1943.
73. Moll, "*Führer-Erlasse*," doc. 222. Registration for conscription was envisaged for men from 17 to 65, for women from 17 to 50; TB, 15 January 1943.
74. TB, 5 January (after a conversation with Lammers) and 15 January 1943.
75. TB, 8 January 1943; see also 17 January 1943.
76. TB, 21 January 1943.
77. On the state of morale, see TB, 3, 4, 8, 9, 13 January 1943. This still relatively stable state of morale is also reflected in *Meldungen aus dem Reich*, 4 January 1943, 4617f.; the reports for 7 January 1943, 4628ff., 11 January 1943, 4650ff., 14 January 1943, 4670ff. reveal an increasing sense of disorientation. On the deterioration in morale, see TB, 15 and 16 January 1943.
78. TB, 17 January 1943. On the deterioration in morale, see 20 and 24 January 1943.
79. TB, 24 January, also 25 and 31 January 1943.
80. TB, 23 January 1943.
81. BAK, ZSg 109/40, VI, 23 January 1943.
82. TB, 24 January 1943.
83. TB, 26 January 1943.
84. TB, 2 and 5 February 1943.
85. TB, 27 January 1943.
86. *RGBl.* 1943 I, 67f.
87. TB, 29 January 1943. At this meeting the final version of the Decree to Release Labor for Deployment in Work Important for the War Effort (*RGBl.* 1943 I, 75f.) was implemented by three edicts of 30 January (R 43 II/662). The final report of the Committee of Three of summer 1944 estimated that 150,000 workers had been released by the closure program (R 3II/664a); Herbst, *Der totale Krieg*, 212ff.
88. TB, 28 January 1943.
89. 7 February 1943, also published in *Aufstieg*, 159–66. Similar views are expressed in the article "Der Blick nach vorne," which was published on 31 January (also published in *Aufstieg*, 151–58).
90. TB, 19, 21, and 23 January 1943.
91. TB, 30 January 1943 on its drafting.
92. *VB* (N), 31 January, "Die Proklamation des Führers am 30. Januar 1943: Deutschlands Antwort: Kampf und Sieg!" (headline). The text of the Goebbels speech was

published on the following day: "Reichsminister Dr. Goebbels im Berliner Sport-palast: 'Wilde Entschlossenheit erhebt unsere Herzen.'"

93. TB, 31 January 1943.

94. TB, 4 February 1943, and 5 February.

95. TB, 5 February 1943. The assessment of the impact of the speech in the *Meldungen aus dem Reich* of 1 Februay 1943, 4732f., is by contrast much less euphoric.

96. *VB* (N), 23–29 January 1943; TB, 25 January 1943: "The situation in Stalingrad is developing more and more into a major national tragedy." See also 26 and 27 January 1943.

97. TB, 31 January/1 February 1943.

98. TB, 3 February 1943.

99. TB, 3 February 1943.

100. TB, 4 February 1943; BAK, ZSg 109, 4 Februar 1943, TP 1. This is confirmed by the *Meldungen aus dem Reich* of 4 February, 4750ff.

101. *Das Reich*, 14 February 1943, "Unser Wille und Weg"; TB, 4 February 1943.

102. TB, 6 February 1943, and 7 February 1943.

103. 1739-PS, published in *IMT* 27, 584ff.

104. TB, 8 February 1943.

105. TB, 13 February 1943.

106. BAB, R 43 II/655, Vermerke Lammers, 6 March, 10 May 1943.

107. TB, 12 February 1943. The *Meldungen aus dem Reich* do not, in any case, confirm this impression. The report of 11 February 1943 shows that the demand for an increase in the war effort was certainly combined with criticism of the regime's policies (4783); see also the reports of 15 February 1943, 4799ff., and 18 February 1943, 4821ff., which give no indication of vigorous calls for "total war."

108. TB, 15 February 1943.

109. TB, 18 February 1943. *Meldungen aus dem Reich*, 11 February 1943, 4783, 15 February 1943, 4799ff., 18 February 1943, 4821ff.

110. TB, 15 February 1943, also 16 and 18 February 1943. On the rally in the Sportpa-last, see Fetscher, *Joseph Goebbels im Berliner Sportpalast 1943*; Kegel, "*Wollt Ihr den totalen Krieg*"; Bohse, *Inszenierte Kriegsbegeisterung und ohnmächtiger Frie-denswille*; Boelcke, "Goebbels und die Kundgebung im Berliner Sportpalast vom 18. Februar 1943"; Moltmann, "Goebbels' Rede zum totalen Krieg am 18. Februar 1943."

111. BAK, ZSg 109/41, VI vom 18. Februar 1943, II. Erläuterungen zur TP.

112. BAK, ZSg 102/42, 18 Februar (M), 10. On the day before the speech he wrote an editorial for *Das Reich*, in which, under the title "Die Krise Europas," he referred to the "danger from Bolshevism" in an equally drastic fashion and attacked "in-ternational Jewry" as the "spiritus rector for the whole of the spiritual and intel-lectual confusion, the ferment of decomposition affecting states and nations": 28 February 1943, in *Aufstieg*, 205–12; TB, 18 February 1943.

113. Text of the speech in *VB* (N), 20 February 1943, also published in Heiber (ed.), *Goebbels Reden*, no. 17.

114. This is noted in particular by Bohse, *Kriegsbegeisterung*, 130ff.

115. In the months before he had still been emphasizing in his editorials that this war was not about "thrones and altars" and that the era of religious wars had finally been left behind. *Das Reich*, 26 August 1942, "Vom Sinn des Krieges," and 18 October 1942, "Der Segen der Erde." See Hockerts, "Kreuzzugsrhetorik," 234ff.

116. TB, 19 February 1943.

117. TB, 14 February, 23 February to 21 March 1943.

118. TB, 20 February 1943, on the reaction at home and abroad.

119. TB, 21 February 1943.

120. TB, 24 February 1943. See also 9 March 1943, according to which Hitler had described the speech as "a psychological and propagandistic masterpiece."

121. TB, 21 February 1943. The *Meldungen aus dem Reich* of 18 February do not, however, comment on his speech, which Goebbels himself noted on the following day (TB, 22 February 1943).

122. TB, 12 December 1942: "Moreover, I have the impression that there is rather too much criticism in the SD reports. Recently my opinion of the SD reporting has not been so positive as hitherto. I shall urge the gentlemen responsible to report in a more objective and factual manner."

123. TB, 22 February 1943.

124. TB, 25 February, also 26 and 27 February.

125. *Meldungen aus dem Reich,* 22 February 1943, 4831.

126. BAB, R 55/603, 27 February 1943, already quoted in Steinert, *Hitlers Krieg und die Deutschen,* 43.

127. TB, 23 February 1943.

128. *VB* (B), 25 February 1943, "Unser Glaube und Fanatismus stärker denn je! Proklamation des Führers zur Gründungsfeier der Partei in München" (headline).

129. TB, 27 February 1943.

130. TB, 11 and 28 February, 17 March 1943; BAB, R 43 II/654a, minutes of the meeting of 10 February 1943 and 16 March 1943. On the discussions of the committee, see Rebentisch, *Führerstaat,* 481ff.

131. BAB, R 43 II/654a, minutes of the meeting of 16 March; TB, 17 March 1943. The decree met with general skepticism from the ministries and in the end was not issued (correspondence on this in R 43II/658).

132. TB, 17 March 1943; BAB, R 43 II/654a, minutes of the meeting of 17 March 1943; Kriegsmaßnahmenverordnung of 12 May 1943, *RGBl.* 1943 I, 290f.

133. See TB, 17 March 1943, compared with the minutes of the meeting of 16 March 1943.

134. TB, 5, 9, 22 March (quotation); BAB, R 43 II/ 658a Führervorlage Goebbels A II 218 of 18 February 1943; here too the note by Lammers on Hitler's decision of 4 March and a letter from Lammers to the responsible Reich ministers re: horseracing of 24 March; see Rebentisch, *Führerstaat,* 490ff.; R 43II/654a, minutes of the meeting of 17 March, where a proposal by Goebbels concerned with this issue was agreed.

135. TB, 11 February 1943.

136. TB, 27 February 1943.

137. TB, 27 February, 1 and 2 March 1943.

138. TB, 9 March 1943.

139. TB, 19 March 1943. On 12 March Goebbels informed Speer, Funk, and Ley about his conversation with Göring (TB, 13 March 1943).

140. TB, 17 March, also 12, 13, 20, 21, and 27 March 1943.

141. TB, 6 March 1943.

142. *Das Reich,* 28 March 1943, "Vom Unrecht im Kriege," also in *Aufstieg,* 228–36.

143. *Das Reich,* 4 April 1943, "Ein offenes Wort zum totalen Krieg," also in *Aufstieg,* 237–42; TB, 23 March, also in 6 March 1943.

144. TB, 18 February 1943.

145. TB, 11 March 1943.

146. This follows the convincing arguments in Gruner, *Widerstand in der Rosenstraße,* 85ff.

147. TB, 9 March 1943.
148. TB, 21 March 1943.
149. TB, 18 April 1943.
150. Minutes of the ministerial briefing, BAK, NL 1118/138, 1 April 1943. However, he was not prepared to accept the suggestion that propaganda should refer publicly to the number of apartments.
151. TB, 18 July, 9 October 1943, 16 March 1944.
152. TB, 7 January 1943; Blank, "Kriegsalltag und Luftkrieg an der 'Heimatfront,'" 391.
153. TB, 16 January 1943; *Tagesberichte,* 16 January 1943.
154. TB, 18 January 1943, and 19 January 1943.
155. Gröhler, *Bombenkrieg,* 121; *Tagesberichte,* 1 March 1943.
156. TB, 3 March 1943; on the removal of the consequences, see 4, 5, 6, and 7 March 1943.
157. TB, 7 March 1944, and 10 March 1944.
158. *VB* (B), 7 March 1943, "Die Haltung der Berliner über jedes Lob erhaben."
159. TB, 22 March 1943.
160. According to the records seen by Goebbels two months later, between 22 June and the end of April 1942 the armed forces had suffered a total of 459,750 fatalities (TB, 14 May 1942).
161. TB, 26 March 1943; see also 27 March 1943.
162. TB, 28 March 1943, also 29 March 1943; Gröhler, *Bombenkrieg,* 121; *Tagesberichte,* 27 March 1943.
163. TB, 30 March 1943; *Tagesberichte,* 29 March 1943.
164. Gröhler, *Bombenkrieg,* 103.
165. TB, 13 March 1943. See also TB, 7, 14, 18, and 20 March, 4, 5, 6, and 7 April 1943.
166. Minutes in BAK, NL 1118/138, 10 April 1943.
167. BAK, ZSg 102/43, 11 April 1943 TP 1; TB, 11 April 1943.
168. TB, 3 June 1943: "The costs of film have been reduced from 1½ million to just over a million. It's clear, therefore, that the goal set by me for film in wartime can definitely be achieved if people have the will and are prepared to put in the necessary resources to do so."
169. Moeller, *Filmminister,* 280.
170. TB, 26 February 1943.
171. TB, 24 December 1943 ("Musik in Salzburg"), also 19 May 1944 ("Heimliche Bräute").
172. TB, 18 November ("Regimentsmusik"), 22 November, 10 December ("Am Abend nach der Oper") 1944.
173. TB, 1 December 1944; see also Moeller, *Filmminister,* 280f.
174. TB, 9 February 1943.
175. TB, 10 January, 27 December 1943 (quotation).
176. TB, 29 March 1943; Moeller, *Filmminister,* 283.
177. Moeller, *Filmminister,* 281ff.
178. TB, 5 March 1944, Moeller, *Filmminister,* 288.
179. TB, 9 May 1944.
180. TB, 10 June 1944; Moeller, *Filmminister,* 290.
181. TB, 25 May 1943, and 7 May 1943 (first entry on the Kolberg project); Moeller, *Filmminister,* 298ff., 309ff.
182. TB, 6 February, 21 April, 6, 12, 14 June, 14 and 15 July 1944.
183. TB, 1, 3, and 12 December 1944.
184. TB, 23 December 1944.

185. TB, 12 February 1944.
186. TB, 19 March 1945.
187. TB, 12 May, 1 June 1942.
188. On his taking on the appointment and his plans, see TB, 4 and 17 April, 6 and 17 May 1943; his further assessment of Liebeneiner's work fluctuated: 28 January 1944, 1 and 3 February, 10, 15, and 16 April, 23 December 1944; Moeller, *Filmminister*, 145ff.
189. TB, 3 August, 15 September 1942 also 27 and 28 February, 4 and 17 April, 12 and 23 May 2, 12, and 24 June 1943; criticism in retrospect also in 24 December 1943; Moeller, *Filmminister*, 127ff.
190. TB, 23 July 1943; also 29 July, 25 August 1943 (address to the heads of production of the film companies).
191. TB, 6 April 1944.
192. TB, 17 March, 18 April 1944; criticism: 16 June, 31 August 1944.
193. Moeller, *Filmminister*, 130ff.; TB, 27 September 1944.
194. TB, 22 May 1943. On light music on the radio during the second half of the war, see Koch, *Das Wunschkonzert im NS-Rundfunk*, 129ff.
195. Bonacker, *Goebbels' Mann beim Radio*, 198f.
196. TB, 5 April 1944.
197. Bonacker, *Goebbels' Mann beim Radio*, 197.
198. BAB, R 55/556, minutes of 30 August. The minutes document further interventions by Goebbels in the music programming, e.g. on 13 September, 11 October 1944.
199. R 55/556, Protokoll vom 24. Oktober 1944; as well as minutes of 31 January 1945.

26. "THE MASSES HAVE BECOME SOMEWHAT SKEPTICAL OR . . . ARE IN THE GRIP OF A SENSE OF HOPELESSNESS"

1. After 22 February 1943 the improvement in the military situation was reflected in the TB.
2. This was the general trend in TB, 7, 13, 16, 20, 23, 26, and 30 March; 3, 9, 18, and 23 April, 1 May 1943.
3. *Das Reich*, 11 April 1943, "Stimmung und Haltung."
4. TB, 2, 4, and 11 April 1943. The remark in the *Meldungen aus dem Reich* of 1 April 1943, according to which many citizens received information via "rumors, slogans, stories told by soldiers on leave, letters from the front and such like" rather than from official channels of information," must have particularly annoyed Goebbels.
5. TB, 17 April 1943.
6. Boberach, introduction to the edition of *Meldungen aus dem Reich*, 36. TB, 12 May 1943: "Himmler is intending to have the SD prepare a special report for me personally, which will basically contain what was hitherto provided for a larger group of recipients."
7. TB, 20 July 1943.
8. TB, 2, 3, 6, and 29 April 1943.
9. Gruchmann, "Korruption im Dritten Reich. Zur Lebensmittelversorgung der NS-Führerschaft."
10. BAB, R 22/5005, Helldorf report of 15 March 1943.

NOTES

11. TB, 22 March 1943; and 17 March 1943.
12. TB, 23 March 1943.
13. TB, 7 May 1943.
14. TB, 19 May 1943.
15. TB, 23 July 1943.
16. BAB, NS 6/344, Anordnung des Führers über die vorbildliche Haltung der Angehörigen an hervorragender Stelle stehender Persönlichkeiten of 28 May 1943; TB, 21 May 1943.
17. TB, 1, 2, 3, and 8 April 1943.
18. TB, 13 April 1943, on the continuing complaints, see also 14–19 April 1943.
19. TB, 13 April 1943, Funk report, 20 April 1943, Ley report.
20. TB, 6 and 7 May (quotation) 1943.
21. TB, 7 May 1943 on the basis of a meeting on the previous day.
22. TB, 6 May 1943, also 24 April 1943.
23. TB, 10 May 1943. See also 22 March 1943: "The Führer also thinks that, for example, we shouldn't ban women from dying their hair."
24. TB, 20 May 1943, and 11 May 1943.
25. TB, 12 May 1943.
26. TB, 27 and 31 March, also 3 April 1943; see also BAK, ZSg 109/42, TP of 1 and 2 April 1943.
27. On the Katyn massacre, see Kaiser, *Katyn.*
28. On the finding of the bodies, see also TB, 9 April 1943.
29. TB, 25 April 1943. On the fighting, see also 2 May 1943. Hermann Fegelein, commander of a Waffen-SS division, who visited him at the beginning of May, confirmed him in his radical views: "Fegelein reckons that he has solved the Jewish question in Warsaw in a very simple and rigorous way" (TB, 2 May 1943).
30. TB, 15, 16, 25, and 29 April 1943.
31. TB, 18 April 1943; on the alleged increase in anti-Semitism in Great Britain, see also 11, 19, and 22 April 1943.
32. The minutes of the ministerial briefings for April (BAK NL 1118/138) contain various warnings from Goebbels not to allow the issue of Katyn to fade away: 17–28 April 1943.
33. Details in Longerich, *Davon,* 268ff.
34. TB, 27, 28, and 29 April 1943.
35. BAB, NS 18/225, Vorlage Tießler, 30 April 1943.
36. BAK, ZSg 109/42, 30 April 1943. See also ibid., 28 April 1943, and 29 April 1943.
37. TB, 8 May 1943.
38. TB, 25 April, 4, 7, 10, and 22 May 1943.
39. Schreiber, "Das Ende des nordafrikanischen Feldzugs und der Krieg in Italien," 1108.
40. *VB* (N), 10 May 1942; *Der Angriff,* 13 May 1942.
41. TB, 9 May 1943.
42. *Das Reich,* "Mit souveräner Ruhe," 23 May 1943. For the official line on the defeat in Africa, see BAK, ZSg 109/42, 13 May 1943, II. Erläuterungen zur TP.
43. TB, 14 May 1943.
44. *DAZ,* 12 May 1943 (M), *VB* (N), 13 May 1943; see also TB, 7 and 10 May 1943.
45. TB, 21 February, 9 May 1943.
46. TB, 10 May 1943.
47. TB, 18 May 1943; on the press reporting, see BAK, ZSg 109/42, 10 May 1943, TP 2; *VB* (B), 11 May 1943, changes in the food rations; *DAZ,* 11 May 1943 (M), adjustment in the food rations.

48. TB, 28 May 1943, and 29 May 1941. *Meldungen aus dem Reich*, 24 May 1943, 5277ff., and 30 May, 5285ff., with a detailed criticism of the press propaganda.

49. TB, 6 June 1943.

50. TB, 25 May 1943.

51. TB, 22 May 1943. Also 30 May 1943: "It's a real catastrophe with Göring. He is staying in his father's castle and simply letting things go whichever way they want."

52. *Das Reich*, 30 May 1943, "Vom Wesen der Krise," and in *Aufstieg*, 279–86; see also TB, 18 May 1943.

53. TB, 14 May 1943.

54. TB, 15 May 1943.

55. TB, 29 May 1943. "Jaques" in the original.

56. See BAK, ZSg 102/42.

57. Details in Longerich, *Davon*, 277ff.

58. TB, 26 May 1943, also: 24, 25, and 26 May 1943. See also his article "Die motorischen Kräfte" in *Das Reich* of 6 June 1943, also published in *Aufstieg*, 307–14; according to it the dissolution of the Comintern was a "Bolshevist-Jewish deception."

59. On the alleged growth of anti-Semitism in Great Britain, see TB, 20 and 22 May, and 6 July 1943, and in the United States, see 4 June 1944.

60. TB, 20 May 1943.

61. The press reported on 18 and 19 May 1943 that the bombing of the dams was the result of a proposal by a Jewish scholar (see, for example, *DAZ* and *VB*). On the bombing, see Gröhler, *Bombenkrieg*, 151ff.; TB, 18–20 May 1943; on the alleged Jewish initiative for it, see 19 May 1943.

62. *VB* (B), 13 May 1943, "Judas Lieblingsplan: Die Hungerpeitsche für Europa" (comment).

63. Details on these issues in Longerich, *Davon*, 277.

64. See *Meldungen aus dem Reich* of 19 April, 5144ff., 30 May 1943, 5290f., as well as numerous other reports on morale, which are discussed in Longerich, *Davon*, 281ff.

65. TB, 19 May 1943; on the visit, see also Hansen, *Knut Hamsun*, 99ff.

66. TB, 23 June 1943. The original of the letter was discovered in Hamsun's papers. Hansen, *Knut Hamsun*, 104.

67. TB, 27 June 1943, also 28 June, 4 July 1943. On the visit, see Hansen, *Knut Hamsun*, 110ff. (on the basis of a note by Hitler's interpreter).

68. Kershaw, *Hitler. 1936–1945*, 738.

69. TB, 28 May 1943, and 30 May 1943.

70. TB, 4 June 1943. Since the previous autumn Goebbels had made several attempts to get German propaganda to offer the prospect of a "European" future. In October and November 1942 he had published two articles for *Das Reich* on the topic of a "New Europe," which, however, basically concentrated on emphasizing Germany's claim as the victorious power to absolute domination ("Das neue Europa," 4 October 1942, "Die Vision eines neuen Europa," 11 November 1942). On 22 January Goebbels had raised this issue with Hitler, who assigned him the task of producing a draft paper (TB, 23 January 1943). In March Hitler permitted Goebbels "to touch on and sketch out the matter" during his next speech in the Sports Palace. TB, 9 March 1943.

71. "Überwundene Winterkrise," published in *Aufstieg*, 287–306; *VB* (B), 7 June 1943, "Bezwingender Eindruck der Kundgebung im Sportpalast—In unerschütterlicher Zuversicht."

72. TB, 6 June 1943.

73. TB, 7 June 1943; also 8, 10, 11, and 12 June 1943.

74. TB, 7 June 1943, and 8 June 1943.

75. SD-Berichte zu Inlandsfragen, 10 June 1943. *Meldungen,* p. 5345.

76. TB, 11 and 18 June 1943.

77. BAB, NS 18/225. The draft of the circular that Tiessler, Goebbels's liaison with Bormann, had composed still stated: "On the Führer's instructions I have launched a propaganda campaign against Jewry, which will continue for months." Significantly, however, in the circular that was finally issued Goebbels no longer referred to Hitler (ibid., Vorlage Tießler an Goebbels, 19 May 1943).

78. BAB, NS 6/344, R 33/43g of 11 July 1943.

79. *Tagesberichte,* 29 May 1943; Gröhler, *Bombenkrieg,* 121; TB, 2 June 1943; and 4, 6, 7 June 1943.

80. Gröhler, *Bombenkrieg,* 121; TB, 14 June 1943 (Bochum).

81. TB, 12, 14, and 15 June 1943.

82. TB, 22 June 1943; a few days earlier he had already indicated that he was convinced that they would "not be able to avoid some kind of compulsory evacuation from particular cities" (TB, 20 June 1942).

83. TB, 2 July 1943, and 8 August 1943.

84. TB, 10 and 11 July 1943.

85. TB, 3 July 1943.

86. *Das Reich,* "Das Denkmal der nationalen Solidarität," 4 July 1943; see also TB, 23 June 1943.

87. TB, 9 July 1943. *Der Angriff,* 10 July 1943, "Dr. Goebbels in Köln."

88. TB, 29 June 1943. The letter survey carried out by his office was equally positive: TB, 10 July 1943.

89. TB, 25 June 1944; BAB, R 43 II/654a, committee meeting of 24 June 1943.

90. TB, 23 January, 10 May 1943.

91. TB, 12 May 1943.

92. See extensive correspondence in BAB, R 55/799 and 1435.

93. He had already promised to do this on 9 May (TB, 10 May 1943). In mid-June Bormann had indicated that Hitler supported Goebbels in this dispute: BAB, R 55/1435, telephone note of 15 June 1943.

94. TB, 1 July 1943; BAB, R55/1435, Lammers to Goebbels on the fact that a rapprochement with Rosenberg had not occurred in the conversation of 28 June, 29 June 1942. On the whole issue, see Reuth, *Goebbels,* 535ff., and Piper, *Alfred Rosenberg,* 604ff.

95. TB, 19 March 1943.

96. TB, 18 March 1943, and 11 June 1943. Schirach, *Ich glaubte an Hitler,* 288 (incorrectly dates the closure to January).

97. TB, 21 and 22 March, 24 April 1943.

98. TB, 9 May 1943.

99. Baldur von Schirach, *Hitler,* 292ff. By contrast Henriette von Schirach's claim that the argument was caused by the critical comments about Jewish persecution that she had made in front of Hitler appears much less plausible (particularly in view of the fact that in September 1942 her husband, Baldur von Schirach, had boasted in the manuscript of a speech that he had "evacuated tens of thousands of Jews from Vienna to the eastern ghettos" (TB, 15 September 1942). Schirach, *Der Preis der Herrlichkeit,* 215ff.; both date the incident to April 1943.

100. TB, 10, 21, and 27 August, also 23 September 1943. Negative comments about Schirach among others in entires for 13 January, 18 April 1944.

101. TB, 21 June 1944.
102. TB, 22 June 1944.
103. TB, 26 June 1943.
104. TB, 6–10 July 1943; Frieser, "Die Schlacht am Kursker Bogen."
105. On the stay in Heidelberg, see TB, 10 July 1943.
106. A similar line is taken in October 1942 in his speech at the gathering of poets in Weimar (TB, 12 October 1942). On 13 June 1943 he had published an editorial in *Das Reich* in which under the heading "Von der Freiheit des Geistes" (On Intellectual Freedom) he emphasized the difference between the valuable work of "intellectual workers" and the subversive activities of "intellectuals," once again strongly attacking the latter. Also in *Aufstieg*, 315–22; TB, 1 June 1943.
107. Published in Heiber (ed.), *Goebbels Reden*, no. 20.
108. Schröder, *Italiens Kriegsaustritt 1943*, 158ff.; see also TB, 12–15 July 1943.
109. Pessimistic also in TB, 16 and 17 July 1943.
110. Frieser, "Schlacht," 174ff.
111. Frieser, "Schlacht," 139ff.
112. TB, 19 July 1943.
113. TB, 21 and 22 July 1943.
114. TB, 18 July 1943; BAK, ZSg 109/43, 17 July 1943, TP 2: "In considering the situation in Sicily, particular attention should be paid to emphasizing the determination of the German troops deployed there to fight and defend their positions."
115. TB, 19 July 1943.
116. TB, 20 and 21 July 1943; *ADAP* E VI, no. 159, Aufzeichnung Schmidt, 20 July 1943; on the meeting, see Kershaw, *Hitler. 1936–1945*, 771.
117. TB, 21 July 1943.
118. TB, 25 July 1943. The information presumably came from the ambassador, Mackensen, who had a conversation with Farinacci on 22 July (*ADAP* E VI, no. 166, report of 22 July 1943).
119. On the meeting of the Grand Council, see Woller, *Die Abrechnung mit dem Faschismus in Italien 1943 bis 1948*, 9ff.; Bosworth, *Mussolini*, 400f.
120. TB, 30 November 1942: "It has come to our ears—so far in any case unconfirmed—that there are circles in Italy who intend to make contact with the enemy or have already done so. These circles are supposed to include Graziani and Badoglio, and above all Volpi. I can entirely believe that of Badoglio and Volpi, particularly the latter."
121. TB, 26 July 1943.
122. TB, 27 July 1943 (for all the meetings on 26 July).
123. On the meetings on 26 July 1943, see Heiber (ed.), *Lagebesprechungen im Führerhauptquartier*, 331.
124. TB, 27 July (quotation) and 28 July 1943.
125. Gröhler, *Bombenkrieg*, 106ff.; Brunswig, *Feuersturm über Hamburg*; Middlebrook, *Hamburg Juli 43*.
126. TB, 26 July 1943.
127. TB, 1 August 1943.
128. TB, 1 August 1943.
129. For example *VB* (B), editorials of 1, 3, and 4 August 1943.
130. TB, 1 August 1942.
131. *VB* (B), 4 August 1943, "Ein Wort zum Luftkrieg"; *Aufstieg*, 400–3.
132. TB, 2 August 1942.
133. TB, 14 August 1942.

134. TB, 3, 4, and 5 August 1943.
135. Girbig, . . . *im Anflug auf die Reichshauptstadt,* 69f.
136. TB, 5 August 1943.
137. TB, 16 and 18 August 1943.
138. TB, 18 August 1943.
139. TB, 10 and 21 August 1943.
140. TB, 21 August 1943. Hölsken, *Die V-Waffen,* 98.
141. TB, 28 August 1943. SD-Berichte zu Inlandsfragen, 26 August 1943 (*Meldungen,* p. 5675).
142. TB, 16 August 1943.
143. TB, 18 August 1943.
144. BAB, NS 18/1125, Vorlage Tießler für Parteikanzlei, 19 August 1943.
145. TB, 12 September, 12 December 1943.
146. TB, 16 August 1943.
147. BAB, NS 18/1071, 28 May 1943. See also BAB, R 55/603, letter from the state secretary to the Reich propaganda offices, 27 February 1943.
148. BAB, R 55/603, 13 September 1943.
149. Gröhler, *Bombenkrieg,* 178.
150. TB, 24 August 1943.
151. TB, 25 August 1943.
152. TB, 26 August 1943, and 19 August 1943.
153. TB, 28 August 1943.
154. TB, 1 September 1943.
155. TB, 2 September 1943; also 7 and 8 September 1943.
156. TB, 1 September 1943.
157. TB, 3 September 1943.
158. TB, 1 September 1943.
159. TB, 4 September 1943.
160. TB, 6 September 1943.
161. This is reflected, for example, in Goebbels's diary entry of 22 July 1943. The main theme is that the Wehrmacht has now gone onto the defensive.
162. TB, 6 August 1943, and already on 3 August 1943 on the impending evacuation.
163. Frieser, "Schlacht," 190ff.
164. Frieser, "Der Rückzug der Heeresgruppe Mitte nach Weißrußland."
165. TB, 10 August 1943.
166. In June 1943 Hitler had already stressed to him that the offices of Propaganda Minister, head of the Party's propaganda and Gauleiter of Berlin should always be held by the same person. TB, 23 June 1942.
167. TB, 13–18 August 1943; on operation "Lehrgang" (course), see Schröder, *Kriegsaustritt,* 263ff.; on the situation in Sicily, see Schreiber, "Ende," 1109ff.
168. TB, 22 August 1943; in general entries from 11 to 24 August 1943. Frieser, "Rückzug," 297ff.; Frieser, "Schlacht," 198.

27. "I HAVE NO IDEA WHAT THE FÜHRER'S GOING TO DO IN THE END"

1. Schreiber, "Ende," 1127, 1118; TB, 4–7 September 1943.
2. TB, 8 September 1943.
3. TB, 10 September 1943, and 11 September 1943; Schröder, *Kriegsaustritt,* 281ff.; Schreiber, "Ende," 1119ff.

4. TB, 10 September 1943 and continuing entries during the coming days; Schreiber, "Ende," 1126ff.

5. *Domarus II,* 2035ff.; TB, 11 September 1943. For Goebbels's reaction to the speech, see TB, 13 September 1943.

6. TB, 13 September 1943; this was similar to his assessment of the situation before the freeing of Mussolini, when he reflected that Mussolini's return to the political life of Italy would not really be in Germany's interest (TB, 11 September 1943).

7. TB, 15 September 1943.

8. TB, 15 September 1943.

9. TB, 17 and 18 September 1943; Schreiber, "Ende," 1130.

10. BAK, ZSg 109/44, 14 September 1943, TP 2, The course of the battle was "favorable," 15 September 1943, TP 2, "Caution" was appropriate, 16 September 1943, IIa, "favorable," 17 September, TP 2, "Caution."

11. TB, 18 September 1943, and 19 September 1943.

12. TB, 19 September 1943.

13. TB, 19 and 21 September 1943.

14. TB, 22 September 1943.

15. TB, 23 September 1943.

16. TB, 2 September 1943. Edda was the illegitimate child of Rachele Guidi and Benito Mussolini (who married in 1915) and was born on 1 September 1910; see Bosworth, *Mussolini,* 74.

17. Frieser, "Die Rückzugsoperationen der Heeresgruppe Süd in der Ukraine," 357ff., 362ff.

18. Frieser, "Rückzug," 301ff.

19. BAB, *NS* 18/264, Aktionsplan der RPL für die Propagandaaktion vom 15. September bis 15. November 1943 (draft). Note from the chief of staff of the head of the Party's Reich propaganda department concerning Bormann's agreement, 17 August 1943. PK-Anordnungen A 55 and 56 of 28 and 29 September 1943 (NS 6/342). See Nolzen, "Die NSDAP, der Krieg und die deutsche Gesellschaft," esp. 162.

20. TB, 1 October 1943, also 9, 22, and 30 October, 12 November 1943.

21. TB, 7 October 1943.

22. See also TB, 29 September 1943 on the conversation with Speer about armaments. On the personnel changes in the Economics Ministry, see Herbst, *Der totale Krieg,* 267ff.

23. See TB, 2 and 19 October 1943.

24. The text of Himmler's Posen speech is published in Smith (ed.), *Heinrich Himmler,* 162ff.

25. *Domarus II,* p. 2045; *VB* (B), 9 October 1943, "Der Führer: Von unserem Willen hängt der deutsche Sieg ab" (headline); TB, 7 and 9 October 1943 (the entry for 8 October is missing).

26. TB, 30 October 1943.

27. TB, 9 November 1943.

28. TB, 30 November 1943.

29. Frieser, "Rückzugsoperationen," 382f.; Frieser, "Das Ausweichen der Heeresgruppe Nord von Leningrad ins Baltikum"; Schönherr, "Der Rückzug der Heeresgruppe A über die Krim bis Rumänien."

30. TB, 26 and 27 November, also 17 December 1942.

31. Gröhler, *Bombenkrieg,* 188; TB, 20 November 1943.

32. Gröhler, *Bombenkrieg,* 188.

33. TB, 15 November 1943.

34. TB, 23 November 1943, edition text supplemented with minor additions.
35. TB, 24 November 1943.
36. TB, 24 November 1943.
37. TB, 24 November 1943.
38. TB, 27 November 1943.
39. TB, 27 November 1943.
40. TB, 28 November 1943, and 30 November 1943.
41. TB, 3 December 1943 (on the arrangement of this group of helpers); see also 28 November 1943.
42. TB, 29 November 1943.
43. *VB* (B), 29 November 1943.
44. See also TB, 26 November 1943.
45. TB, 21 December 1943; BAB, R 43 II/1648, also published in Moll, *"Führer-Erlass,"* no. 288. On the background, see TB, 19 December 1943.
46. TB, 20 December 1943; also 21, 25, and 28 December 1940; Hoffmann had already presented him with initial proposals for his new task at the end of November: TB, 1 December 1943; BAB, R 43 II/669d, Vermerk über die Besprechung of 4 January 1944; Blank, "Kriegsalltag," 392f.; Blank, "Albert Hoffmann als Reichsverteidigungskommissar im Gau Westfalen-Süd 1943–1945."
47. Gröhler, *Bombenkrieg,* 188; TB, 17, 18, 25, and 31 December 1943.
48. TB, 23 December 1943.
49. TB, 25 December 1943.
50. TB, 3 January 1944; *Tagesberichte,* 1 January 1944.
51. Gröhler, *Bombenkrieg,* 188; TB, 21 and 22 January 1944.
52. TB, 29 and 30 January 1944; Gröhler, *Bombenkrieg,* 188.
53. TB, 31 January 1944.
54. TB, 1–9 January 1944.
55. TB, 5 February 1944.
56. *Das Reich,* 13 February 1944; TB, 1 February 1944.
57. TB, 18 February 1944 (difficult to decipher).
58. TB, 4, 10, and 19 February 1944.
59. TB, 19 December 1943, 19 February, 27 April 1944.
60. TB, 24 February 1944.
61. TB, 18 April 1944.
62. Kershaw, *Hitler. 1936–1945,* 797.
63. TB, 28 October 1943; see also 9 November 1943.
64. TB, 29 February 1944.
65. TB, 25 January 1944, also 15 March, 18 April 1944.
66. 15 March 1944.
67. TB, 25 February 1944: "Himmler, like Bormann, keeps trying to establish closer contact with me, which is very agreeable."
68. Concerning lengthy conversations: TB, 27 November 1943 and 18 January 1944; because Speer was in a sanatorium he gave Naumann the task of maintaining these contacts: TB, 6 February, 9 March 1944.
69. Skeptical comments about Ley in TB, 6, 15, and 29 January also 25 February 1944.
70. Führererlaß of 15 August 1943 betr. die Abgrenzung der Zuständigkeiten zwischen dem Reichsministerium für Volksaufklärung und Propaganda und dem Reichsminister für die besetzten Ostgebiete, BAB, R 55/1436, published in Moll, *"Führer-Erlasse,"* no. 262; TB, 28 August 1943.
71. BAB, R 55/1435, Ministeramt an Staatssekretär: no directives received up till now, 21 September 1943.

72. TB, 20 October 1943; see also 22 September, 2 October 1943.

73. Lammers to Goebbels, 27 October 1943, BAB, R 55/1435.

74. On the negotiations, see BAB, R 55/1436, minutes of the meeting in the Ministry of the Eastern Territories, 16 September 1943, Leiter R to Goebbels, 16 September 1943, with drafts from both ministries for the agreement and further relevant correspondence; TB, 12 December 1944.

75. BAB, R 6/11, Abkommen über die Zusammenarbeit in Presse- und Propagandaangelegenheiten zwischen Ostministerium und Propagandaministerium of 20 December 1944.

76. BAB, R 55/440, Erlaß über die Errichtung von Propagandaämtern in den besetzten Ostgebieten of 17 December 1943, in Nachrichtenblatt, 23 December 1943. The diary entry for 15 January 1944 in which Goebbels reports on a further ministerial meeting about the subject suggests further difficulties.

77. TB, 11 and 23 September 1943.

78. TB, 24 February, 4 and 15 March 1944 (quotation). Dobroszycki, *Die legale polnische Presse*, 66; Hoffmann, *NS-Propaganda in den Niederlanden*.

79. Boelcke (ed.), *Deutschlands Rüstung im Zweiten Weltkrieg*, 13–15 May 1943, no. 21, and 30 May 1943, no. 31.

80. TB, 10 May 1943. On Goebbels's ambitions and Hitler's promises, see also TB, 3 January, 14 February, 12 May, 11 June, 11 July, 29 August, 11, 23, and 30 September 1943; see also Uziel, *Propaganda Warriors*, 200ff.

81. TB, 27 October 1943.

82. During 1943 the friction with the Foreign Ministry continued, particularly on account of the dispute over responsibilities for foreign propaganda: TB, 16, 23, 27, and 28 March 1943. They were to continue at the beginning of 1944: TB, 12 and 18 February, 4 and 10 March 1944.

83. Details in Longerich, *Propagandisten*, 227f.; TB, 13 and 14 November 1943.

84. BAK, NL 1118/106, Goebbels letter of 24 November 1943.

85. TB, 9 and 10 December 1943, on the basis of information from Lammers.

86. TB, 1 July, 17 October 1943, also 17 March 1944.

87. TB, 18 (quotation) and 19 April 1944. On the planned changes, see already 26 January 1944.

88. TB, 14 and 24 August 1944; also 23 September, 11 December 1944.

89. TB, 8, 20, and 23 January 1944.

90. TB, 4 and 6 January 1944 (quotation).

91. TB, 7 June, and 9 and 10 June 1944.

92. TB, 20 December 1943.

93. TB, 14 May 1944.

94. TB, 23 December 1944.

95. TB, 21 December 1943.

96. TB, 22 December 1943, 7, 9, and 18 January 1944.

97. TB, 17 February 1944, also 25 January, 17 February 1944, 19 November, 18 and 20 December 1943. He had already given vent to his suspicions in the entry of 26 March 1942: He now wanted "to get Schach closer to me and marginalize Görlitzer more and more." The final appointment to the position of deputy Gauleiter occurred only in January 1945: TB, 4 January 1945.

98. TB, 3 April 1944.

99. TB, 15, 21, and 25 April 1944.

100. TB, 4 May 1944, and 5 May 1944.

101. TB, 17 June 1944.

102. TB, 23 January 1944.

103. TB, numerous entries between 8 February and 4 March 1944. On the feelers, see Wegner, "Das Kriegsende in Skandinavien," 978.

104. TB, 4, 5, and 7 March 1944. *VB* (B), 7 June 1944, "Blutoffensive gegen Finnland" (editorial dated 6 June); *BBZ*, 7 March 1943, "Nervenkrieg im Norden"; BAK, ZSg 109/48, 6 March 1944, TP 1, orders the rest of the press to be cautious; 7 March, TP 1, the comments can be used by the rest of the press. See Wegner, "Kriegsende," 981.

105. See TB, 22 January, 22 March, 7 May 1943.

106. TB, 15 March 1944; Wegner, "Kriegsende," 983.

107. Wegner, "Kriegsende" 978; TB, numerous entries, particularly between 19 March and 25 April 1944.

108. Frieser, "Rückzugsoperationen," 434ff.

109. Frieser, "Rückzugsoperationen," 424ff.

110. Schönherr, "Rückzug," 485.

111. TB, 13 March 1944, and 15 March 1944 on the preparations for the action.

112. TB, 19 March 1944.

113. TB, 20–24 March 1944. On Veesenmayer, see Matic, *Edmund Veesenmayer*.

114. TB, 26, 29 March, 1, 21, 22, and 26 April 1944. On the persecution and deportation of the Hungarian Jews in 1944, see Braham, *The Politics of Genocide;* Gerlach and Aly, *Das letzte Kapitel*.

115. TB, 25 May 1944.

116. TB, 27 April 1944, also 2 and 5 May 1944.

117. TB, 2 August 1944: "Horthy is also of course an unreliable character. He's now [. . .] made the enemy an offer to exchange the Jewish children living in Hungary. Obviously one can't engage in serious politics with such unreliable types." TB, 3 September 1944: "In a radio broadcast the Hungarian Prime Minister has attacked the people in his country who are carping. We might be willing to accept that bit of the speech. But he also declared that the Jewish question was to be solved in a liberal way, which in general we're not happy with. For when one of our allies starts talking about being liberal then he's usually already on the wrong track."

118. TB, 6–11 March 1944. It is clear that these daylight raids did not destroy much housing. Demps, "Die Luftangriffe auf Berlin," 35ff. (table).

119. TB, 11 March 1944.

120. *Tagesberichte,* 24 and 25 March 1944; TB, 25, 26, and 27 March 1944.

121. TB, 22 and 23 January 1944.

122. Boog, "Strategischer Luftkrieg in Europa 1943–1944/45," 367ff.

123. TB, 23 and 26 February, 5 March 1944. On the effects of the raids, see 24 and 25 February 1944, 3, 16, 19 and 22 March, also 20 April 1944.

124. TB, 1 March 1944.

125. TB, 7 March 1944.

126. Boog, "Luftkrieg," 379.

127. In January Goebbels assumed that the "Luftwaffe's retaliation with remote-controlled airplanes" would begin in the middle of February, the A4 (V-2) rockets would be ready for launching in large numbers in the second half of March (TB, 14 January 1944). In March he learned that the flying bomb could be deployed from the middle of April, the A4 was to be deployed in the middle or at the end of April. TB, 9 March 1944; see also 19 March 1944.

128. TB, 18 April 1944, also 27 April 1944.

129. Hölsken, *V-Waffen,* esp. 43f., 64, 68ff., 133f.

130. TB, 3 May 1944.

131. *Tagesberichte,* 20 and 22 April 1944; TB, 21 and 22 April 1944.
132. TB, 26 April 1944; Richardi, *Bomber über München,* 238ff.; Permooser, *Der Luftkrieg über München,* 198ff.
133. Boog, "Luftkrieg," 126ff.; TB, 2, 6, 22, and 24 June 1944.
134. *VB* (B), 27 May 1944; TB, 24 and 25 May 1944.
135. TB, 30 May 1944.
136. TB, 2 June 1944; on the presumed effect of the article abroad, see also 3, 4, and 10 June 1944.
137. Heiber (ed.), *Goebbels Reden,* no. 26, 337.
138. See the figures in Grimm, *Lynchmorde an alliierten Fliegern im Zweiten Weltkrieg.*
139. TB, 22 April 1944.
140. TB, 15 April 1944.
141. TB, 18 April 1944.
142. TB, 27 April. 1944.
143. SD-Berichte zu Inlandsfragen, 25 May 1944, in *Meldungen aus dem Reich,* 6551ff., quotation 6562.
144. TB, 12, 19 (quotation) and 24 May 1944.

28. "VIRTUALLY A WARTIME DICTATORSHIP ON THE HOME FRONT"

1. TB, 6 June 1944.
2. TB, 6 and 3 June 1944.
3. TB, 7 June 1944.
4. TB, 11 December 1943.
5. Heiber (ed.), *Goebbels Reden,* no. 26, esp. 335. On further hints, see Hölsken, *V-Waffen,* 100ff.
6. Steinert, *Hitlers Krieg und die Deutschen,* 433f.
7. TB, 15 and 17 January, 19 February, 9 April, 3 June 1944.
8. TB, 9 and 16 June 1944.
9. The launches should really have begun a few days before but had "gone wrong." TB, 17 June 1944; see also 14 June 1944; on the reasons for the failure, see Boog, "Luftkrieg," 391.
10. TB, 17 June 1944. On the V weapons offensive, see Boog, "Luftkrieg," 380ff.; Hölsken, *V-Waffen,* 126ff.
11. Oven, *Mit Goebbels bis zum Ende,* vol. 2, 18f.; see also TB, 17 June 1944.
12. BAK, ZSg 109/50, 16 June 1944, TP 1; also contains lengthy informative statements on the question of how the notion of retaliation can continue to be utilized; see Hölsken, *V-Waffen,* 103ff.
13. TB, 18 June 1944.
14. BAK, ZSg 109/50, 17 June 1944, TP 1: It was only "the start of the retaliation and the surprise [. . .] that we are preparing"; 20 June 1944, TP 1, the impact depends on the "uninterrupted use of this weapon."
15. TB, 20 June 1944; see also 18 June 1944.
16. TB, 22 June 1944.
17. BAK, ZSg 109/50, 24 June, TP 1, introduction of the term V-1; Hölsken, *V-Waffen,* 106.
18. TB, 20 June 1944; and 23 June 1944.
19. TB, 18 June 1944.
20. TB, 30 June 1944, also 1 and 7 July 1944. See also Hölsken, *V-Waffen,* 197.

21. TB, succession of entries from 18 June 1944.
22. TB, 22 June 1944. On the statistics of hits, see Boog, "Luftkrieg," 397.
23. TB, 23 June 1944.
24. Frieser, "Der Zusammenbruch der Heeresgruppe Mitte im Sommer 1944," 537ff.
25. TB, 22 and 25 June 1944.
26. On the "situation in the East," see the succession of entries from 25 June 1944.
27. Frieser, "Zusammenbruch," 539ff., 545ff., 548ff.
28. Frieser, "Zusammenbruch," 552ff. Goebbels notes the loss of three armies in the entry for 9 July 1944.
29. Frieser, "Zusammenbruch," 563ff.
30. TB, 11 July 1944. Up to a significant gap in the entries from 17 to 22 July there is a succession of entries on the "situation in the East."
31. TB, 15 July 1944.
32. TB, 22 June 1944.
33. TB, 12 July 1944.
34. TB, 2 July 1944.
35. TB, 7–9 July 1944.
36. Das Reich, 23 July 1944; see also TB, 11 July 1944.
37. Heiber (ed.), Goebbels Reden, no. 27, 356f. See also Goebbels's article in Das Reich, 30 July 1944; on the V weapon propaganda in July, see also Hölsken, V-Waffen, 107f.
38. VB (B), 9 July 1944, "Mit allen Mitteln gegen den Feind" (headline). In his speech Goebbels emphasized that it was a matter of "life and death for the nation." TB, 8 July 1944, also 7 and 14 July 1944. On "total war," see in particular his comments on the reviews of letters in 8 and 15 July 1944.
39. TB, 11 July 1944. Speer had made a similar point to Hitler during a meeting on armaments. See Boelcke (ed.), Deutschlands Rüstung, 390, 6 July 1944.
40. TB, 12 July 1944.
41. TB, 13 July 1944.
42. Published in Bleyer, "Pläne der faschistichen Führung zum totalen Krieg im Sommer 1944," 1317ff., 1320ff.
43. TB, 12 and 13 July 1944.
44. TB, 13 July 1944.
45. Longerich, "Joseph Goebbels und der Totale Krieg."
46. TB, 14 July 1944.
47. Richardi, Bomber über München, 268ff.; Permooser, Luftkrieg über München, 249ff.; TB, 13, 14, and 16 July 1944.
48. According to Goebbels's account in his radio address of 26 July 1944, in Heiber (ed.), Goebbels Reden, no. 27, 342f. On the assassination attempt of 20 July, see Hoffmann, Widerstand–Staatsstreich–Attentat; Fest, Staatsstreich. On Goebbels's role on 20 July, see Hoffmann, Widerstand, 529, 539, 593ff.; Reuth, Goebbels, 548ff.
49. Hans Wilhelm Hagen, "Bericht über meine Tätigkeit als Verbindungsoffizier des Wachbataillons 'Großdeutschland' zum Reichsministerium für Volksaufklärung und Propaganda am 20. Juli 1944," in Jacobsen (ed.), "Spiegelbild einer Verschwörung," 12ff.; Remer, "Der Ablauf der Ereignisse am 20. Juli 1944, wie ich sie als Kommandeur des Wachbataillons Großdeutschland erlebte," in ibid., 637ff.
50. In particular in his radio address of 26 July 1944.
51. On this assessment, see Hoffmann, Widerstand, 298.
52. TB, 22 July 1944.
53. Moll, "Führer-Erlasse," no. 340 and 341 (Verfügung V 10/44, BAB, NS 6/347).

54. TB, 23 July 1944; Protokoll der Chefbesprechung of 22 July 1944 in BAB, R 43 II/664a.
55. *RGBl.* 1944 I, 161f.; BAB, R 43 II/664a, Lammers's note on the address, 25 July 1944, here too Goebbels's certificate of appointment, 25 July 1944; on the Führer decree, see Rebentisch, *Führerstaat,* 516f.
56. BAB, R 43 II/664a, Lammers to Goebbels, 26 June 1944. The following were not affected by the decree: the General Buildings Inspector, the General Buildings Councilor for Munich, the Reich Buildings Councilor for Linz, the General Inspector for Motor Transport, the Reich Chancellery, the Presidential Chancellery, and the Party Chancellery.
57. TB, 24 July 1944.
58. Frieser, "Zusammenbruch," 572ff.
59. Schönherr, "Rückzug," 712ff. On the critical military situation on the Eastern Front, see TB, in particular 23 July–2 August 1944.
60. TB, 3 August 1944; Vogel, "Kriegführung," 556ff.
61. Rebentisch, *Führerstaat,* 517f.; BAB, R 43 II/665, General Secretary of the GB to Killy, 1 and 4 August 1944.
62. Heiber (ed.), *Goebbels Reden,* no. 27, 351, 353, 354.
63. TB, 27 and 28 July 1944.
64. BAK, ZSg 109/50, 26 July 1944, TP 1; *VB* (B), 26 July, "Der Führer befiehlt: Entscheidende Verstärkung des Kriegseinsatzes" (headline); 27 July, "Waffen–Hände–Herzen. Reichsminister Dr. Goebbels zieht die Folgerungen aus dem 20. Juli" (headline); TB, 27 July 1944.
65. BAB, R 43 II/665, 28 July 1944; *VB* (B), 28 July, "Dr. Goebbels ordnet an: Keine Scheinarbeit mehr" (headline).
66. TB, 2 August 1944.
67. TB, 4 August 1944 (for the whole meeting); speech published in Heiber (ed.), *Goebbels Reden,* no. 28.
68. BAB, R 43 II/666.
69. BAB, R 43 II/665 (n.d.); published on 24 August, see *Ursachen und Folgen,* vol. 21, no. 3528e; the drafting of the circulars is mentioned in TB, 31 July 1944.
70. BAB, R 43 II/666a, Vermerk Reichskanzlei, 7 August 1944. Telex from Bormann to Goebbels, 8 August 1944.
71. *Ursachen und Folgen,* vol. 21, no. 3528b.
72. TB, 28 July 1944; Dritte Verordnung über die Meldung von Männern und Frauen für Zwecke der Reichsverteidigung vom 28 Juli 1944, *RGBl.* 1944 I, 168.
73. BAB, R 43 II/666b, Goebbels' Führerinformation, 30 July, 2, 8, 11, and 17 August 1944 and press statements (drafts), 5, 12, 19, 26 September, 3 October 1944.
74. TB, 24 August 1944; BAB, R 43 II/666b, Führerinformation, 11 August 1944.
75. TB, 3 November 1944.
76. BAB, R 43 II/665, Bormann to Goebbels, 14 August 1944; R 43 II/666b, Führerinformation A I 465, 17 August 1944.
77. TB, 24 August 1944.
78. TB, 5 October 1944.
79. TB, 24 August 1944.
80. TB, 17 September 1944, and 20 September 1944.
81. BAB, R 43 II/1363, Vermerk of 20 September 1943; further correspondence on this in the file.
82. TB, 10 August 1944; on the Economics Ministry, see Herbst, *Der totale Krieg,* 344.
83. TB, 24 October 1944. At the end of October Goebbels learned that Himmler had no desire to participate in such plans (TB, 1 November 1944).

84. BA 55/614, Rundschreiben of 23 July 1944; see also directives for its implementation in ibid.
85. Kershaw rightly questions the plausibility of these reports. Kershaw, *Der Hitler-Mythos*, 263f.
86. TB, 3 August 1944.
87. TB, 3 August 1944.
88. *VB* (B), 9 August 1944, "Acht Verbrecher vom 20. Juli traf die verdiente Strafe— Das Volk hat sie gerichtet" (headline); TB, 10 August 1944; there are no entries about the days of the trial in the diaries.
89. Ramm, *Der 20. Juli 1944 vor dem Volksgerichtshof,* 449ff. with a survey of the trials.
90. TB, 25 July, 3 August 1944.
91. TB, 16 August 1944.
92. TB, 23 August 1944.
93. TB, 16 August 1944.
94. Vogel, "Kriegführung," 581ff.; TB, 16 August 1944.
95. Vogel, "Kriegführung," 560ff.
96. TB, 22 August 1944.
97. TB, 25 August 1944.
98. TB, 26 and 27 August 1944; Schönherr, "Rückzug," 773ff.
99. TB, 4 and 21 September 1944; on the (foreseeable) developments in Finland, see also 3 August 1944; Wegner, "Kriegsende," 991ff.
100. TB, 10 September 1944.
101. TB, 23 September 1944, see also 2 and 4 November 1944.
102. TB, 17 November 1944.
103. TB, 10 August 1944.
104. TB, 5 September 1944, also 1 and 2 September 1944; BAM, RH 5/126, AHA, Stab II, Stand der Goebbels-Aktion, 29 September 1944, 1 October 1944 and table for the Luftwaffe submission.
105. TB, 27, 29, and 31 August, 1 and 2 September 1944.
106. TB, 3 September 1944.
107. TB, 5 September 1944.
108. TB, 10 September; on difficulties in fulfilling the September quota, see 13, 16, 24, 26, and 27 September 1944.
109. TB, 27 September 1944; 24 September: 244,000.
110. BAM, RH 5/126, AHA, Stab II, Notizen v. 27. November 1944 und v. 23. Januar 1945.
111. TB, 5 October 1944, and 8 October 1944.
112. TB, 30 December 1944.
113. That is clear from BAM, RH 15/126, AHA, Stab II, Stand der Goebbels-Aktion vom 30. Dezember 1944, 1. Januar 1945 und Notiz v. 23. January 1945 concerning the Luftwaffe submission. By contrast Goebbels referred to 685,332 men who had been "transferred" to the Wehrmacht, but noted a deficit of 156,500 men (TB, 30 December 1944).
114. TB, 17 September 1944. Criticism of the Labor Offices already on 31 July, 8 September 1944.
115. TB, 7 October 1944; on 28 September he had noted a figure of 150,000.
116. Gröhler, *Bombenkrieg,* 342f.
117. Gröhler, *Bombenkrieg,* 358.
118. TB, 11 September 1944; Löhr, "Mönchengladbach," 205.
119. Schmidt, *Die Brandnacht; Tagesberichte,* 11 September; TB, 23 September.

120. Gröhler, *Bombenkrieg*, 371; TB, 6 November 1944 (Solingen), TB, 24 October 1944 (Essen).
121. TB, 7 October, 6 December 1944; *Tagesberichte*, 6 October, 5 December 1944 and *Tagesberichte*, 11, 14, 23, 30 October, also 15 and 24 November 1944 about smaller raids, mainly nighttime Mosquito raids by the British.
122. TB, 21–28 September 1944; Vogel, "Kriegführung," 606ff.; Middlebrook, *Arnheim 1944*.
123. Vogel, "Kriegführung," 615; TB, 15 and 17 September 1944.
124. TB, 24 June 1944.
125. TB, 16 September 1944.
126. TB, 17 September 1944.
127. TB, 1, 2, 8, 14, 15, 17, 20, and 23 September 1944.
128. TB, 12 September 1944, and 14 September 1944.
129. TB, 19 September 1944.
130. TB, 30 September 1944.
131. *Der Angriff*, 26 and 30 September 1944. See also *DAZ*, 26 September 1944, "Die Vernichtungsdrohung aus dem Westen" (headline); *VB* (N), 26 September 1944, "Morgenthau übertrifft Clemenceau" (headline); similarly in 27, 28, and 30 September 1944.
132. TB, 3 August 1944.
133. TB, 6 September 1944.
134. TB, 6 June 1944. On Japanese advances, see TB, 11 and 17 June 1944. See Martin, *Deutschland und Japan im Zweiten Weltkrieg*, 196.
135. TB, 10 September 1944; see also 14 September 1944.
136. TB, 13 September 1944.
137. TB, 16 (Stuckart), 17 (Speer), 18 (Naumann) September 1944.
138. TB, 18 September 1944.
139. For the quotations, see TB, 12–18, and 19 September 1944.
140. TB, 20 September 1944.
141. TB, 21 and 23 September 1944.
142. Speer's statement, *IMT* 16, 533.
143. Kershaw, *Hitler. 1936–1945*, 948ff.
144. TB, 23 and 25 September 1944.
145. TB, 23 September 1944.
146. At the beginning of November Goebbels noted that in the foreign press rumors were once more circulating that Germany was trying to make a separate peace with one side or the other. As far as London was concerned, he continued to consider it impossible at the present time to reach a compromise because the English were "too committed to their existing strategy" (TB, 3 and 5 November 1944). During a visit to him at home the Japanese ambassador, Ōshima, once again advocated trying to reach a separate peace with the Soviet Union (10 November 1944). But the diaries do not reveal whether or how Goebbels responded to this initiative.

29. "BUT WHEN WILL THERE BE SOME ACTION?"

1. Hölsken, *V-Waffen*, 142ff., 110.
2. TB, 6 and 24 September 1944.
3. TB, 25 September 1944.

4. TB, 11 November 1944.

5. TB, 5–12 October 1944. There are no entries covering the decisive days of the battle for Aachen. Vogel, "Kriegführung," 615.

6. Frieser, "Die Rückzugskämpfe der Heeresgruppe Nord bis Kurland," 642ff. This is not referred to in the Goebbels diaries because the entries for the period 13–22 October 1944 are missing.

7. TB, 26 October 1944; *VB* (N), 28 October 1944, "Furchtbare Verbrechen in Nemmersdorf"; 29 October 1944, "Das Grauen von Nemmersdorf"; 2 November 1944, "Augenzeugen berichten aus Nemmersdorf. Wie Moskaus Henker toben" (headline). See also *Der Angriff,* 28 October 1944; *Der Freiheitskampf,* 30 October 1944.

8. Weekly activity reports by the head of the propaganda department, BAB, R 55/601, Stichtag 30 October, 7 November 1944.

9. TB, 3 November 1944; see also 22 November 1944. On 24 November he wrote that he wanted "to bring [the Soviet atrocities] to the attention of the public, at least to a certain extent," but this was not evident in the propaganda.

10. This is clear from BAB, R 43 II/666b, press statement, 2 November 1944. The announcement was strongly criticized by the Reich Chancellery because to some extent it was contrary to the facts. (ibid., Vermerk vom 4. November 1944). See also TB, 5 October 1944, where Goebbels complained that the deployment of women in the armaments industry was not going ahead because of Speer's and the industrialists' "laxity."

11. BAB, R 43 II/666b, press statement 10 October 1944.

12. BAB, R 43 II/666b, press statement 2 November 1944, as published, for example, in the *VB* (N), 5 November 1944.

13. TB, 10 November 1944.

14. TB, 11 January 1945.

15. TB, 7 November 1944.

16. TB, 28 November 1944.

17. TB, 29 October, 17 November 1944.

18. TB, 7 December 1944; see also 25 November 1944.

19. TB, 3 November 1944.

20. TB, 16 November 1944.

21. TB, 7 December 1944, and 16 November 1944.

22. TB, 30 September, 30 December 1944; on the continuing poor relationship with the Foreign Ministry, see TB, 31 October, 2, 7, and 11 November 1944.

23. On the investigation of the Foreign Ministry, see TB, 4, 5, and 6 January 1945; on the assignment of investigating the Foreign Ministry to Staatssekretär a. D. Mussehl, see TB, 16 January 1945; on the report produced by Mussehl, see 20 March 1945. On the Ministry of the Eastern Territories, see TB, 16 and 18 March 1945.

24. TB, 27 and 29 September 1944.

25. TB, 4 March 1945; Uziel, *Propaganda Warriors,* 205.

26. TB, 12 and 20 September 1944: During a discussion Speer had become "very insolent"; see also 23, 24, and 26 September, 3, 5, and 10 October 1944.

27. TB, 10 October 1944, and 5 October 1944.

28. TB, 11 and 16 November 1944.

29. TB, 1 December 1944.

30. TB, 4 January 1945.

31. TB, 5, 12, and 19 January 1956; Kunz, *Wehrmacht und Niederlage,* 256ff.; Overmans, *Deutsche militärische Verluste im Zweiten Weltkrieg,* 225.

32. Published in Mammach, *Volkssturm*, 168ff. The decree was dated 25 September 1944. TB, 12 September 1944.

33. TB, 21 September, and 26 September 1944. On the formation of the Volkssturm in Berlin, see 24 and 29 October, 7 November 1944.

34. TB, 13 November 1944; *VB* (N), 14 November 1944, "Geist von 1813—Waffen von 1944. Dr. Goebbels sprach zu den Tausenden Berliner Volkssturmmänner *[sic]*."

35. Kershaw, *Hitler. 1936–1945*, 962; TB, 24 November 1944.

36. TB, 24 November 1944.

37. TB, 30 September, 6 (quotation), 8, 9, and 30 October (after recuperation) 1945; Kershaw, *Hitler. 1936–1945*, 945.

38. Previously: complaints about the lack of a public statement by Hitler: TB, 11, 12, 14, 16, 17, 18, and 30 September, 4, 9, 10, and 13 November, 3 December 1944.

39. TB, 2 December 1944.

40. TB, 23 September 1943.

41. TB, 19 and 21 May 1944.

42. TB, 22 May 1944.

43. TB, 6–8 July 1944. A few months later, at the end of December, Hanke visited the Goebbelses at home in Berlin (TB, 31 December 1944).

44. TB, 4 December 1944.

45. Particularly concerned entries in the TB for 9, 11, 17, 20, 21, 22, and 29 November 1944. On military developments, see Vogel, "Kriegführung," 614ff.

46. TB, 17 and 18 December 1944.

47. TB, 19 December 1944. See the reports of the *VB* (B), which emphasized the offensive on 18 December, but during the following days was cautious in providing details.

48. TB, 19 December 1944.

49. TB, 23 December 1944.

50. TB, 29 December 1944.

51. Vogel, "Kriegführung," 625ff.

52. TB, 21 January 1945.

53. TB, 1 February 1945. On the Soviet offensive, see Lakowski, "Der Zusammenbruch der deutschen Verteidigung zwischen Ostsee und Karpaten," 516ff.

54. *Tagesberichte*, 2 and 7 January; TB, 4, 9, and 10 January 1945.

55. Gröhler, *Bombenkrieg*, 423; *Tagesberichte*, 3 February 1945; on the number of victims, see Demps, "Luftangriffe," 21ff.; TB, 5 and 12 February 1945.

56. Gröhler, *Bombenkrieg*, 400ff.

57. TB, 9 November also 7 and 10 December 1944.

58. However, in agreement with Bormann, Himmler and the relevant military agencies: Erlaß des Führers zur Überprüfung der Wehrmacht, Waffen-SS und Polizei im Heimatkriegsgebiet zur Freimachung von Soldaten für die Front vom 10. Dezember 1944 (Moll, *"Führer-Erlasse,"* no. 377); on the appointment, see TB, 11 December 1944; on taking up the position, see TB, 12, and 15 December 1944; on further activity, see 20, 22, and 29 December 1944.

59. TB, 30 December 1944; see also 3, 11, 18, and 19 January 1945.

60. Overmans, *Deutsche militärische Verluste*, 239.

61. TB, 21 January 1945.

62. TB, 26 January 1945.

63. TB, 7 February 1945; this figure is confirmed by the surviving files of the OKW: According to to Kunz, *Wehrmacht und Niederlage*, 166: BAM, RH 2/923, Notiz für

Reichsbevollmächtigten als Unterlage zur Führerinformation vom 6. Februar 1945.

64. TB, 11 February 1945, also 8 February 1945 concerning Bormann's and Himmler's alleged agreement to his being given this authority.

65. Kunz, *Wehrmacht und Niederlage*, 155.

66. TB, 6 February 1945.

67. TB, 4 January 1945.

68. TB, 23 January 1945.

69. TB, 26 January 1945.

70. TB, 28 January 1945.

71. TB, 30 January, 1 February 1945; Fest, *Speer*, 321f.; Janssen, *Das Ministerium Speer*, 301f.

72. TB, 29 January 1945.

73. TB, 30 and 31 January, 1, 2, and 5 February 1945.

74. TB, 30 January 1945.

75. TB, 11 February 1945.

76. TB, 5 Feburary 1945.

77. TB, 6 February 1945. On the preparations for the defense of Berlin, see also TB, 7, 8, 11, 12, and 13 February 1945.

78. TB, 1 March 1945.

79. TB, 15 March 1945.

80. *Das Reich*, 18 March 1945, "Berlin, Ein Riesenigel."

81. TB, 1 February 1945: He learned from Ley that Hitler had spoken to him in similar terms and Hewel told him that Ribbentrop had tried in vain to get permission from Hitler to put out feelers.

82. TB, 12 February 1945.

83. TB, 13 February 1945.

84. TB, 4, 26, and 29 January 1945.

85. TB, 25 and 29 January, 28 February, 12, 21, 22, and 28 March 1945.

86. TB, 5, 12, and 24 March 1945.

87. TB, 29 January 1945.

88. TB, 1 March 1945.

89. TB, 7 January 1945.

90. *Das Reich*, 21 January 1945, "Die Urheber des Unglücks der Welt."

91. TB, 25 January 1945; see also 26 January 1945.

92. TB, 6 February 1945.

93. TB, 8 and 10 February 1945; Dietrich, *12 Jahre*, 115.

94. Heiber (ed.), *Goebbels Reden*, no. 30; quotations 430, 444, 437, 431f., 446.

95. TB, 2 March 1945.

96. TB, 5 and 12 March 1945.

97. Deutsche Wochenschau, no. 754; *VB* (N), 13 March 1945; TB, 9 March 1945.

98. See the reports in the *VB* (N) for February and March; despite being prominent, the atrocities were not the dominant topic: 9 February 1945, "Bilder des Grauens hinter den Sowjetlinien," 1; 10 February 1945, "Humanitäre Phrasen und grausige Wirklichkeit" (headline) and "Der bolschewistische Blutsumpf"; 20 February 1945, "Moskau deportiert deutsche Arbeiter" (headline); 8 March 1945, "Generaloberst Guderian über die Schandtaten der Bolschewisten: Morden, plündern schänden, sengen" (headline); 10 March 1945, "Tragödien hinter dem Sowjetvorhang," 1; 11 March 1945, "Stalins Gesetz: Mord und Deportation"; 13 March 1945, "Ab nach Sibirien!"; 20 March 1945, "Schwester auf Panzer gebunden."

99. TB, 27 and 28 March 1945.
100. TB, 31 March 1945.
101. TB, 20 and 24 March 1945.
102. TB, 1 February 1945; for criticism of Göring by Hitler, see in particular 4, 15, 16, and 23 January 1945.
103. TB, 1 February 1945, similarly 12 February 1945.
104. TB, 28 February 1945.
105. TB, 31 January, 5 March 1945.
106. TB, 14 March 1945.
107. TB, 14 March 1945. For criticism of Göring by Hitler, see also 21, 22, and 23 March 1945.
108. TB, 22 March 1945.
109. TB, 5 March 1945.
110. TB, 12 and 14 March 1945.
111. TB, 15 March 1945, and 16 March 1945.
112. TB, 3, 13, and 24 March 1945.
113. TB, 14 March 1945, and 15, 23, and 28 March 1945.
114. TB, 28 March 1945.
115. TB, 4 and 28 March 1945. On Hitler's poor health, see also 12 February 1945.
116. TB, 6 February, 22 March 1945.
117. TB, 5 March 1945.
118. TB, 12 March 1945; on Himmler's possible promotion, see 23 January 1945.
119. TB, 8 March 1945.
120. TB, 17, 18, and 22 March 1945.
121. TB, 12 March 1945.
122. TB, 8 April 1945.
123. Ungváry, "Kriegsschauplatz Ungarn," 926ff.; TB, 6–21 March 1945.
124. TB, 9 March 1945; Henke, *Die amerikanische Besetzung Deutschlands,* 347f.
125. TB, 23 and 25 March 1945; Henke, *Besetzung,* 385ff.
126. TB, 25 March 1945.
127. TB, 26 March 1945.
128. TB, 22 March 1945.
129. Gröhler, *Bombenkrieg,* 423; Demps, "Luftangriffe," 21ff.; TB, 19, 20, and 25 March 1945.
130. TB, 14 March 1945.
131. Gröhler, *Bombenkrieg,* 422; TB, 20, 21 (quotation) and 25 March 1945.
132. TB, 15 March 1945.
133. TB, 15 March 1945; *Ursachen und Folgen,* no. 3607f., dated 15 March 1945; see also Fest, *Speer,* 336ff.
134. Moll (ed.), *"Führer-Erlasse,"* no. 394.
135. TB, 28 March 1945.
136. TB, 31 March 1945; *Ursachen und Folgen,* no. 3604c, Durchführungserlaß Hitlers vom 30. März 1945.
137. TB, 28 March 1945; 4 April 1945 (on Bormann): "In the Party too we lack a clear leadership that is rooted in the people."
138. TB, 12, 15, and 16 March 1945.
139. TB, 31 March, 1 and 4 April 1945.
140. TB, 29 March 1945; see also 12 March. On the Werwolf movement, see Biddiscombe, *Werwolf!;* Arendes, "Schrecken aus dem Untergrund. Endphaseverbrechen des 'Werwolf,' " 149–71.
141. TB, 11 March 1945.

142. TB, 29 and 30 March 1945, also 1 April 1945.

143. TB, 1 and 2 April 1945.

144. TB, 31 March 2, 3, and 4 April 1945.

145. TB, 29 March 1945.

146. TB, 1 February 1945.

147. TB, 5 and 6 February 1945.

148. Heiber (ed.), *Goebbels Reden*, no. 30, 435.

149. TB, 5 March 1945.

150. *Das Reich*, 15 April 1945.

151. TB, 30 November 1944: Goebbels found out about the new microfiche process. On the filming of the diaries, see Elke Fröhlich, "Einleitung zur Gesamtedition," in *Die Tagebücher von Joseph Goebbels*, Teil III, Register 1923–1945. Teilband I: Sachregister A–G, 7–178; on the complicated history of the survival of the various parts of the diaries, 36ff.

152. TB, 19 and 30 March 1941.

153. See also TB, 8 April 1945 (resistance).

154. This was reported by Steengracht, the former state secretary in the Foreign Ministry, in a postwar statement; see *IMT* 10, 128.

155. Lakowski, "Der Zusammenbruch," 633ff.

156. Heiber (ed.), *Goebbels Reden*, no. 447, quotations 448, 454, 455.

157. Kershaw, *Hitler. 1936–1945*, 1027ff.

158. Koller, *Der letzte Monat*, 43f.

159. Oven, *Mit Goebbels bis zum Ende*, vol. 2, 308. By contrast, the account by Hans Fritzsche appears implausible because of his desire to exonerate himself. See Springer, *Es sprach Hans Fritzsche*, 28ff.: "Why did you work for me?! Now you're going to get your throat cut" (30).

160. *OKW KTB* IV, 1453.

161. Oven, *Mit Goebbels bis zum Ende*, 22 April 1945, vol. 2, 310f.; LA Berlin, Rep. 058, no. 6012, Statement by Günther Schwägermann, Hannover, 16 February 1948.

162. Kershaw, *Hitler. 1936–1945*, 1034ff.; Joachimsthaler, *Hitlers Ende*, 148ff.; on the battle for Berlin, see Lakowski, "Zusammenbruch," 656ff.

163. *Domarus II*, 2228.

164. Statement by Speer in *IMT* 16, 582f.; Speer, *Erinnerungen*, 485f.

165. *Der Spiegel*, 10 January 1966 (excerpt from Hitler military conferences from 23, 25, and 27 April 1945), 34 (25 April).

166. Ibid., 37 (25 April).

167. Ibid., 39 (25 April). He takes a similar line in the second military conference on 25 April (ibid.).

168. *OKW KTB* IV, 1461ff.

169. Joachimsthaler, *Hitlers Ende*, 185; Registry Office certificate published in *Domarus II*, 2234.

170. *Domarus II*, 2241.

171. Magda reports this in a letter to Harald.

172. On Hitler's suicide, see Joachimsthaler, *Hitlers Ende*, 201ff.; final conversation with Magda according to a statement by Günsche, 221f.

173. Joachimsthaler, *Hitlers Ende*, 233 (statement by Axmann).

174. Kempka, *Die letzten Tage mit Adolf Hitler*, 97f.

SOURCES

1. Elke Fröhlich (ed.), *Die Tagebücher von Joseph Goebbels*, 32 vols. The last volume of text came out in 2006. This work was preceded by a first edition, also edited by Elke Fröhlich, covering the period from 1924 to 1941: *Die Tagebücher von Joseph Goebbels. Sämtliche Fragmente.* In addition, in 1992, Ralf Georg Reuth published a five-volume selection from previously unknown diary texts discovered in Moscow in that year: *Joseph Goebbels, Tagebücher 1924–45.*
2. Osobyi-Archiv, 1363–3.
3. Boelcke (ed.), *Kriegspropaganda 1939–1941.*
4. BAK, ZSg 101, 102 and 109.
5. Semmler (properly "Semler"), *Goebbels;* Borresholm (ed.), *Dr. Goebbels nach Aufzeichnungen aus seiner Umgebung;* Stephan, *Joseph Goebbels;* Oven, *Mit Goebbels bis zum Ende;* Schaumburg-Lippe, *Dr. G.*
6. Riess, *Goebbels.*
7. Fraenkel and Manvell, *Goebbels.*
8. Heiber, *Joseph Goebbels.*
9. Reimann, *Dr. Joseph Goebbels.*
10. Reuth, *Goebbels.*
11. Bärsch, *Der junge Goebbels.*
12. Gathmann and Paul, *Narziss Goebbels.*
13. Thacker, *Joseph Goebbels.*
14. Bering, *Kampf um Namen.*
15. Höver, *Joseph Goebbels.*
16. Barth, *Goebbels und die Juden.*
17. Michels, *Ideologie und Propaganda.*

PHOTO CREDITS

Page 3: Courtesy of The Granger Collection
Page 28: Courtesy of Agentur Karl Hoffkes
Page 51: Courtesy of Art Resource
Page 73: Courtesy of Mary Evans Picture Library
Page 98: Courtesy of The Granger Collection
Page 113: Courtesy of The Granger Collection
Page 131: Courtesy of AKG Images
Page 154: Courtesy of Art Resource
Page 185: Courtesy of AKG Images
Page 205: Courtesy of The Granger Collection
Page 233: Courtesy of Getty Images
Page 250: Courtesy of Ullstein Bild
Page 273: Courtesy of Art Resource
Page 293: Courtesy of The Granger Collection
Page 311: Courtesy of Art Resource
Page 365: Courtesy of Suddeutsche Zeitung Photo
Page 391: Courtesy of Mary Evans Picture Library
Page 429: Courtesy of The Granger Collection
Page 442: Courtesy of The Granger Collection
Page 456: Courtesy of The Granger Collection
Page 479: Courtesy of Mary Evans Picture Library
Page 501: Courtesy of Art Resource
Page 527: Courtesy of The Granger Collection

INDEX

Page numbers in italics refer to illustrations.

"JG" refers to Joseph Goebbels.